Italian Waters Pilot

FRANCE
Genoa
Liguria
Savona
Rapallo
Gulf of Genoa
La Spezia
Marina di Carrara
Livorno (Leghorn)
Ligurian Sea
Toscana
Porto Ferraio
Elba
ITALY
CORSICA
Civitavecchia
See Mediterranean France and Corsica
Rome
Campania
Naples
Ponza
Ischia
Bay of Naples
Capri
Salerno
Porto Cervo
Alghero
Tyrrhenian Sea
Arbatax
SARDINIA
Cagliari
CROATIA
Adriatic Sea
See Adriatic Pilot
Bari
Brindisi
Taranto
Basilicata
Gulf of Taranto
Otranto
Santa Maria di Leuca
Corfu
Calabria
Crotone
Ionian Sea
Ustica
Aeolian Is.
Egadi Is.
Palermo
Trapani
Messina
Reggio Calabria
SICILY
Catania
Strait of Messina
Pantelleria
TUNISIA
Gozo
MALTA
Valletta
Lampedusa
Pelagie Islands
43°
42°
41°
40°N
39°
38°
37°
36°
35°N
8°
9°
10°E
11°
12°
13°
14°
15°E
16°
17°
18°
19°
I. The Ligurian Coast
II. The Tuscan Islands and adjacent mainland coast
III. The Tyrrhenian Sea
IV. Sardinia
V. Sicily
VI. The Ionian
VII. The Southern Adriatic
VIII. Malta

Contents

Italian Waters Pilot

A yachtsman's guide to the west and south coasts of Italy with the islands of Sardinia, Sicily and Malta

ROD HEIKELL

Editor Lucinda Heikell

Imray Laurie Norie & Wilson

Rod Heikell

Rod Heikell was born in New Zealand and sailed hesitantly around bits of its coast in a variety of yachts. He tried racing in the Hauraki Gulf but was really not much good at it. In England he abandoned academic life and for no good reason other than curiosity bought *Roulette*, a 1950s plywood JOG yacht nearly 20ft long, and sailed it down to the Mediterranean. He worked on charter here and delivered yachts until, in ignorance of the scale of the task, he set off to write a yachtsman's guide to Greece. This was followed by guides for other countries in the Mediterranean. He has sailed back and forth between England and the Mediterranean, including a trip down the Danube and on to Turkey in *Rosinante*, an 18ft Mirror Offshore. In 1996 he took his fourth yacht, *Tetra*, to SE Asia and back for the research for *Indian Ocean Cruising Guide*. Apart from sailing the 'wrong' way and back again the 'right' way across the Indian Ocean, he has done four transatlantics on his own yachts and also cruised extensively in other parts of the world on other yachts. He is currently back at the end of a circumnavigation and sailing again in his beloved Mediterranean.

Other books by Rod Heikell

Imray Mediterranean Almanac (editor)
Mediterranean Cruising Handbook
Mediterranean France & Corsica Pilot
Mediterranean Sailing
Greek Waters Pilot
Ionian
West Aegean
East Aegean
Ocean Passages and Landfalls (with Andy O'Grady)
Turkish Waters and Cyprus Pilot
The Turquoise Coast of Turkey
The Danube – A river guide
Yacht Charter Handbook
Indian Ocean Cruising Guide
Dorling Kindersley Eyewitness Companion Sailing (contributor)
Mediterranean Islands (contributor)
Mediterranean Cruising
Sailing in Paradise: Yacht Charter Around the World

Published by
Imray, Laurie, Norie & Wilson Ltd
Wych House St Ives Cambridgeshire PE27 5BT England
✆ +44(0)1480 462114
Fax +44(0)1480 496109
Email ilnw@imray.com
www.imray.com
2011

1st edition 1983
2nd edition 1987
3rd edition 1991
4th edition 1995
5th edition 1998
6th edition 2002
7th edition 2006
Reprinted 2009
8th edition 2011

A catalogue record for this book is available from the British Library.

ISBN 978 184623 332 6

CAUTION
Every effort has been made to ensure the accuracy of this book. It contains selected information and thus is not definitive and does not include all known information on the subject in hand; this is particularly relevant to the plans, which should not be used for navigation. The author believes that his selection is a useful aid to prudent navigation, but the safety of a vessel depends ultimately on the judgement of the navigator, who should assess all information, published or unpublished.

PLANS
The plans in this guide are not to be used for navigation. They are designed to support the text and should at all times be used with navigational charts.

CORRECTIONAL SUPPLEMENTS
This pilot book will be amended at intervals by the issue of correctional supplements. These are published on the internet at our web site www.imray.com and may be downloaded free of charge. Printed copies are also available on request from the publishers at the above address.

This work has been corrected to January 2011

Printed in Singapore by Star Standard Industries Pte

Prefaces

PREFACE TO THE FIRST EDITION

'Morning came with sunny pieces of cloud: and the Sicilian coast towering pale blue in the distance. How wonderful it must have been to Ulysseus to venture into this Mediterranean and open his eyes on all the loveliness of the tall coasts. How marvellous to steal with his ship into these magic harbours. There is something eternally morning – glamorous about these lands as they rise from the sea. And it is always the Odyssey which comes back to one as one looks at them.'

D H Lawrence *Sea and Sardinia*

Most people have a love-hate relationship with Italy. I remember arriving in Camerota on mainland Italy in 1977 and squeezing into the only space between two of the sword-fishing boats that choked the harbour. 'You can't stay there,' one of the fishermen told me, 'it's for another boat arriving soon.' I was shuffled from one berth to another before finally being left alone to sleep after a long trip. When I woke up there was a bottle of wine and a fish sitting in the cockpit, a gift from the fishermen who had caused me the bother. This Janus-like quality of Italy you will encounter again and again. They believe they have a monopoly on scenic beauty, yet while telling you this, can be throwing garbage into the sea or out of a car window. They will point out a beautiful stretch of coastline and in the same breath praise a new development that will ruin it with reinforced concrete and glass monstrosities. They will scream and shout and argue and then turn and *sotto voce* murmur an apology. They have an exaggerated regard for their ancient monuments and the arts but know little about them. The men are vain and flashy. The children are spoilt rotten. The women are temperamental but beautiful. And yet you will leave Italy with regret and with a multitude of fond memories. In Camerota I spent a week talking to the fishermen, going out overnight to lay the long surface nets, I shared their meals and worked their nets. I left with regret and remember Alfio, Giorgio and the *Fabiola* with warmth to this day.

In 1981, after finishing *Greek Waters Pilot*, reading innumerable proofs and working for another season on flotilla, the publishers asked me to do a similar pilot for Italian waters. At the end of the flotilla season I sailed *Fiddlers Green* to Athens and sold her there. I bought a new boat with a name which sounded like a new antibiotic from Ciba-Geigy: *Tetranora*. I have since discovered that the name was born with the boat as she was the fourth boat (*Tetra*) owned by the original owner and she was paid for with a legacy from Aunt Nora. That's one story anyway. Built in 1962 by Cheverton at Cowes she is a ten metre sloop similar to many other craft of the era, the Rustler 31, North Sea 24, Nicholson 32, with all the vices and virtues of craft of this vintage. About the same time I also got crew, secretary and friend in the shapely form of Sharon who sailed with me, helped me maintain the boat, and typed, in often trying conditions, the manuscript for this book. In early 1982 we set off to research *Italian Waters Pilot*. We went first to the southern coast where disaster very nearly curtailed the whole venture. At anchor in the Gulf of Taranto a 15m Italian fishing boat, the skipper blinded by his own bright deck lights, almost ran us down. At 0400 in the morning he scraped our topsides at high speed and, his hydraulic winch standing proud, cut the cap-shroud clean in half. The effect felt something like being dropped from 20 feet onto solid concrete and I was out like a shot, adrenalin pumping, to shout at them to come back. It was resolved amicably, the cap shroud repaired with agricultural wire and bulldog grips, while we were given buckets of fresh fish for the remainder of the time we stayed. When I left the thought of fish was enough to make me feel ill. After the south we circumnavigated Sicily and Sardinia and then headed for Elba and the Ligurian coast. In the autumn we travelled down the mainland coast to the Strait of Messina and arrived in Malta in December running before a *gregale*. It was a busy and tiring season covering so much ground and we were well content to arrive safely in Malta. The autumn weather was not kind to us and we felt battered and bruised after some 3,000 miles exploring and mapping the harbours and anchorages of Italy.

Now it is almost time to leave Malta after committing to paper all I have found and some of what I have felt. As I think back on the previous year and other years spent in Italy, little vignettes come to mind causing a rosy glow to warm my thoughts. Italy is a country of contradictions and idiosyncrasies that can make you laugh for joy at one moment and fume the next. You will never forget it and you will be sorry to leave.

Rod Heikell
Malta
June 1983

PREFACE TO THE EIGHTH EDITION

With the fiscal thunderclouds overhead and everyone tightening their belts for this age of austerity you might think that the financial climate in Italy would mean that fewer people were out on the water, no one was spending on boats, and that there might even be a contraction in the yachting sector. Just the opposite seems to have happened. Italy has seen a boom in yachting with more people sailing, new marinas up and running or under construction with plans for more, Italian boats racing in just about every inshore and offshore series in and out of the Mediterranean, and what seems to be a mass thumb of the nose at the economic meltdown in favour of getting out on the water.

All this activity has not helped those of us on lesser budgets get around the coast without depleting already tight budgets. For this edition we have even had to introduce a new charge band, charge band 6+, for marinas charging over €100 for a 12m yacht in the high season. It used to be that just a few marinas around the Costa Smeralda and the Ligurian coast charged this amount, but now there are more. Many of these are new marinas and I guess that the cost of building a harbour and installing the infrastructure costs more, so in turn some of these new marinas charge a lot more than some of the older established marinas.

For this edition I have put together sections on 'Shoestring Cruising' for the different coasts covered in this book. A general section in the Introduction covers some general advice on getting around the coast and islands and then at the beginning of each chapter there is more specific information. Some caution is advised as things change rapidly. As we were putting this new edition together a new marine reserve was established around Procida and Ischia in the Gulf of Naples. In one stroke some of the anchorages described in the Shoestring section for that chapter were wiped out prompting a quick re-write before the book went to the printers.

Some of you may decry the establishment of marine reserves and the restrictions that imposes on us, but in an age where more of us are out there sailing around and anchoring, I for one believe that the marine environment, both the fauna and flora, do need protection. Rampant over-fishing, too many anchors ploughing the bottom and the toxic effects of boat exhausts not to mention illegal discharges from boats is not doing this enclosed sea any good. The weak attempts at 'self-policing' have not worked. So it has come down to governments to regulate and preserve areas and this does work.

Fortunately there have been fewer changes ashore and the costs of provisioning and eating out are on a par with what they were five or so years ago. It is still a joy to wander around the *panettieri e macellai responsabili candeliere* ashore to stock up on essentials and not-so-essential culinary delights. Italian food in the restaurants still reigns supreme in the Mediterranean and should be indulged. Perhaps like the Italians we need to come out of the accountants closet and spoil ourselves in these days when the press is full of doom and gloom.

One of the ways of getting around the coast on a shoestring entails sailing at the beginning and end of the season around some of the areas which are more expensive. The beginning and end of season has not been helped by marinas extending there high season to cover a longer period and by the introduction of a mid-season either side of high season that is still quite expensive. Sailing around the coast of Italy in April and May and again in late September and October means paying a lot more attention to the weather and to your own pilotage skills when assessing anchorages. It seems common these days to somehow believe that GRIB files will tell you everything you need to know about the weather for the days to come. GRIB files are computer generated and for sea areas like the Mediterranean where there are large land masses in close proximity to the sea and consequently thermal effects that influence the wind, they cannot give you the certainty they might seem to represent. Nor can they give you good information about fronts and squall activity and small local anomalies. Often some old fashioned skill looking at synoptic forecasts and interpreting the isobars and especially those little bumps and unusual patterns to the lines will at least give you a clue to watch the weather and be ready to vacate an anchorage if you have to.

Despite all of this Italy is still Italy. The coasts and islands are still a wonderful cruising area. And you would be foolish to miss it.

Rod & Lu Heikell
London 2010

Acknowledgements

Lu as ever is my shipmate and keeps a tight hand on the toil of adjusting waypoints and taking new ones, refining the pilotage notes, and amending the plans. She is the most wonderful pedantic soul in the world, nearly as pedantic as I am.

We receive a huge amount of feedback from sailors; a vital ingredient as we endeavour to keep up with the rapid development of yacht facilities around the coast. Our grateful thanks to everyone who took the trouble to write and email, with special thanks to Kerr Whiteford, Tim Herbert-Smith, David Youngman on S.Y. *Galloper*, JH Wallace and Dave Kitson who contributed copious perceptive notes and some wonderful photos; many of which you will see in this edition. Also thanks to Luisa Bresciani, Steve Etchells, Nicholas Herdon, Vyv Cox, Isabelle and Joseph Torradellas, Paul and Lorraine Briggs on S.Y. *Moon Monkey*, Graham Adam, Jay Hudson and Yves Rousselin. Peter Stogis, Dick Moore, Doug Roberts and Sara Boys on S.Y. *Mindemoya of Leelanau*, John Heaney and John Hollamby also sent in information. Over many years Jim Parish sent us a steady stream of insightful corrections, but is sadly no longer with us and we will miss his acuity. La Maddalena National Park, Marina di Stintino, Marina di Sant Elmo, Ser-Mar and Aquatica Marina all provided photos and data from Sardinia. Marina Molo Vecchio, Marina di Varazze, Base Nautica Flavio Gioia, Superyacht Services (Viareggio), Marina di Stabia, Marina di Riposto, Cantiere Navale Balsamo and Marina Riva di Traiano also contributed. We have been given kind permission to use photographs from the Italian Government Tourist Board ENIT, and the Malta Tourism Authority.

Also our thanks to the Cruising Association, especially Peggy and Michael Manton who collate and pass on reports from CA members. Likewise Ros Hogbin at the Royal Cruising Club.

Willie Wilson, Elinor Cole, Clare Georgy and all the team at Imray have knocked our plans and text into shape with their customary skill and patience; the mistakes, though, are ours.

As always we look forward to hearing your comments and corrections via Imray.

KEY TO SYMBOLS USED ON PLANS

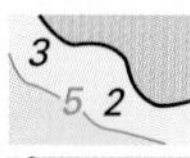 depths in METRES

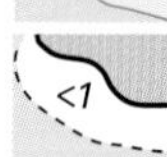 shallow water with a depth of 1m or less

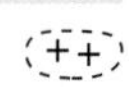 rocks with less than 2 metres depth over them

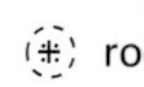 rock just below or on the surface

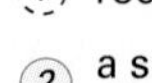 a shoal or reef with the least depth shown

 wreck partially above water

 wreck

dangerous wreck with depth over it

 eddies

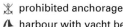

 rock ballasting on a mole or breakwater

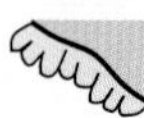 above-water rocks

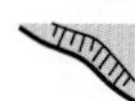 cliffs

 waypoint

 anchorage

prohibited anchorage

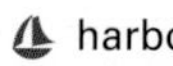 harbour with yacht berths

 yacht harbour/marina

visitors' berths

 fish farm

church

mosque

windmill

wind turbines

chimney

castle

airport

ruins

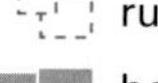 houses/buildings

port authority

port of entry

customs

travel-hoist

 shower

Toilets

water

post office

electricity

fuel

chandlers

tourist information

crane

marshy ground

pine

trees other than pine

yacht berth

local boats (usually shallow or reserved)

beacon

port hand buoy

starboard hand buoy

mooring buoy

Characteristics

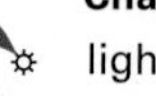 light

lighthouse

F fixed

Fl. flash

Fl(2) group flash

Oc. occulting

R red

G green

W white

M miles

s sand

m mud

w weed

r rock

KEY TO QUICK REFERENCE GUIDES

Shelter
A Excellent
B Good with prevailing winds
C Reasonable shelter but uncomfortable and sometimes dangerous
O In calm weather only

Mooring
A Stern-to or bows-to
B Alongside
C Anchored off

Fuel
A On the quay
B Nearby or delivered by tanker
O None or limited

Water
A On the quay
B Nearby or delivered by tanker
O None or limited

Provisioning
A Excellent
B Most supplies can be obtained
C Meagre supplies
O None

Eating out
A Excellent
B Average
C Poor
O None

Note These ratings are nothing to do with the quality of food served in restaurants, but relate only to the numbers of restaurants.

Plan
- Harbour plan illustrates text

Charges

Charges are for the daily high season rate for a 12m yacht. For smaller or larger yachts make an approximate guesstimate.

1 No charge
2 Low cost, under €25
3 Low–Medium cost, €25–40
4 Medium–High cost, €41–55
5 High cost, over €55–70
6 Very high cost, €70–100
6+ Highest cost, over €100

Introduction

What to expect

Geography

Italy is a long peninsula, jutting nearly 500M SE into the Mediterranean from the Alps. On the W side are the Ligurian and Tyrrhenian seas, at the S end the Ionian Sea, and on the W side the Adriatic. On the western side the Republic of Italy encompasses Sardinia and Sicily, the two largest islands in the Mediterranean. The backbone of the Italian peninsula is the Apennine range of mountains which terminates in the Calabrian massif and the mountains of Sicily.

- The Ligurian coast (or Italian Riviera) runs from the French border to the Magra River and is backed by the Alps rising steeply from the sea. Genoa, Italy's largest commercial port, divides Riviera Ponente (W) and Riviera Levante (E).
- The main Tuscan islands comprise Capraia, Elba, Pianosa, Giglio and Montecristo, and form part of the Tuscan Archipelago Marine Reserve. Much of the adjacent coast is comparatively low-lying.
- The Tyrrhenian Sea covers the area from Civitavecchia to Reggio Calabria in the Strait of Messina. There is a string of offlying islands: Ventotene, Ponza, Ischia Capraia, Procida and Capri. Rome and Naples lie along this coast.
- Sardinia is the second-largest island in the Mediterranean, lying immediately S of Corsica. It is home to the La Maddalena Archipelago Marine National Park and the Costa Smeralda in the N, with a string of harbours and marinas at convenient distances around the coast.
- Sicily, the largest island in the Mediterranean, lies a short hop across the Strait of Messina from the toe of Italy. The smoking bulk of Mount Etna dominates the eastern side of Sicily, and is Europe's most active volcano. Sicily is surrounded by much smaller islands: off the N coast lie Ustica and the Aeolian islands; off the W corner the Egadi Islands; and Pantelleria and the Pelagie Islands lie across the Sicilian channel not far off the Tunisian coast.
- The Ionian is perhaps the least developed part of the Italian coast, with marinas and harbours scattered sparsely along the coast, until you reach the Gulf of Taranto and turn up the heel of Italy's 'boot', and into the Adriatic.
- The Maltese Archipelago, comprising Malta, Gozo, Comino, Cominotto and Filfla, lies just 60M off the SE tip of Sicily, and its strategic importance has been recognised for millennia.

Culture

Art, opera, cinema and architecture, its history, food and language all serve to identify the *Bel Paese* as having a culture quite separate from even its nearest neighbours. Colourful street life, fabulous food and varied landscapes are other reasons why the home of the capuccino is such a popular tourist destination.

Marina, Marine and Yacht Marina

It is easy to be confused when looking at a chart and noting that there are all sorts, of 'Marinas' or 'Marines' along the coast. In Italy 'Marina' (and less commonly the plural 'Marine') is attached to the name of a village when it is located on the coast. Usually it will be the coastal village of the main village further inland. Sometimes it will have a harbour or pier for local boats, but not always. So, for example, along the S coast of Italy you will come across Palizzo Marina, Brancaleone Marina and Bovalino Marina which do not have useful harbours or a harbour at all. Around the corner above Crotone you will come across Ciro Marina and Cariati Marina which do have fishing harbours.

So, if you are looking at a chart, do not assume that there are a whole string of yacht marinas not mentioned. Hopefully any harbours useful to yachts will be in this book.

Marinas, harbours and anchorages

In recent years there have been a large number of new marinas constructed, adding to the numerous established marinas found all around the Italian coast, and more are on the way. The Italians are capable of planning, designing and building a new marina from scratch in a very short time. Most reach full operational standard within three to four years of construction starting. In most marinas you'll find top-class facilities, including shower and toilet blocks, water and electricity connections, satellite TV and internet connections. Allied to these marinas you'll often find a boatyard with lifting facilities and repair services, licensed dealers for popular equipment, and skilled workers. For more details see *Hauling and Boatyards*.

Commercial harbours will often have an area reserved for yachts, although this will vary from the well-organised yacht club pontoon to a length of quay at the end of the breakwater where you must negotiate with the local fishermen for a berth. Some harbours along the W coast are liable to silting and will have a planned programme of dredging every spring to clear the sandbanks created during the winter storms.

Secure and beautiful anchorages are easily found, although in places they may be restricted by fish farms, laid moorings or by marine reserve regulations. Italy now has 30 designated Marine Reserves and two major National Parks with marine restrictions in the waters around the coast. Restrictions apply to yachtsmen on navigation, anchoring, swimming and diving. For details see under *Other Regulations for Yachtsmen*.

Yacht clubs

In many of the harbours there exists a yacht club which leases a part of the harbour and provides facilities for members. Usually there are berths for visiting yachts for which a charge is made. For the most part visiting yachtsmen should not expect the hospitality they encounter from a club in home waters. The clubs vary from small affairs with basic facilities, perhaps an office and cold showers, to luxurious clubs with every facility. The latter often have many members who never go on the water and belong to the club solely for prestige and for the use of the bar and restaurant. If a visiting yachtsman is welcomed by a yacht club, treat it as a bonus.

Ormeggiatori

Literally translated, these are the people who tie up your yacht for you and if necessary fuel, water and clean it. Many of the harbours in Italy have a section of the quay or a basin run by a co-operative of *ormeggiatori* who will charge you for a berth. The co-operative leases the quay or basin and so carries out a legal business.

However, some self-styled *ormeggiatori* do not have the lease of a section of quay and in the words of an Italian friend of mine are simply 'little *mafiosi*'. The problem confronting a yachtsman is whether or not to pay up. Self-styled *ormeggiatori* usually control the water anyway so if you refuse to pay the berthing fee (often negotiable) you may end up simply paying more for water. Even worse, they may be buddies of the port police who will then come along and hassle you. To an extent you must play the situation by ear, but it is always prudent to stay on the right side of even self-styled *ormeggiatori*.

Visitors' berths

With few exceptions most of the marinas and many harbours in this book have visitors' berths. Some marinas have visitors' berths numbered in three figures while others have just a few. There has been some ire expressed over the fact that yachts arriving in the high season cannot find a berth at a chosen marina and there has been some muttering about whether these berths exist at all. All visitors' berths listed in this book are obtained from the marina concerned and the number of visitors' berths is obtained from figures published or given by the marina. In the case of most marinas it is 10% of the total number of berths.

What it is important to remember is that visitors' berths apply equally to Italian boats in transit as well as to boats from outside Italy. I may be stating the obvious, but a visitors berth is for any boat not permanently berthed at the marina in question. The problem is compounded by the fact that Italian owners will often move their boat to a chosen marina somewhere else for two or three months in the high season. While this leaves a berth free in their normal marina where they have a permanent berth (and continue paying for it), it occupies one of the visitors' berths available at the marina where the boat is to be berthed for part of the high season. You don't need too many of these quasi-visiting boats to clutter up visitors' berths in the high season.

In my experience all marina managers will try to squeeze you in whenever it is possible in the high season. Many of them go out of their way to find visiting yachts a berth. If at all possible try to arrange a berth in known crowded marinas in advance. If you intend to base yourself for a week or more in a marina in the high season then book ahead. Many of these marinas have pre-notification forms on their websites which can be printed and posted, or emailed. Alternatively, try to avoid popular parts of the Italian coast in the high season from mid-June to mid-September. The Riviera around to La Spezia, the Tuscan islands, Ponza, the Bay of Naples, the Lipari islands, and northern Sardinia are chock-a-block in July and August. And don't give the marina manager a hard time because none of his 80 visitors' berths are empty.

Charges

A charge is made in all of the marinas and most of the harbours. The charge band system used here applies to the highest season charge which generally runs from July to the end of August. Most marinas have a 'mid' season price band which usually includes May, June, September and October when prices are approximately 20% less than the high season. Low season prices can be as much as 40–50% less than the high season price. A few marinas have no 'mid' season and charge peak prices right through the summer. Most will have deductions for longer-term berths (if they have room), and winter rates are considerably less. Even along the popular marinas on the Riviera and Tuscany good winter rates can be found and it is worth thinking about somewhere along this coast in preference to, say, some of the more remote purpose-built marinas which tend to become ghost towns in the winter.

Charge bands are based on a daily rate for a 12m yacht in the high season:

1	No charge	
2	Low cost	Under €25
3	Low–Medium cost	€25–40
4	Medium–High cost	€41–55
5	High cost	Over €55–70
6	Very high cost	€70–100
6+	Highest cost	Over €100

If a yacht intends to spend some time in a particular marina then it is recommended you phone, fax or email to the marina in question asking for up-to-date berthing charges for the period required. If you are cruising in an area then enquire amongst other yachtsmen as to the charges in any marinas you intend to visit.

All public harbours (Porto Comunale) should by law allow you to tie up on the public section of the quay (*banchina di transito*) free of charge for 24 hours. In practice this does not happen often although some public harbours and even some marinas give you 24 hours' berthing free. In recent years more marinas, especially around the Ligurian coast, seem to have allowed 24 hours free, but in general do not expect it and do not try to argue the case. You will not come off best in the argument and you may find yourself with nowhere to go at all, even if you do decide in the end to pay (see *Ormeggiatori* section above).

Some expensive areas are the southern half of the Riviera, especially around Rapallo; around Rome; around Naples; and around the north and northeast of Sardinia. In most places you can move between cheaper marinas or anchorages in the high season and then explore these more expensive summer areas out of high season with the added bonus that there will be fewer people around.

Shoestring cruising in Italy

In General

Parts of Italy are expensive to cruise in the peak summer season.

Marina prices vary from year to year (and not in line with inflation) and the period of low/mid/high seasons is varied as well. The only way you can find this out is to look on the website for a marina, if there is one, and check that it has been updated with the prices for the current year. Alternatively phone ahead if your Italian is good enough or there is someone in the marina office who speaks English (or your own language if not English). Phoning ahead is especially important where *ormeggiatori* run a section of quay or pontoons. Many now have email which may be easier if you have time.

My advice is to research on the web and plan the route according to prices in marinas and anchorages available. For example you could cruise the Ligurian coast early in the season and then cross to Corsica and Sardinia for the high season where there are a reasonable number of anchorages which avoids high season prices in marinas. Then at the end of the season cross back over to the Italian mainland coast and cruise down it to whatever your destination is. If you are on a tight budget then avoid cruising areas where the only option is a marina or *ormeggiatori*

Anchoring

Where there are options for anchoring most will be free, though in some places the best areas for anchoring have moorings for which a charge is made. Charges for moorings can vary widely but can be very high in the high season. In addition some good anchorages are buoyed off for swimming areas and this means you have to anchor further out where there is less shelter and deeper depths to anchor in.

The anchoring option does mean you will have to judge what wind and sea are doing and also think about safe havens. The prevailing wind directions given are for settled weather and it just needs a few squashed isobars nearby to disturb the normal pattern and give an increased wind strength or to change the wind direction. If an anchorage becomes untenable, and some of them inevitably will, you need to have a plan and a nearby safe harbour in mind along with a bit of prior research on getting to it. In most cases you need to think about harbours in several different directions so you can easily reach another anchorage or harbour without battling for miles to windward.

You will need to have decent anchoring gear. On *seven tenths* (36ft and 7½ tons unladen) we used a 16kg CQR, 60m of 8mm chain and 30m of 14mm nylon rode. On *Skylax* (46ft and 14 tons unladen) we use a 25kg Delta, 80m of 10mm chain and 25m of 16mm nylon rode. To back the main bower anchor up I have always used a Fortress of appropriate size: 4.5kg on *seven tenths* and 9.5kg on *Skylax*. You don't need much chain on these anchors, I use around 2–3m of 8mm or 10mm chain, and the rest is around 35m of nylon three strand of appropriate size. The advantage of using an aluminium anchor like the Fortress as a second anchor is that its easy to load into the dinghy and row or motor out. Its not always that easy to get them up. The Fortress or any Danforth type anchor should not be used as a bower anchor as they are easily fouled by the chain as you swing around.

leased berths in high season and try to do so in low season or at worst in mid-season.

In some harbours you will find that there is a *Banchina di Transito*. This is essentially a free or moderately charged berth for craft in transit. It's important to know that it is not solely for yachts. It may also be full of local craft. There always seems to be some confusion when the locals and even the officials realise that you know of the existence of the *Banchina in Transito* and in some cases officials have ordered yachts to leave the quay. Whether this is from associations with the local *ormeggiatori* or a genuine confusion over whether foreign yachts can use the quay is difficult to know, but probably a bit of both.

It used to be a general rule that the further S you went down the coast of Italy the cheaper marinas and *ormeggiatori* leased quays and pontoons got. That is no longer true and around Sicily and parts of Sardinia some marinas will charge astronomical fees in the high season. Around the Ligurian coast some marinas have very reasonable charges in the low and mid-season. Although not a general rule, it seems that older more established marinas don't charge what new-build marinas charge, possibly because the infrastructure for a new marina costs relatively more these days. It's not a hard and fast rule but might be useful.

Details on cruising on a shoestring can be found at the beginning of each chapter.

GETTING TO ITALY AND GETTING AROUND

Berthing

In all harbours, go stern-to or bows-to the quay with an anchor laid out to hold you off the quay. In the marinas and some yacht club berths there will be laid moorings tailed to the quay or to a buoy which you should pick up. Occasionally marinas will have finger pontoons instead of laid moorings for smaller yachts. In some marinas you will be given some assistance to berth, though more often than not, you will be left to your own devices. It takes some skill to go stern-to, especially if there is a strong crosswind and nearby anchor chains. Always have plenty of fenders out and, when close to the quay, warp the yacht into place rather than using the engine.

For yachts up to 11–12m long it is easier to go bows-to as a yacht can be more easily manoeuvred into a berth when going forward and if ballasting extends a short distance underwater (as it sometimes does) then damage to the rudder is avoided. Moreover, there is a gain in privacy as people on the quay cannot see into the cockpit or the cabin.

Going stern-to or bows-to rather than alongside prevents vermin, particularly cockroaches, from coming on board and avoids damage to a yacht from wash or a surge in the harbour. Even if there is room to go alongside, it is nearly always better to go stern or bows-to.

Gang planks (passerelles)

A gang plank can be an elaborate affair or simply a plank. It is useful to have a pair of small wheels at the outer end of the board so that the end of the board scraping over the quay does not annoy you or your neighbours. A small aluminium ladder can be easily made into a smart passerelle.

Some yachts which always berth bows-to have had stainless steel boarding ladders made up that hang over the pulpit and make getting on and off so much easier.

Chartering

Italy has comparatively few charter yachts in a limited number of bases around the coast. Most fleets are concentrated around the Tuscan coast and islands, northern Sardinia and the bay of Naples, although you'll also find charter boats in northern Sicily and southern Sardinia. Most yacht charters are based on bareboat or skippered charter, and vary from standard 11–15m yachts to 150m superyachts with all the toys. For more details on chartering in Italy refer to Rod Heikell's *Sailing in Paradise* (Adlard Coles Nautica).

Getting to Italy and getting around

By air

Low-cost airlines have transformed the business of air travel in Europe, often offering flights to some destinations for little more than the fee for departure taxes. Likewise, internet booking has become one of the best ways to secure the lowest prices.

If booking some time in advance, low-cost airlines are probably the best bet, as prices are based on a first-come-lowest-price basis. The closer you are to travelling, the higher the price will be, and it can sometimes be better to check prices against the larger airlines' scheduled flights when booking at short notice. Charter flight operators are also a useful place to check for flights only. If you are only flying one way on a charter flight you may find it is sometimes cheaper to buy a return and discard the return part. Within Italy there are regular internal flights between major cities, and to the smaller islands. Flights from London are shown below. Flights from other British/European cities are also widely available.

By ferry

Italy has a comprehensive ferry network, joining major mainland ports to Spain, Morocco, Tunisia, Sardinia, Sicily, Malta, Greece and Turkey. Local ferries service smaller islands in Italian waters. A comprehensive list of services and links to each ferry company is listed on the Italian site below, with English, French and German language versions. Tickets may be booked on various websites in advance, although foot passengers are usually able to book at the port on the day.

www.traghettionline.net

By train

National and local trains service an efficient and relatively cheap rail network. International trains run to Rome and Milan from major European cities including Paris, Munich and Barcelona. The Naples-

Airline	*Destinations*	*Website*
Easyjet	Pisa/Rome/Naples/ Olbia/Cagliari/Palermo	www.easyjet.com
Ryanair	Genoa/Pisa/Rome/ Brindisi/Alghero/ Palermo/Trapani	www.ryanair.com
Alitalia	Most Italian airports via Rome	www.alitalia.com
Meridiana	Pisa/Florence/Cagliari Internal flights to most cities, including Pantelleria/Lampedusa	www.meridiana.it
British Airways	Scheduled flights to major cities	www.ba.com
Lufthansa	Scheduled flights from many European cities	www.lufthansa.com
Bargain Holidays	Package deals/flights only	www.bargainholidays.com
Expedia	Holidays/hotels/car hire and flights	www.expedia.co.uk

Nice mainline serves the west coast. Local and national services run between the major Italian towns and cities.
www.trenitalia.com

By car

National and international car hire companies will be found in most towns and villages around the coast. Prices are comparable with the rest of western Europe.

Yacht facilities

Water

The water is nearly always safe to drink although in some out-of-the-way places it pays to treat it with caution. Some taps may be labelled *aqua non potabile* in which case do not drink the water on any account. In some of the marinas there will be taps for both potable and non-potable water, the latter for washing the boat down – enquire if you are uncertain which is which. If you are uncertain about water quality then some sort of water treatment should be used. Water purifying tablets are cheap and can be bought almost anywhere. Alternatively a little bleach solution or a few grains of potassium permanganate will get rid of most nasties when added to water of doubtful quality.

In restaurants everyone drinks bottled mineral water, an affectation that does not reflect upon the quality of the tap water and a habit not to be encouraged on board as many thoroughly obnoxious plastic mineral water bottles already litter the seas and shores of Italy. A length of hosepipe about 50m long is useful for filling water tanks. A selection of connectors should be carried.

The recent mild and dry winters have caused water shortages in Italy as elsewhere in Europe and the world for that matter. Though many optimistically pin their hopes on a mini-climatic aberration that will right itself in a few years, the evidence for global warming continues to accumulate and if this is so then water poverty in the Mediterranean is going to become a fact of life. Already I see yachtsmen, both local and foreign, surreptitiously washing down their boats when there is a ban on this activity and they have only themselves to blame if they are denied water altogether. If you think I am being melodramatic then let me tell you that in some small ports yachtsman have been denied water. I can see the day when reverse osmosis water-makers become a common piece of equipment on board cruising yachts. Until then I suggest you top up the water tanks whenever you can and refrain from wasting water by washing down the boat in places where there is a water shortage.

Fuel

Where fuel is shown in the pilotage notes as being close to or on the quay I am referring in most cases to diesel fuel. In some cases petrol will also be available, but usually you will have to go to a petrol station in town to obtain it. In some places diesel can be delivered to the quay by tanker.

Electricity

In all marinas and some other harbours it is possible to plug into mains electricity on the pontoon or quay. Most marinas include electricity in the berthing charge so it is worthwhile being equipped to take advantage of it. Unfortunately this will mean a variety of connectors to plug into whatever socket a marina is using and it is really a matter of adapting what you have in the best way possible. Most connections are 220V 50Hz, but some marinas also have 380V. In some of the municipal harbours where electricity and water 'boxes' have been installed the connections can be potentially dangerous and the supply is prone to surges. Turn off any sensitive equipment on board or it may be damaged by the irregular nature of the supply. If you do not have a reverse polarity indicator on your 220V distribution panel, invest a few pounds in a plug-in polarity checker – it will tell you if there are any faults in the shore-side wiring before you use the supply.

When you are away from all-singing and dancing marinas then you will have to rely on generating the stuff yourself. As you get towards southern Italy and around the islands, including parts of Sicily and Sardinia, you must be pretty well self-sufficient for electricity on board and that means totting up your consumption and fitting batteries with sufficient capacity and the means to charge them. Most yachts opt for solar panels or wind generators to top up the charging from the engine alternator. In addition it is worthwhile fitting a 'smart' regulator to the alternator in place of the standard regulators supplied by the manufacturers. It may also be possible to fit two alternators to an engine depending on the relative size of the engine to the boat.

If at all possible don't rely on running a generator to top up batteries and run equipment. There is nothing more irritating than to be near a boat with its generator running in what would be an otherwise tranquil harbour or anchorage. If you really need to pollute the air with engine and exhaust noise and pollute the water with exhaust emissions, please go to a noisy harbour, preferably one that is already suffering from a diesel slick, and stay there to run your generator.

Gas

In most of the larger towns Camping Gaz can be obtained. If a yacht is fitted with Calor Gas type bottles an adaptor can be bought in Italy to take Italian gas bottles. If staying for an extended period and if a lot of gas is used for hot water, heating, or cooking, then it is worth changing over to Italian gas which is comparatively cheap. There are numerous brand names which I have lumped into the generic Italgaz as a convenient shorthand.

Holding tanks

Holding tanks are not yet required by law for private yachts visiting Italian waters, but despite this fact you can still be fined for pumping out a toilet in

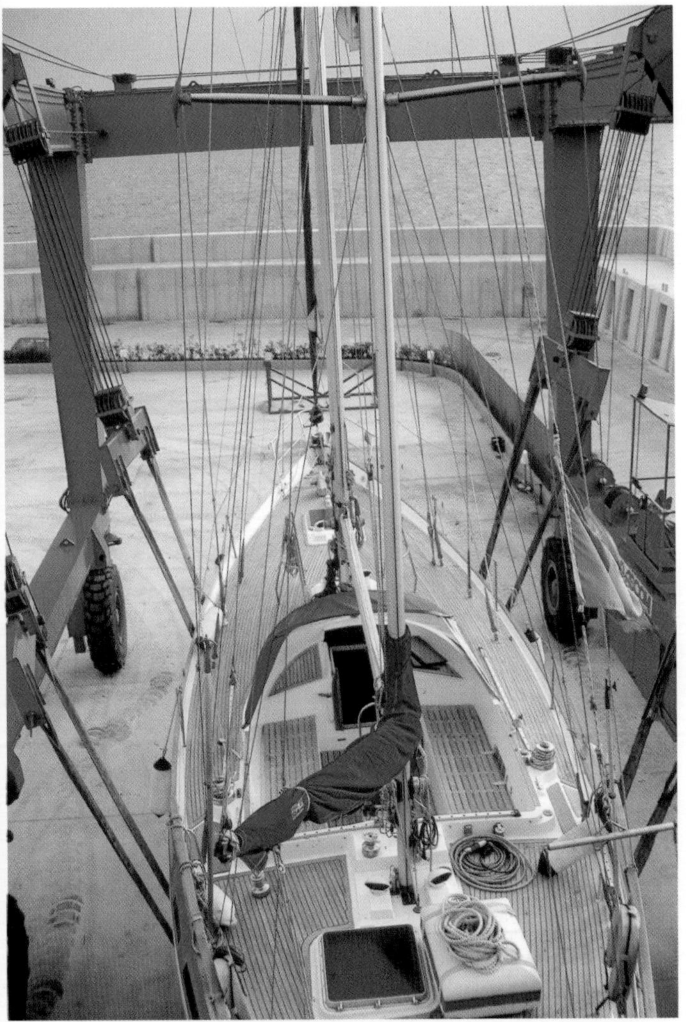

All over Italy there are boatyards where you can be hauled out for the winter. Most are comprehensively equipped

harbour or in an enclosed bay. It is likely that a requirement for holding tanks will be made law at some time in the future.

Any holding tank installation must be able to pump out at sea (the requirement is theoretically three miles offshore) as few marinas and no harbours have pump-out facilities ashore. Every yacht should endeavour to do its bit to keep harbours and anchorages free of black water (toilets as opposed to grey water from showers and sinks) and either use toilets ashore or utilise the holding tank on board. If you are not going three miles offshore then I would suggest that two miles offshore is better than in the harbour or anchorage.

The installation must be installed with odour-free hose, a good-sized vent/breather and preferably a vent filter of which there are several available on the market. The combination of these three ingredients will keep holding tank smells at bay, assuming the rest of the installation is professionally fitted and a stainless steel (or preferably polypropylene) tank is used. The holding tank on my boat is installed in the heads and the toilet pumps through it all the time. To use the holding tank the toilet outlet seacock is closed. To empty the holding tank the outlet is opened and gravity and a bit of pumping do the rest.

Yacht spares

Most yacht spares are easily obtained in Italy or can be ordered at short notice. If you are having small items brought in it is probably best to use a courier company like DHL or Fedex rather than use the postal system which can at times be infuriatingly slow.

Italy manufactures a wide range of yacht fittings and a little research may uncover a similar item or in some cases you will find items manufactured in Italy and re-branded in other countries. This applies particularly to refrigeration systems (many components are manufactured in Italy and bolted together by other companies), engine spares, some electronic items (the two major electronic chart systems, *C-Map* and *Navionics*, are both Italian), paints and varnishes (Veneziani products are world renowned), deck hardware and interior and exterior fittings.

If you are in southern Italy it may be worth waiting until you get to Malta, where there is a good choice of authorised dealers and spares can be easily ordered if they are not in stock.

Antifouling

A yacht bottom fouls more easily in the warm waters of the Mediterranean than it does in more northerly waters. Consequently a more effective antifouling must be used.

Eroding antifoulings made by International Micron, Blakes, Seajet and Hempel's work well as long as your boat is moving and not sitting still at anchor or berthed for long periods, when the build-up of weed and coral worm overcomes the antifouling's ability to erode itself and scrubbing down just takes the antifouling off. Hard scrubbable antifoulings work well and although they tend to foul more quickly than eroding antifoulings, they can be satisfactorily rubbed down without removing all the antifouling.

Locally made antifouling of the soft type is easily found, cheap, and effective – you cannot of course rub it down through the season. Generally for an eight-month season it copes well, with fouling just beginning in the eighth month.

Hauling out

All over Italy there are boatyards which haul out yachts by travel-hoist, crane, or on a patent slipway. Some of the yards cater mostly for local fishing boats while others are equipped to deal with all yacht repairs to a very high standard. In an emergency it is usually possible to find a crane to haul a small to medium size yacht onto the quay in even quite small fishing harbours. The following list of yards are those frequented by foreign cruising yachts. They are not necessarily the best or most comprehensively equipped, simply the most popular.

Liguria

San Remo 30-ton hoist and slipway for larger craft up to 400 tons.

Marina degli Aregai 100-ton travel-hoist.

Porto Maurizio 50-ton travel-hoist. 50-ton slipway. Limited hard standing but right in town.

W-Service (Savona) Hauling facilities for very large yachts.
Marina di Varazze 100-ton travel-hoist.
MA.RI.NA. Service (Genoa) 40-ton travel-hoist. 100-ton hydraulic trailer.
Cantieri Porto di Genova 30-ton travel-hoist and crane. 150-ton slip.
Amico & Co (Genoa) 300 to 510-ton travel-hoists. 200m dry dock.
Santa Margherita Ligure Small and medium size yachts craned onto the hard and slipway for larger craft up to 120 tons.
Lavagna 50-ton travel-hoist and slipway for larger craft up to 300 tons.
Le Grazie 1,000-ton slipway. Most yacht repairs.
Marina del Fezzano (La Spezia) 60-ton travel-hoist.
Marina Porto Lotti (La Spezia) 160-ton travel hoist. Lots of boat building yards nearby.

Tuscan Islands and adjacent coast
Esaom Cesa (Elba) 250/50-ton travel-hoists. Most yacht repairs.
Marina di Carrara Crane up to 150 tons. Slipway. Most yacht repairs. Sympathetic little town with enough facilities nearby.
Viareggio Hoists and cranes up to 1,000 tons. Mostly big yachts undergoing refits here. Yard and facilities are close to town.
Marina Cala di Medici 100-ton travel-hoist.
Etrusca Marina 110-ton travel-hoist. Boatyard part of the Nautor Group.
Marina Punta Ala 90-ton travel-hoist.
Porto Santa Stefano Cantiere dell'Argentario can haul craft up to 400 tons. Open and covered storage and extensive workshops.
Marina Cala Galera 40-ton travel-hoist.

Tyrrhenian Sea
Fiumicino Small and medium-size yachts craned onto the hard.
Fiumare Grande Tecnomar haul yachts up to 300 tons depending on draught. Close to Rome. Also *Darsena Netter* and *Porto Romano*.
Porto Turistico Porto di Roma (Ostia) 400-ton travel-hoist.
Base Nautica Flavio Gioia 50-ton travel-hoist. 400-ton slipway. Good repair facilities. Convivial place.
Salerno Craft up to 500 tons hauled on a slipway. Open and covered storage.

Sardinia
Castelsardo 50-ton travel hoist
Porto Cervo 40-ton travel-hoist. Craft up to 350 tons hauled on a slipway. Open and covered storage.
Olbia Several yards with the capacity to haul yachts up to 150 tons. Extensive repair facilities.
Porto Ottiolu 40-ton travel-hoist.
Santa Maria Navarrese 40-ton travel-hoist.
Arbatax Marina 200-ton travel-hoist.
Motomar Sarda (Cagliari) 50-ton crane. 50-ton slipway for larger yachts.
Marina Torre Grande 65-ton travel-hoist.

Sicily
Marina Porto dell'Etna (Riposto) 160-ton travel-hoist. 45-ton crane. Boat-mover.
Catania 40-ton crane. Slipway up to 150 tons.
Porto Palo Slipway for trawlers, although several yachts have also been hauled here.
Trapani 30-ton travel-hoist.

Ionian/S Adriatic
Sibari 50-ton travel-hoist. Workshops.
Brindisi Marina 100-ton travel-hoist planned, along with boat-mover and small crane.

Malta
Manoel Island Marina 100-ton travel-hoist.
Manoel Island Yacht Yard 30-ton travel-hoist and slipway for craft up to 500 tons. Open storage for 250 small and medium size yachts. Extensive repair facilities.

Wintering afloat

Just as certain yards are popular with cruising yachts, so too certain harbours are popular for wintering afloat.

The following harbours are often used: San Remo, Santa Margherita Ligure, Rapallo, Portoferraio, Marina di Varazze, Genoa, Marina Cala di Medici, Cala Galera, Fiumicino, Porto Turistico di Roma (Ostia), Base Nautica Flavio Gioia (Gaeta), Vibo Valentia, Tropea, Fertilia (Alghero, Sardinia), Sibari, Brindisi Marina, Malta.

Macho man

In recent years there has been an increase in small craft based in Italy and, sad to say, many of these are driven by souls with the money to acquire a boat but none of the wit to learn seamanship and care for others using the sea. I have to say most of these newly acquired craft are motorboats and while some are skippered in a sensible and seamanlike way, others are driven by macho man and all the baggage he carries with him. While I am quite happy for these sad souls to crash around where they affect no-one else, not surprisingly they seem to frequent those places where others are quietly enjoying themselves. Dangerous situations have developed, with craft entering and leaving harbour at high speed creating large amounts of wash as well as posing a danger to any craft manoeuvring within the harbour. Dangerous situations have also arisen with boats navigating around an anchorage at speed where people are swimming or pottering around in dinghies. Often RIBs or water-bikes navigate carelessly and at speed in bays where people are swimming and it should be made plain to anyone doing so that not only is their sport antisocial in such situations, but it is also dangerous should they hit anyone swimming in the water.

In case anyone thinks this is a bit on the heavy side, I should say that a few years ago I was advising in a German case involving serious injury to a yachtsman who was hit by a small speedboat while swimming in Sardinia. The penalties for conviction can be severe and may involve a prison sentence, and in cases where death has occurred, a manslaughter charge can be brought if it is proved that the driver of a craft was acting in an irresponsible and dangerous manner.

Rubbish

The steady increase in man-made disposables found in the oceans and seas of the world is saddening. Around the shores of Italy there has been a steady increase in plastic refuse of all types. Much of it is thrown into the sea by Italians themselves, but shore-based tourists and, unfortunately, some yachtsmen, are also to blame. In nearly every harbour there are containers for litter and it is here and not in the sea that it belongs.

Formalities

- All yachts entering Italy should fly the Italian courtesy ensign. Sardinian or Sicilian ensigns may also be flown when appropriate, below the Italian ensign.
- As part of the EU, any EU-registered yachts, with EU nationals on board, may enter Italy from another EU country without formalities. Such yachts must still be able to produce all necessary documents should they be requested.
- All non-EU yachts, all non-EU nationals, and any yachts entering Italy from a non-EU country, should fly a yellow Q flag and report to the authorities to complete customs and immigration formalities and apply to the Harbourmaster for a *Costituto* (an entry declaration) at the first port. A list of Capitanerie di Porto is shown below.
- Coastguard or Guardia di Finanza vessels may request a spot-check of any yacht cruising in Italian waters. These can be executed briskly, particularly around known smuggling areas, where it is not unusual for a yacht to be stopped and those on board questioned.

Immigration and border controls

The immigration controls outlined below refer solely to the individual. The vessel is considered separately under VAT regulations.

Passports or EU identity cards are required for all those on board the yacht.

European Union

An area consisting of 27 countries, with agreements on trade, security and immigration:

Austria	Germany	Netherlands
Belgium	Greece	Poland
Bulgaria	Hungary	Portugal
Cyprus	Ireland	Romania
Czech Republic	Italy	Slovakia
Denmark	Latvia	Slovenia
Estonia	Lithuania	Spain
Finland	Luxembourg	Sweden
France	Malta	United Kingdom

European Economic Area EEA

An area consisting of the EU countries plus several more with special trade and travel agreements. These 'extra' countries are all part of the Schengen area.

Non EU EEA countries:

Iceland
Liechtenstein
Norway

Switzerland is not in the EEA but has similar agreements

Schengen Agreement

An agreement between European countries which is intended to guarantee free movement of all people between participating countries. Land border controls have been lifted between participating countries, although controls may be imposed for exceptional circumstances. External borders with non-signatory countries and sea borders retain strict border controls. Anybody entering the Schengen area from outside should expect full immigration controls. Not all EU countries are signatories of Schengen, and the agreement includes the non-EU countries listed above.

Capitanerie di Porto

Regional centres are shown in **bold**

LIGURIA
- Imperia
- Savona
- **Genoa**
- La Spezia

TUSCANY
- Marina di Carrara
- **Livorno**
- Viareggio
- Portoferraio (Elba)

TYRRHENIAN SEA
- Civitavecchia
- **Rome/Fiumicino**
- Gaeta
- **Naples/Torre del Greco**
- Torre Annunziata
- Castellamare di Stabia
- Salerno
- Vibo Valentia
- Gioia Tauro
- **Reggio Calabria**

SARDINIA
- Porto Torres
- La Maddalena
- Olbia
- **Cagliari**

SICILY
- **Palermo**
- Milazzo
- Messina
- Augusta
- **Catania**
- Siracusa
- Pozzallo
- Porto Empedocle
- Mazara del Vallo
- Trapani

IONIAN/ADRIATIC
- Crotone
- Taranto
- Gallipoli
- Brindisi
- **Bari**

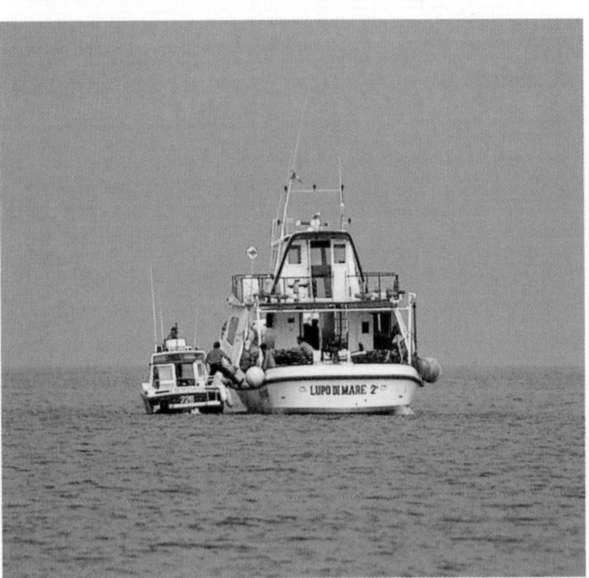

Carabinieri checking a fishing boat. Occasionally you will be stopped at sea and asked to produce your paperwork

EU members not in Schengen:

Ireland	(opted out)
United Kingdom	(opted out)
Cyprus	(due to the partition issue)
Bulgaria	(due to join in 2011)
Romania	(due to join in 2011)

EU citizens, and citizens of Schengen countries may travel and live within any Schengen country on an unlimited basis, but will be considered as a resident of any country where they reside for more than 183 days in one year.

Non EEA passport holders are permitted to stay in the Schengen area for ***up to 90 days in any six month period***. If visitors spend three months within the area, they must leave the area for at least the next three months. Some people will need to obtain a visa on or before arrival. The Schengen visa is a permit to travel within this area once the visa is granted. It is not a work permit.

Those required to obtain a visa are listed in 'Annex I' of the Schengen agreement. The list of visa-exempt countries is listed in 'Annex II'. Visitors from the following countries do not require a visa, but must travel within the restrictions noted above. The list is not exhaustive and if in doubt check the requirements with your embassy.

Australia	Israel
Brazil	New Zealand
Canada	Switzerland
Croatia	USA

In reality, visitors who do not require visas and who are travelling on their own vessel do not appear to have this time limit enforced and many have stayed longer within the Schengen area without penalty, but there is nothing to say that the regulations will not be enforced, and you may be fined for over-staying. Those who can demonstrate that they are travelling through the area are less likely to hit problems than those who stay for long periods within one country.

If you do require a visa (South African or Turkish nationals for example) it is worth applying for a multi-entry visa to assist with travel arrangements. Visas are not readily extended.

Those wishing to stay longer than three months may need to obtain a residence permit.

Selected European country checklist

Country	*EU member*	*EUROZONE member*	*EU VAT area*	*SCHENGEN area*
United Kingdom	✓	✗	✓	✗
Gibraltar	✓	✗[a]	✗	✗
Channel Islands	✗	✗[a]	✗	✗
Portugal	✓	✓	✓	✓
Azores	✓	✓	✓	✓
Madeira	✓	✓	✓	✓
Spain	✓	✓	✓	✓
Ceuta	✓	✓	✗	✗
Melilla	✓	✓	✗	✗
Canary Islands	✓	✓	✗	✓
France	✓	✓	✓	✓
Monaco	✗	✓	✓[b]	✓[b]
Italy	✓	✓	✓	✓
San Marino	✗	✓	✗	✓[b]
Vatican	✗	✓	✗	✗
Malta	✓	✓	✓	✓[c]
Slovenia	✓	✓	✓	✓[c]
Croatia	✗	✗[a]	✗	✗
Montenegro	✗	✓	✗	✗
Albania	✗	✗[a]	✗	✗
Greece	✓	✓	✓	✓
Cyprus	✓	✓	✓	✗
TRNC	✗	✗[a]	✗	✗
Turkey	✗	✗[a]	✗	✗

[a] Euros are widely accepted but not official currency.

[b] De-facto VAT and Schengen countries. In Monaco, French authorities are responsible for import VAT and policing the sea border.

[c] Not signatories to Schengen visa 3rd country lists Annex I and II, so those who need visas may differ from countries listed.

Yacht Registration Documents

Full Part 1 Registration papers (the 'Blue Book') or Part III Registration (Small Ships Register SSR) papers or their equivalent are acceptable.

Insurance

A comprehensive insurance policy for the Mediterranean is not excessively expensive but shop around the various companies to get the best deal. In Italy proof of third party insurance is required and will be examined in many ports. The insurance note must have an Italian translation showing proof of third party insurance or the authorities can hold a yacht in harbour until such proof is obtained. Most insurance companies will provide a translation given sufficient notice.

VAT

Italy, as part of the European Union (EU), comes under EU legislation regarding the implementation of the Single Market Agreement.

EU Registered Yachts

Since 1 January 1993 all yachts registered in EU countries are required to have proof that VAT has been paid or that the yacht is exempt from payment. The only exemption is for yachts built before 1 January 1985 which were in an EU country before 1 January 1993. All yachts built after 1 January 1985, and older craft imported into the EU after 1 January 1993, are liable for VAT payment.

If liable, VAT may be paid in any EU country, but is usually paid in the first country where the yacht enters the EU VAT area, and is subject to a customs

Marine reserves and national parks

Thirty marine reserves (Area Marina Protetta/AMPs) have now been established around the coasts and islands of Italy. In the area covered by this book there are 26 marine reserves and six national parks, some with controlled marine areas.

These nature and marine reserves are intended to protect the natural biodiversity in areas of special interest, and to encourage the widening of knowledge of these sensitive ecosystems. They protect geological and biological environments, birds, fish and mammals, as well as vegetation. One example of intervention in AMPs is the laying of moorings and restricting of anchoring to protect *Posidonia oceanica*, seagrass beds which are an important breeding area for certain fish.

Marine reserves (AMPs) There are three types of restricted zone. The interpretation below is my paraphrasing of the legalese in the Italian original and contains the gist of the regulations. Hopefully I have left nothing out but for a definitive guide refer to the Italian parks website www.parks.it More details are included in the pilotage notes for each AMP.

Zone A *Riserva Integrale*

1. It is prohibited to navigate or anchor in the designated area.
2. It is prohibited to fish in the area.
3. It is prohibited to pollute the area in any way including pumping bilge water or black and grey water.
4. It is prohibited to remove any plant and animal life and to interfere with the mineral strata of the area.
5. Bathing is restricted to designated areas.
6. The area is defined by yellow buoys with × topmarks at the limits of the designated area.

Zone B *Riserva Generale*

1. It is prohibited to carry out any form of fishing without an AMP permit.
2. Navigation and mooring are permitted although there may be specific restrictions at any one reserve.

Zone C *Riserva Parziale*

1. Commercial fishing is prohibited.
2. Sport fishing and scuba diving may be limited in some areas.

Marine reserves have been established in the vicinity of the following areas. New reserves may be created in the future. The zone limits for these areas are shown in the relevant chapter to that area.

LIGURIA
Isola di Bergeggi
Portofino promontory
Cinque Terre

TYRRHENIAN SEA
Secche della Meloria
Secche di Tor Paterno
Isola Ventotene and Santo Stefano
Baia Gaiola
Regno di Nettuno
Punta Campanella (Sorrento Peninsula)
Santa Maria di Castellabate
Costa degli Infreschi and della Masseta

SARDINIA
Isola dell'Asinara
Tavolara/Capo Coda Cavallo (Olbia)
Capo Carbonara
Peninsula Del Sinis and Isola Mal di Ventre (Oristano)
Capo Caccia and I. Piana

SICILY
Capo Gallo – Isola delle Femmine
Isola di Ustica
Isole Ciclopi (Acitrezza)
Plemmirio (Siracusa)
Isole Pelagie
Isole Egadi

IONIAN
Capo Rizzuto (Crotone)
Porto Cesareo (Golfo di Taranto)

ADRIATIC
Torre Guaceto (N of Brindisi)

There have been calls by the WWF for Italy, Malta and Tunisia to establish a marine sanctuary in the Sicily Channel, although no plans were known at the time of writing.

Cetacean sanctuaries
Open sea whale sanctuaries have been set up in the Ligurian Sea and around Sardinia, but no restrictions for yachts are known at this time.

National Parks
There are two national parks with controlled marine areas in Italy covered here, one covering the islands in the Tuscan Archipelago and one covering the La Maddalena Archipelago in N Sardinia. They each have different regulations, and details are given in the pilotage notes for each park. The restrictions are similar to those of the AMPs, with Zones MA and MB restricting access, fishing, diving and anchoring, but the La Maddalena National Park has several additional limitations on navigation, anchoring and swimming in different areas. Yachts wishing to visit the La Maddalena Archipelago must obtain a yacht permit, available at La Maddalena or Palau. Permits may be purchased at daily rate, fortnightly rate or monthly rate. For more details see the section in the pilotage notes on the area.

Islands in the Tuscan Archipelago National Park
Gorgona
Capraia
Elba (land restrictions only)
Pianosa
Montecristo
Giannutri

Islands in La Maddalena National Park
There are four separate island groups in the Park: the La Maddalena group; Isola delle Bisce; Isola Nibanio; and the Isola Mortoriotto group.

Note
It is not uncommon to see yachts and other small craft navigating in restricted zones. In some areas small craft have permission to navigate where larger vessels do not, and others may well be authorised vessels. In any case it is not recommended to navigate in prohibited areas.

For information and links to all the National Parks and Marine Reserves see the website www.parks.it

valuation. If it has been recently purchased, a sales invoice may be useful.

If a VAT paid boat is sold within the EU it retains its status, but if it changes hands outside the EU, it will become liable for VAT as soon as it re-enters the EU. There is also some discussion that VAT becomes liable again if a VAT paid vessel has been outside the EU for longer periods, say three years or more. But as long as you can prove that you owned the boat prior to leaving the EU, and that the vessel had VAT paid status at that time, there should be few problems.

Non-EU Registered Yachts

From 1 July 2002 yachts registered in countries outside the EU and owned by someone who is established outside the EU, are allowed 18 months Temporary Importation (TI) into the EU without incurring VAT liability. At the end of the 18-month period the yacht must leave the EU to discharge its TI liability. Once the TI liability has been discharged by exit from the EU, the vessel may re-enter the EU to begin a new period of TI. There doesn't seem to be an official minimum time that a vessel needs to be out of the EU before it may re-enter to start a new TI period, but it is important that a yacht has established a recognisable time gap, backed up with documentary proof, before attempting to re-enter the EU. For example, proof of clearing customs out of the EU, into and out of a non-EU country, such as Turkey, Tunisia or Croatia, with official documents, and, say, dated berthing receipts from the non-EU country. The lack of an official time limit means that the law is open to a certain amount of interpretation from country to country, and possibly from port to port.

Notes

1. Yachts registered in EU 'non-fiscal' areas, such as the Channel Islands, where the owner is also established, will have similar limitations.
2. Yachts registered in non-EU countries or those such as in Note 1, but with an owner who is an EU resident, have a much more limited TI period of just one month.
3. Yachts registered in EEA countries, such as Norway, are permitted six months sailing, with six months in storage (or out of the EU), in any one year.
4. The Channel Islands, Gibraltar, Ceuta, Melilla and the Canary Islands are not part of the EU VAT area.
5. If a yacht is hauled out and placed under customs bond in an EU country, it is probable that this time will not count against the 18-month limit. Thus a non-EU yacht can remain within the EU for up to two years, as long as it is hauled out and under customs bond for a period of six months. Yacht owners who are not EU nationals must also leave the EU for this 6-month period. It is essential that these terms be agreed with the relevant customs officials before assuming this interpretation of the ruling.
6. Obviously any non-EU nationals' visa obligations must be observed over and above the VAT regulations.

Small Craft Licences

At the time of publication there was no clear EU directive on small craft licences and it appeared to be up to individual countries to determine agreement on what licence or certificate corresponded with what.

The RYA *International Certificate of Competence* (ICC) is generally accepted as a minimum requirement. Check the RYA website for details:
www.rya.org.uk

Radio Licences

All yachts fitted with a VHF radio or SSB radio should carry the appropriate Ship Radio licence. DSC VHF and DSC SSB radios require new Short Range Certificate (SRC) and Long Range Certificate (LRC) user licences. The set must be registered by the national agency (the Radiocommunications Agency-OFCOM in the UK). Following registration a callsign and MMSI (Maritime Mobile Service Identity) number unique to that vessel will be issued.

These details are passed on to the Maritime Mobile Access and Retrieval (MARS) Database and are available to international Search and Rescue centres.
www.ofcom.org.uk

Recreational Craft Directive

On 15 June the Recreational Craft Directive came into existence. The original version of the RCD has undergone numerous amendments, with the latest 2004 directives becoming mandatory from 1 January 2006. The RCD dictates standards for such things as hull construction, gas and electrical installations, steering gear, fuel tanks and hoses, and engine noise and emissions. There are four design categories within the RCD, governing the maximum sea state and wind strength each class is expected to sail in.

A brief summary of the RCD is outlined below.

Category	*Significant Wave Height*	*Beaufort Wind strength*
A Ocean	Exceeding 4m	Exceeding Force 8
B Offshore	Up to and including 4m	Up to and including Force 8
C Inshore	Up to and including 2m	Up to and including Force 6
D Sheltered	Up to and including 0.5m	Up to and including Force 4

- The RCD applies to all recreational craft in the EU between 2·5 and 24m LOA.
- Any craft built after 15 June 1998 must have a CE mark and rating.
- Craft built before 15 June 1998 are exempt, as long as they were in the EU before this date.
- If they were imported into the EU after 15 June 1998 they should apply retrospectively for a Post Construction Assessment to obtain a CE mark.

Port form translation

Name of yacht	*Nome del vascello*
Country of registration	*Paese di registrazione*
Registration number	*Nummero di registrazione*
Registered tonnage	*Peso netto registrato*
Length	*Lungezza*
Beam	*Largezza*
Draught	*Pescaggio*
Type of vessel	*Descrizione del vascello*
Yacht owner	*Nome del proprietario*
Address	*Indirizzo*
Captain of yacht	*Capitano del vascello*
Passport number	*Numero di passaporto*
Crew names and passport nos	*Nomi del equipagio e numeri di passaporti*
Time and date arrival in port	*Ora e data d'arrivo porto*
Last port of call	*Precedente porto*
Next port of call	*Prossimo porto*

The estimated cost for a PCA is £2000–£6000 (in the UK). (This is the main point of contention.)

- Home built craft are exempt if not sold for five years. Historical replicas are also exempt.

It appears that the original brief, to have certain common standards of construction for the EU market so that trade within the EU could be facilitated by one kitemark, has been extended to exclude a large number of craft from being sold on in the EU market.

In practice, however, most EU countries are ignoring the requirements of the RCD regarding retrospective PCAs for the simple reason that it is just not enforceable. For boats built outside the EU before 15 June 1998 and those imported into the EU there are a series of tests which can be applied, but in Italy and throughout most of the Mediterranean this rarely happens in practice.

Port formalities

In some larger ports the authorities may want to see your boat's papers. Other details that may be required are reproduced above in English and Italian.

Other laws for yachtsmen

Smuggling

People who smuggle goods, drugs or people risk hefty jail terms and massive fines as well as the impounding of the vessel. A number of yachts have recently been implicated in high-profile drugs and illegal immigration cases in EU waters. In 2004, during the Athens Olympic games, yachts carrying large quantities of cocaine were intercepted off the Greek coast. They had been tracked right across the Atlantic and Mediterranean from the Caribbean.

In Italy the coasts of Sicily, Pantelleria and the Pelagie islands are often the first landing points for migrants fleeing poverty and persecution in Africa. Unseaworthy boats laden with would-be illegal immigrants regularly ply the brief stretch of water. Hundreds each year fail to make it, as their vessels sink or they are forced overboard by unscrupulous members of smuggling gangs. The wider issues of immigration aside, it is a very real problem for the EU authorities. Increased security around Italy's southern sea border is now the norm. NATO warships and Italian Coastguard high-speed patrol boats police these borders and regularly contact commercial sea traffic. Yachts are rarely contacted but a listening watch on VHF Ch 16 is recommended.

Antiquities

It is prohibited to export antiquities without clearance from the Export Department of the Italian Ministry of Education. An export tax will have to be paid on antiquities exported according to the value of the item.

Underwater fishing

Underwater fishing with scuba equipment is not permitted in Italian waters. However it may be used for pleasure or filming. Only those over 16 years of age are allowed to use a scuba kit or to fish underwater with a mask and snorkel. Underwater fishing is prohibited within 500m of a beach and within 500m of fishing installations and ships at anchor.

When underwater (whether scuba or snorkelling) the presence of a diver must be indicated by a float bearing a red flag with a yellow diagonal stripe. A yacht should keep well away from any area with a buoy indicating that there is a diver down.

Pets

Pets living in the EU with a 'Pet Passport' that contains details of rabies vaccinations, and other preventative treatments, may travel within the EU. The animal should also have a microchip implant to prove its identity. Pets entering the EU from a non-EU country with equal rabies status must have proof of rabies vaccination three months before entering the EU.

Note Sweden, UK, Ireland and Malta require additional preventative treatments for ticks and tapeworms for all visiting pets, and will enforce quarantine restrictions on those arriving from outside the EU.

For more information on pet passports see http://europa.eu/travel/pets/

The source of all local information (Carloforte)

Italy general information

Tourist offices

In the cities and larger towns there will generally be a local tourist office, the *Ente Provinciale Turismo*. These offices can often provide numerous free brochures and maps detailing local itineraries and places of interest as well as helping you with any small problems you may encounter.

Banks and ATMs

Banks are open from 0830 to 1330, Monday to Friday. Credit cards and travellers' cheques are widely accepted. In the cities and larger towns you will have no problem changing money or cashing cheques, but in some out-of-the-way spots it may be difficult to change foreign cash or get cash from a credit card if there is no ATM. Usually something can be sorted out, but if not it pays to carry some cash in euros to get you out of your predicament.

Credit cards (Visa and Mastercard) and charge cards (American Express and Diners) are now widely accepted and can be used for most purchases in shops, supermarkets and restaurants. Cash advances can be obtained in most places with an ATM (Automatic Teller Machine or cash machine, 'hole in the wall machine') with either Visa or Mastercard. There are still some machines which do not take non-Italian credit cards, but generally you should not have too many problems getting cash from an ATM.

Public holidays

Offices, shops and schools are closed all over Italy on the following dates:
1 January (New Year's Day)
Easter Monday
25 April (Liberation Day)
15 August (Assumption of the Virgin Mary)
1 November (All Saints' Day)
8 December (Immaculate Conception)
Christmas Day and Boxing Day

In addition there are many local feast days when offices and shops may or may not be closed. These local feast days and fiestas are celebrated in style with parades and always with fireworks. The latter can be spectacular and often you have one of the best views from your yacht as the firework displays are often staged at the harbour. On more than one occasion the fireworks have been too close for comfort when my yacht has been downwind of the display.

Health and medicines

Throughout Italy there are excellent medical facilities and even in quite small towns a qualified doctor can be found. If a British visitor wants to obtain free or reduced cost treatment under EU reciprocal agreements with Great Britain, then the documentation must be prepared in advance. The old paper form E111 has been replaced with the European Health Insurance Card (EHIC). Application forms are stamped and processed by the post office and the new credit card-sized official-looking EHIC (valid for five years) will be sent to you. This entitles you to free or reduced costs for medical treatment throughout the EEA and Switzerland. (The EEA, or European Economic Area, comprises all the EU countries plus Iceland, Liechtenstein and Norway).

The Italian national health service is the Servizio Sanitaro Nazionale (SSN), and their services are usually free. Emergency services are available through the Guardia Medica. If you have to pay any charges, keep the receipts and apply at the local health authority Azienda Unita Sanitara Locale (ASL) for a refund. Most dentists are private. For prescriptions show your EHIC to the pharmacist; some medicines are free, some have a non-refundable fee. The EHIC does not usually afford discounts for private healthcare.

For more information see the Department of Health website www.dh.gov.uk

In Italy more information is available from the ASL, or in an emergency call 112.

It is definitely worth thinking about private medical insurance if cruising abroad for some time. In most EEA countries, only part of the cost of the treatment will normally be covered and you will have to fork out for the balance.

Specially prescribed drugs should be bought in sufficient quantities in England before departure. Most drugs and medical requisites are freely available in Italy although they may be under other brand names than those common in England. Over the counter medicines are not subject to any discounts.

Drugs

A yacht should not carry illegal drugs such as marijuana or amphetamines, not to mention Class A drugs, on board as the yacht can be seized and confiscated by the *Guardia di Finanza*. Smuggling is rife in Italy and while pleasure yachts are not normally suspected or searched, the risk is not worth the consequences.

Security

While the yachtsman seems to be bothered less with theft in Italy than the land-based tourist, he should be conscious of the possibility of it. In the larger cities and particularly in Genoa, Rome, Naples and Palermo the art of purse-snatching by thieves on motor scooters and cycles is well developed. When walking in the street or market keep a tight hold on purses or cameras and keep them on the side away from the curb. Always lock your boat before leaving it and preferably do not leave a dinghy tied alongside or easily removed articles on the deck or in the cockpit.

Having said this I should say that I have never had anything stolen from my yacht, but I have heard first-hand stories of yachtsmen who have lost (usually small) articles. Another dodge of which to be wary is that of the fisherman who 'saves' your yacht and then puts a salvage claim on it. A friend of mine spent six months in Brindisi fighting a salvage claim after a local fisherman 'saved' his yacht. The service consisted of simply towing the yacht from one quay to another.

Launderettes

In the cities and larger towns laundromats where you do your own laundry can be found, but in most places laundrettes take your laundry in and do it for you. The charges for this service vary enormously so enquire beforehand as to the cost.

Mail

While the Italian postal service is reliable, it is also slow and muddled. Mail sent to a post office to be held poste restante will often be returned to the sender after a short time, although theoretically it should be held for one or two months. Parcels seem to take an age to arrive. The best policy is to have mail sent to a marina with instructions for it to be held until your arrival or to have it sent to some other private address.

Surprisingly, many courier companies cannot guarantee better than five days to places that are away from their main offices. Effectively this means that outside large cities like Genoa, Milan, Rome, Naples, etc. you will not receive courier packages in under five days.

Telecommunications

Landlines

Italy has a good telephone network incorporating direct dialling to anywhere in the world. (Country code 39.) In most places telephone cards are widely available for use in public telephones.

Note When dialling an Italian number from abroad you keep the 0 in front of the area code rather than dropping it as in most other countries.

Fax

Services can be found in the larger towns and cities, either through stationers or print shops or at post offices and public booths.

Mobile phones

Digital cellular phones with GSM (Global System for Mobile Communications) capacity can be used in Italy. Your own service provider will need to have an agreement with the main service providers in Italy (TIM, Omnitel, WIND, Telefonica). EU rulings have forced mobile phone companies to reduce their 'roaming' rates, although costs are still considerably higher than at home – your home allowances will not work abroad. And don't forget that it is still normal for you to be charged to receive calls.

If you are going to spend some time in Italy, it is worth getting a Italian chip with a new phone number for your phone. You can then ask people to call you on your Italian number rather than your home country mobile where the call is costing YOU a lot of money. I use my UK mobile when collecting email and making short calls out. Some Italian chips also allow data transmission at reasonable rates (see below).

If you are planning to spend a lot of time abroad in different countries, it may be worth looking at some new companies who provide a SIM card which can be used in many different countries, but charge very little (often nothing) to receive calls. Call charges are in line with typical local GSM costs, and they operate on a pay-as-you-go basis. Top-ups may be made using the phone or over the internet.

Email and internet access

There are a number of ways of sending and receiving email while cruising in Italy. This guide assumes that you already have an Internet Service Provider (ISP), and are familiar with collecting mail through a mail portal such as Microsoft Outlook. It is also useful to be able to access your mail through the mail server's own webmail facility (i.e. via an internet log-in site, such as Yahoo or Hotmail). The following is a brief round up of ways and means of doing so:

1. **Wireless Internet Access (Wi-Fi) using a laptop computer or Smartphone** Many marinas, hotels, cafés, bars, libraries and internet cafés are installing Wi-Fi networks, some of which are provided free of charge, or unsecured, others require a password. Subscribers may pay a one-off connection charge and/or 'pay-as-you-go' for minutes/hours/days online access. Costs are reasonable for a fast connection, and you don't need to run up unseen bills on your GSM phone. Most new laptops have built-in wireless modems and will 'search' automatically for available Wi-Fi networks. All you need to do is to identify which network you wish to connect to. You can also buy Wi-Fi aerials which enable you to pick up signals at greater distances. Once connected, you can use your own mail portal such as MS Outlook, use a webmail facility, and of course access the internet with very fast broadband connections. It is likely that Wi-Fi technology will continue to develop, and will probably become the standard method of accessing the internet using phones, handheld computers and laptops.
   Note Wi-Fi is a generic term used here to describe all wireless networks.
2. **Using a laptop with a broadband data dongle or phone** Most local phone companies offer pay-as-you-go SIM cards with data capability, which will utilise 3G technology to give you broadband speed if the network is capable. If using a dongle you simply plug in and go. If you use your phone you will need to connect to the computer either using a cable or Bluetooth technology. The advantage of using a phone is that if a 3G network is not available you can also use the GPRS system – not as fast but adequate for email and light surfing. Much is written elsewhere on the ins and outs of both systems, but generally costs are linked to data quantity downloaded/uploaded, and can be arranged on a daily or monthly basis. Shop around the various companies, and in many larger towns the staff will have a good knowledge of the options and will be able to get you what you want. Costs are

generally higher than using Wi-Fi networks, but you have the advantage of being able to use it anywhere where you have a phone signal.

Many people now use a smart phone to access their email accounts, and touch-screen keypads make sending emails easy. The latest phone screens are large enough to be able to usefully use the internet. A 'roaming' EU data add-on to your existing phone contract costs around £10 a month, with a reasonable download limit. Check with your provider as roaming data charges vary enormously.

3. **Internet cafés** Many quite small places have an internet café these days and if you have an internet webmail provider then it takes little time to download and send mail, using a USB stick if you need to save stuff. Costs are usually low and of course connection rates are high with many places on broadband or ASDL connections. As mentioned above, many internet cafés also have a Wi-Fi network, or a cable network which you can use your laptop to connect to.
4. **HF Radio** You can send text based emails and request GRIB files via HF radio and Pactor modem. Data rates are slow, typically less than 4KBPS, but costs for the service are relatively inexpensive and you can send and receive email directly from your boat, anywhere in the world. Annual contracts are around $250US and emails are free to send and receive. A Pactor Modem costs around £650.

For details on systems using satellite phones, HF radio, acoustic couplers and other systems, please refer to the *Mediterranean Cruising Handbook* (Imray).

Voice over Internet Protocol (VoIP)

Using a laptop with a broadband connection and a simple headset, many people are using VoIP to make telephone calls. You need to subscribe to a VoIP provider, and set up an account and username to use the service. Call charges are a fraction of those incurred using a GSM phone, and calls between subscribers of the same provider are free. The only downside for travellers is the need to be connected to a broadband network. Skype is probably the best known service, although there are now many companies offering similar services.

Tropea. Provisioning is a delight all over Italy

Seafood (and other) delights, Ponza

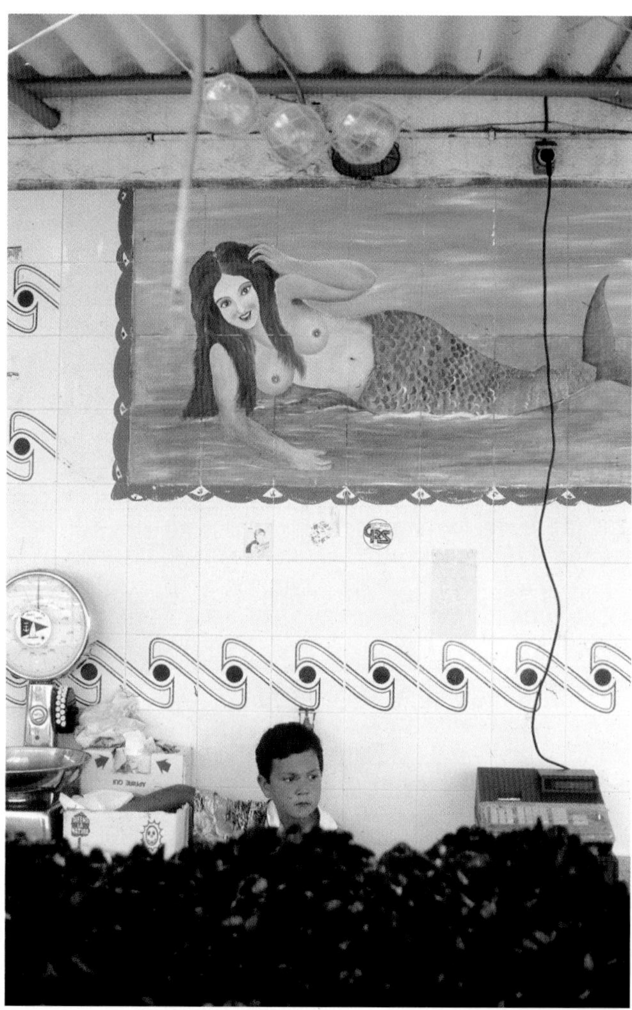

WINE

Italy has always been known as the land of wine. The ancient Greeks called it Oenotria – literally, the country of wine. Today Italy continues to produce a large number of quality wines which, although not always well known, compare well with other good wines from Europe and elsewhere. Until recently, few had received international recognition and only names like Barbaresco, Barolo, Brunello di Montalcino, Chianti, Gattinara, Nobile di Montepulciano, Recioto Amarone Soave and Verdicchio were commonly known.

A large part of the reason for this was the general chaos of Italian legislation concerning verification of appellations – this masked the real quality of Italian wine. In 1992 a revised and much stricter DOC legislation was introduced and this has brought Italian appellations much closer to the essence of the French system.

Vino da Tavola (table wine) is the lowest grade classification. Despite the low classification there are some wines of excellent quality under the category. The reason for this is that some quality wine-makers decided to ignore classifications because of the chaos that ruled over appellations. You should look out for Coltassaia, Ornellaia, Sassicaia, Solaia, Tignanello and Venegazzù.

IGT (Typical Geographical Indication) is the next level up and this wine indicates the name of the area of production and sometimes the names of the grapes used. Examples are Vino Toscano, Frascati and so on.

Above this level comes *DOC (Denominazione di Origine Controllata*: Controlled Denomination of Origin). This is the reliable guarantee of good quality wine.

DOCG (the G stands for *Garantita*, guaranteed) is the top classification and was originally only granted to ten wines from top quality wine areas. Since the 1992 legislation, the difference between *DOC* and *DOCG* has started to disappear. According to current legislation there are 24 DOCGs and 297 DOCs.

Some wines, often whites, do not travel well (Frascati, for example) and should be sampled in their place of origin where they are very good. As a general rule, Italian whites should be consumed within two years. Italian reds on the other hand are generally best when aged. Many Italian reds can take six to eight years of ageing and the better reds up to 10–12 years.

Good wine should never be stored on board a boat. The continuous movement and relatively high ambient temperatures in a boat are contrary to all good wine-cellar principles.

In general Italian white wine can seem a bit bland, although Veneto, Trentino, Campania, Friuli and Sicily have been recommended. Red wines tend to be higher in acid and tannin content than we are used to in French or New World wines. They lack that fruity sweetness, and on their own can taste bitter and dry, but are much better with food.

Perhaps the best known Italian wine is Chianti, but one should keep in mind that widely different qualities of wine come under this label. Only the classico is from the central area and can be recognised by the black rooster on the neck of the bottle (although a few of the top producers do not show it). Chianti from the Siena region (Chianti Senese) is a lighter wine and should be drunk within two years.

Southern Italian wines, although little known, are often of excellent quality, and are often comparable to their better known northern counterparts, and always good value for money.

For reds, look out for the following first-class wines: Aglianco del Vulture, Brindisi Patriglione, Ciro, Duca d'Aragona, Duca Enrico, Salice Salentino, Savuto and Taurasi. Of slightly inferior quality, but still very good and excellent value for money, are Aglianico del Sannio, Alezio, Biferno, Brindisi, Castel del Monte, Ciro, Copertino, Corvo di Salaparuta, Primotivo di Manduria, Solopaca and Squinzano, to name but a few.

A few names for whites: Biancolella, Corvo Colomba Platino, Donnafugata, Falanghina, Falerno del Massico, Forastera, Greco di Tufo, Locorotondo, Regaleali and Solopaca.

Marsala deserves a separate mention. This wine was first produced in 1773 by the Englishman, Woodhouse. During the Napoleonic Wars it replaced port which had become unobtainable in Britain. Nelson and his officers were won over and bought Marsala in sizeable quantities. The better makes of Marsala are still excellent as after-dinner drinks and well worth sampling. Try Marsala by Pellegrino, Donnafugata, Florio Marsala Soleras, Rallo or Vecchio Samperi.

Originally compiled by Andreas R Larsen

Provisioning

Most items are readily available in even quite small towns and local brands are of high quality. Fresh meat, fish and fruit and vegetables are generally of good quality and there will often be a local market with fresh produce, fish and shellfish.

In many of the larger towns there are supermarkets (Canad, Standa, Upim) which have a wide range of goods with all prices clearly marked so you can work out at leisure how much things cost.

Food and wine

Two-thirds of Italy's surface is covered with mountains and hills which, until recently, served to keep one region of Italy isolated from another so that without having to travel great distances one could find differences of custom, dialect and cuisine. When one mentions Italian cooking to foreigners they automatically think of pizza and spaghetti. This is a sad oversimplification because Italian cuisine is as diverse as it is delicious. The centuries during which the country was a collection of separate kingdoms, duchies and republics have given modern Italy as many subtle variations in cuisine as in language.

Italy's historical position at the crossroads of the Mediterranean made it an entry point for foods from Africa and the Near East. Ice cream, sherbert, cane sugar, almond paste and marzipan were introduced by the Arabs. A typical Italian meal, if we could isolate such an animal, now represents the best of a long tradition of cooking with deep roots extending into the past.

One can begin a meal with one of the delicious *antipasti* such as the rosy, thin slices of *prosciutto* (ham), *mortadella*, a kind of Bolognese salami, or *caponata*, the aubergine appetiser from Sicily. The choice of soups ranges from the well known thick vegetable soup, *minestrone*, to the peppery fish stew of Livorno called *caciucco*.

Pasta opens the next course and is the basic Italian staple. There are estimated to be about 100 different pasta shapes, most pasta names being colourful descriptions of shapes, for example: *cannelloni* are 'big pipes', *vermicelli* 'little worms', *farfalle* 'butterflies', *bucatini* 'little holes'. There are many delicious ways pasta can be prepared which range from elaborate lasagne to the simplest *fettucine al cacio e burro*. In Italy, pasta is cooked *al dente*, which means it should be cooked but have some bite to it and should never be the gluey mess sometimes called spaghetti outside Italy.

Veal is the principal meat and is excellent throughout Italy. Veal and chicken, less commonly lamb, beef and pork may simply be grilled, perhaps with an accompanying sauce, or cooked in a casserole in which there may be novel, always delicious, combinations with other ingredients. Fish, now considerably more expensive than it was, may simply be grilled or baked with a sauce or in a casserole. Some of the swordfish dishes in Calabria and Sicily should not be missed. The vegetables are ordered separately and salads are served as a separate course as in France.

Every morning in every town, village and city there is a marvellous aroma of freshly baked bread. There are the golden sticks of *grissini* from the Piedmont, the huge round loaves of Apulia, and the small delicate rolls of Ferrara to name a few.

The variety of cheeses in Italy is almost as great as in France. The best known in Italy are *parmigano*, parmesan, *gorgonzola* and of recent years *bel paese*. *Gorgonzola* is made from whole milk and there are two varieties: green *gorgonzola* which is green-veined having been treated with the mould *penicilium glaucium*, and white *gorgonzola* or *pannerone* which is of the same texture and consistency but not as sweet or hot and not treated with the mould. *Reggiano* is very similar to parmesan cheese, but is more aromatic and highly flavoured. *Parmigiano* or parmesan is the best known of all Italian cheeses and there are at least 18 different varieties. Parmesan improves with age and is at its best when kept for about three years. *Il pecorino romano* is one of Rome's most famous cheeses; made from the whole milk of ewes, it is slightly salty and hot and has a strong characteristic flavour. *La ricotta romana* is another cheese made from the buttermilk of ewes and is eaten either as an ordinary cheese or, like a French cream cheese, with a little sugar. *La mozzarella*, one of the best known cheeses of the province of Napoli, is soft though quite firm and has a mild flavour and should be made from the milk of buffalo cows; it should be eaten when fresh. Finally, *il canestrato* is one of the most famous of Sicilian cheeses; it is made of mixed ewe's and goat's milk and its taste is somewhat hot and quite distinctive; pepper is sometimes added to make it hotter. When fresh it is eaten with bread and when more mature it is used for cooking.

Marine life

The marine life in the Mediterranean is at first disappointing. It is not as prolific or as diverse as you might imagine; there are fewer seabirds than you would see in more northern waters, good eating fish are more scarce and difficult to catch and, in places, the sea bottom can be quite bereft of interest compared to, say, the Red Sea or the Atlantic coast of France. There are a number of reasons for this relative paucity of marine life.

The first is the non-tidal, or nearly so, nature of the sea. This has two effects. First of all there is not the intertidal zone in which a varied and rich marine life exists and contributes to the ecosystem as it does in the Atlantic. The second effect of the absence of tides is that the sea is not turned over by the currents generated by the tides and the water is not, as it were, mixed up. This makes it difficult for plankton, the basis of all marine ecosystems, to live and multiply in great numbers and, indeed, the Mediterranean is a plankton-poor sea and therefore generally poor in marine life. It has always been so and its much vaunted clarity is the result of the absence of 'soupy' plankton obscuring your vision.

The second reason for the paucity of marine life is that the Mediterranean has been fished far longer and more intensively than other seas and it is not surprising that there are not as many fish around as you might have believed. Historically this is nothing new. The Mediterranean is the watery equivalent of marginal land like the prairies or steppes and has never been rich in sea life. The Romans used to complain about poor fish stocks and bad catches and you can hardly say that their fishing methods and craft were over-exploiting the sea.

Although the marine life is initially disappointing, the yachtsman is in a unique position to discover and explore what there is in the Mediterranean. With a snorkel you can potter around the rocky coast and view the underwater life at leisure – at least the water is not so cold that you have to climb out every few minutes to get warm.

Edible Fish

Italy is a country rich in fish and fish recipes. The *Natural History* of Pliny the Elder devoted two books (IX and XXXII) to the classification of fish, and the enigmatic Apicius (born 25AD) devoted a section of one of his cookery books to fish sauces. It is related that the same Apicius heard someone talking about the magnificent prawns to be found in Libya and immediately hired a ship to take him there. He didn't bother to go ashore, so disappointed was he over the small size of Libyan prawns. In the ancient recipes can be found interesting ingredients such as garum, a strong distillation of fish entrails and salt which the Romans used extensively as a condiment. Modern Italian fish recipes that you will encounter successfully combine fish in interesting and artful ways. Alan Davidson in *Mediterranean Seafood* has this to say about his selection of Italian fish recipes:

'... two groups of dishes belong uniquely to Italy – those which combine pasta with seafood, and the seafood pizza dishes. I find both particularly satisfying and harmonious (provided that they are not over-elaborated) and believe the *vermicelli alle vongole*, for example, achieves a smoother fusion between seafood and other food than can ever be managed by the fish and two vegetable formula.'

The following list of edible fish is a brief one and the reader should consult Alan Davidson's *Mediterranean Seafood* for more detailed information.

Tuna *(tonno)* Migrate in the spring and autumn for summer spawning. Firm flesh which is delicious simply grilled or with a sauce.

Swordfish *(pesce spada)* Delicious as a steak simply grilled.

Grouper *(cernia)* Firm white flesh – delicious grilled or baked.

Red mullet *(triglia)* Popular in Roman times when the fish commanded astronomical prices. Tasty, some would say unique, flavour but full of small bones. *Triglie alla Siciliana* combines the fish with an orange sauce.

Sea bream *(orata, dentice, sarago)* Tasty and not too bony.

Flounder and sole *(passera pianuzza, sogliola)* Delicious fried by themselves or with a sauce.

Angel fish, monkfish *(squadro)* Delicious white flesh without small bones.

Shrimps and prawns *(gamberetti and gamberi)* Excellent grilled or in a soup (*zuppa di gamberi*).

Lobster, crawfish and crab (*aragosta, granciporro*) Best eaten cold with a good mayonnaise.

Shellfish Abundant and excellent. The Italians' culinary art with *vongole* (clams or the carpet shell) must be experienced.

Squid *(calamaro)* Delicious fried whole or stuffed.

Octopus *(polpo)* Sometimes a bit tough but always delicious. Often served in a sauce.

Whales and dolphins (cetaceans)

Dolphins are still relatively common in Italian waters and schools of dolphins will often come up to a yacht and play around it. At night the phosphorescence created by dolphins around a yacht is something marvellous to behold. In antiquity the dolphin was mentioned and often depicted in mosaics. Aristotle and Pliny mention it as a friend of man and Herodotus tells of the poet Arion of Lesvos who was thrown overboard by mutinous sailors and rescued by a music-loving dolphin. The modern Italian fisherman is not as fond of the dolphin as his ancestors and it is said that fishermen in Liguria catch and eat it. It used to be dried and sold as *musciame* in Genoa.

There appear to be fewer dolphins today than there were some years ago, but it is difficult to assess numbers accurately as they frequently change their feeding grounds. However, Greenpeace has reported that thousands of striped dolphins have died in recent years because of accumulations of pesticides in their food chain. This accumulation of toxins has probably led to a breakdown in the immune system of the dolphins, leaving them vulnerable to viruses. Following a 10-year moratorium by the UN from 1992, drift netting was banned by the EU from 1 January 2002. According to a WWF report in 2003, drift netting is still practised by French, Italian, Moroccan and Turkish fleets in the Mediterranean. Drift nets are responsible for the accidental deaths and incidental catches of whales, dolphins and marine turtles.

Cetaceans are divided into toothed and non-toothed whales. In the Mediterranean most of the cetaceans seen belong to the toothed whales, which are fish-eaters and so possess teeth to grip their prey. To this class belong the porpoise, pilot whale and killer whale. The common dolphin (*delphinus delphis*) will be commonly seen. Less common are the larger bottle-nosed dolphin (*tursiops truncatus*) and the common porpoise (*phocoena phocoena*). The pilot whale (*globicephala melaena*) is fairly common and grows up to 8·5m long. The bottle-nosed whale (*hyperoodon ampullatus*), Risso's dolphin (*grampus griseus*) and killer whale (*corcinus orca*) have been reported in the Mediterranean. In 1999 the northern hemisphere's first cetacean sanctuary was created in a joint initiative by the governments of Italy, France and Monaco. The reserve, which is twice the size of Switzerland (or 84,000km^2), lies between the French Côte d'Azur, the Ligurian sea, Corsica and Sardinia. Thirteen cetacean species live in this area, including pilot whales, fin whales, sperm whales, common dolphins and bottlenose dolphins.

There have been further calls for Italy, Malta and Tunisia to establish a marine sanctuary in the Sicily Channel.

Dangerous marine animals

In the Mediterranean there are no more dangerous marine animals than you would encounter off the English coast, but the warm sea temperatures mean that you are in the water more often and therefore more likely to encounter these animals.

Sharks Probably the greatest fear of a swimmer, yet in all probability the least to be feared. Films such as *Jaws* and *White Water, White Death* have produced a phobia amongst swimmers that is out of all proportion to the menace. After years of sailing around the eastern Mediterranean I have positively identified a shark in the water on only a few occasions. Fishermen occasionally bring in sharks from the deep water – usually the mackerel shark or sand shark. I have not been able to establish one fatality from a shark attack in Italy and, so far as I know, the total recorded number of fatalities for the Mediterranean is less than a dozen in the last century.

Moray eels Of the family *Muraenidae*, these eels are quite common in the eastern Mediterranean and are often caught by fishermen. They inhabit holes and crevices in rocks and can bite and tear if molested. Usually they will retire and are not aggressive unless wounded or sorely provoked.

Octopus Very shy and do not attack. They have much more to fear from man than man from them.

Stingrays The European stingray (*dasyatis pastinaca*) is common in the Mediterranean. It inhabits shallow waters partially burying itself in the sand. If it is trodden on accidentally it will lash out with its tail and bury a spine in the offending foot. Venom is injected which produces severe local pain, sweating, vomiting, rapid heart beat but rarely death. Soak the foot in very hot water and seek medical help.

Weeverfish Members of the family *Trachinidae*. The two most common are the great weever (*trachinus draco*) and lesser weever (*trachinus vipera*). The dorsal and opercular spines contain venom. When disturbed or annoyed the weever will erect its dorsal fin and attack. The venom injected produces instant pain which spreads to other parts of the body and is very painful. The victim may lose consciousness and death sometimes occurs. There are no known antidotes. Bathe the wound in hot water and seek medical help as soon as possible.

Note When walking in water where stingrays or weevers are thought to be, wear sandshoes and shuffle the feet along the bottom. Do not handle dead weevers or stingrays.

Jellyfish Of all the animals described, the ones you are most likely to encounter are jellyfish. At certain times of the year and in certain places there will be considerable numbers of jellyfish in the water. All jellyfish sting for this is the way they immobilise their prey, but some species have more powerful stings than others and consequently deserve greater respect.

Aurelia aurita The common jellyfish. It has a transparent dome-shaped body with four purple-violet crescents grouped around the centre. Transparent or light violet mouth arms hang below. Up to 25cm in diameter. A light contact with the stings is something like a nettle but prolonged contact can hurt.

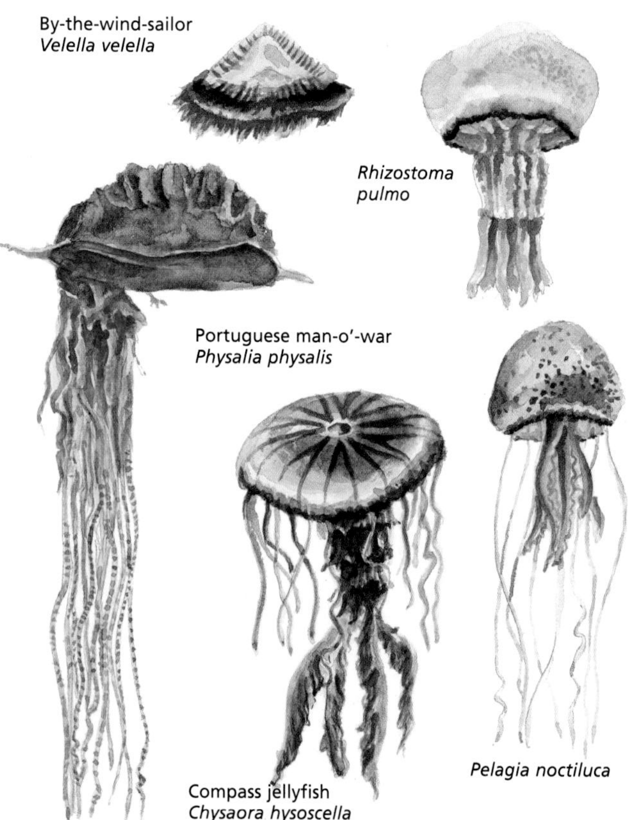

Pelagia noctiluca A mushroom-shaped jelly fish up to 10cm in diameter. It is easily identified being light brown-yellow in colour and covered in 'warts'. It has long trailing tentacles and can inflict severe and painful stings.

Cyanea lamarckii A blue-violet saucer-shaped jellyfish up to 30cm across. It can be identified by the frilly mass of mouth arms underneath. It has long tentacles which can inflict severe and painful stings. There is a brown variety (*cyanea capillata*) which can grow up to 50cm in diameter.

Chrysaora hysoscella Compass jellyfish. Common browny-biscuity coloured 'umbrella' up to 30cm in diameter with brown patches and radiating 'stripes' from the centre. Frilly lobes and tentacles. Can inflict stings although these are usually not severe.

Velella velella By-the-wind-sailor. Flattened oval disc with a gas-filled central float. Silvery float with blue and purple disc and tentacles underneath. In places you can see quite a few of these and they can inflict a severe and painful sting. I've always quite 'liked' their evolutionary stance of having a curved float so that they sail on a beam reach rather than being blown downwind with all the other jellyfish.

Charybdea marsupialis (Mediterranean sea-wasp) A transparent, yellow-red box-shaped 'umbrella' up to 6cm high. Rarely seen but can inflict severe and painful stings.

Physalia physalis (Portuguese man-of-war). Has a large conspicuous float (pneumatophore) above water growing to 30cm long and 10cm wide. Below it stream very long tentacles. Rarely seen but can inflict dangerous stings.

Rhizostoma pulmo Dome-shaped blue-white jellyfish up to 90cm in diameter. Its mouth arms are fused in a grey-green 'cauliflower' mass below the body. It has no long tentacles and is not known as a vicious stinger.

Treatments There are no known antidotes to jellyfish stings but there are a number of ways of obtaining relief. Antihistamine creams have proved useful in some but not all cases. Diluted ammonium hydroxide, sodium bicarbonate, olive oil, sugar, and ethyl alcohol have been used. In general use a weak alkali. A tip which I have not tried but which soun-ds promising is to use meat tenderiser, which apparently breaks down the protein base of the venom. Gloves should be worn when hauling up an anchor in jellyfish-infested water as the tentacles, especially those of *Pelagia*, can stick to the anchor chain.

Bristle worms In some locations numbers of bristle worms, probably of the family *Nereidae*, will be found. They are black and may grow up to 25cm long. The setae can produce a mild irritation similar to a stinging nettle if touched.

Sea urchins In some places on rocky coasts large colonies of sea urchins (*paracentrotus lividus* and *arbacia lixula*) will be found. While they do not have a venom apparatus, the spines penetrate and break off when the urchin is trodden on and are very painful. Care must be taken not to get a secondary infection.

Italian fishing methods

When a fishing boat is sighted a lookout must be kept for floats and lines. Some of the fishing methods could be dangerous to a yacht if you do not understand what is going on and can be bothersome even when you do. The following methods are used:

1. Trawling. The end of the trawl may or may not be marked depending on the depth being trawled. Pair trawling is also practised in places and care is needed not to get between the two pair trawlers.
2. Purse-Seine fishing. Industrial level fishing where large schools of fish – often tuna, can be identified using high tech sonar, encircled and caught with the purse-seine net. Highly efficient way of catching target fish – devastating fish stocks in the Mediterranean.
3. Long-lining. Used in the swordfish and tunny season. Floats with very long lines (often up to 2–3km) are laid in the evening and collected in the early morning.
4. *Mattanza.* Also called *madragues* or *tonnara*, these permanent nets are no longer extensively used and most anchors lie idle except for a number of locations around Sicily and Sardinia. The net is laid vertically for up to a mile and secured by large (wood and iron) anchors. At the seaward end there is a 'T' with an arrangement of nets which has a lifting floor (the *camera de la morte* – literally 'room of death'). The migrating tunny are deflected to the 'T' and thence to the death chamber and when the head man decides sufficient fish have entered, the floor is raised and the struggling fish are gaffed and hauled into waiting boats. Any sharks or swordfish in the chamber must be killed separately, usually by a diver with a spear-gun. The nets are usually laid between March and November and their position marked by buoys or boats carrying lights.
5. *Lampera.* A gas lamp is used to attract fish which are speared, hooked or netted. The bright lamps bobbing up and down in the sea can easily be mistaken for a white flashing navigation light.
6. Surface nets. Used to catch swordfish and tunny. These are laid at night and may be up to 6km in length. The nets extend from the surface down to around 30m. They are generally marked by kerosene lamps or LED strobes at 100–300m intervals, although if there is any sea running these are frequently out of sight, or in the case of the lamps, extinguished. The end of the net is marked by a fixed white lamp or ocassionally a strobe light. The mother ship patrols the net and will guide yachts around the end. Nets are commonly laid around 2100–2300 at night and retrieved around 0500–0600. These nets obviously represent a hazard for yachts sailing at night. They are most common in the sea area between the Bay of Naples and the Strait of Messina and sometimes in the sea area off the toe of Italy. Nets are laid anything from 3–4M to 20–30M off the coast between June and September.

The nets often catch dolphins, who cannot easily detect the nets, and in 1990 the Italian government banned the nets after a public outcry over the hundreds of dolphins known to have been caught in the nets and dumped at sea and in harbour. Public opinion was galvanised when a small sperm whale was caught in a net and freed by divers, all covered live by national television. The government capitulated in 1991 when the fishermen blockaded the Strait of Messina and stopped all ferry and commercial traffic between Sicily and the mainland and through the strait.

The EU banned drift nets over 1·5 miles long in the early 90s, and outlawed the entire practice in 2002. France and Italian fishermen claimed an 'exemption' as they said their nets, some up to six miles long, did not 'drift' as they were weighted along the bottom.

It wasn't until 2007 that the EU formally defined 'drift-netting' to include this type, but the French and Italian governments have persisted in supporting the use of these 'wall of death' nets by issuing special permits and decrees. A €200 million subsidy to encourage Italian drift netters to change their fishing techniques just resulted in the fishermen buying more drift nets.

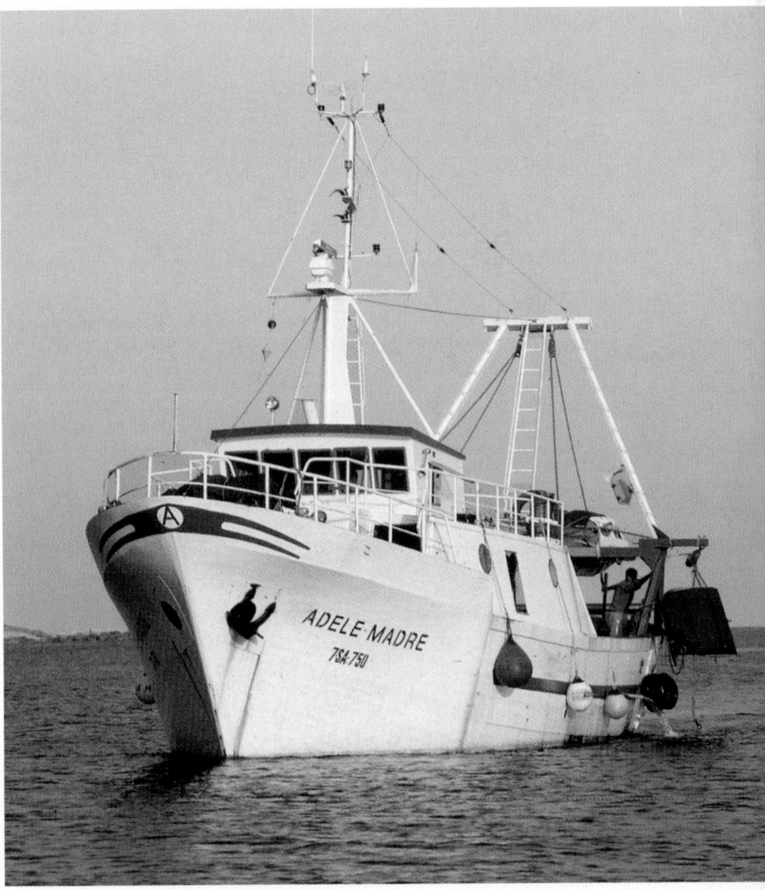

Trawler hauling the drawl net

According to the WWF around 1.5 million tons of fish are caught in the Mediterranean each year, and they claim that destructive and often illegal fishing methods, including bottom trawlers, dynamite, long lines, and drift nets have depleted fish stocks. Use of driftnets is also responsible for the accidental deaths and incidental catches of whales, dolphins and marine turtles. Depleted fish stocks are also reflected in the undersized catch, (83% of all blue-fin tuna and swordfish caught in the Mediterranean are undersized). Is is thought that populations of swordfish and tuna are down by around 90% over the last 30 years.

It is ironic that Italy, a country with the largest number and sea area of Marine Protected Areas, also has one of the most destructive fishing fleets in the Mediterranean.

Support the WWF and Oceana who campaign to stop drift netting in the Mediterranean. www.panda.org www.oceana.org

Fish farms

Unfortunately the requirements for a fish farm are much the same as those for a good anchorage: shelter from strong winds and reasonable depths to anchor the cages. Consequently, a number of coves and bays formerly frequented only by yachts and fishing boats have now sprouted fish farms which may obstruct much of the available space.

Aquaculture is the fastest-growing sector of the world food economy and represents 31% of the total value of EU fish production. Italy alone produces 212,000 tonnes of farmed fish, mainly mussels, clams and trout.

Molluscs such as mussels and clams have been farmed sustainably here for millennia and form an important and tasty part of the Italian diet. You will often see 'strings' of mussel farms around the edge of bays right around Italy's coast.

It is the development of sea-cage fisheries for fin-fish such as salmon, trout, sea bass and sea bream in the Mediterranean that carries more concerns based on environmental, health and sustainability issues. Italy produces 14% (17,000 tonnes) of all EU-farmed sea bream and sea bass (Greece has a 50% share). The continued expansion of captive blue-fin tuna fattening farms in Spain, Malta and Italy is also raising concerns for the viability of wild stocks. Farmed fish has been seen as a solution to the natural poverty in fish in the Mediterranean, but it is becoming evident that these systems are causing more problems than they solve. They threaten the sustainability of wild fish stocks; it takes over five tons of wild fish to produce one ton of farmed sea bass or sea bream. Fish farms pollute the coastal waters with toxic chemicals, and some farmed fish have also been found to be carrying unacceptably high levels of toxic chemicals.

(Figures above have been taken from a paper presented by Don Staniford at the European Parliament's Committee on Fisheries public hearing on *Aquaculture in the EU: Present situation and Future Prospects* (October 2002).

Pollution

The Mediterranean is a closed sea supporting a large population around its shores. It has small tidal differences, with about half of the water lost by evaporation coming from the rivers flowing into it and the other half coming from the Atlantic Ocean flowing in through the Strait of Gibraltar (about one million cubic metres every second).

With the population (resident and visiting) dumping its sewage into the sea and only a small tide to take it away, with rivers dumping industrial waste, and tankers and oil installations causing hydrocarbon pollution, the waters around Italy suffer from some pollution. Some of the worst sewage pollution (and high bacteria count) is found around Genoa, at Ostia near Rome, in the Gulf of Gaeta, and the Bay of Naples (nobody really knows where many of the sewers in Naples are). It should be remembered that mussels grown in the Bay of Naples caused the cholera epidemic there in 1973. Hydrocarbon pollution is at its worst in the Gulf of Genoa, around Fiumicino, around the Bay of Naples, off Augusta in Sicily and off the southeast coast of Sicily, off Cagliari and Porto Torres in Sardinia, and off Crotone and Brindisi.

Up until recently nothing was done about the increasing pollution in the Mediterranean but in 1975 a United Nations Environment committee decided to get together the culturally and politically diverse countries around the Mediterranean and work out a programme to clean up the sea. The Mediterranean Action Plan (MAP) was adopted by all 21 Mediterranean states and the EU. Since 1995 it has been geared to protecting the marine and coastal environment and achieving sustainable development of the coastal regions. It is possible that new protocols will affect yachtsmen in the future.

No thinking yachtsman should ever throw garbage into the sea – especially plastic.

Most Italian harbours now have 'pelicans', small jet-powered boats with two booms which open to collect rubbish. These craft happily potter around the larger harbours and adjacent coast collecting rubbish and though they seem to miss much of it, the government must be applauded for taking concrete action which so many of the other European governments fail to do.

Yachtsmen can be fined for dumping waste oil into a harbour or close to the coast. All charter boats must have holding tanks fitted and in the future it is possible that holding tanks will have to be fitted to cruising boats. The yachtsman may curse the extra cost involved but must acknowledge the necessity of such regulations when so much of the Mediterranean and for that matter the other seas and oceans of the world are threatened by pollution of all types.

www.unepmap.org

History

General

Most people, like me, arrive in Italy without the benefit of a classical education. Homer, Thucydides, Aristotle, Pausanias, Livy, Pliny, Cicero, Virgil, Seneca and Catullus are names we may have heard. Some of their works we may even have read, but do not know of in the way schoolboys of old did. The glories of Greece, the might of Rome, the splendour of Byzantium, the Papacy, the Normans and the Saracens, the Spanish and the French, Garibaldi and the thousand red shirts, these we know of only superficially. In Italy my outstanding difficulty was to put the places inhabited by the ancients, the monuments, castles and forts into some sort of historical order. The following brief history will sort out some of that chaos but for detail and for scholarly wrangling over precise dates and alternative explanations the reader must turn elsewhere.

Prehistoric times

Evidence of life in the Palaeolithic and Neanderthal periods has been found in many places, notably Sicily, the Aeolian Islands, Sardinia and the high promontories along the mainland coast such as Cape Circeo. Minoan and Mycenean influences have been found dating from around the 15th century BC onwards.

Homeric period

The legends recorded by Homer, many of which are founded on fact (see Ernle Bradford's *Ulysses Found*), tell of the influence of Aegean civilisations on Italy. The references to Scylla and Charybdis, the Aeolian Islands, Circeo's Island, Calypso's Island, and so on, can all be traced although the location of many of the sites is disputed.

Magna Graecia

The early Greeks colonised much of Italy: Cumae and Pithecusa (Ischia) in the 11th century BC; Rhegion (Reggio di Calabria), Sybaris and Crotone by the Achaeans, and Taranto in the 8th century BC; Syracuse in 734BC and Selimunte and Acragas (Agrigento) in 650 and 582BC respectively. Together, the settlements in Sicily and southern Italy became known as Magna Graecia and the colonies attracted philosophers like Pythagoras (he settled at Crotone) and produced their own stars (like Zeno). The colonies prospered commercially and fostered the arts. Much great architecture remains from the period. Internecine squabbling eventually led to the downfall of the colonies.

The Etruscans

While the Greeks were colonising the south, the Etruscans were establishing themselves in central Italy from the 8th century BC. They reached their zenith in the 7th–6th centuries BC at which time they occupied the Appenines, Arno, Tiber, Campania and the Po. They were artisans and technicians of some skill, mining iron ore in Elba and planning and building towns of some complexity. Art, sculpture, pottery and goldsmithing, although initially primitive in style, later fused Greek elements with the vigorous Etruscan style. Like the Greek colonies, the Etruscans' downfall came about from internal squabbles between city-states.

The Romans

In 326BC Rome forced the Greeks at Naples into an alliance and the defeat of the Etruscans in 284 gave her southern Italy. Hannibal brought the Second Punic War to Italy and after several victories (especially that at Cannae) looked ready to squash Rome. The Carthaginians were finally defeated by Scipio at Zama in 202 and the fate of all Italy was that of Rome. For nearly 12 centuries, from the foundation of Rome in 753BC through the Roman Republic (509–27BC), the Roman Empire (27BC–AD192) to the decline and later empire (AD284–467), the Romans ruled Italy and most of the known world. The Roman eagle was raised from Britain to Persia and from Africa to Germany. The splendour of Rome spread throughout Europe and was the seed from which western Europe grew.

Constantinople and Rome

The Christian church was broken into two parts in the 5th century AD, the Greek Byzantine tradition rooted in Constantinople, and the Holy Roman Church. The division between eastern and western Christianity endures still, but for some time it was a cause of unrest and bitter argument (cf. Guelphs and Ghibellines). Constantinople was gaining in ascendancy in the 6th century when the Byzantine army under Belisarius occupied much of southern Italy and Sicily. The Roman church was saved by the Lombard invasion. In the 7th century Rome came under the temporal protection of the popes and papal power was sealed with Frankish aid.

Saracens, Lombard, Franks, Normans and Genoa

In Sicily and southern Italy the Saracens had arrived, but Lombard and the Franks held them at bay in most of Italy. In the 10th and 11th centuries there were many independent maritime cities (Naples and

Amalfi. Replica medieval rowing galleys take part in competitions all around Italy

Amalfi were pre-eminent) with constantly changing alliances among themselves and with Lombard and the Byzantines. In the north the Germans squabbled among themselves. The Normans, on their way back from the Crusades, were quick to realise that Sicily and southern Italy were ripe for plucking and soon occupied them. With the defeat of the Saracens, Genoa then became the foremost power in the Mediterranean. Pisa was also ascendant and the two powers were constantly at war. In the Battle of Melloria (1284) the Genoese decisively defeated Pisa and Genoa expanded to become one of the largest cities in medieval Europe. The end of Genoa's maritime supremacy came with their defeat by the Venetians in the war of Chioggia (1378–81). In the south the Hohenstaufen ruled with Frederick II, the bright star in a period of civil and political unrest.

Anjou and Aragon

Italy once more came under a common master when Charles of Anjou defeated Manfred. Under the Angevins, Naples became the important centre. Internecine struggles went on up and down the country until Aragon triumphed in 1442 when Alfonso (the Magnanimous) entered Naples. In 1492 Charles VIII of France invaded Italy and the Spanish, driving them out, became masters of Italy.

Spanish and Austrian rule

Spanish rule was for the most part oppressive, putting heavy taxes on the population and ruthlessly suppressing rebellion. The French attempted to occupy parts of Italy but for the most part were unsuccessful. Spanish rule ended with the War of the Spanish Succession and in 1713 much of Italy was awarded to Austria. Napoleon was crowned King of Italy in 1805 but the Austrians, Russians and English finally defeated the French fleet and the north came under the Austrians and the south under the Bourbons. The occasional tyranny of the Austrians and the wholesale corruption of the Bourbons fuelled Italian rebellion against their foreign masters.

Tropea

THE REGIONS OF ITALY

Italian unity

Giuseppe Mazzini formed the Young Italy movement in 1831 which spurred Italy towards the *Risorgimento*, or revival. Giuseppe Garibaldi led his thousand Red Shirts in 1860 to free the south from Bourbon rule. In 1861 the Kingdom of Italy was proclaimed with Turin as its capital, but it was not until 1870 that Italian unity was complete under the Piedmont monarchy.

1870 to the present day

Italy steadily grew to be a European power, taking colonies in North Africa and strengthening its frontiers. In the Great War, Italy fought with the Allies. A political journalist, Benito Mussolini, wounded on the front, returned home and began organising groups (*fasci*) of workers for social reform. In 1919 these groups formed the Fascist party and fomented disturbances until 1922 when Mussolini was appointed prime minister by King Victor Emmanuel III. Known as *Il Duce*, he waged war against Abyssinia and helped Franco in the Spanish Civil War. In the Second World War he sided with Hitler, although groups of Italian partisans fought against the Germans. Mussolini was captured and shot by partisans near Lake Como in 1945. In 1946 a referendum was held and Italy was declared a republic.

Italy joined NATO in 1949 and the emergent EC in 1958. Post-war Christian Democrat governments oversaw rapid growth right up to the 70s, when high inflation, unemployment, terrorism by the Red Brigades and corruption created political instability. Reforms by the socialist government of Bettino Craxi in the eighties helped to stabilise the economy but were wracked with allegations of corruption. Further reforms and the 'Clean Hands' operation to tackle widespread corruption and Mafia power were implemented by the judiciary in the 90s, and political reforms led to the rise of media mogul Silvio Berlusconi and his Forza Italia party. This controversial character was not only the prime minister; he is also Italy's richest person; he owns AC Milan football club; and, most controversially, he controls vast swathes of the country's newspaper, radio and television production. This surgically enhanced and perma-tanned politician led the party which remained in power for the longest term since the birth of the republic. He continues to fight allegations of tax fraud and bribery, and returned to power in 2008 after a two year stint by Romano Prodi. 2010 has been a difficult year for Mr Berlusconi, but as ever, he fights on.

Technical information

Navigation

A yacht will require no more navigation equipment than would be used around other areas and in all probability will use less in practice.

In a lot of places navigation is about using the Mk1 eyeball and you can often see the next cape, or coast along to where you are going. All the usual instruments (a speed/log, wind strength and direction and a depth sounder come in handy). A GPS repeater is useful for checking things in the cockpit and many yachts now have a full blown chart plotter in a convenient place near the helm.

Most boats will have a VHF. SSB radio has only limited usefulness in the Med compared to other more remote parts of the world where radio nets are more common. Navtex works well in the Med with good coverage in most places. Radar is also a lot more common than it used to be. AIS (Automatic Identification System) is also popular, but along with radar it is an aid to safe navigation, not a solution.

When using GPS and dedicated chart plotters or chart plotters running on a laptop read the caution below carefully. Without doubt GPS is a wonderful aid to navigation as a stand-alone unit or incorporated into a chart plotter, but it does have limitations and some care is needed. Read on.

A word of caution Though many of the charts for Italy have been reissued with substantial corrections by the Admiralty, the problem of re-charting the coast and islands has not yet been addressed and in many cases the latitude and longitude of a particular spot does not correspond to the actual latitude and longitude from satellite positon fixing. In some cases the error can be as much as a quarter of a mile. While you may know your latitude and longitude from a GPS receiver to withing ±20m, the chart on which you are plotting your position (or that on your chart plotter screen), may be accurate only to a quarter of a mile, especially where longitude is concerned. It hardly needs to be said that you should excise great caution in the vicinity of land and hazards to navigation. Eyeball navigation rules OK. See also the section on Waypoints under *About the plans and pilotage.* Most Italian Hydrographic charts use European Datum 1950.

Electronic navigation aids

GPS (Global Positioning System)

The first GPS satellites were launched over 25 years ago. Since then GPS has become the cheapest form of position finding around, with a handheld set now costing less than a decent hand bearing compass. Selective availability (SA) – the function where the (US) military would reduce the accuracy of civilian positioning signals – has been turned off for several years now.

Modern GPS receivers are all multi-channel and can receive from three to twelve signals at any one time and decode them to determine a position. The speed at which a GPS receiver can do a cold start and produce a position is now around 30 seconds. The ease with which we retrieve data has been simplified by software that enables us to scroll through pages and pick out how we want to view the data. From the stream of position data we get speed over the ground, course heading in true and magnetic, distance off course from a waypoint, and a graphic display of our course.

DGPS There are currently no DGPS stations in Italy and in any case now that selective availability has been turned off there is little point in using DGPS add ons.

SDGPS (Satellite Differential GPS) Works by a network of ground reference stations receiving GPS signals and then correcting them for known errors: GPS satellite orbit, clock errors, and transmission errors. A GPS correction signal is then transmitted to geostationary satellites on the same frequency as GPS signals. An accuracy of 1–2m is claimed.

In Europe **EGNOS** (European Geostationary Navigation Overlay Service) is the SDGPS system, which became available in 2005.

WAAS (Wide Area Augmentation System) is the US SDGPS system.

EGNOS/WAAS They are compatible systems and if you buy a WAAS enabled receiver it will recognize EGNOS and vice versa.

GPS Accuracy

SDGPS gives errors of only ±1–3m, and is now the default system in Europe using EGNOS equipped GPS receivers, and in the US using WAAS.

Note some GPS manufacturers recommend that in areas where EGNOS is not available, it may actually improve the accuracy of the unit to disable EGNOS until you are back in range of EGNOS or WAAS satellites. Without SDGPS you can expect an accuracy of ±20m.

The very accuracy of GPS can be misleading and seeing a position to two or three decimal points can induce a false sense of confidence in the user. The problem is simply that we do not have charts accurate enough to make full use of such precise positions. Read over the caution carefully at the end of this section.

Although satellites are turned off for maintenance every now and again and in places coverage by the satellites is not enough to give an accurate position, in my experience these gaps in coverage have never exceeded an hour. Nonetheless it is worthwhile thinking carefully before linking the GPS to the autopilot so that the autopilot is steering a true course relative to currents, tide, etc. or you may end up like the yacht in the Caribbean which hit a reef because the inattentive owner missed the 'Lost satellite reception' warning on his GPS. Without coverage the GPS kept a course using the last data that had arrived from the satellite and without any new data to correct for currents and other errors, steered straight towards a reef.

Note Recent research in the US has revealed problems with corruption of GPS signals by some marine television antennas. A small number of marine TV aerials emit spurious radiation which interferes with the Ll GPS frequency at 1575.42MHz. It is only a problem with land-based broadcast TV; satellite TV antennas operate on different frequencies and are not a problem.

Galileo

The EU alternative to GPS has been approved for start-up costs and operational uses. It has already been agreed that Galileo will be fully compatible with both GPS and GLONASS (the Russian system). In practice this means that receivers can get position data from satellites of all three systems. The first Gallileo satellites were in orbit in early 2006. The project faltered as doubts over the financial viability of Galileo were raised by the consortium, but in April 2008 the European Commission agreed to make €5 billion available to ensure the project's success. Gallileo is now due to be operational in 2013. GLONASS is likely to leapfrog the Galileo project and become operational in the next couple of years. The Chinese sat-nav system 'Compass' is already functioning, but it is not clear whether it will become widely available (or compatible) with existing receivers.

Chart plotters

A number of yachts are fitting dedicated chart plotters which, when interfaced to an electronic position finding system, show a yacht's position on a chart. Dedicated chart plotters are a useful adjunct to the navigation table or cockpit and I use one on *Skylax*. Despite the usefulness of a plotter it does not replace the usefulness of a chart in the cockpit for me. With that old-fashioned paper chart I can put it anywhere, hold it up while looking at a feature or danger to navigation and quickly pan from one side of the chart to the other. You can get irritated with the 'please wait, chart loading' message on chart plotters as you either zoom in or out or pan from one part to another. If the chart plotter is located at the chart table then you must constantly run up and down to check the map against the view above and this can make it difficult to mentally fit the 3D real view to the 2D chart view. A chart in the cockpit lets you constantly scan from one to the other and fit the chart to the real world. In addition, the problems outlined at the beginning of this section on chart accuracy are exacerbated on electronic charts where an electronically derived 'real' position is displayed on a cartographically inaccurate chart.

Laptop computers

Many yachts now have laptop computers on board. There are a number of software packages which reproduce charts and if GPS, radar and the boat instruments are interfaced this can be a useful navigation tool. One of the problems with most systems is that the laptop is not fitted into the navigation area and so is difficult to use when conditions are rough. Most people don't want to risk their laptop slithering all over the place when things get a bit bumpy. If you are contemplating a laptop-based navigation system incorporating charts and instrumentation, then some thought needs to go into securing the laptop on the navigation table or as a modular unit with the screen on a bulkhead and the keyboard secured on the chart table. There are also a number of remote waterproof screens available which can be installed in the cockpit to reproduce the charts, GPS position and other data where it is easy to see when sailing. The following points should be kept in mind when looking at plotting software.

1. You will need to choose between raster and vector charts. Basically, raster charts are scanned originals. Vector charts are redrawn digitally from the original. In practice the best choice is to go for vector charts. They occupy less space on the hard disk, load more quickly and, importantly, can be read when you zoom in or out. Raster charts are scanned at one resolution so when you zoom in or out you lose definition and get a fuzzy pixellated image. That is intensely irritating and the only answer is to buy a large folio of charts, although that means the laptop grinding away to load a chart on a smaller or larger scale. Raster charts also take longer to reload. which is annoying when you are trying to get from one side of the chart to the other on a 15-inch laptop screen.
2. Don't go for a chart plotter that has all the bells and whistles. Even a basic plotter has more than enough for practical navigation and the more you squeeze onto a toolbar the more confusing it gets when conditions are a bit bumpy at sea. Even a basic plotter will insert waypoints, construct routes, let you keep an automatic log off the GPS input and an annotated log as well. Just as most of us never use half of the functions on a word processor, so you will never need to use a lot of the functions on some chart plotters.

   Ease of use and large icons are important when it's blowing half a gale and the boat is bucketing to windward. You don't want to have to work out how to construct a route when the rest of the crew are sick and you are not feeling too bright yourself. And get a mouse for your laptop instead of using the touchpad or that little joystick stuck in the middle of the keys, or every time the boat hits a wave the mouse pointer will shoot across the screen as you twiddle with the touchpad or the miniature joystick.

Handheld computers

are also just starting to gain the processing power necessary to run plotting software. They may become a smaller alternative to a laptop with all the pros and cons (mostly cons), that that brings.

Radar

Now that radar is more compact and more economical with your amps, it can be used as a useful navigation tool. Its great value is in reproducing a map of what is there, rather than a latitude and longitude that you then plot on an (inaccurate) chart. Some are combined with a chart plotter, and may be interfaced with a GPS.

Automatic Identification Scheme

AIS is a vessel-tracking tool using VHF frequency radio transmissions to send and receive information on vessels within that range. Each vessel is shown on a screen as a separate icon with a small data box with information such as:

- Name
- MMSI Number
- Rate of turn
- Course over the ground
- Speed over the ground
- Time of last update.

From 2005 all vessels subject to SOLAS regulations had to be fitted with AIS equipment. A pleasure users' receive-only system has been available for several years now. This enables the skipper to identify shipping in the vicinity, but does not transmit information back to the ships. It is now possible to buy a transmitting Class B AIS unit, which means your vessel is 'seen' on commercial ship Class A AIS units. Both 'receive-only' and Class B systems come either as a stand-alone unit or can be run on a PC or compatible plotter. It's worth mentioning that some commercial vessels are known to turn their AIS transmitters off, and hence will not show up on your receiver.

Routes

In the summer the prevailing winds are predominantly from the NW–W–SW. This is a sea breeze, getting up around midday and dying at night, typically reaching Force 3–5. This means that you can use the wind when you are heading down the coast and it is favourable, or avoid it by leaving early in the morning to make progress northwards before the sea breeze gets up. When planning routes between Sardinia, Sicily and the mainland coast keep an eye on any depressions tracking westwards from Gibraltar, as they can move quickly and generally head either NE or SE across Sardinia or Corsica.

The change in wind direction as the front passes will raise awkward cross-seas, as well as freshening winds. In the Ionian the wind direction is variable throughout, although N–NW winds predominate.

At the beginning of each chapter there is a short section on routes for that area, and routes to and from other areas. There is also a list of Useful Waypoints to facilitate route planning. See the section on Waypoints under *About the plans and pilotage*.

Buoyage

The IALA System 'A' buoyage scheme is being implemented, and yachtsmen can expect to find

Wind direction and frequency

The two most common directions are given for 0800 and 1400 with relevant frequencies. Note the thermal component in most of these statistics.

At Genoa

	Freq 0800		Freq 1400		Calms
Jan	N-NE/49%	E-SE/16%	N-NE/46%	SE-S/28%	12%
Feb	N-NE/51%	E-SE/22%	N-NE/46%	SE-S/32%	11%
Mar	N-NE/41%	E-SE/25%	N-NE/37%	SE-S/37%	9%
Apr	N-NE/36%	SE-S/30%	SE-S/47%	N-NE/24%	8%
May	SE-S/40%	N-NE/35%	SE-S/45%	SW/21%	7.5%
Jun	SE-S/50%	N-NE/22%	SE-S/61%	SW/19%	6%
Jul	SE-S/50%	N-NE/17%	SE-S/69%	SW/16%	5.5%
Aug	SE-S/43%	N-NE/27%	SE-S/64%	SW/10%	7.5%
Sep	N-NE/38%	SE-S/30%	SE-S/59%	N/13%	5.5%
Oct	N-NE/53%	E-SE/22%	N-NE/40%	SE-S/37%	8%
Nov	N-NE/66%	E-SE/13%	N-NE/51%	SE-S/26%	7%
Dec	N-NE/55%	E-SE/17%	N-NE/49%	SE-S/26%	10·5%

At Naples

	Freq 0800		Freq 1400		Calms
Jan	N-NE/38%	SW-W/20%	N-NE/35%	S-SW/25%	14%
Feb	N-NE/40%	S-SW/25%	N-NE/35%	S-SW/34%	11.5%
Mar	N-NE/35%	S-SW/23%	S-SW/48%	N-NE/21%	12%
Apr	N-NE/30%	S-SW/25%	S-SW/57%	W/13%	12.5%
May	N-NE/31%	SW-W/21%	S-SW/51%	W/13%	1.5%
Jun	N-NE/28%	S-SW/16%	S-SW/55%	W/10%	15%
Jul	N-NE/30%	var	S-SW/56%	var	16%
Aug	N-NE/31%	var	S-SW/50%	var	1·5%
Sep	N-NE/27%	var	S-SW/44%	W/12%	16%
Oct	N-NE/34%	var	S-SW/42%	var	1.5%
Nov	N-NE/44%	var	S-SW/36%	N-NE/27%	15%
Dec	N-NE/44%	var	N-NE/33%	S-SW/27%	13%

At Cagliari

	Freq 0800		Freq 1400		Calms
Jan	N-NW/61%	var	N-NW/51%	W/15%	8.5%
Feb	N-NW/63%	var	N-NW/46%	S/13%	7%
Mar	N-NW/49%	SE/12%	N-NW/44%	S-SE/33%	8%
Apr	N-NW/57%	SE/10%	S-SE/41%	N-NW/37%	6.5%
May	N-NW/52%	SE/12%	S-SE/45%	N-NW/32%	6.5%
Jun	N-NW/67%	var	S-SW/52%	N-NW/28%	3%
Jul	N-NW/58%	var	S-SW/52%	N-NW/27%	5.5%
Aug	N-NW/71%	var	S-SW/48%	N-NW/27	7.5%
Sep	N-NW/61%	SE/9%	S-SW/36%	N-NW/36%	6%
Oct	N-NW/56%	SE/9%	W-NW/35%	S-SW/35%	6.5%
Nov	N-NW/54%	SE/9%	N-NW/40%	SE-S/25%	8.5%
Dec	N-NW/54%	W/11%	N-NW/48%	W/14%	10%

Temperature, humidity and precipitation (Naples)

	Av max °C	Av min °C	Highs recorded	Relative humidity	Days 1mm rain	Sea temp °C
Jan	12	4	20	68%	11	14
Feb	13	5	20	67%	10	13
Mar	15	6	25	62%	9	13
Apr	18	9	27	61%	8	13
May	22	12	32	63%	7	15
Jun	26	16	35	58%	4	17
Jul	29	18	36	53%	2	22
Aug	29	18	37	53%	3	24
Sep	26	16	34	59%	5	23
Oct	22	12	29	63%	9	22
Nov	17	9	26	68%	11	19
Dec	14	6	20	70%	12	17

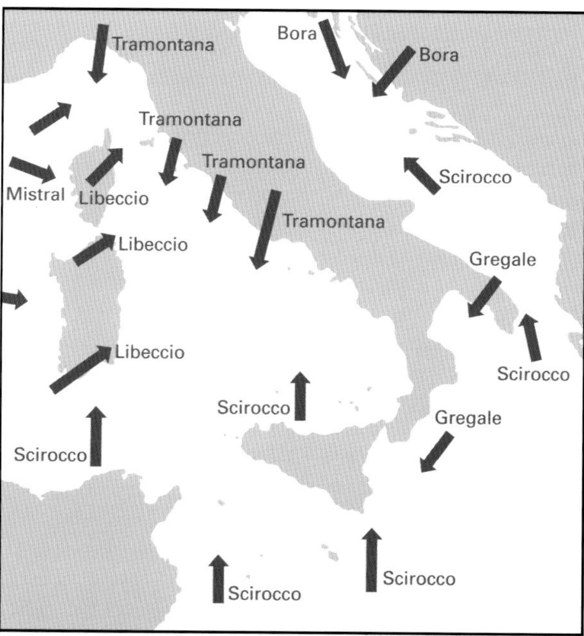

LOCAL WINDS
Note: Winds from N/NW, most common in summer, are not shown. Number of arrows does not indicate frequency.

typical port, starboard and cardinal buoys and beacons. This is the normal European system where green buoys and beacons are left to *starboard* and red to *port* when *entering a harbour*. There may be variations in local marks, for example a simple pole or plastic can may be used to indicate a reef within a bay.

Lights

Areas around commercial ports and marinas are well lit. Major headlands and dangers to navigation also carry appropriate lights, and are as reliable as any in the Mediterranean.

Note Changes to major buoyage or lights are usually reported on Navtex navigation warning messages and at the end of radio weather reports.

Climate and Weather

Wind strength

All wind strengths are described as a force on the Beaufort scale. To calculate the approximate wind speed in knots from its Force, multiply the Force by 5 and then subtract 5 (up to Force 8).

Winds

In the summer winds are predominantly from the NW and the W, although in some areas (the W coast of Italy) land and sea breezes are well developed. As in many other parts of the Mediterranean the complex topography of the area significantly alters winds close to the coast and the wind in one area may be quite different from the wind 20 miles down the coast or out to sea. A list of the local winds is given below.

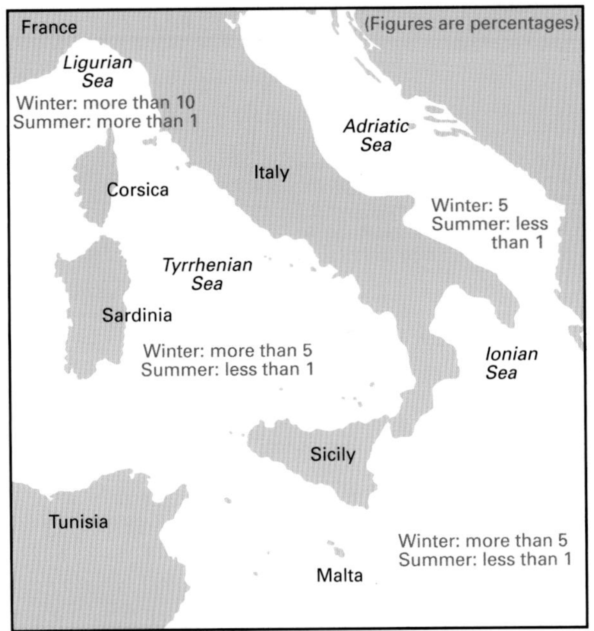

FREQUENCY OF GALES

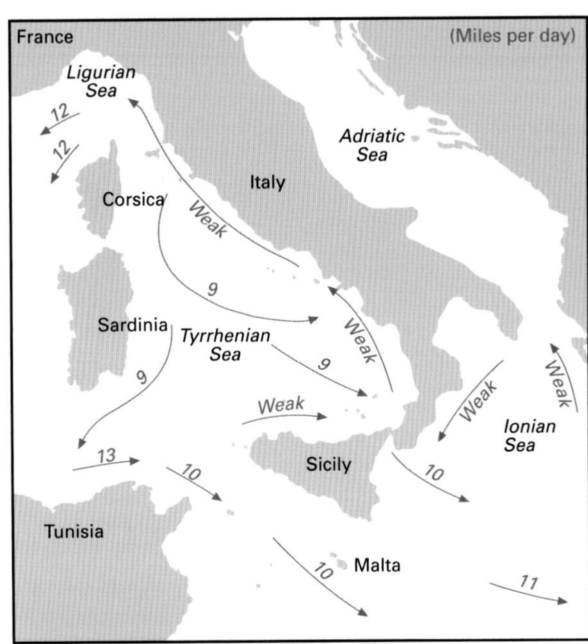

CURRENTS: MAY - JUNE

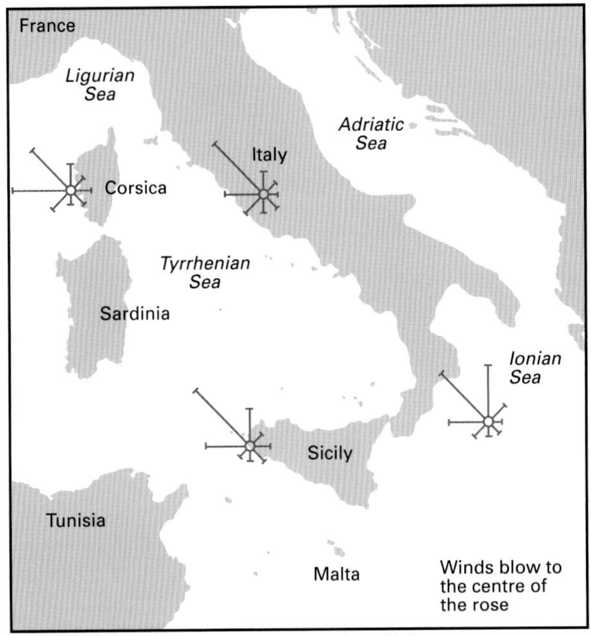

FREQUENCY OF WINDS OVER SEA: JULY

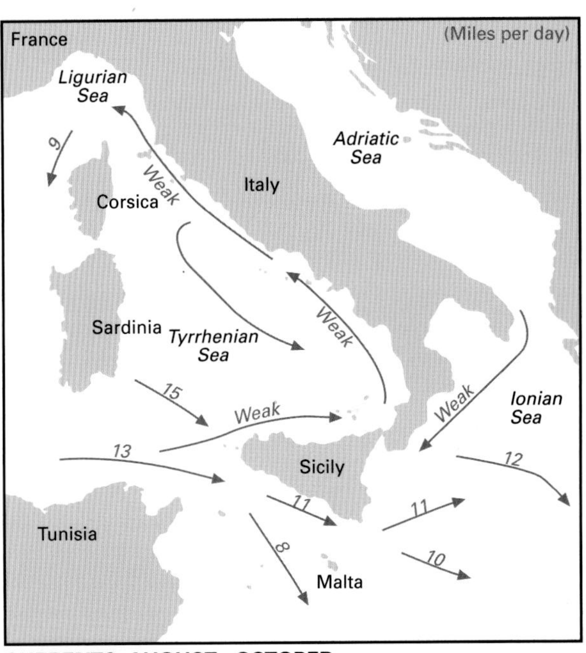

CURRENTS: AUGUST - OCTOBER

Depressions

Depressions originate in the Mediterranean or can enter from the Atlantic, through the Strait of Gibraltar or through the Toulouse gap across the border between Spain and France and into the Golfe du Lion. The depression may then move NE or SE across Sardinia and Sicily. Depressions frequently stop and deepen in the Gulf of Genoa before moving on. Although depressions in the Mediterranean are not large by Atlantic standards, they can nonetheless give rise to violent winds, especially in the winter.

Local winds

Maestrale A corruption of *magistralis*, masterful, describing the gales that frequently blow from the N–NW, but has now been generalised to refer to most winds from this direction.

Libeccio The SW–W wind that blows over Corsica and in the Ligurian and northern half of the Tyrrenhenian sea. It frequently blows at Force 5–8. Accompanied by cloud and often rain in the autumn and winter. Usually lasts 1–4 days.

Ponente West winds.

Tramontana A NE wind which mostly blows in the autumn and winter along the W coast of Italy, principally in the N. It can blow at gale force and there can be severe gusts off high land. Often associated with a depression in the Adriatic and an anticyclone further E. Usually lasts 1–2 days.

Gregale Strong NE wind. Blows principally down

Weather vocabulary

Only the most common terms are given

One *uno*
two *due*
three *tre*
four *quattro*
five *cinque*
six *sei*
seven *sette*
eight *otto*
nine *nove*
ten *dieci*
north nord, *settentrionale*
south *sud, meridionale*
east *est*
west *ovest, ponente*
wind force *forza di vento*
decreasing *diminuzione*
increasing *in aumento*
backing *rotazione a sinistra*
veering *rotazione ovaria*
variable *variabile*
improving *miglioramento*
light *debole*
moderate *moderato*
strong forte
gusty *con raffiche*
gust *colpo di vento*
gale *burrasca*
storm *tempesta*
thunderstorm *temporale*
Often you will hear: *temporale con locali colpi di venti* – local thunderstorms with strong gusts

Sea (*mare*)

choppy *increspato*
heavy *pesante*
rough *agitato, grosso*
calm *tranquillo, calmo*
swell *onda*

Sky (*cielo*)

clouds *nuvole*
cloudy *nuvoloso*
overcast *coperto*

Visibility (*visibilita*)

good *buono*
poor *scarso*
fog (foggy) *nebbioso*
hazy *caliginoso*

Weather (*tempo*)

fine *sereno, bello*
hail *gradine*
heavy *pesante, violento*
intermittent *intermittente*
isolated *isolate*
local *locale*
rain *pioggia*
drizzle *pioggia debole*
snow *neve*

General situation (*situazione*)

anticyclone *anticiclone*
cold front *fronte freddo*
warm front *fronte caldo*
deep *profondo*
depression *depressione*
occlusion *occlusione*
ridge *promontorio*
stationary *stazionario*
trough *saccatura*
coast *costa*
forecast *previsione*

Beaufort scale of wind strength

Sea State	*Beaufort No.*	*Description*	*Velocity in knots*	*Velocity in km/h*	*Term*	*Code*	*Wave height in metres*
Like a mirror	0	Calm, glassy	<1	<1	Calm	0	0
Ripples	1	Light airs Rippled	1–3	1–5	Calm	1	0–0·1
Small wavelets	2	Light breeze Wavelets	4–6	6–11	Smooth	2	0·1–0·5
Large wavelets	3	Gentle breeze	7–10	12–19	Slight	3	0·5–1·25
Small waves, breaking	4	Moderate breeze	11–16	20–28	Moderate	4	1·25–2·5
Moderate waves, foam	5	Fresh breeze	17–21	29–38	Rough	5	2·5–4
Large waves, foam and spray	6	Strong breeze	22–27	39–49			
Sea heads up, foam in streaks	7	Near gale	28–33	50–61	Very rough	6	4–6
Higher long waves, foam in streaks	8	Gale	34–40	62–74			
High waves, dense foam, spray impairs visibility	9	Strong gale	41–47	75–88	High	7	6–9
Very high tumbling waves, surface white with foam, visibility affected	10	Storm	48–55	89–102	Very high	8	9–14
Exceptionally high waves, sea covered in foam, visibility affected	11	Violent storm	56–62	103–117	Phenomenal	9	Over 14
Air filled with spray and foam, visibility severely impaired	12	Hurricane	>63	>118			

the Adriatic and across to Malta. It is particularly dangerous in Malta where it blows into Marsamxett and causes a severe surge. The warning signs are a heavy swell and low cloud with rain. Often blows at gale force. Usually lasts 2–5 days.

Scirocco The hot humid S wind blowing off the Sahara. Most common in southern Italy. It is often accompanied by bad visibility and low cloud. If it rains there will often be 'red rain' containing dust particles from the Sahara. May blow up to gale force. Usually lasts 1–3 days.

Bora A strong N wind similar to the *mistral.* Mainly affects the N Adriatic. Most frequent in winter although it can blow at other times of the year. Oftens blows at gale force. Can last from 2–12 days.

Mistral The wind blowing down the Rhône valley from the N can fan out to blow from the W onto the W coasts of Corsica and Sardinia.

Weather forecasts

Despite the complex topography with high mountains close to the coast, Italian weather forecasts do their best to get it right. In my experience they have been right for 60–70% of the time which, given the complex nature of the area they cover, is an excellent record.

Thunderstorms

These are most frequent in the summer and autumn and may be associated with a cold front or may result from the particular properties of a thermal air mass (a 'heat thunderstorm'). They may occur on successive evenings in some areas depending on thermal conditions. They are more common near the coast than out to sea and although there may be a squall accompanying the thunderstorms, the wind does not usually last for long.

Katabatic winds

Katabatic winds will sometimes blow at night off steep mountain slopes. These winds can sometimes blow at Force 5–6 although usually less. They seldom last longer than 2–3 hours.

Water spouts

Water spouts have been reported in the spring and winter along the Italian Riviera, in the Bay of Naples, around the Aeolian Islands and in the Strait of Messina, and in the Gulf of Cagliari. I have never heard of a yacht suffering damage from one of these spectacular phenomena, but nonetheless I have no desire to encounter one 'in the flesh'.

Fog

The frequency of fog in this area is 2% except in the Gulf of Genoa where it is 2–5%. Radiation fog accounts for most observations and this occurs around dawn, usually clearing by mid-morning. May is the most common month for fog.

In the Strait of Messina a phenomenon known as the Fata Morgana occurs, though I have never seen it. This is a mirage of multiple images seen in the morning where there is a rapid variation of temperature with height in the lowest layers of the atmosphere. Fata Morgana was the fairy or witch Morgana, sister of King Arthur, who was believed by Norman settlers to live in Calabria and to cause these spectacular images.

Visibility

In the summer dust particles suspended in the air may reduce visibility to as little as two miles but rarely less.

Humidity

Is low to moderate in this area. It varies considerably from area to area and with the wind. For example an onshore wind will cause a higher humidity than an offshore one. The *scirocco*, by the time it has picked up moisture during its passage across the sea, has a high humidity which causes discomfort.

Sea temperature

The monthly average values vary considerably. In all cases the temperature is higher the further S you go. In winter (February) the surface temperature is 12·5°C in the N and 14°C in the S (near Sicily). In the summer (August) the temperature is 23°C in the N and 25–26°C in the south.

Swell

Although there is never the large swell encountered in the Atlantic, a heavy swell can build up at times with winds from the W and S, particularly on the W coast of Sardinia, Sicily and Malta. The seas in the Mediterranean are much shorter and steeper than seas around many other areas and should not be underestimated.

Currents

On the whole currents in this area flow to the E or SE with the exception of a weak counter-current flowing up the W coast of Italy towards the N–NW and along the S coast towards the SW. With the exception of the gap between Sicily and Tunisia, the current is generally weak and can be reversed by strong winds from the opposite direction. The accompanying charts give the rates in miles per day for the summer period. For the currents in the Strait of Messina, *see Chapter V, Sicily*.

Sea level

In most of this area the sea level is influenced more by the wind than the tide. The barometric pressure also influences the sea level. With a high barometric pressure and offshore winds the sea level is lowered and conversely with a low barometric pressure and an onshore wind the sea level is raised.

Tides

Tidal differences around the coast vary considerably. On the W coast down to the Strait of Messina the tidal difference is on average around 0·3m (1ft) at springs though mostly less. For all practical purposes this can be ignored except of course for those harbours where 0·3m may put you on the bottom. Onshore or offshore winds can increase or decrease the tidal range. At Elba tidal differences of around 0·5m have been observed.

In the Strait of Messina the tidal difference causes strong tidal streams at springs. The most appreciable rate, up to 4kns at springs, occurs in the narrow section between Punta Pezzo and Capo Peloro. For more detailed information on the Strait of Messina *see Chapter V, Sicily*.

Weather forecasts

VHF frequencies

A continuous automatic weather forecast 'Meteomar' is transmitted on VHF Ch 68. It is updated every six hours and there can be the occasional glitch during the changeover from the old forecast to the new when the forecast is not transmitted. It can in fact be picked up from western

Italy and Malta – Weather forecasts and navigation warnings (including Monaco radio)

All times UTC except where shown. For LT add two hours in summer and one hour in winter.

Station	*VHF/MF*	*Fcast Areas*	*Schedule*
Monaco Radio			
Monaco	20	All French	***Weather forecasts***
	4363/8728kHz	forecast areas	0903, 1403, 1930 LT
	24	Corsican coast	Continuous
Ligurian Sea			
Monte Bignone	07		***Weather forecasts***
Castellaccio	25	Mar di Corsica	0135, 0735, 1335, 1935
Genova	2722kHz	Mar Ligure	***Storm warnings***
Zoagli	27	Tirreno N	On receipt H+03, 33
Monte Nero	61	Mar Ligure	***Navigational warnings***
Livorno	2591kHz	Tirreno N & C (E–W)	0333, 0833, 1233, 1633, 2033
Gorgona	26		
Central Tyrrhenian (N)			
Monte Argentario	01	Tirreno N	***Weather forecasts***
Civitavecchia	1888kHz	Tirreno C (E–W)	0135, 0735, 1335, 1935
T. Chiaruccia	64	Tirreno S (E–W)	***Storm warnings***
Monte Cavo	25	Tirreno N	On receipt H+03, 33
		Tirreno C (E–W)	***Navigational warnings***
			0533, 0933, 1333, 1833, 2333
Central and S Tyrrhenian			***Weather forecasts***
Posillipo	01		0135, 0735, 1335, 1935
Napoli	2632kHz	Tirreno C (E–W)	***Storm warnings***
Capri	27	Tirreno S (E–W)	On receipt H+03, 33
Varco del Salice	62		***Navigational warnings***
Serra del Tuono	25		0533, 0933, 1333, 1833, 2333
Sardinia			
Porto Torres	2719kHz		
Porto Cervo	26	Mar di Corsica	
Monte Moro	28	Mar di Sardegna	
Monte Limbara	85	Tirreno C (E–W)	***Weather forecasts***
Monte Tului	68		0135, 0735, 1335, 1935
Monte Serpeddi	04		***Storm warnings***
Cagliari	2680kHz	Mar di Sardegna	On receipt H+03, 33
Margine Rosso	62	Canale di Sardegna	***Navigational warnings***
Pta Campu Spina	82	Tirreno C & S (E–W)	0303, 0803, 1203, 1603, 2003
Badde Urbara	68	Mar di Corsica	
Osilo	28	Mar di Sardegna	
		Tirreno C (E–W)	
Sicily			
Palermo	1852kHz		
Palermo	81	Tirreno S (E–W)	
Sferracavallo	27	Canale di Sicilia	
Ustica	84		
Cefalu	61		
Forte Spuria	88	Tirreno S (E–W)	
Messina	2789kHz	Ionio N & S	***Weather forecasts***
Capo Lato	86		0135, 0735, 1335, 1935
Augusta	2628kHz	Canale di Sicilia	***Storm warnings***
Siracusa	85	Ionio S	On receipt H+03, 33
Gela	26		***Navigational warnings***
Caltabellotta	82	Canale di Sicilia	0333, 0833, 1233, 1633, 2033
Mazara	2600kHz		
Mazara	25		
Erice	81	Tirreno S (E–W)	
Pantelleria	88	Canale di Sicilia	
Lampedusa	1876kHz		
Lampedusa	25	Canale di Sicilia	
Crecale	87		

Ionian			
Capo Armi	62		***Weather forecasts***
Pta Stilo	84		0135, 0735, 1335, 1935
Crotone	2663kHz	Ionio N & S	***Storm warnings***
Capo Colonna	88		On receipt H+03, 33
Monte Parano	26		***Navigational warnings***
Monte Sardo	68		0333, 0833, 1233, 1633, 2033
South Adriatic			
			Weather forecasts
Abate Argento	05	Ionio N	0135, 0735, 1335, 1935
Bari	2479kHz	Adriatiic S	***Storm warnings***
Bari	27		On receipt H+03, 33
Casa d'Orso	81	Adriatic C & S	***Navigational warnings***
Monte Calvario	01		0333, 0833, 1233, 1633, 2033
MALTA	2625kHz	Maltese waters <50NM	0403, **0803, 1403, 1903**
	04 (Call on 16, 12)		0703, 1103, 1703, 2203

Greece right across to Menorca in the Balearics. It is transmitted using a synthesised voice similar to some US forecasts and gives a forecast for the whole of the Mediterranean, first in Italian and then in English.

Forecast format

The format follows the standard pattern given below:

1. Gale warnings (*avviso*).
2. General situation (*situazione*)
3. A forecast for each sea area or a group of sea areas.
   For broadcasts 0000–1200 UT the forecast is valid to 1800 UT
   For broadcasts 1200–0000 UT the forecast is valid to 0600 UT
   The forecast for each area is given as follows: Wind direction and strength. Sea state. Sky. Visibility. Weather.
   An outlook for a further 12 hours follows.
4. An extended wind forecast for the next 48 hours, in four 12-hour forecasts.

Forecast areas

Mare di Corsica, Mare di Sardegna, Canale di Sardegna, Mare Ligure, Tirreno Settentrionale, Tirreno Centrale, Tirreno Meridionale, Canale di Sicilia, Ionio Meridionale, Ionio Settentrionale, Adriatico Meridionale, Adriatico Centrale, Adriatico Settentrionale.

Additional areas

Alboran Sea, N Balearics, S Balearics, Libyan Sea, Aegean Sea, S of Crete, Levantine Basin.

Note The same broadcast is also transmitted from coastal radio stations in Italian and English at the following times: 0135, 0735, 1335, 1935 UT

Notice of the forecast and VHF channel is given on Ch 16. For the relevant channels for the area see below or look at the coast radio stations given on the introductory map for each chapter. Remember that transmission channels can and do change, so it is worth listening in to Ch 16 to see which channel will be used.

In general it is considered that the Italian forecasts do not give nearly enough detail to be useful, and

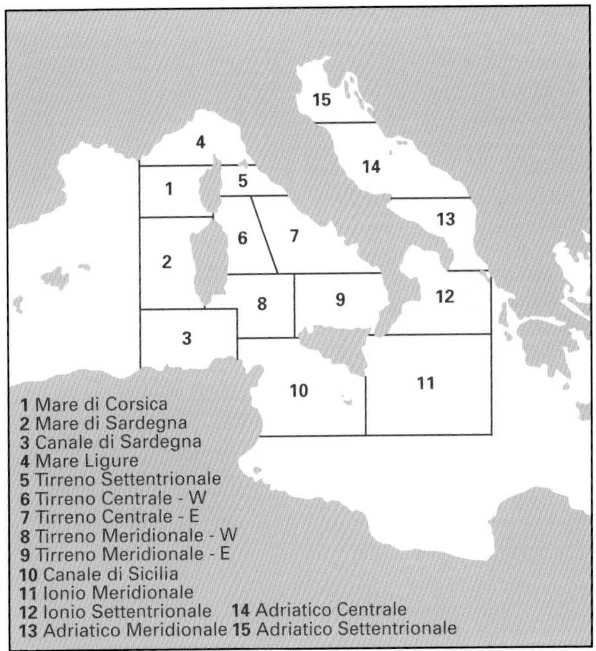

ITALIAN FORECAST AREAS

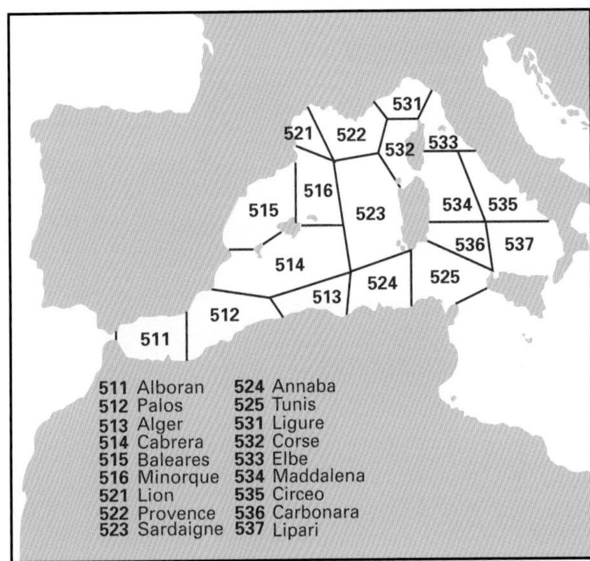

FRENCH FORECAST AREAS

NAVTEX (N4) Transmitters

Country	*Transmitter identification character*	*Freq kHz*	*Times*	*Language used*	*Range NM*	*Status of implementation*
Spain						
Tarifa	G	518	0100, 0500, **0900**, 1300, 1700, **2100**	English	400	Operational
	T	490		Spanish		
Valencia	X	518	0350, **0750**, 1150, 1550, **1950**, 2350	English	300	Operational
(Cabo de la Nao)	M	490	0200, 0600, 1000, 1400, 1800, 2200	Spanish		
France						
La Garde (CROSS)	W	518	0340, 0740, **1140**, 1540, 1940, **2340**	English	250	Operational
	S	490	0300, 0700, **1100**, 1500, 1900, **2300**	French		
Italy						
Roma	R	518	0250, **0650**, 1050, 1450, **1850**, 2250	English	320	Operational
Bari		518		English		Planned
Ancona		518		English		Planned
Trieste	U	518	0320, **0720**, 1120, 1520, **1920**, 2320	English	320	Operational
Sardegna						
La Maddalena		518		English		Planned
Cagliari	T	518	0310, **0710**, 1110, 1510, **1910**, 2310	English	320	Operational
Sicily						
Augusta	V	518	0330, **0730**, 1130, 1530, **1930**, 2330	English	320	Operational
Lampedusa		518		English		Planned
Croatia						
Hvar (Split)	Q	518	**0240, 0640, 1040, 1440, 1840, 2240**	English	150	Operational
Malta						
Malta	O	518	0220, **0620**, 1020, 1420, **1820**, 2220	English	400	Operational
Tunisia						
Tunis		518		English		Planned
Greece						
Kerkyra	K	518	0140, **0540**, **0940**, 1340, **1740**, **2140**	English	280	Operational
Limnos	L	518	0150, **0550**, **0950**, 1350, **1750**, **2150**	English	280	Operational
Iraklion	H	518	0110, **0510**, **0910**, 1310, **1710**, **2110**	English	280	Operational

Weather forecast times shown in bold

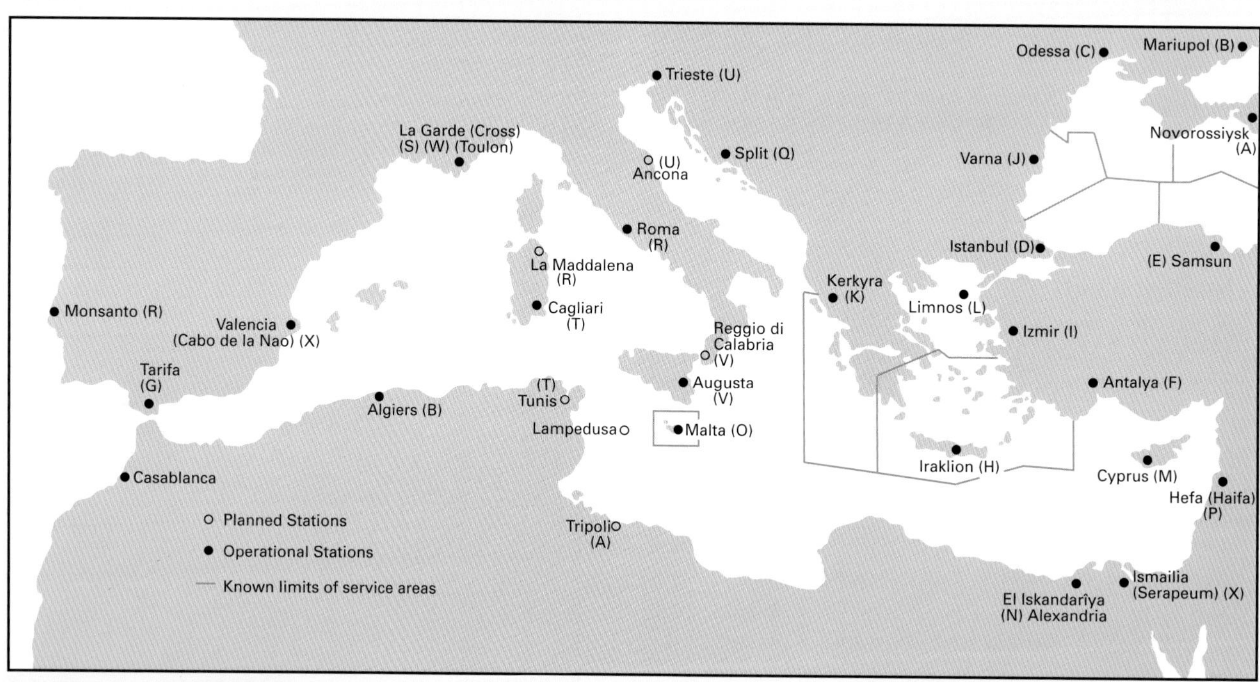

NAVTEX TRANSMITTERS

sailors should consider other radio or email sources, particularly if in exposed or offshore situations.

Monaco radio

Forecasts from Monaco Radio tend to give more detail than the Meteomar, and are particularly useful for the Bonifacio Straits. Broadcast on VHF and SSB in French and English. The VHF forecast can usually be received from Bandol to Genoa and nearly to the N of Corsica. See table for details.

SSB frequencies

The same Meteomar weather forecast is transmitted on MF frequencies in Italian and English at the following times

0135, 0735, 1335, 1935 UT

For frequency details see the table.

Broadcast radio

Weather forecasts (*Bolletini del Mare*) are transmitted in Italian only on broadcast radio at the following times. With a little patience the gist of the forecast can soon be picked up (weather vocabulary in Italian is given below). The bulletins follow the standard format given above for the continuous transmission on VHF Ch 68.

RAI RadioUno 567kHz, 657kHz, 666kHz, 1062kHz, 1332kHz
(1062kHz can be picked up in most places)

Monday–Friday	0545, 0630, 0730, 0835, 1155, 1855, 2310, 2355
Saturday	0545, 0755, 0855, 0935, 1135, 1400, 1955
Sunday	0545, 0705, 0855, 1105, 1255, 1435, 1915, 2125, 2305

General weather bulletins are given regularly through the day at other times and may include gale warnings, but the full *Bolletini del Mare* is only given once a day at 0545.

Television

After the evening news at around 2100 the state television channels (RAI) show a weather forecast with wind direction and force.

Newspapers

The national dailies (*La Stampa, La Repubblica*) have a synoptic weather map from which weather trends can be determined.

Telephone service

Note At the time of writing there are reports that this service has been terminated. Nonetheless I include it in case the system still operates or is resumed.

Anywhere in Italy you can phone 196 and a recorded weather forecast, in Italian and in the same order as above, in fact exactly the same one given on RAI 1°, is played. A new weather forecast is given every 12 hours. The cost is minimal and the call can be made from a public telephone where, for a small sum, you can listen to the forecast going round and round for as long as you like until you get the gist of it.

Marinas and harbours

All marinas and some harbours with yacht berths post a daily forecast which is often printed out from an internet page. Often it includes annotated synoptic maps. The text will usually be in Italian only.

Weather on the Internet

There are a number of services on the Internet which provide up-to-date surface forecasts, text forecasts and satellite pictures. Access to the internet from a boat can be obtained in a number of ways. For a fuller account of the options see the section on telecommunications.

JCOMM GMDSS by Météo France
http://weather.gmdss.org
Official text forecast for GMDSS MSI. Select METAREA III.

Weather Online
www.weatheronline.co.uk/sail.htm
Gives surface wind direction and strength up to a week ahead.

Italian National Meteorological Service
www.meteoam.it
Meteomar text of forecasts as on VHF Ch 68.

Météo France
www.meteofrance.com
Detailed forecasts for coastal and offshore areas in W Med.

Eurometeo
www.eurometeo.com
Gives up to a 3-day forecast with wind strength and sea conditions for all Italian waters.

Sardinian Regional Weather site
www.sar.sardegna.it
Local forecasts for Italian waters.

NEMOC Navy
https://www.nemoc.navy.mil/manual/watch/lamad.gif
Detailed forecast for Bonifacio Strait.

DWD German Weather Forecasting
www.dwd.de
Follow links to Wetter + Klima – Wetter Aktuell – Seewetter – Mittelmeer.
German language site, but easily understood tabled forecasts. Detailed 3-day text forecasts for W Med areas.

Malta Airport
www.maltaairport.com
3-day forecasts, text, graphics and synoptic charts

Navtex

Navtex is part of GMDSS and the system automatically receives MSI (Maritime Safety Information). Receivers can either be stand alone units or use a laptop or chart plotter display. Forecast details and areas covered are usually similar to those given on VHF.

There has been some discussion in the past over message errors and non-recording of messages. In 2005 I experienced no problems with any of the stations listed and received messages at the times given.

The mounting of the aerial for NAVTEX reception is often mentioned as critical. Instructions usually suggest that the aerial is mounted on the pushpit clear of other aerials. Others who have experienced problems have connected the aerial to a shroud for better reception. My NAVTEX aerial is inside the aft cabin where it gets a clear signal.

In areas where there is high ground surrounding the harbour or anchorage some problems can be experienced getting a clear signal, though less than might be expected in my experience.

For the record, I use a NAVTEX Pro Plus with the NAVTEX active aerial.

RTTY Forecasts

It is possible to receive text forecasts using Radio Teletype (RTTY) using either a dedicated receiver (such as the NASA Weatherman or NASA HF3), or an SSB radio linked to a laptop with suitable software. RTTY forecasts for the Mediterranean are available from Hamburg and include a five day outlook which can be a useful alternative to obtaining web forecasts.

Frequencies: 4583, 7646, 10100.8kHz

Times: 0410, 0930, 1015, 1115, 1550, 1610, 2215, 2315

For jargon-free details see Frank Singleton's website http://weather.mailasail.com/Franks-Weather/Home

Weather by Email

Refer also to the section on *Telecommunications* for details on how to retrieve email. This section is intended to provide information on getting forecasts on slow or expensive connections such as dial-up, GPRS or HF radio systems.

Document retrieval using FTP (File Transfer Protocol) is a means of extracting text based weather forecasts from the web, without needing to access the internet. Services such as Saildocs (www.saildocs.com) enable you to 'ask' for a webpage to be sent to your email address as a text only email. Any pictures on the original page are deleted, and the page is reformatted to plain text, so what arrives is a much smaller (read: less kilobytes) text only version of the original.

For example:

Send an email to: query@saildocs.com
Subject: (anything)
Main text: send *http address of webpage*

So to get the GMDSS text forecast for the Eastern Mediterranean from Saildocs type:

Send met.3e
For the Western Mediterranean:
Send met.3w

The link must be exactly as it is on the webpage that you want, with no extra spaces or characters.

More information on Saildocs is available by sending an email to info@saildocs.com, this will return the how-to document (about 5Kb).

Saildocs is provided without charge thanks to the support of Sailmail, a membership-owned radio email service for cruising sailors which operates a network of 13 stations worldwide. For more information on SailMail see their website www.sailmail.com

It is also possible to obtain GRIB files using this system (see below).

Note Obtaining forecasts using phones or email should not replace obtaining MSI (Maritime Safety Information) forecasts using VHF or Navtex. Gale Warnings are disseminated first on official MSI services. Saildocs warns users that the retrieval service is completely automated and therefore is susceptible to changes in URLs or other things which will cause the retrieval to fail.

GRIB weather files

GRIB files are highly compressed weather files which cut download speeds compared to earlier compression formats. They contain all sorts of data though commonly they have information on wind speeds, barometric pressure and rainfall. The files can be downloaded off the internet or received by email and their small size makes them particularly suitable for receiving using slow modems such as HF radio or expensive GPRS connections. You will need a GRIB viewer, although most GRIB services provide these, and the GRIB file free of charge. Subscription services do not seem to offer a great deal more than these, given that the source data for almost all services is the same.

GRIB files obtained solely by email must be requested using specially formatted auto-response email requests, which differ according to the provider. Saildocs is a popular email based GRIB service which uses the Airmail GRIB viewer. See www.saildocs.com or www.siriuscyber.net for more details.

A very useful internet based GRIB service is provided by UGRIB. The software can be downloaded free from the internet, and requests can be easily made by highlighting the area requested on a map, and selecting the resolution, duration and spacing of the files. See www.grib.us for details.

It is important to know that GRIB files are entirely computer generated, and have no human at the helm to interpret data.

These weather files are all fairly broadstroke and do not provide the sort of detailed information found in more dedicated websites for a country or sea area. They provide an overall picture for a large sea area rather than detailed data for short local passages.

Coast radio stations

Coast Radio Italy and Malta – VHF

All stations monitor Ch 16
Traffic lists H+15 UT
R – Call sign *Roma Radio*
P – Call sign *Palermo Radio*

Station		*Manual*	*Auto*	*Autolink*
Ligurian Sea				
Monte Bignone	R	**07**	65	03, 23
Castellaccio	R	**25**	83	
Zoagli	R	**27**	85	
Monte Nero	R	**61**	63	
Gorgona	R	**26**	82	
Elba	R		84	
Tyrrhenian Sea				
Monte Argentario	R	**01**	62	04, 27
T. Chiaruccia	R	**64**	81	
Monte Cavo	R	**25**	65	03, 02
Posillipo	P	**01**	23	
Capri	P	**27**	79	
Varco del Salice	P	**62**		
Serra del Tuono	P	**25**	24	82, 86
Sardinia				
Porto Cervo	R	**26**	88	
Monte Moro	R	**28**	66	24, 87
Monte Limbara	R	**85**	86	07, 23
Monte Tului	R	**83**	86	
Monte Serpeddi	R	**04**	78	05, 26
Margine Rosso	R	**62**	63	
Pta Campu Spina	R	**82**	83	
Badde Urbara	R	**87**	03	
Osilo	R	**26**	61	
Sicily				
Sferracavallo	P	**27**		
Ustica	P	**84**	80	
Cefalu	P	**61**	78	
Forte Spuria	P	**85**	02	
Campo Lato	P	**86**	83	03, 26
Siracusa	P	**85**	81	
Gela	P	**26**	61	
Caltabellotta	P	**22**		
Mazara del Vallo	P	**25**	64	
Erice	P	**81**	65	
Pantelleria	P	**22**		
Lampedusa	P	**25**	85	
Grecale	P	**21**	78	84
Ionian				
Capo Armi	P	**62**	82	
Pta Stilo	P	**84**	65	
Capo Colonna	P	**20**	66	04, 07
Monte Parano	P	**26**	61	
Monte Sardo	P	**27**	02	
South Adriatic				
Abate Argento	P	**05**	62	24, 80
Bari	P	**27**		
MALTA				
Malta Radio		**01, 02, 03, 04, 28**		
Valetta Port Control		**12, 09**		

Coast Radio Italy and Malta – MF/HF

All stations monitor and receive on 2182kHz
Main operating frequency in bold
Traffic lists at 0715, 1115, 1515 All times UT

Station	*Transmit (kHz)*	*Rx*
Genova	1667, 2642, **2722**	
Livorno	1925, **2591**	
Civitavecchia	**1888**, 2710, 3747	
Napoli	**2632**, 3735	
Porto Torres	**2719**	
Cagliari	**2680**, 2683	
Palermo	**1852**	
Messina	**2789**	
Augusta	1643, **2628**	
Mazara del Vallo	1883, 2211, **2600**	
Lampedusa	**1876**	
Crotone	1715, **2663**	
Bari	1771, **2579**	
MALTA		
Malta Radio	2625	
Roma radio – HF	4417,	4125
	6516,	6215
	8779	8255

Weatherfax (WX) broadcasts

Weatherfax services are usually accessed using a HF receiver and appropriate computer and software or a dedicated weatherfax receiver.

For weatherfax station frequencies, transmission times and data please consult:

Imray *Mediterranean Almanac*
Admiralty *ALRS Small Craft NP289*

Or the following websites:
HF-Fax (listing of stations, frequencies and data)
www.hffax.de
Frank Singleton (links and explanations)
http://weather.mailasail.com/Franks-Weather/Home
NOAA (world-wide stations. PDF download)
www.nws.noaa.gov/om/marine/radiofax.htm

Note It seems as if weatherfax transmissions are gradually being phased out as more and more large ships use INMARSAT or internet weather maps. (I should stress this is my opinion and not the official line.)

Satellite weather services

SafetyNET is the MSI service for satellite-based receivers (INMARSAT). The Mediterranean comes under NAV/METAREA III Area of Responsibility covered by the Atlantic Ocean Region – East (AOR–E) satellite footprint.

Forecasts are issued from Greece, with W Med forecasts derived from France at 1000 and 2200 UT.

LIFE-SAVING SIGNALS

SOLAS CHAPTER V REGULATION 29

To be used by Ships, Aircraft or Persons in Distress when communicating with life-saving stations, maritime rescue units and aircraft engaged in search and rescue operations.

Note: All Morse Code signals by light (below).

1. SEARCH AND RESCUE UNIT REPLIES

YOU HAVE BEEN SEEN, ASSISTANCE WILL BE GIVEN AS SOON AS POSSIBLE

Orange smoke flare

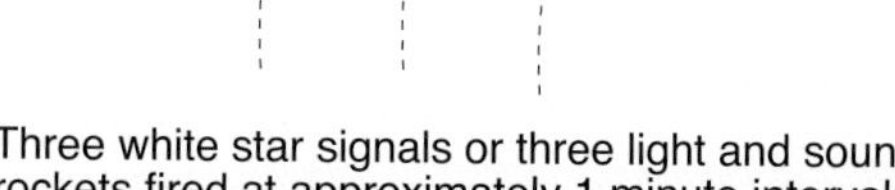

Three white star signals or three light and sound rockets fired at approximately 1 minute intervals

2. SURFACE TO AIR SIGNALS

Note: Use International Code of Signals by means of light or flags or by laying out the symbol on the deck or ground with items that have a high contrast background.

MESSAGE	ICAO/IMO VISUAL SIGNALS
REQUIRE ASSISTANCE	V • • • —
REQUIRE MEDICAL ASSISTANCE	X — • • —
NO or NEGATIVE	N — •
YES or AFFIRMATIVE	Y — • — —
PROCEEDING IN THIS DIRECTION	↑

3. AIR TO SURFACE REPLIES

Note: Use signals most appropriate to prevailing conditions.

MESSAGE UNDERSTOOD

Drop a message. OR Rocking wings. OR Flashing landing or navigation lights on and off twice. OR T — OR R • — •

MESSAGE NOT UNDERSTOOD

Straight and level flight. OR Circling. OR R • — • P • — — • T —

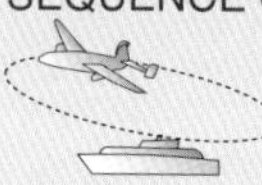

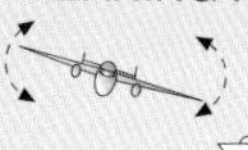

4. AIR TO SURFACE DIRECTION SIGNALS

SEQUENCE OF 3 MANOEUVRES MEANING PROCEED IN THIS DIRECTION

Circle vessel at least once.

Cross low, ahead of vessel rocking wings.

Overfly vessel and head in required direction.

YOUR ASSISTANCE IS NO LONGER REQUIRED

Cross low, astern of vessel rocking wings.

Note: As a non preferrred alternative to rocking wings, varying engine tone or volume may be used.

5. SURFACE TO AIR REPLIES

MESSAGE UNDERSTOOD - I WILL COMPLY

Change course to required direction. OR T — OR Code & answering pendant "Close Up".

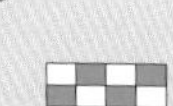

I AM UNABLE TO COMPLY

International flag "N". OR N — •

6. SHORE TO SHIP SIGNALS

SAFE TO LAND HERE

Vertical waving of both arms, white flag, light or flare OR K — • —

LANDING HERE IS DANGEROUS ADDITIONAL SIGNALS MEAN SAFER LANDING IN DIRECTION INDICATED

Horizontal waving white flag, light or flare. Putting one flare/ flag on ground and moving off with a second indicates direction of safer landing.

OR

S • • • Landing here is dangerous.

R • — • Land to right of your current heading.

L • — • • Land to left of your current heading.

Safety and rescue services

SAR organisation

Commando Generale delle Capitanerie di Porto is based in Rome MRCC and co-ordinates SAR operations nationally and internationally through the Guardia Costiera (coastguard). CRS maintain a continuous listening watch on international distress frequencies. They will dispatch an appropriate rescue craft and monitor the operation. The *guardia costiera* operate a range of offshore lifeboats – including large rigid-bottom inflatables capable of 32 knots and operating up to 25M offshore, and all-weather craft capable of 21 knots and operating up to 50 or more miles offshore. The *guardia costiera* can also call in the navy and air force if needed, who operate rescue helicopters, aircraft, and large offshore vessels.

For salvage operations a tug will be called up from the nearest large harbour.

At the beginning of each chapter the relevant coastguard stations are annotated onto the introductory map, with all radio frequencies including DSC capability if applicable.

Roma MRCC
MMSI 002 470 001
DSC VHF Ch 70, 16
DSC MF 2187.5kHz, 2182kHz
DSC HF 4207.5, 6312, 8414.5, 12577, 16804.5 kHz
✆ 06 656 171 *Fax* 06 656 17303
Email roma@guardiacostiera.it
www.guardiacostiera.it

CIRM (International Medical Centre)
✆ 065 923 331/2 *Fax* 065 923 333
Email telesoccorso@cirm.it
www.cirm.it

Palermo MRSC
MMSI 002 470 002
DSC VHF Ch 70, 16
DSC MF 2187.5kHz, 2182kHz
✆ 091 331 538 *Fax* 091 325 519
Email palermo@guardiacostiera.it

Genoa MRSC
✆ 010 241 2222 *Fax* 010 261 064
Email mrsc@mrsc.porto.genova.it

Livorno MRSC
✆ 0586 894 493 *Fax* 0586 826 090
Email compliop@portnet.it

Naples MRSC
✆ 081 244 5111 *Fax* 081 244 5347
Email 4_mrsc@libero.it

Reggio Calabria MRSC
✆ 0965 6561 *Fax* 0965 656 333
Email reggiocalabria@guardiacostiera.com

Cagliari MRSC
✆ 070 605 171 *Fax* 070 605 17218
Email cagliari@guardiacostiera.it

Catania MRSC
✆ 095 747 4111 *Fax* 095 532 962
Email catania@guardiacostiera.it

Bari MRSC
✆ 080 521 6860 *Fax* 080 521 1726
Email bari@guardiacostiera.it

EMERGENCY TELEPHONE NUMBERS
1530 Coastguard (Guardia Costiera, local Capitaneria)
112 Pan-European Emergency number (Police)
113 Police, Red Cross, emergency first aid (Pronto Soccorso)
115 Fire (Pompiere)
118 Ambulance

MALTA

SAR organisation

Malta MRCC is part of Armed Forces Malta (AFM) and co-ordinates SAR operations in Maltese waters assisted by Malta Maritime Authority, Malta Radio and Malta International Airport. Malta Radio maintains a listening watch on international distress frequencies. Several patrol boats are available and a helicopter can be alerted for SAR operations.

For salvage operations a tug will be called from Valetta.

MRCC (AFM) Malta
DSC VHF Ch 70, 16
DSC MF 2187.5kHz, 2182kHz
✆ 21 824 212/809 279 *Fax* 21 809 860

Malta Radio
VHF Ch 16, 01, 02, 03, 04, 28
MF 2182, 2625kHz (0700-1800)
✆ 21 456 767/447 929 *Fax* 21 452 935

EMERGENCY TELEPHONE NUMBERS
191 Police
199 Fire
196 Ambulance

GMDSS (Global Maritime Distress and Safety System)

GMDSS consists of several integrated systems which are now required on all ships with the exception of the following:
Ships other than passenger vessels of less than 300 gross tonnage.
Passenger ships carrying less than six passengers.
Ships of war.
Ships not propelled by engines.
Pleasure yachts not engaged in charter.
Fishing vessels.
The integrated system is composed of the following components:

- **DSC Digital Selective Calling** VHF, MF and HF will utilise DSC for ship-to-ship, ship-to-shore, shore-to-ship and will also generate a preformatted distress signal giving a location position if connected to GPS or any other position finding receiver
- **MSI Maritime Safety Information** NAVTEX and coast radio are the main methods of transmitting Navigation and Met Warnings, Met Forecasts and other urgent safety-related messages. Ship Earth Stations (satellite phones) and HF Radio are also used to receive long range warnings using the SafetyNET Service

Safety Of Life At Sea Regulations (SOLAS)

Since 1 July 2002 skippers of craft under 150 tons have been required to conform to the following SOLAS V regulations. The regulations will almost certainly be applied in piecemeal fashion in the Mediterranean countries. What follows is very much my précis of the regulations and at the time of writing clarification is ongoing.

R19 A radar reflector (3 & 9 GHz) must be exhibited. For vessels over 15m it should be $10m^2$ minimum.
R29 A table of life-saving signals must be available to the skipper/helmsman at all times.
R31 Skippers must report to the coastguard on dangers to navigation including (R32) wrecks, winds of Force 10 or more and floating objects dangerous to navigation.
R33 Vessels must respond to distress signals from another vessel.
R34 Safe Navigation and Avoidance of Dangerous Situations. Vessels must be able to demonstrate that adequate passage planning has been undertaken. Things like weather, tides, vessel limitations, crew, navigational dangers, and contingency plans should be addressed.
R35 Distress signals must not be misused.

- **EPIRB Emergency Position Indicating Radio Beacon** Uses COSPAS-SARSAT international satellites to pick up the 406MHz signal
- **SART Search and Rescue radar Transponders** Portable radar transponders designed to provide a locator signal from survival craft
- **SESs Ship Earth Stations** INMARSAT is currently the main provider of maritime satellite communication systems. SESs may be used to transmit voice messages or to receive Electronic Caller Group (ECG) MSI information.

Of all these it is really DSC which most affects pleasure yachts. All GMDSS equipment had to be fitted to ships by 1 February 1999. Ships are no longer required to keep a listening watch on 2182MHz and will not have to keep a listening watch on VHF Ch 16 after 1 February 2005. It is uncertain yet whether shore stations will likewise stop listening on VHF Ch 16. Ch 70 is now banned for voice transmission and is the designated DSC VHF frequency.

DSC Distress/Safety Calling Frequencies
VHF Ch 70
MF 2187.5kHz
HF 4207.5, 6312, 8414.5, 12577, 16804.5 kHz

SAR co-ordination/on-scene communications
VHF Ch 16, 06 (ship-to-shore/ship-to-ship)
VHF 121.5 and 123.1MHz (Ship-to-aircraft – compulsory for passenger carriers)
MF 2182kHz
HF 3023 or 5680kHz (ship-to-aircraft), 4125kHz (ship-to-shore/ship-to-ship)

About the plans and pilotage notes

Nomenclature

I have adopted the convention, in common with all hydrographic departments, of calling a place by the common Italian name and by the Italian name for the feature described. Thus cape = *capo*, gulf =*golfo*, island = *isola*, and so on. A list of the Italian names and their English equivalents is given in the Appendix.

In some cases I have retained the anglicised version of common place names where there seemed no merit in rigorously adopting Italian names. Thus Sardinia is not Sardegna, Sicily is not Sicilia, Naples is not Napoli. After these anglicised versions I have normally added the correct Italian version and any confusing variations.

Abbreviations

In the pilotage notes all compass directions are abbreviated to the first letter in capitals, as is common practice. So N is north, SE is southeast and so on.

Harbour plans

The harbour plans are designed to illustrate the accompanying notes in the belief that the old adage 'a picture is worth a thousand words' is still true. It is stressed that many of these plans are based on the author's sketches and therefore should only be used in conjunction with official charts. They are not to be used for navigation.

Soundings

All soundings are in metres and are based on low water springs. In the case of my own soundings there will sometimes be up to half a metre more water than the depth shown when the sea bottom is uneven, but in most cases there is for all practical purposes the depth shown. It should be remembered that many of the harbours are prone to silting and while many are kept dredged to a minimum depth, there are others that are not dredged regularly.

For those used to working in fathoms and feet the use of metres may prove difficult at first and there is the danger of reading the depths in metres as the depths in fathoms. For all practical purposes 1m can read as approximately 3ft and therefore 2m is approximately equal to one fathom. As a quick check on the depths in fathoms without reference to the conversion tables in the appendix, it is possible to simply divide the depths in metres by two and that will approximately equal the depth in fathoms: e.g. 3m = 1½ fathoms whereas accurately 3m = 1 fathom 3·8 feet.

Waypoints

Waypoints are given for all harbours and anchorages. The origins of the waypoints vary and in a large number of cases the datum source of the waypoint is not known. Where I have taken waypoints for a harbour or anchorage it has a note after it reading WGS84. All these waypoints are to

World Geodetic Survey 1984 datum, which it is intended will be the datum source used throughout the world. Most GPS receivers automatically default to WGS84.

It is important to note that plotting a waypoint onto a chart will not necessarily put it in the position shown. There are a number of reasons for this:

1. The chart may have been drawn using another datum source. Most Italian Hydrographic charts are still based on European datum 1950. There are many other datum sources that have been used to draw charts.
2. All charts, including those using WGS84, have errors of various types. Most were drawn in the 19th century and have been fudged to conform to WGS84 (the term 'fuzzy logic' could aptly be used).
3. Even when a harbour plan is drawn there is still a significant human element at work and mistakes easily creep in. Yes, I know to my cost.

The upshot of all this is that it is important to eyeball your way into an anchorage or harbour and not just sit back and assume that all those digits on the GPS display will look after you. In the case of waypoints I have taken and which are appended WGS84, the waypoint is indeed in the place shown. In the case of other waypoints it can be derived from the light position, from reports in my files, or from other sources.

In this edition I have also included useful waypoints which are listed at the beginning of the relevant chapter and included on the location maps. As above, any that are appended WGS84 are from my own observations using the radar for distance off and a compass bearing for the direction. Given that some radar distance off readouts can be a bit of a guesstimate, these should be used with every caution. In most cases I have endeavoured to keep a reasonable distance off so that an error of say, 50m, should be unimportant when the waypoint is 0·5M from the land. There are other occasions when I have shaved a cape or islet and the distance off is considerably less.

All waypoints are given in the notation:

degrees minutes decimal place of a minute

It is important not to confuse the decimal place of a minute with the older 60 second notation.

Photographs

Most of the photographs were taken by Rod and Lu Heikell. Many were taken under difficult conditions – when navigating short-handed, in rough weather, under poor light conditions – and consequently the quality is sometimes not all that might be desired.

Bearings

All bearings are in 360° notation and are true.

Magnetic variation

The magnetic variation in Italy is very small, from 01°E in the Ligurian Sea to around 02°30′E in the Ionian. For the relatively short passages normally made around the coast it can be ignored.

Pilotage information

Approach

General notes on the approach including dangers, difficulties, general advice.
Conspicuous Conspics to visually identify where the harbour is.
By night (Only listed if there are specific difficulties associated with a night approach.)
VHF Official and unofficial channels.
Dangers Specific dangers in the approaches including reefs, rocks, bars, currents, traffic, etc.
Note Anything of note in the approach.

Mooring

General note on where and what to look out for.
Data Berths/visitors' berths/max LOA/depths maximum to minimum.
Berths Where and how.
Shelter General note on shelter from the wind and sea.
Authorities Port police, customs, immigration, marina staff and the charge band where known.
Anchorage Any possible anchorages in the harbour or nearby.

Facilities

Services Water/electricity/telephone and TV connections/internet/Wi-Fi/showers and toilets.
Fuel Fuel quay/mini-tanker/service station.
Repairs Travel-hoist or slipway and types of repairs available including chandlers etc.
Provisions
Eating out
Other PO, ATMs, banks, gas, taxis, buses, ferries etc.

General

A general note on anything from the look and feel of the place to ancient or not-so-ancient sites.

Note

Some smaller places and many anchorages will have just a simple description without the standard format above.

Quick reference guide

At the beginning of each chapter there is a summary of important information (prohibited areas, major lights). Following this there is a list of all the harbours and anchorages described in the chapter with a classification of the shelter offered, mooring, and whether fuel, water, provisions and restaurants exist. The charge band group is also included. Compressing information about a harbour or anchorage into such a framework is difficult and more than a little clumsy, but the list can be useful for route planning and as an instant *aide-mémoire* to a harbour.

Le Grazie, Rada di La Spezia

I.

The Ligurian Coast

The Ligurian coast sweeps in a semicircle from the Franco-Italian border round to Genoa and then down to the Gulf of La Spezia. This is the Italian Riviera and at its heart is Genoa which divides the Riviera in two: the Riviera di Ponente which runs west from Genoa to the French border; and the Riviera di Levante which runs south and east from Genoa to the Gulf of La Spezia. Both are famous for their natural beauty, although the Riviera di Levante is wilder and more imposing than its softer sister coast.

The very name *Riviera* immediately conjures up an image of a coastal resort blessed by a mild climate and lapped by the blue Mediterranean in which the beautiful people dabble their toes. The image is correct except that today everyman mingles along with the beautiful people. As far as I can ascertain the word riviera comes from the French *rivière* which means not only a river, but a necklace of precious stones and such a description is apt, since the region is not only geographically beautiful but also picturesque. Villages and towns of a distinctive Ligurian style of architecture are dotted along the coast like gems in a necklace fastened by the chain of the Mediterranean.

In such a popular resort area it is pleasing to see so few of the reinforced concrete monstrosities that masquerade in the name of architecture. Only in the residential area around Genoa does the disease really take root.

Genoa is both the geographical and historical pivot of Liguria. The harbour and installations stretch for something like 12 miles along the coast, making it the second largest seaport in the western Mediterranean after Marseille. Nearly half of all Italian trade passes through the city and an important shipbuilding industry flourishes here. Perhaps the best known shipyard is Ansaldo which has built many ships for the Italian navy.

Genoa's sons include Christopher Columbus and Andrea Doria and its former wealth and power determined events in the western and eastern Mediterranean between the 12th and 14th centuries and again between the 16th and 17th centuries. The old Latin saying, *Genuensis, ergo mercata* (Genoese, therefore a merchant), describes the city and its inhabitants as well today as it did in the past.

The yachtsman sailing along the Ligurian coast will mostly encounter purpose-built marinas, except for a few commercial harbours, fishing ports and anchorages along the Riviera Levante. The severe mountain backdrop shorn off at the sea allows for few natural harbours, with the notable exceptions of the Gulf of Marconi and La Spezia.

Weather patterns on the Ligurian coast

In the summer the prevailing winds in this area are not strong and are often variable in direction. The most common winds along the Riviera Ponente are from the SW or SE and the wind strength is generally less than Force 4. Along the Riviera Levante the winds are mostly from the NW or W and again are usually less than Force 4. At night and in the early morning, light northerlies blow off the coast. There are numerous days of calm weather. In the summer, gales are rare although they do occur. In the spring and autumn the winds are variable with no one direction prevailing over another.

In the winter, northerlies predominate but the wind to be feared is the *libecchio*, the SW wind which causes a heavy sea and is usually accompanied by squalls and heavy rain. The *libecchio* may also blow in the summer, but not with any frequency. Squalls are particularly bad at Rapallo and La Spezia. Along the Riviera Levante, a wind known locally as a *provenza* may blow from the NNW with considerable strength.

The *mistral*, originating in the Golfe du Lion, has moderated considerably by the time it reaches the Ligurian Sea and does not normally blow with any strength, although a heavy sea may be felt. In the Ligurian Sea a fall in pressure may mean that a cold front is developing in the Golfe du Lion, and the consequent depressions will then probably move E into the Ligurian or SE to the Tyrrhenian Sea. Often such a depression will linger in the Golfe du Lion or the Ligurian Sea, bringing unsettled weather to these areas before moving on. A yacht should be careful of the wind veering to the N from where it will blow with some violence.

Shoestring cruising along the Ligurian Coast

Anchorages
There are not a lot of good natural anchorages around the Ligurian coast although there are a number that can be used in settled weather.

Riviera Ponente

Along the Italian Riviera from the French border to Genoa the coast is fairly straight and there are just a few anchorages off some of the marinas where you can anchor and get a bit of shelter from the presence of the marina itself in settled weather. The wind here is generally a sea breeze blowing from the S–SE onto the coast although it can also blow from the SW at times. It usually dies in the evening and there may be a light land breeze at night blowing off the coast.

Harbours and marinas
San Remo in the Porto Communale.

Imperia Porto Maurizio in the old basin.

Oneglia Imperia Levante where you may or may not be allowed to stay.

Marina di Alassio but check on prices.

Isolotto Gallinara.

Finale Ligure but check on prices.

Savona in Darsena Vecchia.

Sestri Ponente in Genoa (this is about the only really affordable option for Genoa but check on prices).

Anchorages
(*most of these are marked in the pilot*)

Under the entrance to Marina degli Aregai.

North of Imperia Maurizio outside the northeast breakwater.

Just south of Diano Marina there is a breakwater you can anchor north or south of.

East of Andora off the shingle beach.

Just north of the entrance to Finale Ligure.

On the north or south side of Capo di Noli.

North of the entrance to Arenzano.

None of these anchorages are tenable in onshore winds, although it is worth bearing in mind in the summer that the onshore sea breeze will usually die in the evening and a light offshore land breeze will kick in. There will still be swell rolling into these anchorages but at least there will be good shelter nearby.

Riviera di Levante

From Genoa down the coast to Marina di Carrara there are a few more options for anchoring compared to the Riviera di Ponente. The sea breeze here is from the SW or even W in places. There may be a land breeze blowing offshore at night.

Harbours and Marinas

Camogli has a Banchina di Transito but it will often have local boats on it.

Santa Margherita Ligure.

Lavagna but check on prices.

Le Grazie.

Bocca di Magra although prices vary from one catwalk/yard to another.

Anchorages
(*most of these are marked in the pilot*)

Golfo Marconi You can anchor in several coves around Golfo Marconi depending on wind and sea. Some of the coves up from Portofino are now buoyed off for swimming areas, but you can anchor off near the entrance clear of the buoys. Just N of the entrance to Santa Margherita Ligure clear of the moorings is fairly well sheltered in settled weather. The best place is up around Rapallo at the head of the gulf, though the authorities here are not keen on you anchoring. If you get there late-ish you may not be bothered. Anchor off on the E side. You can also anchor in a cove on the E side opposite the marina.

Sestri Levante The anchorage at Sestri Levante is good in settled weather although most of the area is occupied by permanent moorings or anchoring restrictions in the season. You can also try off Baia del Silenzio on the S side.

Cinque Terra The Cinque Terra is spectacular and worth a visit in calm weather. There are several bays that are suitable in settled weather though there invariably seems to be some swell coming in. Try Riva Trigoso, Levanto, and Vernazza.

Golfo di la Spezia This large bay or small gulf provides some of the best anchorages along this coast and you can usually find somewhere to anchor in and around the gulf whatever the weather. The anchorages off Ile Palmaria, in Le Grazie, at San Terenzo and off Lerici are favourites.

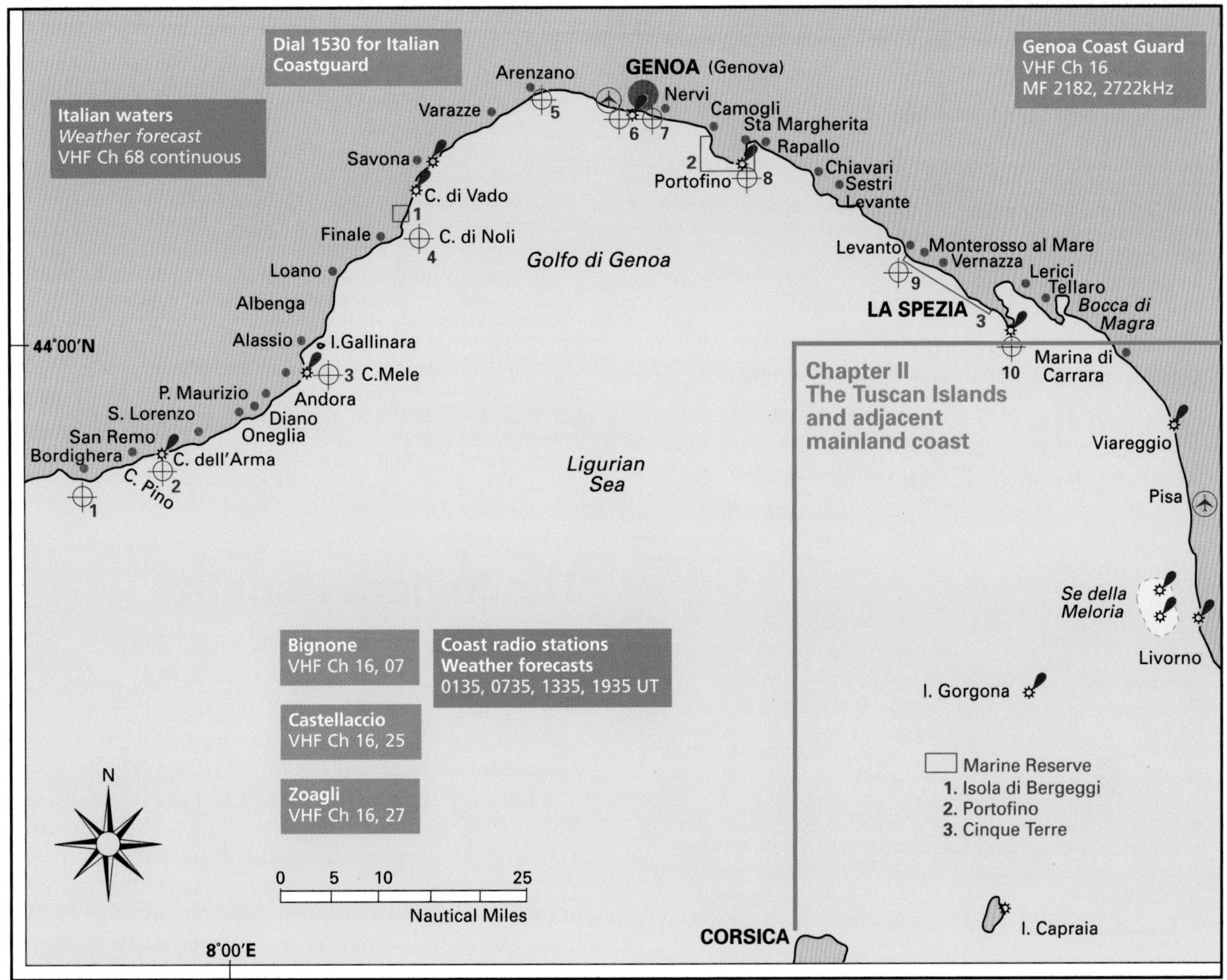

LIGURIAN COAST

USEFUL WAYPOINTS

⊕1 1M S of Capo S. Ampeglio
43°45'·45N 07°40'·4E
⊕2 1M S of Capo dell'Arma
43°48'·0N 07°49'·9E
⊕3 1M E of Capo delle Mele
43°57'·7N 08°11'·1E
⊕4 1M E of Capo Noli
44°11'·55N 08°26'·8E
⊕5 1M S of Capo Arenzano
44°22'·65N 08°41'·5E
⊕6 Genoa approaches – W
44°23'·75N 08°48'·95E
⊕7 Genoa approaches – E
44°22'·95N 08°56'·3E
⊕8 1M S of Pta di Portofino
44°16'·9N 09°13'·1E
⊕9 1M W of Pta Mesco
44°08'·0N 09°36'·5E
⊕10 1M S of I. Del Tino
44°00'·6N 09°51'·0E

Data

PROHIBITED AREAS AND MARINE RESERVES

La Spezia
Anchorage is prohibited southward of a line joining Punta del Varignano and Punta di Calandrello; within approximately 100m of the shore or the pierheads between Molo Cantiere Ansaldo and Molo dei Pagliari; in a triangular area extending about 350m E from the NE corner of Darsena Duca degli Abruzzi; and in all areas where there are mussel beds. Anchoring and fishing are prohibited in an area extending S from Diga Foranea and ESE from the NE side of Isola di Palmaria.

Marine reserves (Area Marina Protetta – AMPs)
There are three marine reserves with restricted areas.
1. **Isola di Bergeggi**
2. **Portofino promontory**
3. **Cinque Terre**

See the introduction for an explanation of the restricted areas. The extent of the marine reserves is described in the appropriate part of this chapter.

Currents

Currents in the Ligurian Sea are variable and for the most part set along the coast. Along the Riviera Ponente the current sets mostly to the SW although a strong *libecchio* may stem it. When the current along the Riviera Levante reverses from the SW to SE a change of weather is probable. Along the Riviera Levante the current generally sets to the N, although northerly winds in the summer frequently result in little or no current. In harbour a rise in the sea level generally indicates an approaching depression and the onset of bad weather.

MAJOR LIGHTS

Capo dell'Arma Fl(2)15s50m24M
Porto Maurizio Iso.4s11m16M
Capo delle Mele Fl(3)15s94m24M
Capo di Vado Fl(4)15s43m16M
Lanterna (Genoa) Fl(2)20s117m25M
Airport (Genoa) Oc.3s10m12M
Punta Vagno LFl(3)15s26m16M
Punta di Portofino Fl.5s40m16M
Rapallo Fl.3s9m9M
I. del Tino Fl(3)15s117m25M
Rada di La Spezia (entrance on 306°) Ldg Lt
Front Fl.WRG.3s21m8-6M
297°-G-305.3°-W-306.8°-R-315°
Pegazzano *Rear* 0.56M from front Iso.4s48m16M

Quick reference guide

	Shelter	*Mooring*	*Fuel*	*Water*	*Eating out*	*Provisions*	*Plan*	*Charge band*
Ventimiglia Marina (planned)							•	
Bordighera	B	A	O	A	B	B	•	2
Capo Pino	C	A	O	B	C	C	•	
San Remo	A	A	A	A	A	A	•	1/3/4
Marina degli Aregai	A	A	A	A	C	C	•	4
Marina di San Lorenzo al Mare	A	A	A	A	C	C	•	4
Porto Maurizio	B	A	A	A	A	A	•	4
Oneglia	B	AB	A	A	A	B	•	1/2
Diano Marina	A	A	O	A	A	A	•	2
Marina di Andora	B	A	A	A	B	B	•	4/5
Alassio Marina	A	A	A	A	O	C	•	3
I. Gallinara	B	AB	O	O	O	O	•	
Loano	A	A	A	A	A	A	•	2/3
Finale Ligure	A	A	A	A	C	C	•	3
Savona	A	A	A	A	A	A	•	2/3
Varazze Marina	A	A	A	A	B	A	•	6
Arenzano	A	A	O	A	B	B	•	3
Genova								
Sestri Ponente	B	A	B	A	B	B	•	2/3
Marina Genova	A	A	A	A	B	C	•	6
Fiera di Genova	B	A	A	A	A	A	•	3
Abruzzi	A	A	A	A	A	A	•	3
Marina Molo Vecchio	A	A	B	A	A	A	•	5
Marina Porto Antico	A	A	A	A	A	A	•	4
Nervi	C	A	O	O	B	B	•	
Camogli	B	A	B	A	B	A	•	
San Fruttuoso	C	C	O	O	O	C	•	
Portofino	B	AC	A	A	C	A	•	6+
Paraggi	C	C	O	O	C	B	•	
Santa Margherita Ligure	A	A	A	A	A	A	•	4
Rapallo	A	A	A	A	A	A	•	6+
Chiavari	A	A	A	A	A	A	•	5
Lavagna	A	A	A	A	A	B	•	5
Sestri Levante	B	AC	A	A	A	A	•	1/2
Baia del Silenzio	C	C	O	O	A	A	•	1
Levanto	C	C	O	O	C	C	•	1
Monterosso al Mare	C	A	O	A	C	C	•	
Vernazza	B	A	O	A	C	C	•	
Portovenere	A	A	A	A	C	B	•	6+
Le Grazie	B	AC	A	A	B	B	•	
Fezzano	B	A	B	A	C	C	•	5
Marina Mirabello	A	A	A	A	A	B	•	6+
La Spezia	A	A	A	A	A	A	•	3/4
Porto Lotti	A	A	A	A	C	C	•	5
San Terenzo	C	C	O	O	C	C	•	
Lerici	B	A	A	A	B	A	•	4
Bocca di Magra	A	AB	A	A	C	C	•	4/5

Routes

Most yachts will be day-hopping around the coast and given the numbers of marinas and harbours at relatively short intervals, there are no obvious routes to take except a preference for where the next stop will be.

Yachts on passage to or from Corsica and the Riviera and Tuscan Islands need to keep an eye on the weather. If a depression is hovering in the Gulf of Lion or thereabouts, it may decide to zoom over to the Gulf of Genoa and will often sit there and deepen. The Genoa lee cyclone can bring unsettled weather and strong winds. In the Gulf of Genoa and adjacent waters things can get stirred up with very uncomfortable cross seas. While things are not usually too bad in the summer, care is needed in the spring and autumn and especially in the winter. Make sure you have a good weather window before crossing to or from Corsica or the Riviera and Tuscan Islands.

The Riviera Ponente

VENTIMIGLIA

The existing harbour is busy with fishing boats, and it is unlikely to have room for yachts. It is open SSW–W and has maximum depths at the entrance of 2m, with less than 1m for much of the inside.

A plan for the new marina, 'Cala del Forte' on the site of the existing fishing harbour, is shown below. The original project to build a *porto turistico* at Ventimiglia began 20 years ago. Many designs have been rejected, but the latest plan purports to be the most eco-friendly marina in Europe. Work is due to start in Spring 2010, and the project is scheduled to take 4–5 years.

Approach

Ventimiglia lies on the E side of Capo Mortola, three miles beyond the border with France, at the mouth of the Roya river.

Mooring

Data (when marina completed) 350 berths. 50 visitors' berths. Max LOA 45m. Depths 2–6m.

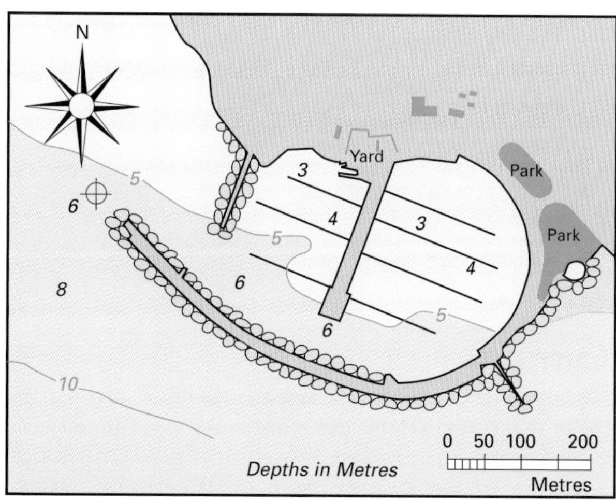

VENTIMIGLIA CALA DEL FORTE MARINA (planned layout)
⊕43°47'·3N 07°35'·8E

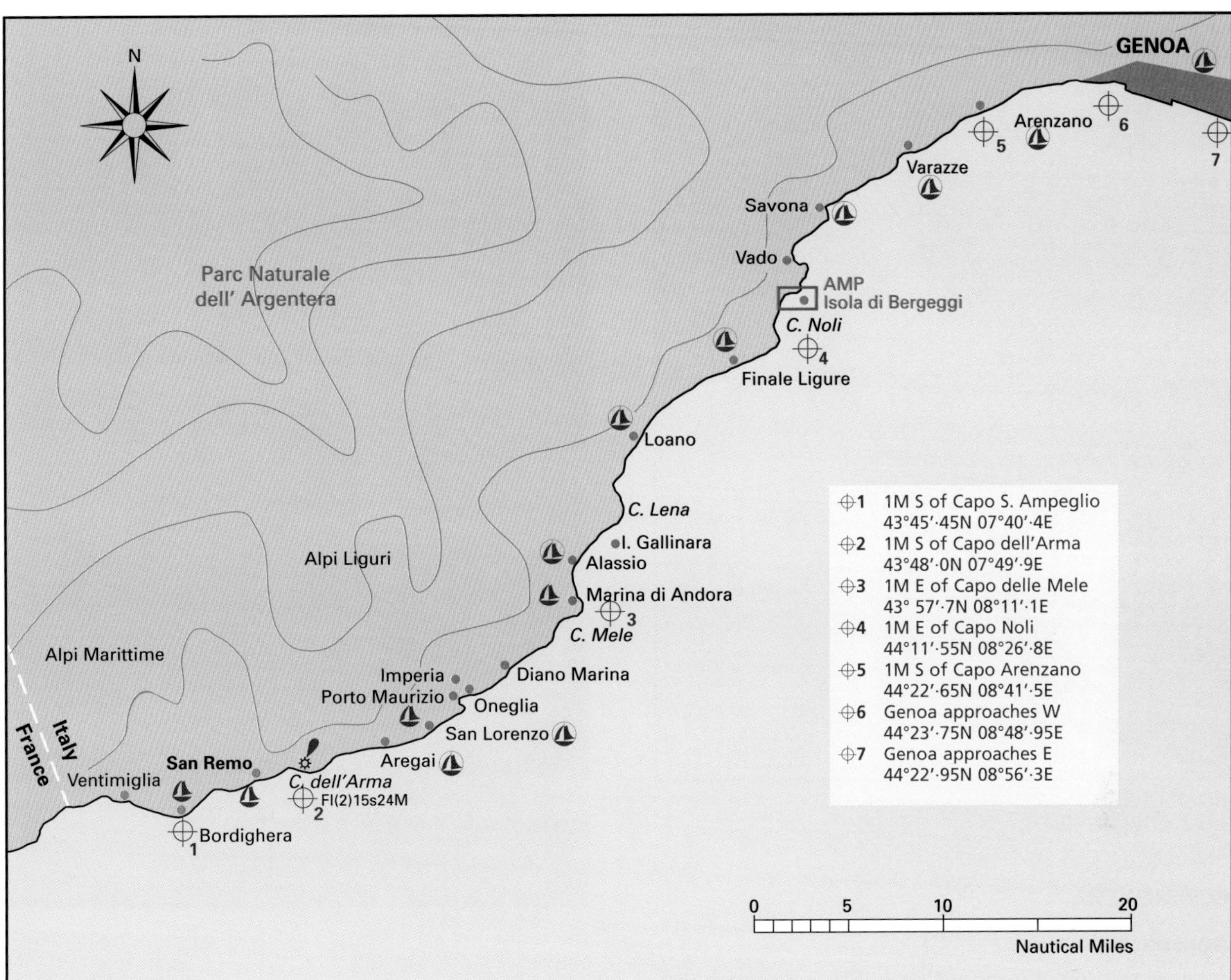

RIVIERA PONENTE

Shelter The new marina should provide good all-round shelter.

Authorities Marina staff.
www.caladelforte-ventimiglia.it

Facilities

When completed the marina will have all the usual facilities, including hauling, storage and repairs services and shore-side recreational facilities. Good shopping and restaurants in the town. Open-air market on Fridays.

Further details will be included in subsequent supplements to *Italian Waters Pilot* at www.imray.com

General

Ventimiglia town has a charming medieval old quarter, with a maze of narrow streets and 11th-century church buildings; Roman ruins including an open-air theatre, and close by are the Balzi Rossi prehistoric cave dwellings, and the Hamburg Botanical Gardens.

Food and Wine

Liguria consists of a luxuriantly fertile strip of land producing citrus fruit, wines, chestnuts, olives and olive oil in abundance and, in the Ligurian hills, mushrooms grow profusely. A variety of dishes are based on mushrooms and there is a famous old country recipe, though I have never seen it on a menu, in which small birds are individually roasted on large wild red mushrooms found in the district. It sounds to me like a lot of small bones to pick over.

Anchovies are used in sauces, salads and stuffings and sometimes in unexpected ways. There are *crostini di provatura*; croutons of bread and melted cheese with a sauce of anchovies cooked in butter, a combination that works well. Ligurian pizza or *sardenara* differs from the more commonly found pizza in that the top dressing of cheese is omitted and the filling consisting of tomatoes, onions, olive oil, basil, seasonings, black olives and anchovies. Ligurian *pesto*, a paste of basil, garlic, oil, pine nuts and sharp cheese, and said to be the best in Italy, is often mixed into a vegetable soup. *Pesto* is also excellent with lasagna and other types of pasta.

Liguria does not produce much wine and none of the best Italian vintages. Its white wines are probably the most notable, especially the heavy and sweet white wines of the Cinque Terre.

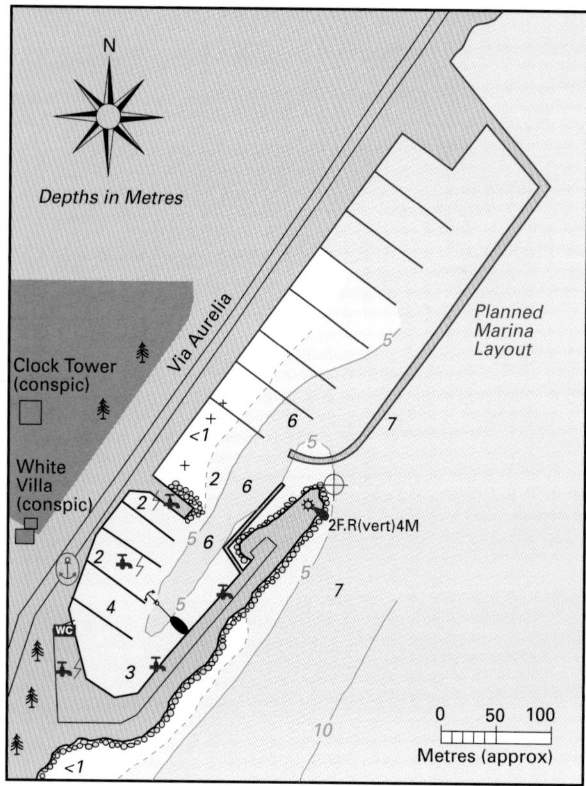

BORDIGHERA
⊕43°46´·8N 07°40´·7E

The ravine just after Menton in France which is the border between France and Italy

BORDIGHERA

Approach

A small harbour on the E side of Capo Ampeglio. A clock tower and a white villa with a tower behind the harbour are conspicuous.

VHF Ch 16, 09 (0700–1900). CB Ch 2.

Mooring

Data 250 berths. Max LOA 20m. Depths 2–5m.

Berth Where directed. The harbour is normally crowded and it is not uncommon for visitors to be turned away (San Remo is the nearest safe harbour in Italy). Visitors normally go on the pontoon at the entrance.

Shelter It can be uncomfortable on the outer pontoon with the normal SE sea breeze. A surge develops with S–SE gales.

Authorities YC staff. Charge band 2. Bordighera Capitaneria
☎ 0184 265 656

Note A marina for vessels 10–30m LOA, Marina di Sant'Ampeglio is planned for here, and the planned final form is shown on the plan. No completion dates were available at the time of writing.

Facilities

Services Water and electricity at or near every berth.
Fuel About 250m from the harbour.
Repairs Small slipway. 15/25-ton cranes available.
Provisions Good shopping in the town.
Eating out Good restaurants nearby.

Riviera of Flowers

The Riviera Ponente is also known as the 'Riviera of Flowers', a name derived from the fact that as much as 70% of the horticulture along the coast is devoted to flower growing. The business started with Ludwig Winter, a German landscape architect, who set up a horticultural business and showed that flowers could be cultivated for profit by exporting them to northern Europe. He also designed the elegant Hanbury Gardens near Ventimiglia. Others soon followed his lead and today flower growing is big business. The flower market in San Remo is near the harbour and well worth a visit to see exotic blooms of all varieties on sale.

Bordighera looking NNW *Roberto Merlo*

History

The region takes its name from the Liguri who peopled the area about 700BC, although there is plenty of evidence to show that the area has been occupied since Neanderthal times. For the most part the story of Liguria revolves around the fortunes of Genoa. As early as 500BC Genoa was trading with the Greeks and Etruscans. By 300BC the Romans were eyeing the province and took it in 222BC. They built many forts, a fine harbour at Genoa, and the Via Aurelia to link Rome and France (the coastal road still follows the original Roman road). The Carthaginians sacked Genoa in 205BC but the Romans rebuilt the city which flourished until the fall of the empire. Genoa and other Ligurian ports like Savona, Camogli and La Spezia continued to develop, but without the unifying hand of Rome there was much dissension and feuding. In AD936 the Saracens destroyed the city.

The Genoese epoch

After the sacking of Genoa the Pope persuaded the Ligurian cities to stop feuding amongst themselves and Genoa and Pisa combined forces to oust the Saracens in 1148. As soon as the Saracens were driven back, Genoa and Pisa resumed their warring and Genoa slowly gained territory to become one of the largest and most powerful cities in Europe, supplying not only the Crusaders with ships and stores, but at the same time trading with the East. Like Venice, Genoa's main competitor, the Genoese set up colonies in Sicily, Greece, Syria and North Africa.

On the home front constant feuding and bickering weakened the city, the enduring problem being the internecine struggle between supporters of the papacy and followers of the Holy Roman Empire of Byzantium. The former were the Guelph families and the latter the Ghibellines. Despite the constant feuding, all the families amassed huge fortunes and built elegant palaces in Genoa and along the Ligurian coast. At this time the Genoese (and the Venetians) made some of the finest sea charts in the world, the 'portulan' charts, accurately mapping the seas and coast. Innovative features such as rhumb lines and compass roses enabled accurate courses to be steered and pilotage notes and sketches of cities and ports also appear on these early charts. The Genoese introduced marine insurance and founded large banks which were to endure after Genoa's fortunes had declined. In the war of Chioggia (1378–81) the Venetians defeated Genoa, ending their maritime power. In the late 14th and 15th centuries the French and the Milanese occupied Genoa and internal revolts pushed the city further into decline until 1528.

Mercantile Genoa

On 13 September 1528 Admiral Andrea Doria entered the city and restored peace. By an arrangement with the Holy Roman Emperor, Charles V, he managed to secure Genoa's independence, thus beginning a further period of prosperity for the city. The city's banks expanded throughout the western world and in time the Genoese became merchant bankers to the known world. Christopher Columbus, a native of Genoa, had discovered the Americas in 1492 in an expedition financed by the Spanish. The Genoese reaped the rewards of their hero indirectly since much of the wealth returning from the New World was processed through Genoese banks. In 1608 Genoa was declared a free port and it was not until the end of the 17th century that the financial renaissance went into decline. After this Genoa lost her independence and was in turn ruled by the French, the Austrians, by the French again and finally, in 1815, by the kingdom of Sardinia.

Unification of Italy

As Italy struggled towards unification after 1814, Genoa again played an important role. The patriot Giuseppe Mazzini was Genoese, but the most illustrious son of the time was without doubt Giuseppe Garibaldi. He set sail in May 1860 with his thousand 'Red Shirt' volunteers to free Sicily and southern Italy from the Spanish. Garibaldi did much to spur Italy on to unification in 1861. Genoa was badly damaged in the Second World War, but was rebuilt and has prospered and now the only invaders who come to her shores are peaceful – the thousands of tourists who flock to the Riviera every year.

General

The harbour is a wonderful spot if you can find space to squeeze in. It is a peaceful place, a piece of the old Riviera in a wooded corner of the bay with tall palms dotted about among the fine old villas on the slopes behind.

MARINA BAIA VERDE

Approach

A new marina under construction on the old tunnel excavation dump near the village of Ospedaletti, between Bordighera and Capo Pino. Due to open 2012.

All data given below is for the finished marina.

Mooring

Data 390 berths. Max LOA 33m.

Berths Go stern or bows-to where directed. Laid moorings.

Shelter It looks to provide good all-round shelter, although strong southerlies may make some berths uncomfortable.

Authorities Marina staff.
✆ 0184 292 308 *Fax* 0184 252 999
www.baiaverde.net

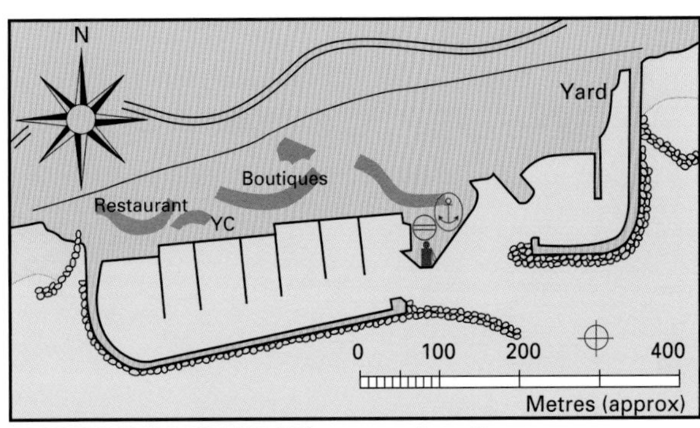

MARINA BAIA VERDE (When completed)
⊕43°18'·0N 07°42'·7E

Facilities

Services Water and electricity (220/380V). Wi-Fi. Showers and toilets. Pump-out.
Fuel On the quay
Repairs Boatyard with travel-lift, hardstanding and undercover storage is planned.

General

The project also has plans for residential and commercial development including a yacht club, other sporting and beachfront facilities.

CAPO PINO

Approach

A small harbour lying immediately E of Capo Nero.

Mooring

Data 20 berths. Max LOA 7m. Depths <1–3m.

The harbour is very small and you would be lucky to find a berth here.

Facilities

Water and WC ashore. Shops and restaurants nearby.

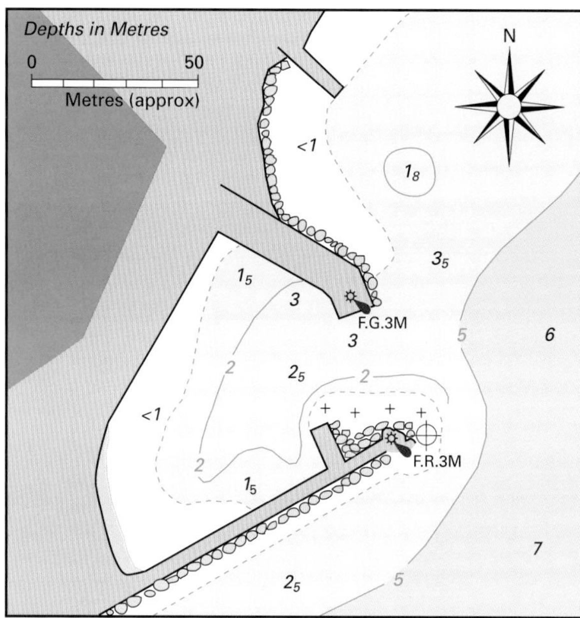

CAPO PINO
⊕43°47´·9N 07°44´·6E

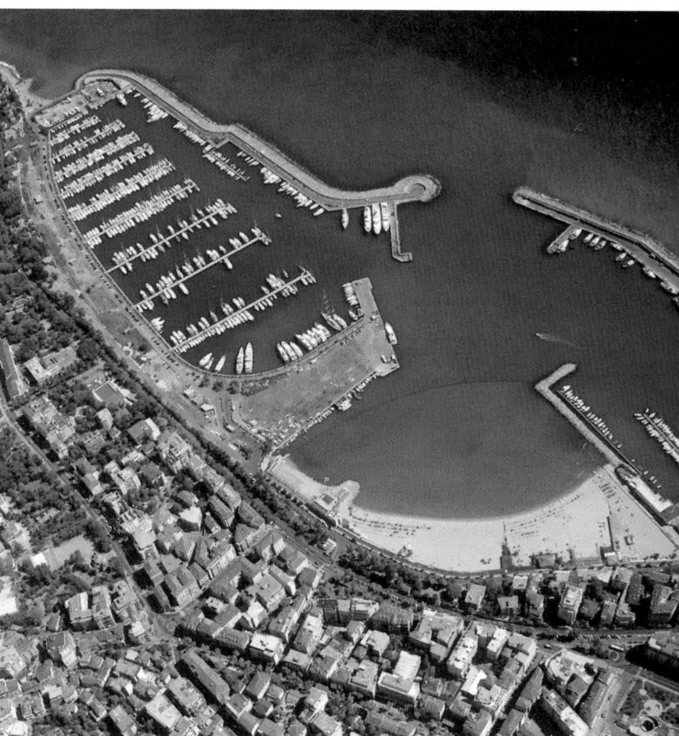

San Remo looking SE *Roberto Merlo*

SAN REMO

BA 351
Italian 51

Approach

This large harbour lying nearly 12 miles from the Franco-Italian border is currently the best harbour to make for when coming from France to Italy.

Conspicuous The lighthouse on Capo dell'Arma is conspicuous from the W and east. The large town on

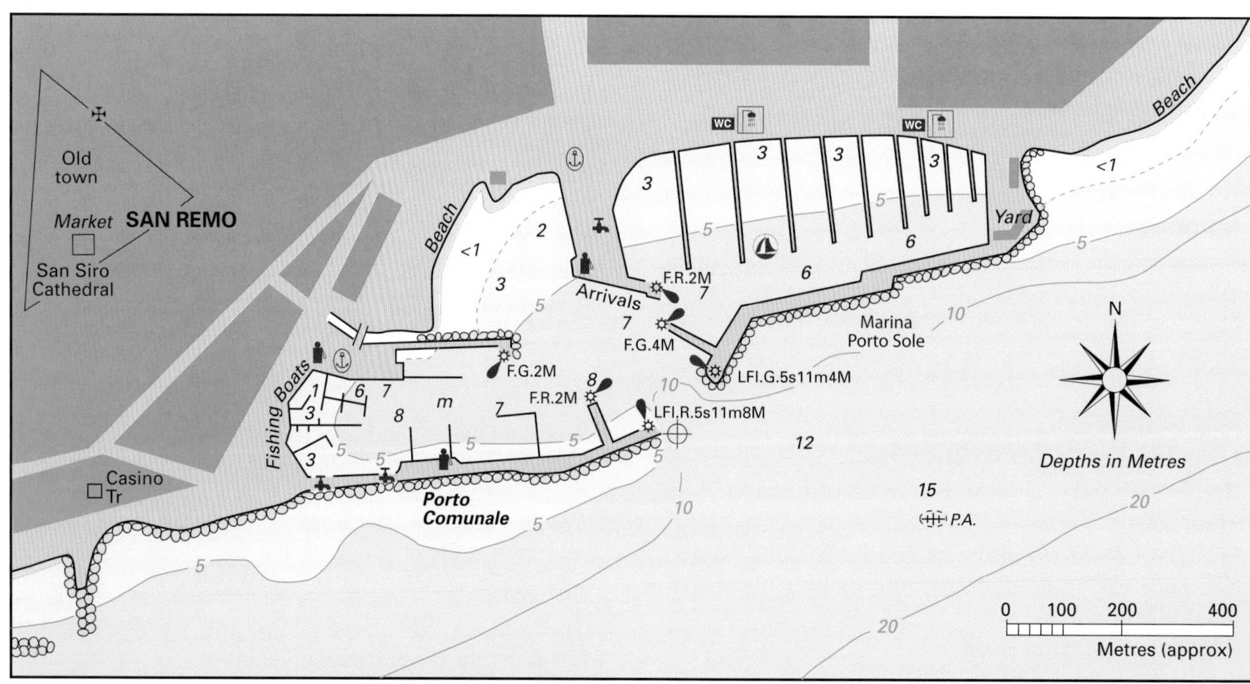

SAN REMO - PORTO COMUNALE AND MARINA PORTOSOLE
⊕43°48´·9N 07°47´·3E

San Remo. The outer breakwater and entrance to Portosole

the slopes rising up from the coast will be seen from the distance and, closer in, the huddle of houses of the old town sandwiched between the newer multi-storey buildings can be identified. Closer in, the long breakwaters and the masts of the yachts inside are easily identified. The entrance is difficult to see until close to.

By night Use the light on Capo dell'Arma Fl(2)15s50m24M until the lights at the entrance are picked up.

VHF Porto Comunale Ch 16, 14 (office hours). Portosole Ch 09, 16 (24 hours). CB Ch 02.

Danger A wreck has been reported approximately 0·2M (two cables) ESE of the entrance to San Remo.

Mooring

Porto Comunale (Porto Vecchio)

Data 12 visitors' berths. Max LOA 30m. Depths 1–7m.

Berth Where directed or wherever there is room. These berths are commonly crowded and you may have difficulty finding a berth. Berths are short-term, normally with a limit of three days. Transit berths on the S breakwater outside the fuel berth.

Shelter Generally good, although S–SE gales cause a surge.

Authorities Harbourmaster. Customs. YC staff in Porto Communale. Charge band 3.

Porto Communale ✆ 0184 505 531

Portosole

Data 800 berths. 90 visitors' berths. Max LOA 90m. Depths 2·5–7·5m.

Berth Where directed. Laid moorings tailed to the quay.

Shelter Good all-round shelter.

Authorities Marina staff. Customs. Charge band 3/4.

Portosole ✆ 0184 5371 *Fax* 0184 53741
www.portosolesanremo.it

Facilities

Services Water and electricity (220 or 380V) at every berth in Portosole, and at most berths in Porto Comunale. Shower and toilet blocks at Portosole. Wi-Fi at Portosole.

Fuel On the quay at the entrance to Portosole.

Repairs A 30-ton travel-hoist and 15/30-ton cranes at Portosole. A 750-ton platform lift and slipways at Portosole. Cranes can lift small to medium size yachts at Porto Comunale. Mechanical and engineering repairs. GRP and wood repairs. Electrical and electronic repairs. Sailmakers. Chandlers.

Provisions Excellent shopping for all provisions in the town behind Porto Comunale. Market near the San Siro Cathedral on Tuesday and Saturday.

Eating out Excellent restaurants, trattorias and pizzerias on the waterfront and in the town. A number of fine restaurants dating from the 'good old days' in San Remo still offer the best cuisine and service assuming you have the cash or the plastic to pay for it.

Other PO. Banks. ATMs. Italgaz and Camping Gaz. Hire cars. Buses and trains to Genoa.

General

Before the second world war San Remo was the haunt of the rich, and renowned for its fine hotels and restaurants offering service in the 'grand manner' and for its casino where large sums could be lost or won. Today the casino and San Remo have succumbed to tourism *en masse* and now one no longer needs a dinner jacket or even a tie to gamble in the casino. But the vestiges of the era remain and the elegant villas and hotels confer the charm of a once-exclusive resort on the town. Many of the large elegant super-yachts still base themselves here as a quick stroll around the marina will show.

Behind the Porto Vecchio near the San Siro cathedral is the original San Remo flower market, claimed to be the largest in the world. The bulk of Monte Bignone, hunched behind the town, is now a designated Parc Naturale, and from the top there is a panoramic view along much of the French as well as the Italian Riviera.

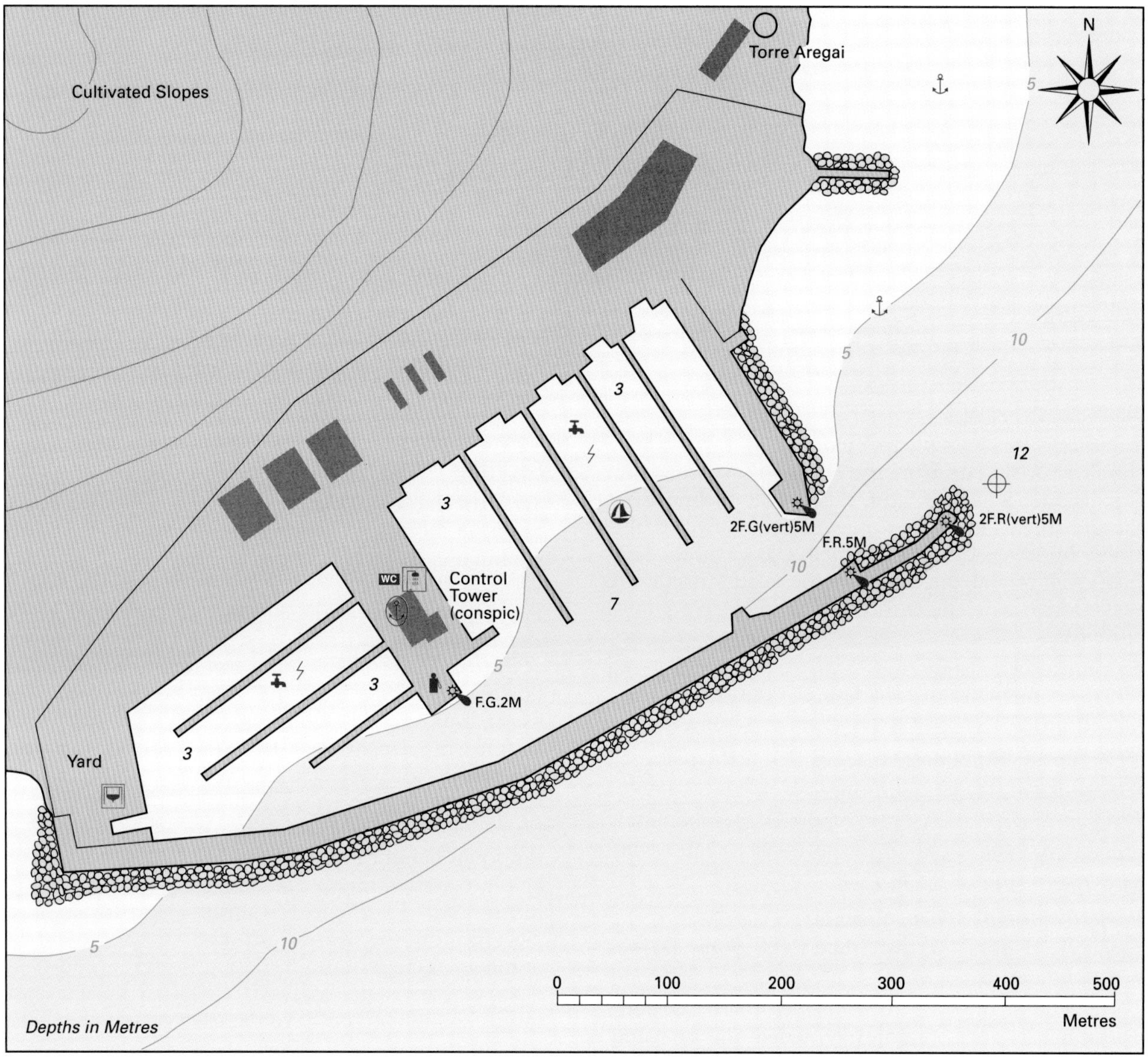

MARINA DEGLI AREGAI
⊕ 43°50′·31N 07°55′·07E WGS84

ARMA DI TAGGIA

⊕ 43°49′·9N 7°52′·6E

A small harbour just inside the mouth of Torrente di Taggia on the E side of Capo dell'Arma. A small yacht could investigate it in calm weather. On no account should it be entered in onshore winds. There are reported to be 1·5–2m depths over the bar at the entrance and 1–2·5m depths in the small basin just inside the entrance on the port side.

Cantiere Diurno ✆ 01844 87010

The town of Taggia is famed for the quality of its olive oil.

MARINA DEGLI AREGAI

A large marina immediately E of Punta San Stefano.

Approach

The outer breakwater under the slopes off Punta San Stefano will be seen from the E and SW. The tall, banded control tower (beige and ochre bands) within the marina is conspicuous.

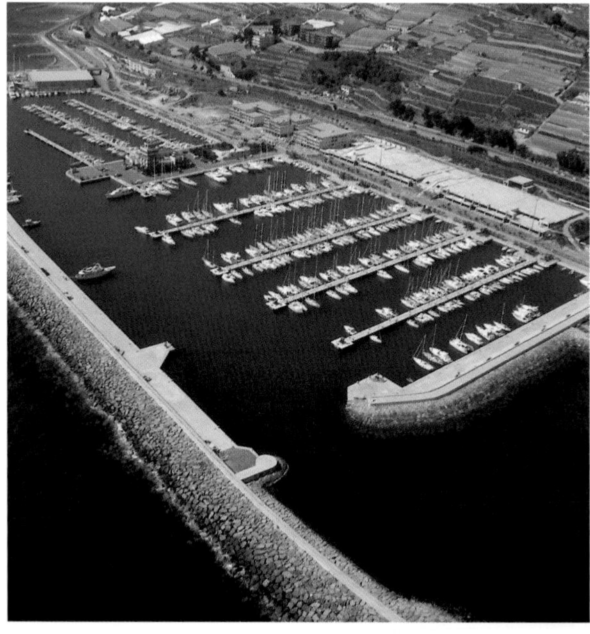

Marina degli Aregai looking SW *Marina degli Aregai SpA*

By night Inside the central quay is spot-lit.

VHF Ch 09 for the control tower.

Mooring

Data 990 berths. 73 visitors' berths. Max LOA 40m. Depths 3–10m.

Berth Report to the central pier to be allocated a berth.

Shelter Good all-round shelter.

Authorities Harbourmaster. Marina staff. Charge band 4.

Marina degli Aregai ✆ 0184 4891 *Fax* 0184 489 200
Email info@marinadegliaregai.it
www.marinadegliaregai.it

Cantieri degli Aregai ✆ 0184 489 213 *Fax* 0184 481 011

Anchorage It is possible to anchor off to the N of the entrance in 4–8m. The anchorage is exposed and only suitable in calm weather.

Facilities

Services Water and electricity at every berth. Wi-Fi. Shower and toilet block. Laundrette.

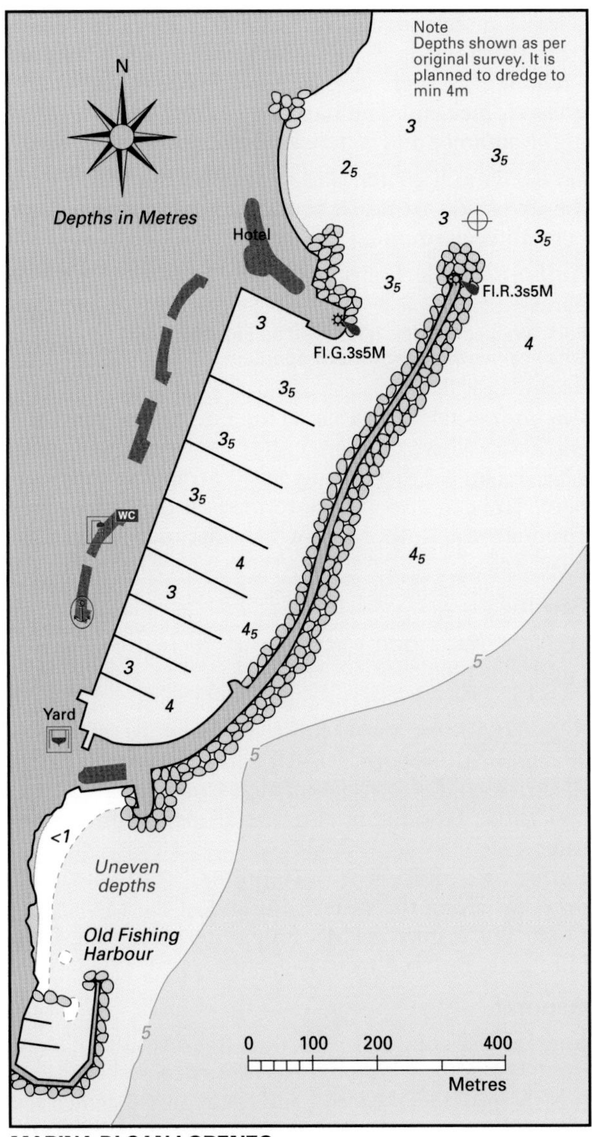

MARINA DI SAN LORENZO
⊕43°51′·58N 07°58′·34E WGS84

San Lorenzo: the new marina under construction in late 2005. The old fishing harbour can be seen top right

Fuel On the end of the central pier.
Repairs 100-ton travel-hoist. Most yacht repairs can be carried out or arranged here.
Provisions Minimarket. It is a fair hike to the village above for shopping.
Eating out Restaurants and bars at the marina.

General

The marina is now established with all facilities and is a useful stop along the coast. It also has good facilities if you want to base yourself here or leave a yacht for the winter. Nice is not too far away to the west and Genoa is just along the coast road to the east.

Note There have been some reports of GPS anomalies around this area.

MARINA DI SAN LORENZO AL MARE

Approach

The marina lies close N of the small shallow fishing harbour, approximately halfway between Marina Degli Aregai and Imperia. A church is conspicuous on a small promontory between the harbour and the marina.

VHF Ch 09, 16.

Mooring

Data 360 berths. 36 visitors' berths. Max LOA 20m. Depths 3–5m.

Shelter The marina provides good all-round shelter, although entry may be difficult with strong onshore winds.

Authorities Marina staff. Charge band 4.

Marina di San Lorenzo al Mare ✆ 0183 91773
Fax 0183 931418
Email info@marinadisanlorenzo.it
www.marinadisanlorenzo.it

Facilities

Services Water and electricity (220V). Wi-Fi. Showers and toilets. Pump-out.
Fuel Fuel quay.

Repairs Slipway. Boatyard facilities to be developed.
Other Café, bar, restaurant to open in the marina. Some provisions available in the village.

General

The marina is now open, and the commercial premises are being developed.

The small town of San Lorenzo al Mare dates back to Roman times, but it wasn't until the 16th century that Genoese protection meant the town could better defend itself from Saracen invasion. Split by the San Lorenzo river, the E side of the town was much influenced by Porto Maurizio, while the W side, with more maritime associations, was founded by the lords of Lengueglia. The old town centre has been renovated and pedestrianised in recent years, and is a pleasant place to stroll around.

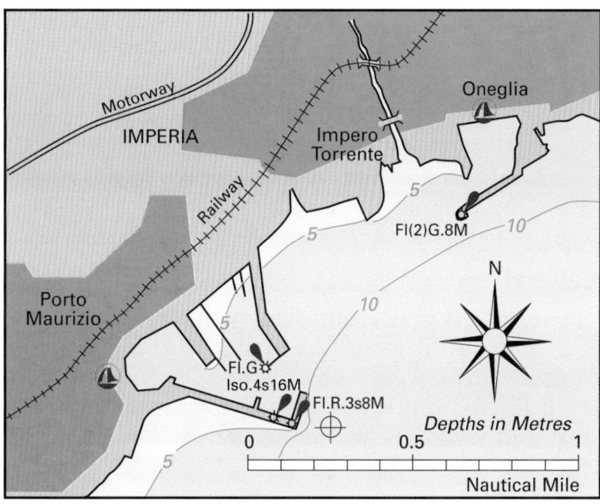

IMPERIA
⊕43°52′·49N 08°01′·78E WGS84

Yacht berths on the S quay in Porto Maurizo, Imperia Ponente

IMPERIA

The city of Imperia is divided by the Impero Torrente into two districts of Porto Maurizio and Oneglia.

PORTO MAURIZIO (Imperia Ponente)

BA 351
Italian 52

Approach

Conspicuous From the W the pastel coloured houses of the old town clustered on the promontory are easily identified. The cathedral tower and cupola in the town and the long breakwater with a small white lighthouse near the extremity are conspicuous. Closer in, the entrance is easily identified.

VHF Ch 09, 16 (24hr).

Note Major work expanding the N side of the harbour is almost complete.

Mooring

Imperia Mare
Data (when complete) 1,300 berths. 50 visitors' berths. Max LOA 90m. Depths 2–8m.

Berth Go stern-to where directed. Larger yachts go stern-to the S quay in the inner harbour. For most yacht berths there are laid moorings tailed to the quay to pick up. The harbour can be very crowded in the summer and it may be difficult to find a berth.

Shelter Good shelter, and should be improved with the extension to the E breakwater. Yachts are kept here all year round.

Authorities Harbourmaster and customs. Charge band 4.

Port Turistico ✆ 0183 60977 / 0183 667 453
Email ormeggiatori@portodimperia.it
www.portodimperia.it

Anchorage It is possible to anchor to the N of the entrance where shown. This anchorage is quite exposed and if there is any swell around it rolls into here. You can also anchor to the S of the breakwater although the authorities will sometimes get you to move on.

Facilities

Services Water and electricity at all berths. Shower and toilet block.
Fuel On the quay in the inner basin.
Repairs 50-ton travel-hoist. Slipway to 50 tons. Mechanical repairs. GRP and wood repairs. Electrical and electronic repairs. Chandlers.
Provisions Good shopping for all provisions in the town.
Eating out Excellent restaurants, trattorias and pizzerias along the waterfront and in the town.
Other PO. Banks. ATMs. Italgaz and Camping Gaz. Hire cars. Bus and train to Genoa.

General

Imperia is a comparatively new town resulting from the 1923 unification of Porto Maurizio and Oneglia. It is the provincial capital and the regional centre for olive oil production. It also claims to be the regional centre for pasta and just outside Imperia at

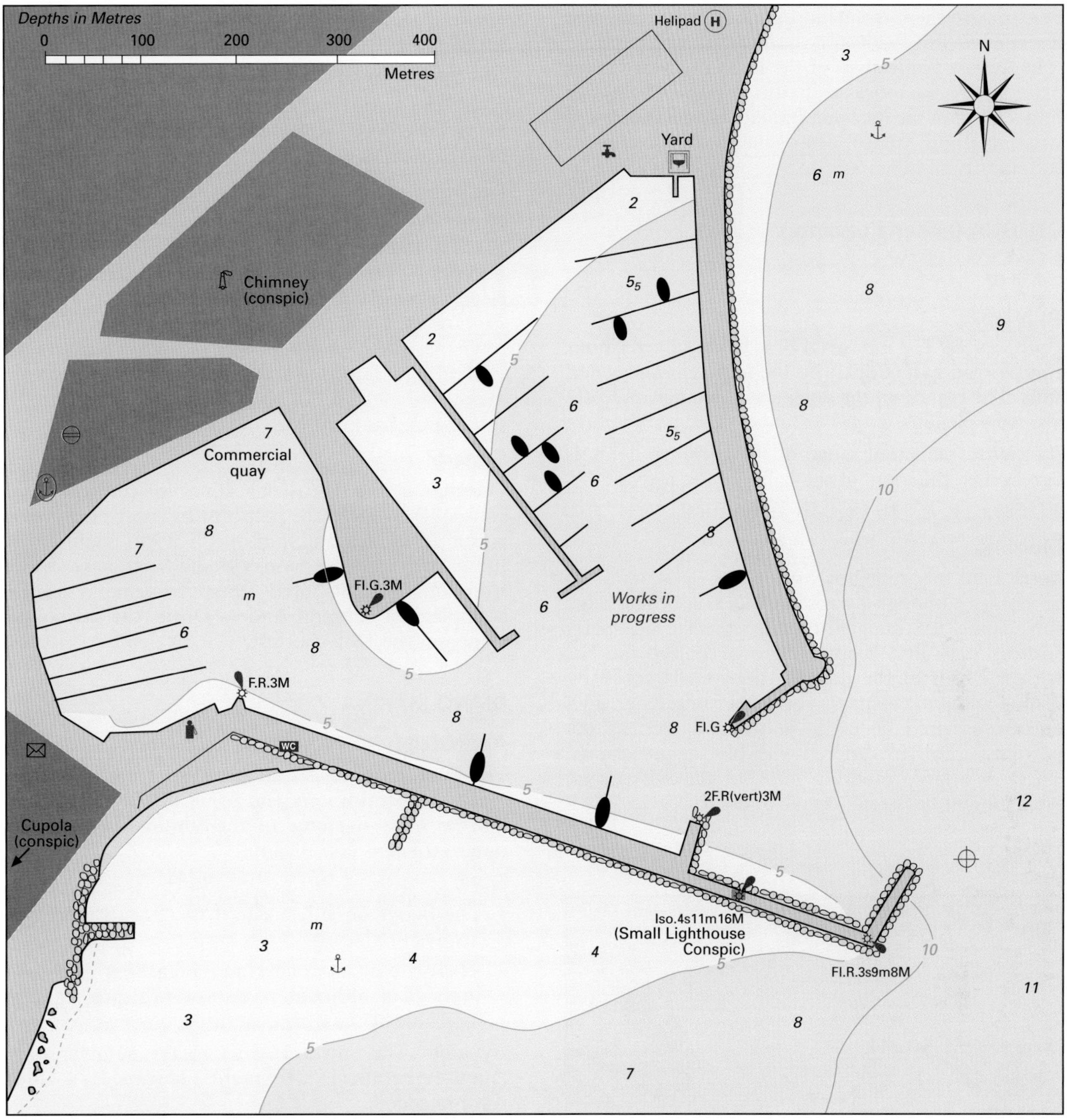

PORTO DI IMPERIA
⊕43°52´·51N 08°01´·76E WGS84

Looking NE across Porto Maurizo. This area has since been re-developed and new pontoons offer more berths

Pontedassio there is the museum of the Agnesi pasta firm devoted to the history and varieties of pasta.

In August the festival of the Palio del Mare takes place in which a mock sea battle is staged. If you can find a berth in the harbour, Imperia is a relaxed place with a good boaty atmosphere and excellent restaurants and bars ashore.

ONEGLIA (Imperia Levante)

BA 351
Italian 52

Approach

Conspicuous The industrial zone behind the harbour can be readily identified by the large chimneys and silos. The cranes on the dock and the outer mole are also conspicuous.

By night The actual range of the entrance lights is less against the loom of the lights of the town.

VHF Ch 11, 12, 16 for port authorities.

Mooring

Berth Laid moorings for local boats lie around the SE corner, although care is needed as a broad ledge runs along the quay just under the surface here. Visitors may find a space here or in the far NE corner. Much of the quay in between is taken by fishing and workboats. If you need to use your own anchor, a trip line might be a good idea as the bottom is probably littered with blocks and chains. There is a large mooring buoy in the NE corner, which might be useful to take a line to.

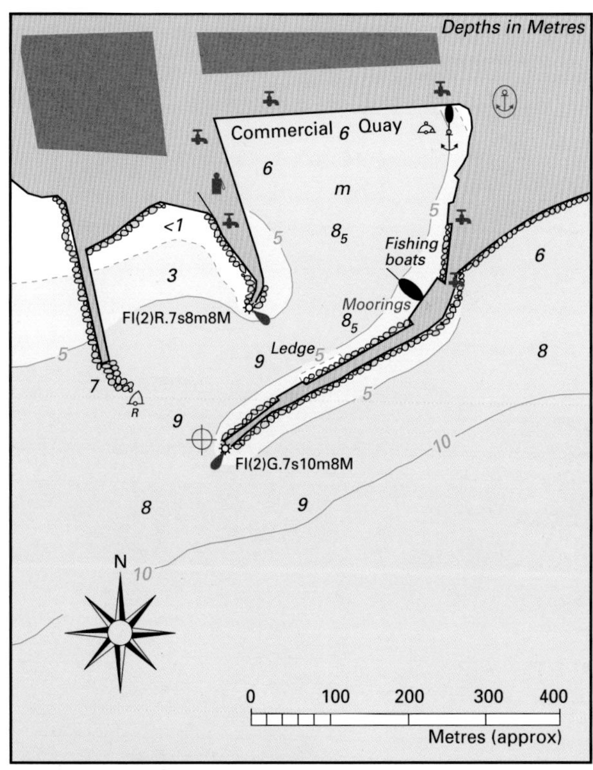

ONEGLIA - IMPERIA LEVANTE
⊕43°53´·02N 08°02´·46E WGS84

Shelter Good, although strong S–SW winds cause a surge. Gales from the S may make it untenable.

Authorities Port police and customs.

Note The basin immediately W of the harbour is being developed, which might increase the number of yacht berths here.

Facilities

Water On the quay.
Fuel On the quay.
Repairs There are numerous mechanical and electrical workshops near the harbour.
Provisions Good shopping for provisions in the town.
Eating out Trattorias and pizzerias a short distance away.
Other PO. Bank. ATM.

General

Oneglia is the industrial zone for Imperia and consequently lacks the polish of its sister port. Yet it is not an unpleasant spot and if Porto Maurizio is full in the summer you may find a berth here. Apart from olive oil, its other claim to fame is as the birthplace of Admiral Andrea Doria, the saviour of Genoa in the 16th century.

DIANO MARINA

Approach

The small harbour is difficult to spot until closer in when the breakwaters and some of the craft inside will be seen. A statue of the Virgin Mary on the outer groyne is conspicuous.

Note

1. The buoys on either side if the entrance are not always in place.
2. There are plans to develop the harbour as shown in the plan, although no dates for the project were available at the time of writing.

By night The entrance is lit in the summer only (June–September). A night entrance is not recommended.

VHF Ch 16, CB Ch 15.

Mooring

Data 270 berths (550 when completed). 12 visitors' berths. Max LOA 14m. Depths <1–2m.

Berth Where directed. The harbour can be crowded in the summer. Laid moorings tailed to the quay.

Shelter Generally good although strong onshore winds create a surge.

Authorities Harbourmaster. Charge band 2.
Capitaneria ☎ 0183 490 273 / 4

Anchorage There is a long groyne running E out from Capo Berta, ½M S of the harbour. A yacht may be able to tuck in under here where there looks to be a decent lee from S–SW winds.

Facilities

Services Water and electricity near every berth. Showers and toilets.

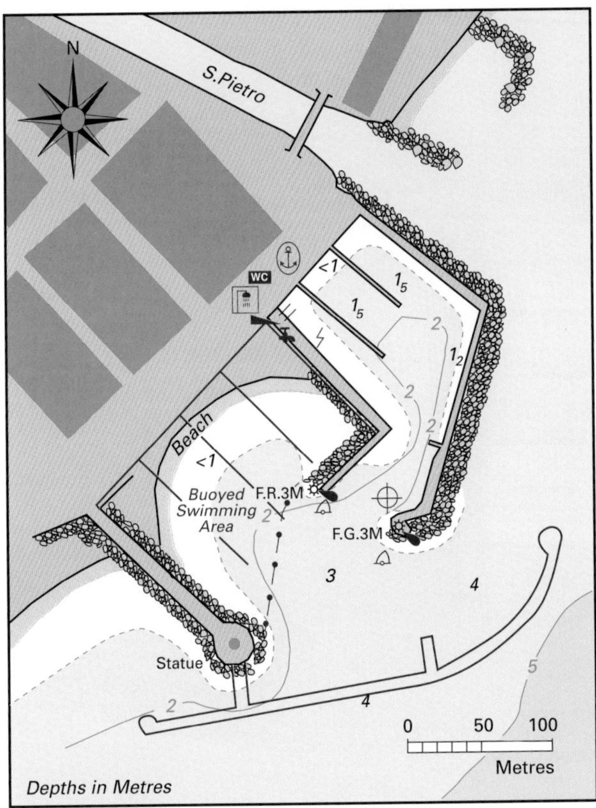

DIANO MARINA
⊕43°54´·53N 08°05´·16E WGS84

Fuel In the town about 300m away.
Repairs 15-ton crane.
Provisions Minimarkets in the town.
Eating out Numerous restaurants including some good ones further back from the waterfront.
Other PO. Bank. ATM.

General

The harbour is pleasantly located in the small resort town which has ancient associations reflected in the name. The Romans took over an ancient Ligurian cult associated with the forests and eventually substituted the name of their goddess of the woods and hunting: Diana. The town was devastated by an earthquake in 1887, but more recently posed in the role of glamorous seaside cousin to Diano San Pietro in Annie Hawes' *Extra Virgin*.

Diano Marina looking SE across the crowded basin

SAN BARTOLOMEO

A small harbour lying one mile NE of Diano Marina. It is mostly occupied by private berth-holders and it is unlikely you will find a berth here. Depths inside are mostly less than 2m so only shallow draught craft will be able to berth here.

Data 170 berths. Limited visitors' berths mostly relying on permanent berth holders being away. Max LOA 15m. Depths 1–2m.

Porto turistico ✆ 0183 40921
✆ /*Fax* 0183 408 089
Email info@sanbart.it
www.sanbart.it

Facilities

Services Water and electricity at or near every berth. Showers and toilets. Provisions and restaurants nearby.

Note Beach stabilising works are in progress to the SW of the harbour.

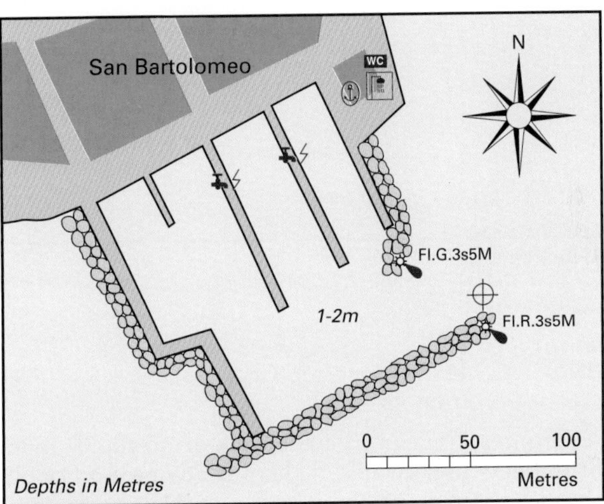

SAN BARTOLOMEO
⊕43°55´·18N 08°06´·45E WGS84

MARINA DI ANDORA

Approach

Conspicuous The marina lies under the pine-covered slopes on the S side of Capo Mele, at the E end of the town. The high apartment blocks of the town are conspicuous and, closer in, the outer mole is easily identified.

By night Use the light on Capo delle Mele Fl(3)15s94m24M.

VHF Ch 09, 16 (0800–1900). CB Ch 32.

Dangers With onshore winds there is a confused swell at the entrance.

Mooring

Data 800 berths. Max LOA 18m. Depths <1–4m.

Berth Where directed. There are laid moorings tailed to the quay. Yachts should still make for the inner basin unless directed into the new E basin.

Shelter Good all-round shelter now the breakwater has been extended and beefed up. The surge which E–SE winds used to cause should hopefully be absent now.

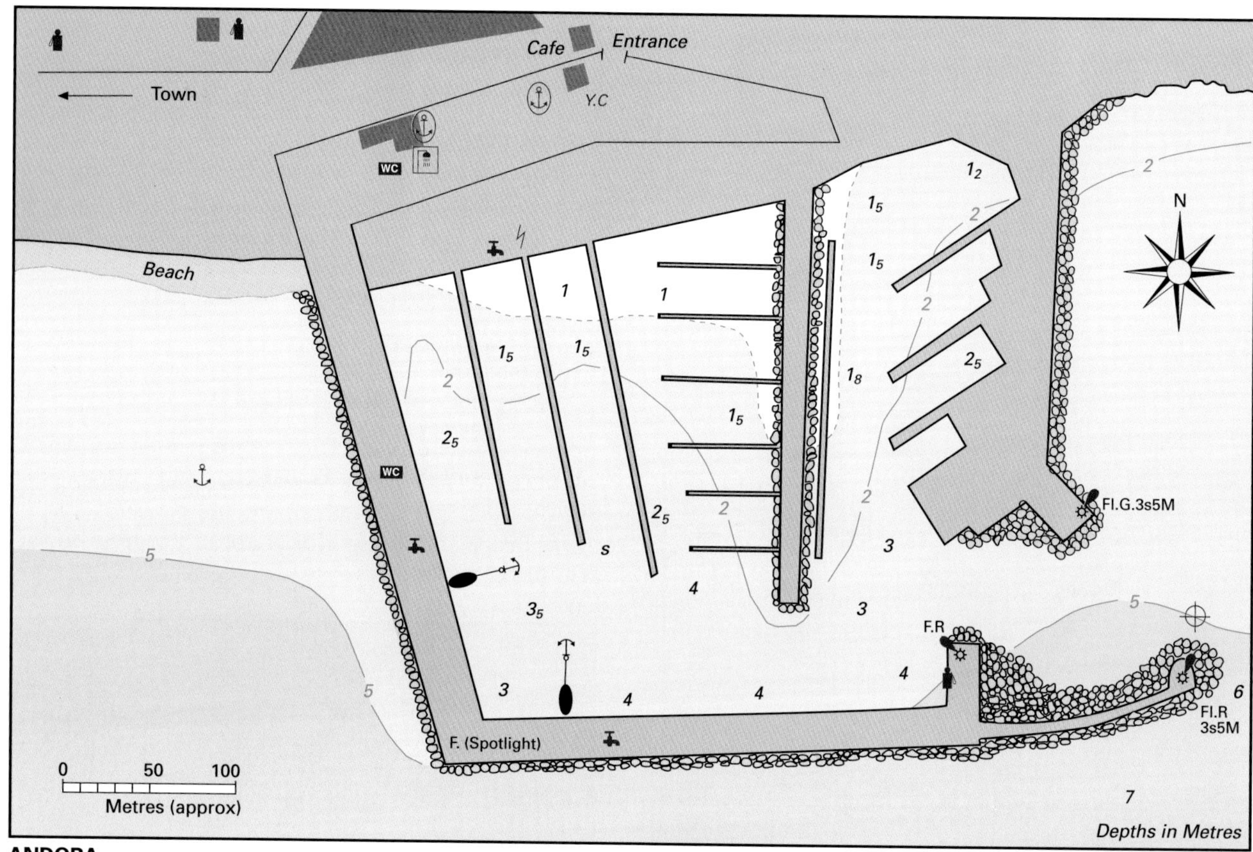

ANDORA
⊕43°57´·04N 08°09´·56E WGS84

Authorities Harbourmaster. Charge band 4/5.
Capitaneria ✆ 0182 88899

Anchorage You can try anchoring off to the W or E of the new breakwater. If there is any ground swell around it seems to be exacerbated around Andora and it can be extremely uncomfortable. The bottom is sand and gravel, not everywhere good holding.

Note The harbour is prone to silting, so care must be taken of the depths, especially at the entrance.

Facilities

Services Water and electricity (220V) at or close to most berths.
Fuel On the S quay just inside the entrance.
Repairs A 30-ton crane. Yachts are craned onto the hard on the W quay. Mechanical repairs. Chandlers.
Provisions Most provisions can be obtained in the town.
Eating out Restaurants, trattorias and pizzerias along the waterfront.
Other PO. Bank. Italgaz and Camping Gaz.

General

In contrast to other resorts along the coast, Andora lacks lustre, with only a shingle and sand beach and tall apartment blocks looking like so many oversized cornflake packets. Yet the harbour is a sympathetic place, a little lacklustre itself, but all the better for it. Why the marina charges super-marina prices for what are pretty ordinary facilities is an odd Andoran eccentricity.

Marina di Andora looking SW across the entrance

On the slopes around the bay there are stylish villas to remind you that this is still the fashionable Italian Riviera. In the approach from the W to Andora the medieval village of Cervo perched on the steep slopes near the coast stands out and if you want to visit this unspoiled though hardly unknown picturesque spot, Andora is the closest safe harbour to it.

ALASSIO

Approach

The harbour lies approximately one mile NE of Alassio town on the N side of Capo San Croce.

Conspicuous Isolotto Gallinara 1½ miles ENE of Alassio harbour is easily identified. A jetty and tower on the beach are conspicuous and, closer in, a small chapel on the tip of Capo San Croce is conspicuous.

Note A fish farm in the W approaches off Capo San Croce is poorly marked.

Alassio looking NE across Isolotto Gallinara and beyond to Capo Lena

MARINA DI ALASSIO
⊕44°01´·15N 08°11´·68E WGS84

VHF Marina *Ormeggiatori* Ch 09, 16.

Dangers There can be strong gusts off the mountains in the approaches to the marina.

Mooring

Data 400 berths. Visitors' berths. Max LOA 35m. Depths 2–5m.

Berth Call ahead to arrange a berth. Where directed. There are laid moorings tailed to the quay.

Shelter Excellent.

Authorities Harbourmaster and marina staff. Charge band 3.

Marina di Alassio ✆ 0182 645 012 *Fax* 0182 648 655
Email info@marinadialassio.net
www.marinadialassio.net

Anchorage In calm weather a yacht can anchor off the town SW of Capo San Croce, or further S off the suburb town of Laigueglia. A special mark (yellow × topmark) buoy marks an obstruction in the approaches, but is easily seen and is lit Fl.Y3s.

Facilities

Services Water and electricity at or near to all berths.
Fuel On the quay at the entrance.
Repairs 35-ton crane. Yachts are craned onto the hard on the W side of the harbour. Mechanical repairs. A boatyard within the marina can carry out most GRP and wood repairs.
Provisions In Alassio town about one mile away.
Eating out There is a café bar and restaurant in the marina and others in Alassio town.
Other ATM in the marina. Bicycle hire. PO. Banks in Alassio town.

General

Alassio town is a popular tourist resort boasting many good hotels, restaurants and bars. It is famous not only for its fine old buildings and towers, but also for its *muretto* (little wall), where the signatures of famous visitors such as Sophia Loren, Winston Churchill, Frank Sinatra and Ernest Hemingway, are reproduced on ceramic tiles incorporated in the wall. Every August the Festival of Muretto including a beauty contest is held, and presumably the winner gets to include her hand-print among those of the rich and famous.

On a more prosaic level, the disco in marina can get noisy!

Isolotto Gallinara

This is a private island with a small harbour on the NW side. A tower and several buildings on the island are conspicuous. Although the harbour is private there seems to be no objection to yachts using it overnight.

Berth stern or bows-to the S or E quay. The W mole is encumbered with underwater rocks. You are not allowed to go ashore and explore the island. Alternatively anchor off to the W or E of the small harbour depending on the wind direction in 8–12m. Shelter in the harbour is good although open to the NE.

There are, of course, no facilities.

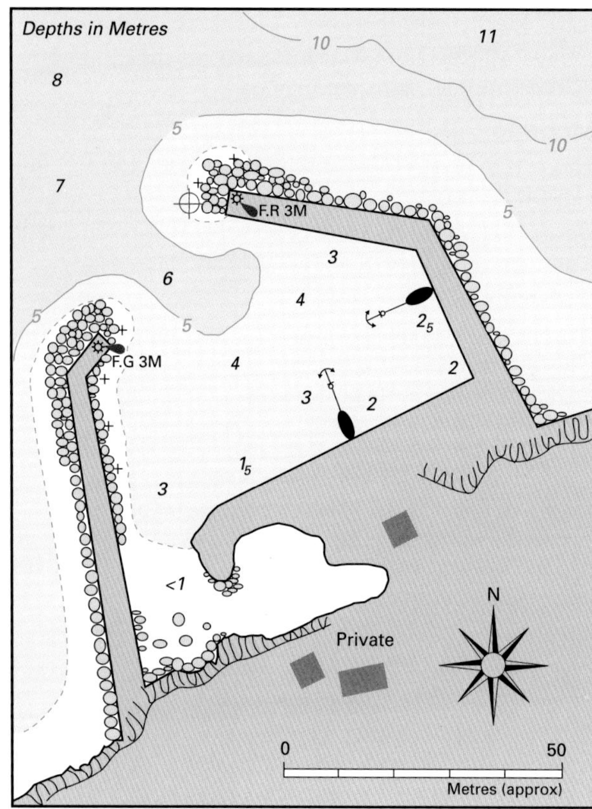

ISOLOTTO GALLINARA
⊕44°01´·6N 08°13´·5E

Weather note

According to the Admiralty *Pilot*, 'should the southern sky become obscured by heavy cumulus clouds with grey strata, strong southerly winds may be expected.'

MARINA DI LOANO

Approach

Conspicuous A large cathedral with a verdigris cupola behind the harbour, and a pavilion and tower at the root of a rough pier extending approximately 200m immediately S of the harbour, are conspicuous. Closer in, a hotel sign behind the harbour and the outer mole are conspicuous.

By night The works inside the harbour are lit (occas) by Fl.Or or Fl.R. light buoys. When the works are complete additional lights will be established inside. The effective range is less against the lights of the town behind.

VHF Ch 09, 16 (*Porto Loano*).

Note Care is needed of work going on expanding the marina. Care needed in the immediate approaches and in the outer harbour.

Mooring

Data 1,000 berths. 100 visitors' berths. Max LOA 40m. Depths 1·5–3m.

Berth Where directed. When the expansion of the harbour is finished it is likely that space for visitors will be allocated in the outer basin. There are laid moorings tailed to the quay at present.

Loano looking NNE across the marina towards the entrance

The old town of Loano was once part of the Doria family estate

Shelter Good shelter with the new outer breakwater.

Authorities Harbourmaster and harbour attendants. Charge band 2/3 (although this is likely to increase on completion of the harbour works).

Capitaneria ☏ 019 666 131
Marina di Loano ☏ 019 675 445 *Fax* 019 669 264
Email info@marinadiloano.it
www.marinadiloano.it

Facilities

Services Water and electricity at every berth. Wi-Fi.
Fuel In the outer basin.
Repairs A 70-ton travel-hoist and cranes up to 25 tons. Mechanical repairs. GRP and wood repairs. Electrical and electronic repairs. Chandlers. In the NW corner of the harbour there is a large boatyard which can attend to all yacht repairs.
Provisions Good shopping for all provisions in the town. Market on Fridays.
Eating out Restaurants, trattorias and pizzerias along the waterfront and in the town.
Other PO. Banks. ATMs. Italgaz and Camping Gaz.

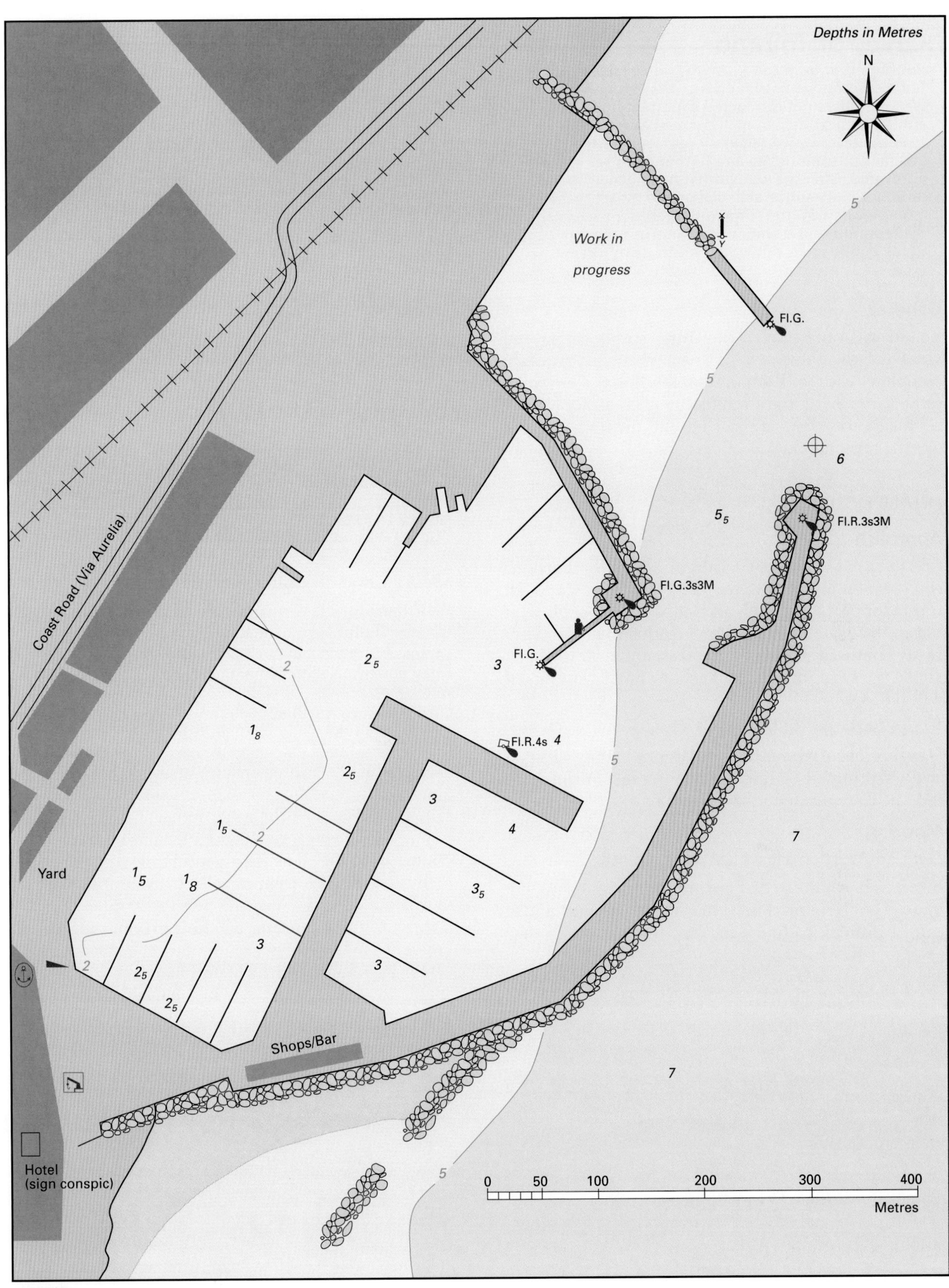

LOANO
⊕44°08´·15N 08°16´·34E WGS84

Caves of Toirano

Not far inland from Loano are the remarkable caves of Toirano. Although known prior to the Second World War, they were not considered important by anthropologists despite early remains found there. In 1944 the caves were used as air raid shelters and it became apparent there were further caves yet to be discovered. After the war, further huge underground caverns with beautiful stalagmites and stalactites were found, along with the remains of prehistoric bears and the footprint of a Neanderthal man. The caves are open to the public and a visit is well worth the effort.

General

Loano was once part of the Doria family estate and what is now the town hall was the family palace complete with a Roman mosaic floor. The town retains much of the architecture and grace of six centuries ago and is a pleasant and picturesque spot worth stopping at.

FINALE LIGURE

Approach

Conspicuous A tower on a bluff above the harbour is conspicuous. However, a tower on Capo di Caprazoppa to the SW and another on a bluff at Varigotti to the E are identical to this tower and are easily confused. Closer in, the restaurant on the bluff above the harbour and the harbour breakwater itself will be seen.

VHF Ch 16, 69 (0600–1900).

Dangers The harbour has silted since earlier surveys, and without dredging depths will continue to reduce. Care needed in the approaches.

Mooring

Data 550 berths. Max LOA 18m. Depths 2–4·5m.

Berth Where directed. Laid moorings tailed to the quay. The harbour is very full in the summer and it can be difficult to find a berth.

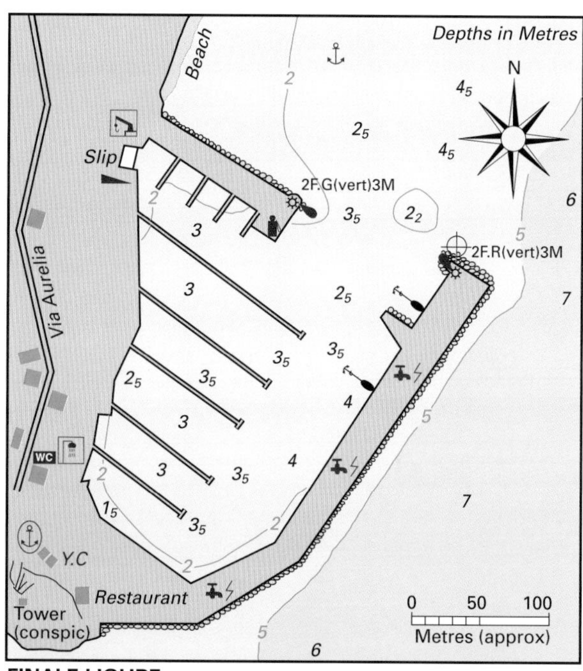

FINALE LIGURE
⊕44°10′·51N 08°22′·34E WGS84

Shelter Good all-round shelter.

Authorities Harbourmaster and marina staff. Charge band 3.

Capitaneria ☎ 019 690 985 *Fax* 019 690 959
Email porto.finaleligure@tin.it
www.porto.sv.it

Circolo Nautico ☎ 019 601 640

Facilities

Services Water and electricity at every berth on the quay.
Fuel On the end of the inner mole.
Repairs Cranes up to 40 tons available. Yachts are craned onto the quay. Most mechanical repairs.
Provisions In the town about 20 minutes' walk to the west.
Eating out Restaurant at the harbour. Others in Finale.
Other PO. Bank and ATM in Finale.

Finale Ligure looking NW towards Capo Noli

General

The town of Finale is an unassuming seaside town with some fine old architecture. In the 14th century when most of the towns along the coast surrendered their independence to Genoa, Finale did not and under the Marquis of Savona turned to Spain for help, thereby obtaining a foothold for the Spanish in Italy. Not until 1713 did Genoa obtain Finale and then for less than a century. The surrounding hills are extensively cultivated with the vine and a fine white wine, Lamassina, is produced locally. The harbour is a peaceful spot tucked under a rocky headland away from the noise and bustle of downtown Finale.

Capo di Noli

An old signal station on the cape is conspicuous. In calm weather or light southerlies a yacht can find some shelter on the N side of the cape off the medieval village of Noli.

It is quite deep for anchoring until close in, and not suitable with normal onshore breezes.

ISOLA DI BERGEGGI

Two miles N of Capo di Noli and one mile S of Capo di Vado, Isola di Bergeggi lies close in to the coast; a large wedge-shaped rocky islet covered in olive trees.

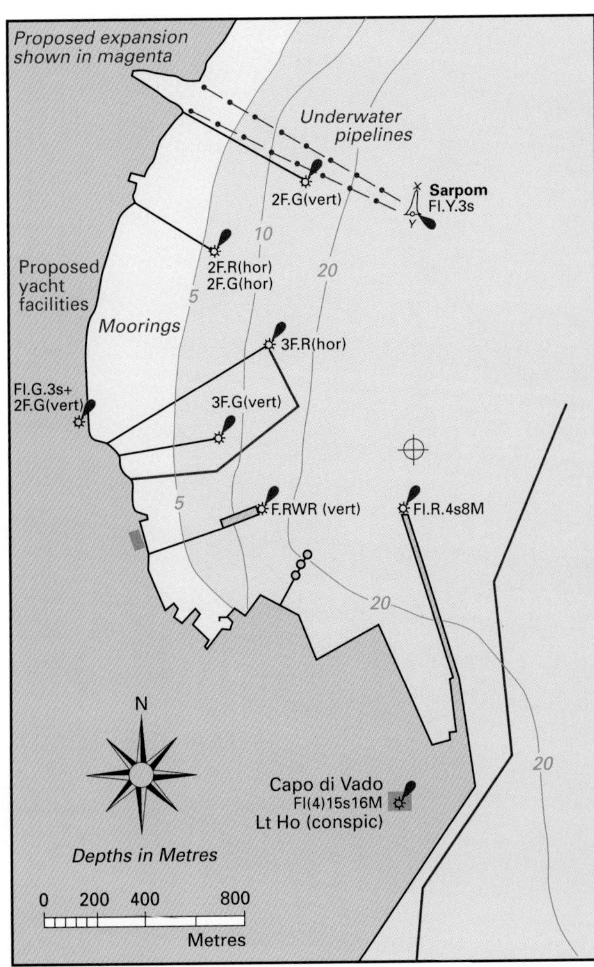

VADO LIGURE
⊕44°16'·1N 08°27'·2E

The Island is now designated as an Area Marina Protetta, which covers the island and adjacent coast. The SE side of the island lies in Zone A of the AMP and as such is out of bounds to all unauthorised vessels.

In Zone B anchoring is prohibited, but yachts may navigate within the zone and use AMP mooring buoys. Anchoring is permitted in Zone C, although there is little shelter anywhere from the normal sea breeze.

VADO LIGURE

The harbour and jetties for Vado Ligure Oil Terminal lie just E of the lighthouse at Capo di Vado. The harbour is not for yachts.

In light offshore winds you may find some shelter immediately N of the oil terminal jetties where there are convenient depths of around 3–6m to anchor in. Make sure your anchor light is up and working as it can be busy with supply and work boats even at night.

Care must be taken of laid moorings for local boats close in. Along the shore are small jetties and boatyards with hauling facilities for yachts and fishing boats. Ferries for Corsica run from Vado Ligure.

Note There are plans to expand the port and to improve facilities for yachts here, although no details are available yet.

SAVONA

BA 350
Italian 53

Approach

Conspicuous The large town is conspicuous from some distance off. From the S the lighthouse on Capo di Vado (a building and white tower 34m high) is conspicuous. Off Vado and off Savona, there are always a number of ships at anchor. At Vado the oil refinery with tall chimneys and storage tanks are conspicuous. Two chimneys with red and white bands stand out. A number of jetties for discharging oil are also prominent. Approaching Savona, a very tall silo at the harbour is conspicuous and, closer in, the harbour breakwaters and large cranes and gantries are easily identified.

By night Use the light on Capo di Vado Fl(4)15s43m16M. The oil loading jetties of Vado Ligure in the SW of the bay are lit.

VHF Ch 13, 16 for port authorities. Ch 09 for yacht berths.

Dangers With strong southerlies there is a reflected swell off the new S breakwater. In gale force winds this causes a cross swell for some distance off which can be dangerous for small craft. In such conditions stand out to sea and approach the port from a SE direction.

Note Work is in progress extending the commercial harbour quays. Work is also planned to begin on the proposed yacht basin on the NW side of the entrance. Care is needed especially if entering at night.

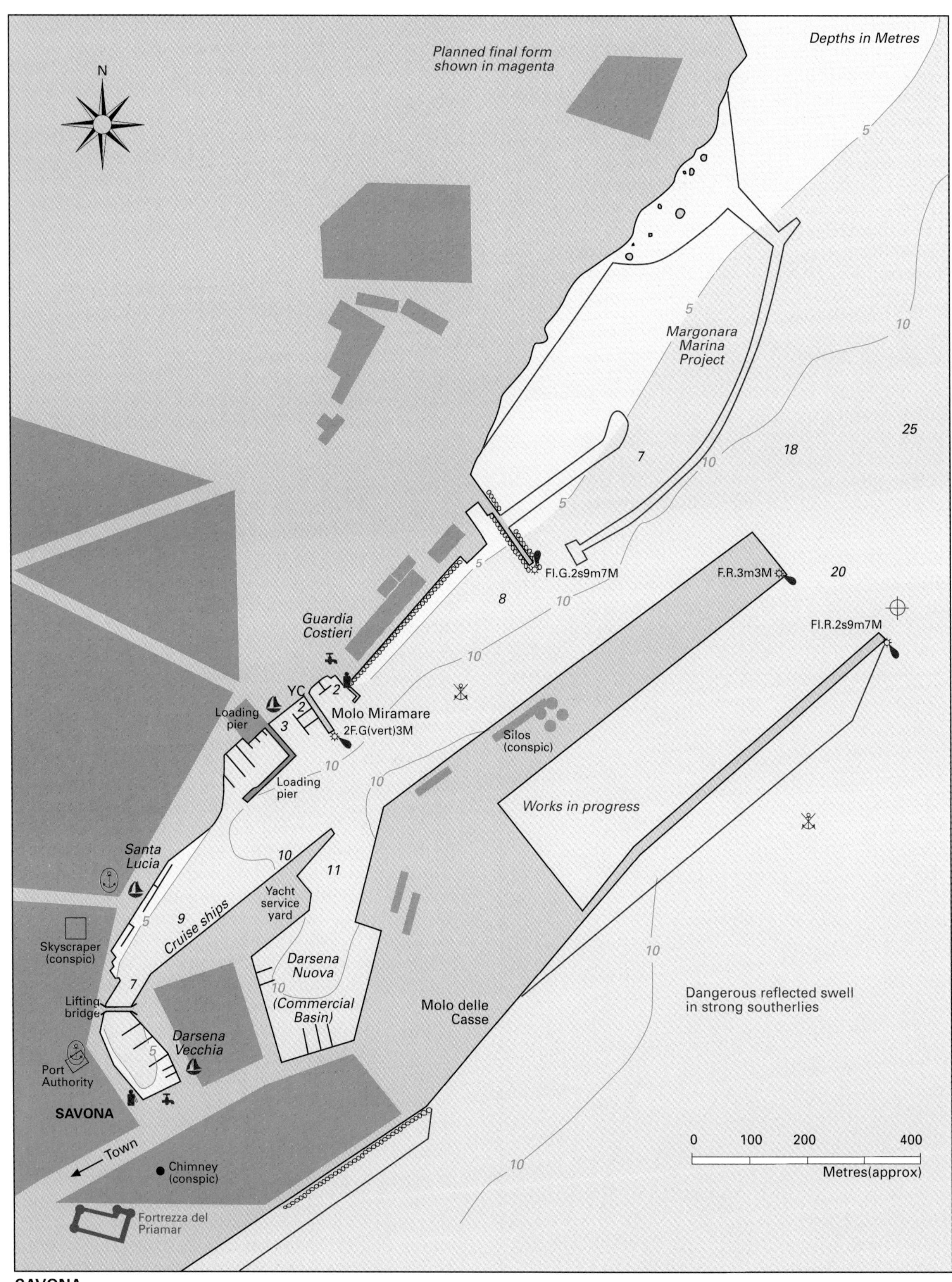

SAVONA
⊕44°19´·06N 08°30´·33E WGS84

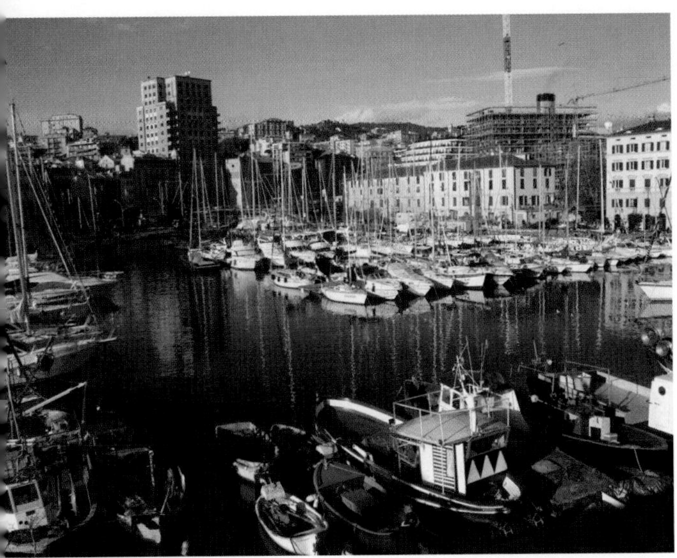

Savona. Darsena Vecchia looking N towards the lifting bridge at the entrance

Mooring

Assonautica and the port authority co-ordinate most visitors' yacht berths in Savona. There are berths in Miramare, a YC near the coastguard offices; pontoon Santa Lucia opposite the cruise ship berths; and berths in the Darsena Vecchia.

Data 300 berths. 25 visitors' berths. Max LOA 20m. Depths 4–9m.

Molo Miramare At the yacht club. It is very crowded here and the surroundings are industrial.

Santa Lucia Pontoon near the entrance to Darsena Vecchia. Most berths will suffer from wash caused by the cruiseships manoeuvring onto their berths opposite.

Darsena Vecchia The old basin right in the middle of town. Yachts must wait for the lifting bridge to open at the entrance to the Darsena Vecchia.

The bridge opening times are:

Monday–Friday Every hour on the half hour i.e. 0630, 0730, 1730, 1830 etc.

Saturday and Sunday Every half hour i.e. 0700, 0730, 0800 etc. Yachts may call ahead on VHF Ch 09 to request opening.

It is crowded in here but with persistence you should find a berth. Laid moorings tailed to the pontoons.

Shelter Good at Molo Miramare and Santa Lucia although there can be wash from passing craft. All-round shelter in Darsena Vecchia.

Authorities Port authorities. Club officials at the YC and harbourmaster at Darsena Vecchia. Charge band 2/3 at Darsena Vecchia.

✉ Assonautica Savona, Associazione Provinciale per la Nautica da Diporto, Via Baglietto 1, 17100 Savona
✆ 019 821 451 *Fax* 019 833 6805
Email info@assonauticasavona.it
www.assonauticasavona.it
Savona Port Authority S.V. Port Services ✆ 019 855 4345
Fax 019 827 399
Email svport@portosavona.net
www.porto.sv.it

Facilities

Services Water and electricity (220V) on the quay in Darsena Vecchia, Santa Lucia and Molo Miramare.
Fuel Near the quay in the SW corner of Darsena Vecchia and at Molo Miramare.
Repairs Yachts can be craned out at the yacht club. Boatbuilders and technical services in the port. W-Service offers technical services and haul-out facilities at the entrance to Darsena Nuova.

W-Services ✆ 019 848 5379 *Fax* 019 848 7527
Email mail@w-service.com
www.w-service.com

Engineering and electrical workshops in the town. Chandlers and hardware shops. Towards Vado Ligure there are several yards where a yacht can be hauled.
Provisions Excellent shopping for all provisions in the town.
Eating out Restaurants, trattorias and pizzerias in the town.
Other PO. Banks. ATMs. Italgaz and Camping Gaz. Hire cars. Bus and train to Genoa.

General

Savona is the fifth-largest port in Italy, handling mostly oil and coal. Although the dock area is drab and industrial, the town centre a short distance away is a sophisticated shopping area replete with elegant boutiques and smart cafés. Many medieval buildings have been restored along the cobbled streets. The arcaded 'high street', the Via Paleocapa, leads to the Leon Pancaldo Tower erected to the sailor from Savona who was one of Magellan's navigators on the first round-the-world voyage in 1520. Magellan's voyage of 42,000 miles, 22,000 of these across waters never before sailed upon by Europeans, makes Columbus' voyage across 8,000 miles of sea look a doddle – yet it is Columbus and the names of his ships that are remembered. Pancaldo was evidently one of those who made it back again on the *Vittoria*, as he is recorded as sailing from Cadiz by way of the Strait of Magellan in order to reach Peru in 1537–8.

Savona. Yacht club pontoons on Molo Miramare

I. THE LIGURIAN COAST

VARAZZE

Approach

This new marina, built to replace the original harbour, lies on the N side of Capo dell'Olmo, close W of Varazze town.

Conspicuous From the S and E a red brick villa and tower and an autostrada bridge behind the harbour are conspicuous. From the W neither the harbour nor Varazze town will be seen until close to.

VHF Ch 09, 16.

Mooring

Data 800 berths. 70 visitors' berths. Max LOA 35m. Depths 3·5–6m.

Berths Go stern or bows-to where directed. Laid moorings tailed to the quay. Motor boats will use the S side of the marina, and sailing yachts will be directed to berths to the N of C pontoon. The basin in the N of the marina belongs to the Baglietto boatyard.

Shelter There looks to be excellent all-round shelter in the marina.

Authorities Marina staff. Charge band 6 (June–September).

✉ Marina di Varazze, Via Savona, 17019 Varazze, SV
✆ 0199 35321 *Fax* 0199 353250
Mooring ✆ 338 364 1506
Email olga.grassi@marinadivarazze.it
www.marinadivarazze.it

Facilities

Services Water and electricity (220/380V). Telephone and TV connections. Wi-Fi. Showers and toilets.
Fuel On the quay at the E side of the entrance.
Fuel ✆ 348 995 7411
Repairs 100-ton travel-lift. Hard-standing and covered storage facilities. Most repairs can be arranged. Sailmaker. Chandler.

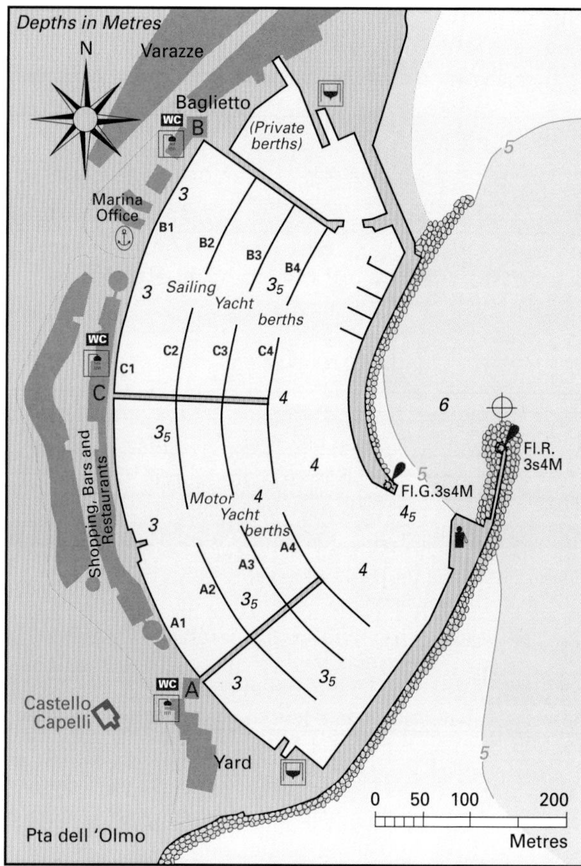

MARINA DI VARAZZE
⊕44°21'·16N 08°34'·27E WGS84

Provisions A supermarket is planned for the marina. Good shopping in Varazze town, about 10 minutes' walk from the marina.
Eating out Bars and restaurants are planned for the marina. Good restaurants and pizzerias in the town.
Other In the marina: ATM. Laundry. Newspapers. Electric carts and bicycle hire. In the town: PO. Banks. ATMs. Italgaz and Camping Gaz. Hire cars. Bus and train to Genoa.

General

Varazze town is a major tourist resort, though it retains a relaxed old-world atmosphere. Tall palms line the beach and the old town seems wreathed in greenery and flowers. The marina is a short distance from the town, and has been designed with panache. Timber and glass pavilions with verdigris roofs stand on stilts with elevated walkways around the quays. Boutiques and apartments will complement the usual café-bars, *gelateria* and restaurants. The idea of splitting the marina berths into strictly sail and motor sections seems like a good idea – a bit of boat apartheid won't harm anyone and hopefully I won't be near a generator running all night. Unfortunately the prevelance of motorboats in this area means segregation is not always possible.

Note When there are strong NE winds blowing all along the Riviera, the Admiralty *Pilot* states that there is little or no wind off Varazze.

Marina di Varazze looking NE. Note the shallows off the point to the N of the marina *Marina di Varazze*

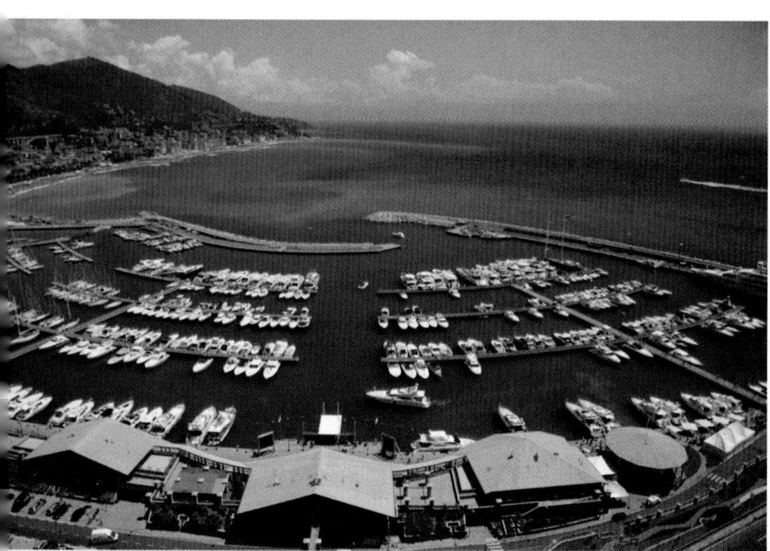

ARENZANO

Approach

The harbour is tucked behind Capo Arenzano.

Conspicuous A large brown apartment block behind the harbour and the outer mole is conspicuous.

VHF Ch 09.

Dangers The harbour has always had problems with silting, and a sandbank used to obstruct part of the entrance. Recent improvements to the breakwaters and extensive dredging have improved things here, but yachts should approach with caution.

Mooring

Data 185 berths. Max LOA 18m. Depths 1·5–4m.

Berth Go stern or bow-to the outer breakwater. There are laid moorings at most berths.

Shelter Good all-round shelter.

Authorities Harbourmaster and marina staff. Charge band 3.

Capitaneria ✆ 010 912 4537

Facilities

Services Water and electricity at or near most berths.
Fuel In the town about 150m away.
Repairs Cranes up to 20 tons. Mechanical repairs. Other minor repairs. Chandlers.
Provisions In Arenzano town about 15 minutes' walk along the waterfront.
Eating out Café bars and restaurants close to the harbour. More in the town.
Other PO. Bank and ATM in the town.

General

Arenzano is the last of the Riviera resorts before the industrial sprawl of Genoa is encountered. If you can get in here it is a private, almost snooty little place, with a calm and peace much removed from the noise and hustle and bustle of Genoa.

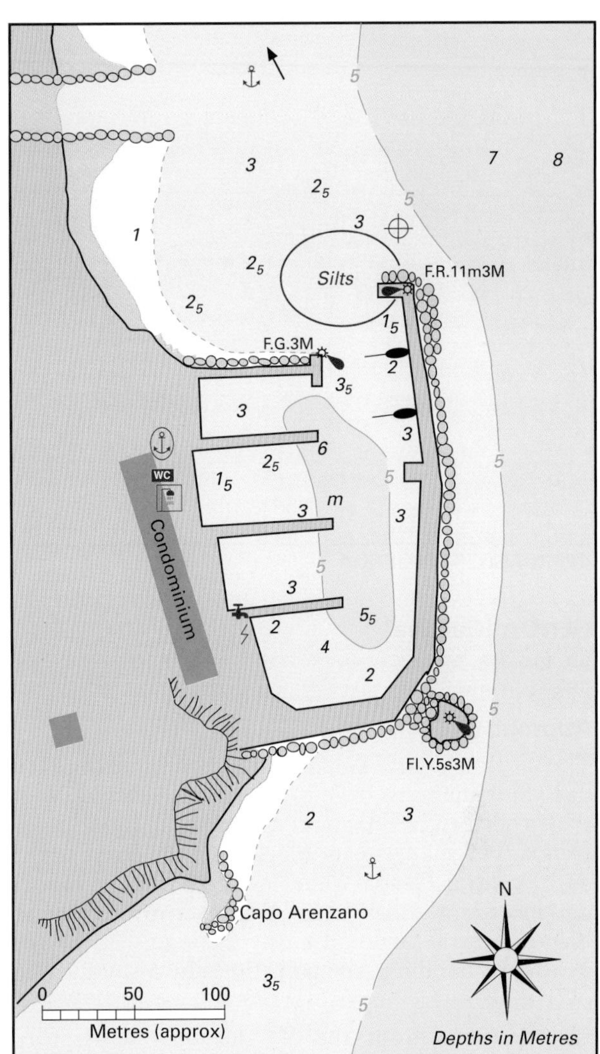

ARENZANO
⊕44°23´·99N 08°41´·28E WGS84

Arenzano looking WSW
Roberto Merlo

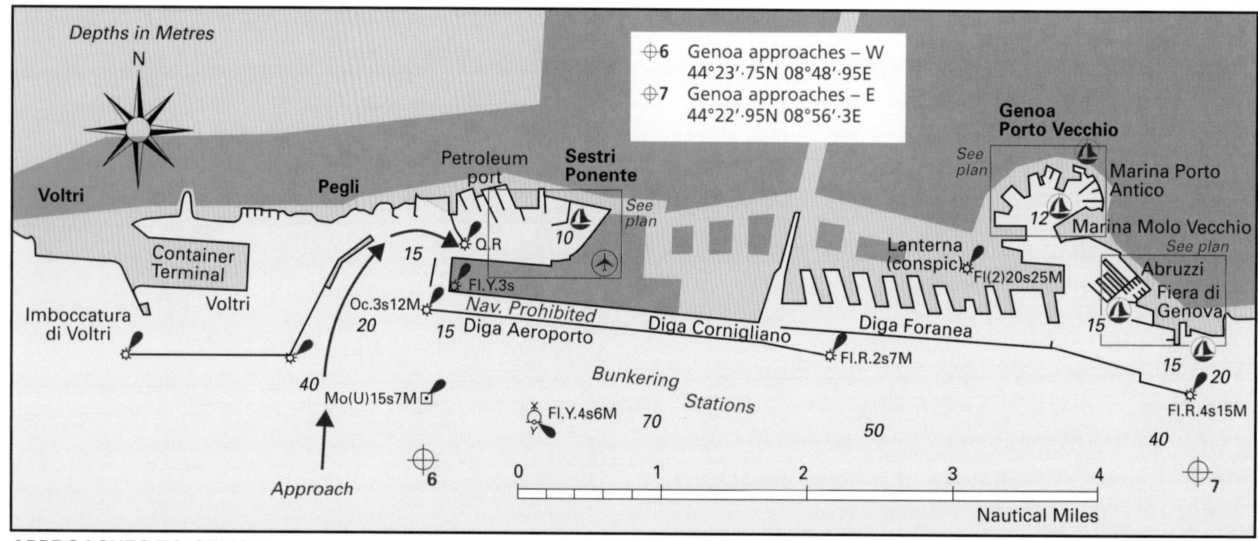

APPROACHES TO GENOA

GENOA (Genova)

BA 354, 355, 356
Italian 54 and 55

Approach

The city of greater Genoa extends in an unbroken line along the coast from Voltri, about 1½ miles W of the airport, to Nervi, about two miles ESE of central Genoa. Large apartment blocks line the coast to the W of central Genoa while fewer apartment blocks and more large villas extend E from central Genoa to Nervi. Central Genoa is easily distinguished by the density of buildings and sometimes by a smog cloud over it.

Conspicuous From the W the busy Cristoforo Colombo airport can be identified from the numerous aircraft landing. Closer in, the oil tanks at the petroleum port are conspicuous and the W end of Diga Aeroporto will be easily identified. From the SE the large buildings of the exhibition centre on the N side of the entrance are conspicuous as is the tall Lanterna lighthouse (117m/380ft high).

By night Use Lanterna lighthouse Fl(2)20s117m25M and Oc.R.1.5s119m10M. It is difficult to make out many of the lights against the loom of the city lights behind.

VHF

Port authorities Ch 11, 16 (24/24).
Sestri Ponente Ch 16, 11, 67 (0700–1900).
Marina Genova Aeroporto Ch 71.
Abruzzi Ch 16, 11 (0700–1900).
Fiera di Genova Ch 74 (0830–1830).
Marina Porto Antico Ch 71.
Marina Molo Vecchio Ch 71.

Dangers

1. Genoa is an extremely busy port and a good lookout must be kept for other craft entering and leaving the harbour.
2. With strong onshore winds there is a considerable reflected swell off the long breakwaters protecting the various basins. The effects of this reflected swell may be felt up to a mile and more off. At either entrance there can also be a confused swell and care must be taken with strong onshore winds.
3. Off Diga Aeroporto there are two oil bunkering stations with floating hoses around them. A yacht should keep well clear of them by day and night. The platforms are lit Mo(U)Y.15s7M.

Prohibited Area It is prohibited to navigate or moor inside Diga Aeroporto.

Genoa looking E over the commercial docks to Porto Vecchio
Roberto Merlo

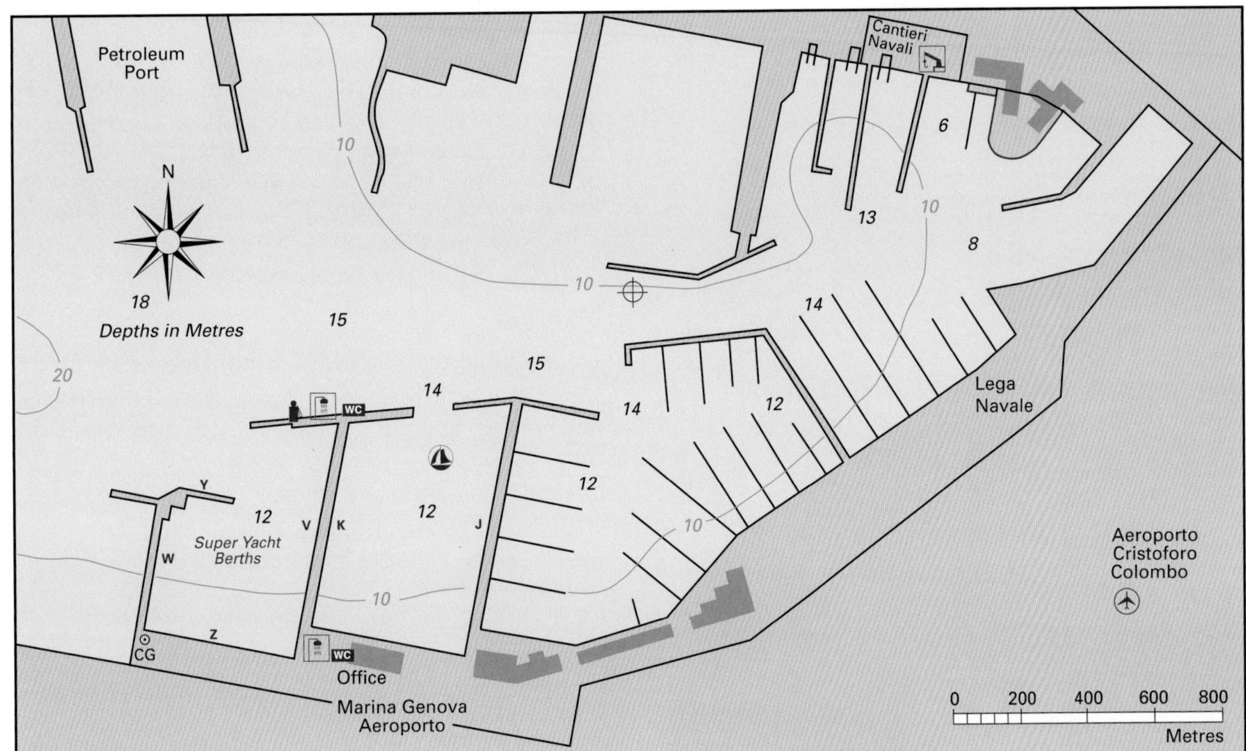

SESTRI PONENTE
44°25´·05N 08°50´·5E

Genova Sestri Ponente

Approach

The channel past the end of the airport runway and into the basin is marked with buoys and beacons. Care should be taken of commercial shipping entering and leaving in the narrow channel.

Note Vessels with air height over 4m must keep close to the Voltri breakwater when approaching Sestri Ponente. From the end of the breakwater head towards the elbow of the Sestri Ponente N breakwater, then S across to the S breakwater and along to the marina. Keep clear of commercial vessels at all times.

VHF Ch 67 (Lega Navale/Cantieri Navali).

Mooring

Data 475/150 berths. Max LOA 25/45m. Depths 2–10m.

Berth

Lega Navale berths are on pontoons around the basin. Finding a spare berth depends on the permanent berth-holder being away.

Cantieri Navali berths on two pontoons on the N quay. Laid moorings tailed to the quay.

Shelter Good shelter although there can be some wash from passing craft.

Authorities Harbourmaster. Charge band 2/3.

Lega Navale ✆ 010 651 2654

✉ Cantieri Navali di Sestri, Via Cibrario 3, Genova Aeroporto ✆ 010 651 2476 *Fax* 010 651 2282
www.cantierisestri.it

Facilities

Services Water and electricity near all berths.
Repairs (Cantieri Navali) 400-ton hydraulic trailer. 50-ton crane. Hard-standing and covered workshops. Most repairs can be arranged. Specialists in GRP, West System, electronics and stainless steel work.
Provisions The yard is in the industrial area of Sestri Ponente, on the 'wrong' side of the railway. It is a 15-minute walk to the main coast road, and the town lies on the N side of it.
Eating out Local restaurants in Sestri. More in the city centre.
Other PO. Banks and ATMs in Sestri. Buses and trains into Genoa. Cristoforo Colombo International Airport is adjacent to the yard.

Marina Genova Aeroporto

A new project to regenerate the entire area adjacent to the airport began in 2006. The marina is now open but work continues ashore.

VHF Ch 71.

Mooring

Data 500 berths. Max LOA 90m. Depths 2–15m.

Berths Some berths in the S part are available. Work continues on the N side and shoreside.

Shelter Good shelter at most berths.

Authorities Marina staff. Charge band 6.

✆ 010 614 3420
Email info@marinagenova.it
www.marinagenova.it

Facilities

Services Water and electricity (220/380V). Wi-Fi. Pump-out.

Fuel Fuel dock ✆ 010 614 3453

Repairs Boatyards nearby.

Other As for Sestri Ponente.

Genova Porto Vecchio

Approach

Yachts must approach the marinas in Porto Vecchio using the E entrance (Bocca Levante). Yachts should keep to the N side of the channel, and must not impede the progress of commercial shipping.

Genoa Porto Vecchio looking E across Marina Porto Antico
Marina Porto Antico

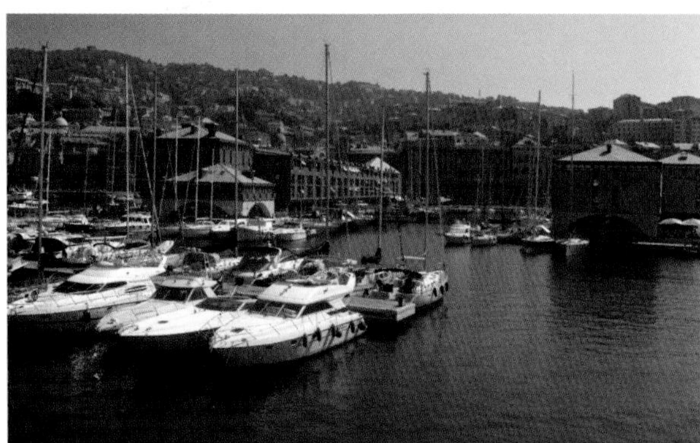

Fiera di Genova

Fiera di Genova is the first marina in the approaches to Porto Vecchio. The basin is part of a large exhibition centre, home to the Genoa Boatshow in October each year. Marina RR Genoa Yacht Services, is a technical service company based in Fiera di Genova. Marina Service, part of Marina Porto Antico, operates the berths here.

VHF Ch 74 for Marina Service (0830–1830).

Mooring

Data 450 berths. Max LOA 20m. Depths 4–7m.

Berth Where directed. Space is tight inside the basins and yachts should not enter until directed. Laid moorings.

Shelter Good all-round shelter.

Authorities Harbourmaster. Charge band 3.

Marina Service ✆ 010 251 8552 (for details see entry for Marina Porto Antico).

✉ Marina RR, Via Pone Reale, 2/4 Piano, 1624 Genova
✆ 010 24981 *Fax* 010 249 8200
Email info@marinarr.com

✉ Fiera di Genova, Piazzale JF Kennedy 1, 16129 Genova
✆ 010 53911 *Fax* 010 539 1270
Email fierage@fiera.ge.it
www.fiera.ge.it

Facilities

Services Water and electricity (220V) at all berths. Telephone connection. Toilets and showers. Laundry. Telephone and fax services.

Fuel On the quay (0830–1730).

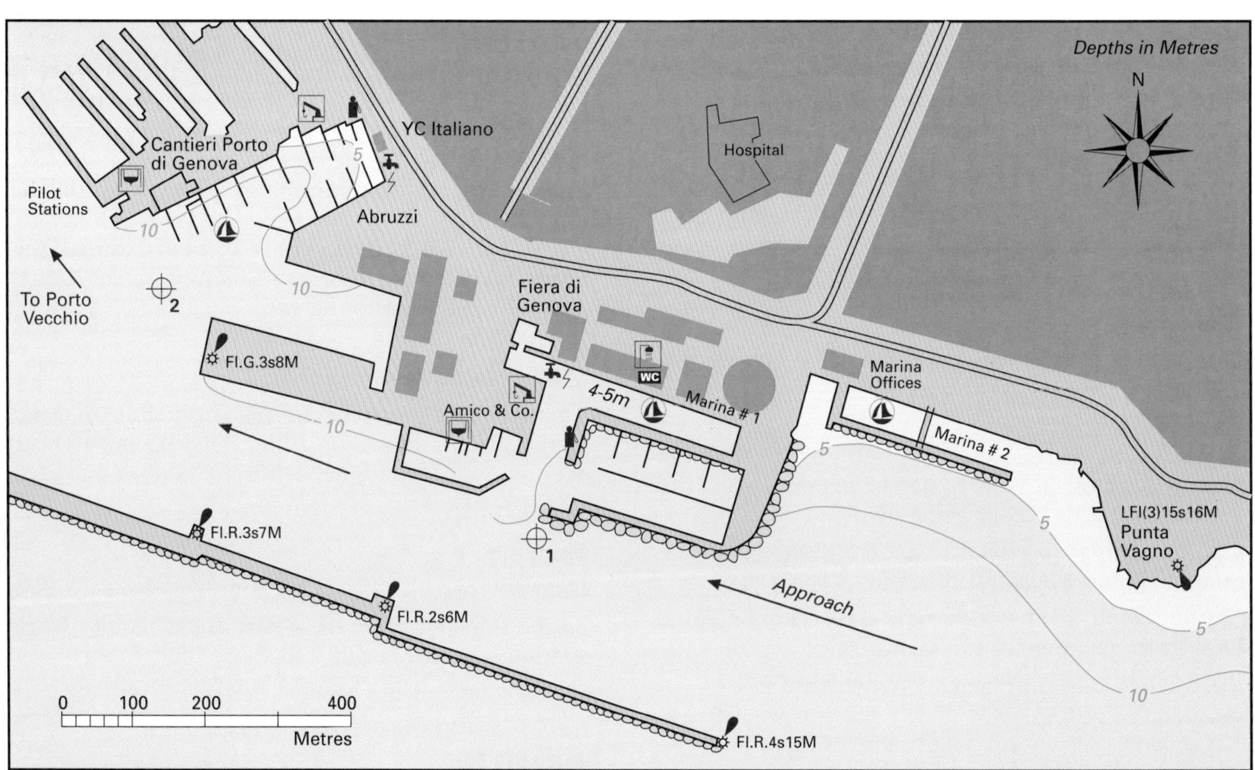

GENOA: MARINA FIERA DI GENOVA AND MARINA ABRUZZI
⊕1 44°23′·6N 08°56′·15E
⊕2 44°23′·85N 08°55′·55E

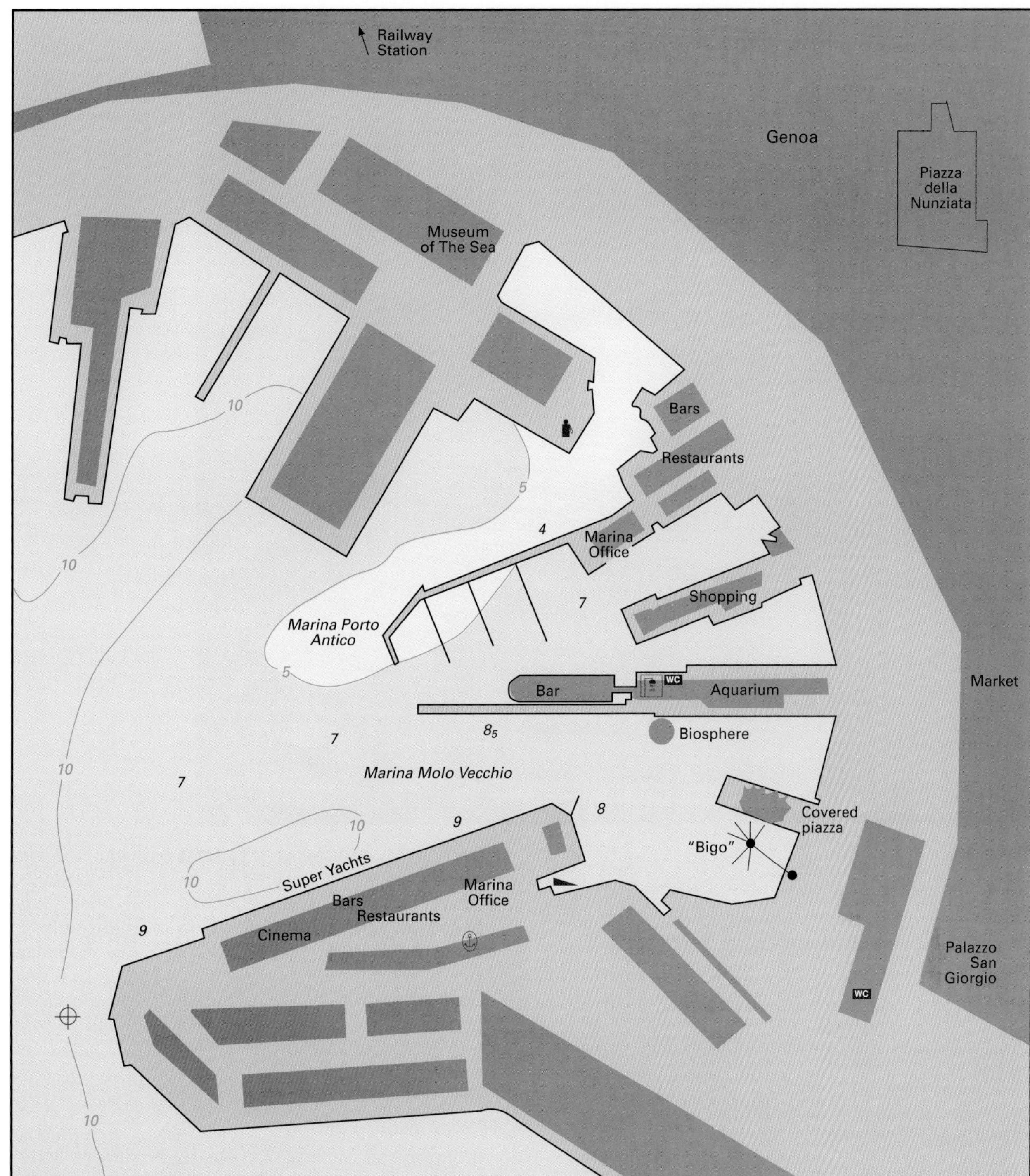

PORTO VECCHIO Marina Porto Antico and Marina Molo Vecchio
⊕44°24′·44N 08°55′·12E WGS84

Repairs 300-ton travel-lift (planned). 60m dry dock. Most repairs including engineering, electronics, painting, upholstery and joinery. Chandlers.
Provisions All provisions available in Genoa (see below).
Eating out Club bar and restaurant at the marina (see also below).

Abruzzi

Properly Duca degli Abruzzi, the basin lies 600m beyond Fiera di Genova in the approach to Porto Vecchio. The main pilot station is on the N side of the entrance to the basin. Yacht Club Italiano and Lega Navale control most of the berths in the basin.

VHF Ch 11, 16 for YC Italiano and Lega Navale (0700–1900).

Marina Molo Vecchio with, 'Bigo', a lifting viewing platform, and the adjacent aquarium *Marina Molo Vecchio*

Mooring

Data 300 berths. Max LOA 30m. Depths 3–10m.

Berth Where directed. Laid moorings. Finding a vacant yacht club berth is difficult in the summer.

Shelter Good shelter.

Authorities Harbourmaster. Charge band 3.
YC Italiano ✆ 010 246 1206
Email info@yci.it
www.yci.it
Lega Navale ✆ 010 246 1201
Email segreteria@leganavalegenova.net
www.leganavalegenova.it

Facilities

Services Water and electricity at most berths. Toilets and showers.
Fuel On the quay (0800–1800).
Repairs 30-ton crane. 150-ton slipway. Most repairs can be arranged.

Cantieri Porto di Genova has a yard and pontoon on the NW side of the basin. 30-ton travel-hoist. 30-ton crane. Most repairs and refit facilities. Covered workshops.

✉ Cantieri Porto di Genova Srl, Via al Molo Giano, 16128 Genova Porto ✆ 010 246 2061 62 63 *Fax* 010 267 033
Email info@cantieriportodigenova.com
www.cantieriportodigenova.com

Note The Luna Rossa (Prada) Challenge for the America's Cup is backed by the Yacht Club Italiano. Founded in 1997, Team Prada on their boat *Luna Rossa* won the Louis Vuiton Cup in 2000, only to lose in the final to the NZ *Black Magic* defender. After a disappointing campaign in 2003, the Luna Rossa team were back in the hunt for the 2007 America's Cup, but had their work cut out to win the right to challenge the Swiss holders Alinghi.
www.americascup.com
www.lunarossachallenge.com

Marina Molo Vecchio

The marina uses the quay on the N side of Molo Vecchio and around the E side of the harbour to the pontoon off the Aquarium.

VHF Ch 71 for Marina Molo Vecchio and Amico & Co.

Mooring

Data 160 berths. Visitors' berths. Max LOA 150m. Depths 6–10m.

Berths Super-yachts berth stern-to along Molo Vecchio. Other berths on the pontoon W of the Biosphere. Smaller yachts may be directed to berths along the quay N of the Aquarium. Laid moorings throughout. Marina staff will assist mooring.

Shelter Good shelter.

The large aquarium and Biosphere are adjacent to both marinas in Genoa's Porto Vecchio

Authorities
Harbourmaster. Marina staff. Yacht Agency. Charge band 5.

✉ Marina Molo Vecchio, Calata Molo Vecchio, Modulo 3, 16128 Genova ✆ 010 27011 *Fax* 010 270 1200
Email mmv@mmv.it
www.mmv.it

Pesto Yacht & Ship Agency ✆ 010 270 1305
Fax 010 270 1200
Email pesto@pesto.it
www.pesto.it

Facilities

Services Water and electricity (220/380V 16–250A). Telephone and satellite TV. ISDN internet. Wi-Fi. Toilets and showers. Pump-out facilities.
Fuel By tanker, or on the quay in Porto Vecchio.
Repairs Amico & Co. near Fiera di Genova provide complete repair or refit services. 300/510-ton travel-hoists. 200m dry dock. Covered workshops and controlled environment paint sheds. All electronic, engineering, joinery, GRP and wood repairs. Project management. Agents for Awlgrip, Caterpillar, Boero and Northern Lights.

✉ Amico & Co., Via dei Pescatori, 16128 Genova
✆ 010 247 0067 *Fax* 010 247 0552
Email amico.yard@amicoshipyard.com
www.amicoshipyard.com

Marina Porto Antico

The marina pontoons lie immediately N of Marina Molo Vecchio.

VHF Ch 74 for Marina Porto Antico (0830–1830).

Mooring

Data 280 berths. Visitors' berths. Max LOA 55m. Depths 3–8m.

Berths Stern or bows-to. Laid moorings. Larger yachts are directed to the N side of the pontoons. Marina staff will meet you in a RIB and will assist with mooring.

Shelter Good shelter.

Authorities Harbourmaster. Marina staff. Charge band 4.

✉ Marina Porto Antico, Molo Ponte Morosini 28, 16126 Genova ✆ 010 251 8552 *Fax* 010 251 8536
Email mpa@marinaportoantico.it
www.marinaportoantico.it

Facilities

Services Water and electricity at all berths. Toilets and showers.
Fuel On the quay adjacent to the marina.
Repairs Marina RR Genoa Yacht Services haul-out and repair facilities in Fiera di Genova (see entry for details).

Genoa

Provisions Excellent shopping for all provisions. Excellent fresh fruit and vegetables market and fish market near the waterfront.
Eating out Excellent restaurants, trattorias and pizzerias of all categories near the waterfront.
Other PO. Banks. ATMs. Italgaz and Camping Gaz. Internal and international flights. Hire cars. Buses and trains to all destinations.

General

If you are in one of the central yacht harbours (everywhere except Sestri Ponente) you are right in the middle of town and close to everything you could need. In fact, you don't have to stray far into the city as the whole port area has been revived and there are more than enough shops, boutiques, cafés and restaurants to occupy your time close at hand.

Marina Porto Antico looking W across Porto Vecchio, Genoa
Marina Porto Antico

I. THE LIGURIAN COAST

Christopher Columbus

Cristoforo Colombo was born in Genoa in October 1451 to a family of wool weavers. As a boy he worked on the loom and later went to sea. In 1476 he went to Lisbon and joined his younger brother Bartholomew in chart making before making several voyages to Iceland, Madeira and Africa – on the last he was the master of a Portuguese ship. Columbus now moved back to Lisbon to promote the idea that it was possible to sail west to the Orient rather than around the treacherous Cape of Good Hope. The latter route was the Portuguese hope and they were soon to attain their goal.

For 10 years Columbus attempted to get backing for the venture, but Portugal, France and England all turned him down. Eventually Ferdinand and Isabella in Spain supplied the vessels and men he required and the concessions to trade and future power he demanded.

The ships on this first voyage were the caravels, *Pinta* and *Nina*, supplied by Isabella, and a Galician caravel, the *Santa Maria*, chartered by Columbus. These ships were the typical small trading ships of the day rigged as either caravel rotunda (square-rig on the two forward masts and a lateen-rigged mizzen) or caravel latina (lateen-rigged on two masts). The *Nina* was originally caravela latina but it was later changed. The *Pinta* and *Nina* were 58′ and 56′ overall respectively and the *Santa Maria* was 95′ overall. Although there were good maps (portulans) of the Mediterranean, north Atlantic and parts of Africa and India, there was as yet no knowledge of a continent between Europe and the Orient going westward. The notion that Columbus was trying to prove the world was round is entirely unfounded, as most educated Europeans already regarded the world as a sphere.

Columbus set off to sail along latitude 28°N believing he would reach Japan. However, his idea of distances was wildly wrong as he estimated the distance from the Canary Islands to Japan as being 2,400 miles whereas it is in fact 10,600 miles. On 12 October 1492 he made landfall in the Bahamas at an island he named San Salvador. He then sailed southwest with an Arawak Indian pilot, still hoping to discover Japan, but instead discovering more of the Bahamas and Cuba. Later he discovered Hispaniola (Haiti) where he established a garrison before returning to Spain. From the Indies he took back Indian slaves, parrots, gold nuggets and tobaccos (as the Indians called cigars). He is also credited with bringing back syphilis from the Indies, but this we now know to have existed in Europe for a long time already.

In 1493 he made a second voyage with 17 vessels and numerous men and supplies to colonise the Indies. He made a landfall at Dominica, encountering the cannibal Carib Indians, and then continued on to the Leeward Islands, the Virgin Islands and Puerto Rico. Returning to Haiti he found his garrison had been wiped out so he shifted its location to the north coast. He then journeyed westward, still believing he was on the Chinese coast, and discovered Jamaica. On 10 March 1496 he set out to return to Spain to restore his declining political fortunes.

In 1498 he set out on his third voyage to explore further south of the Antilles. On 31 July he landed on Trinidad and then continued on to Venezuela to be the first European to land on the American continent. He now realised he was on a new continent, an *otro mundo* (other world) unknown to the Greeks, yet he still believed it to be close to Asia. Returning to Spain he set about equipping a fourth voyage which sailed from Cadiz in 1502 and made a landfall at Martinique after a 21-day passage. Crossing to the mainland he skirted the coast of Nicaragua and Costa Rica and eventually anchored off Panama, disappointed not to have found a passage to Japan. He did not realise that the Pacific Ocean was only a short distance away. Returning to Spain in late 1504 he died 18 months later, a virtually forgotten man, bitter and frustrated at having failed to find China or Japan, although he believed he was very near to them, and snubbed and ignored by the Spanish court.

Looking back we now recognise Columbus as one of the greatest seamen of his time. Although his celestial navigation was not always accurate, his dead reckoning and pilotage in unfamiliar waters strewn with coral reefs was superb. His handling of the small caravels, often riddled with worm, undermanned and short of supplies, was an outstanding feat in itself. On his first voyage he had discovered America (John Cabot did not reach Newfoundland until 1497) and on his subsequent voyages he had discovered more islands and coastline than anyone except Magellan. If Genoa had only listened to her explorer son she would have become an even richer and more powerful city-state.

Around Marina Molo Vecchio the old warehouses have been sympathetically revamped by the architect Renzo Piano into commercial offices with shops, restaurants and cafés at ground level. Around Marina Porto Antico there are more shops, cafés and restaurants and a good chart agent. Head away from the sea and there are yet more facilities, and all these have been designed with pedestrians in mind so that you can wander around aimlessly and at will without dicing with the *Tifosi* (of the Ferrari persuasion) on the overhead bypass road.

The city has ancient associations and was probably founded by the Etruscans in the 8th–7th century BC. Greeks settled here in the 6th century, and it prospered until the Carthaginian War, when it was invaded in 209BC. The Romans rebuilt it and its present name possibly derives from this time when it was called Janua after Janus, the Roman two-headed god that traditionally guarded a Roman gate or door. After the fall of the Roman Empire it declined until medieval times when its inhabitants started building up its trading fleet and the Genoese voyaged throughout the Mediterranean, especially to the eastern Mediterranean to load up with spices and fine cloth for the increasingly prosperous city. Its rise to mercantile stardom would eventually bring it into conflict with other Italian maritime republics, especially Pisa and Venice, and these three powerful mini-states were often at war and squabbling over far-away bits of territory. A good number of the castles and forts around the Levant and down through Corsica and Sardinia are Genoese in origin or were at least occupied by the Genoese at some time.

Many of the crusaders were shipped from Genoa to the Levant and Richard Coeur de Lion left from here on his way to the Crusades. It is interesting to speculate that the patron saint of England, St George, may well have been introduced by King Richard I. On voyage down the coast a storm beset his ship and he implored the captain to pray to his saint for deliverance and then, as the storm increased in fury, pledged to adopt the saint as his own. That saint was St George (see entry on San Fruttuoso below). After the crusades Genoa allied with Byzantium and traded throughout the Black Sea. At the end of the 13th century Genoa defeated both Pisa and Venice and became the significant sea power in the western Mediterranean.

Genoa was at the forefront of the Renaissance and wealthy patrons attracted artists to the city, and architects (notably Alessi) designed some of the fine palazzos in the city. After the Renaissance it slowly declined, though it has always been an important city, and remains Italy's largest port.

With the rehabilitation of the port area and some sympathetic new buildings, the large aquarium foremost amongst these, the port area is really a wonderful place from which to explore this city, and a relaxed place to return to when you have had enough of the traffic and noise of Genoa central. In October the Genoa Boat Show takes place around Fiera di Genova and berths are limited in and around Genoa.

The Riviera Levante

Note In high season berths right around the coast here are much in demand. In harbours *ormeggiatori* will often try to squeeze 'just one more' in, although equally some will try to fill their berths with only the biggest yachts possible. There are frequent regattas throughout the summer, when marina berths will be reserved for participants, although sometimes the berths are not obviously occupied. There is no simple answer to getting a place; in some places it pays to call ahead; in others you're better to find yourself a berth and then report in. In some places you may find short-term berths are free.

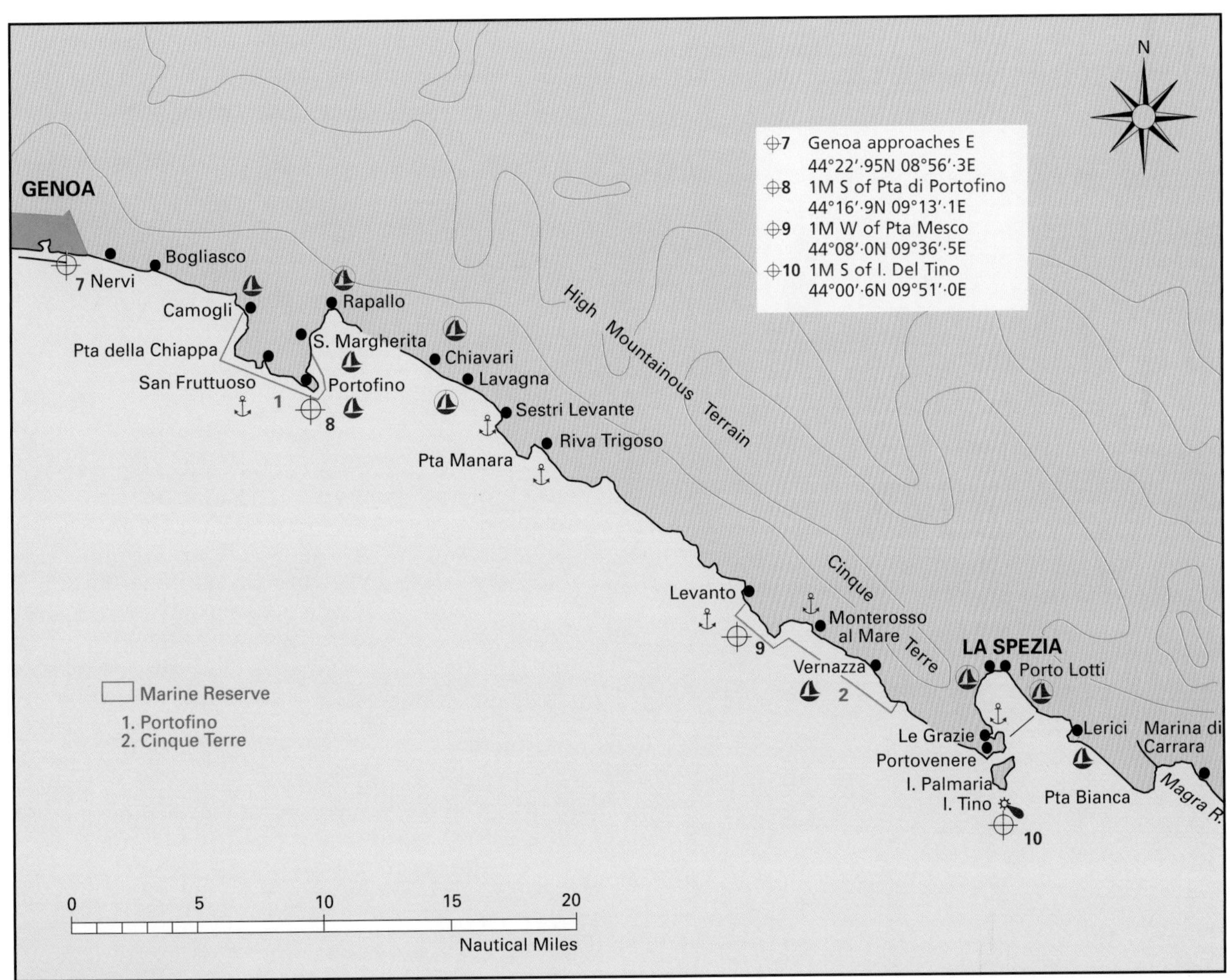

RIVIERA LEVANTE

NERVI

A very small harbour situated to the E of Genoa. There are 1·5–2m depths in the entrance close to the end of the mole. It is suitable for very small craft drawing 1m and less provided you keep close to the end of the mole and berth on the mole itself. Much of the harbour has less than 1m depths and part of it is obstructed by a sandbank (see plan). It should not be entered with onshore winds. Restaurants and bars ashore.

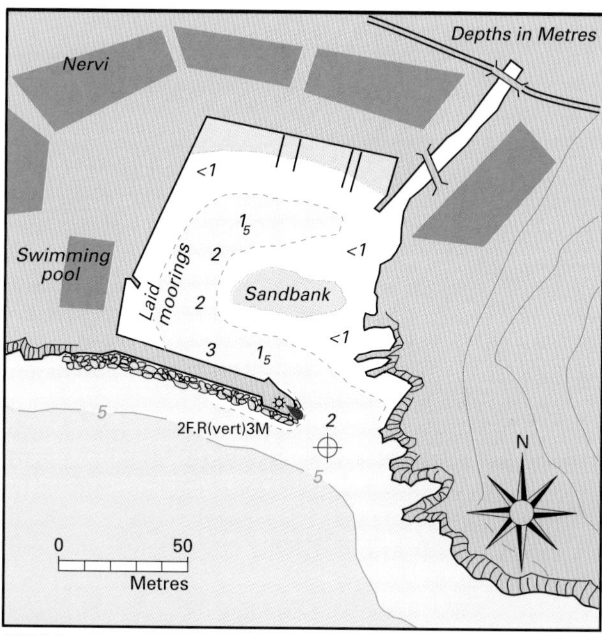

NERVI
⊕ 44°22′·92N 09°01′·90E

BOGLIASCO

⊕ 44°22′·61N 09°04′·13E

A small harbour situated just over two miles E of Nervi. A green cupola is conspicuous in the town. Most of the inner part of the harbour sheltered by a short outer mole has less than 1m depths. In calm weather anchor just under the outer part of the mole in 3m and take a long line to the mole if possible. Restaurants ashore.

RECCO

⊕ 44°21′·55N 09°08′·4E

A small harbour has been constructed around the mouth of a *torrente*, less than ½M N of Camogli. The entrance is open S, with a miniature harbour on the E side. Depths are mostly 1–2m, and it is liable to silt.

The small craft harbour at Nervi *Gino Cianci, FOTOTECA ENIT*

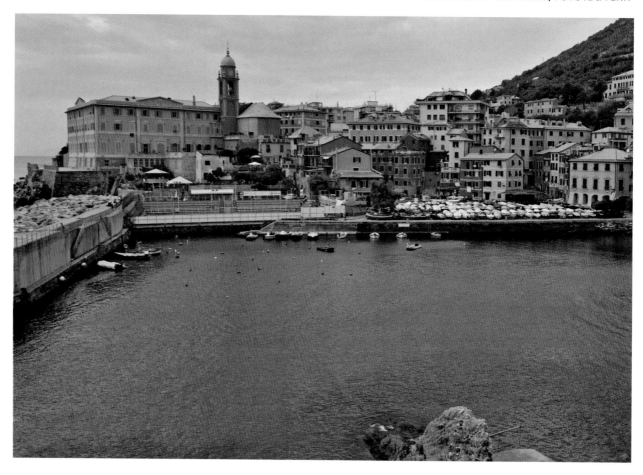

CAMOGLI

Approach

The harbour lies at the bottom of wooded slopes two miles N of Punta della Chiappa.

Conspicuous The tall old houses, 6–7 storeys high, fringing the harbour, and a chateau-like villa at the root of the mole, are conspicuous.

VHF Ch 16.

Dangers

1. In strong S and W winds a swell heaps up at the entrance and care is needed. With onshore gales the entrance could be dangerous.
2. Up to 100m to seaward of the mole there are numerous above and below-water rocks.

Mooring

Data Max LOA 12m. Depths 2–4m.

Berth Most of the craft in the harbour are moored fore and aft right across the inner basin. A yacht should go bows-to the outer part of the mole where shown. This part of the mole is reserved for visiting yachts with a sign on the wall denoting the space: *Ris imbarcazioni in transito*. Care must be taken of the ballasting extending underwater from the quay so go bows-to rather than stern-to if possible.

Shelter Good in settled weather. With strong onshore winds there can be a surge in the harbour.

Authorities Harbourmaster and customs.
Capitaneria ✆ 0185 770 032

Facilities

Water On the quay in the inner basin.
Fuel On the quay near the entrance, but underwater ballasting extends off the quay.
Repairs Minor mechanical repairs only. Chandlers
Provisions Good shopping for provisions nearby.

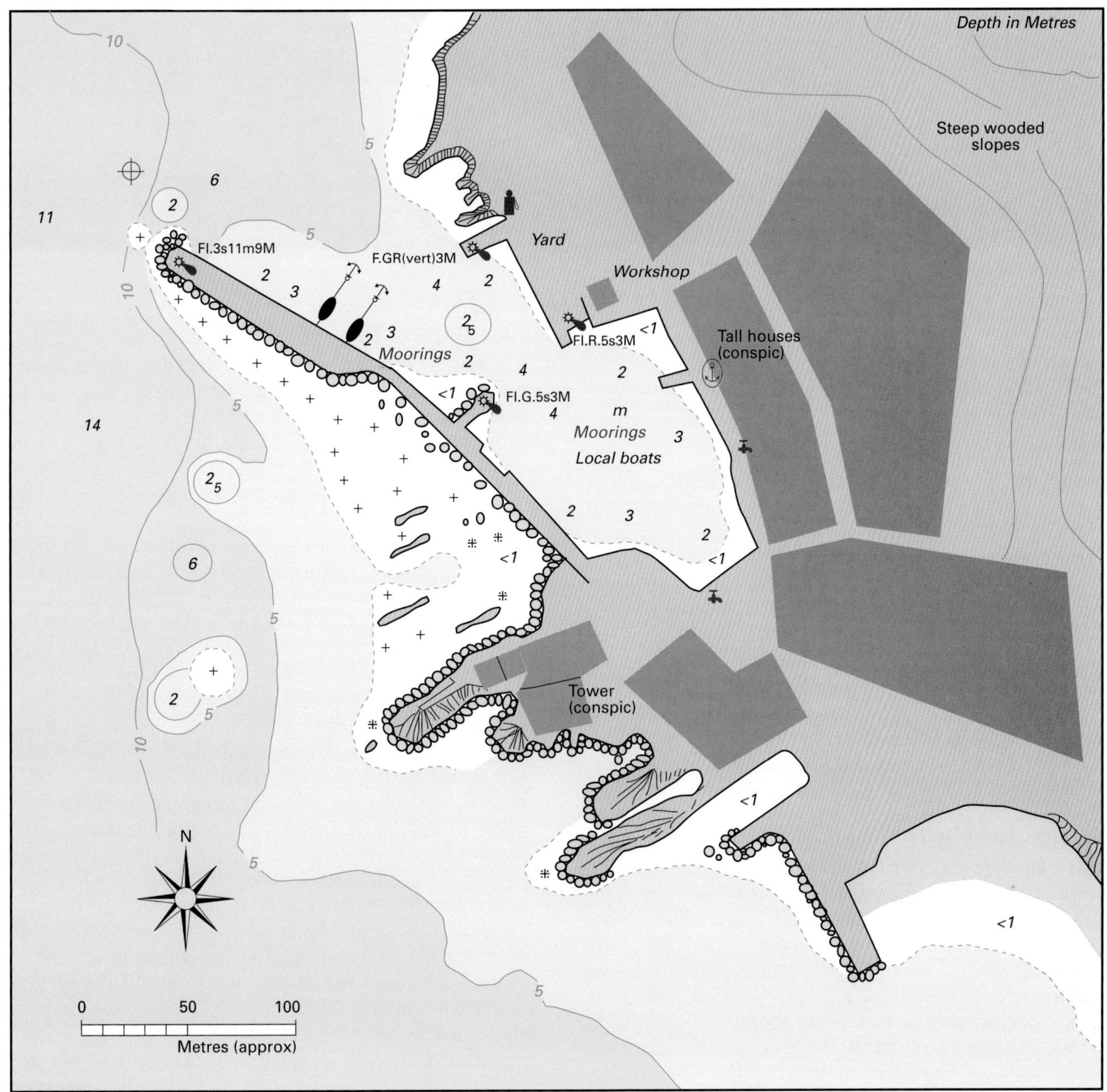

CAMOGLI
⊕ 44°21´·1N 09°08´·9E

Camogli looking SE *Roberto Merlo*

Eating out Restaurants, trattorias and pizzerias along the waterfront.
Other PO. Bank. ATM. Italgaz and Camping Gaz. Bus to Genoa.

General

Camogli is a gem. The tall old houses of burnt umber and sienna and the old fishing harbour at the foot of the steep wooded slopes make a visit well worthwhile despite difficulty in finding a berth. Camogli once supported a large trading fleet numbering nearly a thousand vessels, but the coming of steam turned trade and prosperity elsewhere. The large houses around the harbour were built in its heyday in the 19th century and though the fleet exists no longer, the town still has a strong association with the sea.

The Instituto Cristoforo Columbo, a nautical school established in 1874, is still here and in the museum there are numerous models and paintings of the sailing fleet. Today tourism has returned a little of that prosperity, although some of the male population are said still to be deep sea fishermen going as far as the South Atlantic. The name Camogli is apparently a corruption of *Casa delle Moglie*, which were the communal houses the fishermen installed their wives in while away at sea – presumably to ensure no landlubbers whisked them off and assaulted their virtue. Charles Dickens summed up Camogli in these words '... the saltiest, roughest, most piratical little place'.

SAN FRUTTUOSO

On the S side of Punta della Chiappa is the small cove of San Fruttuoso sheltered from all but strong southerlies. A church with a prominent cupola in the abbey of Capodimonte at the head of the cove is conspicuous. There is a corridor for navigation through the marine reserve which may be buoyed in places.

A yacht should anchor fore and aft as there is limited swinging room, or better still anchor off the NE corner and take a line ashore. There are 5–6m depths in the middle and 2m depths until close in. The E bay is administered by *ormeggiatori* who may restrict anchoring, or may levy a charge. A small quayed area is reserved for tripper boats.

A friend, Jan Roos, when diving in this bay was surprised to find a statue of Christ some 4m high in the water in the position shown. Inscribed on the base of the statue is: *Il Cristo degli Abissi*. The tiny village has long been famous for its monastery and the vaults of the Doria family, and the statue was perhaps placed here by this illustrious family. The church and monastery have recently been restored.
Legend has it that Richard the Lionheart shipped from Genoa and soon after was caught in a terrible storm. The Lionheart trembled and prayed for deliverance to the nearest sacred object which was the Genoese patron saint mounted on the poop rail, promising that if delivered from the tempest he would make the saint patron of England. The saint

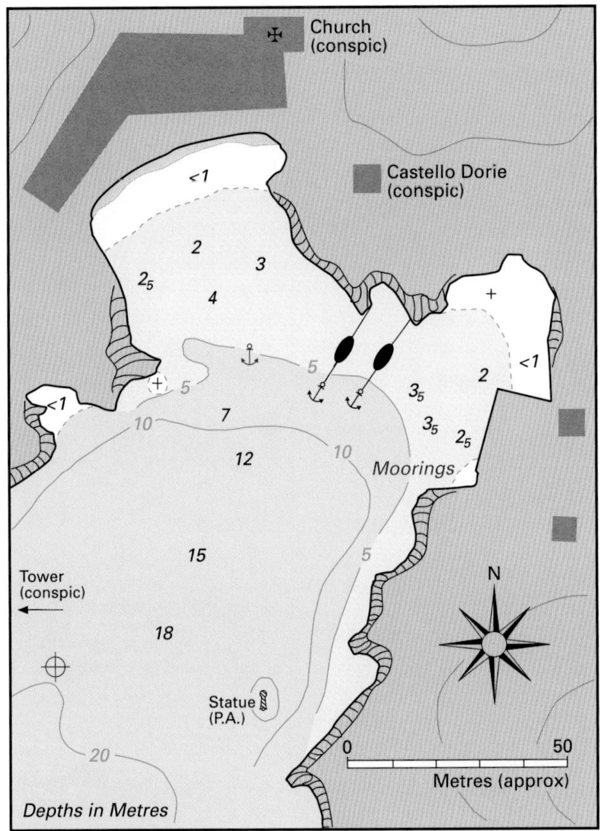

SAN FRUTTUOSO
⊕ 44°18′·85N 09°10′·45E

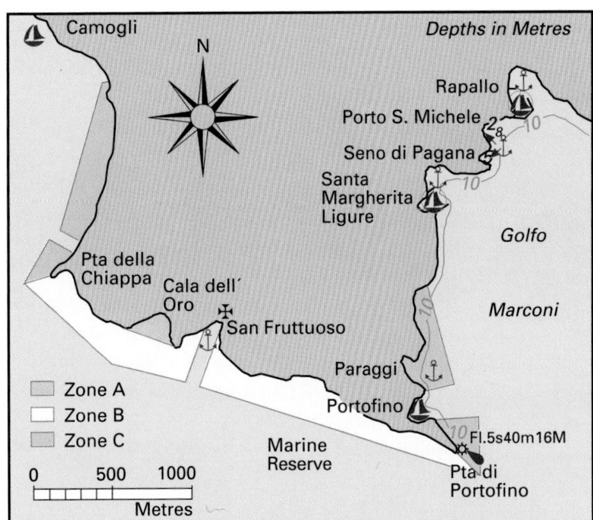

PORTOFINO MARINE RESERVE AND GOLFO MARCONI

was St George. The king was saved, coming ashore at San Fruttuoso.

For active walkers there is a footpath around to Portofino and the Basillica di San Giorgio where the saint is supposed to be buried – about a two-hour walk.

Golfo Marconi

BA 1998
Italian 58

The gulf, named in honour of Guglielmo Marconi who conducted some of the first radio transmission experiments near here, is considered one of the most beautiful in Liguria. On the west side of the gulf the exclusive harbours of Portofino, Santa Margherita Ligure and Rapallo grace the coast whilst on the east Chiavari and Lavagna are large marina complexes.

Weather note

According to the Admiralty *Pilot*, 'an exceptionally clear atmosphere and light clouds scattered high above the mountains around Rapallo and Chiavari are said to presage fresh north-easterly winds'. With winds from anywhere in the W there are strong gusts off the high land on the west side of the gulf.

Portofino Marine Reserve

Established in 1997 in the waters surrounding the Portofino promontory, the area is subject to the following regulation:

Zone A
Navigation, stopping, anchoring, mooring, swimming, fishing and diving prohibited.

Zone B
Navigation under sail or with oars permitted.
Motor vessels up to 7.5m and sailing vessels up to 10m can navigate at speeds up to 5kns.
Mooring only on mooring buoys in the following areas: Cala degli Inglesi, S. Fruttoso (right side), Punta Chiappa.
Free anchoring prohibited.
Swimming permitted.
Sport fishing is subject to official authorisation.
Accompanied diving permitted; unaccompanied only with permission.

Zone C
Navigation and fishing are subject to the same regulations as Zone B. Swimming permitted.
Anchoring is permitted in regulated zones at the discretion of the reserve authorities of the particular area.
Subaqua activities do not need authorisation and are free of charge.

✆ 0185 289 649
Email amp.portofino@parks.it
www.riservaportofino.it

PORTOFINO

Approach

The harbour is on the E side of Punta Portofino.

Conspicuous The lighthouse (a white building and tower) on Punta Portofino is conspicuous and the inlet is approximately half a mile NW of the point. On the S side of the entrance a castle is conspicuous.

VHF Ch 12.

Mooring

Data approx. 220 berths. Eight visitors' berths. Max LOA 70m. Depths 1–4m.

Berth Yachts are on fore and aft moorings or you can go on the quay. Larger yachts may have to anchor with a long line ashore. There are only eight moorings reserved for visitors and at times, especially at weekends, these will all be booked up in

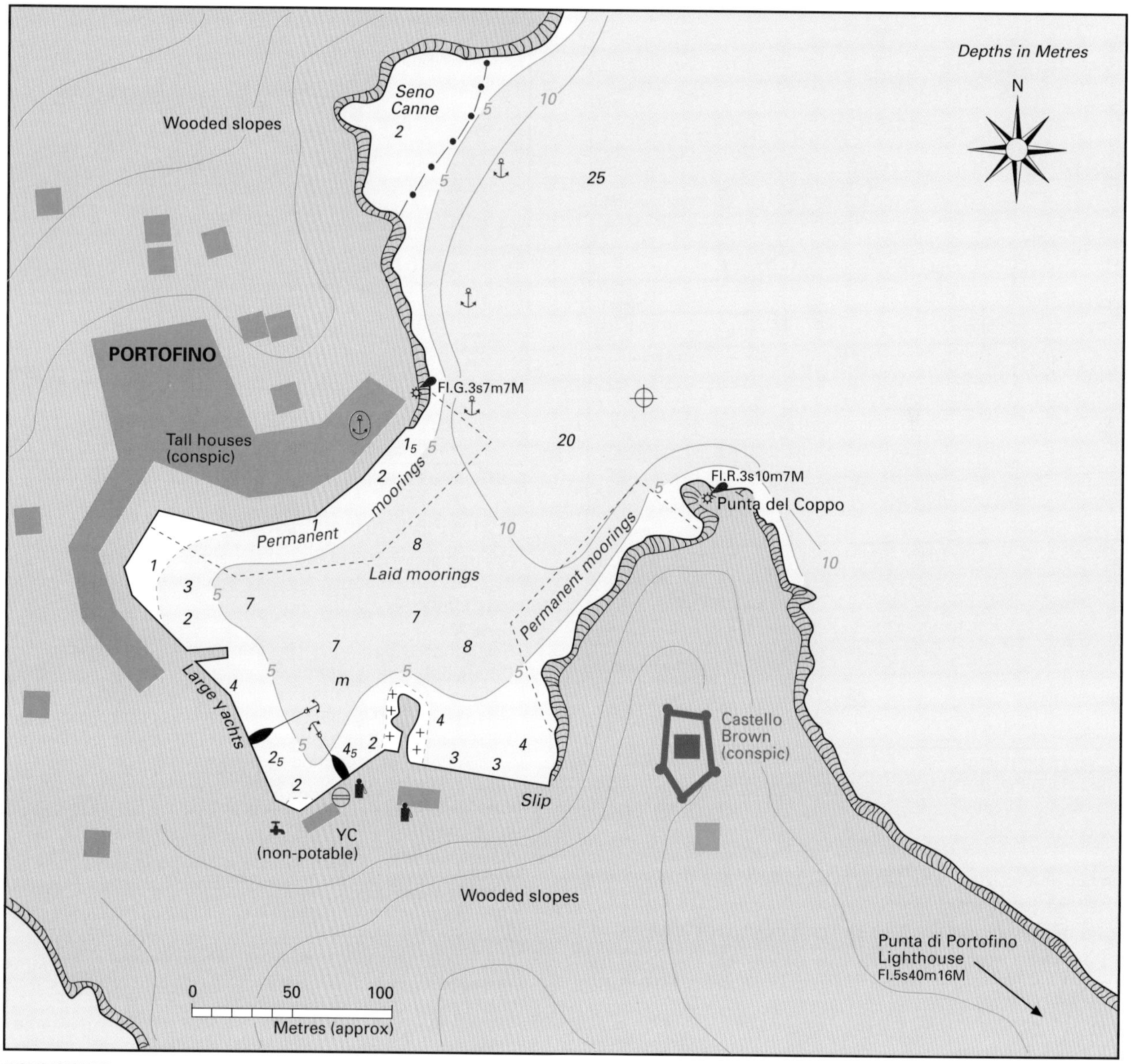

PORTOFINO
⊕44°18´·25N 09°12´·8E

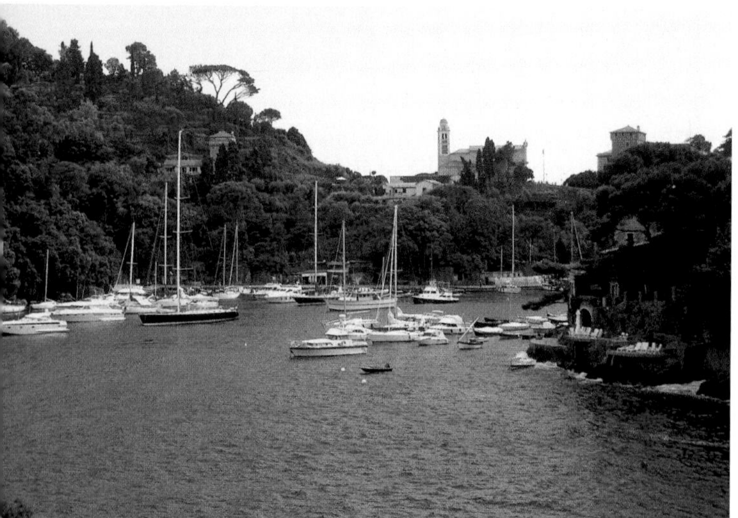

Portofino looking SW into the entrance

advance. In the summer the harbour is very popular and it can be difficult to find a berth, so you should probably reckon on having an alternative plan.

Shelter Good, although there can be an uncomfortable swell in here especially with easterly winds. In strong NE winds care is needed and it may be prudent to go to the head of the gulf.

Authorities Harbourmaster and customs. Charge band 6+.

Portofino Marina ✆ 0185 269 580
www.marinadiportofino.com
Capitaneria ✆ 0185 269 040
Ormeggiatori Renzo ✆ 0185 269 388

Anchorage In calm weather a yacht can anchor on the N side of the entrance up to Seno Canne with a long line ashore in 10–20m on mud and weed. It is a short dinghy ride into Portofino and the water is clean enough to swim here. At times Seno Canne is roped off with small buoys as a swimming area, but it is usually possible to anchor off beyond the buoys or to the S of the cove.

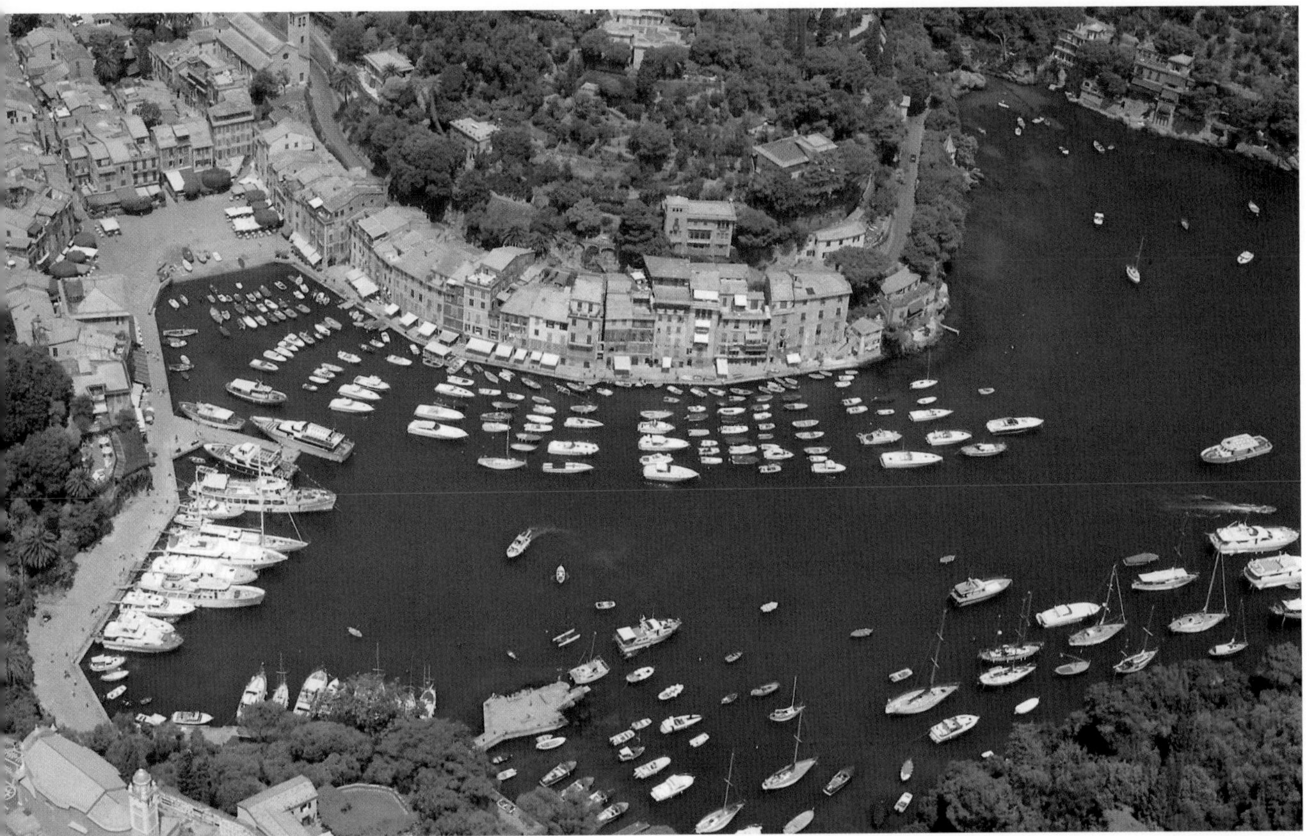

Portofino looking north *Roberto Merlo*

Facilities

Services Water on the quay. There is potable and non-potable water here so check before you fill your tanks. Electricity can be connected. Shower and toilet block.
Fuel On the quay.
Provisions Limited. Good shopping in Santa Margherita Ligure about 5km away.
Eating out Restaurants and trattorias.
Other For most services you will have to go to Santa Margherita Ligure about 5km away.

General

It has been said that while anyone can visit Portofino, few can stay here. It is an aristocrat of a resort for the rich and a favourite of the jet set. It is beautiful, elegant and sophisticated and the yachtsman is one of the lucky few who can stay here if a berth is available.

The castle on the ridge is known locally as 'Castello Brown' after a British Consul General at Genoa in the 19th century who bought it and renovated it to live in as his residence. It remained in the family until the 1960s when it was given to the Commune di Portofino. The Basillica di Santa Giorgio on the ridge above the harbour is said to contain the body of St George and has marvellous views into the bargain.

SENO DI PARAGGI (Zone C)

A bay immediately N of Portofino. Open to the E–SE, it offers good shelter in settled weather. In the summer much of the bay is roped off for swimmers so you will have to anchor in 15–20m outside the line of buoys. Depending on the wind and sea the best place is probably on the SW with a long line ashore. The bottom is sand and weed, mediocre holding in places. It is about a 1km walk around to Portofino and about 2kms to San Margherita Ligure.

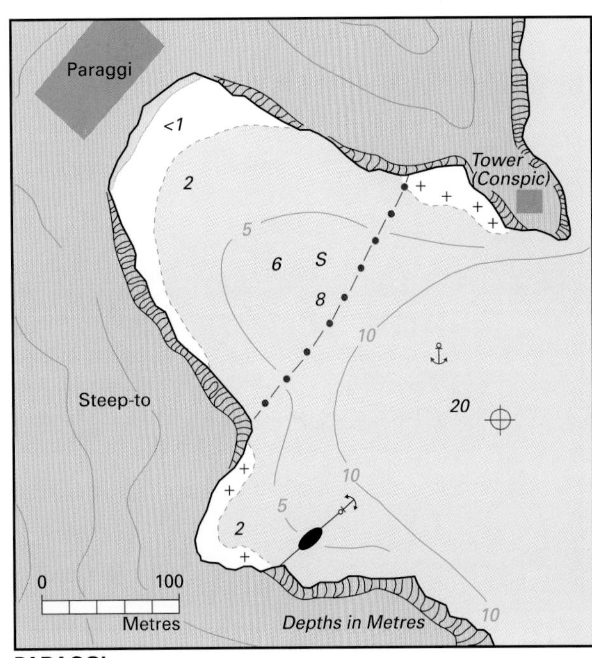

PARAGGI
⊕44°18′·5N 09°12′·7E

SANTA MARGHERITA LIGURE

Approach

The harbour lies approximately 1½ miles N of Portofino.

Conspicuous The elegant buildings around the harbours are easily identified, particularly the Hotel Imperiale, a large white building.

VHF Ch 11, 16 (24/24 in the summer, 0800–1900 October–May).

Note Work is in progress extending the sea wall.

Mooring

Data 350 berths. 50 visitors' berths. Max LOA 60m. Depths 2–10m.

Berth Go stern-to the mole where directed. There are numerous concessions controlling berths. Laid moorings tailed to a buoy or to the quay. Larger yachts use their own anchors. The bottom is mud and good holding. Cantieri Sant'Orsola has a pontoon on the N side with visitors' berths. Laid moorings.

Shelter Good all-round shelter. Many boats are wintered afloat here.

Authorities Harbourmaster and customs. Marina staff. A charge is made.

Ormeggiatori Giorgio & Giuliano ✆ 0185 205 453
Societa Gestioni Portuali ✆ 0185 288 893
IBS Yachting Point ✆ 0185 288 408 *Fax* 0185 284 470
Email santamargherita@ibsgroup.it
www.ibsgroup.it
Cantieri Sant Orsola ✆ 0185 282 687
Capitaneria ✆ 0185 287 029

Anchorage A yacht can anchor off to the N of the marina in 3–6m on mud, good holding.

Facilities

Services Water and electricity at or near all berths. Telephone connection to some berths. A shower and toilet block.
Fuel On the outer mole and on the W quay.
Repairs Crane up to 30 tons. Yachts can be hauled onto the hard by the harbour. All mechanical and engineering repairs. Wood and GRP repairs. Electrical and electronic repairs. Chandlers.
Provisions Good shopping nearby for all provisions. Fish market near the harbour and a general market on Friday mornings.
Eating out Excellent restaurants, trattorias and pizzerias along the waterfront. A friend recommends a local dish allegedly only found here – a kind of vegetable ravioli with a walnut sauce.
Other PO. Banks. ATMs. Italgaz and Camping Gaz. Hire cars. Bus to Genoa.

General

Santa Margherita Ligure is an elegant upmarket resort – a suburb of sophisticated Rapallo just round the corner. On the slopes above are the villas of the

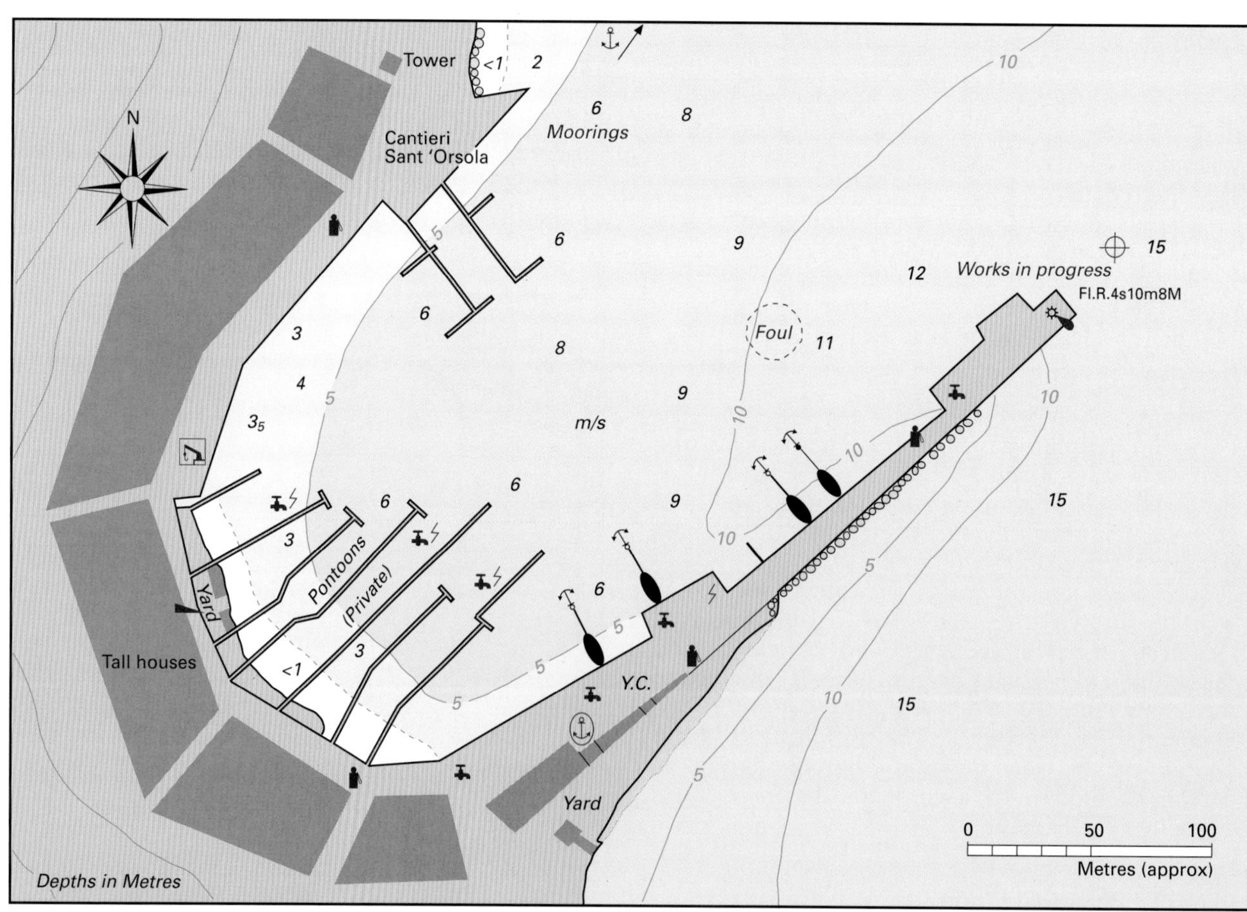

SANTA MARGHERITA LIGURE
⊕ 44°19´·9N 09°13´·1E

Santa Margherita Ligure *Vito Arcomano, FOTOTECA ENIT*

rich and very rich from the northern inland cities. Down around the harbour there is a more workaday atmosphere and it is really a thoroughly likeable spot.

The village takes its name either from Santa Margherita d'Antiochia whose remains are ensconced in the church of the same name, or for those of a secular mind, from the white-flowering bush, the *margherita*, which can be seen everywhere.

Seno di Pagana and Porto San Michele

Between Santa Margherita Ligure and Rapallo there are two small coves, one above the other, where a yacht can anchor in settled weather. Both are open to the E and SE. In Pagana anchor in 6–8m on sand and weed. In San Michele, immediately N and the larger of the two coves, anchor in 5–9m on sand and weed, good holding. In the SW corner of San Michele there is a yard with a short quay. It is just over a kilometre to Rapallo, where there are provisions and restaurants.

Santa Margherita Ligure looking south. New pontoons on the NW quay are not shown *Roberto Merlo*

RAPALLO (PORTO PUBLICO AND CARLO RIVA)

Approach

The harbour lies at the head of the Golfo Marconi about one mile NE of Santa Margherita Ligure.

Conspicuous The elegant houses around the bay and the harbour breakwater are easily identified. The Castello standing on a rock N of the harbour is conspicuous.

By night Use the main light on the elbow of Carlo Riva Fl.3s9m9M.

VHF Ch 09 for Carlo Riva. Ch 16 for Porto Publico (0830–1730).

Mooring

Carlo Riva

Data 400 berths. Max LOA 40m. Depths 3–7m.

Berth Where directed.

Shelter Excellent.

Authorities Marina staff. Charge band 6+ (May–September).

Carlo Riva ✆ 0185 6891 *Fax* 0185 63619
Email info@portocarloriva.it
www.portocarloriva.it

Note Visitors' berths are often full in July and August. The Porto Publico adjacent to the marina is full of pontoons with local yachts on them and there are no places here.

Anchorage In settled weather a yacht can anchor safely at the head of the bay which is open only to the south. Care needs to be taken, particularly at night, of the numerous moorings around the bay. Anchor in 2–5m on mud, good holding.

Facilities

Services Water and electricity at every berth. Telephone connections at most berths. A shower and toilet block.
Fuel At the extremity of the inner (W) mole. There are 3m depths alongside.
Repairs A 40-ton travel-hoist and cranes up to 48 tons. Mechanical repairs. Some wood and GRP repairs. Electrical and electronic repairs. Sailmakers. Chandlers.
Provisions Most provisions can be obtained in the marina. Better shopping in the town about 10 minutes' walk away.
Eating out Restaurant at the marina and others in the town.
Other PO. Banks. ATMs. Italgaz and Camping Gaz. Hire cars. Bus to Genoa.

General

Nestled at the head of the gulf under steep wooded slopes, Rapallo is a picture postcard sort of place. The original medieval village has been overlaid with Baroque and Rococco and neo-Baroque, though all in the most genteel way, all this is framed by green slopes and rock faces on three sides and by the blue Mediterranean on the other.

It was discovered by the wealthy after the First World War and became a popular resort with them.

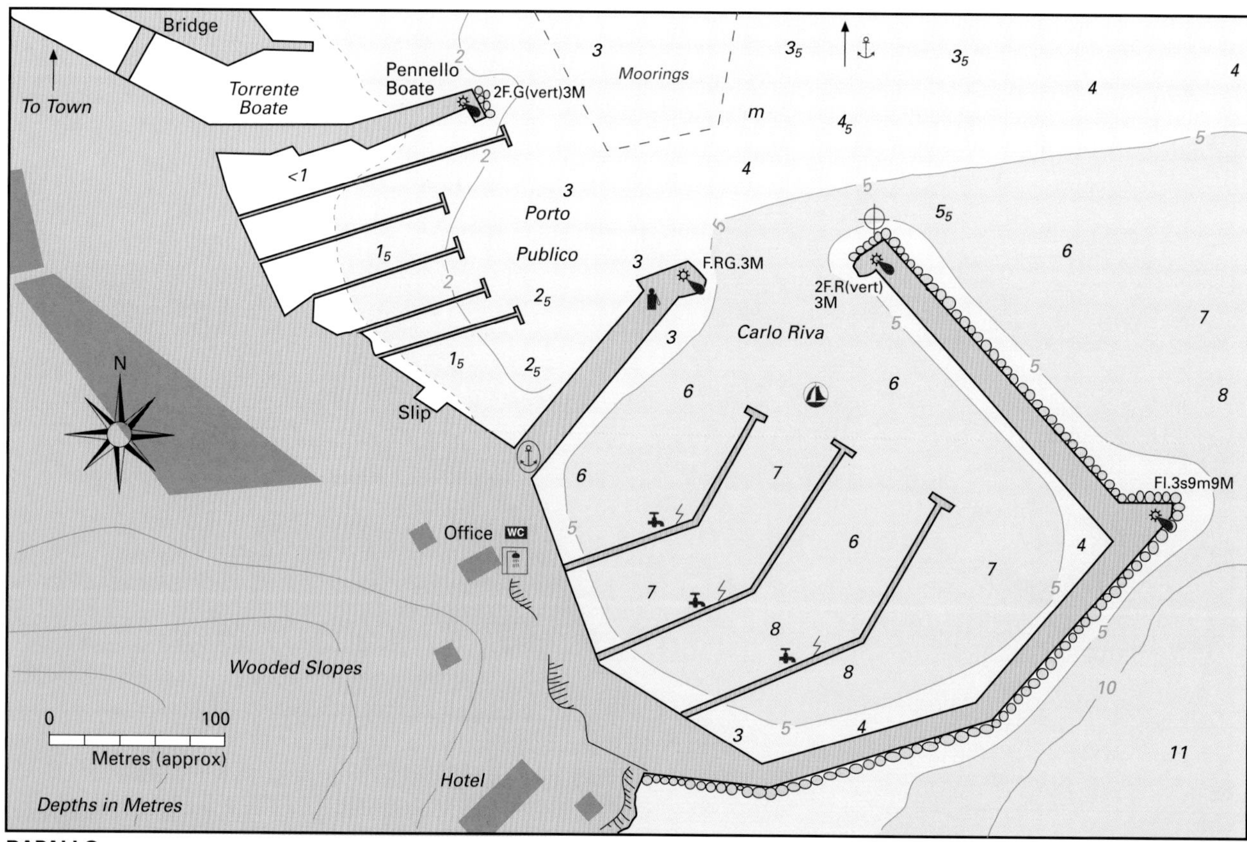

RAPALLO
⊕44°20´·65N 09°14´·0E

Rapallo looking SSW *Roberto Merlo*

At this time Rapallo was also in the news as an international meeting place: in 1917 the wartime allies conferred here; in 1920 Italy and Yugoslavia debated and settled territorial rights here; and in 1922 Russia and Germany signed a peace pact.

Today Rapallo is still pretty much an up-market sort of place and you get the feeling in the marina that you should have got all matching fenders and perhaps a new sail-cover this season.

Rapallo looking east

CHIAVARI

Approach

This large marina lies approximately four miles SE of Rapallo.

Conspicuous The town behind and two black cupolas are conspicuous. The harbour breakwaters and the masts of the yachts inside are easily identified.

VHF Ch 10 for the marina (24hr).

Danger With strong onshore winds there is a heavy swell at the entrance making it difficult and possibly dangerous to enter. With gale force winds a yacht should not attempt to enter or leave the harbour.

Note

1. Several small buoys mark the port side of the channel into the harbour. The buoys cannot always be relied upon to be in position, but the approach is straightforward whether or not they are there.
2. The harbour is prone to silting and depths are decreasing in both the entrance and the harbour itself.

Mooring

Data 460 berths. 40 visitors' berths. Max LOA 25m. Depths 2·5–4·5m.

Berth An attendant will direct you to a place and assist you to berth. Laid moorings. If the marina is full there may be room to go stern-to on the outer breakwater, although shelter is not as good here.

Shelter Good, although southerlies can cause a surge in the harbour.

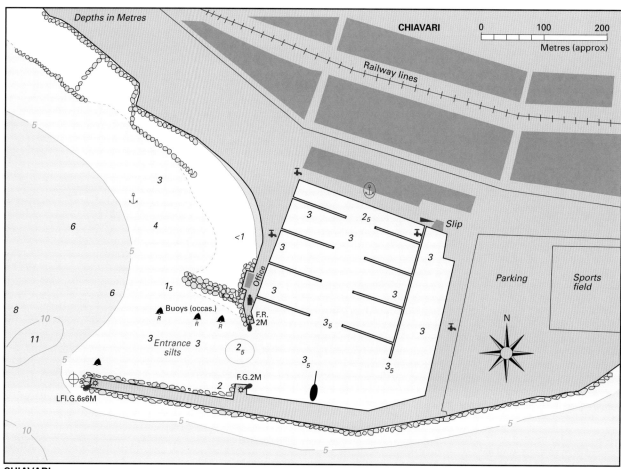

CHIAVARI
⊕ 44°18´·7N 09°18´·95E

Chiavari looking SE with Lavagna in the background and Sestri Levante top

Authorities Harbourmaster and marina staff. Charge band 5 (July–August).
Marina Chiavari ✆ 0185 364 081 *Fax* 0185 376 007
Email info@marina-chiavari.it
www.marina-chiavari.it

Facilities

Services Water and electricity at every berth. Telephone connections at some berths. Shower and toilet block.
Fuel At the extremity of the inner (W) mole.
Repairs (*Alaggi* Chiavari) 50-ton travel-hoist and cranes up to 25 tons. Hard standing area nearby. Mechanical repairs. Electrical and electronic repairs. GRP and wood repairs. Sailmakers. Chandlers.
Alaggi Chiavari ✆ 0185 310 044
Provisions Good shopping for all provisions in the town.
Eating out Restaurants, trattorias and pizzerias in the town.
Other PO. Banks. ATMs. Italgaz and Camping Gaz.

General

Chiavari is undistinguished rather than unattractive. Perhaps it is their proximity to Rapallo that cause Chiavari and nearby Lavagna to look a little dowdy at first glance. Once beyond the waterfront, though, the old town of Chiavari is really quite charming. Chiavari is pronounced *Kee-av-ah-ree*. The same spelling but pronounced in the English way means something quite different and should never be used – if you get my drift.

LAVAGNA

Approach

This huge marina complex lies less than a mile SE of Chiavari. A fish farm lies 0·5M SW of the marina entrance.

Conspicuous A steeple in the town is conspicuous but the long outer mole and the forest of masts within are the most conspicuous objects on the coast.

VHF Ch 09, 16. CB Ch 31.

Dangers Strong southerlies cause a confused swell at the entrance which makes entry difficult and sometimes dangerous. With gale force winds from the S there are breaking waves at the entrance and a yacht should not attempt to enter or leave under these conditions.

Mooring

Data 1,600 berths. 160 visitors' berths. Max LOA 50m. Depth 2–5m.

Berth Where directed. There are laid moorings tailed to the quay or a buoy.

Shelter Good, although strong southerlies make some berths uncomfortable.

Authorities Harbourmaster, customs, and marina staff. Charge band 5.

Porto di Lavagna ✆ 0185 312 626 / 364 192
Fax 0185 300 211
Email reception@portodilavagna.com
www.portodilavagna.com

Facilities

Services Water and electricity at every berth. Telephone connections to some berths. Shower and toilet blocks.
Fuel On the quay near the entrance.
Repairs A 50-ton travel-hoist and cranes to 55 tons. Slipways up to 325 tons. All mechanical and engineering repairs. GRP and wood repairs. Electrical and electronic repairs. Sailmakers. Chandlers. Backing onto the marina are a number of established boatyards that build new craft and can carry out all repairs and alterations. Among the more well known yards are Cantiere Sangermani, Cantiere Al Mare, and Cantiere Lavagna.
Other PO. Banks. ATMs. Italgaz and Camping Gaz. A shopping centre, restaurants and bars within the marina complex.

General

The town of Lavagna lies behind the railway line that runs along the waterfront. The marina and the town are unremarkable, being virtually a continuation of nearby Chiavari, but the concentration of good yards in the vicinity of the marina make it a useful place to winter if major repairs or alterations are needed.

SESTRI LEVANTE

Approach

The harbour lies under a headland connected by a narrow isthmus to Sestri Levante town.

Conspicuous The town of Sestri Levante lying under wooded slopes is readily identified from the N but

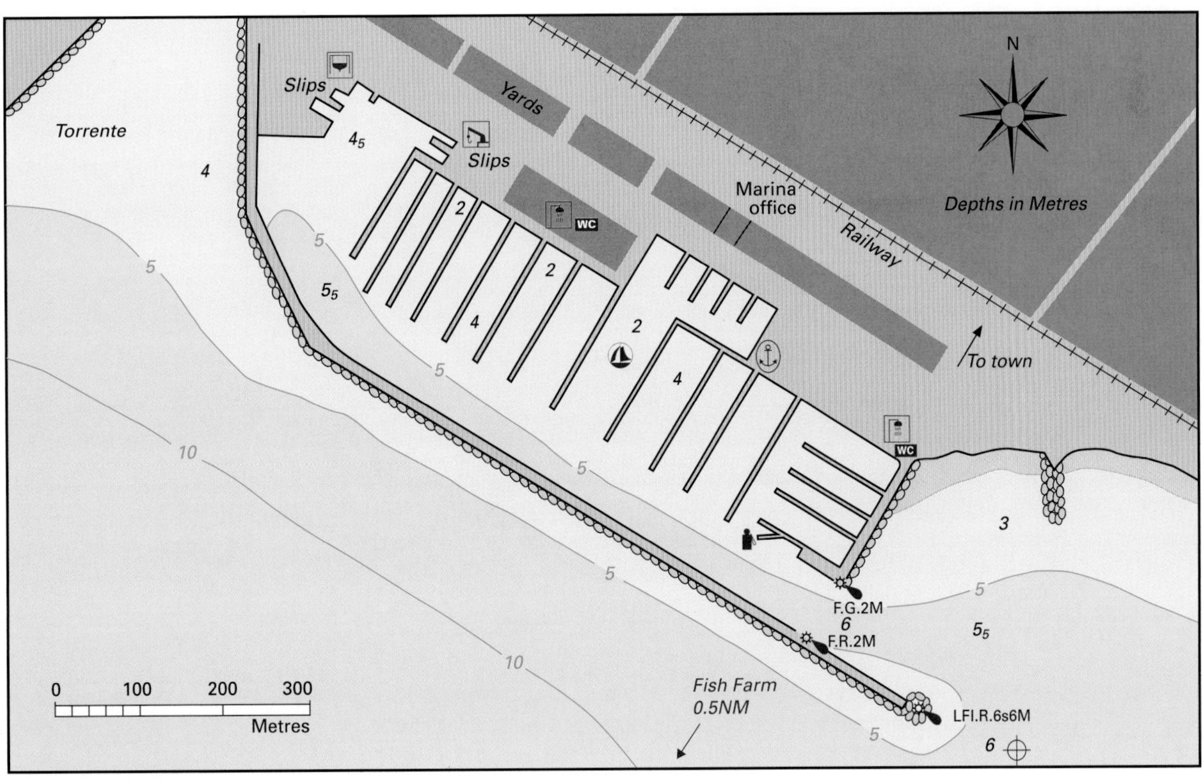

LAVAGNA MARINA
⊕44°18′·15N 09°20′·6E

cannot be seen until closer in from the south. The headland and a hotel on it are conspicuous and closer in, the harbour mole is easily identified.

Mooring

Data 125 berths. Four visitors' berths. Max LOA 20m. Depths 2–15m.

Berths Go stern-to where directed or wherever there is room. Laid moorings at a few berths. There is often a slight swell in the bay which can make berths here uncomfortable. Smaller yachts may be able to pick up a vacant mooring in the bay. You may find room to anchor, but see the note below. The bottom is sand or mud and good holding.

Note There are now restrictions on anchoring in the bay. From 1 May to 30 September anchoring is prohibited in the areas marked on the plan.

Shelter Good. Although the bay is completely open to the N, winds from this direction are reported not to blow home. Local yachts are wintered afloat on permanent moorings.

Authorities Harbourmaster. Charge band 1/2.
Capitaneria ✆ 0185 41295

Facilities

Water On the fuel quay.
Fuel On the quay near the root of the mole.
Repairs Cranes up to 10 tons available. Small craft are craned onto the quay. Mechanical repairs. Chandlers.
Provisions Good shopping in the town about 15 minutes' walk away.
Eating out A restaurant is open on the quay in the summer. Others in the town.
Other PO. Banks. ATMs. Italgaz and Camping Gaz.

Sestri Levante looking N from the root of the mole

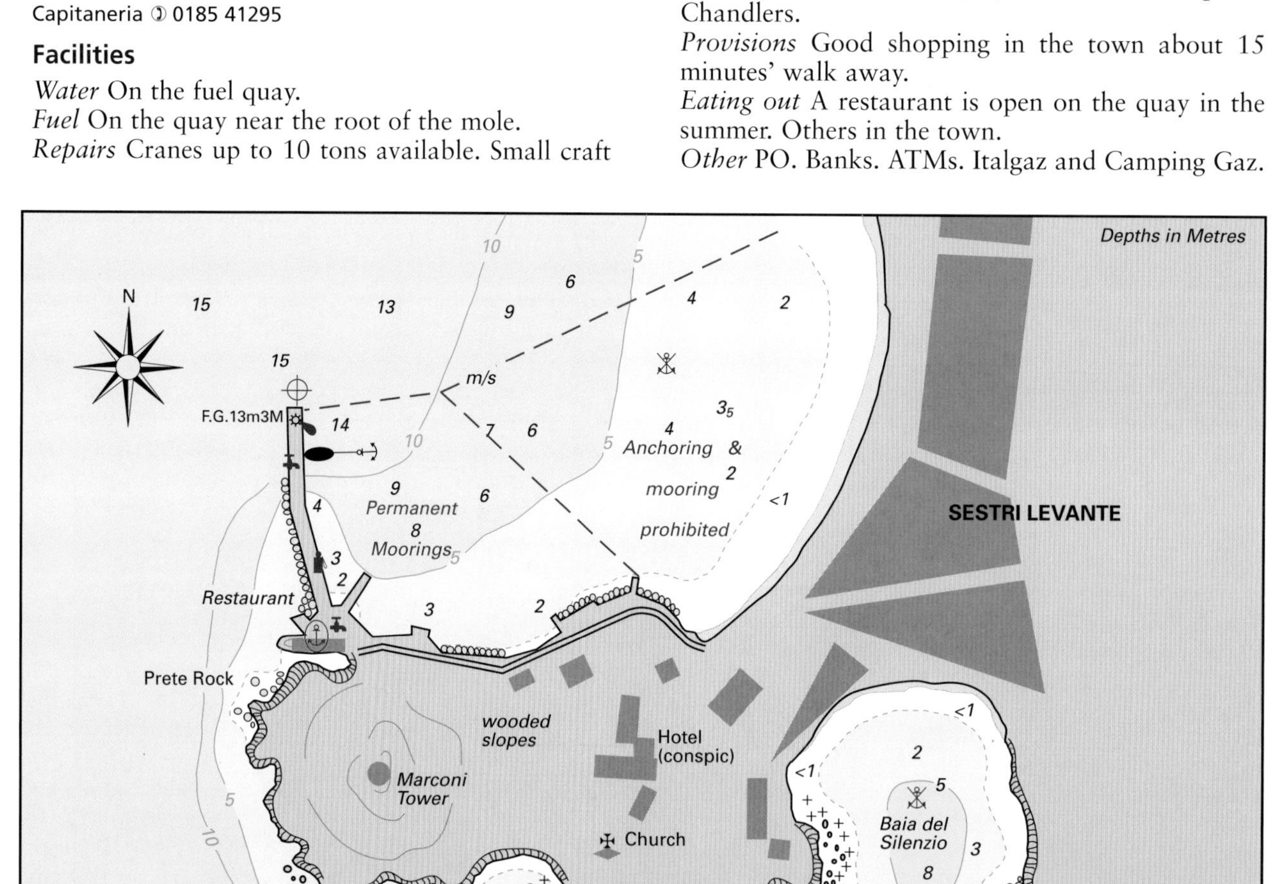

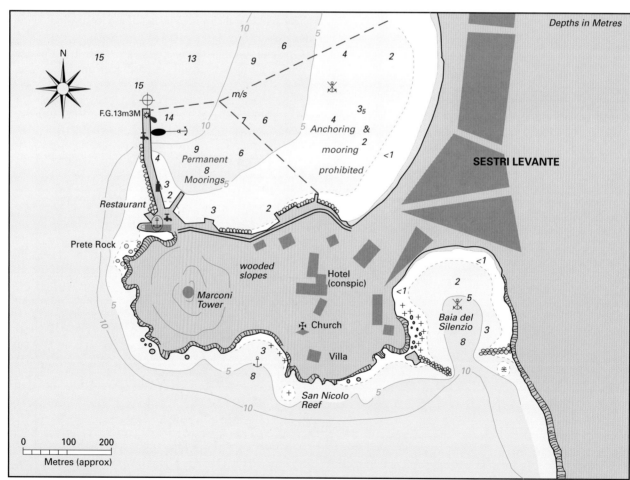

SESTRI LEVANTE
⊕ 44°16´·35N 09°23´·1E

General

The promontory with a public garden on top and the old town straddling the isthmus combine to make this an appealing and attractive place. It is surprisingly peaceful, even in the summer, and of an evening the promontory is a marvellous place to take a post-prandial stroll, especially if there is some swell working its way around into the bay causing you to roll at anchor. In the tower on the promontory, Marconi conducted his early experiments with radio transmissions, hence its name: Torre Marconi.

Note There have been plans to build a marina here for some time but work has not started to date and there are no indications that it will in the near future.

Baia del Silenzio

Note From 1st May to 30th September anchoring is prohibited in the bay.

On the S side of the promontory there is a cove with a rough breakwater built out from either side. A yacht can anchor in the middle, although a stern anchor may be needed because of the local boats moored there. It is a useful anchorage in northerlies, but in southerly winds a heavy swell rolls in.

It is also possible to anchor in light winds in a cove to the W of Baia del Silenzio. If there is any ground swell around it inevitably rolls into here.

Riva Trigoso

A large bay under Punta Manara approximately 2M SE of Sestri Levante. The bay is completely open to the S, but in calm weather or a light offshore breeze is a useful stop. Anchor in 5–10m on sand and weed keeping clear of the pipeline.

Provisions and restaurants ashore.

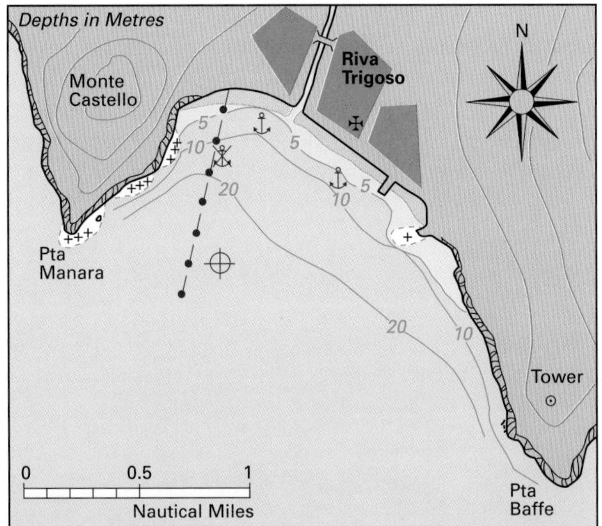

RIVA TRIGOSO
⊕44°15´·0N 09°25´·2E

Framura

Off Framura railway station, a yellow two-storey building, is Chiama Rock which lies just off the coast. A breakwater has been built between the S end of the islet and the coast to form a small harbour. Although there are good depths inside, the entrance is rock-bound and should not be negotiated without local knowledge. For small craft it offers good shelter.

Cinque Terre

Between Sestri Levante and the Gulf of La Spezia lies the mountainous area known as the Cinque Terre – the five lands which historically were five remote villages. Until comparatively recently the only way of getting to the villages along the coast was by boat or on foot. For the most part the land rises abruptly from the sea and the two harbours in this region, Monterosso al Mare and Vernazza, are built out from the cliffs and rocks at the bottom of steep slopes. The region is known for its wines, particularly a sweet white wine called Sciacchetra, although one wonders how vines are cultivated on slopes that often appear to be almost vertical.

In spite of efforts to preserve this Unesco world heritage site, collapsing terraces and soil erosion are close to irreversibly changing the nature of these slopes. The latest initiative is to lease parcels of land to individuals and in return the new owner pays nothing, but is obliged to cultivate the land according to a plan drawn up by the park. This includes rebuilding the web of stone walls criss-crossing the slopes, and to cultivate traditional crops of organic lemons and basil as well as vines on the restored terraces.

Levanto

Just over five miles NNW of Punta Mesco is the small bay of Levanto with a village at the head. Care must be taken of a reef, Secca della Perla, with 1m over it, approximately 400m SE of the N entrance point.

There is a small harbour at the S end of the bay, but the best place to be is at the N end. Anchor in 2–4m off a small fishing boat harbour. Alternatively anchor at the S end of the bay in 4–6m. The bottom is sand, rock, and weed, generally adequate holding. The bay can only be used in settled weather being completely open to all sectors west.

Ashore in the town most provisions can be found and there are several restaurants.

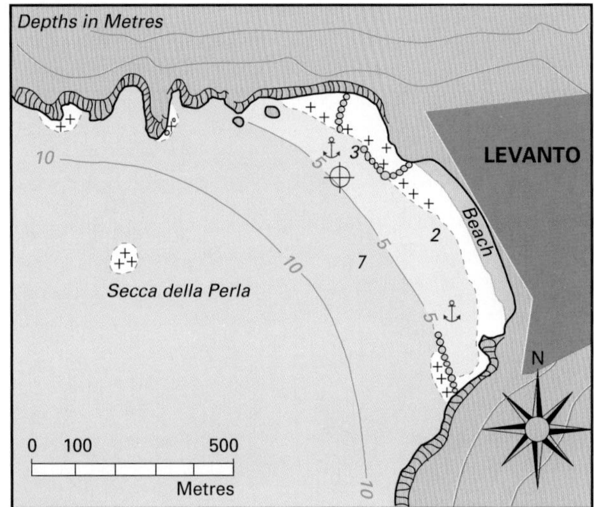

LEVANTO
⊕44°10´·3N 09°36´·2E

MONTEROSSO AL MARE (Zone B/C)

Approach

Two small harbours in a bight about one mile NE of Punta Mesco. Both are mostly shallow and suitable in settled weather only.

Conspicuous On a rocky bluff a large square tower is conspicuous. On the E side lies one harbour (Monterosso Levante) below the village of Monterosso al Mare and on the W side under a large white villa lies the other harbour (Monterosso Ponente).

By night There are no lights and entry at night would be hazardous. Yellow buoys mark the boundaries of Zones A and B. Light characteristics for buoys in Zone A are Fl.Y.5s2M/Fl(2)10s2M and Zone B Fl.Y.5s2M/Fl.Y.3s2M.

Danger With strong onshore winds there is a reflected swell off the cliffs causing a confused sea. Moreover, neither harbour is tenable under these conditions.

Mooring

Both harbours are much used by local boats in the summer and a yacht will have to squeeze in wherever there is room or sufficient depths. In Monterosso Levante a yacht will not be able to go up close to the quay but must hang off on long lines. Alternatively anchor off in 5–6m off Monterosso Levante. Care is needed near the extensive reef off Monterosso Levante. The bottom is sand and rock, adequate holding. AMP moorings are provided in Monterosso Ponente.

MONTEROSSO

Shelter With moderate offshore winds the harbour offers adequate shelter, but with strong winds from any direction a yacht should be prepared to move out. Winds from the S cause a heavy swell to roll in, often in advance of the wind itself.

Facilities

Water A tap on the quay in Monterosso Ponente.
Fuel None nearby.
Provisions Basic provisions in the village.
Eating out Restaurant at Monterosso Ponente and in the village.

General

Although the shelter is not good, Monterosso al Mare is well worth a visit. The village of pastel houses and twisting lanes under steep slopes is exquisite and the mountainous backdrop grand.

VERNAZZA (Zone C)

Approach

This small harbour lies 1·5 miles to the SE of Monterosso al Mare.

Conspicuous The hamlet on the hillside is easily identified. Two towers in it are conspicuous: a square bell-tower high up and a round tower with cupola at the edge of the harbour.

VHF Ch 16.

Caution Care should be taken with strong onshore winds.

Mooring

The harbour is very small and there is room for perhaps only four or five yachts among the local boats. Go stern or bows-to the outer end of the mole, though care should be taken of the ballasting which extends a short distance underwater. The bottom is sand with some rocks and is generally good holding.

Shelter Good shelter, although strong NW–W winds send in some swell and there is a reflected swell off the cliffs near the entrance.

Pastel coloured houses and gothic church at Vernazza
Vito Arcomano, FOTOTECA ENIT

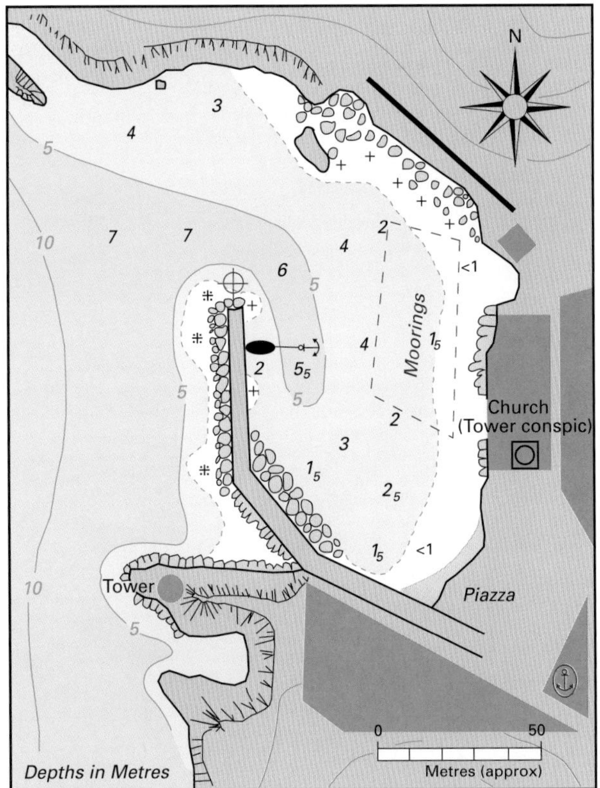

VERNAZZA
⊕ 44°08′·1N 09°40′·0E

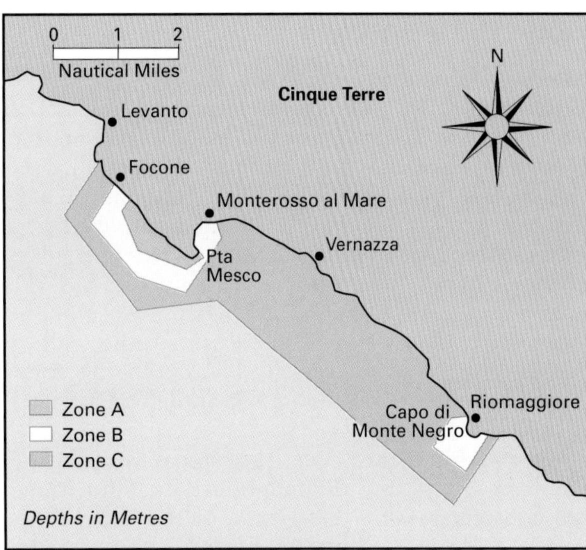

CINQUE TERRE MARINE RESERVE

Cinque Terre Marine Reserve

This marine reserve was established in 1997 and covers the sea area along the coast between Levanto and Capo di Monte Negro (Riomaggiore).

Zone A
Motor navigation, anchoring, mooring and all types of fishing are prohibited. Transit by small craft without motors permitted (limited numbers, at the discretion of the authorities).

Zone B
Small craft are permitted to navigate up to a speed of 8kns.
Mooring is allowed exclusively in zones defined by the reserve authorities. Swimming and diving permitted.
Small-scale fishing permitted only to resident commercial fishermen.
Sport fishing permitted with fixed lines and rods.
Underwater fishing prohibited.

Zone C
No limits on small craft navigation. Max LOA 24m. Sport, commercial and underwater fishing are regulated by the authorities.

✆ 0187 760 31 *Fax* 0187 760 061
Email info@parconazionale5terre.it
www.parconazionale5terre.it

Note Mooring buoys have been laid in several bays through the park and are administered by MarPark. They may be booked in advance through MarPark or Yachtlife. Charges €30 (12hrs) €60 (24hrs) up to 50ft LOA.

Monterosso	15 buoys (eight for <50 feet)
Vernazza	15 buoys (10)
Riomaggiore	20 buoys (eight)

MarPark booking ✆ 0899 100 001 Office ✆ 0833 970 111
Fax 0833 970 160
Email info@marpark.com

Yachtlife booking
www.yachtlife.it/YL-marpark/MP-en1.html

Facilities

Water A tap at the root of the mole.
Provisions Basic provisions in the hamlet.
Eating out A number of restaurants and trattorias.

General

Lying at the mouth of a steep-sided valley, Vernazza is another gem of the Cinque Terre. One side of the harbour is cliff, and on the other side are the pastel houses of the hamlet interrupted by the stark Gothic church of Santa Margherita d'Antiochia. If you can get in here the setting is wonderful and is worth a small amount of discomfort.

Moorings are now available at Riomaggiore
Vito Arcomano, FOTOTECA ENIT

I. THE LIGURIAN COAST

Golfo di La Spezia

The gulf is entered between Isola Tino and Capo Corvo about five miles to the E, and extends about 5½ miles NW to the port and town of La Spezia. Rada di La Spezia is the inner part of the gulf, protected by a breakwater about 1·2 miles long which extends across the mouth of the gulf leaving a channel free for navigation at either end. The gulf is everywhere mountainous and attractive. Rada di La Spezia is the principal Italian naval base and the large harbour in the NW corner of the gulf is exclusively for naval vessels. Photographing some parts of the naval installations in Rada de La Spezia is prohibited.

Approaching the Gulf the signal station on Palmaria Island and the lighthouse on Tino Island are conspicuous. On the E side of the gulf Monte Sagro, 1,749m (5,738ft), Monte Attissimo, 1,589m (5,213ft) and Monte Pania della Croce, 1,859m (6,100ft) can easily be identified. Once into the gulf, the breakwater, Diga Foranea, is just above water but is easily identified by its raised ends, the light structures on each end and two masts near the centre. Within Rada di La Spezia there are numerous buoys, most of which are reserved for naval vessels and to which it is prohibited to tie up. The buoys are unlit so caution must be exercised when moving within the roadstead at night.

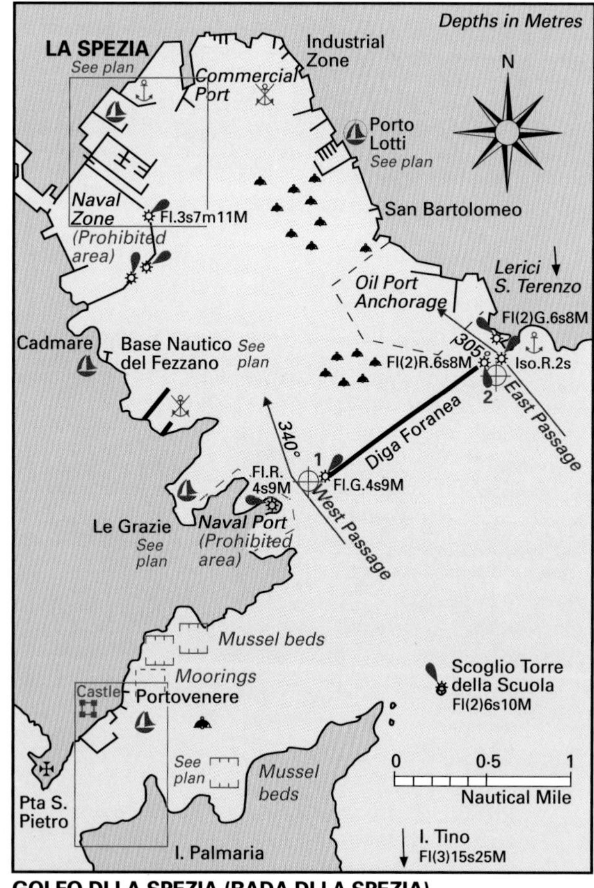

GOLFO DI LA SPEZIA (RADA DI LA SPEZIA)
⊕1 44°04'·1N 09°51'·4E
⊕2 44°04'·8N 09°52'·8E

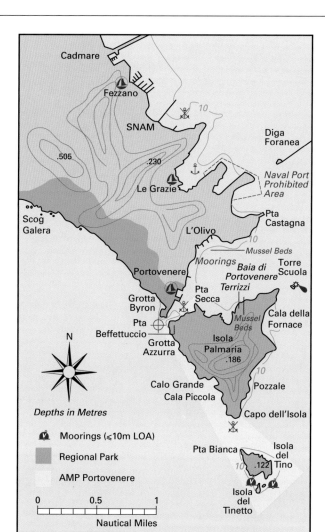

PARCO NATURALE REGIONALE DI PORTO VENERE
⊕44°02'·8N 09°49'·9E

Parc Naturale Regionale di Porto Venere

Although not part of the national AMP network, this regional AMP has similar restrictions:

- Max speed 6 knots
- Use moorings where available≤
- I. Tino/Tinetto only open to vessels ≤10m LOA
- No anchoring between Pta Secca and Pta Beffettuccio, and S of Capo dell'Isola
- No mooring off I. Tinetto unless authorised

PORTOVENERE

Approach

The harbour lies on the E side of Punta San Pietro. A yacht can proceed through Passaggio di Portovenere between the mainland and Isola Palmaria where there are least depths of 2·4m (8ft) at the bar across the E end. There are overhead cables between Punta San Pietro and Isola Palmaria with a minimum height of 24·4m (80ft).

Conspicuous Tino and Palmaria Islands are easily identified. The lighthouse on I. Tino (a white round tower on a large building), a grey church and campanile on Punta San Pietro, and the castle behind Portovenere are all conspicuous. The village and harbour are easily identified.

Looking S past the pontoons and harbour at Portovenere with Isola Palmaria left of picture

By night Use the light on I. Tino (San Venerio) Fl(3)15s117m25M and, closer in, the light on Scoglio Torre della Scuola Fl(2)6s16m10M.

VHF Ch 09, 16.

Dangers

1. *Mooring buoys* Off the SE side of Isola Palmaria there are a number of unlit mooring buoys. There is also an unlit mooring buoy approximately one third of a mile E of Portovenere.
2. *Mussel beds* To the N of the harbour there are extensive mussel beds and a yacht should avoid venturing into this area.
3. *Prohibited area* To the E of I. Tino there is a prohibited area used by the navy. This does not cover the channel between I. Tino and Isola Palmaria which has good depths and is free of dangers except for the mooring buoys to the SE of Isola Palmaria.
4. *Torre Scuola* Is situated just off the reef on the NE tip of Isola Palmaria. It is easily identified.
5. *Tinetto reef (Scoglio del Tinetto)* Above and below-water rocks extend for approximately one quarter of a mile S from the southern tip of I. Tino.

Mooring

Data 32 visitors' berths. Max LOA 50m. Depths 1–4m. Pontile Ignazio 45 berths. Max LOA 25m.

Berth Where directed on the S mole. The berths available for visitors seem to change from year to year. Charter yachts are based here during the summer, with some berths reserved for changeovers. In the summer the harbour is popular and it is difficult to find a space in which case head for Le Grazie or anchor off in the bay on Isola Palmaria opposite. Laid moorings tailed to the quay.

Pontile Ignazio is a single pontoon lying to the N of the fuel berth, N of the harbour. Laid moorings at all berths.

Note In calm weather a yacht can anchor in the bay to the NE taking care to avoid the mussel beds. The bay is open to the south.

Shelter Good in the harbour. The pontoons to the N of the harbour should be reasonably sheltered from the normal summer sea breeze, although they may

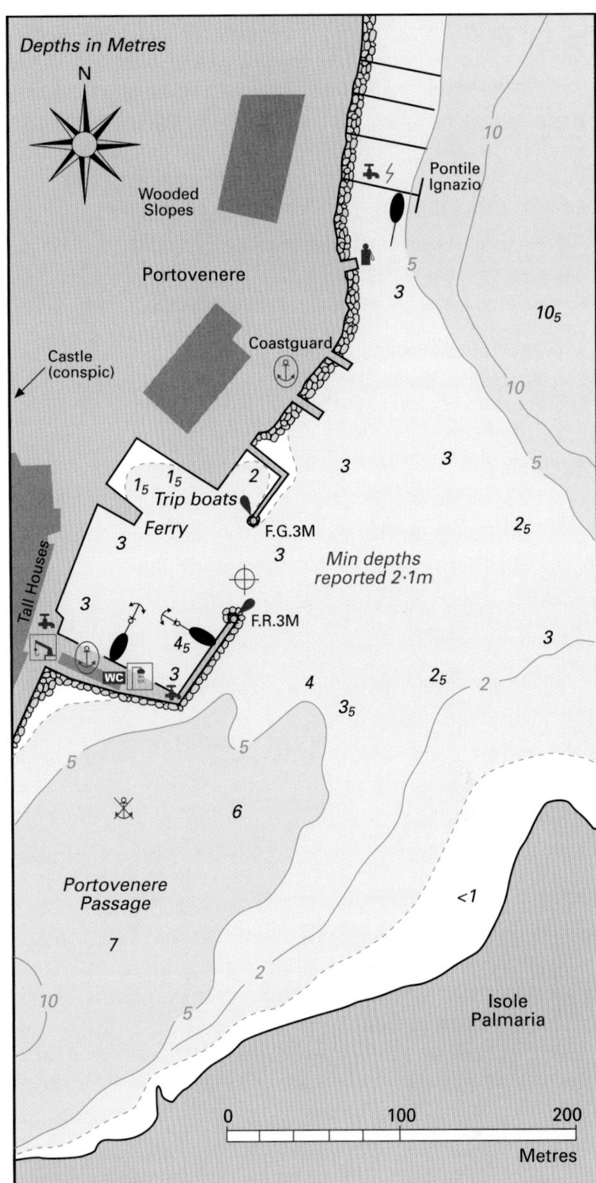

PORTOVENERE
⊕44°03′·05N 09°50′·3E

Portovenere harbour

be subject to wash from the numerous tripper boats, ferries, and other craft. In unsettled weather some care is needed, and with strong winds, particularly from the NE, some berths may be rather exposed. Shelter is also good in the anchorage under Isola Palmaria and in fact some of the tripper boats are left on moorings here throughout the winter.

Authorities Harbourmaster. Charge band 6+.

Capitaneria ✆ 0187 790 768

Porto Venere Marina Misenti ✆ 0187 793 042
Email portodiportovenere@alice.it
www.portodiportovenere.it

Pontile Ignazio ✆ /*Fax* 0187 791 364
Email info@pontileignazio.org
www.pontileignazio.org

Facilities

Services Water and electricity (220/380V) on the quay. Showers and toilets.
Fuel On the quay close to Pontile Ignazio.
Repairs 5-ton crane available. Limited mechanical repairs only. Le Grazie with its repair facilities is nearby.
Provisions Most provisions. Good fresh fish from stalls at the harbour.
Eating out Restaurants and trattorias.
Other PO. Bank. ATM.

General

The village and harbour are picturesque, although the slate grey buildings and castle on slate grey rock take on the aspect of a black and white photograph – especially at dusk. On closer inspection, the tall houses are painted in subdued pastel hues but the two churches are black and white striped marble affairs.

Byron had some affection for Portovenere and a plaque records his now famous swim from Portovenere to Lerici thus:

> 'GROTTA BYRON
> This Grotto was the inspiration of Lord Byron.
> It records the immortal poet who as a daring
> swimmer defied the waves of the sea from
> Portovenere to Lerici.'

(I suspect if he were alive now the caustic Byron would make an acerbic comment on the rather pompous language describing his swim.)

One story handed down to me about Byron and attributed to a recent mayor of La Spezia goes something like this: 'The reason for his Lordship's swim – which he did several times – was an establishment in Lerici in which he kept two ladies. Of course you understand that on walking up the beach at Lerici the noble lord had to rest awhile before visiting the ladies.' Sounds a wonderfully Italian story to me.

ISOLA PALMARIA

Yachts can anchor on the NE corner of Isola Palmaria though care is needed of numerous permanent moorings in the area. The anchorage is more secure than it looks and boats are left on moorings here over the winter. About halfway along the sheer cliffs of the island there is the Grotta Azzura, a sea cave of some beauty. It should only be attempted in calm weather as the roof is very low – any swell would squash a dinghy against the roof of the cave.

LE GRAZIE

BA 118
Italian 60

Approach

Le Grazie lies just inside the western entrance to Rada di La Spezia. It should not be confused with Seno del Varignano, a cove immediately SE of Le Grazie, which is a prohibited military area.

Conspicuous The light structure on the W end of the breakwater (Diga Foranea), a stone tower, is conspicuous. The old stone fort off Punta Santa Maria, on the W side of the entrance, should be left to port. A number of large buildings on Punta del Varignano are conspicuous and Le Grazie lies just round this point.

By night Although the entrance to Le Grazie itself is not lit, the western entrance to Rada di La Spezia is.

VHF Ch 16.

Dangers

1. Care should be taken of a shoal extending about 100m from Punta Santa Maria (minimum depth 3m) and a shoal extending about 50m from Punta del Varignano (less than 1m depths).
2. In Le Grazie the SE side of the bay is a military zone where anchoring is prohibited. On the NW side there are numerous laid moorings with mussel beds near the extremity of the point.
3. Prohibited area: Seno del Varignano is a military area and should not be entered. Anchoring is prohibited on the S side of Punta Santa Maria (in Seno della Castagna), in Seno del Varignano, around the extremity of Punta del Varignano and on the SE side of Le Grazie.

Mooring

Berth Go stern or bows-to the town quay in the SW corner or anchor in the bay. Care must be taken along this quay as the rock ballasting extends underwater in places. Go bows-to or choose where

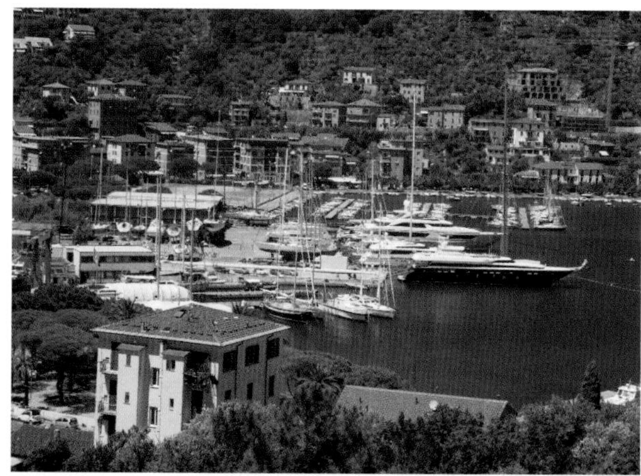

Le Grazie town quay. *See also photo page 42*

you go stern-to with care. The bottom is mud and good holding.

Shelter Good all-round shelter although easterlies kick up a slop across Rada di La Spezia.

Authorities Harbourmaster and customs.
Ormeggiatori ☎ 0187 793 042

Anchorage Anchor off the town clear of the moorings in 6–8m. Good holding on mud.

Facilities

Services Water and electricity (220/380V). Shower and toilet block. Self-service laundry on the quay.
Fuel On the quay nearby.
Repairs Several yards at the head of the bay carry out all types of work. Crane up to 10 tons. Slipways reported to be able to take craft up to 1,000 tons subject to draught. Most repairs can be arranged.
Cantiere Valdettaro Srl, Via Libertà 12, 19022 Le Grazie di Portovenere
☎ 0187 791 687 *Fax* 0187 798 037
Email info@valdettaro.it
Provisions Good shopping for most provisions.
Eating out Good restaurants, trattorias and pizzerias nearby.
Other PO. Bank. ATM. Italgaz and Camping Gaz. Bus to La Spezia and Portovenere.

General

Le Grazie is a peaceful spot with just enough old Ligurian-style buildings to lend it charm and just enough work going on in the boatyards so that it is not precious. It is a fair hike around into town at La Spezia, but there are enough shops in Le Grazie itself and some pleasant eateries down near the quay. A number of large yachts have refits here and you could get worse than a winter in Le Grazie.

MARINA DEL FEZZANO

Approach

The pontoons of the marina lie just NW of the oil jetty in Seno di Panigaglia.
VHF Ch 09, 16.

Mooring

Data 250 berths. Max LOA 25m. Depths 3–7m.
Berth Where directed. Laid moorings.

Shelter Although the situation of the pontoons looks a little exposed, shelter is reported to be good. With strong winds from the east I would be a little worried as there is no sheltering breakwater.

Authorities Harbourmaster. Charge band 5 (May–September).

✉ Marina del Fezzano Srl., Via dei Cantieri 19020, Fezzano di Portovenere ☎ 0187 790 103 *Fax* 0187 790 513
Email info@marinadelfezzano.it
www.marinadelfezzano.it

Facilities

Services Water and electricity at all berths. Showers and toilets.

LE GRAZIE
⊕44°04′·11N 09°50′·34E WGS84

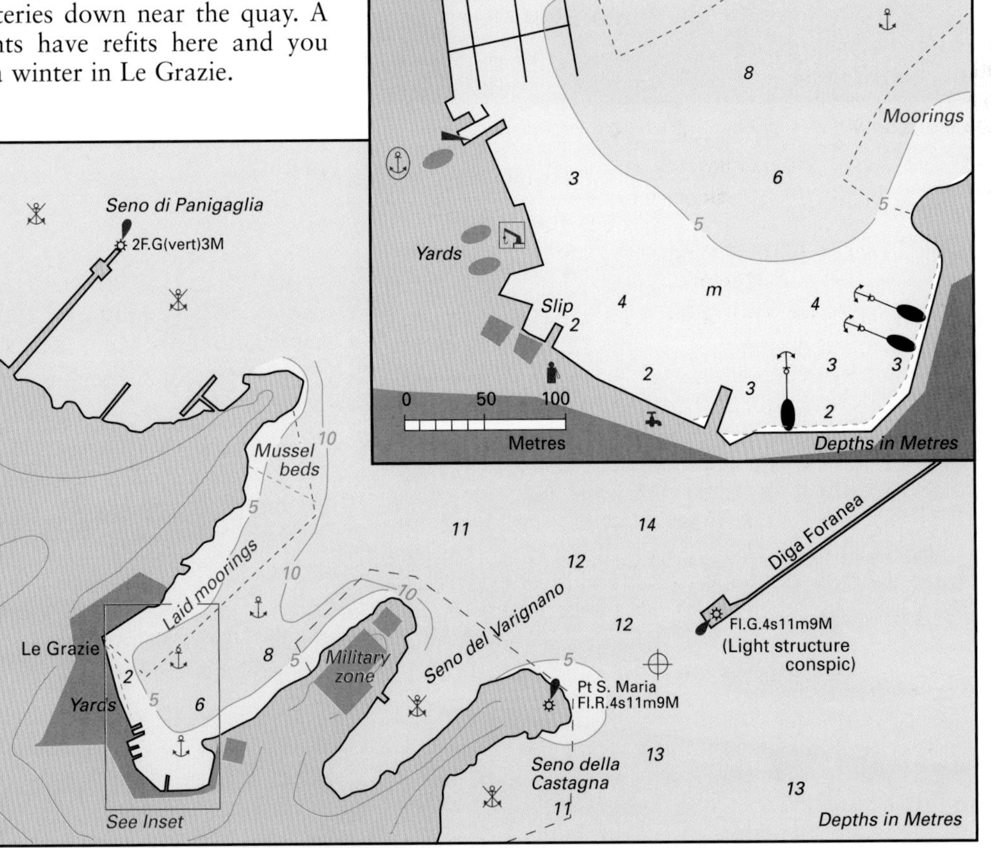

LE GRAZIE AND WESTERN APPROACHES TO RADA DI LA SPEZIA
⊕44°04′·0N 09°51′·25E

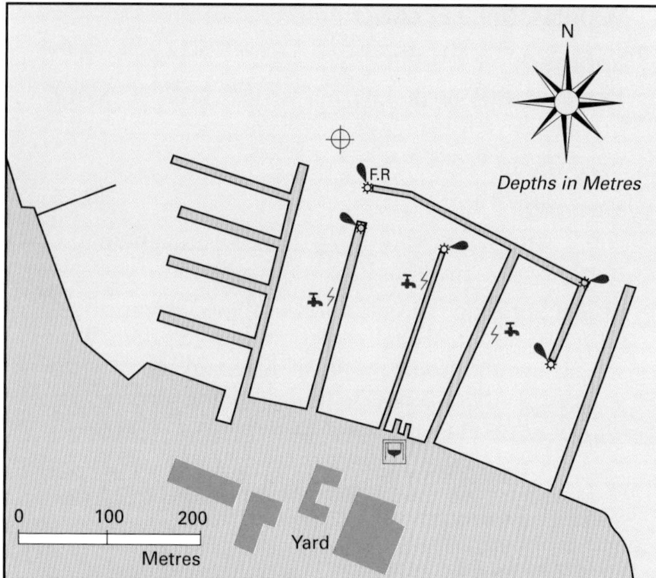

BASE NAUTICA DEL FEZZANO
⊕44°04'·9N 09°49'·9E

Marina del Fezzano looking SE towards Portovenere passage

Repairs 60-ton travel-lift. 60-ton crane. Covered workshops. Specialist paint facilities. Mechanical and engineering work. Wood and GRP repairs. Electrical and electronics services.

Other Buses into La Spezia.

PORTO MIRABELLO MARINA

Approach

A new marina nearing completion in La Spezia, in the NW of the harbour. The marina opened in May 2009.

Conspicuous The buildings of the commercial harbour are easy to identify once past the outer breakwater. The entrance to the marina lies close N of the Darsena Duca Degli Abruzzi.

VHF Ch 73, 16.

Mooring

Data 470 berths. LOA 14–100m. Depths 3·5–12m.

Berths Go stern or bows-to where directed. Marina staff will assist you. Laid moorings tailed to the quay.

Shelter Good all-round shelter.

Authorities Marina staff. Charge band 6+

✆ 0187 778 108, *Fax* 0187 732 102
Email info@portomirabello.it
www.portomirabello.it

Facilities

Services Water and electricity (220/380V). Wi-Fi. Showers and toilets. Pump-out.

Fuel Fuel on the quay.

Repairs 160-ton travel hoist. Large covered workshop. Most repairs can be arranged.

Other Bicycle, scooter and car hire. Helipad. Shops, bars and restaurants under development in the marina.

Yachts in the new Marina Mirabello

LA SPEZIA COMMERCIAL HARBOUR

BA 118
Italian 59

Approach

The commercial harbour lies at the head of Rada di La Spezia. The approach is straightforward by day or night. From the W passage through the outer breakwater (Diga Foranea) steer 340° and from the E passage steer 305° for the commercial port.

Conspicuous Once into Rada di La Spezia it is difficult to identify exactly where the harbour is. Three tall chimneys with red and white bands behind the town are conspicuous from some distance off. Steer on these for the commercial port. Closer to, a row of silos on the quay, the harbour moles and entrance are easily identified.

VHF Ch 09, 11, 12, 14, 16 for Port authorities. Ch 14 for pilots. Ch 71 for *Assonautica* A. de Benedetti.

Mooring

Data (*Assonautica*) 600 berths. 60 visitors' berths. Max LOA 14·5m. Depths 2–4m.

Berth Stern or bows-to on the pontoons where directed. There are also reports of visitors' berths available on Molo Mirabello in the commercial port. Yachts must call the Capitaneria on VHF Ch 16 before entering the commercial port.

Shelter Good shelter in A. de Benedetti.

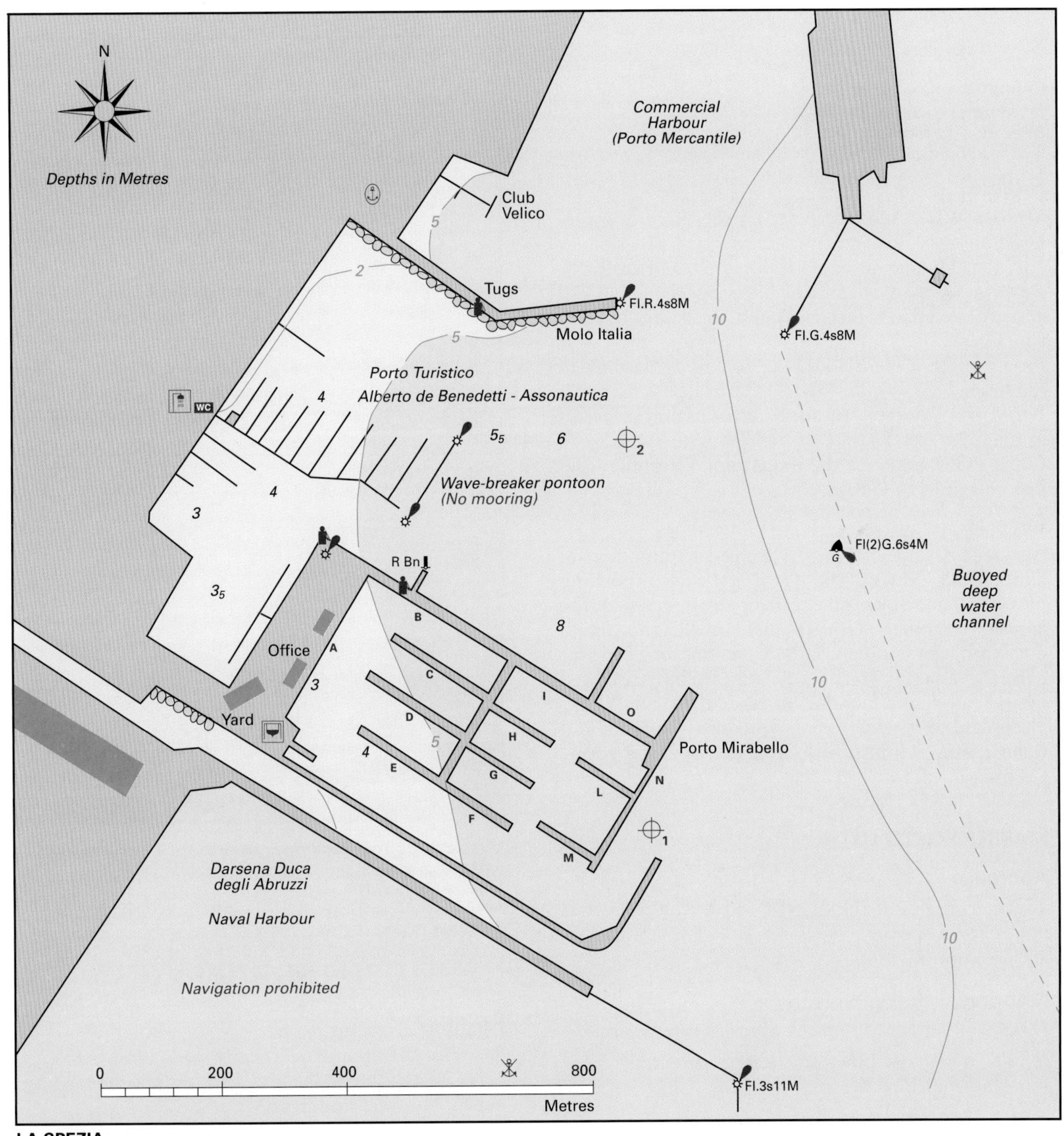

LA SPEZIA
⊕1 44°05′·81N 09°49′·94E WGS84
⊕2 44°06′·19N 09°50′·08E WGS84

Assonautica pontoons at La Spezia

Authorities Harbourmaster. Customs and immigration. Charge band 3/4.
Assonautica ✆ /*Fax* 0187 770 229 / 728 263
Email asso_sp@libero.it
www.assonauticasp.it www.porto.laspezia.it

Facilities

Services Water and electricity on the quay. Showers and toilets.
Fuel On the quay at Molo Italia Porto Mirabello.
Repairs Mechanical and engineering repairs. GRP and wood repairs. Electrical and electronic repairs. Chandlers.
Provisions Excellent shopping for all provisions in the town.
Eating out Good restaurants, trattorias and pizzerias in the town.
Other PO. Banks. ATMs. Italgaz and Camping Gaz. Bus and train to Genoa.

General

Although La Spezia town is fringed by commercial and military docks, the town itself is a bustling pleasant place. It has an excellent naval museum (the Museo Technico Navale just inside the naval dockyard) containing a large collection of maritime exhibits, among which is Atlanta, a bare-breasted figurehead found floating in the Atlantic in 1864. She is said to bewitch sailors who gaze upon her and to have caused four suicides to date, the last a young German naval cadet in 1944.

MARINA PORTO LOTTI

Approach

The marina lies at the eastern end of the industrial docks at La Spezia.

VHF Ch 09.

Mooring

Data 500 berths. Max LOA 80m. Depths 3–8m.

Berth Stern or bows-to where directed. Laid moorings tailed to the quay.

Shelter Good shelter.

Authorities Harbourmaster. Marina staff. Charge band 5.

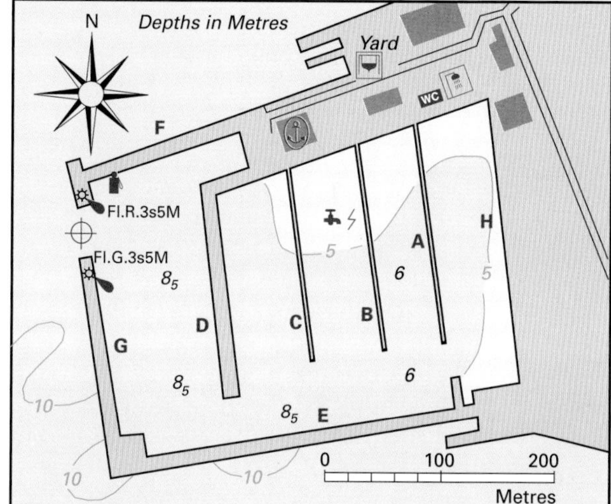

PORTO LOTTI
⊕44°05´·75N 09°51´·5E

Marina Porto Lotti looking S towards the W entrance to Rada di La Spezia and beyond to I. Palmaria
Marina Porto Lotti

✉ Marina Porto Lotti, Viale S. Bartolomeo 394, 19126 La Spezia ✆ 0187 5321 / 532 203 *Fax* 0187 532 245
www.portolotti.com

Facilities

Services Water and electricity (220 and 380V) at every berth. Telephone and TV connections possible. Wi-Fi. Showers and toilets.
Fuel On the inner mole near the entrance (0800–2000).
Repairs 160-ton travel-hoist. 50/12/7-ton cranes.

Covered storage ashore. All GRP, steel and wood repairs. Sail repairs. Electrical and electronic repairs.
Provisions Minimarket. It is a longish walk to other shops.
Eating out Restaurant. Stroll along to the waterfront at La Spezia for a good choice of all types of restaurant.
Other ATM. Bus into town. Taxis. Helipad. Health Centre. Swimming pool.

General

This is very much an up-market marina, a bit of an oasis tucked into the commercial docks. It is a rather a hike into town, though it is walkable and you can always get a taxi back after dinner.

LA SPEZIA SHIPYARDS

There are several large ship-builders on the E side of the harbour. Many of these have a number of berths, although they are usually reserved for those using the yard facilities.

Cantieri Navali di La Spezia

Data 120 berths. Max LOA 25m. Depths 5–9m.

Facilities

100-ton-travel-hoist. All repairs. Specialist covered workshops.
✆ 0187 520 937
www.cnlaspezia.com

Navalmare

Data 160 berths. Max LOA 40m. Laid moorings.

Facilities

350-ton hoists. Major ship, superyacht and commercial projects.
✆ 0187 562 042
www.navalmare.it

SAN TERENZO

At the eastern entrance to Rada di la Spezia there is the bay of San Terenzo, partially sheltered by a stone breakwater. The large castle on an escarpment behind is conspicuous. Anchor in 4–8m outside the breakwater. The anchorage is completely open to the SW but otherwise there is good shelter. The bottom is mud and good holding. Restaurants nearby and provisions can be obtained ashore.

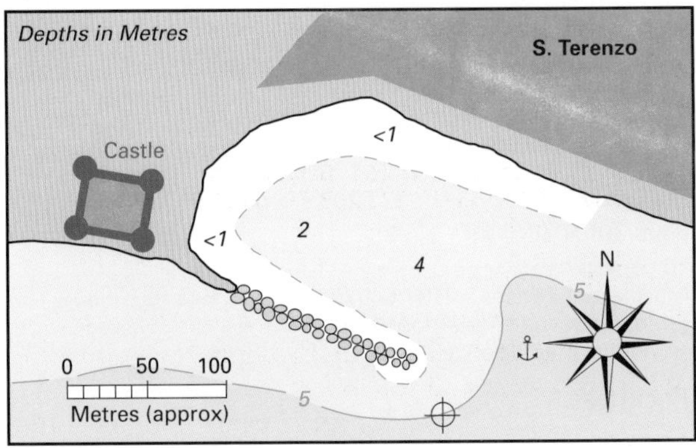

SAN TERENZO ⊕44°04′·8N 09°53′·1E

LERICI

BA 118
Italian 909/25

Approach

The harbour lies in the eastern approach to Rada di la Spezia.

Conspicuous A castle on a rocky promontory is conspicuous from some distance off. Closer in, the harbour mole is easily identified.

Caution Local craft are on permanent moorings behind the mole and constitute a hazard at night.

Mooring

Data Max LOA 25m. Depths 1·5–9m.

Berth Go stern or bows-to on the YC pontoon if a berth is available. Otherwise pick up a fore and aft mooring of an appropriate size in the bay. Water-taxi will bring you ashore. There is little room to anchor behind the breakwater, but in calm weather anchor outside the moorings in 9–12m. The harbour is very congested in the summer with large numbers of craft on permanent moorings. The bottom is mud and good holding. Care needed of swimmers in the bay.

Shelter Good shelter in the summer. However, the bay is open to the NW for over a mile to Diga Foranea and a considerable slop can be set up with winds from this direction. Strong winds from the SW cause a surge.

Authorities YC staff, *ormeggiatori*. Charge band 4.

Facilities

Water On the quay.
Fuel On the quay.
Repairs Crane up to 10 tons. Limited mechanical repairs. Chandlers.
Provisions Good shopping for provisions ashore.
Eating out Restaurants, trattorias and pizzerias nearby.

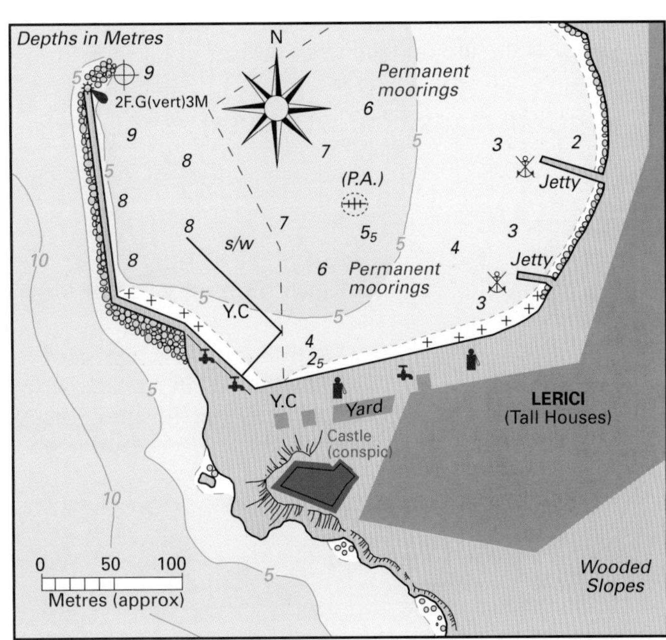

LERICI
⊕44°04′·4N 09°54′·4E

I. THE LIGURIAN COAST

Lerici looking SW. With all the laid moorings there is limited room to anchor behind the breakwater

Other PO. Bank. ATM. Local ferries to Portovenere and La Spezia.

General

The village at the foot of wooded slopes is delightful. Lerici has a Tuscan air to it and, indeed, it was a Pisan town until the Genoese seized it in 1256. The castle on the promontory was originally Pisan but was rebuilt by the Genoese in the 16th century. It remains an excellently preserved piece of medieval military architecture. Lerici was an early runner in the tourist business, attracting among others Dante (he mentions Lerici in the Divine Comedy), Byron, Leigh Hunt and Shelley.

Lerici to Tellaro

Between Lerici and the village of Tellaro, about 1·5 miles to the SE, there are several miniature coves where a small yacht can anchor in calm weather. Care must be taken of above- and below-water rocks close to the coast in the vicinity of the coves. In all of the coves the water is quite deep until close-to and you will be anchoring in 7–10m on sand, rock, and weed. There are no facilities ashore.

BOCCA DI MAGRA (MAGRA RIVER)

BA 118
Italian 115

Approach

This river reaches the sea on the E side of Capo Corvo, the ridge of hills which form the eastern side of the Gulf of La Spezia.

Conspicuous The river mouth lies at the junction of the high ridge to the W and the low plain to the east.
By night A yacht should not attempt to enter the river at night on account of the dangers outlined below.

VHF Ch 08, 16 for Porticciolo, 09 for Ar-Nav, 16 for Marina del Ponte.

Dangers

1. The channel and the depths in the channel are constantly changing. A yacht drawing more than 2m should not attempt to enter the river. (Although local yachts drawing 2m happily come and go and run aground.) The channel on the W side has depths of 2m, although it is reported to silt sometimes to just 1·5m. The sandbank in the middle of the river mouth is easily identified.
2. The river should not be entered in moderate and strong onshore winds when there is a confused swell and breaking crests.

Note A considerable number of yachts are permanently moored in the river and in the summer a local yacht coming or going will show the channel.

Mooring

Porticciolo
Data 230 berths. 30 visitors' berths. Max LOA 30m. Depths 2–4m.

Ar-Nav
Data 80 berths. Max LOA 35m. Depths 2–3m.

Marina del Ponte
Data 35 berths. LOA 10–22m. Depths 2–4m.

Berth Where directed inside the basin at the W side of the entrance to Bocca do Magra. Laid moorings. Further up the river there are a number of riverside quays, pontoons, trots and two small basins.

Marina del Ponte has pontoon berths just to seaward of the bridge. Care is needed in the approaches as the centre of the river appears to be silting badly just off the pontoons. In spring 2010 the sandbank was just breaking the surface here, although with care shallow draft yachts can still access the berths. Call ahead for the latest advice.

Marina 3B is past the road bridge so only motor boats which can clear the bridge will be able to get up to it. It is really a matter of negotiating a berth where you can with one of the clubs or associations. In general there should not be too much of a problem finding a berth for smaller yachts under 10m.

Shelter Excellent although large logs floating downstream with the current are an occasional hazard.

Note

1. A current of up to 3kns, but usually less, can run in the river so a yacht must have sufficient power to overcome this.
2. Yachts generally berth bows-to as the river bank shelves gradually.

Authorities Marina staff. Charge band 4/5.

⊠ Porticciolo di Bocca di Magra, Ameglia Servizi Turistici
✆ 0187 608 037 *Fax* 0187 609 649
Email info@amegliaservizi.it
www.amegliaservizi.it

www.portoboccadimagra.it

Ar-Nav
✆ 0187 65204
Email info@ar-nav.it
www.ar-nav.it

Marina del Ponte ✆ 0187 64670 *Fax* 0187 648 093
Email info@marinadelponte.it
www.marinadelponte.it

Facilities

Services Water and electricity at most berths. Showers and toilets.

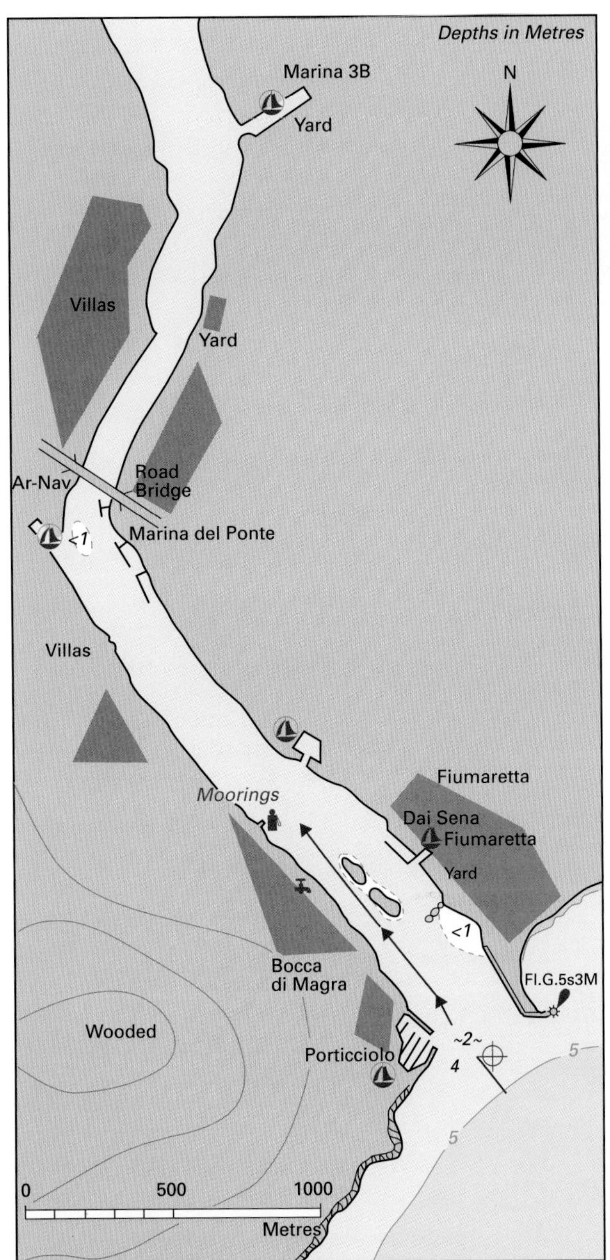

BOCCA DI MAGRA
⊕44°02´·7N 09°59´·4E

The entrance to the Magra River looking NE from the slopes on the S side. A strong southerly is heaping up at the entrance but a few yachts are still coming and going

Shelley's death

It was from the Casa Magni in Lerici that Shelley set out on the tragic sailing trip that ended his life. We know little about the actual event. Shelley set out to sail to Leghorn (Livorno) with Captain Daniel Roberts who had built the boat (though Edward Trelawney may have had a hand in its design) and two friends. They arrived there safely and five days later set out to return to Lerici. The demonic Trelawney, a shadowy figure in this whole business, saw them off. A sudden storm blew up off Viareggio, as a *temporale* can along this coast, and the boat was seen to sink off Viareggio. Trelawney's account is that the boat was rammed by some Italians who believed that the amorous Byron who had been busy seducing their wives was aboard, but then Trelawney was notorious for his inaccuracies. The bodies were not washed up until 10 days later on 17 July 1822. Trelawney, Byron and Leigh Hunt who were in Leghorn hurried down and made the funeral arrangements – the bodies had to be cremated because of the quarantine laws. Trelawney is supposed to have snatched Shelley's heart from the flames to give to Mary Shelley. On the last house that Shelley lived in, the Casa Magni, there is this moving inscription from one of his last letters.

'I still inhabit this divine bay, reading Spanish dramas, sailing and listening to the most enchanting music. My only regret is that the summer must ever pass.'

Fuel On the quay.
Repairs Some repairs can be arranged. Various cranes and slips at several yards. 150-ton travel-hoist at Ar-Nav.
Provisions Some provisions at Bocca di Magra and Fiumaretta.
Eating out Restaurants and bars at Bocca di Magra and Fiumaretta.

General

Although the entrance to the river is difficult, once inside the effort is well worthwhile. Tall trees line the river banks and this leafy haven is reminiscent of the inland waterways of France.

Pontoon berths in the Bocca di Magra. Note the sand bar in the centre of the fairway

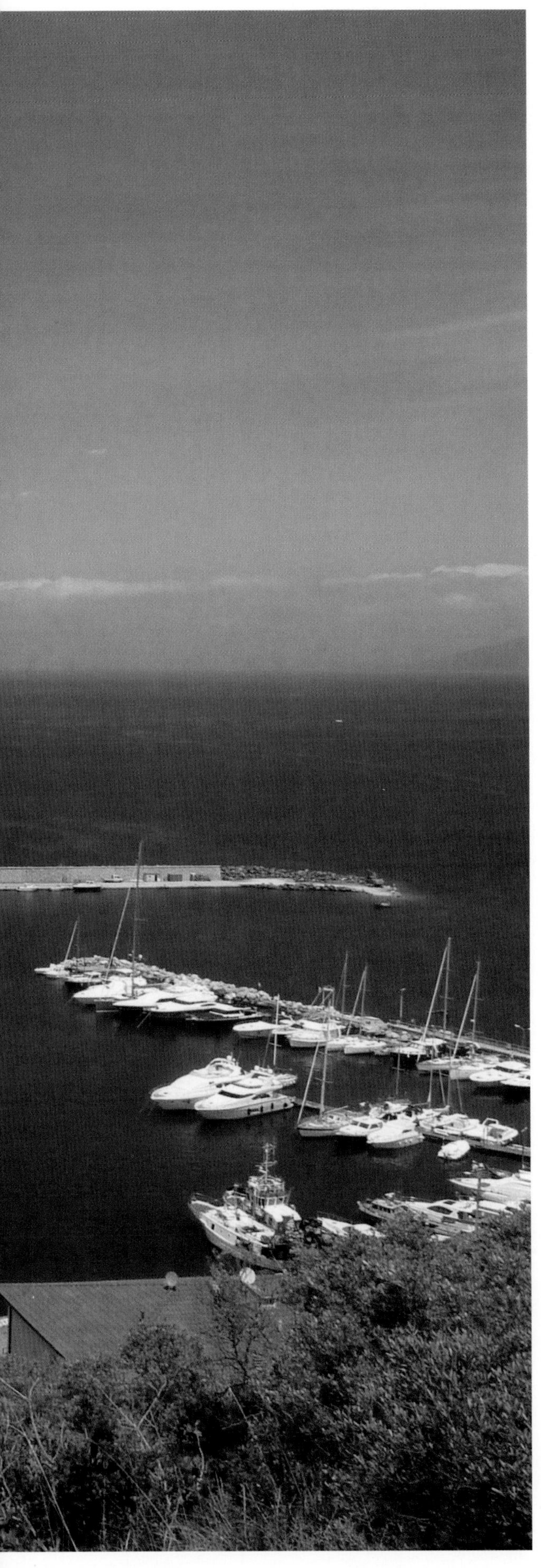

II.

The Tuscan islands and adjacent mainland coast

The Tuscan Islands dot the sea between Italy and Corsica. They are the mountain peaks of the continent of Tyrrhenia which sank into the sea in the Quarternary Era leaving a chain of islands across the western Mediterranean: the Balearics, Sardinia, Corsica and the Tuscan Islands all belong to this group. The Tuscan archipelago consists of Gorgona, Capraia, Elba, Pianosa, Montecristo, Giglio and Giannutri. With the exception of Pianosa and Giannutri, they are all mountainous islands rising sheer from the sea and there are generally good depths close to the coast. The mainland coast opposite the islands is by contrast mostly marshy land except for several promontories which project from the flat land and look like islands from afar.

The Tuscan archipelago is a popular cruising ground for yachts and in the summer can be crowded. The patchwork of islands between Corsica and the mainland provides conveniently spaced stepping stones for the passage between Corsica and Italy. However you may end up staying longer than you planned, seduced by the charm of these islands. Foreign yachts heading further south often get no further than Elba and use Portoferraio as a base for exploring the Ligurian Coast, Corsica, Sardinia and the adjacent mainland.

Routes

Yachts hopping down the coast have a pretty straightforward route going N or S with maybe a few excursions into the Tuscan Islands. Some yachts will often choose to cross to Corsica from France and then hop across to the Tuscan Islands and the Italian coast. On the east coast of Corsica either Macinnagio or Bastia are good jumping off points for Capraia or Elba.

All these routes are straightforward and it is really only a matter of picking a weather window to make the hops across. In the summer it will often be lack of wind that is the problem rather than too much.

Porto delle Valle in Santo Stefano

USEFUL WAYPOINTS

⊕1 1M W of Marina di Carrara
44°01'·6N 10°01'·1E
⊕2 5M W of Secche della Meloria (S) light tower
43°32'·8N 10°06'·7E
⊕3 3M W of Secche di Vada light
43°19'·2N 10°18'·0E
⊕4 1M N of N end of I· Capraia
43°05'·2N 09°49'·5E
⊕5 1M S of S end of Capraia
42°59'·2N 09°48'·7E
⊕6 1M N of Pta Polveraia (Elba/NW corner)
42°48'·6N 10°06'·6E
⊕7 0·5M N of Scoglietto (Elba/Portoferraio approach)
42°50'·18N 10°19'·7E
⊕8 1M S of Pta dei Ripalti (Elba/SE corner)
42°41'·25N 10°25'·5E
⊕9 1M W of I. Palmaiola
42°51'·9N 10°27'·0E
⊕10 1·5M W of Punta Ala
42°48'·1N 10°42'·3E
⊕11 1M W of Talamone
42°33'·1N 11°07'·0E
⊕12 0·5M of Pta Lividonia (Monte Argentario)
42°27'·2N 11°06'·3E
⊕13 0·5M S of Pta di Torre Ciana (Monte Argentario)
42°21'·0N 11°09'·0E
⊕14 1M N of Pta del Fenaio (I. del Giglio)
42°24'·2N 10°52'·9E
⊕15 1M S of Pta del Capel Rosso (I. del Giglio)
42°18'·2N 10°55'·3E
⊕16 1M S of Punta del Capel Rosso (I. di Giannutri)
42°13'·3N 11°06'·6E
⊕17 1M N of Pte del Marchese (I. Pianosa)
42°39'·0N 10°04'·9E
⊕18 1M S of Pta Brigantina (I. Pianosa)
42°33'.2N 10°05'·5E
⊕19 1M W of Scoglio Africa
42°21'·4N 10°02'·6E
⊕20 1M N of I. di Montecristo
42°22'·0N 10°18'·8E
⊕21 1M S of I. di Montecristo
42°17'·8N 10°18'·8E

Weather patterns

The prevailing wind in the summer is from the W–NW and rarely blows at gale force. There will frequently be SE winds around Capraia, Elba and the mainland coast down to Giannutri, and frequent periods of calm. Often there will be a light W or SW wind at night. If a depression passes northwards through the Gulf of Genoa, a SW wind (the libeccio) will blow with considerable force. In the spring and autumn there are frequent local squalls around the islands, usually easily spotted as a ragged black line of cloud, though they do not normally last for long.

Shoestring cruising in the Tuscan Islands and adjacent coast

If you are cruising S down from the Ligurian coast there are few anchorages until you get to the Tuscan Islands. Even around the islands and the adjacent coast there are not as many useable anchorages as you might imagine.

Tuscan Islands

Harbours and marinas

Around the Tuscan Islands ***Porto Capraia, Marina di Campo and Cavo*** are reasonably priced though check in advance during high season. Marinas around ***Portoferraio and Porto Azzuro*** on Elba are now very expensive in the high season. ***Giglio Marina*** is good early and late season.

Anchorages

Capraia At Porto Capraia there are fore and aft moorings at a reasonable price.
Elba Around Elba the best anchorages are along the S coast at Golfo di Campo, Golfo della Lacona and Golfo Stella. You can anchor on the SW side of Portoferraio although there have been problems reported here and yachts have been moved along. You can also anchor off in the bay at Porto Azzurro clear of the moorings.
Giglio Around Giglio there are anchorages on the W and E coast depending on wind and weather. Cala Canelle and Cala Capazzollo on the E side are usually good in settled weather.
Giannutri Around Giannutri anchoring is much restricted by the marine reserves and Cala Schiavone is really the only practical place.

Mainland Coast

Harbours and marinas

Marinas in this patch of Italy can be very expensive in high season and even mid-season. The following marinas and harbours/catwalks are more reasonably priced than others in the vicinity, though you are better off here in low or mid-season compared to high season prices.
Marina di Carrara is usually welcoming and not too expensive. The town ashore is also just great.
Bocca d'Arno further down the coast has catwalks off some of the yards you can go alongside at a reasonable price. You will not be able to get in or out of the river with strong onshore winds.
Livorno Try the YC pontoon in ***Porto Mediceo***
Castiglione della Pescaia although you need to be careful of the bar at the entrance.

Anchorages

Off the S side of Livorno (just off Nazzaro Saura). You may be asked to move.
Torre del Romito In settled weather anchor off the small harbour or just E.
Castiglioncello Anchor on the N or S side of the point depending on wind and sea.
Porto Baratti The S end of the bay is best clear of the moorings.
Punta Ala Anchor on the side of the point with northerlies.
Forte Rochetta Anchor on the S side with northerlies.
Cala di Forno Reasonable shelter from southerlies.
Talamone Reasonable shelter from northerlies and light westerlies.
Monte Argentario There are a number of useful anchorages around the promontory. Pozzarello just E of Santo Stefano has adequate shelter in southerlies. Cala Grande, Cala del Bove and L'Isolotto provide some shelter from southerlies or northerlies. Pick the most useful as they are all close together. Off Marina di Cala Galera you can anchor off the N breakwater and get some shelter from westerlies.

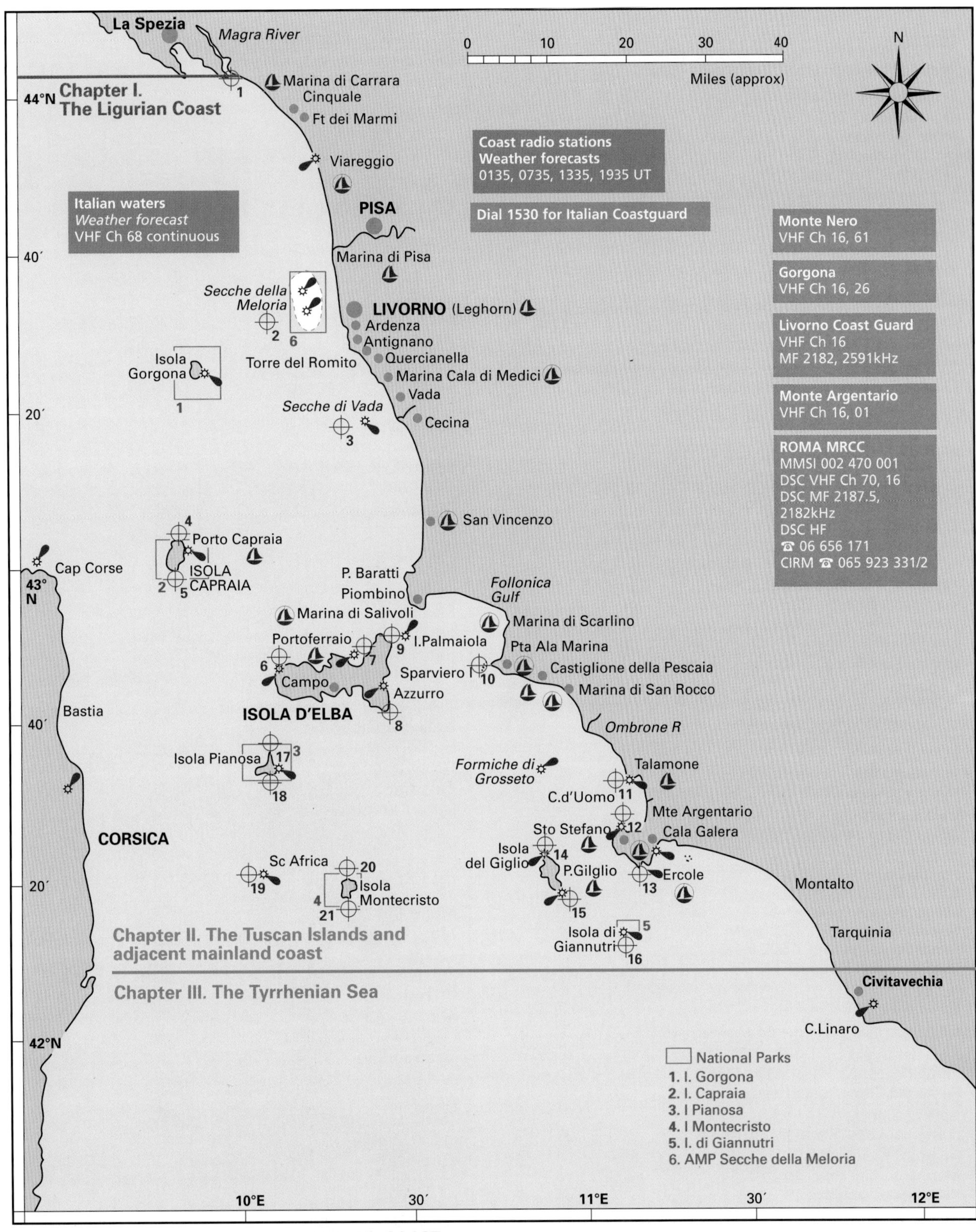

TUSCAN ISLANDS AND ADJACENT MAINLAND COAST

Data

PROHIBITED AREAS AND NATIONAL PARKS

Tuscan Archipelago National Park

The Tuscan Archipelago National Park authority regulates access and activities on part or all of all the islands, including Elba. Only restrictions applying to yachtsmen are listed below.

1. ***Isola Gorgona*** It is prohibited to approach within two miles or to land anywhere on the island without permission from the authorities. A national park with maritime areas has been created around the island and the only access to Cala dello Scalo is on a course of due W.
2. ***Isola Capraia*** A national park with maritime areas has been created around the island and the only access to Porto Capraia is on a course of due W.
3. ***Isola Pianosa*** A former prison island, it was declared a National Park with maritime areas in 1997. All navigation, anchoring, fishing and diving is prohibited within 1M of the island.
4. ***Isola Montecristo*** A national park with maritime areas has been created around the island. Navigation, anchoring, fishing and diving is prohibited within 1,000m.
5. ***Isola di Giannutri*** A national park with maritime areas has been created around the island. There are access channels to Cala Maestra and Golfo Spalmatoi.

Tuscan Archipelago National Park
Via Guerrazzi 1, 57037 Portoferraio
✆ 0565 919 411 *Fax* 0565 919 428
Email parco@islepark.it www.islepark.it

Marine Reserves *Area Marina Protetta (AMP)*

6. ***Secche della Meloria*** A new reserve around the reef off Livorno. The most sensitive parts of the reef are within Zone A of the reserve.

MAJOR LIGHTS

Isola Gorgona
Punta Paratella (Maestra) LFl.10s105m9M

Isola Capraia
Punta del Ferraione LFl.6s30m16M

Isola d'Elba
Portoferraio, Forte Stella Fl(3)14s63m16M
Capo Focardo Fl(3)15s32m16M
Monte Poro Fl.5s160m16M
Marina de Campo Fl.3s34m10M
Punta Polveraia LFl(3)15s52m16M
I. Palmaiola Fl.5s105m10M

Isola Pianosa
Pianosa Fl(2)10s42m16M

Scoglio Africa. Formiche de Montecristo Fl.5s19m12M

Isola del Giglio
Punta del Fenaio Fl(3)15s39m16M
Punta del Capel Rosso Fl(4)30s90m23M

Isola di Giannutri
Punta del Capel Rosso Fl.5s61m13M

Adjacent mainland
Marina de Carrara Fl.3s22m17M
Viareggio Fl.5s30m22M

Secche della Meloria
N end: Fl(2)10s18m10M
S end: Q(6)+LFl.15s18m12M
Livorno Fl(4)20s52m24M
Secche di Vada Fl(2)10s18m12M
Porto Baratti Fl.3s75m9M
Piombino (La Rocchetta) Fl(3)15s18m11M
Punta Ala Marina Fl.2s12m7M
North Rock (Formiche di Grosseto) Fl.6s23m11M
Talamone Fl(2)10s30m15M
Punta Lividonia Fl.5s47m16M
Forte La Rocca LFl.WR.7s91m16/13M
Marina Cala Galera Iso.WR.2s10m10/7M

Quick reference guide

	Shelter	*Mooring*	*Fuel*	*Water*	*Eating out*	*Provisions*	*Plan*	*Charge band*
Isola Capraia								
Porto Capraia	A	A	A	A	C	C	•	5
Isola d'Elba								
Portoferraio	A	A	A	A	A	A	•	6
Esaom Cesa	A	A	O	A	C	C	•	5
Edilnautica	A	A	B	A	C	C	•	5
Magazzini	C	AC	O	B	C	C	•	
Cala Bagnaia	C	C	O	O	O	C	•	
Nisporto/Nisportino	C	C	O	O	O	C	•	
Capo Vita anchorage	O	C	O	O	O	O		
Cavo	B	A	A	A	C	C	•	
Rio Marina	C	A	B	A	C	C	•	
Senno d'Ortano	C	C	O	O	C	C	•	
Porto Azzurro	A	A	A	A	A	A	•	5/6
Cala del' Innamorata	O	C	O	O	C	C		
Morcone	O	C	O	O	O	C		
Golfo Stella	C	AC	O	O	C	C	•	
Golfo della Lacona	B	C	O	O	C	C	•	
Marina di Campo	B	AC	A	A	B	A	•	4
Cavoli	C	C	O	O	C	C		
Barbatoia	C	C	O	O	C	C	•	
Marciana Marina	B	A	A	A	B	A	•	4
Procchio	C	C	O	O	C	C	•	
Isola del Giglio								
Giglio Porto	A	A	B	A	B	B	•	4
Cala Canelle	C	C	O	O	C	O		
Cala Capazzollo	C	C	O	O	O	O		
Seno Campese	C	C	O	O	C	C	•	
Isola di Giannutri								
Cala Spalmatoi	B	C	O	O	O	C	•	
Cala Maestra	O	C	O	O	O	C		
Mainland coast								
Marina di Carrara	A	A	A	A	B	B	•	2/3
Cinquale	A	A	B	A	O	O		
Forte dei Marmi	O	BC	B	O	B	B		
Viareggio	A	A	A	A	A	A	•	6
Marina di Pisa	A	AB	A	A	B	B	•	2/3
Livorno	A	A	A	A	A	A	•	3/4
Nazario Saura	B	A	A	A	C	C		
Ardenza	C	A	O	O	C	C	•	
Antignano	O	A	B	A	B	B	•	
Torre del Romito	O	C	O	O	O	O	•	
Quercianella	C	A	O	O	C	C	•	
Chioma	O	A	O	O	O	O		
Rossana	C	AC	O	O	O	O		
Castiglioncello	C	C	B	B	B	B	•	
Marina Cala di Medici	A	A	A	A	B	A	•	6
Vada	O	AB	B	O	O	O		
Cecina Mare	A	A	A	A	O	C	•	2
San Vincenzo	A	A	B	A	B	B	•	6+
Porto Baratti	C	C	O	O	O	C	•	
Marina di Salivoli	A	A	A	A	C	C	•	6
Piombino	B	A	B	A	C	C	•	

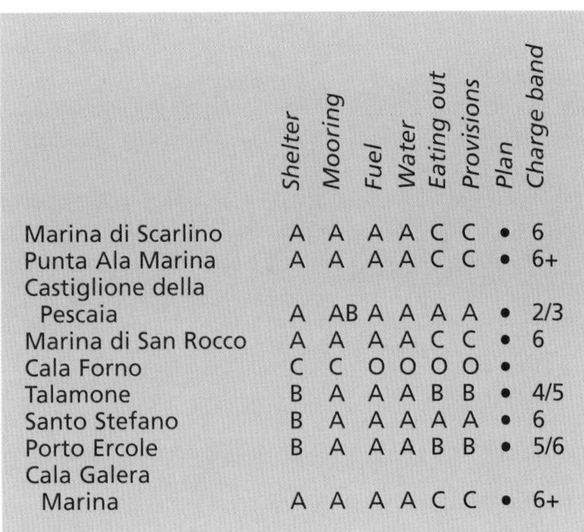

	Shelter	Mooring	Fuel	Water	Eating out	Provisions	Plan	Charge band
Marina di Scarlino	A	A	A	A	C	C	•	6
Punta Ala Marina	A	A	A	A	C	C	•	6+
Castiglione della Pescaia	A	AB	A	A	A	A	•	2/3
Marina di San Rocco	A	A	A	A	C	C	•	6
Cala Forno	C	C	O	O	O	O	•	
Talamone	B	A	A	A	B	B	•	4/5
Santo Stefano	B	A	A	A	A	A	•	6
Porto Ercole	B	A	A	A	B	B	•	5/6
Cala Galera Marina	A	A	A	A	C	C	•	6+

The Tuscan Islands

Isola Gorgona

The northernmost island of the group, it lies about 18 miles WSW of Livorno. It is hilly (255m/837ft high at Punta Gorgona) with a small settlement and minuscule harbour on the E side of the island at Cala dello Scalo. The island is a National Park and landing is prohibited except at Cala dello Scalo.

Isola Capraia

The northwesternmost island of the group situated approximately 16 miles E of Cap Corse, the northernmost cape of Corsica. It is often used as a stepping stone for yachts en route from Corsica to Elba. It is a mountainous island reaching 447m (1,467ft) at its northern end at Monte Arpagna. It is

Pta Zenobito (Capraia) looking NE. Note conspicuous tower

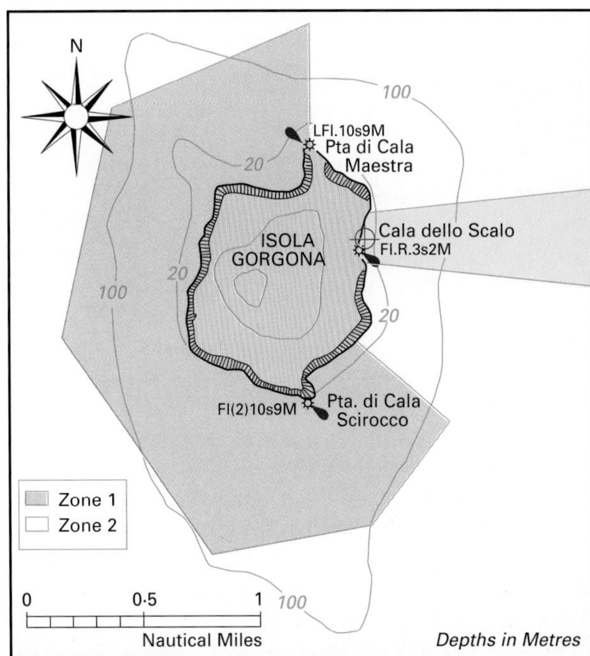

ISOLA GORGONA ⊕ 43°25'·7N 09°54'·6E

Isola Gorgona National Park

Part of the Tuscan Archipelago National Park since 1996, and a former penal colony, the island's waters are now a marine reserve.

Zone 1

Access, navigation, short- and long-time stays, anchoring, any kind of fishing and diving prohibited.

Zone 2

Extends up to 3M from the coast. Commercial, sport and underwater fishing prohibited. Access only via the channel to Cala dello Scalo. Anchoring and diving are regulated.

Tuscan Archipelago National Park
✆ 0565 919 411 *Fax* 0565 919 428
Email parco@islepark.it
www.islepark.it

easily identified when sailing from Corsica. The island is steep-to and everywhere rocky, covered with maquis, and little cultivated except for the terraced slopes on the coast.

The island was at one time a prison island and landing was prohibited on parts of the island. The prison buildings remain and can be visited.

PORTO CAPRAIA

Approach

Conspicuous Capo Ferraione (Ferrajone) lighthouse, a white square tower and the fort on Capo Ferraione are conspicuous. From the S and E the harbour and village will not be seen until you have opened the bay. Once into the bay the light tower at the entrance and the harbour breakwater are easily identified.

By night Use the light on Capo Ferraione LFl.6s30m16M.

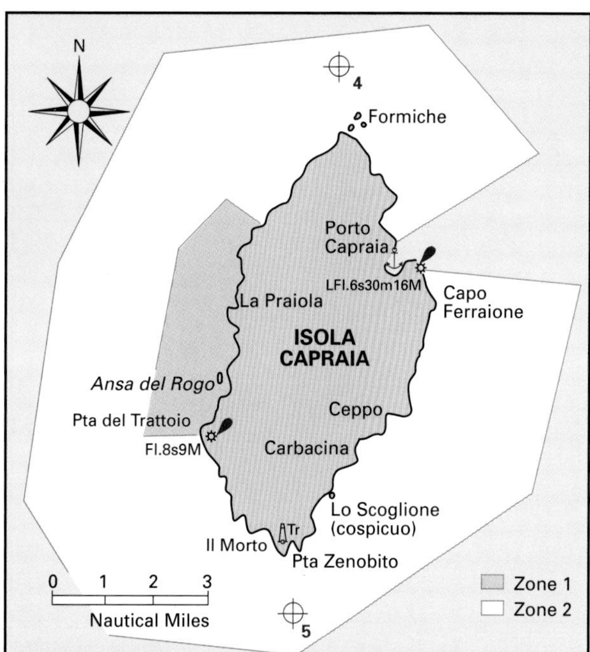

ISOLA CAPRAIA

⊕**4** 1M N of N end of I. Capraia 43°05'·2N 09°49'·5E
⊕**5** 1M S of S end of Capraia 42°59'·2N 09°48'·7E

Isola Capraia National Park

Part of the Tuscan Archipelago National Park since 1992, the island and its waters are now also a marine reserve.

Zone 1
Covers the area from Punta della Manza to Punta del Trattoio.
Access, navigation, short- and long-time stays, anchoring, all types of fishing and diving prohibited.

Zone 2
Extends up to 3M from the coast. Commercial, sport and underwater fishing prohibited.
Only access is via channel to Porto Capraia. Anchoring and diving are regulated.

✆ 0565 919 411 *Fax* 0565 919 428
Email parco@islepark.it
www.islepark.it

Mooring

Berth Go stern or bows-to where possible. Laid moorings at most berths. The bottom is sand and silt and not everywhere good holding. In the summer the harbour is very crowded and you may have to pick up a mooring outside the harbour.

Even early in the season it can be busy with Italian yachts escaping the mainland for the weekend.

Shelter Good shelter inside although there are gusts with strong W–NW winds and a bothersome surge with strong NE winds. Strong winds in the Ligurian Sea to the north can cause a large swell which makes a night on the moorings uncomfortable.

Authorities Port police and customs. Harbourmaster. Charge band 5.

Anchorage In settled weather a yacht can anchor off outside the harbour, beyond the moorings. Anchor in 8–10m in the bight on the S of the bay on sand and weed, good holding once through the weed. It can be fairly rolly in here and it may pay to anchor fore and aft with the bows into the swell.

Porto Capraia looking east *John Clift*

Facilities

Services Water and electricity on the quay (the conduit runs along the quay at water level). Water may be rationed in the summer.
Fuel On the quay though it can be difficult to get in the summer.
Provisions Most provisions can be found though the village is much dependent on supplies brought in by ferry.
Eating out Restaurants and bars.
Other Ferry to the mainland. Bank. ATM.

General

Capraia is known to have been settled in Roman times and on the outskirts of the village above the harbour there are the ruins of a large Roman villa. Later it was settled by monks who over time slipped into what Pope Gregory the Great called 'unorthodoxy and loose behaviour'. He sent an armed force to put them back on the orthodox path. Early on in his life Boswell inadvertently spent some time here. In 1765 when the ship Boswell was travelling in from Corsica to Genoa encountered a northerly gale, it put into Capraia and Boswell went ashore. He stayed with the Franciscan friars and wrote a detailed description of the island.

Like most of the Tuscan Islands, the island was ravaged for several centuries by pirates. Nelson captured it for a short time but did not retain it for long. Today, the islanders enjoy a modest income from a little tourism. It is possible to take a tour of the old prison buildings from Porto Capraia.

Anchorages around Capraia

Around the southern end of the W and E coasts are a number of anchorages that can be explored in settled weather. The authorities allow access to the southern end of the island, but not to the northern end.

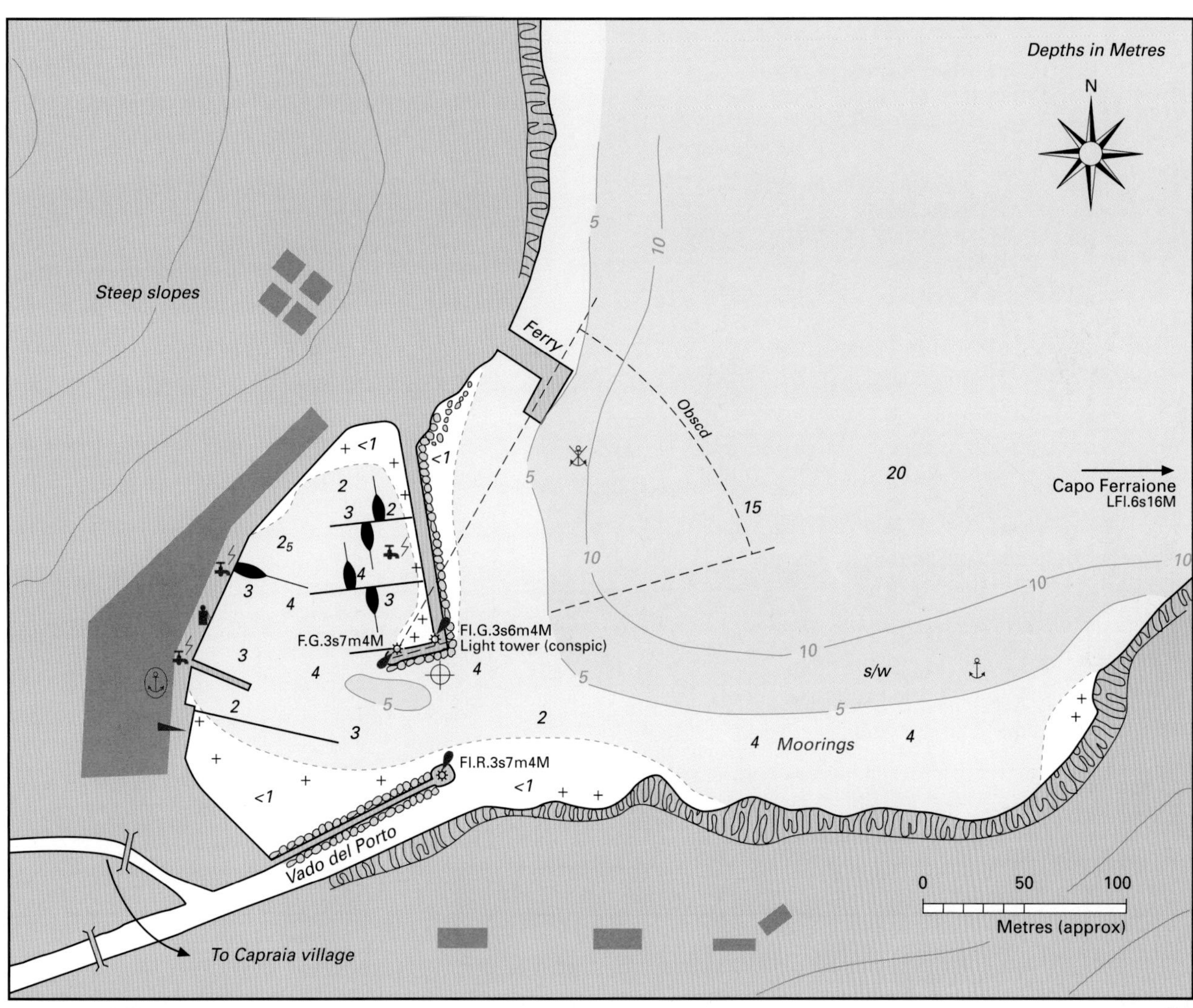

PORTO CAPRAIA
⊕43°03´·1N 09°50´·35E

Note All these anchorages are in the Zone 2 area around Isola Capraia. This means navigation is permitted and permission to anchor can be obtained, or play it by ear and in the summer if the locals are anchoring do likewise. It is prohibited to fish in the area.

The two anchorages at Anse del Rogo and La Praiola described in earlier editions are in the Zone 1 area where navigation and anchoring are prohibited.

Ansa Ceppo

A bay under Pta Civitata open to the S and east. Anchor in 5–8m on sand.

Carbacina

A cove just SE of Ceppo. Open S and east. Anchor in 10–14m.

Lo Scoglione

A cove immediately S of Carbacina named after the rock on its S side, Lo Scoglione. Anchor in 9–20m: the bottom comes up quickly.

Il Morto

A bay on the W side of Pta Zenobito. The tower on Pta Zenobito is conspicuous if you are coming from the W or east. Open S–SW. Anchor in 10–15m on sand and rock.

Isola d'Elba

Local magnetic anomalies

Are reported to be frequently encountered off the coasts of Elba, especially off the NE coast. These are no doubt caused by the substantial iron deposits around the island.

Well known as the subject of the Napoleonic palindrome, 'Able was I ere I saw Elba', the Admiralty *Pilot* describes Elba as 'the largest, richest and most beautiful island of the Archipelago Toscano', and it is difficult to improve on the description. It is everywhere mountainous with the highest part in the W of the island culminating in Monte Capanne (1,019m/3,343ft). Its coast is much indented and there are numerous attractive harbours and anchorages. The slopes are extensively terraced and the island is always green even in the middle of

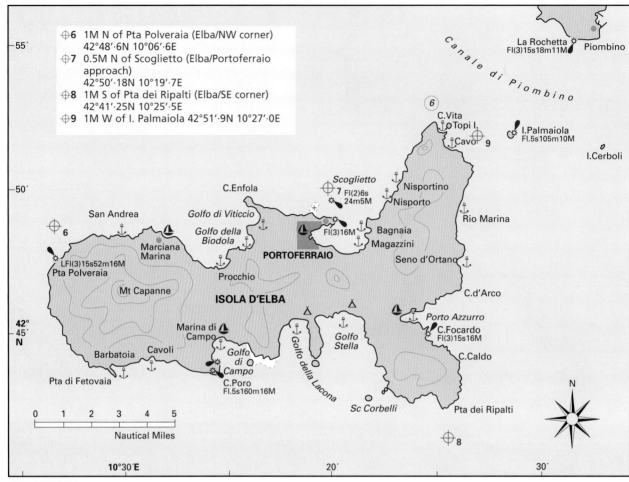

⊕6 1M N of Pta Polveraia (Elba/NW corner) 42°48'·6N 10°06'·6E
⊕7 0.5M N of Scoglietto (Elba/Portoferraio approach) 42°50'·18N 10°19'·7E
⊕8 1M S of Pta dei Ripalti (Elba/SE corner) 42°41'·25N 10°25'·5E
⊕9 1M W of I. Palmaiola 42°51'·9N 10°27'·0E

ISOLA D'ELBA

summer. Palms, eucalyptus, cedars and pine grow everywhere and olives and vines are cultivated. The local Elban DOC wine, both Elba Bianco and Elba Rosso is excellent, although it can be hard to get hold of.

In ancient times Elba was important for the easily obtained iron ore on the east coast. As early as the 6th century BC the Etruscans were open-cast mining at Capo Calamita and between Rio and Cavo. The last mine on the E coast only closed in 1984. In the middle ages Elba was preyed upon by pirates, who operated fleets as large as any small duchy. In May 1564 a pirate fleet of 42 sail was sighted off Elba. In the 17th and 18th centuries the fleet anchorage of Portoferraio was coveted by France, Spain, Italy and England. Nelson described it as 'for its size the most complete harbour in the world'.

Scoglietto and mini-lighthouse in the approaches to Portoferraio

At the end of the 18th-century England occupied Elba for two years and in 1814 the exiled Napoleon arrived. With him came a number of soldiers, 100 grenadiers and light infantry and 600 others including Polish lancers, and a 'navy', the brig *Inconstant*. His principality included Pianosa and he sailed around Elba and across to Pianosa, constructed roads and modernised Portoferraio, all the time no doubt brooding over how he was to get back to France. On 26 February 1815, he embarked on the *Inconstant* and, evading the naval patrols, sailed to France. You can visit Napoleon's house, the Villa dei Mulini in Portoferraio, where he lived a rather spartan life, almost as if he never expected to be long in Elba. The villa contains an Egyptian room with scenes from the Egyptian campaign and a handwritten inscription by Napoleon: 'Napoleon is happy everywhere.' His country house was three miles away in San Martino. Elba became part of united Italy in 1862.

PORTOFERRAIO

BA 131
Italian 72

Approach

Straightforward by day and night.

Conspicuous Scoglietto Rock and the small stone lighthouse on it is easily identified. The walls of the citadel and the lighthouse on Forte Stella are conspicuous. Once into Rada di Portoferraio the yacht harbour is easily located.

By night Unless familiar with the approach a yacht should keep to seaward of Scoglietto at night.

VHF Ch 11, 16 for port authorities. Ch 12 for pilots. Ch 09 for Darsena Medicea.

Dangers

1. By day a yacht can pass inside Scoglietto with due caution. Secca di Capo Bianco is once again marked with a N cardinal beacon, lit Q.3M.
2. A yacht should give way to the numerous ferries entering and leaving the harbour.
3. With strong southerlies there are gusts off the high land into Rada di Portoferraio.

Mooring

Data 150 berths. 15 visitors' berths. Max LOA 50m. Depths 3–10m.

Berth Call ahead for a berth. Port staff will come out

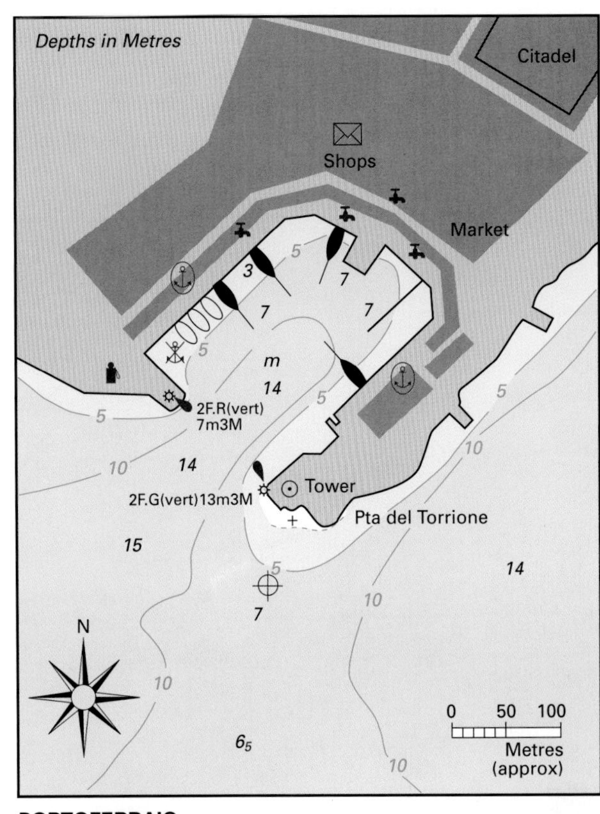

PORTOFERRAIO
⊕42°48′·6N 10°19′·8E

Zone A - C and Access Channel: Anchoring, diving, sailing water-skiing, jet skis, canoes, wind surfing and fishing is prohibited

Speed limit: 4 Knots in Zones A and C

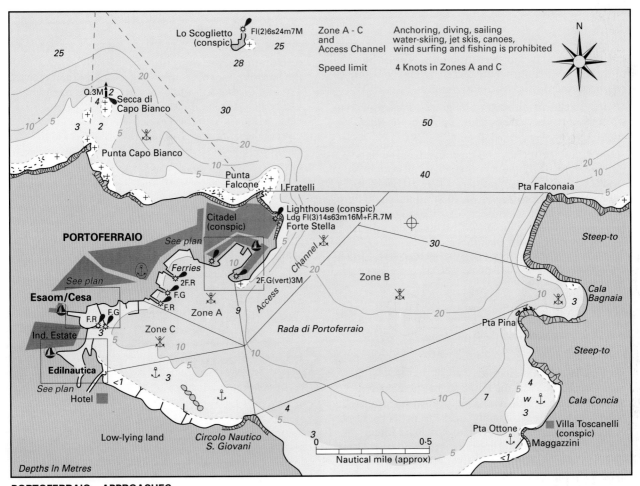

PORTOFERRAIO – APPROACHES
⊕42°48′·9N 10°20′·75E

II. THE TUSCAN ISLANDS AND ADJACENT MAINLAND COAST

Portoferraio looking SW

to meet you and assist mooring. Laid moorings tailed to the quay. Go stern-to on the NW or SE side of the yacht harbour where directed. The NW side is reckoned the noisier of the two quays.

Shelter Excellent although SW gales (*libeccio*) blow strongly into the harbour and cause a considerable slop.

Authorities Port police and customs. Charge band 6. Portoferraio is a *porto turistico,* although you wouldn't believe it sometimes when accosted for a fee by the local *ormeggiatori*. In summer yachts are only allowed a maximum of one night in the Darsena Medicea. Outside of high season you may be able to negotiate a bit longer.

⌧ Cosimo De'Medici Srl, Cala Mazzini, 37 Portoferraio, Elba
✆ 0565 944 024 / 914 121 *Fax* 0565 945 355
Email cosimomedici@virgilio.it

Ormeggiatori ✆ /*Fax* 0565 914 352
Email ormeggiatorielba@tiscalinet.it

Capitaneria ✆ 0565 914 000
Email porto.ferraio@capitaneria.isoladelba.it

Facilities

Services Water and electricity at all berths.
Fuel On the quay at the entrance to the basin.
Repairs There is little available at Portoferraio itself, however the extensive facilities at the yards in the W of Rada di Portoferraio are close by. Chandlers.
Provisions Excellent shopping for all provisions close to the harbour. Good covered market just behind the harbour on Fridays.
Eating out Excellent restaurants, trattorias and pizzerias close to the harbour. Although the restaurants on the waterfront have lovely views across the harbour, the incessant traffic destroys their charm. Try one of those in the alleys behind the harbour.
Other PO. Banks. ATMs. Italgaz and Camping Gaz. Gas cylinders can be refilled here. Hire cars and motorbikes. Buses around the island. Ferries to Piombino.

Portoferraio Old Port looking N into the entrance
John Clift

Punta Falcone looking south

General

Few people fail to fall in love with Portoferraio. Behind the harbour the 18th-century buildings in shades of cream and ochre are tucked under the craggy 16th-century citadel, built originally by Cosmino I, Duke of Florence. The warrens of alleys and staircases are lined with dwellings, shops and restaurants and occasionally lead to unexpected views of the sea behind. You should climb to the citadel walls at least once to watch the sunset and the sea below turning liquid red and sepia as it washes over the rocks and reefs. Even the grubby ferries from Piombino fit into the picture in the half-light at dusk. Without doubt Portoferraio is at its best in the spring or autumn when there are fewer tourists, but it should not be missed even at the height of summer. I can't imagine why Napoleon ever left.

West side Rada di Portoferraio

You can anchor on the SW side of Rada di Portoferraio clear of the ferry turning area and clear of the fairway into the two harbours here. East of the hotel on the S side has been reported to be a good spot. The bottom comes up fairly gradually and you can usually anchor in 2–5m. The bottom is mud and excellent holding. It is not always the most comfortable at anchor. If it blows from the north or east a fair amount of chop is pushed into the western corner. Added to that is the wash from the ferries and other craft coming and going from Portoferraio. If you need to get into town the best thing to do is take your dinghy across as it is a long dreary walk through some pretty depressing industrial suburbs otherwise.

Note Yachts left at anchor in the no-anchoring zones may be moved, at the owner's expense.

ESAOM CESA

Approach

This marina lies immediately W of the commercial port in the NW corner of Rada di Portoferraio.

Conspicuous A large concrete hangar behind the marina is conspicuous. The entrance is difficult to pick out until you are close to it.

VHF Ch 09 (0600–2200).

Mooring

Data 150 berths. 20 visitors' berths. Max LOA 40m. Depths 2·5–5m.

Berth Where directed. There are finger pontoons or laid moorings tailed to the quay, or mooring buoys off the quay for visiting yachts.

Shelter Good all-round shelter.

Authorities Port captain and marina staff. Charge band 5.

Marina ✆ 0565 919 311
Cantiere Esaom Cesa ✆ 0565 919 273 / 919 311
Fax 0565 917 397
Email marina@esaom.it
www.esaom.it

Note Immediately S of the ferry quays, NE of Esaom Cesa, is another basin used primarily as a charter yacht base. At weekends it is busy, but during the week visiting yachts may find a berth. It is less crowded than in Portoferraio and offers better shelter from the afternoon sea breeze. Water and electricity on the quay. No facilities. Supermarket nearby. A charge is made.

Facilities

Services Water and electricity at or near every berth.
Fuel In Portoferraio basin.
Repairs 250 and 50-ton travel-hoist. Open and covered storage ashore. Mechanical and engineering repairs. GRP and wood repairs. Some fine wood construction and reparation carried out here. Electrical and electronic repairs. Sail repairs. Life-raft servicing. Chandlers.
Provisions Supermarket nearby.
Eating out In Portoferraio.
Other ATM. Italgaz and Camping Gaz. Hire cars near the commercial port.

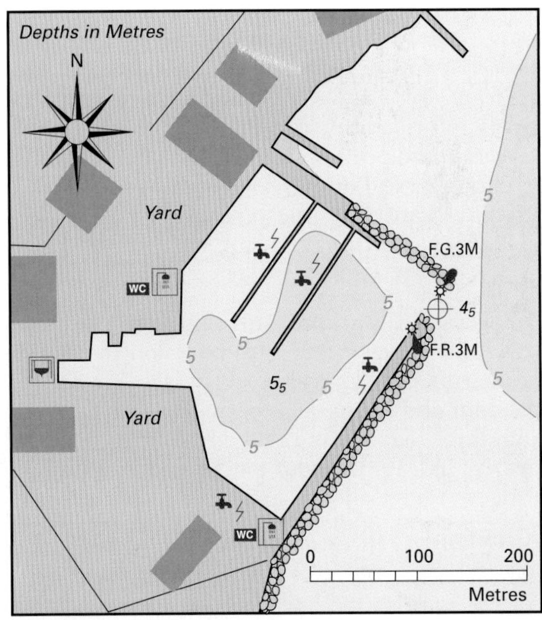

ESAOM CESA
⊕42°48′·5N 10°19′·07E

General

You wouldn't come here for the surroundings which, although pleasant enough in the marina itself, are pure industrial just outside the gates. Rather this is somewhere to have work done on the boat or a secure base port for exploring Elba. The yard, Cantiere Esaom Cesa, carries out high quality work on yachts and is often refitting old classics.

EDILNAUTICA MARINA

Approach

This marina lies immediately S of Esaom Cesa and is part of the same group. Care is needed in the approaches as there are shallows off the coast immediately S of the entrance. Proceed parallel to the outer breakwater of Esaom Cesa through the somewhat indistinct entrance. There is a sign on the S side of the entrance welcoming you to Edilnautica Marina.

VHF Ch 09.

Mooring

Data 100 berths. Max LOA 15m. Depths 2–4m.
Berth Where directed. There are finger pontoons or laid moorings tailed to the quay.

Shelter Excellent all-round shelter.

Authorities Port captain and staff. Charge band 5.
✆ 0565 919 309 / 311

Anchorage Anchor off outside the moorings in 4–6m on sand, good holding.

Facilities

Services Water and electricity at or near every berth. The water is reported to be non-potable. Showers and toilets.
Fuel In Portoferraio or large amounts can be delivered by tanker.
Repairs Travel-hoist and slipways. A large hard standing area ashore. Extensive repair facilities which are part of Esaom Cesa. Mechanical and engineering repairs. GRP and wood repairs. Electrical and electronic repairs. Chandlers.
Provisions Some provisions available at the marina. Better shopping in Portoferraio.
Eating out A canteen in the yard.
Other Italgaz and Camping Gaz.

General

As at Esaom Cesa, the surroundings here are industrial. However a few local boats on the N side of the marina and up the creek on the S side add some colour and life to the otherwise grimy factories surrounding the marina. As a secure base or somewhere to leave the boat for the winter it is ideal, but it doesn't have a lot of appeal as a spot to visit.

San Giovanni

⊕ 42°48'·2N 10°19'·45E

On the S side of Rada di Portoferraio, almost immediately opposite Portoferraio basin, a rough mole shelters a small harbour for local yachts. Although there are 2m depths in the entrance, these quickly shallow up to 1–1·5m off the catwalk. The depths in here are irregular and caution is needed. Local craft are kept on laid moorings under the mole with some craft berthed stern-to the catwalk which belongs to a local *circolo nautico*.

If you can get in here or even anchor off outside, the small village ashore has a lot of charm. Most provisions can be found and there are several restaurants ashore.

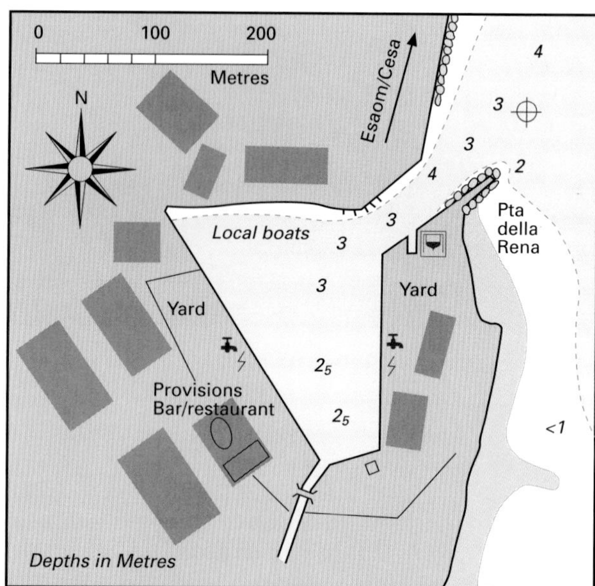

EDILNAUTICA MARINA
⊕42°48´·46N 10°18´·98E

Magazzini

Under Punta Ottone in the SE corner of Rada di Portoferraio. The Villa Toscanelli immediately NE stands out well. A short mole shelters the small harbour which is very shallow. Although there are depths of 2m off the end of the mole, most of the harbour is 1m or less deep. The bottom is covered in weed and is poor holding. In calm weather anchor off the beach in 2–4m. Ashore restaurants open in the summer.

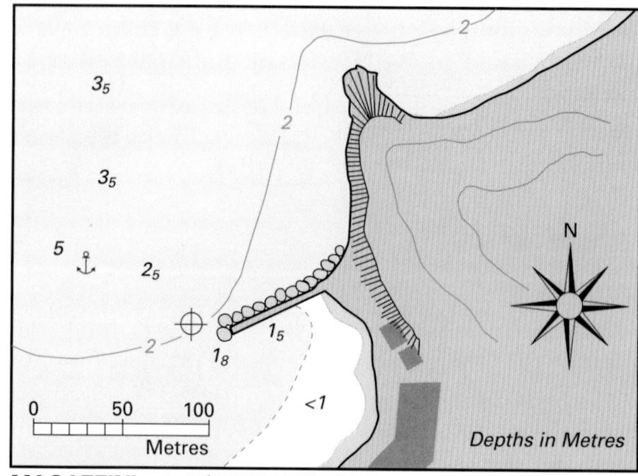

MAGAZZINI ⊕ 42°48´·0N 10°21´·5E

Cala Bagnaia

Note It is currently prohibited to anchor in this bay (see plan on page 111).

A U-shaped bay on the E side of Rada di Portoferraio. Open to the W and NW. There are numerous permanent moorings in the bay. Reasonable shelter except in strong N–W winds.

Restaurants ashore open in the summer.

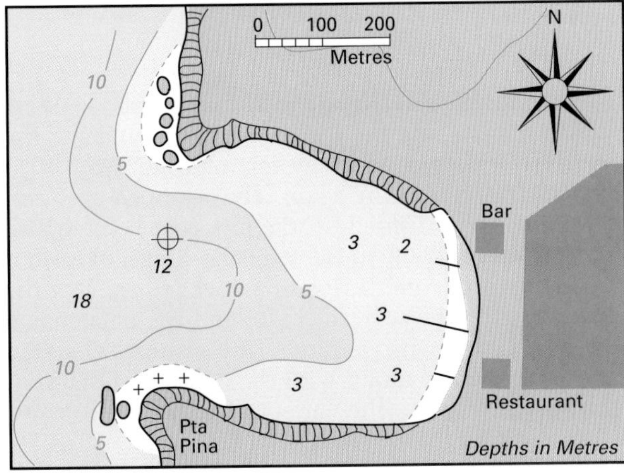

CALA BAGNAIA
⊕42°48'·65N 10°21'·5E

Nisporto and Nisportino

Two small coves lying 1·5 miles N of Cala Bagnaia. Anchor in 5–10m. The coves are open to the W–NW, but shelter is adequate in settled conditions. There are a few villas about the slopes and a pizzeria in Nisporto, the more southerly of the two coves.

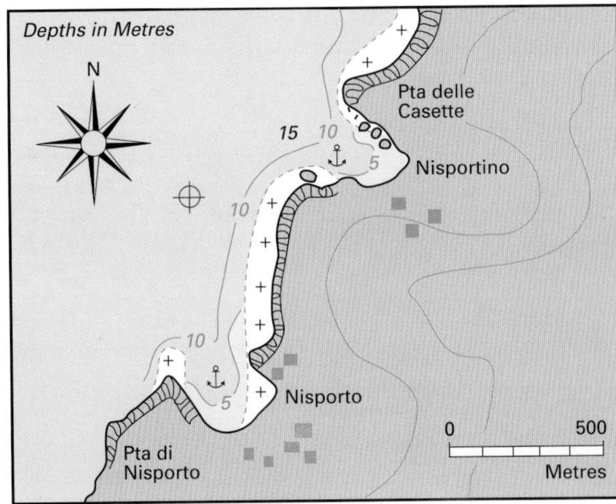

NISPORTO AND NISPORTINO
⊕42°49'·9N 10°22'·6E

Capo Vita

On the ridge running down to Capo Vita a large monument is conspicuous. On the E side of Capo Vita there is a delightful anchorage under Topi islet suitable in calm weather. Anchor in 5m on sand – good holding.

ISOLA PALMAIOLA

⊕9 1M W of I. Palmaiola 42°51'·9N 10°27'·0E

In settled weather it is possible to anchor in the lee of the island. Useful as a lunch stop, but not as an overnight anchorage.

CAVO

Approach

The small harbour lies on the E side of Capo Vita.

Conspicuous Isola Palmaiola, which is easily distinguished, lies about two miles due E of the harbour. The monument on Capo Vita and the houses of the small village are readily identified.

VHF Ch 16.

Mooring

Data 230 berths. 40 visitors' berths. Max LOA 15m. Depths <1–2·5m.

Berth The harbour is mostly shallow and there is only room for small or medium-size yachts. Go stern-to where directed or wherever looks likely.

Shelter Good although strong NE winds send in a heavy swell.

Authorities Harbourmaster. *Ormeggiatori.*

Anchorage In calm weather or light offshore winds it is possible to anchor off to the N of the harbour. Anchor in 3–5m on weed over a sandy bottom. It may take more than one attempt to penetrate the weed. There always seems to be a bit of swell running

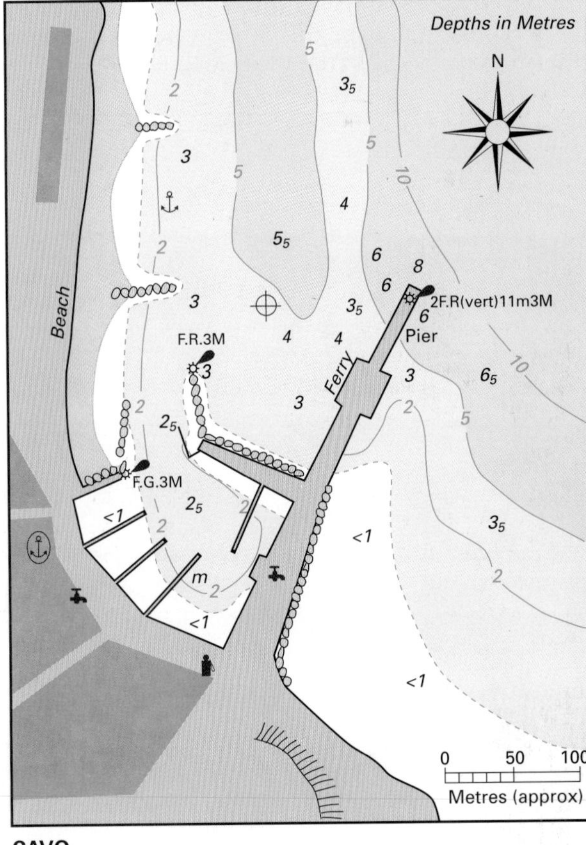

CAVO
⊕42°51'·6N 10°25'·4E

here so it is not always the most comfortable place to be.

Facilities

Water On the quay.
Fuel On the quay in the S corner of the basin although it shallows up here.
Provisions Basic provisions in the summer.
Eating out Restaurants in the summer.
Other PO. Bank. ATM. Ferry to Piombino and Portoferraio.

General

A pleasant village in a delightful setting under green slopes with a long sandy beach running around the bay. The latter attracts large numbers of holiday-makers in the summer.

RIO MARINA

Approach

A small harbour under the scarred slopes of the old open-cast mines behind the village.

Conspicuous The scarred slopes and the tall 18th-century buildings in the village are conspicuous from some distance off. The tower on the elbow of the mole and that at the root of the mole stand out well.

Mooring

Data 100 berths. 15 visitors' berths. Max LOA 15m. Depths <1–4m.

Berth Go stern-to the pontoon in the SE corner of the harbour. Laid moorings at all berths.

Shelter Reasonable shelter although northerlies send in a considerable swell. Strong northerlies and easterlies make the harbour untenable.

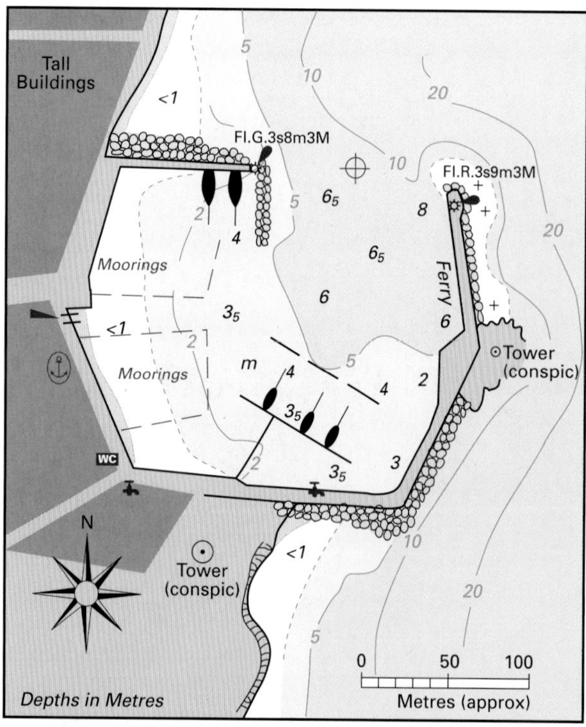

RIO MARINA
⊕42°48´·9N 10°25´·8E

Authorities Harbourmaster.
Ormeggiatori ✆ /*Fax* 0565 914 352

Facilities

Water On the quay
Fuel In the town about 250m away.
Provisions Most provisions can be found in the summer.
Eating out Restaurants and bars in the summer.
Other PO. Bank. Ferry to Piombino and Portoferraio.

General

An attempt has been made to attract holiday-makers to Rio Marina, but the scarred slopes behind and the red dust in the air with any sort of wind deter most visitors from returning again. The last open-cast iron ore mine on the island, in the hills just behind Rio, was closed in 1984, so the sea is no longer stained a haematite red from the loading docks to the S of the port. Despite the scarred hinterland the place has a quaint charm with a tatty 18th-century elegance scattered around along with the dust. A museum in the village displays the variety of mineral wealth to be found on Elba.

SENNO D'ORTANO

A small cove sheltered from the S by I. d'Ortano. Open to the east. At the N end of the cove there is a sandy beach at the bottom of a gorge cutting down through the hills. Anchor off the beach in 4–8m on sand, rock and weed, indifferent holding. Care is needed of the pipeline running out from the beach. With care, a yacht can anchor at the S end under I. d'Ortano. Care is needed of the rocky patches extending up to 100m off the coast and the islet in the southern corner. Anchor in 5–6m on a rocky bottom, poor holding.

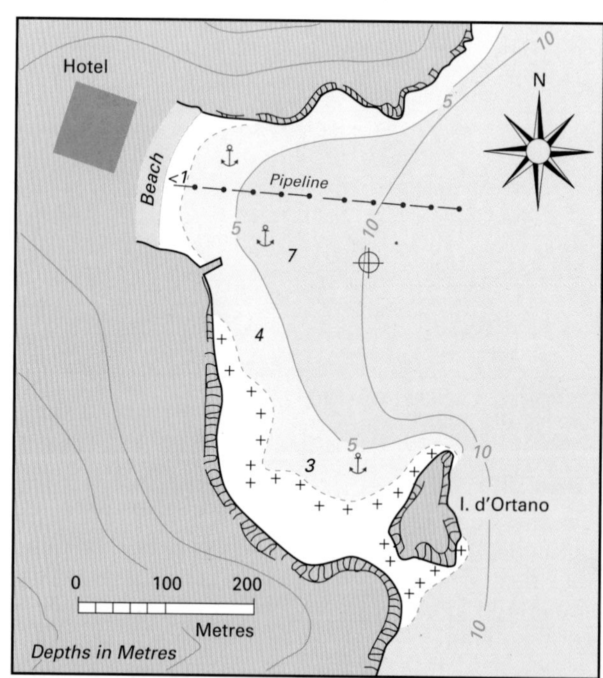

SENNO D'ORTANO
⊕42°47´·0N 10°26´·0E

The shelter from the prevailing southerlies in this southern corner is generally better than in the northern half of the bay. Ashore behind the beach there is a hotel complex with a restaurant, bar and minimarket.

PORTO AZZURRO

BA 131
Italian 913/05

Approach

The harbour lies on the SE corner of Elba.

Conspicuous On the N side of the bay two large modern hotels are conspicuous. On the S side Fort Focardo and the light tower within it are conspicuous. The citadel standing atop a rocky promontory immediately E of the harbour, and a church and spire within the citadel, are also conspicuous.

Mooring

Data 190 berths. Approx 25 visitors' berths. Max LOA 20m. Depths 2–7m.

Berth Go stern-to on the quay or pontoon where convenient. In the summer a couple of bossy *ormeggiatori* may assist you to berth. There are several concessions in the harbour. The harbour can be very crowded in the summer and it is often worthwhile anchoring off for the night and coming in mid-morning when some of the boats will have left. Some laid moorings, otherwise use your anchor. The bottom is mud and sand, good holding.

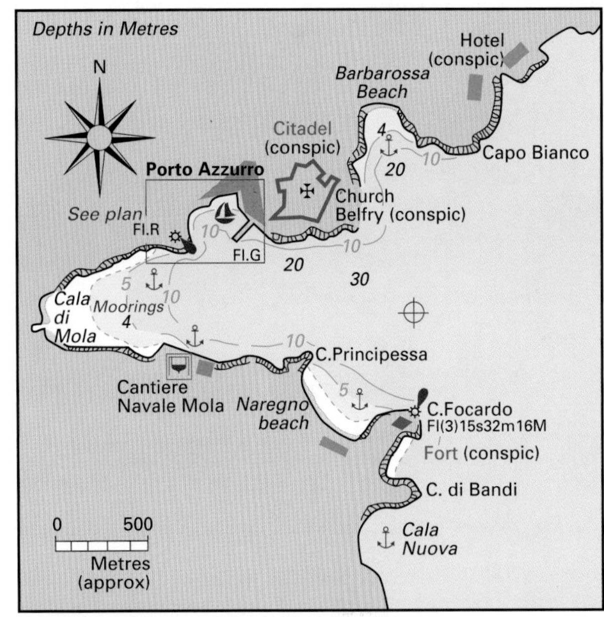

PORTO AZZURRO APPROACHES
⊕42°45´·6N 10°24´·6E

Shelter Excellent shelter although with a strong scirocco there is a surge in the harbour, more bothersome than dangerous. A number of boats are wintered afloat here.

Authorities Harbourmaster and customs. Charge band 5/6 (August).

Balfin Marina ✆ 0586 899 827 / 0565 951 102
Email info@balfinsrl.it
www.balfinsrl.it

Pontile Giovanni Messina ✆ 339 441 9634

Porto Luna Pontoon ✆ 0565 921 158 / 335 787 8832
Email portoluna@tiscali.it

Porto Azzurro looking SW. Note the pontoon layout has changed

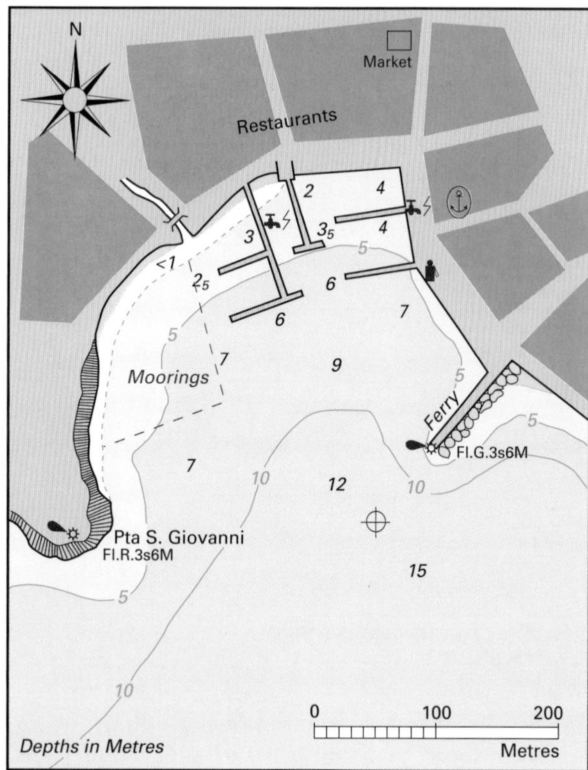

PORTO AZZURRO
⊕42°45'·7N 10°23'·9E

Facilities

Services Water and electricity on the quay. You will have to find the 'waterman' who will make a charge.
Fuel On the quay (0800–1930).
Repairs Cantiere Navale Golfo di Mola boatyard on the S side of the bay. 200-ton travel-lift. Most repairs. Limited mechanical repairs in the village. Chandlers.
C.N Mola ✆ 0565 968 692
Email info@golfomola.it
Provisions Good shopping for provisions. A supermarket and small covered market in the village.
Eating out Good restaurants and pizzerias although many are open for the summer only.

General

Crowded it may be, but Porto Azzurro is a gem. The citadel above was built by the Spanish in the middle of the 16th century. In the 19th and 20th centuries it was a prison for hardened criminals, both the political and mafioso type, and the original name of the fortress, Longone, has always been associated with criminals in Italy. The name of the village was changed to Porto Azzurro to break this association and attract tourists to this beautiful spot and, judging by the numbers of tourists arriving here in the summer, the ploy has worked wonderfully well.

ANCHORAGES AROUND PORTO AZZURRO

There are several anchorages around the large bay.

Barbarossa Beach The cove on the E side of the citadel above Porto Azzurro. The prevailing SE winds send a swell in here, but in northerlies or in calm weather it is a pleasant anchorage. Unfortunately moorings and a dive boat jetty in the NE corner leave very little room to anchor now.

Cala di Mola At the head of the bay. Moorings occupy much of the SW corner. The very end of the bay is shallow, but you can anchor 500m off the head in 4–8m on mud keeping clear of the ferry turning area. Good holding except in the NW corner where it is weedy. Good shelter, although there is some swell with S–SSW winds. There may be room to go stern-to among the charter yachts on the quay off the boatyard on the S side of the bay. It can be uncomfortable with any swell. Water and electricity. A charge may be made.

Naregno Beach Anchor under the lee of Capo Focardo in 6–12m on sand outside the buoyed swimming area. There is normally a reasonable lee from the prevailing southerlies here. A hotel and restaurant-bar ashore.

Porto di Cala Nuova

A large bay under Capo di Bandi which lies immediately S of Capo Focardo. The fort on Focardo is conspicuous. At the S end of the bay lies I. dei Topi. The bay is really only tenable in calm weather as the prevailing wind sends a swell in here. Anchor in any of the small coves in 5–10m. There are no dangers except close to the coast. The best anchorage is in the cove under Topi islet. There are some nice little beaches here and a wilderness of pine forest on the slopes around.

Cala del'Innamorata (Palazzo)

A small cove lying immediately N of the Isolotti Gemini. Care must be taken of the Scog. Corbelli and of the reef running SW from Isolotti Gemini in the southern approaches to the cove. Anchor in 2–4m on a sandy bottom. Open to the W–NW. Restaurant ashore.

Punta Morcone anchorage

A larger bay lying immediately N of Cala del'Innamorata. Anchor where convenient in 2–5m on a sandy bottom. Open to the W and really only suitable in calm weather. Small hotel and several restaurants ashore.

Golfo Stella

A large bay lying on the E side of Capo della Stella. Villas have been built on the slopes around the gulf and there are several camping grounds near the shore.

In calm weather or light SE winds, a yacht can anchor in the NE corner off Lido Beach but there is an uncomfortable swell with E winds. Anchor in 5–10m on sand.

At Ansa di Margidore in the NW corner there is a rough stone breakwater and a pontoon used by local boats. A small yacht can anchor fore and aft or anchor with a long line to the breakwater, although it is often crowded here. This NW corner is particularly attractive and behind the breakwater you have protection from all but strong southerlies. There are several camping grounds where provisions can be obtained and several restaurants close to the neck of the headland.

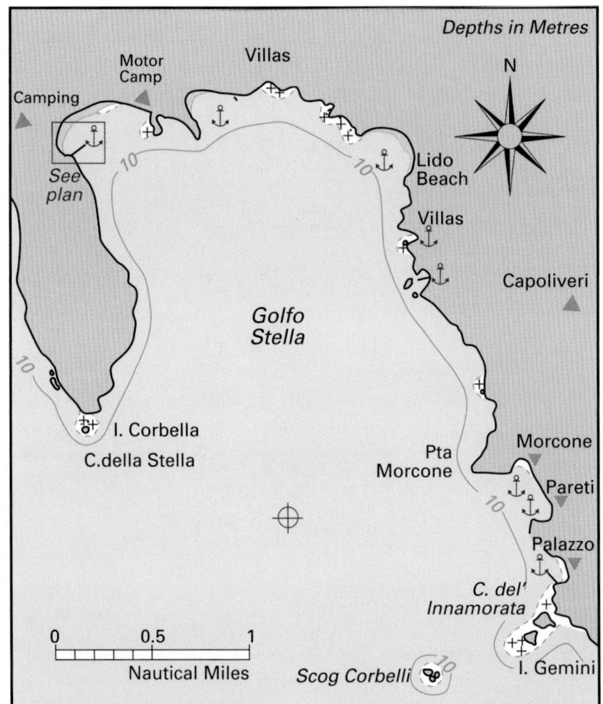

GOLFO STELLA
⊕ 42°43′·8N 10°20′·7E

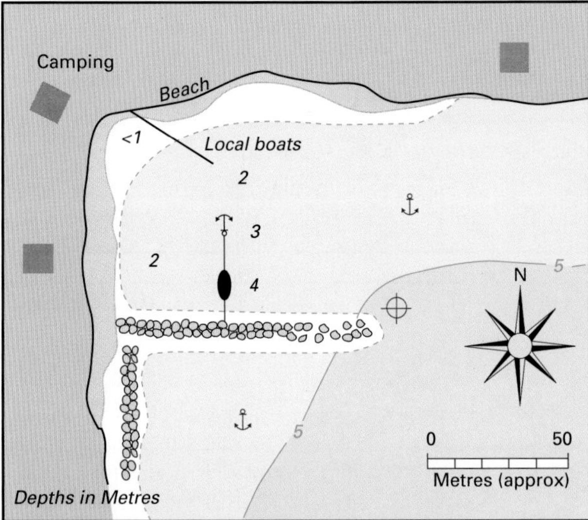

ANSA DI MARGIDORE (Golfo Stella)
⊕42°45′·6N 10°19′·3E

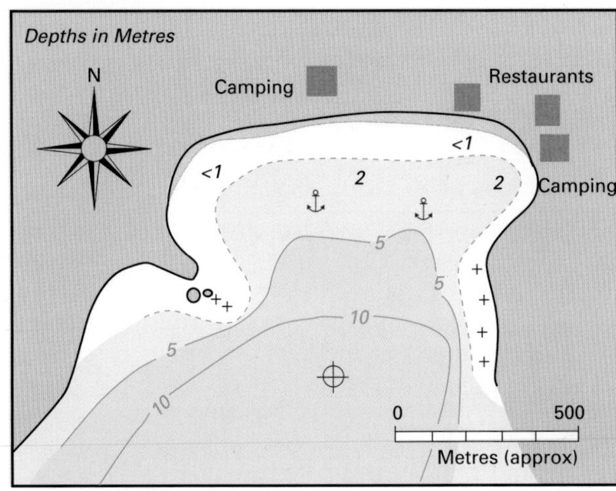

GOLFO DELLA LACONA
⊕ 42°45′·1N 10°18′·2E

GOLFO DELLA LACONA

A large bay on the W side of the promontory that terminates in Capo della Stella. Anchor where convenient at the head of the bay in 3–7m on a gently sloping sandy bottom. The best place here is tucked into the NE corner. Open only to the south. Numerous hotels and camping grounds ashore where you can find basic provisions and numerous restaurants scattered around the shore.

MARINA DI CAMPO

Approach

A small harbour on the W side of Golfo di Campo. The solid rock promontory dropping sheer into the sea at Capo Poro is easily identified.

Conspicuous The light structure on Capo Poro is not conspicuous, but the high promontory is. From the W and S the village and harbour of Marina di Campo cannot be seen. However the village of San Pietro di Campo, a tower in Pila and two villages on the slopes above the harbour are conspicuous. Closer in, the tower above the harbour and the harbour mole are visible.

By night Use the light on Capo Poro Fl.5s160m16M although the actual range appears to be about half the stated range. Closer in use the light immediately S of the harbour Fl.3s34m10M (range again about half of that stated).

Mooring

Berth Go stern-to the outer mole. Laid moorings at most berths. Mooring buoys outside the harbour for visitors. Large yachts may have to anchor off. The bottom is sand with a few rocks – good holding
Shelter Better than it looks but strong SE winds would make the harbour uncomfortable and possibly untenable with a southerly gale.
Authorities Harbourmaster and customs. *Ormeggiatori* administer berths and moorings. Charge band 4.
Anchorage Anchor off to the N of the harbour outside the buoyed swimming area in 4–7m on sand. The anchorage is open to southerlies although light southerlies tend to lift over the land leaving just a bit of uncomfortable slop rolling in. With moderate N–E winds the anchorage is reasonably secure.

Facilities

Services Water and electricity boxes on the quay, but you need to find someone switch them on. Alternatively a public fountain in the square nearby.
Fuel On the end of the inside mole (0800–1900).
Repairs 50/5-ton cranes. Limited mechanical repairs. Chandlers.
Provisions Good shopping for provisions. Supermarket near the river. Ice from the fish market.
Eating out Good restaurants, trattorias and pizzerias.
Other PO. Banks. ATMs. Buses to Portoferraio.

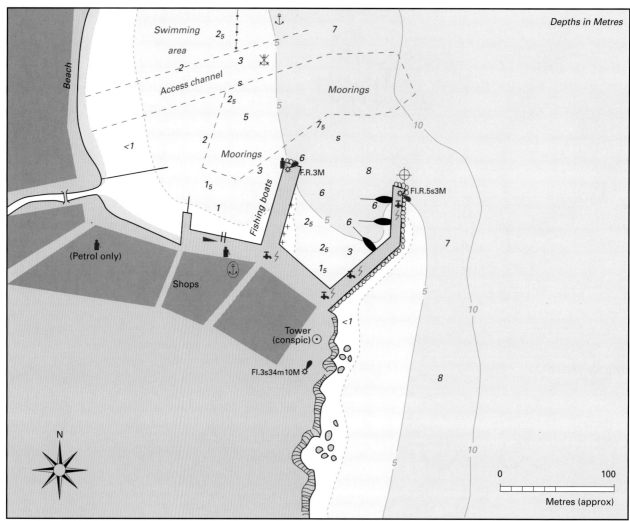

MARINA DI CAMPO
⊕42°44´·55N 10°14´·35E

General

Lying on the edge of a cultivated plain and hemmed in by mountains, Marina di Campo is an attractive and popular tourist resort. At the harbour you are close to the old part of town and away from the activity on the beaches further around the bay. The inner harbour is packed with trawlers adding a touch of colour and chaos to the place. Good fresh fish can be obtained at the fish market nearby.

Cavoli

⊕ 42°44′·2N 10°11′·0E

A U-shaped bay immediately W of Punta Cavoli. Open only to the south. The E half of the bay has a line of buoys across it in the summer marking off the bathing area. Local boats are kept on laid moorings around the rest of the bay. Anchor where possible in 3–5m. Restaurants and bars ashore.

Barbatoia (Fetovaia)

A bay tucked under the E side of Punta Fetovaia. The shelter is not as good as it might appear on the chart. Anchor in 2–8m where convenient. A number of local boats are kept here on permanent moorings in the summer. Although not well sheltered, it is a

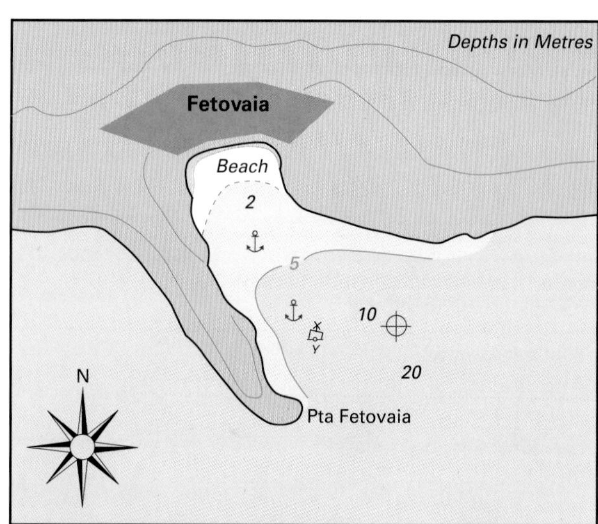

GULF OF BARBATOIA – FETOVAIA
⊕42°43´·6N 10°09´·5E

picturesque place and well worth a visit in settled weather. Restaurants and bars ashore.

San Andrea

⊕ 42°48′·5N 10°08′·5E

A bay and holiday resort approximately two miles W of Marciana Marina. Much of the bay is a restricted area and yachts should enter on the W side of the bay and anchor in a buoyed off area. The bay is entirely open to the N and really only suitable in calm weather. There is a short quay but it is mostly rock-bound. Restaurants and bars ashore.

MARCIANA MARINA

Approach

The harbour is not easy to identify from seaward as the rock breakwater blends into the coast.

Conspicuous The large elegant houses of the village and the tower near the root of the mole are conspicuous.

By night A beacon off the pontoon on the SW side is lit F.R but should not be relied on.

VHF Ch 16 and Ch 09 for Circolo della Vela.

Mooring

Data 150 berths. Max LOA 30m. Depths <1–7m.

Berth Go stern or bows-to the quay in the NW corner or stern or bows-to the pontoon on the S side of the harbour. Alternatively you may find a berth on the YC pontoon or on the concession pontoons off the breakwater. There are laid moorings at administered berths. If you have to use your own anchor there are numerous permanent mooring chains on the bottom, but they can usually be seen by day. The bottom is mud and clay over rock – generally good holding.

Marciana Marina looking west

Shelter Normally adequate in the summer. With fresh NE–E–SE winds it can be uncomfortable and with gales from the NE–E–SE the harbour can be untenable.

Authorities Harbourmaster. Club attendants on the pontoons. Charge band 4.

Circolo della Vela ✆ 0565 99027 *Fax* 0565 904 325
Email segreteria@cvmm.it
www.cvmm.it

Facilities

Services Water and electricity at most berths.

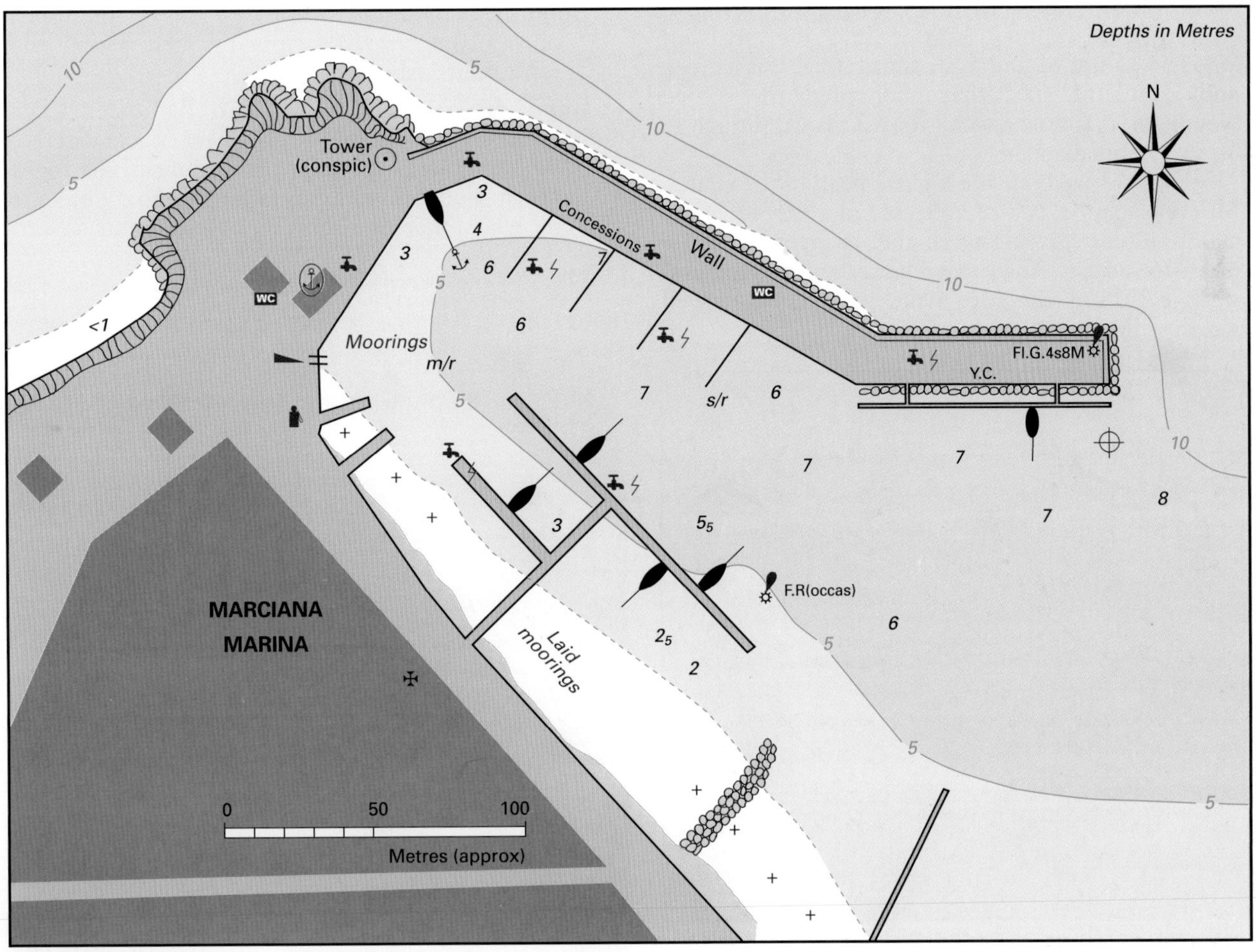

MARCIANA MARINA
⊕42°48´·5N 10°11´·9E

Marciana Marina looking south. Note more pontoons are now in place

Fuel On the quay although it is shallow off the quay.
Repairs A 50-ton crane available. Mechanical repairs. Chandlers.
Provisions Good shopping for provisions. Fish market. Ice factory near the village.
Eating out Good restaurants, trattorias and pizzerias.
Other PO. Banks. ATMs. Bus to Portoferraio.

General

This was once the fashionable quarter for a country residence in Elba and it is pleasing to this day: elegant 19th-century houses line the seafront amongst palms, oleanders and magnolia. It is a green and colourful spot that enchanted the exiled Napoleon. It is now a small tourist resort, though in no way spoiled.

Behind the harbour the highest peak in the island, Monte Capanne, can be ascended in a *cabinovia*, an aerial railway carrying small and, to my mind, quite precarious cages. The rugged hinterland around and the view from the top make an excursion well worthwhile.

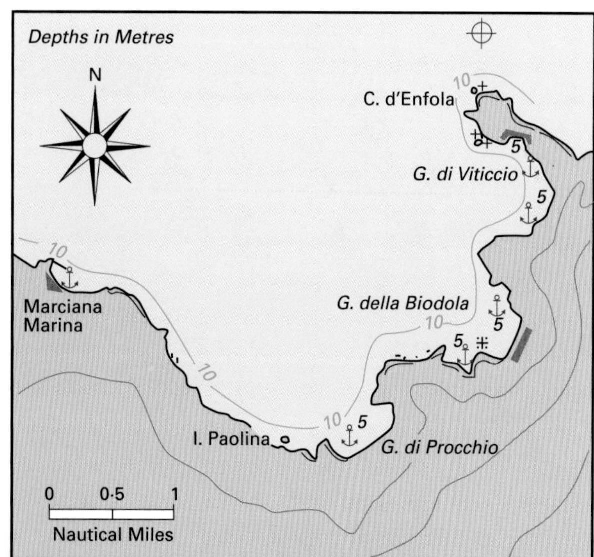

MARCIANA MARINA TO CAPO D'ENFOLA
⊕42°50′·25N 10°15′·8E (0·5M N of C. d'Enfola)

GOLFI DI PROCCHIO, BIODOLA, VITICCIO

To the E of Marciana Marina there are three bays affording reasonable shelter in settled weather.

Golfo di Procchio Anchor in 7–9m on sand outside the buoyed swimming area. A sandy beach ashore hemmed in by rock. The site of ancient Cervinia, where copper and iron was smelted, is nearby. Immediately to the W is an islet, christened locally as Isola Paolina, because, it is said, Pauline the sister of Napoleon, used to bathe here.

Golfo della Biodola Anchor in 6–8m off the beach outside the buoyed swimming area. Hotel and restaurants ashore.

Golfo di Viticcio The bay directly under Capo d'Enfola. Anchor in 4–10m where convenient. No swimming area, perhaps on account of the rocky beach. Under the isthmus joining Capo d'Enfola to the island there is a short pier. Restaurants ashore.

Elba. Golfo di Viticcio between Marciana Marina and Capo d'Enfola

Elba. Golfo della Biodola between Marciana Marina and Capo d'Enfola

Elba. SW corner of Golfo di Procchio between Marciana Marina and Capo d'Enfola

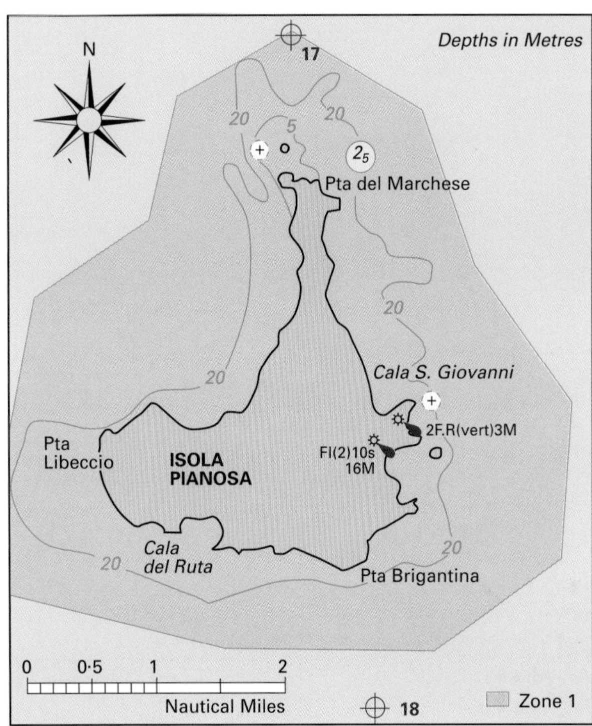

ISOLA PIANOSA

⊕17 1M N of Pte del Marchese (I. Pianosa)
42°39'·0N 10°04'·9E
⊕18 1M S of Pta Brigantina (I. Pianosa)
42°33'·2N 10°05'·5E

Isola Pianosa National Park

A prison island until 1997, Isola Pianosa is now part of the Tuscan Archipelago National Park.

Zone 1
Access, navigation, stopping, anchoring, fishing, swimming and diving prohibited within 1M.

✆ 0565 919 411
Email info@islepark.it
www.islepark.it

Isola Pianosa

In contrast to the other islands in the Tuscan archipelago, Pianosa is a low barren island nowhere more than 30m (100ft) high. From seaward you will see the buildings on the island before you sight the island itself. The only harbour is the small rock-bound harbour at Cala San Giovanni. The island is a National Park and all unauthorised vessels are prohibited to navigate within 1M of the island.

Formiche di Montecristo

⊕19 1M W of Scoglio Africa 42°21'·4N 10°02'·6E

A bank with an above-water rock, Scoglio Africa, on it, lying about 10 miles W of Isola Montecristo. Although Scoglio Africa is only just above water, the light tower on it, a round stone tower 15·8m (52ft) high, is conspicuous. A light is exhibited: Fl.5s12M.

Note The current in the vicinity of Formiche di Montecristo sets towards the E and can be quite strong at times. Although it is not reported anywhere, several yachts have experienced a magnetic anomaly in the vicinity of Formiche di Montecristo. On passage from Corsica to the Tuscan Islands this magnetic anomaly coupled with the E-going current can give you some headaches over your navigation.

Isola di Montecristo

A high conical island that dominates the seascape. Its highest point is at Picco del Segnale (648m/2126ft) and it slopes down more or less evenly to the sea. The island is a nature reserve and although there are no totally sheltered anchorages, there are several deep bays affording some shelter depending on the wind and sea. It is said to be infested with adders. Why Alexandre Dumas should have chosen Montecristo for *The Count of Montecristo* is not known, but his great 19th-century thriller has imbued the island with an aura that can still be felt. HM Denham records that a

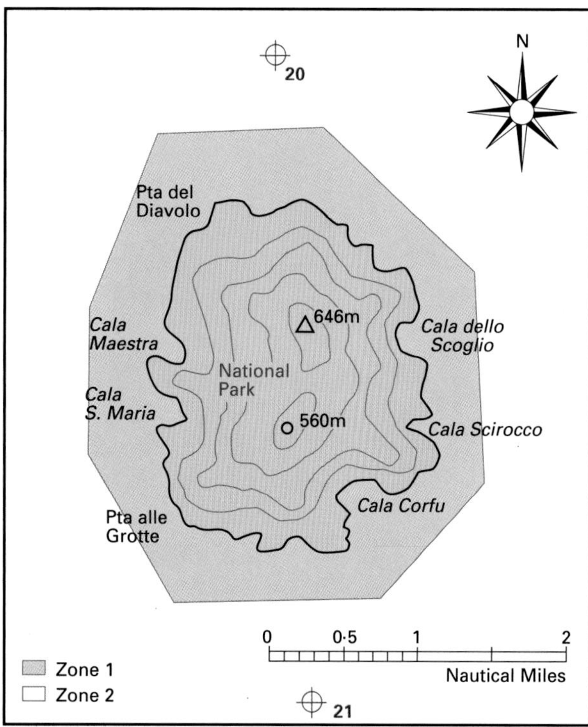

ISOLA DI MONTECRISTO

⊕20 1M N of I. di Montecristo
42°22'·0N 10°18'·8E
⊕21 1M S of I. di Montecristo
42°17'·8N 10°18'·8E

Isola di Montecristo National Park

Zone 1
Access, navigation, short- and long-time stays, anchoring, fishing, swimming and diving prohibited within 1,000m.

Zone 2
Extends up to 3M from the coast. Fishing regulated by park authorities.

Forest Warden ✆ 0566 40019 Park office ✆ 0565 919 411
Email info@islepark.it
www.islepark.it

number of eccentric individuals, including an Englishman who styled himself 'The Count of Montecristo', went to live on the island at the end of the last century.

Note The island is officially designated a nature reserve and, as such, anchoring and landing is prohibited, except in case of an emergency and with permission from the authorities in Elba. The wardens of the island take their job very seriously and will turn yachts away. This should be borne in mind if you are making a longish passage and expecting to find shelter for the night. I have retained the plans in the book as it might be necessary some time for a yacht to find refuge in bad weather.

Caution There can be violent gusts and wind-shifts up to a mile off the island. Care needed.

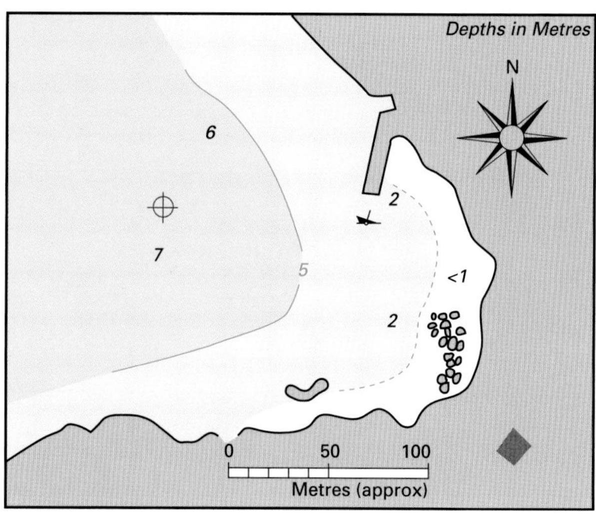

CALA MAESTRA
⊕42°20'·3N 10°17'·5E

Cala Maestra

A small cove on the W side. There is a small mole on the N side of the cove, but it is too shallow to use. Anchor in 5–7m. Open to the NW–W.

Cala Santa Maria

A bay immediately S of Cala Maestra. Anchor in 5–12m. Open to the NW–W. Immediately below Cala Santa Maria there is the small cove of La Mendolina open only to the west.

Cala Corfu

A deep bay on the SE side of the island. It is very deep until close to the shore. Open to the S and east.

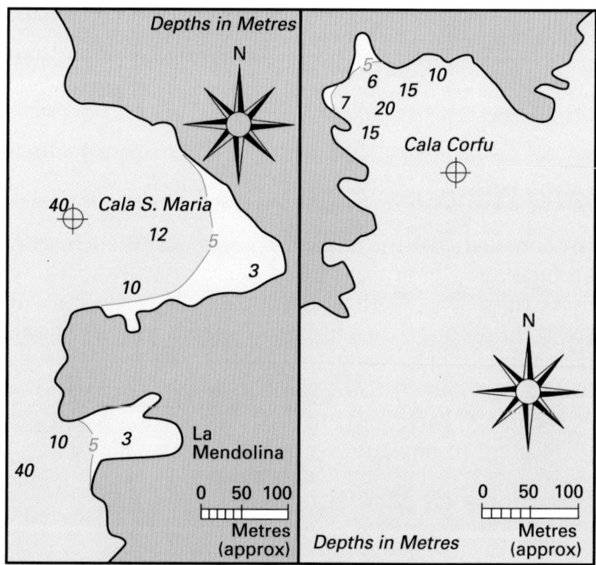

CALA SANTA MARIA
⊕42°19'·7N 10°17'·4E

CALA CORFU
⊕42°19'·1N 10°19'·2E

Isola del Giglio

A mountainous island lying approximately 25 miles E of Montecristo and separated from the mainland by a channel about eight miles across. Its coasts are steep-to and it rises to 498m (1,634ft) at Poggio della Pagana in the middle.

The harbour is on the NE coast where most of the population lives, but the old Aragonese walled village of Giglio (Castello) is still inhabited. Castello, some 400m (1,300ft) up the side of the mountain, was the refuge when pirates raided the islands. The old castle and walled village, all narrow alleys and crenellated walls, is well worth a visit. Isola del Giglio means literally 'the island of the lily': apparently it is covered with lilies in the spring.

⊕14 1M N of Pta del Fenaio (I. del Giglio) 42°24'·2N 10°52'·9E
⊕15 1M S of Pta del Capel Rosso (I. del Giglio) 42°18'·2N 10°55'·3E

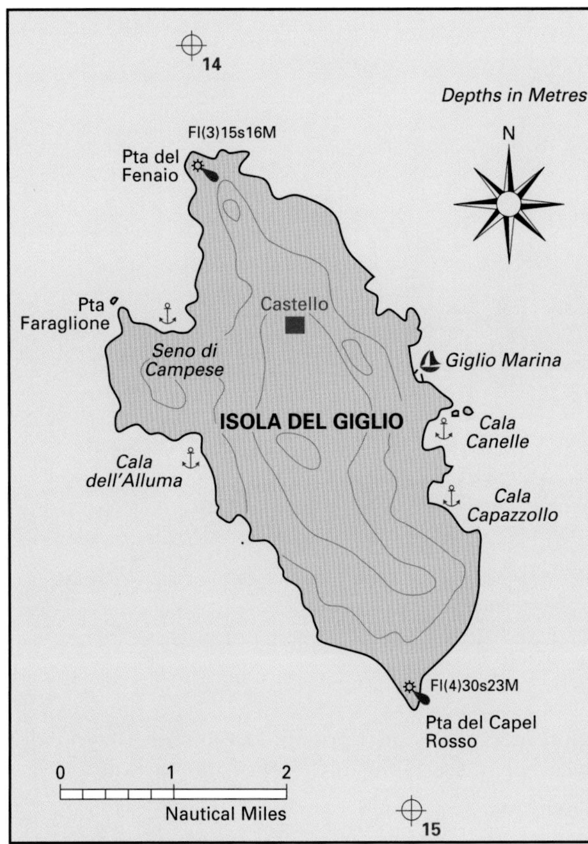

ISOLA DEL GIGLIO

GIGLIO PORTO (Giglio Marina)

Approach

Although the harbour is difficult to locate from the N and S, the castle and village of Castello are conspicuous.

Conspicuous Castello is easily identified. Closer in, the houses of Giglio Marina and the harbour moles will be seen.

VHF Ch 16 (0800–1300).

Mooring

Data 150 berths. 20 visitors' berths. Max LOA 20m. Depths <1–5m.

Berth Go stern or bows-to where directed. Most visitors' berths are on the N side of the outer pontoon. Laid moorings tailed to the pontoon. The harbour is very crowded in the summer and many berths are reserved for the summer months. The *ormegiatori* will let you know whether there is a berth with much shouting and waving. The large mooring chains on the bottom can normally be seen so if you need to the anchor can be placed safely away from them. If you do foul the chains there will be a local who makes a living from freeing fouled anchors.

Giglio Marina looking west

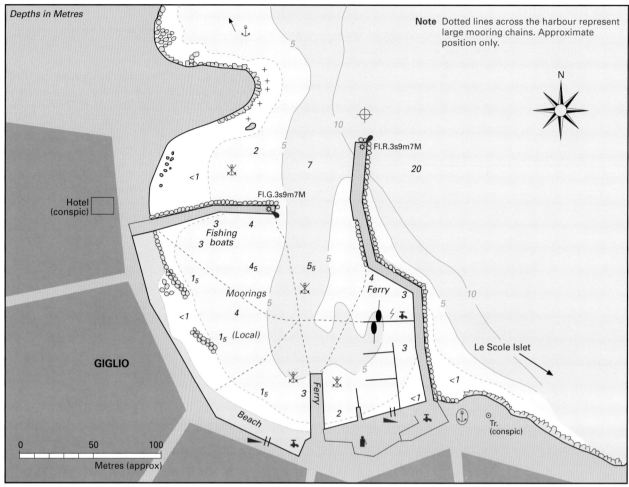

Depths in Metres

Note Dotted lines across the harbour represent large mooring chains. Approximate position only.

N
Fl.R.3s9m7M
Fl.G.3s9m7M
Hotel (conspic)
Fishing boats
Moorings
(Local)
Ferry
Le Scole Islet
GIGLIO
Beach
Tr. (conspic)
0 50 100
Metres (approx)

GIGLIO MARINA
⊕42°21′·65N 10°55′·2E

Shelter Good all-round shelter although even moderate N–NE winds make it uncomfortable.

Authorities Harbourmaster. *Ormeggiatori.* Charge band 4.

Ormeggiatori ☎ 0564 809 517

Anchorage In settled weather a yacht can anchor in Cala Canelle immediately S of the port under Le Scole rocks. Anchor at the head of the bay which is quite deep. It is also possible to anchor off in calm weather in the bight to the N of the harbour.

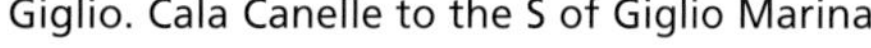

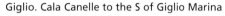

Giglio. Cala Canelle to the S of Giglio Marina

Facilities

Service Water and electricity (220V) on the quay. Water reported non-potable.

Fuel Close by on the waterfront.

Repairs 8-ton crane. Limited mechanical repairs. Chandlers.

Provisions Good shopping for provisions on the waterfront.

Eating out Restaurant and pizzerias in the summer.

Other PO. Bank. ATM. Ferry to Santo Stefano. Occasional buses to Castello.

General

The small harbour and village is picturesque. Tourism has revived the island's flagging economy but the inhabitants seem intent on making sure that the tourists don't despoil the island, with signs everywhere telling you not to drop litter, pick wild-flowers, or even make too much noise – Hooray Henries should stay away from here. Though tourism makes Giglio lively enough in the summer, in the winter it all closes down, wonderfully so. A bus runs approximately every hour to Castello and it repays the effort to make the trip. The energetic can walk up a footpath instead.

OTHER ANCHORAGES

South of Giglio Marina are two anchorages suitable in settled weather. In Cala Canelle anchor in 6–10m and in Cala Capazzollo in 5–10m. A sand over rock and weed bottom in both bays. Open SE.

Seno di Campese

A large bay on the NW of the island. Care should be taken of a reef with just 2m over it in the northern approaches. Faraglione rock and the tower at the NE end of the beach will be seen. Anchor in 3–8m off the beach on a sandy bottom, good holding.

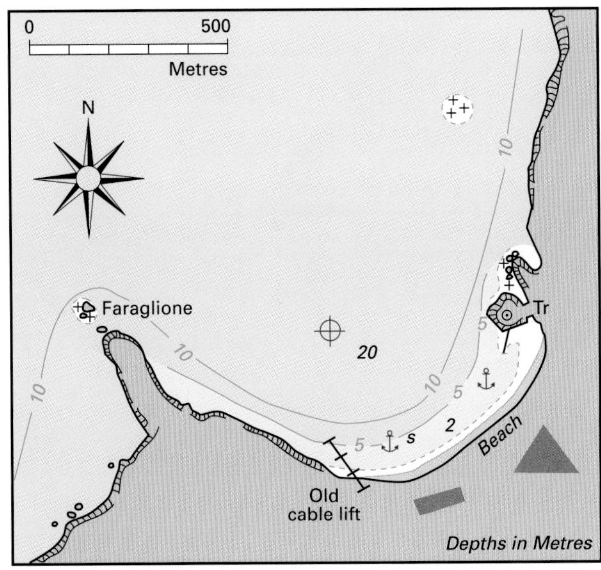

SENO DI CAMPESE
⊕42°22′·2N 10°52′·4E

Open to the W–NW but good shelter from southerly swells.

A holiday village and villas have been built around the slopes. Restaurants and bars open in the summer. Artisan food shops and a supermarket. Bus to Giglio.

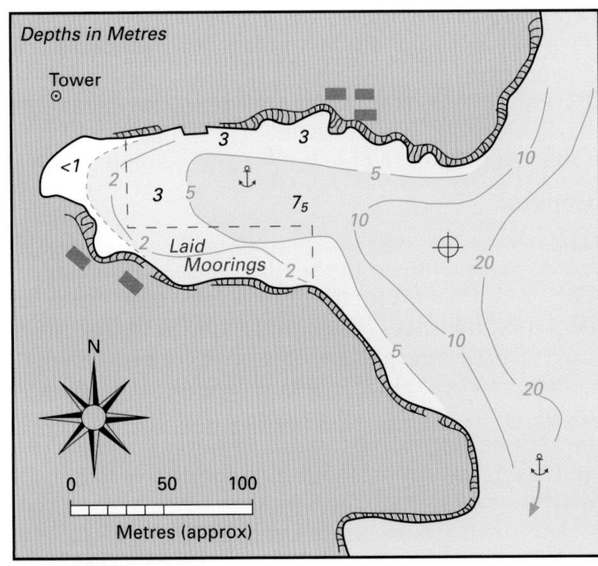

CALA SPALMATOI
⊕42°15′·15N 11°06′·5E

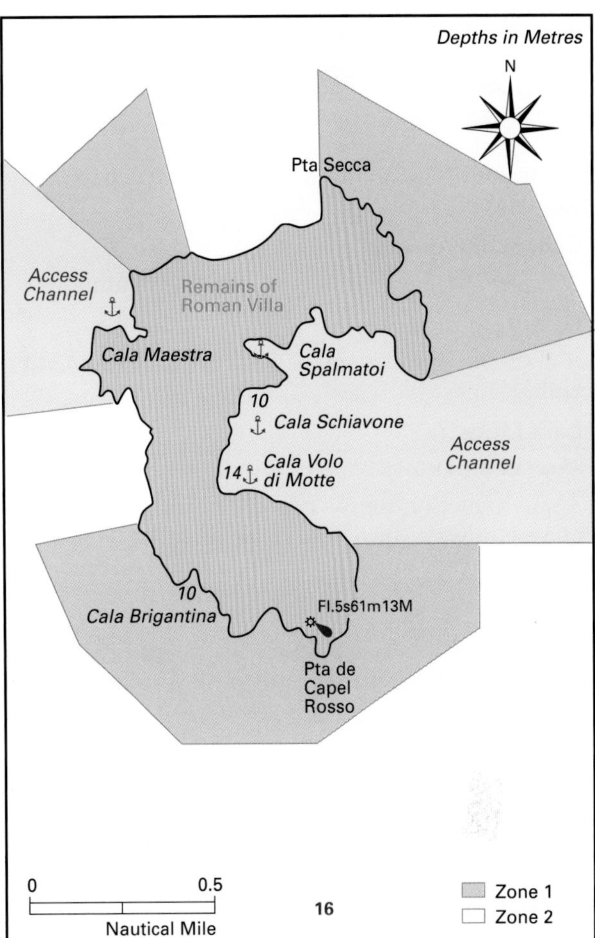

ISOLA DI GIANNUTRI

⊕16 1M S of Punta del Capel Rosso (I. di Giannutri)
42°13′·3N 11°06′·6E

Isola di Giannutri National Park

Part of the Tuscan Archipelago National Park since1996, the island and its waters are now a marine reserve.

Zone 1
Access, navigation, short- and long-time stays, anchoring, fishing, swimming and diving prohibited. Two access channels for vessels, to Cala Maestra and Golfo Spalmatoi.

Zone 2
Extends up to 3M from the coast. Fishing regulated by park authorities.

Isola di Giannutri

The southernmost and smallest island of the Tuscan archipelago, Giannutri is situated about 8½ miles SE of Isola del Giglio. It is barren and comparatively low-lying with the highest point, Punta Mezzogiorno (93m/305ft) near the southern end. Until recently it was barely inhabited, but villas and a development at Cala Spalmatoi have been built in the last few years. There are several anchorages on the E side suitable for yachts.

Cala Spalmatoi

A cove on the E coast offering good shelter from all but strong SE–E winds. Anchor in 5–8m where possible. The bottom is sand and rock, not everywhere good holding. There are numerous laid moorings for small craft obstructing the head of the inlet and you must tuck yourself in where you can. Ashore at the 'summer village' there is a hotel and restaurant. The path to Cala Maestra passes the Roman villa ruins.

Cala Schiavone

A rather deep and open cove just S of Spalmatoio.

Cala Volo di Motte

A deep and open bay in the SW corner of Spalmatoio Gulf.

Cala Maestra

⊕ 42°15'·3N 11°05'·5E

A small inlet on the W side of the island. The small quay is always busy and a yacht must anchor off where possible and take a line ashore. The bottom is sand with some rocks and not always good holding. Restaurant ashore.

Immediately N of Cala Maestra is a ruined Roman villa overlooking the sea. It is a pleasant walk from Cala Maestra to the villa, said to have been the property of Nero's mother.

The adjacent Tuscan coast: Marina di Carrara to Monte Argentario

MARINA DI CARRARA

BA 118
Italian 61

Approach

Conspicuous There are usually a number of cargo ships anchored off the harbour. A large apartment block immediately E of the harbour, the harbour moles, and cranes and loading gantries within the harbour are all conspicuous.

VHF Ch 12, 15, 16 for port authorities. Ch 16, 06 for Club Nautico.

Mooring

Data 250 berths. 10 visitors' berths. Max LOA 30m. Depths 3–8m.

Berth Go stern-to where directed at the yacht club. There are laid moorings tailed to the pontoons.

Yachts are also kept on moorings near the entrance to the harbour.

Shelter Good, although southerlies send in an uncomfortable swell. Local boats are wintered afloat.

Authorities Harbourmaster and customs. Club helpers who are friendly and helpful. Charge band 2/3.

Club Nautico di Carrara Marina ✆ 0585 785 150
Fax 0585 785 364
Port Authority ✆ 0585 787 205 *Fax* 0585 788 346
Email info@portauthoritymdc.ms.it
www.portofcarrara.it

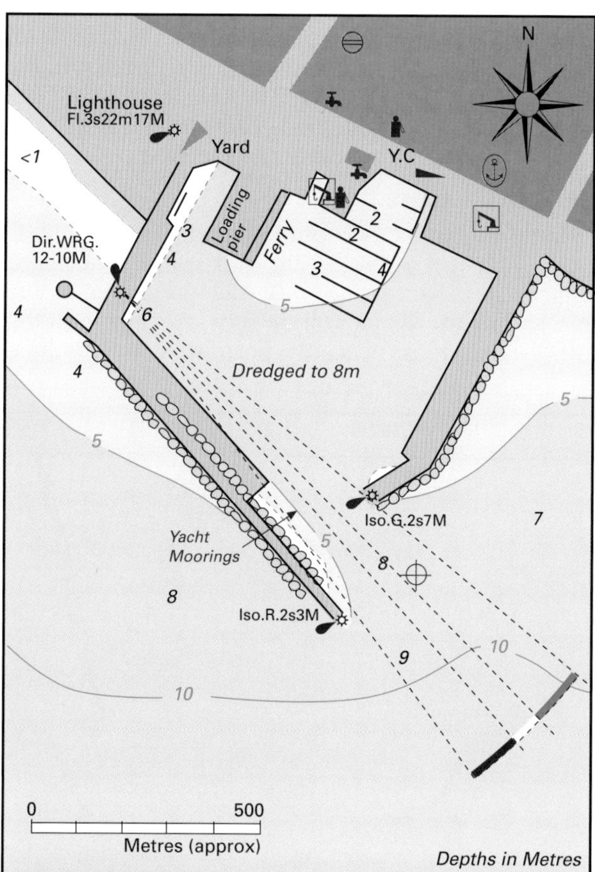

MARINA DI CARRARA
⊕44°01´·62N 10°02´·61E WGS84

Facilities

Services Water and electricity at or near most berths. For potable water use the tap near the entrance to the harbour compound. Showers and toilets at the clubhouse.

Fuel On the quay nearby.

Repairs Cranes up to 150 tons. Larger yachts can be hauled on a slip in the N corner. Good repair facilities at the harbour. Mechanical and engineering repairs. Electrical and electronic repairs. GRP and wood repairs. Sailmakers. Chandlers.

Provisions Good shopping for provisions in the town nearby.

Eating out Restaurants and pizzerias near the harbour, others in the town.

Other PO. Bank. ATM. Italgaz and Camping Gaz.

General

The harbour is used for the shipment of the Carrara white marble mined in the hinterland. Michelangelo favoured Carrara marble and it is still much in demand. In his day chisels and wooden wedges were used to prise out the marble whereas today dynamite splits the rock along natural fissures. The marble industry is much in evidence around Carrara, everything from tombstones and statues to chess sets and ashtrays in the souvenir shops are made of marble.

The town itself is a pleasing low-key resort with some elegant old buildings lining the grid-like

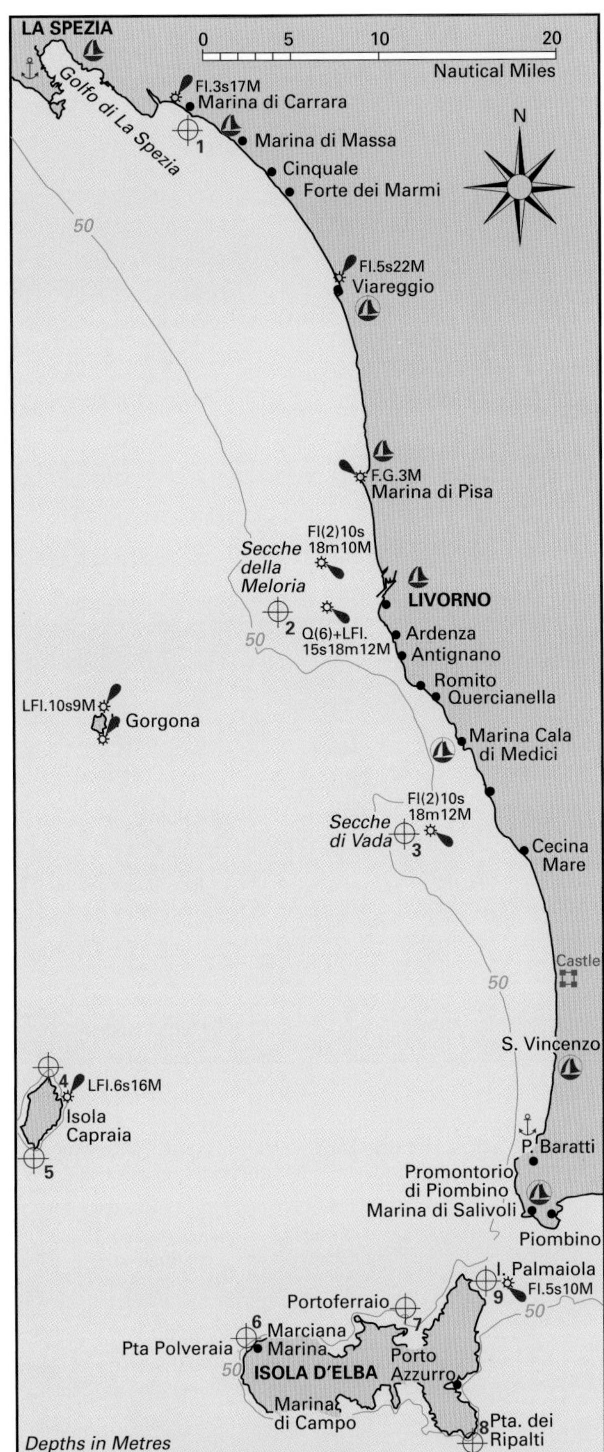

MARINA DI CARRARA TO PIOMBINO

streets. Also in Marina di Carrara are the original headquarters of two of the leading electronic chart producers, C-Map and Navionics.

Marina di Massa

⊕ 44°00'·3N 10°05'·8E

A pier off a seaside resort which can be used in calm weather. The end of the pier is lit 2F.GR(vert)3M. There are mostly 2–3m depths either side of the pier. Restaurants ashore.

⊕**1** 1M W of Marina di Carrara
44°01'·6N 10°01'·1E
⊕**2** 5M W of Secche della Meloria (S) light tower
43°32'·8N 10°06'·7E
⊕**3** 3M W of Secche di Vada light
43°19'·2N 10°18'·0E
⊕**4** 1M N of N end of I. Capraia
43°05'·2N 09°49'·5E
⊕**5** 1M S of S end of Capraia
42°59'·2N 09°48'·7E
⊕**6** 1M N of Pta Polveraia (Elba/NW corner)
42°48'·6N 10°06'·6E
⊕**7** 0.5M N of Scoglietto (Elba/Portoferraio approach)
42°50'·18N 10°19'·7E
⊕**8** 1M S of Pta dei Ripalti (Elba/SE corner)
42°41'·25N 10°25'·5E
⊕**9** 1M W of I. Palmaiola 42°51'·9N 10°27'·0E

Cinquale

⊕ 43°58'·6N 10°08'·4E

A small shallow harbour in the Cinquale canal about six miles SE of Marina di Carrara. New *porto turistico* pontoons lie further up the canal, beyond two bridges, and protected by a wave-breaker pontoon. There are reported depths of 1·5–2m at the entrance but depths are less inside. The entrance is lit F.R.7m3M/F.G.7m3M. The small basin inside is entered through a lock-gate and only light displacement power boats are moored inside.

Data 240 berths. Max LOA 12m. Depths 1–1·5m.

Water and electricity at all berths. Fuel quay.

Forte dei Marmi

⊕ 43°57'·2N 10°09'·8E

A summer resort about 13 miles from Marina di Carrara. A pier extends from the beach with depths of 5m at the extremity and 2–3m for most of its length. The extremity of the pier is lit F.R.6m3M. In calm weather a yacht can go alongside. Provisions and restaurants ashore.

VIAREGGIO

Approach

The harbour lies about six miles SE of Forte dei Marmi. The coast is everywhere flat with continuous beach backed by pine forest.

As part of the 'Safe Sea Net Harbour System' introduced in December 2009, all vessels over 300GRT are required to contact a local ship agent 24hrs in advance of their arrival, or at the earliest opportunity, for entry and berthing arrangements.

Conspicuous The large hotels bordering the beach in the vicinity of Viareggio are conspicuous, particularly one which has two square towers (Hotel Reale). A large travel-hoist in one of the yards is also conspicuous. Closer in, the harbour breakwaters are easily identified.

By night The entrance lights can be difficult to pick up against the loom of the town lights (including some bright neon lights) behind.

VHF Ch 16 for port authorities/harbourmaster Ch 12, 16 for the marina (24hr).

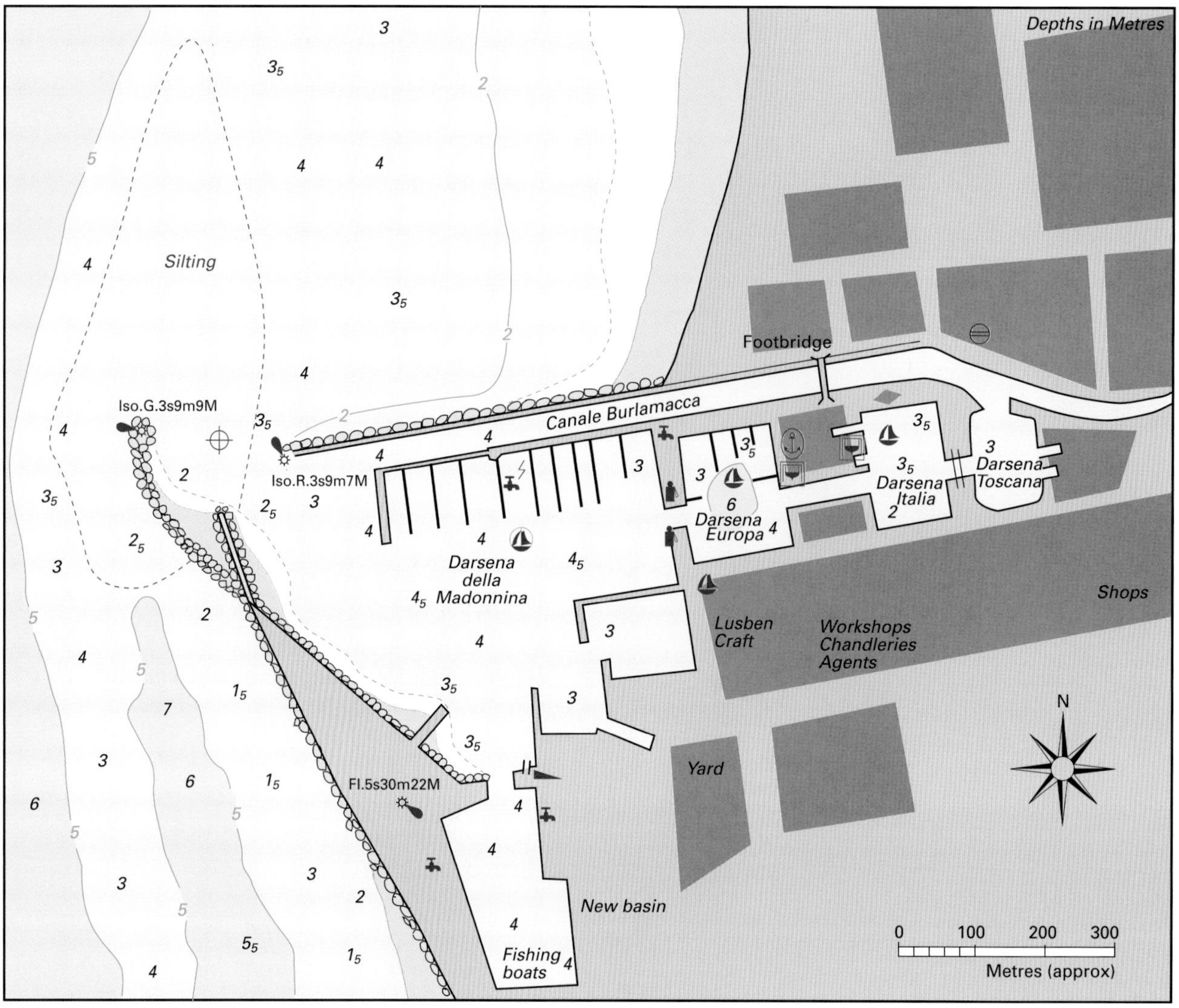

Depths in Metres
Silting
Iso.G.3s9m9M
Iso.R.3s9m7M
Canale Burlamacca
Footbridge
Darsena della Madonnina
Darsena Europa
Darsena Italia
Darsena Toscana
Shops
Lusben Craft
Workshops Chandleries Agents
Fl.5s30m22M
Yard
New basin
Fishing boats
N
0 100 200 300
Metres (approx)

VIAREGGIO
⊕43°51´·7N 10°14´·1E

Viareggio looking NE across the entrance, with Viareggio Porto Marina berths and Darsena Europa beyond *Superyacht Services*

Dangers With strong westerlies and particularly southwesterlies (*libeccio*) there is a heavy swell at the entrance. Extreme caution is needed when entering or leaving under these conditions.

Note The harbour approaches are gradually silting. Yachts need to take care in the immediate approaches where the sand bar has least depths of 3m in places. The sand bar extends for at least 600m NNE from the end of the breakwater. Approach should be made on a course due E towards a conspicuous hotel on the shore. When the light Iso.R.3s9m7M bears 220° turn towards the entrance, keeping close to the E side when entering. It is recommended that yachts with a draught of 2·5m plus call up on VHF Ch 16 to request a pilot.

Mooring

Data 1,800 berths. 80 visitors' berths. Max LOA 85m. Depths 2–4m.

Berth Yachts up to 18m LOA should head for Viareggio Porto marina in Darsena della Madonnina. Yachts may also find a berth in Darsena Europa, or alongside in Canal Burlamacca. Superyacht Services can arrange berths for 24–70m LOA. Lusben Craft may also have berths. Otherwise arrange a berth through the yacht agents.

Shelter Excellent.

Authorities Port police and customs. Marina staff. Charge band 6 in the marina (Viareggio Porto). Charge band 6 at Lusben Craft. A charge may be made in Canal Burlamacca.

Marina Viareggio Porto ✆ 0584 32033
Email prenotazioni@viareggio-portospa.it
www.viareggioporto.com

Superyacht Services Yacht Agency ✆ 328 057 9847
Fax 0584 943 080
Email info@superyachtservices.it

Vannucci Yacht & Ship Agents ✆ 0584 46553
Email info@agenziavannucci.it

Lusben Shipyard ✆ 0584 380 1400

Facilities

Services Water and electricity (220/380V) at or near all berths. Wi-Fi. Toilets and showers. Pump-out.

Fuel On the quay at the entrance to Darsena Europa.

Repairs Craft up to 60m long and up to 1,000 tons can be hauled and stored under cover. Four travel-lifts up to 600 tons. Mechanical and engineering repairs. Electrical and electronic repairs. GRP and wood repairs. Sailmakers. Chandlers. Repairs of all kinds to a very high standard can be carried out in a number of yards. The yards of Perini Navi and Lusben (Azimut/Benetti) are probably the two best known yards.

Provisions Good shopping for all provisions. Excellent fish stalls at the harbour.

Eating out Good restaurants, trattorias and pizzerias nearby and in the town.

Other PO. Banks. ATMs. Italgaz and Camping Gaz. Hire cars.

Darsena Europa looking NE towards the Alpi Apuane mountains

Drop nets at the mouth of the Arno River

General

Viareggio is a popular and crowded summer resort. It is renowned for its carnival (late January to March) when there are colourful parades and masquerade balls. But for the yachtsman the fascination of Viareggio must lie in the two boatyards of Perini Navi and Lusben Craft. Between them these two build some of the largest and most luxurious yachts in the world. Several years ago most of the large craft made here were steel, but the new generation of super cruisers are mostly being built with aluminium superstructures to keep the weight down. Increasingly large yachts in GRP are also being built.

The amount of money involved is staggering to ordinary mortals like me, and on a boring day motoring down this coast I worked out that in a whole season I use something like one-third of the daily (yes, daily!) fuel consumption of a friend who runs a comparatively small 22m Benetti. Not only that, but for my one-third consumption I cover ten times the distance he does, not counting the distances I sail, though at a more modest 5kns compared to his 20.

Note GPS anomalies have been reported in this area.

MARINA DI PISA (BOCCA D'ARNO)

Approach

Marina di Pisa is the name of the town on the south bank of the river Arno which runs down through Pisa to the sea.

Conspicuous The entrance to the river can be difficult to identify. Breakwaters extend from either side of the river mouth and arrayed along both walls are large drop-nets on gantries. On the south side of

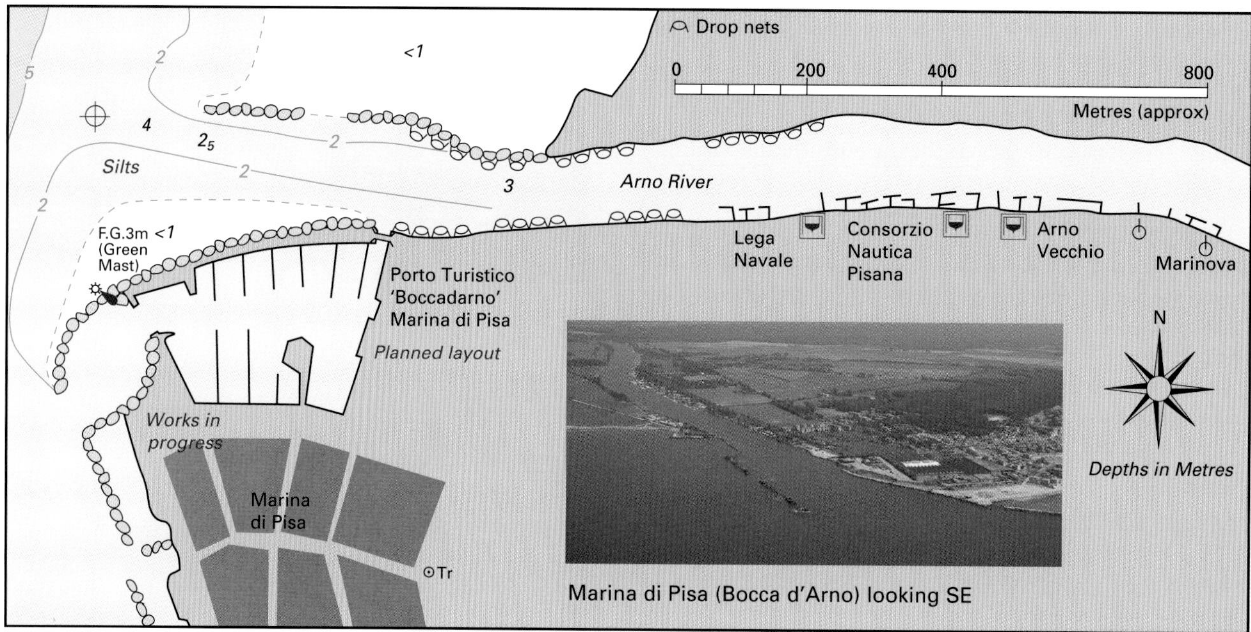

Marina di Pisa (Bocca d'Arno) looking SE

MARINA DI PISA
⊕43°40'·8N 10°16'·2E

the river mouth the town of Marina di Pisa is easily identified and on the river bank a large factory building is conspicuous.

Work is due to start on the new Boccadarno Marina (*see below*) on the S bank, and part of the development involves the redevelopment of the land where the factory stands. Expect work in progress on the S side of the approaches to the river.

By night A F.G.6m3M is exhibited at the extremity of the S breakwater, but a yacht should enter the river with caution on account of the dangers outlined below.

VHF Ch 16.

Dangers

1. There are usually depths of 3–4m on the N side of the river mouth and for some distance upstream. However it is reported that depths may sometimes be reduced to as little as 2m when prolonged strong onshore winds cause the entrance to silt. (The strong current flowing seawards clears the silt away when the onshore winds cease.) The position of the navigable channel varies from year to year. For some years now the channel is reported to be closer to the N side than the south.
2. With onshore winds there is an ugly swell at the river mouth and with strong winds there are breaking waves. A yacht should not attempt to enter or leave under these conditions.

Navigation upstream

In the river a current of up to 3kns, but usually less, may flow downstream and a yacht should have sufficient power to overcome this current. About 500m upstream, cables are stretched across the river and from them drop-nets are suspended. The estimated height from river to cable is about 18m (59ft) although near either bank of the river there is slightly more owing to the droop of the cables in the middle. To add to the problem, yachts must look out for the nets themselves – usually they will whoosh up out of the water when the net operator sees a yacht coming. Approximately 3½ miles upstream a bridge crosses the river and air height underneath this is perhaps 4·5m (15ft).

Mooring

Data c.500 berths. Visitors' berths. Max LOA 15m (Marinova) to 20m (Arnovecchio). Depths 2·5–3·5m.

Along the S bank of the Arno there are numerous small T-shaped catwalks and pontoons. Both Marina Arnovecchio and Marinova have been recommended, but there are many others. There are currently no visitors' berths at Lega Navale. Laid moorings at most berths.

Shelter Excellent inside the river. The only hazard may be logs floating downstream.

Authorities Harbourmaster. Charge band 3.

Marina Arnovecchio ✆ 050 35030 / 348 234 4136
Email limqg@tin.it

Marinova (Mauro Favati) ✆ 050 355 88 / 050 310 037
Fax 050 357 37
Email marinova@alice.it

Cantiere Fontani ✆ 050 960 075

Lega Navale ✆ 050 36652

Facilities

Water and electricity at most berths. Fuel at Lega Navale. Showers and toilets at most bases. A number of travel-lifts and cranes at the yards. Some places have a small café bar, or it is about half a mile into Marina di Pisa where there are numerous restaurants and bars and good shopping for provisions. Excellent fish stalls on the S bank of the river mouth.

The unmistakable 'leaning tower' of Pisa

General

The river Arno is a pleasant place with tall trees growing over the river banks. It is a completely safe place to leave a yacht if a visit to Pisa and the famous leaning tower is planned and many yachts overwinter afloat and ashore here.

The 'Leaning tower of Pisa' was finally completed in 1319 as the *campanile* or bell tower for the adjacent cathedral in Piazza del Duomo, and its tendency to tilt became apparent even before it was completed.

The tower was closed for a decade when remedial work to improve stability took place. Soil extraction proved the most successful technique, 'righting' the tower by 45cm, and the tower reopened at the end of 2001.

It is about 11km into Pisa and buses run there from Marina di Pisa: enquire locally for the times.

A visit to Pisa should be made not only to see the infamous tower, but also to see a city that was the hub of the empire that vied with Genoa and Venice for Mediterranean real estate. The tower itself is a little austere, really just an adorned version of all those Pisan watchtowers dotted around the coast that make such good conspics. The Piazza where it stands is a wonderful example of a particularly Pisan twist on Romanesque architecture. The cathedral, the tower, and surrounding buildings bring a vibrancy to the Romanesque with different coloured marbles and little turreted balconies. You should allot a bit of time for just wandering around after you have taken the usual photo of friends holding up the leaning tower.

PORTO TURISTICO BOCCADARNO

A new marina development, just beginning, on the S bank of the entrance to the Arno river. All data below is for the completed project.

Approach

The entrance to the river is difficult to identify until close to. The town of Marina di Pisa along the coast to the S is easily seen.

Mooring

Data 475 berths. Max LOA c.20m. Depths 3–5m.

Shelter Should provide good all-round shelter.

Authorities Marina staff.

Boccadarno Porto di Pisa ✆ 050 36142
www.portodipisa.it

Facilities

All marina facilities can be expected.

General

The project to build a marina here has gone through many incarnations and designs over the last decade or so, but it looks as if things are moving now, and construction is starting, although no completion dates are available yet.

Meloria Reef (Secche della Meloria)

This is a large patch of reefs and shoal water lying off Livorno. It is marked by towers on the N and S side. The N tower, round, white, 20m (66ft) high Fl(2)10s18m10M lies about four miles NW of Livorno. The S tower, round, black with a yellow top, 17m (5ft) high Q(6)+LFl.15s18m12M, stands on rocks about three miles W of the port. There is also a square unlit tower near the S tower proper. The E side of the reef is marked by an E cardinal buoy, BYB, and lit Q(3)10s5m7M. Shoal water over the area varies in depth between 5·5m and 0·9m (18–3ft) with breaking seas in strong southerlies and westerlies.

Currents

In the summer with NW winds a strong S-going current sets down between Meloria Reef and the coast. Conversely with persistent southerlies a N-going current sets to the N between the reef and the coast.

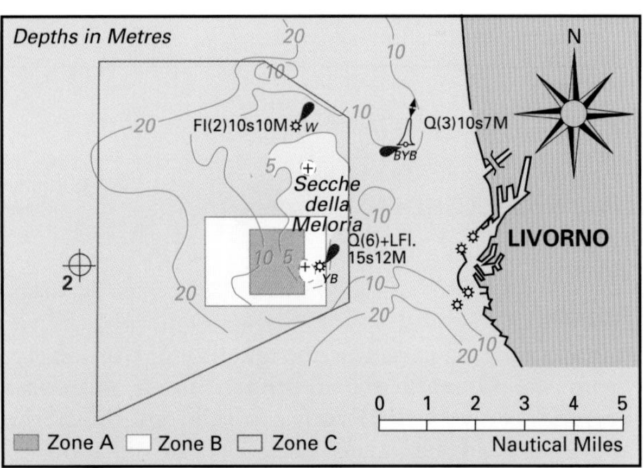

APPROACHES TO LIVORNO (SECCHE DELLA MELORIA)

⊕2 5M W of Secche della Meloria (S) light tower
43°32′·8N 10°06′·7E

AMP Secche della Meloria

The most sensitive parts of the reef are now protected and lie within Zone A of the reserve, where all unauthorised navigation is prohibited.

In Zone B navigation by jet skis and motor boats is restricted. Maximum speed 5kns. Anchoring and mooring is restricted.

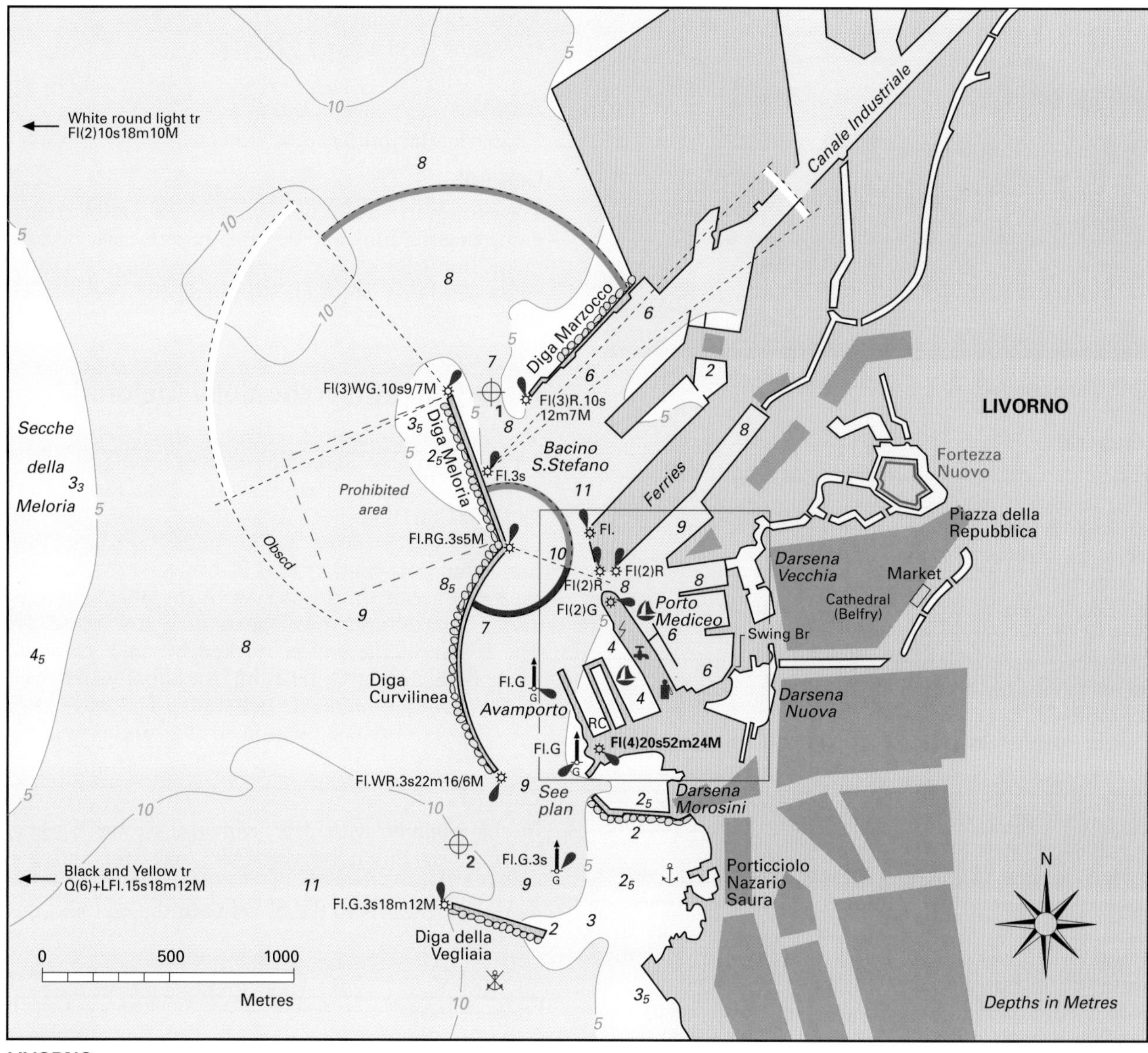

LIVORNO
⊕ **1** 43°33′·45N 10°17′·4E
⊕ **2** 43°32′·45N 10°17′·3E

LIVORNO (LEGHORN)

BA 119
Italian 62

Approach

In the approach care must be taken of Meloria Reef. From the N make the approach along the coast keeping between ½–1½ miles off. From the S the approach can be made between ESE around to south. Entrance into the harbour can be through either the N or S entrance.

Conspicuous The towers at the N and S ends of Meloria Reef have already been mentioned and stand out well. From the N the tall chimneys and storage tanks of the oil refinery immediately N of Livorno are conspicuous. From the S a number of radio masts on the coast are conspicuous. In the port the lighthouse (a round tower 52·4m (172ft) high), the grain silos, and the cranes within the harbour are conspicuous.

By night Use the main light in the Avamporto Fl(4)20s52m24M. The flare(s) from the oil refinery to the N of the harbour also show up well.

VHF Ch 10, 16 for port authorities. Ch 14 for pilots. Ch 09 for the YC.

Danger With strong SE winds a confused swell occurs at the entrances to the outer harbour.

Mooring

Data 120 berths. Visitors' berths. Max LOA 30m. Depths 3–6m.

Berth Go stern or bows-to the YC pontoon in Porto Mediceo. Alternatively try Porto Mediceo pontoons in the SE corner. Circolo Nautico Vela may also have a short-term berth on the pontoon in the SW corner. Larger yachts may find a berth at Lusben (Azimut/Benetti) also in the SW corner. There are laid moorings tailed to the quay or a small buoy at most berths.

Shelter The pontoons in Porto Mediceo offer good all-round shelter, although berths here are subject to wash from ferries and fishing boats. With moderate onshore winds there is a bit of surge at some berths, more uncomfortable than dangerous.

Livorno looking SE

Looking NW across the yacht berths in Porto Mediceo, Livorno

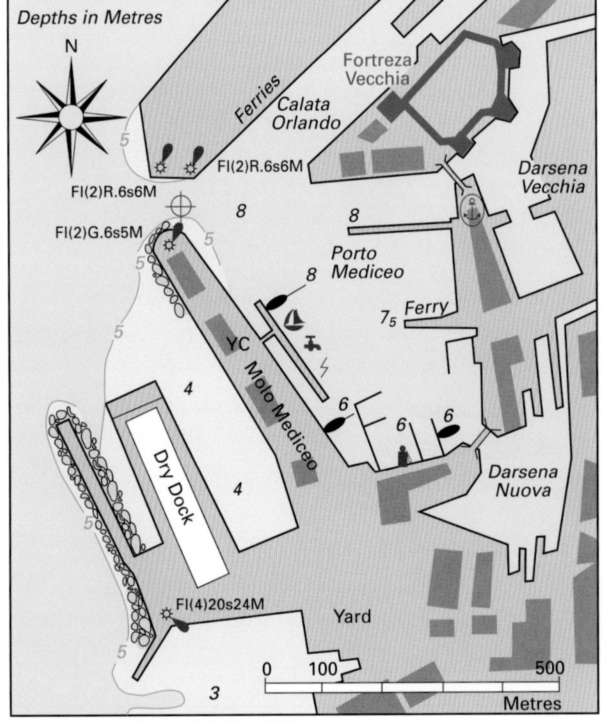

PORTO MEDICEO (LIVORNO)
⊕43°33′·1N 10°17′·8E

Authorities Harbourmaster and customs. Charge band 3/4.

Yacht Club Livorno ✆ 0586 807 354
Porto Mediceo ✆ 0586 887710
Livorno Port Authority ✆ 0586 249 465 / 411
Fax 0586 249 514
Email info@porto.livorno.it

Note Darsena Vecchia is used by fishing boats and some local yachts. There are no places for visiting yachts.

Facilities

Services Water and electricity at or near most berths.
Fuel On the quay in Porto Mediceo.
Repairs Cranes up to 40 tons and slipways up to 500 tons. Mechanical and engineering repairs. GRP and wood repairs. Electrical and electronic repairs. Sailmakers. Chandlers.
Provisions All provisions can be obtained in the town, a short walk away. Excellent indoor and outdoor markets.
Eating out Restaurants, trattorias and pizzerias in the town.
Other PO. Banks. ATMs. Hospital. Italgaz and Camping Gaz. Hire cars. Bus to Genoa.

General

Livorno is a large industrial port, shipping mostly bulk cargo and petroleum, but in Porto Mediceo you are tucked away from the worst of the industrial quarter. The port and the town have important historical associations and parts of the town, including the old harbour, have fine 16th- and 17th-century buildings. Cosimo I de'Medici built a canal to link Livorno and Pisa in 1573 and began work on the harbour. In 1620 the Porto Mediceo, Port of the Medicis, was completed under Cosimo II. The two 15th–16th-century explorers Amerigo Vespucci (who gave his name to America) and Giovanni da Verrazzano, were both sons of this city, and it was from here that Shelley left on his fateful last voyage back to Lerici.

With much of the city destroyed during the last war, Livorno is in part a modern city, while the many old merchants houses lining narrow canals around the Nuova Venezia quarter lend it an air of aged elegance. It is well worth a wander around, using the canal as a route, taking in the market, Piazza della

Repubblica (the largest bridge in Europe) and the Nuovo Fortrezza. For the Natural History museum and aquarium you will need to take a bus or taxi.

Porticciolo Nazario Saura

⊕ 43°32′·35N 10°18′·05E

In the S of the outer harbour there is the small harbour of Nazario Saura. The approaches and the port are very shallow (1m and less in places) and even small yachts are not advised to enter without local advice. It is crowded with the local boats of the yacht club there. (See plan for Livorno.)

ARDENZA

Approach

A small and mostly shallow harbour approximately two miles S of Livorno. The approach to the harbour should be made on a course of due E to avoid shoal water to the N and south.

CB Ch 30, 31, 32.

Danger Care is needed of the shoal water and the reef on the N side of the entrance.

Mooring

Data 260 berths. 30 visitors' berths. Max LOA 10m. Depths <1–1·8m.

Berth Where directed.

Shelter Strong onshore winds cause a surge but otherwise good shelter.

Authorities Harbourmaster. A charge is made.

Facilities

Water Near every berth.
Fuel About 500m from the harbour.
Repairs 10-ton crane. Mechanical repairs. Livorno is nearby.
Provisions Minimarket nearby.

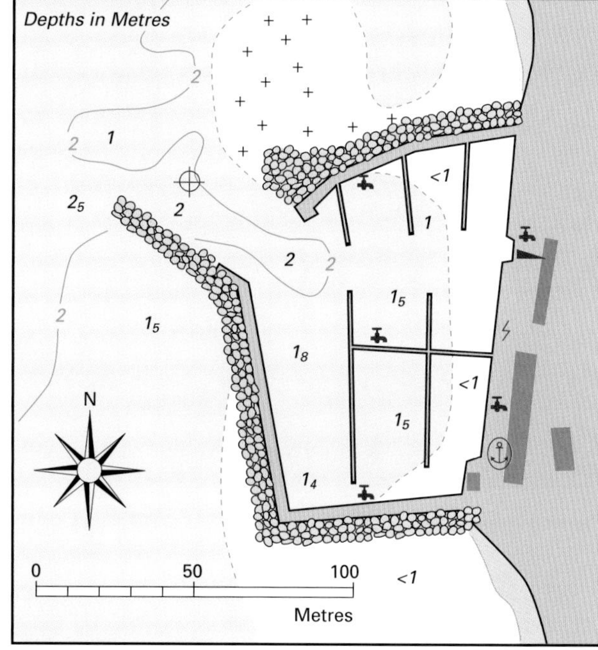

ARDENZA
⊕43°31´·0N 10°18´·9E

ANTIGNANO

A small shallow harbour approximately 3·5 miles S of Livorno. There are 1·5m depths in the entrance and the depths inside are less. With onshore winds there are breaking waves across the entrance and it is positively dangerous to enter or leave.

Water on the quay. Provisions and restaurants nearby.

Data 230 berths. Max LOA 9m. Depths <1–2m.

Ardenza looking ESE

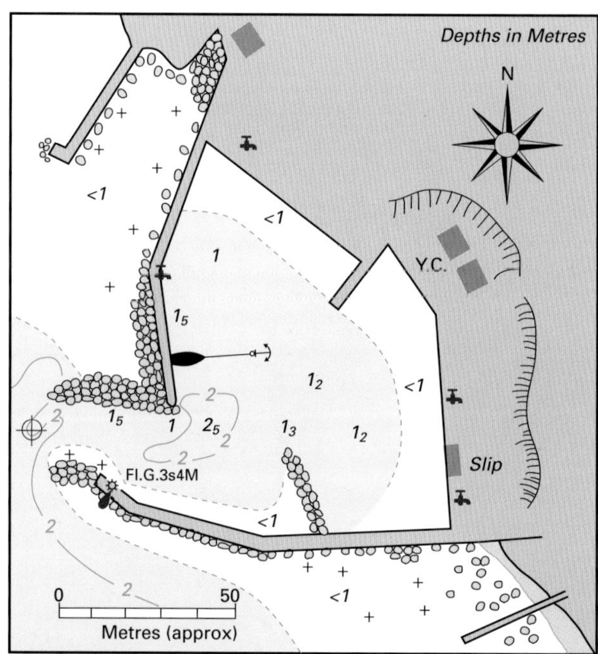

ANTIGNANO
⊕43°29´·7N 10°24´·6E

TORRE DEL ROMITO (CASTEL SONNINO)

A miniature harbour six miles S of Livorno. A castellated tower, a square tower, and a chimney in the bay are easily identified. The harbour is very small and usually crowded, but in settled conditions a yacht can anchor in the bay. The bottom is sand over rock, average holding only, and really only suitable as a lunch stop.

QUERCIANELLA

About 0·5 miles SE of Torre del Romito at Quercianella a rough mole gives some shelter from W winds. The end of the mole is lit F.R.7m3M. Only at the outer end of the mole is there sufficient depth for a small yacht to go bows-to with long lines onto the mole.

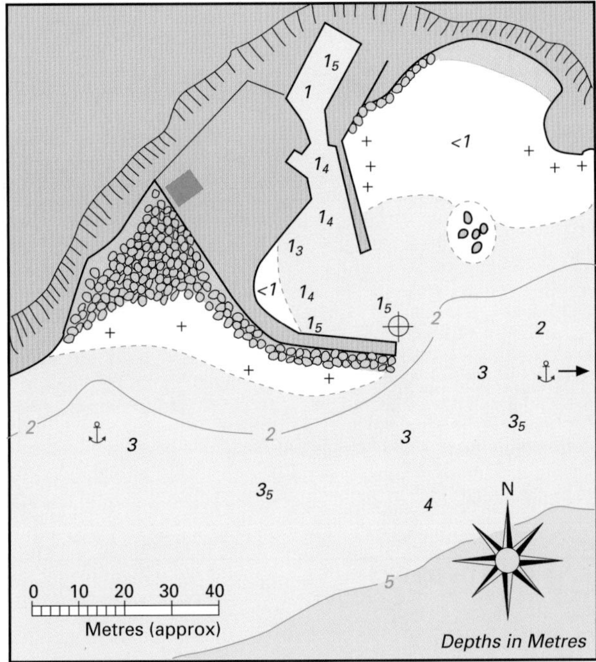

TORRE DEL ROMITO
⊕43°22'·5N 10°21'·5E

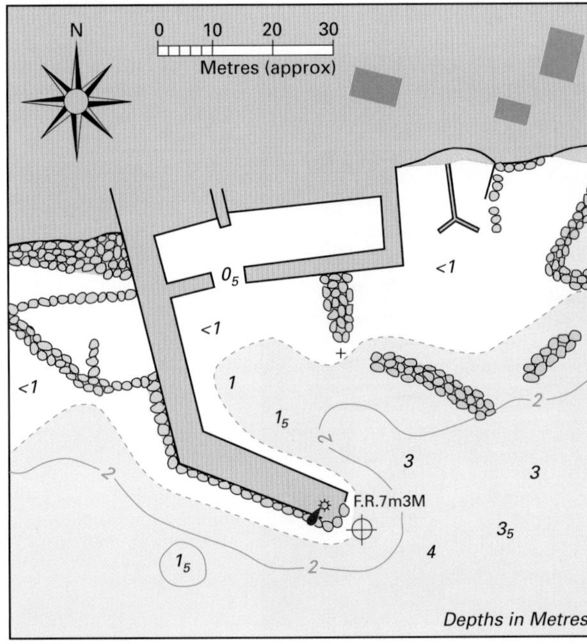

QUERCIANELLA
⊕43°27'·5N 10°21'·8E

Chioma

⊕ 43°26'·75N 10°22'·8E

This is a very small and shallow inlet protected by a rough breakwater. There are 1m depths in the entrance and 1–1·5m depths inside. The entrance should not be attempted with moderate or strong onshore winds.

Rossana

⊕ 43°26'·72N 10°22'·9E

Lies immediately S of Chioma. A rough breakwater provides some shelter from S winds. The approach should be made from the W as a reef with some above-water rocks extends from the coast in a westerly direction immediately N of the entrance. Although there are 4m depths in the entrance and 2m depths in the middle, most of the harbour is very shallow and rock-bound.

CASTIGLIONCELLO

On the S side of Punta Castiglioncello (on which there is a tower) there is a small harbour. Although there are 2m depths in the entrance most of the

Punta Castiglioncello looking SE

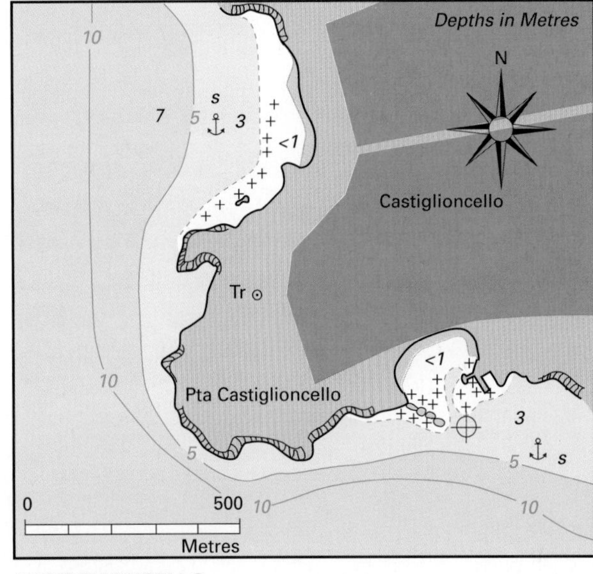

CASTIGLIONCELLO
⊕43°24'·15N 10°25'·3E

harbour is shallow and rock-bound. However a yacht can anchor on the N or S side of the headland depending on the wind direction. On the N side anchor in 4–5m on sand. Care needs to be taken of above- and below-water rocks off the coast. On the S side anchor off the tiny harbour in 5–8m on sand. Both anchorages are tenable only in settled weather. Provisions and restaurants in the village ashore.

MARINA CALA DE MEDICI (Rosignano Solvay)

Approach

This large new marina lies S of Castiglioncello, off the town of Rosignano Solvay. The high wall of the outer breakwater is easily identified. Care is needed in strong SW–NW winds as you will need to turn side on to the waves as you enter. Once inside there is good shelter and flat water.

Conspicuous The large industrial installations and long loading pier at Vada to the S of the marina are conspicuous.

VHF Ch 09 (24hr).

Dangers Secche di Vada lies in the S approaches to the marina (see below).

Mooring

Data 650 berths. 65 visitors' berths. Max LOA 40m. Depths 3–8m.

Berth Where directed. Marina staff will assist mooring. Laid moorings tailed to the quay.

Shelter Good all-round shelter inside the marina.

Authorities Marina staff. Charge band 6 (July–August).

✉ Marina Cala de Medici, Viale Trieste 6, 57013 Rosignano Solvay, Livorno ✆ 0586 795 211 / 348 311 1888
Fax 0586 764 553
Email info@calademedici.net
www.calademedici.net

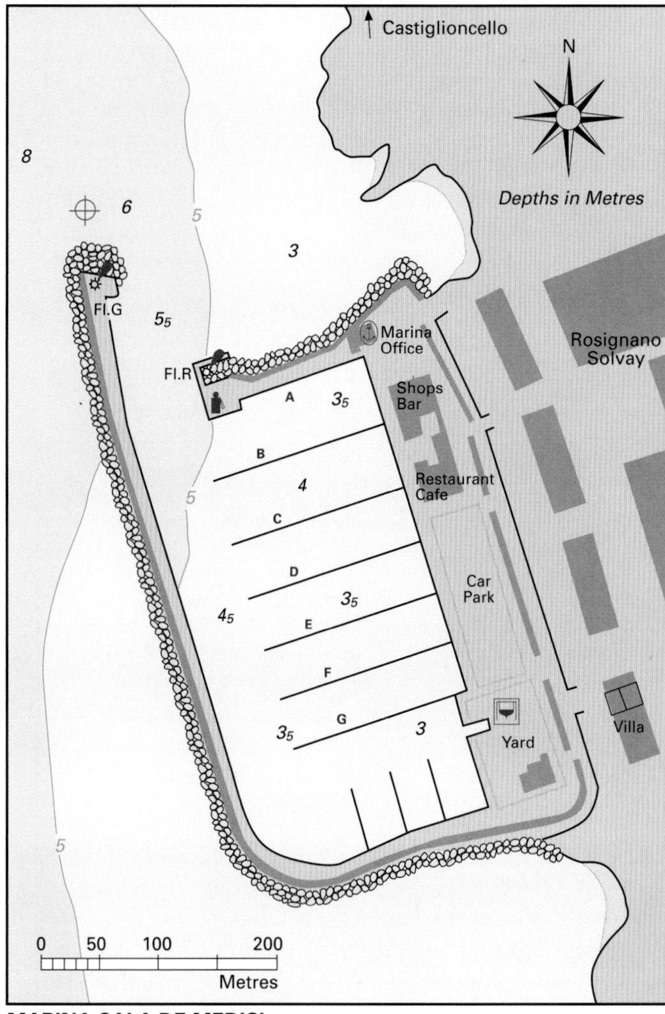

MARINA CALA DE MEDICI
⊕43°23'·84N 10°25'·41E WGS84

Marina Cala di Medici looking NNW across to Castiglioncello *MCDM*

Facilities

Services Water and electricity (220/380V). TV and telephone connections. Internet. Wi-Fi. Showers and toilets. Self-service laundry. Pump-out facilities.
Fuel Fuel on the quay near the entrance. (0900–1200 and 1430–1800).
Repairs 100-ton travel-lift. Hydraulic trailer. Max LOA 35m. Carpentry and teak deck repairs. Mechanical and electrical engineering. Electronics and painting services.
Cantiere Cala de Medici ✆ 0586 795 225
Email cantiere@calademedici.net
Provisions Good shopping in the town. The supermarket in the town will delivery to the marina.
Eating out Bars and restaurants in the town. Cafés and restaurants planned for the marina.
Other PO. Banks. ATMs. Buses. Trains to Livorno and Rome. Pisa airport 40km.

General

The new marina has got off to an impressive start, with all services well established, and events from music concerts to foodie evenings filling the calendar. Yacht Club Cala de Medici organises yacht and dinghy regattas throughout the summer. The marina is also host to the Rotta del Vino (Wine Route), a week of gourmet food and wine and racing, in September each year.

The modern town of Rosignano Solvay was developed during the early 20th century as part of an industrial development. It is a pleasant enough place and its famous white sandy beaches draw in the masses every summer. For something more historic take a bus up to Rosignano Marittimo, the medieval village on the hill beyond the new town.

Vada Reef (Secche di Vada)

⊕3 3M W of Secche di Vada light 43°19'·2N 10°18'·0E

Just over five miles SW from Marina Cala de Medici, and 4½ miles off the coast S of Vada, shoal water extending off the coast between Rosignano and Cecina Mare culminates in the Secche di Vada. There are least depths of 2·1m (7ft) over the reef and it is marked by a black round tower with a red band and lit Fl(2)10s18m12M. There are least depths of 7–8m reported in the fairway between the reef and the shore, but the prudent course is to keep to seaward of the reef.

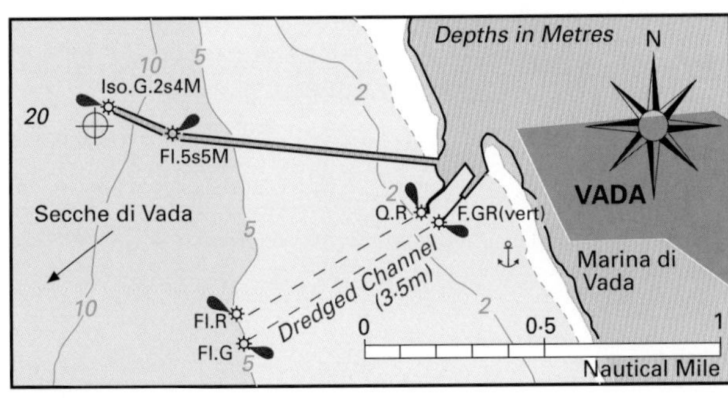

VADA
⊕43°21'·3N 10°25'·4E

VADA

A commercial port with a long pier and a basin. A buoyed channel dredged to a minimum depth of 3·5m leads into a basin. The harbour is for commercial shipping only, and yachts should not attempt to enter.

To the S of the commercial harbour there are several detached breakwaters off the coast with local boats on moorings behind the breakwaters. Depths in here are variable between <1–1·5m.

CECINA MARE

Just inside the narrow entrance at the mouth of the river Cecina there is a small basin. The entrance silts so take great care when attempting to enter. Recent dredging has restored minimum depths of 1·5–1·8m. With strong onshore winds a yacht should not attempt to enter as big seas heap up at the entrance.

VHF Ch 09, 16 (office hours). CB Ch 31.

Data 400 berths. visitors' berths. Max LOA 12m. Depths 0·5–1·5m. Charge band 2.

Services Water and electricity. Fuel. 10-ton crane. Charge band 2.

Circolo Nautico Foce Cecina ✆ 0586 622 763 *Fax* 0586 622 765
Email info@circolonauticofocececina.it
www.circolonauticofocececina.it

Marina di Cecina looking east

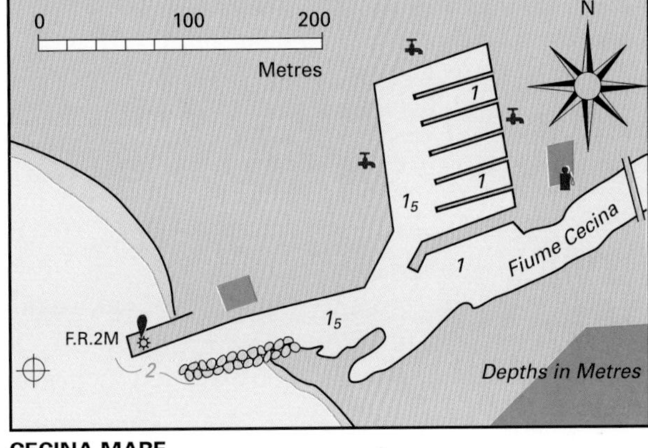

CECINA MARE
⊕43°18'·18N 10°29'·18E WGS84

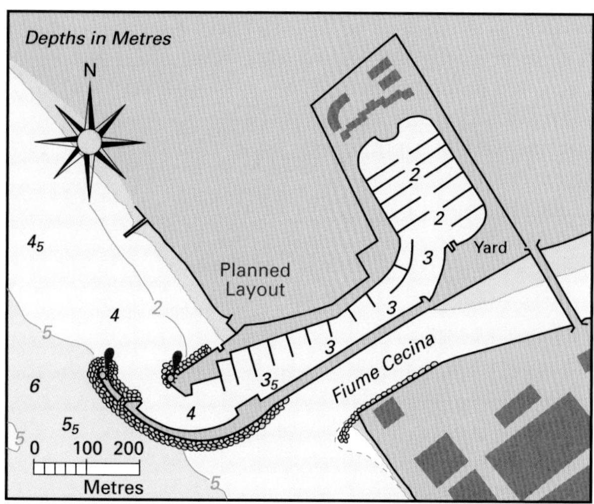

PLAN OF PROPOSED NEW MARINA DE CECINA

Marina de Cecina

There are plans to develop a new *porto turistico*, Marina de Cecina, on the site of the existing basin at Cecina Mare. No dates are available yet, but the proposed marina details and the layout is shown here. The new plan aims to separate the marina from the river, eliminating problems with silting, and to build breakwaters out from the entrance to offer protection from onshore winds, allowing access in most conditions.

Data c.900 berths. Visitors' berths. Max LOA 15m. Depths 3–4·5m. Boatyard and hauling facilities. Leisure and sporting facilities.
Circolo Nautico Spa ✆ 0586 620 602 *Fax* 0586 622 765
Email Info@circolonauticospa.it
www.circolonauticospa.it

MARINA DI SAN VINCENZO

A new marina about 16 miles S of Vada.

Approach

The marina lies on the site of the old shallow basin off the town of the same name.

Conspicuous The buildings of the town are easily seen. Closer in the breakwater can be identified.

VHF Ch 09.

Dangers With moderate and strong onshore winds there are waves breaking across the entrance and onto the adjacent beach. Yachts must turn beam onto the surf to enter the marina. Having watched a yacht do this, thankfully successfully, in about 15–20 knots of onshore wind I can see little to recommend it.

Mooring

Data 350 berths. Max LOA 27m. Depths 3–4·5m.

Berths Stern or bows-to where directed. Laid moorings tailed to the quay.

Shelter Once inside there is good all round shelter in the marina.

Authorities Marina staff. Charge band 6+.
Marina di San Vincenzo ✆ 0565 702 025 *Fax* 0565 705 467
Email porto@marinadisanvincenzo.it
www.marinadisanvincenzo.it

Facilities

Services Water and electricity (220/380V). Wi-Fi. Showers and toilets. Pump-out (to be completed).

Fuel Fuel quay (to be completed).

Repairs 75-ton travel-lift. Repairs can be arranged at the yard. Chandler.
✆ 0565 704 717
Email sanvincenzo@golfomola.it

Provisions Good shopping in the town.

Eating out Bars, cafés and restaurant in the marina. More in the town.

General

The marina is complete, and already fairly full, and the infrastructure is not far behind. The quality of fittings are very high, and the modern buildings stylish, but I for one am delighted to see the original café bars and tiny shops along the quay have survived and thrived in the make-over from silting small-craft harbour to very smart yacht marina.

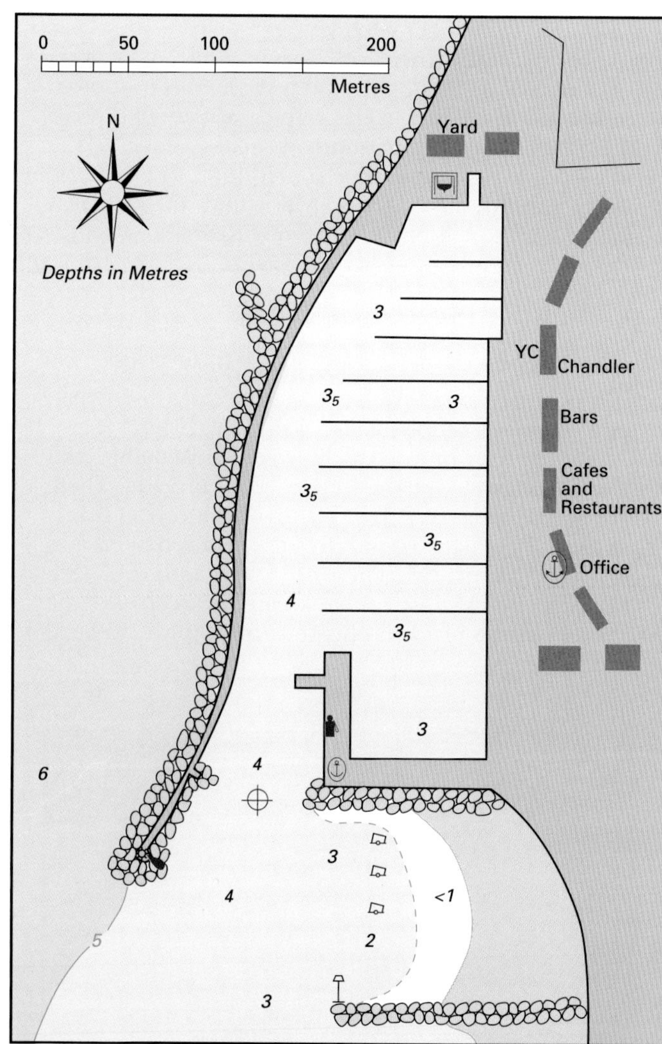

MARINA DI SAN VINCENZO
⊕43°05'·90N 10°32'·21E WGS84

Porto Baratti looking E into the S corner of the bay. Anchoring is prohibited in the N of the bay

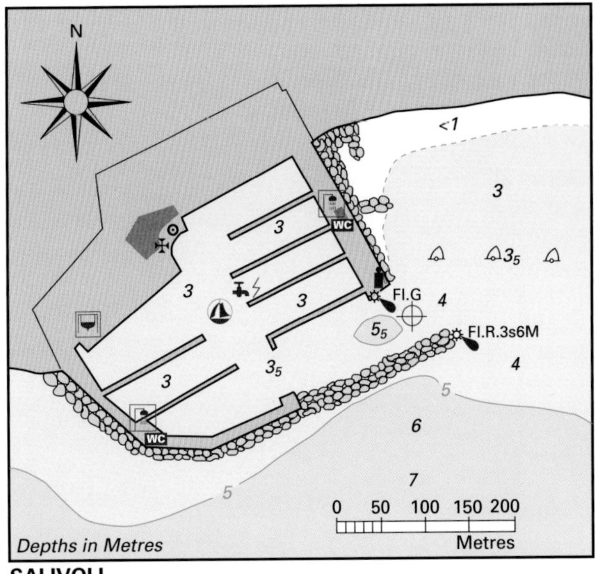

SALIVOLI
⊕42°55'·98N 10°30'·47E WGS84

PORTO BARATTI

About 5½ miles S of San Vincenzo lies Porto Baratti, a large bay with a beach around the shore. It is prohibited to anchor in the N of the bay. In the S of the bay there are numerous permanent moorings. Anchor N of these or try to find a spot closer in clear of moored boats. The bottom is sand, generally good holding. The bay is open between W to NW but affords good shelter from southerlies.

The bay is a delightful spot and one of the few usable anchorages along this coast. A restaurant ashore. Behind the beach there are the remains of an Etruscan necropolis.

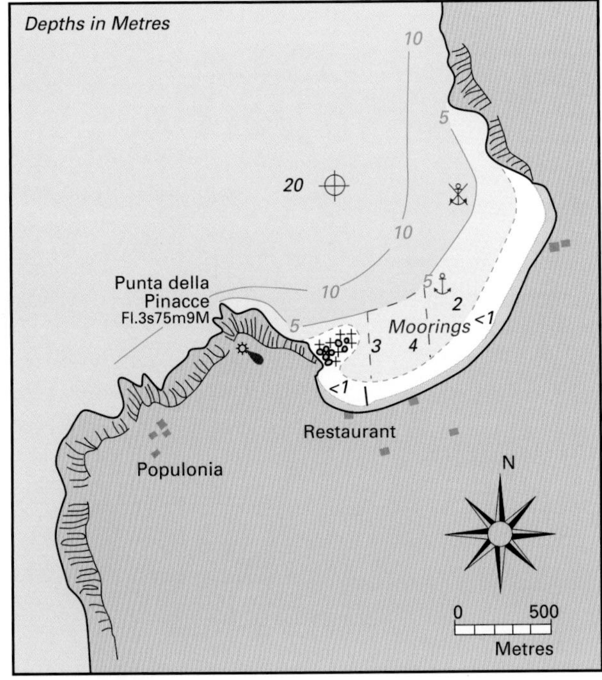

PORTO BARATTI
⊕43°00'·0N 10°30'·3E

SALIVOLI

Approach

A *porto turistico* just S of Piombino.

VHF Ch 16, 09 (0800–2000).

Mooring

Data 450 berths. 30 visitors' berths. Max LOA 18m. Depths 2·5–4m.

Berth Where directed. Laid moorings tailed to the quay.

Shelter Good all-round shelter.

Authorities Harbourmaster and marina staff. A charge is made.

Marina di Salivoli ✆ 0565 48091 / 42809 *Fax* 0565 42824
Email info@marinadisalivoli.it
www.marinadisalivoli.it

Facilities

Services Water and electricity at all berths. Shower and toilet block.
Fuel On the quay.

Marina di Salivoli looking SE

Repairs 80-ton travel-lift. 70-ton crane. Repairs can be arranged.
Provisions Minimarket.
Eating out Restaurant and bar.
Other Bank. ATM. Yacht club.

General

Although it sits under the cloud generated at Piombino, the marina seems somehow insulated from it all most of the time. The port is usefully situated along this stretch of coast and should be used in preference to Piombino.

Piombino looking east

PIOMBINO

BA 131
Italian 71

Approach

Straightforward.

Conspicuous The numerous high chimneys in the vicinity of the harbour make identification easy. The constant coming and going of ferries to Elba also make the port and the entrance easy to find.

By night Use the light on La Rochetta Fl(3)15s18m11M.

VHF Ch 14, 16 for port authorities. Ch 12 for pilots.

Caution Care must be taken of the ferries to Elba which have right of way in the approaches and the harbour itself.

Mooring

Berth Go stern-to or alongside in the SW basin of the harbour. The bottom is mud and good holding.

Shelter Good although strong NE winds send in a swell. Wash from the constant coming and going of the ferries.

Authorities Harbourmaster and customs.

Note Yachts are not normally welcome in the harbour and it should only be used in extremis.

Facilities

Water On the quay.
Other Taxis to the town. Ferries to Elba.

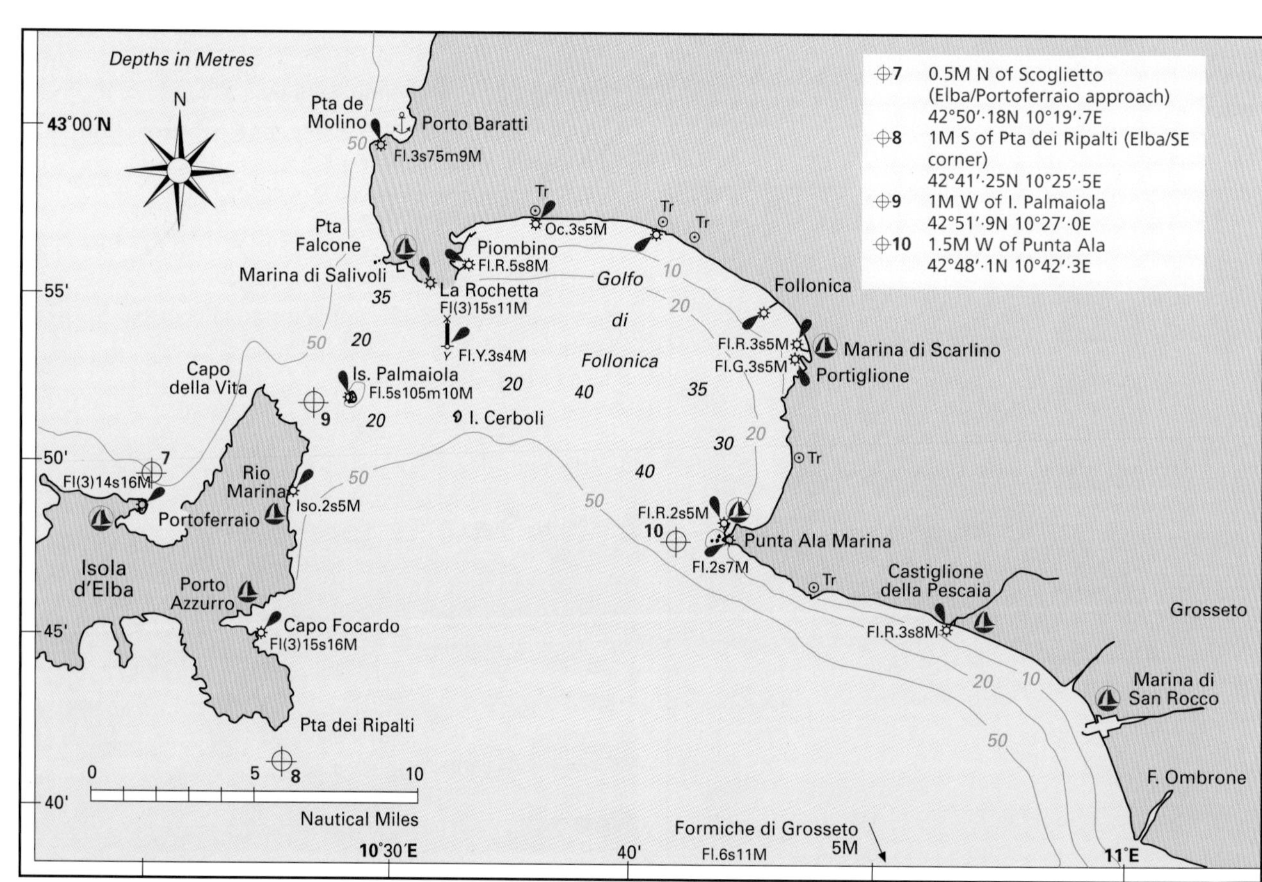

CANALE DI PIOMBINO

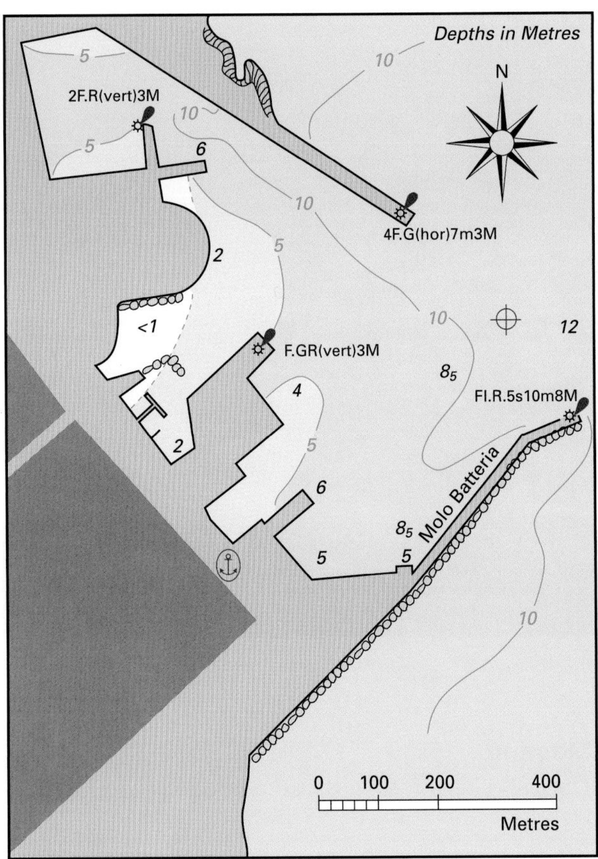

PIOMBINO
⊕42°55′·9N 10°33′·1E

General

Piombino is a useful harbour in an emergency, but the surroundings can only be described as industrial and if the wind is in the wrong direction you get the smell of the oil refinery up your nose to go with the industrial landscape.

Golfo di Follonica

From Piombino the coast trends in a wide curve to Punta Ala about 11 miles to the SE. The shores of the gulf are low and marshy and there are numerous chimneys and industrial plants in the northern half of the gulf.

Care is needed when passing through the strait between Elba and Piombino and into the gulf. It is always busy with commercial ships, either on passage or at anchor in the roads, and ferries plying between the islands and the mainland.

MARINA DI SCARLINO

A marina on the S side of the entrance to Portiglione Canal.

Approach

Marina di Scarlino lies in the E corner of Golfo di Follonica, some 11M E from the Canale di Piombino. The coast around the gulf is low-lying, and the chimneys of industrial plants are easy to see against the shore. The N shore of the gulf is shallow, with depths under 20m nearly 2M off the coast in places. With onshore winds the sea heaps up over here, and care is needed in the final approaches to the marina.

Conspicuous The control tower, a sandstone brick tower with a hexagonal roof and reflective glass, is easily identified.

By night Shoal water off the entrance to the Portiglione canal is marked with red buoys (lit Fl.R5s), and the marina entrance is lit, but a night entry, particularly with strong onshore winds, is not recommended.

VHF Ch 72.

Dangers The area around the mouth of the Portiglione canal and the marina entrance appears to be liable to silting, particularly after winter storms, although the marina entrance is dredged and buoyed. Deep-draught yachts should call ahead for advice if in any doubt. With strong onshore winds care is needed when entering the marina, but it is more difficult than dangerous.

Mooring

Data 950 berths. Visitors' berths. Max LOA 40m.

Berth Marina staff will direct you to a berth. Finger pontoons, and laid moorings tailed to the quay for larger yachts (>12m).

Shelter Good all-round protection inside the marina.

Authorities Marina staff. Charge band 6.

✉ Marina di Scarlino, Localita Puntone 58020, Scarlino
✆ 0566 866 302 *Fax* 0566 866 252
Email info@lamarinadiscarlino.it
www.lamarinadiscarlino.it

Facilities

Services Water and electricity (220/380V) at all berths. Showers and toilets.
Fuel Fuel on the quay (0800–1200 and 1500–1900).

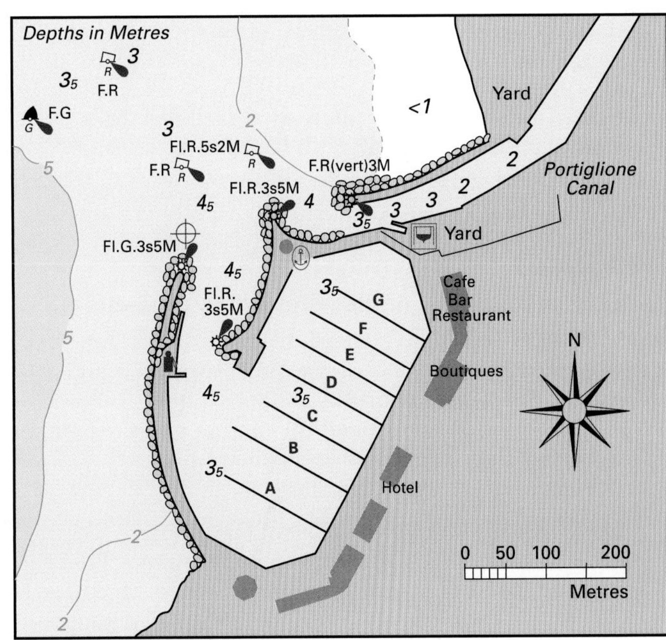

MARINA DI SCARLINO
⊕42°53′·23N 10°46′·84E WGS84

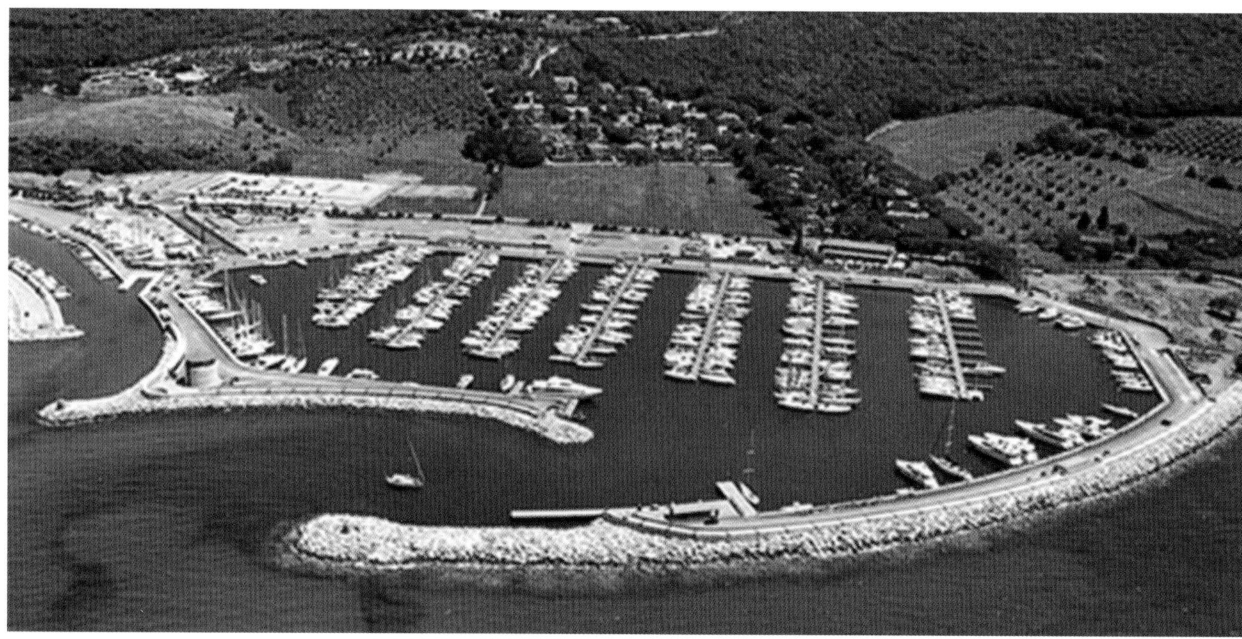

Marina di Scarlino and the entrance to Portiglione canal *Marina di Scarlino*

Repairs Yacht Service (part of the Nautor Group) operate in the yard along the S side of the canal. 100-ton travel-lift. 30-ton crane. 40-ton hydraulic trailer. Repair facilities including carpentry, mechanical, electrical and electronics. Steel and GRP repairs. Painting facilities. Chandlers. B&G and Simrad dealers.

LAMDS Yacht Services ✆ 0566 867 031 *Fax* 0566 867 047
Email info@lamdsyachtservice.it

Provisions Shops under construction in the marina. Bakery and minimarket in the village 200m away.

Eating out Hotel restaurant in the marina. More planned. Other restaurants nearby.

General

This marina is now well established, with charter fleets based here and a growing number of yachts wintering afloat and ashore here. The final phase of apartments, boutiques and shops are now complete. It is an agreeable place, with good facilities, friendly staff and an active yacht club based here.

PUNTA ALA MARINA

Approach

This marina lies in the SE corner of Golfo di Follonica.

Conspicuous Sparviero islet with a tower on it and a square tower on Punta Ala are conspicuous. Closer in, the development around the marina and the light towers at the entrance are easily identified.

VHF Ch 09, 16 (0830–2000).

Dangers Care should be taken of Scogli Porcellini, a group of above and below-water rocks, off Punta Ala. The passage between Sparviero islet and the outermost rock of the Porcellini group is straightforward by day with depths of 12m in the fairway. The passage should not be attempted at night.

Mooring

Data 895 berths. 90 visitors' berths. Max LOA 28m. Depths 1·8m–4m.

Berth Go stern or bows-to where directed. There are laid moorings tailed to the quay and you will be assisted to berth. Visitors' berths usually on the two pontoons near the entrance.

Shelter Excellent.

Authorities Harbourmaster and marina staff. Charge band 6+.

Punta Ala Marina Control Tower ✆ 0564 922 784
Office ✆ 0564 922 217 / 785 *Fax* 0564 921 086 / 923 212
Email info@marinadipuntala.com
www.marinadipuntala.com

Scogli Porcellini off Punta Ala marina looking east

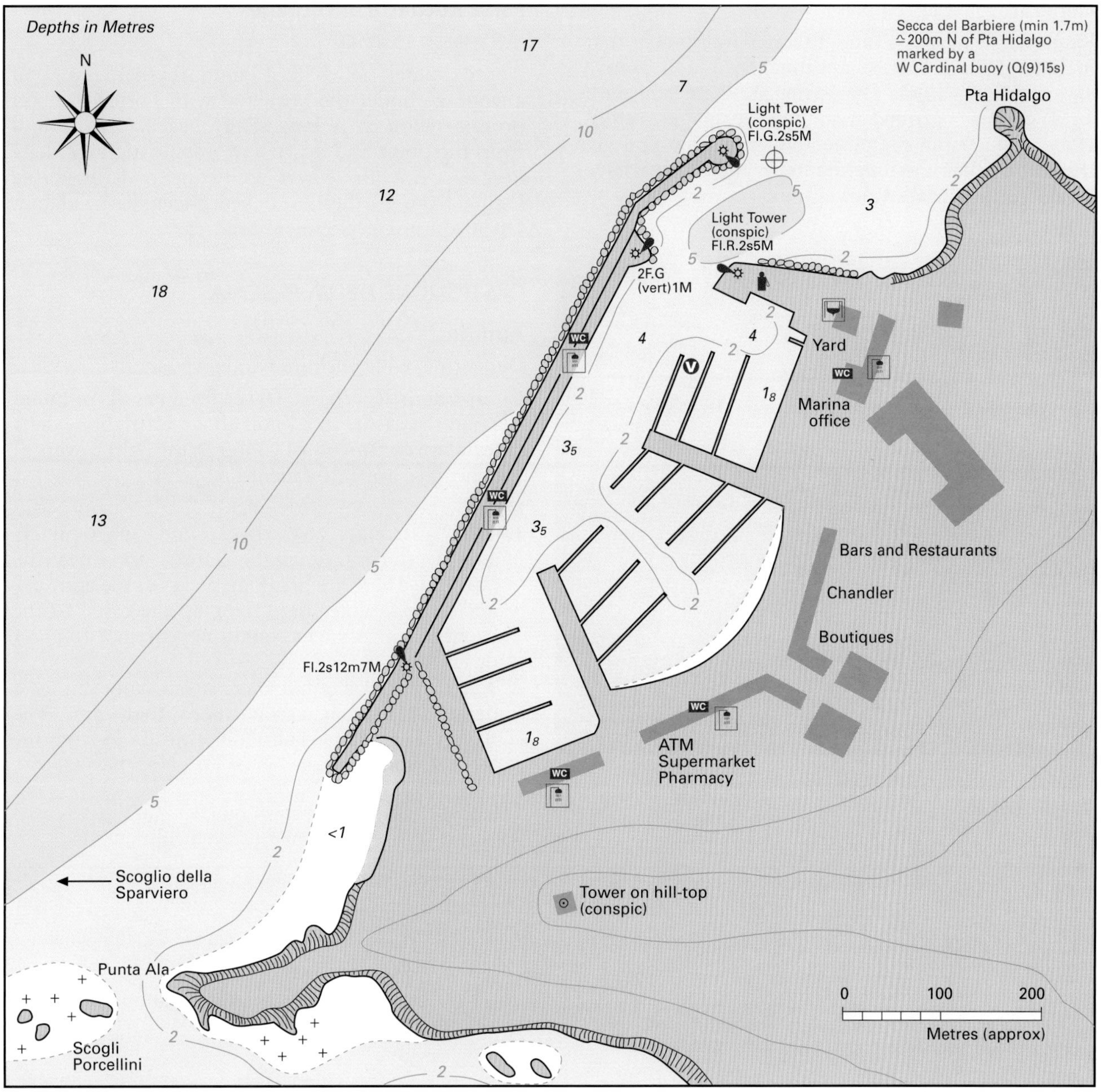

Depths in Metres
N
Secca del Barbiere (min 1.7m) ≏200m N of Pta Hidalgo marked by a W Cardinal buoy (Q(9)15s)
Pta Hidalgo
Light Tower (conspic) Fl.G.2s5M
Light Tower (conspic) Fl.R.2s5M
2F.G (vert)1M
Yard
Marina office
Bars and Restaurants
Chandler
Boutiques
Fl.2s12m7M
ATM
Supermarket
Pharmacy
Scoglio della Sparviero
Tower on hill-top (conspic)
Punta Ala
Scogli Porcellini
0 100 200
Metres (approx)

PUNTA ALA MARINA
⊕42°48´·5N 10°44´·2E

Punta Ala looking ENE

Facilities

Services Water (both potable and non-potable) and electricity at every berth. Telephone and Satellite TV connections available. Shower and toilet blocks. Internet access.
Fuel On the quay at the entrance (0800–1300 and 1400–1800).
Repairs A 100-ton travel-hoist. 40-ton crane. Hard standing ashore. Mechanical repairs. GRP and wood repairs. Electrical and electronic repairs. Chandlers.
Cantiere Punta Ala ✆ 0564 922 761
Email info@cantierenavaletoscana.com
Provisions Supermarket.
Eating out Restaurants and bars open in the summer.
Other Yacht club. ATM. Pharmacy. Information office. Exchange facilities.

General

Punta Ala is part of a large leisure development that includes several hotels, apartments, a golf course and a riding school. The setting is wonderful with wild country around and the Scogli Porcellini running out from the point, but somehow you get the feeling that the inhabitants of the marina have insulated themselves from all this.

Forte Rochetta anchorage looking east

Forte Rochetta anchorage

⊕ 42°46'·5N 10°47'·6E

Approximately 3½M SE of Punta Ala there is a good anchorage under the headland with Forte Rochetta prominent on it. A long sandy beach runs around from the point and down towards Castiglione della Pescaia. Anchor where convenient. Reasonable shelter from northerlies tucked under the headland. Open south. Development ashore.

CASTIGLIONE DELLA PESCAIA

Approach

Dangerous with onshore winds.

Conspicuous Rocchetta Tower 3½ miles SE of Punta Ala and the castle on a knoll above Castiglione della Pescaia are conspicuous. Closer in the light towers at the entrance are easily identified.

Dangers

1. With strong westerlies, and particularly southwesterlies, it is dangerous to enter the harbour. There are breaking waves at the entrance and considerable surge right up the canal to the yacht basin. A yacht should not attempt to enter or leave.
2. The entrance silts but there are usually 2m least depths. There is rarely more than 3m. The navigable channel is about one-third out from the S breakwater.

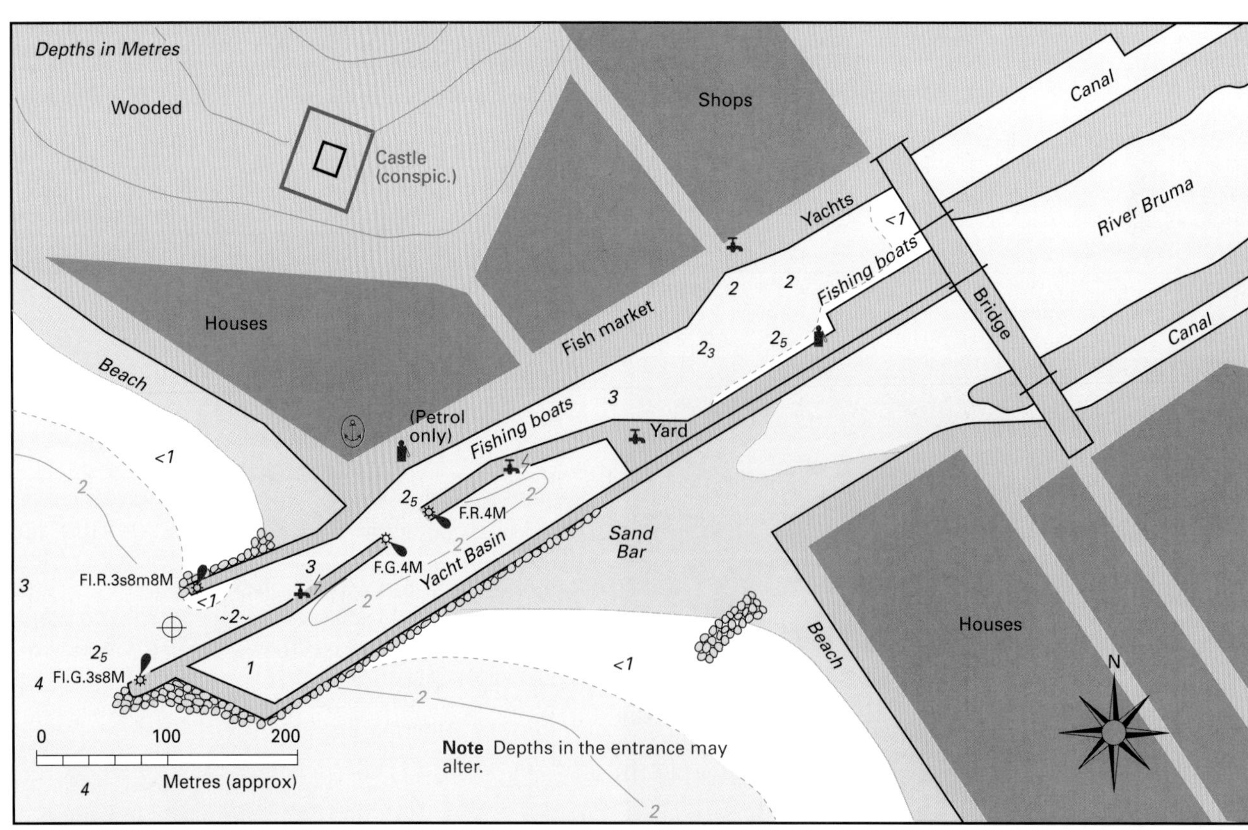

CASTIGLIONE DELLA PESCAIA
⊕42°45'·66N 10°52'·76E WGS84

Castiglione della Pescaia looking east
Gino Cianci, FOTOTECA ENIT

The entrance to the canal at Castiglione della Pescaia. Strong onshore winds cause dangerous breaking waves in the entrance

Mooring

Data Max LOA 13m. Depths 0·5–2·5m.

Berth Go stern or bows-to in the canal or in the basin. There are laid moorings tailed to the quay or to a small buoy in both the canal and the basin.

Shelter Excellent although strong westerlies send a lumpy swell into the canal which affects some of the berths in the basin, more uncomfortable than dangerous.

Authorities Port police and customs. *Ormeggiatori* in the yacht basin. Charge band 2/3.

Facilities

Services Water on the quay in the canal and the basin. Electricity on the quay in the basin.
Fuel On the quay in the canal. The first pump has petrol only, but the second has diesel.
Repairs Cranes up to 15 tons. Slipway up to 25 tons. Mechanical and some engineering repairs. GRP and wood repairs. Chandlers.
Provisions Good shopping for all provisions. Small market in the town. Excellent fish market on the N bank of the canal. Ice at the fish market.
Eating out Good restaurants, trattorias and pizzerias. A small restaurant-bar at the basin.
Other PO. Banks. ATMs. Italgaz and Camping Gaz. Hire cars. Buses to Rome.

General

A bustling fishing port with a growing tourist population attracted to the nearby sandy beaches. Castiglione della Pescaia is a thoroughly likeable small town. The harbour is always crammed full of trawlers adding a colourful air and the throb of powerful diesels, not to mention the wash, when these boats enter and leave at high speed with typical Latin machismo. The castle standing over the town is a private residence and not open to visitors.

MARINA DI SAN ROCCO (Il Porto della Maremma, Marina di Grosseto)

A new marina in the Canal San Rocco, off the town of Marina di Grosseto, 5½M ESE from Castiglione della Pescaia.

Approach

Entry dangerous with onshore winds.

Conspicuous The control tower and the breakwaters will be seen when closer in.

VHF Ch 09, 16.

Dangers
1. With strong onshore winds (over Force 5) it is dangerous to enter the marina. There are breaking waves and surf in the entrance and a yacht should not attempt to enter or leave. Entry is not easy with even moderate onshore winds.
2. The entrance is liable to silting, and regular dredging maintains depths at 2·5–3m. Yachts drawing more than 2m should call ahead to ensure there are sufficient depths.

Mooring

Data 560 berths. 56 visitors' berths. Max LOA 14m. Depths <1–3m.

Berths Stern or bows-to where directed. Larger yachts (11–14m) use the basin on the N side of the entrance. Laid moorings tailed to the quay or to buoys.

Shelter Good all-round protection inside the marina although there can be a bit of a surge with onshore winds.

Authorities Marina staff. Charge band 6 (July–September).
Marina di San Rocco Control tower ☎ 0564 330 027
Office ☎ 0564 330 075
Fax 0564 330 903
Email info@marinadisanrocco.it
www.marinadisanrocco.it

Facilities

Services Water and electricity (220V) at all berths. Telephone and satellite TV connections. Showers and toilets.
Fuel On the quay near the entrance.
Repairs 20-ton crane. GRP and sail repairs. Some mechanical repairs. Chandlers.
Provisions Most provisions can be found in the town.
Eating out Café bar and restaurant in the marina. More in the town.
Other Bank. ATM. Pharmacy.

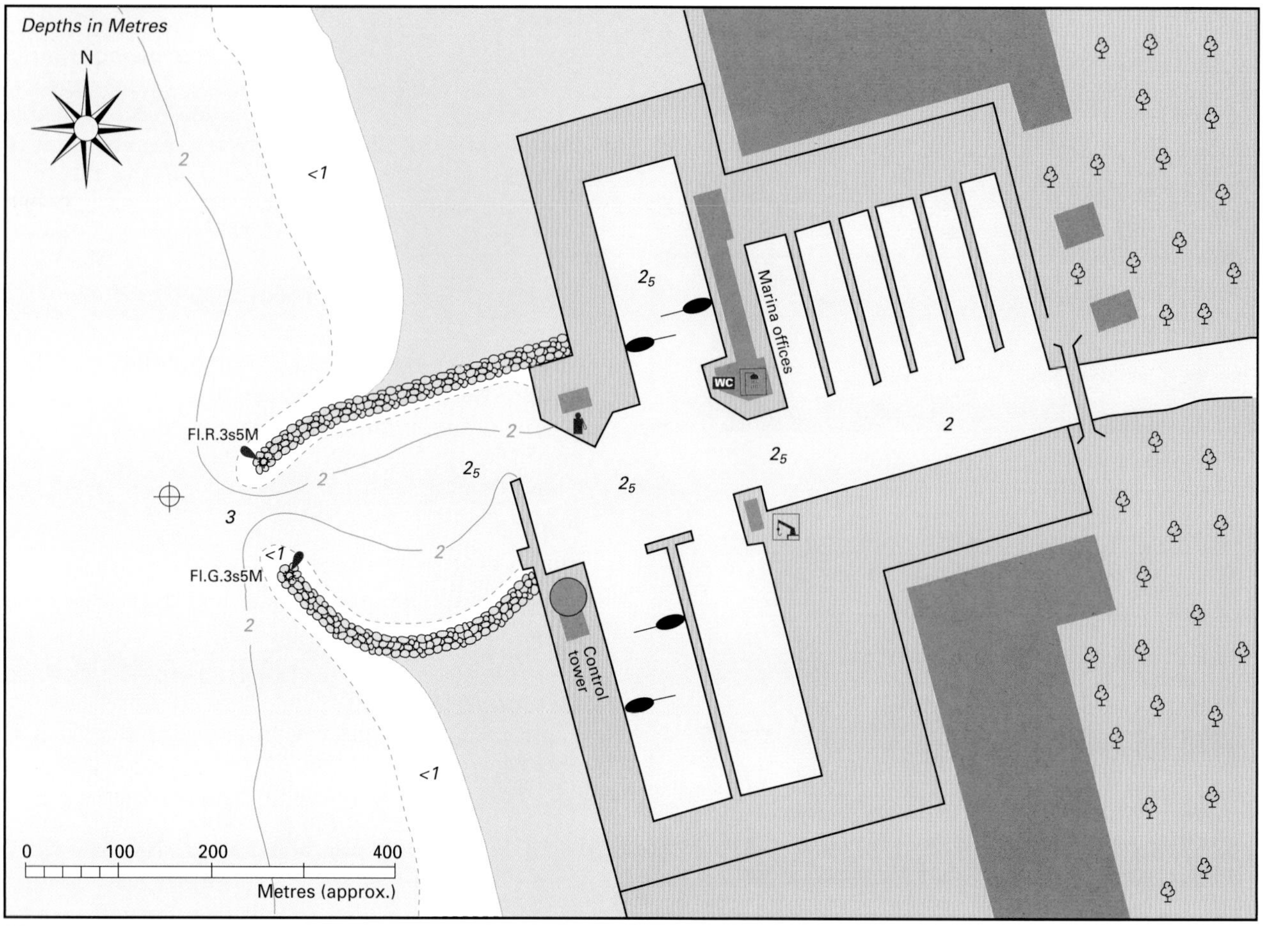

MARINA DI SAN ROCCO
42°42′·79N 10°58′·83E WGS84

General

The marina is adjacent to the resort town of Marina di Grosseto. Beaches stretch either side of the marina, thick with the sunbathing bodies of Italians and northern Europeans. Inside the marina you are insulated from this, and it provides a good base from which to explore inland. The provincial capital Grosseto, with its 13th-century church, lies 5M inland. Further N you'll find the site of excavations of the Etruscan city of Roselle, dating back to the 3rd century BC.

Marina di San Rocco looking west. Strong onshore winds can make entry dangerous, though once inside shelter is good

Cala di Forno (Forno Cove)

A small cove lying four miles SE of the Ombrone river. A tower stands on the headland on the S side. Anchor in 3–4m on a sandy bottom. The cove shallows near the beach. Open to the W–NW. The cove at the bottom of a valley is a delightful spot with pine around the beach at the head.

Note After heavy rain the sea off the mouth of the Ombrone river is discoloured for several miles out by the silty fresh water flowing out.

Cala di Forno looking east

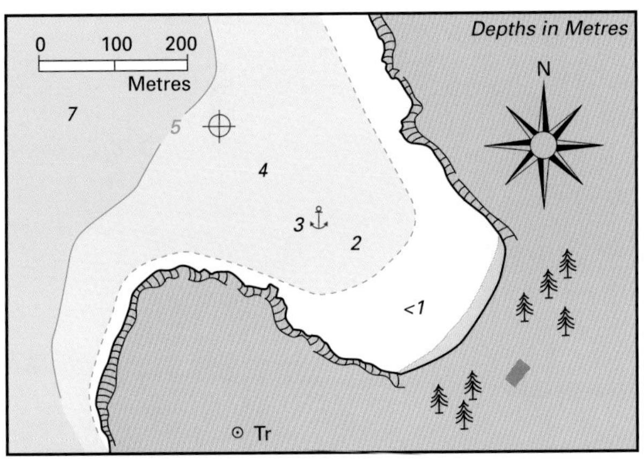

CALA DI FORNO
⊕42°37′·0N 11°05′·0E

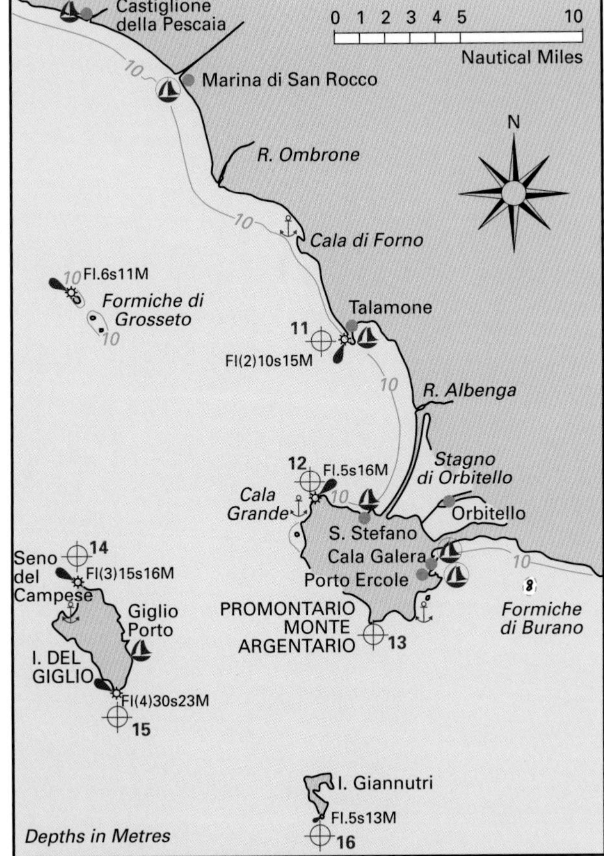

CASTIGLIONE DELLA PESCAIA TO ISOLA DI GIANNUTRI

⊕**11** 1M W of Talamone
42°33′·1N 11°07′·0E
⊕**12** 0.5M N of Pta Lividonia (Monte Argentario)
42°27′·2N 11°06′·3E
⊕**13** 0.5M S of Pta di Torre Ciana (Monte Argentario)
42°21′·0N 11°09′·0E
⊕**14** 1M N of Pta del Fenaio (I. del Giglio)
42°24′·2N 10°52′·9E
⊕**15** 1M S of Pta del Capel Rosso (I. del Giglio)
42°18′·2N 10°55′·3E
⊕**16** 1M S of Punta del Capel Rosso (I. di Giannutri)
42°13′·3N 11°06′·6E

Formiche di Grosseto

Formiche di Grosseto light 42°34′·6N 10°53′·0E

A group of rocks lying about seven miles SW of the Ombrone river. The rocks are North Rock (Formica Maggiore), Middle Rock and South Rock. The group extends about 1½ miles SE from North Rock on which there is a conspicuous light tower (a round white tower) 23m (75ft) high. Light characteristic Fl.6s23m11M. The Admiralty *Pilot* warns that in gales there are overfalls for over half a mile S of South Rock.

TALAMONE

Approach

From the distance Capo d'Uomo looks like an island, being higher than the surrounding land.

Conspicuous From NW the tower, fort and village at Talamone will not be seen until close in. From the S, the tower, fort and a belfry in the village are conspicuous.

By night Use the main light on the cape Fl(2)10s30m15M.

Dangers In the approach a yacht must keep about 400m off Capo d'Uomo and the coast before turning due W into the harbour. Care is needed of the shallow ledge on the N side of the harbour where numerous yachts are on laid moorings.

Mooring

Data Max LOA 14m. Depths <1–5m.

Berth Go stern or bows-to where directed or wherever there is room. Laid moorings at some berths. The bottom is mud and good holding.

Shelter Is better than it looks and good with SW winds. However strong SE winds must raise a sea here.

Authorities Harbourmaster. Charge band 4/5.

Facilities

Services Water and electricity at some berths.
Fuel On the quay.
Provisions Most provisions can be obtained in the village.
Eating out Restaurants in the summer.
Other PO. Banks. ATMs. Bus to Orbitello.

General

The town is named after Telamon, the Greek hero who took part in the hunt for the Calydonian Boar and who sailed with Jason and the Argonauts in search of the Golden Fleece. He also gave his name to the sculptured figures adorning the columns of Greek temples (*telamones*). I'm not sure why the village is named after Telamon, but the medieval walled village is an interesting warren of alleys and stone houses. The low-key aspect of Talamone lends it a quiet charm away from some of the bigger resorts.

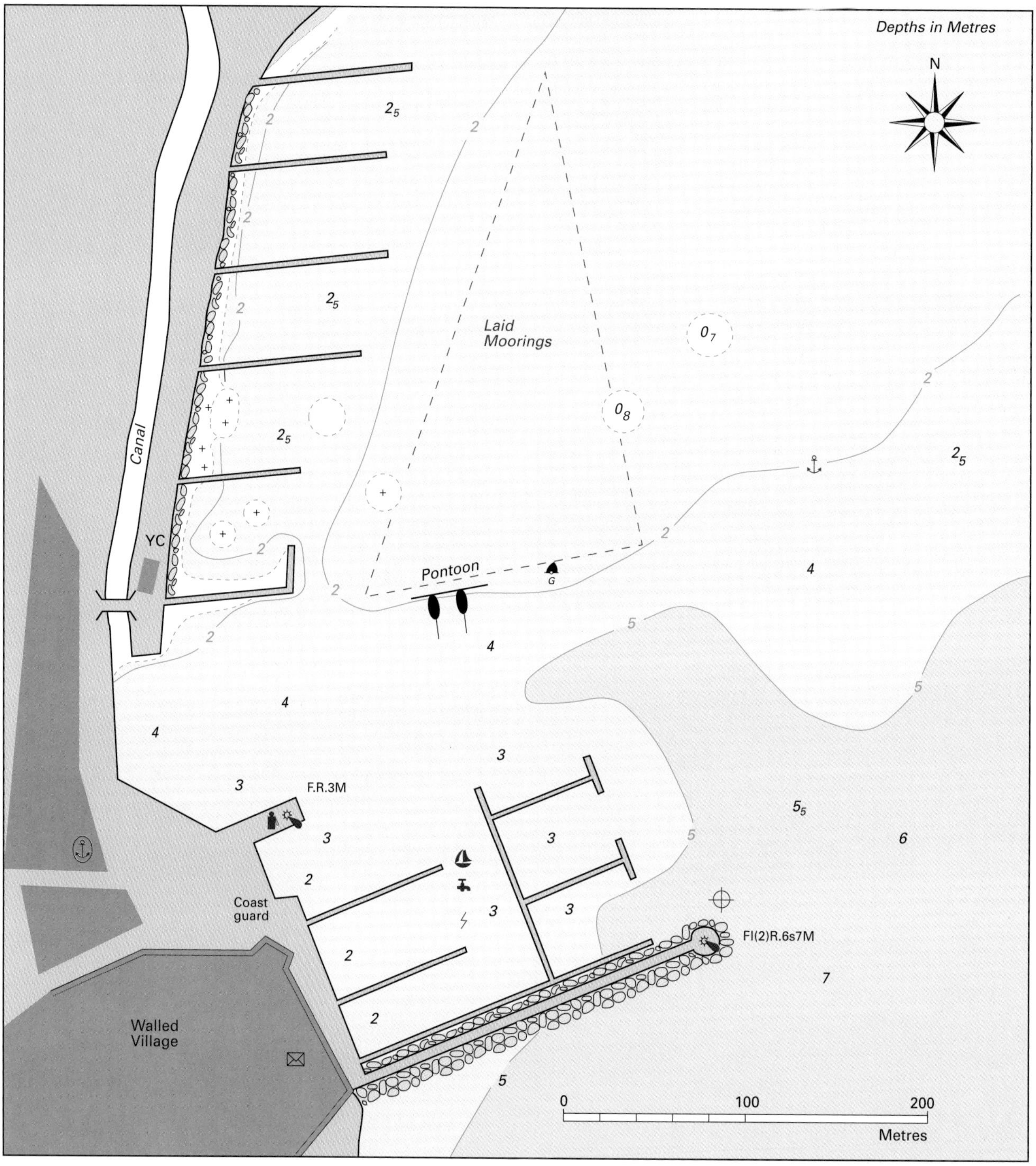

TALAMONE
⊕42°33′·21N 11°08′·26E WGS84

Talamone looking ENE across Capo d'Uomo to the harbour. The shallow area can clearly be seen

Monte Argentario

The Promontorio del Argentario, known colloquially as *Monte Argentario*, consists of a high conical mountain which used to be an island about a mile off the coast. The silt brought down by the river has, over time, reached out to connect Monte Argentario to the mainland with a series of sandbars. The enclosed shallow waters within the sandbars is called the Stagno di Orbitello – *stagno* means a pond or tank, and comes from the same Latin root (*stagnum* – a pool) from which we get 'stagnate'. The medieval city of Orbitello is on a small peninsula projecting into the stagno from the mainland. The peninsula once contained a major air force seaplane base. There is a railway station at the end of the Orbitello peninsula and trains run frequently to Rome.

Santa Liberata

⊕ 42°26'·0N 11°09'·5E

On the NE side of Monte Argentario, a canal leads to Orbitello. At the entrance to the canal two training walls direct the flow of water out to sea and there is a detached breakwater off the NE side of the entrance. On the W side of the W wall there are 1–1·5m depths where small craft go alongside. The entrance to the canal is obstructed, but small craft use the canal.

Santa Liberata just E of Santo Stefano looking ESE

Pozzarello

⊕ 42°26'·1N 11°08'·6E

A large open bay on the N coast of Promontorio del Argentario. The bay is open N, but may be suitable for an lunch stop in settled weather. SW–W winds will probably send in an uncomfortable swell. With any N in the wind yachts should head for Porto Santo Stefano or Talamone. There are moorings for local craft in the N of the bay, but a yacht may find depths suitable for anchoring to the S of the moorings. A small pontoon off the beach is only suitable for dinghies.

SANTO STEFANO

BA 131
Italian 74

Approach

The tall Argentario peninsula is easily identified against the flat land surrounding it.

Conspicuous From the N a monument on the hill behind the harbour and the tall houses on the slopes are conspicuous. From the W and S the harbour and town cannot be seen until around Punta Lividonia. The lighthouse on Punta Lividonia, a white tower on a two storey dwelling, and a white crenellated villa nearby, are conspicuous.

By night Use the light on Punta Lividonia Fl.5s47m16M.

VHF Ch 14, 16 for port authorities (winter 0700–1900/summer 0700–2300). Ch 12 for pilots. Ch 16 for pontoon berth (Porto Domiziano) in Porto del Valle.

Mooring

Data 205 berths. 20 visitors' berths at Porto Domiziano. Max LOA 35m. Depths 3–10m.

Berth In settled weather go stern or bows-to in Porto Vecchio. Otherwise proceed to Porto del Valle and go stern or bow-to where directed on the pontoon marina (Porto Domiziano). You may be able to find a berth at the club in the NE corner or off the yard in the S corner, though it is unlikely. Porto del Valle is very crowded in the summer and it is difficult to find a berth here as most of the town quay space is reserved for fishing boats. The bottom is mud and good holding.

Between Porto del Valle and Porto Vecchio lies a large field of moorings, available to visiting yachts. The moorings are managed by MarPark, and can be booked in advance.

MarPark booking ✆ 0899 100 001 Office ✆ 0833 970 111
Fax 0833 970 160
Email info@marpark.com

Shelter Good shelter, much improved with the breakwater extension in moderate westerlies and northerlies.

Authorities Harbourmaster and customs. Charge band 6.

Porto Domiziano ✆ 0564 810 845 *Fax* 0564 815 063
Email info@portodomiziano.it

Facilities

Services Water and electricity at most berths.
Fuel On the quay in Porto del Valle.
Repairs The Cantiere Navale del'Argentario can haul yachts up to 400 tons on a patent slip. Mechanical and engineering work (including stainless steel fabrication). GRP and wood repairs and fabrication to a high standard. Many large yachts come here in the winter to be refitted. A limited number of yachts can be stored ashore in the open and under cover. Electrical and electronic repairs. Chandlers.
Cantiere Navale del'Argentario ✆ 0564 814 063

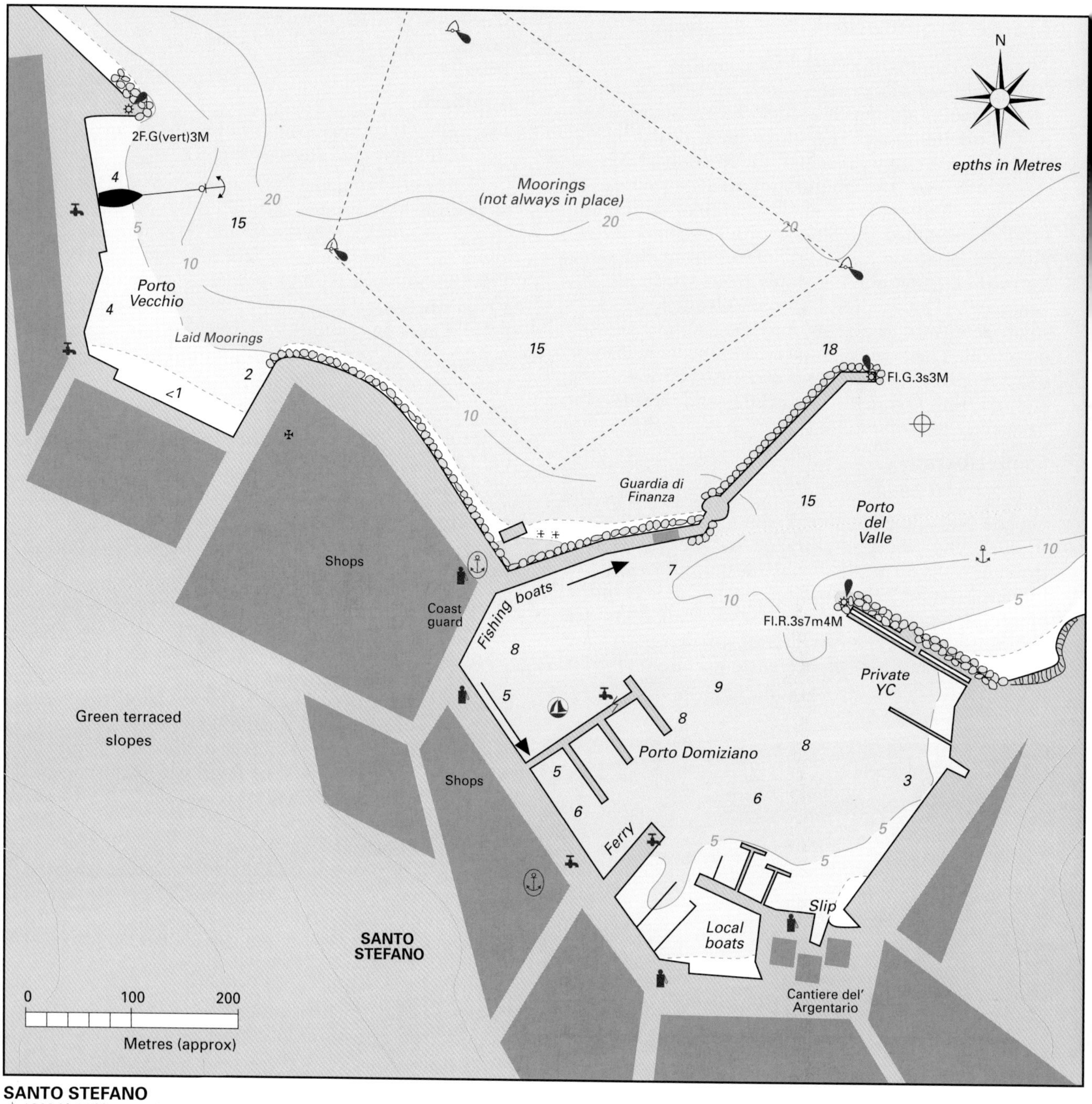

N
epths in Metres
2F.G(vert)3M
Moorings
(not always in place)
Porto
Vecchio
Laid Moorings
Fl.G.3s3M
Guardia di
Finanza
Porto
del
Valle
Shops
Coast
guard
Fishing boats
Fl.R.3s7m4M
Private
YC
Porto Domiziano
Green terraced
slopes
Shops
Ferry
Local
boats
Slip
SANTO
STEFANO
Cantiere del'
Argentario
0 100 200
Metres (approx)

SANTO STEFANO
⊕42°26'·29N 11°07'·49E WGS84

Porto delle Valle in Santo Stefano looking NW

Porto Vecchio looking NW

Provisions Good shopping for all provisions. Excellent fish market on the quay. Ice from the fish market.
Eating out Excellent restaurants, trattorias and pizzerias.
Other PO. Banks. ATMs. Italgaz and Camping Gaz. Buses to Orbitello. Trains to Rome/Pisa from Orbitello. Ferry to Giglio.

General

Santo Stefano is a large fishing port and a popular yacht harbour. The Cantiere Navale del'Argentario is well known for the quality of its work and a number of 'one-off' yachts are built every year – beautiful expressions in wood that can be seen in the water being fitted out. They also carry out rejuvenation work on old classics, work that often entails more work than building from new.

The tall elegant buildings around the harbour have mostly been rebuilt after extensive damage in the second world war. One thing they didn't do was divert the sewers from Porto del Valle. It can get very pongy in the summer and you may be better off going to Porto Vecchio.

Around Monte Argentario

The submerged mountain peak of Monte Argentario, joined by low marshy land and several brackish lagoons to the mainland, is a conspicuous feature whether coming from the N or south. In calm weather it is pleasant to potter around under the steep slopes as there are considerable depths right up to the coast nearly everywhere. In rough weather a yacht should keep a good distance off as there is a wicked reflected swell off the steep-to coast. There are several anchorages between Santo Stefano and Porto Ercole that can be used according to the wind direction or in calm weather.

Cala Grande

⊕ 42°26'·00N 11°05'·5E

Lies close SSW of Pta Lividonia. The old signal station on Pta Cala Grande that shelters the bay from the S will be seen. Open N and west. Anchor in 10–20m in the SE corner or off the beach on the E in 5–10m. The bottom is sand and weed.

Cala del Bove

⊕ 42°25'·0N 11°05'·3E

Lies S of Cala Grande. The islet, L'Argentarola, immediately N of the anchorage is easily identified. There are 8–12m least depths between the islet and the coast. Anchor in 10–20m in the SE corner.

Cala Grande on Monte Argentario looking SSE

II. THE TUSCAN ISLANDS AND ADJACENT MAINLAND COAST

L'Isolotto anchorage on Monte Argentario

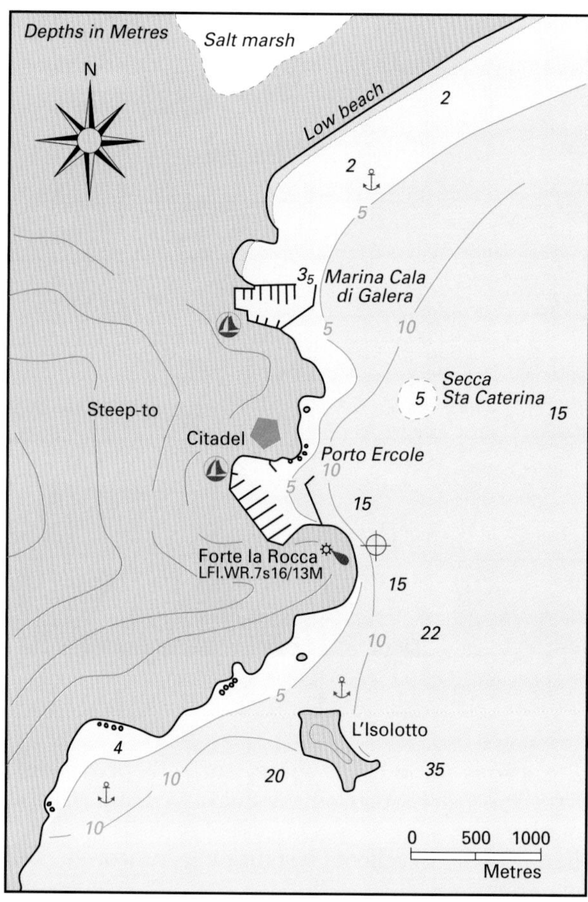

PORTO ERCOLE AND CALA GALERA – APPROACHES
⊕ Forte La Rocca light 42°24'·3N 11°14'·0E

L'Isolotto

⊕ 42°22'·7N 11°12'·0E

Between L'Isolotto and the coast there is a strip of shoal water bordering the coast where a yacht can anchor in calm weather. Good holding on sand.

PORTO ERCOLE

Approach

Conspicuous There are forts everywhere. On the S entrance Forte La Rocca and a white lighthouse within is conspicuous. On the N entrance a large citadel is conspicuous. The village cannot be seen from seaward.

Porto Ercole looking WNW

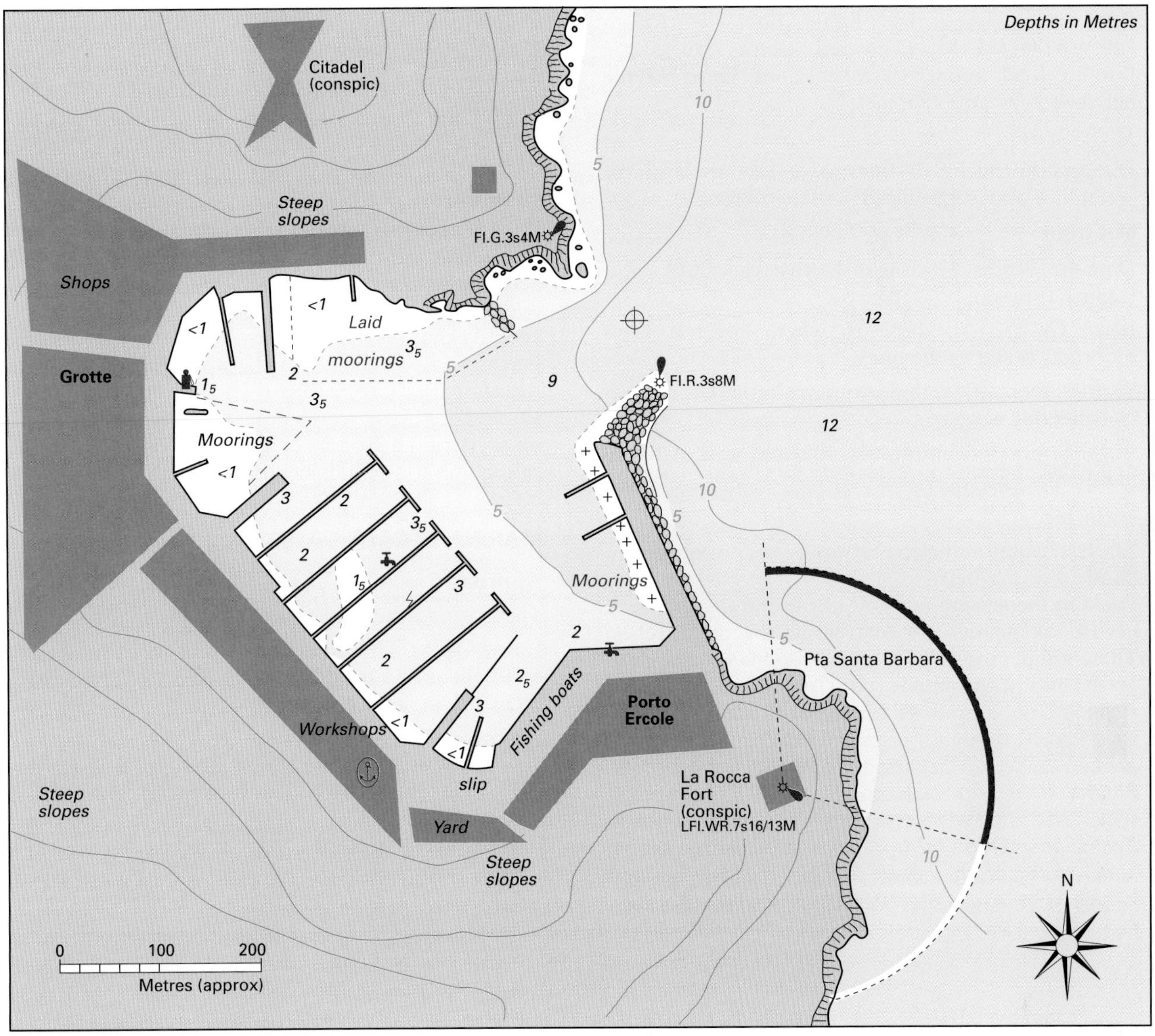

PORTO ERCOLE
⊕42°23´·63N 11°12´·64E WGS84

Porto Ercole looking N towards Grotte

By night Use the light on La Rocca LFl.WR.7s16/13M. (The red sector covers the Burano Reef about 4½ miles E of Porto Ercole between 177° and 285°).

VHF Ch 16.

Dangers Formiche di Burano, a low rock above water, lies about 4½ miles E of Porto Ercole.

Mooring

Data 400 berths. 10 visitors' berths. Max LOA 24m. Depths 1–6·5m.

Berth Go stern or bows-to where directed. Laid moorings tailed to the quay.

Shelter Good although prolonged southerlies cause a considerable surge.

Authorities Harbourmaster. Marina staff. Charge band 5/6.

Facilities

Services Water and electricity at or near every berth. Showers and toilets.
Fuel On the jetty directly W of the entrance. Care is needed as depths are uneven in the approaches. There are depths of 1·5m alongside the low catwalk on the end of the jetty.
Repairs Cranes up to 40 tons. A 500-ton slipway for larger craft, though it is mostly fishing boats which are hauled here. Mechanical and engineering repairs. Electrical repairs. Chandlers. The yard mostly specialises in trawler repairs, but can haul yachts.
Provisions Good shopping for all provisions. Supermarket in the village at the top of the hill and a small but good fish market on the waterfront. Ice from the fish market.
Eating out Good restaurants, trattorias and pizzerias.
Other PO. Bank. ATM. Italgaz and Camping Gaz. Bus to Orbitello.

General

Porto Ercole is a thoroughly likeable fishing port that has capitalised on its assets and now accommodates yachts as well, but is not overrun or overawed by them. The village of Porto Ercole is actually that on the southern slopes above the yacht berths and the village on the northern slopes (with the shops) is Grotte. Between the two villages the slopes are thickly wooded. It is well worth the climb up to Forte La Rocca for the view over the sea and salt marsh to the hills behind.

MARINA DI CALA GALERA

Approach

The marina is situated about ½ mile N of Porto Ercole.

Conspicuous The outer mole and yacht masts are easily identified from Ercole.

VHF Ch 09, 16.

Mooring

Data 700 berths. 80 visitors' berths. Max LOA 50m. Depths 2·5–5m.

Berth Call ahead for a berth. There are five agencies (listed under *Authorities* below) which control

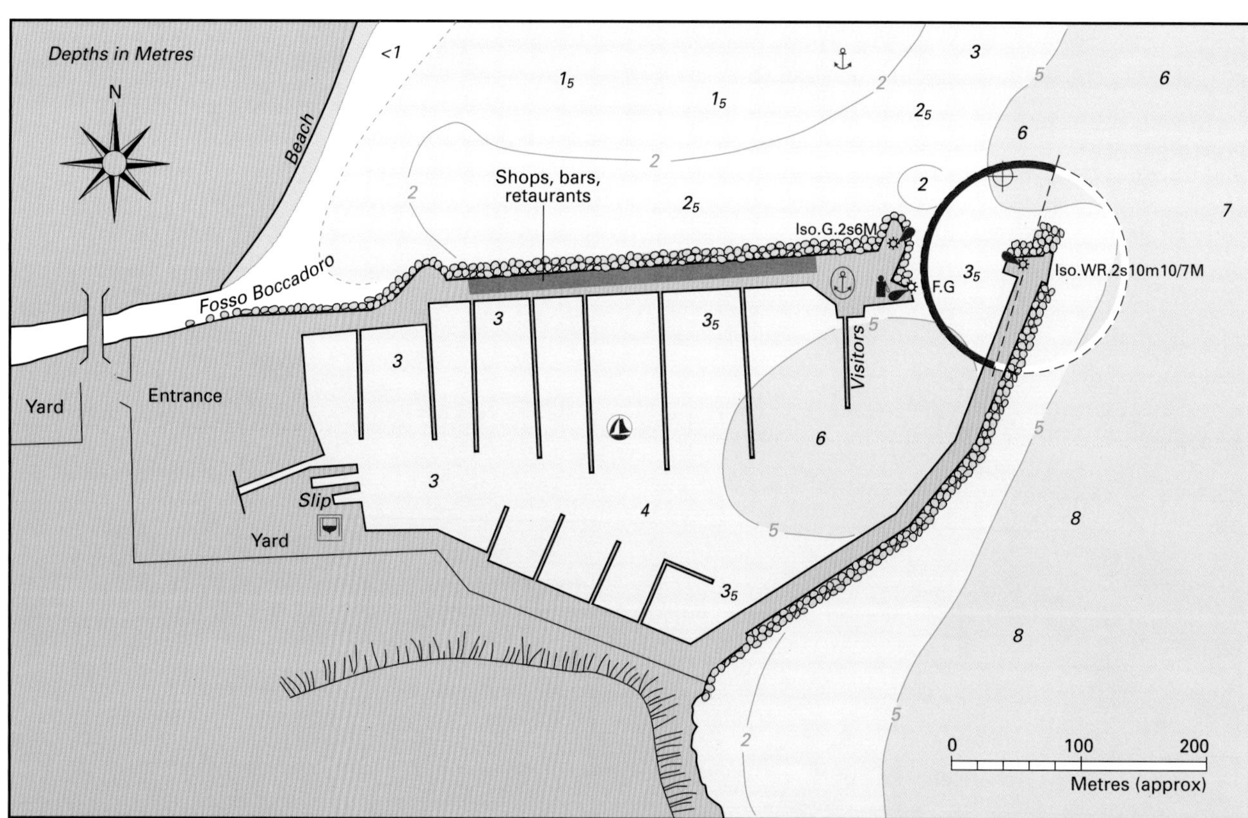

MARINA DI CALA GALERA
⊕42°24'·16N 11°12'·41E WGS84

Cala Galera looking NW

berths in the marina. The marina does not arrange visitors' berths.

Once you have been allocated a berth a marina attendant will normally scoot out in an inflatable to assist you. In the summer the marina is very crowded and a yacht may have difficulty getting a berth. There are laid moorings with a line tailed to the quay.

Shelter Excellent. Many yachts are wintered afloat here.

Authorities Port police. Marina staff. Charge band 6+ (July–August).

Marina Cala Galera ✆ 0564 833 010
Email marinacg@tiscalinet.it
www.marinacalagalera.com

Agencies
Claudio Mare ✆ 0564 830 135
Covemar ✆ 0564 833 131
Immobiliare Nautica ✆ 0564 832 344
IMS ✆ 0564 832 138
Scott Marina ✆ 0564 832 540

Anchorage In light offshore winds a yacht can anchor to the N of the marina under the sand bar blocking off Stagno di Orbitello. The bottom slopes gently to the shore and you can nose in slowly to drop the anchor in convenient depths. This is quite a peaceful anchorage and a good place to watch the birdlife on the stagno. With strong winds from any direction a large swell rolls in.

Facilities

Services Water and electricity at every berth. Telephone connections to some berths. Shower and toilet blocks.
Fuel On the quay.
Repairs An 80-ton travel-hoist. Slipway up to 200 tons. Hard standing ashore. Mechanical and engineering repairs. GRP and wood repairs. Electrical and electronic repairs. Sailmakers. Chandlers.
Provisions Small supermarket in the marina.
Eating out Restaurant, pizzeria and snack bar.
Other Exchange facilities. ATM. Hire cars. Shuttle to Porto Ercole every 15 minutes.

General

With its proximity to Rome, Cala Galera is a popular place for the inhabitants of that city to keep their boats. From the noise and chaos of Rome, the peaceful wooded setting of the marina must be a godsend. A yacht club in the marina, the Circolo Nautico e della Vela Argentario, has a restaurant and bar facilities and a summer and winter racing programme.

The coast between Promontorio Argentario and Civitavecchia

A narrow coastal plain backed by mountains runs around a large bay for nearly 30M, with the industrial city of Civitavecchia lying 5M N of Capo Linaro at the southern end.

Note Along the coast between Cala Galera and Civitavecchia are several power stations. There are prohibited areas around them and a yacht should not attempt to approach the quayed areas and piers off the stations. The installations are lit as follows:

Montalto di Castro power station
42°20'·7N 11°31'·1E Fl.Y.5m1M and Fl.Y.4m1M

Torre Valdaliga power station
42°07'·4N 11°45'·2E Fl.Y.3s6m5M; Fl(3)Y.10s10m5M; Fl.Y.3s10m4M and Fl.Y.2s10m4M.

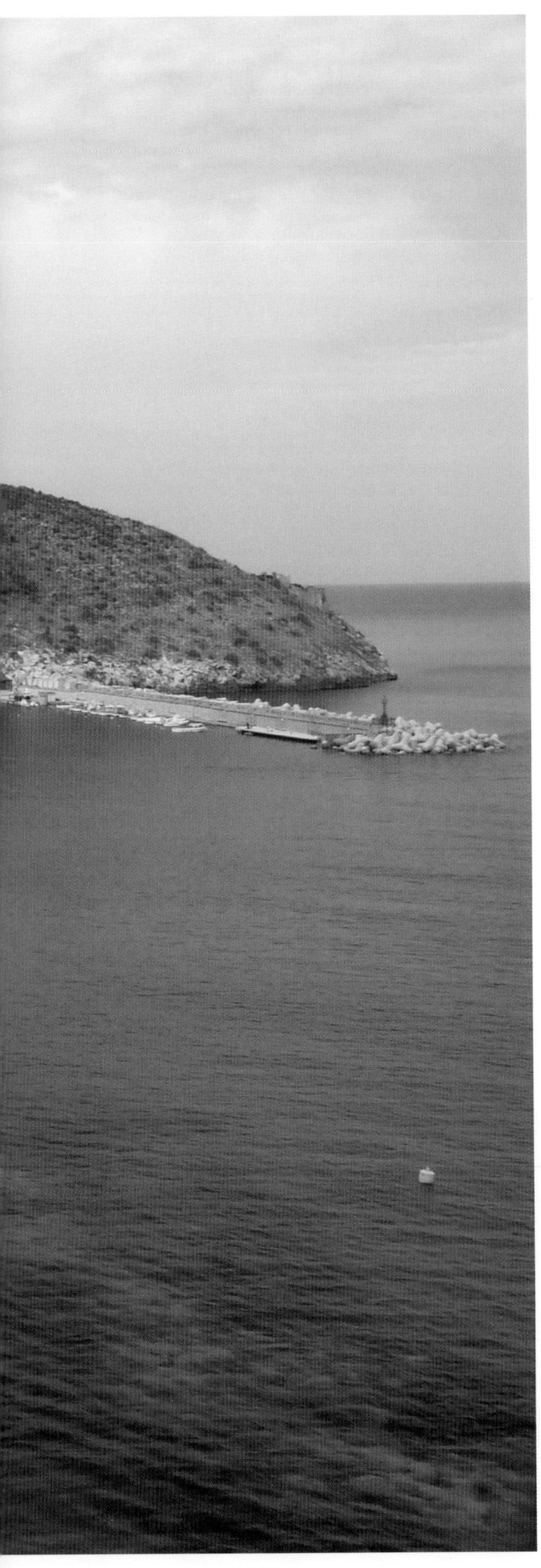

III.

The Tyrrhenian Sea

This chapter covers the mainland coast from Civitavecchia to Reggio di Calabria. It also covers the Pontine Islands (Ponza and Ventotene) and the islands in the Bay of Naples (Procida, Ischia and Capri). It covers four provinces: Lazio (Civitavecchia to the Gulf of Gaeta), Campania (the Bay of Naples to Capri), Basilicata (which has only an 18 mile seaboard on the Tyrrhenian and another 27 mile seaboard in the Gulf of Taranto) and Calabria (Maratea to Reggio). The historical sites along the coast are many and of diverse origin. The reader is advised to consult his choice of guide books which are similarly plentiful and of diverse origin.

Porto Palinuro

Routes

Yachts hopping down the coast have a pretty straightforward route going N or S. From the Bay of Naples some yachts will choose to go directly down to the Aeolian Islands or Sicily. The Aeolian Islands are a popular destination in the summer and can get very crowded. By following the coast around from Capo Palinuro and on down to Vibo Valentia and Tropea you will have one of the best cruising grounds in Italy to yourself. This high mountainous coastline is wonderful with a good scattering of little visited harbours along its length.

When going north a fairly common route to Sardinia is to coast up to the Bay of Naples and then cross to Ponza to wait for a weather window to cross to the northeastern corner of Sardinia. Olbia or Porto Cervo are both useful places to make for. Some care is needed on this crossing if there are weather systems around as you will frequently encounter some large cross-seas which can make the crossing uncomfortable (and in some cases very uncomfortable). The last time I crossed the boat pounded so much into the cross-seas that I blew out a sonar transducer. If you are making the reverse crossing from Sardinia to the Italian coast it is probably best to head for the Bay of Naples where there is a good selection of safe harbours.

USEFUL WAYPOINTS

⊕**1** 1·5M W Capo Linaro
42°01'·65N 11°47'·0E

⊕**2** 1M W Fiumicino
41°46'·2N 12°11'·6E

⊕**3** 1M W Capo d'Anzio
41°26'·6N 12°36'·1E

⊕**4** 1M S Capo Circeo
41°12'·3N 13°04'·1E

⊕**5** 1M N Capo Negro (I. Zannone)
40°59'·3N 13°03'·4E

⊕**6** 0·3M S Punta della Guardia (I. Ponza)
40°52'·30N 12°57'·24E WGS84

⊕**7** 0·8M S Monte Orlando
41°11'·39N 13°34'·69E WGS84

⊕**8** 1·5M N Pta d'Eolo Ventotene
40°50'·2N 13°26'·0E

⊕**9** 1·5M W Scoglio di S.Martino
40°47'·89N 13°59'·98E WGS84

⊕**10** 2M W Pta Imperatore (I. Ischia)
40°42'·6N 13°48'·5E

⊕**11** 0·1M S Capo Miseno
40°46'·49N 14°05'·33E WGS84

⊕**12** 2M W Pta Carena (I. Capri)
40°32'·1N 14°09'·2E

⊕**13** 0·25M W Pta Campanella
40°34'·12N 14°19'·07E WGS84

⊕**14** 1·6M W Pta Licosa
40°15'·05N 14°51'·73E WGS84

⊕**15** 0·25M W Capo Palinuro
40°01'·45N 15°15'·64E WGS84

⊕**16** 0·5M S Pta Iscoletti
39°58'·64N 15°25'·20E WGS84

⊕**17** 1M W Capo di Bonifati
39°32'·70N 15°51'·99E WGS84

⊕**18** 0·5M W Capo Vaticano
38°37'·12N 15°48'·87E WGS84

⊕**19** 1·75M E Capo Peloro
38°15'·86N 15°41'·42E WGS84

⊕**20** 0·3M W Pta Pezzo
38°13'·88N 15°37'·72E WGS84

Data

Marine Reserves and Prohibited Areas

There are eight separate areas along the coast of the Tyrrhenian Sea now protected under Marine Reserve status. For details of these areas refer to the special plans throughout the chapter.

1. ***Secche di Tor Paterno Marine Reserve*** A shoal area (least depth 18m) between Ostia and Anzio has been designated a Zone B Marine Reserve.
2. ***Ventotene Marine Reserve*** Isola S. Stefano is in a Zone A except for part of the N coast. The W and SE coast of Ventotene are in Zone B. The N and E coast including Cala Rossano are in Zone C.
3. ***Baia Marine Reserve*** An underwater marine reserve (Parco Sommerso) has been established off Baia.
4. ***Gaiola Marine Reserve*** An underwater marine reserve (Parco Sommerso) has been established off Punta Gaiola, between Nisida and Capo Posillipo.
5. ***Sorrento Peninsula Marine Reserve*** Scoglio Vervece and Vetara are in a Zone A. Isoletti Galli, Isca up to Capo Scannato and the area around Pta Campanella, including Seno di Ieranto, are under Zone B. Zone C covers any part of the coast from Capo di Sorrento to Pta Germano, not already listed above.
6. ***Regno do Nettuno (Neptune's Kingdom) Marine Reserve*** covers the Isole Flegree, with comprehensive zoning and restrictions on navigation and mooring. Two new Marine Protected Areas within the Cilento and Diano Valley National Park:
7. ***Santa Maria Castellabate Marine Reserve*** covers the coast from Pta Tresino to Pta dell'Oligastro, with special protected areas where unauthorized navigation is prohibited, around both capes and over the Secche di Licosa.
8. ***Costa degli Infreschi e della Massetta Marine Reserve*** runs around Pta Iscoletti from Camerota to Pta del Monaco S of Scario, with Zone A protection around Pta Iscoletti

MAJOR LIGHTS

Civitavecchia (Monte Cappucini) Fl(2)10s125m24M
Fiumicino Fl.3s20m11M
Capo d'Anzio Fl(2)10s37m22M
Capo Circeo Fl.5s38m23M
Gaeta (Monte Orlando) Fl(3)15s185m23M
Formia Fl.WR.3s11m11/8M

Isole Pontine
Zannone (Capo Negro) Fl(3)10s37m12M

Ponza
La Rotonda della Madonna Fl(4)15s61m12M+F.R.55m9M
Punta della Guardia Fl(3)30s112m24M+Fl.R.5s96m8M
Ventotene (Porto Nicola) Fl.5s21m15M

Ischia
Punta Imperatore Fl(2)15s164m22M
Porto d'Ischia Fl.WR.3s13m15/12M
Castello d'Ischia LFl.6s82m16M

Capo Miseno Fl(2)10s80m16M
Porto di Napoli Fl(3)15s25m22M
Portici Fl.3s16m11M
Castellammare di Stabia Fl(2)10s114m16M
Capri Punta Carena Fl.3s73m25M
Capo d'Orso Fl(3)15s66m16M
Agropoli Punta Fartino Fl(2)6s42m16M
Capo Palinuro Fl(3)15s206m25M
Scario Fl(4)12s24m15M
Capo di Bonifati Fl(2)10s63m15M
Paola Fl(3)15s53m15M
Capo Suvero Fl(2)10s58m16M
Vibo Valentia Marina Fl.WG.5s17m15/12M
Capo Vaticano Fl(4)20s108m24M
Scilla Fl.5s72m22M
Punta Pezzo Fl(3)R.15s26m15M

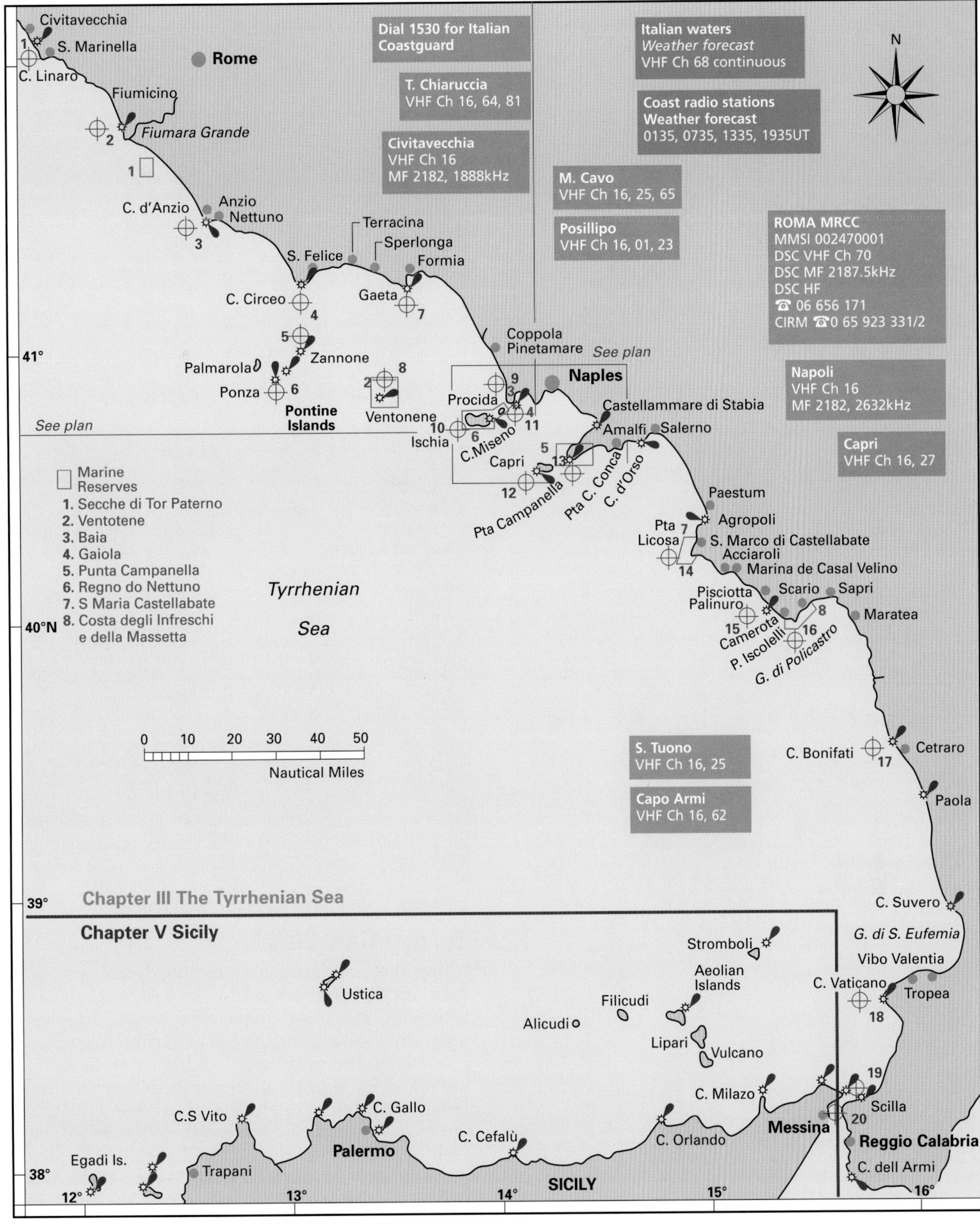

THE TYRRHENIAN SEA – CIVITAVECCHIA TO REGGIO DI CALABRIA

Quick reference guide

	Shelter	Mooring	Fuel	Water	Eating out	Provisions	Plan	Charge band
Mainland coast								
Civitavecchia	A	A	A	A	A	A	•	
Riva di Traiano	A	A	A	A	B	B	•	5
Santa Marinella	B	A	B	A	B	A	•	3/4
Fiumicino	A	AB	A	A	A	A	•	5
Fiumare Grande								
Darsena Netter	A	A	A	A	C	C	•	
Marina Porto Romano	A	A	A	A	C	C	•	5/6
Tecnomar	A	AB	O	A	C	C		3
Nautilus Marina	A	AB	O	A	C	C		3
Porto Turistico di Roma	A	A	A	A	B	B	•	5
Anzio	A	A	A	A	A	A	•	1/4
Nettuno	A	A	A	A	A	A	•	5
San Felice Circeo	A	A	A	A	C	C	•	6
Badino	C	B	O	A	C	C		
Terracina	A	AB	A	A	A	A	•	
Sperlonga	O	C	B	B	C	C	•	
Gaeta								
Porto S Maria	B	A	B	B	B	B	•	
Base Nautica Flavio Gioia	A	A	A	A	A	A	•	5/6
Caposele	B	A	A	A	C	C	•	
Formia	B	A	A	A	A	A	•	1/4
Scauri	C	A	B	A	C	C	•	
Pineta Mare	A	A	A	A	B	C	•	4
Pontine Islands								
Ponza Harbour	B	AC	A	A	B	A	•	1/6+
Cala di Feola	C	AC	O	O	C	C	•	
Cala dell'Acqua	C	C	O	O	O	O	•	
Ventotene Harbour	A	A	B	B	C	B	•	3/4
Cala Rossano	B	AC	A	A	C	B	•	1/4
Bay of Naples								
Acquamorta	B	AC	O	O	O	C	•	
Porto Miseno	A	C	B	B	C	C	•	2/3
Baia	B	A	A	A	C	C	•	3/4
Pozzuoli	A	A	A	A	B	B	•	5/6
Bagnoli	B	C	B	B	B	B		
Nisida	B	A	A	A	B	B	•	
Posillipo	B	A	O	A	C	C		
Sannazzaro	A	A	A	A	A	A	•	6+
Santa Lucia	A	A	A	A	A	A	•	4/5
Molosiglio	A	A	B	A	A	A	•	
Marina Vigliena	A	A	A	A	A	A	•	6+
Portici	B	A	B	A	B	C	•	
Torre del Greco	B	A	A	A	B	B	•	4
Torre Annunziata	B	A	A	A	A	B	•	
Castellammare di Stabia	B	A	A	A	A	A	•	
Marina di Cassano	C	AC	O	O	C	C	•	
Sorrento	C	AC	A	A	A	A	•	
Marina della Lobra	B	A	O	B	O	O	•	
Senno di Ieranto	C	C	O	O	O	O	•	
Procida								
Procida Marina	B	A	A	A	B	A	•	6
Cala di Corricella	C	C	O	O	B	C	•	
Chiaiolella	B	A	A	A	C	C	•	4/5
Vivara I anchorage	B	C	O	O	O	O		
Ischia								
Porto d'Ischia	A	A	A	A	A	A	•	5
Casamicciola	B	A	B	A	A	A	•	4
Lacco Ameno	O	AC	B	A	B	B	•	
Forio d'Ischia	O	C	B	B	B	B	•	
Sant'Angelo D'Ischia	B	A	O	B	C	B	•	6
Castello d'Ischia	C	C	O	O	B	B	•	
Capri								
Marina Grande	B	A	A	A	B	A	•	6+
Mainland Coast								
Positano	O	C	B	B	B	B		
Amalfi	C	A	A	A	A	B	•	2/5
Cetara	C	A	O	B	C	C	•	
Salerno	A	A	A	A	A	A	•	2/3
Agropoli	B	A	A	A	B	C	•	4
San Marco di Castellabate	C	B	O	A	C	C	•	
Agnone	B	A	O	B	C	C	•	
Acciaroli	B	AB	A	A	C	C	•	1/4
Marina di Casal Velino	B	A	O	O	O	O	•	
Palinuro	C	AC	O	O	C	C	•	4/5
Camerota	A	A	B	A	B	B	•	5
Scario	A	A	O	B	C	C	•	1/3
Policastro	B	A	O	A	O	O	•	
Sapri	B	AC	A	B	B	B	•	1/3
Maratea	A	A	B	A	B	C	•	4
Cetraro	B	A	O	A	C	C	•	1/3
Vibo Valentia	A	AC	A	A	B	B	•	3
Tropea	B	A	A	A	A	A	•	4
Gioia Tauro	A	BC	O	B	O	O	•	2
Bagnara Calabra	B	AB	O	A	B	B	•	1/2
Scilla	C	AC	B	A	B	B	•	1/2
Reggio di Calabria	B	AB	A	A	A	A	•	3

Weather patterns in the Tyrrhenian Sea

Along the mainland coast the winds are generally light in the summer with sea and land breezes producing the most predictable winds. The wind generally blows from the SW–SE at between Force 2–5 in the afternoon and dies down at sunset. At night and in the early morning there may be a light E–NE wind but it rarely gets above Force 2. There are frequent days of calm weather especially in the Gulf of Salerno and the Gulf of Policastro. In places the wind may be more westerly. Towards the Strait of Messina the prevailing wind is from the NE or SW blowing up or down through the Strait of Messina. At Reggio di Calabria winds from the NE account for 50% of all wind observations in July and August.

In the spring and autumn there are frequently short-lived thunderstorms and associated strong winds. In the winter, gales can be from the NW or the south. Close to the coast there can be vicious squalls, especially near Ponza, the Gulf of Salerno, the coast between Capo Palinuro and Reggio di Calabria and in the Strait of Messina (see *Chapter V, Sicily*).

Shoestring cruising in the Tyrrhenian Sea

Civitavecchia to Bay of Naples

Marinas and harbours

Civitavecchia The old inner basin is usually crowded and near impossible to get into.

Riva di Triano A better bet than Civitavecchia and reasonably priced in early and late season. Moreover it is run by a proper sailor.

Fiumocino Try up the canal or in the basin.

Fiumare Grande In the Fiumare Grande some of the yacht marinas/yards here charge pretty high prices and you need to pick and choose carefully. They are also full to bursting.

Porto Turistico di Roma at Ostia is expensive in the high season, but has reasonable rates out of season and has been used by boats to winter over.

Anzio has some cheap options as well as expensive ones and in calm weather you can always anchor off.

Terracina Difficult to find a place although the fishermen are usually friendly and you may be able to tie alongside a fishing boat in the river. Wonderful town ashore.

Formia Until the proposed marina is built you should be able to find a berth inside the old harbour.

Ventotene Reasonable if you can get in, but best early or late season.

Anchorages

Santa Marinella Usually tenable in light winds although any swell makes it a bit rolly.

Anzio Although it looks quite protected, there is often a big swell rolling in out of all proportion to the wind.

Sperlonga Delightful anchorage depending on wind and sea.

Rada di Gaeta The anchorage N of Flavio Gioia is usually tenable. You can also try N of Porto Salvo S of the pipeline.

Scauri In settled weather anchor between the breakwater and the small harbour.

Ponza Around the Pontine Islands there are several anchorages on the W side of Ponza. You can anchor in Ponza itself and although it is shown on some charts as a no anchoring zone, in practice yachts do anchor here. Keep well clear of the channel used by the ferries. The Guardia Costiera patrol the area and will soon let you know if you can stay or not.

Ventotene Anchor off the old harbour in calm weather, though it will still be rolly.

Bay of Naples

Harbours and marinas

Acquamorto You can anchor in here if there is room clear of the moorings. It is likely to be developed soon.

Around the islands you may be able to go on the fuel quay in Porto d'Ischia after closing hours or haggle with the *ormeggiatori* in the harbour. Forio d'Ischia and Sant'Angelo are also possibilities. Avoid Capri in the high season and mid-season.

Anchorages

In the Gulf of Naples you can anchor in Porto Miseno where there is good shelter, off Baia under Fortino Tenaglia, and on moorings in Senno di Ieranto.

Procida Several anchorages on the S side of Procida at Corricella and under I. Vivara, but AMP restrictions apply.

Ischia Under Castello there is a reasonably sheltered anchorage though it can be a bit rolly. Depending on wind and sea try anchoring E of Porto D'Ischia, off Lacco Ameno, just N of Forio and under the promontory at Sant Angelo. AMP restrictions apply.

Capri The anchorages around Capri are very exposed and for calm weather only.

Bay of Naples to the Messina Strait

A lot of yachts skip over to the Lipari islands from here, but it is well worth following the coast around where there are delightful spots.

Harbours and marinas

Amalfi Reasonable out of high season on the end of the mole near the fuel station.

Salerno Has some cheaper options on the pontoons. Check around the various pontoons for the best price.

Agropoli Reasonable out of high season.

San Marco di Castellabate Not easy to find a berth but usually free or reasonable.

Agnone San Nicola Reasonable and there is usually space.

Acciaroli Reasonable although prices go up in high season. Usually being dredged early season.

Marina del Casal Velino You need great care over depths and in calm weather only. Reasonable.

Marina di Scario Reasonable and wonderful.

Policastro Reasonable.

Sapri Reasonable in early and late season.

Cetraro Good value.

Vibo Valentia Reasonable on either of the two catwalks and a convivial place to boot.

Tropea Tropea is reasonably priced and has been used to winter over.

Gioia Tauro A bit of an odd place in the huge commercial harbour but reasonable.

Bagnara Calabra Another odd place though usually free with a tip for the locals who 'help' tie you up.

Scilla Room for a little one on the quay, otherwise pick up a visitors' mooring with a moderate price from the local *ormeggiatori*. Amazing location.

Reggio di Calabria The inner basin is usually full but alongside in the commercial harbour is free.

Anchorages

Isolotti Galli to Positano Local boats anchor off the Galli islands and in Cala di Punta di Sogno and at Positano, but these are all quite exposed anchorages.

Salerno Try anchoring off to the W of Porto Mausuccio Salernitano although you may be asked to move. There are reasonably priced pontoons close by.

Punta Licosa Exposed anchorage at Oligastro.

Capo Palinuro Enchanting anchorage on the SE side but often swelly.

Sapri Anchor in the bay according to wind and sea. Can be a bit rolly.

Isola di Dino Anchor off the N or S side depending on wind and sea. Local boats are kept on moorings on the N side.

Future developments

Below is a list of planned developments, with approximate number of berths when completed, and completion dates if available:

Port	Type	Berths	Date
Civitavecchia (Porto del Tirreno)	*Dev*	c.400	
Riva di Traiano Marina	*Ext*	1,050	
Fiumicino (Porto della Concordia)	*New*	1,050	2015
Anzio	*Ext*	860	
Gaeta Base Nautica Flavio Gioia	*Ext*	+400	
Formia (Porto di Levante)	*New*	1,045	2015
Marina Vigliena	*Dev*	850	2013
Salerno (Marina Arechi)	*New*	1,000	

Future projects:

Santa Marinella	*Ext*	500
San Felice Circeo	*Ext*	
Foce del Fiora (Montalto di Castro)		600
Terracina	*Ext*	500
Sperlonga (Lago Lunga)	*New*	300
Formia (Pineta di Vindicio)	*New*	630
Ladispoli	*Dev*	400
Ponza	*Dev*	500
Ventotene	*Dev*	
Bagnoli (Porto Turistico)	*New*	350
Salerno (Porto Turistico)	*Ext*	c.200
Diamante (Porto Turistico)	*New*	180

Note Not all of these projects have completed the planning process which can take some time, with no guarantee of success.

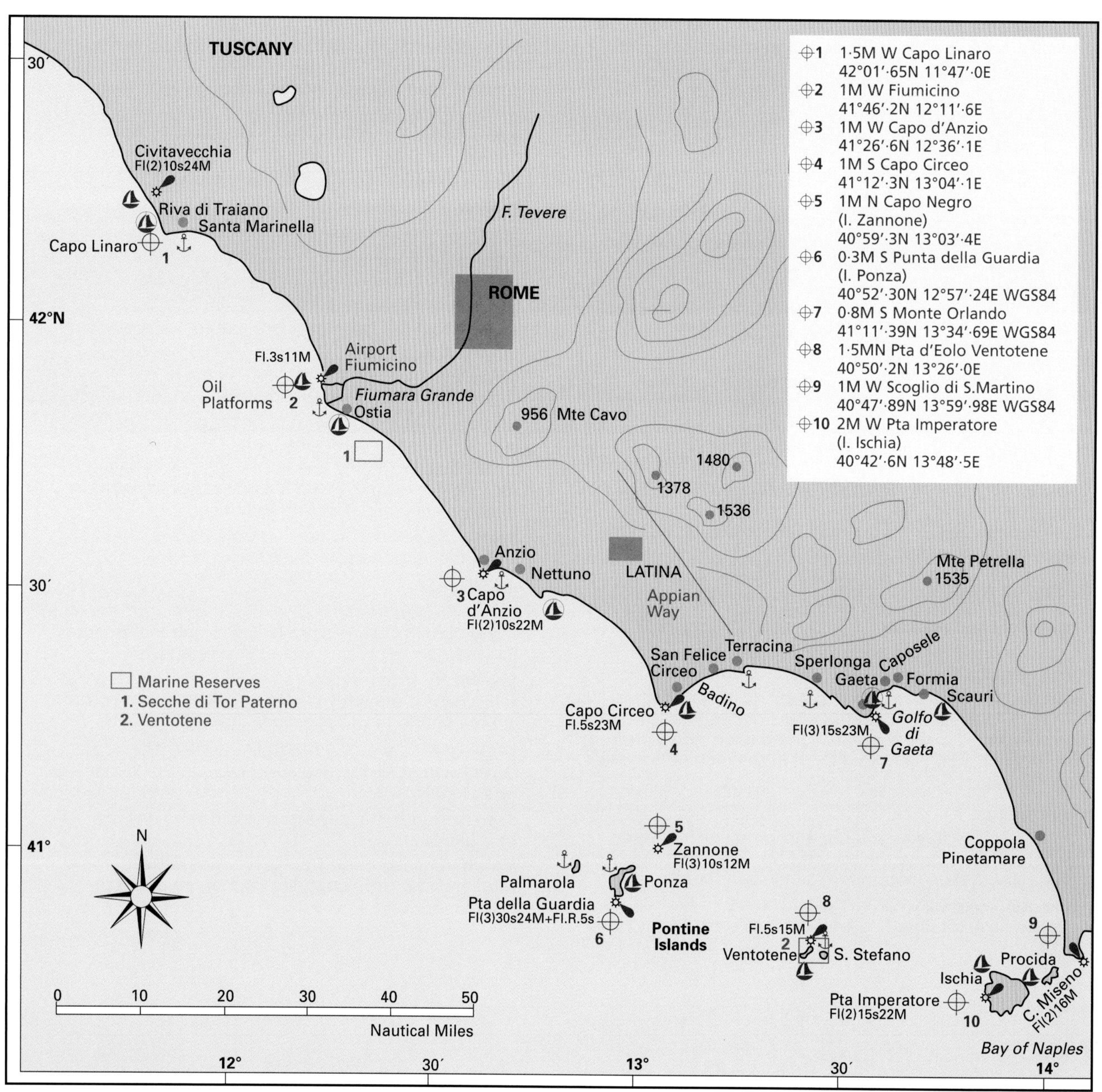

CIVITAVECCHIA TO THE BAY OF NAPLES

CIVITAVECCHIA
BA 907
Italian 76

Approach

The large commercial harbour and city are easily spotted on the low-lying coastal plain.

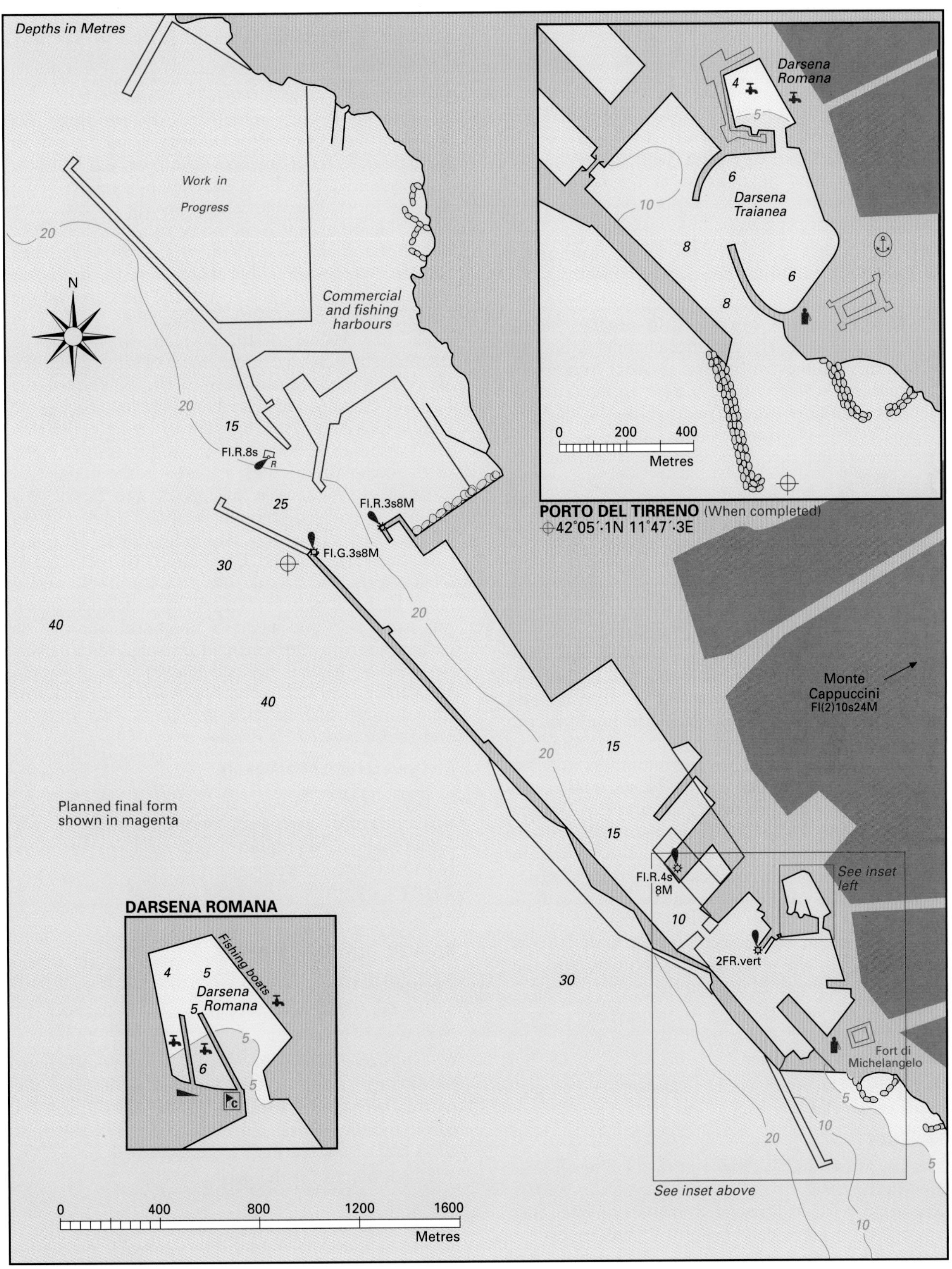

CIVITAVECCHIA
⊕42°06′·4N 11°45′·75E

Conspicuous A tall chimney with red and white bands close N of the harbour and a number of smaller chimneys within the harbour area can be seen from a considerable distance. Within the harbour a number of cranes and silos and the berthed cargo ships are also conspicuous. Closer in, the outer breakwater and the entrance are easily identified. The lighthouse in the town itself is also easily spotted.

Note Development works to the outer harbour are on-going.

By night Harbour extension works are lit with Fl.R.8s buoy and Fl.G.4m8M at the head of the mole. Light characteristics and positions are likely to change as work progresses.

VHF Ch 06, 15, 16 for port authorities (0700–1900). Ch 14 for pilots.

Dangers

1. Major expansion works are in progress in the outer port area. The entrance channel is buoyed, but the channel will move as work progresses. Eventually there will be a new entrance to the Porto Storico in the SE corner of the harbour, which is the entrance yachts should use. Until then extreme care is needed when approaching the port.
2. With strong onshore winds there is a confused swell at the entrance: troublesome but not dangerous.

Mooring

Data Max LOA 50m. Depths 4–8m.

Berth Proceed through the narrow entrance to Darsena Romana. It is very crowded in this inner basin and a yacht will normally have to go bows-to the stern of another yacht on the W quay. A berth may be found at the club berths on the pontoons out from the S side. The bottom is mud (and the anchors of other yachts). There are laid moorings tailed to the pontoons at the club berths. Larger yachts may be able to find a berth on the pontoon in Darsena Traianea. The 'Porto del Tirreno' project aims to restore the structure of the inner port to the time of Emperor Trajan in the early second century, complete with curved breakwaters. There will be yacht berths and trip boat berths in the two basins. No start date for the project is available at the time of writing, but the planned final form of Porto del Tirreno is shown as an inset to the plan.

Shelter Excellent in Darsena Romana. The berths in Darsena Traianea are subject to the wash from fishing boats and ferries.

Authorities Harbourmaster and customs. A charge is made at the club berths.

Facilities

Services Water and electricity at the club berths.
Fuel In the town.
Repairs A yard in Darsena Romana can haul craft up to 200 tons on a patent slipway. Small yachts can be craned onto the quay. Mechanical and engineering repairs. Electrical repairs. Chandlers.
Provisions Good shopping for provisions in the town. Good wet fish shops close to the fishing quay. Ice on the fishing boat quay.
Eating out Restaurants in the town.
Other PO. Banks. ATMs. Italgaz and Camping Gaz. Buses and trains to Rome. The railway station is adjacent to Darsena Romana. Ferries to Sardinia, Sicily and Tunisia.

General

The harbour and immediate surroundings are industrial and grimy and Darsena Romana, cut off by high walls from any cooling breeze, is a hell-hole in the summer. One local yachtsman has described it as the most horrible place on the coast, only excusable because it is the home of *sambucca*. Once out of the docks, (a difficult process from Darsena Romana where you will probably have to climb over several other yachts and then walk right around the basin), the town is really quite likeable.

The new vision for the port appears to include rescuing the inner harbour from its industrial limbo. Work is already under way in the N part of the harbour creating new ferry berths and expanding the commercial area. It is intended to create pedestrian areas around the Porto Storico, and to restore many of the original buildings, perhaps in the manner of Genoa's renaissance a few years ago. Until this project is realised, though, you are better off in Marina Riva di Traiano, two miles to the SSE.

In the reign of the Emperor Trajan (Traiano), Civitavecchia was made the port for Rome and a large harbour was built here. It continued as an important port into medieval times and much of the decaying fortifications around Darsena Romana was designed by Michelangelo. Stendhal was appointed Consul here in 1821, a post which left him much free time during which he wrote *Mémoires d'un Touriste* and *La Chartreuse de Parme*.

Civitavecchia Lega Navale

⊕ 42°05′·1N 11°47′·9E

A miniature harbour about 1·5M SE of Civitavecchia. Maximum depths of 1·2m and max LOA of 6·5m.

VHF Ch 09.

RIVA DI TRAIANO MARINA

Approach

A marina lying approximately two miles SSE of Civitavecchia harbour.

Conspicuous From the N the most conspicuous object after those at Civitavecchia harbour is the marina breakwater itself and, closer in, the control tower for the marina. From the S, the old tower at the S end of the marina can be identified.

VHF Ch 09, 16 for the marina (24hr).

Dangers

1. The coast around the entrance is fringed by above and below-water rocks. The approach should be made on a course of E–NE. At the entrance a red

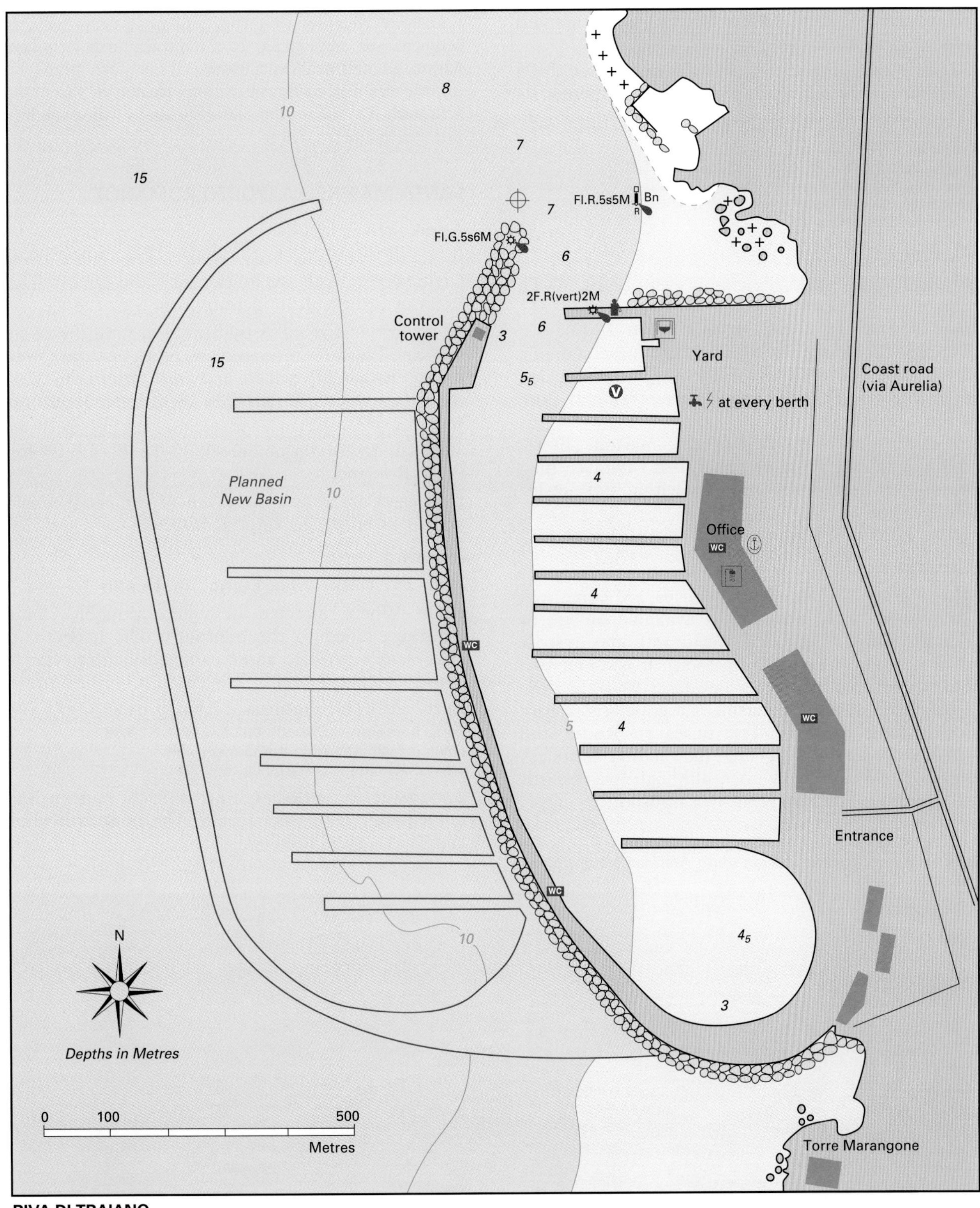

RIVA DI TRAIANO
⊕42°04′·01N 11°48′·58E WGS84

pillar beacon Fl.R.5s5M marks the port side of the channel into the marina. A line of red buoys (occas) mark the port side of the channel.

2. With strong onshore winds, a swell piles up in the approaches making entry difficult. With an onshore gale, entry may be dangerous.

Mooring

Data 1,180 berths. 110 visitors' berths. Max LOA 42m. Depths 2–5m.

Berth If possible call or email in advance for a berth. Call on VHF on approaching the marina. The friendly, knowledgeable management will always try to accommodate visitors even though the marina is full to bursting. Berth where directed. There are laid moorings tailed to the quay.

Shelter Good all-round shelter although an onshore swell produces an irritating surge at some berths.

Authorities Harbourmaster and marina staff. Charge band 5.

Porto Turistico Riva di Traiano ✆ 0766 580 193
Fax 0766 500 696
Email direzione@rivaditraiano.com
www.rivaditraiano.com

Facilities

Services Water and electricity at every berth. Wi-Fi. Shower and toilet blocks. Launderette.
Fuel On the quay at the entrance (0800–2000).
Repairs 100-ton travel-hoist. Large hard standing area. Mechanical repairs. GRP and wood repairs. Electrical and electronic repairs. Canvas and sailmakers. Chandlers.
Provisions Mini-market in the marina. Better shopping about 500m away towards Civitavecchia.
Eating out Restaurants and bars within and outside the marina.
Other Hire cars. Italgaz and Camping Gaz.

General

The marina and ancillary services are now well established, with most things available on-site or nearby. (Some shops and restaurants may restrict their opening times out of season). It is about two hours to Rome by bus, or one hour by train from Civitavecchia, and the marina is a good secure base for visiting the city. The buses to Rome and Civitavecchia stops outside the marina gates. A number of boats overwinter, although live-aboards will find it easier with their own transport.

Despite the fact that the marina is very busy, it remains the best place to break the trip between Monte Argentario and Rome. There are plans to double the size of the marina as shown in the plan, although it is still in the planning stage and work has not started yet.

SANTA MARINELLA (PORTO ROMANO)

Approach

A small yacht harbour lying seven miles from Civitavecchia and two miles E of Capo Linaro. The harbour is difficult to identify from the distance.

Conspicuous The villas built right around the coast on Capo Linaro will be seen and, closer in, the tower of the Castello Odescalchi and a convent to the W of the villa are conspicuous. The breakwater shows up well.

VHF Ch 16 for Locomare (0800–1630). Ch 09 for Porto Romano.

Dangers Care should be taken of the shoal water and rocks bordering Capo Linaro.

Mooring

Data 285 berths. Max LOA 15m. Depths 1·5–5m.

Berth Where directed or where possible. Laid moorings tailed to the pontoons. The harbour is always very crowded and it can be difficult to find a berth.

Authorities Harbourmaster. Charge band 5.

Porto Romano ✆ 0766 513 005 *Fax* 0766 518063
Email info@marinadisantamarinella.com
www.marinadisantamarinella.com

Anchorage In settled weather a yacht can anchor immediately E of the harbour. The bottom is mud and sand – good holding.

Marina Riva di Traiano looking south *Marina Riva di Traiano*

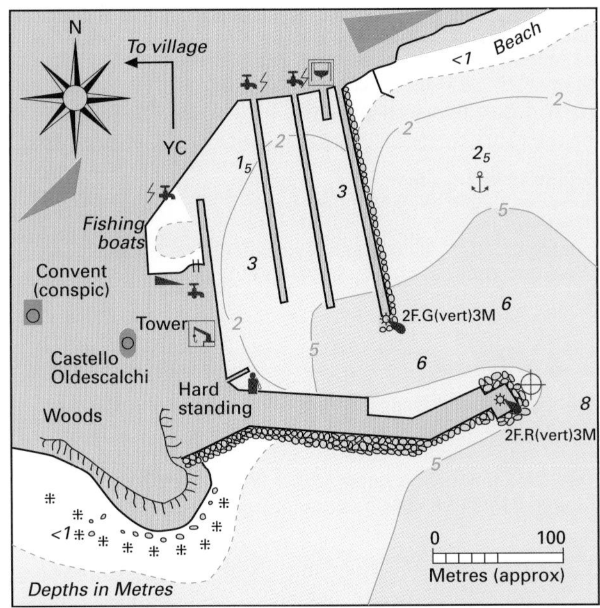

SANTA MARINELLA
⊕42°02′·07N 11°52·46E WGS84

Facilities

Services Water (not potable) and electricity on the pontoons. Care needed of uneven depths.
Fuel On the quay.
Repairs 40-ton travel-lift. A 20-ton crane. Mechanical repairs.
Provisions Most provisions can be bought in the village which is a short walk up the hill.
Eating out Restaurants and cafés in the marina, more in the town.
Other Bank, ATMs and PO in the town.

General

From Capo Linaro, the shores of the bay are lined with the villas and hotels to which the modern Romans escape at weekends. The harbour is packed with yachts registered in Rome (as are many of the other harbours close to the capital) and it can be difficult to find a berth here – a pity, as the small harbour and its setting are most attractive. The marina is under the management of Porto Romano Spa, who have a marina in Fiumara Grande.

Campo di Mare

⊕ 41°59′·4N 12°00′·3E

A small harbour has been built in the mouth of the river. There are two small basins on either bank, and short breakwaters extend out to the NW. The entrance is shallow and liable to silt. Max LOA c.10m.

FIUMICINO

BA 906
Italian 75

Approach

Fiumicino Canal lies close S of Rome's Leonardo da Vinci Airport.

Conspicuous The planes constantly taking off and landing at the airport are a useful guide to the whereabouts of the canal. Closer in, the control tower and large buildings of the airport and the buildings of Fiumicino itself are useful. On the shore by the entrance a large white storage tank and the girder light tower on the S bank are conspicuous. Closer in, the light structures at the entrance will be seen.

By night A Fl.WG at the airport on the N side of the canal has a good range.

VHF Ch 12, 16 for port authorities (Roma Radio 24/24). Ch 12, 16 for pilots.

Dangers

1. Two oil discharging platforms are situated about 2½ miles SW and three miles WSW of the entrance to the canal. These platforms are low-lying with masts exhibiting Mo(A)Y.4s3M/2Fl.R.5s&4s and a Fl.Y.2s3M respectively. It is prohibited to anchor within a radius of three miles around the entrance to Fiumicino because of the underwater pipe lines from the discharge platforms. The limit of the restricted area where anchoring and fishing are prohibited is shown in the approach plan.
2. The entrance and canal are liable to silt, and are dredged periodically. Dredging was due to take place in 2010. If in doubt about depths call Darsena Traiano for the latest advice.

Santa Marinella Marina looking SE towards the entrance

Looking W past the entrance to Darsena Traiano to the mouth of the Fiumicino Canal

3. Plans to build a new commercial harbour have been on the board for several years now. The latest plan is shown on the approach plan, and will provide a large harbour for fishing boats, ferries and other commercial shipping. When the fishing boats can use the new harbour, it is intended to develop further yacht berths in the canal. The recently extended S breakwater is complete, and work on the new harbour is due to start soon.
4. There is always a current running W out of the canal which turns to the NNW to run parallel to the coast. In the spring, autumn and winter, especially after heavy rain, the current can reach an appreciable rate: often 3–4 knots with rates up to 6–7 reported. Considerable overfalls occur at the entrance and it is advisable to enter the canal at a good speed. Allowance must be made for leeway with the current turning NNW. With strong onshore winds there can be breaking waves at the entrance and it can be dangerous to enter.
5. In the spring, autumn and winter, after heavy rains, there is a lot of debris washed out to sea from the canal and Fiumara Grande. Large trees and similar debris which could cause damage to a yacht will be found floating far out to sea off Fiumicino.

Note Yachts over 20 tons must engage a pilot before entering the canal.

Mooring

Data (Darsena Traiano) 120 berths. Max LOA 15m. Depths 1–3·5m.

Berth Proceed up the canal and berth in Darsena Traiano. There are laid moorings tailed to the pontoons. Yachts intending to stay for an extended period can proceed past the footbridge and the road bridge and berth off yards on both sides of the canal.

Bridge opening times:
Summer 15/06–30/09 Monday–Friday 0945, 1130, 1900
Weekends/holidays 0830, 1130, 1900
Winter 01/10–14/06 Monday–Friday 0700, 1130, 1600
Weekends/holidays 0900, 1130, 1600

Shelter Excellent.

Authorities Harbourmaster. Customs. Club attendants. Charge band 5.

Co-operativa del Porto di Traiano (Darsena Traiano)
✆ /*Fax* 0665 82361
Email cooperativa.traiano@tiscalinet.it
Tre Effe Elle (Fulvio's boatyard) ✆ 0665 029 392 / 4
Mobile 335 717 8584

Note
1. The N side of the canal is reserved for fishing boats. Work boats use the S side and any large yachts directed here by the harbourmaster. The basin is very crowded in the summer and a berth can be difficult to find although normally everyone is somehow fitted into a place.
2. Development of Porto Turistico di Fiumicino (Isola Sacra) is expected to add a futher 1,400 berths to this area. See entry below.

Facilities

Services Water and electricity in the basin.
Fuel On the quay in the basin.

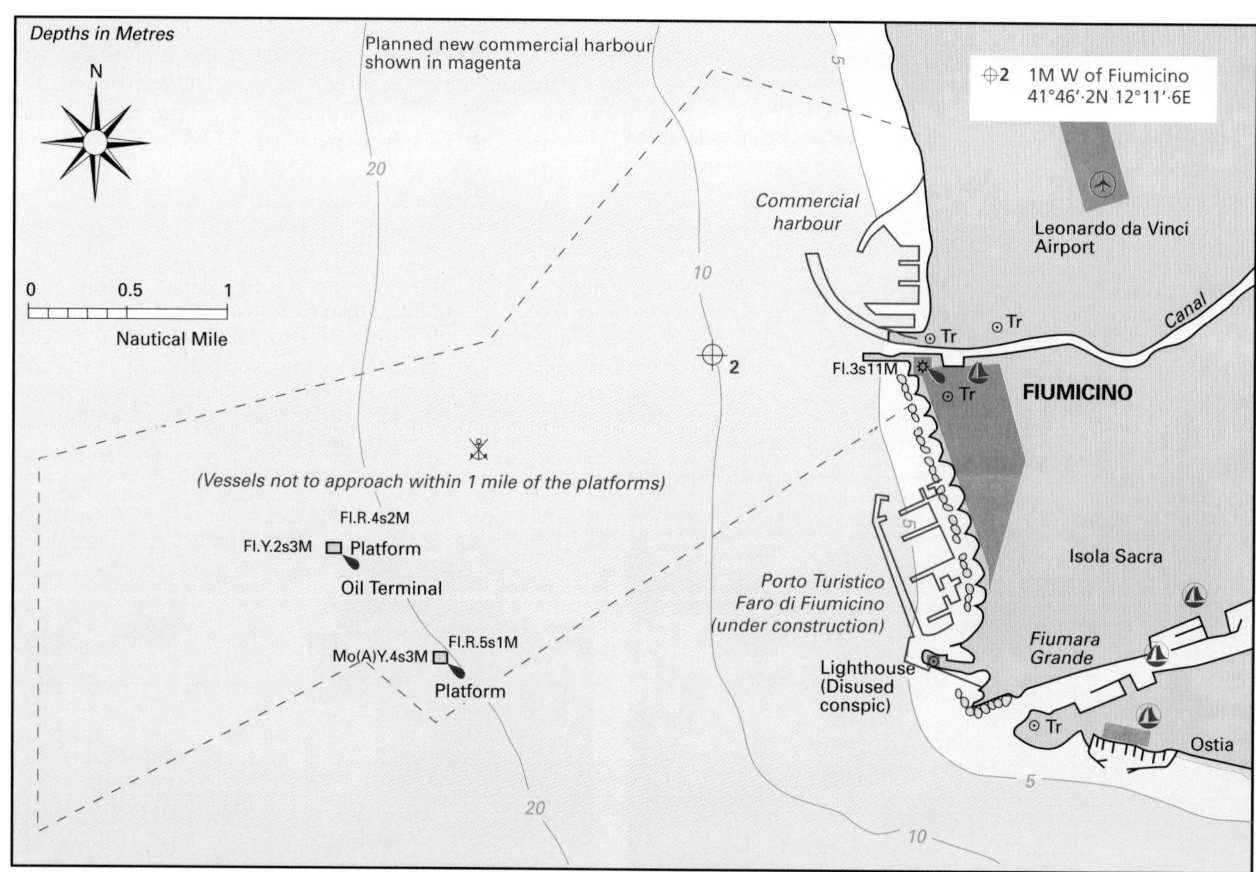

APPROACHES TO FIUMICINO AND FUMARA GRANDE

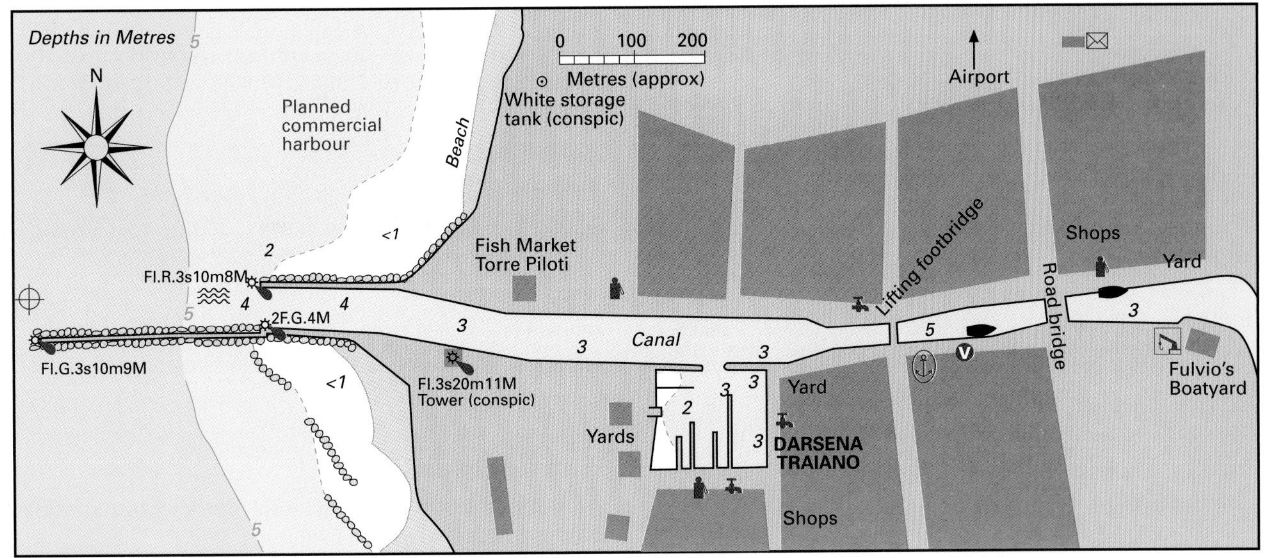

FIUMICINO
⊕41°46′·3N 12°12′·8E

Repairs A 15-ton travel-hoist. Cranes up to 30 tons. Slipways up to 50 tons. There are numerous excellent yards around the basin and in the upper reaches of the canal. Mechanical and engineering repairs. GRP and wood repairs. Electrical and electronic repairs. Sailmakers. Chandlers. Repairs of all types can be carried out to a very high standard in the yards around. One-off yachts are built and the interior work is to a standard seldom seen today.

Tre Effe Elle (or Fulvio's boatyard) lies on the S bank beyond the road bridge. Max 12-ton crane. Mooring and storage.

Il Mare in Rome (Via di Ripetta 239, Roma ✆ 063 612 091) has an excellent stock of all sorts of nautical books and charts.

Provisions Excellent shopping for all provisions. Supermarket close by. Fish market on the N bank of the canal. Ice.

Eating out Good restaurants, trattorias and pizzerias. Several excellent fish restaurants.

Other PO. ATM. Italgaz and Camping Gaz. Gas bottles can be filled here. Hire cars. Buses and train to Rome. The British Consulate is near the Spanish Steps adjacent to Porto Pia. Internal and international flights from Leonardo da Vinci airport.

Note In the canal it is recommended you keep a yacht securely locked up at all times.

General

This is a convenient port to Rome. Trains run from the station on the N bank or you can take a taxi or bus to the airport and get a train from there. Numerous boats have wintered in the upper reaches of the canal and the surroundings are not unattractive except for the noise from the airport.

The ruins of Ostia Antica are nearby to the SE and are certainly worth a visit.

Fiumicino Canal looking E past the footbridge

MARINA DEL FARO
PORTO TURISTICO DI FIUMICINO
(PORTO DELLA CONCORDIA)

A new marina under development between Fiumicino and Fiumare Grande that is now in the construction stage. The project was officially started in February 2010, with a planned completion date of 2015. The outer breakwater is already in place. The shoreside development will include commercial and residential buildings, including bars and restaurants, yacht club, sports club, hotel and apartments, as well as the usual marina and boatyard facilities.

Data 1,050 berths (1st phase 2012). 1,445 berths (completed). Max LOA c.60m.
www.portodellaconcordia.it

FIUMARA GRANDE

Approach

About two miles S of Fiumicino lies the entrance to Fiumara Grande.

Conspicuous The disused lighthouse on the N side of the entrance and a large square tower a short distance inland on the S side of the river are conspicuous.

Dangers In strong onshore winds the entrance to Fiumara Grande can be dangerous with breaking waves as the wind pushes against the outgoing current.

Note A sand bar forms at the entrance to the river and a central channel is dredged periodically to 3–5m. At times port and starboard poles mark the channel, but if in doubt contact any of the marinas for details. In the summer there are usually yachts coming and going to show the navigable channel.

In Fiumara Grande there are three yacht basins: Porto di Roma on the S bank, Porto Romana and Darsena Netter on the N bank. Approximately 1M upriver is an island which should be left to starboard if proceeding towards Rome. There are a number of catwalk berths and boatyards on the S bank of the river.

CANTIERI DI OSTIA

⊕ 41°44'·5N 12°14'·55E

A boatyard with limited berths. Home to Canados boat builders.

VHF Ch 16.

Data Max LOA 20m. Depths 1·5–3m.

Facilities Water and electricity. 60-ton slipway. 12-ton crane. Most yacht repairs.

PORTO ROMANO

A new marina on the N bank immediately downstream of Darsena Netter.

Note A floating barrier is placed across the entrance at night and during strong onshore winds. Do not attempt to enter the marina without calling ahead.

VHF Ch 73.

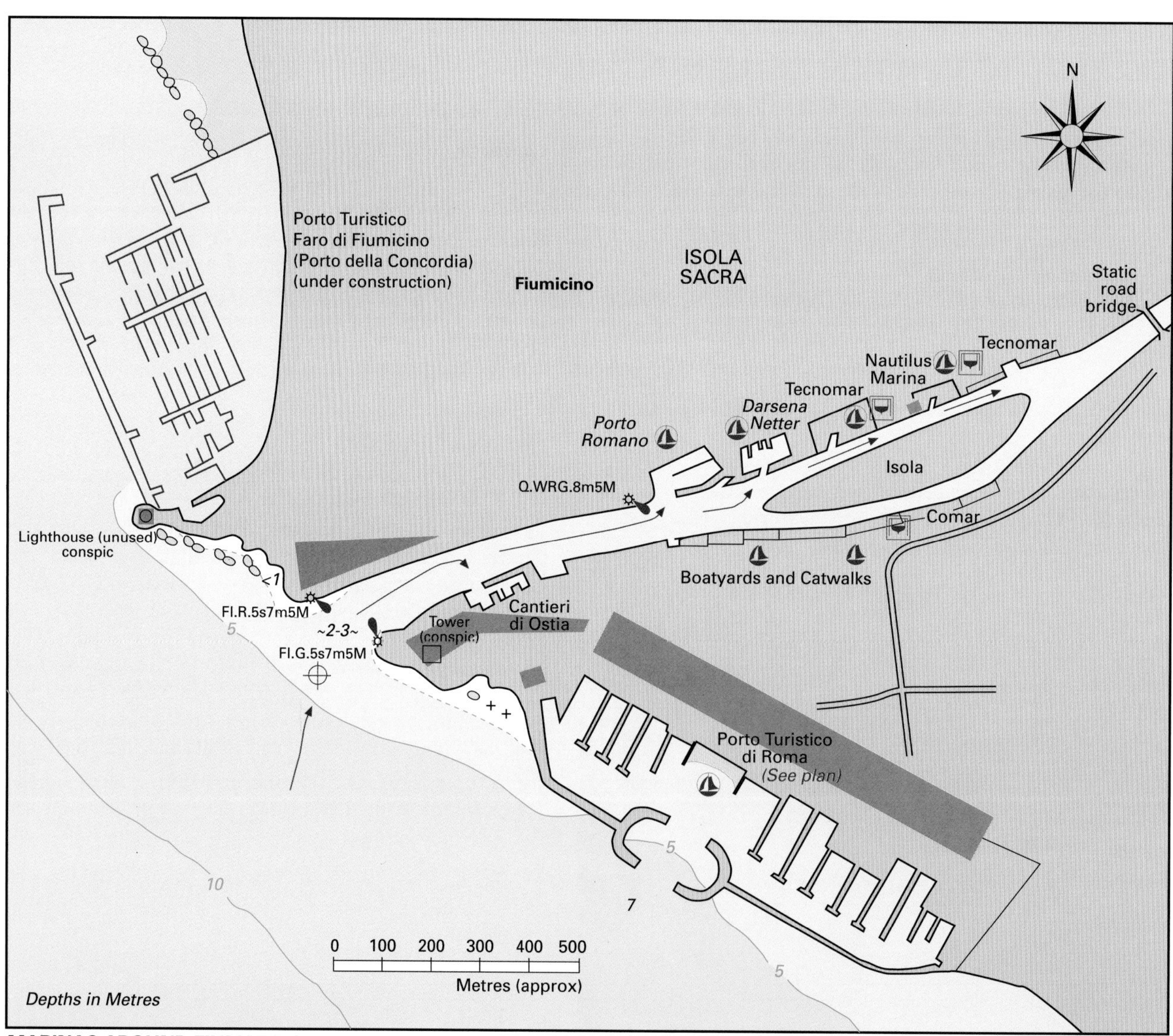

MARINAS AROUND FIUMARA GRANDE
⊕ 41°44'·34N 12°13'·58E WGS84

Yacht berths and boatyards on the S bank of the river

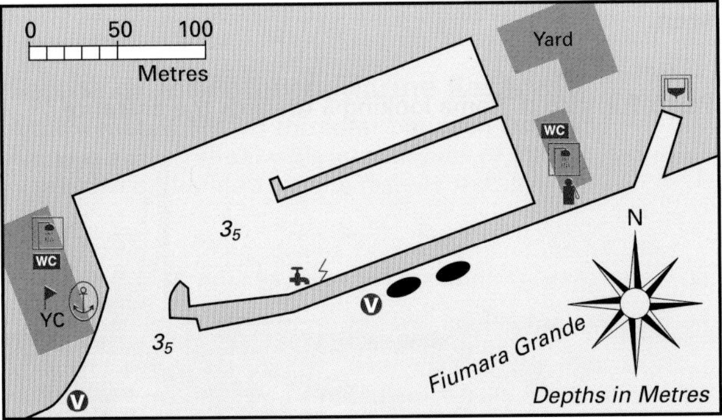

PORTO ROMANO
⊕41°44´·6N 12°15´·2E

Data 200 berths. 100m visitors' quay. Max LOA 50m. Depths 3·5m. Mooring posts inside the basin. Visitors' berths are alongside the outer wall (100m), or inside if berths are available.

Authorities Marina staff. Charge band 5/6.
Porto Romano (Yacht Club Tevere) ✆ 06 650 2651
Fax 06 652 2724
Email marina@portoromano.com

Facilities

Services Water and electricity. Showers and toilets.

Fuel Fuel on the quay.

Repairs 75-ton travel-hoist. Some repairs at the yard.

Other Restaurant and bar, fitness centre and swimming pool at the yacht club.

DARSENA NETTER

⊕ 41°44'·7N 12°15'·44E

The marina and yard lies on the N bank just off the island in the Tiber.

VHF Ch 16.

Data 70 berths. 10 visitors' berths. Max LOA 30m. Depths 3–4·5m.

Facilities

Services Water and electricity. Toilets and showers. Fuel quay. 150-ton slipway. 30-ton travel-hoist. Most yacht repairs. Restaurant and bar. Telephone.

Rome

I will not even begin to attempt to describe what to see and not to see in Rome when whole bulky guide books are devoted to this great city. It cannot be seen in a day or two and at first it is a baffling and confusing city. It has no readily identifiable character and no real reason for being there at all, except that it always has been from Etruscan times to the present. It has had artistic and architectural wonders bestowed upon it by the Etruscans; it was a virtual storehouse of stolen Greek statuary; the Romans themselves bestowed fine monuments and buildings by the hundreds; it was adopted in turn by the Catholic church and showered with gifts by the Papacy; Raphael, Michelangelo and Da Vinci adorned it; and Goethe, Stendhal, Hawthorne and Byron have written of its grandeur.

All these layers are mixed up without a coherent pattern and, for this reason, Rome can be the most infuriating city in the world to explore. It is a gigantic jigsaw puzzle incorporating written history and many works of art and it all has to be picked over at leisure. If you are here for a short time I suggest you buy a map/guide-book and tarry over a few selected sights within handy walking distance of each other, interspersed with frequent stops at cafés to catch your breath and watch the frenetic modern-day Romans hurtling around Rome's choked roads. To hurry over Rome is to get naught but a fleeting glance of an old maid's make-up.

'O thou new-comer who seek'st Rome in Rome
And find'st in Rome nothing thou can'st call Roman;
Arches worn old and palaces made common
Rome's name alone within these walls keeps home.'

Rome Joachim du Bellay, trans. Ezra Pound

The Colloseum in Rome was the largest amphitheatre ever built in the Roman Empire
Vito Arcomano, FOTOTECA ENIT

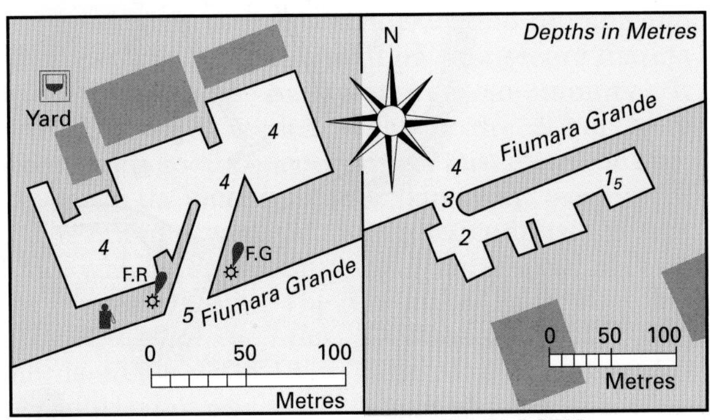

DARSENA NETTER **CANTIERI DI OSTIA**

✉ Netter Italia, Via Monte Cadria 135, 00054 Fiumicino
✆ 06 652 1966 / 7 *Fax* 06 658 1615
Email netter@faronet.it
www.netter.it

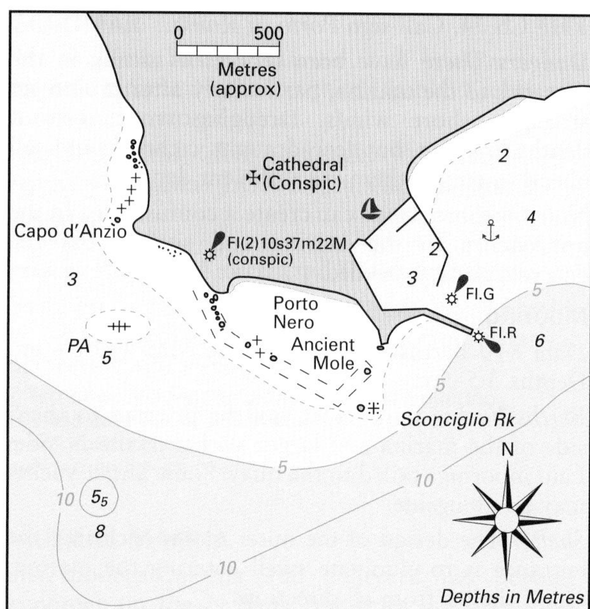

ANZIO APPROACHES

ANZIO

BA 906
Italian 7, 77

Approach

Between Ostia and Anzio there are long sandy beaches popular with wind and kite surfers, and associated development along the foreshore.

Care must be taken of the numerous above and below-water rocks off Capo d'Anzio, the remains of an ancient Roman harbour, in the approaches.

Conspicuous From the N the lighthouse and dwelling on Capo d'Anzio and the cathedral and tower in the town are conspicuous. From the S a building looking something like a mini-Empire State Building at Nettuno is conspicuous. The buildings of Anzio and the outer breakwater are easily identified when closer in.

Anzio inner harbour looking north

Anzio lighthouse

VHF Ch 11, 16 for port authorities (24hr).

Dangers

1. The remains of Nero's ancient harbour, above and below-water obstructions, extend some 500m from the coast.
2. With southerly gales it is impossible to enter or leave the harbour. There are breaking waves at the entrance over the bar (approximately 5m line). After weathering a southerly gale in here the swell still rolling in reduced the depths at the bottom of the troughs by 2½m at the entrance when I eventually left.
3. The entrance continues to silt, with a sandbank that builds up, running out northwards from the end of the breakwater. Keep close to the green buoys at the entrance. The harbour is dredged periodically. Local ferries and fishing boats should show the way in, but if in any doubt call the port.

Note

1. A fish farm has been established close off Capo d'Anzio, marked with yellow buoys. Care needed if approaching at night.
2. The planning stages of the harbour development continues, with the final design to include 860 yacht berths in the inner basin; fishing boat, ferry, ro-ro and military berths in the outer basin, along with a fish warehouse and market, boat hauling and repairing facilities, yacht club and a fuel quay.

Mooring

Data Depths <1–5m.

Berth The harbour is always crowded. The inner yacht basin, dubbed a 'marina', is crowded but a yacht can sometimes find a berth off the yard near the entrance. A pontoon off the W wall has four

The entrance to Anzio showing the breaking waves along the sandbar after a strong southerly has been blowing

Yacht berths and boatyards on the S bank of the river

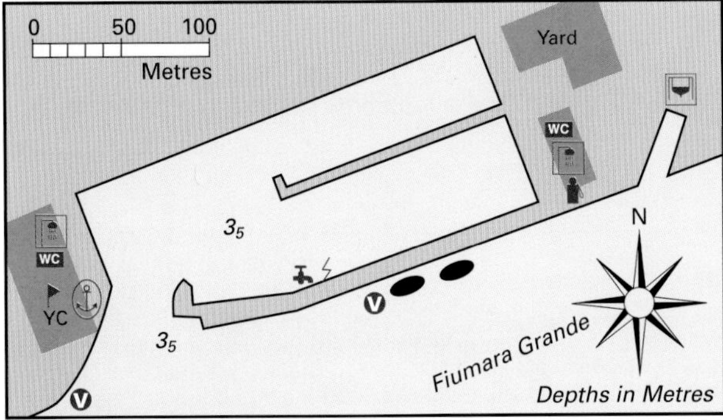

PORTO ROMANO
⊕41°44′·6N 12°15′·2E

Data 200 berths. 100m visitors' quay. Max LOA 50m. Depths 3·5m. Mooring posts inside the basin. Visitors' berths are alongside the outer wall (100m), or inside if berths are available.

Authorities Marina staff. Charge band 5/6.
Porto Romano (Yacht Club Tevere) ☎ 06 650 2651
Fax 06 652 2724
Email marina@portoromano.com

Facilities

Services Water and electricity. Showers and toilets.

Fuel Fuel on the quay.

Repairs 75-ton travel-hoist. Some repairs at the yard.

Other Restaurant and bar, fitness centre and swimming pool at the yacht club.

DARSENA NETTER

⊕ 41°44′·7N 12°15′·44E

The marina and yard lies on the N bank just off the island in the Tiber.

VHF Ch 16.

Data 70 berths. 10 visitors' berths. Max LOA 30m. Depths 3–4·5m.

Facilities

Services Water and electricity. Toilets and showers. Fuel quay. 150-ton slipway. 30-ton travel-hoist. Most yacht repairs. Restaurant and bar. Telephone.

Rome

I will not even begin to attempt to describe what to see and not to see in Rome when whole bulky guide books are devoted to this great city. It cannot be seen in a day or two and at first it is a baffling and confusing city. It has no readily identifiable character and no real reason for being there at all, except that it always has been from Etruscan times to the present. It has had artistic and architectural wonders bestowed upon it by the Etruscans; it was a virtual storehouse of stolen Greek statuary; the Romans themselves bestowed fine monuments and buildings by the hundreds; it was adopted in turn by the Catholic church and showered with gifts by the Papacy; Raphael, Michelangelo and Da Vinci adorned it; and Goethe, Stendhal, Hawthorne and Byron have written of its grandeur.

All these layers are mixed up without a coherent pattern and, for this reason, Rome can be the most infuriating city in the world to explore. It is a gigantic jigsaw puzzle incorporating written history and many works of art and it all has to be picked over at leisure. If you are here for a short time I suggest you buy a map/guide-book and tarry over a few selected sights within handy walking distance of each other, interspersed with frequent stops at cafés to catch your breath and watch the frenetic modern-day Romans hurtling around Rome's choked roads. To hurry over Rome is to get naught but a fleeting glance of an old maid's make-up.

'O thou new-comer who seek'st Rome in Rome
And find'st in Rome nothing thou can'st call Roman;
Arches worn old and palaces made common
Rome's name alone within these walls keeps home.'

Rome Joachim du Bellay, trans. Ezra Pound

The Colloseum in Rome was the largest amphitheatre ever built in the Roman Empire
Vito Arcomano, FOTOTECA ENIT

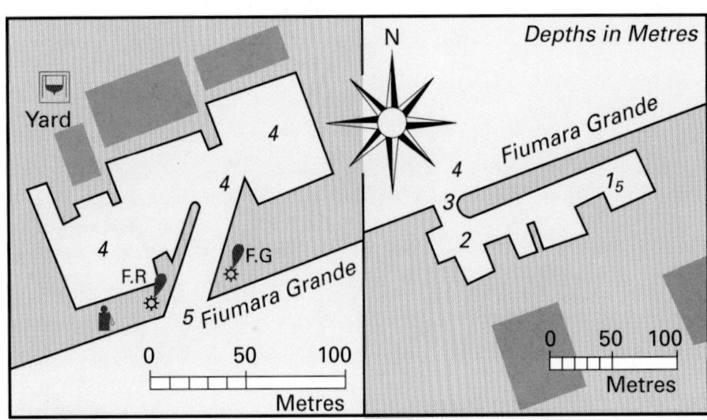

DARSENA NETTER **CANTIERI DI OSTIA**

✉ Netter Italia, Via Monte Cadria 135, 00054 Fiumicino
☎ 06 652 1966 / 7 *Fax* 06 658 1615
Email netter@faronet.it
www.netter.it

TECNOMAR

This well-established marina and boatyard lies beyond Darsena Netter on the N bank. Yachts are hauled out or stored afloat.

Data 200 berths rafted alongside. 50 places ashore. Depths 4–5m. Max LOA c.45m. Charge band 3.

Facilities

Services Water and electricity. Toilets and showers.

Travel-lift and slipway up to 300-tons. Most repairs for GRP, wood or steel. Mechanical and electrical engineering and rigging service.

✉ Tecnomar, Via Monte Cadria 73, 00054 Fiumicino
✆ 06 658 0691 *Fax* 06 658 0646
Email info@tecnomar.net
www.tecnomar.net

NAUTILUS MARINA

This modern marina and boatyard lies beyond Tecnomar on the N bank. Facilities are good and prices in line with other yards along the river.

Data c.100 berths rafted alongside. 30 places ashore. Depths 4–5m. Max LOA c.45m. Charge band 3.

Facilities

Services Water and electricity. Toilets and showers. Restaurant. Security.

50-ton travel-lift. Most engineering, electrical and mechanical repairs. Paint shop. West System. Osmosis treatment. No owners' or contractors' work permitted.

✉ Nautilus Marina, Via Monte Cadria 127, 00054 Fiumicino
✆ 06 658 1221 *Fax* 06 658 2285
Email info@nautilusmarina.com
www.nautilusmarina.com

Note There are various other small yards and clubs along the banks of the river which may have berths for visiting yachts.

PORTO TURISTICO DI ROMA – OSTIA

This huge new complex dominates the coast in the southern approaches to Fiumara Grande. The unusual shape of the outer moles and the 'beach' inside are designed both to improve protection from any onshore swell and, coupled with a pumping plant, to maintain high water quality within the marina.

Approach

Conspicuous Immediately N of the marina the tower and disused lighthouse around the entrance to Fiumara Grande are conspicuous. Closer in, the Roman-style control tower on the N side of the entrance and other buildings of the marina will be seen.

Porto Turistico di Roma looking S towards the entrance

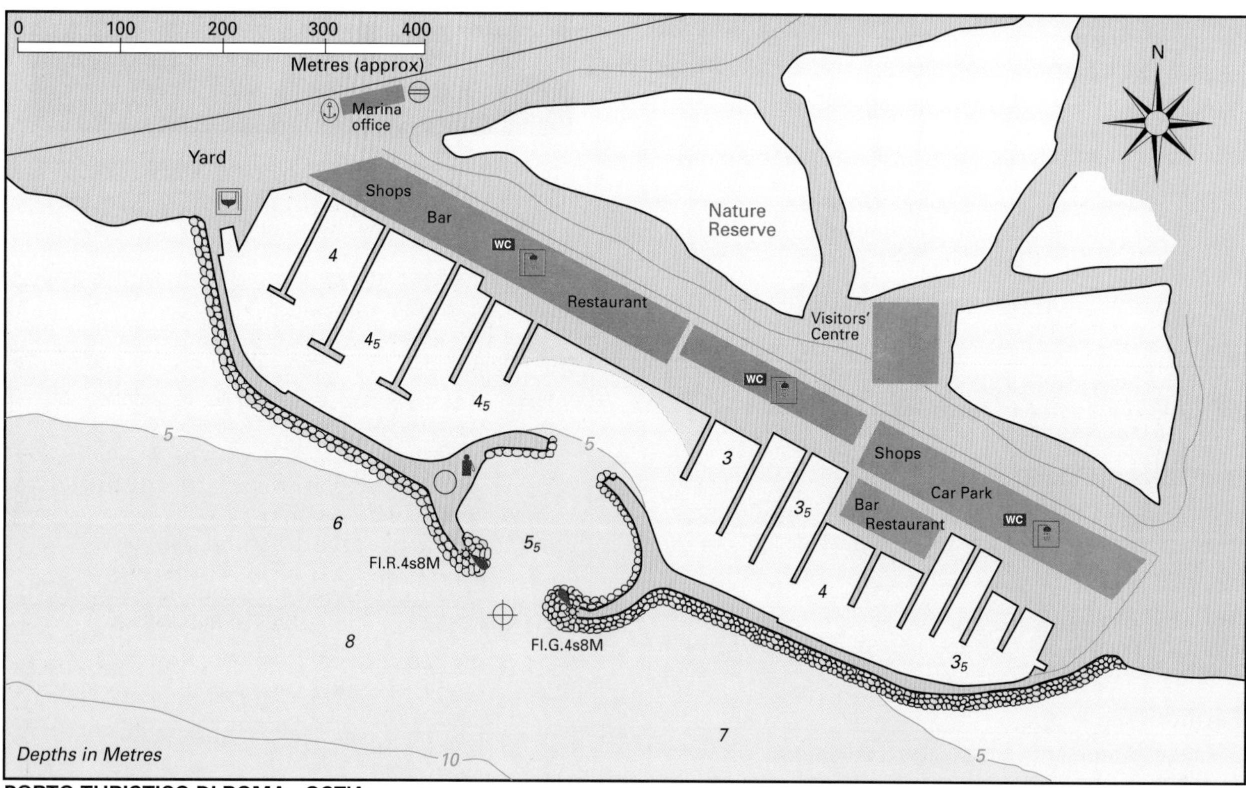

PORTO TURISTICO DI ROMA - OSTIA
⊕41°44'·1N 12°14'·6E

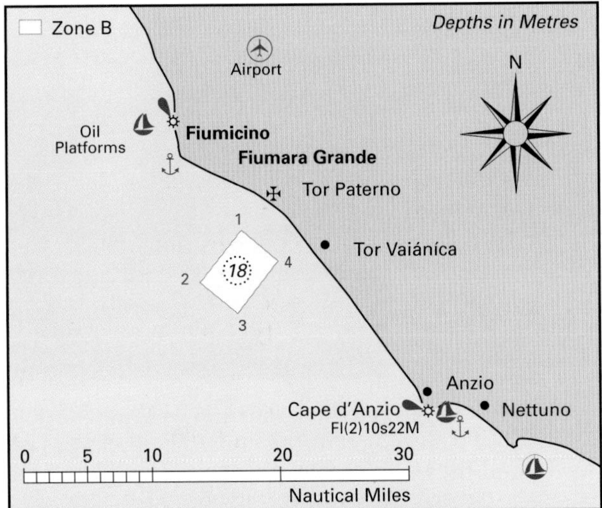

SECCHE DI TOR PATERNO MARINE RESERVE

Secche di Tor Paterno Marine Reserve

Approximately 5M off the coast between Ostia and Anzio is a rocky shoal with least depths of 18m. It has now been designated marine reserve status

Zone B

Unauthorised fishing, diving, navigation and anchoring prohibited. The area as shown in the plan is bounded by the co-ordinates:

1. 41°37'·3N 12°20'·5E
2. 41°35'·8N 12°18'·0E
3. 41°34'·5N 12°19'·5E
4. 41°36'·0N 12°21'·9E

It is marked on each corner with yellow buoys × topmark.

✆ 0635 405 310 *Fax* 0635 491 519
Email torpaterno@romanatura.roma.it
www.ampsecchetorpaterno.it

Ostia Antica

The Roman settlement dating from 4BC, is around 2km away from Porto Turistico di Roma. Excavations have revealed a cosmopolitan town and port believed to have had a population of around 100,000. The fall of Rome and ravages of malaria took their toll and Ostia Antica was soon forgotten and buried in the silt brought down the Tiber, only to be unearthed again at the beginning of the last century. Much remains of the ancient town and there is an excellent museum mapping out the rise and fall of the port. The designers of the new marina Porto Turistico di Roma are said to have been inspired by the original Roman port. Note: closed on Mondays.

Theatre and the traders' square at Ostia Antica
Vito Arcomano, FOTOTECA ENIT

VHF Ch 74. Call sign *Porto di Roma*.

Dangers There have been reports of silting in the entrance to the marina, particularly after prolonged strong onshore winds. Dredging work restores depths to 4–5m, but deep-draught yachts should call ahead to ensure there are sufficient depths.

Note Onshore winds can create a confused sea in the approaches to the marina and surf across the entrance; care is needed.

Mooring

Data 810 Berths. Visitors' berths. Max LOA 60m. Depths 3·5–5m.

Berths Yachts under 15m will be directed to the S side of the marina and larger yachts to the N side. Laid moorings tailed to the quay. Some larger yachts may go alongside.

Shelter The design of the outer moles enclosing the entrance is to eliminate swell entering the marina. Good shelter from all directions.

Authorities Harbourmaster. Customs.
Charge band 5.

✆ 06 561 88236 *Fax* 06 561 88243
Email direzione.porto@portodiroma.it
www.portoturisticodiroma.net

Facilities

Services Water and electricity (220/380V) at every berth. Telephone connection on request. Shower and toilet blocks.

Fuel On the quay on the N side of the outer port.

Repairs Cantieri Navali Rizzardi operates the yard in the marina. 400-ton travel-hoist. Most yacht repairs can be carried out in the yard. Winter storage. Chandlers.

CN Rizzardi ✆ 06 561 88280 *Fax* 06 561 88281
Email gbiamonte@rizzardi.com

Provisions A supermarket within the marina. Other supermarkets nearby in Ostia.

Eating out Three restaurants and bars. Restaurants along the waterfront in Ostia.

Other Bank. ATM. PO and banks in Ostia. Regular bus to the metro/rail station to get into Rome. Taxis.

General

Porto Turistico di Roma is now up and running and is developing a good reputation as a secure marina with a growing overwintering community. It provides much needed yacht berths 20km from Rome with good connections via bus, metro or taxi. Leonardo da Vinci airport is 9km away.

The brand new marina is in stark contrast to Ostia Lido, which until recently was a fairly seedy area on the fringes of Rome. The film-maker Paolo Passolini (*The Canterbury Tales*, *Decameron*, *Salo*) was murdered nearby in 1975. Battered to death by a 17-year-old who was later caught driving the film-maker's Alfa Romeo, Passolini's body was dumped in waste land behind what is now the marina. Today the area is being developed by the marina as a nature reserve, managed by the LIPU (Italian League for the Protection of Birds).

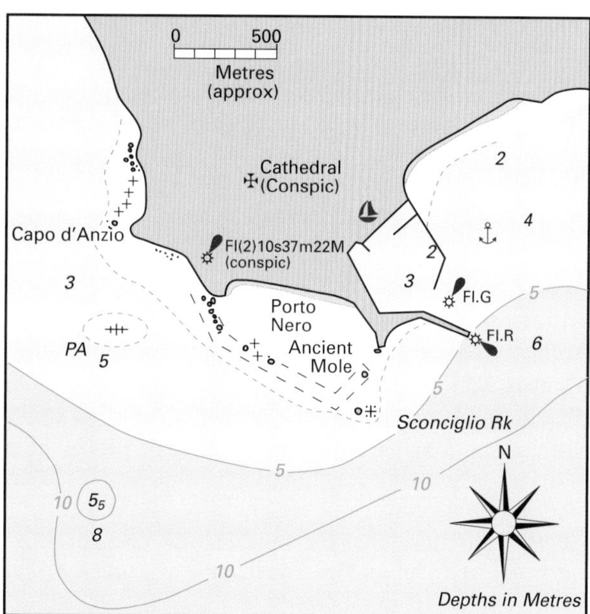

ANZIO APPROACHES

Anzio lighthouse

ANZIO

BA 906
Italian 7, 77

Approach

Between Ostia and Anzio there are long sandy beaches popular with wind and kite surfers, and associated development along the foreshore.

Care must be taken of the numerous above and below-water rocks off Capo d'Anzio, the remains of an ancient Roman harbour, in the approaches.

Conspicuous From the N the lighthouse and dwelling on Capo d'Anzio and the cathedral and tower in the town are conspicuous. From the S a building looking something like a mini-Empire State Building at Nettuno is conspicuous. The buildings of Anzio and the outer breakwater are easily identified when closer in.

VHF Ch 11, 16 for port authorities (24hr).

Dangers

1. The remains of Nero's ancient harbour, above and below-water obstructions, extend some 500m from the coast.
2. With southerly gales it is impossible to enter or leave the harbour. There are breaking waves at the entrance over the bar (approximately 5m line). After weathering a southerly gale in here the swell still rolling in reduced the depths at the bottom of the troughs by 2½m at the entrance when I eventually left.
3. The entrance continues to silt, with a sandbank that builds up, running out northwards from the end of the breakwater. Keep close to the green buoys at the entrance. The harbour is dredged periodically. Local ferries and fishing boats should show the way in, but if in any doubt call the port.

Note

1. A fish farm has been established close off Capo d'Anzio, marked with yellow buoys. Care needed if approaching at night.
2. The planning stages of the harbour development continues, with the final design to include 860 yacht berths in the inner basin; fishing boat, ferry, ro-ro and military berths in the outer basin, along with a fish warehouse and market, boat hauling and repairing facilities, yacht club and a fuel quay.

Mooring

Data Depths <1–5m.

Berth The harbour is always crowded. The inner yacht basin, dubbed a 'marina', is crowded but a yacht can sometimes find a berth off the yard near the entrance. A pontoon off the W wall has four

Anzio inner harbour looking north

The entrance to Anzio showing the breaking waves along the sandbar after a strong southerly has been blowing

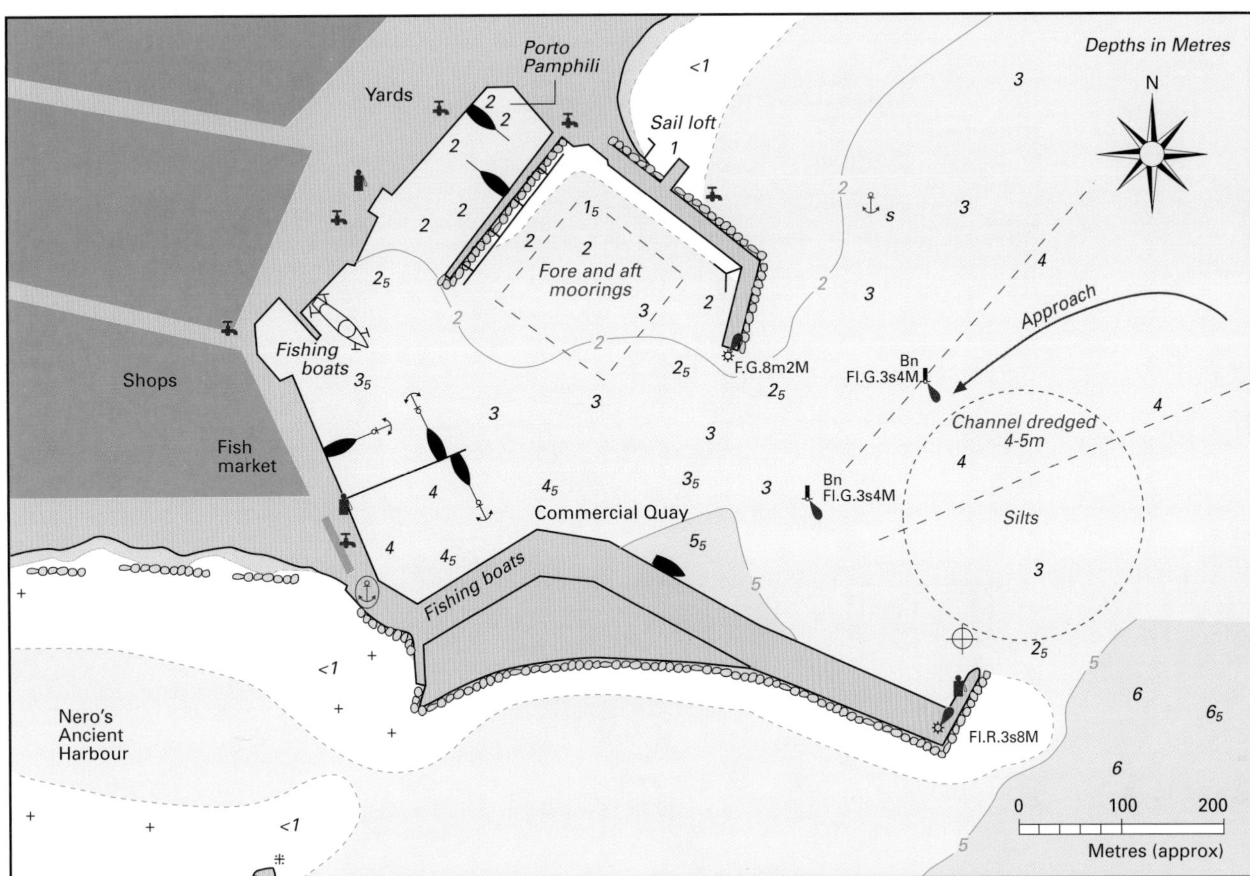

ANZIO
⊕41°26´·62N 12°38´·29E WGS84

visitors' berths, but it is not always in place. There may also be a berth on the commercial quay if a space is free and the harbourmaster tolerant or you may be able to negotiate a berth on the N mole. Under the N mole the whole area is taken up with fore and aft moorings, so there is nowhere to anchor. If no berths are available then it is a matter of anchoring off outside if conditions are suitable or going to Nettuno Marina across the bay.

Shelter Good all-round shelter in the inner basin although strong southerlies cause a surge. Good in the outer harbour although southerlies cause a surge.

Authorities Harbourmaster and customs. *Ormeggiatori* in the inner basin where a charge is made. Charge band 1/4.

Anchorage In settled weather or light northerlies a yacht can anchor off to the NE of the harbour in 2·5–3m depths on sand. Even light southerlies or westerlies cause an uncomfortable swell here.

Facilities

Water On the quay
Fuel On the quay at the S end of the W breakwater. Depths uneven.
Repairs Slipways up to 300 tons. Mechanical and engineering repairs. GRP and wood repairs. There are several yards in the inner basin that carry out good quality work. Electrical repairs. Sailmakers. Chandlers.

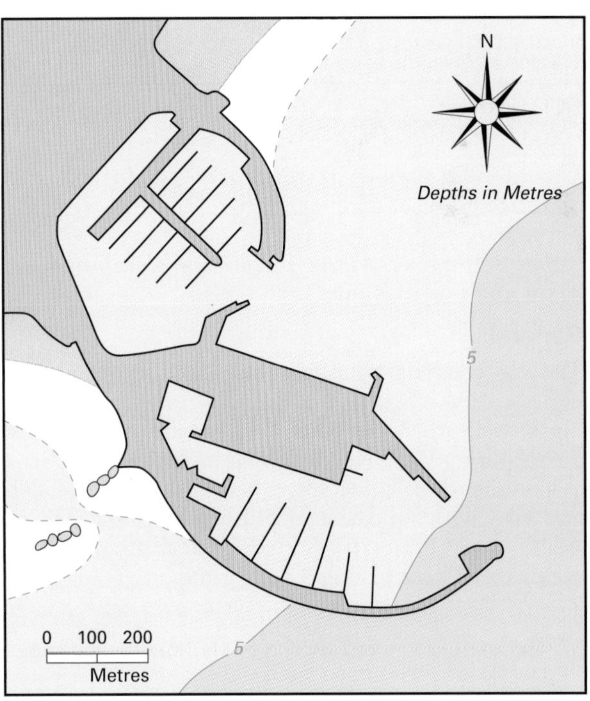

ANZIO - PLANNED DEVELOPMENT

Provisions Excellent shopping for all provisions. Supermarket nearby. Fresh fruit and vegetables and fresh fish markets in the town near the harbour. Ice from the fish market.

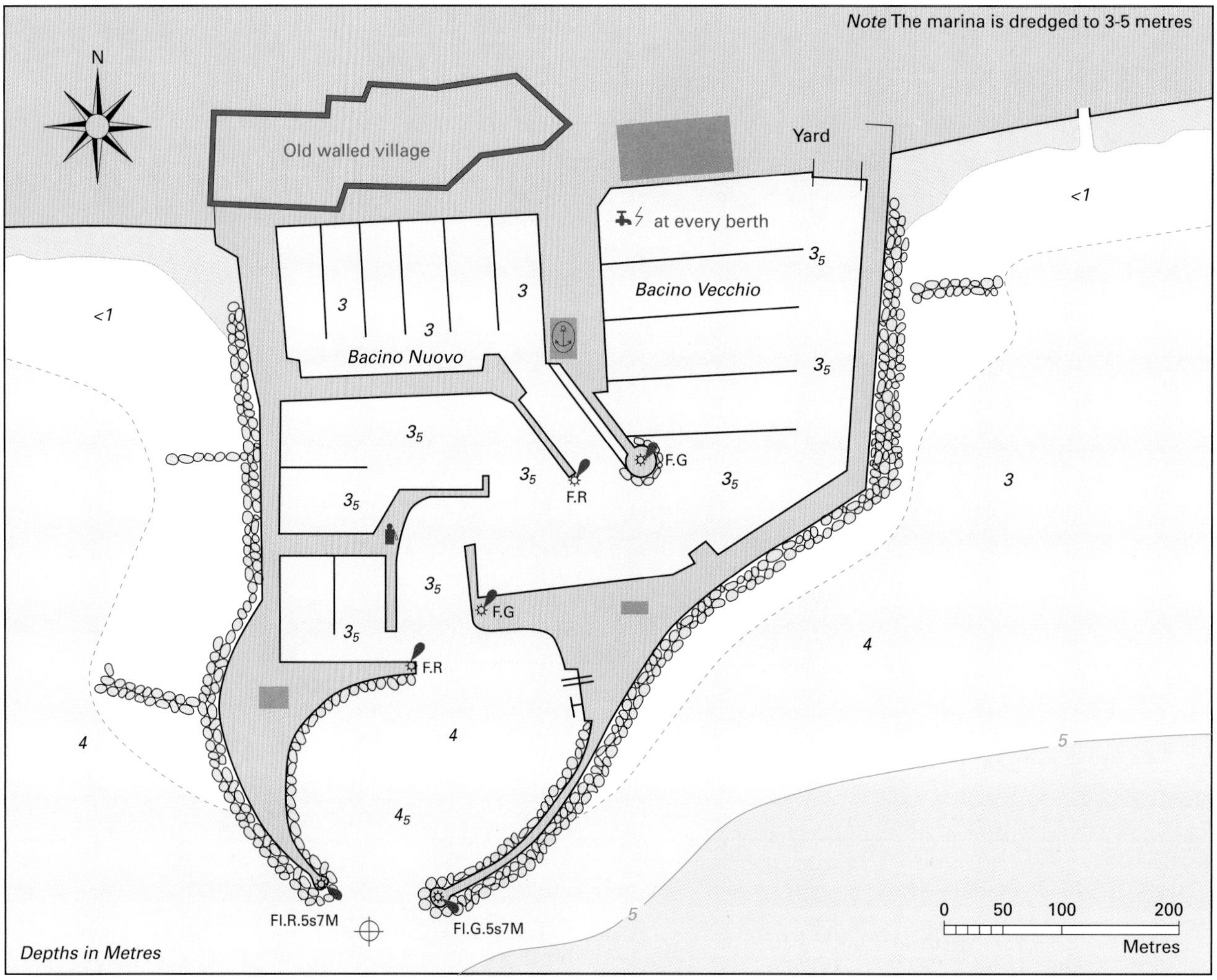

NETTUNO
⊕41°27´·05N 12°39´·6E

Eating out Good restaurants, trattorias and pizzerias. Several excellent fish restaurants near the harbour.
Other PO. Banks. ATMs. Italgaz and Camping Gaz. Train and bus to Rome.

General

The crowded harbour is a headache, especially in high season when one is being shunted from one place to another, but when finally berthed, Anzio is a charming place. The old town near the harbour is a bustling thoroughly alive place, smelling of fish and busy with a purpose of its own. During carnival, Anzio reverberates to fireworks and all of Rome seems to be here having a good time.

The town has been completely rebuilt since the war, when so much of it was devastated during the Allied landings prior to the attempt to turn the Gustav line and the assault on Casino. The British and American military cemeteries are close by, near Aprilia and Nettuno respectively.

From a much earlier period the ruins of Nero's port of Antium are visible off the beach. Then as now, Antium was a popular Roman resort and both Caligula and Nero were born here.

Note There are plans to greatly expand the yacht facilities at Anzio along the lines shown. The plan is in the proposal stages and has yet to be approved before construction begins.

The approach to Nettuno looking north. Note the mini-Empire State Building conspicuous in the approaches

Nettuno Marina looking S out to the entrance

Nettuno Firing Range

A firing range E of Nettuno extends out over the adjacent coast. When in use naval patrol boats control an exclusion zone at least 10M off the coast. Check with Anzio or Nettuno port offices.

NETTUNO

A marina 1·3 miles to the NE of Anzio off the seaside resort of Nettuno.

Approach

Conspicuous From Anzio a building looking like a mini-Empire State Building is conspicuous E of the marina. From the S the tower on Foce Verde is conspicuous and, closer in, the mini-Empire State Building will be seen. The breakwater and entrance are easily identified.

VHF Ch 09, 16 for the marina (0800–2000).

Caution With strong onshore winds a swell piles up in the approaches making entry difficult and possibly dangerous in an onshore gale.

Mooring

Data 970 berths. 80 visitors' berths. Max LOA 40m. Depths 2–5m.

Berth Where directed. There are finger pontoons or laid moorings at all berths. For a berth also try Sailing Yachts (English spoken).

Shelter Good shelter in the inner basins. Shelter should be much improved with the new extension to the breakwaters now completed, although berths in the outer basin are likely to suffer from uncomfortable surge in moderate to strong southerlies. Pay attention to warps and if possible get a berth in the inner basin.

Authorities Harbourmaster and marina staff. Charge band 5.

✆ 06 980 5404 *Fax* 06 988 1780
www.marinadinettuno.it

Sailing Yachts ✆ 0698 05372
Email info@sailingyachts.it

Facilities

Services Water and electricity at all berths. Shower and toilet block.
Fuel On the quay.
Repairs A 50-ton travel-hoist and a 50-ton slipway. Mechanical repairs. GRP and wood repairs. Electrical and electronic repairs. Sailmakers. Chandlers.
Provisions Good shopping for provisions nearby.
Eating out Restaurants and pizzerias.
Other PO. Bank. ATM. Italgaz and Camping Gaz. Hire cars. Bus and train to Rome.

General

Built under the old walled village on a low rocky promontory, the marina offers excellent facilities and the bonus of being close to the life and cheer of the village.

The second world war American cemetery is here, with some 7,400 dead from what turned out to be the militarily inept assault on Monte Casino and the attempt to turn the Gustav line. The Anglo-American force held the line with great losses until a combined general offensive took Rome nearly six months later on 4 June 1944.

Rio Martino

⊕ 41°22'·9N 12°54'·8E

A river port suitable for shallow draught craft. A sandbank at the entrance restricts depths to less than 1m. The entrance is lit F.R/F.G. Water and fuel in the basin.

SAN FELICE CIRCEO

Approach

The high promontory of Monte Circeo (541m/1,775ft) is easily distinguished, looking like an island against the low-lying land around it.

Conspicuous Monte Circeo stands out well. Closer in, the communications towers on the summit and the white lighthouse tower on Capo Circeo are conspicuous. From the N and W the harbour will not be spotted until close to it.

San Felice Circeo looking SE from Monte Circeo

By night A night approach is not recommended because of the dangers outlined below.

VHF Ch 09, 16 for Circeo yacht harbour (Co-operative Ormeggiatori Circeo).

Dangers

1. With strong winds there can be a confused reflected swell off Capo Circeo and strong gusts off the high land. With strong onshore winds the entrance would be dangerous with breaking waves in the immediate approaches.
2. The sandbank extending in a northeasterly direction from the outer breakwater must be avoided. Over the years the extent and position of the sandbank has changed and it appears that overall depths in the approaches are decreasing. On my first survey the sandbank was comparatively small and the depths in the immediate approaches were 4–5m. Now the sandbank covers a much larger area and the depths in the immediate approaches have decreased to 2·5–3m. The sandbank and the entrance is periodically dredged (2010), but it is safe to say that overall depths are decreasing and will continue to do so although the depths in the harbour proper remain much the same. Even the locals appear to forget about the sandbank and I have seen local yachts go hard aground when attempting to cut the corner into the harbour.

A 2·5–3m channel has been dredged through the sand bar running E from the entrance. The position given on the plan is approximate only. The channel is marked by port and starboard-hand buoys.

Mooring

Data 380 berths. Max LOA 20m. Depths 0·5–4m.

Berth Go stern or bows-to where directed or in a free space in the outer part part of the harbour. There are laid moorings tailed to the quay. This is a busy marina with few spare berths. The pontoons are low in the water and make getting on and off difficult if bows-to. Yachts have reported anchoring fore and aft inside the breakwater on the S side of the entrance, where there may be suitable depths for shallow draft craft following dredging, but this area silts quickly and depths of less than 1m are the norm.

Shelter Good all-round shelter although strong easterlies must make the berths on the S breakwater uncomfortable. Local yachts are wintered afloat here.

Authorities Harbourmaster. *Ormeggiatori.* Charge band 6.

Co-operative Ormeggiatori Circeo ✆ 0773 547 336
Fax 0773 546 184
Email info@circeoprimo.it
www.circeoprimo.it

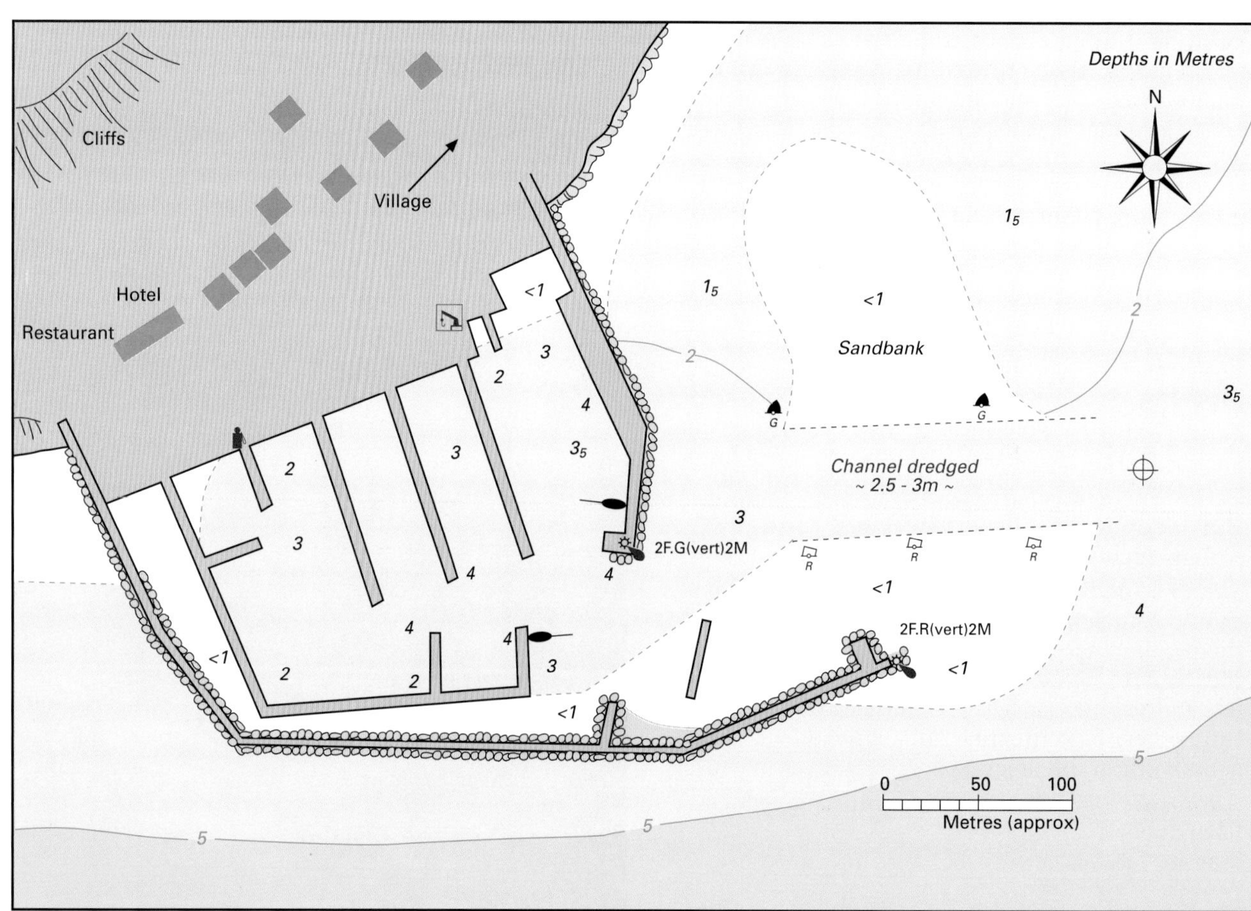

SAN FELICE CIRCEO
⊕41°13´·5N 13°05´·9E

Facilities

Services Water and electricity near most berths. Toilets (poor).
Fuel On a pontoon on the W side.
Repairs A 40-ton travel-hoist. Cranes up to 40 tons. Mechanical repairs. Electrical repairs. Chandlers.
Provisions Most provisions can be obtained at the harbour or in the village, a pleasant 30-minute walk away.
Eating out Restaurants and pizzeria at the harbour.
Other Irregular bus service to Rome.

General

Monte Circeo is generally identified with Aeaea, home of the enchantress Circe with whom Odysseus lingered for a year during his travels. Odysseus and his men reached Circe's island after escaping from the Laestrygonians and beached their ship on its shores. Members of an exploratory party commanded by Eurylochus were turned into wild animals by Circe's magic. Odysseus, protected by Hermes, went to Circe with these instructions from his ancestor god:

> 'When Circe smites you with her wand, draw your sword from your side and spring at her as if you meant to take her life. Now she will fall before you in terror and invite you to her bed. Do not hesitate to accept the favours of the goddess...'

And so he did, and his issue was believed to be Telegonus. His men were changed back to human form and the whole party spent a year there 'getting good meat to eat, and plenty of wine to drink', not to mention the attractions of Circe and her handmaidens.

The promontory, which was once an island, is a spectacular spot with sheer cliffs rising straight up from the harbour to 571m (1,855ft). On the summit are the remains of a Temple to the Sun and around the slopes are the massive walls of the ancient city of Circeii. The place has a mystery about it still and the harbour and small village nearby are one of the most pleasant places to tarry along this coast.

Foce Sisto

⊕ 41°15'·8N 13°09'·0E

A small boat harbour in the river Sisto. Depths between 1–2m and max LOA 6m.

Badino

⊕ 41°16'·8N 13°12'·1E

A small canal harbour at the mouth of Portatore river. Although there are 3m depths inside the canal there are barely 1m depths over the bar at the entrance. Once inside there is good shelter.

Water and electricity can be connected. 20-ton crane. Provisions and restaurants nearby.

Data 50 berths. Max LOA 12m. Depths 1–1·4m at the entrance.

Terracina looking S over the rock pillars to the N of the harbour *Sandro Bedessi, FOTOTECA ENIT*

TERRACINA (PORTO CANALE)

Approach

The harbour lies at the bottom of a promontory easily distinguished against the low-lying land between Monte Circeo and Monte St Angelo.

Conspicuous The high promontory with the arches of the Roman temple on it, is conspicuous from some distance off. Closer in, the town and a quarry behind it (quarry scars conspicuous) are easily identified. The harbour breakwater and the light structure are easily spotted.

VHF 14, 16 for port authorities (0700–1900).

Dangers

1. With strong onshore winds there are breaking waves and a confused swell at the entrance.
2. A sandbank extending N from the S breakwater obscures most of the entrance to the harbour, and further silting has significantly reduced depths inside. Leave the S breakwater well to the W and

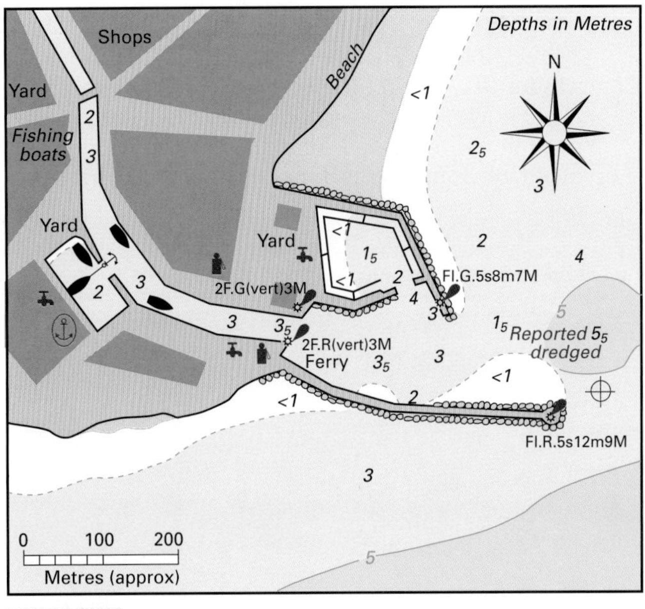

TERRACINA
⊕41°16′·96N 13°15′·73E WGS84

approach from the N, keeping close to the N breakwater. Recent dredging has restored depths of 5–6m in the entrance, with 3–4m inside. The plan remains with least depths shown, and extreme caution is needed when entering as silting will continue to reduce depths in between dredging operations.

Mooring

Data 110 berths in the outer basin. 70 berths in the canal basin. Max LOA 14m. Depths <1–4m in the outer basin/<1–3m in the canal basin.

Berth A large number of fishing boats use the harbour and it can be difficult to find a berth. You can usually find a space to go alongside on the S side of the canal near the inner basin. It may also be possible to find a berth in the outer basin.

Shelter Excellent shelter in the canal and inner basin.

Authorities Harbourmaster and customs. *Ormeggiatori* in the inner basin and yacht harbour.

Note If the sea-level rises and remains high in the harbour then strong winds can be expected.

Facilities

Water On the quay.
Fuel On the quay.
Repairs Cranes up to 20 tons and a 100-ton slipway. Mechanical and engineering repairs. Electrical repairs. Chandlers. The yard here deals mostly with fishing boats and repairs are basic.
Provisions Excellent shopping for all provisions. Fresh fruit and vegetable market near the canal. Ice from the fish market.
Eating out Good restaurants, trattorias and pizzerias in the town and along the waterfront. Fish co-operatives on the waterfront with self-service restaurants serve a number of seafood dishes. The facilities are basic but the fish is as fresh as it comes and it's great value.
Other PO. Banks. ATMs. Italgaz and Camping Gaz. Bus to Rome.

General

Terracina is a lively fishing port under the shadow of Monte St Angelo. It lies at the point where the Appian Way reaches the coast and the remarkable rock monolith, Pisco Montano, was cut through to a depth of 36m by the Emperor Trajan to make an easier path for the Appian Way, which formerly went over the summit of Monte St Angelo. Terracina was a favourite seaside resort for the Romans and the Emperor Galba (ruled AD68–69) was born here.

The temple on Monte St Angelo, so conspicuous from seaward, is the temple of Jupiter Anxurus, possibly also Venus Obsequens, and earlier possibly the site of the temple of Feronia, the ancient Goddess of the Forest. In the square of the old village is the Cathedral of San Cesario, an architectural palimpsest incorporating part of a Roman temple with construction from the 9th, 12th, 14th and 17th centuries – you can get all your history in one here with this Heath Robinson piece of architecture.

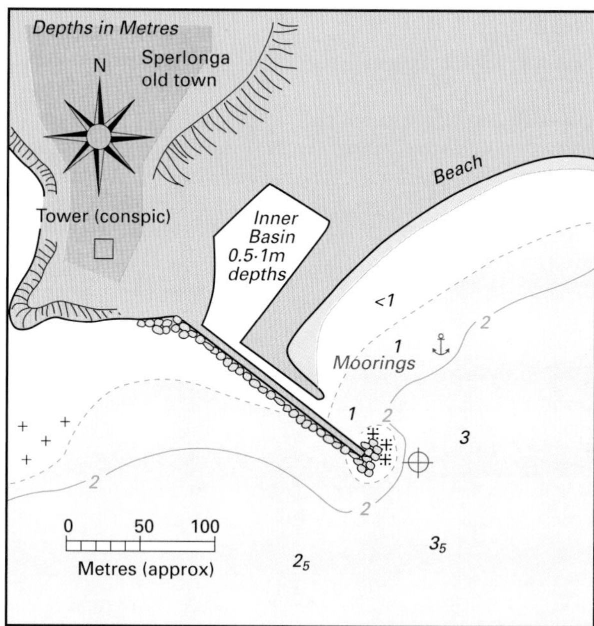

SPERLONGA
⊕41°15′·1N 13°26′·2E

Approaches to Gaeta looking north

Canale Sta Anastasia

⊕ 41°17′·3N 13°20′·5E

Roughly halfway between Terracina and Sperlonga the Sta Anastasia canal links Lago di Fondi to the coast. With maximum depths of 1·2m and max LOA of 6m it is limited to all but small boats. The entrance is prone to silting and a road bridge a short distance up the canal limits its usefulness.

Sperlonga

An old village on a rocky headland (with the new quarter behind) and a square medieval watch tower above the small harbour. The harbour is too shallow except for craft drawing less than 1m, but a yacht can anchor in the bay with offshore winds or in calm weather. The old town is a picturesque spot atop the rocky bluff.

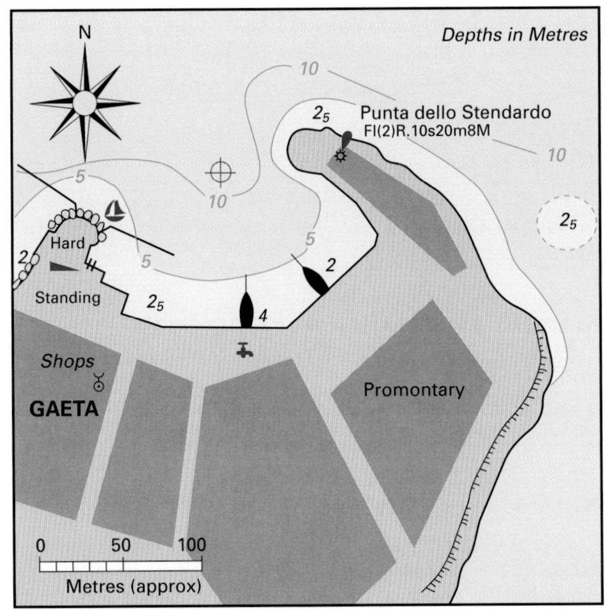

PORTO SANTA MARIA
⊕41°12′·7N 13°35′·2E

Rada di Gaeta

BA 906
Italian 78

Approach

The tall rocky promontory with cliffs dropping into the sea is unmistakable.

Conspicuous The promontory with the town of Gaeta built across the isthmus is easily identified. On the isthmus a chimney and a bell-tower are conspicuous. On Monte Orlando the lighthouse and a large round water reservoir are conspicuous.

VHF Ch 11, 16 for Gaeta port authorities. Ch 12, 16 for pilots.

Dangers Within Rada di Gaeta there are numerous unlit mooring buoys which are a danger to navigation within the roadstead at night. Care is also needed of the mussel beds in the bay.

PORTO SANTA MARIA

Approach

This small basin lies close W of Punta dello Stendardo.

VHF Ch 11, 16.

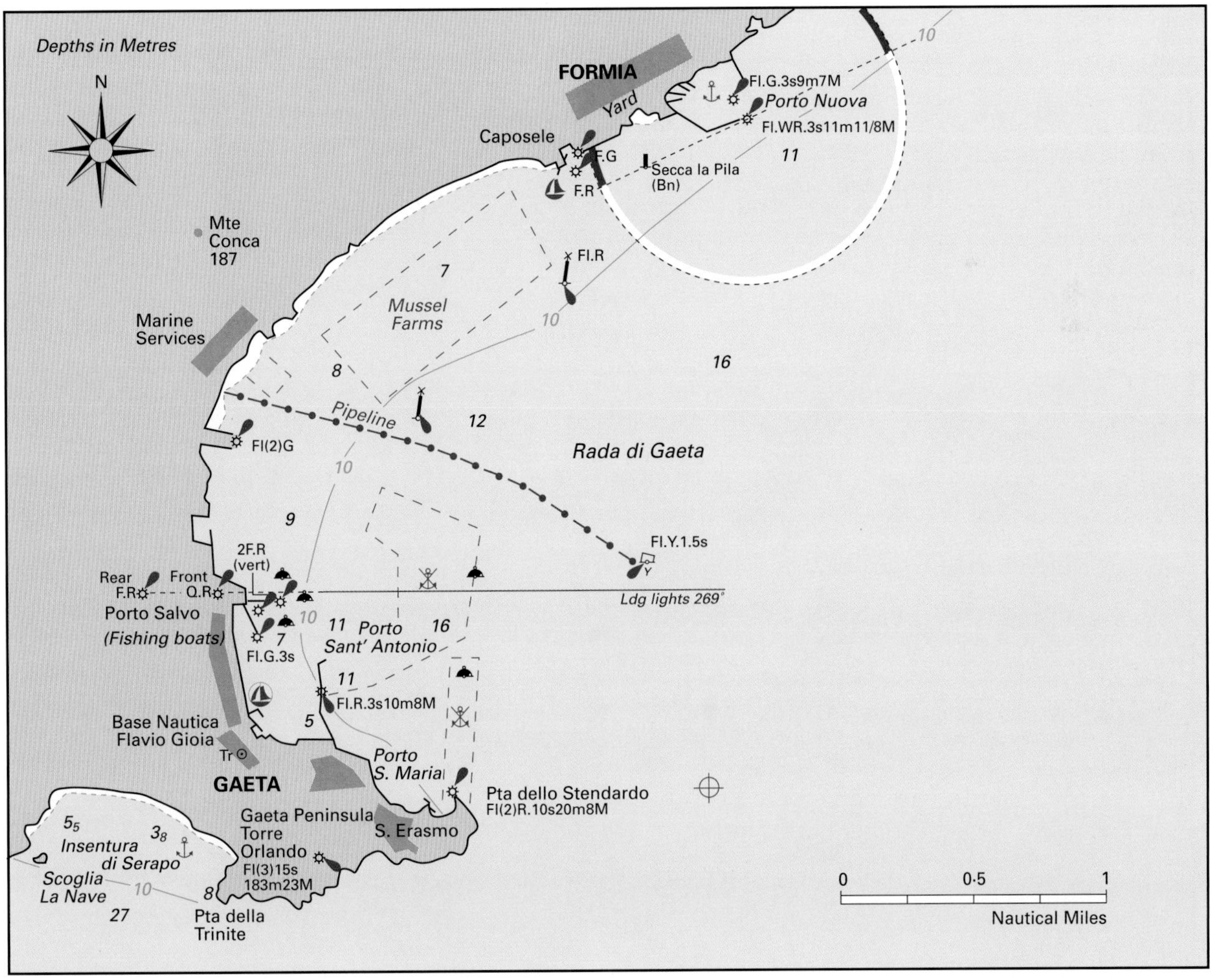

RADA DI GAETA
⊕1M E of Pta dello Stendardo 41°12′·62N 13°36′·54E WGS84

Classic yachts moored in Porto Santa Maria during a regatta
Base Nautica Flavio Gioia

Mooring

Berth Where directed or convenient. It is usually difficult to find a berth in here as most are occupied by local boats.

Shelter Normally adequate in the summer although it is open N–NW across Rada di Gaeta. The wash from fishing boats and other craft is bothersome.

Authorities Ormeggiatori. A charge may be made.

Facilities

Water On the quay.
Provisions Most provisions can be found in the old village to the west.
Eating out Restaurants nearby.

MARINA BASE NAUTICA FLAVIO GIOIA

Approach

The marina lies on the W side of Porto Sant'Antonio.

VHF Ch 09 for Base Nautica Flavio Gioia (24/24).

Note A yacht should keep well away from the breakwater and installations at Porto Sant'Antonio which are classified as a military area. It is prohibited to berth anywhere except for Base Nautica Flavio Gioia.

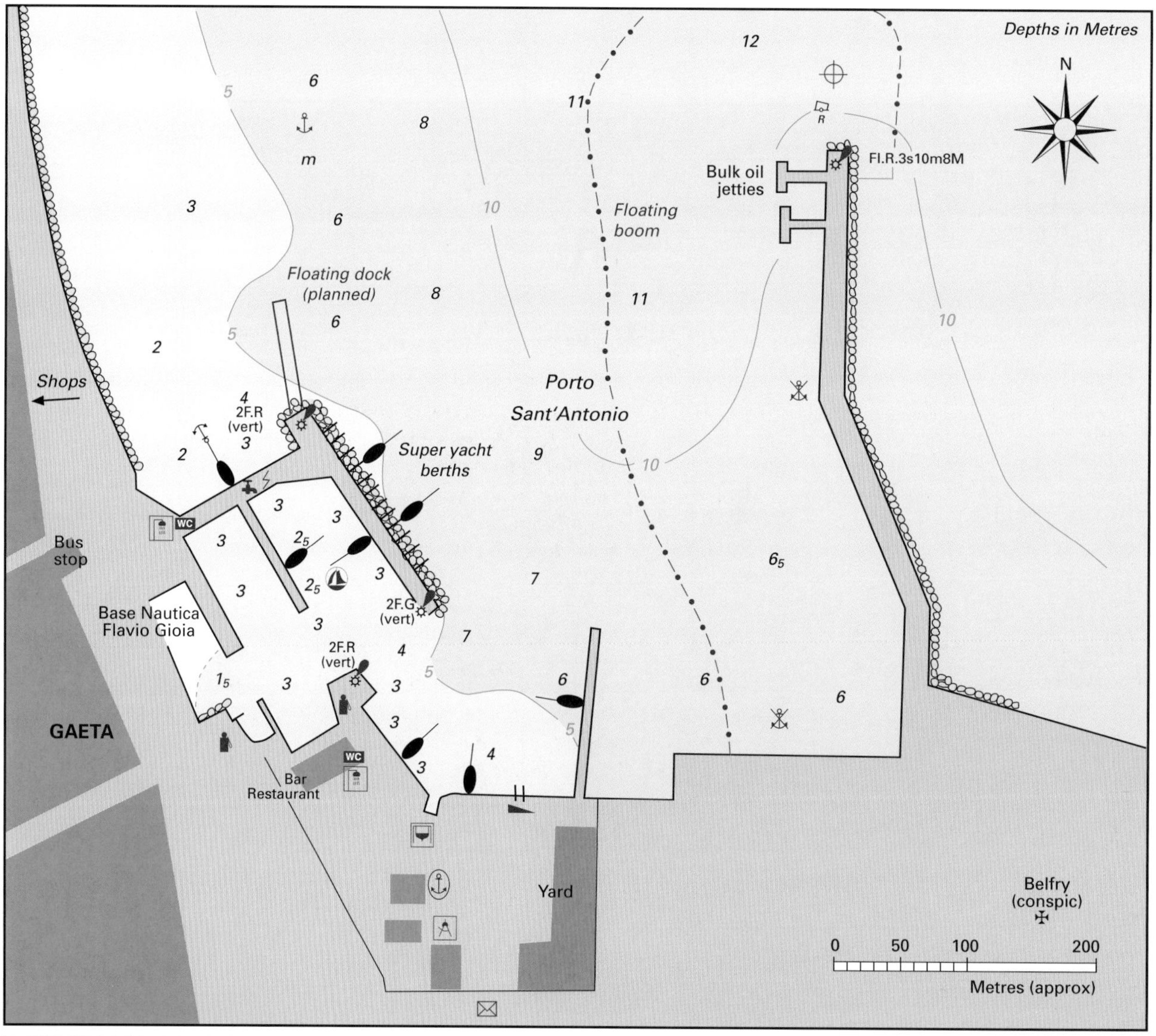

BASE NAUTICA FLAVIO GIOIA
⊕41°13´·09N 13°34´·70E WGS84

Base Nautica Flavio Gioia looking SW across the isthmus of the Gaeta peninsula *Base Nautica Flavio Gioia*

The new superyacht berths along the outer breakwater at Base Nautica Flavio Gioia are available from May to October *Base Nautica Flavio Gioia*

Mooring

Data 250 berths. Visitors' berths. Max LOA 60m. Depths 2–6m.

Berth Where directed. Laid moorings tailed to the quay.

Shelter Good all-round shelter.

Authorities Harbourmaster and marina staff. Charge band 5/6.

Base Nautica Flavio Gioia ✆ 0771 311 013 / 14
Fax 0771 464 580
Email info@basenautica.com
www.basenautica.com

Note There are plans to extend the marina to the N, as shown on the plan, but this is still in the planning stage and has yet to be approved before construction begins.

Facilities

Services Water and electricity (220/380V) at every berth. Telephone connection at some berths. Showers and toilets.
Fuel Fuel quay at the entrance.

Gaeta specials

Some excerpts from *Anna's Guide*

Tiella is a local speciality pizza. Looking much like a savoury pie, there are various fillings such as octopus, mussels, spinach or broccoli. Buy a slice or the whole pie, but get there before midday or you'll miss out.

Mozzarella is made locally from buffalo milk – the best time to buy it fresh is in the afternoon.

Fresella is a crunchy bread that will keep on board for a month or so. The recipe below is Anna's:

Panzanella
Moisten the *fresella* with water in a bowl until it is softened but not mushy.

Add olive oil, salt, Gaeta olives and basil.

Add chopped fresh tomatoes and toss lightly.

Leave for an hour for the bread to absorb all the flavours.

Repairs 100-ton travel-hoist. 400-ton slipway, 50-ton trailer. 9-ton crane. Large area of hard standing (250 places). Covered yards. Controlled environment paint shed. Rigging service. Mechanical and engineering repairs (Volvo Penta agent). Electrical and electronic repairs (Raymarine agent). GRP and wood repairs. Sailmaker. Chandlers.
Provisions Excellent shopping in Gaeta. Ice available.
Eating out Restaurant/bar. Good restaurants, trattorias, and pizzerias in the town.
Other PO. Bank. ATM. Italgaz and Camping Gaz. Buses to Formia and then trains to Rome.

General

Base Nautica Flavio Gioia is a family run business that has become popular with cruising yachtsmen. Most people who come here will bump into Anna or her brother sooner or later. Anna is a fount of knowledge, from the best place to buy your *tiella* for lunch, to train times to Rome or Naples. She has also put together a comprehensive guide to the area for the increasing numbers of yachties overwintering here. The marina is only a short walk from Gaeta town, and a 10-minute walk into Gaeta old town.

The old village on the promontory between Porto Santa Maria and Porto Sant'Antonio was so severely damaged in the second world war that it was virtually abandoned afterwards and a new town was built on the isthmus connecting the promontory and the mainland.

The old quarter around the harbour of Porto Santa Maria is a wonderful place: the streets and vaulted passageways and winding steps rise steeply up the medieval village built on and around the promontory. Winding lanes hemmed in by high walls and stone buildings hide the sea below and you could be many miles from the coast and a few centuries removed just a short distance from the harbour. The cathedral (originally built in 1106 but rebuilt in the 17th and 18th centuries) and the 10th-century church of San Giovanni a Mare are worth looking at, or just wander at will.

Between Gaeta and Caposele are a number of boatyards and small private basins, including Halcraft Cantieri Navali.

CAPOSELE

Approach

In the approaches there is shoal water and Pila Rock to avoid. The harbour itself is very small and care is needed when entering and berthing.

Conspicuous The town of Formia with a grey cupola and the tower on the waterfront are easily identified. Closer in, the beacon on Pila Rock can be identified and the harbour breakwater will be seen.

By night The entrance is lit F.G.4m2M/F.R.4m2M. The lights in line on 323° lead clear of Secca la Pila on the W side. Note that Secca la Pila is not lit.

VHF Ch 10, 16 for the harbourmaster.

Dangers Care should be taken of Secca la Pila and the shoal patch immediately NE of the entrance (see harbour plan).

Mooring

Data 130 berths. Max LOA 12m. Depths <1–2m.

Berth Go stern or bows-to where directed. The small harbour is invariably crowded and much of it is too shallow for even small yachts – it can be difficult to find a berth in the summer. There are laid moorings.

Shelter Good although strong southeasterlies send in some swell.

Authorities A yacht club administers the berths and a charge is made.

Facilities

Services Water and electricity at or near most berths.

Fuel On the quay.

Repairs Small yachts can be craned onto the quay. Mechanical repairs.

Provisions In Formia.

Eating out Restaurants nearby.

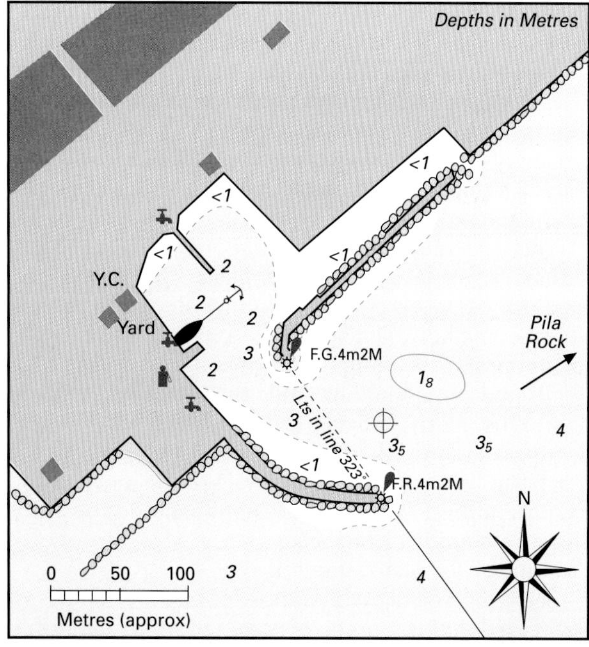

CAPOSELE
⊕41°15´·0N 13°36´·0E

Other Most facilities are in Formia about 30 minutes' walk away.

General

A pleasant peaceful spot if you manage to get a berth. Caposele was the ancient Roman harbour for Formia and parts of it have been incorporated into the yacht harbour.

FORMIA (PORTO NUOVO)

Approach

This large harbour lies close E of Caposele.

Conspicuous The medieval white tower immediately E of the harbour stands out from the buildings of Formia. Closer in the harbour breakwaters are easily identified.

VHF Ch 16, 10 (Locomare Formia 0800–2000).

Mooring

Data 500 berths. Max LOA 30m. Depths <1–7m.

Berth At present try and get a berth on the end of the E mole or on the end of one of the pontoons running out from the shore. The planned 'Marina di Mola' development off the outer breakwater seems to have been shelved in favour of a new project, 'Porto di Levante'. This marina will be built to the E of the main harbour in two phases and will include a full service boatyard. Work is as yet sporadic, and no completion dates are available, but the project details are listed below, and the planned final form is shown on the plan.

Shelter Good all-round shelter although strong southerlies, especially southeasterlies, cause a surge. The prevailing breeze blows briskly right across the harbour onto the berths in the NE corner so ensure your anchor is well in if you are here. It dies down in the evening.

Authorities Port police and customs. Charge band 1/4. It has been reported that mooring rates can fluctuate depending on who you see there.

Facilities

Water On the quay.

Fuel A fuel quay near the ferry berth.

Repairs Just W of the harbour there is a large yard. Crane up to 24 tons and slipways up to 40 tons. Mechanical and engineering repairs. Some GRP and wood repairs. Electrical repairs.

Provisions Good shopping for all provisions in the town.

Eating out Good restaurants, trattorias and pizzerias in the town.

Others PO. Bank. ATM. Italgaz and Camping Gaz. Bus and train to Rome and Naples. Ferries to Ponza and Ventotene.

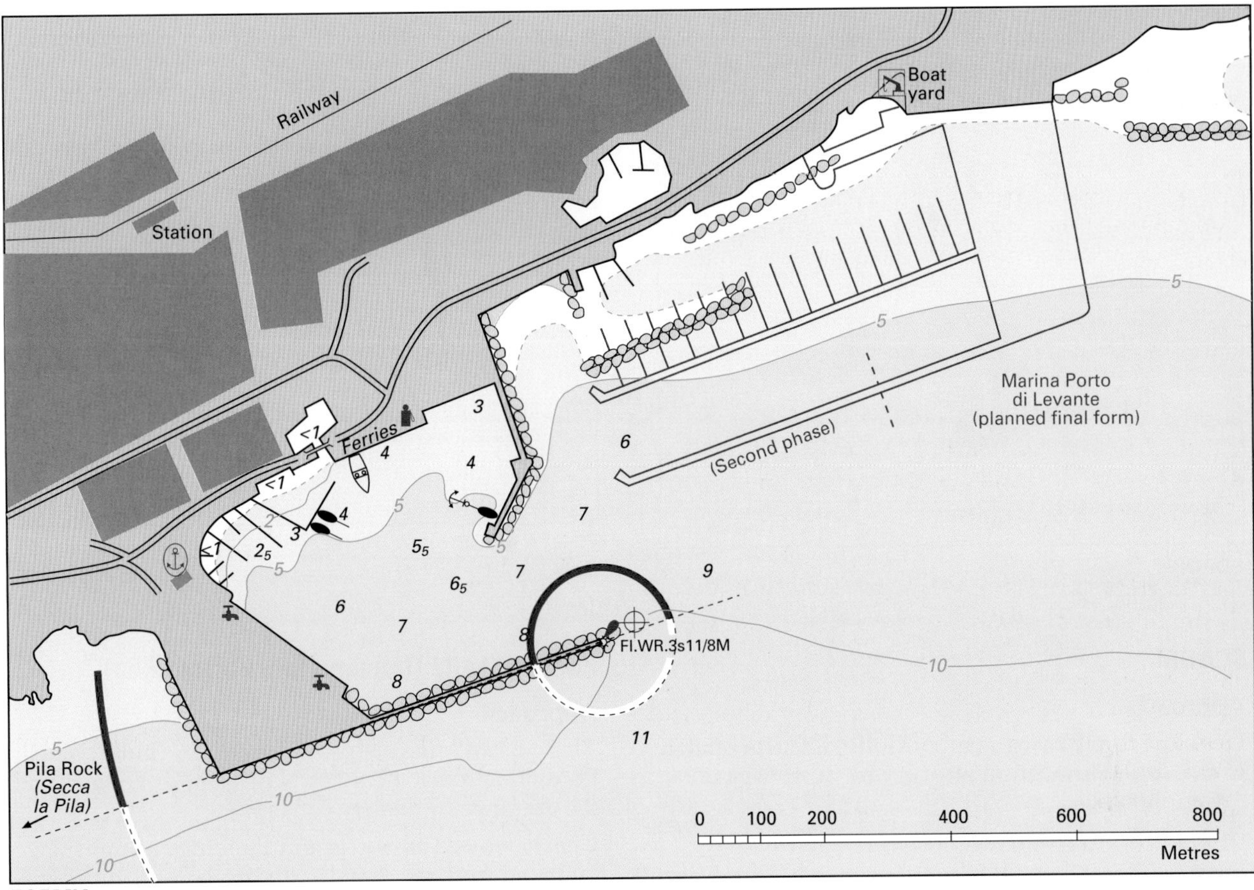

FORMIA
⊕41°15´·22N 13°36´·96E WGS84

Yacht berths on the pontoons in the NW corner of Formia harbour

MARINA PORTO DI LEVANTE

Data (when open) 750 berths (1st phase). 1,300 berths (completed). Max LOA 15m. Depths 1–5m.

Facilities Water and electricity at all berths. Showers and toilets. Travel-lift and repair facilities.

www.portodilevanteformia.it

General

Formia was a popular seaside resort for the Roman aristocracy, indeed it was the prime residential area along this coast apart from Naples. However few interesting sites remain. It was also once renowned for its wine and in the hinterland there are the remains of Roman smallholdings scattered about the slopes. Cicero was killed here in his villa in 43BC by Antony's soldiers. After the murder of Julius Caesar, Cicero denounced Mark Antony and was subsequently tracked down to his villa here and was himself murdered in turn. On the waterfront the remains of a Roman villa are labelled 'Cicero's Villa', but then it is inevitable that any large remaining villa would *have* to be that of Cicero.

The town is a pleasant workaday place that makes few concessions to tourism and seems happy instead transporting them all over to Ponza and Ventotene by ferry.

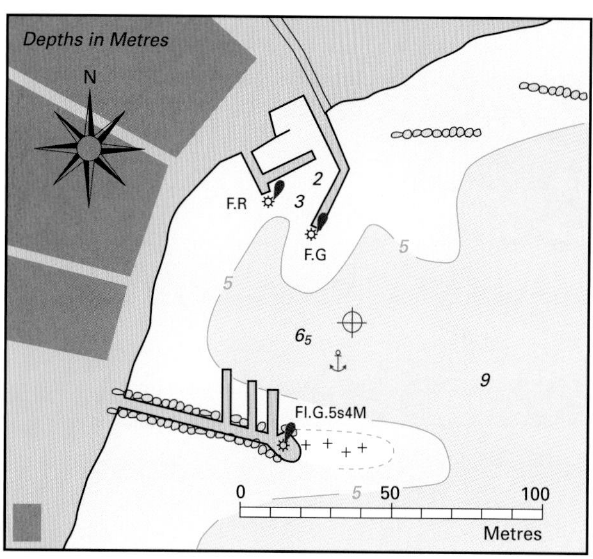

SCAURI
⊕41°15´·2N 13°42´·1E

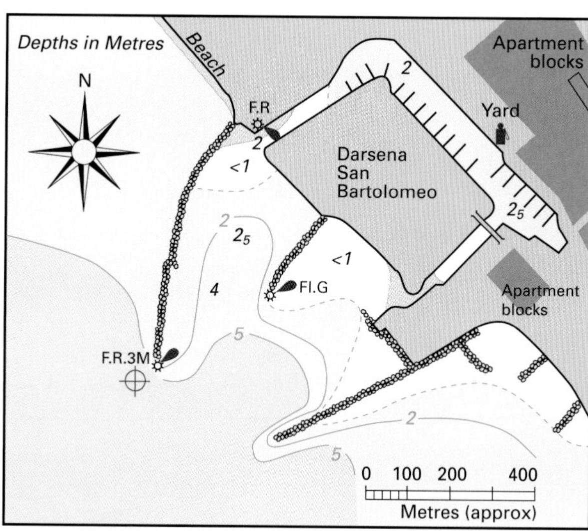

PINETA MARE
⊕40°59´·1N 13°58´·2E

SCAURI

Approach

Lies close to the eastern end of Golfo di Gaeta on the E side of a low promontory with a conspicuous tower on it.

By night A night approach is not recommended.

Dangers A reef extends for approximately 25m from the end of the W mole.

Mooring

Data 90 berths. Depths 0·5–2m in the E basin.

Berth Only small and comparatively shallow draught craft will be able to get into the basin. Most craft will have to anchor off in 5–7m between the mole and the basin.

Shelter Adequate in the basin. The anchorage is only suitable in calm weather.

Authorities Ormeggiatori. A charge is made.

Facilities

Services Water and electricity in the basin.
Provisions Most provisions in Scauri.
Eating out Restaurants nearby.

Scauri looking S from the beach

PINETA MARE (Darsena San Bartolomeo)

Approach

This marina lies approximately 23 miles SE of Formia, and just 12 miles N of Isola di Procida and the entrance to the bay of Naples.

Conspicuous The hotels and buildings of the village built on the flat coastal strip are conspicuous. It is difficult to identify the breakwaters until close to.

Note The harbour continues to silt. In 2010 the harbour was completely inaccessible to all but small craft. Fishing boats and charter yachts have left, and motor yachts from the yard here are obliged to leave by road transport. Although a dredger is stationed in the harbour, we understand that there are no plans to dredge and that the harbour is closed to all vessels. The plan is retained in case the situation changes.

Caution With onshore winds a considerable swell piles up in the approaches and entrance, making entry difficult. In an onshore gale entry could be dangerous.

General

Originally built in 1984 by the Coppola family, this project has suffered from numerous setbacks, not least that the original development was illegal, but the biggest problem with Pineta Mare was always going to be the rapidity with which the entrance silts up. The 2006 plan for a 1,200 berth porto turistico appears to have met with opposition from environmental groups, concerned about how beaches to north and south have been affected. It seems that there are no new plans for the place, and it already has something of a forgotten air about it.

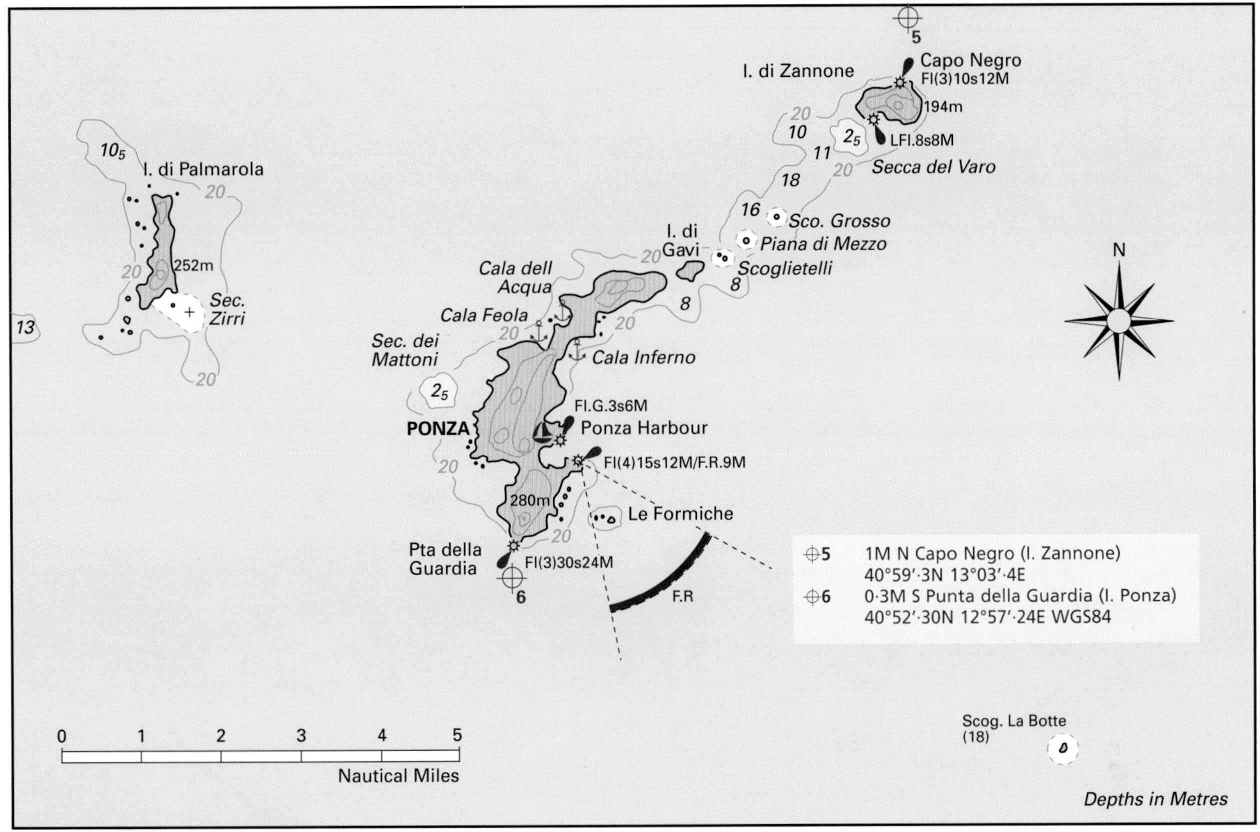

ISOLE PONTINE - NW GROUP

The Pontine Islands

The Pontine Islands are five islands in two distinct groups: Ponza, Zannone and Palmarola forming the NW group situated between 15 and 20 miles S of Capo Circeo; and Ventotene and Santo Stefano situated about 30 miles SSE of Capo Circeo and 18 miles WNW of Ischia. The islands are the crests of volcanic craters, though of two different chains. Ponza, Zannone and Palmarola belong to a volcanic chain extending over to Anzio, while Ventotene and Santo Stefano are linked geologically to the volcanic area in the Bay of Naples.

The anchorage at Ponza town looking NNE to Ravia Rock

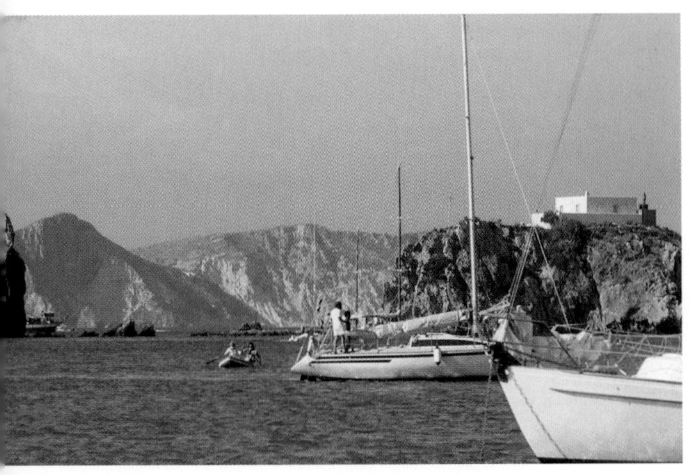

The Northwest Group

Isola Ponza

The largest island in the archipelago, famed for its beauty, is a long jagged crescent with the highest part, Monte della Guardia (280m/918ft) in the south. It is well cultivated and produces a reasonable local wine. The main town is Ponza, arranged in a semi-circle around the harbour. Being close to Rome, Ponza is a popular resort and in July and August it teems with tourists, both local and foreign.

The island was inhabited in Palaeolithic times and later by the Volscians, an early pre-Roman people. In 313BC the Romans colonised the island and Augustus built a villa here. In later years it became an island of exile playing host to, among others, the demented Caligula's brothers and his sister Agrippina, who was the mother of Nero. After the demise of Rome, Ponza was ravaged by pirates until the Bourbons attempted to resettle the island in the early 19th century. Somehow the colony survived to cash in on late 20th-century tourism.

PONZA HARBOUR

Approach

The island is fringed with above and below-water rocks and the approach to the harbour is best made in daylight.

Conspicuous Ile di Zannone, the steep-to island (194m/630ft) three miles NE of Ponza is easily identified. The lighthouse on Pta della Guardia (a

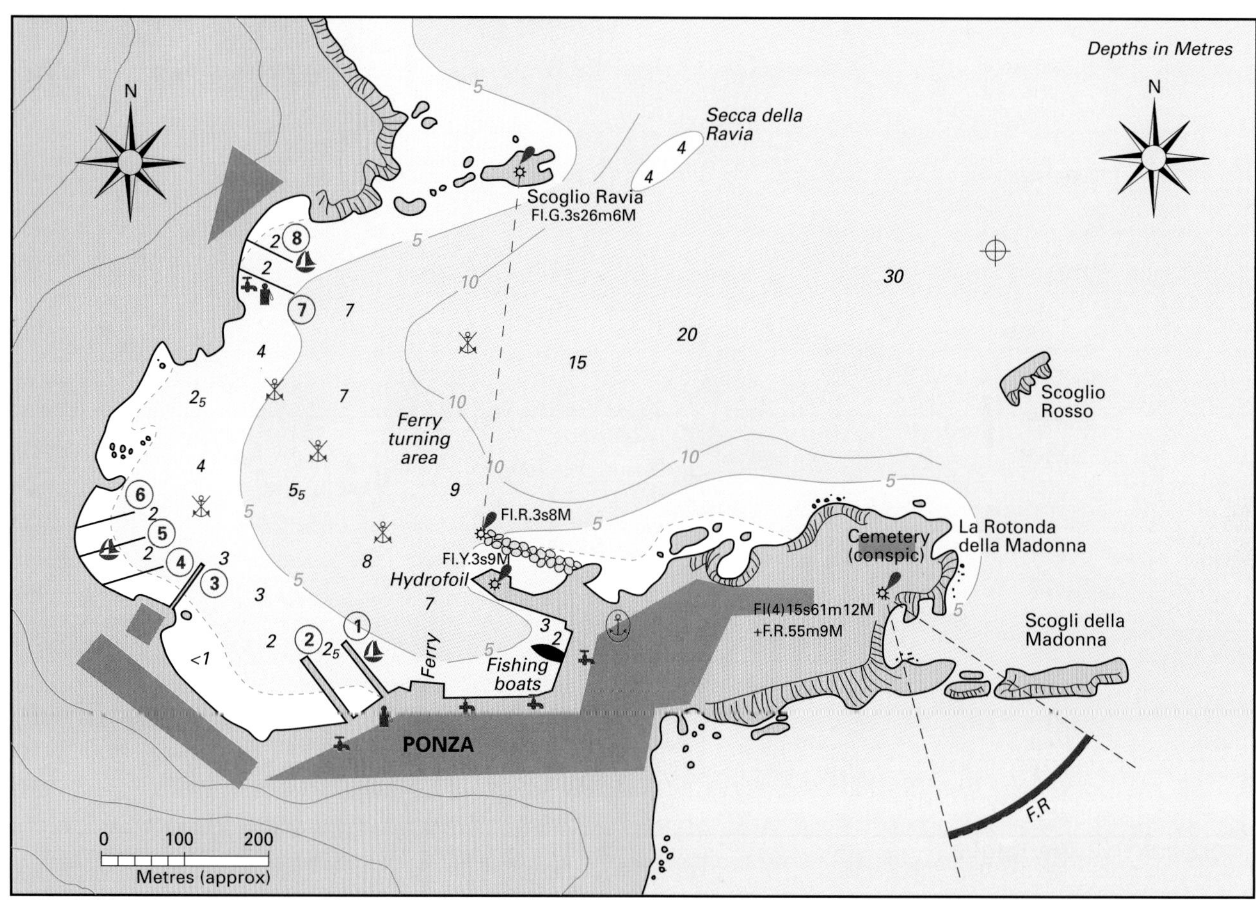

PONZA
⊕40°54´·06N 12°58´·24E WGS84

white tower on a dwelling) is conspicuous. The splash of white buildings which is Ponza town on the S of the island makes identification straightforward. The cemetery and the lighthouse on La Rotonda della Madonna and the red cupola of the cathedral in the town are conspicuous. Closer in, the harbour is readily identified.

By night Many of the rocks in the approach are not lit but with care an approach can be made by night. Use the light on La Rotonda della Madonna Fl(4)15s61m12M/F.R.55m9M. The F.R is visible over 301°-341° covering Secche Le Formiche.

VHF Ch 14, 16 (Locomare Ponza 0700–1900).

Dangers Numerous rocks and reefs encircle the island and care must be taken when navigating around the coast.

Mooring

There are several mini-marinas around the bay which essentially consist of pontoons running out from the shore. You can negotiate a berth at one of these or try your luck getting a berth on the E side of the harbour. The latter is unlikely as the harbour is crammed to overflowing with fishing boats and local boats or yachts.

The hydrofoil berth tends to be free overnight, 1800–0800.

The following is a list of each pontoon around the bay. All have laid moorings at most berths. Depths vary but generally it is only the outermost berths which have sufficient depths for most yachts. Max LOA c.25m. Larger yachts by arrangement.

1. *Ponzamare*
   VHF Ch 09 ☎ 0771 80679 / 809 678 *Fax* 0771 820 184
   Email ponzamare@ponzamare.it
   www.ponzamare.it
2. *Ciccio Nero*
   VHF Ch 10, 11 ☎ /*Fax* 0771 80697
   Email info@ciccionero.it
   www.isolaponza.it
3. *Gennarino al Mare*
   ☎ 0771 80071
4. *Enros*
   VHF Ch 12, 16 ☎ 0771 80012 / 339 830 9246
   Email nauticaenros@tiscali.it
   www.nauticaenros.it
5. *Ecomare*
   VHF Ch 68 ☎ 338 204 6081
6. *La Fenicia*
   ☎ 338 926 6716
7. *Cantieri Parisi*
   ☎ 0771 80544 / 333 796 2895 *Fax* 0771 809 669
   Email info@cantieriparisi.it
   www.cantieriparisi.it
8. *Cantiere Nautico Porzio*
   ☎ /*Fax* 0771 809 830
   Email info@cantierenauticoporzio.com

Shelter Better than it looks on the plan and in normal settled summer weather the harbour and the bay provides good shelter. With strong NE winds a swell rolls into the harbour.

The lighthouse and cemetery on La Rotonda della Madonna on the entrance to Ponza looking south

Ponza town looking from the anchorage

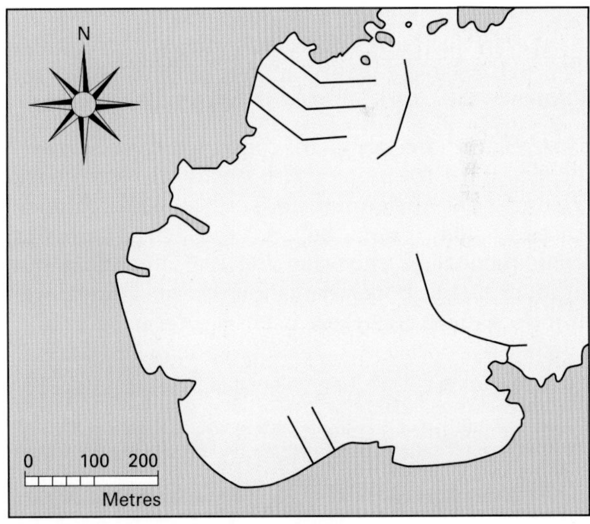

PONZA: PLANNED DEVELOPMENT

Authorities Harbourmaster and customs. Charge band 6+.

In July and August prices anywhere in Ponza are extremely high. €10 per metre quotes are not unusual here. Outside these months prices drop, a little.

Note Throughout July and August Ponza harbour overflows with boats of all shapes and sizes. This has led to problems with boats anchoring in the ferry turning area. Because of this the anchoring area from 01/04–30/09 is strictly limited to a buoyed zone. Anchoring is not really advisable outside the bay. Even in calm weather a swell creeps around the point and makes it very uncomfortable except if you are tucked well in. Close N of Scoglio Ravia there are adequate depths and you are not too far from town. It may be that at times other yachts are anchored outside the zone. Play it by ear, and only contemplate anchoring if someone else is, and also if you can tuck in so close as to be in no way obstructing the ferry.

Facilities

Services Water on the quay in the harbour and water and electricity at the mini-marinas. Not all have potable water. Water may be rationed in the summer. Laundry services.

Fuel On the quay near the harbour, but it is too shallow for all but very shallow draught craft to berth at the fuel quay. Fuel is also available on the Pontile Parisi in the NW side of the bay.

Repairs Slipways up to 180 tons at Cantiere Nautico Porzio in the bay. Mechanical repairs. The yard carries out repairs to fishing boats and is unversed in the finer arts of yacht maintenance. 16-ton crane at Enros. Most of the other pontoons can arrange for minor repairs.

Provisions Good shopping in the town. Good fish market near the quay. Ice is available from the latter. Provisions and a supermarket in the village on the N side of the bay.

Eating out Good restaurants, trattorias and pizzerias, although many are open only for the summer.

Other PO. Bank. ATM. Italgaz and Camping Gaz. Ferry to Anzio, Terracina, Formia and San Felice Circeo, Naples.

Ponza. Punta della Guardia looking west

General

The harbour and small town are picturesque with pastel rose, ochre, blue, and white houses under green slopes and the fishing boats providing splashes of bright colour on the waterfront. Around the coast the rock pinnacles and cliffs have been eroded into fantastic and wonderful shapes; a geological feast of metamorphosed rock twisted and compressed every which way and then eroded by the wind and sea to further the effect. I don't exaggerate: the rock formations are spectacular.

Ponza is a popular resort and its population increases dramatically in the summer. Around the summer solistice, when the Festival of San Silverio is celebrated, Ponza erupts into life. Ten days of celebration culminate in a huge midnight firework display in the bay – before anchoring was prohibited you had to make sure you were not anchored too close.

Note There are plans to construct two detached breakwaters to protect the anchorage at Ponza. Planning permission has not yet been granted and I suspect may not be if the environmental consequences of enclosing the bay are taken into account. Let us hope permission is turned down even if it does mean that there is less shelter here.

Stunning white cliffs in Cala dell'Acqua
Vito Arcomano, FOTOTECA ENIT

Cala Inferno

⊕ 40°55'·18N 12°58'·26E WGS84

A cove lying 2·5 miles NNE of Ponza harbour. It is surrounded by white cliffs, from which it takes its name from the intense reflection of the sun. Anchor in 3–6m on sand, although be aware that yachts may need to move when the water or the fuel boat comes in here. Care needed of a wreck, just breaking the surface, in the N of the bay. In settled weather there are numerous other anchorages along the E coast where a yacht can anchor.

Cala dell'Acqua

A small bay lying on the NW side of the island. It can be used in calm weather – the prevailing breeze sends a swell in, making it uncomfortable and possibly untenable in the summer. The bay is fringed with above and below-water rocks. Anchor where convenient. The wharf in the NE corner has now been removed. On Punta del Papa which forms the N side of the *cala* a British cargo ship carrying German prisoners of war foundered with the loss of most on board.

Note There are plans to develop a 500 berth marina here, but no further details are available and it is likely to come under scrutiny by the environmental lobby.

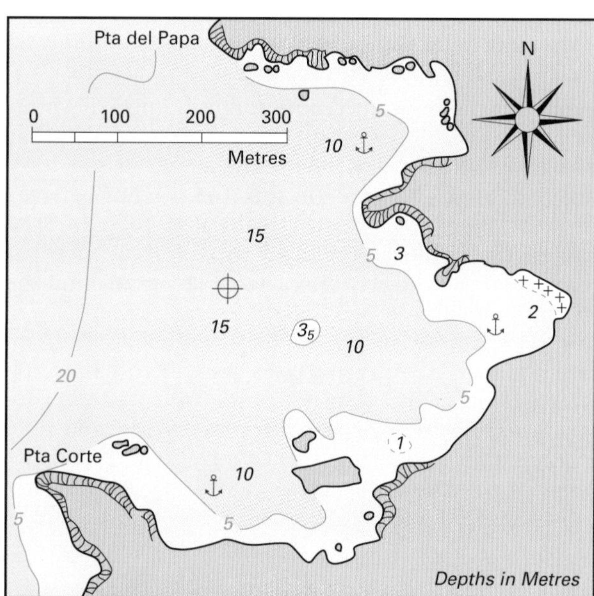

CALA DELL'ACQUA
⊕40°55′·5N 12°57′·9E

Cala di Feola

A cove lying immediately S of Cala dell'Acqua. A short mole provides some protection from westerlies though it can become very uncomfortable and may become untenable with any wind from the west. Care needs to be taken of underwater debris off the end and inside the short mole. With gales from almost any direction, but particularly from the W through to N, there is a heavy scend into here making it unsafe. A yacht should leave at the merest hint of bad weather.

Anchor in 5–8m in the bay taking care of the numerous permanent moorings in the SW corner.

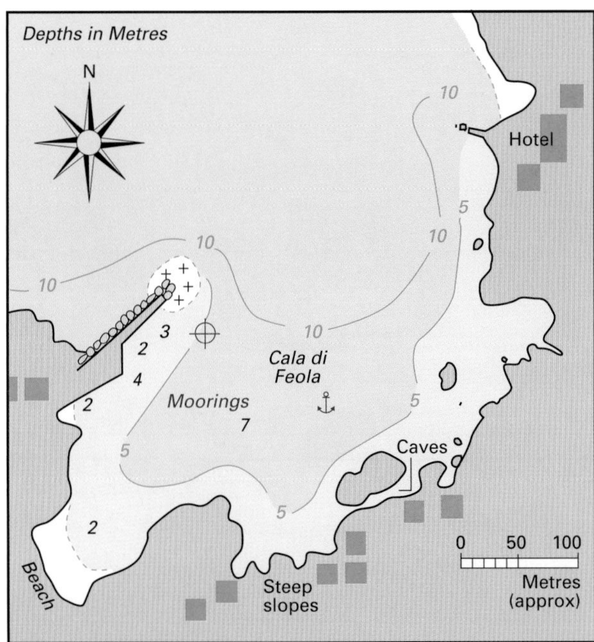

CALA DI FEOLA
⊕40°55´·2N 12°57´·7E

Moderate to good holding. Restaurant nearby. About five minutes' walk up the hill you can catch a bus to Ponza town. Between Cala di Feola and Cala dell'Acqua there is a natural spring that was frequented by the Romans. In the bay there are some interesting sea caves and natural rock tunnels that can be explored by dinghy.

Isola Palmarola

The most westerly island of the group, it is fringed by above and below-water rocks and caution is required when navigating around it. Yachts sometimes anchor in a cove on the S of the island or a cove partially protected by two islets on the NW. A restaurant opens in the summer months.

Note Navigation should be carried out in daylight owing to the numerous rocks and reefs around the coast.

Isola Zannone

A small round island situated 3½ miles NE of the northern tip of Ponza. In calm weather a yacht can anchor on either side of Capo Negro. The island is a nature reserve where it is said mouflon, the wild sheep once common in Europe and now rare, flourish.

Between Isola Ponza and Isola Zannone

Along a line drawn from Isola di Gavi on the NW corner of I. Ponza, to Punta Varo on I. Zannone, lies a narrow chain of rocks and reefs. Above-water rocks along the S section are easily seen by day in calm weather. The N part of the three-mile chain is mostly free of dangers with least depths of 11m, except for Secca del Varo (minimum 2·4m), which lies just over 500m (¼M) SW of Pta Varo on I. Zannone.

The Southeast group

Isola Ventotene

The largest of the southeastern group of the Pontine Islands. The island rises to 139m (456ft) in the S at Monte dell'Arco. It is sparsely covered in *maquis* and prickly pear and not a lot else. In Roman times the island was called Pandataria and, like Ponza, several notable undesirables were exiled here: Julia, daughter of Caesar Augustus; Nero, son of Germanicus; Octavia, wife of Nero; and Flavia, grand-daughter of Domitan. Julia, famous for her adulterous ways, was exiled here by her own father. Far from the gossip of Rome, she had a large and sumptuous villa built and entertained her lovers more or less in private. Her second husband, Agrippa, a right hand man in Augustus' campaigns, is thought to be the architect behind the tiny harbour hewn from the rock. Octavia the wife of Nero was exiled on the island at the request of his mistress Poppea Sabina. Later Nero had her killed on the island and her head was allegedly presented to Poppea.

The island acquired its present name in the Middle Ages from the winds that swept across its barren surface. Like Ponza it was colonised by the Bourbons. Both Ventotene and nearby San Stefano were penal settlements until quite recently. Under Mussolini, those of a persuasion other than Fascist were incarcerated here and on San Stefano.

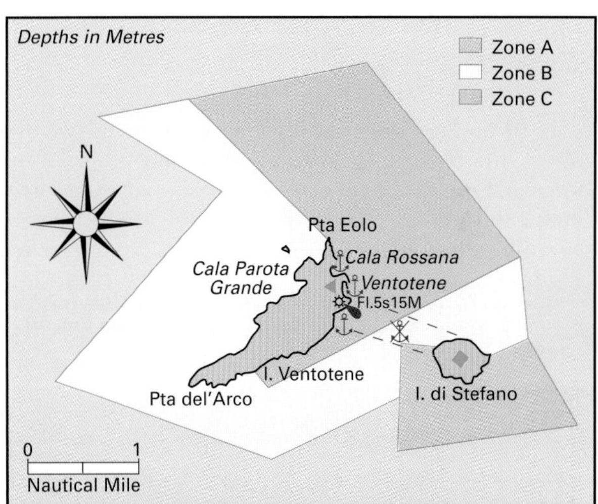

ISOLA VENTOTENE AND MARINE RESERVES

Ventotene Marine Reserve

In 1997 a marine reserve was established in the sea area around the islands of Ventotene and Santo Stefano. The area is divided as follows:

Zone A
Navigation, access and short- and long-time stays prohibited.

Zone B
Within 500m of the coast navigation, overnight stays and access are prohibited to motor vessels.

Zone C
Commercial and sport fishing prohibited.

Capitaneria ✆ 0771 85291 Commune ✆ 0771 85014

VENTOTENE HARBOUR
(Cala Rossano, Porto Nicola, Porto Vecchio)

Approach

The harbour lies on the NE corner of the island.

Conspicuous The large fort-like building on San Stefano is conspicuous. The white and ochre buildings of the small village are easily identified and the lighthouse tower at the entrance to the small harbour is conspicuous.

VHF Ch 16.

Dangers The entrance to Porto Vecchio is very narrow and a yacht should have everything ready for berthing before entering. Once into the entrance a yacht must make a 90° turn to starboard.

Note The starboard mole at the entrance to Cala Rossano has been damaged by storms. The remains were marked by a green buoy (not lit), in 2004.

Mooring

Porto Vecchio (Porto Nicola)
Data Max LOA 12m. Depths 1–3m.

Berth Go bows-to the quay on the W side taking care of the rocky ledge bordering the quay. If the W side is full go stern or bows-to the E side. Care is needed of rocks which protrude underwater for some distance in places. Laid moorings at most berths. The bottom is thin mud and not good holding.

Shelter Good shelter although there is a surge with NE winds.

Authorities Harbourmaster. *Ormeggiatori*. Charge band 4.
Giro (Enrico) ✆ 0771 85122

Note In bad weather fishing boats and local yachts take a line right across the harbour and tie it to the other side. A yacht entering should be wary of such lines criss–crossing the harbour.

Ventotene. Porto Vecchio looking NE. Porto Vecchio was originally an old Roman galley port literally carved out of the rock

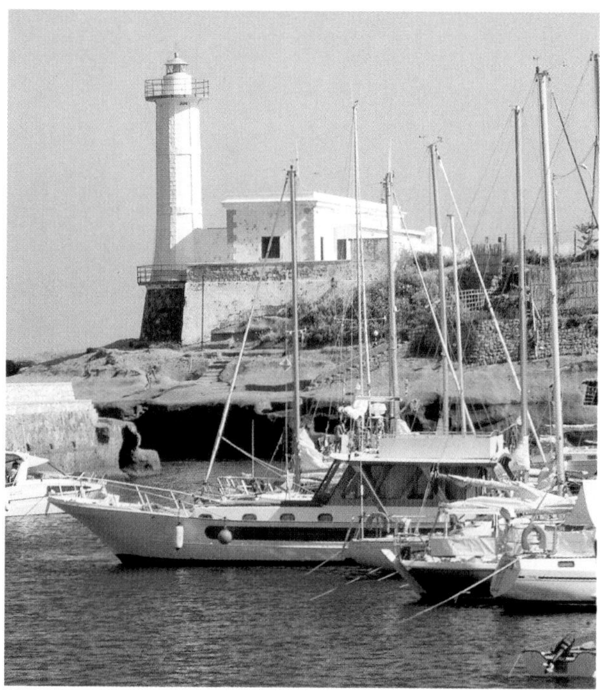

Porto Vecchio on Ventotene looking S to the lighthouse

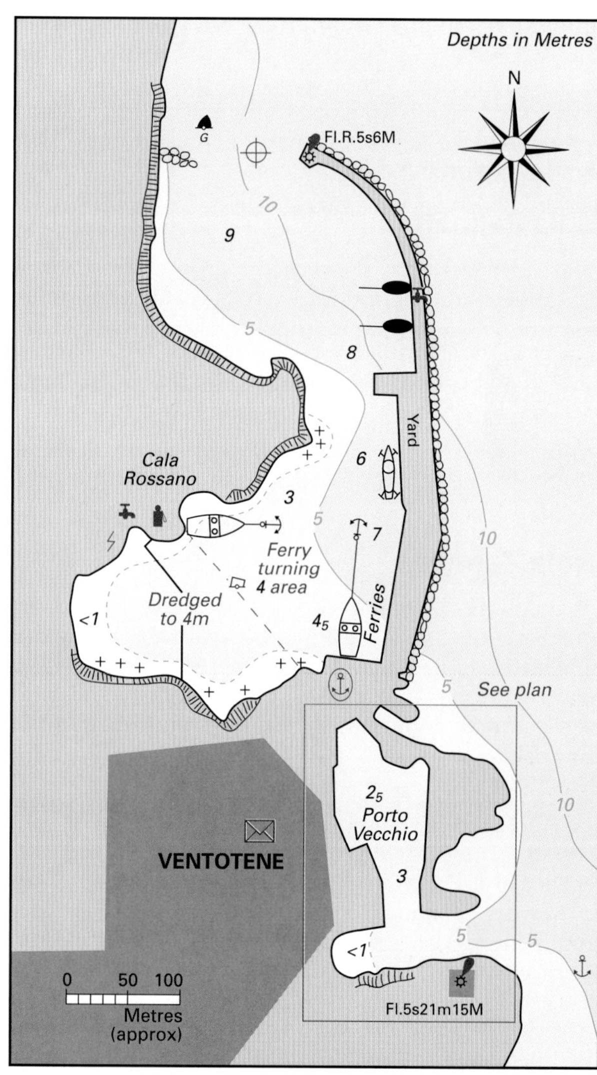

VENTOTENE – CALA ROSSANO AND PORTO VECCHIO
⊕40°48′·24N 13°26′·01E

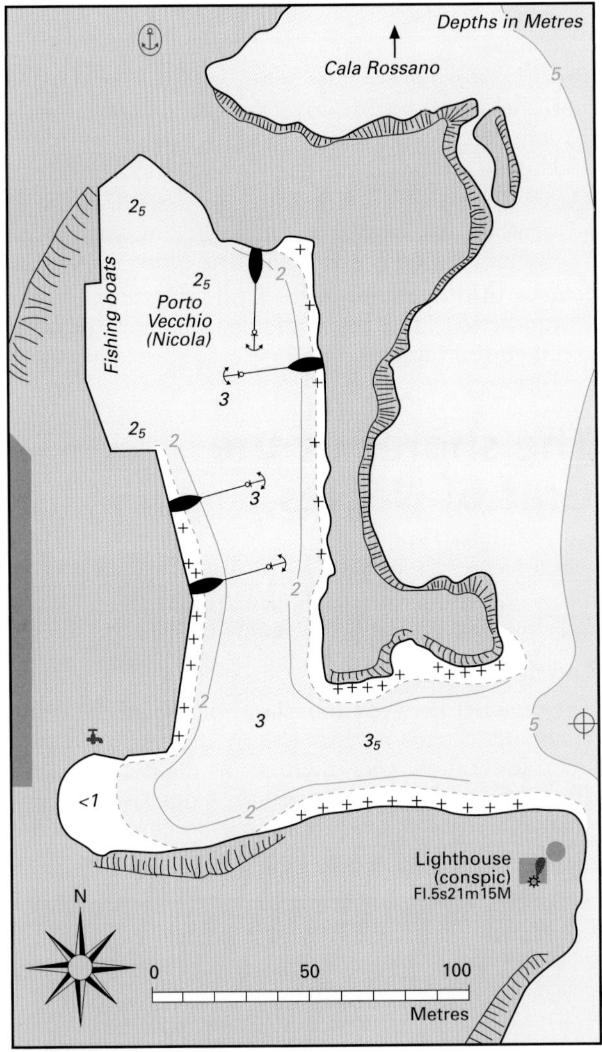

VENTOTENE – PORTO VECCHIO
⊕40°47′·8N 13°26′·1E

Cala Rossano (Porto Nuova)
Data Depths <1–6m.

Berths Go stern or bows-to on the S pontoon if there is space. The pontoon off the NW corner is not always in place. This area is reported to have been dredged to 4m. Laid moorings tailed to the pontoon. There are also new yachts berths with laid moorings tailed to the quay on the inside of the breakwater in the outer harbour. Go stern or bows-to where directed. Occasionally you may be permitted to berth overnight on the ferry/hydrofoil quay (1730–1000). Go alongside where convenient, but don't depend on being allowed to stay here. Alternatively anchor fore and aft in the W side of the harbour, clear of the pontoons. Anchoring is prohibited in the ferry turning area marked on the plan.

Shelter Good shelter although NE winds cause a surge, more uncomfortable than dangerous although northerly gales cause a dangerous surge. Some wash from ferries at berths near the entrance.

Authorities Harbourmaster. Charge band 1/4.

Note There are plans to increase the number of yacht berths in Ventotene to 180. No further details were available at the time of writing.

Facilities

Services Water tap on the quay. Water and electricity on the pontoons. However, there is a shortage of water in the summer and it may be turned off.
Fuel Near the quay in Cala Rossano. Anchor with a long line ashore to take on fuel.
Provisions Most provisions can be bought in the village.
Eating out Restaurants and pizzerias.
Other PO. Bank. ATM. Ferry to Formia.

General

The old Roman galley port excavated from the native tufa and the galley sheds dug into the rock behind are a marvel of Roman engineering. Whether Julia's husband, Agrippa or another, ordered the construction, there are few other Roman harbours like this executed quite as neatly. As well as the harbour, the Roman engineers constructed two underground aqueducts to supply the town with water. The present day village is a pleasant low-key place that sees an onslaught of tourists in July and August, but is otherwise fairly quiet.

Anchorages

In settled weather a yacht can anchor off outside the harbour in 8–12m on sand and rock. It can be a bit rolly here, but is usually safe. Alternatively anchor in the bay immediately SW of the lighthouse where there is slightly better shelter. Care is needed of rocks lying off the coast, but the water is clear enough to identify hazards.

San Stefano

A round steep-to island about one mile E of Ventotene Island. It was at one time a penal colony and it gives every impression of being a 'Devil Island'. There are no sheltered landing places and in any case most of the coast lies in a Zone A area of the Marine Reserve.

San Stefano, the 'Devil Island' across from Ventotene

Yacht harbours around the Gulf of Naples

Finding somewhere safe and convenient to leave your yacht when visiting Naples and Pompeii is a bit of a headache. Many of the visitors' berths in marinas around the Bay of Naples are pre-booked; sometimes weeks in advance. Marinas a little further afield are more likely to have berths available, and with good ferry and train connections, are good bases for day trips to the city and surrounding attractions. The following are harbours in which you can leave a boat:

Sannazzaro (Mergellina) Molo di Luise on the breakwater offers superyacht berths.

Marina Vigliena When finished this new marina will offer berths to yachts in transit.

Marina di Stabia A new marina close to Vesuvius where a yacht can be left safely.

Casamicciola On Ischia. The harbour is well protected from the prevailing winds and there are usually fellow yachtsmen around who can keep an eye on your yacht while you are away. Regular ferries and hydrofoils to Naples from Casamicciola or Porto d'Ischia.

Porto d'Ischia is well protected, but it is difficult to find a secure berth here. If you do, this is an excellent place to leave a yacht for a visit to Naples.

Procida Marina provides a safe and sheltered place to leave a yacht now the *porto turistico* is complete. Frequent ferry and hydrofoil services to Naples.

Capri Reasonable protection in settled summer weather and there are usually fellow yachtsmen around. Regular ferries and hydrofoils to Naples.

Salerno Although not in the Gulf of Naples a yacht can be left in safety at the 'marina' and the train taken to Pompeii.

The shores of the Gulf of Naples

BA 914, 915 and 916
Italian 83, 84, 95 and 130

There are numerous harbours around the gulf but only some are suitable for yachts.

Canale di Procida

The channel between the island of Procida and the mainland. Shoals extend a short distance on either side. In mid-channel there is a shoal (Secca del Torrione) with least depths of 4·6m over it and patches with 5–6m. A S cardinal beacon marks the shoal and a light is exhibited: Q(6)+LFl.15s. Care

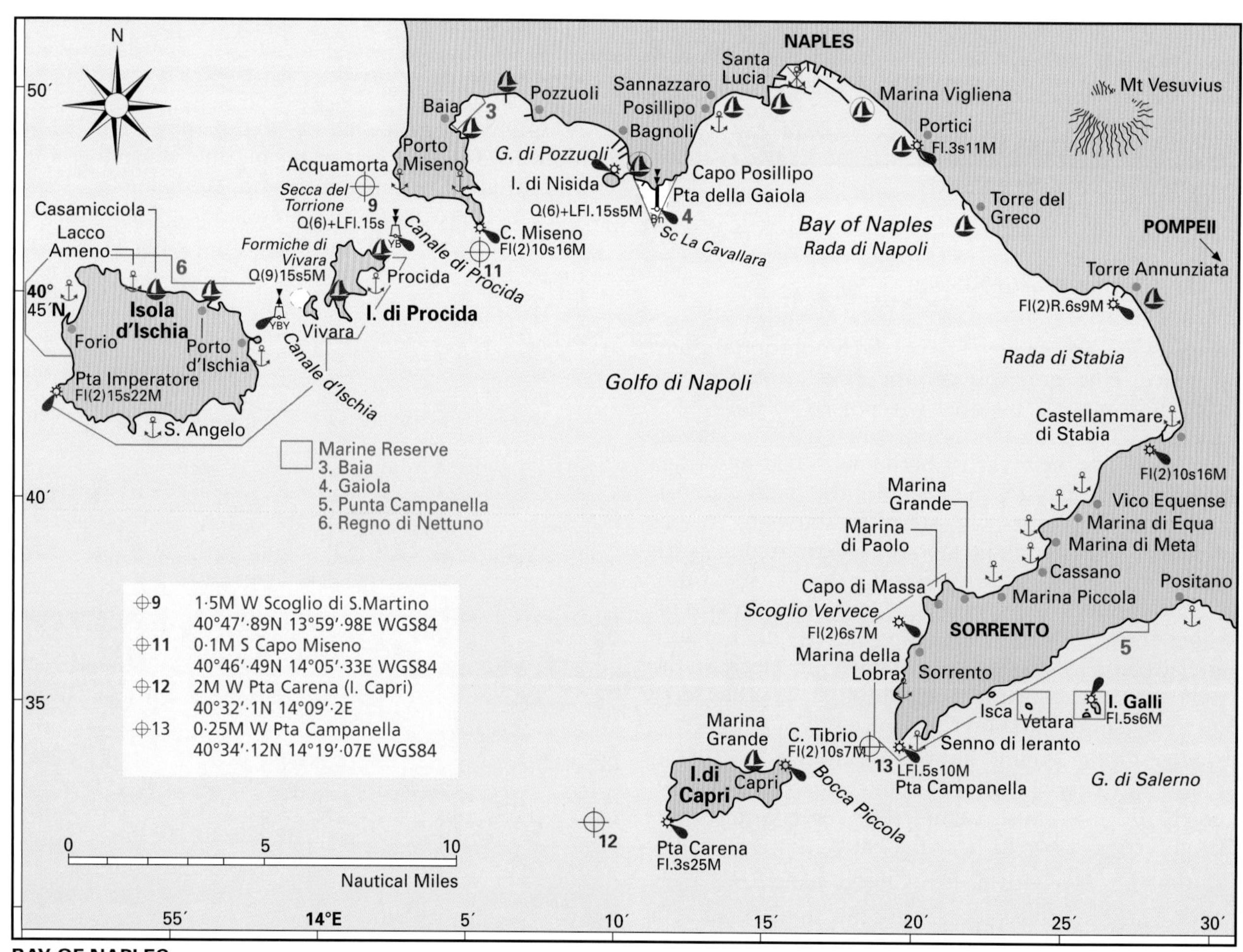

BAY OF NAPLES

Acquamorta looking N towards Punta di Torrefumo

should be taken as the light characteristic appears to be changed sometimes. There are least depths of 9·4m in the channel apart from Secca del Torrione. The current in the channel sets westward but is not normally appreciable.

Caution A wreck with a least depth over it of 5m is reported to lie in position 40°46´·6N 14°02´·0E.

ACQUAMORTA

Approach

A harbour under Punta di Torrefumo on the NW side of Canale di Procida. The large square tower on Scoglio San Martino, built on a rocky islet joined to the coast by a causeway, is conspicuous. Closer in, the breakwater shows up well.

Mooring

Data Depths <1–6m.

Berth Where directed or anchor off.

Shelter West through S winds cause a surge which could make parts of the harbour untenable if they blow with any strength.

Facilities

None nearby.

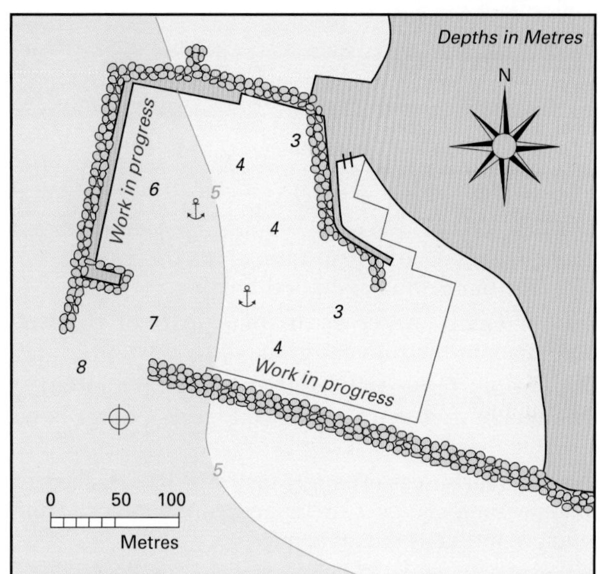

ACQUAMORTA
⊕40°47´·4N 14°02´·5E

PORTO MISENO

BA 916
Italian 83

Approach

The almost land–locked bay under Capo Miseno on the W side of Golfo di Napoli. The approach and entrance is between extensive mussel beds off the coast which mostly consist of blue plastic barrels with the seed mussels hanging off them. Enter the bay along the buoyed channel and leave the beacon to port. The buoys are not always in place, but there is also a leading line on a beacon on the shore with a house behind on a bearing of about 296°.

By night A night approach is not recommended.

Mooring

Most of the bay is taken up with laid moorings where yachts moor fore and aft and these moorings are the property of one or other of the clubs here. You can anchor to the N of the moorings or

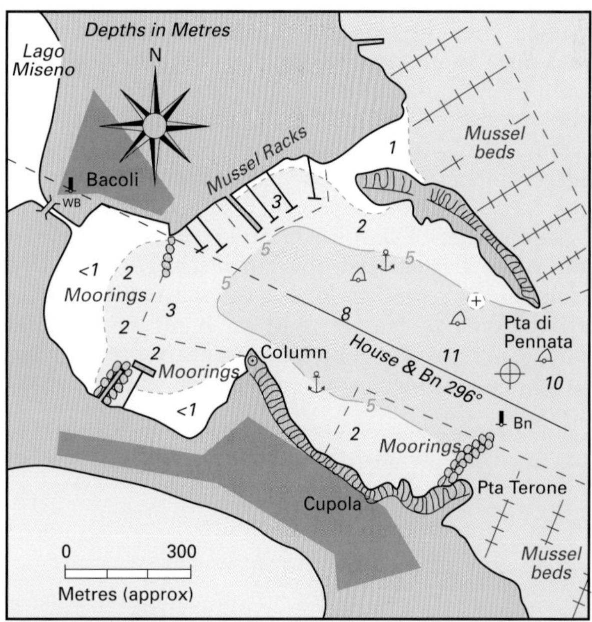

PORTO MISENO
⊕40°47´·33N 14°05´·48E WGS84

Capo Miseno looking S over the mussel beds in the approaches to Porto Miseno

immediately W of the moorings off the S entrance. The bottom is mud and good holding.

Shelter Good shelter in the inner part of the bay. Adequate in the summer in the outer part.

Authorities Ormeggiatori. If you pick up a mooring you will be accosted for a variable sum. Charge band 2/3.

Note In early season buoys may not be attached to the mooring chains. Care is needed when anchoring and a trip line is recommended.

Facilities

Provisions and a few restaurants ashore in Bacoli.

General

Capo Miseno is part of an ancient crater and is named after the trumpeter of Aeneas. The harbour was once an important Roman galley port originally built by Agrippa in 41BC. It was from here that Pliny the Younger watched the devastating eruption of Vesuvius in AD79 which destroyed Pompeii and Herculaneum. The much maligned Tiberius, he of the debauchery on Capri, died here in AD27.

The village of Bacoli is a poor cousin of some of the other flashier suburbs but has a good deal of charm for all that. In lots of ways it is more like a village outside Naples than an outer suburb and once you have visited the centre a few times the local grocer and greengrocer will greet you like old friends.

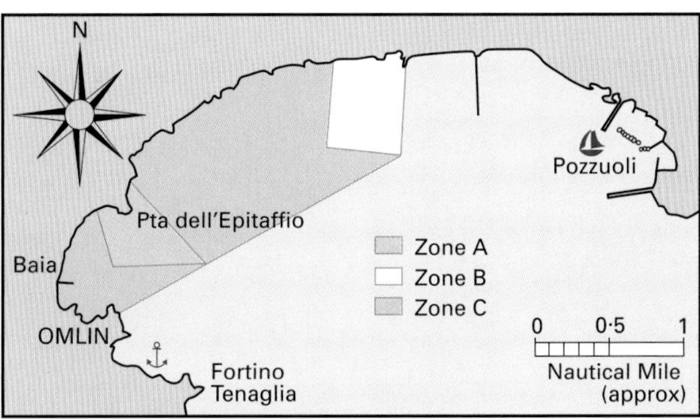

BAIA UNDERWATER (AMP) RESERVE

Baia Marine Reserve

An underwater marine reserve (Parco Sommerso) has been established off Baia to protect ancient remains on the seabed. The area has been divided into zones as shown on the plan.

Zone A
Navigation, anchoring, fishing, diving prohibited.

Zone B
Fishing without a permit prohibited.

Zone C
Commercial fishing prohibited.

✆ */Fax* 081 523 5992 / 372 3760
Email info@areamarinaprotettabaia.it
www.areamarinaprotettabaia.it

BAIA

BA 916
Italian 83

Approach

Lies just under two miles N of Porto Miseno. There are some 3m patches close to the 5m line in the approaches.

By night There is only the light on Fortino Tenaglia Iso.R.4s13m8M. A night approach should be made with caution.

VHF Ch 16.

Mooring

Data 200 berths. Depths <1–4·5m.

Berth Where directed. Laid moorings tailed to the pontoons.

Shelter Normally adequate in the summer although strong SE–E winds must make berths uncomfortable and possibly untenable in some cases.

Authorities Harbourmaster and staff. Charge band 3/4.

Anchorage Yachts can anchor in the bight under Fortino Tenaglia. The bottom is mostly mud and good holding. Better shelter than it looks here, although it is open to the NE–E–SE. The anchorage in the bay falls within the AMP and it is reported that anchoring here is now prohibited.

Facilities

Services Water and electricity near most berths.
Fuel On the quay in the marina and on the yard quay.

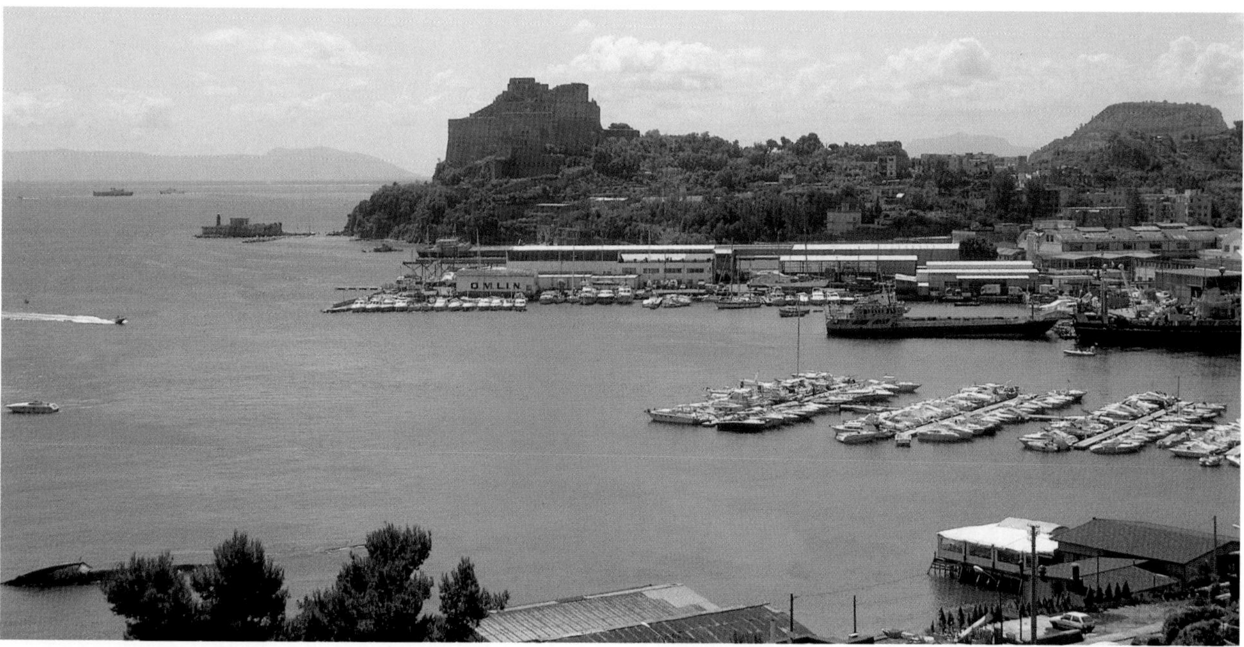

Baia looking SE

Repairs The large yard (Cantiere OMLIN) has a slipway up to 250 tons and a 60-ton crane. Most yacht repairs including GRP, wood and steel work.
Provisions Minimarkets nearby.
Eating out Restaurants and bars nearby.
Other PO. Italgaz. Buses and taxis into Naples.

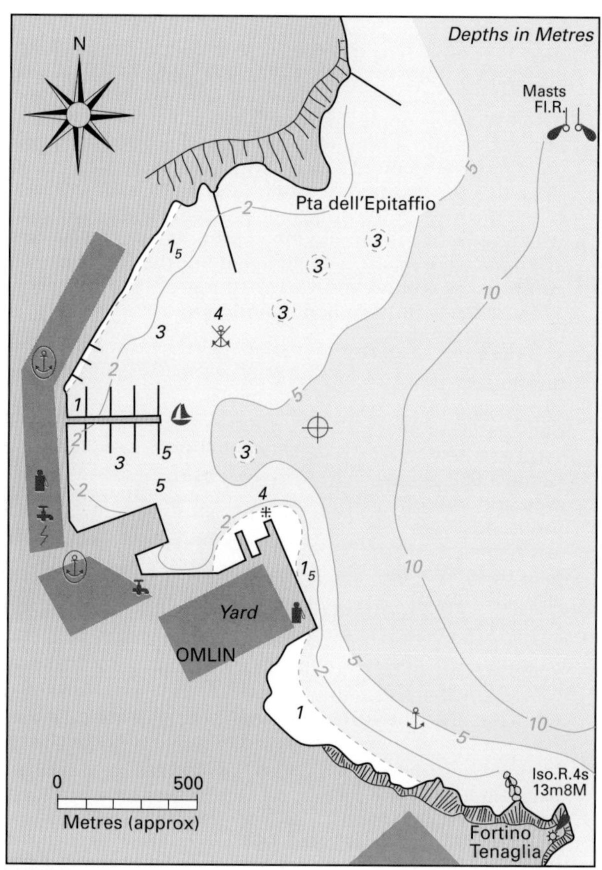

BAIA
⊕40°49'·0N 14°04'·7E

General

Baia is now a safe place to leave a yacht if you want to venture into Naples. There are buses from the coast road behind the marina or take a taxi.

Baia is said to take its name from Baios, the navigator of Odysseus. Most of the extensive villas and palaces that graced the shores in Roman times have been submerged as, in the last 2,000 years, the land has subsided. From ancient maps it is thought the shore probably extended as much as 900m further to seaward. Numerous archaeological finds have been made on the seabed.

It was from Baia that Caligula built his bridge of ships and rafts across to Pozzuoli so that he could exclaim how he had ridden across the water from one city to another. The voluptuary Caligula (commonly thought to be mentally unbalanced by both ancient and modern historians) subsequently made his horse a consul. Here also Nero murdered his mother Agrippina and brutally suppressed the conspiracy of Piso. The Temple of Diana and the Imperial Palace close by are open to visitors.

Port Julius

Little remains of the ancient port built by Agrippa but some of the tunnels of the defence complex still remain.

POZZUOLI (MARINA DI MAGLIETTA)

BA 916
Italian 83

Note The region around Pozzuoli has been subject to severe earth movements and consequently the soundings for the harbour can only be approximate. From my first soundings twenty years ago depths appear to have decreased by around 1m.

The Italian government began evacuating the inhabitants in 1984 for fear of a major 'quake. In

Naples

Naples: a bay lapped by the blue Mediterranean and hemmed in by the islands of Capri and Ischia. Naples: the town spread fan-wise around the palm-lined shores and behind the lower rubble-strewn slopes of Vesuvius that preserved Roman life under hot ash at Herculaneum and Pompeii. Naples: the city of song and gaiety, of sadness and poetry, full of noisy and vivacious Neopolitans, the intellectual and commercial heart of the south. The appellations are well known throughout the world. For 200 years and more guide-books have praised the place and the setting. Whoever coined the phrase; 'See Naples and die', probably didn't count on it becoming the ironic epitaph of this great city. For the yachtsman it is difficult to see Vesuvius for the smog and the clear blue waters are polluted with oil and plastic. He will find it difficult to leave his yacht close to Naples without wondering if it will still be there, or at least intact, when he returns. Yet despite these words apparently condemning the place for yachtsmen cruising here, I would add that if you omit the Gulf of Naples from your list of harbours deemed desirable to stop at, then you will miss much indeed.

There is something about Naples that you must experience for yourself. Perhaps it is the richness and vitality of the life. There is intense fervour that is applied to everything from politics to the way pizza must be cooked. Add to this the incomparable sites of Herculaneum and Pompeii, the treasures from these sites housed in the National Museum, the treasures of 13th-century Renaissance art and the art of the 17th century in the National Gallery and one understands the complexity of the place. Among the skyscrapers and the 'throwaway' apartment blocks are churches and castles and monuments from all ages, but it must be that the inhabitants of a city on the slopes of an active volcano pay scant attention to their environment, to the sea and land about, on the tacit understanding that tomorrow it may all be destroyed if Vesuvius so much as burps. Strange too, to find industry spreading its ugly web over Roman villas and ancient harbours, changing the landscape and seascape from the once beautiful to the instantly forgettable – but somehow not quite obliterating it, so that the landscape familiar to Virgil, Augustus, Tiberius and Nero can still be faintly picked out.

'We were in Anacapri. The whole bay of Naples lay at our feet encircled by Ischia, Procida, the pine-clad Posilipo, the glittering white line of Naples, Vesuvius with its rosy cloud of smoke, the Sorrento plain sheltered under Monte Sant'Angelo and further away the Appenine mountains still covered with snow. Old Mastro Vincenzo was still hard at work in his vineyard, digging deep furrows in the sweet-scented soil for the new vines. Now and then he picked up a slab of coloured marble or a piece of red stucco and threw it over the wall, '*Roba di Timberio*', said he. I sat down on a broken column of red granite by the side of my new friend. '*Era molto dura*', it was very hard to break, said Mastro Vinzeno. At my feet a chicken was scratching in the earth in search of a worm and before my nose appeared a coin. I picked it up and recognised at a glance the noble head of Augustus, '*Divus Augustus Pater*'. Mastro Vinzenzo said it was not worth a '*baiocco*', I have it still.'

The Story of San Michele Axel Munthe 1928

The city of Naples spread under the bulk of Vesuvius
Paolo Ghirotti, FOTOTECA ENIT

Brief history

Naples was founded in 900BC as Parthenope by Rhodian navigators. In 600BC Cumaen colonists established Neapolis by the old settlement and with Greek immigrants from Khalkis and Athens it soon outstripped the original colony. In 326BC the Romans conquered it and it fast became a centre of learning and art within the Roman Empire. Among its citizens it numbered Lucullus, Virgil (he wrote the *Georgics* and the *Aeneid* here), Augustus, Tiberius (on Capri), Statius, and Nero. Pliny the Elder died in the eruption of Vesuvius which destroyed Herculaneum and Pompeii in AD79. After the fall of the Roman Empire from 568 to 1130 it was ruled by dukes owing allegiance to Byzantium. In 1139 it became part of the Norman kingdom of Sicily. It then became Hohenstaufen and later part of the House of Aragon. The Spanish ruled for two centuries from 1504 until 1707 after which it was briefly under the rule of the Archduke Charles of Austria. In 1734 the infant Charles of Bourbon seized Sicily and Naples and founded the Neopolitan Bourbon dynasty. Bourbon rule ended with Garibaldi's occupation in 1860. After the inattention of her foreign rulers, (Naples was a densely populated slum, albeit a picturesque one), much was done to improve sanitation and rebuild the city. It was heavily bombed in the Second World War, thus negating many of the improvements made.

Despite the large industrial belt and extensive rebuilding since the war, the city remains a poor one compared to her northern rivals and crime is endemic. Several years ago the workers in the city went on strike when the mayor attempted to clamp down on crime and gang activities and to stop the almost traditional smuggling of cigarettes and other goods. In the city itself, there is the age-old problem of scugnizzi, slum children who survive through crime and have developed the skill of purse-snatching from scooters to a high art. Remember when wandering the streets to conceal your valuables.

Pompeii

Buried by a layer of pumice (lapilli) and ash in AD79, the ruins of Pompeii give a large scale, unique and vivid idea of a Roman town. Some 2,000 perished at Pompeii (the population at the time was estimated at 20,000) and the buildings were buried so that only the tops protruded. Pliny the Elder, the eminent naturalist and Admiral of the fleet at Misenum, died in the eruption, overcome by the hot gases when he went to help the inhabitants escape. Half-hearted attempts were made to build again but the frequent earthquakes around Vesuvius discouraged reconstruction. In 1748 excavations were begun and have continued to this day. Unfortunately the 1980 earthquake that caused so much damage in southern Italy (some 3,000 people died and tens of thousands were left homeless in piles of rubble) has virtually closed Herculaneum and about half of Pompeii. One of the custodians there estimates that the earthquake had caused more damage in Pompeii than did Vesuvius in the eruption that covered it.

The forum at Pompei
Vito Arcomano, FOTOTECA ENIT

Pompeii is easily reached on the Circumvesuviana railway from Naples central railway station. Trains leave on the half hour. The regular train to Salerno also stops at Pompeii Villa dei Misteri, but it is more convenient on the Circumvesuviana. You should put aside a day at the very least to visit Pompeii.

Pozzuoli looking SW across the marina. Note the S breakwater has since been extended

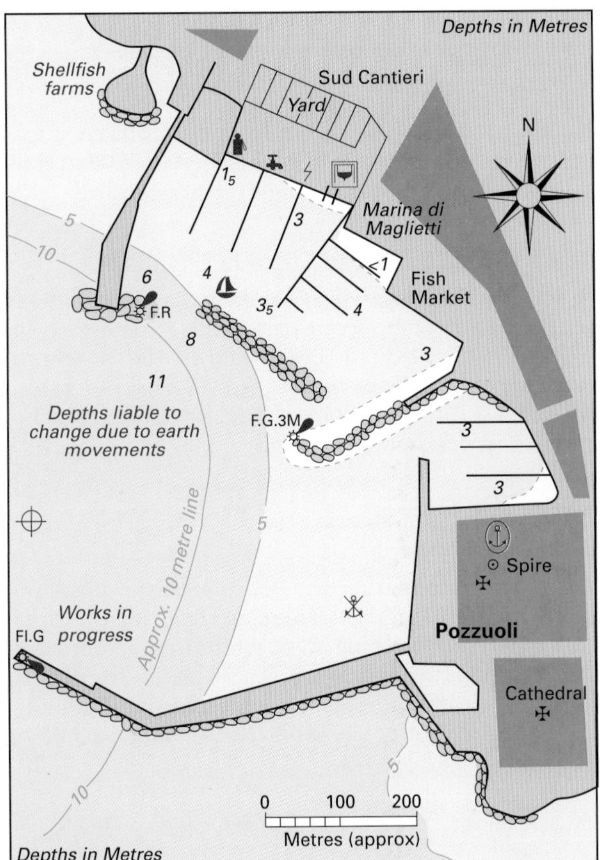

POZZUOLI
⊕40°49′·26N 14°06′·75E WGS84

recent years the earth movements have died down and everyone has returned, but it is likely that sometime in the future it will all happen again.

Approach

The harbour lies in the NE corner of Golfo di Pozzuoli. A yacht should head for Marina di Maglietta off the yard in the N of the harbour. Use the NW entrance. It is unlikely that you will find a berth in Pozzuoli fishing harbour to the south.

VHF Ch 16, Ch 09 (Pozzuoli 0800–2000), Ch 72 (Marina di Maglietta/Sud Cantieri).

Mooring

Data 150 berths. Max LOA 50m. Depths 1–5m.

Berth Where directed. Laid moorings tailed to the quay. Very limited visitors' berths.

Shelter Good all-round shelter.

Authorities Harbourmaster and marina staff. Charge band 5/6.

Sud Cantieri ✆ 081 526 1140 *Fax* 081 526 7034

Facilities

Services Water and electricity at all berths. Toilets and showers.
Fuel On the quay but depths off it are relatively shallow so enquire first.
Repairs Large yard ashore with 40/80-ton travel lifts and slipway capable of taking large craft. All yacht repairs can be carried out.
Provisions Good shopping in Pozzuoli up the hill to the east.
Eating out Restaurants in Pozzuoli.
Other PO and banks in Pozzuoli. ATMs. Italgaz. Buses and taxis into Naples.

General

Pozzuoli was called Puteoli in Roman times and became the most important port for Rome. Accordingly it was decorated with sumptuous buildings befitting the trade and wealth passing through it and many of these remain. The theatre, the Serapeum or Macellum, amphitheatre and the remains of several temples are close to the harbour.

The land about is constantly rising and falling in a 'slow earthquake' which in 1970 raised the ground by 75cm in six months. Over the centuries it is estimated that the level of the land may have been lowered and raised again by as much as 5½m. This whole area from Pozzuoli to Miseno is the Phlegrean Fields, a huge area of hot springs and suphur pits that is fuelled by the hot magma somewhere underneath. Many vulcanologists believe the next eruption in the Naples area will occur here and that it will be much greater than the eruption of Vesuvius in AD79.

Bagnoli

⊕ 40°48'·4N 14°10'·0E (F.G.3M)
BA 916
Italian 83

A commercial town lying about two miles E of Pozzuoli. There is a new pedestrian pier and several loading piers extending off the shore but they are not for yachts.

A request to build a 350-berth *porto turistico* for Bagnoli has been put forward. No details were available at the time of writing.

ISOLA DI NISIDA

BA 916
Italian 130

Approach

The islet of Nisida, joined by a causeway to the mainland, is easily identified. A yacht should head for the pontoons on the N side of the causeway.

Mooring

Data 400 berths. Max LOA 25m. Depths 5–6·5m.
Berth Where directed. Laid moorings tailed to the quay.

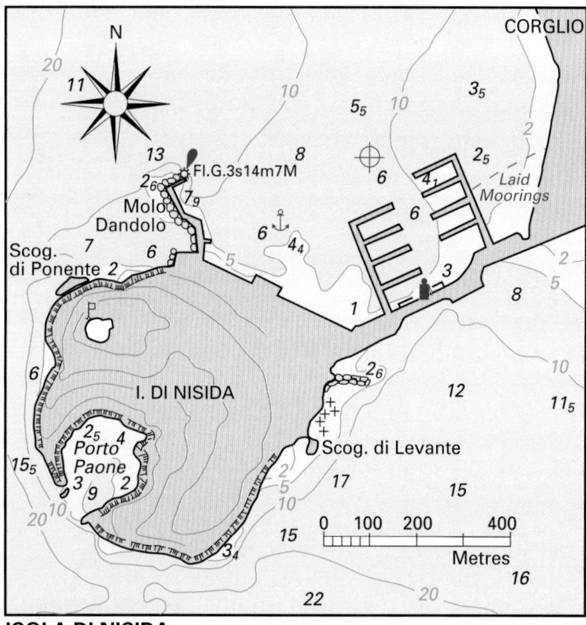

ISOLA DI NISIDA
⊕40°47′·9N 14°10′·1E

Shelter Good shelter although the harbour is open NW–N.
Authorities Harbourmaster. *Ormeggiatori*. The two sets of pontoons are run by two different groups: Onda Azzura and SENA. A charge is made.
Nisida Marina ✆ 081 762 0021
Onda Azzura ✆ 081 570 8000

Facilities

Services Water and electricity at all berths.
Fuel Fuel quay on the N side of the causeway.
Provisions and restaurants nearby.

General

Nisida was called Nesis in Roman times and it was here that Portia committed suicide, allegedly by swallowing hot burning coals, after the Battle of Philippi in which her husband Brutus (along with Cassius) was defeated by Antony and Octavian. Prior to this Brutus and Cassius had hatched their plan to murder Caesar on the islet.

Porto Paone

⊕ 40°47'·5N 14°09'·6E

A small cove on the S end of Isola di Nisida. A small yacht may be able to anchor inside with a long line ashore. There are mostly 3–6m depths with 8–10m in the entrance.

Secca della Gaiola and Secca la Cavallara

A reef extends SSE from Punta della Gaiola. The southern part of it, Secca La Cavallara, is awash in places. A S cardinal buoy marks the southern extremity of the reef. It is lit Q(6)+LFl.15s5M. From the reef to Capo Posillipo the coast is bordered by above and below-water rocks.

POSILLIPO

⊕ 40°49'·25N 14°13'·1E

A small private marina situated N of Capo Posillipo (40°48′·1N 14°12′·5E). There are apartment blocks and hotels surrounding it. A white monument near the entrance is conspicuous. There are 2–3m depths near the extremity of the mole decreasing gradually to 1m at the root of the mole. Most of the basin has

Nisida looking SE towards the islet and marina on the N side

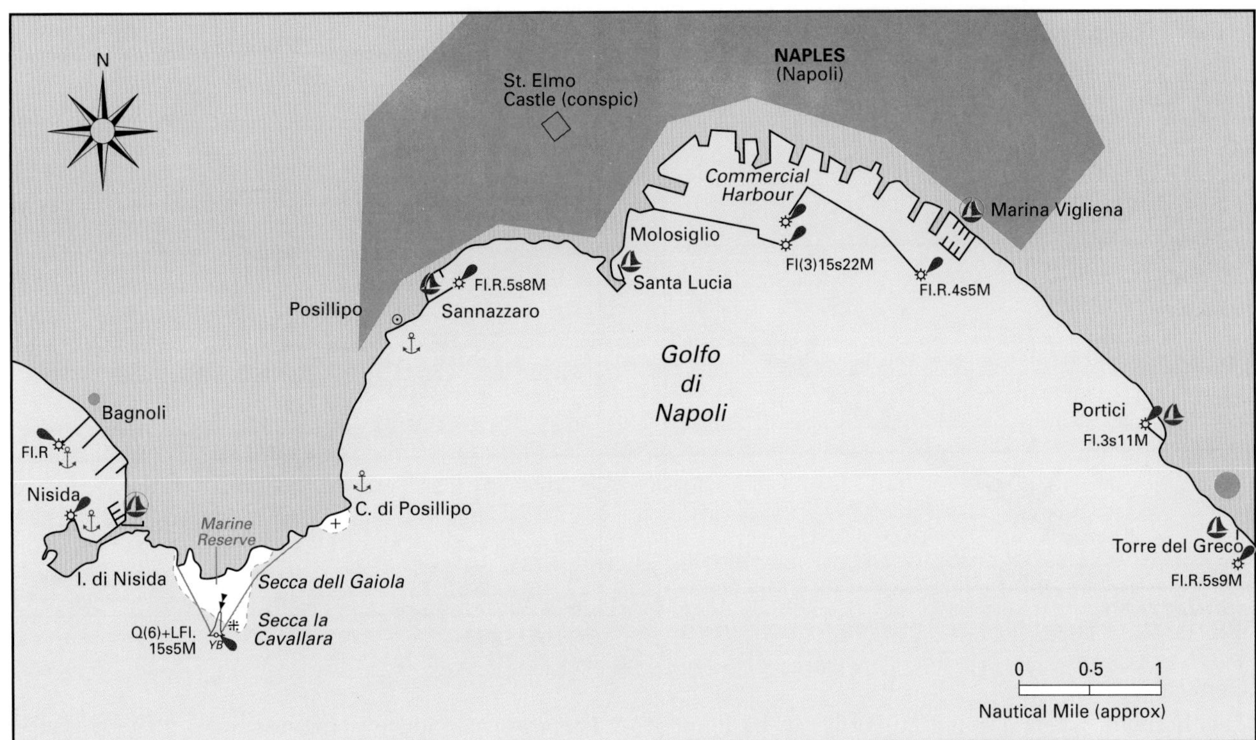

NAPLES APPROACHES

2m plus depths. It is usually crowded with local yachts. Water on the quay. Restaurants nearby but shops are some distance away.

SANNAZZARO (MERGELLINA)

Approach

This large harbour lies on the W side of Rada di Napoli. The coast about it is covered in apartment blocks but it is not difficult to locate the harbour.

VHF Ch 09 for Marina Molo Luise.

Dangers Care is needed of hydrofoils and other craft using the harbour.

Mooring

Data Max LOA 75m. Depths <1–8m.

Berth Go stern-to where directed. Care should be taken of the ballasting off the mole as it protrudes a short distance underwater in places. Laid moorings. Large yachts may need to use their own anchors.

Shelter Good shelter although strong NE–E winds may make it uncomfortable.

Authorities Harbourmaster and customs. Charge band 6+.

Marina Molo Luise ✆ 081 963 3396 *Fax* 081 963 3333
Email luise@luise.it
www.luise.it

Anchorage Anchoring is reported to be permitted to the NE of the harbour. Anchor in 7–10m, good holding once the anchor bites.

Facilities

Fuel and water on the quay. Shops and restaurants close by.

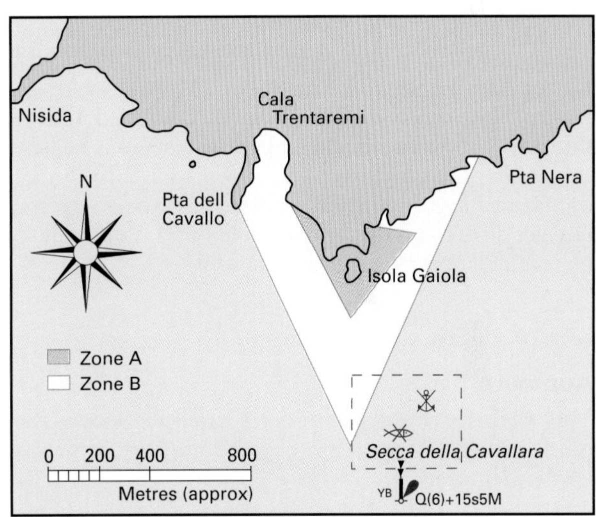

GAIOLA UNDERWATER RESERVE

Gaiola Marine Reserve

An underwater marine reserve (Parco Sommerso) has been established off Punta Gaiola, between Nisida and Capo Posillipo. The area has been divided into zones as shown on the plan.

Zone A
Navigation, anchoring, fishing, diving prohibited.

Zone B
Fishing without a permit prohibited.
✆ */Fax* 081 372 3760
Email sanc@interbusiness.it
www.areamarinaprotettagaiola.it

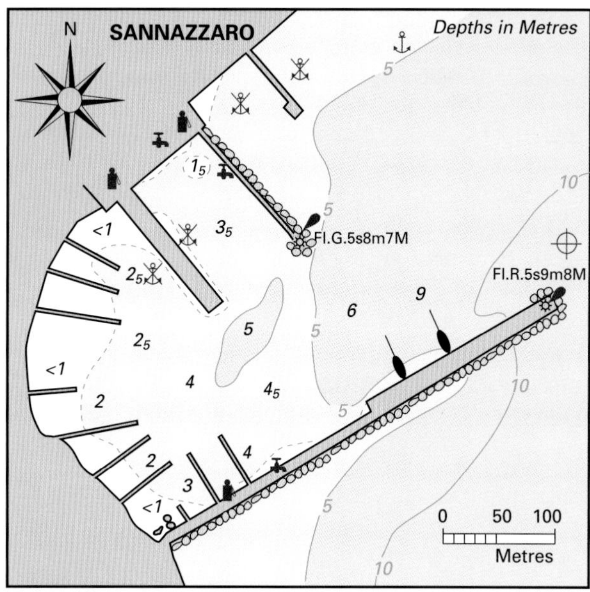

SANNAZZARO
⊕40°49´·7N 14°13´·6E

General

This harbour, where a managed berth can be found for a stay near Naples, is popular with large yachts. Here you are about as close to the centre of Naples as you can get in a yacht. Close by is the quarter of Santa Lucia (essential sunset viewing), Castel Nuovo and Castel Sant'Elmo, the Carthusian Monastery of St Martin and the National Museum crammed full of things Greco-Roman. The Naples Aquarium is nearby to the NE and is said to contain more than 200 species of marine life from the Bay of Naples. Having seen the bay get dirtier and dirtier over time I find it difficult to believe 200 species can now live in it.

SANTA LUCIA

Approach

This yacht harbour lies under Castell del'Uova, the old fortified village on a rocky promontory, which is easily identified.

VHF Ch 77.

Mooring

Data 150 berths. Max LOA 25m. Depths 2–5m.

Berth Where directed. The Coop Ormegiatori Luciani di Napoli controls berths here. Most berths are private and it is reported to be difficult and expensive to get a berth here.

Shelter Good shelter although southerly winds are reported to cause a surge.

Authorities Coop. *Ormeggiatori* Luciani. Charge band 4/5.
✆ 081 764 5517 *Fax* 081 764 8842
Email orm.slucia@tiscali.it or ormeggiatori1@virgilio.it
www.ormeggioslucia.com

Facilities

Services Water and electricity at or near all berths.
Fuel On the quay and at the yard.
Repairs 15-ton slipway and 10-ton crane. Most repairs can be carried out.

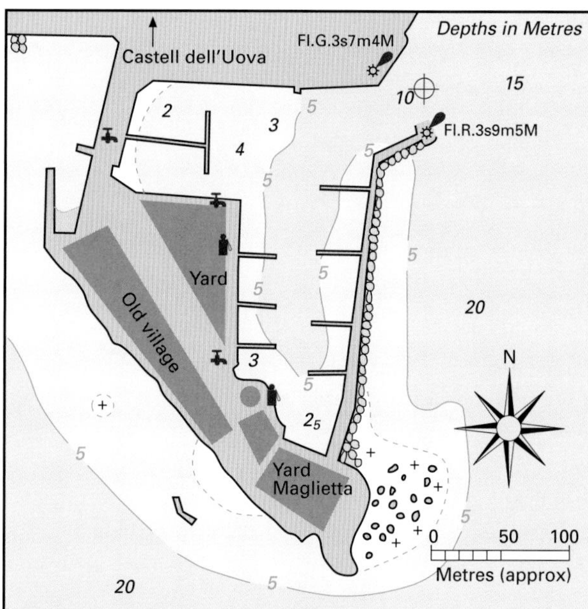

SANTA LUCIA
⊕40°49´·8N 14°15´·1E

Provisions Good shopping nearby.
Eating out Restaurants and bars nearby.

General

This was originally an island, Megaris, until joined by a causeway. The harbour takes its name from the nearby area of Santa Lucia, popularly said to be the Santa Lucia immortalised in song. Castell del'Uova above was once a prison and is now a barracks. It is a short walk to the centre of Naples.

MOLOSIGLIO

A small private yacht harbour close NE of Santa Lucia. It is always crowded and it is all but impossible to find a berth.

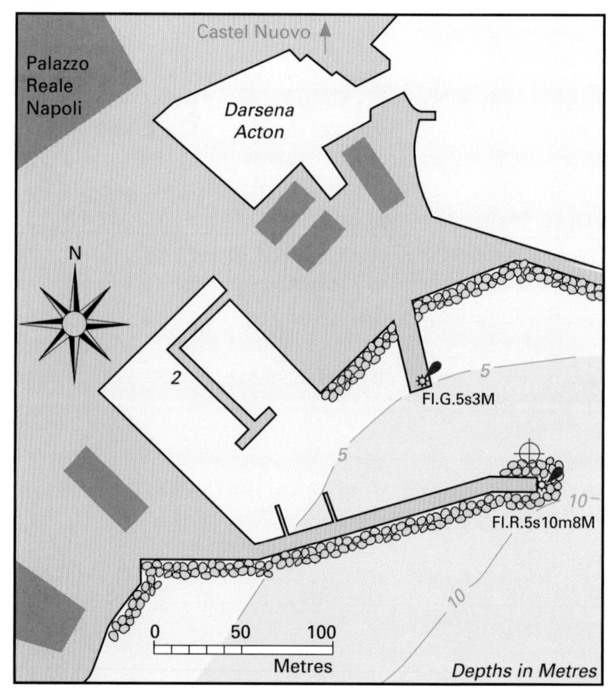

MOLOSIGLIO
⊕40°50´·0N 14°15´·4E

Data 150 berths. Max LOA 14m. Depths 2–5m.

Authorities Lega Navale Italiana ✆ 081 551 1806. Circolo Canottieri Napoli ✆ 081 551 2331.

NAPLES COMMERCIAL HARBOUR

This large harbour was established in Greek and Roman times and greatly developed by Charles II of Anjou. It was extensively damaged in the Second World War but has now been rebuilt and is the second most important port in Italy, handling the greatest number of passengers. The waterfront is being smartened up and Darsena 'Acton' is being developed for yachts and tourist vessels. No further details are available yet.

VHF Ch 11, 16 for port authorities (24hr). Ch 12 for pilots.

Note It is reported that GPS signals will be lost in the vicinity of Naples commercial port.

MARINA VIGLIENA (PORTO FIORITO)

A marina just SE of Naples commercial port.

The original marina is being re-developed and expanded. At present transit berths are limited. The project is due to be completed in 2012/13. The plan and data below is for the completed marina.

Approach

Head just to the SE of the commercial port where the cranes and derricks are conspicuous.

Note Commercial traffic has priority at all times.

VHF Ch 16, 72.

Mooring

Data 850 berths. LOA 12–80m. Depths 4–10m.

Berth Where directed. Laid moorings tailed to the quay.

Shelter Good shelter although some berths may be uncomfortable with strong southerlies.

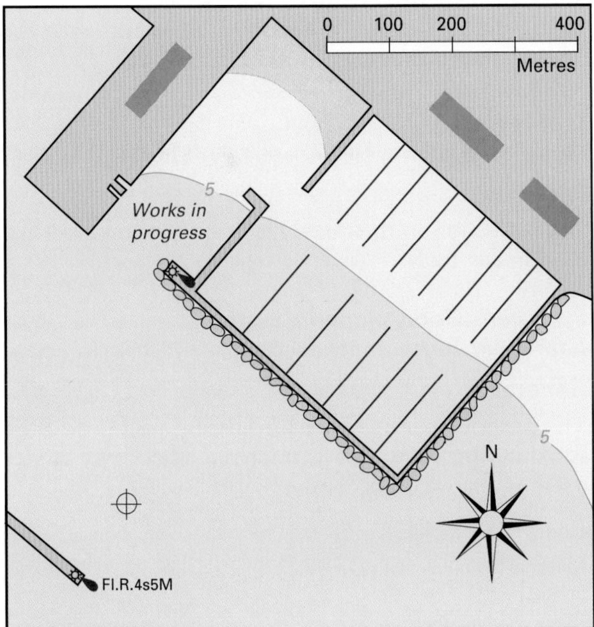

MARINA VIGLIENA
⊕40°49'·6N 14°18'·0E

Authorities Harbourmaster and marina staff. Charge band 6+.

Porto Fiorito ✆ /*Fax* 081245 7531
Email info@marinavigliena.it
www.marinavigliena.it

Cantiere Navale Partenope ✆ 081 752 9017
Fax 081 752 4017
Email cantierepartenope@tin.it
www.cantierepartenope.it

Facilities

Services Water and electricity at every berth. Toilets and showers. Wi-Fi.
Fuel On the quay.
Repairs 50-ton travel-lift. Most yacht repairs can be carried out.
Provisions Good shopping nearby.
Eating out Numerous restaurants of all types nearby.
Other Close to the centre of Naples and all its facilities.

PORTICI

A small commercial and fishing port about four miles SE of Naples. A silo and chimney near the harbour are conspicuous. Berth near the end of the mole if there is room. Fishing boats occupy most of the available space. Water on the quay. Restaurant nearby. The harbour is oily and sooty and the surroundings mostly industrial.

VHF Ch 11, 16 for port authorities (0700–1900).

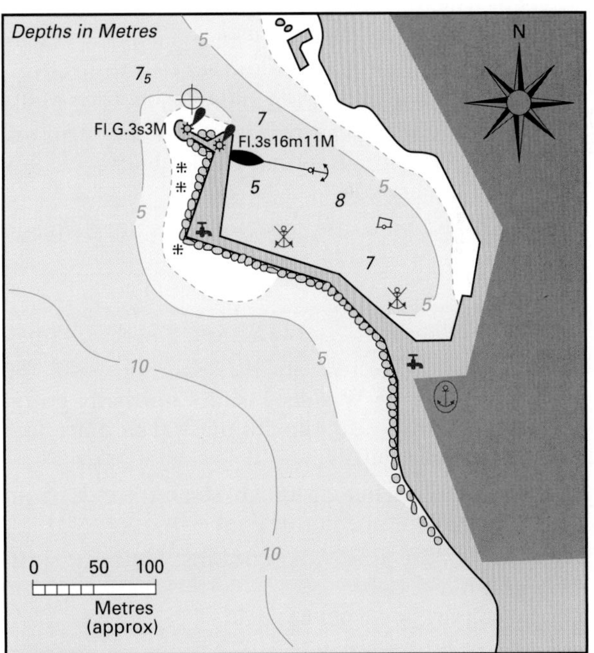

PORTICI
⊕40°48'·7N 14°20'·0E

TORRE DEL GRECO

BA 916
Italian 914, 26

Approach

A large harbour lying two miles SE of Portici. A chimney close to the root of the outer mole is conspicuous. Closer in, the outer mole and the light

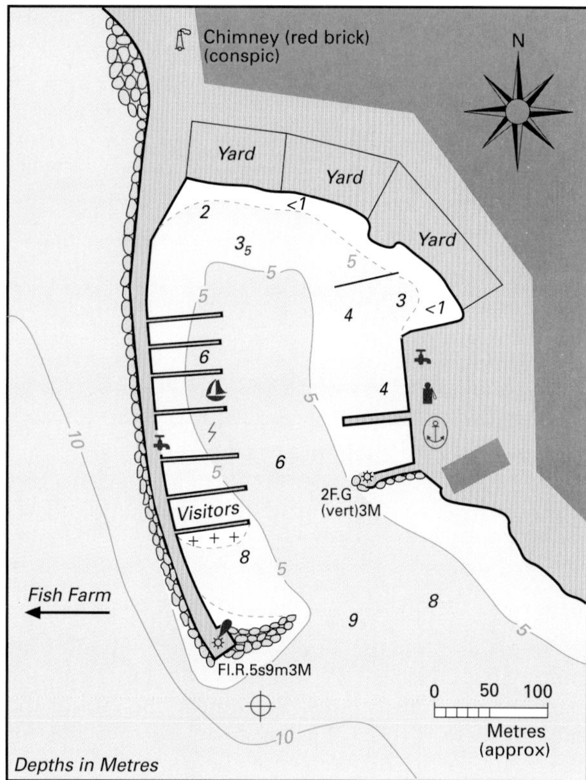

TORRE DEL GRECO
⊕40°47´·0N 14°21´·8E

tower at its extremity are easily identified. Entry can be difficult with strong SE winds.

VHF Ch 14, 16 for port authorities (0700–1900).

Note A fish farm is reported approximately ½ a mile W of the entrance. The perimeters of the farm are marked by four unlit special marks buoys (yellow with a × topmark).

Caution GPS signals are reported to be unreliable in this area.

Mooring

Data c. 500 berths Max LOA 15m. Depths 2–8m.

Berth Where directed on the pontoons off the breakwater on the W side. Visitors normally go on the first pontoon near the entrance. There are laid moorings to pick up.

Shelter Good shelter although strong winds from S–W can make it uncomfortable.

Authorities Port police and customs. Harbour staff. Charge band 4.

Circolo Nautico Torre ✆ 081 881 9150

Facilities

Services Water at or near most berths. Electricity connection possible.
Fuel On the quay.
Repairs A 5-ton crane. Mechanical repairs. GRP and wood repairs in the yard. Electrical and electronic repairs. Chandlers.
Provisions Good shopping in the town. Fish shop in harbour.
Eating out Restaurants and pizzerias.
Other PO. Banks. ATMs. Italgaz and Camping Gaz. Buses and trains to Herculaneum and Pompeii.

General

The modern town is the most populous in the province after Naples. The area around the harbour is not the most salubrious, and security has been reported to be minimal. Lock up well if you leave your boat here. Sitting close to Vesuvius, it comes as no surprise that it has many times been destroyed by lava and earthquakes. It is a convenient place from which to visit Herculaneum, Pompeii and Vesuvius although security at the yacht harbour has reportedly lapsed so check before leaving your boat here.

1. *To see Herculaneum.* Take bus No. 255 from the port. About 3km away.
2. *To see Pompeii.* Take the Circumvesuviana railway from Torre del Greco. The train station is about 20 minutes' walk inland from the port. The train stops at the ruins themselves (Scavi).
3. *To see Vesuvius.* Take the Circumvesuviana railway to Herculaneum station (Ercolano). Here a shuttle bus takes you most of the way up. It is about 20 minutes' further walk to the summit.

TORRE ANNUNZIATA

BA 916
Italian 94

Approach

A large commercial harbour nearly five miles SE of Torre del Greco. The wheat silos at the harbour are conspicuous.

VHF Ch 16, 13, 15 (0700–1900).

Mooring

Data 100 berths. Max LOA 10m.

Berth Head for the pontoons at the NW end and berth where directed. Laid moorings.

Shelter Normally adequate shelter although strong southerlies can make it uncomfortable and even the afternoon sea breeze causes a bit of slop.

Authorities Harbourmaster and customs. *Ormeggiatori.*

Circolo Nautico Torre Annunziata ✆ 081 536 4318

Facilities

Service Water on the quay. Electricity at some berths.
Fuel In the town.
Repairs 20-ton crane.
Provisions Good shopping ashore.
Eating out Restaurants ashore.

General

The harbour is not really for visiting yachts and the surroundings are not attractive. The town styles itself as the regional 'pasta centre'.

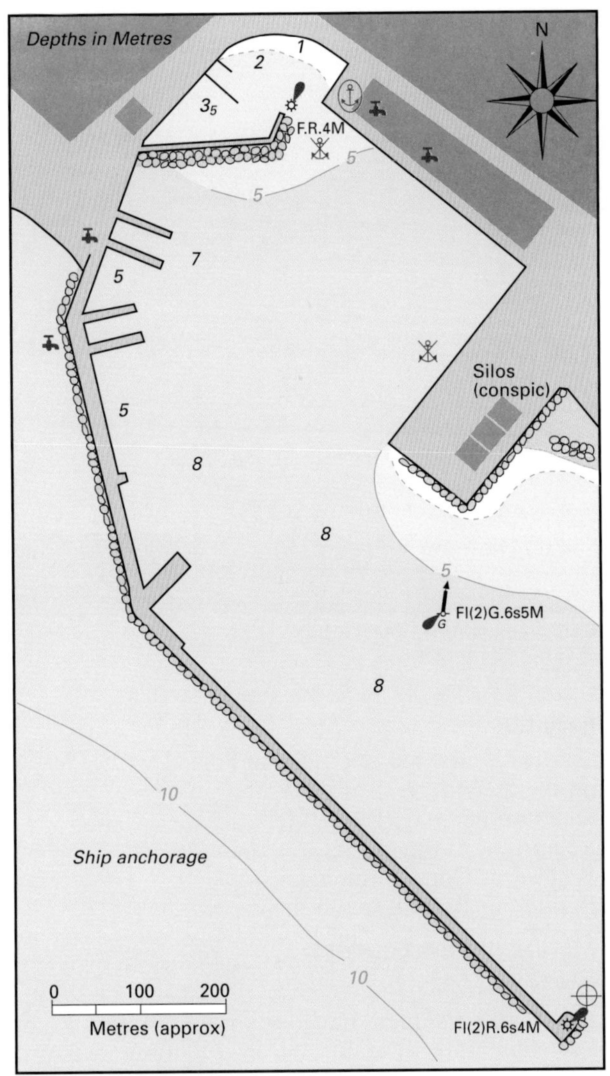

TORRE ANNUNZIATA
⊕40°44´·5N 14°27´·2E

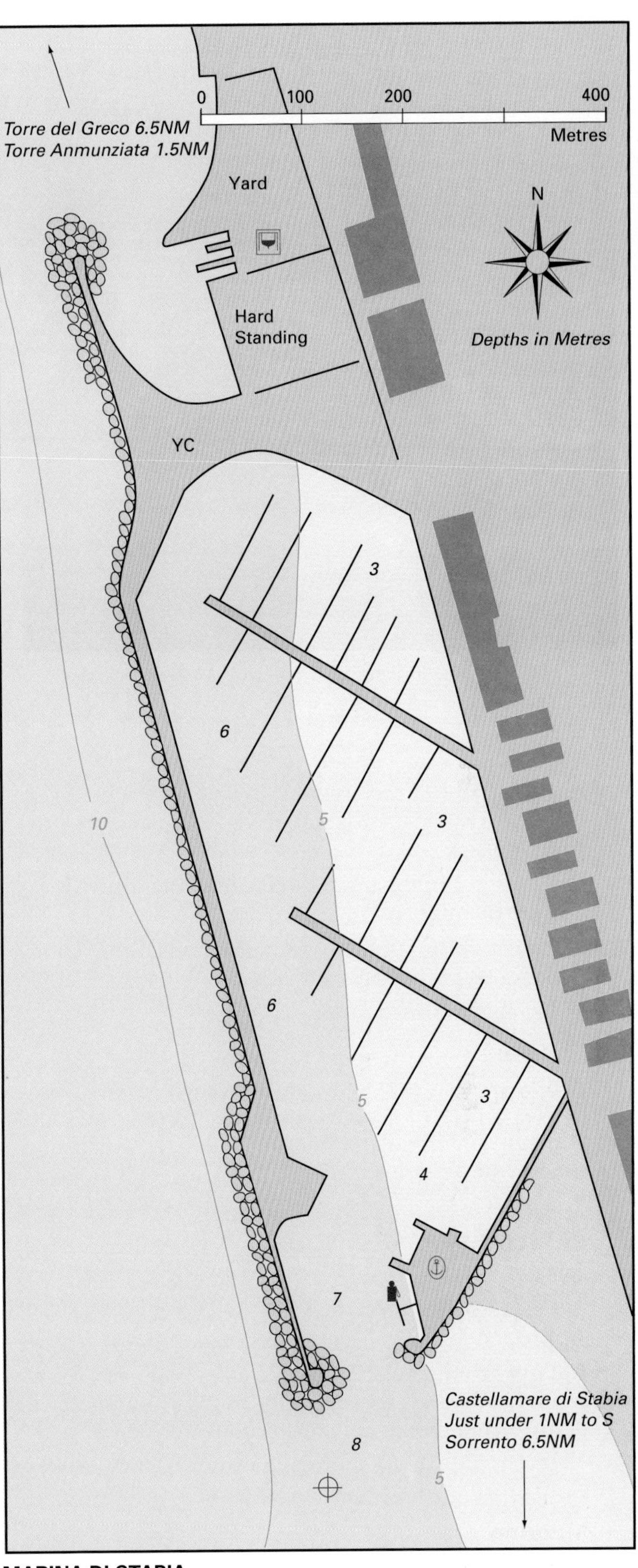

MARINA DI STABIA
⊕40°42′·9N 14°28′·4E

MARINA DI STABIA

Approach

A new marina now completed lying 1·5M S of Torre Anunziata (6·5M S of Torre del Greco), and 1M N of Castellamare di Stabia (6·5M NE of Sorento).

VHF Ch 69.

Mooring

Data 685 berths. Max LOA 80m. Depths 3·5–6m.

Berths Where directed. Stern or bows-to with finger pontoons. Laid moorings for larger yachts.

Shelter Good shelter.

Authorities Marina staff. Charge band 6.
Marina di Stabia ✆ 081 871 6871 *Fax* 081 872 7963
Email info@marinadistabia.it
www.marinadistabia.it

Facilities

Services Water and electricity (220/380V). Showers and toilets. Launderette. Wi-Fi being installed.

Fuel On the quay.

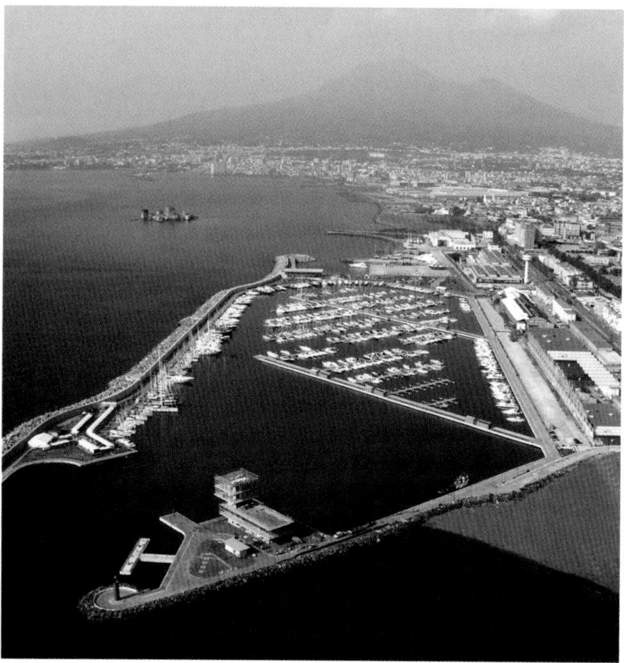
Marina di Stabia looking N to Vesuvius *Marina di Stabia*

Repairs 220-ton travel-lift. Slipways for yachts over 40m. Workshops and paint sheds. Most repairs can be organised.

Provisions Mini-market under construction. More outside the marina.

Eating out BBQ area, bar, restaurant and Yacht Club under construction in the marina.

Other Bus to Castellamare di Stabia.

General

A new marina providing much needed berths close to the centre of Naples, and the historic sites of Pompeii and Ercolano, sitting under the imposing shadow of Vesuvius.

CASTELLAMMARE DI STABIA

BA 916
Italian 95

Approach

A large commercial port 3½ miles SSE of Torre Annunziata. Several tall silos and a number of derricks and cranes are conspicuous.

VHF Ch 11, 16 for port authorities (0700–1900). Ch 72 for Porto Davide.

Mooring

Data 200 berths. Max LOA 30m. Depths 1·5–10m.

Berth Try at Porto Davide; the pontoon berths on the E side of the entrance or at the pontoons at the S end.

Shelter Open N–NE.

Authorities Harbourmaster and customs. *Ormeggiatori.*

Porto Davide ☎ 081 871 0107

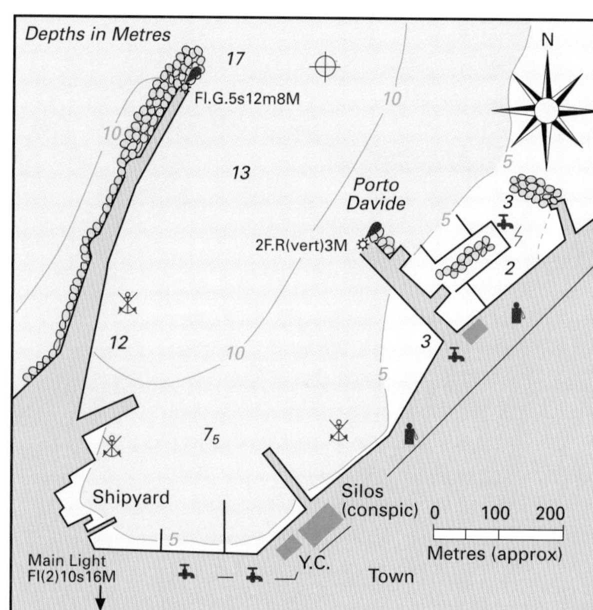

CASTELLAMMARE DI STABIA
⊕40°42′·2N 14°28′·6E

Facilities

Services Water and electricity in Porto Davide. Water on the quay.

Fuel On the quay.

Repairs 5–50-ton cranes.

Provisions Good shopping ashore.

Eating out Restaurants nearby.

Marina di Vico Equense

⊕ 40°40′·1N 14°25′·8E

A small fishing harbour two miles S of Castellammare di Stabia. Steep-to cliffs and Banco Santa Croce shoal can cause confused seas around Capo d'Orlando. Scoglio Marguerita lies to the NW of the harbour. There are 0·5–3·5m depths in the harbour, but it is not really suitable for yachts.

Marina di Equa

⊕ 40°39′·7N 14°25′·0E

A small and mostly shallow harbour approximately three miles SW of Castellammare di Stabia. A small yacht might find shelter in here though it is normally crowded with local boats. Open to the north.

Marina di Meta

⊕ 40°38′·8N 14°24′·4E

A small harbour lying under Punta Gradelle about two miles SW of Equa.

MARINA DI CASSANO

A small harbour lying just over a mile NE of Sorrento. The quayed part of the mole is normally used by fishing boats but a berth can sometimes be found. The harbour should only be used in calm weather.

A new yacht harbour to the W of Marina di Cassano is being developed, with pontoons and further laid moorings.

Data 188 berths. Max LOA 14m. Depths 2·5–8m.

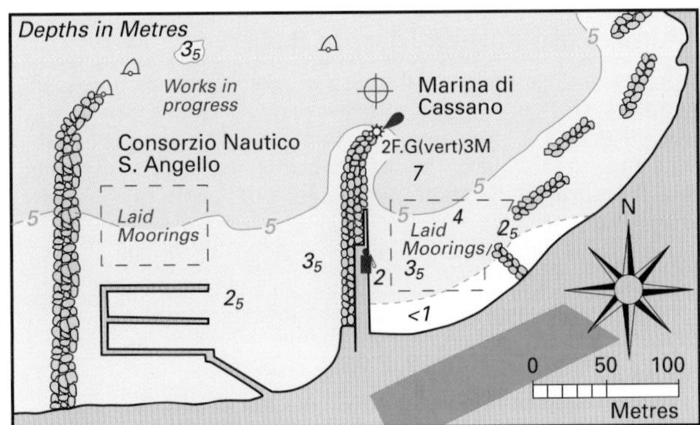

MARINA DI CASSANO
⊕40°38′·4N 14°24′·1E

Authorities Consorzia Nautico Sant Agnello VHF Ch 16.
Five Marine Service ✆ 081 878 8564
Marina di Vico Equense ✆ 081 878 8436

Sant Agnello di Sorrento

⊕ 40°38′·0N 14°23′·4E

A very small and shallow harbour that is usually full of local boats. Shelter appears good if you can get inside.

SORRENTO (MARINA PICCOLA)

BA 916
Italian 131

Approach

The town of Sorrento standing on a plateau which drops sheer into the sea can be identified by the elegant red building on the cliff-top above and closer in, by the high harbour wall.

Note Work is in progress extending the outer breakwater and building a new breakwater on the E end of the harbour.

By night The Fl.G.3s5M at the end of the original breakwater is not in operation during the current works, but a Fl.G buoy marks the extremity of the extension. On completion the Fl.G.3s5M will be at the head of the extended breakwater.

VHF Ch 16, 13.

Mooring

Data 250 berths. Max LOA 15m. Depths 0·5–5m.

Berth Go stern or bows-to where possible, keeping clear of the ferry quay.

Shelter Good shelter in settled weather.

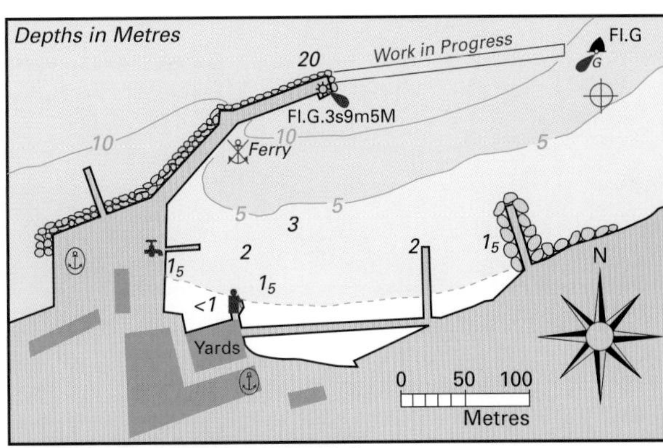

SORRENTO - MARINA PICCOLA
⊕40°37′·8N 14°22′·9E

Authorities Co. Port Sorrento.
✆ 081 807 2582 *Fax* 081 878 6760
Email coport@libero.it
www.coportsorrento.com

Anchorage In calm weather it may still be possible to anchor to the E of the harbour in 2–5m on a sandy bottom. Care must be taken of numerous laid moorings.

Facilities

Services Water and electricity on the quay.
Fuel On the quay (0730–2030) ✆ 081 807 1593.
Repairs Small crane. Limited repairs only.
Provisions in the town.
Eating out Restaurants at the harbour and in the town.

General

The town above is charming and the countryside round about noted for its citrus orchards, though tourism has long been the prime earner and not oranges and lemons. Sorrento was the 'Surrentum' of the Romans, a resort famed for its scenery and climate. In the 19th century it was a popular winter resort for northern Europeans.

Sorrento Marina Grande

⊕ 40°37′·7N 14°22′·1E

A small and mostly shallow harbour. Untrue to its name, it is not large at all.

Marina di Puolo

⊕ 40°37′·55N 14°20′·8E

A breakwater extending in a NE direction for approximately 100m. Laid moorings.

Punta di Montalto at the bottom of the Sorrento peninsula looking west

Elegant buildings atop the cliffs in Marina Piccola, Sorrento
Gino Cianci, FOTOTECA ENIT

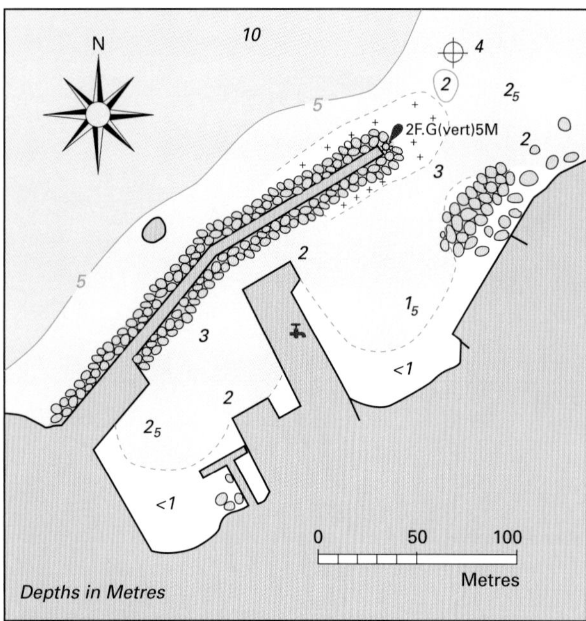

MARINA DELLA LOBRA
⊕40°36´·6N 14°20´·1E

MARINA DELLA LOBRA (Massa Lubrense)

Approach

A small harbour under Punta di Vacca. The entrance is rock-bound and great care is needed. A night approach should not be made.

Mooring

Berth Go stern or bows-to the quay taking care of depths and underwater rocks or anchor and take a long line to the breakwater.

Shelter Good shelter although strong NE winds may cause problems.

Data 100 berths. Max LOA 14m. Depths <1–3m.

Authorities Co. Marina Lobra.
✆ 081 808 9380

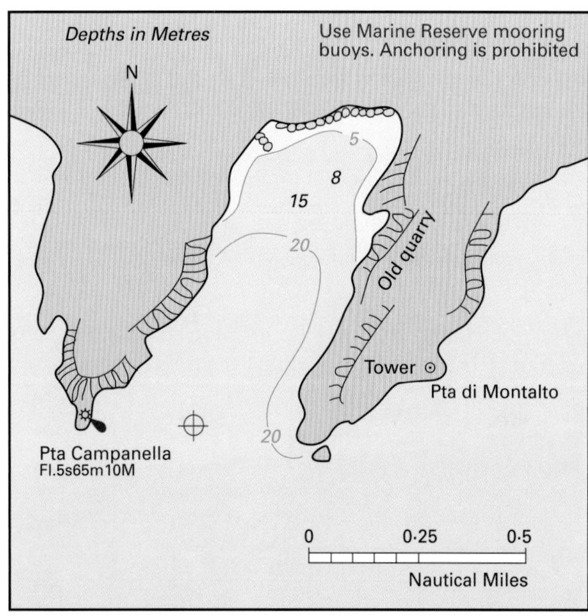

SENNO DI IERANTO
⊕40°34´·12N 14°19´·82E WGS84

Punta Campanella Marina Reserve

This marine reserve, established in 1997, extends between Capo di Sorrento and Punta Germano, and includes Vervece, Isca, Vetara and the Isole Galli. The perimeter of the reserve is marked by yellow buoys, some of which are lit. Transit appears to be permitted, but caution is advised.
The area is divided as follows:

Zone A
Swimming, navigation, anchoring and mooring prohibited.

Zone B
Motor navigation prohibited except for access to regulated mooring buoys in the transit channel (max. speed 5kns). Anchoring and fishing prohibited.

Zone C
Sail and motor navigation permitted (max. speed 10 knots) only for access to controlled moorings and anchorages. Unregulated anchoring prohibited.
✆ 081 808 9877
www.puntacampanella.org

PUNTA CAMPANELLA MARINE RESERVE
⊕1 40°34´·12N 14°19´·07E WGS84 (0·25M W of Pta Campanella)
⊕2 40°34´·29N 14°26´·06E WGS84 (0·5M S of I. Galli)

Facilities

Water on the quay.
Repairs Some mechanical and electrical repairs.
Provisions Most provisions nearby.
Eating out Restaurants nearby.

Senno di Ieranto (Zone B)

A large bay under Punta Campanella. It provides useful shelter at the S end of Golfo di Napoli. Authorised mooring buoys have been laid in the bay, and yachts should use these instead of anchoring. Good shelter in the summer and the daily sea breeze blowing into the Gulf of Naples does not blow home. Attractive surroundings.

The bay lies within the Punta Campanella Marine Reserve. It within Zone B and specific restrictions apply.

The islands in Golfo di Napoli

On the NW side of the gulf are the Flegree Islands (Isole Flegree) comprising Procida, Vivara (joined to Procida by a bridge) and Ischia. On the southern side of the gulf is Capri. The northern group of Ischia and Procida are part of a huge volcanic chain that includes Ventotene and the Phelagrian Fields on the mainland. Capri belongs geologically to the Sorrento peninsula. The islands are described separately.

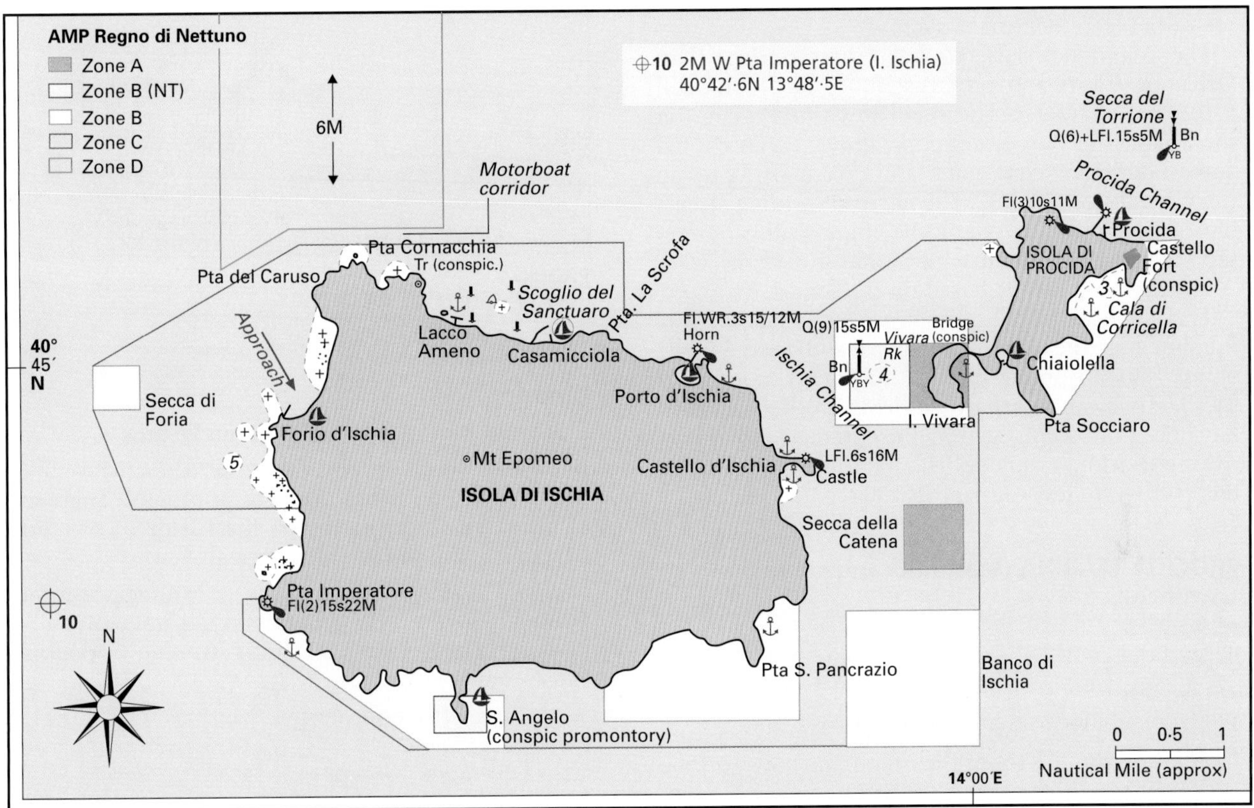

ISCHIA AND PROCIDA (FLEGREE ISLANDS)

AMP Regno do Nettuno (Neptune's Kingdom Marine Reserve)

Regulations

Zone A
All unauthorised navigation, fishing, swimming, diving, anchoring and mooring prohibited.

Zone B
Navigation and mooring by sailing yacht and motor boats at less than 5 knots permitted subject to authorization. Diving subject to authorization. Contact the AMP for permission. Swimming and rowing permitted.
Anchoring prohibited except for residents. Most fishing (except gill netting) prohibited.

Zone B(NT) Special zones for diving. Authorized guided diving permitted. Swimming, rowing, electric drives and sailing permitted. All un-authorised navigation, fishing, swimming, diving, anchoring and mooring prohibited.

Zone C
Navigation by sailing yacht permitted. Jet skis, planing boats and boats at over 10 knots require authorization. Anchoring prohibited between 1st June and 30th September, except for residents. Anchoring out of season permitted with authorization. Mooring and some fishing permitted with authorization. Diving permitted with authorization.

Zone D
Cetacean Sanctuary. Jet skis, planing boats and boats at over 10 knots are prohibited. Most authorized fishing and diving permitted.

Notes
1. Rules are not as stringent for residents, so you may see vessels in areas where visitors are not permitted.
2. Most visitors will require authorization in advance before entering Zone B. PDF forms requesting permission are available to download on the website. Contact the AMP for details and authorization.
3. Fees and authorization depend on LOA, engine emissions, holding tanks and type of anti-fouling.
4. Within 300m of the coast the maximum speed is 5kns.
5. Within 600m of the coast the maximum speed is 10 knots.
6. Jet skis and water-skiers may only transit the AMP perpendicular to the coast.
7. Access to sea caves restricted to rowed boats or inflatables.
8. Discharge of black or grey water or solid waste is prohibited.
9. Anchoring prohibited in posidonia beds or areas of coral, overnight, or close to mooring buoys.
10. Yachts may only pick up designated mooring buoys, and not take those reserved for dive or trip boats.

✉ Area Marina Protetta Regno di Nettuno, Piazza municipio 9 80075, Forio, NA
✆ */Fax* 081 333 2941 *Email* info@nettunoamp.it
www.nettunoamp.org

Flegree Islands

Isola di Procida

A small low-lying island (greatest elevation: 115m/377ft) close to the northwestern end of Golfo di Napoli. I. Vivara off the SW corner of Procida is connected to it by a bridge. The island is composed of four craters now so eroded by the sea that they are difficult to identify as such.

The island has suffered less from tourism than Ischia or Capri and retains a noisy and colourful Procidean character. The small town of Procida on the N coast has an oriental air about it: flat-roofed cubic houses in white, pink and cream rising up to the Castello on the hill. The narrow winding streets have a medieval aspect and the countryside about is terraced and cultivated with orchards and the vine. A large fishing fleet is based on the island.

There is little to tell of ancient settlements: it was inhabited in the Neolithic period and used by the Romans as a hunting reserve, and apart from raids by the Turks and Barbarossa (in 1544) life seems to have been uncomplicated by the comings and goings of civilisations outside the island. Even today comparatively few tourists visit here.

PROCIDA MARINA (Marina Grande, Sancio Cattolico)

BA 908, 916
Italian 131, 913/01

Approach

Conspicuous The fort and several cupolas sitting high up on the NE tip of the island and town on the saddle of the ridge nearby are conspicuous. A white cupola at the harbour and the harbour breakwaters are easily identified.

VHF Ch 11, 16 for port authorities. Ch 06 for Marina di Procida (24/7).

Dangers Care is needed of the constant stream of ferries and hydrofoils coming and going.

Castello on the eastern end of Procida looking SW

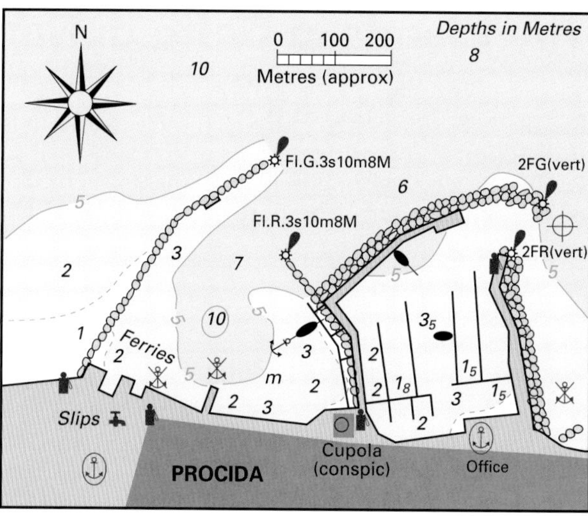

PROCIDA
⊕40°46´·12N 14°02´·02E WGS84

Mooring

Data 490 berths. Max LOA 30m. Depths 1–4m.

Berth Go stern or bows-to in Procida Marina (E basin). Laid moorings tailed to pontoons. There are also limited yacht berths on the E side of the ferry harbour along the wooden catwalk.

Shelter Good shelter from the prevailing westerlies although strong NW winds make it uncomfortable in here. The ferries constantly coming and going cause some wash in the W basin.

Authorities Harbourmaster. Marina staff. Charge band 6.

Marina di Procida ✆ /*Fax* 081 896 9668
Email info@marinadiprocida.191.it

Facilities

Services Water and electricity (220/380V) at all marina berths. Toilets and shower cabins. Laundry nearby.
Fuel On the quay (0800–1900).
Repairs 500-ton slipway and 10-ton crane. Mechanical and engineering work.
Provisions Good shopping nearby.
Eating out Restaurants nearby and at Castello.
Other Bank. ATM. Ferries to Ischia and Naples.

General

The town around the ferry port, known variously as Procida Marina, Marina Grande, Sancio Cattolico, the latter often abbreviated to Sant'Co, is a faded, patchy lived-in town with pastel houses and narrow alleys, none of it tarted up for the tourists as Ischia and Capri have been. Above, the town of Corricella on the ridge is more of the same, a riot of pastel colours and peeling paint, well worth a visit. There are some good fish restaurants at Sant'Co or over the hill on the waterfront at Corricella.

This is a safe place to leave a yacht with good ferry and rail connections to Pompeii.

Procida Marina looking south

Cala di Corricella (Zone B)

An anchorage under the NE tip of the island. Castello fort on the steep-to tip of the island is conspicuous. Cala di Corricella is the northern cove of the bay and Cala di Sant Antonio the southern cove. A sandy spit with some rocks with a least depth of 3m over it divides the bay into two. Both offer good shelter except from the S–SE. The bottom is sand and good holding. In Cala di Corricella two breakwaters shelter local fishing boats.

Note This anchorage lies within Zone B of the AMP. Restrictions apply.

Proceed with care through the E or middle passages behind the breakwaters. The area in here is pretty much full of laid moorings and probably the best thing to do is anchor and take a line to the breakwater. Alternatively you may be able to pick up a mooring, but enquire first. If all else fails you can anchor off outside the breakwaters in calm conditions. Be sure to carry an anchor light as there is much coming and going in the evening and early morning.

The setting here is wonderful under Castello and there are restaurants and bars ashore.

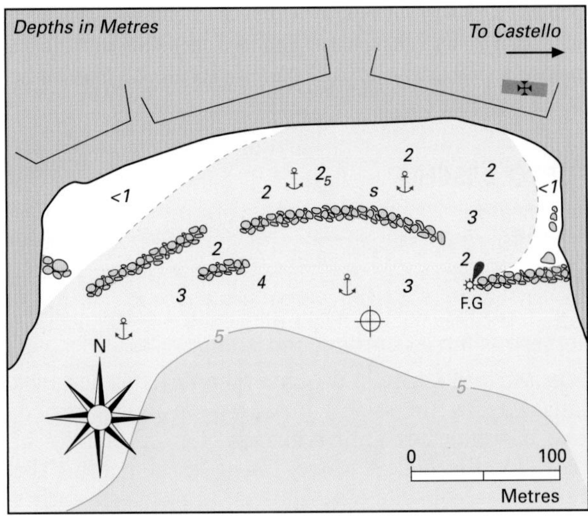

CORRICELLA
⊕40°45´·5N 14°01´·9E

CHIAIOLELLA

Approach

A small harbour on the S of the island. The bridge between Procida and Vivara is easily identified and in the closer approaches a small square tower on the W side of the entrance will be seen. Care is needed in strong southerlies when a swell piles up in the approaches and the entrance.

VHF Ch 11, 16. Ch 11 for Procida Yachting Club.

Mooring

Data Max LOA 30m. Depths 1–5m.

Berth Stern or bows-to one of the pontoons. Laid moorings tailed to the quay. Several yacht clubs and co-operatives have their own pontoons and quay

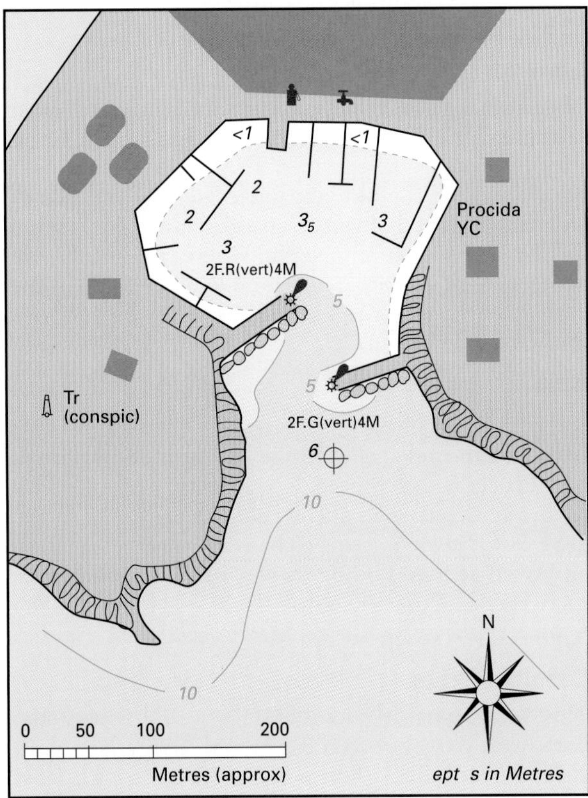

CHIAIOLELLA
⊕40°44´·7N 14°00´·4E

The approaches to Chiaiolella looking north

space. It is invariably busy, although one or other of them can usually squeeze just one more in, particularly if you call in advance.

Shelter Good shelter although southerlies cause a surge.

Authorities Ormeggiatori. Charge band 4/5.

Sta Margherita ☏ 081 896 8074
Meditur ☏ 081 810 1934
Procida Yachting Club ☏ 081 810 1481
Email info@procidayachting.it
www.procidayachting.it

Facilities

Services Water and electricity on the pontoons.
Fuel On the quay (0800–2000).
Repairs 30-ton crane. Limited repairs only.
Provisions Most provisions can be found.
Eating out Restaurants nearby.
Other Buses to Procida.

General

The little harbour and its surroundings are most attractive and much frequented by local yachts and tripper boats in the summer. The bay of Vivara next door is one of the old volcanic craters of the island. Vivara, reached by the pedestrian foot-bridge nearby, is a nature reserve where the birds are protected – if you are going for a wander do so in the early evening when it is cooler as it can be very hot in the middle of the day.

Isola Vivara (Zone A/C)

⊕ 40°44'·6N 14°00'·0E

A yacht can find shelter in the bay formed by Vivara and Procida S of the bridge. Anchor in 5–10m on sand and weed. The anchorage is open only to the S–SE but it always seems to be very rolly in here with any swell around finding its way in. With southerlies there is reasonable shelter on the N side of the bridge.

Note AMP restrictions apply.

Canale d'Ischia

This is a narrow channel (1¼ miles across the narrowest part) between Ischia and Vivara Island. In it lies Vivara Reef (Formiche di Vivara) with least depths of 4m (13ft) over it. It is marked on its western side by a W cardinal beacon Q(9)15s5M.

Isola d'Ischia

Isola d'Ischia is the largest of the islands in the Gulf. It is a collection of craters and ancient lava flows, but these are difficult to identify under the lush semi-tropical vegetation. In the 5th century BC violent eruptions and earthquakes caused the Greek colony to evacuate it. The last eruption was in AD1301. There are numerous hot water springs, many of them with bathing establishments, indicating that there is still subterranean activity.

In mythology the island was believed to be the dwelling place of Typhoeus or Typhon, a hundred-headed monster said to be the father of the Chimaera and the Hydra. Vanquished by Zeus along with the other giants, he expressed his fury at Zeus by eruptions and earthquakes. (He is also said to dwell under Etna). The island was colonised early on, around 750BC, by Greeks from Evia who called the island Pithecusa referring to the fine clay (*pithos*) used for pots found on it. The colonists soon moved on when the volcano at Montagnone just SW of Ischia town erupted. The Romans called the island Aenaria or Iarime as Aeneas is supposed to have stopped here to repair his ships.

The name Ischia is said to be a corruption of *insula* (simply 'the island'). The Saracens occupied it in the 7th and 8th centuries, the Pisans in the 12th century and thereafter it followed the fates and fortunes of Naples. From antiquity it has been famed for its hot mineral springs and strict conditions are laid down for drinking or bathing in them. The majority of the springs show traces of radioactivity and are reputed to be especially beneficial in the treatment of arthritis and rheumatism.

Although not as well known, the island's beauty rivals that of Capri: steep high mountains rising to Mount Epomeo (788m/2,586ft) are covered in lush semi-tropical vegetation. Bishop Berkeley described it in a letter to the Pope in 1717 as 'an epitome of the whole earth', and European travellers, among them Ibsen, Gladstone, and Edward Lear, praised its beauty. Today it is much visited by tourists and also has a considerable permanent foreign population. There are several harbours around the island and although the main harbour, Porto d'Ischia, is mostly taken up with ferries and yachts permanently moored there, the island can be explored from the other harbours.

PORTO D'ISCHIA

BA 908, 916
Italian 82

Approach

The harbour is not easy to locate except by the numerous ferries coming and going.

Conspicuous Castello d'Ischia on an islet joined by a causeway to the island proper is easily identified. The harbour lies approximately 1·5 miles NW of Castello d'Ischia. A tower on a knoll behind the harbour is conspicuous. Closer in, a church with a red cupola immediately E of the entrance, the harbour breakwater and the red light tower on the end of the breakwater are easily located.

By night Use the light on the end of the main breakwater Fl.WR.3s15/12M. The red sector covers the detached breakwater immediately N of it and is visible over 127°–197°. The detached breakwater occasionally has a weak F exhibited on its eastern end.

VHF Ch 13 Circomare Ischia. Ch 74 for Portosalvo Marina.

Dangers

1. The detached breakwater is easily seen by day but not by night.
2. Ferries and hydrofoils are constantly coming and going and a yacht must take care not to obstruct their path. I have seen so many near misses that I cannot believe that a yacht has not been sunk yet by one of the ferries or hydrofoils.

Mooring

Data 200 berths. Max LOA 50m. Depths 2–10m.

Berth Go stern-to the quay on the SW or on the E wherever there is room or wherever you can negotiate a berth. Marina Portosalvo runs the three S pontoons on the E side. The harbour is very crowded all year round and yachts are regularly two out from the quay. If you arrive late you may be able to stay on the fuel quay for the night. The bottom is mud and good holding.

Shelter Excellent all-round shelter. The fast ferries cause a dangerous amount of wash, in spite of complaints.

Authorities Port police and customs. Local *ormeggiatori* who will demand a fee, sometimes reasonable and sometimes exorbitant, but always open to haggling. Marina staff (co-op). Charge band 5.

Portosalvo Marina ✆ 081 333 4070 ✆ /*Fax* 081 333 1252
Email marina.portosalvo@libero.it
Gruppo Ormeggiatore Battellieri ✆ 081 981 419

Anchorage In calm weather a yacht can anchor off to the E of the entrance just behind the stone breakwaters that shelter the beach. It is technically a prohibited anchorage here, but local yachts and boats anchor with apparent immunity. Anchor in 5–8m on sand. It is a short row to the beach and the town.

Facilities

Service Water and electricity on the quay, in the marina and on the fuel quay. Toilets and showers in the marina.

Fuel On the quay in the NW corner (minimum depth 2m).

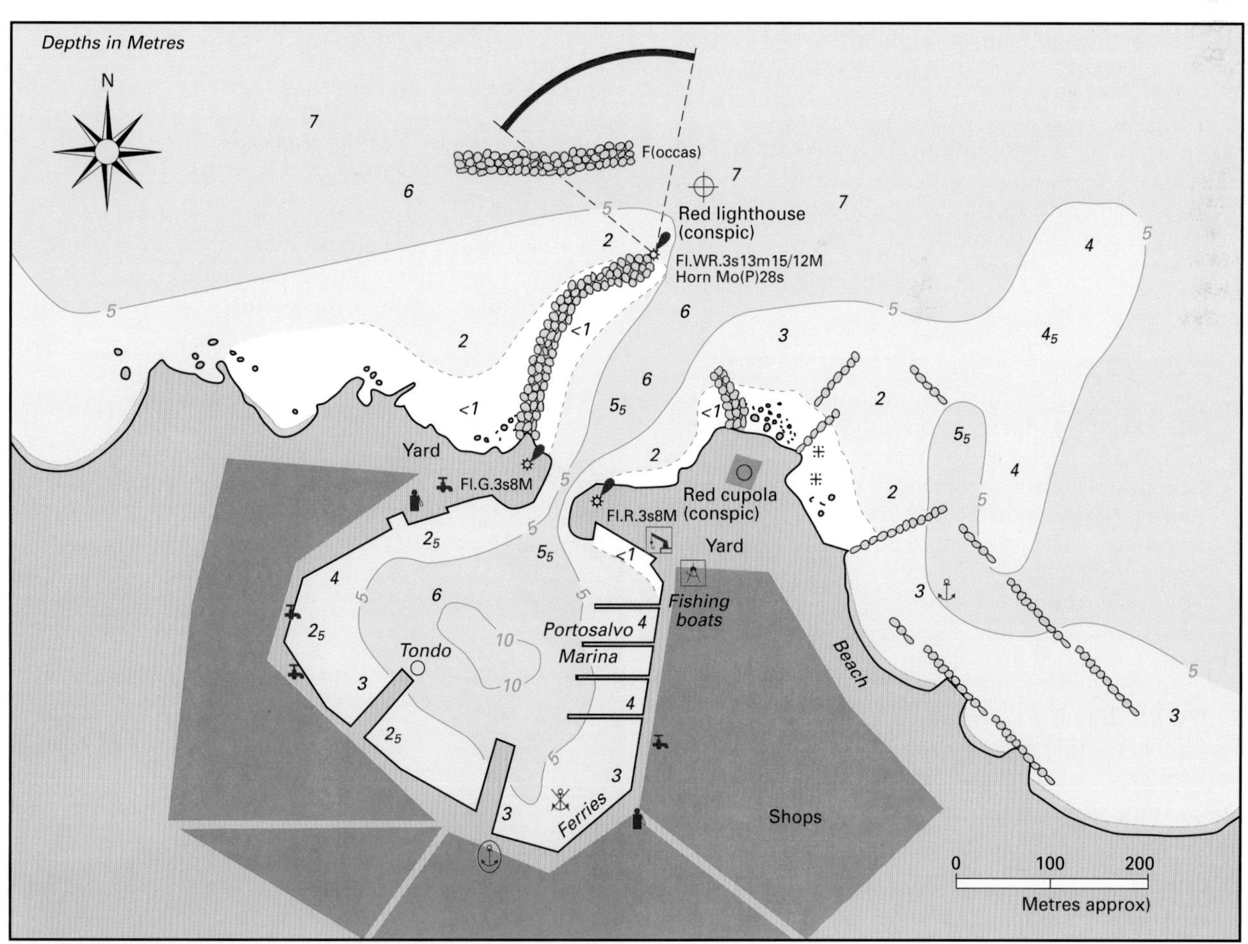

PORTO D'ISCHIA
⊕40°44′·9N 13°56′·6E

Repairs Several yards that can haul yachts up to 150 tons subject to draught. All types of repairs can be carried out to a good standard. Chandlers.
Provisions Good shopping for all provisions in the part of the town E of the port. Ice can be ordered.
Eating out Excellent restaurants, trattorias and pizzerias.
Other PO. Bank. ATMs. Italgaz and Camping Gaz. Hire motor-bikes and cars. Regular buses around the island. Ferries to Naples and Pozzuoli.

General

Ischia is a wonderful place, but in the summer the harbour is a nightmare. The perfectly sheltered harbour surrounded by white- and rose-washed houses and lush vegetation is a gem. There are numerous ferries, hydrofoils and catamaran ferries rushing back and forth and tourists everywhere even in winter, yet Ischia is not blemished on account of this and my memories of it are always warm ones. Pliny records how there was once a small town where the harbour now is, but an earthquake caused the land to subside and become a lake, the Lago del Bagno. In 1854 during the reign of Ferdinand II a channel was cut through the narrow strip of land separating it from the sea and it became the present Porto d'Ischia.

CASAMICCIOLA (MARINA ARAGONESI)

This is the logical place to make for when you give up trying to get a berth in Porto d'Ischia.

Approach

A large harbour lying about 1½ miles W of Porto d'Ischia. The harbour moles are easily identified from the east. From the W the mushroom-shaped rock at Lacco Ameno can be identified.

VHF Ch 09, 16. Ch 08 for Marina di Casamicciola.

Dangers

1. From the E care is needed to avoid the shoal water off Pta della Scrofa just E of the harbour.
2. From the W care must be taken of the reef, Secca del Sancturio, lying approximately half a mile NW of the harbour. The reef and an area around it, marked by four yellow pillar buoys, is now a nature reserve where anchoring and fishing are prohibited. The reef is marked by a conical yellow N cardinal buoy, not always in place. The approach to the port should be made on a course of around due south.
3. There is a shallow patch with approximately 1·8m over it about where shown on the plan. Yachts drawing more than 1·6–1·7m should keep closer to the E breakwater where depths are greater.

Note With strong northerlies a swell piles up in the approaches to the harbour making entry difficult.

Mooring

Data 100 berths. Max LOA 30m. Depths 1–7m.

Berth Go stern or bows-to on the new pontoons where directed. There are laid moorings tailed to the pontoon at most berths.

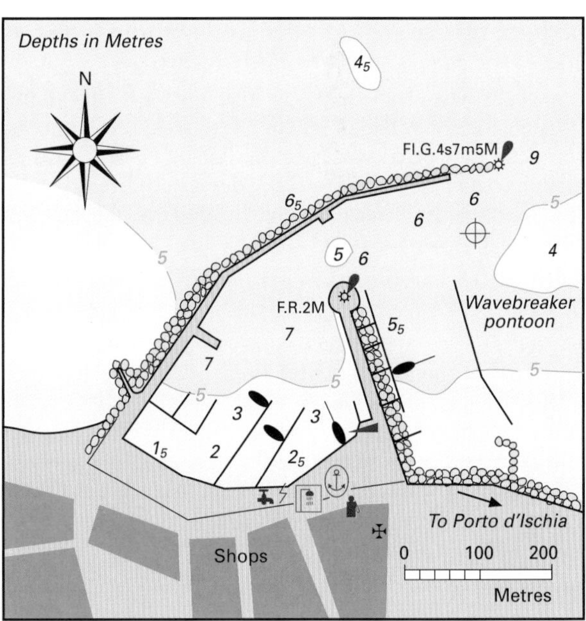

CASAMICCIOLA
⊕40°45´·1N 13°54´·7E

Shelter Good shelter from the prevailing winds. Strong northerlies may cause some discomfort in here.

Authorities Harbour staff. Charge band 6+.
Casamicciola Marina ✆ 081 507 2545 / 333 888 7975
Fax 081 99 41 52
Email info@marinadicasamicciola
www.marinadicasamicciola.it
Aragonesi Marina ✆ 081 980 686
www.caladegliaragonesi.it

Facilities

Services Water and electricity at or near every berth. Showers and toilets. Pump-out facilities.
Fuel Available from a station just behind the quay.

Casamicciola looking E onto the yacht quay

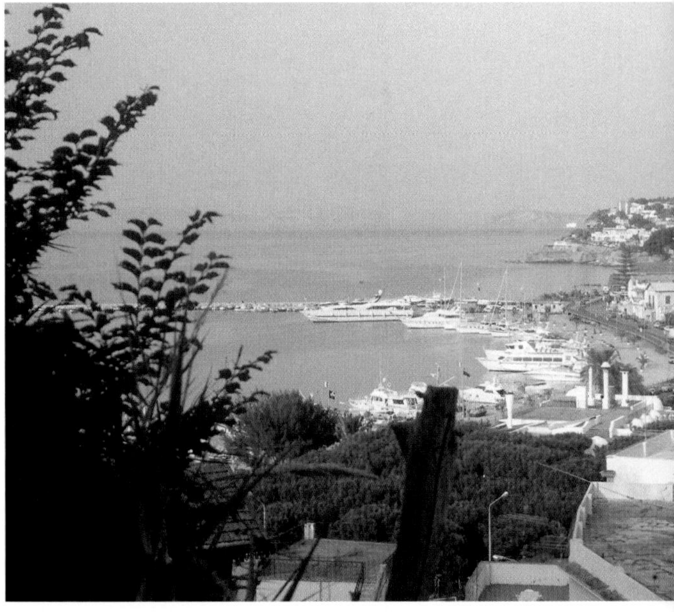

Repairs A 10-ton crane. Limited hard standing. Some mechanical repairs. Chandlers.
Provisions Good shopping nearby.
Eating out Restaurants nearby. The restaurant Zurosta in a back street behind the marina has excellent food although the surroundings are plain.
Other PO. Bank. ATM. Italgaz and Camping Gaz. Ferries and hydrofoil to Naples.

General

The harbour and the village is a pleasant unpretentious place after the hurly-burly and boutiques of Porto d'Ischia. Henrik Ibsen spent a summer in a villa here writing *Peer Gynt*. Most of the buildings are comparatively new after Casamicciola was flattened in the 1883 earthquake. The thermal spa here is said to be the hottest on the island at over 63°C (180°F) and you will need a doctor's certificate (obtained locally) if you are contemplating trying it. Porto d'Ischia is about 35 minutes' pleasant walk away or there are buses.

Scoglio del Sanctuario (Zone C)

A rock with a depth of 2·4m (8ft) over it and shoal water around it lies about 640m (3½ cables) NW of the entrance to Casamicciola. It is marked by a yellow N cardinal conical buoy. Four yellow pillar buoys mark off a marine reserve around it.

Lacco Ameno (Zone C)

A small harbour lying three quarters of a mile W of Casamicciola. A pier partially sheltered by a rough stone breakwater provides some shelter, but the harbour is really only suitable in calm weather. Any swell running rolls in here. Pietra del Lacco or Il Funghi, a distinctive mushroom-shaped rock at the E end of the breakwater is conspicuous. Berth on the E side of the pier where there are good depths. There are laid moorings for local fishing boats on the W side. Alternatively anchor off to the W of the pier. Fuel near the quay. Good shopping for provisions and restaurants nearby.

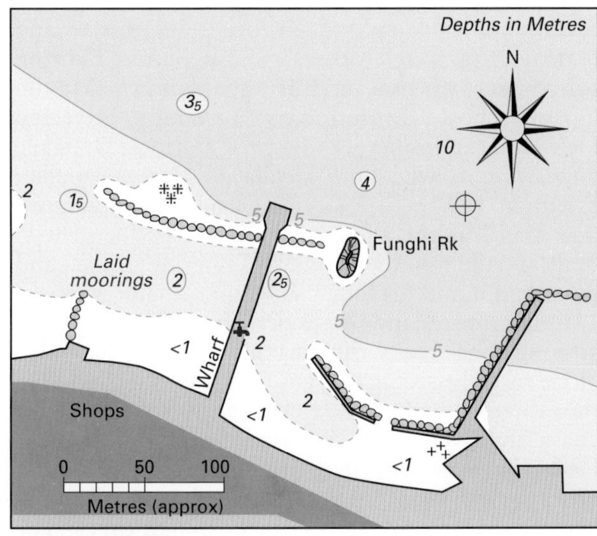

LACCO AMENO
⊕40°45′·3N 13°53′·4E

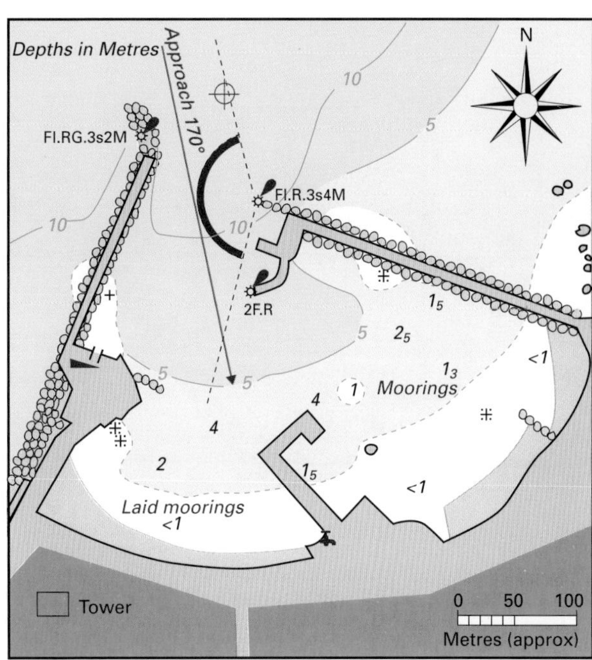

FORIO D'ISCHIA
⊕40°44′·5N 13°51′·5E

FORIO D'ISCHIA

Approach

A large open harbour on the W coast. The entrance is fringed by reefs and shoal water with the safe approach along 170°. The sea breaks on Scoglio Camerata, the reef on the W side of the approach to the harbour.

Mooring

Anchor with a long line to the E breakwater or go stern or bows-to the central pier if there is room. The bottom is sand and rock, not everywhere good holding.

Shelter Adequate in the summer although the harbour is open NW–N and could be untenable with strong winds from this direction.

Facilities

Water on the pier. Fuel in the town. Provisions and restaurants ashore.

Caution

The W coast of Ischia is fringed with above- and below-water rocks and a yacht should keep a prudent distance off (¾ mile is recommended) when proceeding along the coast.

SANT'ANGELO D'ISCHIA

Approach

A small harbour on the E side of Punta Sant'Angelo which is a high steep-to promontory connected to Ischia by a low sandy isthmus. The white houses of the village of Sant'Angelo built into a cliff are conspicuous. The entrance can be difficult to identify from the distance but, closer in, the outer breakwater will be seen.

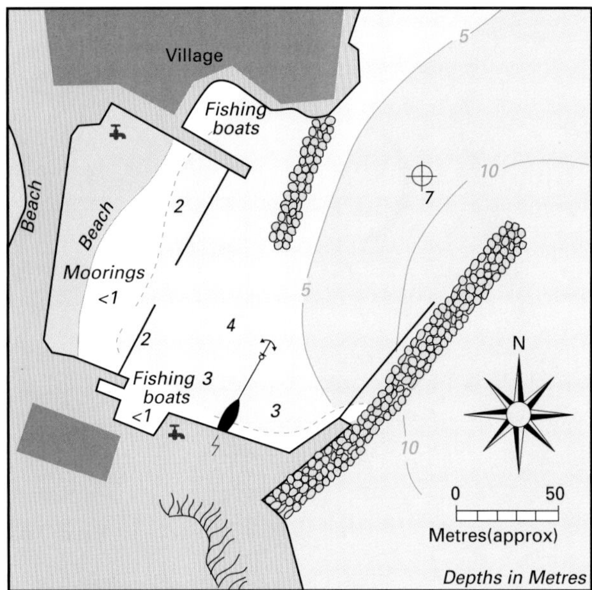

SANT'ANGELO
⊕40°41´·8N 13°53´·8E

Dangers With strong S–SE winds there is a confused swell at the entrance and waves break across the entrance.

Mooring

Data c.20 visitors' berths. Max LOA 50m. Depths <1–4m.

Berth Go stern or bows-to the quay taking care of the depths which are uneven in places. Laid moorings tailed to the quay. The day ferry uses the short pier at the N end.

Shelter Good shelter in the summer. South winds cause a surge.

Authorities Harbourmaster. *Ormeggiatori.* Charge band 6.

Anchorage The bay to the west of Punta Sant'Angelo can be a useful day anchorage. Holding is good in sand but is subject to wash from passing craft and landing is not encouraged on beaches run by the locals.

Note This anchorage is in Zone B/B(NT) and AMP restrictions apply.

Ischia Yacht ✆ 081 999 102 *Fax* 081 999 150
Email info@ischiayacht.it
www.ischiayacht.it

Facilities

Water and electricity (220/380V) on the quay. Toilets and showers. Provisions and restaurants in the village.

General

Sant'Angelo is a popular summer resort with good beaches close by and thermal springs inland. The villages of white Cyclades-style houses clinging to the steep cliff are attractive. Along the adjacent coast, breakwaters have been built to stop the sea eroding the stratified cliffs although part of the road leading to Sant'Angelo looks doomed already.

Castello d'Ischia (Zone C)

On the NE coast, Castello d'Ischia is an islet with an Aragonese castle on it (conspicuous) connected to the mainland by a causeway. A yacht can anchor on either side of the causeway according to the wind. Care should be taken of Scoglio di Sant' Anna, a group of above- and below-water rocks off the coast about a quarter of a mile S of the causeway. The southern side (La Marinella) gives reasonable shelter from the prevailing summer winds although it can be a bit rolly in here. Anchor in 4–10m on sand, mud and weed. With southerlies, anchor on the N side of Castello d'Ischia in 3–6m on sand. In summer areas are sometimes buoyed off for swimming on either side of the causeway but there is still room to anchor. Good in settled weather, but with a land breeze blowing out of the Bay of Naples an uncomfortable chop is sent in here. It is a short walk into Ischia town for supplies.

Note Anchoring is prohibited in the S bay due to underwater cables. An underwater cable runs into the N part of the bay near position 40°43´·75N 13°57´·86E WGS84 – care needed.

Isola di Capri

The pearl of the Bay of Naples and surely the most famous island in Italy. It is mountainous, with a precipitous limestone coast pockmarked by caves and fissures and eroded into fantastic natural sculptures. The island was occupied in prehistoric times and later by the Greeks and Romans. Augustus exchanged it for Ischia and built roads and aqueducts, but the fame of the island began with Tiberius and his alleged voluptuary activities publicised in the writings of Tacitus and Suetonius. The stories of the orgies, the brutality, the splendour and the horror of Tiberius' 10 years' residence on the island have been largely discounted by modern historians, but the stories persist and have infused the island with a mysterious air.

Many celebrities have been attracted to it; the list of famous residents and visitors is impressive and features, among others, Emil von Behring (discoverer of the tetanus inoculation); Maxim Gorky whose revolutionary university attracted Lenin and Stalin here; the writer Norman Douglas; Gracie Fields who built a villa at Marina Piccolo; Friedrich Krupp, the German arms manufacturer; and Axel Munthe, the eccentric Swedish doctor who built a villa on the ruins of Tiberius' villas and described it and his life in *The Story of San Michele*.

Today the island is under siege from tourists although thankfully the harbour is left pretty much alone by sight-seeing tourists. It is worth a trip to see the famous Blue Grotto, a marine cavern on the NW coast that was once a nymphaeum of Tiberius. Under 2m of water, there are niches, platforms and apses carved out of the rock, indicating that the land had subsided considerably since Roman times. The normal way to visit the grotto is to take a launch from Marina Grande. On arrival you transfer to a

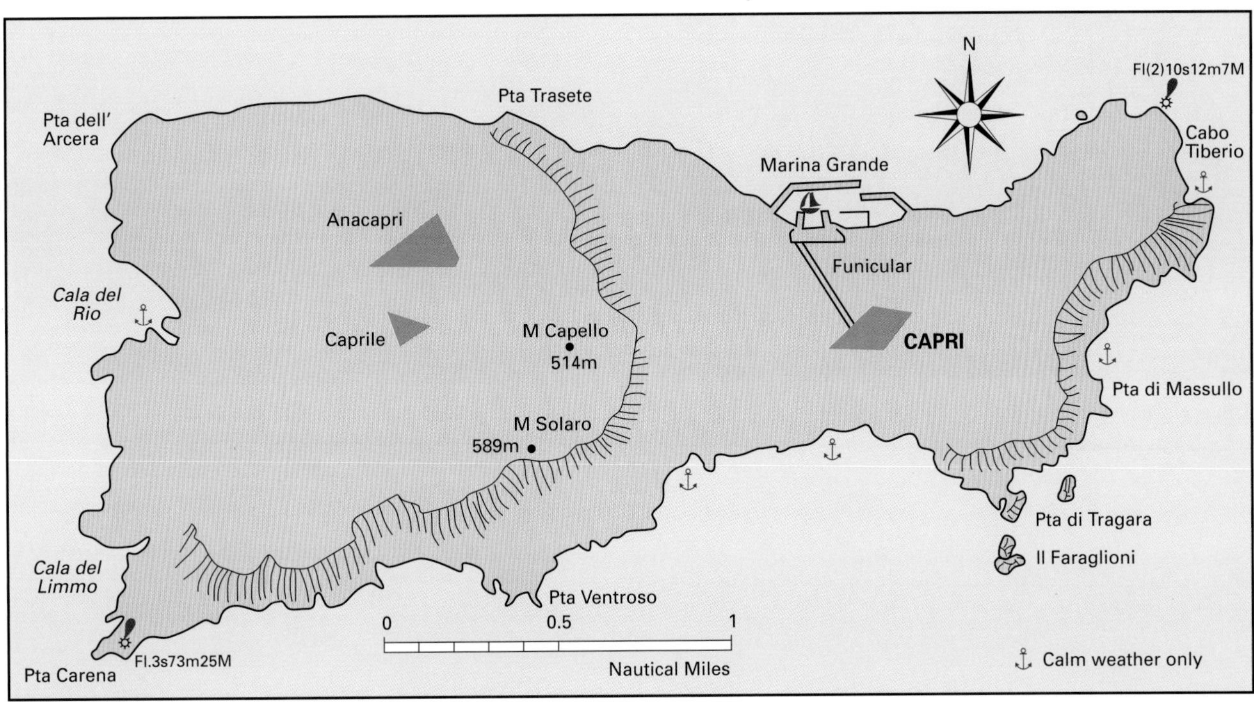

ISOLA DI CAPRI

dinghy (an extra charge) to enter the grotto. In settled weather it is possible to do the first part in a yacht, leaving someone on board to potter around and going in by dinghy.

CAPRI MARINA GRANDE

BA 908
Italian 913, 01

Approach

From the N a yacht should make for the saddle between the two summits at either end of the island.

Conspicuous Make for the lowest point in the saddle with the buildings of Capri on it and, closer in, the harbour moles and the light towers at the extremities can be easily identified.

VHF Ch 14, 16. Ch 71 for *porto turistico*.

Dangers Ferries and hydrofoils are constantly coming and going and a yacht should give way to them.

Mooring

Data 300 berths. Visitors' berths. Max LOA 65m. Depths 3–10m.

Berth Go stern or bows-to in the E basin. There are laid moorings.

Shelter Good although strong northerlies raise a sea inside. The wash from the ferries is also bothersome.

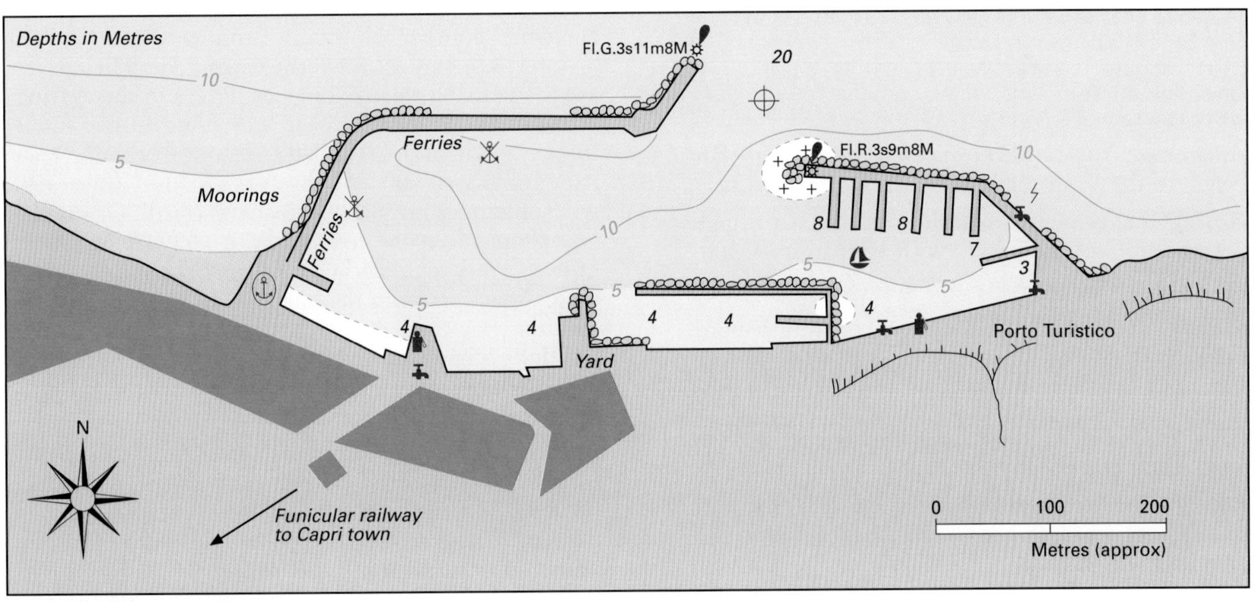

CAPRI MARINA GRANDE
⊕40°33′·6N 14°14′·7E

The approaches to Marina Grande looking SE

Marina Grande looking down from Capri

Authorities Harbourmaster and customs. Charge band 6+.

Porto Turistico ✆ 081 837 8950 *Fax* 081 837 5318
Email prenotazioni@portoturisticodicapri.com

Gruppo Ormeggiatori Capri ✆ 081 837 7158

Tecnomar Boat Capri ✆ 081 837 9659 *Fax* 081 838 9117
Email info@tecnomarcapri.com

Luise Associates ✆ 348 386 8538 *Fax* 081 963 3333
Email capri@luise.it
www.luise.com

Anchorage Yachts have reported anchoring off the beach to the W of the harbour in settled weather.

Note In many places in Italy it is illegal to anchor within 300m of the beach, with fines up to €300.

Facilities

Services Water and electricity at or near most berths.
Fuel On the quay.
Repairs Crane up to 20 tons. Limited hard standing on the quay. Some mechanical repairs. Chandlers.
Provisions Basic provisions can be obtained nearby. A supermarket in Capri.
Eating out Excellent and often expensive restaurants of all types everywhere. The cheaper places are around the harbour.
Other PO. Bank. ATM. Italgaz and Camping Gaz. Ferries to Naples.

General

You have to visit Capri at least once, and by yacht one avoids the worst excesses of mass tourism. Several years ago the numbers of tourists on Capri were getting so bad that the authorities decided to curb the number of ferries running from Naples. Scooters are banned from the town and all deliveries are made using electric buggies. Prices in the marina are dramatic in the high season, around €145 a night for a 12m yacht in 2010 (add 50% at weekends!), so if possible visit out of season when the authorities will sometimes not bother to charge at all. Or maybe you should join the tourists on a ferry. A funicular railway runs regularly up to Capri town and buses go to Anacapri from the harbour. If you are an Axel Munthe fan then a visit to his villa (open to the public) with its numerous artefacts and a breathtaking view make it well worth the trek to Anacapri.

'After five long summers' incessant toil from sunrise til sunset San Michele was more or less finished, but there was still a lot to be done in the garden. A new terrace was to be laid out behind the house, another loggia to be built over the two small Roman rooms which we had discovered in the autumn. As to the little cloister court I told Mastro

Capri. Yacht pontoons in Marina Grande *Kerr Whiteford*

Nicola we had better knock it down, I did not like it any more. Mastro Nicola implored me to leave it as it was, we had already knocked it down twice, if we kept on knocking down everything as soon as it was built, San Michele would never be finished. I told Mastro Nicola that the proper way to build one's house was to knock everything down never mind how many times and begin again until your eye told you that everything was right. The eye knew much more about architecture than did the books. The eye was infallible, as long as you relied on your eye and not on the eye of other people. As I saw it again I thought San Michele looked more beautiful than ever. The house was small, the rooms were few but there were loggias, terraces and pergolas all around it to watch the sun, the sea and clouds – the soul needs more space than the body.'

The Story of San Michele Axel Munthe

Isola Faraglioni

The pillars of rock emerging from the sea on the SE corner of the island that feature in most photographs of Capri. In calm weather it is possible to anchor in the cove to the N of Isola Faraglioni though it is very deep. Anchor in 15–25m on sand and rock. Alternatively just tour around Isola Faraglioni and motor through the largest arch. Apparently every destroyer in the Italian navy has a photo of itself steaming through the largest arch at 30 knots so beware of local motorboats emulating the navy when you make your run.

Marina Piccola

⊕ 40°32′·4N 14°14′·3E

An open anchorage about 0·6 miles NE of Punta Ventroso. In settled weather anchor in 8–10m on a sandy bottom off the restaurant built on rocks near the shore. Gracie Fields' villa is built on the slopes above here.

Bocca Piccola

The channel between Isola di Capri and the mainland. A current often runs N or S through here according to the wind direction and may reach a rate of 2kns. It causes a bothersome popple in the channel, but once clear of it this sea will usually disappear.

Capri to the Strait of Messina

The coast from the Gulf of Naples south to the Strait of Messina has a number of attractive and little-visited harbours. Many yachts opt to head straight from the Gulf of Naples to the Lipari Islands, perhaps breaking the voyage at Acciaroli or nearby. For the yachtsman who is not in a hurry to go south there are a number of secure and interesting harbours along the mainland coast.

Note Seas in Golfo di Salerno become amplified when a SW swell is running, raising an uncomfortable sea around the gulf.

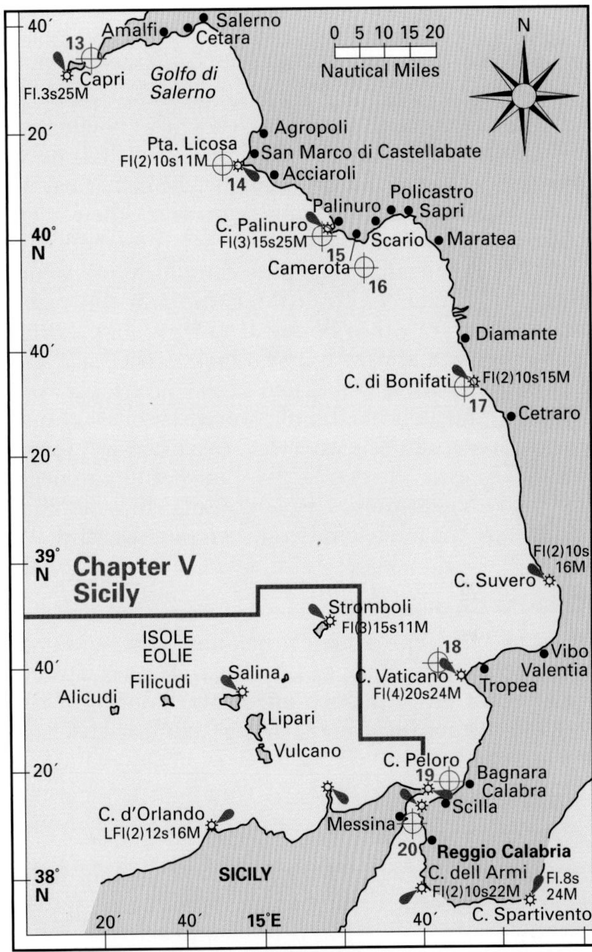

CAPRI TO THE STRAIT OF MESSINA

⊕13 0·25M W Pta Campanella
40°34′·12N 14°19′·07E WGS84
⊕14 1·6M W Pta Licosa 40°15′·05N 14°51′·73E WGS84
⊕15 0·25M W Capo Palinuro
40°01′·45N 15°15′·64E WGS84
⊕16 0·5M S Pta Iscoletti
39°58′·64N 15°25′·20E WGS84
⊕17 1M W Capo di Bonifati
39°32′·70N 15°51′·99E WGS84
⊕18 0·5M W Capo Vaticano
38°37′·12N 15°48′·87E WGS84
⊕19 1·75M E Capo Peloro 38°15′·86N 15°41′·42E WGS84
⊕20 0·3M W Pta Pezzo 38°13′·88N 15°37′·72E WGS84

Isolotti Galli

This group of small islands lies five miles E of Punta Campanella. The latter is easily recognised by a girder tower on it painted in black and white bands. Vetara lies 1½ miles W of I. Galli, the largest island in the group, and Isca Rock about one mile WNW, close to the mainland coast. In calm weather it is possible to anchor off the islands in 10–25m. The most popular anchorage with local boats is between I. Galli and La Castelluccia, the islet W of I. Galli.

Note All these islets lie within the Punta Campanella Marine Reserve. Only Vetara is within a Zone A (prohibited to navigate or anchor), but specific restrictions may apply to navigation or anchoring anywhere around the islets. For details of the areas covered see the plan on page 210 and details in the *Introduction*.

The Galli Islands are commonly accepted to be the islands of the Sirens of which Circe warned Odysseus:

'You will come to the Sirens, they who bewitch all men. Whoever sails near them unaware shall never again see his wife and children once he has heard the Siren voices. They enchant him with their clear songs, as they sit in a meadow that is heaped with the bones of dead men, bones on which still hangs their shrivelled skin. Drive your ship past this place, and so that your men do not hear their song, soften some beeswax and with it seal their ears. But if you yourself should wish to listen to the Sirens, get your men to bind you hand and foot with ropes against the mast-step. In this way you may listen in rapture to the voices of the two Sirens. But should you begin to beg your comrades to unloose you, you must make sure that they bind you even more tightly.'

The Odyssey, Book 12

Cala Punta di Sogno

A small bay approximately halfway between Punta Capanella and Positano. In settled weather a yacht can anchor off or pick up one of the mooring buoys off the restaurant ashore. The restaurant has been recommended.

Positano

⊕ 40°37'·4N 14°29'·1E

An open anchorage off the town about eight miles ENE of Punta Campanella suitable in settled weather only.

AMALFI

BA 908
Italian 914/33

Approach

The harbour is difficult to identify from seaward. It is situated at the bottom of a gorge running down through the steep cliffs.

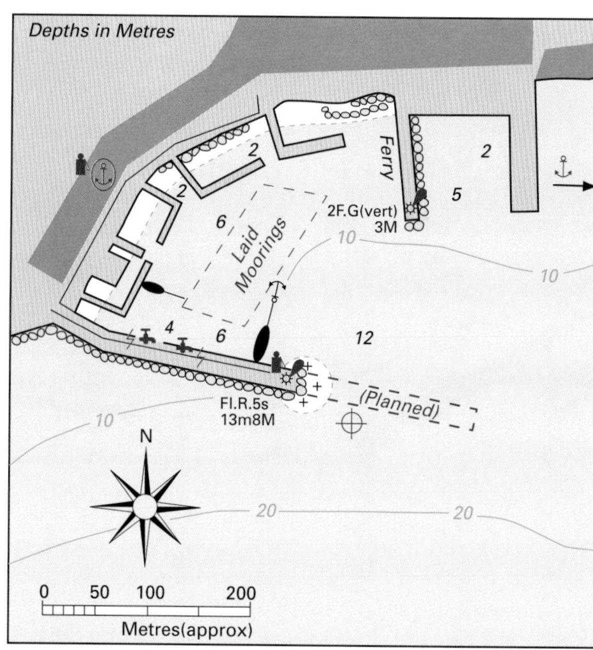

AMALFI
⊕40°37´·79N 14°36´·05E WGS84

Conspicuous The arched gallery of the cemetery and the cupola of the cathedral are conspicuous and, closer in, the harbour moles will be identified.

VHF Ch 14, 16 (0700–1900).

Dangers

1. With strong northerlies, particularly the *tramontana* (NE) there are violent squalls off the high land. A yacht should proceed to Salerno in such weather.
2. Care must be taken of the rocks and rubble extending a short distance off the extremity of the outer (S) mole.

Mooring

Data 300 berths. Max LOA 40m. Depths <1–10m.

Berth Go stern-to the outer mole. A small section near the fuel quay is a public quay. After this berths

The approaches to Amalfi looking north

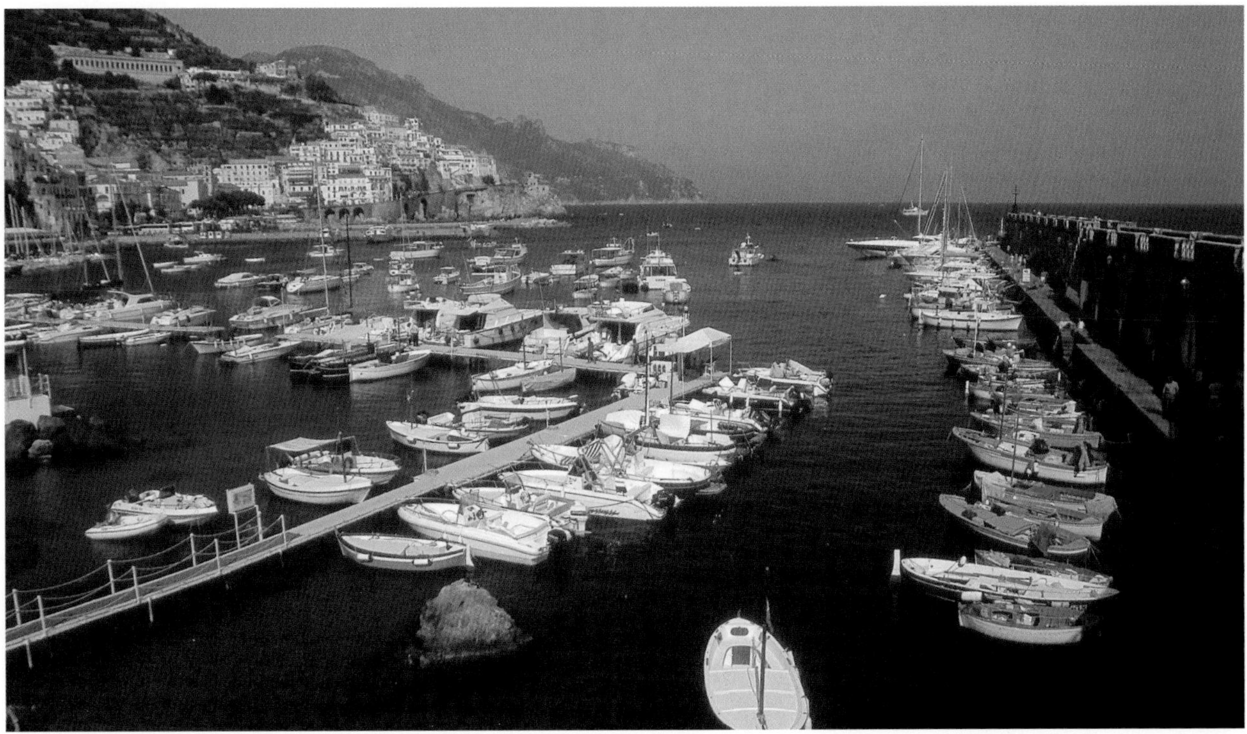

Amalfi harbour looking E from the root of the mole

are private with laid moorings. The ballasting extends a short distance underwater in places so care must be taken when close to the quay. Helpful *ormeggiatori* seem pretty equitable and when the quay is full may suggest returning after the fuel quay closes to berth there.

Shelter Good in settled weather but, with strong southerlies, a swell rolls in and, with strong northerlies, there are violent squalls off the high land. Tripper boats and other craft cause a lot of wash across the harbour. Even moderate westerlies cause quite a surge on the outer breakwater, but it's more uncomfortable than dangerous.

Authorities Port police and customs. *Ormeggiatori*. Charge band 2/5.

Aniello Esposito ✆ 338 219 3421

Pontile Coppola (SW corner) ✆ /*Fax* 089 873 091
Mobile 339 422 4484
Email info@amalfimooring.com
www.amalfimooring.com

Il Faro (assistenza nautica) ✆ 338 999 8710
Email amalfifuture@inwind.it

Facilities

Services Water and electricity (0700–2300) on the quay.
Fuel On the quay (0800–2000).
Repairs 15-ton crane. Mechanical and electrical repairs. Chandlers.
Provisions Good shopping in the town.
Eating out Restaurants, trattorias and pizzerias.
Other PO. Bank. ATM. Buses to Naples.

General

The setting is spectacular and the town colourful and attractive. It's a place where you could equally be moored next to an 80m superyacht or a 10m cruising yacht. The town was a prosperous trading centre from the 6th century AD under Byzantium and handled much Oriental trade. It amassed much wealth, supporting a large merchant fleet comparable to that of Genoa and Pisa. Its maritime laws, the *Tavole Almalfitane*, were accepted by most of the powers trading in the Mediterranean and were in effect as late as 1570, even though Amalfi was no longer a maritime power.

The hospital of St John the Almoner was maintained in Jerusalem by merchants from Amalfi and it was from this that the crusader Knights built the Order of St John which was to have so much influence on the history of the Mediterranean. In the piazza near the harbour there is a statue to Flavio Gioja who popularised the use of the newly introduced compass from China to Europe in the early 14th century. It is believed that the fleur-de-lis which traditionally marks north on the compass was the inspiration of Gioja, who used it in honour of the King of Naples.

Cetara

A small harbour lying nearly a mile after Capo d'Orso. The harbour is home to a fleet of anchovy fishing boats. They fish in the Atlantic and are generally away from spring until July. During this time there is plenty of room to go stern or bows-to where convenient. From July onwards the harbour is busy and only small yachts will be able to find a berth. The harbour is gradually being improved,

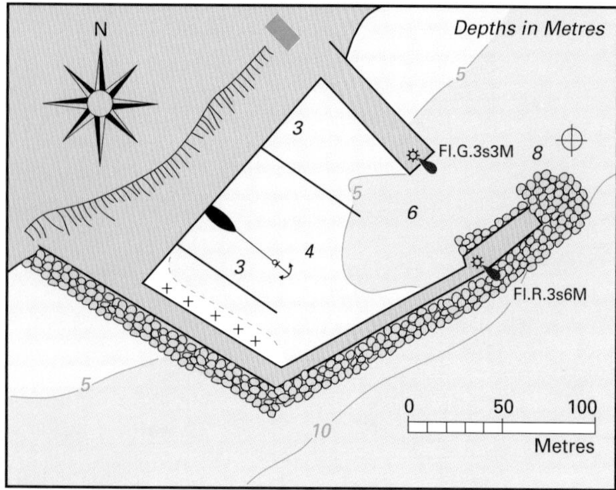

CETARA
⊕40°38´·8N 14°42´·3E

with a new breakwater extension and improved quays, although care is needed as there is underwater rubble and rocks off the quay in places.

Provisions and restaurants in the village.

SALERNO

BA 907
Italian 96

Approach

Straightforward by day and night. The large town is easily identified at the head of Salerno Roads.

Conspicuous A large framework cross on the hill NW of the harbour and the castle on the hill behind the town are conspicuous. Large apartment blocks line the waterfront. The harbour moles of Porto Nuovo are easily identified but the smaller Porto Turistico (Porto Masuccio Salernitano) won't be seen until closer in.

VHF Ch 11, 16 for port authorities. Ch 14, 16 for pilots. Ch 16 for Masuccio Salternitano.

Mooring

Data
Porto Nuovo Depths 5–10m.
Santa Teresa 600 berths (when completed). Max LOA c.15m. Depths 2–7m.
Porto Turistico Max LOA 15m. Depths 2–5m.

Berth A yacht should first try in Porto Nuovo for a berth.

1. ***Porto Nuovo*** Go stern or bows-to the pontoons on the W side of Molo di Levante. Care needed of a floating boom in two parts in front of the pontoons. The 'entrance' between the booms is lit with small red lights. Good all-round shelter, although southerly gales make it uncomfortable.
2. ***Santa Teresa*** On the NE side of Molo di Levante in the area off Santa Teresa beach, a new 600 berth marina is being developed. New breakwaters are being constructed, and work continues in the area. As the development continues it is likely that the pontoon layout will change. At present the pontoons are run by helpful *ormeggiatori*.

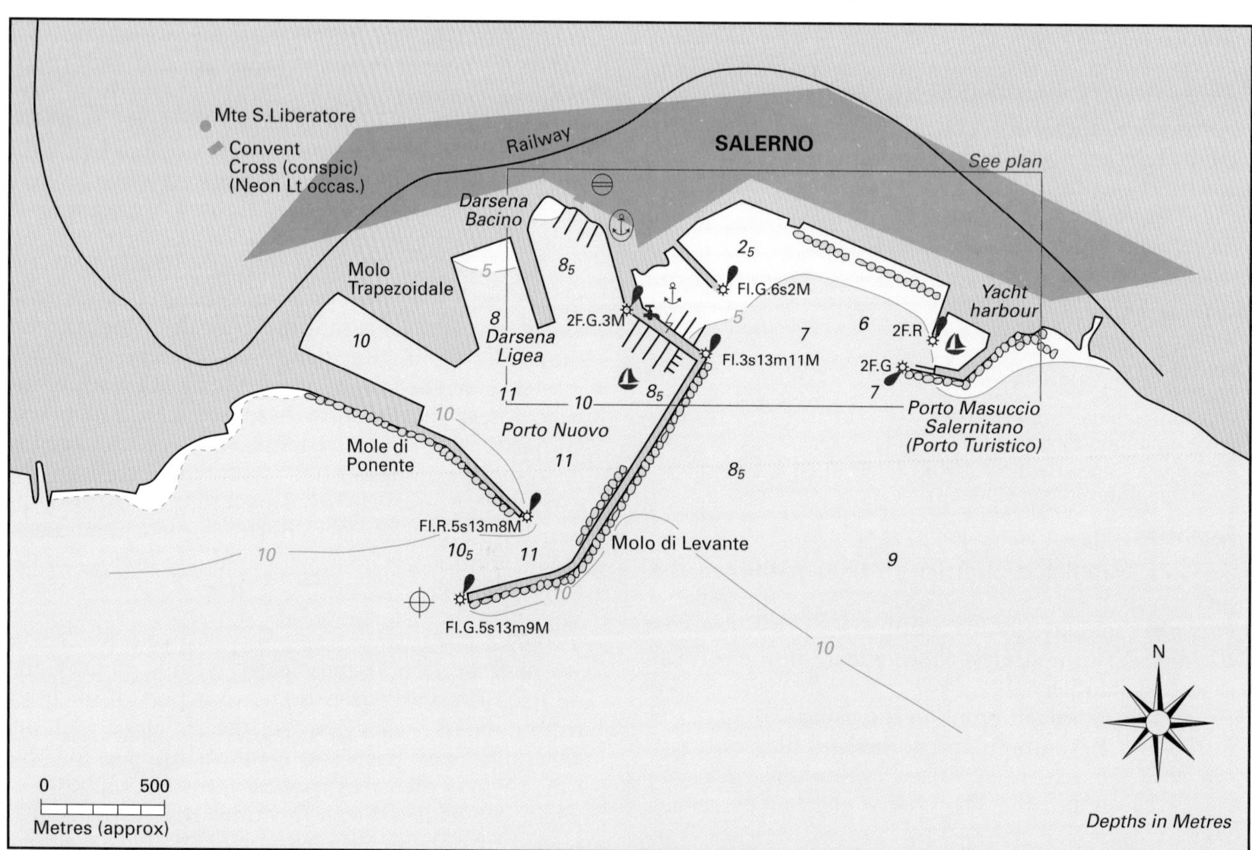

SALERNO APPROACH
⊕40°39´·9N 14°44´·5E

Salerno Porto Nuovo looking E with Porto Masuccio in the background

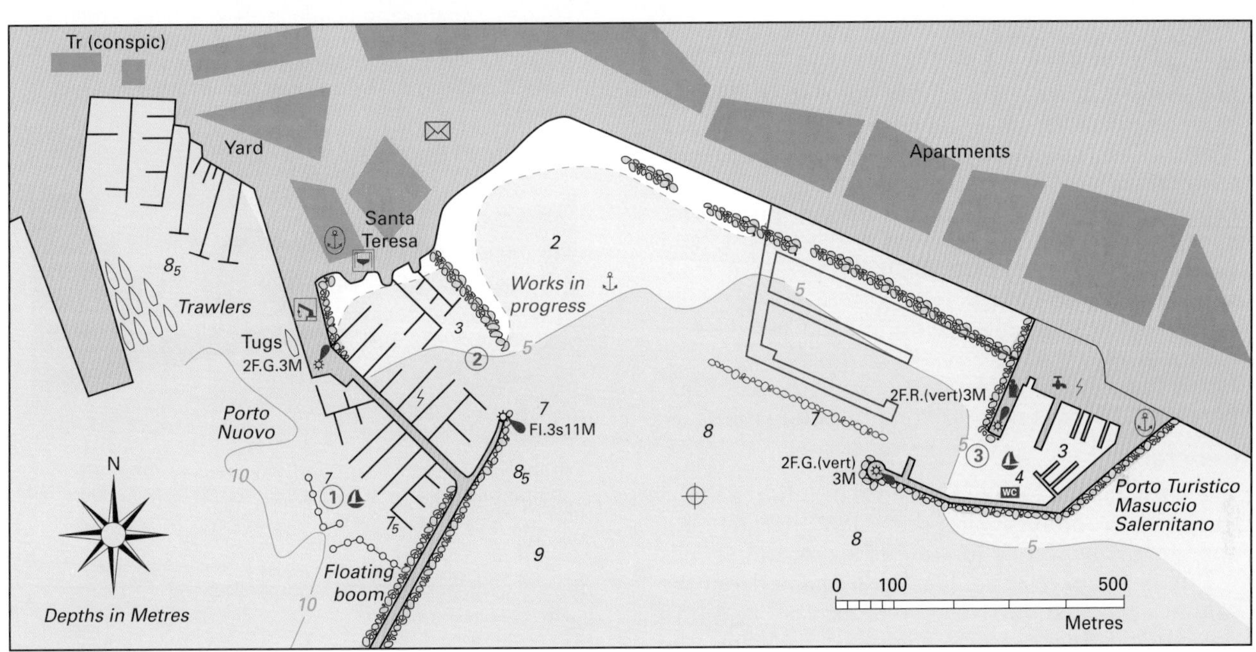

SALERNO
⊕40°40′·3N 14°45′·6E

3. ***Porto Turistico Masuccio Salernitano*** Go stern-to wherever you can find a spot. It is very crowded with local boats and difficult to find anywhere to berth in here. Shelter is good in settled weather, but in strong northerlies it becomes only just tenable. With strong northerlies there are violent gusts off the hills and if the wind goes around to the W a surge can build up. With strong southerlies there is a violent surge and waves break at the entrance although things have improved with the breakwater extension.

   Note There are plans to double the size of the marina, as shown in the plan, but no start dates for the project are available.
4. Future plans There are plans to develop two more harbours in the area to the SE of the porto turistico. The first is in the Pastena area, and will include berths for fishing boats. The second is 'Marina d'Arechi', details of which are given below.

Anchorage Anchor off the beach between Santa Teresa and the Porto Turistico in fair weather. Care needed as a dinghy has been reported stolen overnight.

Authorities Harbourmaster and customs.

Ormeggiatori. Charge band 3.

Gruppo Ormeggiatori ✆ 089 241 201

Club Velico Salernitano ✆ 089 236 235

Facilities

Services Water at the berths in Porto Nuovo, at the berths outside the NE corner and in the Porto Turistico. Electricity near some of these berths.

Fuel On the quay in Porto Turistico (0800–1900).

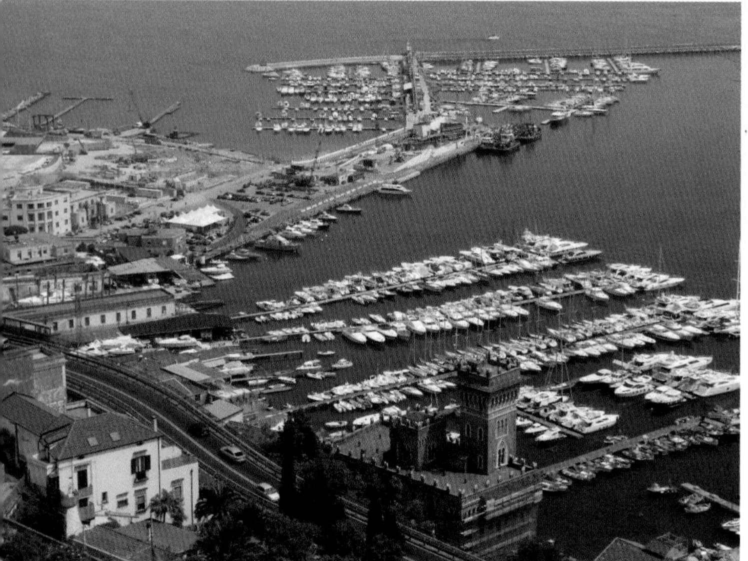
Yacht berths in Porto Nuovo with the new marina at Santa Teresa under construction left of picture

Repairs A 30-ton crane and slipways up to 150 tons in Porto Nuovo. Travel-lift at Santa Teresa. Mechanical and engineering repairs. GRP and wood repairs. Electrical and electronic repairs. Sailmakers. Chandlers.
Provisions Excellent shopping for all provisions. Supermarkets and a fresh fruit and vegetable and fish market in the town about 15 minutes' walk away from Porto Nuovo.
Eating out Restaurants, trattorias and pizzerias in the town.
Other PO. Banks. ATMs. Italgaz and Camping Gaz. Hire cars. Bus and train to Pompeii and Naples.

General

The setting in the Gulf of Salerno is beautiful and the town a crumbling (in the old quarter) but continually interesting mixture of sights and sounds – almost a mini-Naples. It takes its name from the salty sea (*sal*) and the river Irno to the east. Its gift to the Middle Ages was its school of medicine, the Civitas Hippocratica, which endured for over a thousand years and reached its zenith in the 12th century. The town was much damaged in the Second World War when the Allies landed from seaward in 1943. Salerno is a suitable place to leave a yacht for a visit to Pompeii, a journey of 30–40 minutes by rail.

Note According to the Admiralty *Pilot*, when Capo d'Orso is hidden by clouds or mist, SE–S winds are likely. When Punta Licosa is clearly visible, N winds are probable. Squalls from N–NE are usually preceded by sheets of cloud on the mountains above Agropoli.

MARINA D'ARECHI

A new marina under development approximately 3M SE of porto turistico Masuccio Salernitano.

Paestum

Said to be the finest Greek architecture in Italy, the ruins of the town have stood in majestic solitude for over a thousand years. The city was founded by Greeks from Sibaris in the 6th century BC as Poseidonia (the city of Neptune), which was latinised to Paestum by the Lucanians in the 4th century. The Romans took it in 273BC. The city was eventually abandoned as malaria took its toll and in AD877 it was sacked by the Saracens. Until the 18th century the city lay abandoned although it was shown on sea charts as a mark for mariners – Genoese *portulans* showed it. The site, comprising the town wall and four gates, and numerous towers, baths, a theatre, and two groups of Doric temples (dedicated to Athene and Neptune), can be visited from Salerno or Agropoli (it is open from 0900–1600 and an entrance fee is charged).

The ruins are now surrounded by much modern development and numerous hotels. If you squint your eyes the setting is quite spectacular with the mountains in the distance (Shelley said of it: '... the effect of the jagged outline of the mountains through groups of enormous columns on one side, and on the other the level horizon of the sea, is inexpressibly grand.') and the temples rival those to be found anywhere. In settled weather it is possible to anchor off the ruins to go ashore to visit them, though it would be prudent to leave someone on board in case the weather changes suddenly.

Ruins at Paestum. There are two virtually complete temples at the site *Vito Arcomano, FOTOTECA ENIT*

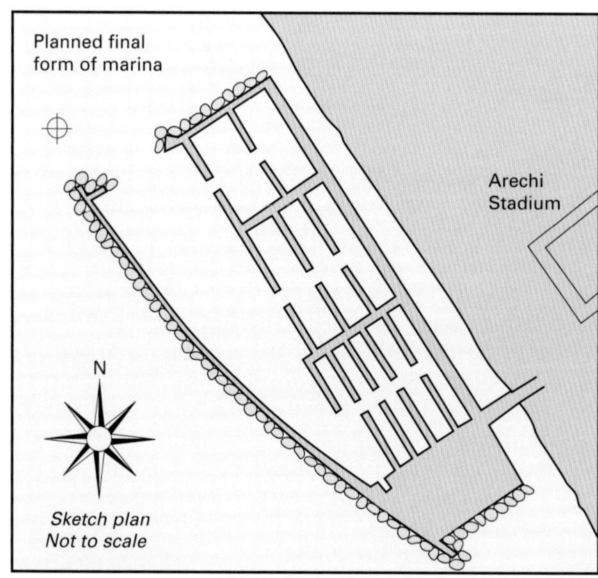

MARINA D'ARECHI
⊕40°38'·2N 14°49'·2E

Agropoli looking NE out of the entrance

It is still in the planning stage, with a completion date of 2012, but work had not started at the time of writing. The data and plan refer to the completed project.

Data 1,000 berths. Max LOA 50m.

Facilities Water and electricity at all berths. Wi-Fi. Showers and toilets. Pump-out. Fuel quay. Travel-lift and repair facilities.

Other Restaurants, bars, shops, yacht club, fitness club.

Marina d'Arechi ✆ 089 278 8801 *Fax* 089 278 8808
Email info@marinadarechi.com
www.marinadarechi.com

AGROPOLI

Approach

The nearest safe harbour to Paestum, situated under a rocky promontory on which the town of Agropoli is built.

Depths in Metres
N
Lighthouse (conspic.) Fl(2)6s42m16M
10
7
Fl.G.5s5M
5
Punta Fortino
6
Old town (conspic)
2F.R(vert)3M
Moorings
2_5
2
<1
3
New town
0 100 200
Metres(approx)
Square tower

AGROPOLI
⊕40°21´·28N 14°58´·98E WGS84

Conspicuous It can be difficult to determine exactly where the harbour is from the north. Closer in the old town atop the promontory and the lighthouse, a square crenellated tower, will be seen. The harbour mole and a square tower at the root of the mole, are easily identified.

Mooring

Data c. 500 berths. Max LOA 40m. Depths <1–6m.

Berth Visiting yachts may be able to find a spot on the end of the mole. Go stern or bows-to where convenient. The bottom is mud and said to be of the 'galvanising stripping' variety. If there are no berths here negotiate a berth at the pontoons off the SW corner. Laid moorings.

Shelter Good shelter except from the NE. I have ridden out a NE gale here but not comfortably and would not like to do so again.

Note There are plans to develop a further 450 berths here. No details were available before going to print.

Authorities Harbourmaster. Club representatives. Charge band 4.

Porto Turistico Consorzio Euromar ✆ 0974 824 545
Fax 0974 824 710
Email euromar@oneonline.it
Yachting club Agropoli ✆ 338 542 6082 (outer pontoon)
Canottieri Agropoli ✆ 0974 821 884 (next pontoon)
La Rosa dei Venti ✆ 368 322 3182

Facilities

Services Water and electricity at or near most berths.
Fuel On the quay in the SW corner (0800–2000).
Repairs 36-ton crane. Mechanical and some other repairs can be arranged. Chandlers.
Provisions Good shopping in the town. The supermarket in town will deliver to the boat.
Eating out Restaurants of all types nearby in the town.
Other PO. Banks. ATMs. Italgaz. Bus to Salerno and tours to Paestum can be arranged.

General

The harbour is an attractive place with the rocky promontory and the medieval village rising steep-to

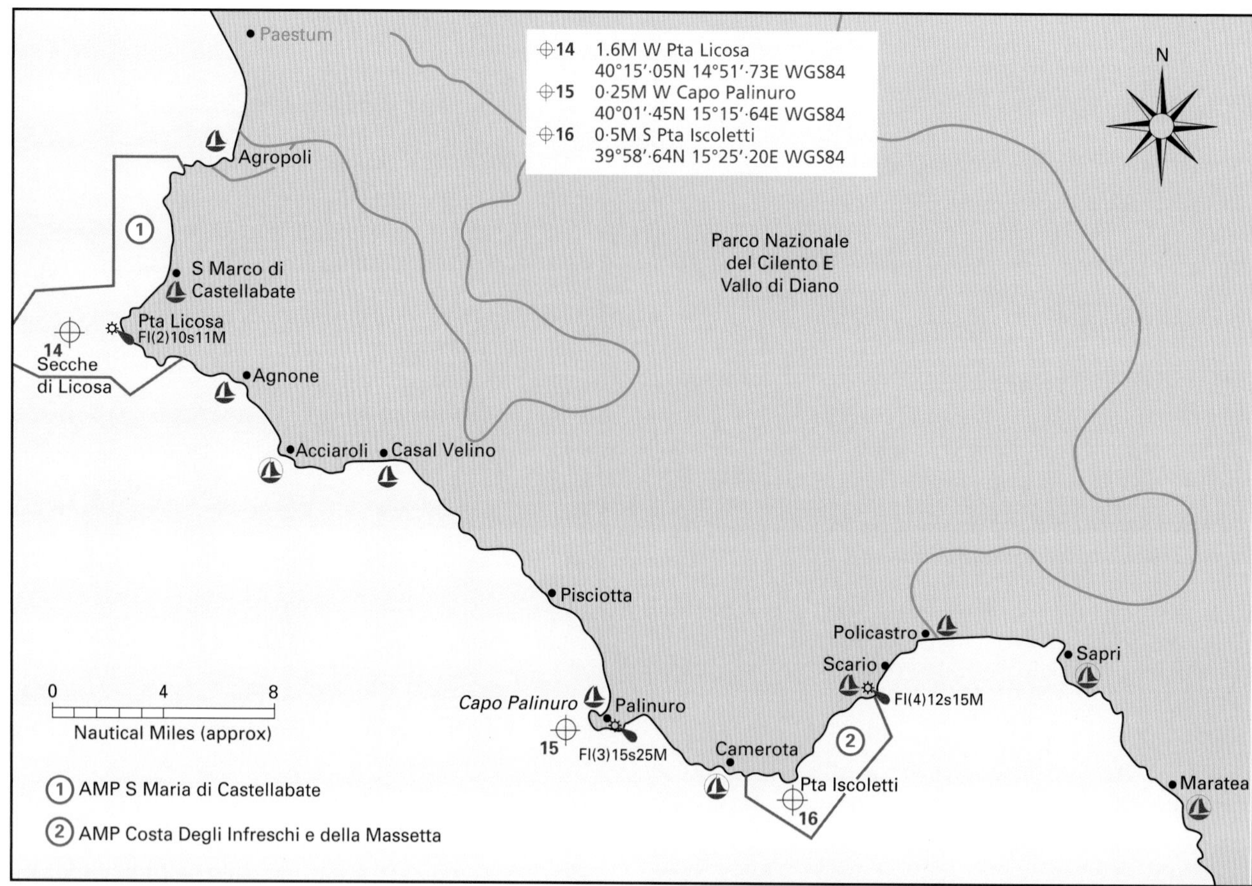

AGROPOLI TO MARATEA

PARC NAZIONALE CILENTO E VALLO DI DIANO (Cilento and Diano Valley National Park)

The low-lying land runs down the coast from Salerno to Agropoli, and abruptly meets the Karst landscape of the Cilento and Diano Valley National Park. Limestone geology, underground streams and aquifers, caves and deep valleys are all typical features of a Karst landscape. Add to that the extraordinary mountain villages perched atop many of the peaks, and the sheer rugged cliffs plunging down to the sea. It is a stunning part of the coast, and a trip inland following savagely steep and winding lanes and paths, while not for the faint hearted, is not to be missed.

There are two new Marine Protected Areas within the National Park.

AMP Santa Maria Castellabate covers the coast from Pta Tresino to Pta dell'Oligastro, with special protected areas where unauthorized navigation is prohibited, around both capes and over the Secche di Licosa.

AMP Costa degli Infreschi e della Massetta runs around Pta Iscoletti from Camerota to Pta del Monaco S of Scario, with Zone A protection around Pta Iscoletti *(see above)*.

Zone A All unauthorised navigation, fishing and diving is prohibited.

Zone B Navigation by jet skis and motor boats is restricted. Maximum speed 5 knots up to 300m off the coast. Max 10 knots 300–600m off the coast. Anchoring and mooring is restricted.

Zone C Maximum speed 10 knots. Fishing restricted.

For further details see www.cilentoediano.it

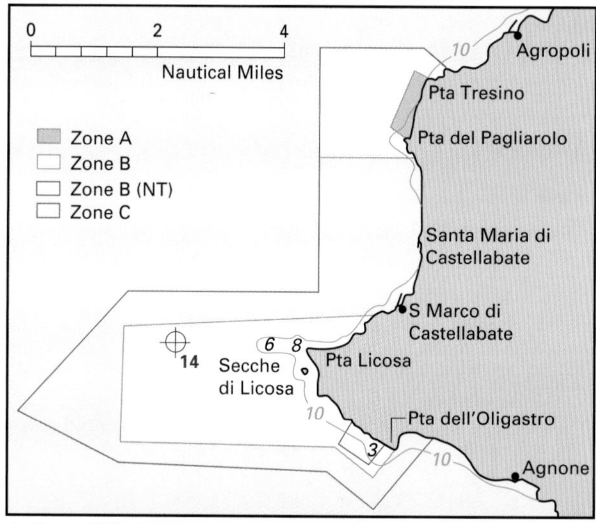

AMP SANTA MARIA DI CASTELLABATE

⌖14 1.6M W Pta Licosa 40°15'·05N 14°51'·73E WGS84

The crowded, small harbour at San Marco di Castellabate

on the west. The name Agropoli is said to be a corruption of Acropolis, betraying the town's Greek origins. It is a convenient harbour to leave your yacht for a visit to Paestum about eight miles away.

SAN MARCO DI CASTELLABATE

Approach

A small fishing harbour lying two miles S of Punta Pagliarolo.

Conspicuous The hamlet behind the harbour with a large building and tower on the ridge above can be identified close in. The exact location of the harbour is not easy to spot.

Dangers

1. In the approach from the SW care should be taken of the above and below-water rocks fringing the coast. Off Pta Licosa across to I. di Licosa there is a reef only just above water in places. Secche di Licosa is a reef with 6m least depth over it lying WNW of I. di Licosa. A yacht should stay well off Pta Licosa before making the approach to San Marco di Castellabate.
2. In strong NW to SW winds there are breaking waves across the entrance and a yacht should not attempt to enter the harbour.
3. In bad weather fishing boats take their lines across to the other side of the harbour making it dangerous to enter.

Mooring

Data Depths <1–3·5m.

Berth The harbour is nearly always crowded with trawlers and small craft on moorings, but a berth can usually be found somewhere on the outer mole. The fishermen are helpful.

Shelter Good in settled weather but in strong westerlies the swell is reflected off the cliffs into the harbour making it very uncomfortable.

Anchorage In calm weather anchor off in the bay outside the harbour, taking care of numerous isolated shoal patches.

Facilities

Water Tap on the quay.
Fuel On the quay.
Repairs Travel-hoist.
Provisions Most provisions can be obtained locally. Ice is delivered to the fishing boats.
Eating out Restaurants and bars nearby.

General

The village and the small harbour are attractive and the hinterland wooded and green. In the sea nearby there is said to be the remains of a Roman breakwater carved out of rock.

Punta Licosa

The point itself is not easy to make out from a distance, but I. di Licosa, the islet lying off it, is easily identified by the white light tower on it 12m high (Fl(2)10s11M). Care needs to be taken of the reef lying between the islet and the point. Normally the sea can be seen breaking on it. Approximately one mile WNW of the islet there is a reef, Secche di Licosa, with 6m least depth over. Shoal water fringes the coast nearby. With any sea running a yacht should keep well off Pta di Licosa as a heavy sea heaps up here. On the islet there are reported to be the remains of ancient walls and in the waters around several ancient shipwreck sites have been located.

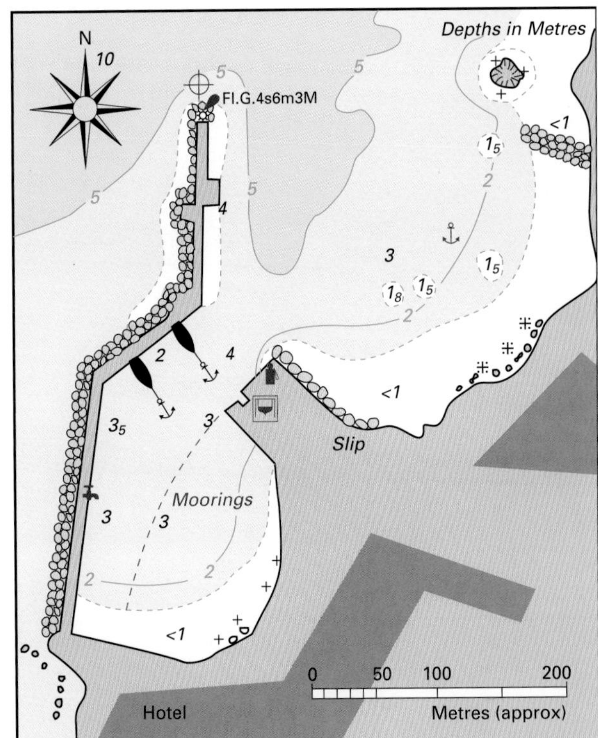

SAN MARCO DI CASTELLABATE
⊕40°16´·27N 14°56´·07E WGS 84

Oligastro

⊕ 40°13'·9N 14°56'·45E

A calm weather anchorage under Punta Licosa. A hotel resort ashore with some facilities. Holding and shelter indifferent.

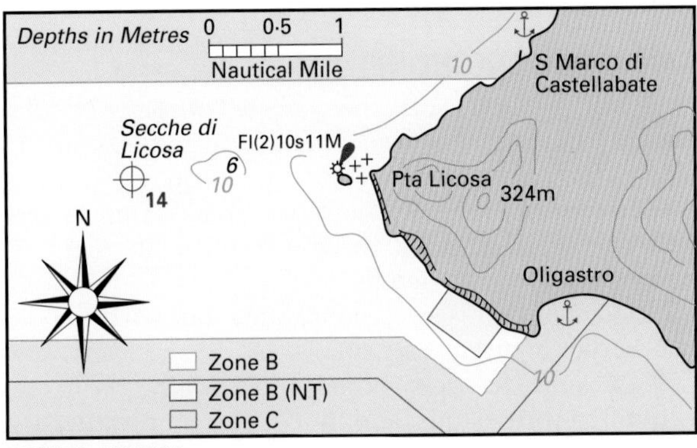

PUNTA LICOSA

⊕14 1.6M W Pta Licosa
40°15'·05N 14°51'·73E WGS84

San Nicola looking SE towards the village

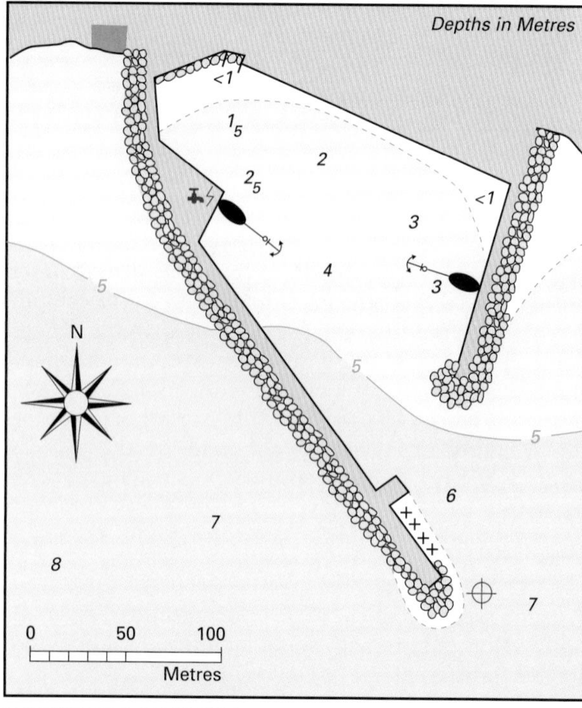

SAN NICOLA (AGNONE)
⊕40°13´·05N 14°59´·22E WGS84

SAN NICOLA (AGNONE)

A small harbour off the village of San Nicola roughly halfway between Pta Licosa and Acciaroli. The harbour shallows towards the N quay.

Go stern or bows-to the outer breakwater or the end of the inner mole where convenient. Care is needed of irregular depths.

Good shelter in settled conditions, but with strong southerlies a surge is set up.

Water and electricity boxes on the quay.

Limited provisions and a couple of restaurants ashore.

For better shopping, bars and restaurants walk around the harbour to the bustling village on the hillside.

ACCIAROLI

Approach

A fishing harbour 7½ miles SE of Punta Licosa. Care must be taken of the shoal water and reefs in the approaches.

Conspicuous A large square Norman tower and a church and spire at the root of the outer mole are conspicuous. On the coast immediately S of the harbour an arched bridge is also conspicuous. Closer in, the town and harbour are easily identified. A white statue of the Madonna is conspicuous on the end of the mole.

By night The light at the extremity of the outer mole Fl.WR.3s6/4M shows the safe approach on the white sector (346°–126°) with the red sector (293°–346°) covering the reefs in the southern approaches. A W cardinal beacon now marks the Secca Vecchia and is lit Q(9)15s. The sectored light listed on the coast has not been working for several years and appears to have been removed.

Dangers The two reefs lying in the southern approaches, Secca Vecchia (least depth 2m) and Secca del Generale (sea breaks on it), may be avoided by approaching the head of the outer mole on a course of due E before turning hard to port to enter.

Both reefs are now marked with beacons.

Note The harbour entrance is subject to silting. Dredging in 2010 will restore depths of 4–6m in the outer harbour, and 2–3m alongside the breakwater. In between dredging, depths in the entrance can go down to 2–3m, with less along the S end of the breakwater. Care is needed as silting will continue unless dredging takes place.

Mooring

Data Max LOA 20m. Depths 2–6m.

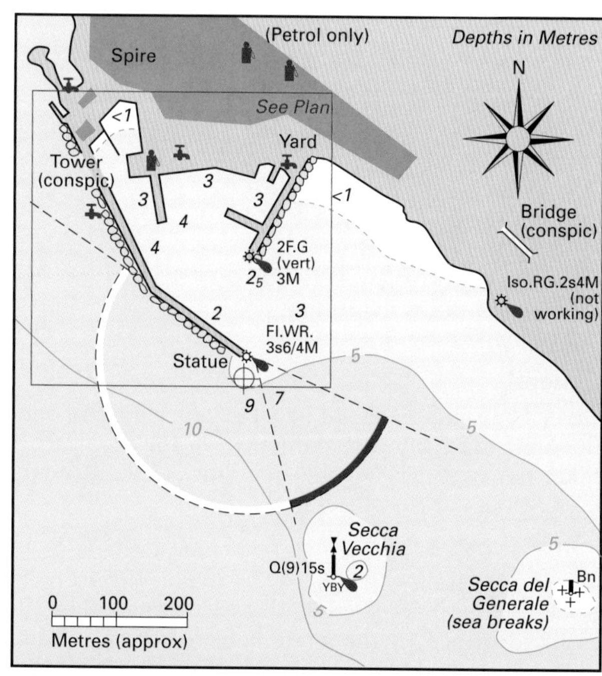

ACCIAROLI APPROACH
⊕40°10´·50N 15°01´·66E WGS84

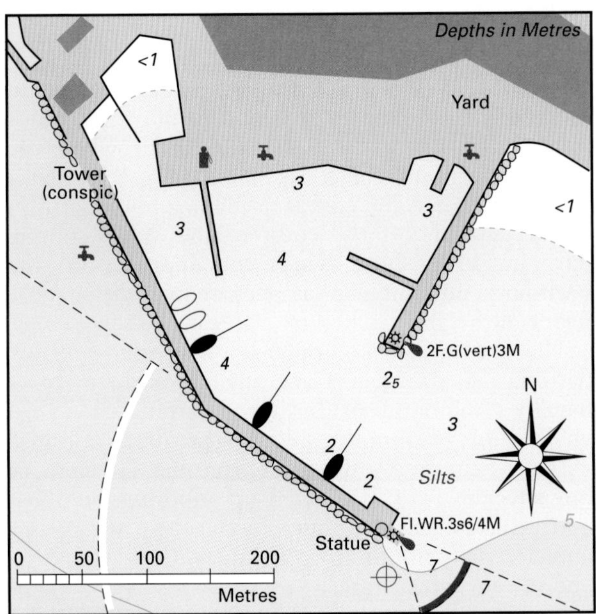

ACCIAROLI
⊕40°10´·50N 15°01´·66E WGS84

Berth Major development works along the breakwater are almost complete. Go stern or bows-to along the breakwater. Laid moorings at most berths. The town quay is much used by fishing boats. The bottom is soft mud and the holding is bad in places. Yacht berths may also be found on either of the pontoons.

The new stub quay at the end of the breakwater should be left clear for the new ferry service.

Shelter Good shelter in settled weather but south-westerlies cause a surge inside. The breakwater has been considerably beefed up, and as part of the development this quay is now lined with offices and storage buildings that provide greater protection from winter storms, which had been known to shift huge boulders over the quay here.

Note A number of permanent mooring buoys are for the fishing boats on the town quay. When a number of boats are tied to a buoy the combined pressure on it pulls the buoy under the water and it cannot be seen. Care needed.

Authorities Harbourmaster. Charge band 1/4.

Facilities

Services Water and electricity at all berths. Showers and toilets almost completed on the quay.
Fuel On the quay.
Repairs A 15-ton crane and 16-ton slipway. Hard standing in the yard. Mechanical repairs. GRP and wood repairs. Electrical repairs. Yachts can be stored ashore.
Provisions Good shopping for provisions. Good fishmonger.
Eating out Restaurants, trattorias and pizzerias on the waterfront and in the village.
Other PO. Bank. ATM. Bus to Salerno.

General

The harbour and the village around it has always been a gem, and the recent make-over of both has only improved it. As well as the porticoed buildings along the yacht quay and car-free streets, in the

Acciaroli looking NW into the inner harbour

Acciaroli looking SW

narrow streets of the village you'll find boutiques and bars as well as pescherias and mini-markets. Acciaroli is said to have been one of Hemingway's favourite places in Italy and it is easy to see why: the landscape and seascape provide a vista of ever-changing patterns and colours. The rocky coast slopes right up to the village to give the impression that the whole has grown from the reefs and sea snarling at the coast.

On a visit here I got talking to a local yachtsman whose family lives here and who grew up here, and I mentioned Hemingway. The yachtsman asked his parents, grandparents, uncles, aunts – No! nobody here ever saw the great man in Acciaroli. However, in one of the hotels here there is a room where Hemingway is supposed to have stayed and where he is also supposed to have got the inspiration for *The Old Man and the Sea*. It's a pity nobody told the owners or whoever penned the blurb that his Nobel Prize winning novel was conceived and set in Cuba. Moreover the hotel was built well after the novella was published in 1952. Well, if Hemingway didn't come here then he should have done – he would have liked it.

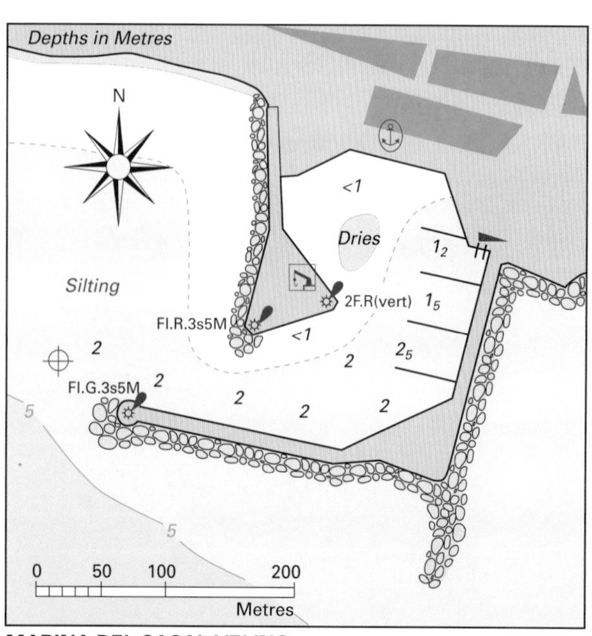

MARINA DEL CASAL VELINO
⊕40°10´·48N 15°07´·04E WGS84

MARINA DEL CASAL VELINO

A small fishing village and resort lying at the head of the bay SE of Acciaroli. A large square tower on an escarpment near the coast is conspicuous but is not to be confused with the more prominent tower to the S of the harbour. The coast here is fringed by rocks and shoal water and care is needed. A buoy marks a rocky outcrop off the coast to the WNW of the harbour. In onshore winds the approach to the harbour is difficult as a sea piles up over the shallow water in the approaches.

The harbour is constantly silting and is periodically dredged. Generally speaking there is usually a minimum of 2m in the entrance, but if in any doubt reconnoitre by dinghy first, and use extreme caution if any swell is running. Go stern or bows-to the S or E quay. Laid moorings at most berths. Good shelter inside. Fuel in the town. Water and electricity points along the quay. Good shopping and restaurants ashore.

Marina di Pisciotta

⊕ 40°06'·1N 15°13'·7E

A very small and rock-bound harbour suitable for a small shallow draught yacht to explore in settled weather. A large stone building in the hill village

Pisciotta looking SW

Marina del Casal Velino looking east

above it is conspicuous. The harbour and entrance are difficult to spot until close to. Because of the shoal water in the approach care is needed and in onshore winds even very small yachts should not attempt to enter.

Like many harbours along the coast it is liable to silt, and between dredging depths can reduce to less than 1m. A catwalk at the entrance may be useful in calm weather, but it offers no shelter from wind or sea.

No facilities in the harbour. In the bustling village up on the hill there is a mini-market, visiting vegetable and fish trucks and a pizzeria.

PALINURO

Approach

The cliffs of Capo Palinuro dropping sheer into the sea are easily identified. The harbour lies on the N side of the cape.

Conspicuous The white tower of the signal station, the lighthouse, and a radio mast on the cape are conspicuous. From the N the houses and hotels at Palinuro village will be seen. From the S the village and harbour cannot be seen until right around the cape.

Dangers

1. On the E side of the bay there is a wreck which now does not break the surface.
2. Care is needed, especially at night, because of the numerous craft on moorings inside the harbour.

Mooring

Berth Go stern or bows-to the new quay where directed. The quay is normally crowded with fishing boats but a berth can usually be found. Laid moorings tailed to the quay at most berths. Holding is uncertain on sand, rock and weed. If possible call ahead for a berth. The stub quay on the end of the breakwater should be kept clear for the ferry. Care is needed of the numerous laid moorings behind the mole.

Shelter Open to the north. With strong westerlies there are violent gusts and a swell works its way around into the anchorage. In the event of deteriorating weather a yacht is advised to go to Camerota or Acciaroli.

Authorities Co-operative. Charge band 4/5.
Co-op. Palinuro Porto, Pepoli Gerardo ✆ 0974 931 604
Mobile 339 877 6562
Email info@palinurocoop.com
www.palinurocoop.com

Facilities

Services Water and electricity at most berths. Wi-Fi.

Fuel In Palinuro village.

Repairs 15-ton crane. Some repairs can be arranged.

Other Restaurant, cafés and bars around the beach. Shops and restaurants in Palinuro village about a mile away.

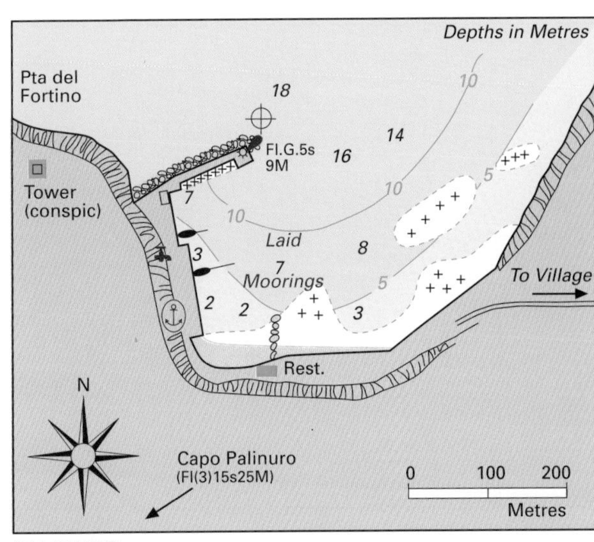

PALINURO
⊕40°01´·93N 15°16´·61E WGS84

General

The cape is named after Palinurus, the helmsman of Aeneas' ship who fell overboard and was washed ashore here to be murdered by the natives. In the *Aeneid*, Palinurus tells his story when his spirit tries to cross the Styx, but is refused because he has had no proper burial. Palinurus explains how he was exhausted after the battle with Scylla and Charybdis and fell asleep and then overboard, taking the tiller and part of the stern with him. Sybil can only tell him he will not be forgotten and that a shrine will be erected to him. Near the harbour there are ruins locally attributed to Palinurus.

Palinuro village itself situated above the sandy beach is a growing tourist resort though, apart from a few tripper boats, they intrude little on the cape.

Note According to the Admiralty *Pilot*, when the summit of Mte Madonna della Stella and Mte Bulgheria (Bulgaria), the highest mountains in the vicinity, are covered in cloud, NW winds are likely, but if the cloud forms lower down leaving the summits bare, then S winds are likely.

Palinuro harbour looking west. *See also page 158*

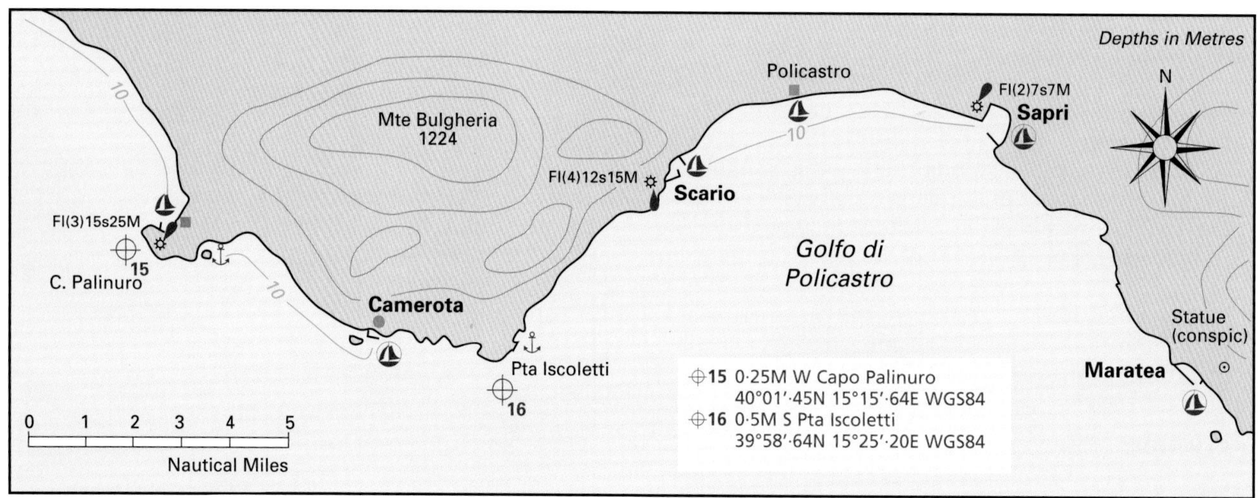

CAPO PALINURO TO MARATEA

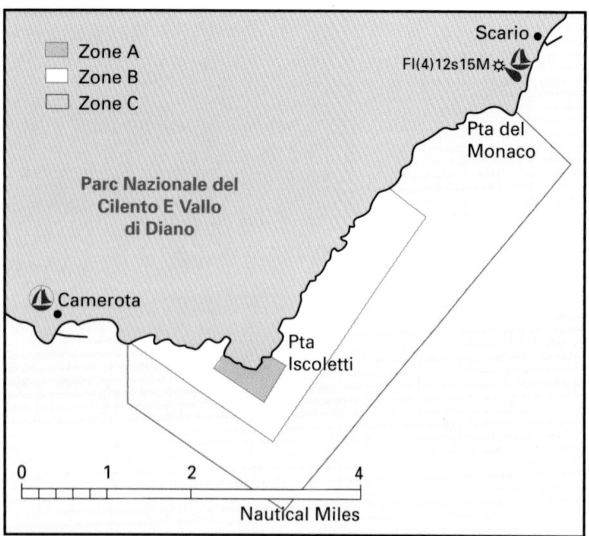

AMP COSTA DEGLI INFRESCHI E DELLA MASSETTA

AMP COSTA DEGLI INFRESCHI E DELLA MASSETTA

Zone A All unauthorised navigation, fishing and diving is prohibited.

Zone B Navigation by jet skis and motor boats is restricted. Maximum speed 5 knots up to 300m off the coast. Max 10 knots 300–600m off the coast. Anchoring and mooring is restricted.

Zone C Maximum speed 10 knots. Fishing restricted.

For further details see www.cilentoediano.it

Capo Palinuro and lighthouse looking SE

Capo Palinuro

The steep-to cape is an impressive place and with deep water right up to it in most places you can chug around close to the cliffs in calm weather. In heavy weather the swell rebounds off the cliffs to give a bad cross-swell for some distance off. In settled weather there is an attractive anchorage on the SE side off the beach under a rocky islet. Anchor in 4–6m on sand. A camping ground ashore.

CAMEROTA (MARINA DI CAMEROTA)

Approach

The Admiralty *Pilot* states that there are 2–4m depths in the channel between I. del Camerota and the mainland, but I have encountered uneven depths of less than 2m. Shoal water also extends to seawards of the islet and I would advise a yacht to keep well to seaward of the islet.

Conspicuous I. del Camerota and a square tower to the W of the harbour are easily identified from the west. The town and harbour will not be seen until you are around I. del Camerota. From the S, the village of Camerota on the hillside and numerous apartment blocks in Marina di Camerota are conspicuous. Closer in, Castello Marchelase behind the harbour and the harbour moles are easily identified.

VHF Ch 16, 09 (Marina di Camerota).

Dangers

1. With strong southerlies there is a confused swell at the entrance making entry difficult.
2. In the winter the entrance silts with southerly gales. The new N breakwater seems to have made little difference, and the new ferry quay here is unusable due to silting. A dredger is kept here more or less on a permanent basis, and a narrow channel into the harbour is maintained with depths of 3–5m. Deep draught yachts should call ahead for advice.

Note Approximately 1M SE of the harbour lies a fish farm in position 39°59´·3N 15°23´·1E. It is marked on the N side by two yellow buoys (lit Fl.Y), and on the S side by numerous unlit buoys, some with heavy floating lines attached.

Mooring

Data c.400 berths. Max LOA 25m. Depths <1–4m. Depths in the entrance 3–5m.

Berth Go stern or bows-to the pontoons where directed. Laid moorings are tailed to buoys or to the pontoons.

Shelter Good all-round shelter although prolonged southerlies cause a surge – bothersome but not dangerous.

Authorities Harbourmaster. Charge band 5.
Marina di Camerota 'La Marina de il Leone di Caprera'
✆ 0974 939 813 *Fax* 0974 939 184
Email: info@portodicamerota.it
www.portodicamerota.it

Facilities

Services Water and electricity on the pontoons. Shower and toilet block.
Fuel On the town quay.
Repairs An 18-ton crane available. 200-ton travel-hoist. Mechanical repairs.
Provisions Good shopping for all provisions nearby.
Eating out Restaurants and pizzerias nearby.
Other PO. Bank. ATM.

Camerota looking south

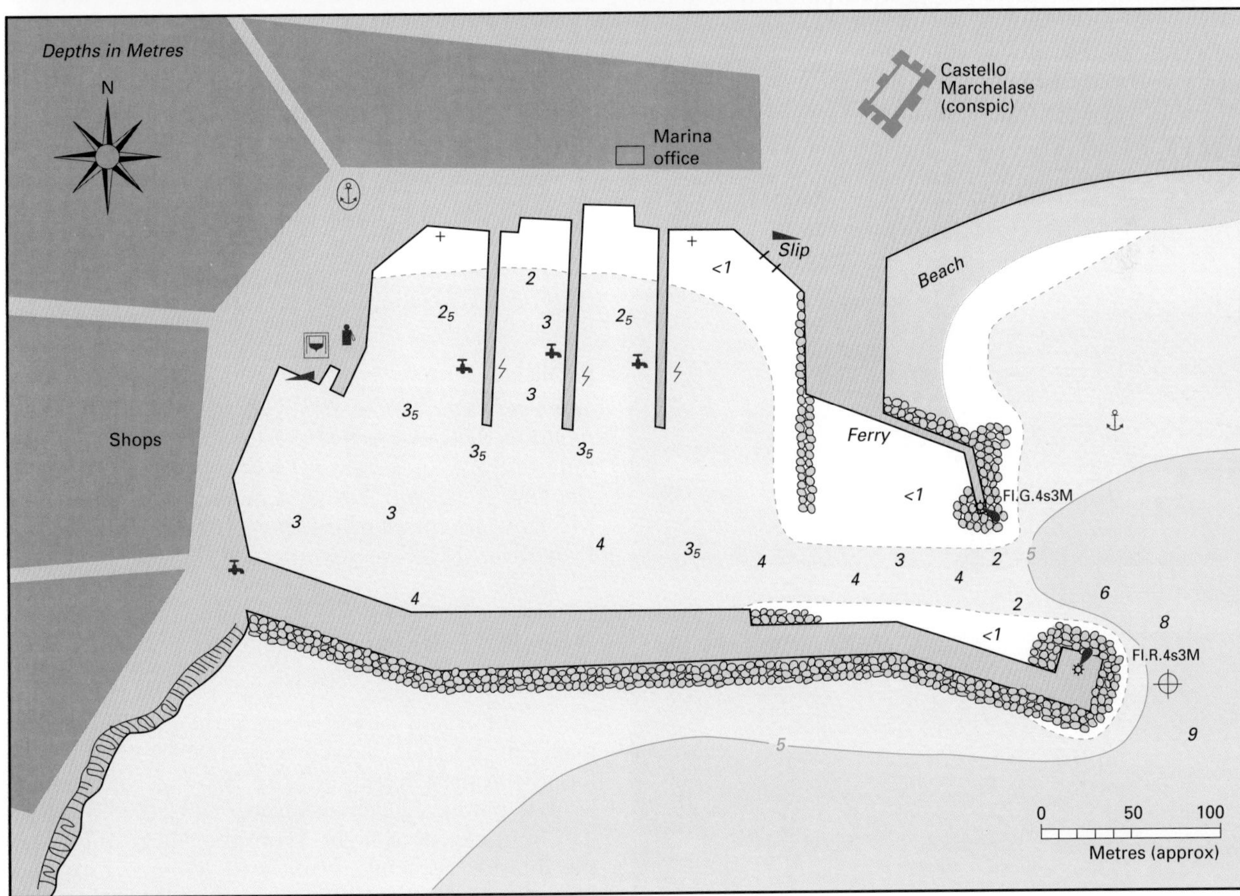

MARINA DI CAMEROTA
⊕39°59´·87N 15°22´·78E WGS84

General

Marina di Camerota is not the most architecturally inspired spot, but the spectacular coast nearby and the friendly locals make up for that. At one time sword-fishing boats from southern Calabria and Sicily made it their base in the summer, but now fewer boats use the harbour though with much longer nets.

Punta Iscoletti

The point with a square fort on it is easily identified. All along this coast, between Camerota and Sapri, watchtowers are perched at strategic points. Just NE of Punta Iscoletti there is an attractive cove with two forks used by local boats. Inside the cove is a ring of mooring buoys for visitors. Restaurant/bar ashore. Shelter looks good from all but easterlies. A little further up the coast towards Scario, a spectacular ravine cuts down through the mountains to the sea.

This area is part of the Cilento and Diano Valley National Park, and Punta Iscoletti lies within the AMP Costa Degli Infreschi e della Massetta, with restrictions on navigation and anchoring. *See plan for details.*

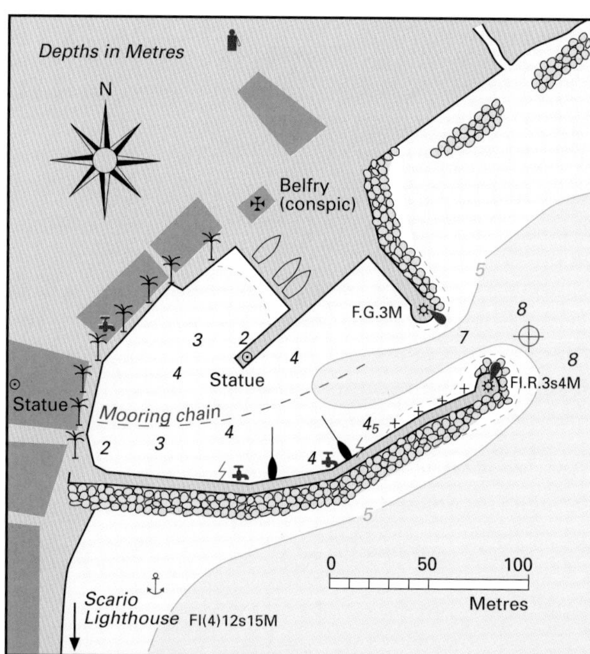

MARINA DI SCARIO
⊕40°03´·15N 15°29´·72E WGS84

MARINA DI SCARIO

Approach

From the SW the village and harbour will not be seen until you are into the bay. The fort on Pta Iscoletti and the tower on the escarpment S of the town are conspicuous. From the S and SE the buildings of the village will be seen. The lighthouse at the SW end of the harbour and the church tower in the village are conspicuous.

Approach to Scario looking NNW

Scario harbour looking WSW from the entrance

Note In the summer three conical yellow buoys (× topmark/light Fl.3s) mark a tunny net laid in the Golfo di Policastro off Scario and Sapri. It is a bottom net and not a hindrance to navigation.

Mooring

Data 60 berths. Max LOA 30m. Depths 2–5m.

Berth Go stern or bows-to the quay on the inside of the mole. Laid moorings at most berths.

Shelter Good all-round shelter. Strong southerlies cause a surge, more uncomfortable than dangerous. Sometimes a current seems to flow through the entrance from the E, perhaps the current circulating around the head of Golfo di Policastro, or from one of the rivers that flow into the sea nearby.

Authorities Harbourmaster. *Ormeggiatori*. Charge band 1/3.

Facilities

Services Water can be arranged.
Fuel On the outskirts of the village or delivered by mini-tanker.
Repairs A 25-ton crane. Limited hard standing. Mechanical repairs possible.
Provisions Most provisions can be found in the village.
Eating out Restaurants and pizzerias nearby.
Other PO. Italgaz and Camping Gaz.

General

The harbour and village is one of the most delightful places in the gulf – a picture-postcard sort of place. Pastel-coloured houses line the harbour front shaded by date palms. The church tower rings the hour and half hour except at night. From the village and coast the interior rises up abruptly to wooded hills and valleys with streams running down to the sea even in the summer. The village sees some tourism, though

Policastro looking ESE towards the entrance

not too much, something which may well change in the future – I hesitated before including details of Scario in previous editions.

POLICASTRO

Approach

A small harbour approximately 2½M NE of Scario. The houses of the resort village and the harbour breakwater are easily recognised.

Dangers The entrance is silting, with depths of less than 2m before dredging.

Mooring

Data 50 berths. Max LOA 15m. Depths <1–2·5m.

Berth Go stern or bows-to the outer breakwater just past the solid square pier.

Shelter Good shelter although strong southerlies are said to cause a surge.

Authorities Ormeggiatori.

Facilities

Water Locally from the café or restaurant near the harbour.
Repairs 25-ton travel-lift and 30-ton crane.
Provisions In the village directly up from the harbour.
Eating out Several restaurants including a good local trattoria/pizzeria close by the harbour.

General

Policastro is a low-key local resort and, like its neighbour Scario, well worth a visit. The harbour has recently been smartened up, and is likely to open soon as a Porto turistico with associated charges.

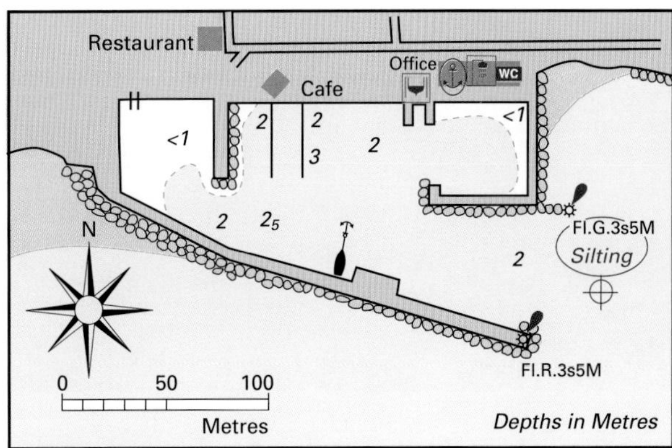

POLICASTRO
⊕40°04´·23N 15°31´·64E WGS84

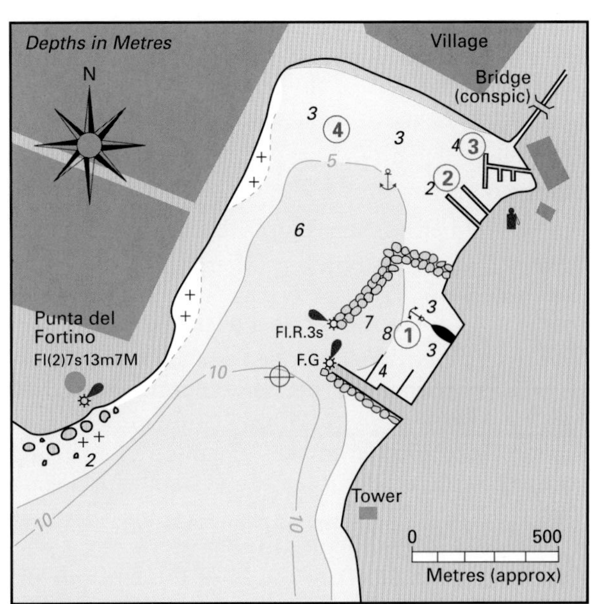

SAPRI
⊕40°03´·7N 15°37´·0E

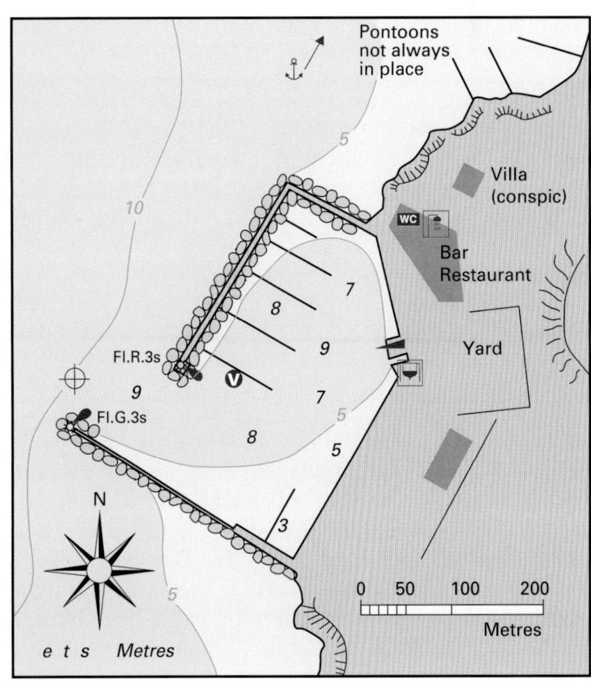

SAPRI
⊕40°03′·92N 15°37′·49E WGS84

SAPRI

Approach

A large bay in the NE corner of Golfo di Policastro. From the W the bay is readily identified and the breakwater shows up well. From the S it is difficult to determine just where the bay is. A town on a sandy beach to the WNW of the bay can be identified. A dun-coloured church and a square tower in

The new harbour at Sapri looking NW across the bay

the town will be identified. Closer in, rocks off the coast immediately S of the entrance to the bay will be seen.

VHF Ch 16.

Mooring

Data c.300 berths. Max LOA 40m. Depths 3–9m.

Berth Go stern or bows-to where directed in the harbour. Most visitors' berths are on the outer pontoon. Laid moorings tailed to the pontoons.

Note To the N of the harbour there are three simple catwalk/pontoons run by San Giorgio and Base Nautica Mandola, but they are not always in place.

Shelter Good shelter in the harbour. With strong northerlies there are violent gusts and with strong southerlies a swell rolls in to the bay though there is some shelter behind the breakwater.

Anchorage Anchor off to the N of the harbour off the beach at the head of the bay.

Authorities Club representatives. Charge band 1/4.

Sapri Ormeggiatori Toni ✆ 338 700 5750 / 0973 605 536
S. Giorgio (pontoons) ✆ 0973 603 305
Base Nautica Mandola (pontoons) ✆ 0973 391 358.

Facilities

Services Water and electricity (220V) at all berths.
Fuel On the pontoon at Base Nautica Mandola.
Provisions Good shopping in the town although it is a long walk. Take the dinghy over to the beach off the village.
Eating out Restaurant above the E side of the bay and in the village.
Other PO. Bank. ATM.

General

Sapri is a small mostly local resort town with most of its charm lying in the bay and its surroundings. It achieved brief fame in 1857 when Carlo Piscane landed here with a small group to foment an insurrection against the Bourbons. It failed and the group was harried and killed by Bourbon troops aided by the local peasants. As if in shame the light is called Carlo Piscane. Otherwise Sapri has sat here in the corner of the gulf pretty much out of things and it is none the worse for that.

MARATEA

Approach

Conspicuous The white statue of Christ with arms outstretched on the precipitous bluff above the harbour is conspicuous from some distance off. From the N it can be difficult to determine the exact location of the harbour until close to as the breakwater blends into the rocks behind. From the S the small hamlet by the harbour will be seen.

By night The statue of Christ is sometimes lit at night.

VHF Ch 16, 06.

Caution With onshore winds a swell piles up at the entrance, though once inside it is calm.

Mooring

Data 250 berths. Visitors' berths. Max LOA 35m. Depths 2–7m.

Berth Go stern or bows-to where directed. There are laid moorings tailed to the pontoons. Free berths stern or bows-to on the W breakwater, keeping clear of berths reserved for fishing boats. It is very tight in the harbour for manouevring.

Shelter Good all-round shelter although strong southerlies cause a surge.

Authorities Harbourmaster and customs. Harbour attendant. Charge band 4.

Porto Turistico Maratea ✆ 0973 877 307 / 871 056

Facilities

Services Water and electricity at or near every berth. Water on fuel quay.
Fuel On the quay.
Repairs 18-ton crane. 40-ton travel-hoist. Some mechanical repairs.
Provisions Most provisions can be obtained locally. Better shopping in Fiumicello village about 4km away, with supermarket, fruit and veg stalls and a butcher.

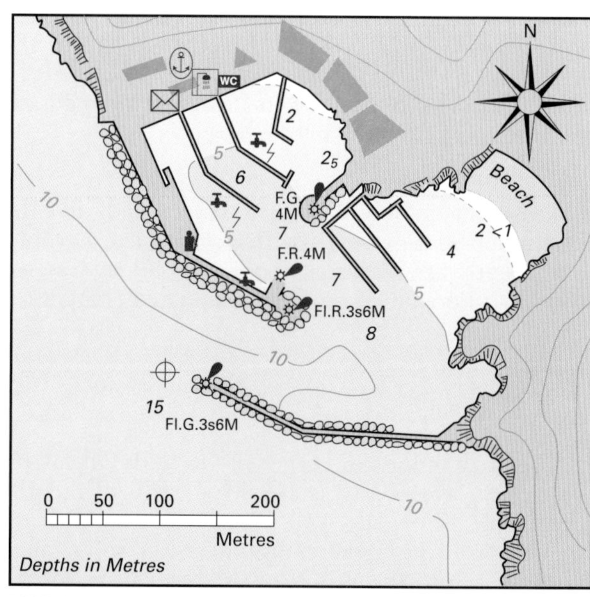

MARATEA
⊕39°59´·21N 15°42´·40E WGS84

Maratea looking NW

Eating out Restaurants and pizzeria around the harbour.
Other PO. Bank in Fiumicello village. Irregular bus service to Maratea village.

General

A great deal of effort has been spent turning the old fishing harbour into a tasteful and unspoiled yacht harbour. The rocks and a grotto on the N of the inner harbour have been left intact. In the outer harbour the rocky coastline and the beach have been enclosed by the breakwaters. The old houses of the fishing hamlet remain and, while some of them have been converted into expensive restaurants with neon signs, at least no new architectural intruders ruin the look of the place. It has not been easy. The breakwaters were partially destroyed in a winter storm when construction began, but they have been built up higher and stronger than the originals so that now they completely block out the view of the sea outside.

Torre Caino

A small rocky promontary just under 3M S of Maratea makes a popular lunch stop for local boats in calm weather. Anchor in the cove on the N side, just under the squat tower above the cliff.

Isola di Dino

A slab-sided islet lying approximately seven miles S of Maratea. In calm weather local fishing boats anchor on either side of the islet, depending on breeze and swell. The beach and town of Praia a Mare on the mainland just to the north. The passage between the island and the shore is shallow and rock strewn and should not be attempted. There are reported to be a number of caves similar to Capri's Blue Grotto around it.

Just over a mile to the S is the small town of San Nicola Arcella, where local boats anchor in the bay with what looks like reasonable shelter from southerlies tucked right in behind the headland.

Isola di Cirella

An islet lying approximately 11 miles S of Isola di Dino. It is readily identified by the tower on its summit.

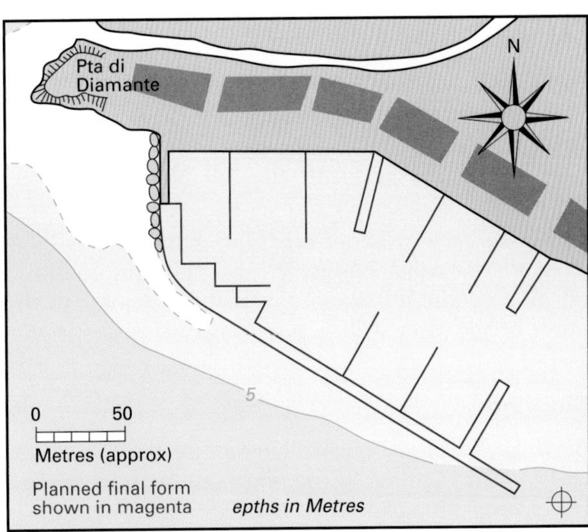

DIAMANTE
⊕39°40'·44N 15°49'·25E WGS84

DIAMANTE

Approach

The ruined harbour lies directly under Punta di Diamante off the town of Diamante. The buildings of the town are easily identified.

Note Problems with planning permission have delayed the development of the porto turistico. The plan and data given below is for the finished marina. Work is due to start in 2010, but no completion dates were available at the time of writing. Currently there is little here save a damaged breakwater, and as yet has nothing to recommend it for yachts.

VHF Ch 16.

Mooring

Data (When completed) 180 berths. Max LOA 12m. Depths 1–3m.

Berth Where directed on the pontoons. Care is needed as the depths are irregular.

Shelter Reasonable shelter, although with southerlies some berths may be uncomfortable.

Authorities Harbourmaster. A charge will be made.

Anchorage In calm weather a yacht could anchor off the town to the SE. Open S and west.

Facilities

Services Water and electricity near most berths on the pontoons.
Fuel In the town.
Provisions Good shopping for provisions in the town.
Eating out Restaurants in the town.
Other PO. Bank.

CETRARO

Approach

The harbour lies about three miles SSE of Capo Testa, a dark rocky spur projecting from the beach. Care needed of gusts off the hill N and E of the town.

Conspicuous A viaduct on Capo Bonifati N of the harbour is conspicuous, as is the dun-coloured hospital on the hill above the harbour. Closer in the outer breakwater will be seen.

VHF Ch 16.

Mooring

Berth Go stern or bows-to where directed. There are laid moorings tailed to the pontoons at most berths. If berthing alongside care is needed as fendering is difficult: the concrete jetty is cut away beneath the quay, and low topsides may get caught under the ledge, particularly if there is a surge in the basin.

Shelter Good all-round shelter although southerly gales cause a surge which can trap and damage yachts alongside.

Authorities Harbourmaster. Capitaneria. Guardia Costiera may wish to check your papers. Charge band 1/3.

Anchorage In calm weather it may be possible to anchor outside the inner N mole.

Facilities

Services Water and electricity at most berths. Showers and toilets.

Repairs 10-ton crane. Some repairs can be arranged.

Provisions About 500m away.

Eating out Restaurants and cafés, and sea-food pizzeria near the harbour.

General

Cetraro has been transformed into a *porto turistico*. The pontoons have been put in and moorings laid, and the surrounding concrete buildings are mellowing. The harbour is becoming a focal point for the village, with more restaurants and cafés springing up in the vicinity, and locals taking their *passegiata* past the yacht berths and along to the fishing boats on the far quay.

Note There are no harbours suitable for any but very small yachts on the coast between Cetraro and Vibo Valentia. There are a few small villages on the coast with maybe a handful of fishing boats including Paola, Amantea and Gizzeria. The new *porto turistico* at Amantea and the breakwaters of a fishing harbour under construction between Amantea and Capo Suvero (39°02´·2N 16°05´·5E) offer limited shelter. These villages may have restaurants or shops, but otherwise offer little or no shelter to those who stop.

Cetraro looking SW from the slopes behind

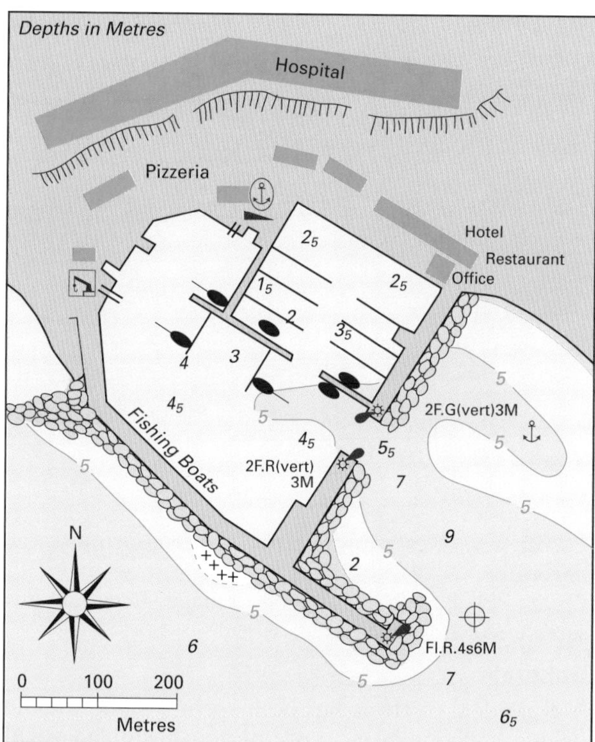

CETRARO
⊕39°31´·44N 15°55´·28E WGS84

AMANTEA

A *porto turistico* has been built to the S of the town of Amantea. It is mostly full with small local boats, and visiting yachts should not depend on finding a berth here.

Approach

VHF Ch 16.

Mooring

Data c.200 berths. Max LOA 15m. Depths reported 2–4m.

Berths Go alongside on the wedge-shaped quay or inside the S breakwater. Alternatively there may be room for smaller yachts to go stern or bows-to on one of the pontoons.

Shelter Adequate shelter, although southerlies will make some berths uncomfortable and possibly untenable.

Authorities Harbourmaster.
✆ 0982 48565 / 347 093 0081
Email portoamantea@virgilio.it

Facilities

Water and electricity at most berths. Fuel on the quay. 25-ton crane.

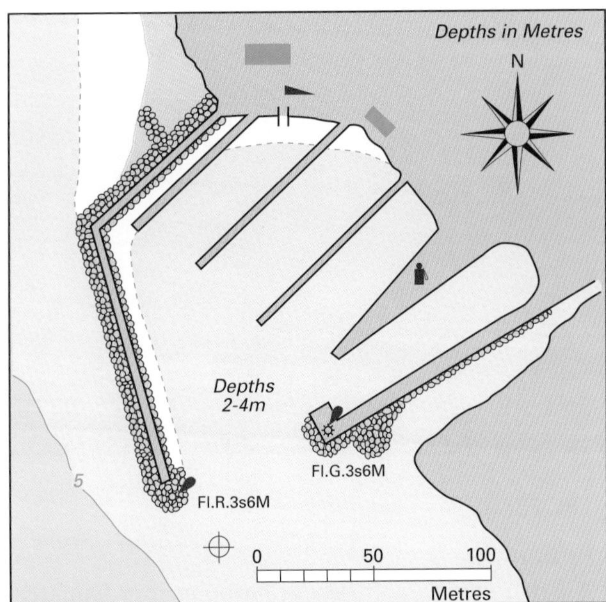

AMANTEA
⊕39°03´·0N 16°05´·5E

General

This new *porto turistico* is one of a number of harbour developments in Calabria, but its small size limits its usefulness to smaller yachts only.

Pizzo

⊕ 38°44'·1N 16°09'·4E

Approximately 2½M NE of Vibo Valentia a short breakwater extends from the coast at Pizzo. Depths inside it are mostly less than 1m and in any case it affords little shelter.

VIBO VALENTIA MARINA

Approach

A commercial and fishing port at the southern end of Golfo di Sant'Eufemia.

Conspicuous A number of chimneys and oil storage tanks within the harbour are conspicuous. Two large viaducts are also conspicuous in the approach from the north. The entrance lies about 1·5 miles W of them. Closer in, the town and the harbour breakwater are easily identified.

By night From the N the bright lights around the harbour obscure the main light on the N mole so it has about half its stated range.

VHF Ch 11, 16 for port authorities (0700–1900). Ch 14 for pilots (0700–1900). Ch 16, 10 for Stella del Sud. Ch 12, 16 for Marina Carmelo.

Note With southerlies there are gusts off the high land around the harbour.

Mooring

Vibo Valentia has two well-run marinas.

1. ***Marina Stella del Sud*** A long dog-leg pontoon. Laid moorings tailed to the quay. Berth stern or bows-to where directed. Max LOA 35m. Depths 2–6m. Stella del Sud is an Italian/Canadian family-run marina. English is spoken and everyone is helpful. Impromptu barbecues add to the friendly atmosphere. Charge band 3.
   ✆ 0963 573 202
   Email stellasud@tin.it
   www.marinastelladelsud.it
2. ***Marina Carmelo*** The catwalk and pontoons immediately E of Stella del Sud. Berth where directed. Friendly and helpful. Charge band 3.
   ✆ 0963 572 630
   Email info@marinacarmelo.it
   www.marinacarmelo.it

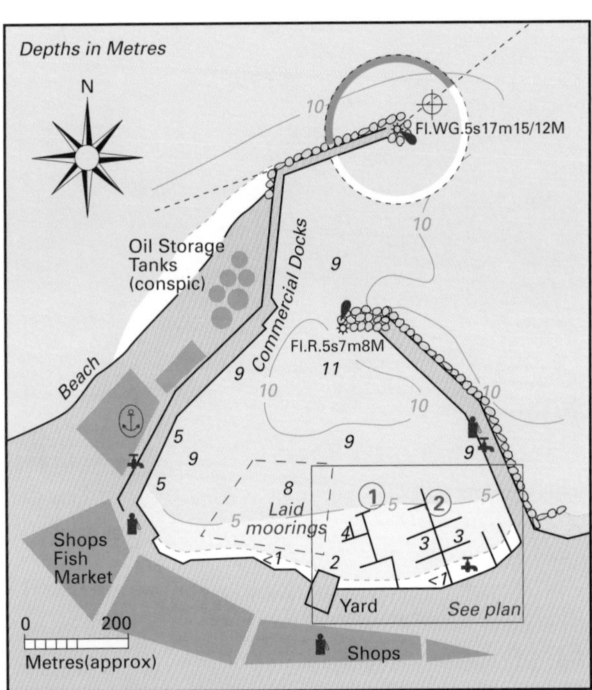

VIBO VALENTIA MARINA
⊕38°43´·22N 16°07´·79E WGS84

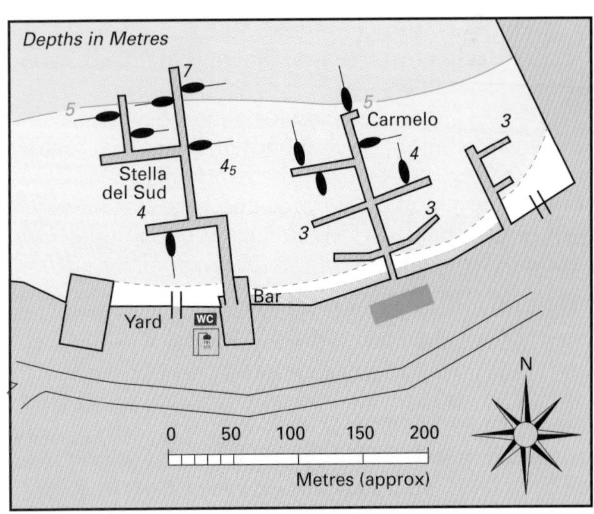

MARINA STELLA DEL SUD & MARINA CARMELO

Shelter Good all-round shelter although strong westerlies are said to cause a surge. A number of yachts are kept here all year round on permanent moorings, and at the marinas.

Vibo Valentia looking NNW *Sandro Bedessi, FOTOTECA ENIT*

Authorities Harbourmaster and customs. Staff at the 'marinas'. Charge band 3.

Facilities

Services Water and electricity (220/380V). Telephone and fax. WC and showers. Laundry. Wi-Fi (Stella). Weather forecast. Bar.
Fuel On the quay on the E breakwater.
Repairs A 24-ton crane and 30-ton slipway at the yard. Mechanical repairs. Some GRP and wood repairs. Chandlers.
Provisions Good shopping for all provisions. Several excellent fishmongers in the town. Ice from a factory in the SW corner or from the fishmongers.
Eating out Good restaurants and pizzerias nearby.
Other PO. Bank. ATM. Italgaz and Camping Gaz. Train to Rome. Lamezia international airport 20km.

General

Apart from the oil installation on the W side of the harbour, this is an attractive and friendly place. The slopes behind are wooded and there are good sandy beaches nearby. There is little left in this sleepy little town to remind you that this was once ancient Greek Hipponium and an important naval base in Roman times. Even in the 18th century it was renowned as a centre of learning.

Today it is a small provincial Calabrian town where everyone takes a siesta in the hot afternoon and oil is more important than the university.

TROPEA

Approach

A small marina and fishing harbour approximately 11 miles W of Vibo Valentia. The town of dun-coloured houses on a rocky bluff just W of the harbour is easily identified.

VHF Ch 16, 09 for marina.

Dangers

1. Caution is needed when navigating between Tropea and Capo Vaticano as there are unmarked above and below-water rocks some distance offshore. A yacht is recommended to keep 1–1·5 miles off the coast.
2. The harbour is prone to silting and depths have reduced in the entrance and the basin. Care is needed in the final approach and entrance. At present there are around 5m depths off the outer breakwater. See plan for details.

Mooring

Data 620 berths. 70 visitors' berths. Max LOA 60m. Depths <1–4m.

Berth Go stern or bows-to where directed. Laid moorings tailed to the quay.

Shelter Good shelter in the inner basin.

Authorities Capitaneria. Marina staff.
Charge band 4.
✆ 0963 61548 *Fax* 0963 607 029
Email info@portoditropea.it
www.portoditropea.it

Capo Vaticano looking north

The approaches to Tropea looking SE towards the old town on the summit

Tropea looking E from the old town

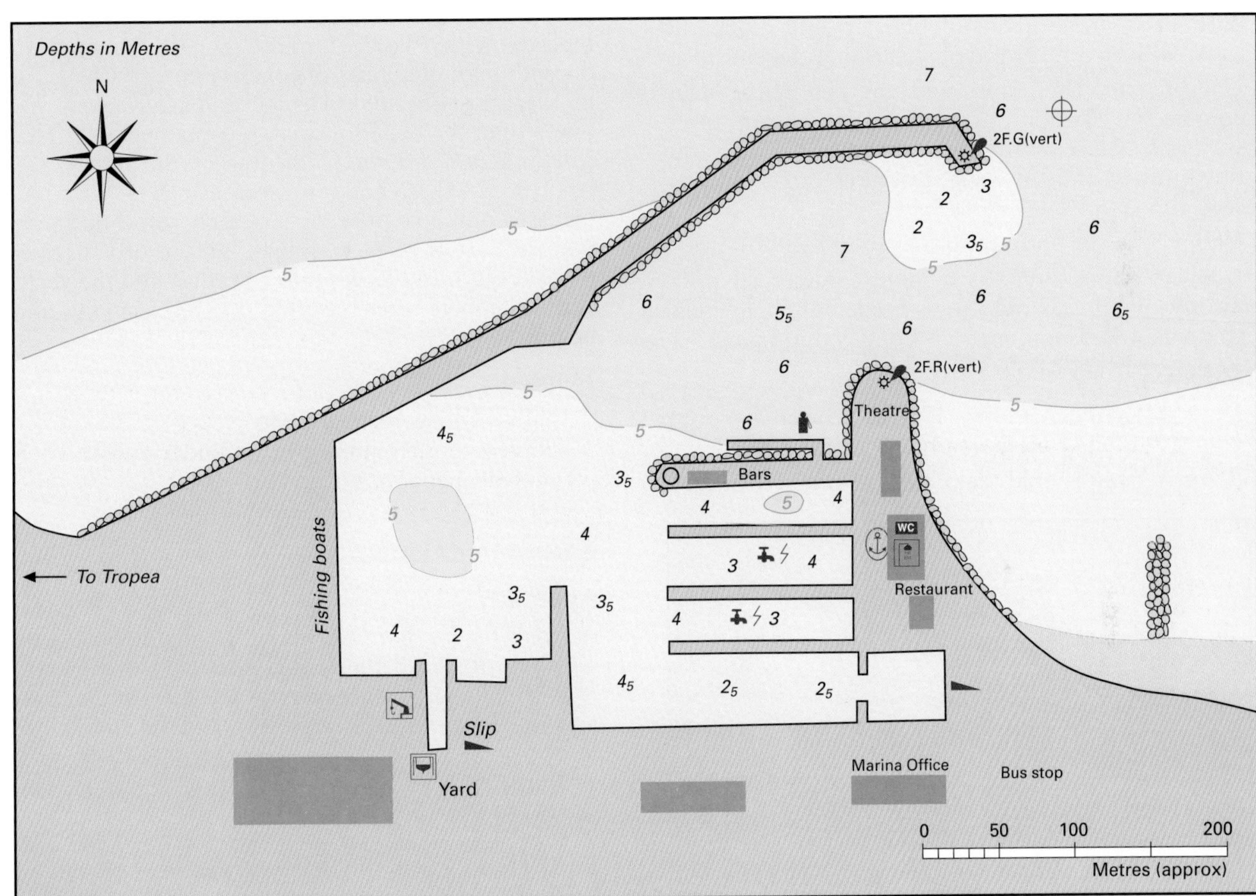

TROPEA
⊕38°41′·04N 15°54′·39E WGS84

Facilities

Services Water and electricity (220/380V) points. Wi-Fi. Internet. Showers and toilet block. Laundry facilities.
Fuel On the quay (0700–2100) where shown.
Repairs 50-ton travel-hoist and 40-ton crane. The yard is now operating, but fairly limited repairs possible at present.
Cantiere Navale ✆ 0963 61885
Email info@cantieretropea.it
www.cantieretropea.it

Provisions Shops close to the harbour. More extensive provisions in the town.
Eating out Bars and restaurant planned for the harbour. More choice in town.
Other Banks, PO, Camping Gaz and Italgaz, taxis. Minibus to town centre.

General

The town and the setting are picturesque and don't let the thought of climbing nearly 200 steps deter you from visiting it. Narrow streets lead to *piazze* bustling with locals and tourists alike. Pastel-coloured houses cling to the clifftops and churches seem to grow from the rock itself. It is a busy town in a low-key sort of way, and is well worth the climb up from the harbour.

The marina is now established, with most shoreside facilities in place and a developing repair yard. Marina staff are reported to be friendly and efficient, and a number of yachts have overwintered here. It is a base for the Guardia Costieri, and has even been used as the location for a new Italian TV drama series based on 'real-life' coastguard activities.

GIOIA TAURO

Approach

Gioia Tauro is a large commercial harbour lying approximately 12 miles S of Capo Vaticano. The harbour is dredged out of the flat land along the coast with two breakwaters protecting the entrance.

Conspicuous The cranes and gantries in the huge commercial harbour are conspicuous from some way off. Closer in by the ballasting along the breakwaters and the light structures can be clearly seen.

VHF Ch 16 for port authorities (0800–2000).

Dangers Gioia Tauro is a large commercial port, mostly containers, and care is needed of commercial shipping and fishing trawlers coming and going.

Mooring

Data Max LOA 20m. Depths Outer harbour 12·5–20m. Inner basin 3–4m.

Berth A yacht should make for the inner basin. The YC here has a pontoon where you may find a berth. Laid moorings.

Shelter Good all-round shelter. The high walls enclosing the basin mean it is almost too sheltered as little wind gets in to cool things down.

Authorities Harbourmaster. *Ormeggiatori*. Charge band 2.

Facilities

Services Water and electricity in the inner basin.
Fuel Can be delivered by arrangement.
There is a bar in the inner basin clubhouse and a restaurant a short walk away. Gioia town is about 30 minutes' walk away – take a taxi in the summer. Trains to Naples and Rome from the town.

General

Why the fertile orange and olive groves in the high risk earthquake zone around Gioia Tauro were replaced with 50km^2 of industrial park has more to do with mafia interests in concrete construction and in turn the Christian Democrat party's quest for funds than the need for a large container port. This *catedrale nel deserto* (cathedral of the desert) lay empty for years, and only recently has 'Europe's biggest container port' at last seen some business. Not the sort of place you might go out of your way to visit, but it is a useful port of refuge and the yacht club members are reported to be friendly and helpful.

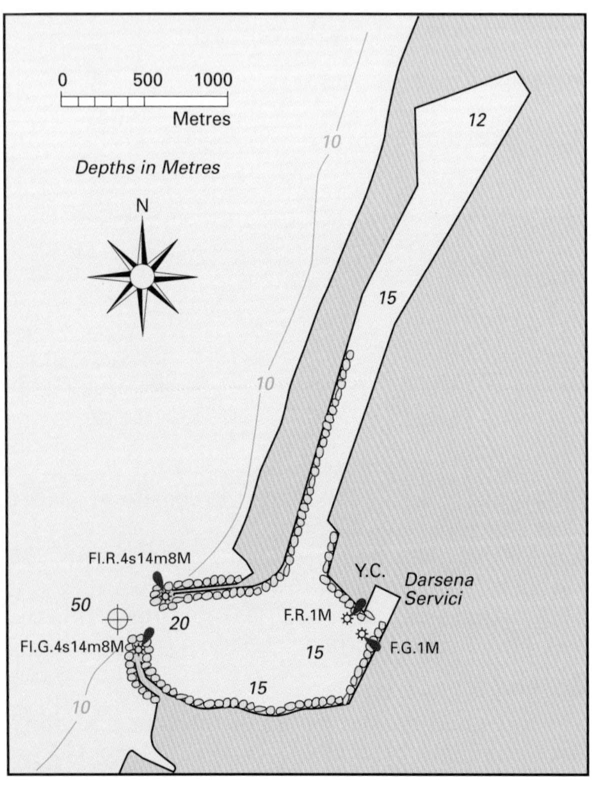

GIOIA TAURO
⊕38°26′·66N 15°53′·32E WGS84

Taureana

⊕ 38°21′·5N 15°50′·1E

A small harbour reported to be under construction off the village of Palmi.

BAGNARA CALABRA

Approach

A small fishing harbour about 10 miles S of Gioia Tauro. A tower at the root of the outer breakwater is conspicuous. The breakwater blends into the coast and the entrance is difficult to make out until close to.

VHF Ch 16, 11.

Mooring

Berth Stern or bows-to or alongside the outer end of the outer breakwater, or just inside on the E quay.

Bagnara Calabra looking S from the entrance

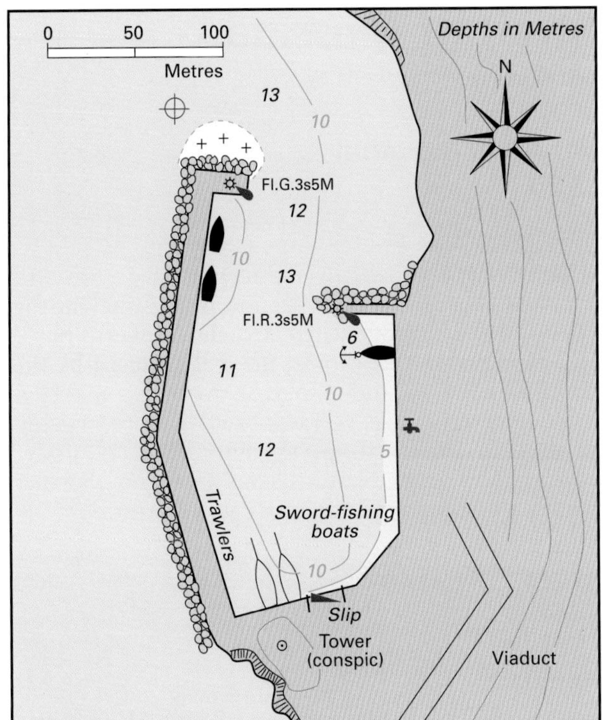

BAGNARA CALABRA
⊕38°18´·06N 15°48´·88E WGS84

Shelter Good shelter.

Charge band 1/2.

Facilities

Water On the quay.
The village is about 15 minutes' walk to the S of the harbour. Market on Tuesday. Café bar nearby.

General

The fishing harbour is conveniently placed outside the N entrance of the Strait of Messina and is a useful alternative to Scilla or Reggio di Calabria.

Bagnara Calabra is predominantly a fishing port, though it is usually possible to find a berth here. You may find some enterprising youngster waves you in, ties you up, and then damands a few euros – best to pay up as you never know who dad is. It's a friendly sort of place set under the steep slopes of the Aspromontes of Calabria and you will often see the distinctive sword-fishing boats of the area in here.

SCILLA

Approach

The harbour, lying under a rocky bluff, can be difficult to identify.

Conspicuous From the N follow the coast until the craggy rock bluff with a fort on top can be identified. Closer in, the short harbour mole will be seen.

Note The whirlpool famous in antiquity is no longer situated here. An earthquake in 1783 changed the topography of the sea bottom so that the whirlpool is barely a ripple today.

Mooring

Entering the harbour, care must be taken of the underwater debris off the extremity of the mole. A winter storm knocked part of the mole into the water and successive storms have compounded the damage.

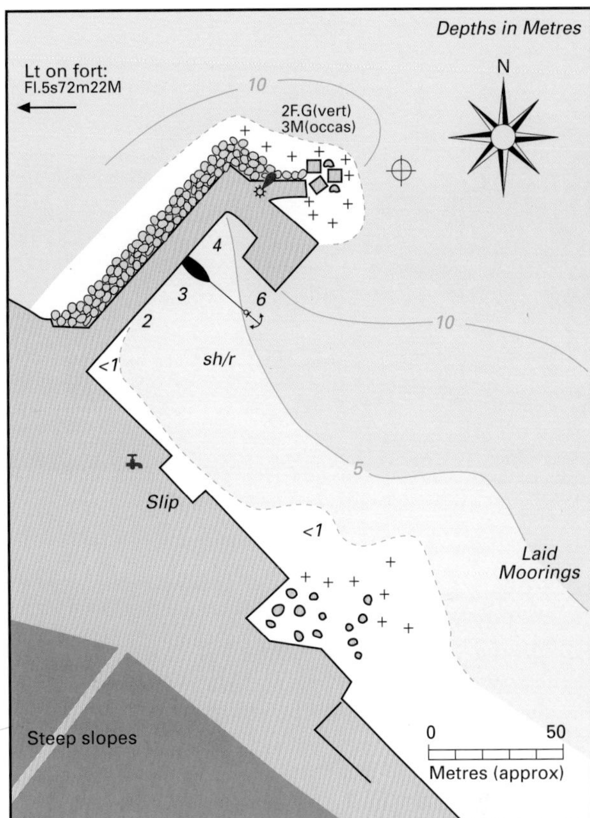

SCILLA
⊕38°15´·43N 15°43´·01E WGS84

Berth Go stern-to the quay taking care of more debris underwater close to the quay. The bottom is shingle and rocks – bad holding. There are also numerous large permanent mooring chains fouling the bottom.

Alternatively pick up one of Giovanni's mooring buoys for visiting yachts. Make sure you do not have a fishing boat moorings before you go ashore.

Giovanni Arena ✆ 338 9713 413
Email giovarena@libero.it

Shelter Is better than it looks but the harbour is really only suitable in settled weather.

Charge band 1/2.

The approaches to Scilla looking SW

Visitors moorings at Scilla *David Youngman*

Facilities

Water Tap on the quay.
Fuel In the village on top of the hill.
Provisions Limited provisions from a shop near the beach. Good shopping in the village at the top of the hill.
Eating out Restaurant and pizzeria on the beach, others in the village.
Other PO. Bank. Bus to Reggio di Calabria at the village.

General

The harbour and fishing village around the coast are most attractive. The fishermen's cottages are built at the water's edge with their fishing boats moored at the 'back door'. Winding staircases lead up the rocky promontory to the village on the top. From the summit the view straight down to the harbour or to the beach on the other side, onto which yet more fishing boats are hauled, is splendid. From here too you can get a good view of the northern approaches to the Strait of Messina. On the top of the crag there is a cave reputed to be that where Scilla dwelt and plucked sailors from passing ships with her seven snapping jaws.

> 'Then Skylla made her strike,
> whisking six of my best men from the ship.
>
> I happened to glance aft at ship and oarsmen
> and caught sight of their arms and legs, dangling
> high overhead. Voices came down to me
> in anguish, calling my name for the last time.
>
> A man surfcasting on a point of rock
> for bass or mackeral, whipping his long rod
> to drop the sinker and bait out,
> will hook a fish and rip it from the surface
> to dangle wriggling in the air
>
> so these
> were borne aloft in spasms towards the cliff.'
>
> *The Odyssey* transl. Robert Fitzgerald

Strait of Messina

See notes in Chapter V, Sicily.

VILLA SAN GIOVANNI

BA 992
Italian 145
⊕ 38°13'·1N 15°38'·0E

A large harbour used by the ferries which cross to Messina. There is a short section of the quay at the N end of the harbour where a yacht can berth but it is very exposed and, worse, the wake caused by the constant comings and goings of the ferries makes it most uncomfortable. A yacht is advised to proceed to Reggio di Calabria. A new basin is under construction to the N of Villa San Giovanni. Further details were not available as we go to print.

REGGIO DI CALABRIA

BA 992
Italian 145

Approach

Between Villa San Giovanni and Reggio di Calabria the coast is built-up and it can be difficult to locate exactly where the harbour is. The ferries and hydrofoils using the harbour are a useful clue to its identification.

Conspicuous A belfry in the town is conspicuous and, closer in, several large warehouses by the harbour and the outer breakwater can be identified.

VHF Ch 11, 16 for port authorities (24hr). Ch 09 for yacht harbour.

Dangers When the tidal stream is running strongly against the wind there is a nasty chop in the approaches to Reggio. Violent gusts also blow down in the approaches.

Mooring

Data Basin: Max LOA 15m. Depths 3–5m.

Berth Turn into the yacht harbour at the N end of the commercial harbour. Go stern or bows-to wherever there is room or where directed on the outer half of the mole. There are laid moorings tailed to the quay. You should not use your own anchor. Berths are difficult to find in July and August, but you may get a berth when charter boats are out.

It is also possible to go alongside the E quay in the commercial harbour. However I have noticed in the past that some very big rats inhabit the warehouses here. Shelter is not as good in the commercial harbour as in the yacht harbour and strong NW winds make it untenable.

Shelter Good shelter. However with moderate to strong winds from the NW there is a considerable surge in here.

Note There are plans to increase the number of yacht berths here by 350. No details were available at the time of writing.

Authorities Harbourmaster and customs. Club attendant. Charge band 2/3.
Dario ✆ 0965 47914

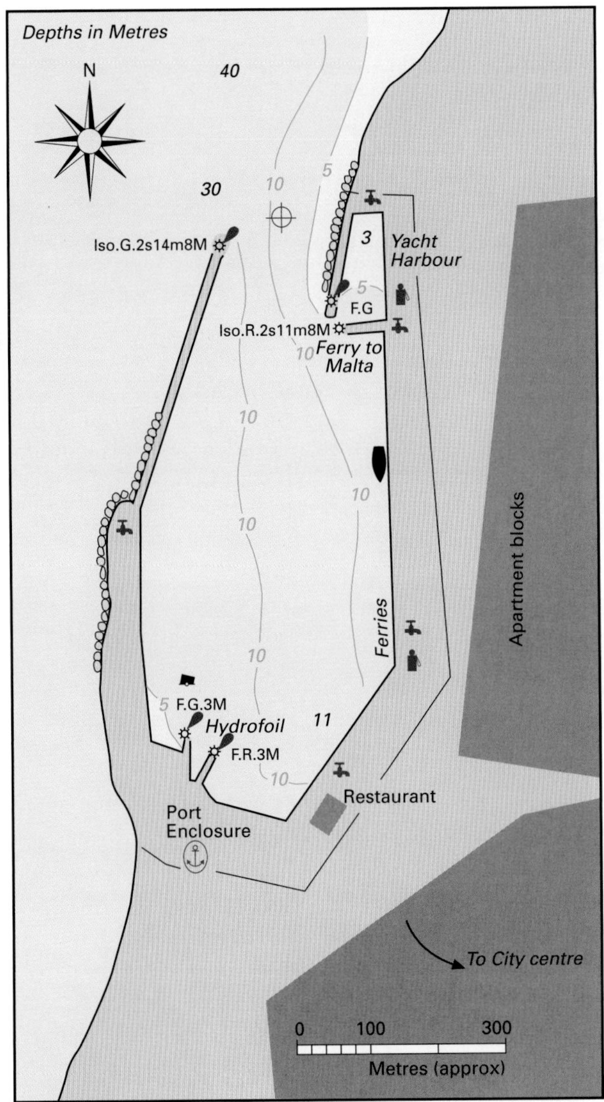

REGGIO DI CALABRIA
⊕38°07′·70N 15°39′·00E WGS84

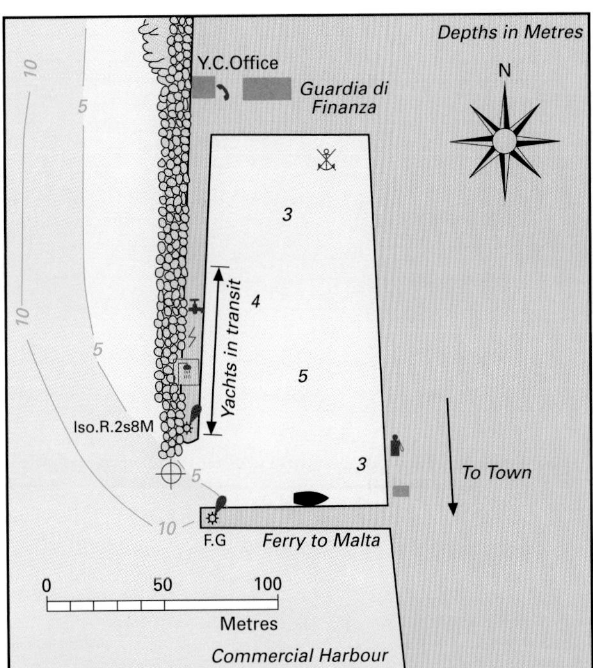

REGGIO DI CALABRIA: YACHT HARBOUR
⊕38°07′·64N 15°39′·09E WGS84

Facilities

Services Water and electricity at or near every berth. The water has been reported non-potable, but has been fine when I used it. Showers and toilets ashore.
Fuel On the quay in the yacht harbour.
Repairs A small yard nearby can haul small to medium-size yachts. Mechanical repairs.
Provisions Excellent shopping in the town about 15 minutes' walk away. In the summer it is a long hot dusty walk to get supplies. Ice can be ordered at the harbour.
Eating out Good restaurants, trattorias and pizzerias in town.
Other PO. Banks. ATMs. The club office will sometimes change money. Metered telephone calls can be made from the club office. Italgaz and Camping Gaz. Hire cars. Ferries to Messina, Siracusa and Malta.

General

Reggio is not the most attractive place but it is the safest and most convenient harbour on the E side of the Strait. Throughout history, if war or pirates did not ravage the town then an earthquake would flatten it. The last severe earthquake in 1980 killed 5,000 and seriously damaged every house that was not completely destroyed. It was heavily bombed in the second world war and most of the buildings of low aspect and reputed to be earthquake-proof (cf. Messina) date from the post-war period. The town is also reputed to be one of the principal recruiting grounds for the Calabrian Ndrangheta. That said, the town has a certain charm and an excellent museum where the Greek bronze statues (Bronzi di Riace) are exhibited.

Saverio, taxi-driver, sometime *ormeggiatori*, fixer and supplier of liquid victuals and morning croissants, has been around Reggio for at least 25 years. In my experience he has the cheapest slabs of beer and can find some excellent *parmigiano reggiano*. Say hello to him – he is a part of Reggio and most of us who travel down this way have looked forward to seeing him here over the years.

The yacht basin at Reggio di Calabria looking S towards the entrance

IV.

Sardinia (Sardegna)

After Sicily, Sardinia is the largest island in the Mediterranean and, for most people, it is a giant question mark in the middle of the sea. Some will know of the Aga Khan's development of the Costa Smeralda, some of the bandits that occasionally make the headlines, and some of the strange stone fortresses called *nuraghs* dating from around 1000BC. Sardinia is a mysterious island for most people, a dark undiscovered place that is a part of Italy yet apart from it, an island colonised but never dominated, a Christian land that exudes paganism; and, for the yachtsman, a cruising ground difficult to better in the western Mediterranean. It is one of my favourite islands and the best part of Italy, if indeed it can be called a part of Italy at all.

The island has an area of 9,300 square miles, nearly three times the size of Corsica, and a population of almost 1½ million. It lies 112 miles from the Italian mainland, seven miles from Corsica and 120 miles from north Africa. There are approximately 1,150 miles of coastline if you count all the bumps and bays along the way. A large part of it is hilly and mountainous with the principle range running from north to south down the east coast. The highest peaks are in the Gennargentu range with the highest, Punta la Marmora, reaching 1,834m (6,017ft). Another massif lies in the southwest corner in the Iglesias mining area.

Much of the land is bare rock, useless for agriculture. In the summer it can be very hot and dusty, almost a desert except for stunted *maquis* and prickly pear. In contrast there are woods, mostly holm oak and cork oak, on the east and southwest coasts. The cork oak is cultivated for its valuable bark and interesting souvenirs are fashioned from it.

The Sardinians, like the Sicilians, consider themselves Sards first and Italians second. The island enjoys some autonomy (but not enough, you will be told) yet you feel farther away from Italy than actual geographical distance suggests. The Sards are an independent people, close to Sard tradition and the soil; they are less exuberant, more reserved, and quite unlike the more transient populations of Europe. You won't feel 'at home' quickly but you will be captured, not by bandits, but by the magic of the land and people that seem of another age.

Alghero, looking NE over the town
Aquatica Marina

'It was too lost in the sea to play an important role, too far from the enriching contacts that linked Sicily, for example, with Italy and Africa. Mountainous, excessively divided, a prisoner of its poverty, it was a self-contained world with its own language, customs, archaic economy, and persuasive pastoralism – in some regions remaining as Rome must have found it long ago.'

The Mediterranean World in the Age of Philip II
Braudel

It is changing, but Braudel's words could be used to describe much of Sardinia in the 21st century.

History

Neolithic

The Nuraghese period of Sardinian history has only recently been receiving serious attention. Enduring features of the culture are the many *nuraghs* still standing: great truncated cones of stone blocks built without mortar and serving part as dwelling place and part as fortress. They bear some resemblance to the *Toreen* towers of Corsica, the *talayots* of the Balearics, and the *tholoi* of Mycenae. The earliest date back to 1500BC and the largest extant nuraghs have three central floors and a complex of towers, fosses and galleries. Most *nuraghs* are found inland and on elevations from 160 to 330m (500 to 1,000 feet). There are many examples, with some 7,000 *nuraghs* remaining from an estimated 30,000 sites. *Nuraghs* near to safe harbours can be found at Alghero: Maiori and Tempio di Palmavera; Arzachena: Albucciu; Olbia: Cabus Abbas; and Cala Gonone: Serra Arrios.

Also of interest are the 'tombs of the giants', burial tombs in the shape of a ship, in the hold of which the dead were laid. Associated with the Nuragh culture are numerous artefacts: stone and obsidian tools and small bronze sculptures of original and intriguing design. Statues of warriors, chiefs, shepherds, animals and ships can be found in the museum at Cagliari and replicas can be bought in many of the tourist shops.

Nuragh inland from Porto Torres

Phoenicians

The Phoenicians provided the first written history of the island. Numerous architectural remains can be found on San Pietro and Sant' Antioco Island, including the enclosures where children were sacrificed to Baal and Tanit. An interesting aside is a slight similarity between Maltese and Sard words where the *x* is pronounced as *sh:* the Maltese language claims some of its origin from Phoenician, and perhaps so may the old Sard language.

Romans

238BC. Between the first and second Punic Wars the Romans landed and eventually conquered the coastal regions. The Sards retreated to the eastern mountains and established themselves there, an area the Romans called Barbaria after the wild inhabitants they could never fully conquer. Roman architecture can be found all around the coast but the best examples are at Cagliari, Nora (Capo Pula), Sant' Antioco Island, Tharros and Porto Torres. Over the centuries a rise in the sea level has covered whole districts of some of these ruins, particularly Nora, Tharros and Olbia. At Nora and Tharros in calm weather the ruins can be seen beneath the sea.

Middle Ages

Until the Genoese and the Pisans arrived, Sardinia was ravaged, like so much of the Mediterranean, by the Vandals, Byzantines, Saracens and Arabs. The indigenous Sards retreated from the shores to the mountains and only under the rule of the Pisans and later the Aragonese and Spanish did life become more ordered. The poverty of Sardinia has meant that much of the Romanesque style of architecture introduced by the Pisans has remained virtually unadulterated by later generations and many fine examples are to be found, especially the churches.

Modern history

In 1708 Cagliari surrendered to the English fleet and Sardinia was ceded to Austria. In 1720, after the Treaty of London, Sardinia came under the sway of the Dukes of Savoy and it has since remained a part of Italy. In the 19th century a network of roads was begun, but Sardinia remained very much a forgotten part of Italy. To Nelson it was anything but unimportant. HM Denham writes at length on Nelson and the various anchorages utilised when blockading the French in 1804. Nelson attempted to persuade the British government to annex the island, writing to Lord Hobart: 'If we could possess one island, Sardinia, we should want neither Malta nor any other; this which is the finest island in the Mediterranean possesses harbours fit for arsenals and of a capacity to hold our Navy within 24 hours sail of Toulon'. Nelson used the anchorages at La Maddalena (Agincourt Sound in the vicinity of Palau and the fleet anchorage between Caprera and the Saline Gulf), Aranci Bay, Cape Pula, Palmas Bay,

Carloforte and Oristano. Yet, despite Nelson's knowledge of the coast, he never stepped ashore during this whole period in order not to violate the neutrality of the Kingdom of Sardinia in the Anglo-French war.

In 1948 Sardinia was granted political autonomy. In the post-war period the swamps were drained to rid the island of malaria; up until the Second World War Sardinia was the worst affected area of Italy. In the 1960s the Aga Khan began developing the Costa Smeralda and other Italian and international development companies have followed his lead. As yet development is largely confined to the NE of the island and it remains one of the least spoilt islands in the western Mediterranean.

Bandits

From Roman times, the rugged slopes under the Supramonte, the backbone of Sardinia, have been home to people unwilling to conform to outside influences. The Romans were unable to quell them and called them Barbarie – consequently the region became known as Barbagia – an indication of the nature of the people. Mostly shepherding families, they were not averse to rustling sheep, not from neighbours you understand, but those of the next valley perhaps. Resulting feuds turned bloody and escalated, occasionally entire families would be annhililated. Some commentators draw parallels with the revenge and protection operations of mafia groups, but most tend to romanticise them more.

During the post war years the 'bandits', partly driven by similar independence demands as their Corsican counterparts, diversified into kidnapping of wealthy individuals, or their children, for ransom. The odd tourist coach also was targeted. Mesina Graziano 'the Scarlet Rose' with his cult Robin Hood ethos, daring prison breaks and womanising reputation, became the most notorious bandit of all.

High up in the hills, Orgosolo is the village most associated with Sard banditry, and until he was murdered in 2007, was home to the octagenarian poet Peppino Marotto. His murder, as the old man fetched his morning paper, marked the end of a 50-year vendetta. Since the 1960s and 70s many of the dull grey walls of the village houses have been painted with murals in Cubist style, originally to celebrate the 30th VE anniversary. They have been much added to, and carry various messages of local and world events, some bright, some brooding, some carry the lyrics of the late poet, and the whole is attracting tourists to the 'bandit village'. In reality, unless you are a Rothschild or royalty, there is little chance you will be kidnapped, and for me the journey up the narrow zig-zag roads was far more threatening than the friendly locals.

Folklore

Locked in by its poverty, Sardinia has a strong religious tradition and there are numerous interesting festivals. Perhaps the best known and most spectacular is that held on 1 May in honour of Sant' Efisio at Cagliari. Three centuries ago Sant' Efisio interceded to stop the plague and a vow was made to honour this intercession every year. Thousands turn out in national and other elaborate costumes reminiscent of the Middle Ages: mounted knights, jugglers and harlequins accompany the gilded coach containing the saint's effigy. Other festivals are the Cavalcade at Sassari (May), the festival of the Redeemer at Nuoro (29 August), the Candelieri at Sassari (14 August), the Ardia, a highly

Shoestring cruising in Sardinia

Marinas and harbours

Marinas in Sardinia can be very expensive in the high season. Even some superyachts think twice about berthing in marinas around the Costa Smeralda. Marinas on the E coast S of Capo Coda Cavallo are reasonable as are a number of marinas on the S coast. There are also some reasonable deals at Oristano and Alghero on the W coast and in places like Castelsardo on the N coast.

Basically it is a matter of finding out what the high season charges are and working out a strategy from there. You can cruise most of the coast using just anchorages with maybe a few stops in marinas over the longer stretches in places like Porto Torres, Castelsardo and Cala Mangiavolpe on the N coast, Olbia, La Caletta, Arbatax, and Porto Corallo on the E coast, Cagliari and Porto Teulada on the S coast, and Carloforte (on the public quay), Portoscuso, Torre Grande, and Alghero (on the town quay or negotiate at the pontoons) on the W coast.

Anchorages

Around Sardinia there are good anchorages in the N and S and some down the W and E coasts.

North coast

On the N coast there are numerous anchorages around the coast and off-lying islands. Some of these around the La Maddalena group are now designated as marine reserves and you can only pick up moorings for which a charge is made. There are still sufficient anchorages around La Maddalena and Caprera so that you do not have to use moorings, though you should take care not to anchor on Posidonia sea grass which is the habitat the moorings are preserving. A cursory look at the pilot will show you that you can pretty much traverse the whole northern coast using anchorages and there are enough places affording good shelter for this not to be a problem even in bad weather. If it does blow up in an unsuitable anchorage there are useful marinas nearby.

East coast

On the E coast there are again a good selection of anchorages as far as Capo Coda Cavallo S of Olbia. After that the coast straightens out and there are few good anchorages until you turn the corner at Capo Carbonara. You can anchor off Arbatax and try Frailis and Pira in calm weather.

South coast

On the S coast you can anchor off near the entrance to Villasimius and then there is not much until Malfatano and Teulada (it shallows quickly in the bay to the N).

West coast

On the W coast anchoring in Carloforte is now sadly prohibited. Try anchoring just S of Calasetta although depths come up quickly. From here it is a long haul up to Oristano where you anchor under Capo San Marco although some swell tends to creep around into the anchorage. Going N there is Bosa Marina and then Porto Conte where the best anchorage is usually N of Porto Conte Marina.

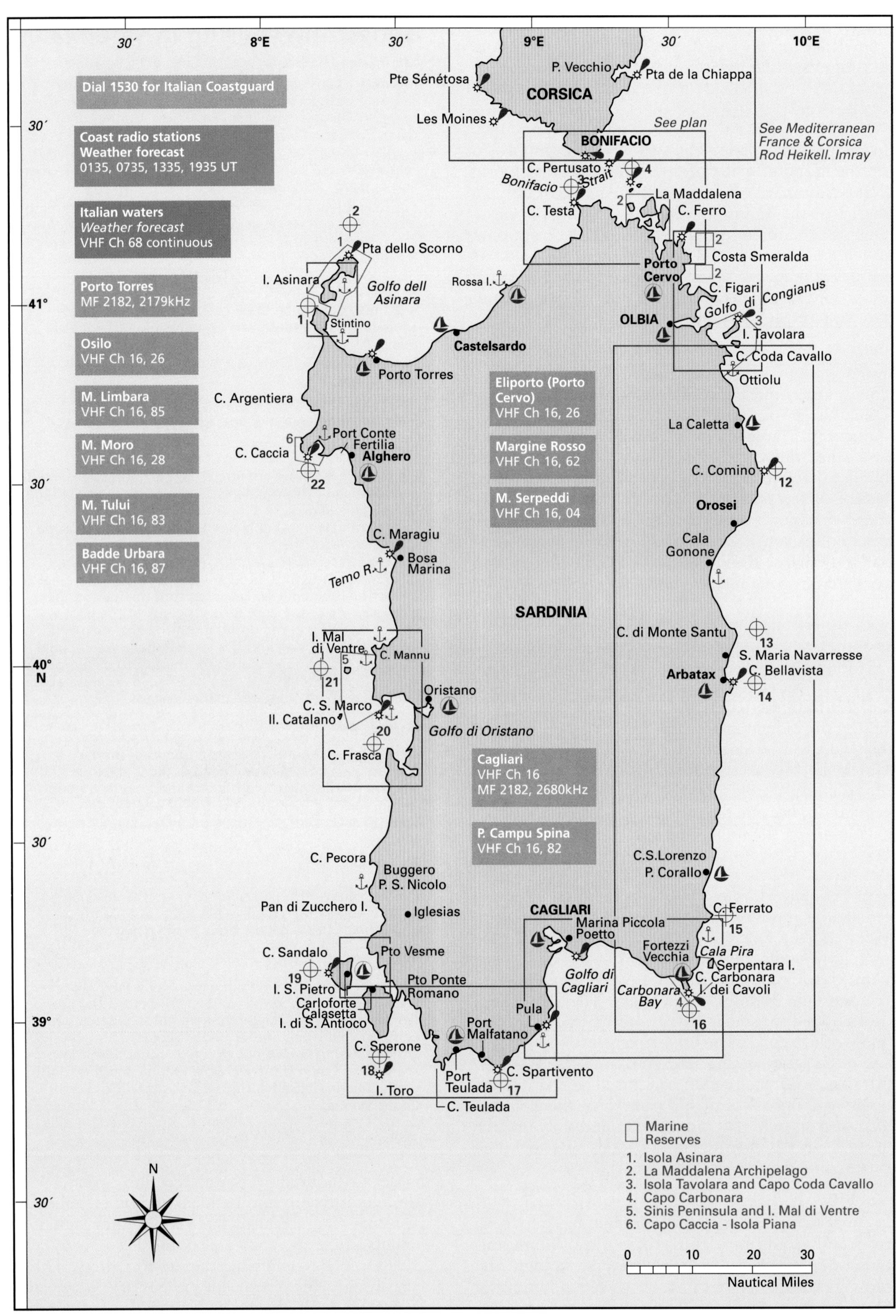

Dial 1530 for Italian Coastguard
Coast radio stations
Weather forecast
0135, 0735, 1335, 1935 UT
Italian waters
Weather forecast
VHF Ch 68 continuous
Porto Torres
MF 2182, 2179kHz
Osilo
VHF Ch 16, 26
M. Limbara
VHF Ch 16, 85
M. Moro
VHF Ch 16, 28
M. Tului
VHF Ch 16, 83
Badde Urbara
VHF Ch 16, 87
Eliporto (Porto Cervo)
VHF Ch 16, 26
Margine Rosso
VHF Ch 16, 62
M. Serpeddi
VHF Ch 16, 04
Cagliari
VHF Ch 16
MF 2182, 2680kHz
P. Campu Spina
VHF Ch 16, 82
CORSICA
SARDINIA
BONIFACIO
See plan
See Mediterranean France & Corsica Rod Heikell. Imray
Bonifacio Strait
Golfo dell Asinara
Golfo di Oristano
Golfo di Congianus
Golfo di Cagliari
Carbonara Bay
Marine Reserves
1. Isola Asinara
2. La Maddalena Archipelago
3. Isola Tavolara and Capo Coda Cavallo
4. Capo Carbonara
5. Sinis Peninsula and I. Mal di Ventre
6. Capo Caccia - Isola Piana
Nautical Miles

USEFUL WAYPOINTS

⊕1 1M W of Capo Falcone
40°58'·3N 08°10'·7E

⊕2 5M N of Pta della Scorno light – I. Asinara
41°12'·1N 08°19'·1E

⊕3 1M N of Capo Testa light
41°15'·6N 09°08'·7E

⊕4 1M N of light on Isola Razzoli
41°19'·4N 09°20'·4E

⊕5 0·2M N of Pta Sardegna light
41°12'·61N 09°21'·77E WGS84

⊕6 Capo d'Orso - Pta Fico Fairway
41°10'·65N 09°25'·82E WGS84

⊕7 2M N of Pta Galera – I. Caprera
41°16'·9N 09°27'·8E

⊕8 Bisce Channel Mid-Channel
41°09'·57N 09°31'·63E WGS84

⊕9 1M E of light on I. Mortoriotto – Costa Smeralda
41°05'·2N 09°38'·5E

⊕10 1M E of Capo Figari
40°59'·7N 09°41'·2E

⊕11 1M N of Pta Timone – I. Tavolara 40°56'·5N 09°44'·2E

⊕12 0·4M E of Capo Comino light
40°31'·77N 09°50'·37E WGS84

⊕13 1M E of Capo di Monte Santu
40°04'·6N 09°45'·8E

⊕14 0·25M E of Capo Bellavista light
39°55'·78N 09°43'·33E WGS84

⊕15 1M E of Capo Ferrato light
39°17'·9N 09°39'·4E

⊕16 2M S of Secca di S. Caterina – Capo Carbonara
39°03'·0N 09°29'·7E

⊕17 1M S of Capo Spartivento
38°51'·49N 08°50'·69E WGS84

⊕18 2M N of I. del Toro
38°53'·64N 08°24'·58E WGS84

⊕19 2M W of Capo Sandalo – I. S. Pietro 39°08'·8N 08°10'·8E

⊕20 3M W of Capo Frasca
39°46'·1N 08°23'·5E

⊕21 3M W of I. Mal di Ventre
39°59'·5N 08°14'·3E

⊕22 1M S of Capo Caccia
40°32'·6N 08°09'·8E

Data

NOTE

This chapter is arranged clockwise around the island as follows:

1. **North coast**: Isola Asinara to Capo Ferro
2. **East coast**: Capo Ferro to Capo Carbonara
3. **South coast**: Capo Carbonara to Capo Sperone
4. **West coast**: Capo Sperone to Isola Asinara

MAJOR LIGHTS

North coast

I. Asinara (Punta Dello Scorno) Fl(4)20s80m16M
Porto Torres LFl(2)10s45m16M
Capo Testa Fl(3)12s67m22M
I. Razzoli. NW point Fl.WR.2.5s77m19/15M
I. Santa Maria. Punta Filetto Fl(4)20s17m10M
Punta Sardegna Fl.5s38m11M
Capo d'Orso Fl.3s12m10M
I. Monaci Fl.WR.5s24m11/8M
Capo Ferro Fl(3)15s52m24M & Oc.R.5s8M. Vis 189°-203°

East coast

Olbia I. Bocca LFl.5s24m15M Horn Mo(B)30s
I. Tavolara. Punta Timone LFl(2)10s72m15M
Capo Bellavista Fl(2)10s165m26M+F.R.145m6M
Capo Comino Fl.5s26m15M
Capo Carbonara Fl.7.5s120m23M

South coast

I. Cavoli Fl(2)WR.10s74m11/8M
Capo Sant'Elia Fl(2)10s70m21M
Capo di Pula Fl(4)15s48m11M
Capo Spartivento Fl(3)15s81m18M
Porto Ponte Romano Fl.5s23m15M

West coast

I. San Pietro. Capo Sandalo Fl(4)20s134m24M
Portoscuso La Ghinghetta Rk Fl(2)WR.10s12m11/8M
I. Piana Fl(2)WR.8s18m7M
Capo Frasca Fl.6s66m11M
Gran Torre Fl.R.5s18m8M
Capo San Marco Fl(2)10s57m22M & LFl.R.5s55m12M
Mal di Ventre Islet Fl.WR.6s26m11/8M
Capo Mannu Fl(3)15s59m15M
Porto Conte Capo Caccia Fl.5s186m24M

PROHIBITED AREAS

See also Marine Reserves below

North coast

1. *La Maddalena* It is prohibited to navigate or berth at the Italian naval base E of Cala Gavetta.
2. *Isola San Stefano* It is prohibited to enter the naval base on the NE corner of San Stefano.

East coast

Tavolara Isola The NE part of the island is a military area. Anchoring prohibited.

South coast

Punta Zari to Isola Rossa At times it is prohibited to anchor in the waters around Capo Teulada and navigation close to the coast may sometimes be prohibited.

West coast

Golfo di Oristano The southern part of the gulf is a firing range. Anchoring prohibited and navigation sometimes prohibited.

MARINE RESERVES (Area Marina Protetta – AMPs) AND NATIONAL PARKS

1. ***Isola Asinara*** A marine nature reserve surrounds the island, including the Fornelli Passage. The outer limits of Zone C lie some 3M N of Pta dello Scorno and 3M W of Pta Salippi on the W coast. On the E coast Zone B/C runs from Pta Negra SW for 2.5M before running around Rada della Reale N to Pta dello Scorno.
2. ***La Maddalena Archipelago National Park***
   All the islands in the archipelago are enclosed by Zone C of the Marine Reserve, leaving one access channel into Cala Gavetta and another which runs between I. S. Stefano, I. La Maddalena and I. Caprera. A third channel runs between I. Pecora and I. Bisce.

   The Southern part of the National Park covers I. Nibani, I. dei Poveri and the area around I. Soffi, I. Mortoris and I. Mortoriotto.

   The restrictions are extensive and complicated, and are detailed in a full section within the pilotage notes for the area.
3. ***Isola Tavolara and Capo Coda Cavallo Marine Reserve***
   The extent of the Marine Reserve (Zone C) runs from Capo Ceraso to just N of Pta d'Ottiolu on the Sardinian coast, and encloses Isola Tavolara and I. Molarotto. Zone A covers the NE corner of I. Tavolara and the sea surrounding I. Molarotto.
4. ***Capo Carbonara Marine Reserve***
   The marine reserve Zone C runs from I. Serpentara around the coast to Capo Boi. The W side of I. Serpentara is in Zone A. The E coast of the island, along with Secca di Berni and the area around Capo Carbonara and I. dei Cavoli are in Zone B.
5. ***Sinis Peninsula and Isola Mal di Ventre Marine Reserve***
   The boundary of Zone C runs from immediately W of Torre Grande SW to 1.5M S of Capo San Marco, E to 08°14 .0E and N to 40°01 .9N (around Il Catalano and I. Mal di Ventre) before rejoining the coast S of Capo Sa Sturaggia. Zone A areas:
   1. W side of I. Mal di Ventre
   2. Il Catalano
6. ***Capo Caccia – Isola Piana Marine Reserve***
   A reserve covering the area from Capo Galera, past Capo Caccia and Isola Piana and up to Punta delle Gessiere, including Porto Conte.

Quick reference guide

	Shelter	Mooring	Fuel	Water	Eating out	Provisions	Plan	Charge band
North coast								
Ancora YC	B	A	O	A	C	B	•	
Stintino	A	AC	A	A	B	B	•	5
Porto Torres	A	AB	A	A	A	B	•	4
Castelsardo	B	A	B	A	A	B	•	4
Porto Marina Isola Rossa	B	B	A	A	B	B	•	4
La Colba Baia (Capo Testa)	O	C	O	O	O	O	•	
Reparata Baia (Capo Testa)	B	C	O	O	O	O	•	
S. Teresa di Gallura	A	AC	A	A	B	B	•	5
Porto Quadro	O	C	O	O	O	O		
Baia Marmorata	O	C	O	O	O	O		
Porto Pozzo	B	C	O	B	C	C	•	
Liscia	C	C	O	O	O	O	•	
Porto Pollo	B	C	O	O	O	O	•	
Porto Rafael YC	B	AC	O	A	O	O	•	
Palau	A	A	A	A	B	A	•	5
G. delle Saline	C	C	O	A	O	O		
Cala Bitta	A	AB	O	A	O	C	•	
Cannigione	A	A	A	A	B	B	•	5
Poltu Quatu	A	A	A	A	C	C	•	5
Liscia di Vacca	O	C	O	O	O	C	•	
I. Razzoli								
Cala Lunga	C	C	O	O	O	O	•	
Cala Giorgio Marina	C	C	O	O	O	O		
I. Santa Maria								
Cala Santa Maria	C	C	O	O	O	O	•	
I. Budelli								
Cala Sud	C	C	O	O	O	O		
I. Spargi								
Cala d'Alga	C	C	O	O	O	O		
Cala Corsara	C	C	O	O	O	O		
Cala Ferrigno	C	C	O	O	O	O		
I. La Maddalena								
Cala Gavetta	A	A	A	A	A	A	•	5
Marina del Ponte	B	A	O	B	B	B	•	5/6
Cala Nido d'Aquila	C	C	O	O	O	O		6+
Cala Francese	B	C	O	O	O	O	•	
Stagno Torte	O	C	O	O	O	O	•	
Porto Massimo	A	A	O	A	C	C	•	6+
Cala Spalmatore	B	C	O	O	O	C	•	
I. San Stefano								
Cala Villamarina	B	BC	O	O	O	O	•	
I. Caprera								
Porto Garibaldi	B	C	O	O	O	O	•	
Cala Stagnali	B	C	O	O	O	O		
Porto Palma	B	C	O	O	O	O	•	
I. Porco	C	C	O	O	O	O		
Cala Portese	O	C	O	O	O	O		
Cala Brigantine	C	C	O	O	O	O		
Cala Coticcio	B	C	O	O	O	O	•	
East coast								
Cala Granu	O	C	O	O	O	O		
Porto Cervo	A	A	A	A	B	A	•	6+
G. Pero	O	C	O	O	O	O		
Porto Liccia	O	C	O	O	O	O		
Romazzino	C	C	O	O	O	O		
Cala di Volpe	B	C	O	O	C	O	•	
I. Mortorio anchorages	O	C	O	O	O	O		
Cala Petra Ruja	O	C	O	O	O	O		
Marina di Portisco	A	A	A	A	B	B	•	6+
Porto di Cugnana	C	C	O	O	O	O	•	
Porto Asfodelli	B	A	O	A	C	C	•	
Porto Rotondo	A	A	A	A	C	B	•	6+
Porto Oro	A	A	O	A	C	C		
Punta Marana	A	A	A	A	C	C	•	5
G. di Marinella	O	C	O	O	O	O		
C.N Marinella	B	A	O	A	O	C		
YC Vela Blu	B	A	O	A	O	C		
Golfo Aranci	C	AC	A	B	C	C	•	1/3
Baia Caddinas	A	A	O	A	O	C	•	
Olbia	A	AB	A	A	A	A	•	6+
Liscia delle Saline	C	C	O	O	O	O		
Porto Costa Corallina	B	A	O	B	O	C		
Porto Istana	C	C	O	O	O	O		
Porto della Taverna	C	C	O	O	O	O		
Cala Coda Cavallo	B	C	O	O	O	O		
Porto Brandinghi	B	C	O	O	O	O	•	
Marina di Puntaldia	A	A	A	A	C	C	•	5
Ottiolu	A	A	A	A	C	C	•	5
La Caletta	A	A	A	A	C	B	•	4
Cala Gonone	B	A	O	A	C	B	•	4
Sta Maria Navarrese	A	A	A	A	C	C	•	4
Arbatax	A	AB	B	A	B	B	•	4
Porto Frailis	C	C	O	B	O	C	•	
Porto Corallo	A	A	O	A	C	C	•	4
Cala Pira	O	C	O	O	O	O	•	
Porto Giunco	O	C	O	O	O	O		
South coast								
Villasimius	A	A	A	A	C	C	•	5/6
Baia Carbonara	C	C	O	O	O	O		
Marina de Capitana	A	A	A	A	C	C	•	4
Marina Piccolo Poetta	A	A	A	A	A	A	•	4/5
Cagliari	A	A	A	A	A	A	•	5
Perd'e' Sali	B	A	A	A	B	B	•	5
Cala Verde	A	A	O	A	C	C	•	4/5
Porto Malfatano	B	C	O	O	O	O	•	
Porto Teulada	A	A	B	A	O	O	•	5
Porto Ponte Romano	A	B	B	A	C	C	•	1
West coast								
Calasetta	A	A	B	A	C	C	•	5
Carloforte	A	A	A	A	A	A	•	3/5
Porto Vesme	B	B	B	B	C	C	•	
Portoscuso	A	A	B	A	B	C	•	4
Buggeru	B	AB	O	A	C	C	•	
Golfo di Oristano								
Capo S. Marco	C	C	O	O	O	O		
Porto Turistico Torre Grande	A	A	A	A	O	C	•	4
Torre Grande	C	C	O	O	C	C		
Porto d'Oristano	A	BC	O	A	O	O	•	
I. Mal di Ventre	O	C	O	O	O	O		
Bosa Marina	B	AC	B	A	A	B	•	4
Temo river	A	B	A	B	B	B	•	
Alghero	A	A	A	A	A	A	•	5
Fertilia	A	A	B	A	C	C	•	5
Porto Conte Marina	B	A	A	A	C	C	•	5

Routes

Routes around Sardinia are often part of a passage either E-going or W-going. Yachts leaving from the Balearics or Spain will often head for either the Strait of Bonifacio and one of the harbours around the northern coast of Sardinia or head for the SW corner of Sardinia, usually Carloforte. It is best to time the arrival by day, especially in the Strait of Bonifacio, as there are a lot of dangers to navigation around. A night approach is possible at Carloforte, though you should be cautious. Yachts heading W will often leave from Palermo or Capo San Vito heading for the SE corner of Sardinia, usually somewhere like Villasimius or Cagliari. There are enough well lit places here to make a night approach feasible. Alternatively yachts on the W coast of Italy will often leave from around Gaeta or Ponza heading for somewhere like Porto Cervo or Olbia. If heading for the Strait of Bonifacio again it is best to time the arrival for daylight hours.

From the S of Sardinia it is also possible to head for Tunisia, often heading for Ile de la Galite, Bizerte or one of the marinas on the SE side of Cap Bon.

Yachts sailing around Sardinia will usually do two sides of the rectangle, as it were. So yachts might arrive from the W in the Strait of Bonifacio and potter around the N and E coasts before jumping off to Sicily or might arrive from the E and potter up the E and N coasts before leaving for points further W. Few yachts cruise the W coast although there is no good reason not to.

dangerous horse race at Sedilo (6 and 7 July), and the Sartilla, a medieval procession and jousting match at Oristano (carnival time).

Fishing

The great *mattanzas*, the long permanent tunny nets that were a navigational hazard off parts of the coast, are no longer laid in the numbers they once were. Various reasons are given: the tunny have changed their migration route so they no longer pass close to the coast; pollution and over-fishing have drastically reduced the numbers of tunny; the cost of laying and supervising the *mattanza* is now prohibitive and industrial methods of catching tunny such as purse-seine netting and long-lining, make the *mattanza* redundant. The *mattanza* nets are now laid in just a few places on the SW coast.

The decline of the Northern Blue Fin tuna, *Thunnus thynnus*, to the point of extinction, is largely down to massive over fishing by commercial ships using the latest technology, both legal and illegal, to ensure the maximum (short-term) return on their investment. Lack of political will to curb quotas, and the fact that quotas are regularly exceeded, means this magnificent fish will not be around much longer. Best estimates put it at around 10 years. The laying of the *mattanzas* is viewed by conservation groups as an acceptable traditional method of catching tuna, where selection is possible and numbers are limited. It is also becoming an attraction to tourists who want to see the drama and machismo of the Rais (head fisherman) and the teamwork of the Tonnarotti. This year Italy banned its purse-seiners from joining the annual month-long bluefin fishing season, and has recently indicated it will support a vote on the immediate worldwide ban on the trade in Bluefin tuna. It remains to be seen whether this ban will become reality.

For more information on fisheries and sustainability see
www.endoftheline.com
www.wwf.panda.org
www.slowfood.com/slowfish

Compared with the mainland coast there are few fishing boats, large or small, in Sardinia. Most of the trawlers operating from the south and east coasts are from the mainland. In the north long-lining trawlers operate from Porto Torres from June until October before returning to mainland Italy.

There is good underwater fishing in the seas around Sardinia, though remember you are not allowed to spear fish using bottles.

Food

The saffron crocus is cultivated in Sardinia so, not surprisingly, this spice features in a number of dishes. A minute amount is used to flavour and colour dishes of semolina, rice, fish and even tripe. Semolina, although not peculiar to Sardinia, is quite popular especially in *sa simbula fritta* and *su farri*. An unusual pasta popular in Sardinia is *malloreddus*, small dumplings with sausage meat. *Paella,* which is served with delicious sauces of seafood and flavoured with saffron represents the Spanish influence which is very strong on the west coast of Sardinia. A typical Sardinian dish also of Spanish descent is *faina* made from *garbanzos*; these are thick pancakes which are made from chick pea flour and fried in oil.

Some of the more typical Sardinian dishes which you are likely to encounter are: *pane de gherda*, flaky pastry patties of cheese, bacon and onion; *su pilaf*, rice with sauce of lobster, prawns or octopus; *cullingio mis*, a kind of ravioli filled with cheese and meat; and *buttarigia*, compressed dried bass or mullet eggs seasoned with olive oil and lemon.

Seafood around Sardinia is abundant and the local fish soup called *ziminu* which theoretically should have 12 different varieties of fish in it, but rarely has, should not be missed. Lobster is recommended (if you are feeling extremely rich on the night) especially when cooked in a sauce of its own eggs. So also is catfish stewed in a sauce of oil, pine nuts, garlic, nutmeg, bread crumbs and vinegar. However, you will be lucky to find these exotic dishes on the average restaurant menu. Around most of the coast mainland dishes have been adopted by the restaurants, though with the good local ingredients available you will not be disappointed by them.

There are many excellent cheeses such as *pecorino sardo*, a hard sheep's milk cheese, *gioddù*, similar to the Greek *feta* and *sù casu marzu*.

Some of the best known sweets are: *sabada* a soft cheese rolled in pastry, *pardulas*, *zippulas* and *coccias de saba*.

Sardinia produces wine of good quaffable quality and is noted for its dessert wines, especially the honey-coloured Vernaccia of Oristano. Normal reds and whites include Anghelu Ruiu (red) and Torbato (white) from Alghero and Aleatico and Cannonau.

North coast – Isola Asinara to Capo Ferro

The N coast of Sardinia between Isola Asinara and Capo Ferro forms the S side of the Bonifacio Strait. It is bordered by numerous islands which are in turn bordered by even more numerous rocks and reefs. The Bonifacio Strait (Bocche di Bonifacio) is used by a large number of merchant vessels and ferries as well as pleasure craft and it is also the graveyard of considerable numbers of them. The latter fact has caused the authorities to ban ULCCs and VLCCs and there are now moves afoot to ban all tankers carrying oil or other products which could damage the waters and coast if there was an accident or a spill. The Bonifacio Strait has an evil and well-deserved reputation in a strong *libeccio* or *mistral* and yachtsmen attempting to cruise around these waters for the first time are well advised to exercise some caution. To temper this harsh warning I will add that the northern coast and offlying islands offer a superb cruising ground with numerous attractive anchorages and safe harbours. It should not be missed.

Weather patterns on the north coast

In the summer, winds from the NW predominate and blow through the Strait from the NW–W with considerable strength, often getting up to Force 5–6. Off Isola Asinara there are frequently calms when it is blowing strongly further N and E in the Strait. Around La Maddalena there are frequently SE and SW winds. With NW winds, a long sea rolls in whereas easterlies kick up a short chop. Winds in spring are most frequent from the NW and NE and again blow with some strength. In autumn, winds are predominantly from the NW and SE. At this time a moderate SE wind can quickly reverse and blow very strongly from the NW, sometimes at gale force. In winter the worst gales are generally from the NW and NE. A *mistral* sends very heavy seas into the Strait.

Currents

Currents in the Strait follow the prevailing winds but are diverted by the numerous islands and headlands. The currents are variable in direction and strength, but since most navigation in the Strait is of the 'eyeball' variety, they can generally be ignored.

Isola Asinara

This bleak island lies off the NW extremity of Sardinia separated by the Fornelli Passage. There are four groups of hills on the island of no great height, the highest being Monte Scomunica on the N end at 408m (1,339ft). The coast is everywhere rocky with low cliffs.

A national park since 1997, Asinara also became a marine reserve in 2003. The reserve area covers the whole island and the surrounding waters. The island has been in relative isolation for over a century. It

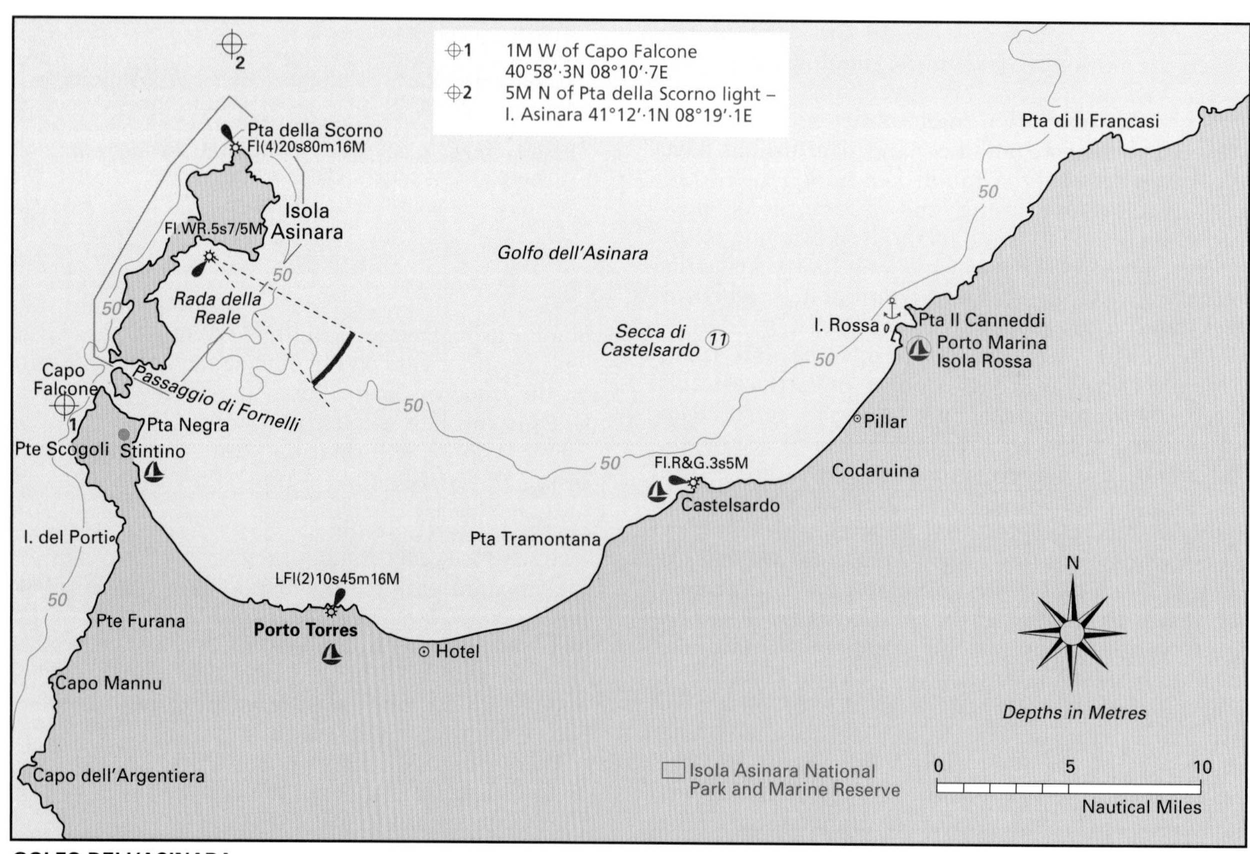

GOLFO DELL'ASINARA

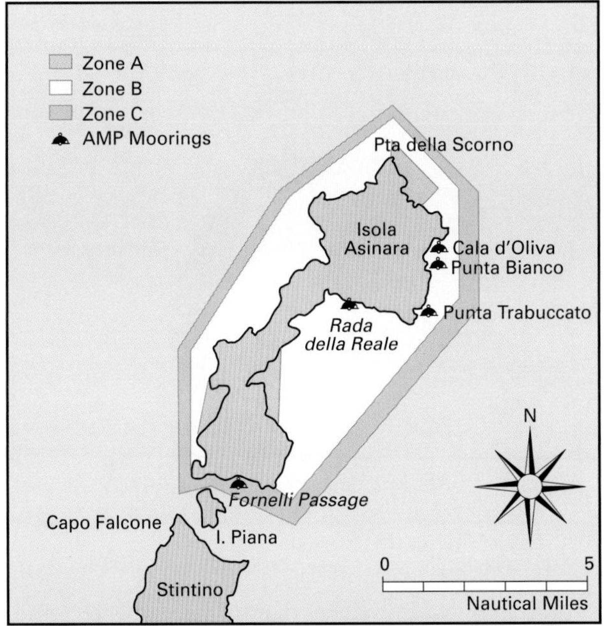

ISOLA ASINARA NATIONAL PARK AND MARINE RESERVE

Isola Asinara National Park and Marine Reserve

In 2003 the island became a marine reserve and navigation in surrounding waters is subject to regulation except in emergencies or when authorised. Landing on Isola Piana is prohibited.

At present there are three areas classified as Zone A:

- the area to the NE of Punta dello Scorno
- Cala Scombro di Dentro on the east coast
- Cala Scombro di Fuoro on the west coast, between Punta Pedra Bianca and Punta Agnadda.

The rest of the marine reserve area is Zone B and C.

At the time of writing the following regulations were in force, but they may be subject to change in the future.

Zone A
Navigation, short- and long-time stays, anchoring, mooring, swimming, diving, any kind of fishing prohibited.

Zone B
Permitted: swimming, diving, navigation under sail and with oars. Mooring is allowed in areas with mooring buoys laid out by the park authorities. Any type of motor navigation is prohibited.

Zone C
Navigation under sail and with oars permitted. Motor boats subject to regulation by park authorities. All types of fishing prohibited.

Fees €3.50/m

Asinara Marina VHF Ch 74 ✆ 079 512 290 / 348 691 3528
Email info@cormoranomarina.it

✆ 079 503 388
Email parco@asinara.org
www.parcoasinara.org

has been a quarantine island, then a first world war POW camp, and later a 'super-prison' for organised crime until the prison closed and the reserve was established.

Fornelli passage

This shallow passage (least depth 3m) between the NW corner of Sardinia and Isola Asinara is a useful short-cut saving over 20 miles compared to

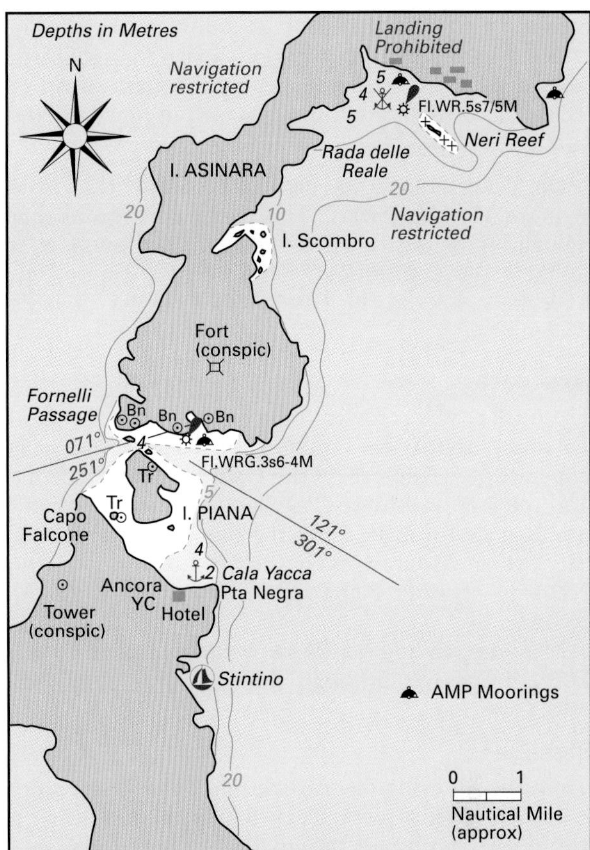

FORNELLI PASSAGE

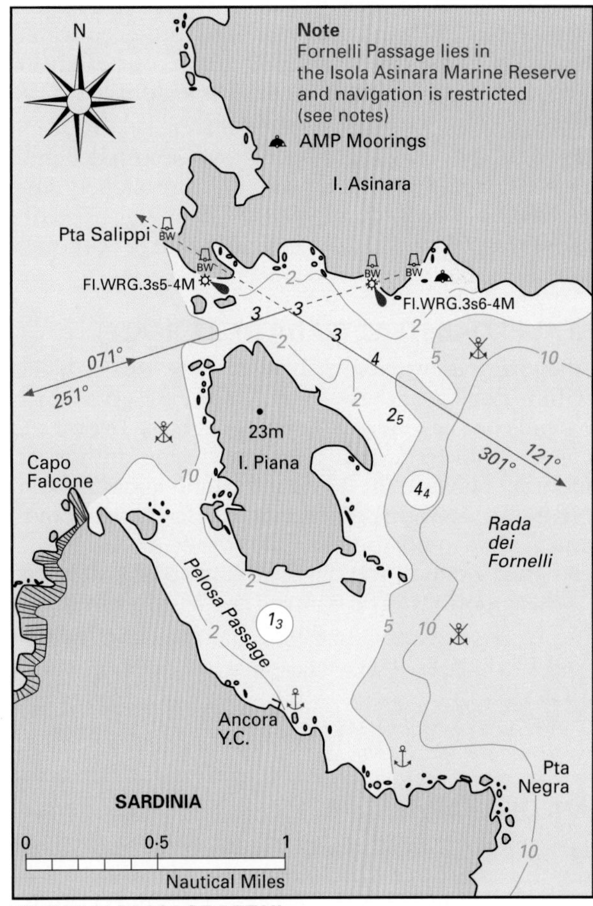

FORNELLI PASSAGE DETAIL

rounding Isola Asinara itself. It should not be used in strong westerly or easterly winds when the swell will reduce the effective depths. A tidal stream of up to 2kns may flow through the passage but normally the current is negligible.

Note The passage is partially within the Isola Asinara Marine Reserve. This technically means that navigation is restricted in this area, though it is unlikely the authorities will object. Park moorings have been laid in the bay on the S coast of Isola Asinara.

Approach

From the W, a tower on the summit of Capo Falcone, about one mile S of its extremity, is conspicuous. A tower on the E side of Capo Falcone and the fort on Monte Castellaccio on Isola Asinara are also useful in locating the passage. From the E the fort on Monte Castellaccio and a tower on the NE side of Isola Piana are useful in locating the passage.

Masonry leading marks show the passage through Fornelli Passage although they are difficult to see until close in.

Passage

From the W, bring the leading marks (two off-white masonry beacons with black bands) into transit on about 071° until past the small islet off the NW end of Isola Piana. The islet must be left to port. When the second set of leading marks are in transit turn onto about 121° and continue until into deep water. From the E, use the reciprocals of the courses given. The least depth of 3m is just off the small islet at the western entrance to Fornelli Passage.

By night The passage is lit by two sectored lights: Fl.WRG.3s6-4M show the E approaches and Fl.WRG.3s5-4M for the W side. The white sectors show the safe channel through the passage, although a night passage is not recommended.

REALE ROADSTEAD (RADA DELLE REALE)

Anchoring is prohibited in Rada delle Reale. It lies within Zone B of the Asinara Marine Reserve which extends out beyond the Neri Reef at least 1M off the coast. Mooring is only permitted using authorised mooring buoys in the N of the bay and in bays on the NE coast. Navigation is restricted (see notes above) and Cala Scombri in the SW corner of the bay is classified Zone A, where all navigation is prohibited.

The moorings area is open E–SW. Moorings can be booked through Porto Torres Cormorano Marina. Charge band 3.

VHF Ch 74.

✆ 079 512 290, *Mobile* 348 691 3528
www.asinaramarina.com

ANCORA YACHT CLUB

Just under 1M W of Pta Negro there is a small private harbour sheltered by a breakwater approximately 150m long. There are reported to be mostly 2m depths inside going down to 1m but silting may well reduce depths here. Water and electricity on the quay. The harbour has been constructed privately but visitors can usually find a berth on the end of the breakwater. The club is a friendly place and the setting really quite beautiful.

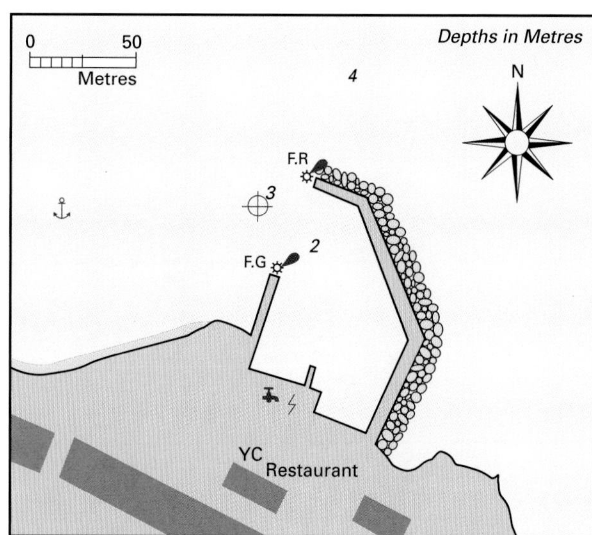

ANCORA YACHT CLUB
⊕40°57´·6N 08°13´·1E

Anchorage

In fine weather a yacht can anchor off the hotel in Cala Yacca. The bottom is sand – good holding. Ashore there is a fine sandy beach. Strictly speaking it is prohibited to anchor here but in the summer the authorities don't seem to bother you. Bear in mind you could be moved along.

STINTINO

A small fishing village about 2½ miles S of Fornelli Passage.

Approach

Conspicuous The white houses of the village are easily identified. Several chimneys in the vicinity are conspicuous. The outer breakwater is easily identified.

Dangers Care is needed of the reef and shoal water off the promontory. It is marked by a black and white truncated pyramid beacon and should be left to port if you are headed up to Porto Mannu.

VHF Ch 09 for Marina di Stintino. Ch 73 for Circolo Valera Stintino.

Mooring

Stintino Marina
Data 270 berths. 50 visitors' berths. Depths 2–11m. LOA 12–40m.

Porto Mannu
Max LOA 20m. Depths 2–2·5m.

Berth Yachts should head for the new marina under the breakwater, or Porto Mannu. Stern or bows-to where directed. Laid moorings tailed to the quay.

Note Porto Minore is largely for fishing boats and local boats.

Shelter Good shelter.

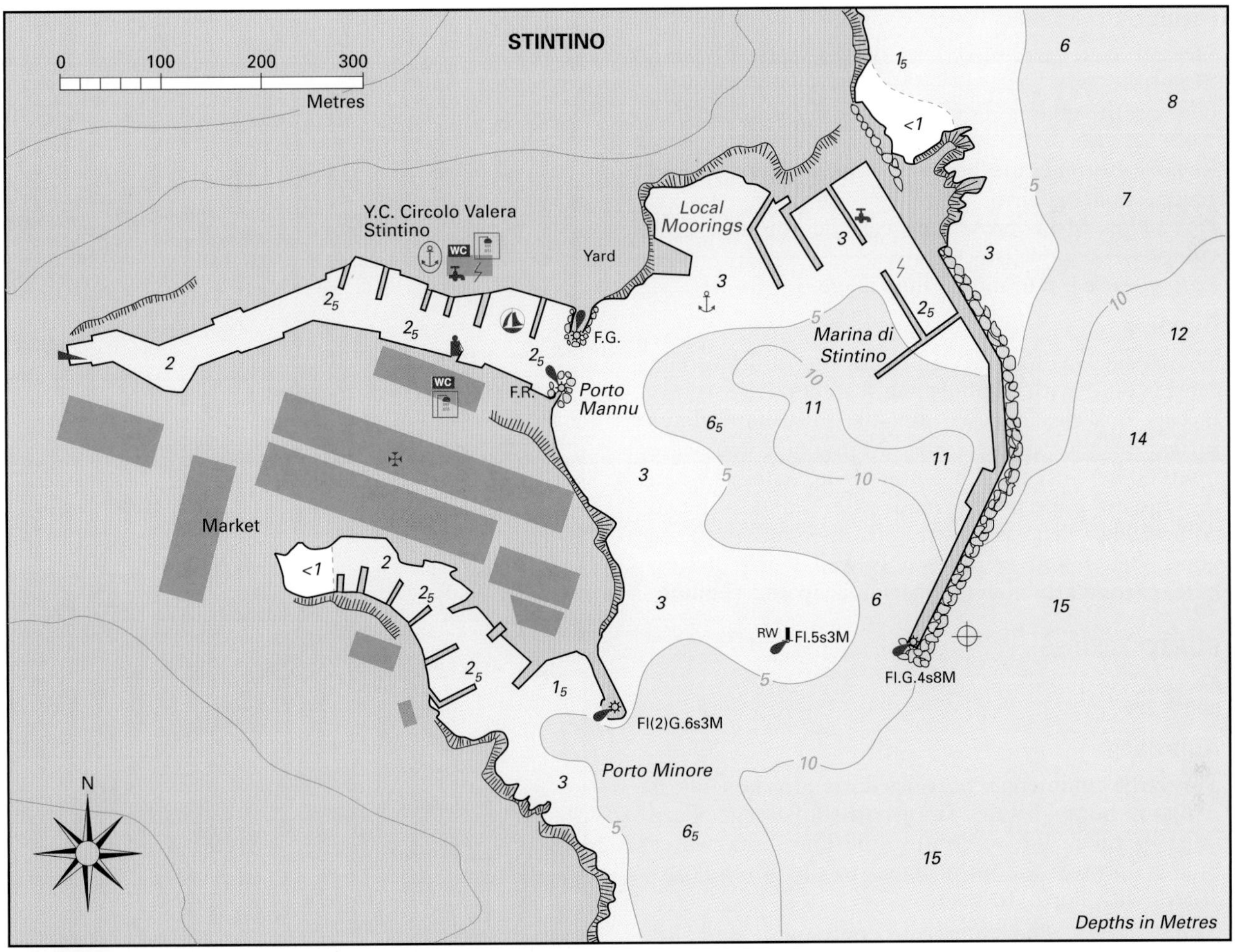

STINTINO
⊕40°56′·1N 08°14′·0E

Stintino looking SW *Marina di Stintino*

Authorities Harbourmaster. *Ormeggiatori*. Charge band 5 (July–August).
Circolo Nautico Porto Torres (N quay) ✆ 079 523 519
Nautilus (S quay) ✆ 079 523 721
Stintino Marina ✆ 334 740 4583
Email marinadistintino@alice.it

Anchorage There is little room for anchoring in suitable depths, although there may be room outside local moorings in the N of the harbour. The bottom is sand and rock, mediocre holding. Good shelter in settled weather but open south.

Facilities

Services Water and electricity on the quay. WC and showers.
Fuel On the quay in Porto Mannu.
☎ 079 523 118
Repairs 40-ton crane. Slipway. Some mechanical and general boat repairs.
Provisions Most provisions can be found in the village.
Eating out Restaurants in the village.

General

The village was formerly an important tunny fishing centre but, with diminishing catches, the tunny factory has closed down and the inhabitants have turned to the tourist trade. Many of them were resettled here in the 19th century from Asinara when the Italian government made the island a penal colony. The village is an attractive spot and given the good shelter and facilities it is well worth a stop here, particularly now the marina is up and running.

PORTO TORRES

BA 1202
Italian 286

Approach

This large commercial port lies deep into the Gulf of Asinara about 11 miles SE of Fornelli Passage. Care must be taken not to confuse the long breakwater built to protect the oil terminal to the W of Porto Torres with Porto Torres itself.

Conspicuous The numerous chimneys and oil storage tanks of the oil refinery immediately W of the harbour are conspicuous. There are usually several tankers anchored off the oil terminal. Closer in, the buildings of Porto Torres and the outer harbour mole are easily identified.

VHF Ch 09, 12, 14, 16 for port authorities (0800–2100). Ch 12, 16 for pilots. Ch 74 for Cormorano Marina/Marina di Porto Torres.

Porto Torres looking SE into the inner basin
Note: Pontoons in outer basin have been changed
Carlo Delfino

APPROACHES TO PORTO TORRES
⊕40°52′·0N 08°23′·1E

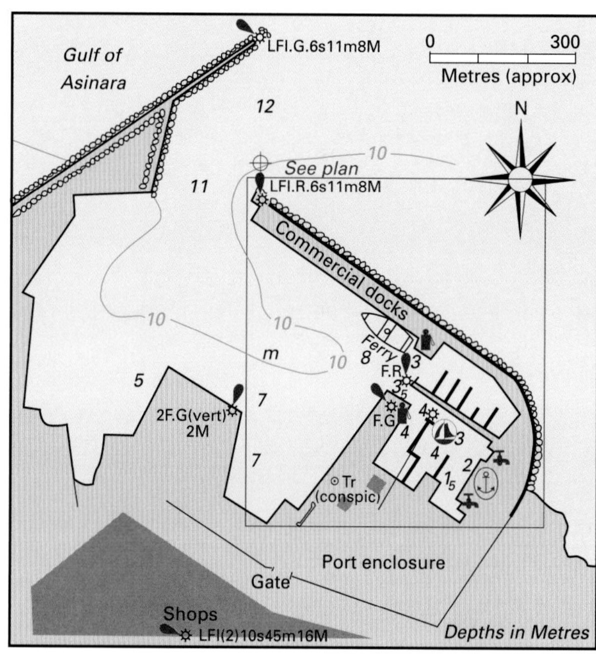

PORTO TORRES
⊕40°50′·69N 08°23′·95E WGS84

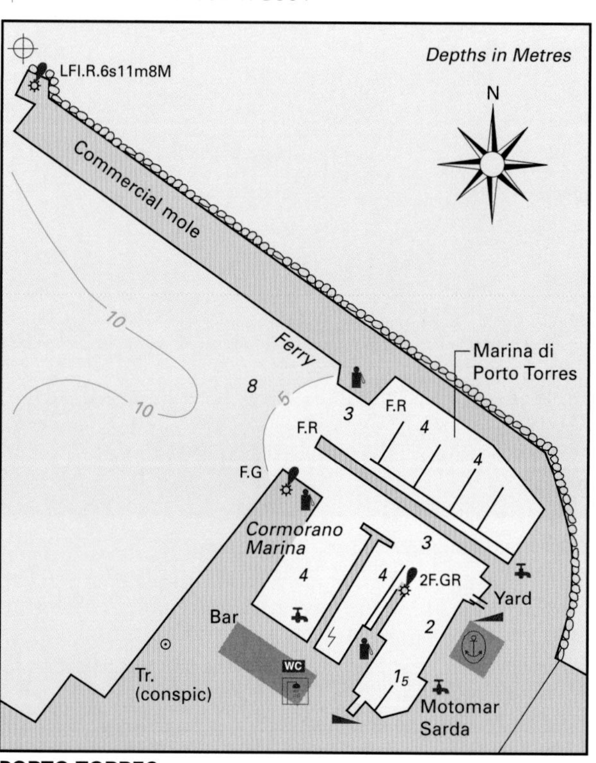

PORTO TORRES
⊕40°50′·69N 08°23′·95E WGS84

Note Care must be taken not to confuse the lights of Porto Torres with the lights of the oil terminal to the west. The breakwater sheltering the oil terminal is lit Fl(3)G.10s4M. There are also leading lights for the oil terminal piers and several flares are conspicuous.

Caution With strong onshore winds there is a reflected swell off the oil terminal breakwater. A yacht is advised to keep at least half a mile off.

Mooring

Data
Cormorano Marina 150 berths. Max LOA 30m. Depths 3–7m.
Marina Porto Torres 200 berths. Max LOA 40m. Depths 4–5m.

Berth Stern or bows-to in Cormorano Marina or Marina Porto Torres where directed. Laid moorings tailed to the quay.

Shelter Good shelter.

Authorities Harbourmaster. Customs. Marina staff. Charge band 4 (June–September).
Cormarano Marina ✆ 079 512 290 / 349 245 3887
Fax 079 515 250
Email info@cormorano.com
www.cormoranomarina.it

Marina di Porto Torres ✆ 079 512 290 / 503 873
Email info@marinadiportotorres.it

Facilities

Services Water and electricity at or near every berth in the marina berths. WC and showers. Wi-Fi.
Fuel On the quay.
Repairs Crane to 50 tons and 200-ton slipway. Engineering, mechanical and electrical repairs can be carried out. Hauling and storage ashore in La Darsena.
Motomar Sardo ✆ 079 514 885

Provisions Good shopping for all provisions in the town. Excellent fresh fish can be found. Ice is delivered to the fishing boats in the harbour.
Eating out Bar in marina. Restaurants, trattorias and pizzerias in the town.
Other PO. Banks. ATMs. Hospital. Italgaz and Camping Gaz. Hire cars. Ferries to Genoa, Civitavecchia and Olbia. Alghero international airport 20km.

General

With the vast oil terminal sited next door no one could describe Porto Torres as attractive, but the town itself is pleasant enough and the harbour bustles and buzzes with ferries, tugs, cargo ships and fishing boats. In Roman times this was Turris Libyssonis, an important port and town. In the Middle Ages it flourished as the capital of the Giudicato of Torres, but from then on it went into decline and, until its revival this century, as an oil terminal and port, it had been quietly rotting away. Instead of rebuilding the old town the inhabitants have simply built a new town by the harbour.

CASTELSARDO

Approach

The harbour lies to the W of the village of Castelsardo.

Conspicuous The village of Castelsardo on a rocky promontory, a belfry on the seaward slope and a castle on the summit of the promontory are conspicuous. Closer in, the breakwater of the harbour and the ruined tower at the entrance are easily identified.

Note With strong NW–N winds a heavy swell is reported to pile up at the entrance making entry difficult.

VHF Ch 09.

Mooring

Data 500 berths. Max LOA 28m. Depths 1–5m.

Berth Stern or bows–to where directed. Laid moorings tailed to the quay. Free overnight berth W of the fuel quay reported.

Shelter Good shelter.

Authorities Harbourmaster. Charge band 4.
Dock ✆ 079 471 339 Office ✆ 079 479 010 *Fax* 079 479 174
Email info@portodicastelsardo.com

Facilities

Services Water and electricity. Shower and toilet block.

Fuel Fuel on the quay.

Repairs A 50-ton travel-hoist. A 15-ton mobile crane can be arranged. Many repairs can be arranged. Chandlers in the marina.
North Sails agent Technomarine ✆ 388 618 5412

Castelsardo looking NE

IV. SARDINIA

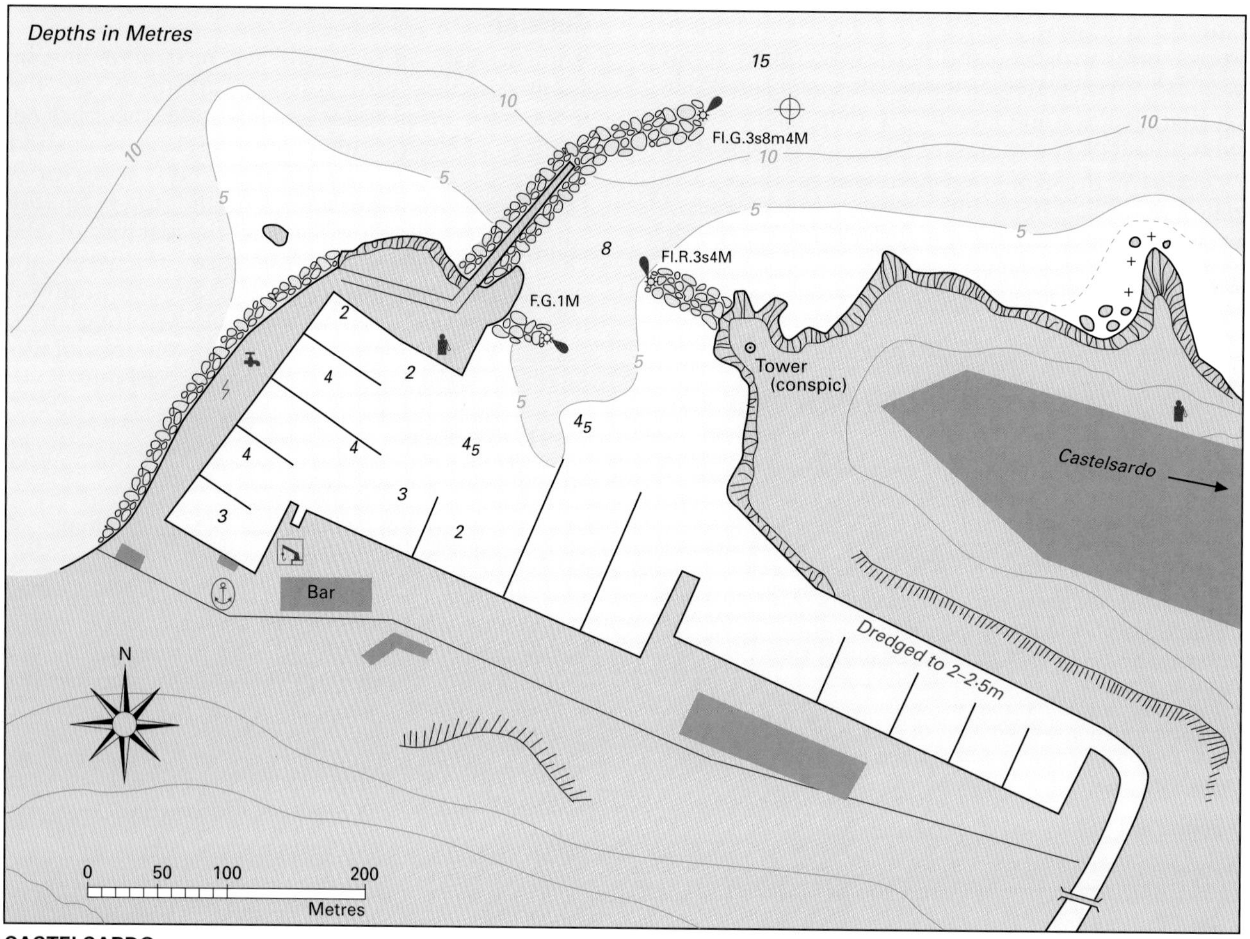

CASTELSARDO
⌖ 40°54´·97N 08°42´·28E WGS84

Provisions Supermarket in the marina. Most provisions can be found in the village about 20 minutes' walk away. Alternatively take your dinghy across to the tower or the town beach to shorten the trip.

Eating out Bar in marina. Restaurants and pizzerias in the town. The restaurant Fo-Fo in the Hotel Riviera has been much recommended for its fresh fish, although prices are quite high.

Other PO. Bank. ATM. Italgaz and Camping Gaz. Car hire. Bus to Porto Torres.

General

Castelsardo is a delightful old fishing village built in tiers up the rocky promontory. Steep alleys wind up to the castle at the summit. The village was originally called Castelgenovese from the period when the castle was the principal defence for the Genoese along the N of Sardinia. The belfry conpicuous from seaward belongs to the 11th-century cathedral of San Antonio Abate which incorporates some Doric and Corinthian columns in its construction. The town is known for its basket-weaving, but more striking are the distinctive carpets on sale in the village which are presumably woven locally. Take your dinghy across the harbour to the tower, or further around to the beach to shorten the walk into town.

PORTO MARINA ISOLA ROSSA (Marina Trinita d'Agultu)

About nine miles NE of Castelsardo lies Isola Rossa opposite a low promontory with a tower on it.

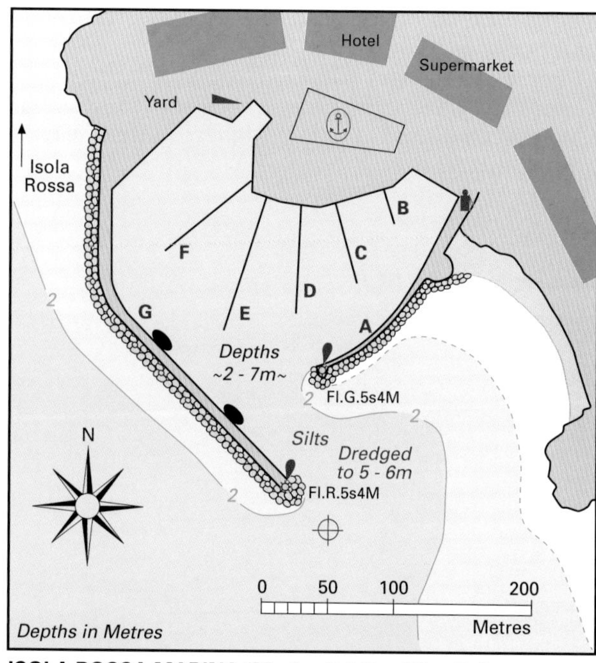

ISOLA ROSSA MARINA (Marina Trinita d'Agultu)
⌖41°00´·6N 08°52´·3E

Approach

This new marina lies on the mainland to the SW of Isola Rossa. The passage between the island and the mainland is wide and free of dangers, with minimum depths 12–14m.

Conspicuous From the N the tower on the promontory will be seen. The marina will not be seen until you are through the passage between the island and the mainland. From the S the tower lies directly behind the marina, but the breakwaters of the marina will be seen.

VHF Ch 16, 09.

Note The marina is regularly dredged to 5–6m. Care needed of silting in the approaches (2–3m depths are reported).

Mooring

Data c. 150 berths. Max LOA c.20m. Depths 2·5–6m.

Berths Visiting yachts go alongside the inside of the breakwater.

Shelter Reasonable shelter from the prevailing wind.

Authorities Marina staff. Charge band 4 (July–August).

Porto Marina Isola Rossa ✆ 079 694 184 *Fax* 079 694 177
Email info@portoisolarossa.com
www.portoisolarossa.com

Anchorage In settled weather a yacht can anchor on either side of the promontory opposite Isola Rossa where shelter can be found from all but westerly winds (unfortunately the most common winds here). Anchor in 5–10m on sand where convenient.

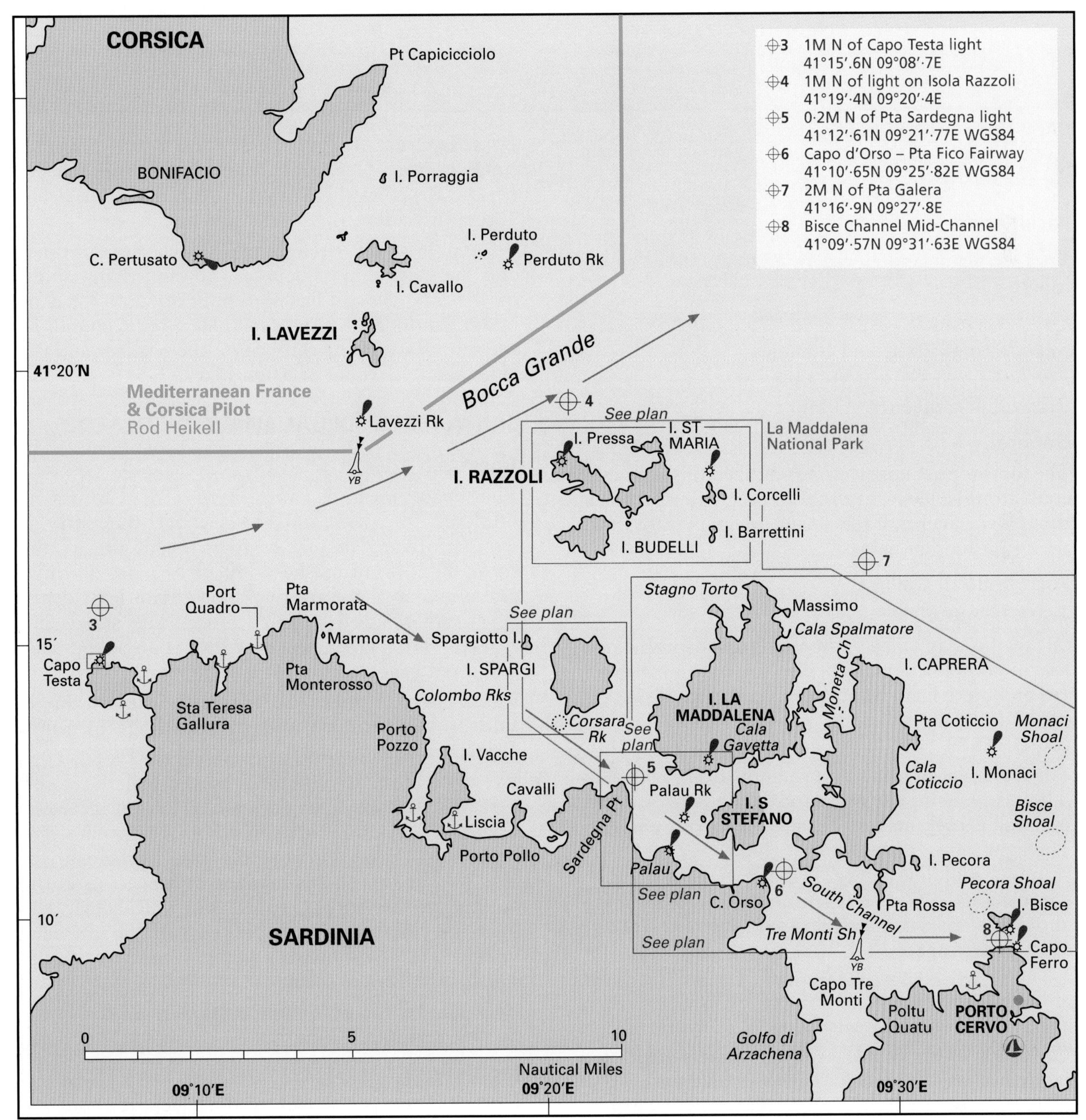

BONIFACIO STRAIT

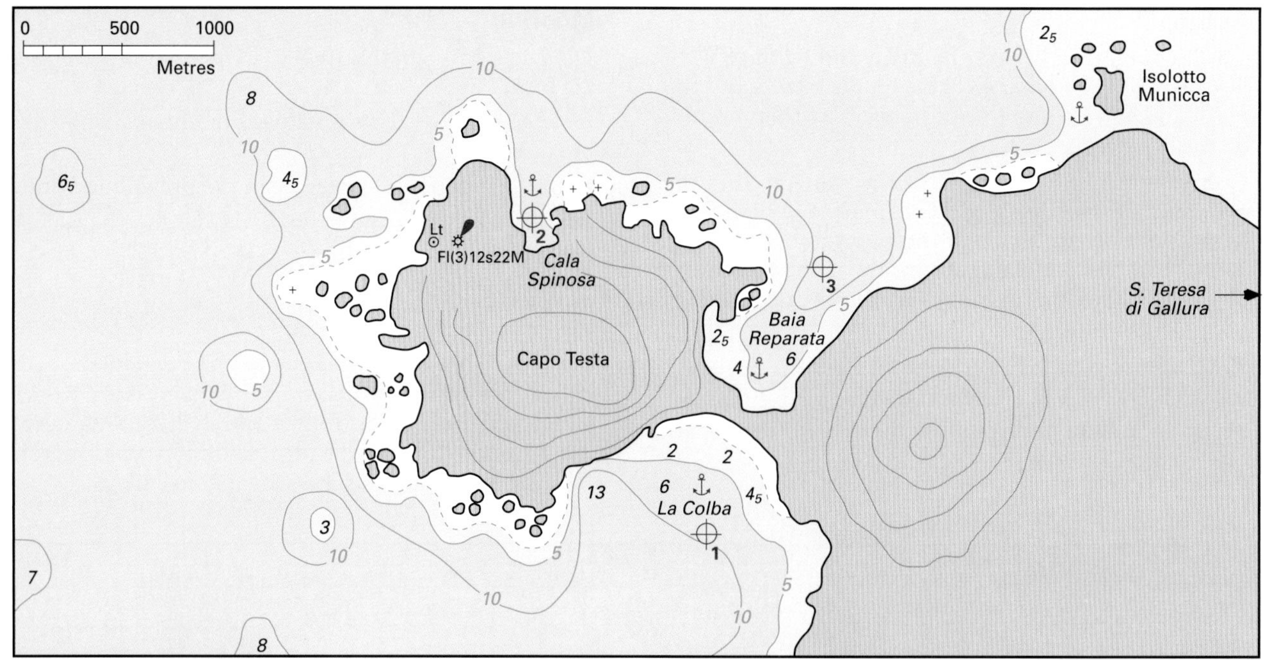

CAPO TESTA ANCHORAGES
⊕1 41°13′·9N 09°09′·5E
⊕2 41°14′·8N 09°08′·9E
⊕3 41°14′·5N 09°10′·0E

Facilities

Services Water and electricity (220V). Showers and toilets.

Fuel On the quay (depths c.2·5m).

Repairs Small crane and chandler.

Other Supermarket with most provisions nearby. Restaurants and bars. ATM.

General

The local tourist authority has dubbed this stretch of coast from Isola Rossa to Palau the 'Costa Paradiso' though you will find few locals or even visitors who refer to it by that name.

Portobello di Gallura

⊕ 41°07′·5N 09°01′·2E

Off the holiday village ashore there is a stubby mole for the complex. Depths behind are only a little over 1m and there is no room for visiting yachts.

CAPO TESTA

The extremity of a rugged promontory connected by a low isthmus to the mainland. The fantastic wind-sculptured rock makes the cape easily recognisable. The lighthouse, a low white square tower on a two-storeyed building (67m/219ft above sea level), is conspicuous. The cape is fringed with rocks, mostly above water, and a yacht should exercise caution close to the cape.

There are several anchorages around the cape although some areas are buoyed off for swimming and the bays are busy with craft of all types.

La Colba On the S side. Anchor where shown on a sandy bottom, over rock. Mediocre holding.

Cala Spinosa Anchor in 10m on a sandy bottom, excellent holding.

Baia Reparata Anchor where shown in 4–6m on a sandy bottom. Open only to the north. Mini-market nearby. Restaurant ½M to the north. 2M walk to Sta Teresa di Gallura.

Capo Testa has been quarried since Roman times and there are said to be a few columns lying about on the cape. A road has been built down to the cape and it is no longer a secluded place, but resounds to the sounds of happy throngs on the beaches and the less palatable sound of water-bikes.

SANTA TERESA DI GALLURA (LONGOSARDO)

Approach

The coast around Santa Teresa di Gallura is bordered by rocks and shoal water, but entry is straightforward in fair weather. From the W the rocks off I. Municca should be given a good offing, and closer in there are two shoals with least depth 3·5m either side of the entrance. The shoals are marked with a green beacon with a triangle topmark and a red beacon with a square topmark.

Conspicuous A tower (Torre Longosardo) on the W side of the entrance and the buildings of Santa Teresa are conspicuous.

By night Entry is difficult. Use the light on Capo Testa Fl(3)12s22M for an approach from the west. There are leading lights Oc.R.4s3M (front) and Fl.R.4s7M (rear) showing the safe passage in on 196·5°. The two shoals marked with beacons in the approaches are lit Fl.G.4s3M and Fl.R.4s3M. The light on Pta Corvo on the E side of the entrance Fl.WR.3s10/8M shows the safe passage between the shoals in the white sector (164°-184°).

VHF Ch 16 for port authorities. Ch 12 for Porto Turistico Santa Gallura.

Mooring

Data 600 berths. Max LOA 40m. Depths 1–6m.

Berth Stern or bows-to where directed. The first

pontoon is private. The rest are part of the Porto Turistico. Laid moorings tailed to the quay.

Shelter Good shelter although with strong NW–W winds there are gusts off the high land on the W side. With prolonged northerlies a surge is set up.

Authorities Harbourmaster. *Ormeggiatori.* Charge band 5 (July–August).

✆ 0789 751 936 *Email* info@portosantateresa.com
www.portosantateresa.com

Anchorage In calm weather it is possible to anchor in the bight on the W side near the entrance. The anchorage is exposed to winds from the N–NE–ENE, but has been used on occasion. There is a concrete path up to the village from the anchorage.

Facilities

Services Water and electricity at or near most berths. WC and showers.

Fuel On the E quay.

Repairs 100-ton travel-lift. 20-ton crane. Small yachts are craned onto the quay in the S creek. Mechanical repairs. Chandlers on the quay.

Provisions Good shopping in Santa Teresa about 10 minutes' walk uphill from the port.

Eating out Good restaurants at the harbour, others in Santa Teresa.

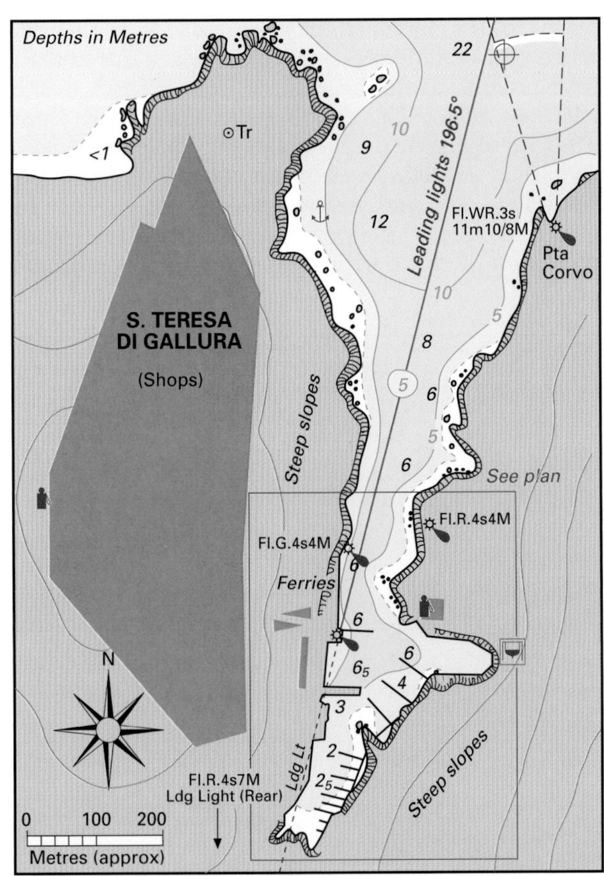

SANTA TERESA DI GALLURA
⊕41°14′·7N 09°11′·8E

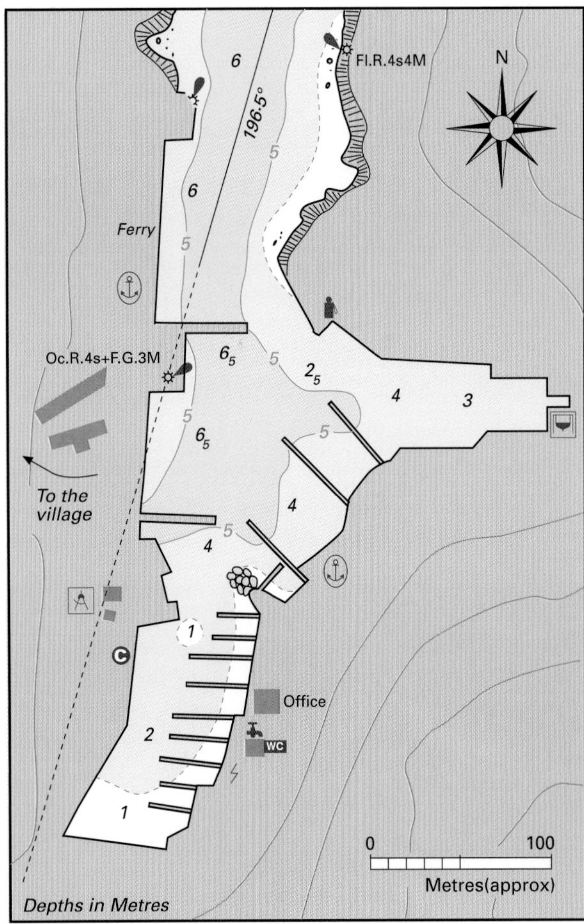

SANTA TERESA DI GALLURA

Other PO. Banks. ATMs. Italgaz and Camping Gaz. Buses to Palau. Ferry to Bonifacio.

General

The town was named after Queen Maria Teresa when a colony from Piedmont was established here in the 19th century. The village is unassuming and the harbour below a peaceful spot except for July and August when it is packed with yachts and holidaymakers en route from or to Corsica.

Porto Quadro

⊕ 41°15′·2N 09°12′·6E

A bay adjacent to Santa Teresa with a large and hideous hotel complex on the shore. Care must be taken of the above- and below-water rocks on either side of the entrance. The bay is open to the NW–W.

Note In the vicinity of Santa Teresa and Porto Quadro a W-going current of 2–3 knots has been reported during prolonged E winds.

Baia Marmorata

⊕ 41°15′·2N 09°14′·7E

Lies about ½ mile S of Punta Marmorata which is easily identified by a beacon on it which stands out well. The bay is open between N and E and NW winds are reported to send a swell in. There is a large hotel complex ashore.

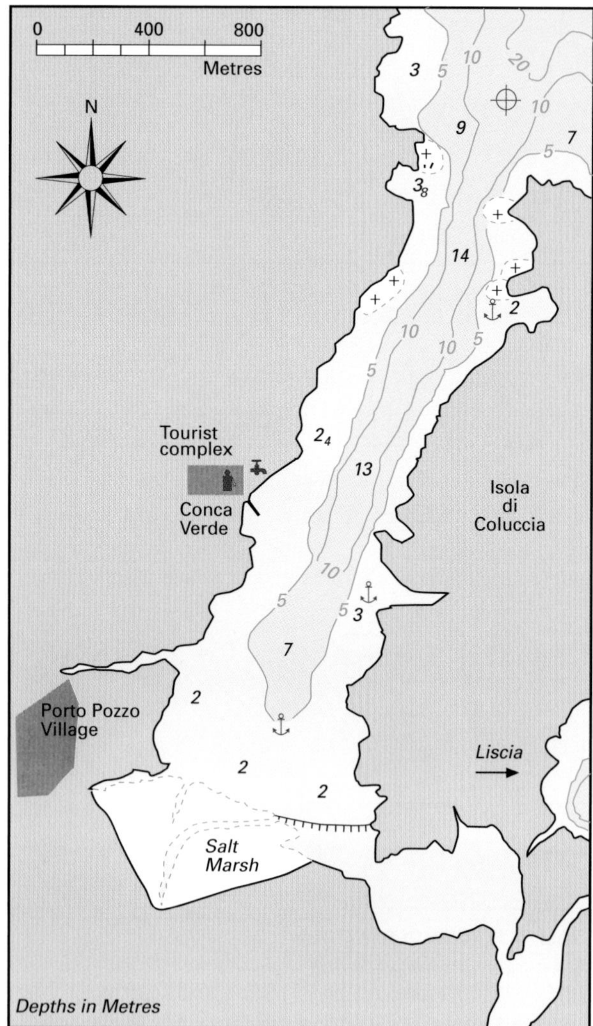

PORTO POZZO
⊕41°13′·3N 09°17′·1E

PORTO POZZO

A long inlet about three miles SE of Punta Marmorata. The beacon marking the northern extremity of Scoglio Paganetto stands out clearly. A yacht should enter the inlet and anchor near the head in about 2–5m. The bottom is mud and weed and the holding is suspect. As the bottom shelves gently to the shore it is impossible to anchor near the small hamlet of Pozzo.

Some provisions in the village and simple trattorias, and a beach restaurant.

On the W side of the inlet there is a large tourist village, Conca Verde, with a small jetty off it. You can anchor off here in 2–3m. There are reported to be 2–4m depths off the outer end of the jetty. Water available on the jetty. Holiday village ashore and some facilities including a restaurant and bar. Fuel currently unavailable.

LISCIA

A large bay on the E side of Isola di Coluccia. Anchor on the W side of the bay in 3–10m on a sandy bottom, good holding. Depths come up quickly close into the shore. The shelter here is

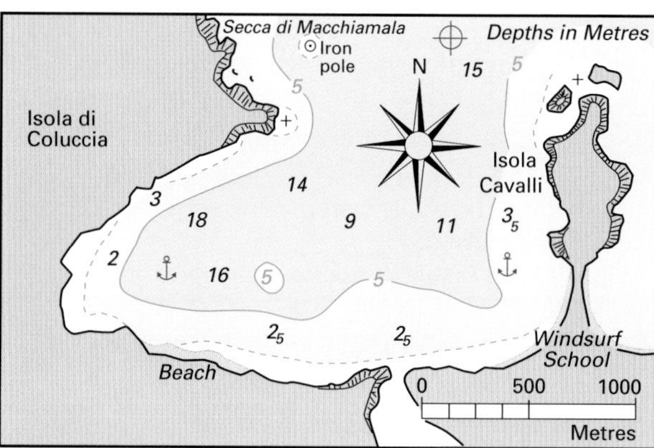

LISCIA
⊕41°12′·5N 09°18′·6E

reported to be better than it looks and is tenable, even with N winds. Good holding. If it gets uncomfortable you can move to Porto Pollo nearby. In calm weather there is a delightful anchorage on the E side under Isola Cavalli. Good beach around the shore.

PORTO POLLO (PUDDU)

A well sheltered bay adjacent to Liscia. The entrance is somewhat difficult to identify from seaward. There is a small hotel on the W side of the entrance and another on the slopes above the southern shore. A yacht can anchor behind the islet.

Some care is needed in the approach. Keep to the middle of the channel until you are due W of the islet when you should keep close to the beach rather than to the islet to avoid the shallows off the S side of the islet (see plan). The depths come up quickly from 10–15m to just over a metre off the S side of the islet so care is needed. The bottom is bad holding, hard sand and rock, and you will need some patience to ensure you get your anchor securely in. With westerlies there are strong gusts into the bay over the

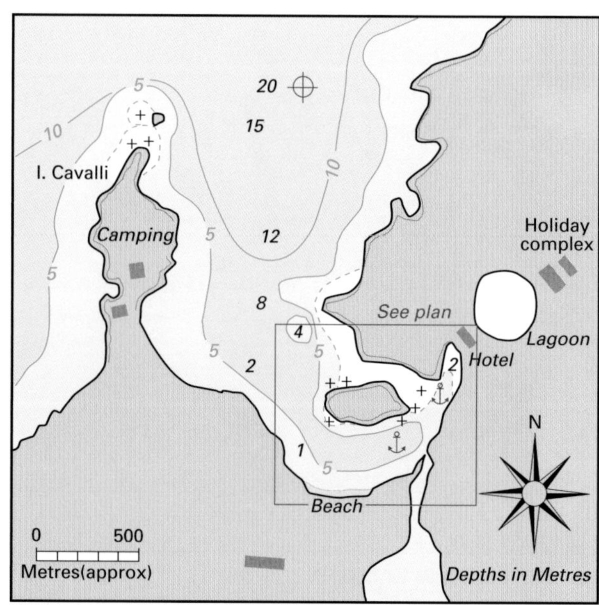

PORTO POLLO APPROACH
⊕41°12′·4N 09°19′·7E

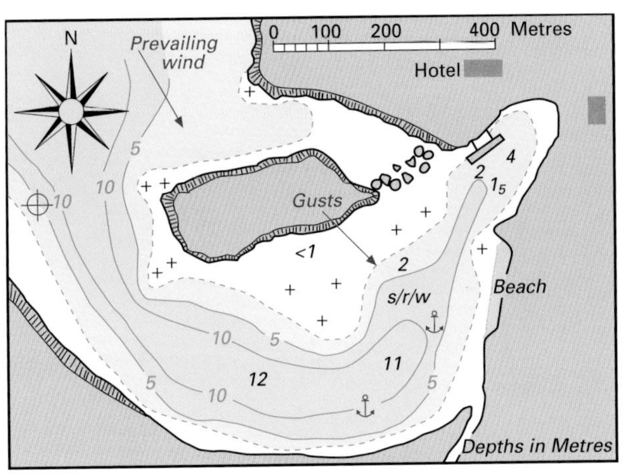

PORTO POLLO ⊕41°11′·5N 09°19′·7E

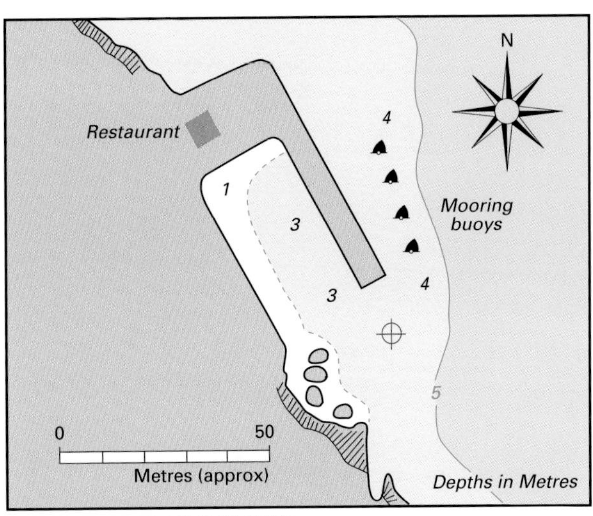

PORTO RAFAEL YACHT CLUB
⊕41°11′·7N 09°21′·8E

islet and a second anchor may be needed. With care, small yachts can get right up to the pontoon in the E corner.

A number of hotels have been built around the shores, but do not intrude overly much on the bay and it remains a delightful, if windy, place. There is only windsurfer pollution here, though this is much to be preferred to water-bike pollution and, like flies and wasps, they return home after dark.

Porto Rafael Yacht Club

A very small private harbour about ¾ miles S of Punta Sardegna. Large yachts moor outside the breakwater while smaller yachts berth inside. In the bay *Mezzo Schiffo* holding is unreliable on weed, as the name suggests (half bad!). VHF Ch 09. Water and electricity. Restaurant and bar ashore.

Pontile Punta Stroppello ✆ 335 547 8438

PALAU

Approach

Straightforward by day and night.

Conspicuous The town of Palau is easily identified. The light structure, a white tower with a green band on Punta Palau, is conspicuous. Behind Palau three huge apartment complexes are conspicuous. Ferries are constantly running between Palau and La Maddalena and are useful for locating where the harbour is. A yacht should keep well out of the way as they always seem to travel at 'full ahead'.

VHF Ch 09.

Note A W cardinal beacon marks the underwater rock on the E side of the entrance into Palau. Topmarks replaced with red ball (occas). It is lit VQ(9)10s4M.

The approaches to Palau looking south

Palau looking north *Carlo Delfino*

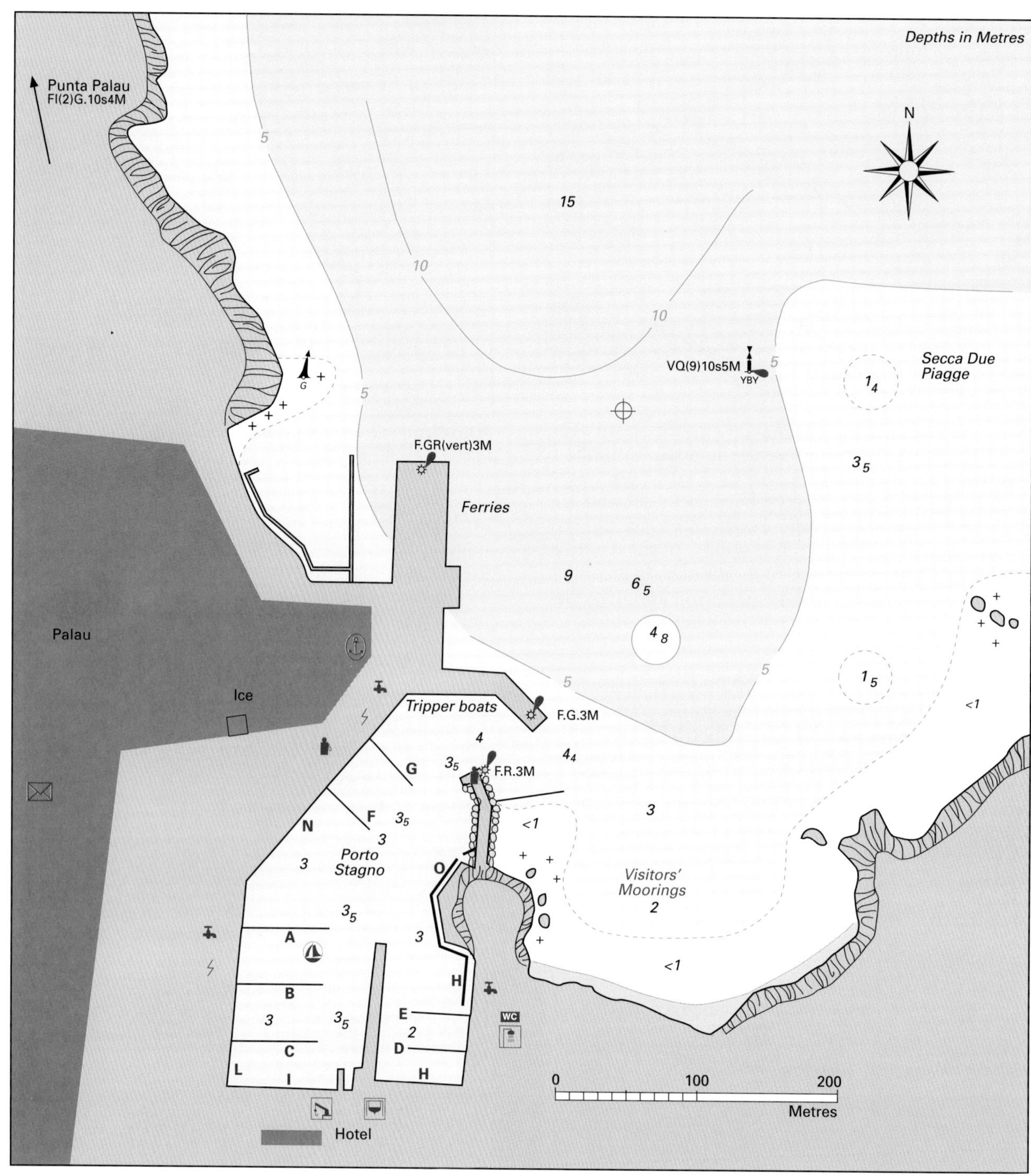

PALAU
⊕41°10′·96N 09°23′·25E WGS84

Mooring

Data 400 berths. Max LOA 18m. Depths 2–4m.

Berth Stern or bows-to where directed or where convenient. Laid moorings tailed to the quay. Visitors' moorings have been laid in the bay immediately E of the harbour.

Shelter Good all-round shelter although strong NE winds might make it uncomfortable. Yachts are wintered afloat here.

Authorities Harbourmaster and customs. *Ormeggiatori*. Charge band 5.

✆ */Fax* 0789 708 435 *Email* portoturistico@palau.it

Note La Maddalena National Park permits can be obtained at an office near the ferry terminal.

Facilities

Services Water and electricity at or near every berth. The water is reported to be non-potable (though I have drunk it with no perceptible ill effect) and is also in short supply so it may be turned off at times in the summer. Shower and toilet block.

Fuel On the quay (0800–1200/1530–1900).

Repairs 50-ton travel-hoist and a 15-ton mobile crane. Mechanical repairs. Chandlers.

Provisions Good shopping for all provisions. Market on Friday. Ice from a stall on the quay.

Eating out Numerous restaurants, trattorias and pizzerias.

Other PO. Bank. ATM. Italgaz and Camping Gaz. Ferries to La Maddalena and Porto Vecchio, Corsica. Train to Sassari.

General

At one time a small farming village, Palau today is a comparatively modern town which also serves as the mainland ferry port for La Maddalena. It is not an offensive place, but it seems not to have any centre or architectural cohesion and one gets the feeling that if the ferries to La Maddalena didn't run from here, Palau would have no purpose on the coast.

Golfo delle Saline

⊕ 41°09'·7N 09°25'·4E

This large bay lies about one mile S of Capo d'Orso. It gives good protection from westerlies but is open to easterlies. Attractive setting with much windsurfing and dinghy sailing in the summer. There is a short mole in the NE corner of the bay which appears to be private. There is also a sailing school pontoon on the S side.

Golfo di Arzachena

This deep bay has two harbours in it: Cala Bitta on the E side near the entrance and Cannigione on the W side. The normal summer winds are a land breeze blowing out of the gulf in the morning and a sea breeze blowing in during the afternoon. Villas now line the western shores of Arzachena, and are beginning to spread to the E side too.

Tre Monti Shoal

A beacon BRB marks the shoal (least depth 5m) approximately ¾M N of Capo Tre Monti. The beacon is an isolated danger mark showing Fl(2)8s5M with topmark ⁑.

Porteddu

⊕ 41°07'·8N 09°26'·2E

A tiny cove under Punta Arzachena. A small pontoon is used by a shore-based sailing school. Care needed of the reef marked by a flag (occas). It is also possible to anchor in the bight directly under Punta Arzachena.

Note It is prohibited to anchor in the bay NW of Punta Arzachena.

Zui Paulu

⊕ 41°07'·43N 09°26'·59E WGS84

The anchorage under the islet of Zui Paulu where a 'stick-figure' statue stands guard on the beach. Care needed of an unmarked dangerous rock reported approximately 50m SW of the statue in position 41°07'·5N 09°26'·6E. There is a good lee from NW–W winds. Anchor in 3–5m on sand, good holding. Restaurants and bars ashore.

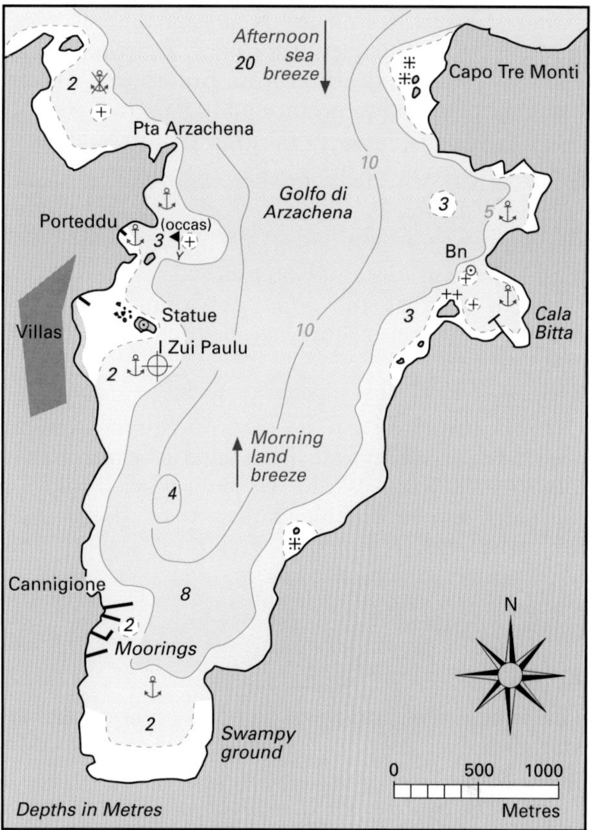

GOLFO DI ARZACHENA
⊕41°07'·43N 09°26'·59E WGS84

CALA BITTA

Approach

At the head of the bay there is a hotel/apartment complex which is conspicuous.

By night There are no lights and a night approach is not recommended.

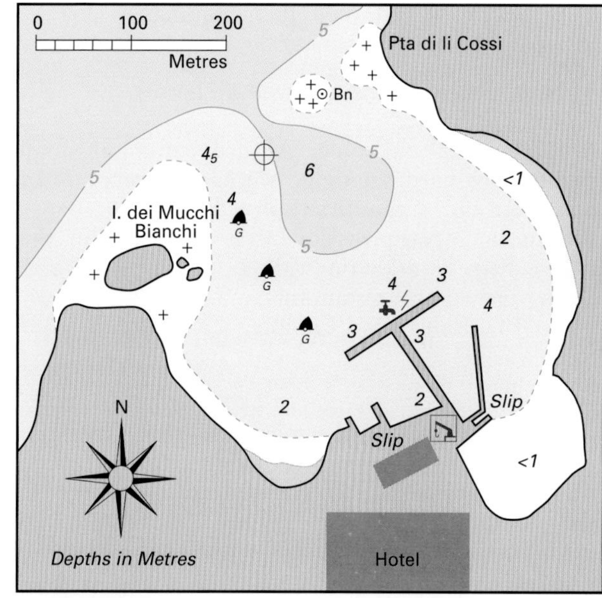

CALA BITTA
⊕41°07'·74N 09°27'·93E WGS84

Dangers A reef lies on the N side of the entrance, marked by a concrete 'fence-post' beacon. Rocks and shoal water extends N from Isolotti dei Mucchi Bianchi, making the entrance quite narrow.

Data 180 berths. Max LOA 30m. Depths 1·5–3m.

Berth Where directed or where convenient. Good all-round shelter.

Facilities Water and electricity at or near most berths. Restaurants and bars ashore.

Unlike most of the other development on this coast, the hotel ashore is in the pour-and-fill concrete style.

Anchorage You can anchor in the bay to the N of Cala Bitta around Pta di li Cossi. Anchor in 4–5m on a sand and weed bottom. The shelter is better than it looks on the chart. With NW winds a swell rolls in, normally uncomfortable rather than dangerous, otherwise shelter is good. Wonderful scenery and unobtrusive architecture ashore.

CANNIGIONE

Approach

The village of Cannigione and the mole are easily identified.

By night The end of the mole is lit F.G.7m3M.

VHF Ch 11, 16 Sardomar (0700–1900).

Mooring

Data 400 berths. Max LOA 25m. Depths 1–4m.

Berth Go stern or bows-to where directed or convenient. Laid moorings.

Shelter Adequate shelter in the summer.

Authorities Harbourmaster. Charge band 5.
Sardomar ✆ 0789 88422
Email coop.sardomar@tiscali.it

Anchorage Anchor off in the S of the bay, although care is needed with the prevailing afternoon sea breeze blowing down into the gulf. The bottom is hard mud, rock and weed, poor holding.

Facilities

Services Water and electricity at all berths.
Fuel On the quay.
Repairs A 12-ton crane. A yard can haul small yachts onto hard standing. Mechanical repairs can be carried out. Chandlers (Volvo dealer).
Provisions Most provisions can be found in the village. Street market on Fridays.
Eating out Several restaurants.
Other PO. Italgaz and Camping Gaz. Laundry. Bus to Palau.

General

The small village is charming and the hinterland fertile and green, in marked contrast to the barren rocky landscape so often encountered elsewhere. In the summer the town is full of life in an unsophisticated (compared with Porto Cervo), enjoyable way.

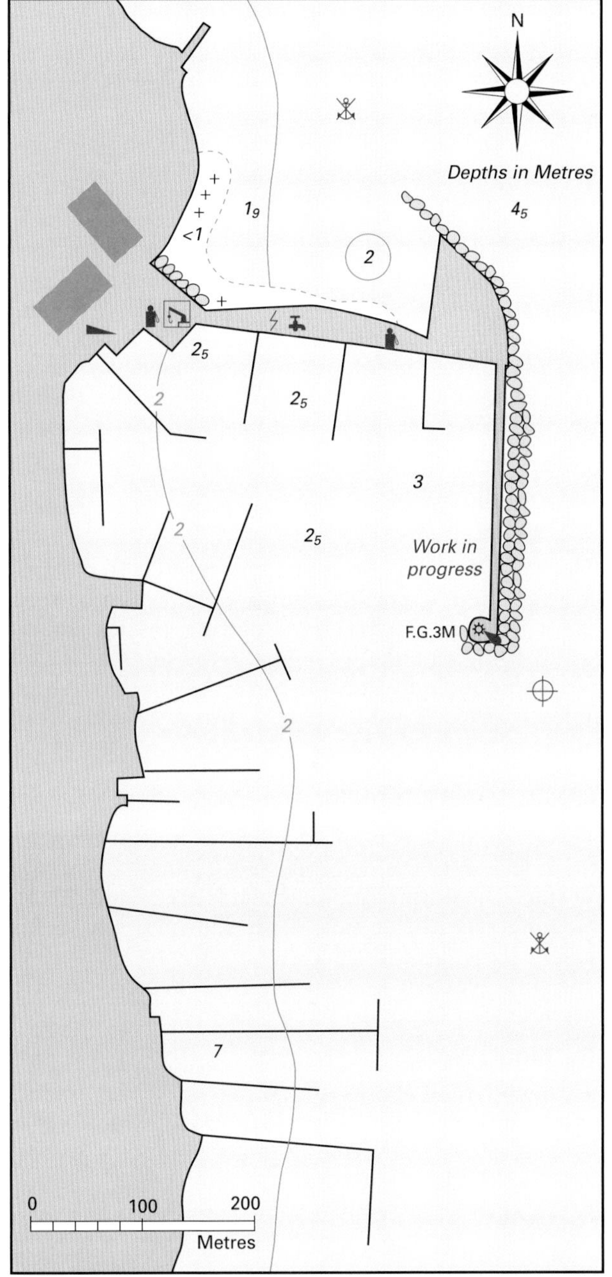

CANNIGIONE
⊕41°06´·4N 09°26´·7E

POLTU QUATU (Marina dell'Orso)

A marina that has been built in the deep inlet immediately E of Capo Tre Monti.

Approach

The marina is difficult to see from the E and W until you are at the entrance. The control tower looks like a periscope and is conspicuous. Once here the masts of the yachts inside and the apartments built around the marina will be seen.

VHF Ch 09, 16.

Mooring

Data 450 berths. 50 visitors' berths. Max LOA 35m. Depths 2–4m.

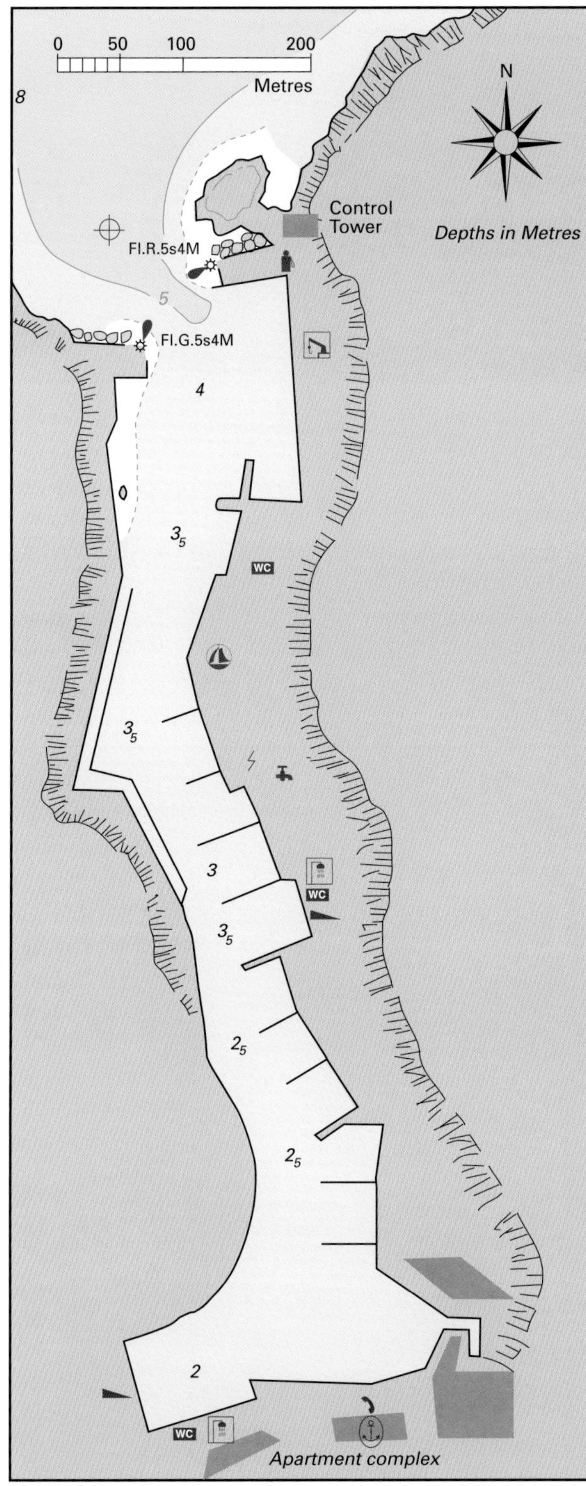

POLTU QUATU
⊕41°08′·6N 09°29′·7E

Berth Where directed. There are laid moorings tailed to the quay.

Shelter Good all-round shelter.

Authorities Harbourmaster and marina staff. Charge band 5.

Facilities

Services Water and electricity at every berth. There is both potable and non-potable (for washing the boat down) water. Telephone and television connections. Showers and toilets.
Fuel On the quay.
Repairs 30/15-ton cranes. Hard standing on the quay. Limited mechanical repairs.
Provisions A minimarket.
Eating out Restaurants and bars ashore.
Other Hire cars.

General

The marina was built as part of an apartment complex ashore, a low aspect development similar to others around this coast. There is nothing wrong with the place, but nor is there an especially good reason to visit unless you plan to base yourself here or the other harbours nearby are full in the summer months. Being shut in by the rocks around it is something of a suntrap, ideal in the early spring and late autumn, but a little stifling in summer.

LISCIA DI VACCA

Lies on the W side of the promontory that ends in Capo Ferro. It is open to the NW–N but otherwise offers reasonable shelter. Anchor in 5–10m where convenient. The bottom is sand and weed: bad holding. The shores are fringed by above and below-water rocks so care must be taken when close in. The water here is crystal clear and ashore there is the Hotel Pitrizza, a monument to the policy of the Costa Smeralda Consortium which maintains strict control over development. The Hotel Pitrizza is difficult to see even from quite close in so well does it blend into the landscape. It is a small but very private and very expensive hotel (the staff outnumber the guests) where the casual drink is unobtainable.

The reef in the bay is marked by a beacon on a concrete base.

Note There have been plans to build a yacht basin here for some time, but to date nothing has happened.

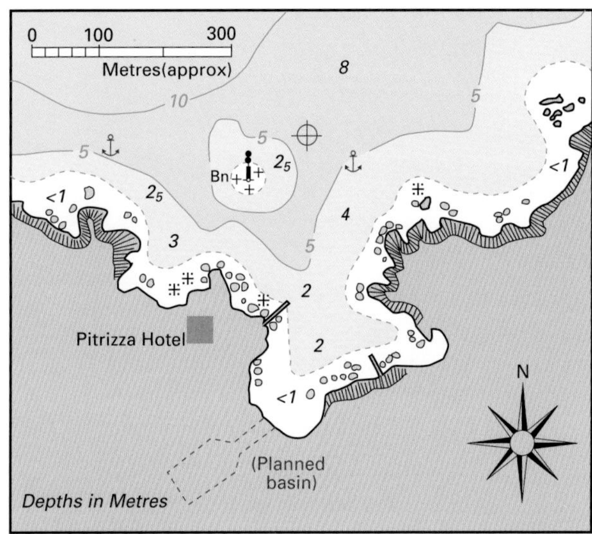

LISCIA DI VACCA
⊕41°08′·6N 09°30′·7E

IV. SARDINIA

La Maddalena archipelago

This group of islands lies on the S side of the Bonifacio Strait. On the N side lies Corsica and the islands off its southern tip. The islands are all composed of red granite and for the most part are bare of vegetation except for *maquis*. In nearly all cases the islands are surrounded by above and below-water rocks and caution must be exercised when navigating in their vicinity. There are seven principal islands divided into two groups: the northern group consisting of Razzoli, Santa Maria and Budelli and the southern group consisting of Spargi, La Maddalena, Santo Stefano and Caprera.

Cala Santa Maria (Zone MB)

Note With moderate to strong winds there are strong gusts off the lee side of the islands.

For information on Corsica and the islands on the N side of the Strait of Bonifacio see Rod Heikell's *Mediterranean France and Corsica.*

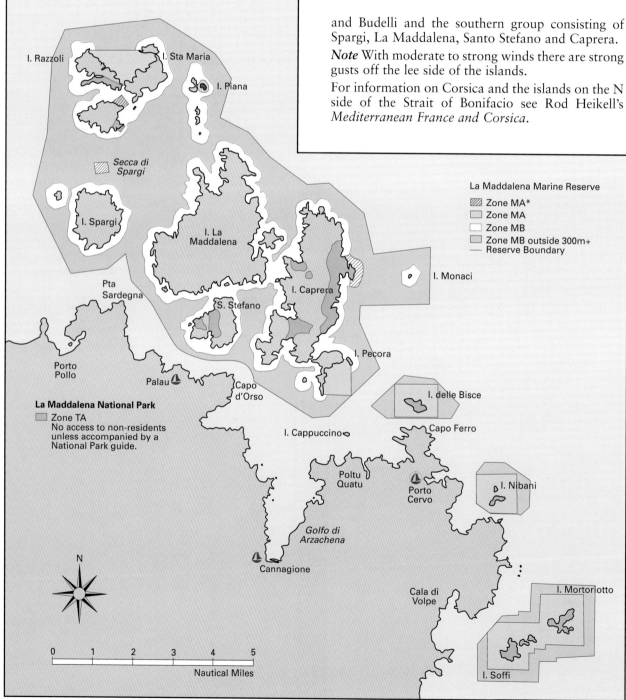

La Maddalena Marine Reserve
Zone MA*
Zone MA
Zone MB
Zone MB outside 300m+
Reserve Boundary

La Maddalena National Park
Zone TA
No access to non-residents unless accompanied by a National Park guide.

LA MADDALENA NATIONAL PARK AND MARINE RESERVE

La Maddalena Archipelago National Park and Marine Reserve

A vast marine reserve, divided into zones which differ from those in other AMPs.

For more details and the latest park regulations see www.lamaddalenapark.it/download/documenti/zonizzazione/zonizzazione-2010-alta.pdf

Zone MA* (special protection)

In addition to the restrictions of Zone MA
All navigation, anchoring, mooring, swimming, fishing and diving is prohibited.

There are three Zone MA* areas:
1. Porto Madonna (N end of Dead Man's Reef Passage)
2. Spiaggia Rosa (Pink Beach)
3. Punta Coticcio

Zone MA
Navigation, temporary stopover. Mooring and anchoring are prohibited.

5% of moorings are reserved for residents and locals from the Comune di La Maddalena.
Swimming permitted.
No anchoring.
No fishing.
No SCUBA diving.
No rubbish.
No pump-out of any sort.
No interfering with nesting sites.

Zone MB within 300m of the coast
Free anchoring is allowed within 300m from the coast only with a permit, and clear of posidonia (sea grass) beds. From 1st June to 30th September anchoring overnight is not permitted, but those with a permit and a holding tank, and using a buoy, are permitted to stay.

Note
1. Care is needed as not all buoys are laid in sufficient depths for many yachts.
2. Anchoring in a bay where there are mooring buoys is prohibited and subject to a fine of €50.
3. Residents with holding tanks are permitted to anchor overnight.

Where there are no such buoys, free anchoring is allowed. In order to protect the environment and respect the park you are required to anchor on sandy banks, avoiding areas where the seabed is covered with *praterie di Posidonia* (sea grass).
SCUBA diving by special permit only.
Sport fishing by special permit only.
No jet-skis or water-skis within 300m of the coast.
No rubbish.
No pump-out of any sort.
No interfering with nesting sites.

Zone MB >300m from the coast
Passage and navigation, short- and long-time stays and anchoring are unregulated.
Free anchoring is permitted more than 300m from the coast without a permit.
Jet-skis and water-skis only permitted from 0800–1200 and 1700–1900.

Other regulations for the La Maddalena Marine Reserve

Motor navigation in the park area is limited to 7kns within 300m of the coast where navigation is permitted, 15 knots in the other zones beyond 300m.

Automatic bilge pumps must be turned off.

All types of amateur and commercial fishing are banned inside Zone MA. In Zones MB, sport fishing is permitted for residents, while non-residents over 16 years must purchase a permit from the park authorities or from sports shops.

Underwater fishing is permitted in Zone MB for residents only from 1 September to 30 June. Outside this period non-residents may also fish in the waters of La Maddalena, but at a charge (€52 per month).

Unaccompanied diving using breathing apparatus is permitted for non-residents, but a payment must be made to the park authorities, as follows:

€5 for a single dive

€75 for a pass valid until the end of the current year.

Important note
Because of the complexity of the rules governing the use of the marine reserve and the fact that they are subject to frequent changes, it is important to check information at the archipelago's tourist offices, or refer to the contacts below.

La Maddalena Archipelago National Park and Marine Reserve permits
To navigate within the Zones MA and MB of the Marine reserve between 1 May–31 October, non-resident yachtsmen must obtain a permit of navigation. This permit also allows the free use of mooring buoys within the park. Fees can be paid on arrival to a relevant park official, at the park's main office or at other designated offices, at authorised tourist ports, and also via the website by credit card or PayPal. Those without a permit will pay a 40% surcharge.

Yacht length metres	*Day permit € per m*	*2 week permit €*	*Monthly permit €*
8–10	2	130	250
11–13	2	165	320
14–16	2	195	380
17–20	3	460	900
20–24	4	760	1500

Note Sailing yachts can claim a 40% discount on the above rates (ie the daily rate for a 12m yacht is €14.40 (€1.20/m)

✉ Parco Nazionale Arcipelago La Maddalena, Via G.Cesare 7, 07024 La Maddalena ✆ 0789 790 211 *Fax* 0789 720 049
Email info@lamaddalenapark.it
www.lamaddalenapark.it
www.lamaddalenapark.net (English/French)

The Northern group

These islands have few inhabitants and little in the way of vegetation or water. There are lots of tripper boats churning around, but they all disappear at sundown.

Isola Razzoli

The northwesternmost of the group, it is low (the highest point reaches 65m/213ft), barren and uninhabited. On the NW extremity a light is exhibited: Fl.WR.2.5s77m19/15M. The red sector covers Iles Lavezzi between 092°–137° and Isola Santa Maria and Corcelli and Barrettini islets between 237°–320°.

The light tower and lighthouse behind are conspicuous. There are three bays providing good shelter:

Cala Lunga (Zone MB <300m)

On the W side of the island. Care must be taken of the above and below-water rocks at the entrance, but particularly on the S side. Pick up a mooring or anchor in 3–4m on a sand and rock bottom. Open to the W but otherwise good shelter. Note that the S shores of the bay are in Zone TA of the National Park. No access without a guide.

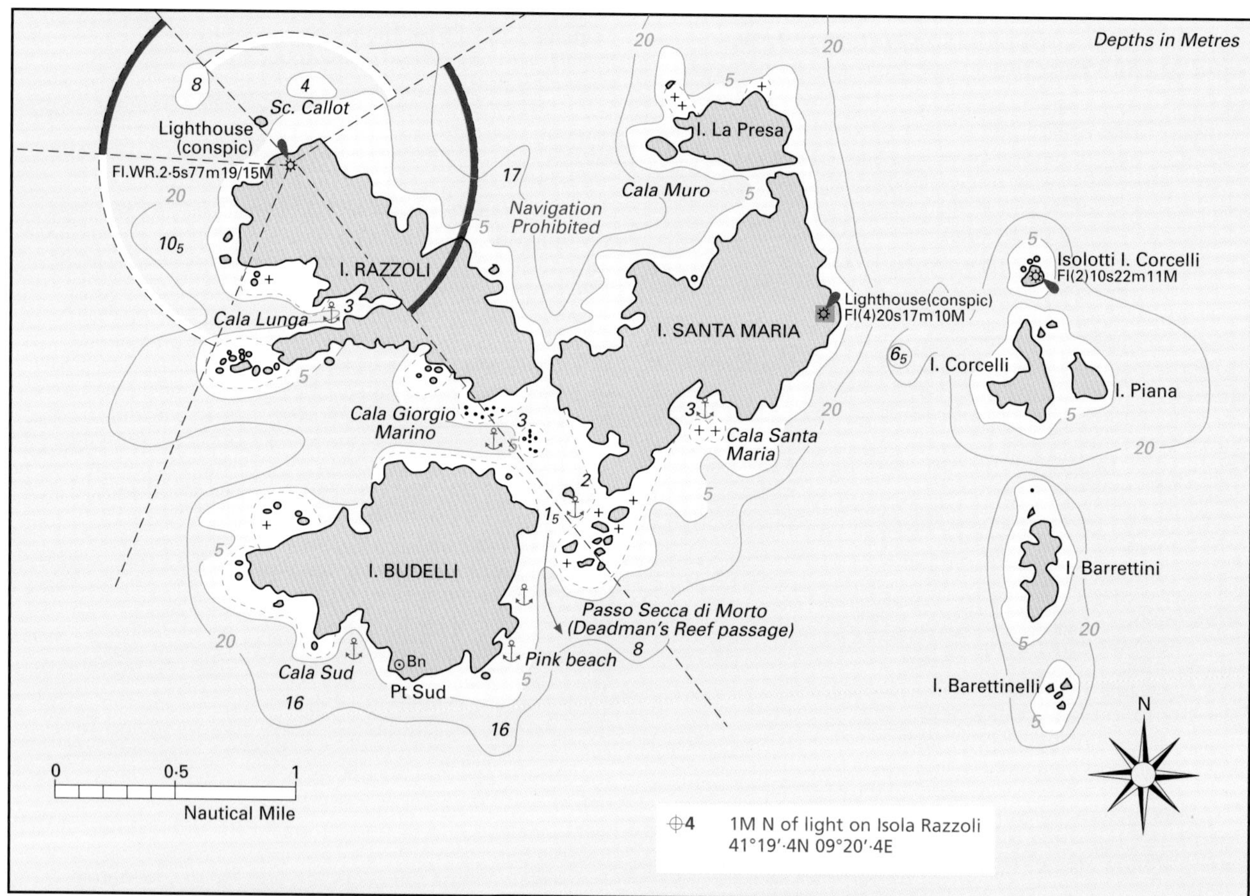

LA MADDALENA NORTHERN GROUP
⊕41°19′·4N 09°20′·4E IM N of I. Razzoli lighthouse

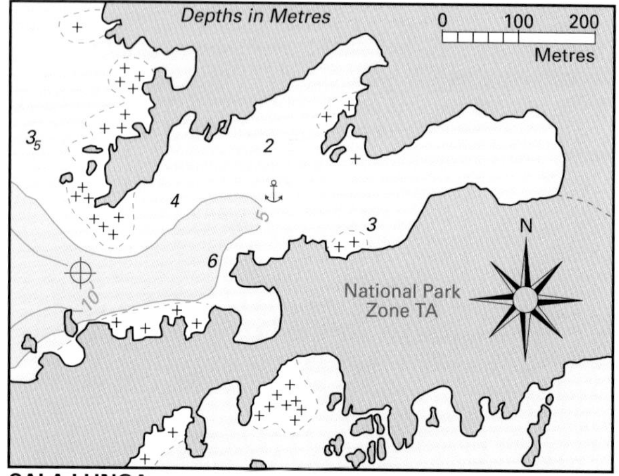

CALA LUNGA
⊕41°17′·9N 09°20′·5E

Cala Giorgio Marino (Zone MB <300m)

On the S side of the island, is a bay sheltered by all three islands of the northern group. Anchor off the southern shore in 3–5m on a sandy bottom. The holding has been reported to be indifferent. Care should be taken of rocks fringing the shore. Open to the W but otherwise good shelter.

Note The park authority has laid around fifteen mooring buoys in the bay in order to protect the sea grass (*Posidonia*) and other vegetation on the sea bottom. Use of these buoys is free to those holding a Marine Reserve permit. More buoys have been laid in many other bays around the Marine Reserve, although care is needed as not all buoys are laid in sufficient depths for many yachts. It should be noted that anchoring on *Posidonia* beds is prohibited and subject to a fine of €50.

Deadman's Reef Passage (Zone MA*/MB <300m)

A transit parallel to the coast and outside the market buoys through Zone MA* is permitted at a max of 3kns. Yachts anchor in and around the southern entrance to this passage although care is needed threading your way into it. Anchor where convenient on sand and some rock. Good shelter from the prevailing wind in quite wonderful surroundings.

Looking SW along Cala Cavalieri across Passo Secca di Morto
La Maddalena National Park

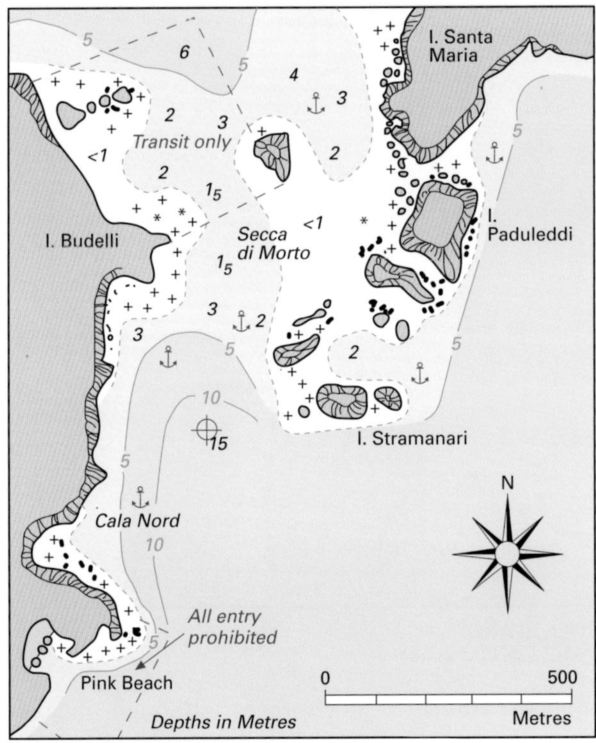

DEADMAN'S REEF PASSAGE TO PINK BEACH
⊕41°16´·93N 09°21´·66E WGS84

The area off the NE corner is in Zone MA* although swimming and access to rowing boats is permitted.

The rest of the area is in Zone MB.

Isola Santa Maria

Lies immediately E of Isola Razzoli from which it is separated by Passo degli Asinelli. I. La Presa, with reefs extending for a short distance N, lies close off the N side of Isola Santa Maria. Off the E side there are the Corcelli islets, I. Barrettini and I. Barrettinelli. The passage between these islets and Santa Maria is free of dangers except for a 6·5m shoal patch. A light is exhibited on the E side of Santa Maria from an impressive lighthouse (a circular tower with a cupola and a two-storeyed building) showing Fl(4)20s10M. A light is also exhibited from a white stone tower on a rock immediately N of I. Corcelli Fl(2)10s11M. There are two bays on the island providing some shelter depending on the wind and sea.

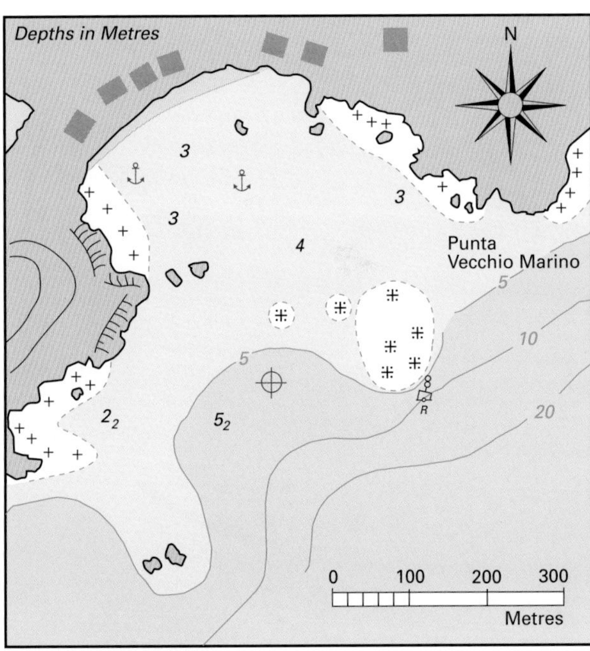

CALA SANTA MARIA
⊕41°17´·34N 09°22´·38E WGS84

Cala Muro (Zone MA)

⊕ 41°18'·3N 09°22'·3E

On the NW tip under I. La Presa.

Note This anchorage lies within Zone MA of the Marine Reserve, and all navigation is now prohibited.

Cala Santa Maria (Zone MB <300m)

On the SE side. Care must be taken of two reefs in the entrance. Anchor in 3–4m on a sandy bottom. Open to the S and east. Good sandy beach and wonderful rocky surroundings.

Isola Budelli

Lies close S of Razzoli and SW of Santa Maria. It is separated from the latter by Passo Secca di Morto ('Dead' or 'Deadman's' passage) through which there is a shallow (1·5m) rocky passage close to Isola Budelli. It is now within Zone MA* and all navigation is now prohibited.

There are three anchorages:

Cala Sud (Zone MB <300m)

⊕ 41°16'·7N 09°20'·6E

On the SW side immediately W of Punta Sud on which there is a beacon. It offers indifferent shelter in 5–8m on a sandy bottom.

Pink Beach (Spiaggia Rosa) (Zone MA*)

On the SE side there is a small cove. Much of the cove is now buoyed off and all access is prohibited, including swimming. The cove takes its name from the pink colour of the sand and is a beautiful little spot.

Cala Nord (Zone MB <300m)

Just N of Pink Beach there is a bight used by yachts and yachts also anchor in the entrance to Deadman's Reef Passage. Use park authority mooring buoys.

The pink beach is now completely protected and buoyed to prevent access *La Maddalena National Park*

The Southern group

These islands are larger and greener than the northern group. There are numerous anchorages and the sea is everywhere a crystal clear turquoise and aquamarine over a rock and sand bottom.

Nelson spent a few months here waiting for the French to come out before the Battle of Trafalgar. He could not land on Sardinia because the Kingdom of Sardinia was theoretically neutral, instead he busied his men charting the area and firing off letters to the Ministry explaining how this northern end of Sardinia would make a superb naval base. His letters had little effect and in the end Malta was chosen as the British naval base in the Mediterranean after Gibraltar. His death at Trafalgar robbed him of the chance to press his case in London and much later it was to be the Americans who acted on his wisdom and established a naval base on Sant Stefano.

Isola Spargi (Zone MB <300m)

The westernmost of the southern group lying just under a mile W of La Maddalena and just over a mile N of Diego Point on Sardinia. The island is rocky and hilly rising to 155m (509ft) at its summit. Off its southern tip lies Secca Corsara (least depth 3m/10ft) marked by a S cardinal beacon and a light Q(6)+LFl.15s5M. A small islet, Spargiotto, lies off the NW corner of Spargi.

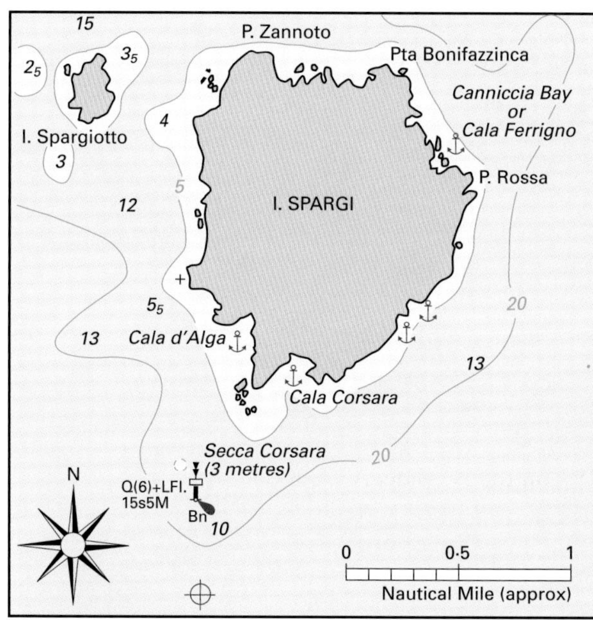

ISOLA SPARGI
⊕41°12´·9N 09°20´·2E

There are three anchorages although in the summer yachts anchor all along the E coast wherever there are convenient depths.

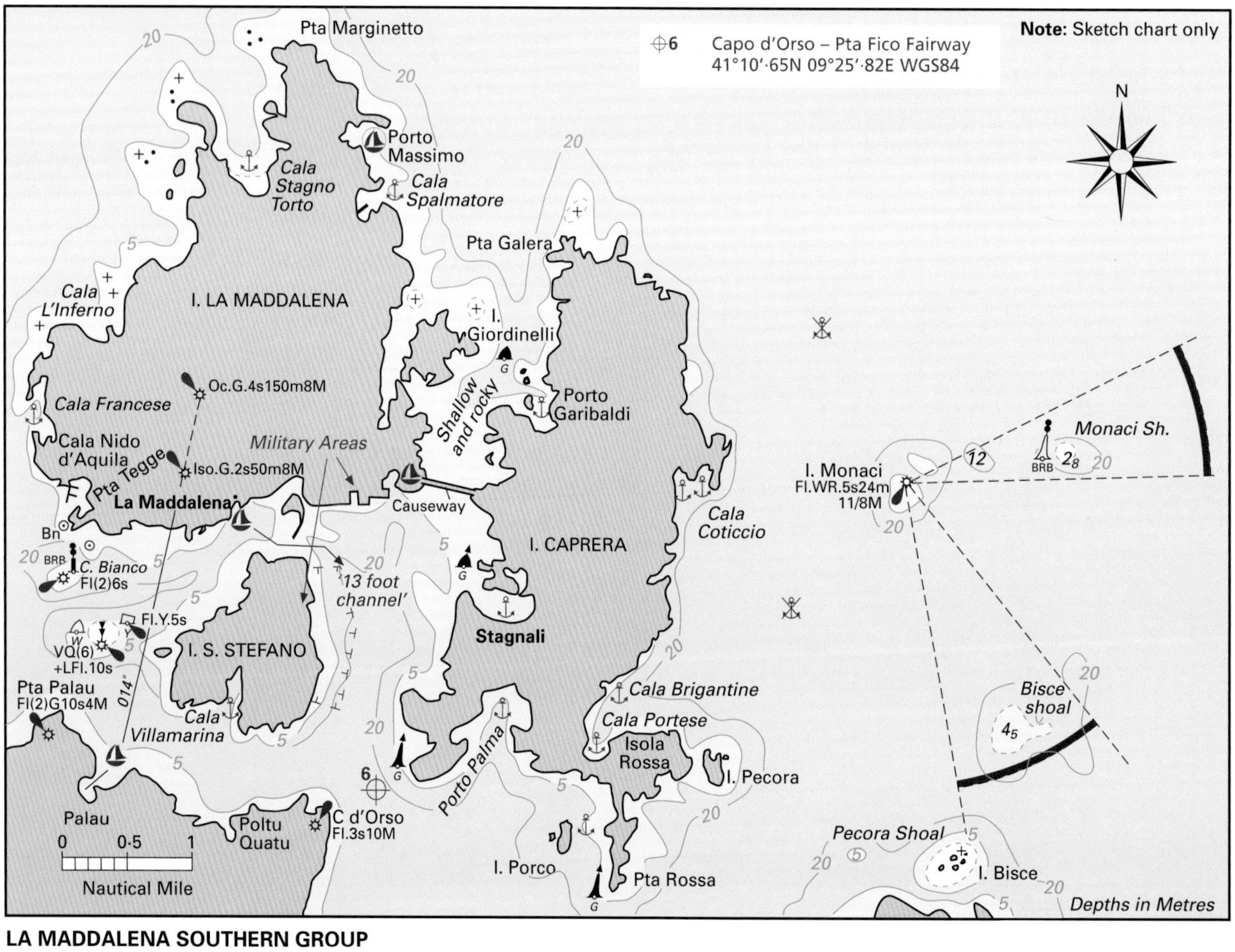

LA MADDALENA SOUTHERN GROUP

Cala d'Alga

⌖ 41°13'·8N 09°20'·2E

Lies on the W side of the southern tip of the island. Care should be taken of offlying rocks in the middle of the bay. Anchor in 3–5m on a sand and rock bottom. Open to the W and south.

Cala Corsara

⌖ 41°13'·7N 09°20'·5E

Lies on the E side of the southern tip. Open to the E and south. Good shelter from W–NW. Anchor clear of the buoyed area off the beach on sand.

Cala Ferrigno

⌖ 41°14'·7N 09°21'·5E

Lies on the NE side. A white house on the shore and a short quay below make identification easy. There are many rocky outcrops and a small yacht should only attempt to reach the quay in calm weather and with someone in a dinghy going ahead to con the way in. There are 4–5m depths at the end of the quay but little room to manoeuvre because of the rocky outcrops. Open only to the east. The cove is delightful. There is only the house and a well ashore.

Isola La Maddalena (Zone MB <300m)

The largest of the La Maddalena archipelago and the only one which supports a sizeable population. Although a stony island, there are cultivated patches and some forested areas giving the granite a green coat in places. It is hilly at the southwestern end (153m/535ft) and at its northern end (84m/276ft). Its coast is much indented and there are numerous anchorages offering good shelter. The coast is everywhere fringed by a rocks and caution is needed when navigating inshore.

Western approaches

The approach to the south coast and to La Maddalena harbour is obstructed by above and below-water rocks. There are three approaches into the strait between La Maddalena and Isola Santo Stefano.

North Passage The S coast of Isola La Maddalena is fringed by a rocky bank which extends as much as ¼ mile offshore in places. The extremities of the rocky bank are marked by stone beacons which are easily identified. Off Punta Tegge, the SW tip of La Maddalena, lies a rock, Scoglio Bianco (White Rock) with a pyramidal beacon, 16·2m (53ft) high, on it. NNW of Scoglio Bianco lies a detached shoal with a small (3m high) beacon on it. A red buoy with ■ topmark lies about 240m SE of Scoglio Bianco and marks the extremity of Secca di Forte Tegge (Forte Tegge Reef) which extends from the coast. About ¼ of a mile S of Scoglio Bianco lies Secca di Mezzo (Middle Reef) with a red and black beacon on it, topmark ⁑. A light is exhibited on the beacon: Fl(2)6s5M. Nearby is a WRW (faded) masonry beacon. North Passage between the two reefs is deep and free of dangers in the fairway.

Mezzo Passo (Middle Passage) Lies between Secca di Mezzo and Secca del Palau lying about 0·5M SE.

Mezzo Passo looking across Secca di Mezzo to Scoglio Bianco pyramidal beacon behind

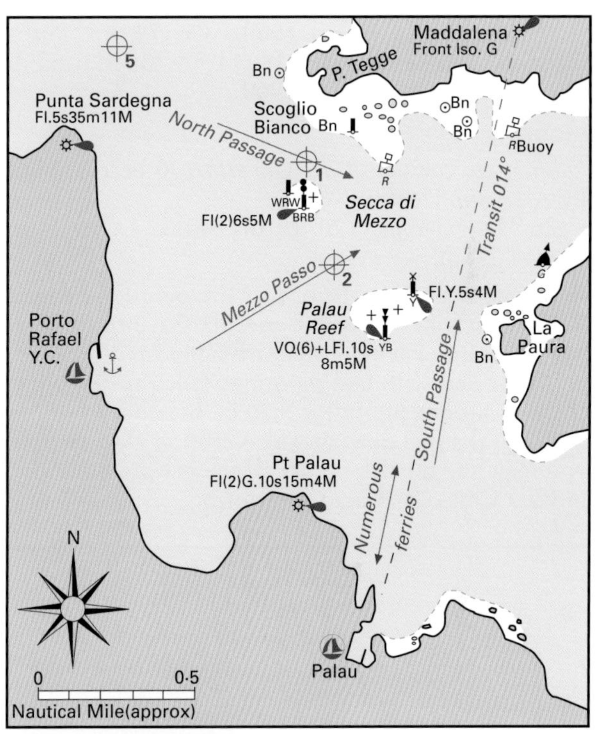

MADDALENA CHANNEL
⌖1 41°12'·33N 09°22'·99E WGS84
⌖2 41°12'·04N 09°22'·86E WGS84

Secca del Palau is a rocky shoal with three large above-water rocks. It is marked by a S cardinal beacon and a yellow beacon with a basket and x topmark. The S cardinal is lit VQ(6)+LFl.10s5M. Mezzo Passo is the most commonly used channel and there are good depths in the fairway.

South Passage Lies between Secca del Palau and the western edge of I. La Paura off Isola Santo Stefano. A concrete beacon with a bronze sculpture atop is situated on the western edge of La Paura. The conical buoy shown about 300m NNE of La Paura is small and difficult to see. In the roadstead between La Maddalena and Isola Santo Stefano are several large unlit mooring buoys. South Passage is the one most frequently used by the ferries running between La Maddalena and Palau.

LA MADDALENA (CALA GAVETTA AND CALA MANGIAVOLPE)

Approach

Despite the numerous above and below-water rocks fringing the approaches, the approach is straightforward.

Conspicuous Once into the roadstead the leading marks below Fort Camicio (in transit 066·2°) show the way. However the marks are not really necessary. The buildings of La Maddalena are easily identified. If in doubt one of the numerous ferries coming or going will enable you to pin-point the harbour.

By night Leading lights on the slopes to the W of La Maddalena show the way (014°) through South Passage: Front Iso.G.2s8M/Rear Oc.G.4s8M. Care must be taken of the unlit mooring buoys in the approaches.

VHF Ch 11, 16 (0700–1900). Ch 74 for Porto turistico Cala Gavetta. Ch 16, 11, 09 for Marina di Cala Mangiavolpe (0700–1900).

Mooring

Data Porto turistico Cala Gavetta 130 berths. Max LOA c.16m. Depths 2–8m.
Cala Mangiavolpe 120 berths. Max LOA 24m. Depths 2–6m.

Berth Stern or bows-to one of the pontoons where directed or where possible in Cala Gavetta or Cala Mangiavolpe. The pontoons are signposted for LOA and provided with laid moorings tailed to the quay. If the pontoons are full it may be possible to find a berth on the fuel quay in Cala Gavetta, alternatively you may find a berth on one of the private pontoons in Cala Chiesa or Cala Camiciotto.

Cala Gavetta looking SW towards Isola Santo Stefano
La Maddalena National Park

Shelter Good all-round shelter although the numerous ferries cause some wash as they go past.

Cala Mangiavolpe is open S–ESE and is exposed to the wash of all the passing ferries.

Note There are more pontoons in Cala Camicia beyond I. Chiesa, but this is part of the military area and entry is prohibited.

Authorities Harbourmaster and customs. *Ormeggiatori*. Charge band 5.
Porto turistico ☎ 0789 730 121
Email cgavetta@yahoo.it
Marina di Cala Mangiavolpe ☎ 333 563 0553
Email calamangiavolpe@yahoo.it
Cala Mangiavolpe, Ecomar ☎ 338 637 8256
Email ecomar_@yahoo.it
Soc Genesa ☎ 0789 731 125

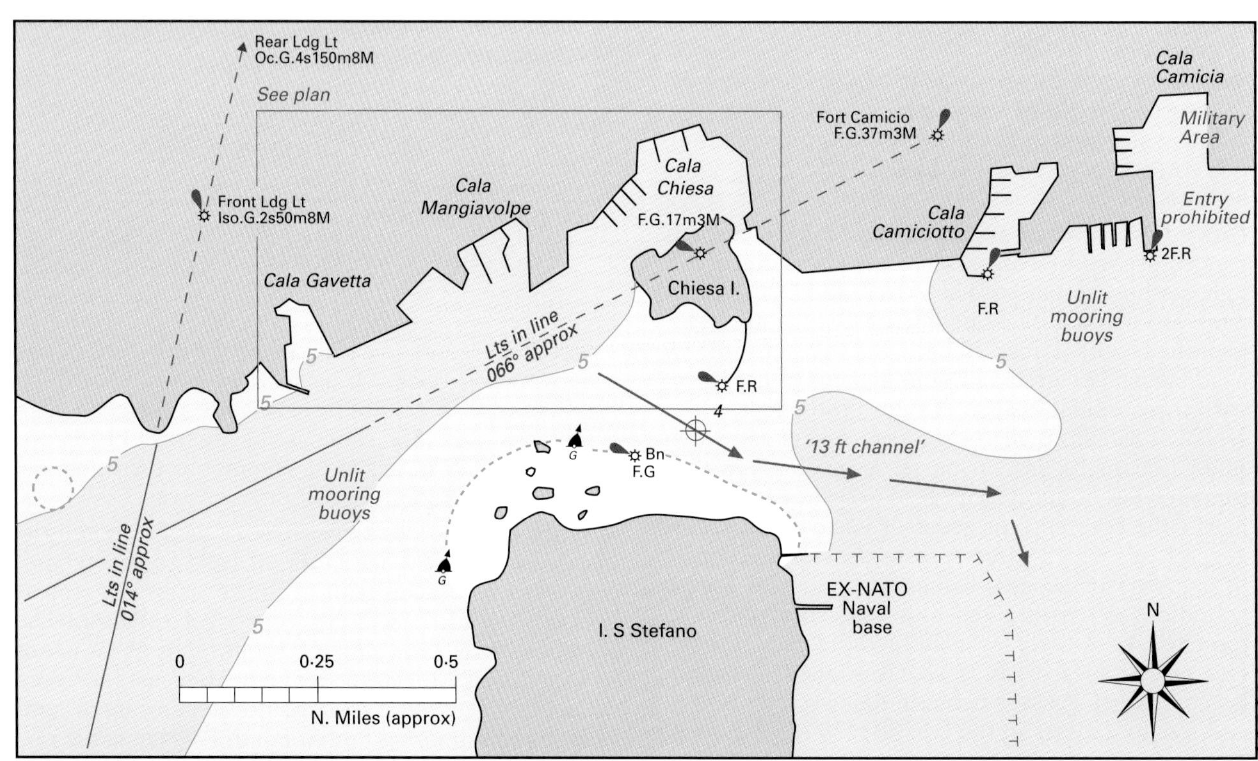

LA MADDALENA - APPROACHES AND '13 FOOT CHANNEL'
⊕41°12´·58N 09°24´·99E WGS84

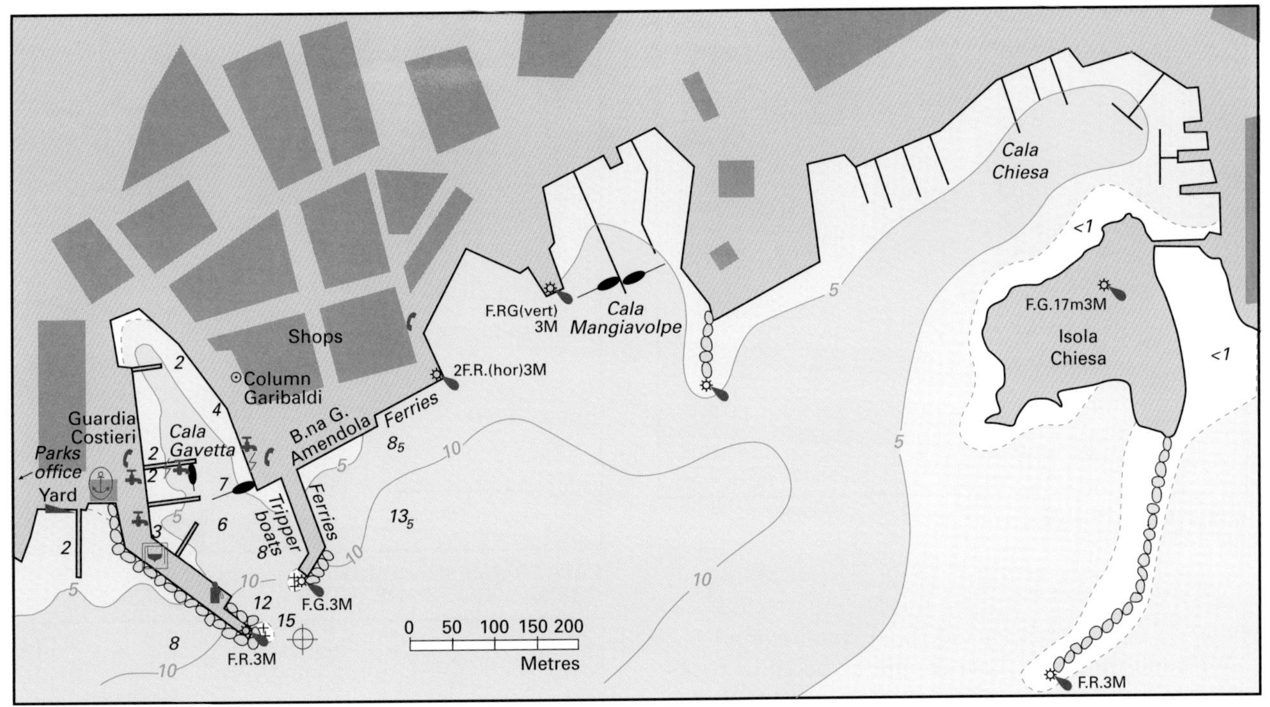

LA MADDALENA
⊕41°12′·60N 09°24′·31E WGS84

Facilities

Service Water and electricity at most berths on the quay. Toilets and showers (0800–1100/1700–2100).
Fuel On the quay.
Repairs A 20-ton crane and 10-ton slipway. Yachts are hauled onto hard standing by the quay. Engineering and mechanical repairs. Chandlers. Sailmaker.
Provisions Good shopping for all provisions. Covered market in the town. Bigger market on Wednesdays.
Eating out Excellent restaurants, trattorias and pizzerias.
Other PO. Bank. ATM. Italgaz and Camping Gaz. Gas bottles can be filled at one of the chandleries near the waterfront. Ferries to Palau.

General

La Maddalena is an ideal base for exploring the archipelago. Around Isola La Maddalena and the two adjacent islands there are enough anchorages for a busy week of gunk-holing – to explore everywhere thoroughly will take you longer. The La Maddalena Park Office is in the town, 100m or so W of the W side of the harbour. From its opening in 1973, the NATO base on Santo Stefano bestowed a prosperity on the islands, though strangely it was little spoiled because of it. The presence of nuclear submarines, and possible links to higher incidences of lymphatic cancer drove a local campaign for answers, and perhaps the final straw came on 2003 when a US nuclear submarine hit Monaci shoal. Local people recall hearing a load explosion, but it took three weeks for the crash to be revealed. The last US naval ship left Santo Stefano in September 2007, and the base was closed in January 2008. Many US navy sailors remember the place and the people with real warmth, but many of the locals feel more than ready to stand on their own and move on. With the protected land and waters of the National Park already secure, it is hoped that the Sards will take as sensible an approach to developing the old military areas for tourism. In the summer it attracts a large number of tourists from the hotels on the mainland who come on day trips, but by evening they have all departed.

Chiesa passage ('13ft channel')

To the E of Cala Mangiavolpe lie the numerous piers and the buildings of the Italian navy. Isola Chiesa is a low rocky island with a rough breakwater extending S from it for about 260m. The N end of Isola Santo Stefano is fringed by above and below-water rocks, two green conical buoys mark the edge of the shoals off the NW coast of the island and a green conical beacon marks the S side of the channel leading between the breakwater from Isola Chiesa and Isola Santo Stefano. There are least depths of 4·3m (13ft) in the fairway of this channel. The channel is lit at the extremity of the breakwater F.R and at the beacon F.G. Passage through here is more straightforward in practice than it appears on paper.

MARINA DEL PONTE

Beyond the military docks of Cala Camicia, at the W end of the Maddalena–Caprera causeway, a new marina is under construction.

Approach

From Cala Gavetta or Cala Mangiavolpe, pass through the Chiesa Passage, past the military docks and around Pta Moneta. From the S the approach up Rada di Santo Stefano is straightforward. The marina lies immediately to the W of the pass in the causeway.

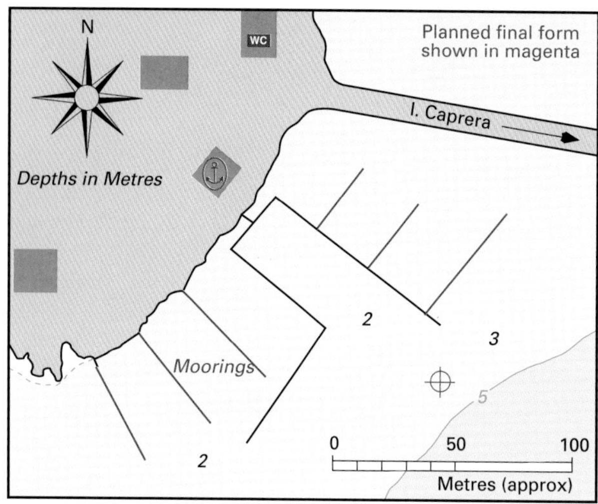

MARINA DEL PONTE
⊕41°12′·9N 09°26′·4E

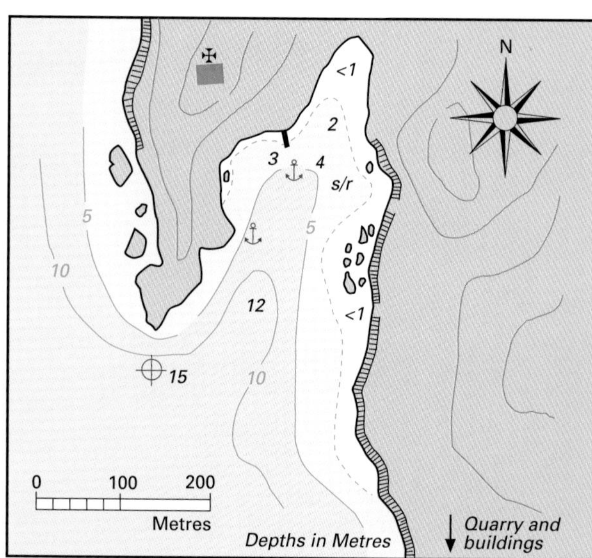

CALA FRANCESE – N END
⊕41°13′·49N 09°22′42E WGS84

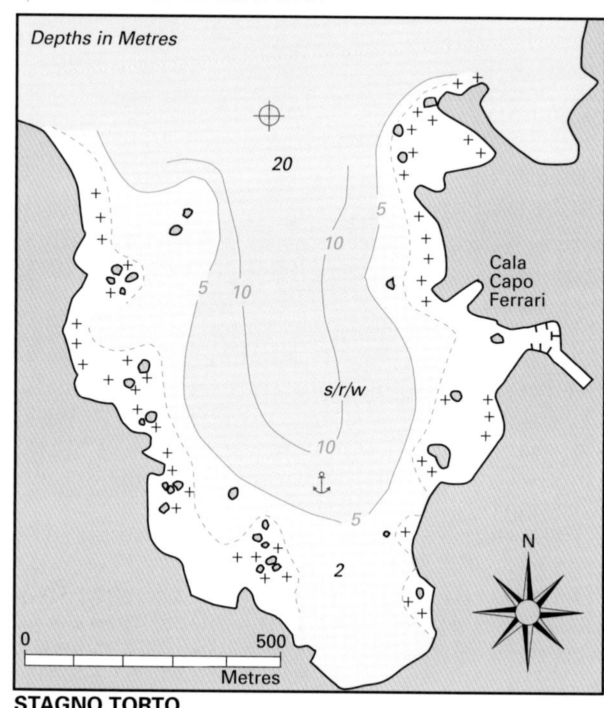

STAGNO TORTO
⊕41°15′·5N 09°24′·6E

Dangers Offlying rocks and shoal water extend out all around the coast. Care should be taken of rocks off Pta Moneta, and isolated rocks over ¼M W of I. dell Aglio.

Mooring

Data 120 berths. Max LOA 18m. Depths 1–6m reported. Water and electricity on the quay.

Berth Where directed. Laid moorings tailed to pontoons.

Shelter Good shelter except from southerlies.

Authorities Marina staff. Charge band 5/6.

✆ 368 553 858
Email marinadelponte@tiscalinet.it

Marina Nido d'Aquila

41°12'·90N 09°22'·92E

Pontoon berths on the W shores of Cala Nido d'Aquila on the SW corner of Isola Maddalena.

Approach

Care needed off off-lying rocks off Punta Tegge. The bay is everywhere rocky and mostly shallow.

VHF Ch 09, 16.

Mooring

Data 100 berths (300 planned). Max LOA 20m. Depths 1–4m.

Berth Where directed. Care needed for those drawing more than 1·8m. Laid moorings tailed to pontoons.

Shelter The bay is open S–W. Reasonable shelter in settled summer conditions.

Authorities Marina staff. Charge band 6+ (July–August).

✆ 334 710 9642 / 0789 720 053
Email info@marinanidodaquila.it
www.marinanidodaquila.it

Facilities

Services Water and electricity. Showers and toilets planned.

General

A low-key marina in wonderful surroundings outside the bustle of La Maddalena town.

Cala Francese

Lies on the W coast. The southern end of the bay has numerous above and below-water rocks. An old quarry and buildings will be seen here. The northern end offers better shelter and more room. Anchor in 4–10m on a sand and rock bottom. There is a small pier in the NW corner to which a yacht can take a line. The setting is attractive but the beach a bit scrappy. It is about a half-hour walk to La Maddalena for supplies.

Stagno Torto (Cala Capo Ferrari)

A large bay on the N coast. In calm weather or when the wind has a southerly component this bay can be

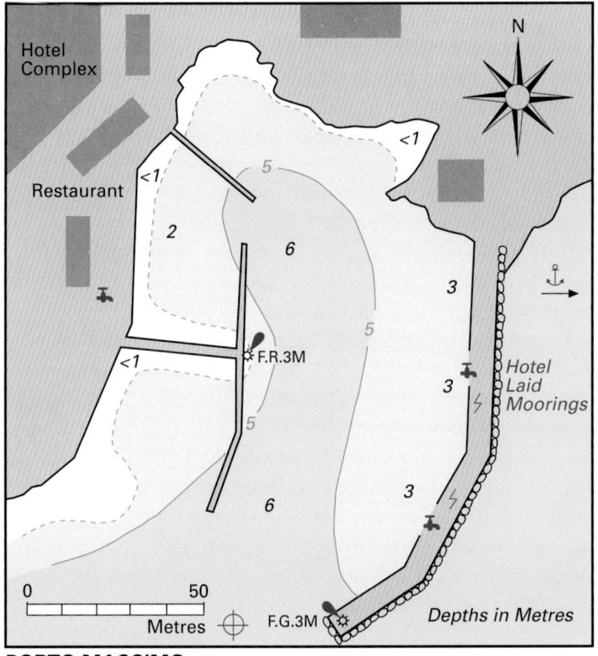

PORTO MASSIMO
⊕41°15´·4N 09°25´·6E

used. If the wind goes into the N then the bay should be vacated. Care is needed of the numerous above and below-water rocks around the edge of the bay. Anchor in 4–10m where convenient. The bottom is sand and weed with some rock, good holding once the anchor is in.

Cala Capo Ferrari, the narrow inlet in the E side of the bay, has several pontoons suitable for very small motorboats.

PORTO MASSIMO (PORTO LUNGO)

A private marina associated with a hotel complex.

Approach

It is difficult to see exactly where the marina is from the north. From the E, the hotel complex ashore is easily identified.

VHF Ch 09, 16 (0700–1900).

Porto Massimo looking north

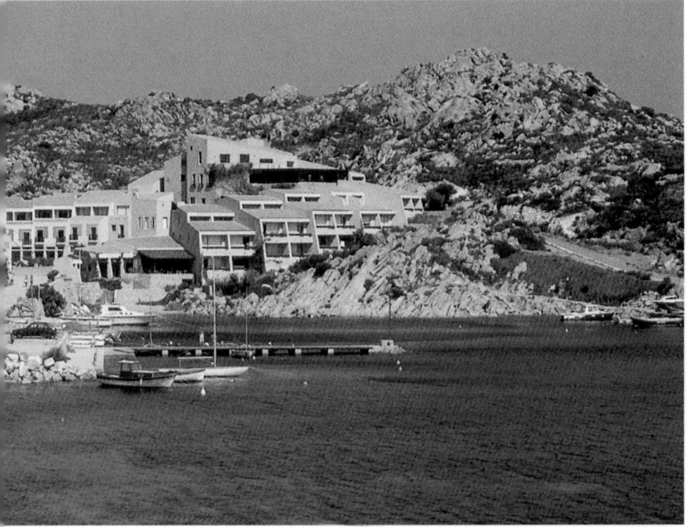

Mooring

Data 200 berths. Max LOA 35/50m. Depths 1–5m.

Berth Where directed. Laid moorings tailed to a buoy or the quay. Laid moorings E of the breakwater. Park authority buoys within the bay.

Shelter Good shelter although it is open S for a short distance.

Authorities Harbourmaster and marina staff. Charge band 6+ (July–August).
ITAS ✆ 079 734 033 / 348 885 7973 / 347 686 9901
Fax 0789 721 039
www.portomassimo.it

Facilities

Services Water and electricity (220/380V) at every berth. Showers and toilets.
Repairs 10-ton crane.
Eating out Restaurant and bar.

General

The setting is exquisite and the water crystal clear, but for my money the hotel complex and marina lack something: vitality, life, colour? Well, something anyway.

CALA SPALMATORE (ZONE MB)

Lies immediately S of Porto Massimo. The above-water rocks on the N side of the entrance are easily identified. Proceed into the bay and pick up a mooring at the southern end in 3–4m or at the northern end off the beach in 4–5m. Park authority mooring buoys. The bottom is sand and rock, good holding. There is a pier running out from the W shore which has 4m at its extremity. The rest of the pier is bordered by underwater rocks. Good shelter in the bay although NE–E winds make it uncomfortable and it can become untenable. If it blows strongly from the E one can move around to Porto Massimo.

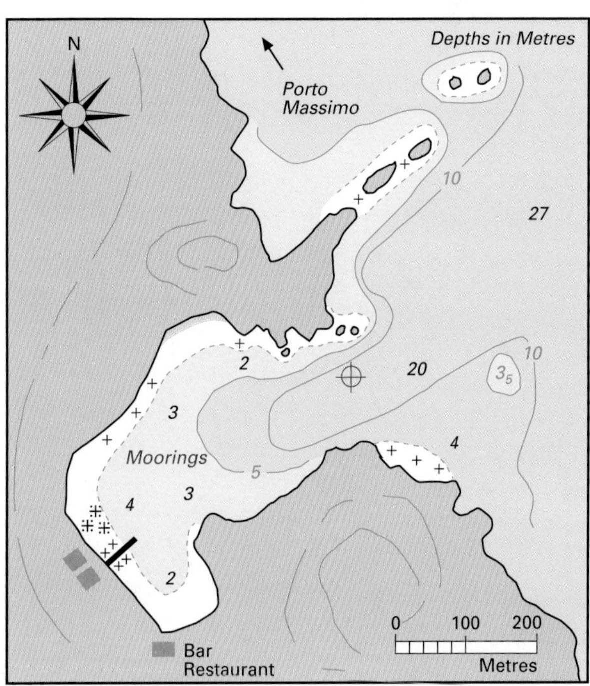

CALA SPALMATORE
⊕41°15´·0N 09°26´·0E

Restaurant and bar ashore. The bay is exquisite with a sandy beach and clear, clear emerald water.

CALA PETICCHIA (MARINA DEI GIARDINELLI)

⊕ 41°13'·65N 09°26'·3E

A small marina under development between Isola Giardinelli and Isola Maddalena. Pontoons in place. Approach from the N keeping well clear of the rocks off Punta Rossa. The bay is everywhere shallow and rock- bound. At present looks limited to smaller shoal draft craft. Further development underway.

✆ 349 451 9072 / 339 279 0126
Email info@calapeticchia.it

Moneta passage

There are several coves and bays in the passage between Isola La Maddalena and Isola Caprera which, while beautiful, are rock-bound. A yacht should explore this area only in calm weather and with someone conning in the bows. There are numerous wrecks, big and small around this coast, and these should serve as a warning to inattentive souls when navigating around here.

Isola San Stefano

A comparatively flat and mostly barren island. It is highest on the western side (100m/330ft) sloping down to the east. The northern end of the island is a military area and anchoring nearby and landing are prohibited. There is only one good anchorage at Villamarina on the S coast.

Cala di Villamarina (Zone MB/TA)

The green light structure on the E side of the entrance and a white house near the head of the inlet are conspicuous. Care should be taken of the above and below-water rocks fringing the entrance. A yacht can go either alongside or stern-to the quay or anchor out and take a line ashore. A local excursion boat uses the quay on some days so you may have to move off in the morning. Good all-round shelter. There are no facilities ashore but in the quarries behind the inlet lies an unfinished statue – the head and arms are finished but little else.

The shore at the head of the bay lies within Zone TA of the National Park. Access is prohibited unless accompanied by a park guide.

I originally (and incorrectly) identified the statue as that of Garibaldi, but as Richard Williamson in correspondence with Alessandro Olschki has pointed out, it could not possibly be Garibaldi because he does not have a beard! It could well be Domenicio Millelire (1761–1827), a native of Sardinia who was instrumental in seeing off Bonaparte when he landed on San Stefano intending to capture the archipelago. Apparently as a *nocchiere* of the Sardinian navy he would have worn a hat that looks like the sou'wester on the statue. Millelire was awarded a gold medal and a submarine in the Italian navy was subsequently named in his honour. I have recently been advised that it is in fact Admiral Ciano, a First World War naval hero. His son married the daughter of Benito Mussolini and became leader of the Fascist movement. He resisted Italy's entry to the Second World War and to that end mounted a coup in 1943, only to be executed for treason. My thanks to W Musker for solving the puzzle.

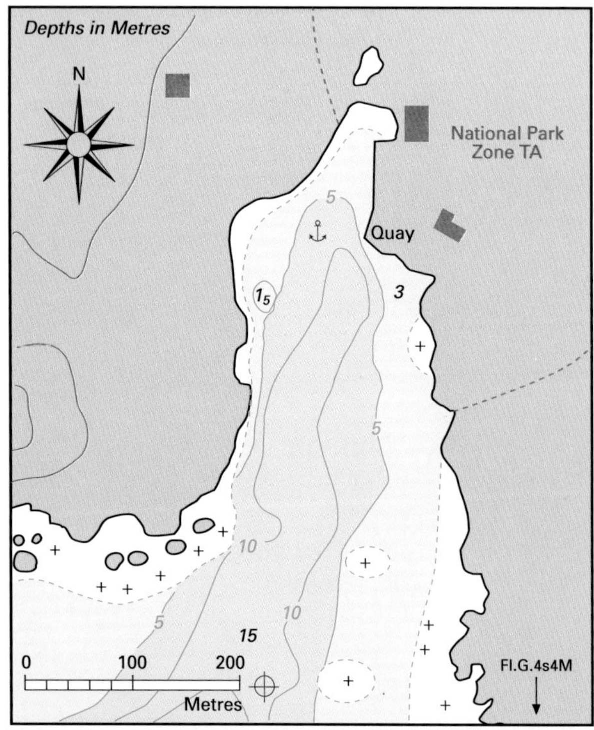

CALA DI VILLAMARINA
⊕ 41°11'·3N 09°24'·4E

Isola Caprera

The easternmost island of the archipelago is hilly and scrubby. It rises up to 212m (696ft) in the centre. It is connected on its western side to Isola La Maddalena by a causeway. A number of reefs and islets fringe the island. A reef extends for about half a mile N of the NW tip. About 1·3 miles E of Punta Coticcio lies I. Monaci with a stone tower on it at a height of 24m/79ft from which a light is exhibited Fl.WR.5s11/8M: the red sector covers Secca dei Monaci (246°-268°) and Secca delle Bisce (317°–357°). About 1·2 miles ENE of I. Monaci lies Secca dei Monaci marked by a conical buoy with a • topmark. About two miles SSE of I. Monaci lies Secca delle Bisce with a least depth over it of 4·6m

In the northeastern part of Rada di Santo Stefano there are numerous above- and below-water rocks.

Isola Caprera *De Agostini Picture Library, FOTOTECA ENIT*

Also in Rada di Santo Stefano are numerous large unlit mooring buoys.

Most of the island is a nature reserve and is a thoroughly pleasant place to walk around though parts of it are now a Zone TA, where access is prohibited unless accompanied by a park guide. Garibaldi spent the last years of his life in exile on Caprera after his part in the unification of Italy and his adventures in South America. His house, the *Casa Bianca*, built along South American lines, and his tomb are preserved as a memorial by the Italian government. After his death in 1882, his daughter, Donna Celia, lived on here. You can see his old red shirt, the saddle of his horse, numerous old photographs and other memorabilia. The house and tomb lie about three-quarters of a mile E of the causeway.

Porto Garibaldi (Zone MB<300m/TA)

A bay in the Moneta Passage on the NW side of Isola Caprera. Care needs to be taken of the above and below-water rocks in the vicinity. Anchor where shown in 4–5m on a sand and rock bottom, good holding. Keep one eye on the wind though; if it turns to the NW this anchorage is untenable and should be vacated. At the head of the bay there is a Club Med holiday village which at times can be a bit obtrusive – it depends on your inclinations.

CALA STAGNALI (Zone MB<300m/TA)

⊕ 41°12′·1N 9°27′·0E

A large bay opposite the northern tip of Isola Santo Stefano. Care must be taken of the numerous above and below-water rocks at the entrance and at the head of the bay. Anchor in 2m depths on sand and rock. A small-craft harbour is for local boats only. The lagoon that opens to the N is too shallow for even small yachts. There are numerous ruined buildings ashore and a hotel complex. This is reported to be the headquarters of the nature reserve. Ashore is a geological museum and the dolphin research centre.

Leading marks (white marks by houses) on 139° show the safe passage, lit F.G.3M/F.G.3M. A green buoy with ▲ topmark and a BW beacon mark the S side of the channel.

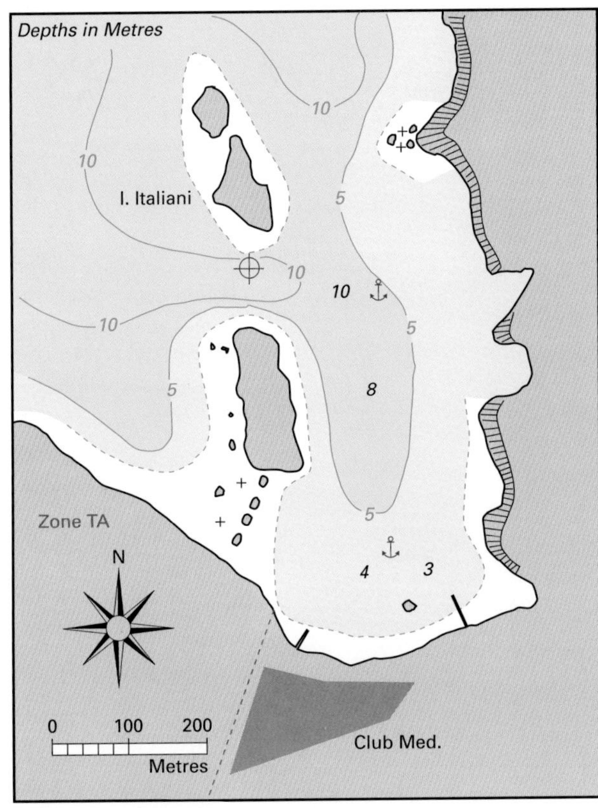

PORTO GARIBALDI
⊕41°13′·6N 09°27′·4E

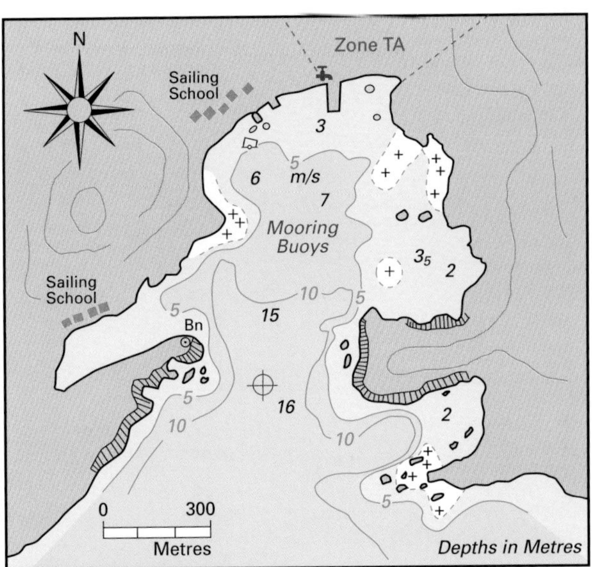

PORTO PALMA
⊕41°11′·1N 09°26′·9E

Porto Palma (Zone MB<300m/TA)

The restrictions on anchoring in Porto Palma have now been enforced and yachts must use park authority mooring buoys only. Care must be taken of above and below-water rocks fringing the coast and of two reefs on the E side of the bay with just over 1m of water over them.

There are two sailing schools on the W side of the bay, but no facilities to speak of. Good all-round shelter can be found somewhere in the bay depending on the wind direction. The cove on the E side of the bay is recommended as the best place to be if a swell is rolling into the anchorage at Porto Cervo and you need to move on.

Isolotto Porco (Zone MB<300m/TA)

⊕ 41°10′·3N 09°27′·9E

To the E of this island, which is S of Isola Caprera, there is an attractive anchorage. Care should be taken of rocky outcrops.

Cala Portese (Zone MB<300m/TA)

⊕ 41°11′·2N 09°28′·1E

On the N side of Isola Rossa. Park authority mooring buoys have been laid here. Open to the NE and with strong northerlies or easterlies a swell rolls in.

Uncomfortable with W wind that brings a NE swell.

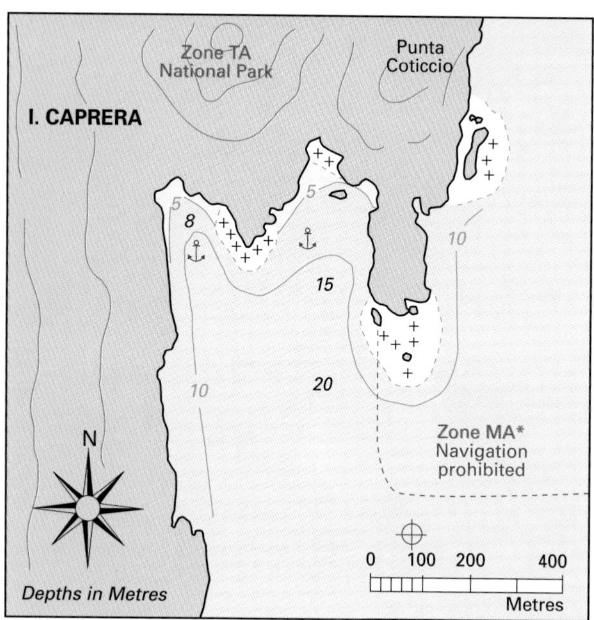

CALA COTICCIO
⊕41°12´·7N 09°29´·2E

Cala Brigantine (Zone MB<300m/TA)

⊕ 41°12′·3N 09°28′·7E

A small inlet just over a mile N of Isola Rossa. Care must be taken of above and below-water rocks fringing the entrance. Gusts into the cove with strong westerlies.

Cala Coticcio (Zone MA/MB<300m/TA)

(Known locally as **Tahiti Bay**)

Actually two coves which lie on the S side of Punta Coticcio. It is very deep except close-to and the holding is suspect on sand and rock. With strong westerlies there are gusts from different directions so it is advisable to take lines ashore. There are rocky outcrops running out from the shore so care is needed.

In the summer this is a popular day anchorage for the 'Riva' set and can be crowded. The more easterly of the two coves is the best, so if it is crowded wait in the W cove until the 'Riva' set depart for Porto Cervo and then move to the E cove. Beautiful surroundings. Buoyed swimming area. Good snorkelling. No facilities.

Bisce Channel

The channel between Isola delle Bisce and Capo Ferro is deep and clear of dangers in the fairway. On the S and particularly the SE side of Isola delle Bisce above and below-water rocks fringe the coast. By day the rocks are easily seen. The main lighthouse on Capo Ferro, a white circular tower on a two-storeyed building (52m/140ft high), is easily identified and exhibits two lights Fl(3)15s24M and Oc.R.5s8M, the latter covering Bisce Shoal (Secca delle Bisce) and Monaci Shoal (vis 189°–203°). There is a second white tower on the NE corner of Capo Ferro: Fl.R.3s8M.

East coast: Capo Ferro to Capo Carbonara

In cruising terms the northern tenth of the east coast is in complete contrast to the remaining nine tenths. From Capo Ferro to Capo Coda Cavallo there are numerous anchorages and harbours. From Ottiolu, the last of the NE group of harbours to Capo Carbonara (over 110M in a straight line) there are only five safe harbours and several exposed anchorages. Along most of the coast, mountains rise sheer from the sea and while it is a spectacular coast to sail, it is also a daunting and inhospitable one. Only the coast between Capo Ferro and Capo Coda Cavallo breaks up into a tangle of reefs and islands to provide both safe anchorages and hazards to navigation.

The description of Pausanias some 2,000 years ago remains largely true for the greater part of the coast: 'An unbroken chain of impassable mountains, and if you sail along the coast you will find no anchorage on this side of the island, while violent but irregular gusts of wind sweep down to the sea from the tops of the mountains.'

The two light structures on Capo Ferro are conspicuous in the E approaches to the Bisce Channel *Paul Donnerup*

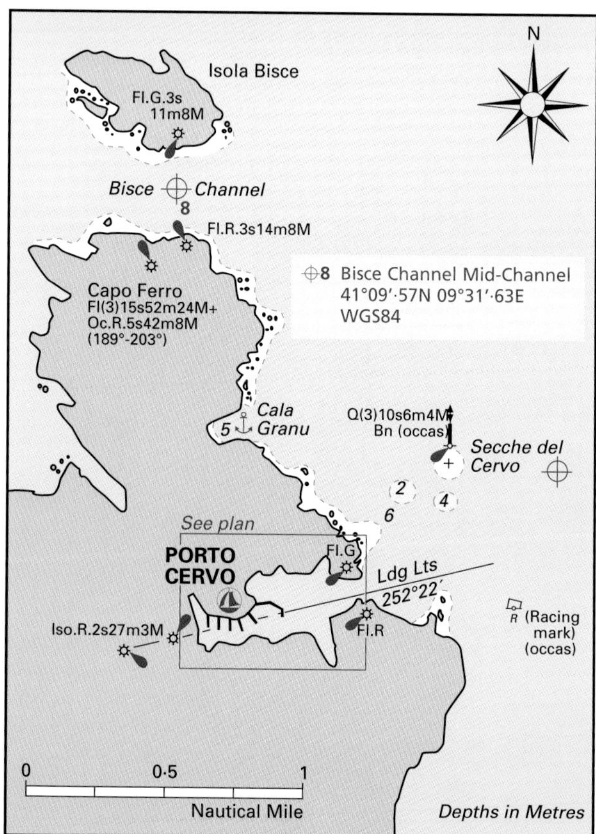

BISCE PASSAGE AND APPROACHES TO PORTO CERVO
⊕0·15M E of Beacon 41°08´·64N 09°32´·91E WGS84

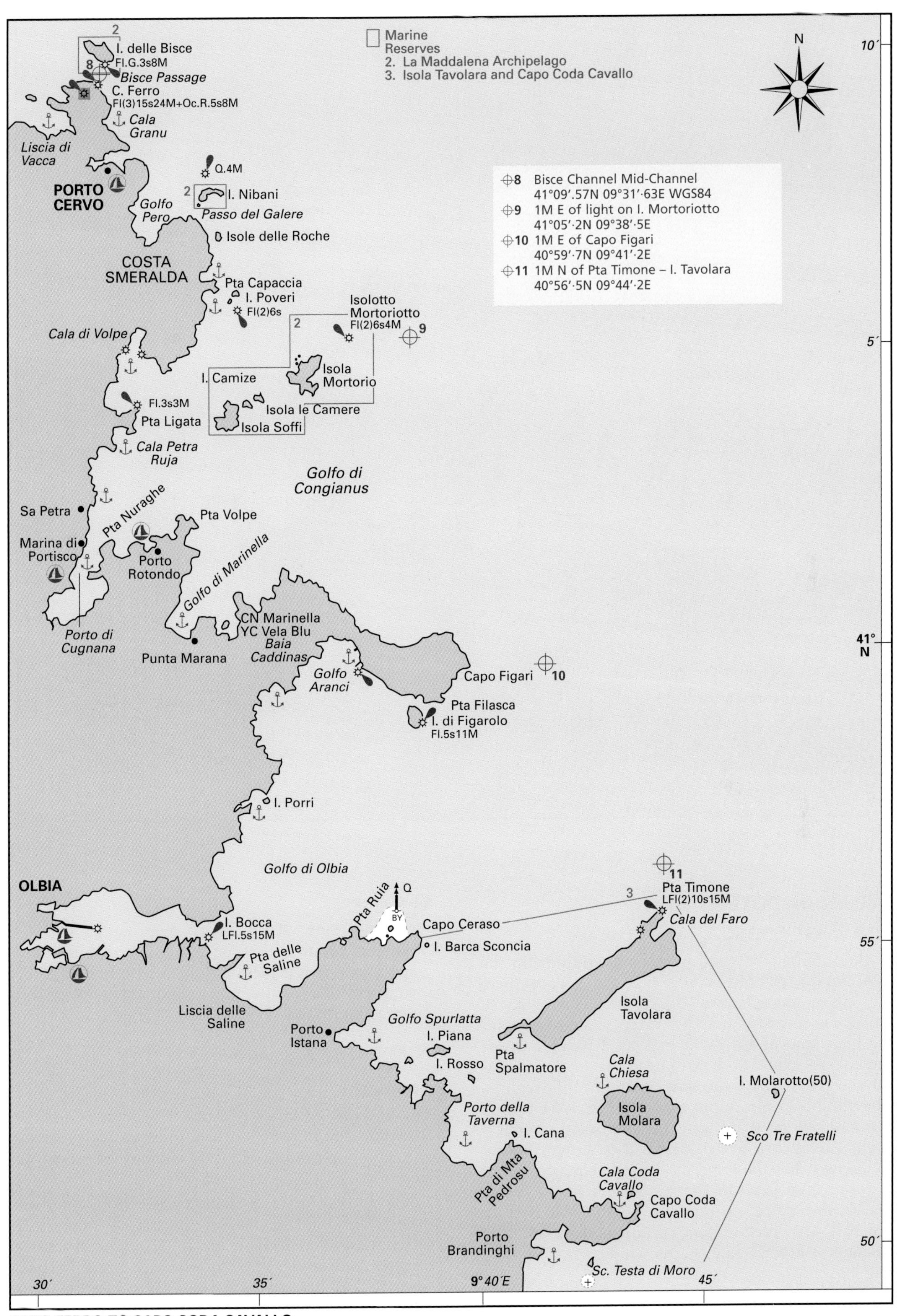

CAPO FERRO TO CAPO CODA CAVALLO

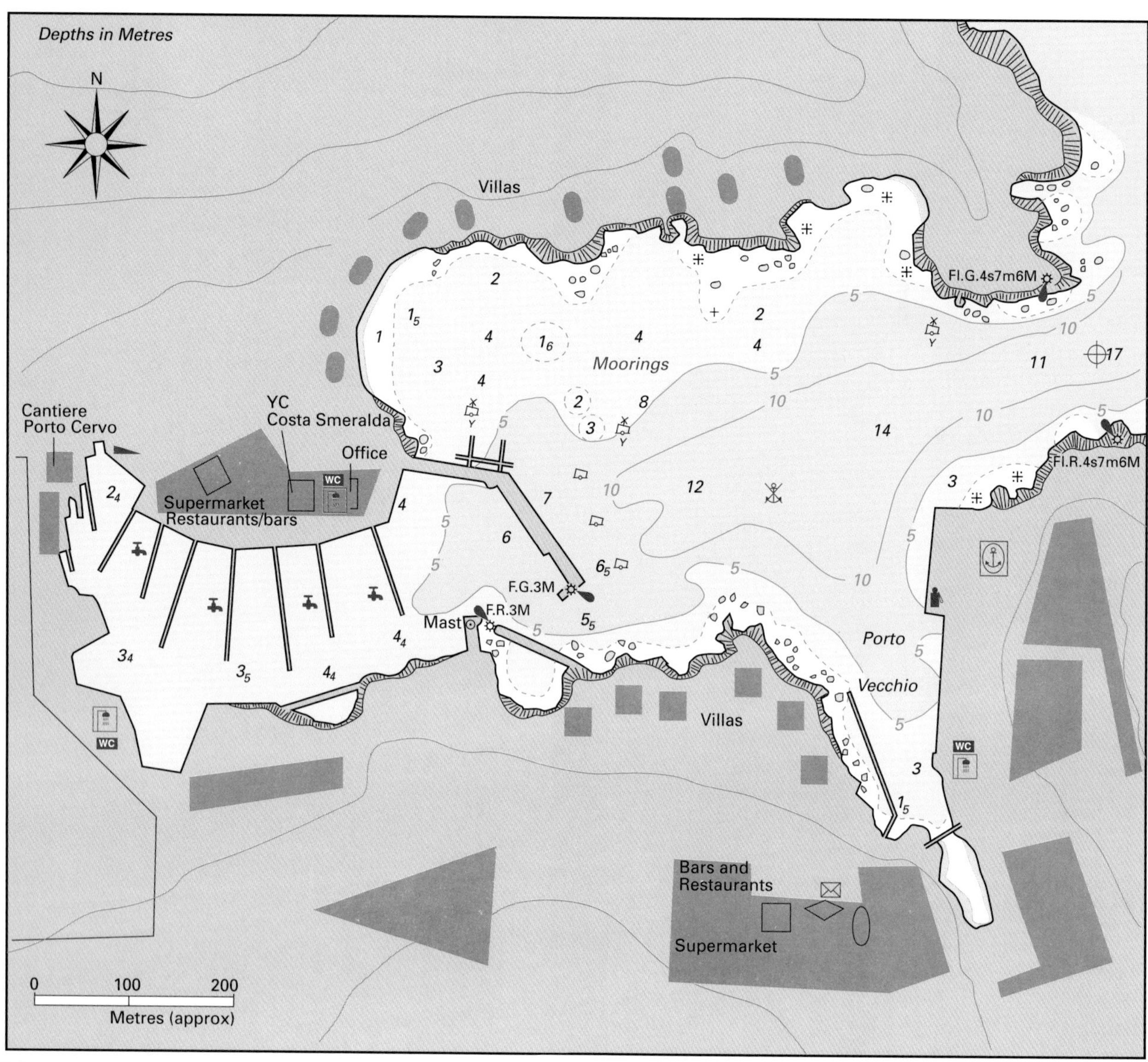

PORTO CERVO
⊕41°08′·24N 09°32′·34E WGS84

Weather patterns on the East coast

In the summer the wind is predominantly from the NW, but it rarely blows more than Force 4 and there are often many days of calms. However, as Pausanias records, there are often violent gusts off the high land and a yacht making a passage down the E coast would do well to keep two or three miles off the coast where the wind will be more regular. The wind may also blow from the NE or SE and in this case the eastern massif lifts the wind so that a yacht sailing close to the coast will get little wind but all the sea that the wind has raised. The occasional *scirocco* may blow in the summer raising a heavy sea. In the spring, autumn and winter, winds from the NW also predominate although there are also frequent southerly gales in the winter.

Cala Granu

⊕ 41°08′·7N 09°31′·8E

A small cove situated about two-thirds of a mile S of Capo Ferro. It is a pleasant lunch-stop before going into Porto Cervo and much frequented by power boats from there.

PORTO CERVO

Approach

The harbour entrance is difficult to identify for the first time, but in summer the numerous craft coming and going pin-point it. Care should be taken of Cervo Rock.

Conspicuous Until the yacht is lined up to enter the inlet you will not see the buildings around the shore or the masts of the yachts inside. The light structures on either side and a building (the race control office) on the S side help. With strong NW winds there are gusts out of the inlet and off the surrounding hills so it is wise to motor into the harbour.

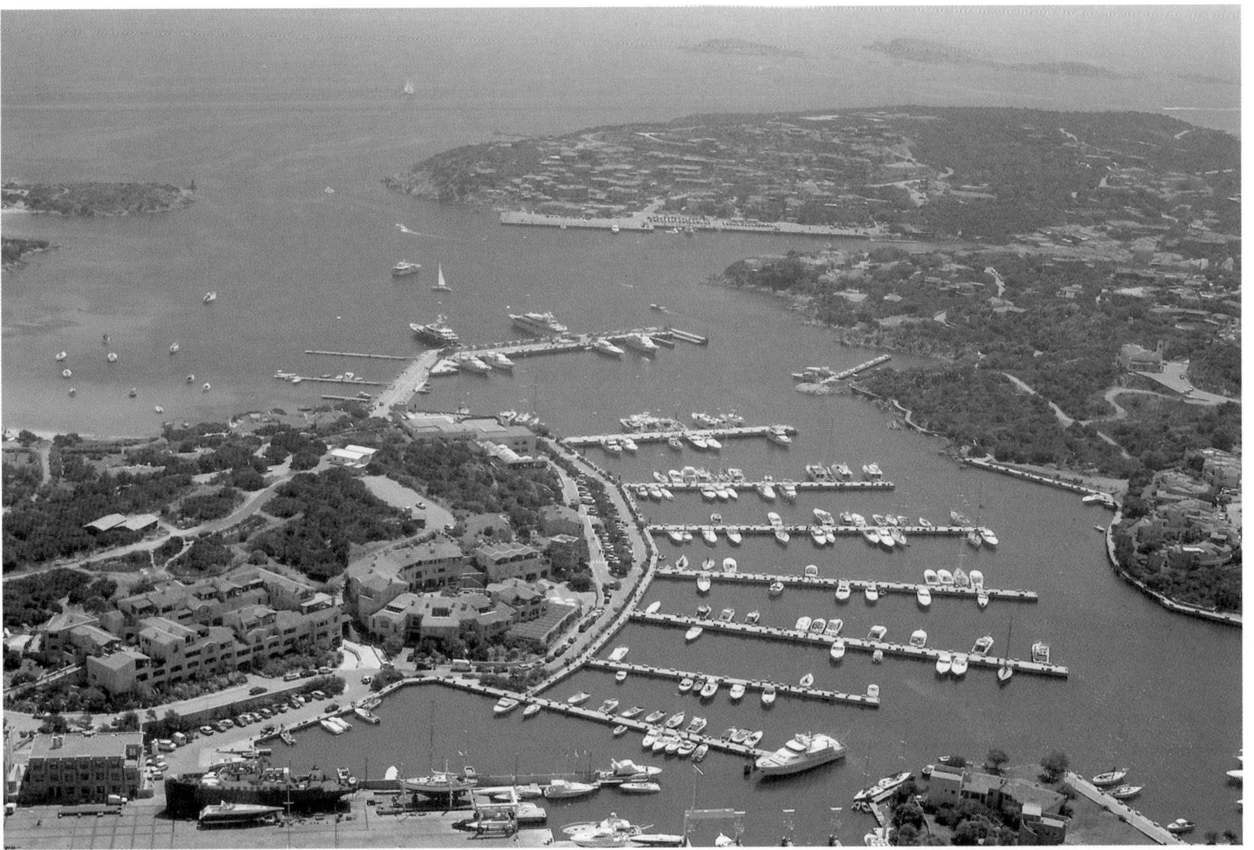

Porto Cervo looking E out to the entrance *Carlo Delfino*

By night Cervo Rock (Secche del Cervo) is lit in the summer (1/6 to 30/9) Q(3)10s6m4M. Leading lights on 252°22′ *Front* Iso.R.2s27m3M, *Rear* Oc.R.4s47m3M.

VHF Ch 09, 16 (call sign *Cervo Radio*).

Note Care needs to be taken in Porto Vecchio and off the marina at night as there are a number of large unlit mooring buoys in the vicinity.

Dangers

1. Cervo Rock (Secche del Cervo) Lies 0·6 mile NE of Porto Cervo. It is marked by an E cardinal beacon Q(3)10s4M (summer only). Both the light and the 'beacon' are difficult to see if the sea is disturbed. There is a safe passage (6m deep) between the rock and the coast, but the prudent course is to keep to seaward of the rock.
2. Inside Porto Cervo there are several isolated shoal patches on the W side of the mooring zone. They can be difficult to spot in anything other than a flat calm.

Note From May to September there is often a large cylindrical red buoy in position off the S entrance to Porto Cervo. This does not mark a danger to navigation, but is the finish line for the numerous yacht races going on throughout the summer.

Mooring

Data 700 berths. 100 visitors' berths. Max LOA 100m. Depths 1·5–8m.

Berth Go stern-to in Porto Vecchio immediately to port just inside the entrance, or in Porto Cervo Marina, where directed. There are laid moorings tailed to the quay or to a buoy. Marina staff will assist you to berth.

Note In July and August every berth will inevitably be full and the harbour packed to capacity.

Shelter Excellent.

Authorities Customs. Harbourmaster and marina staff who will help you to do or find anything and everything. Porto Cervo is not a cheap marina and a substantial charge is made. Charge band 6+.

Porto Cervo Marina ✆ 0789 905 605 / 610
Fax 0789 911 583
Email info@marinadiportocervo.com

Anchorage On the N side of the harbour the anchoring zone is now laid with 10 moorings.

They may be booked in advance through Porto Cervo Marina, MarPark or Yachtlife. Charges €75 (12hrs) €150 (24hrs) up to 15m LOA.

MarPark booking ✆0899 100 001
Email info@marpark.com
Yachtlife booking
www.yachtlife.it/YL-marpark/MP-en1.html

Anchoring is prohibited in the vicinity of the moorings. There may be room for catamarans or shoal draft craft close in.

Care needs to be taken of the shoal patches here. The bottom is sand and weed with some rocks, mostly good holding. The anchorage affords good shelter except in E–SE winds which send a considerable swell into here. With strong winds from this direction it may be necessary to move out. The logical place to make for is somewhere around the La Maddalena group or the adjacent coast. The E side of Porto Palma, Cannigione, and Palau all afford good shelter from E–SE winds.

Facilities

Services Water and electricity (220 and 380V) at every berth. Telephone and television connections. Shower and toilet blocks. Self service laundry in the marina.

Fuel On the quay in Porto Vecchio (0800–1300 / 1430–1900).

Weather forecast Daily weather forecast in English posted at the marina office. A weather forecast is also available on VHF Ch 88.

Rescue service A tugboat, the *San Marco*, can attend emergencies at sea. Fire fighting and service craft for harbour emergencies.

Repairs The Cantiere Porto Cervo can carry out almost all the repairs needed by a yacht. It operates a 40-ton travel-hoist and craft up to 350 tons can be hauled on a patent slip. Covered and open storage is available. All types of mechanical, engineering, wood, GRP and steel repairs are carried out. Surveys. Extensive chandlery. 24-hour security.

Provisions Two supermarkets, one in the marina and one near Porto Vecchio.

Eating out A range of restaurants. Numerous bars of all types in the marina and near Porto Vecchio (summer only).

Other PO, Bank and ATM in Cervo village. Costa Smeralda medical centre near Porto Vecchio. Italgaz and Camping Gaz service. Dry cleaning service at the Mach petrol station. Shops and boutiques from the best quarters of Rome and Milan. Hire cars.

Note Many of the facilities are available only in the summer. In the winter many of them are not available and one yacht reported having trouble even finding a mechanic.

General

Porto Cervo is the yachting hub of the Consorzio Costa Smeralda and one of the first parts of the Costa Smeralda to be developed beginning in the 1960s. It cost millions of dollars to build; a millionaires' playground that looks like an ethnic fishing village grown big, and it works – at least, it works architecturally. Without doubt Porto Cervo is a gem of environmentally sympathetic architecture, buildings honed to the contours of the land to create a landscape that adds to rather than detracts from the beauty of the bay, though it dates a little now. There is no convenience architecture clumsily conceived and hastily erected here but it works in the same way as a Hollywood film set. The architecture really has little to do with Sardinia, rather it is a sanitised idea of what Italian rustic architecture should be.

In July and August the beautiful people arrive; movie legends and rock stars like Bruce Willis and Mick Jagger rub shoulders with royalty and celebrities, the rich and super-rich show off their new floating toys worth millions of pounds, the hangers-on and the minions run around in circles disappearing up their own nautical specifics, and Porto Cervo hums and buzzes with activity. The international jet set arrive and Porto Cervo is a living place, albeit of the very rich and their entourage. When they depart one gets the feeling that the plugs have all been pulled out and a cardboard cut-out film set remains. Nonetheless, Porto Cervo has to be

Costa Smeralda

The Consorzio Costa Smeralda was formed in March 1962 by a group of six property owners in the region headed by the Aga Khan. From the beginning the consortium laid down strict requirements that the land should be developed only in a tasteful and environmentally pleasing fashion. A panel of leading architects and planners was commissioned to draw up a master plan for the area (which has since been added to) and the result is a harmonious landscape probably unique in the world. Every effort has been made to blend the architecture – the buildings, signs, lighting, gardens, roads, pavements, harbours with the land and its traditions to preserve its beauty. (The Hotel Pitrizza at Liscia di Vacca has its roof covered in grass so that it is difficult to pick it out even when close to it.) The Costa Smeralda has become the playground of the very rich and the envy of other resorts, even some close to it.

Costa Smeralda Yacht Club

Founded in 1967, the Costa Smeralda YC is based at Porto Cervo. Over the years it has established an international reputation as the promoter of major sailing and powerboat events in the local waters. The Week of the Straits was held for the first time in 1972 and in 1973 the club hosted the One Ton Cup. In 1978 the first series of the Sardinia Cup was held and by 1982 this biannual event had become one of the major Mediterranean events, ranking with the Admiral's Cup and the American SORC. The Swan World Cup is run concurrently with the Sardinia Cup on alternate years to the Admiral's Cup. The great interest in 12m racing and the Americas Cup prompted the Yacht Club Costa Smeralda to mount its own challenge in 1983 when the club's boat *Azzura* came third in the first Louis Vuitton Cup Challenge. The club hosted the 12m championships in 1984 and since then regattas have been staged at YCCS as training for potential Americas Cup teams. In the Americas Cup of 1987 two challengers, *Azzura* and *Italia,* travelled to Fremantle only to be outclassed, returning to Italy to lick their wounds. In 1992 Italian fortunes and pride were restored by the victory of *Il Moro di Venezia* in the Louis Vuitton Cup, only to be beaten in the final by *America 3*. 1999 saw Patrizio Bertelli's Prada team in an epic Louis Vuitton Challenge series. They claimed victory over 10 rivals in Auckland, but again the Cup eluded them in a one-sided final with New Zealand's *Black Magic*. In October 2002 there were again two Italian challengers, with Mascalzone Latino joining Prada in Auckland. Mascalzone Latino ('Latin Rascals') was a popular syndicate in the Viaduct Harbour in the Louis Vuitton series, though never really figured in the top rankings. Patrizio Bertelli's Prada Team fared a little better, but have never managed to recapture their 1999 form. With the 'Swiss' Alinghi victory in 2003 the Cup returned to Europe for the first time since leaving the Isle of Wight in 1851. And the latest challenge takes the 'Auld Mug' back to the USA. A new format of the Louis Vuitton trophy using TP52s has brought the America's Cup circus to several northern European and Mediterranean venues (including Porto Cervo).

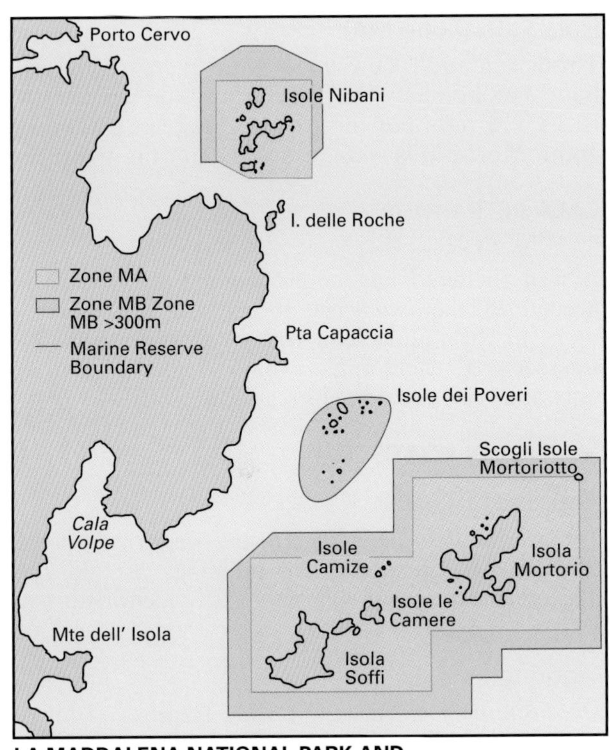

LA MADDALENA NATIONAL PARK AND MARINE RESERVE - SOUTH EXTENSION

La Maddalena Archipelago National Park and Marine Reserve

(South Extension)

The southern section of the park includes Isole Nibani, Isola Mortorio and Mortoriotto, Isolitti Camize, Isole Le Camere and Isola Soffi.

Zone MA
All navigation, stopping, fishing and diving are prohibited.

Zone MB within 300m of the coast
Free anchoring is allowed within 300m from the coast, clear of Posidonia seagrass, only with a permit, except in specific areas designated by the park authorities where areas may be roped off or where mooring buoys are supplied.

Zone MB over 300m from the coast
Transit and navigation are permitted. Max speed 15kns.

For regulations applying to the use of the park and its marine reserves, see the section on La Maddalena National Park on page 273.

seen at least once and the yachtsman is lucky to be able to drop in to see it.

Golfo Pero

⊕ 41°07'·2N 09°32'·8E

A large bay close S of Porto Cervo. In calm weather or light W–S winds it makes a pleasant anchorage. Care is needed of the reef off the S entrance marked by a beacon and of above and below-water rocks off the coast.

The most popular anchorage is off the beach in the south. Anchor in 3–5m on sand, rock and weed, not everywhere good holding.

Passo del Galere

⊕ 41°08'·20N 09°34'·08E WGS84
0·25M E of light on NW of I. Nibani

The passage between I. Nibani and the adjacent coast and I. Rocche is not easy to distinguish until close to it. It should only be used by day. There are good depths (11m) in the fairway and in good weather the passage is a useful short cut. The light structure on the N end of I. Nibani, a N cardinal beacon, is conspicuous Q.21m4M.

Porto Liccia and Romazzino

Porto Liccia on the N side of Punta Capaccia and Romazzino on the S side are popular day anchorages for the Cervo set. Care must be taken of the Capaccia Rocks on the S side of Punta Capaccia which are easy to see in calm weather, but difficult to spot if the sea is disturbed, although the sea does break over the rock, making identification easier.

Isolotti Poveri

⊕ 41°05'·87N 09°34'·52E WGS84
Fairway between Pta Capaccia and Isolotti Poveri

This group of islets lies immediately SE of Punta Capaccia. They are low, reddish and surrounded by rocks and reefs. The light structure on the most southerly of the group is conspicuous Fl(2)6s4M.

An E cardinal marks the NE extremity and is lit Q(3)10s4M.

Cala di Volpe

A long and mostly shallow bay with the Hotel Cala di Volpe at the head. To the S Punta Ligata is lit Fl.3s11m3M.

Cala di Volpe looking in from the entrance

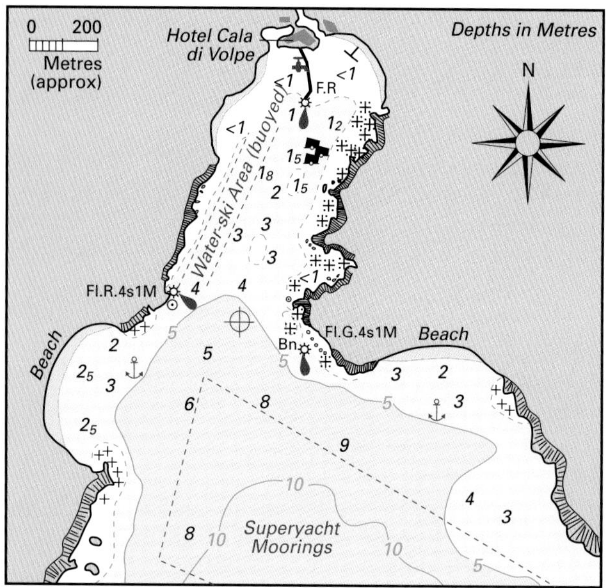

CALA DI VOLPE
⊕41°04´·89N 09°32´·38E WGS84

Note The beacons in the approaches are not always in place. Care needed of an underwater rock to the N of the white buoy close S of the rocks on the S side of the entrance in position 41°05´·03N 09°32´·43E WGS84.

With local moorings taking much of the space there is no longer any anchoring room within the N cove. The bay is now laid with 19 moorings for vessels up to 300ft LOA. Anchoring is prohibited in the vicinity of the moorings and anchoring in the bay is restricted in high season. You may be asked to move by the coastguard. The bottom is sand and good holding. Open to the south.

Moorings may be booked in advance through Porto Cervo Marina, MarPark or Yachtlife. Charges €75 (12hrs), €150 (24hrs) up to 15m LOA.

MarPark booking ✆ 0899 100 001
Email info@marpark.com

Yachtlife booking
www.yachtlife.it/YL-marpark/MP-en1.html

It is a long row to the hotel where one can buy a drink at the bar. The setting is exquisite: the extensive dappled shallows turn the bay into an emerald and turquoise patchwork quilt in which it is very nearly possible to see your anchor from the hotel.

Isola Mortorio (Zone MA)

⊕ 9 1M E of light on I. Mortoriotto 41°05′·2N 09°38′·5E

A rugged bare island surrounded by above and below-water rocks. Anchoring is now prohibited anywhere around the islands here. There are park authority mooring buoys in the S cove which may be used from sunrise to sunset. Yachts should purchase a park permit if navigating within the national park marine reserve. See page 273 for details.

Isolotti Mortoriotto, NE of Isola Mortorio, has a light structure, a white conical tower which is conspicuous Fl(2)6s10m4M.

Isola Soffi (Zone MA)

This island and I. Le Camere N off it are rugged red lumps of granite. The islands are surrounded by rocks and reefs but the passage between I. Camize and I. Mortorio is straightforward in calm weather.

CALA PETRA RUJA

⊕ 41°03′·5N 09°32′·3E

A well sheltered bay under Punta Ligata. Care is needed of the extensive above and below-water rocks in the middle and rocky outcrops from the sides. A small yacht might explore it in calm weather only and with considerable caution.

MARINA DI PORTISCO

Approach

The marina is located close to the western entrance to Porto di Cugnana. The buildings around the marina and the breakwater are easily identified.

VHF Ch 16, 69.

Mooring

Data 600 berths. Max LOA 90m. Depths 2–10m.

Berth Where directed. Large yachts berth on the outer mole. There are laid moorings tailed to the quay.

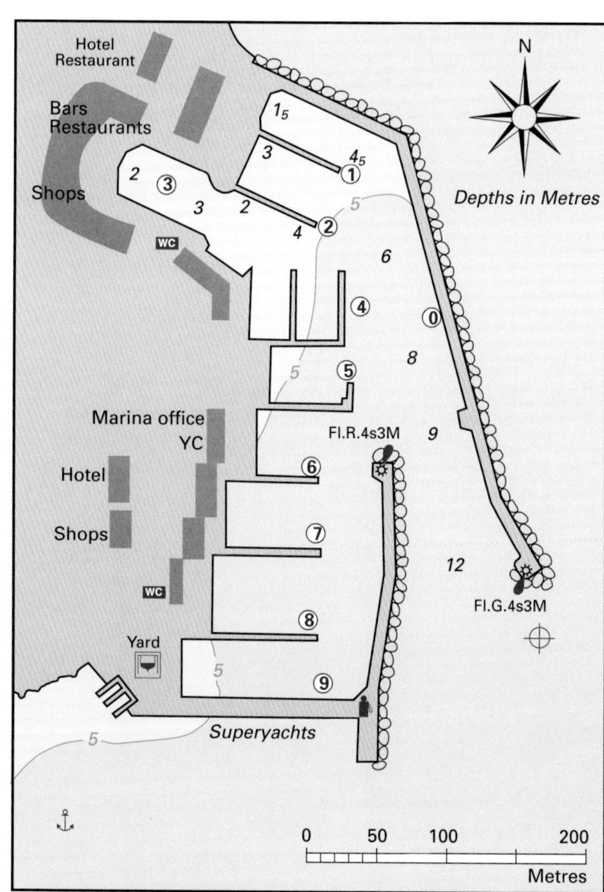

MARINA DI PORTISCO
⊕41°01´·92N 09°31´·62E WGS84

Portisco looking ESE with Porto Rotondo top right

Shelter Good all-round shelter although strong southerlies might make some berths uncomfortable.

Authorities Harbourmaster and marina staff. Charge band 6+.

☎ 0789 33520 *Fax* 0789 33560
Email info@marinadiportisco.com
www.marinadiportisco.com

Facilities

Services Water and electricity (220/380V) at every berth. Wi-Fi. Shower and toilet block. Laundry.
Fuel On the quay.
Repairs 70-ton travel-lift. Yachts can be hauled onto hard standing. Mechanical repairs.
Provisions A supermarket.
Eating out Restaurant and bars.
Other PO. Bank. ATM. Car rental. Olbia international airport 20km.

General

Tucked into the western entrance of Porto Cugnana, Portisco is an intimate sort of place which doesn't just cater for super-yachts. The marina has proved popular, with some yachts basing themselves here for the summer season. Ashore you can find most things you need, and if not Olbia is around 20km away.

Porto di Cugnana

A yacht can anchor in Porto di Cugnana where shelter is reported to be better than it looks. There are sometimes gusts off the high land but little swell enters. Anchor in 2–5m where convenient according to the wind direction. The bottom is sand and weed, good holding.

Note Anchoring is prohibited in an area where an underwater cable crosses the bay. See plan for details.

Porto Asfodeli

A small port off the hotel and apartment complex on the E side of Porto di Cugnana. Depths are mostly fairly shallow <1–2·5m. VHF Ch 09. Berth where directed. Water and electricity available. Fuel can be arranged. Restaurant ashore.

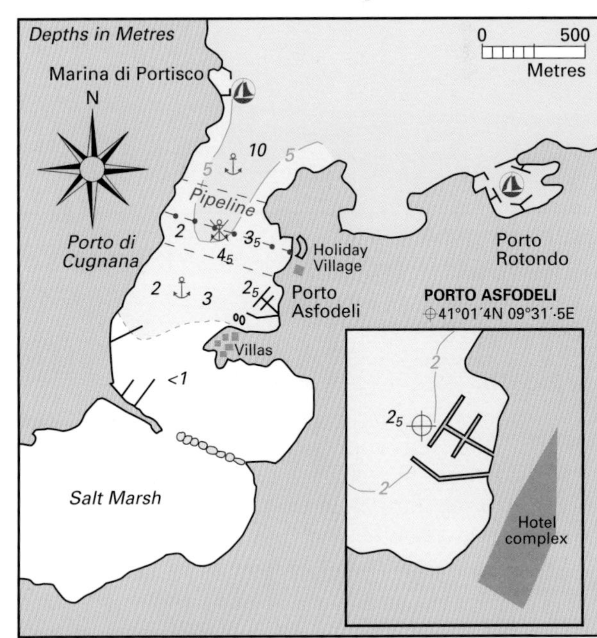

PORTO DI CUGNANA

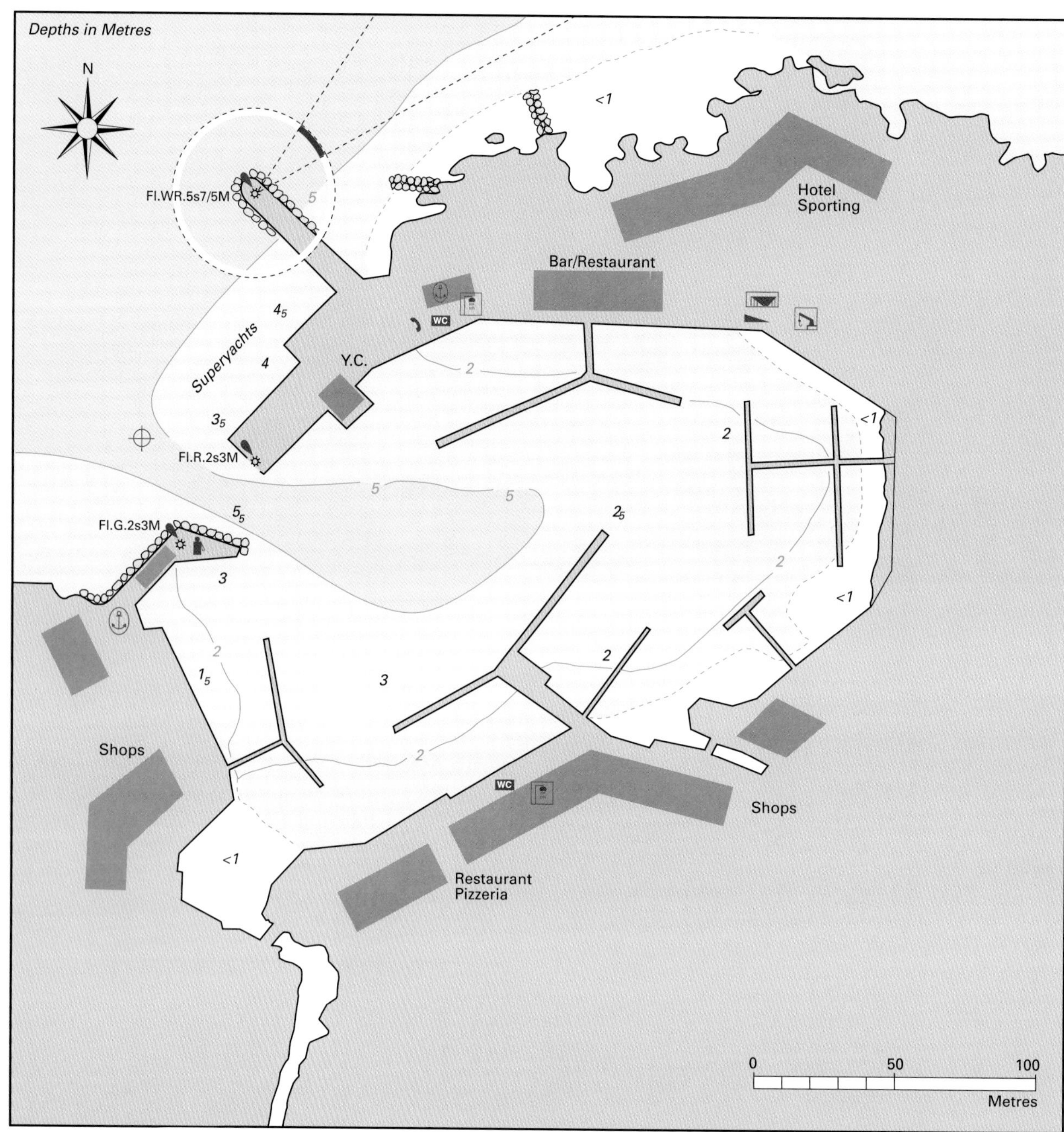

PORTO ROTONDO
⊕41°01´·84N 09°32´·52E WGS84

PORTO ROTONDO

Approach

Conspicuous The large hotel complex behind the marina (the red roof is conspicuous) is easily identified, but the entrance to the marina itself is difficult to see until close to it. The entrance is very narrow and with W–NW winds gusting across Golfo di Cugnana care should be taken in the approach to the marina.

By night Use the light on the breakwater on the E side of the entrance Fl.WR.5s7m7/5M (215°-R-240°).

VHF Ch 09 (24hrs).

Note

1. It is prohibited to sail into the marina.
2. Work has been completed developing the outer N breakwater into a superyacht quay. There are eight berths with electricity (220/380V 120/250A), water and pump-out facilities for yachts up to 70m.

Mooring

Data 640 berths. Eight superyacht berths. 63 visitors' berths. Max LOA 50m. Depths 1·5–4·8m.

Berth Go stern or bows-to where directed by the marina attendant who will assist you to berth. There are laid moorings tailed to the quay or a buoy.

Porto Rotondo looking south. Note that this does not show the new super-yacht berths on the outer breakwater

Shelter Excellent although strong NW winds cause a little chop.

Authorities Marina staff. Charge band 6+ (July–August).

✆ 0789 34203 *Fax* 0789 34368
Email marinaportorotondo@tiscali.it
www.marinadiportorotondo.it

Facilities

Services Water and electricity (220/380V) at every berth. WC and showers.
Fuel On the quay.
Repairs A 20-ton crane. Slipway up to 45m LOA. Hard standing. Mechanical repairs. Winter storage service for boats afloat and ashore.
Cantieri Costa Smeralda ✆ 0789 381 104 *Fax* 0789 381 492
Email info@cantiericostasmeralda.com
Provisions Supermarket nearby open all year round.
Eating out Restaurant and pizzeria, the latter open all year round.
Other Exchange possible in the hotel. Medical centre. Gas bottles can be delivered. Shops and boutiques open in the summer only. Olbia international airport 15kms.

General

Porto Rotondo, although not part of the Consorzio Costa Smeralda, is modelled on that idea. It is a pleasing and attractive marina with friendly staff. Yacht Club Porto Rotondo has staged a number of regattas, including the J22 World Championship and J24 European Championship. Racing and associated events go on throughout the summer, but the end of season Porto Rotondo Classic Regatta is one not to miss.

Porto Oro

⊕ 41°00′·8N 09°33′·35E

A miniature basin dredged out of the coast and protected by a short breakwater. The entrance is lit F.G/F.R. VHF Ch 09. The basin is private, but there may be a berth free for visitors. Call up on VHF to check first. Depths are 1·5–3m.

Water and electricity near all berths. Fuel can be arranged. Restaurant and bar.

PUNTA MARANA (Porticcioli Marinella)

Approach

The harbour is situated in the SE corner of Golfo di Marinella. The buildings around the marina are

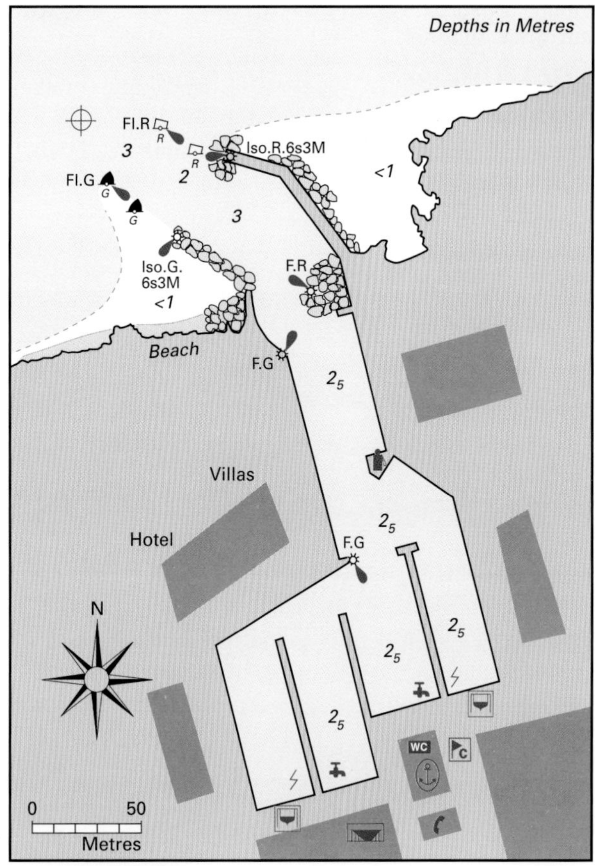

PUNTA MARANA
⊕41°00′·3N 09°33′·5E

Punta Marana

easily identified. A narrow channel marked by two pairs of small red and green buoys marks the entrance channel. There are least depths of 2m in the channel over a rocky ledge.

Dangers The entrance channel and entrance proper are too small for most yachts to turn round so a yacht must be committed to enter once into the entrance channel.

VHF Ch 09, 16.

Mooring

Data 300 berths. Max LOA 14m. Depths 2–2·5m.

Berth Where directed. Laid moorings.

Shelter Good shelter.

Authorities Harbourmaster. Charge band 5.
☏ 0789 32088 *Fax* 0789 32089

Facilities

Services Water and electricity at every berth.
Fuel On the quay.
Repairs 40-ton crane possible. Minor repairs.
Eating out Restaurant and bar.

Golfo di Marinella

⊕ 41°02′·51N 09°33′·79E WGS84
0·25M N of the N cardinal beacon on Pta Cannigione

On the W side of the gulf there are several small coves suitable as day anchorages. On the E, on either side of Punta Sabina, there are anchorages open only to the north. Care must be taken of the reef immediately N of Punta Sabina and the extensive reef in the bay on the W side of the point. Care must also be taken of the reefs off Punta Cannigione. A distinctive modern house and tower lie on the point. A N cardinal beacon (occas) marks the extent of the reefs. It is lit Q.5m4M.

Circolo Nautico Marinella

⊕ 40°00′·5N 09°34′·6E

A T-pier running out from the SE side of Isola di Marinella. There are 2–2·5m depths reported off the end. Water and electricity. Bar ashore.

Yachting Club Vela Blu

⊕ 41°00′·2N 09°34′·6E

Basically a jetty running out from the coast in a NE direction. 0·5–2m depths reported off the jetty. VHF Ch 09. Laid moorings. Water.

Capo Figari

⊕**10** 40°59′·7N 09°41′·2E
1M E of Capo Figari

A high (340m/1,115ft) prominent rocky peninsula that drops sheer into the sea at its eastern end. This

Golfo di Marinella

Capo Figari looking SE

great lump of rock often simply stops W–NW winds so that you may be wallowing off it in a confused sea. In this case it is best to motor around it until you pick up the wind (usually gusting around the neck) again. The passage between Capo Figari and I. Figarolo is free of dangers with good depths in the fairway.

GOLFO ARANCI

BA 1211
Italian 322

Approach

The harbour is tucked up inside the NE corner of Golfo Aranci. It is easily identified by the buildings of the town and the cranes at the commercial docks.

Mooring

Berth Yachts should see if they can find a berth in the fishing harbour to the N although it is normally crammed full of trawlers and local boats. If not, anchor off to the N of the fishing harbour.

Shelter Good shelter in the fishing harbour. The anchorage is open NW–W–S.

Authorities Harbourmaster. Charge band 1/3.

Facilities

Water On the quay.
Fuel On the quay.
Repairs 30-ton crane. Limited mechanical repairs.
Provisions Most provisions can be found.
Eating out Restaurants ashore.

BAIA CADDINAS

Approach

A very small marina in the NW corner of Golfo Aranci. The harbour breakwater is easily identified but the entrance is difficult to spot until close in. The entrance channel marked by four pairs of small red and green buoys turns sharply to starboard into the narrow entrance.

VHF Ch 09 (0700–2000).

Mooring

Data 100 berths. Five visitors' berths. Max LOA 15m. Depths <1–3m.

Berth stern or bows-to where directed. Laid moorings tailed to the quay or a buoy.

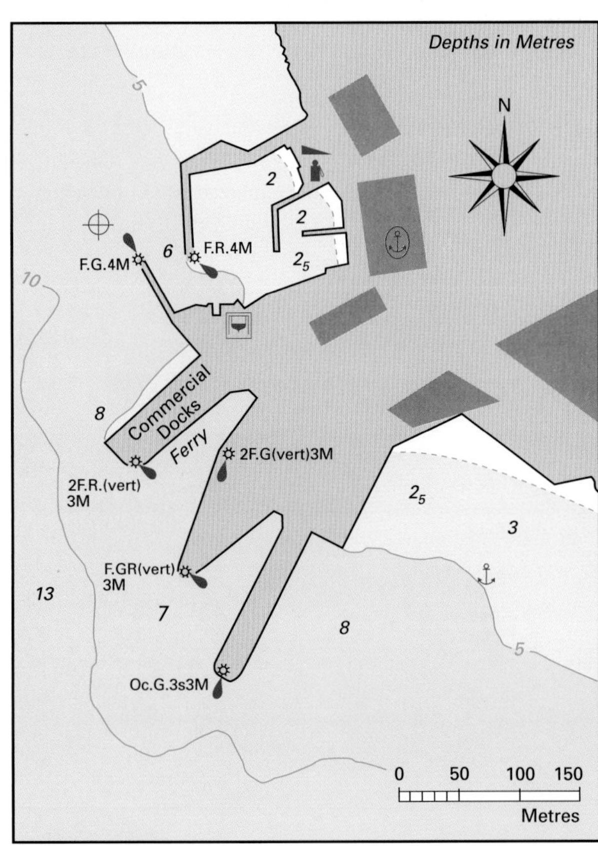

GOLFO ARANCI
⊕40°59′·6N 09°37′·1E

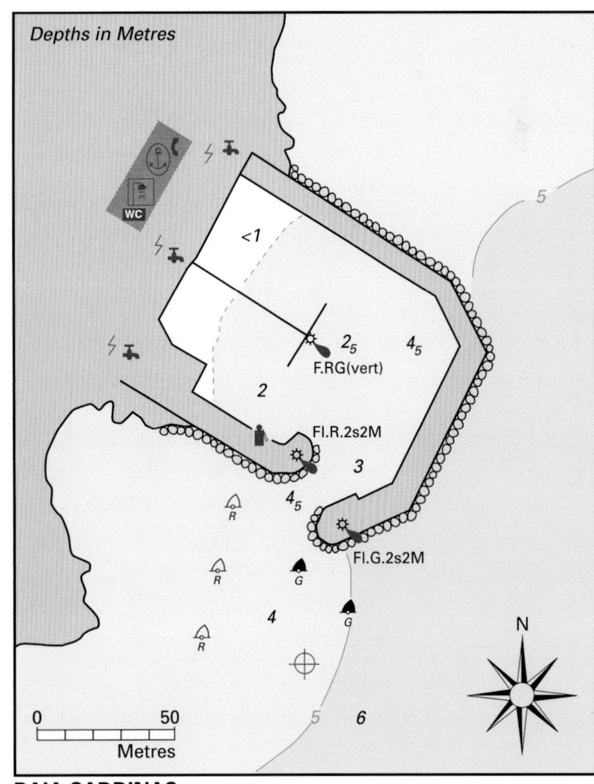

BAIA CADDINAS
⊕40°59′·7N 09°36′·2E

The lighthouse at the entrance to Olbia

Shelter Good shelter.
Authorities Harbourmaster. A charge is made.
Porto Turistico ✆ 0789 46813

Facilities

Services Water and electricity at or near all berths.
Fuel On the quay near the entrance.
Repairs 20-ton crane. Limited repairs.
Eating out Restaurant and bar ashore.

Isola di Porri anchorage

⊕ 40°57′·4N 09°35′·1E

A yacht can find good shelter from all but southerlies in the bay on the W side of Isola di Porri. The bottom is sand and rocks and good holding. Care should be taken of Porri Reef (least depth 3·4m) lying about half a mile S of I. di Porri.

OLBIA

BA 1210
Italian 318

Approach

Conspicuous The easily recognised massifs of Capo Figari and Isola Tavolara stand out on either side of the entrance to Golfo di Olbia. The NE end of Isola Tavolara has a girder communications mast (red and white bands) which is conspicuous. Once into Golfo di Olbia it can be difficult to pinpoint exactly where the channel is until the lighthouse (a white square tower on a two-storey dwelling) is identified. Once into the channel, the approach is straightforward by day or night although some care is needed in the final approach on the S side of the long central mole. A yacht should make for the new marina in the S approaches or the yacht harbour shown on the plan near the town centre.

By night Use the light on Isola della Bocca at the entrance to the bay LFl.5s24m15M. The first pair of beacons at the entrance to the channel (270°) are lit Fl.G.5s5M/Fl.R.5s5M. Beacons marking the channel down to the commercial pier are also lit. A pair of lights Fl.G.5s/Fl.R.5s and a beacon on the S of I. Mezzo Fl.G.3s show the channel to the S of the pier. The entrance to Circolo Nautico Olbia is not lit.

VHF Ch 11, 16 for Port Authorities. Ch 09 for Marina di Olbia. Ch 12 Circolo Nautico Olbia.

Dangers

1. Off Capo Ceraso and Punta Ruia there are numerous rocks extending up to nearly half a mile

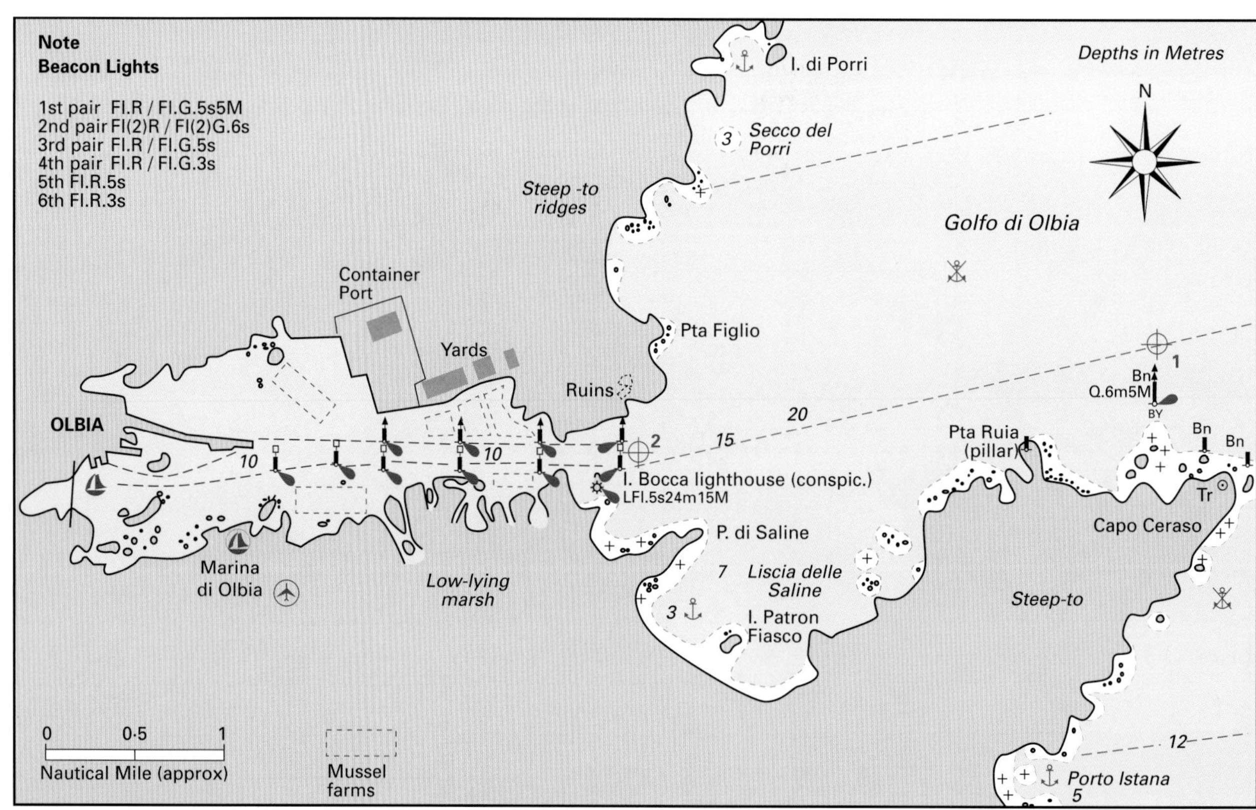

OLBIA - APPROACHES
⊕1 40°55′·77N 09°38′·03E WGS84 0·2M N of Capo Ceraso beacon
⊕2 40°55′·39N 09°34′·39E WGS84 Between 1st bns of entrance channel

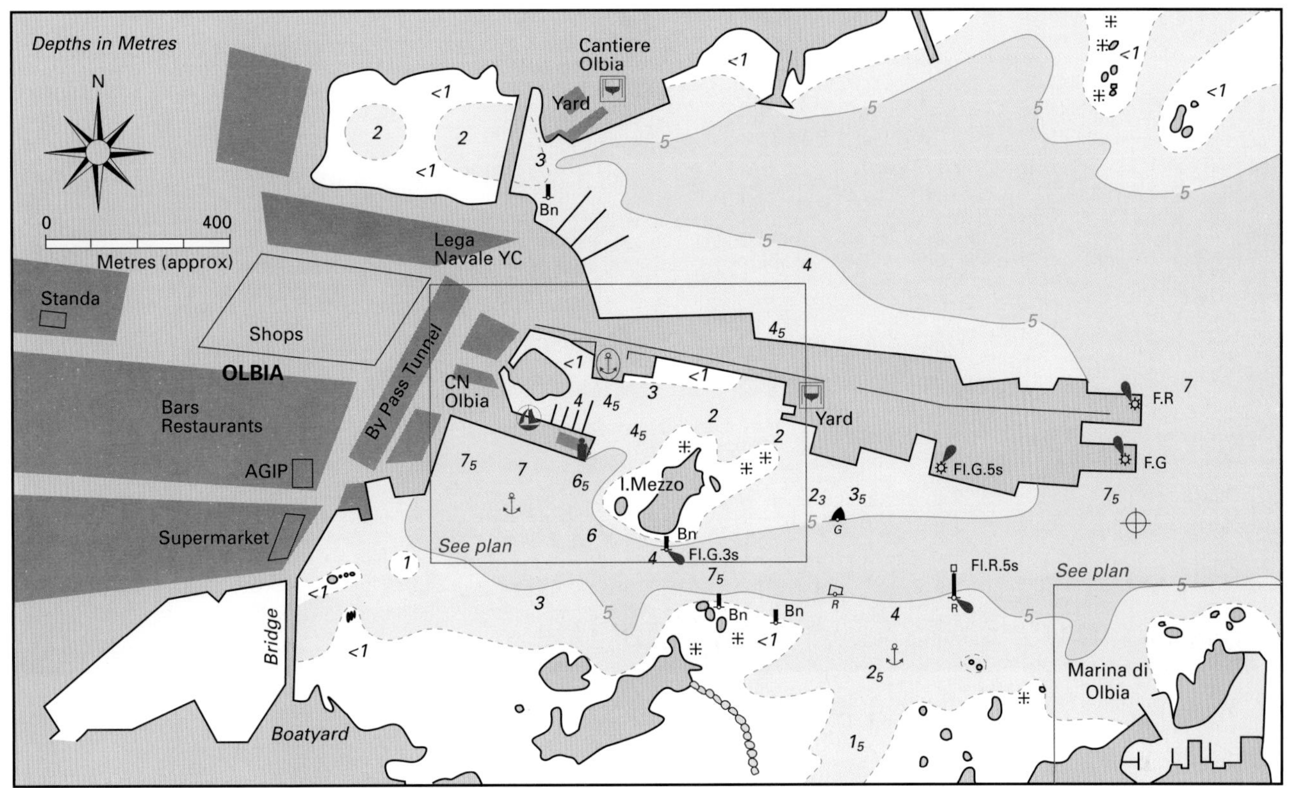

OLBIA
⊕40°55'·22N 09°31'·44E WGS84

offshore. The reef with Isoletto Barco Sconcia on it is marked at its extremity by an E cardinal buoy. One mile to the W lies Punta Ruia and midway between the point and the cape, a reef off some islets extends northwards. It is marked at its extremity by a N cardinal buoy and exhibits a Q.6m5M.

2. A reef extends a short distance off Punta delle Saline.
3. Merchant vessels regularly use Olbia and they have right of way in the channel.

Note There are mussel farms on either side of the main channel.

MARINA DI OLBIA

A new marina on the southern shores of the harbour, close to Olbia airport.

Approach

Follow the buoyed channel in past the ferry quays until you 'open' the marina entrance.

Dangers Care needed of numerous above and below-water rocks close to the entrance.

VHF Ch 09.

Mooring

Data 270 berths. Max LOA 60m. Depths 3–5m.

Berths Where directed. Laid moorings tailed to the quay.

Shelter Good all-round shelter in the marina.

Authorities Marina staff. Charge band 6+

IBS Yachting Point Marina di Olbia ✆ 0789 645 030
Fax 0789 645 063
Email marinadiolbia@ibsgroup.it

Facilities

Services Water and electricity (220/380V). Wi-Fi. Showers and toilets. Laundry.

Fuel On the quay.

Repairs IBS Servizi can arrange most repairs.

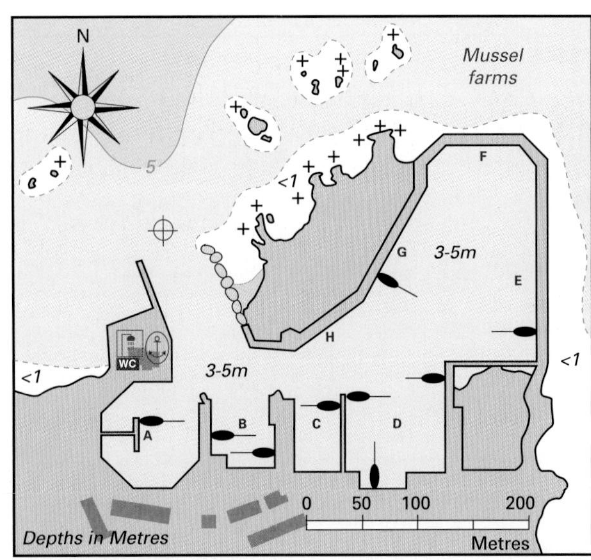

MARINA DI OLBIA
⊕40°55'·0N 09°31'·4E

The new marina in the southern approaches to Olbia *IBS Marina di Olbia*

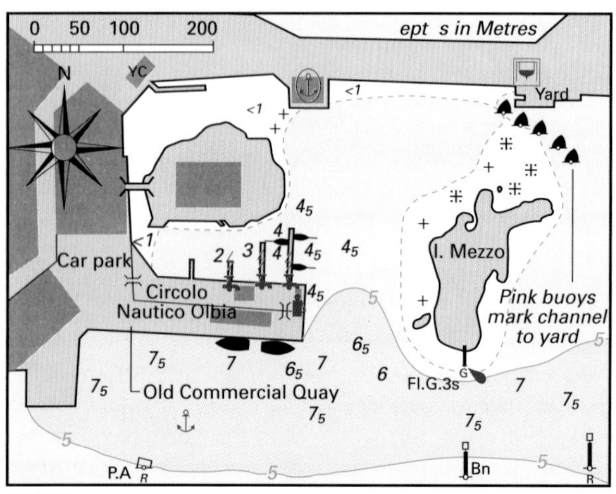

OLBIA

Olbia alongside berths on the old commercial docks

OLBIA TOWN

1. *Old Commercial quay* Most yachts moor alongside the old commercial quay to the W of I. Mezzo. The quay wall is quite high which makes getting on and off difficult and mooring rings are scarce. It is a bit run-down and derelict here, but you are close to town. The Guardia Costieri will sometimes ask you to move, but will usually allow yachts to anchor off S of the commercial quay.

Shelter Good all-round shelter.

Authorities Harbourmaster and customs, although they won't usually bother you.

Note

1. There have been several reports of break-ins and theft from yachts anchored off.
2. It is likely that this area will be redeveloped and in the future it is possible that you will not be able to berth here. At present there is no work going on.

2. *Circolo Nautico Olbia* A small, friendly club marina close to the town.
   Data 200 berths. Max LOA 25m. Water and electricity at all berths. Fuel on the quay. Bar.
   Shelter Good all-round shelter.
   Authorities Harbourmaster. Charge band 2/3.
   Circolo Nautico Olbia ✆ 0789 26187.
3. *Olbia Lega Navale* A private yacht club at the root of the N side of the pier. Not usually welcoming to visitors.
4. *Cantiere Olbia* A repair yard with small quay to the N of Lega Navale.
5. A repair yard on the S side of the pier near I. Mezzo. It has small pink buoys leading into the quay.

Facilities

Services Water and electricity
Fuel On the quay near Circolo Nautico Olbia.
Repairs As well as the yards mentioned above, there are more on the N side of the Olbia entrance channel. Access is possible via narrow channels through the vast mussel farms.

Many can carry out mechanical, electrical, wood and GRP repairs.

Cantieri Costa Smeralda (also in Porto Rotondo)
☎ 0789 57087 *Email* info@cantiericostasmeralda.com

Olbia Boat Service 160-ton travel-hoist. VHF Ch 16, 09
☎ 0789 53060 *Email* obs.obs@tiscali.it

CS Nautica Crane ☎ 0789 57497
Nausika 50-ton travel-hoist ☎ 0789 57181
Sailmaker (Lomar) in Via Roma ☎ 0789 23728.

Provisions Excellent shopping in the town for all provisions. There is a town plan just outside the harbour gates to help you orientate yourself. A market in the town and a supermarket by the harbour. Evening street markets.
Eating out Good restaurants, trattorias and pizzerias in the town.
Other PO. Banks. ATMs. Hospital. Italgaz and Camping Gaz ☎ 0789 36380. Hire cars. Ferries to the Italian mainland. Internal and international flights from the airport nearby.

General

In complete contrast to the wonders to the north, Olbia is a chaotic and somewhat grubby town, but it fairly hums and bustles with life. Architecturally undistinguished it may be, but after the sophistication and elegance of the Costa Smeralda and its imitators, Olbia is a pleasant surprise and, more importantly, a wholly living community.

It was founded by the Carthaginians (as Olvia) and prospered as the best natural harbour on the east coast. When the Romans arrived it further increased in power, but declined thereafter with the arrival of the Goths and Vandals. Over the centuries its buildings were picked over for building materials by the Sards and at some time it was renamed Terranova Pausanias. Mussolini renamed it Olbia in 1939. In 2001, during the construction of a new road tunnel under the harbour, the sunken wrecks of 26 ships were discovered. Included in the finds was an oak mast from the 1st century AD, hulls from the 5th century, and more vessels from Medieval times. Work continues on their restoration both in Olbia and Cagliari, with a fine collection and historical information exhibited in the new archaeological museum, finished in 2003, on the island near the Circolo Nautico, very close to where the discoveries were made.

Liscia delle Saline

⊕ 40°54'·8N 09°35'·2E

A large bay under Punta delle Saline immediately E of Isola della Bocca and the entrance channel to Olbia with a salt marsh around its southern shores. Open to the north.

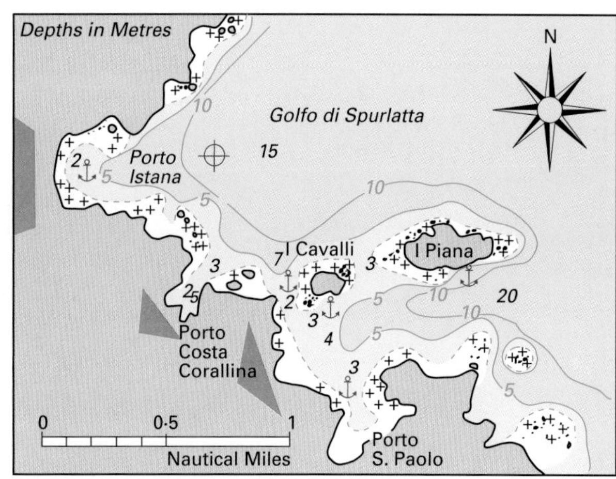

GOLFO DI SPURLATTA
⊕40°53'·5N 09°37'·8E

Porto Istana (Zone C)

A bay in the westernmost part of Golfo di Spurlatta. Care must be taken of the reef in the N of the bay and around the western and southern sides. AMP authority mooring buoys lie in 3–5m on a sandy bottom. Open only to the east. Great care must be taken of above and below-water rocks in the general area.

Porto Costa Corallina (Zone C)

A small private harbour to the S of Porto Istana. Care needed of rocks and shoal water off the entrance to the bay. Call ahead to enquire before entering the harbour.

Data Max LOA 10m. Depths <1–2m.
☎ 0789 36680

Porto San Paolo (Zone C)

⊕ 40°52'·5N 09°38'·55E

A small private harbour associated with development ashore in the N of Porto della Taverna. It is not for visiting yachts. There are reported to be 150 berths up to a maximum of 10m LOA and depths of 1–2m in the basin.

VHF Ch 72.

Isola Tavolara (Zone C)

A narrow solid chunk of granite whose silhouette, once seen, is unmistakeable. It is everywhere steep-to except at its southwestern end where a low spit of land extends for about ¾ of a mile. The NE part of

Isola Tavolara looking NW

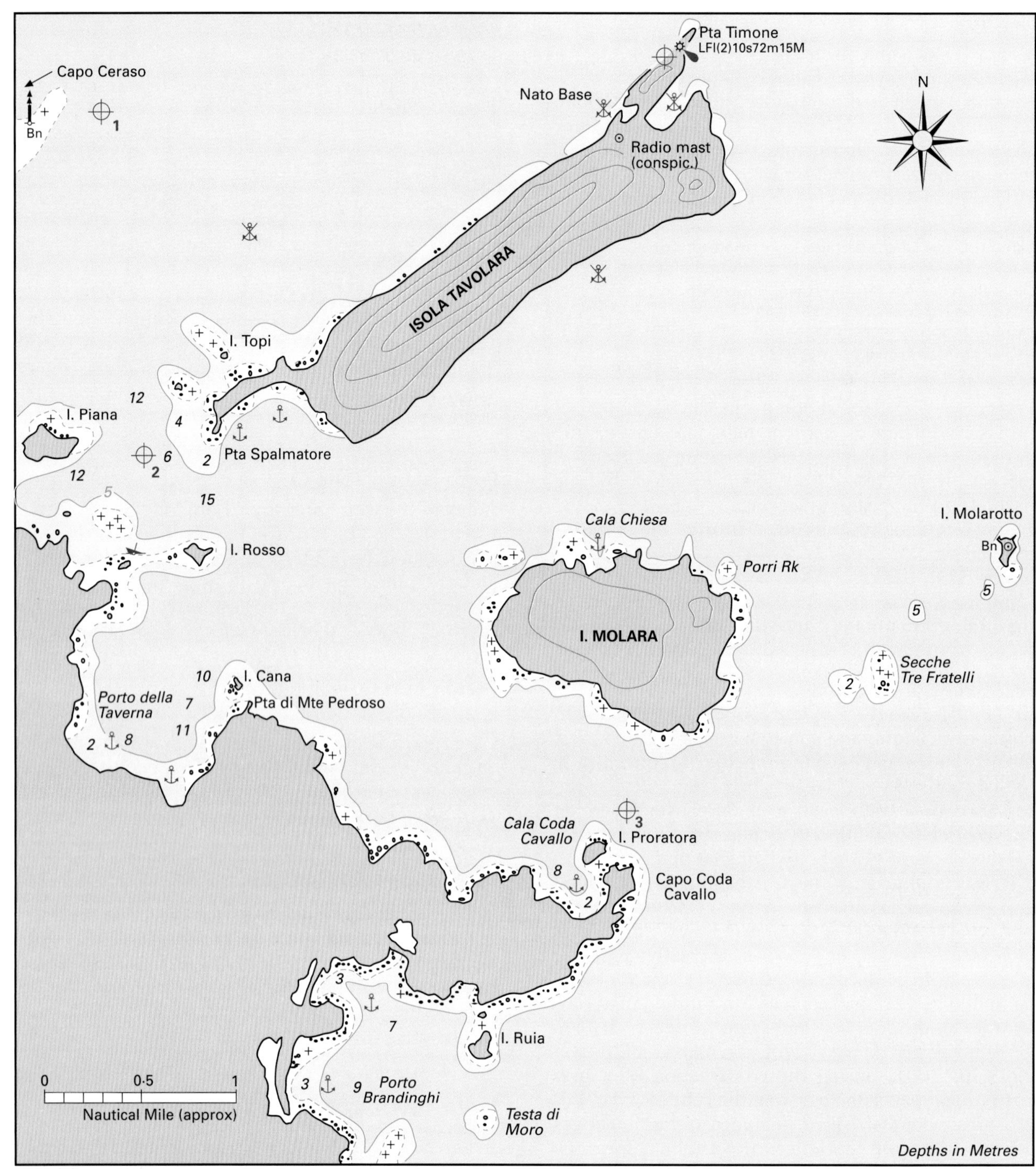

ISOLA TAVOLARA TO PORTO BRANDINGHI
⊕1 40°55´·32N 09°39´·36E WGS84
⊕2 40°53´·27N 09°39´·64E WGS84
⊕3 40°51´·03N 09°43´·71E WGS84

the island is a military zone and falls within Zone A of the AMP. On the SW end a yacht can pick up an AMP authority mooring buoy if available. There are a number of houses ashore and a restaurant open only in the summer.

Dangers At Punta Spalmatore, off the N and W end of the spit, there are numerous islets, above and below-water rocks, and shoal water. Caution must be exercised when navigating in this area.

Isola Molara (Zone B)

A high granite island lying just over one mile S of Isola Tavolara. It is fringed by above and below-water rocks. On the N side Cala Chiesa affords shelter from southerlies. It is deserted ashore. To the E of Isola Molara lies Secche Tre Fratelli (The Three Brothers Reef) and to the NE of the reef is I. Molarotto. Yachts may pick up an AMP authority mooring buoy off the SW corner.

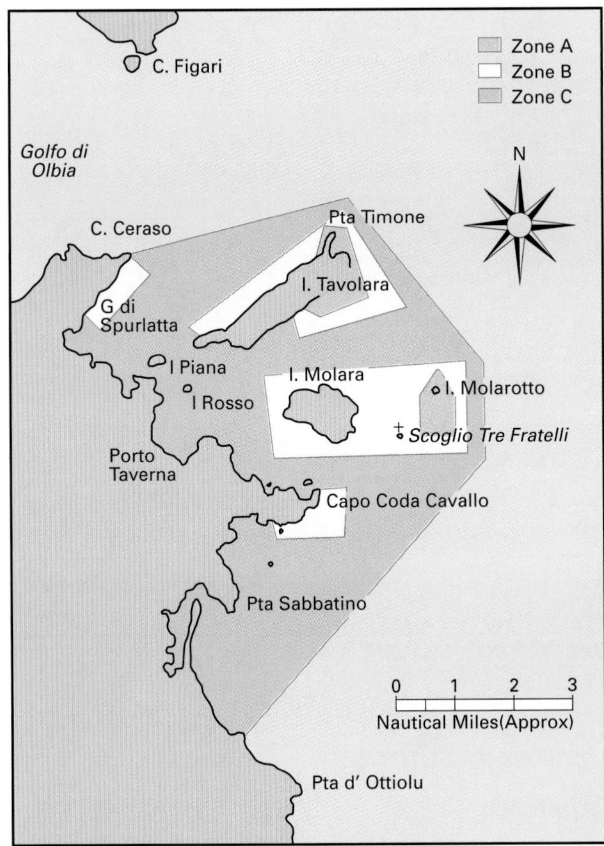

ISOLA TAVOLARA & CAPO CODA CAVALLO MARINE RESERVE

Isola Tavolara and Capo Coda Cavallo Marine Reserve

Established in 1998, this marine reserve covers the area from Capo Ceraso to Punta di Isuledda, near San Teodoro.

The area is currently divided as follows:

Zone A
This area is marked by lit yellow buoys.
Navigation, short- and long-time stays, swimming and all types of fishing are prohibited. Guided diving trips permitted on prearranged routes.

Zone B
All fishing prohibited.
Navigation is permitted, speed limit 10 knots.
Mooring permitted only on mooring buoys laid out by the authorities. Authorised diving trips permitted.
Swimming allowed.

Zone C
Navigation is not subject to any regulations, but mooring is restricted to authorised mooring buoys.
Diving and sport fishing with static lines and rods permitted.

Porto della Taverna (Zone C)

⊕ 40°51′·8N 09°40′·0E

A large bay open to the north. It should be entered between Isolotto Rosso and Isolotto Cana. A reef and shoal water connect Isolotto Rosso to the coast. The wreck of a ship lies on the reef and is conspicuous. Pick up an AMP authority mooring buoy where convenient. A number of villas have been built on the slopes around the shore.

Cala Coda Cavallo (Zone C)

⊕ 40°50′·6N 09°43′·1E

An attractive bay situated on the W side of Capo Coda Cavallo. AMP authority mooring buoys. There is a small quay in the bay. Open only to the NW. If it should blow from this direction a yacht can go around into Porto Brandinghi. The land around the bay is being developed.

Porto Brandinghi

A large bay with several attractive coves in it. Care must be taken of Testa di Moro rock just awash in the entrance to the bay. The rock, as its name suggests looks just like a man's head. (Testa di Moro translates as the Moor's head.) Anchor where convenient, although the cove in the northern corner is the best. Anchor here in 3–5m – good holding. Open only to the SE. A number of hotels and villas have been built around the shores of this attractive bay.

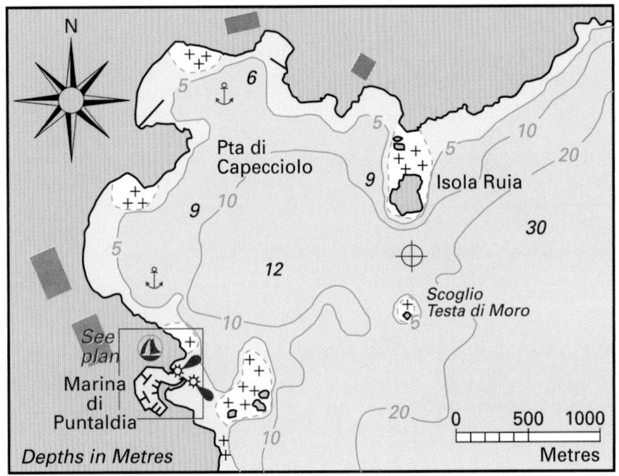

PORTO BRANDINGHI
⊕40°49′·4N 09°42′·5E

The conspicuous wreck of the ship on the reef near I. Rosso

IV. SARDINIA

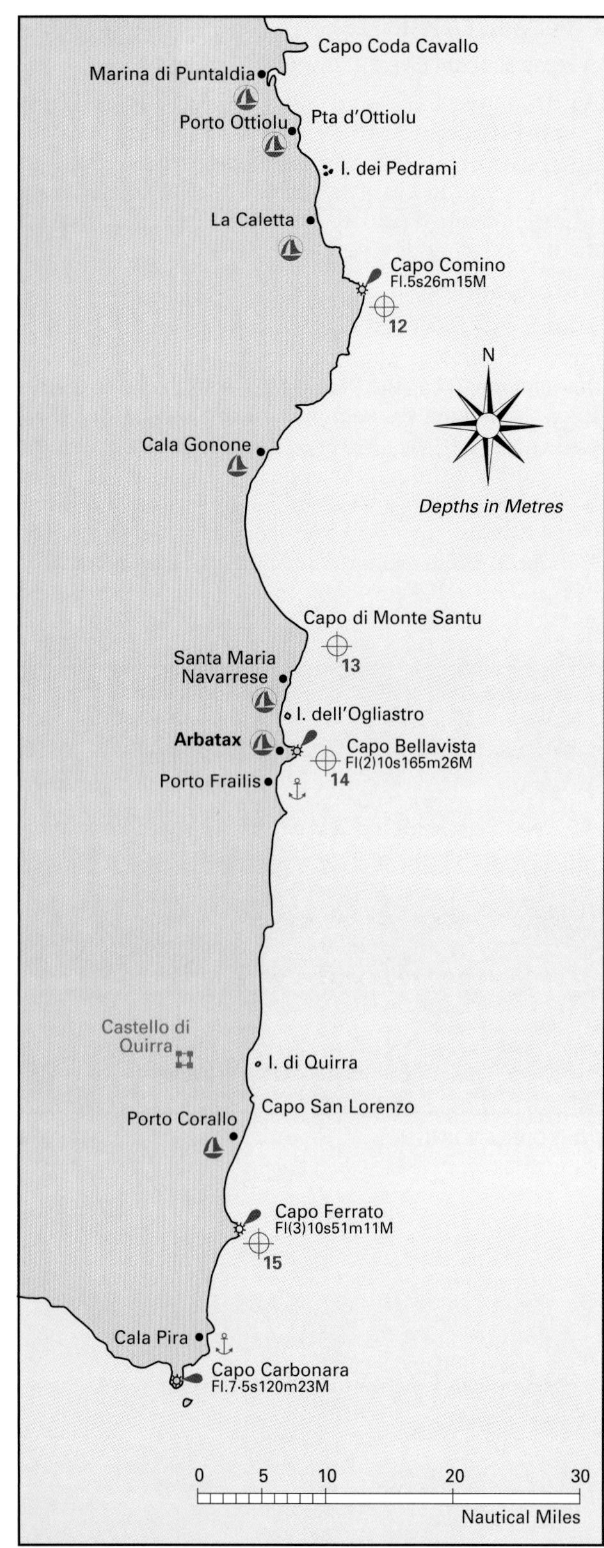

CAPO CODA CAVALLO TO CAPO CARBONARA

⊕**12** 0·4M E of Capo Comino light
40°31'·77N 09°50'·37E WGS84
⊕**13** 1M E of Capo di Monte Santu
40°04'·6N 09°45'·8E
⊕**14** 0·25ME of Capo Bellavista light
39°55'·78N 09°43'·33E WGS84
⊕**15** 1M E of Capo Ferrato light
39°17'·9N 09°39'·4E

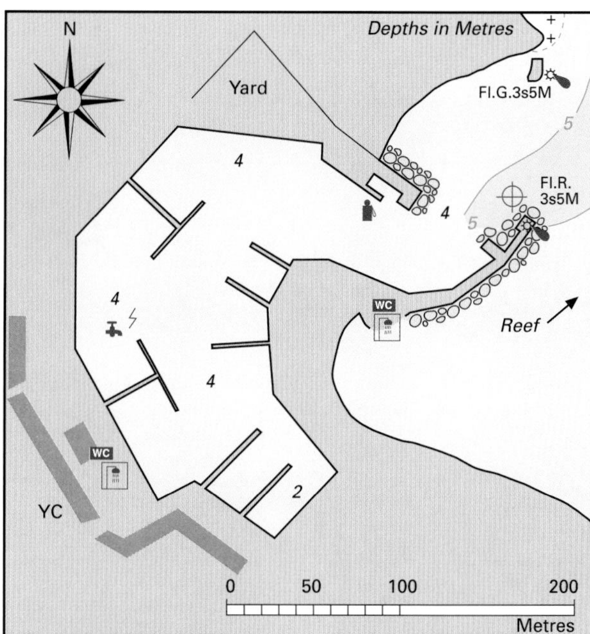

MARINA DI PUNTALDIA
⊕40°49'·0N 09°41'·5E

MARINA DI PUNTALDIA

Approach

The marina has been dredged out of the low-lying coast. Once into Porto Brandhingi the location of the marina in the SW corner of the bay is easily established.

VHF Ch 09.

Dangers Care is needed of the group of above and below-water rocks immediately E of the marina. The approach should be made from the N before turning to starboard into the marina itself.

Mooring

Data 380 berths. Max LOA 20m. Depths 2–4·5m.

Berth Where directed. There are laid moorings tailed to the quay.

Shelter Good all-round shelter.

Authorities Harbourmaster and marina staff. Charge band 5.

✆ 0784 864 589 *Fax* 0784 864 594.

Facilities

Services Water and electricity at all berths. WC and showers.
Fuel On the quay at the entrance.
Repairs Crane and hardstanding. Mechanical and other yacht repairs can be organised.
Provisions Minimarket.
Eating out Restaurant and bar.

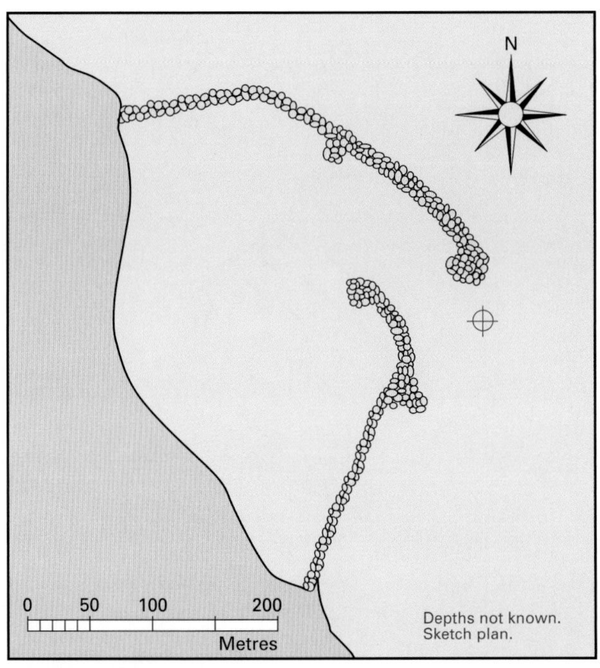

PORTO DI SAN TEODORO
⊕40°46′·8N 09°40′·7E

Porto di San Teodoro

A new *porto turistico* is under construction roughly halfway between Marina di Puntaldia and Porto Ottiolu, at the SW boundary of the Capo Coda Cavallo AMP. The breakwaters are complete, but as yet there are no quays or infrastructure. At present the harbour is used by small local boats on moorings. Care is needed as reefs and shoal water extend off the coast in places here. No completion dates or details were available at the time of writing.

PORTO OTTIOLU

A marina lying approximately ¾ of a mile S of Punta Ottiolu.

Approach

With little other development along this stretch of coast the buildings and harbour at Ottiolu are easily identified. From the N the marina won't be seen until you are almost due E of the entrance.

VHF Ch 09, 16.

Dangers Entry should be made from the NE to avoid Isolotto Ottiolu and the reef connecting it to the shore. When leaving do not attempt to cut in between I. Ottiolu and the coast, but keep well to seawards of the islet and reef.

Mooring

Data 405 berths. 45 visitors' berths. Max LOA 30m. Depths 3–6m.

Berth Where directed. There are laid moorings tailed to the quay.

Shelter Good all-round shelter.

Authorities Harbourmaster and marina staff. Charge band 5.

✆ 0784 846 211

Facilities

Services Water and electricity at every berth. A shower and toilet block.
Fuel On the quay.
Repairs A 40-ton travel-hoist. Mechanical repairs.
Provisions Most provisions can be obtained.
Eating out Restaurants and bars in the summer.
Other PO. Bank. ATM.

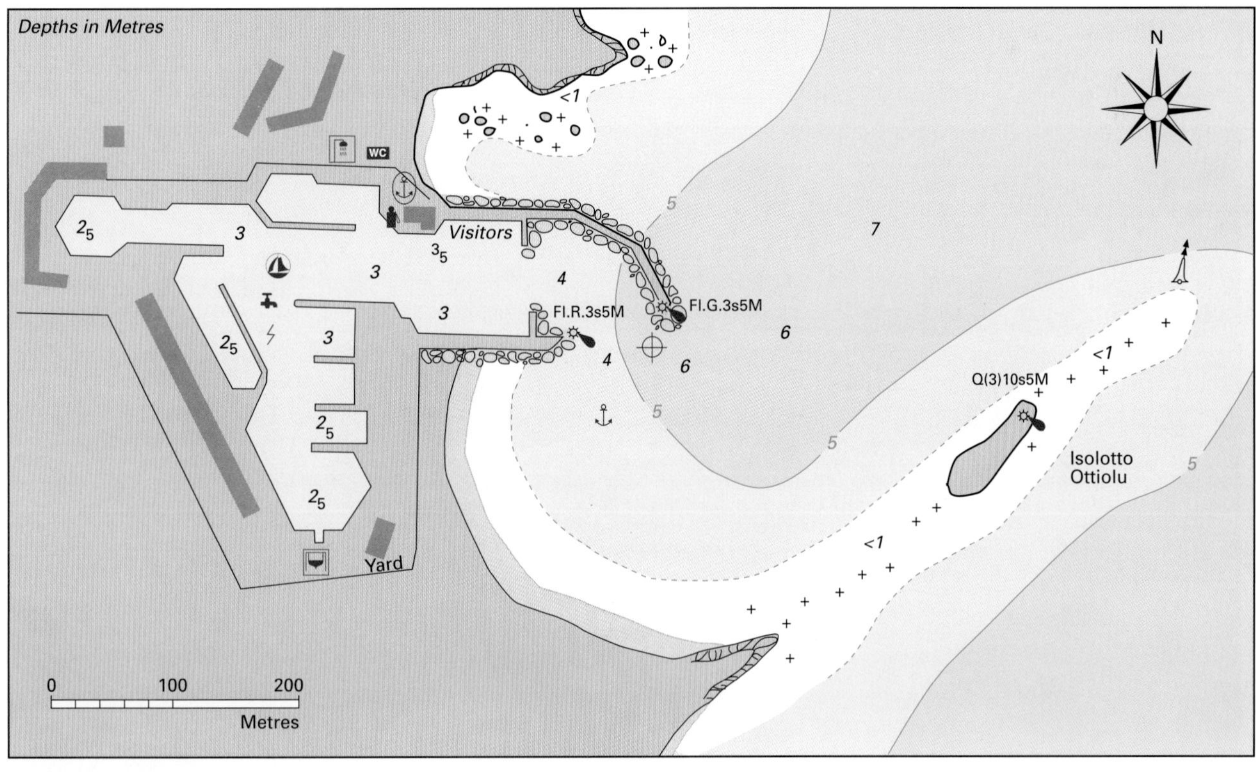

PORTO OTTIOLU
⊕40°44′·3N 09°42′·9E

General

The most southern (so far) of the lookalike Costa Smeralda imitators to open. This stretch of coast is just as beautiful as that to the north and the beaches every bit as good, so it is not surprising that the chain of marinas in the NE is extending S down this coast.

Pedrami Rocks

⊕ 40°41'·11N 09°46'·75E WGS84
0·5M E of outer reef

The Pedrami Rocks extend nearly 1¼ miles eastwards from the coast. Only the outermost rocks are above water and they can be difficult to make out from a distance. Although there is a shallow passage between the rocks and the coast it is only prudent to keep well to seaward of them.

LA CALETTA

Approach

The harbour lies about 4½ miles S of the Pedrami Rocks and six miles N of Capo Comino.

Conspicuous The village of Posada built on a hummock and a square tower in it to the NW of La Caletta are easily identified. Closer in, the buildings of La Caletta and San Giovanni tower on the foreshore are conspicuous. The tower is in need of a coat of paint and looks grey rather than white.

By night A night approach is possible with care.

VHF Ch 16.

Dangers Pedrami rocks: see note above.

Mooring

Data 300 berths. Max LOA 18m. Depths 1–5m.

Berth Go stern or bows-to wherever there is room or where directed. Berths on left side of the pier are council run, and those on right side are run by the yacht club. It is reported that the pontoon inside the SW side of the T-pier is not part of the marina and as such may be used, albeit with no facilities. Likewise the outside of the T-pier, although this is not suitable with any S–SE winds.

Shelter Good shelter although strong S–SE winds cause an uncomfortable surge.

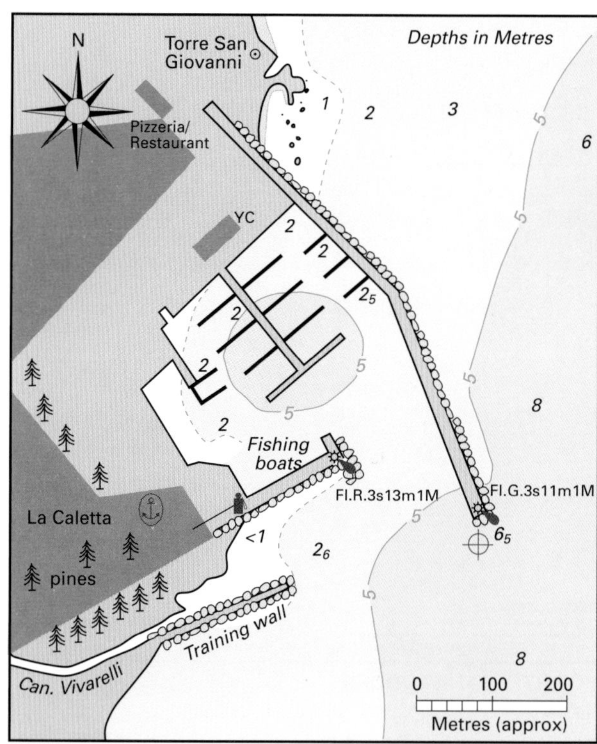

LA CALETTA
⊕40°36'·6N 09°45'·4E

La Caletta looking SSW (new pontoons have been added since the photo was taken) *Carlo Delfino*

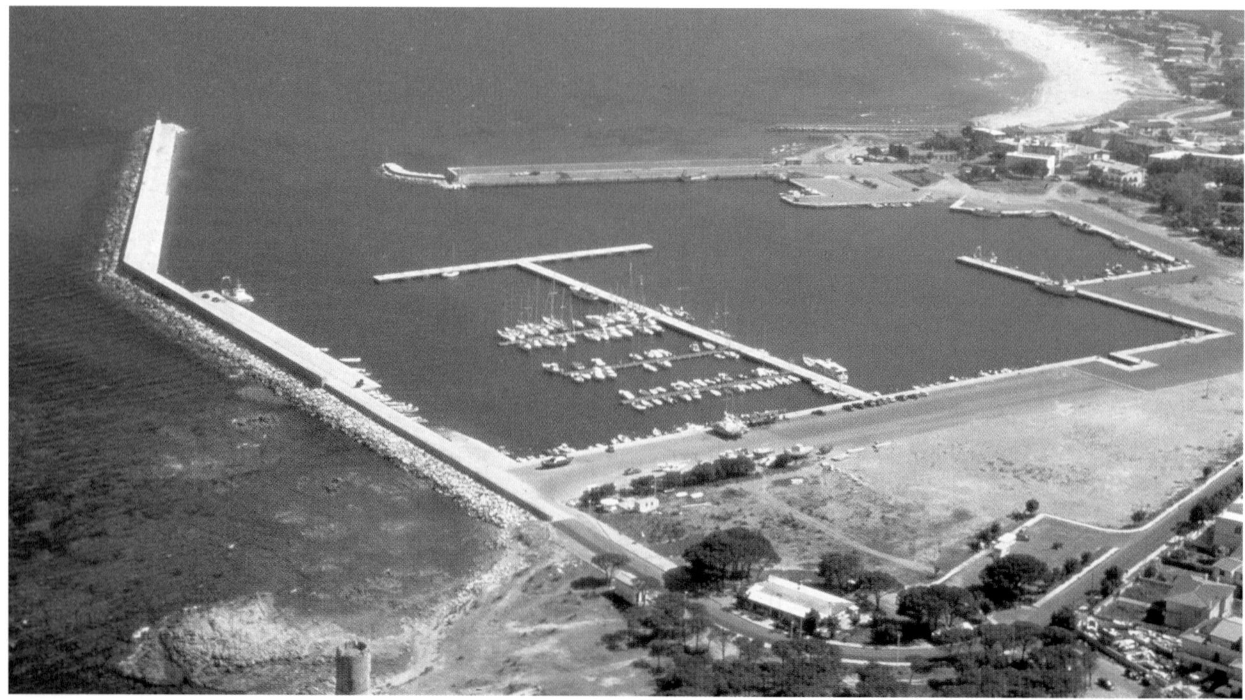

Authorities Harbourmaster. CN charge band 4. Council berths charge band 5.
Circolo Nautico La Caletta ✆ 0784 810 631
Email info@circolonauticolacaletta.it

Facilities

Services Water and electricity at marina berths.
Fuel On the quay.
Repairs Minor mechanical repairs only.
Provisions Most provisions can be obtained locally.
Eating out Restaurants, although some are only open in the summer. *La Nuova Torre* restaurant/pizzeria near the marina is worth a visit.
Other PO. Bank. ATM. Pharmacy. Camping Gaz in Siniscola or Santa Lucia. Infrequent bus to Siniscola and Santa Lucia. Bus to Nuoro.

General

Once a small timber port, La Caletta is now becoming a small resort servicing the adjacent coast. Standing at the edge of a cultivated plain, it is a pleasing, friendly place well worth stopping at on the trek down the east coast. Siniscola, connected by an infrequent bus service, is an old agricultural town gradually adapting to the new-found tourism going on around it: an interesting place once renowned for its folk costumes.

La Caletta Porto Vecchio

Mr LSA Hammick reports that five miles to the S of La Caletta is the old port which was destroyed by the authorities to prevent its use by smugglers. He says it is in a long inlet fringed by rocks with depths of around 1·5m. There are no leading marks to get in or out. In calm weather a very small yacht could investigate. 'A marvellous place for a picnic in absolutely settled weather and dreamy on a full moon night', he says.

Note The coast between Capo Comino and Cala Gonone is mostly low-lying land bordered by sandy beaches. There are several villages and resorts along the coast with their own small fishing harbours and beaches protected by breakwaters. None of these appear suitable for anything but very small yachts, and may be worth investigating in calm weather. Once round Pta Nera di Osalla the land rises and the buildings of Cala Gonone can be seen.

S of Orosei River

⊕ 40°21'·59N 09°42'·92E WGS84

Marked by a yellow beacon with x topmark.

N and S of a quarry on Punta Nera di Osalla

⊕ 40°19'·81N 09°40'·88E WGS84

Depth 4m in the entrance.

Capo Comino

⊕ 12 0·4M E of Capo Comino light
40°31'·77N 09°50'·37E WGS84

In calm weather a yacht can anchor off the N side of the cape. Care is needed of above and below-water rocks. Reasonable shelter from SW–NW but with even moderate winds from almost any direction a swell will roll around into here.

Cala Gonone looking in from the entrance

CALA GONONE

Approach

Lies approximately 18 miles SW of Capo Comino.

Conspicuous The lighthouse on Capo Comino, a white three-storey building with a short tower, is readily identified. The buildings of Cala Gonone are easily identified. Closer in, the numerous villas and hotels behind the harbour and the outer breakwater can be identified.

VHF Ch 16.

Dangers With offshore winds there are strong gusts and with onshore winds a confused swell at the entrance.

Mooring

Data Max LOA 12m. Depths 1–5m.

Berth The harbour is usually full of fishing or tripper boats. You may find a space on the S end of the

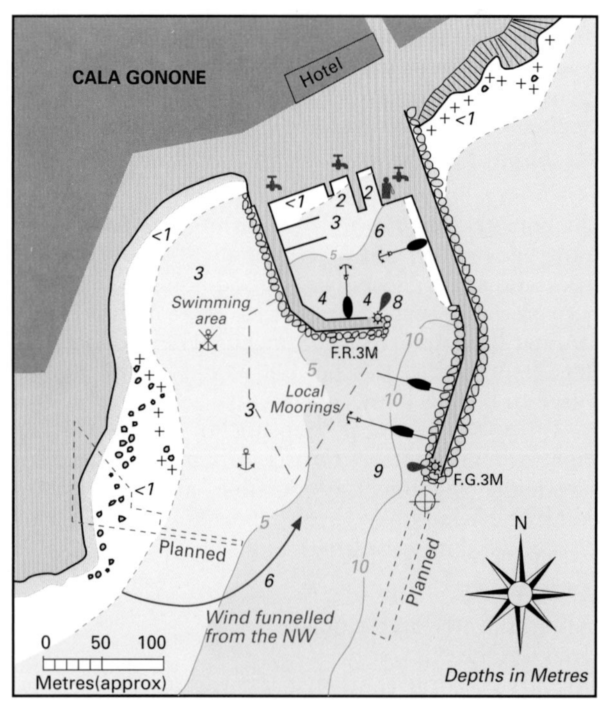

CALA GONONE
⊕40°16´·84N 09°38´·33E WGS84

Cala Gonone looking north *Carlo Delfino*

breakwater where there are landing stages with laid moorings. Bottom is sand and rock, generally not good holding.

Shelter Generally fair, although wash from tripper boats can be annoying. It has been reported that strong northwesterlies can get diverted by the high land and end up blowing into the harbour. This funnelling effect has caused considerable damage to yachts moored off the breakwater. When the planned improvements to the harbour are made the shelter will be improved.

Authorities Harbourmaster. Charge band 4.

Anchorage In the summer you will probably have to anchor off. Much of the area around the harbour is now buoyed off, and space is limited. The bottom is rock and sand, generally not good holding so it may pay to set a second anchor. If there is any wind around keep an eye on the anchor. The anchorage is tenable in settled weather but would not be a good place to be in a blow.

During the day local boats anchor off the beaches right around Golfo di Orosei. In settled weather an overnight stay might be possible, although strong katabatic winds have been reported, gusting up to Force 7 and more at times.

Facilities

Services Water on the quay.
Fuel On the quay.
Repairs A 9-ton crane and slipway up to 20 tons. Mechanic in Dorgali.
Provisions Most provisions can be obtained.
Eating out Restaurants and bars open in the summer.
Other PO and Bank in Dorgali (10km away).

General

Cala Gonone is being developed as a tourist resort right in the middle of one of the wildest and most rugged parts of Sardinia. Cala Gonone village is built on the slopes of an extinct volcano, Monte Codula Manna, and is surrounded by limestone mountains covered by holm-oak forests. The scenery is majestic and if the weather permits you to leave your yacht in safety a visit inland is worthwhile. Near Dorgali at Serra Orrios lies the largest and most complete Nuraghic village and at Grotta di Ispinigoli the world's second-highest stalagmite (38m/125ft) can be found. Phoenician jewellery and human bones were also found in the cave, possibly as a result of Nuraghic burials or sacrifices.

SANTA MARIA NAVARRESE (Marina di Baunei)

Approach

The marina lies at the S end of a range of cliffs where the high ground joins the beach.

Conspicuous The Genoese tower to the S of the entrance is conspicuous. Isola dell'Olgiastra is easily identified just 1M to the SE, and closer in the outer breakwaters will be seen.

By night Use the light on Capo Bellavista (Arbatax) Fl(2)10s165m26M.

VHF Ch 16, 74.

Note There can be a lumpy swell at the entrance with onshore winds.

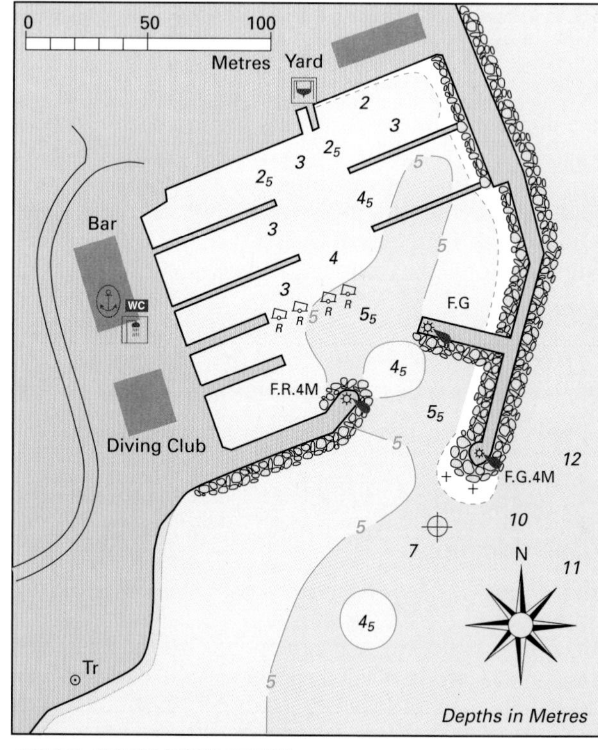

SANTA MARIA NAVARRESE
⊕39°59´·37N 09°41´·68E WGS84

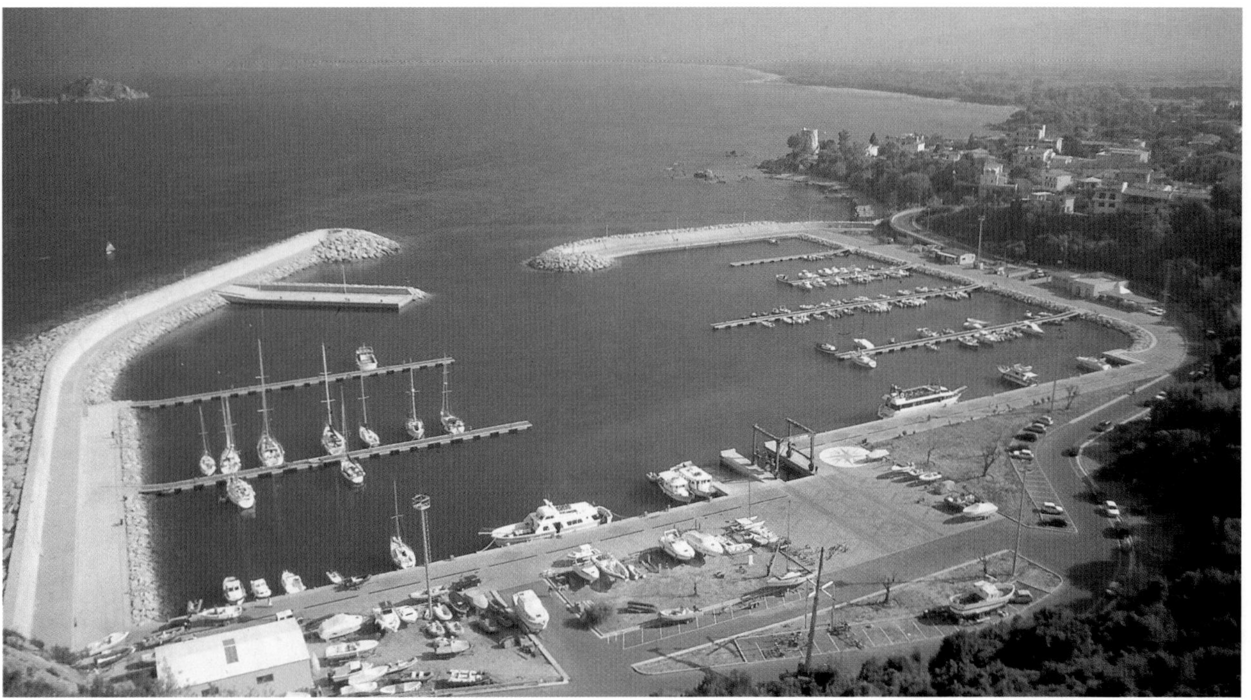

Santa Maria Navarrese looking SSE

Mooring

Data 340 berths. Max LOA 30m. Bigger yachts should call ahead. Depths 2–5m.

Berths The W side of the marina is filled with small local boats. Marina staff will come to meet you in a RIB and assist mooring. Moor stern or bows-to on the E side where directed. Laid moorings tailed to the quay.

Shelter Good all-round shelter.

Authorities Marina staff. Charge band 4.

✆ 0782 614 020 *Fax* 0782 614 198
Email marinabaunei@tiscalinet.it
www.portosantamaria-baunei.it

Facilities

Services Water and electricity at all berths. Shower and toilet block. Self service laundry planned.
Fuel 2M S at Arbatax.
Repairs 40-ton travel-lift and 15-ton crane. Yamaha/Yanmar workshop and store. Some repairs possible.
Provisions In the village up the hill most provisions can be obtained.
Eating out Café/bar in the marina. Several restaurants and bars in the village.
Other PO and gas (Camping Gaz/Italgaz) in the village. ATMs. Taxis and hire cars.

General

This secure and friendly new marina is now an excellent place to leave a boat in order to explore the surrounding Gennargentu National Park, but you don't necessarily have to go far. The *bellavista* at the top of the hill beyond the village gives a wonderful view over Isola dell'Oligastra towards Arbatax.

Boat trips up the coast to the Grotto delle Bue Marine (the grotto of the Sea-Ox) run from the marina. It is a sad irony that due mainly to human disturbance it is now devoid of the Mediterranean Monk Seals that originally drew the tourists here.

Isola dell'Olgiastra

⊕ 39°58′·59N 09°42′·77E WGS84 0·15M E of the island

Isola dell'Olgiastra lies approximately halfway between Santa Maria Navarrese and Arbatax. The passage between the island and the coast has least depths of 8m, but should only be attempted in good weather with a large-scale chart. In calm weather yachts can anchor off the W and NW sides. Good holding with sand and weed in around 5–8m.

ARBATAX

BA 1210
Italian 316

Approach

Conspicuous Capo Bellavista lighthouse (a white square crenellated tower and dwelling) standing on a rocky promontory can be identified from some distance off. A number of chimneys and large buildings behind the harbour are also conspicuous from the north. From the S, Torre San Geminiano is conspicuous on the promontory immediately S of Capo Bellavista. Closer in, the breakwaters and the buildings of Arbatax are readily identified.

By night Use the light on Capo Bellavista Fl(2)10s165m26M and F.R.145m6M. The red sector 164°-177·5° covers Isola dell'Ogliastra.

VHF Ch 11, 16 for port authorities (0700–1900). Ch 09 for marina.

Dangers With offshore winds there can be savage gusts down into Golfo Tortoli.

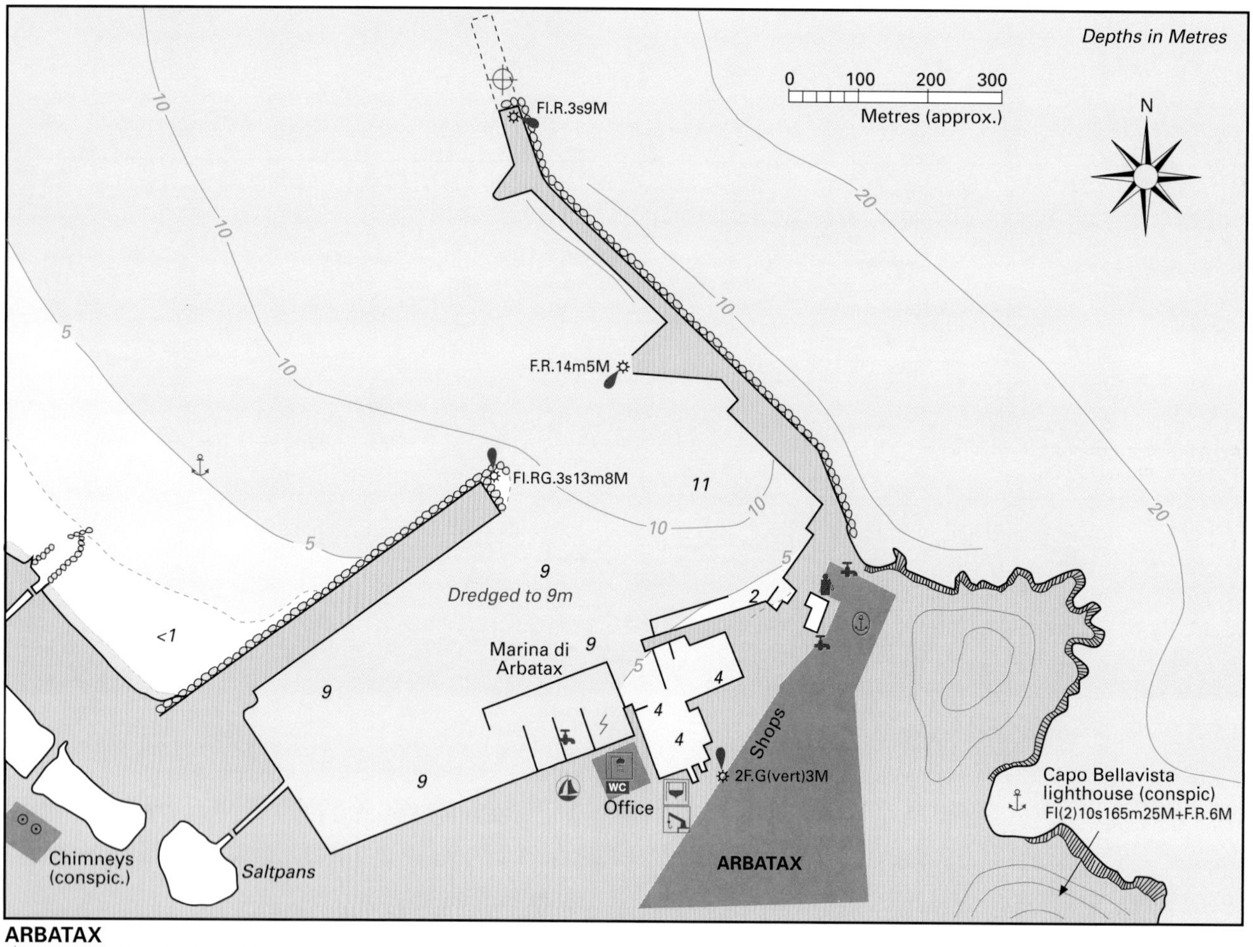

ARBATAX
⊕39°56′·76N 09°42′·08E WGS84

Mooring

Data 400 berths. Max LOA 50m. Depths 4–10m.

Berth Yachts should head for the marina where you will be shown to a berth. Laid moorings tailed to the quay.

Shelter Good all-round shelter although gusts off the mountains cause a slop in the harbour.

Arbatax looking WSW over the basin. (Note Marina di Arbatax is not complete here) *Carlo Delfino*

Authorities Port police and customs. Marina staff. Charge band 4.

Marina di Arbatax ☎ 0782 667 405 *Fax* 0782 664 359
www.marinadiarbatax.it

Anchorage Yachts can anchor off the beach N of the W breakwater. Good holding on sand, although at night a swell penetrates, making it quite rolly.

Facilities

Services Water and electricity in the marina. Toilets and showers in the marina.

Fuel From a station near the quay.

Repairs 200-ton travel-hoist. Chandlers near the quay. A yard in Tortoli on the coast to the west. Mechanical and some yacht repairs can be carried out here.

Provisions Small supermarket near the quay. Ice can be ordered from Tortoli.

Eating out Restaurant by the marina. Several restaurants in the village.

Other Pharmacy. Camping Gaz from the chandlers. Irregular bus service and train to Tortoli.

General

A friendly and helpful marina has been developed here in the heart of this busy commercial harbour.

The port is being developed for the pulp and plywood factories behind and can take vessels up to 10,000 tons. A new facility builds offshore gas rigs

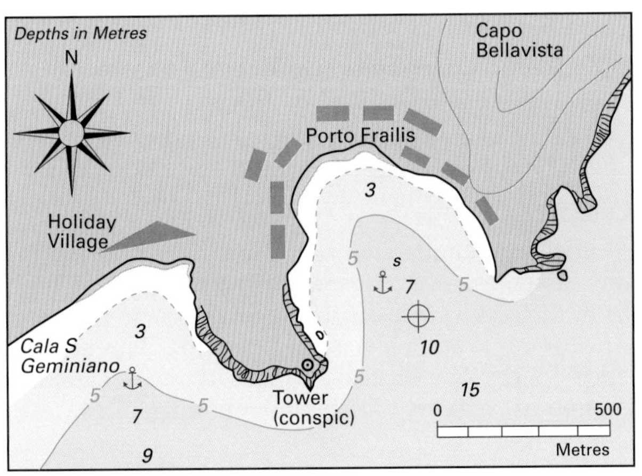

PORTO FRAILIS
⊕39°55′·5N 09°42′·8E

for export worldwide. The mountains surrounding the harbour are magnificent. At the foot of the massif there is a thin belt of flat land bordered by a long white sandy beach and the sea. The craggy red granite promontory sheltering the harbour is extensively wooded and a pleasant place to walk around on a hot summer's day. Just over the saddle of the promontory from the town there is a pleasant cove suitable for bathing.

Porto Frailis

A cove on the S side of Capo Bellavista. The lighthouse on Capo Bellavista (Fl(2)10s165m26M) is visible from some way off. On the S side the tower (Torre San Geminiano) on the rocky spur and the holiday village will be seen.

Anchor in 7–10m on sand outside the buoyed swimming area. Open south. The cove is useful in settled summer weather although there can be a strong katabatic wind off the land at night. The bottom is sand, good holding. The vast holiday village ashore has a fortissimo line in beach entertainment. Jet skis and pedalos churn the waters. A peaceful place this isn't.

Cala San Geminiano immediately W of Porto Frailis is not as well sheltered and the holding appears to be suspect on rock and weed with much of the bay now buoyed off for swimming. Water and a restaurant at the holiday village.

Isola di Quirra

⊕ 39°31′·5N 09°39′·1E

5M N of Porto Corallo the river Quirra carves a valley down from the Barbagia mountains to the sea. In the hills the Castello di Quirra provides a useful landmark and Isola di Quirra will also be seen. The passage between the island and the coast is free of dangers. Passing one-third of the distance between the island and the shore will give least depths of 12m. To the E of the island shoal water extends out for some way and should be given a good offing.

PORTO CORALLO (MARINA DI VILLAPUTZU)

Approach

From the N Capo San Lorenzo with a tower on it is easily recognised. Close to the harbour a tower is conspicuous. To the N of the harbour a development of barracks-like apartments and villas on the hill will be seen.

VHF Ch 74, 16 for Marina di Villaputzu.

Dangers

1. A dangerous wreck lies just off the coast S of the entrance to the marina in position 39°24′·7N 09°38′·5E.
2. The entrance tends to silt and is dredged periodically.
3. Shallow water extends out some distance to the S of the entrance.
4. Care is needed with strong onshore winds when a considerable swell piles up at the entrance.

Mooring

Data 350 berths. Max LOA 30m. Depths 3–6m.

Berth Marina staff will usually show you to a berth on the W side of the harbour. The E side is crowded with fishing and local boats. Moor stern or bows-to or alongside where directed. Laid moorings tailed to the quay.

Shelter Good shelter in the summer. Strong S winds would probably make things uncomfortable.

Authorities Charge band 4.

Marina di Villaputzu ✆ 393 923 8334 / 8909
Email marinadivillaputzu@tiscali.it
www.marinadivillaputzu.it

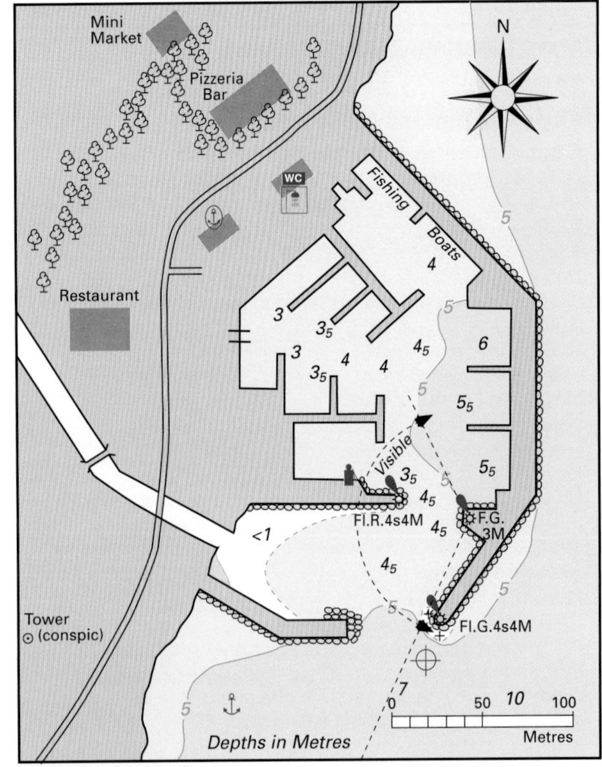

PORTO CORALLO
⊕39°26′·4N 09°38′·4E

Facilities

Services Water and electricity at most berth. Toilets and showers.
Fuel On the quay.
Repairs 50-ton travel-lift. Slip and 15-ton crane. Some repairs may be possible.
Provisions Minimarket in the camping ground.
Eating out Restaurant near the harbour. Restaurant/pizzeria in the camping ground.
Other Infrequent bus service. Bank, PO and shops in the tourist development to the north.

General

The harbour is being developed as a *porto turistico* by the local commune although at present only a few cruising yachts and fishing boats use it. The setting is wonderful and the harbour conveniently sited to break the journey along the E coast of Sardinia.

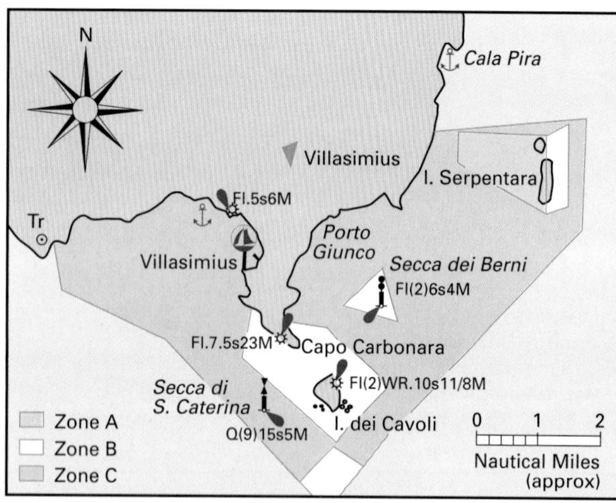

CAPO CARBONARA MARINE RESERVE

Capo Carbonara Marine Reserve

Established in 1998, this marine reserve stretches from Isola Serpentara to Capo Boi, the western extremity of the Golfo di Carbonara. At present the area is divided as follows:

Zone A
Access, navigation, short- and long-time stays, swimming, and all types of fishing prohibited.
Guided diving trips are permitted and are regulated by the authorities.
(Note that this restricts navigation between Isola Serpentara and the coast).

Zone B
Free anchorage prohibited.
Navigation is permitted but only at max 10 knots.
Mooring permitted only on moorings provided by the authorities.
Sport and commercial fishing are allowed with previous authorisation.

Zone C
Navigation is unrestricted.
Anchorage permitted exclusively in marked zones and mooring only allowed in officially designated zones.
Fields of mooring buoys are to be laid out in certain areas to protect *Posidonia* (sea grass).

✆ 070 790 234 *Fax* 070 790 314
Email info@ampcapocarbonara.it
www.ampcapocarbonara.it

Capo Ferrato

⊕ 15 1M E of Capo Ferrato light 39°17'·9N 09°39'·4E

Reasonable shelter from light S–SW winds on the N side of the cape. Anchor in 5m on sand, with a stern anchor to hold you into the swell.

Cala Pira

A small cove under Punta Cappuccini. A tower on the eastern side is conspicuous when approaching from the south. Just off the headland there is a reef. Anchor in 5–8m on a sandy bottom. The cove is open to the S and east. Ashore there is camping ground in pleasant wooded surroundings.

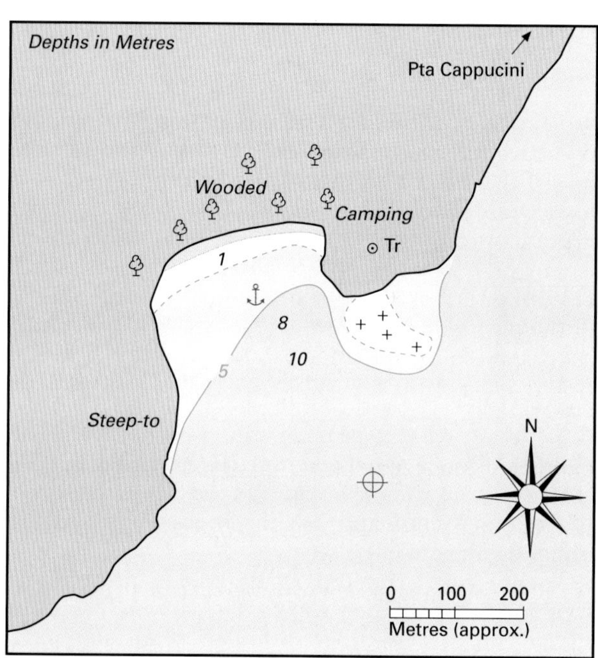

CALA PIRA
⊕39°10'·1N 09°34'·5E

Porto Giunco (Zone C)

An exposed anchorage under Pta Molenti. The beacon with ⁝ topmark marking Secca del Berni is reported to have lost the topmark. It is lit Fl(2)6s4M.

South coast: Capo Carbonara to Capo Sperone

Like the west coast, this coast has a reputation for being a very windy spot. The reputation is partly true, especially around Isola Sant' Antioco and in Golfo di Cagliari. Yet the coast offers a cruising ground of considerable beauty to the yachtsman patient enough to wait for settled weather and there are plenty of safe harbours in which to find refuge should you get caught out.

Weather patterns on the South coast

In the summer, winds are predominantly from the NW but SW winds are also common. Off Sant' Antioco and in Golfo di Cagliari there is often a SW wind by the afternoon and it can blow up to Force 5–6. In the spring, autumn and winter winds are commonly from the NW or NE although there are also southerly gales in the winter. With strong southerlies a heavy sea sets onto the coast. With strong winds from any quarter there is always a confused sea off Capo Sperone and Capo Carbonara. Thunderstorms seem to home in on Golfo di Cagliari, but they seldom last longer than two to three hours.

VILLASIMIUS (FORTEZZA VECCHIA)

The small harbour previously here has been much enlarged into a marina with all facilities.

Approach

From the S and E the waters around Capo Carbonara are shallow, with Secca dei Berni and Secca di Santa Caterina either side of I. dei Cavoli. Secca dei Berni is marked by a beacon with a ⁝ topmark and Secca di Santa Caterina is marked by a W cardinal buoy.

Conspicuous The lighthouse on Capo Carbonara, a round white tower is conspicuous from some distance off. Once around into the bay a villa development to the S will be seen. Closer in the breakwaters and buildings (with red roofs) will be identified.

By night Use the light on Capo Carbonara Fl.7.5s23M and the light on Isola dei Cavoli Fl(2)WR.10s11/8M. The red sector covers Secca di Santa Caterina on 073°-093°. The W cardinal buoy on Secca di Santa Caterina is lit Q(9)15s5M. The N side of Golfo di Carbonara is lit Fl.5s6M.

VHF Ch 16, 09 for Marina Villasimius.

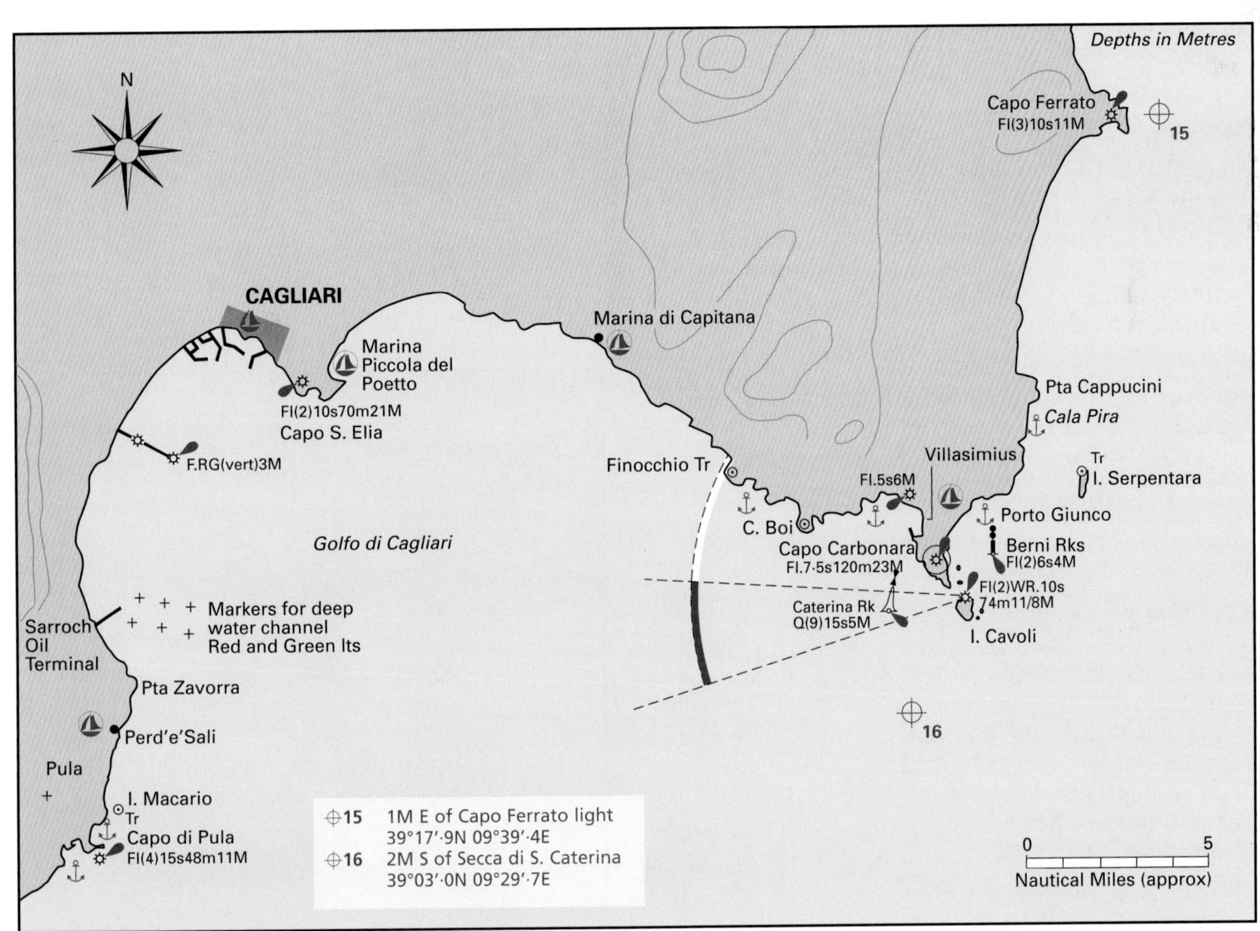

CAPO FERRATO TO CAPO DI PULA
⊕**15** 39°17′·9N 09°39′·4E 1M E of Capo Ferrato Light
⊕**16** 39°03′·0N 09°29′·7E 2M S of Secco di S. Caterina

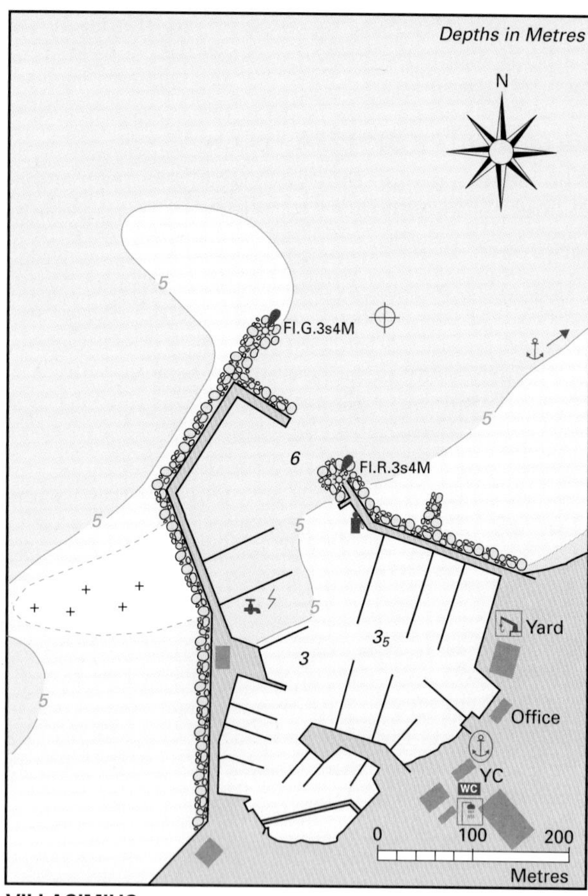

VILLASIMIUS
⊕39°07´·41N 09°30´·23E WGS84

Mooring

Data 750 berths. Visitors' berths. Max LOA 25m. Depths 1–6m.

Berth Where directed. Laid moorings tailed to the quay. The marina generally has plenty of visitors' berths, although it is busy at weekends with local boats from Cagliari.

Shelter Good all-round shelter.

Authorities Harbourmaster and marina staff. Charge band 5/6 (July–August).

✆ 070 797 8006 *Fax* 070 797 137
Email info@marinavillasimius.it
www.marinavillasimius.it

Anchorage No anchoring within 200m of the marina entrance, or the shore.

Facilities

Services Water and electricity (220/380V) at all berths. Wi-Fi. WC and showers. Pump-out. Laundry/laundrette.
Fuel On the quay (summer only).
Repairs Hauling max 30-tons/20m LOA. Chandler. Limited mechanical repairs.
Cantiere Nautico ✆ 070 797 8007
Provisions Mini-market in the marina in the summer.
Eating out Restaurant and bar in the summer. Also *pizzeria* near the campsite.
Other ATM. Pharmacy. Car hire. Camping Gas. Shuttle bus to Villasimius town.

General

At last the infrastructure ashore in the marina has been completed, with something for most people including bars and cafés, supermarket, chandlers and boutiques. It has been recommended as a friendly place with the staff eager to please and win customers. Out of season, though, many of the shops are closed, and it can seem a bit deserted.

Baia Carbonara (Zone C)

Depending on the wind, anchor on the W or E side of the bay. The bottom is sand and rock, indifferent holding. Marine reserve mooring buoys are planned and should be used in preference to anchoring. The large bay is most attractive and a popular summer lunch-stop for local yachts.

MARINA DI CAPITANA (Porto Armando)

BA 1983
Imray M9
Italian 45

Approach

A harbour approximately halfway between Villasimius and Cagliari.

Conspicuous A white bat silhouette 300m N of the entrance is conspicuous. The marina breakwater and yachts inside can be seen from a few miles away. Approximately 1M W of the marina a concrete water tower is conspicuous.

VHF Ch 16, 74.

Mooring

Data 446 berths. 90 visitors' berths. Max LOA 27m. Depths 3m.

Berths Visitors normally go on the pontoon just E of the fuel quay. Laid moorings tailed to the quay.

Shelter Good all-round shelter.

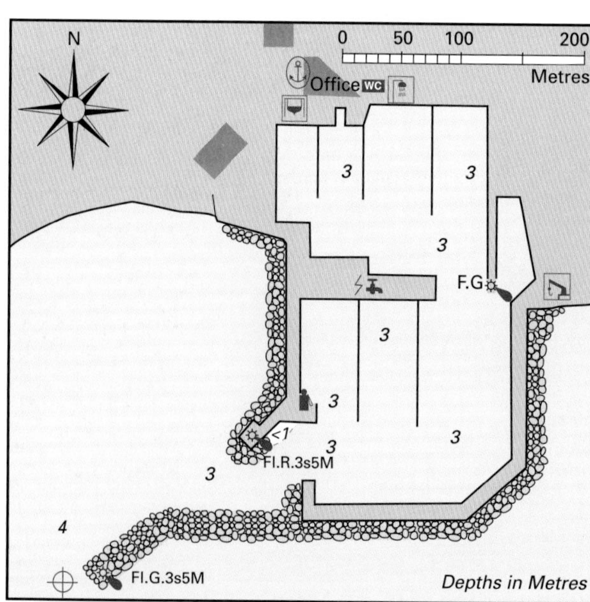

MARINA DI CAPITANA
⊕39°12´·28N 09°17´·95E WGS84

Marina di Capitana looking E into the marina from the entrance

Authorities Harbourmaster and marina staff. Charge band 4.
Marina di Capitana ☏ 070 805 460
Email marinadicapitana@tiscali.it
www.marinadicapitana.it

Facilities

Services Water (not potable) and electricity at or near every berth. WC and showers. Holding tank pump-away.
Fuel On the quay at the entrance (ring bell for service).
Repairs 40-ton travel-hoist. Hardstanding. Mechanical and other repairs now established.
Provisions Supermarket nearby (300m).
Eating out Restaurant, pizzeria and bar.
Other Telephone. Bus to Cagliari.

General

The marina is reported as a friendly and helpful place to visit or over-winter. Space ashore is limited and most yachts winter afloat.

MARINA PICCOLA DEL POETTO

Imray M9

Approach

Conspicuous Capo Sant'Elia is conspicuous. The marina lies on the E side of the cape. Behind the marina the apartment complex looks a little tatty, but the buildings around the marina and the harbour moles are easily distinguished.

VHF Ch 16, 74.

Mooring

Data 300 berths. Max LOA 18m. Depths 2–3m.

Berth Stern or bows-to where directed. Laid moorings tailed to the quay or buoys. The marina is usually crowded with local boats and it can be difficult to find a berth.

Shelter Good although strong N–NW winds send in some swell.

Authorities Harbourmaster and marina staff. Charge band 4/5.

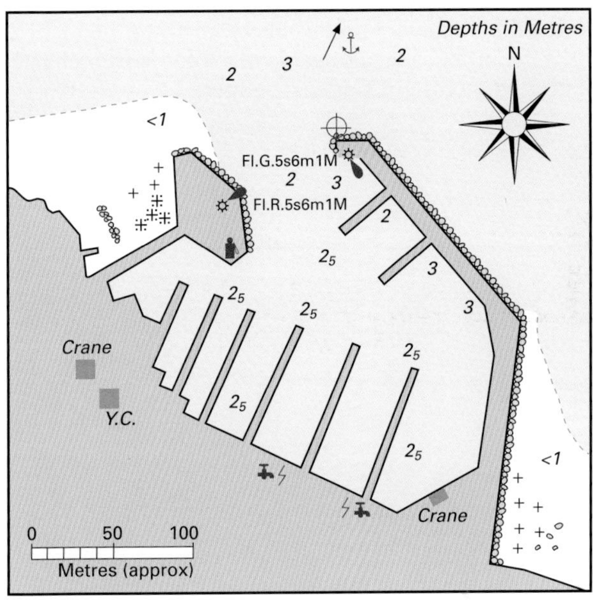

MARINA PICCOLA DEL POETTO
⊕39°11´·6N 09°09´·8E

Capo Sant'Elia looking NE

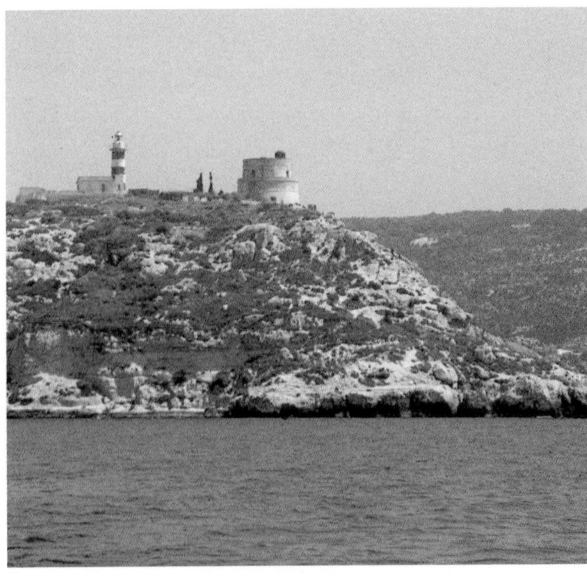

IV. SARDINIA

Facilities

Services Water and electricity at or near every berth. Basic portocabin WC and shower facilities.
Fuel On the quay near the entrance.
Repairs A 15-ton crane and 50-ton mobile crane. Slipway up to 3 tons. Mechanical repairs. Some general yacht repairs.
Provisions Limited, but Cagliari is a short distance away.
Eating out Restaurant, pizzeria and snack bar at the harbour.
Other Buses to Cagliari (15 minutes), or it is about 30 minutes' walk.

General

The fine sandy beach, the Poetto, stretching eastwards along the coast, is crowded with locals and tourists in the summer months. It has little to do with old Cagliari, looking like something deposited here from Florida alongside the old world charm and architecture of Cagliari proper.

CAGLIARI

BA 1208
Italian 311

Approach

Straightforward by day and night.

Conspicuous Capo Sant'Elia, a white chalk promontory, stands out against the surrounding flat land and looks like an island from the distance. From the S the oil port and installation, particularly the chimneys, are conspicuous. Closer in, the lighthouse and the signal tower of Capo Sant'Elia and the buildings of Cagliari are conspicuous. In the city a large church to the E and two cupolas in the centre are conspicuous. The entrance to the harbour is not immediately obvious by day until close in.

By night Once into Golfo di Cagliari use the light on Capo Sant'Elia Fl(2)10s21M. From the S the lights of the oil terminal, particularly the Fl.3s6M and the F.R&G(vert)3M, and a flare, are conspicuous.

VHF Ch 11, 16 for port authorities (0700–1900 call sign *Cagliari Radio*). Ch 09, 12, 16 for pilots. Ch 74 for Marina di Sant'Elmo. Ch 13 for Marina del Sole. Ch 74 for Marina Portus Karalis.

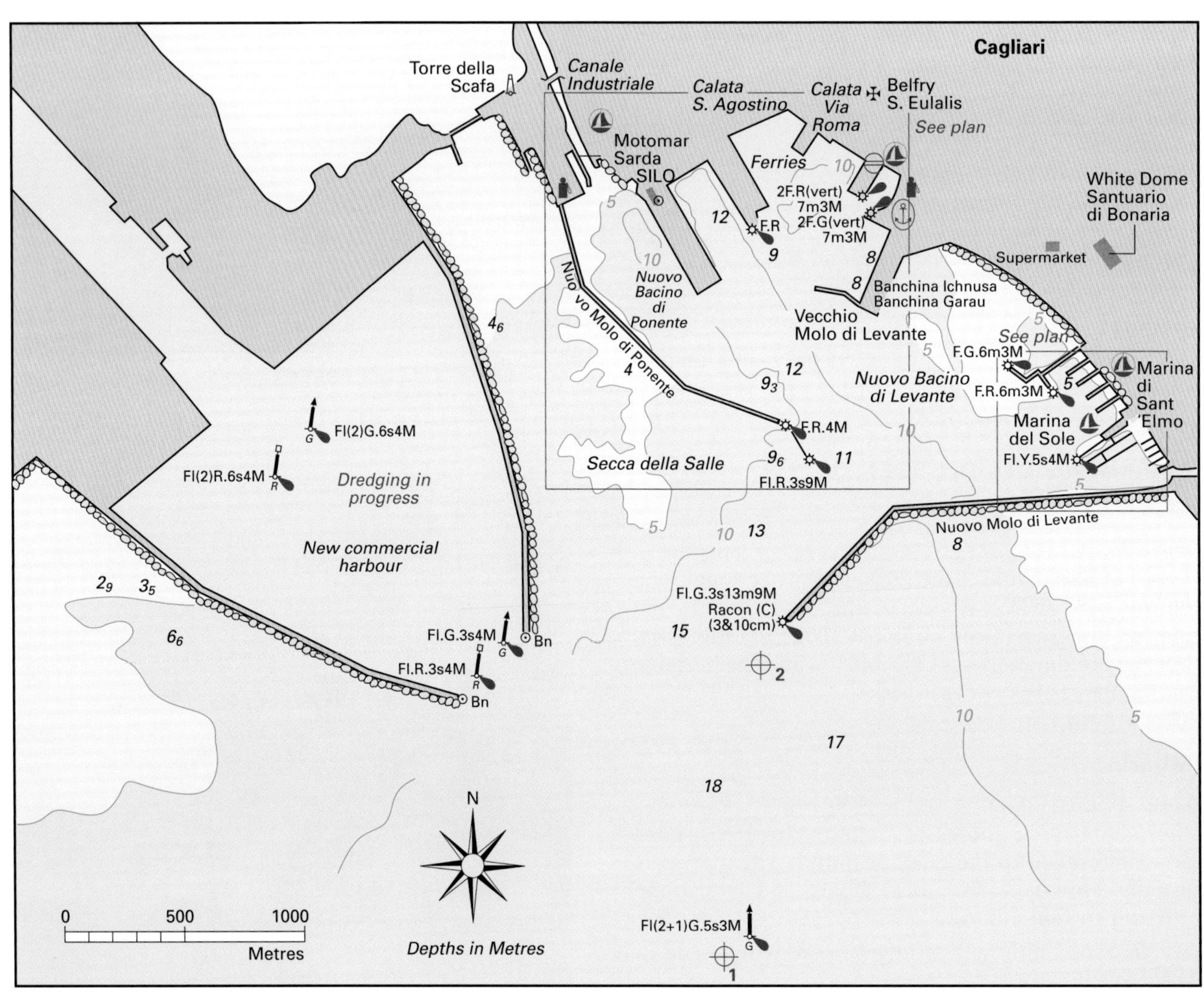

CAGLIARI
⊕1 39°11'·00N 09°06'·50E WGS84
⊕2 39°11'·60N 09°06'·48E WGS84

Dangers There are always tankers anchored off the oil terminal. By day these present no problem but at night, in combination with the lights of the terminal, there may be problems identifying what is where. The prudent course is to keep well off the oil terminal.

MARINA DEL SOLE

Approach

This friendly family-run marina lies in the SE corner of the harbour. The pontoons of the marina lie on the end of the short mole close N of Nuovo Molo di Levante.

VHF Ch 13.

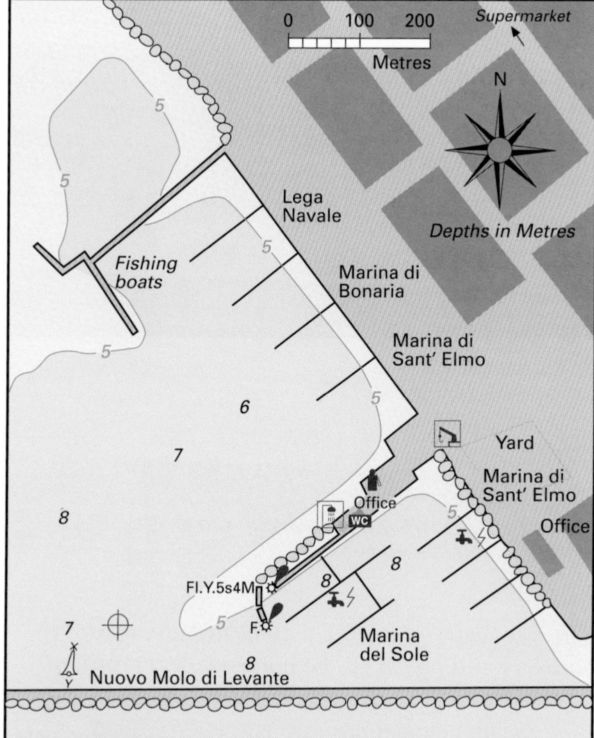

CAGLIARI: Marina del Sole and Marina di Sant' Elmo
⊕39°12'·0N 09°07'·5E

The pontoons of Marina di Sant'Elmo in the SE corner of Cagliari harbour. Note the dry dock has been removed
Marina di Sant'Elmo

Cagliari looking ENE into the entrance

Mooring

Data 220 berths. 30 visitors' berths. Max LOA 20m. Depths 5–8m.

Berths Go stern or bows-to where directed. Marina staff in a RIB will meet you and assist mooring. Laid moorings tailed to the pontoons.

Shelter Excellent shelter, although there may be some slop on the outer berths.

Authorities Harbourmaster. Marina staff. Charge band 5.

✆ 070 308 730 *Fax* 070 383 7951
Email marinadelsole@tiscali.net.it
www.marinasole-santelmo.com
www.approdomarinasole.com

Facilities

Services Water and electricity (220V). Portacabin toilets and showers. Self-service laundry.
Fuel Can be delivered. Note the fuel pump nearby is duty free for fishing boats only.
Repairs Cantieri del Sole. 40-ton crane. Mechanical, electrical, GRP and wood repairs.
Other Bar. Bus service into town passes outside the marina.

MARINA DI SANT'ELMO

Approach

A single pontoon between Marina di Bonaria and Marina del Sole. Four pontoons along the shore inside Marina del Sole. The passage behind Marina del Sole into the two inner pontoons is narrow but free of dangers.

VHF Ch 74.

Mooring

Data 300 berths. 50 visitors' berths. Max LOA 18m. Depths 1·5–9m.

Berths Visiting yachts are directed to the new pontoons behind Marina del Sole. Berth where directed. Marina staff will assist mooring. Laid moorings tailed to the quay.

Shelter Excellent all-round shelter.

Looking NE across Nuovo Molo di Levante and the pontoons of Marina di Sant'Elmo and Marina del Sole *Marina di Sant Elmo*

Authorities Marina staff. Charge band 5.
✉ Marina di St'Elmo, (Enrico Deplano), Via Roma 93, 09124 Cagliari, Sardinia
✆ 070 344 169 / 328 978 1391 *Fax* 070 344 156
Email marinasantelmo@yahoo.it
www.marinasantelmo.it

Facilities

Services Water and electricity (220V) at all berths. A clubhouse with toilets, showers, changing rooms and laundry facilities. Pump-out.
Repairs 35-ton crane. GRP and wood repairs. Mechanical and electrical repairs. Over-winter storage.
Other Clubhouse with bar and restaurant with a terrace facing the sea, 12 guest-rooms and a luxury suite being developed. Bus service into town passes outside the marina.

MARINA PORTUS KARALIS

Approach

Pontoon and quay berths in the inner harbour.

VHF Ch 74.

Mooring

Data 140 berths. LOA 18–100m. Depths 8–15m.

Berths Where directed. Laid moorings.

Shelter Excellent all-round shelter.

Authorities Marina staff. Charge band 6+ (July–August).
Portus Karalis ✆ 070 653 535 *Fax* 070 640 4898
Email portuskaralis@gmail.com

Facilities

Services Water and electricity (220/380V). Wi-Fi. Showers and toilets (to be completed). Pump-out. Laundry.

Repairs Technical assistance can be arranged.

Other Close to town centre.

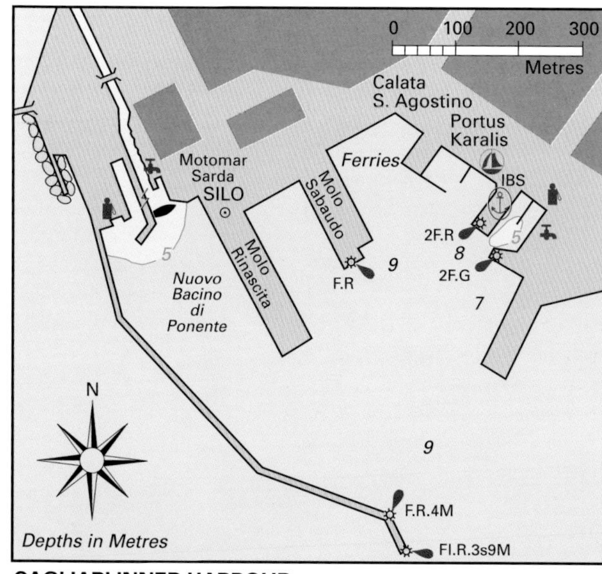

CAGLIARI INNER HARBOUR

IBS Yachting Point Cagliari

Operates within Marina Portus Karalis.

VHF Ch 74.

Data 18 berths. Max LOA 40m. Depths 6–9m. Charge band 6.

IBS Yachting Point ✆ 070 662 355 *Fax* 070 640 1838
Email giambattista.angioni@ibsgroup.it

Marina Di Bonaria

Private pontoon marina N of Marina del Sole.

Data Max LOA 30m. Depths 1·5–7m. Laid moorings. Water and electricity (220V).

✆ 070 300 240

Motomar Sardo

Small marina in NW corner of the main harbour.

Data 50 berths. Max LOA 35m. Depths 1·5–5m. (dredged recently). Laid moorings.

Services Water and electricity (220V).

Fuel On the quay opposite (see below).

Repairs 50-ton crane. Slipway. Some repairs.

✆ 070 665 948 fax 070 653 501

Cantiere Navale di Ponente

Fuel quay (depths 4m). 30-ton travel-hoist. Most repairs can be arranged.

✆ 070 662 290

Facilities (Cagliari)

Repairs A 50-ton mobile crane. Slipway up to 50 tons. Mechanical and engineering repairs. Electrical repairs. Electronic repairs. Some GRP and wood repairs. Sailmakers. Chandlers.
Provisions Most provisions can be found nearby. Two supermarkets to the NE of the S marinas. Use the underpass to cross the autostrada.
Eating out Excellent restaurants, trattorias and pizzerias in the town. Try the N side of Via Roma.
Other Banks. ATMs. PO. Hospital. Italgaz and Camping Gaz at Marina del Sole. Hire cars. Buses to major towns. Ferries to Genoa, Naples, Sicily and Tunisia. Internal and international flights.

General

The change from clear blue to greeny-brown water in the approaches tells of the industrial nature of much of the harbour. Cranes and derricks and modern concrete blocks form the skyline, but nestled in amongst this is the elegant old town of Cagliari. Recently it has been going through something of a make-over in the centre. Buildings are being cleaned up and pedestrian access is improving. The marinas 'del Sole' and 'Sant'Elmo' provide excellent visitors' berths, albeit a rather hot and dusty hike from the town centre. But don't let this put you off getting into town. The newly-developed inner harbour provides more berths including superyacht facilities.

Of Phoenician origin, the city and harbour were important to the successive waves of invaders: the Carthaginians, Romans, Pisans and the Spanish. The architecture of the Spanish dominates the centre of the city and much of it has been renovated so that there are many fine old buildings set on tree-lined boulevards. The city itself is the most cosmopolitan and sophisticated in Sardinia. Despite the modern buildings and the streets choked with cars, despite the oil terminal to the W and the outlying industrial suburbs, Cagliari is one of my favourite 'big town' harbours. The archaeological museum is one of the best in Sardinia, particularly for its *Nuragh* artifacts, and is well worth a visit.

'And suddenly there is Cagliari: a naked town rising steep, steep, golden-looking, piled naked to the sky from the plain at the head of the formless hollow bay. It is strange and rather wonderful, not a bit like Italy. The city piles up lofty and almost miniature, and makes me think of Jerusalem: without trees, without cover, rising rather bare and proud, remote as if back in history, like a town in a monkish, illuminated missal. One wonders how it ever got there. And it seems like Spain – or Malta; not Italy.'

D H Lawrence *Sea and Sardinia*

Sarroch Oil Terminal

This oil terminal in the SW of Golfo di Cagliari is conspicuous by day and night. By day, the chimneys and buildings of the refinery are conspicuous and by night numerous lights and a flare have a good range. Care should be taken of three pairs of beacons marking the deep water channel into the jetty. There are often a number of large tankers anchored off the refinery and workboats going back and forth.

Lights Pontile Saras No.2 leading lights front 2Iso.R.2s(vert)11m3M, rear 2Oc.R.4s(vert)28m3M. Jetty 2F.G(vert)11m3M. Oil terminal Fl.3s 27m6M.

PERD'E' SALI

BA 1990
Italian 45, 46

Approach

A harbour under Punta Zavorra. Isola San Macario with the tower atop in the S approaches is conspicuous and the breakwater will be identified closer in.

By night A night entry is not recommended.

VHF Ch 15, 16, 74 0600–1900 (Call sign *Sarroch*). Also Sarroch pilot on Ch 06, 11, 12, 14, 16 for advice on the approach.

Dangers

1. Depths in the entrance are subject to silting. Depths of 3–5m in the approaches, but it quickly shallows once round the end of the breakwater, with least depths of 1·3m in the inner entrance. The deepest channel with min 1·7–1·8m lies close to the fuel quay.
2. From the N stay at least 500m off the E mole before turning into the harbour.
3. From the S pass to the E of Isola San Macario (with a conspicuous Nuragh tower on it) before heading for the harbour.

Perd'e' Sali looking NE *Carlo Delfino*

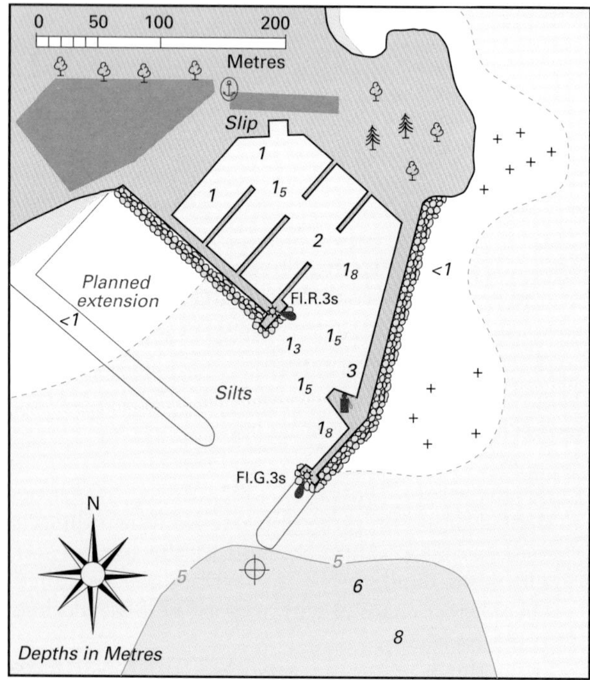

PERD'E' SALI
⊕39°01'·70N 09°02'·00E WGS84

4. With strong E–SE winds care is needed as a swell piles up at the entrance.
5. The harbour has plans to expand, but there is no sign of work starting at present.

Mooring

Data 200 berths. Limited visitors' berths. Max LOA 12–14m. Depths 1–3m.

Berth Where directed. There are laid moorings tailed to the pontoons. There is very little space to manoeuvre between mooring lines and pontoons once inside. The marina is crowded with motor boats and it may be wise to call in advance for a berth and advice on depths.

Shelter Reported to be good.

Authorities Harbourmaster. Charge band 5.
Saromar ✆ 070 925 3145

Facilities

Services Water and electricity at all berths.
Fuel On the quay.
Repairs 45-ton travel-lift/5-ton crane can haul out onto hardstanding. Mechanical and some other repairs can be arranged.
Provisions Minimarket in the village. Better shopping in Sarroch.
Eating out Bar in the marina. Restaurant and bar in the village. Others in Sarroch and San Pietro.
Other Taxi can be arranged to Sarroch and San Pietro.

General

The harbourmaster here has been recommended as a helpful sort who will attempt to make your stay here a friendly one. Sarroch, around 5km and San Pietro around 3km away, have some additional facilities and from there you can get into Cagliari.

Capo di Pula

⊕ 38°59'·03N 09°01'·67E WGS84 300m E of Capo di Pula

The tower on Isola San Macario and the tower on Capo di Pula are conspicuous from some distance. A yacht wishing to visit the ancient city of Nora can anchor on either side of the headland. Local boats usually choose the W side where there is a large bay, with good shelter from the NE–SE. Care is needed of above and below-water rocks and ruins from the ancient city, which have become submerged some distance off the coast. Holding is good in patches of sand on the W side of the bay, away from the rocks and weed found closer in towards the promontory.

In S–SW winds anchor on the N side of the headland, again taking care of underwater ruins off the coast. The best place to be is tucked into the NW corner. Anchor on sand, good holding. Further out there is more rock and weed, and indifferent holding. There is a restaurant and bar ashore.

The ruins of the ancient city are easily identified when rounding the cape. The ruins of the Punic-Roman city; the Romans took it over from the Phoenicians, is worth a visit to wander around the streets, many with sewers running underneath, a temple to Tanit, and mosaics on the floors of some of the villas.

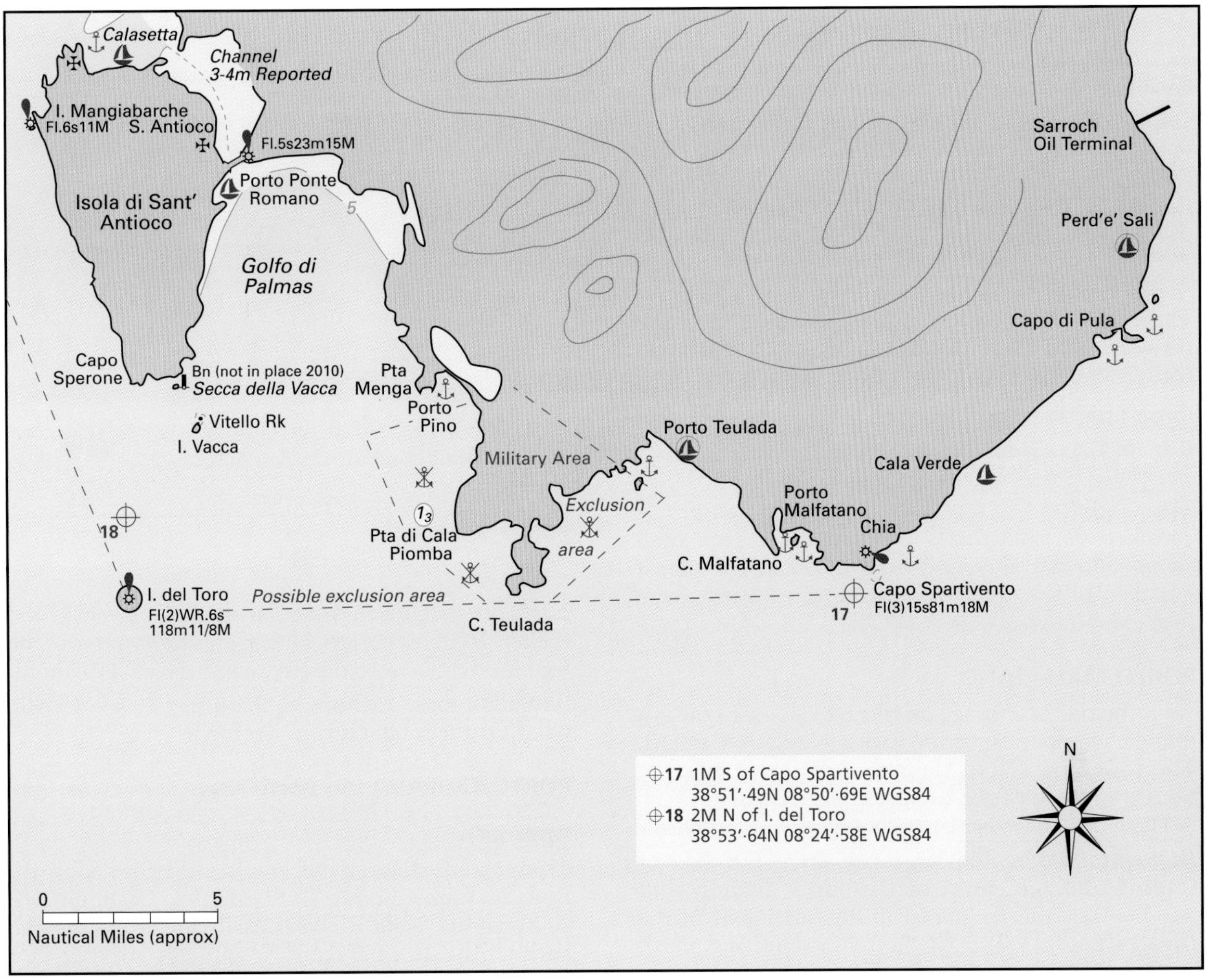

⊕17 1M S of Capo Spartivento
38°51′·49N 08°50′·69E WGS84
⊕18 2M N of I. del Toro
38°53′·64N 08°24′·58E WGS84

0 5
Nautical Miles (approx)

CAPO DI PULA TO ISOLA S. ANTIOCO
⊕**17** 38°51′·6N 08°50′·7E 1M S of Capo Spartivento
⊕**18** 38°52′·6N 08°24′·6E 1M N of I. del Toro

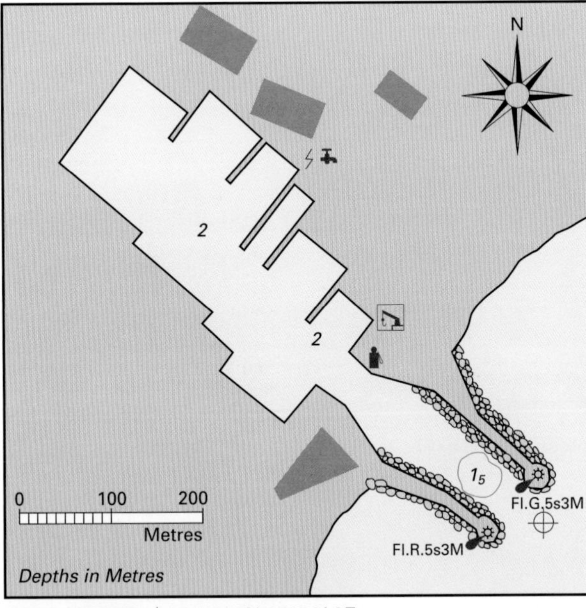

CALA VERDE ⊕38°56′·0N 08°56′·3E

CALA VERDE

Approach

A small private harbour approximately five miles NE of Capo Spartivento. The harbour is dredged out of the land with two breakwaters protecting the entrance. The entrance is difficult to pinpoint, but a white crane near the entrance will be seen.

VHF Ch 10 (*Curimar*).

Dangers

1. Rubble has fallen into the entrance from the breakwaters effectively reducing the depths to 1·5m although it is possible to get in with care with 1·6–1·7m draught. Care needed.
2. With onshore winds a swell piles up at the narrow entrance and care is needed lining up to go in.

Mooring

Data 100 berths. Eight visitors' berths. Max LOA 12m. Depths 2m. Entrance 1·5m.

Berth Stern or bows-to where directed. Laid moorings.

Shelter Good shelter.

Authorities Harbourmaster. Charge band 4/5.
☎ 070 921 214.

Facilities

Services Water and electricity near most berths.
Fuel On the quay.
Repairs 6-ton crane.
Eating out Restaurant and bar.

Chia

⊕ 38°53'·0N 08°52'·8E

There are calm weather anchorages along the coast between Cala Verde and Capo Spartivento. Not really suitable for anchoring overnight.

Capo Spartivento

⊕**17** 1M S of Capo Sportivento
38°51'·49N 08°50'·69E WGS84

The lighthouse on the prominent cape is conspicuous from the W but cannot be seen by a yacht following the coast from the east. Care must be taken of the 4m shoal extending seawards from the cape proper.

PORTO MALFATANO

An attractive anchorage on this rocky coast that is a popular weekend spot for yachts based at Cagliari. The tower on Capo Malfatano and a number of houses to the E of the bay are conspicuous.

There are a number of anchorages:

Porto Malfatano The large bay on the E side of Capo Malfatano. Most of the bay is shallow, but good shelter can be gained in the outer half of the bay. Anchor in 3–6m. The bottom is mud and weed, reasonable holding once through the weed.

I. Teredda Anchor on either side depending on the wind and sea in 3–8m. The bottom is mud, sand and weed, reasonable holding.

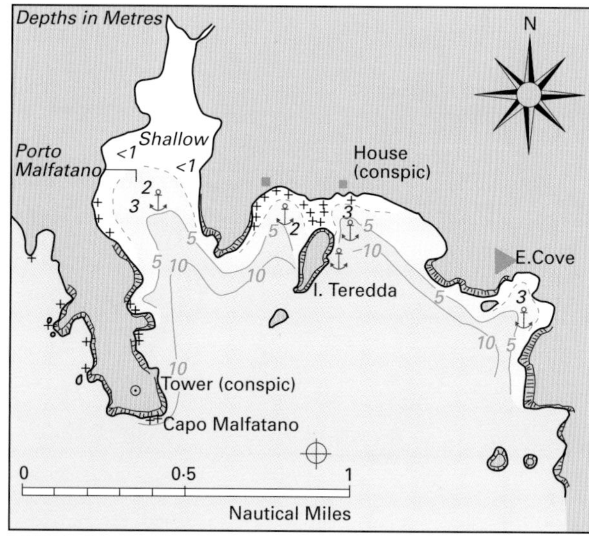

PORTO MALFATANO
⊕38°53'·87N 08°48'·79E WGS84

East cove Anchor in 4–6m on sand and weed. Good shelter from easterlies, although the wind can be funnelled down into the bay out of the valley behind.

In all of these anchorages there may be a katabatic wind off the mountains in the night.

PORTO TEULADA (Su Portu Nou)

Approach

Conspicuous A large red hotel to the SE and Torre Budello immediately NE of the harbour are conspicuous. Isola Rossa is easily identified but the harbour breakwater can be difficult to pick out against the surrounding land.

VHF Ch 16, 09 for Teulada Marina.

Porto Teulada looking E towards the entrance, works in progress before pontoons were installed

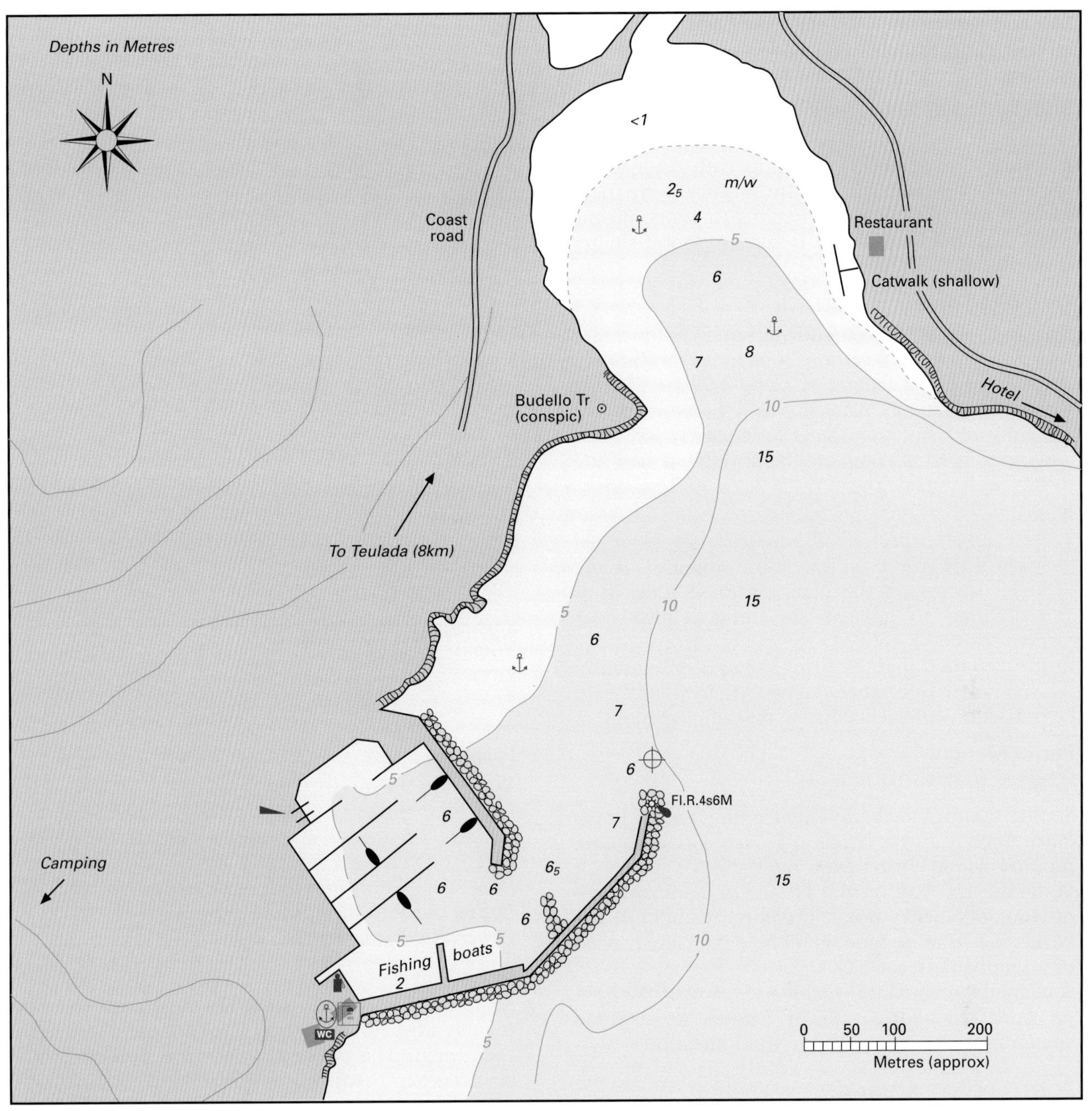

PORTO TEULADA
⊕38°55´·67N 08°43´·41E WGS84

Mooring

Data 250 berths. Max LOA 30m. Depths 1–4m.

Berth Go stern or bows-to or alongside where directed. Laid moorings tailed to the pontoons.

Shelter Good all-round shelter although strong NE winds might make it uncomfortable.

Authorities Marina staff. Charge band 5.
✆ /*Fax* 070 928 3705
Email info@teuladamarina.it

Facilities

Services Water and electricity (220/380V). Wi-Fi. Toilets and showers. Pump-out.

Fuel Fuel on the quay.

Other Over the hill to the SW there is a camping site with a small shop and a bar. The village of Teulada is 8km inland; a bus service operates from the harbour. A mobile *cantina* arrives daily and provides snacks and drinks at the harbour.

The restaurant, La Mezza Luna, will pick up and return guests.
✆ 070 927 0440

General

It is difficult to know why this large harbour was built here – the locals claim it was built for the fishermen. A small patrol boat for policing the prohibited area is kept here. In the last year or two the harbour has been developed to become a *porto turistico* for the area. Most of the basic structure is now in place and the infrastructure ashore is being developed.

Budello tower anchorage

Anchor in the large bay to the NE of Teulada harbour. Care is needed as depths come up quickly once into the bay. The bottom is thick weed over sand. It may take several attempts to penetrate the weed, and holding can be uncertain. Good shelter from all but southerlies.

Prohibited area

An area in which anchoring and fishing are prohibited, and navigation sometimes prohibited, exists from Punta Pinetto to Capo Teulada to Isola Rossa. The Teulada peninsula is a firing range for the army and is often in use. Consequently a yacht is advised to heed the limits of the prohibited area and to stay well outside them.

Note

1. At times the prohibited zone may be extended when there are naval operations going on to the limits shown on the plan. At these times it is prohibited to navigate in the extended area between 0600–1800.
2. It is reported that the firing range is only used in November/December, and there are no restrictions to yachts during the summer months.

Punta Menga

⊕ 38°57′·4N 08°36′·15E (Porto Pino)

Settled weather anchorage under the cape in Porto Pino. Anchor off the beach in 5–10m. Good holding on sand. Good shelter from the E–N–NW but open W–S–SE. The bay on the N side of Punta Menga offers good shelter from SE winds. Anchor off the beach in 5–10m on sand, good holding. Care needed of a sandbank in the bay.

In calm weather local yachts use many of the bays on both sides of Golfo di Palmas as daytime anchorages, depending on the wind direction.

PORTO PONTE ROMANO

Approach

A line of buoys marks the dredged channel leading into the harbour.

Conspicuous The buildings around the harbour and the cranes are easily distinguished. The lighthouse, a white building with a black band, is conspicuous. Closer in, the buoys marking the channel will be seen.

VHF Ch 14, 16 (0700–1900).

Mooring

Berth Go alongside the quay on the E side of the pier where shown.

Shelter Good shelter from the N and W but open to the south. In the event of strong southerlies it would be better to find a berth on the W side of the pier.

Authorities Harbourmaster and customs. Charge band 1.

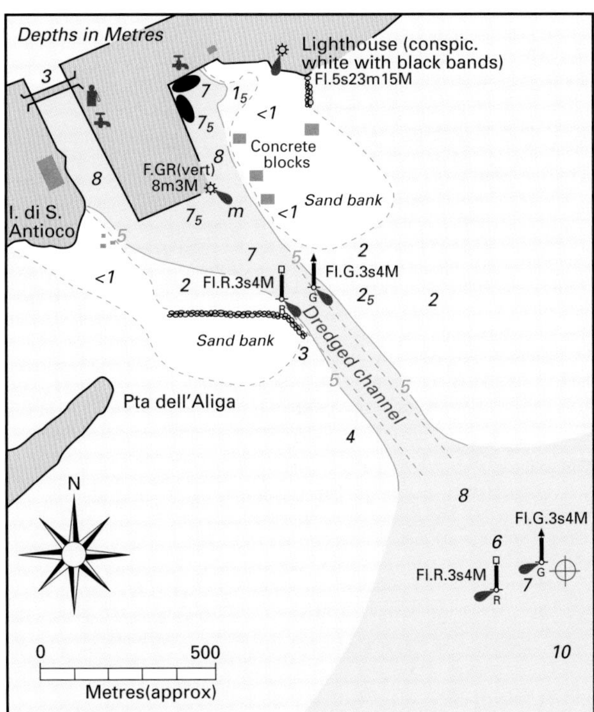

PORTO PONTE ROMANO
⊕39°02′·7N 08°29′·0E

Facilities

Water On the quay.
Fuel Near the quay approximately 250m away.
Repairs A 40-ton mobile crane available. Mechanical repairs.
Provisions Good shopping for most provisions.
Eating out Restaurants and pizzerias.
Other PO. Bank. Italgaz. Buses to Calasetta.

General

Although the harbour is not the most attractive, the town is a friendly rambling place not often visited by yachtsmen. The causeway over the shallow water between Sant' Antioco and mainland Sardinia was started by the Carthaginians and completed by the Romans. Sant' Antioco town, approximately 1½ miles N of Ponte Romano, is on the site of the original Sulcis (established by the Carthaginians as their first colony in Sardinia) and claims to have been continuously inhabited for some 2,600 years. However the visitor will have to scratch around to find this ancient pedigree – the best place is at the Punic-Roman necropolis on the outskirts – in what is for all intents and purposes a modern town.

West coast: Capo Sperone to Isola Asinara

The west coast of Sardinia has a number of harbours and anchorages of outstanding beauty yet it is cruised less than the other coasts. It is not as mountainous as the east or south coasts except between Capo Pecora and Capo Altano in the Iglesias mining area, but most yachtsmen avoid it, touching only at the southern or northern ends on passage from the Balearics or France. It has a reputation for heavy seas, particularly if a mistral is blowing, and such a reputation is deserved if even moderate westerlies blow. For the yachtsman prepared to encounter such weather, this solitary coast can offer magnificent scenery and enchanting harbours.

Weather patterns on the west coast

In the summer the wind is predominantly from the W–NW but it rarely blows above Force 4–5. There are frequent days of calms and a yacht should choose to motor slowly along the coast rather than waiting for wind. Around Isola di San Pietro and Isola di Sant'Antioco the wind is frequently from the SW. In the spring, autumn and winter the wind is again mostly from the W–NW but there are also SE winds in the autumn. With a *mistral*, exceptionally heavy seas pound the west coast and it is wise to stay in harbour a day or two after the wind has died down to allow the sea to calm.

Isola di Sant' Antioco

A rocky island with a forbidding rock-bound coastline except for the NE coast which is bordered by shallow saltpans extending to the mainland opposite. The island is connected to the mainland by a causeway. There are three harbours on the island, Calasetta on the NW corner, Sant' Antioco on the E coast and Porto Ponte Romano on the artificial isthmus. Local yachts are also kept on moorings to the S of Calasetta where the shelter is better than it might appear on the chart.

Off the southern tip of the island there are three small islets: Vitello, Vacca and Toro meaning 'calf', 'cow' and 'bull' respectively. Secca della Vacca is a reef extending offshore one mile E of Capo Sperone and is marked by a beacon (missing 2010). Vitello is a small islet immediately N of Isola Vacca which lies two miles SE of Capo Sperone. Isola Vacca is steep-to and rocky as is Isola Toro, lying 5½ miles S of Capo Sperone.

Note Off Capo Sperone and on the SW coast of Isola di Sant' Antioco there is often a heavy confused swell. In bad weather the seas in this area can be dangerous and it is wise to keep well off the cape. Proceeding along the W coast of Isola di Sant' Antioco the lighthouse on I. Mangiabarche is conspicuous.

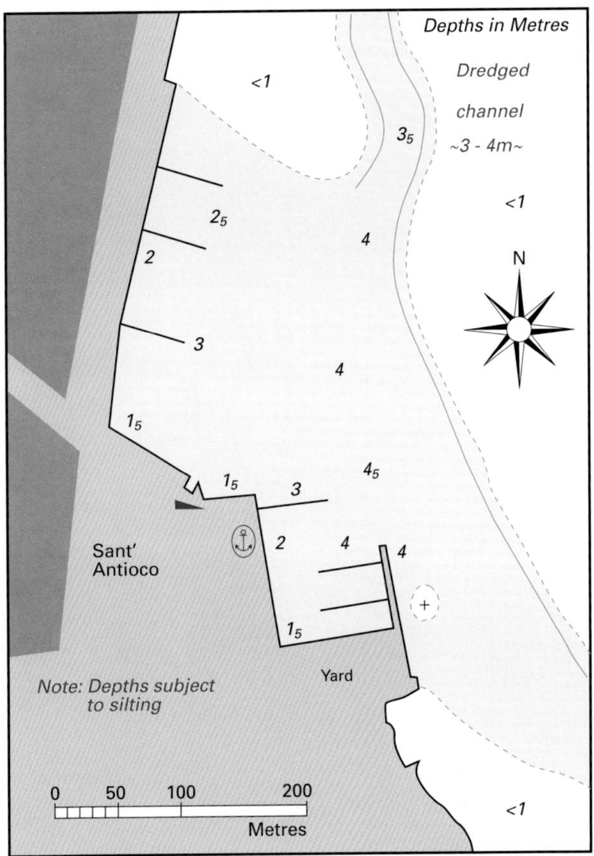

SANT 'ANTIOCO

SANT' ANTIOCO

Approached from the N past Punta Dritta, a small harbour lies to the N of the isthmus, off the town of Sant' Antioco. There are depths in the harbour of 2–4m and following dredging maximum depths in the approach channel from Punta Dritta are reported to be 3–4m. The channel down through the salt marshes can be quite tricky, and should only be attempted in calm weather. Yachts could investigate with caution, as silting is likely to reduce depths again.

Data 113 berths. Max LOA 18m. Depths 1–4m.

VHF Ch 16, 64.

Gest. Solkimar ✆ 349 139 3324

CALASETTA

Approach

The small town and harbour is tucked behind the NW corner of Isola di Sant' Antioco.

Conspicuous The village saddling the promontory is easily identified. An Aragonese tower in the village is conspicuous. Ferries regularly ply between Carloforte and Calasetta.

By night A night approach is not easy and should be made with due care and attention.

VHF Ch 74, 16 (0700–1900) for Calasetta Marina.

Dangers The N cardinal beacon marks the edge of the channel into the harbour and must be left to starboard when approaching the harbour.

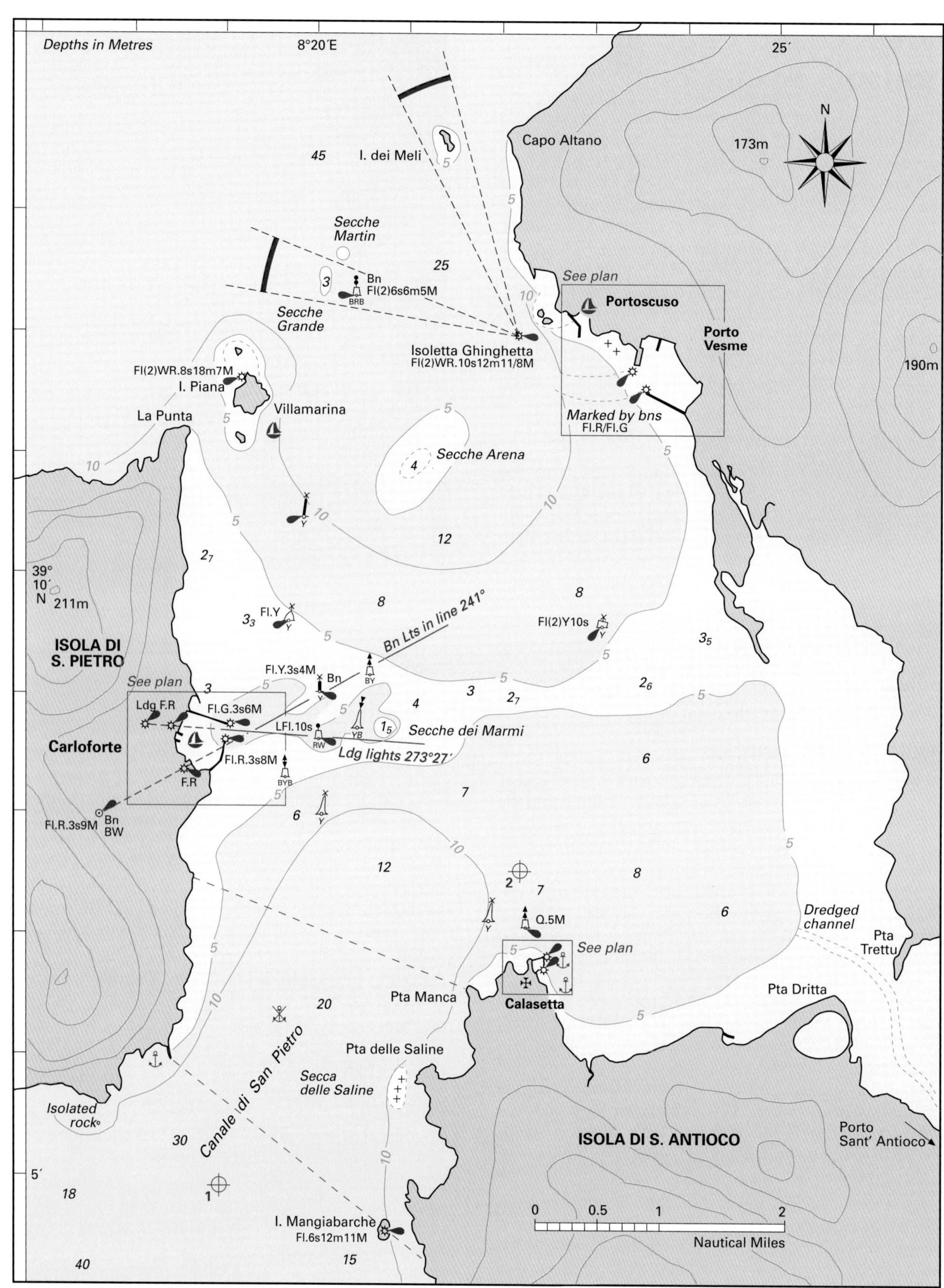

SAN PIETRO CHANNEL (CANALE DI SAN PIETRO)
⊕1 39°04´·86N 08°18´·84E WGS84
⊕2 39°07´·22N 08°22´·00E WGS84

Mooring

Data 300 berths (when completed). 55 visitors' berths. Max LOA 20m. Depths are irregular <1–5m.

Berth The Porto Turistico is now open after several years without much happening. Some pontoons are in place, with more to come. Work continues on the N quay and travel-hoist bay. Go stern or bows-to where directed. Laid moorings.

Shelter Good shelter although strong E–SE winds raise a considerable chop across the bay.

Authorities Harbourmaster and customs. Marina staff. Charge band 5.

Calasetta Marina ✆ /*Fax* 0781 88083
Email info@portocalasetta.it
www.portocalasetta.it

Anchorage Anchor off to the S of the commercial quay where convenient in depths of 2–4m. Good shelter from SE–SW winds, and good holding on mud, rock and weed.

Facilities

Services Water and electricity. Toilets and showers. Water on the quay in the fishing harbour.
Fuel Near the quay in the NW corner of the harbour.
Repairs Limited mechanical repairs.
Provisions Most provisions can be obtained. There is a minimarket near the harbour.
Eating out A restaurant near the harbour and another at the hotel.
Other PO. Bank. ATM. Italgaz and Camping Gaz. Regular ferry to Carloforte.

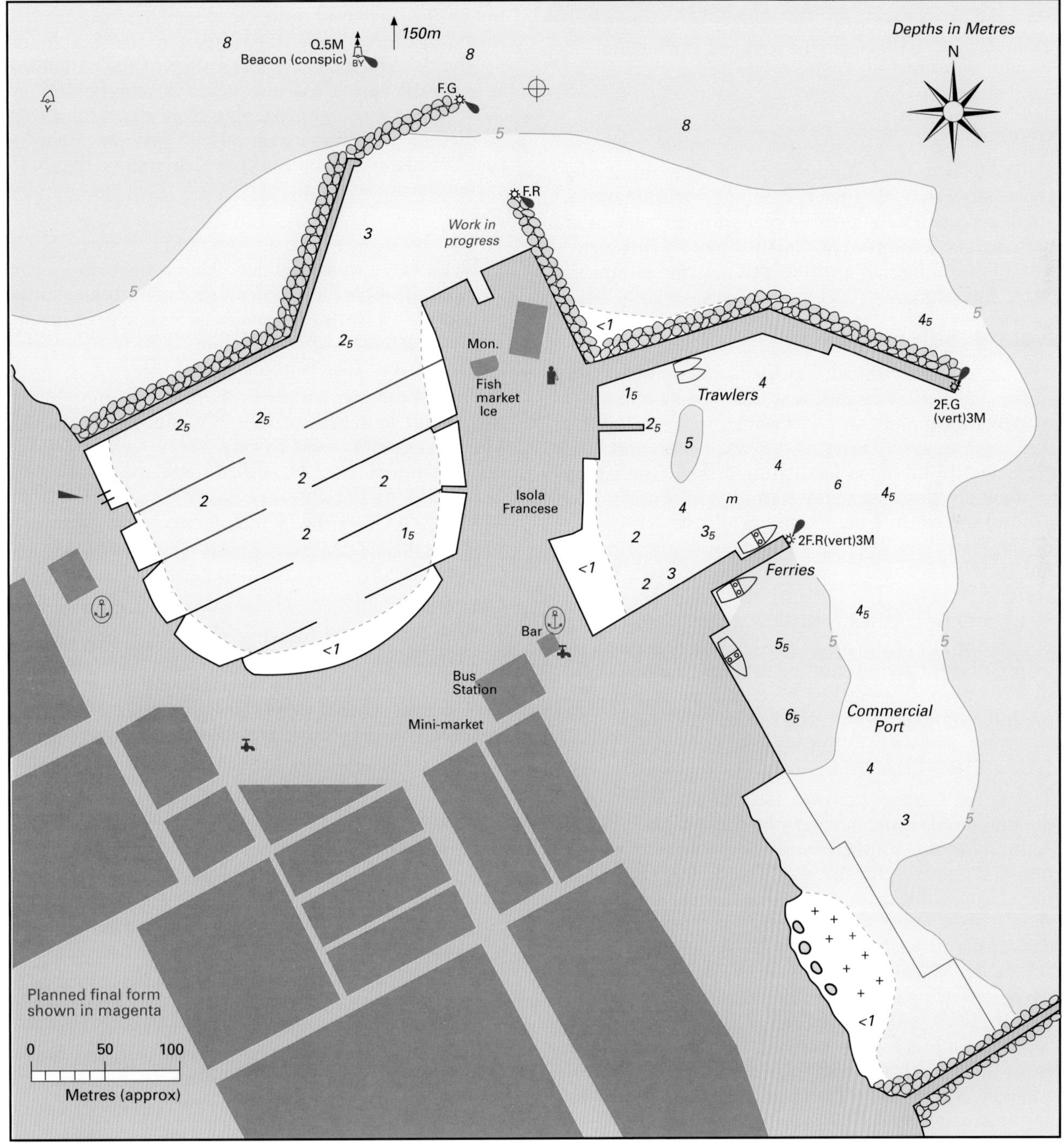

CALASETTA
⊕39°07′·01N 08°22′·43E WGS84

Calasetta looking SW before the pontoons of the Porto Turistico were installed *Carlo Delfino*

General

Calasetta is a dusty rambling place, something of a cross between a ferry port, a fishing harbour, and a small resort. It is a likeable place for no particular reason. It was founded in the 12th century but seems not to have figured prominently in the affairs of Sant' Antioco.

Isola di San Pietro

The jagged rocky island that forms the seaward side of the San Pietro Channel. It is indented by a number of coves and inlets, some of which make delightful day anchorages depending on the wind and sea. Care should be taken navigating around the island as there are numerous above and below-water rocks around the coast. Isola Piana lies off the NE corner of San Pietro, the old tunny fishery on it and another old fishery on the NE corner of Isola di San Pietro are conspicuous. The channel between Isola di San Pietro and Isola Piana is shallow and a yacht should not attempt to negotiate it. The island takes its name from St Peter (patron saint of fishermen) who is said to have been shipwrecked here and to have taught the inhabitants how to catch tunny.

SAN PIETRO CHANNEL

This is the channel between Isola di San Pietro and the mainland in the northern half and Isola di Sant' Antioco at the southern end. The southern end is free of dangers in the fairway. The middle section of the channel due E of Carloforte has a number of shoals obstructing the channel, none of which are dangerous to yachts drawing 2m or less except for Secche dei Marmi. Yachts drawing 3m or more must navigate with care in the channel. At the northern end of the channel a yacht can pass on either side of Secca Grande which is marked by a beacon and is easily identified. Care should be taken of the reef running NW of Isola Piana as the outermost rocks are only just awash.

CARLOFORTE

BA 1202
Imray M9
Italian 297

Approach

The approaches off the harbour are shallow and it can be disconcerting making an approach through waters in which you can clearly pick out every feature on the sea bottom. The buoys in the approaches cannot always be relied upon to be in place.

Conspicuous From the N, the chimney and buildings of Porto Vesme and the old tunny fishery on Isola Piana are conspicuous. Closer in, the town of Carloforte and the breakwaters are easily identified. The buoys marking the channel into Carloforte are not easy to see until quite close in. There is a transit into Carloforte with a passage on the S side of Secche dei Marmi: the white belfry of the cathedral is in transit with a BW chequered beacon behind on 273·5°. For those approaching from the N two BW banded beacons line up on 241·9°. Also in transit is the Y beacon (× topmark) which marks the NW extremity of the shoal.

Note

1. The N transit was in operation before the S breakwater was extended. This transit no longer leads through the entrance to the harbour, but it does give a transit to pass N of Secche dei Marmi.
2. The entrance to the fishing harbour is very narrow and care is needed.

By night Both transits are lit, but these leading lights should not be relied on. The NW side of Secche dei Marmi is lit Fl.Y.3s4M (Y bn). The W side of Secche dei Marmi is lit LFl.10s6M (RW beacon). The Fl.R.3s8M at the entrance is only visible on 221-251° which clears the N side of Secche dei Marmi.

VHF Ch 11, 16. Marine Sifredi Ch 15. Marinatour Ch 09.

Dangers

1. With a *mistral* blowing there can be a large confused swell in the San Pietro Channel and yachts drawing 3m or more should pay attention to depths when a big swell is running.
2. Secche dei Marmi is the only real danger in the immediate approaches to Carloforte with 1·5m least depths.

Mooring

Note Some of the yacht berths around the harbour are made very uncomfortable by the near constant wash from ferries and other craft, particularly in the busy summer period. There are a number of places for visiting yachts.

1. ***Public Transit quay*** Visiting yachts can berth stern or bows-to on the public quay where there is room. No laid moorings or services although they may be installed in the future. Stays notionally restricted to 48 hours.

   Data c.20 berths. Max LOA c.20m. Depths 2·5–6m. Charge band 3.

2. *Marine Sifredi* A new marina at the root of the N mole.
   Data 250 berths. Two additional pontoons in the S of the harbour. Max LOA 50m. Depths 2–5m. Laid moorings tailed to the quay. Water and electricity (220/380V). Wi-Fi. Showers and toilets. Charge band 5.
   ☎ 0781 857 008 *Fax* 0781 857 228
   Email info@marinesifredi.it
   www.marinesifredi.it
3. *Marinatour Marina di Carloforte* Operates the pontoon immediately S of Marine Sifredi.
   Data 100 berths. Max LOA 40m. Depths 5m. Laid moorings. Water and electricity at all berths. Charge band 5.
   ☎ /*Fax* 0781 854 110
   Email marinatour@carloforte.net
   www.carloforte.net/marinatour
4. *Marine Service Yacht Carloforte* Pontoon in the S of the harbour.
   Data 50 berths. Max LOA c.25m. Depths 1–5m. Laid moorings. Water and electricity. Showers and toilets. Laundry. Charge band 5.
   ☎ 0781 856 533 / 338 203 8746
   Email marine.service@tiscali.it
   www.carloforte.net/marineservice
5. *Lega Navale* Private YC immediately S of the river.
   ☎ 0781 855 618

Note Anchoring is now prohibited within the harbour. Yachts arriving after dark may be permitted to anchor overnight, but will be asked to move to a berth the next morning.

Shelter Good from the prevailing summer winds although there can be a surge in the harbour with a prolonged *mistral*. Open to the E–SE although shelter from the SE is better in the S end of the harbour.

Authorities Harbourmaster and customs. *Ormeggiatori*. Marina staff.

Facilities

Services Water and electricity at or near most berths. The water has been described as non-potable, but I have never encountered problems drinking it. Separate taps are used to provide water for washing boats.

Fuel On the quay in the fishing harbour and in the town. The fishing harbour appears to be silting, with least depths around the fuel quay down to 1·8m.

Repairs 70-ton travel-hoist. A 30-ton mobile crane

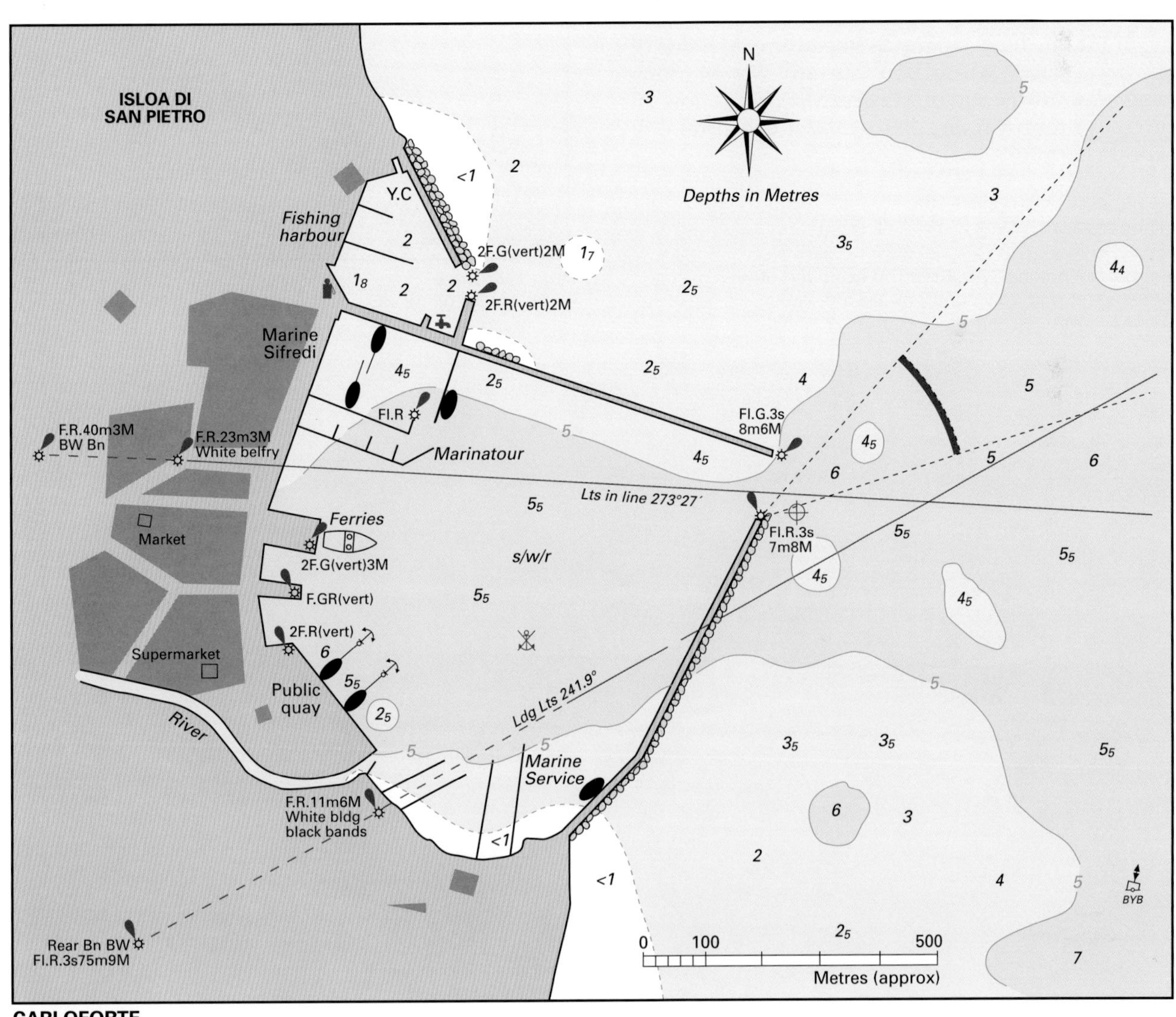

CARLOFORTE
⊕39°08´·7N 08°19´·0E

and a 20-ton slipway. Mechanical repairs. Electrical repairs.
Provisions Good shopping for provisions. Supermarket near the river in the town. If moored in the S of the harbour it is possible to take a tender up river and moor up outside the supermarket. There is a covered market for fresh produce and fish stalls in the town.
Eating out Good restaurants, trattorias and pizzerias on the waterfront and in the town.
Other PO. Bank. ATM. Italgaz and Camping Gaz. Ferries to Calasetta.

General

The setting is pleasing and so is the town. Elegant pastel-coloured houses with wrought iron balconies line the streets running back from the spacious, palm-lined boulevard along the sea-front. It could be somewhere in Liguria and in a way it is. The inhabitants of San Pietro are of Genoese extraction and their dialect is said still to be Genoese. They were settled here from a Genoese colony in North Africa in 1738 to escape Tunisian persecution and named Carloforte after Carlo Emmanuello of Savoy who effected the migration. Fifty years later they were abducted by Tunisian pirates and the Sardinian government had to pay to get its colonists back again. At one time a tunny fishing centre, and one of the few places where you can still see working *mattanzas*, at the end of May each year. It is now an attractive tourist resort that retains a delightful old-world charm.

Isola Piana

VILLAMARINA

The island is a private resort. On the SE side of the island there is a small harbour protected by a short breakwater. The approaches are rock-bound and it is shallow.

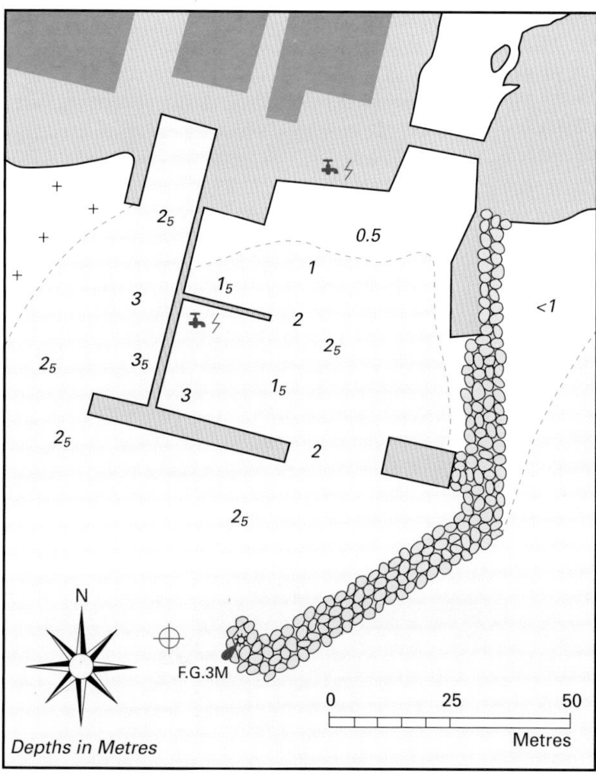

VILLAMARINA
⊕39°11′·3N 08°19′·5E

Carloforte looking SSW. Note the extended outer breakwater and new pontoons are not shown
Carlo Delfino

Data 77 berths. Visitors' berths on the outer pontoon. Max LOA 20m. Depths <1–2·5m.

VHF Ch 72.

You can try to find a berth here, but don't rely on getting one.

PORTO VESME

BA 1202
Italian 294

Approach

This large commercial port lies in the NE corner of San Pietro Channel.

Conspicuous The numerous tall chimneys and the buildings of the power station are the most conspicuous features in the San Pietro Channel.

By night Use the light on Scoglio La Ghinghetta Fl(2)WR.10s12m11/8M (100°-R-116° and 153°-R-165° over I. dei Meli and Secche Grande). The approach channel is lit by beacons Fl.G.3s5m4M/ Fl.R.3s5m4M (x2).

VHF Ch 12, 16 for port authorities (0700–1900). Ch 12 for pilots.

Mooring

Berth It can be difficult to find a place to berth if the commercial quay is in use, but there is usually somewhere or someone to go alongside on the W mole.

Shelter Good although a *scirocco* sends in a considerable swell.

Facilities

Water On the quay
Fuel In the town.
Repairs A 20-ton mobile crane. Mechanical repairs.
Provisions Basic provisions.
Eating out Limited.

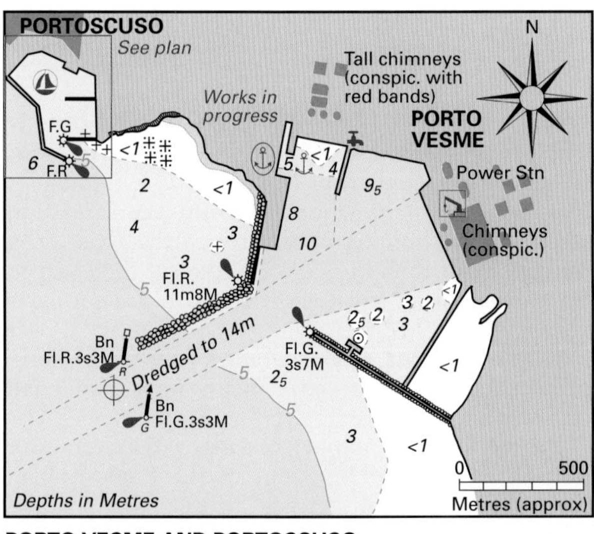

PORTO VESME AND PORTOSCUSO
⊕39°11′·4N 08°23′·1E

General

The setting is an industrial wasteland and not for yachts. You will most likely be directed to Portoscuso where there are proper facilities for yachts.

PORTOSCUSO

Approach

A yacht harbour immediately NW of Porto Vesme. The outer breakwater is easily identified.

By night Use the light on Scoglio La Ghinghetta Fl(2)WR.10s12m11/8M.

VHF Ch 09, 16 for Portoscuso Locomare.

Mooring

Data 300 berths. Depths 2–3·5m.

Berth Stern or bows-to where directed or convenient. Laid moorings or finger pontoons at most berths.

Shelter Good shelter.

Authorities Harbourmaster. *Ormeggiatori*. Charge band 4.

Saromar ✆ 0781 507 248

Facilities

Services Water and electricity points.
Repairs 3-ton slipway. Limited mechanical repairs. Small chandlery.
Provisions Most provisions can be found.
Eating out Restaurants ashore.

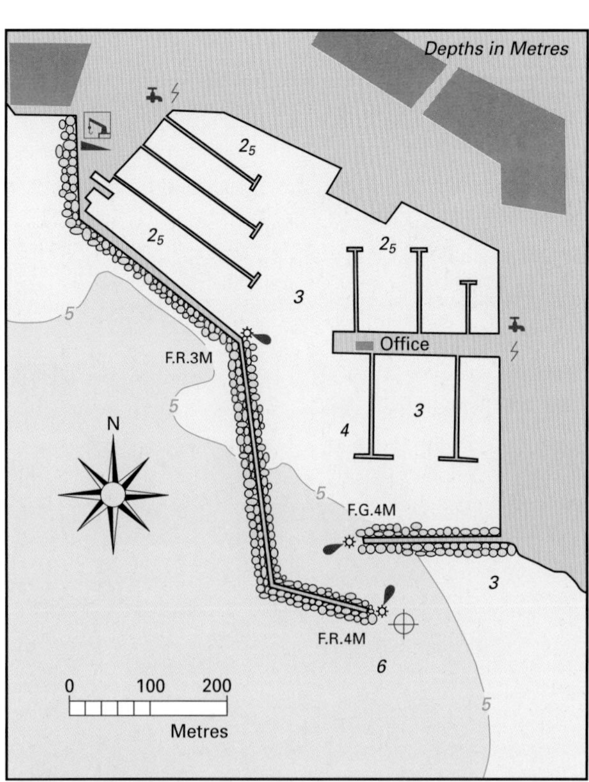

PORTOSCUSO
⊕39°12′·0N 08°22′·9E

General

Portoscuso provides a secure berth in this part of the world and the village ashore is pleasant despite its proximity to the industrial ghetto next door at Porto Vesme.

Isola Pan di Zucchero ('Sugar-Loaf')

This precipitous rock juts out of the sea under Punta Masulas and is conspicuous from seaward.

BUGGERRU

Approach

A small harbour in the large bay between Punta S. Nicolo and Capo Pecora. The houses of the village and the harbour breakwater are easily identified in the SE corner of the bay.

VHF Ch 16.

Dangers Depths in the entrance have reduced significantly, with least depths of 1·2m. It is likely that without dredging depths will decrease further.

Work in progress reinforcing the breakwaters. Depths in entrance 3–6m. Depths inside just 1m. Dredging likely as part of the works.

Mooring

Data 300 berths. Max LOA 10m. Depths <1–4·5m.

Berth Where directed or where convenient.

Shelter Good shelter although strong W winds may cause a surge.

Anchorage In calm weather anchor off the beach under Capo Pecoro, N of Buggeru. Good holding on sand in 5–8m. A peaceful spot in crystal clear water.

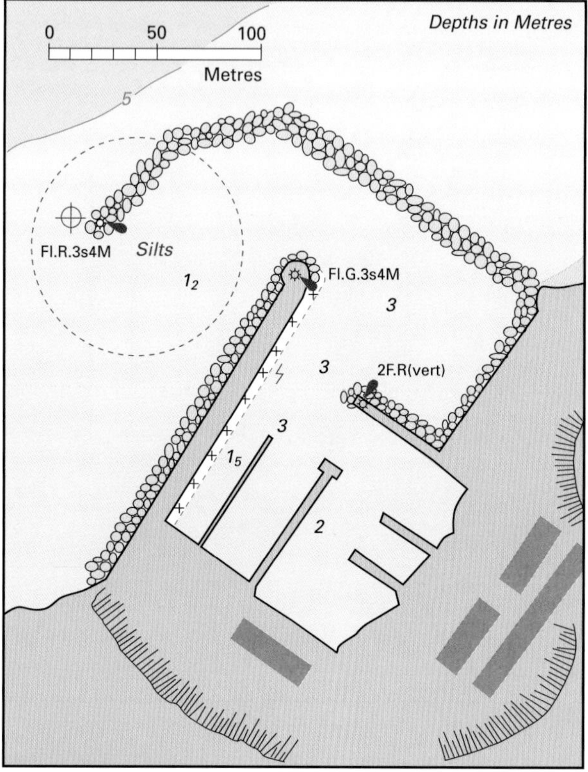

BUGGERRU
⊕39°24´·1N 08°23´·8E

Facilities

Water and electricity. Showers and toilets. Fuel can be arranged. Limited provisions in the village. Bank.

General

The setting is spectacular under steep slopes and the harbour conveniently sited along the coast between Carloforte and Golfo di Oristano. It will be a shame if Buggerru is permanently limited to shallow draught yachts only. And yes, the name is correct!

Golfo di Oristano

This large gulf lies very nearly halfway along the west coast. The gulf is entered between Capo San Marco and Capo Frasca 5½ miles south. These two capes are prominent mostly because the land around the edges of the gulf is low-lying. Capo San Marco looks like an island from the distance being joined to the mainland by a narrow isthmus. A white circular tower (Torre San Giovanni di Sinis) and the lighthouse (a two-storeyed building surmounted by a circular tower in all 15·5m high) are conspicuous on the cape. On Capo Frasca a girder tower painted in red and white bands and the lighthouse (a white squat building with a single black band) are conspicuous.

An area around Capo Frasca and the southern part of the gulf is a prohibited zone for anchoring and fishing. Navigation may also be prohibited at times and enforced by a navy patrol boat. It is part of a firing range belonging to the air force and is often in use. It is somewhat disconcerting to be in the run-up zone outside the prohibited area and see four jets screaming down out of the sky onto a target in the vicinity of Capo Frasca, let alone to be in the prohibited zone itself.

Care needed of tunny net laid across the NW corner of the gulf.

Once in the gulf, a yacht can find shelter in one of four places.

1. Under Capo San Marco.
2. Torre Grande anchorage.
3. In Oristano Commercial Harbour.
4. Marina Torre Grande.

CAPO SAN MARCO ANCHORAGE (Zone C)

The bay immediately NE of San Giovanni di Sinis tower is protected from NW–W–SW winds but is otherwise open. Anchor in 3–4m on sand and weed – good holding once through the weed. You must be N of the N tower or 500m off the coast to be outside the Zone C AMP, where anchoring is restricted.

Within the AMP mooring buoys have been laid to protect the posidonia beds. Anchoring is prohibited on the posidonia.

On the S side a number of villas have been built and on the N side the ruins of the Punic-Roman town of Tharros can be seen. Most of the artifacts are in the museum in Oristano.

The small village of San Giovanni di Sinis is a short walk away and basic provisions can be obtained there.

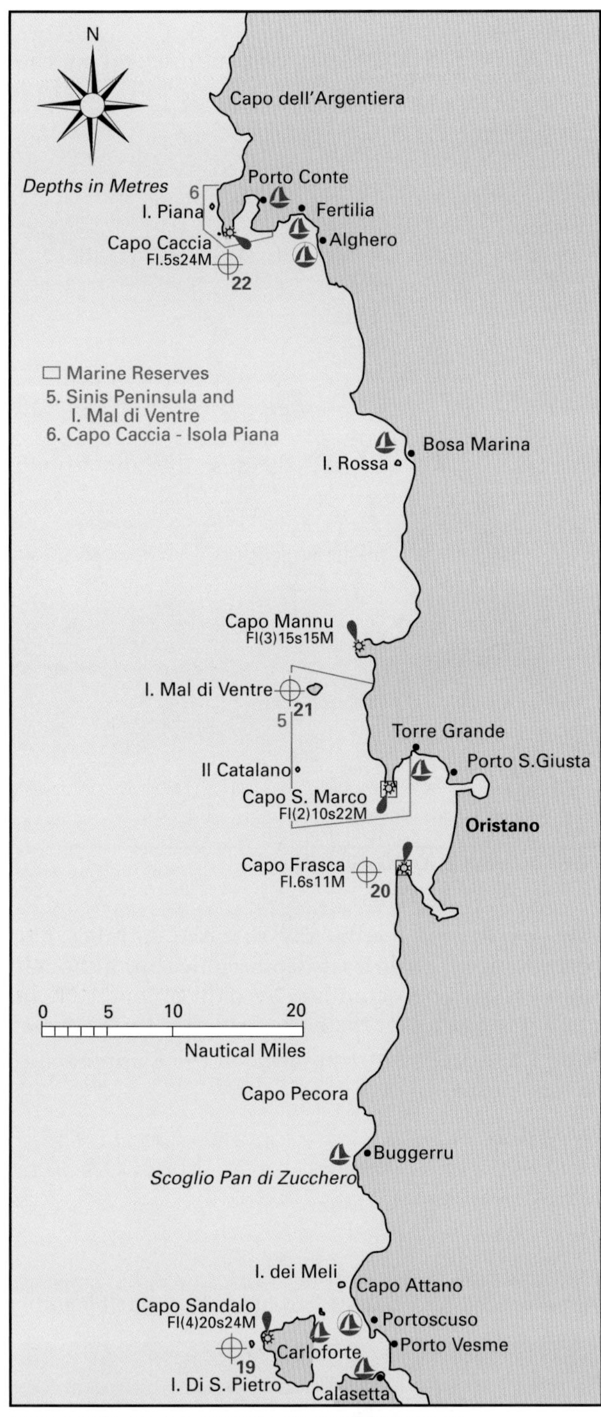

CAPO SANDALO TO CAPO DELL'ARGENTIERA

⊕19	2M W OF Capo Sandalo 39°08'·8N 08°10'·8E
⊕20	3M W of Capo Frasca 39°46'·1N 08°23'·5E
⊕21	3M W of I. Mal di Ventre 39°59'·5N 08°14'·3E
⊕22	1M S of Capo Caccia 40°32'·6N 08°09'·8E

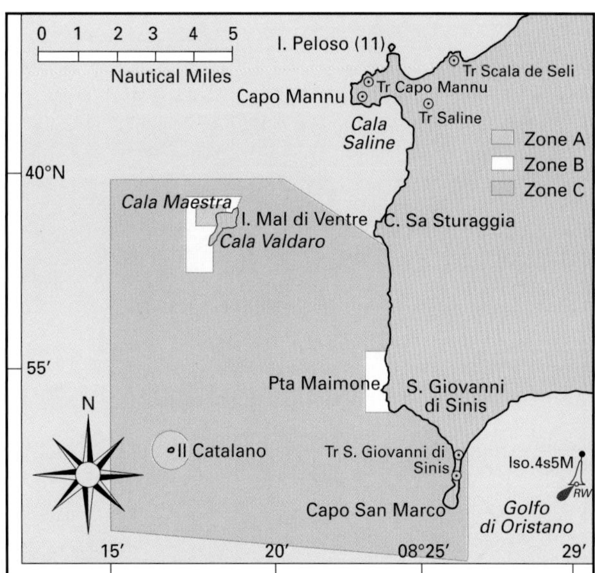

PENISOLA DEL SINIS AND ISOLA MAL DI VENTRE MARINE RESERVE

Sinis Peninsula and Isola Mal di Ventre Marine Reserve

Since July 2003 the new perimeter of this marine reserve is as shown above.

The protected areas are regulated as follows:

Zone A
Navigation, access and short- and long-time stays anywhere prohibited.
Swimming and all fishing prohibited.

Zone B
Navigation parallel to the coastline and any kind of unauthorised fishing prohibited.
Navigation permitted in controlled areas.
Swimming and sport fishing (with nets) permitted.
(Includes Cala Maestra and Capo San Marco anchorage).

Zone C
Sport and commercial fishing permitted, as well as nautical activities authorised by the authorities.

✆ 0783 290 071 *Fax* 0783 391 097
Email info@areamarinasinis.it
www.areamarinasinis.it

PORTO ORISTANO (SANTA GIUSTIA)

Approach

The large commercial harbour is on the E side of the gulf immediately S of Fiume Tirso. The approach channel is marked with buoys and dredged to 13m. The channel runs on a course of 130°.

Conspicuous A 'mushroom' water tower near the harbour, the large storage building in the harbour and the harbour breakwater are conspicuous.

By night Use the beacon in the approach to the channel Iso.4s5M. The channel buoys are lit Fl.R.3s (x4) and Fl.G.3s (x3).

VHF Ch 16, 12.

Mooring

Go alongside the quay in the E basin where there is room or where directed. Work is in progress developing the inner basin. Mooring or anchoring in the vicinity may be restricted.

Ormeggiatori ✆ 0783 74159

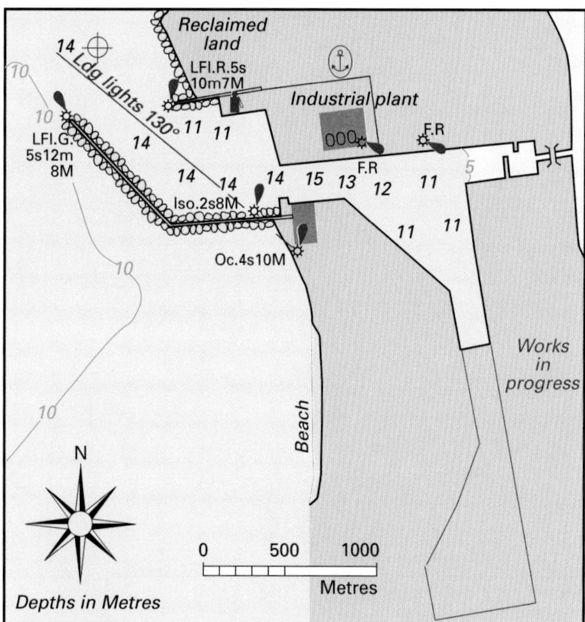

PORTO ORISTANO - SANTA GIUSTIA
⊕39°52'·1N 08°31'·9E

Tecnomar (of Fiumicino, Rome) are reported to be opening a marina and shipyard in the basin here.
Email info@tecnomar.net
www.tecnomar.net

Facilities

Tecnomar shipyard

Services Water and electricity. Showers and toilets.
Repairs 1,200-ton floating dock. 30-ton crane. Large shipyard and 50m covered yard. Sea rescue. Steel repairs, carpentry and mechanical repairs.
Other Restaurant and bar. Internet and email.

General

The large harbour was completed comparatively recently and seems little used. The shores of the gulf are described by the Admiralty *Pilot* as 'mostly low and sandy and behind them are extensive lagoons and marshes, rendering the neighbourhood unhealthy.' The locals seem to disagree as the shores are lined with row upon row of beach huts.

PORTO TURISTICO TORRE GRANDE (Marine Oristanesi)

A harbour approximately 1M W of Torre Grande.

Approach

The large tower in the NE corner of the gulf is conspicuous. The yacht harbour has been constructed to the E of it where the Stagno di Cabras empties into Golfo di Oristano. Make the approach towards the marina from the SE to avoid the shallows around the coast and then turn to follow the outer breakwater in to avoid the shallows on the N side of the entrance.

By night Illuminated red and green buoys show a channel in towards the entrance to the marina. The fish farm in the S approaches is poorly lit.

VHF Ch 09, 16.

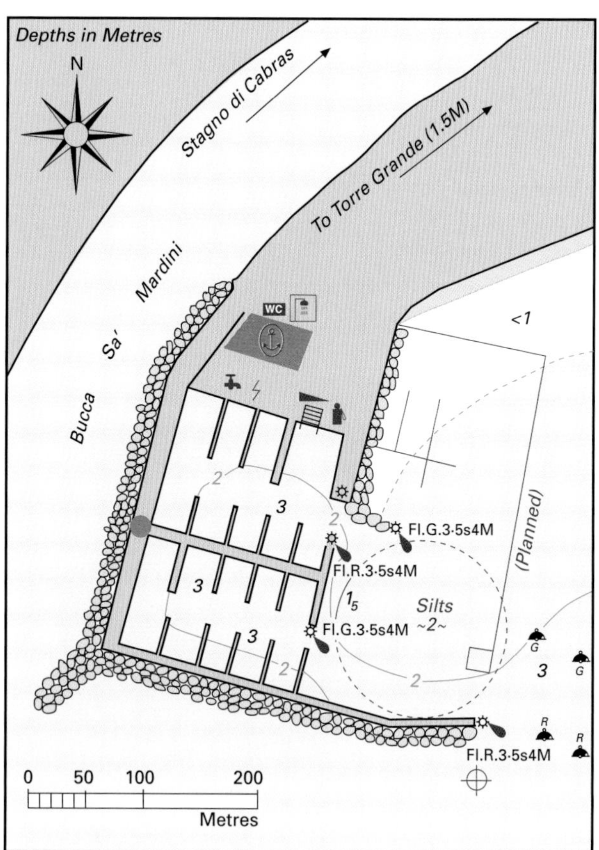

PORTO TURISTICO TORRE GRANDE
⊕39°54'·3N 08°29'·4E

Dangers Recent reports say that the entrance has been dredged, with least depths now 2m, although silting is likely to continue to reduce depths. If in doubt try calling up the harbourmaster for advice.

Note Care needed of fish farms in the S approaches to the marina.

Mooring

Data 400 berths. Visitors' berths. Max LOA 30m. Depths 1·5–3m.

Porto Turistico Torre Grande looking east *Carlo Delfino*

Berth Where directed or convenient. Visitors' berths are usually along the inside of the breakwater. Laid moorings.

Shelter Good shelter.

Authorities Harbourmaster. Marine staff. Charge band 4.

✆ */Fax* 0783 22189
Email marineoristanesi@marineoristanesi.it
www.marineoristanesi.it
Circolo Nautico ✆ 0783 210 172

Facilities

Services Water and electricity at all berths. WC and showers.
Fuel On the quay in the N basin (depths 1·8m reported).
Repairs 65-ton travel-hoist. Hardstanding. Mechanical and other repairs can be arranged.
Provisions In Torre Grande.
Eating out Restaurant/bar (July–August only).
Other Bus to Torre Grande.

General

The developers hope to attract yachts to this area with the construction of the marina and an increasing number of cruisers are now based here. It is a bit remote though the setting is attractive.

Torre Grande

⊕ 39°54′·4N 08°31′·0E

A yacht can anchor off Torre Grande to the E of the marina itself in settled weather. A light is exhibited here Fl.R.5s18m8M. Anchor in 3–4m off the small village. The anchorage is tenable with NW–N–E winds. In the summer there is a restaurant open at Torre Grande and another to the W around the bay. The large town of Oristano is some 7km inland.

Isolotto Mal di Ventre (Zone A/B/C)

('Stomach-ache' Island)

This low scrubby island lies approximately four miles W of Punta Catalanetto. Off the NE end a reef (above and below-water rocks) extends N for about one mile. A light is exhibited on the summit Fl.WR.6s26m11/8M. Local yachts often anchor in a shallow bight in 3–4m at the SE corner of the island. The island is now part of the marine reserve, and so restrictions to anchoring and fishing apply.

Capo Mannu

⊕ 40°02′·1N 08°22′·7E Capo Mannu light

Capo Mannu is a low (47·8m/157ft) rocky peninsula connected by a low sandy isthmus. A light is exhibited on the cape Fl(3)15s59m11M. A yacht can anchor on either side of the isthmus in settled weather and find shelter from all but strong westerlies. Anchor outside the moorings on sand, good holding. Both bays have magnificent beaches – indeed much of the coast to the S is fronted by beautiful and often deserted sandy beaches. Late night disco and small supermarkets ashore. The Stagno di Sale Porcus nearby is reported to be one of the few remaining summer habitats of the European crane.

Bosa Marina looking N with the entrance to Fiume Temo above Isola Rossa. Note the new detached breakwater is not shown here *Carlo Delfino*

BOSA MARINA PORTO COMMERCIALE

Approach

The harbour is behind Isola Rossa.

Conspicuous Isola Rossa and the breakwater running S from it are easily identified. On Isola Rossa, Rossa Torre and the rather dilapidated white three-storeyed lighthouse are conspicuous.

VHF Ch 16, 14 (0800–2000).

Dangers

1. With the prevailing NW winds there are strong gusts in the vicinity of Bosa Marina.

Note A new breakwater is under construction running in a curve across the entrance to Fiume Temo.

Mooring

Berth Go stern or bows-to one of the pontoons on the W side of the bay, S of the river mouth. Laid moorings tailed to buoys.

Shelter Good shelter from the normal NW winds, although the swell works its way around into the bay making a very uncomfortable surge, even after the wind dies. Open to the south.

Authorities Ormeggiatori. Charge band 4.

Circolo Nautico Bosa ✆ 0785 376 174
R. Pirisi ✆ 0785 375 550

IV. SARDINIA

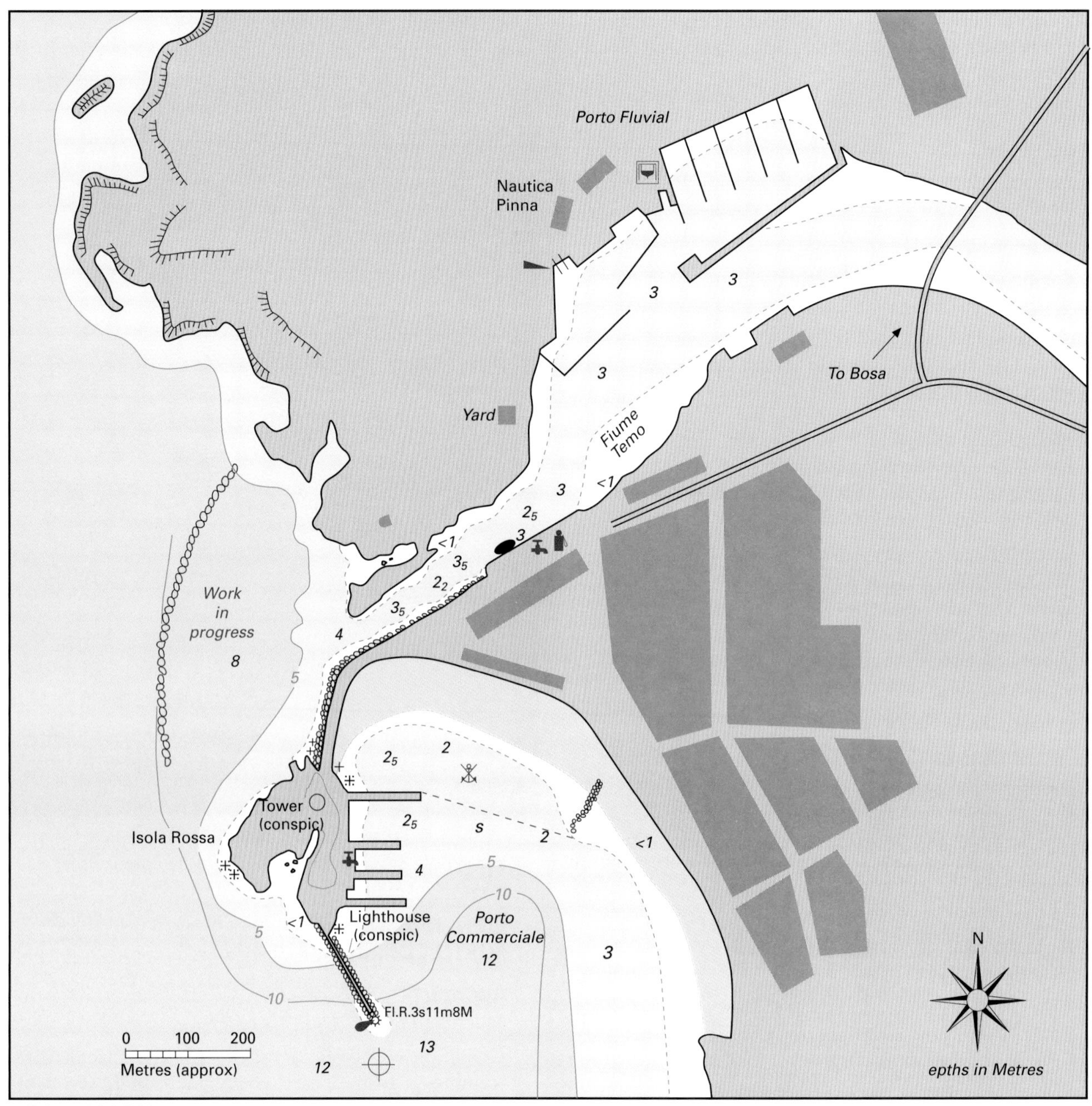

BOSA MARINA
⊕40°17′·0N 08°28′·5E

Anchorage Anchor in the bay in 3–6m. The bottom is sand and weed, good holding. Some swell inevitably penetrates and it can be quite rolly at anchor. Open south. Anchoring is prohibited N of a line from the end of the N pier to the end of the rough semi-submerged mole in the NE corner.

Fiume Temo – Porto Fluviale

Approach

Immediately N of Isola Rossa, Fiume Temo is navigable for approximately 800m as far as the road bridge. With onshore winds (NW–W–SW) blowing there are breaking waves at the entrance. With a Force 4 or more blowing onshore it is dangerous to enter the river. Once the new breakwater is complete then approaches in onshore winds should be possible with care. The channel up to the Porto Fluviale is not buoyed and not lit. There is a minimum depth of 2·2m in the channel although there are mostly 3m depths.

VHF Ch 09, 73.

Note A new breakwater is under construction running in a curve across the entrance to Fiume Temo. Care needed in the approaches to the river during construction. Approach from the S keeping close to Isola Rossa.

Mooring

Data 200 berths. Max LOA 25m. Depths 1·5–3m.

Berths Nautica Pinna is an established boatyard with pontoon berths in the river. Go stern or bows-to in Nautica Pinna or in the new basin. Laid moorings tailed to the pontoons.

Shelter Excellent all-round shelter. *See note on Dangers, above.*

Authorities Ormeggiatori.

Nautica Pinna ✆ 0785 373 554 / 331 806 3356
Email info@nauticapinna.it

Il Porticciolo di Bosa ✆ 0785 375 550

Facilities

Services Water and electricity on the pontoons. Showers and toilets.
Fuel On the quay in Fiume Temo for fishing boats only. The *ormeggiatori* will deliver jerrycans back to the pontoons.
Repairs 65-ton travel-lift. A slipway up to 10 tons. The boatyard in the Fiume Temo can haul yachts and carry out some repairs. Mechanical repairs.
Provisions Basic provisions can be obtained. Better shopping in Bosa about 2km up the river.
Eating out Restaurants and pizzerias are open in the summer.
Other Bosa is a sizeable town and there is a PO and bank there.

General

The fine sandy beach attracts large numbers of tourists in the summer but in the winter it is deserted. A number of fine old stately villas are clustered around the deserted railway station and no doubt Bosa Marina was an outer suburb of the Alghero European refugee belt. One feels there is perhaps a tale or two hidden in the dying shadows of the villas and their overgrown gardens.

ALGHERO

BA 1202
Italian 911/05

Approach

Straightforward by day and night.

Conspicuous The old walled town of Alghero flanked by modern suburbs is easily identified. In the old town a belfry and cupola are conspicuous. Isoletto della Maddalena 800m to the NNW of the entrance is easily identified. The light structure on it, a white tower with a black band is conspicuous. Closer in, the outer breakwater is easily identified.

By night Isoletto della Maddalena is lit Fl.R.5s4M.

Dangers Fish pen in position 40°33´·7N 08°16´·0E, approximately 1¾M due W of the entrance to the port. It is lit by flashing white 'fairy lights', and is not easily seen.

Note With the prevailing NW winds there is a confused swell at the entrance, more bothersome than dangerous.

VHF Ch 16. Ch 09 for Marina di Sant Elmo. Ch 74 for Aquatica. Ch 09 for Ser-Mar.

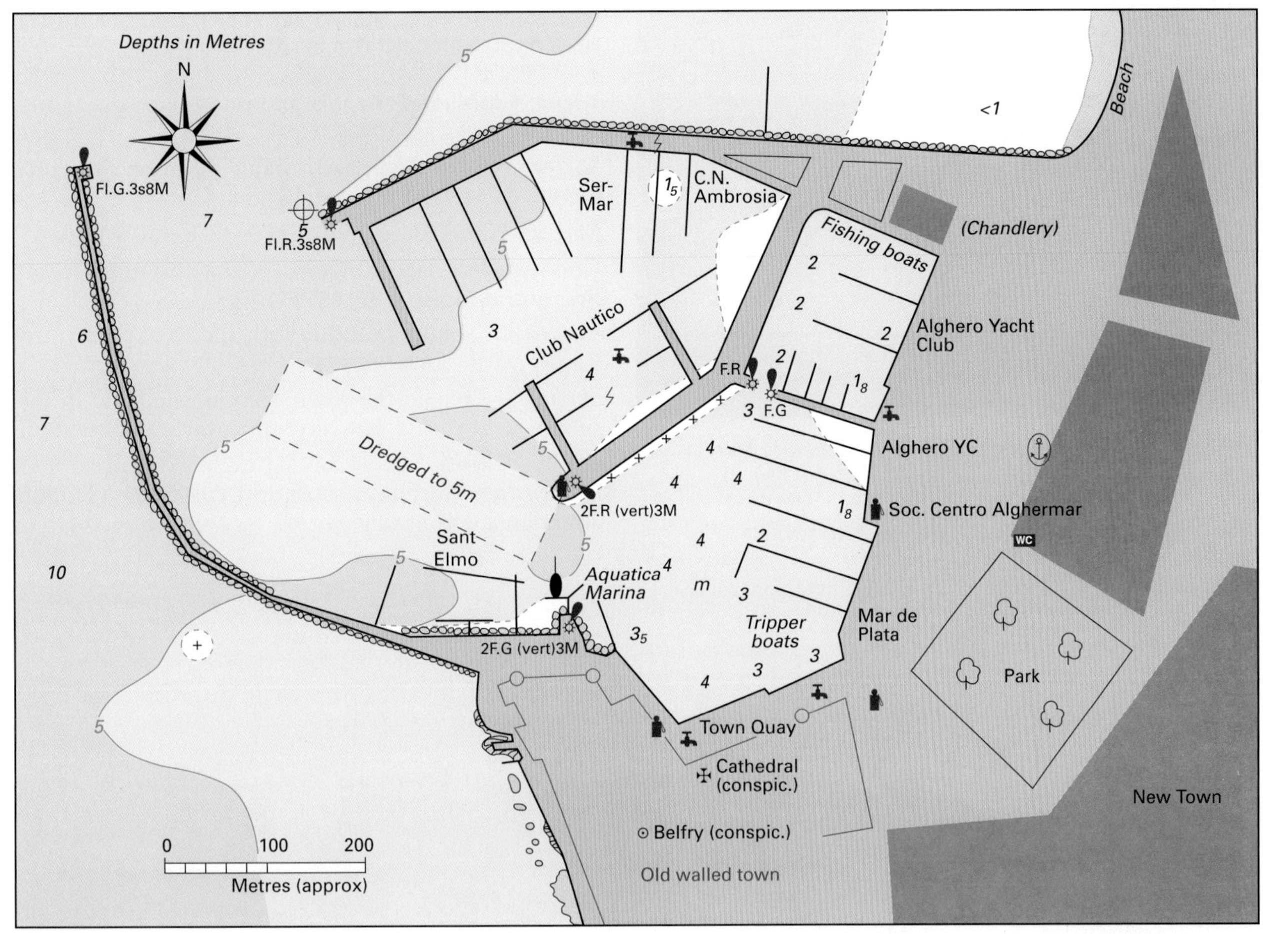

ALGHERO
⊕40°33´·87N 08°18´·49E WGS84

Visitors' berths on the town quay at Alghero

Alghero inner harbour and walled town *Aquatica Marina*

Yacht berths under the cathedral and walled town in Alghero *Marina di Sant'Elmo*

Mooring

Data 2,500 berths. Visitors' berths. Max LOA 25m. Depths 1–5m. Depths are irregular.

Berth There are several options for yachts in transit: the town quay under the cathedral, or various marina pontoons around the harbour. You may be able to negotiate a berth at one of the YC pontoons around the harbour, although spaces are usually taken with local boats. Most berth managers offer assistance with RIBs. Laid moorings at all berths.

Town Quay c.30 berths. Depths 3–5m. Max LOA 50m. Charge band 5.

Porto di Alghero ☎ /*Fax* 079 989 3117 ☎ 339 732 9921
Email info@portodialghero.com
www.portodialghero.com

Aquatica Marina A 60 berth pontoon and service company adjacent to the town quay. Max LOA 60m. Laid moorings.

Manager Fabrizio Goldoni ☎ 079 983 199 or 348 130 3966
Email info@aquaticamarina.com
www.aquaticamarina.com
Atlantis Agency ☎ /*Fax* 079 976 686

Marina di Sant Elmo 100 berths. Max LOA 60m. Depths 3–5m. Charge band 5.

Marina di Sant Elmo ☎ /*Fax* 079 980 829 ☎ 333 221 4342
Email info@marinadisantelmo.it
www.marinadisantelmo.it

Ser-Mar Pontoon in the N of the harbour. 120 berths. Depths 1·5–3·5m. Yachts overwinter here. Repairs yard. Charge band 5.

Manager Federico Crisafulli ☎ 347 772 0544 *Fax* 079 978 413
Email fecrisa@tiscalinet.it or info@ser-mar.it
www.ser-mar.it

Yacht Club Alghero Six pontoons in the inner harbour. ☎ 079 952 074

Society Centro Alghermar Single pontoon near fuel quay.

Mar de Plata Three pontoons N of the town quay.

Club Nautico Two concrete piers with pontoons off the central mole. ☎ 079 986 958

Ambrosia Single pontoon off the N breakwater. Repair yard. ☎ 079 952 179

Shelter Shelter on the town quay is adequate in the summer, but can be very uncomfortable with a strong *mistral*.

Authorities Harbourmaster and customs. YC club attendants and *ormeggiatori*.

Facilities

Services Water and electricity (220/380V) at or near all berths. Wi-Fi available. Showers, toilets and laundry at Ser-Mar. Showers and laundry at YC.
Fuel Near the quay. Large quantities from a fuel point on the town quay in the S corner.
Repairs A 15-ton crane and a 50-ton mobile crane available. Yachts are craned onto the quay in the inner basin. Mechanical and engineering repairs. Electrical and electronic repairs. Some GRP and wood repairs. Sailmakers (Fois who are agents for Ratsey and Lapthorn). Chandlers.
Provisions Good shopping for all provisions. Large *Standa* supermarket in the town. Ice from the 'fish shop' on the town quay.
Eating out Excellent restaurants, trattorias and pizzerias in the old town. The Spanish influence can be seen in the cuisine and *paella* is on every menu.
Other PO. Banks. ATMs. Internet cafés. Hospital. Italgaz and Camping Gaz. Hire cars. Tripper boats to Neptune's Grotto. Internal and international flights from the airport nearby (transfers by Ser-Mar).

General

The town was founded by the Dorias in the 12th century and then conquered by Pedro IV of Aragon, becoming Catalan two centuries later. Today it preserves the flavour of a Spanish town and some of the older fishermen still speak Catalan. The walled town incorporates a Gothic style cathedral, Gothic chapels and old towers. Bright tiles decorate the old houses and porches and many of the streets have kept their Spanish names. The setting in what is locally known as the Golfo del Corallo is enchanting with sandy beaches and, behind, rolling wooded hills.

Before the first world war, Grand Admiral von Tirpitz owned a large estate to the north of Alghero and after the war European refugees fled here and built some of the grand villas to be seen around the town. All in all, one of my favourite spots in Sardinia.

FERTILIA

Approach

The yacht berths lie at the head of Rada di Alghero at the entrance to Stagno di Calich. A steeple is conspicuous in the cluster of buildings around the river mouth.

Fertilia looking S to the entrance

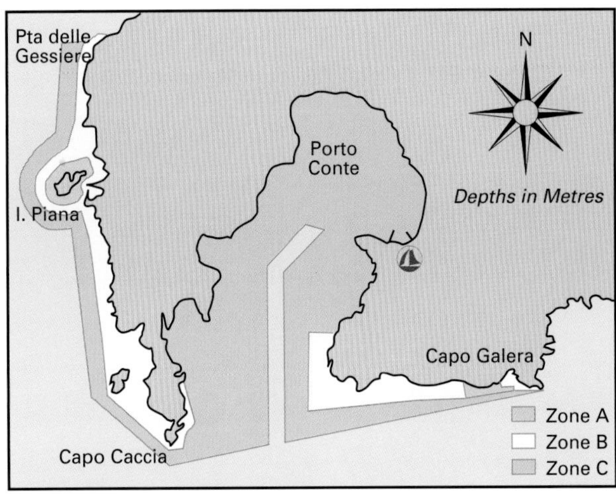

CAPO CACCIA - ISOLA PIANA

Capo Caccia – Isola Piana Marine Reserve

A recently established reserve covering the area from Capo Galera, past Capo Caccia and Isola Piana and up to Punta delle Gessiere, including Porto Conte.

Zone A
Navigation, access, anchoring, mooring, swimming, diving, fishing of any sort all prohibited.
Access only by AMP wardens or authorised research teams.

Zone B
Permitted activities:
Navigation under sail or with oars and by motor boat (speed limit 5kns).
Anchoring in authorised designated areas.
Mooring in specific authorised areas on AMP mooring buoys.
Swimming and diving (except in underwater caves, which requires authorisation).
Sport fishing with net and line (in limited numbers and subject to marine reserve rules).
Underwater fishing is prohibited.

Zone C
Permitted activities:
Navigation with or without motor up to 10 knots.
Navigation with or without motor in the access channel to Porto Conte and landings.
Mooring in specific authorised areas on AMP mooring buoys.
Anchoring in specific zones designated by the reserve authority.
Free anchoring only for boats using a mazzere (an anchor made of local stone).
Subaqua diving and swimming.
Sport fishing with net and line (only if authorised and subject to marine reserve rules).
Underwater fishing is prohibited.

Comune di Alghero ✆ 079 997 816 *Fax* 079 997 819
Porto Conte Branch office ✆ 079 998 551 / 548/543
Fax 079 998 415
Email info@ampcapocaccia.it
www.ampcapocaccia.it

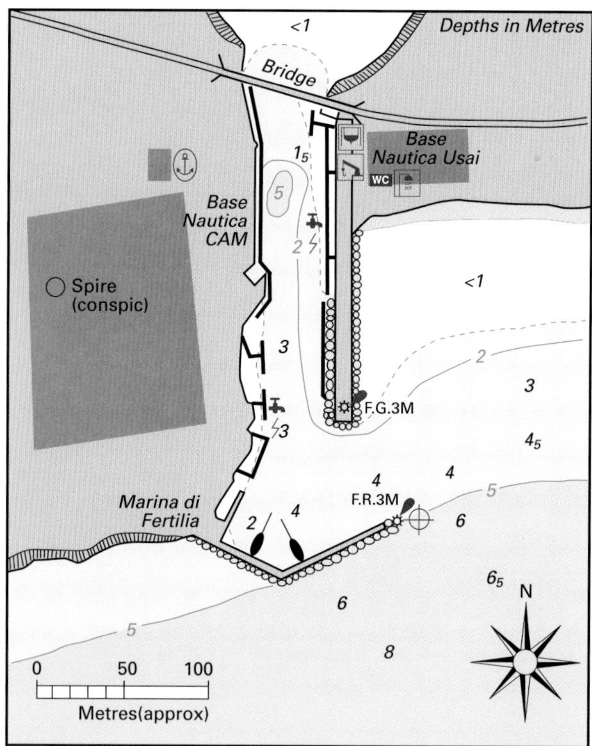

FERTILIA
⊕40°35′·5N 08°17′·3E

Note Poorly lit fish pen in the approaches (see *Alghero, Dangers*, above).

VHF Ch 16.

Mooring

Base Nautica Usai is on the E side. Base Nautica CAM is on the W side. Marina di Fertilia operates along the S breakwater.

Data c.300 berths. Visitors' berths. Max LOA 30m. Depths <1–4m.

Berth Stern or bows-to where directed. Laid moorings.

Shelter Good shelter in the summer.

Authorities Harbourmaster. Charge band 4/5.

Base Nautica Usai
Cesare Usai
✆ 079 930 233 *Fax* 079 930 088
Email basenauticausai@tiscalinet.it
www.basenauticausai.it

Base Nautica CAM ✆ 338 722 2440

Marina di Fertilia ✆ /*Fax* 079 930 002 *Mobile* 349 1943 022 (English spoken)
Email info@marinadifertilia.it
www.marinadifertilia.it

Note Base Nautica Usai is more a boatyard with moorings than a marina. Prices for short-term (overnight) berths are very high, but for longer-term stays (monthly or longer) the rates become more competitive. Its proximity to Alghero airport has made it a popular over-wintering spot, although the yard may not suit everyone.

Facilities

Services Water and electricity at most berths. Showers and toilets. Wi-Fi. Laundry.
Fuel About 100m away. Delivery can be arranged.
Repairs 60-ton travel-hoist. 10–40-ton cranes. Most repairs can be arranged.
Provisions Most provisions can be found.
Eating out Restaurants ashore.
Other Alghero International airport 2km. Car rental. Taxis.

General

The small harbour is pleasantly situated and a quiet alternative to bustling Alghero.

PORTO CONTE (Zone C)

BA 1202
Italian 292

This large almost landlocked bay is entered between Capo Caccia and Punta del Giglio. The steep sheer cliffs of Capo Caccia with a lighthouse atop are easily recognised from some distance off. A yacht can find shelter from all winds somewhere in the bay. The following anchorages offer good shelter:

Calla del Bollo On the W side. A large hotel complex around the northern side of the cove is conspicuous. Anchor in 4–10m on sand and weed. With even light winds some swell will be pushed in here. Restaurant ashore. A yacht can also anchor in the southern end of the cove under Punta del Bollo.

Cala Tramariglio On the W side. Anchor off in 3–5m on sand and weed or go stern-to the end of the pontoon.

Data 80 berths. Max LOA 12m. Depths <1–2m (pontoon).

Facilities Water. Restaurant.

Porto Conte At the head of the bay in 2–3m. There is a large hotel complex ashore.

Cala Torre del Conte On the E side. Anchor in 2–3m on sand and weed.

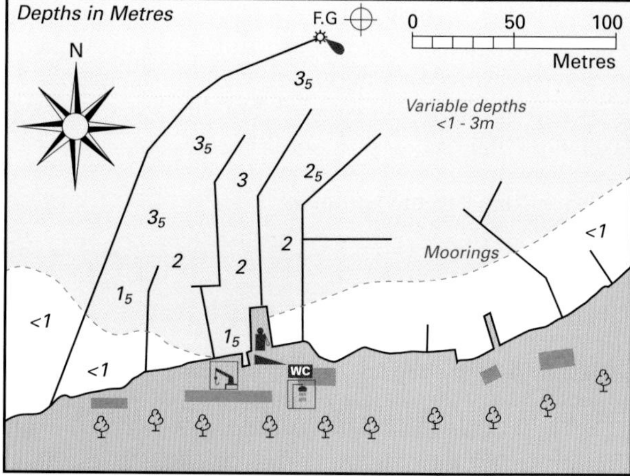

PORTO CONTE MARINA
⊕40°35′·7N 08°12′·8E

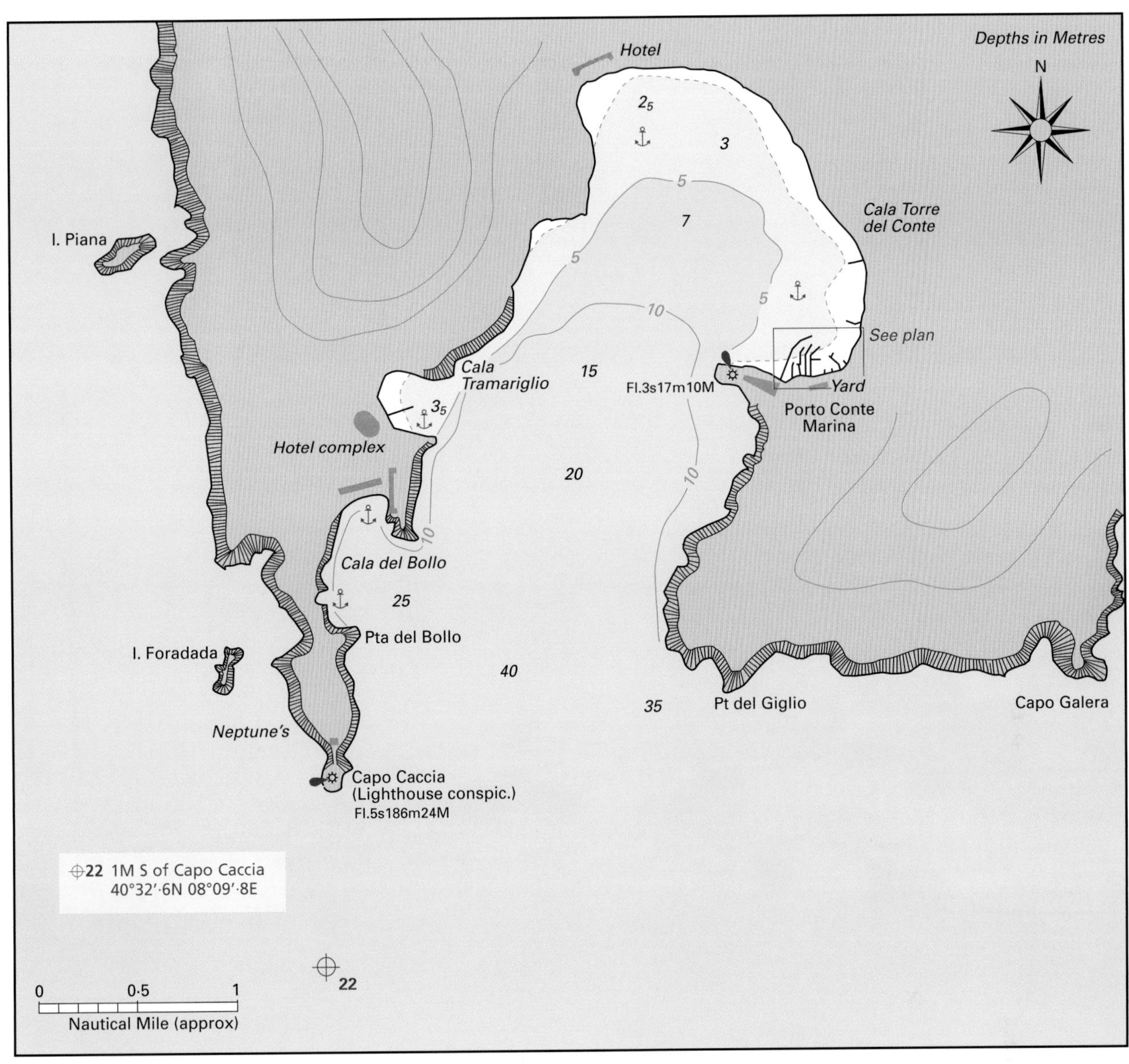

PORTO CONTE

PORTO CONTE MARINA

Approach

The catwalks and pontoons are tucked into the S corner of Cala Torre del Conte.

VHF Ch 09, 16.

Mooring

Data 350 berths. 10 visitors' berths. Max LOA 20m. Depths 1–3·5m.

Berth Where directed.

Shelter Good shelter in the summer. Fetch across the bay with NW–W winds.

Authorities Harbourmaster. Charge band 5.

✆ /*Fax* 079 942 013
Email info@portocontemarina.it
www.portocontemarina.it

Facilities

Services Water and electricity. Showers and toilets.
Fuel Fuel quay (depths 1·5m).
Repairs 30-ton crane. Yard ashore.
Provisions Some provisions available.
Eating out Restaurant, pizzeria and bar ashore.

Note There are often strong gusts off the high land on the W side of the bay. Strong southerlies send a swell into the bay and during such weather the best anchorage is in Cala Torre del Conte.

General

The bay is a spectacular spot. The impressive limestone cliffs and wooded hinterland enclose the clear blue water. In the limestone cliffs there are numerous caves of which the most famous is Neptune's Grotto. This can be reached by local boat from Alghero or a yacht can anchor in Cala del Bollo and its crew walk around the cliffs to the staircase, the Escala del Cabirol (Mountain-goat's staircase), which descends to the Grotto. It is possible to sail around to the Grotto but there is nowhere secure to leave a yacht. It is fascinating to sail, (or more likely, motor, as the wind is flukey close to the cliffs), along near to the cliffs and between the islets where there is everywhere deep water.

V.

Sicily

'Cold, fresh wind, a blue-black, translucent, rolling sea on which the wake rose in snapping foam, and Sicily on the left; Monte Pellegrino, a huge inordinate mass of pinkish rock hardly crisped with the faintest vegetation, looming up to heaven from the sea. Strangely large in mass and bulk Monte Pellegrino looks: and bare, like a Sahara in heaven: and old looking. These coasts of Sicily are very imposing, terrific, fortifying the interior. And again one gets the feeling that age has worn them bare: as if old, old civilisations had worn away and exhausted the soil, leaving a terrifying blankness of rock, as at Syracuse in plateau, and here in great mass.'

D H Lawrence *Sea and Sardinia*

History

The history of Sicily is rich and varied. It consists mostly of successive waves of invaders occupying the island and leaving cultural influences which have blended in often fascinating ways such as the unique Arabic-Norman architecture of the Middle Ages. The island's name is derived from a fairly insignificant mainland tribe, the Sicela, who migrated here in about 1000BC. Soon after this the first Greek colonists arrived.

The Greeks

The first Greeks were Chalcedians from Evia who founded Naxos about 735BC. In 734 the Corinthians arrived and founded Syracuse which was to become the most important city in Magna Graecia. While the Greeks continued to colonise eastern and southern Sicily, the Phoenicians colonised western Sicily.

The Phoenicians were succeeded by the Carthaginians and it was inevitable that there would be conflict between the Greeks and the west coast colonies. The conflict erupted in the Battle of Himera in 480BC when the Greeks trounced the Carthaginians. In 413BC, Athens challenged the power of Syracuse and it in turn was defeated by the city that was to dominate Magna Graecia for two centuries. One of the Greek names for the island was

Santa Maria Salinas looking N into the S basin
Kerr Whiteford

Trinacaria, 'the three-cornered island', symbolised by a head with three running legs nearly identical to the symbol for the Isle of Man. The three-legged flag is often used as the national flag of Sicily to this day. The Romans' growing power bit into the Greeks' hegemony, but Hieron II of Syracuse threw in his lot with the Romans during the first Punic War and Syracuse was left a free city-state when Rome occupied Sicily.

The Romans

In the Second Punic War, Syracuse sided with Carthage, and the Romans, having defeated the Carthaginians, sacked Syracuse and destroyed much of the Greek architecture. Under the Romans the importance of Sicily declined and much of the land was awarded as *latifundia* and was worked by slaves for absentee landlords. The Christians began to arrive about AD100 and Rome suffered an uneasy few centuries with them until its decline and the arrival of the Barbarians. Belisarius briefly reoccupied the island for Byzantium until the Arabs arrived.

The Arabs

The Arabs conquered North Africa and moved onto Sicily, landing at Mazara del Vallo in AD827. They made Palermo their capital and did much for local agriculture by improving irrigation methods and introducing new crops: citrus fruits, cotton, sugar cane and pistachio nuts.

The Normans

Back from the Crusades, these soldiers of fortune took the south of Italy and then stormed through Sicily. Under Roger and Robert de Hauteville, the knights had secured Sicily by 1091 and were responsible for many buildings still standing to this day. The Normans were sympathetic conquerors and their architecture reflects this in their synthesis of the Norman and Arabic forms. The Norman line ended with the infant King William III, disposed of by Henry of the Swabian house of Hohenstaufen, in turn succeeded by his son Frederick I of Sicily and later Frederick II of Germany and the Holy Roman Empire. Frederick is the star of Sicily and indeed of the Middle Ages. An intelligent, artistic and able ruler, he promoted the arts and had the title Stupor Mundi (the Amazement of the World) bestowed upon him. Frederick was succeeded by his bastard son, Manfred, who reigned for a short time before being defeated in battle by Charles of Anjou. The Angevin rule of Charles was cruel and repressive and resulted in the War of the Vespers in which the Sicilians were aided by Spain under Peter of Aragon.

The Spaniards

The four centuries of Spanish rule were not beneficial for Sicily. Characterised by indifferent and corrupt rulers who favoured the rich, Sicily became a forgotten province of Italy until the Sicilians, with nothing left to lose, revolted against the weak King Ferdinand in 1848.

Garibaldi

Garibaldi landed at Marsala in 1860 with his 'Thousand' and decisively defeated the Bourbons. But the unification of Italy in 1870 was not beneficial for Sicily which, together with southern Italy, was literally forgotten by the new government. After the Second World War in 1946, the Sicilians were granted some autonomy by Rome and development began, albeit slowly.

The Mafia

The word 'mafia' is thought to be an Arabic word meaning 'a refuge' and was first used during the Arab conquest when some Sicilians moved to secret places inland where they became bandits. The Mafia, as a group for protecting the weak and the poor, continued during the Norman occupation to the Spanish period in which it became more powerful and assumed a more sinister role. It specialised in 'protection' and blackmail and the code of silence, the *omerta*, ensured its survival and growth. The mass emigration from Sicily in the late 19th century introduced the mafia to America where it still flourishes. Although its power in Sicily was broken by Mussolini in the 1920s, it revived after the war and has grown to blight the ordinary life of Sicilians.

In recent years the families have feuded among themselves for control of the drug market – much heroin and cocaine passes through the island and, despite the governments efforts to clamp down on the mafia, it flourishes still, though the tourist hears and sees little of it. The families figure in most of the scandals that come to light: development funds that have mysteriously disappeared, crooked construction deals, and general graft and bribery in everyday Sicilian affairs. It is not just Sicily that is blighted by the mafia, but all of Italy including the north where it was recently disclosed that the mafia have substantial holdings in some of the banks in Milan and Turin. Yet, as I say, the visitor will see and hear little of this.

Shoestring cruising in Sicily

Sicily is a good option for summer cruising as long as you plan it well. There are sufficient anchorages and cheaper harbours to make it around the island without too much damage. However numerous harbours are being upgraded into marinas and the prices can be high in the summer. Outside of marinas prices are generally reasonable though where *ormeggiatori* have concessions then in high season prices can be extortionate.

Marinas and harbours

North coast

Along the N coast you may be able to negotiate a berth at Castellamare del Golfo which has reasonable charges. Palermo main harbour needs some polite haggling, but lots of us have negotiated quite reasonably priced berths in here even if the surroundings are a bit mucky (the city more than makes up for it). San Nicola L'Arena and Capo d'Orlando (if you can get in) are reasonably priced.

East coast

Along the E coast Naxos, Acitrezza and Catania on the outer harbour berths are all reasonably priced.

South coast

Porto Empedocle, Mazzara del Vallo, and Marsala are all reasonably priced.

West coast

On the W coast it is a matter of seeing what price you can get in Favignana and Trapani. In Trapani there will be one or two reasonably priced deals going on the various pontoon berths, alternatively pick up a mooring buoy.

Anchorages

North coast

On the N coast there is a pretty precarious anchorage N of San Vito Lo Capo (it is prohibited to anchor in the bay now) and then it is a fairly long haul to the anchorage under Porticello. After that there is Cefalu and then the anchorages around the Lipari Islands. Some care is needed around the islands in the anchorages as many of them are exposed and in unsettled weather you will need to be careful.

East coast

Down the E coast the first useful anchorage is at Taormina although it can be rolly in here. After that it is a bit of a long haul to Brucoli where there is an open anchorage. A bit further on the anchorage under Capo Santa Croce off Augusta is a better anchorage with good shelter in Augusta if it blows up. Down the coast there is a good anchorage in Siracusa with all-round shelter.

South coast

Along the S coast try Porto Palo although it is crowded and the bottom foul in places. You can no longer anchor in Licata as they are building a marina here, but in calm weather you anchor just E of the harbour. At Mazaro del Vallo there is quite a good anchorage outside the harbour where some protection is gained from the long breakwater.

West coast

The moorings at Trapani have been free up to now. There are also a number of anchorages around the Egadi Islands where shelter can usually be found from one or other direction.

Note There have been lots of dinghy theft around Sicily and you should hoist it up on deck. Leaving it in the water, even with a chain or cable locking it onto the boat, is no guarantee it won't be stolen.

Weather patterns in Sicily

In the summer the normal winds encountered around the Sicilian coast vary considerably so each coast is considered separately.

North coast

The prevailing summer wind is from the NW. It gets up in the morning and blows Force 3–4 before dying down again at night. Sometimes it may blow from the SW and further towards the Strait of Messina it may blow from the NE. A weak current sets eastward at less than one knot but it is easily reversed by strong winds from a contrary direction. With strong winds and gales from the N a heavy swell descends on the N coast, especially around Capo San Vito.

Strait of Messina

See the section on the Strait for weather patterns and currents.

East coast

The normal wind is a sea breeze from the S–SE. It gets up in the morning and blows until dusk at about Force 4–5. Often it will blow all night without letting up. Winds from the NE are also common and are accompanied by a sea-state in excess of what might normally be expected.

South coast

The normal wind here is a sea breeze from the SW which gets up in the morning and dies down at night. It normally blows no more than Force 4 and there are frequent days when there is little or no wind at all. Towards the W coast the wind blows more from the west. Southerly gales cause a heavy swell on this coast but are rare in summer.

West coast

The normal summer wind here is from the NW although it sometimes backs to the west. Along the coast and in between the Egadi Islands a current which sometimes runs at over one knot sets towards the NE and the prevailing wind blowing from the NW causes a confused sea even when the wind is light. Sailing around the islands this is very noticeable: there may be a confused sea in one place and yet, around a headland where the current is deflected, there can be an almost calm patch of sea. The sea caused by the current is more annoying than dangerous.

Winter

Over all of Sicily, gales are most often from the W–NW although there may be occasional gales from the NE (*gregale*). In the spring and autumn the *scirocco* may also blow with some strength and the moisture it picks up in its passage over the sea from Africa bathes Sicily in a soporific humidity.

It is said that if the *scirocco* blows for more than three days all inexplicable 'crimes of passion' are excused.

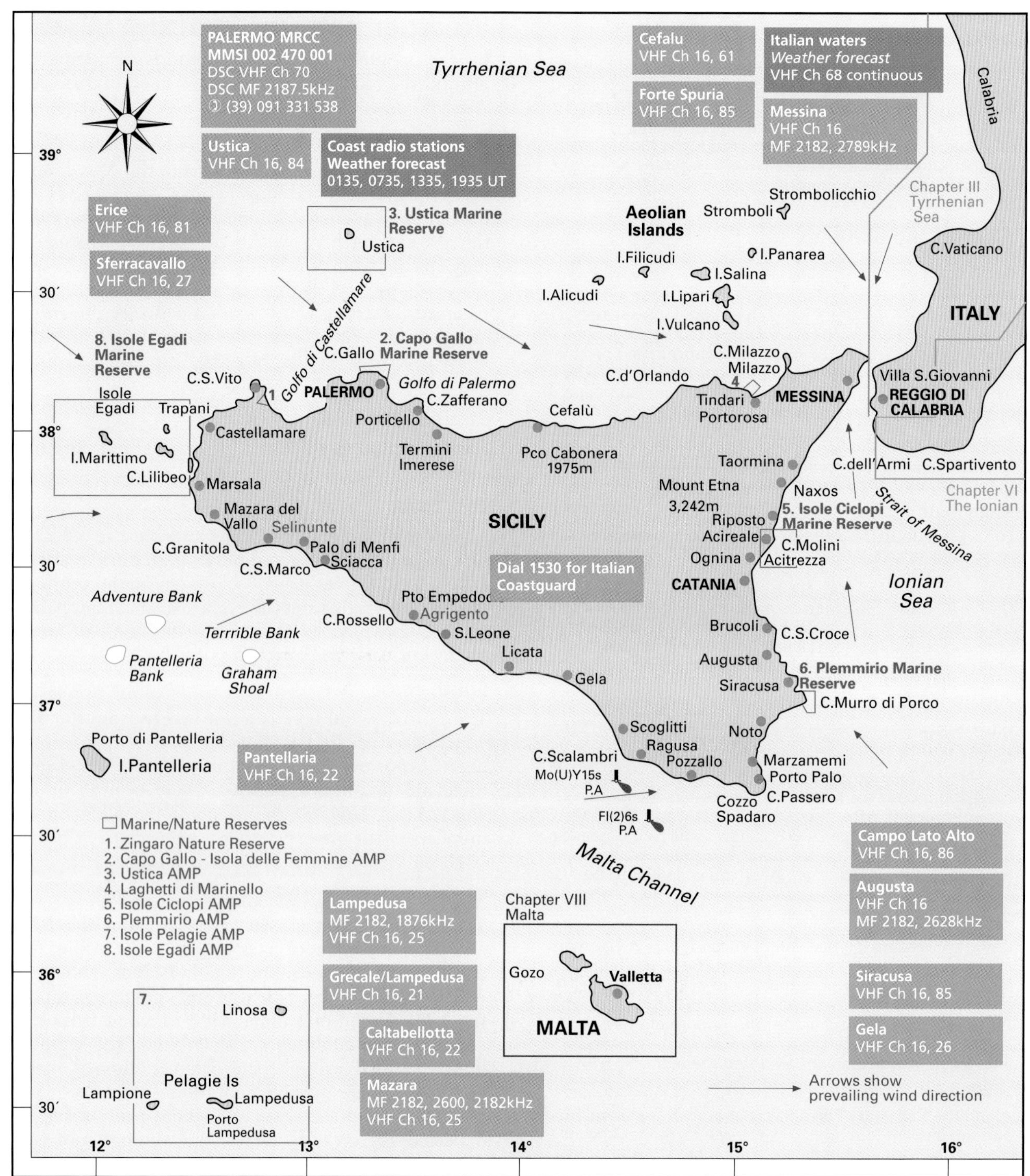

PALERMO MRCC
MMSI 002 470 001
DSC VHF Ch 70
DSC MF 2187.5kHz
(39) 091 331 538
Tyrrhenian Sea
Cefalu
VHF Ch 16, 61
Forte Spuria
VHF Ch 16, 85
Italian waters
Weather forecast
VHF Ch 68 continuous
Messina
VHF Ch 16
MF 2182, 2789kHz
Calabria
Ustica
VHF Ch 16, 84
Coast radio stations
Weather forecast
0135, 0735, 1335, 1935 UT
Erice
VHF Ch 16, 81
Sferracavallo
VHF Ch 16, 27
3. Ustica Marine Reserve
Ustica
Aeolian Islands
Stromboli
Strombolicchio
Chapter III Tyrrhenian Sea
I.Filicudi
I.Panarea
I.Salina
I.Alicudi
I.Lipari
I.Vulcano
C.Vaticano
ITALY
8. Isole Egadi Marine Reserve
Golfo di Castellamare
2. Capo Gallo Marine Reserve
C.Gallo
C.Milazzo
Milazzo
C.d'Orlando
C.S.Vito
Isole Egadi
Trapani
PALERMO
Golfo di Palermo
C.Zafferano
Porticello
Tindari
Portorosa
MESSINA
Villa S.Giovanni
REGGIO DI CALABRIA
Cefalù
Castellamare
I.Marittimo
C.Lilibeo
Marsala
Termini Imerese
Pco Cabonera 1975m
Taormina
C.dell'Armi
C.Spartivento
Mount Etna 3,242m
Naxos
Chapter VI The Ionian
5. Isole Ciclopi Marine Reserve
Strait of Messina
Mazara del Vallo
Selinunte
SICILY
Riposto
Acireale
C.Molini
Acitrezza
C.Granitola
Palo di Menfi
Sciacca
C.S.Marco
Ognina
CATANIA
Dial 1530 for Italian Coastguard
Ionian Sea
Adventure Bank
Pto Empedocle
Agrigento
C.Rossello
S.Leone
Terrrible Bank
Brucoli
C.S.Croce
Pantelleria Bank
Graham Shoal
Licata
Gela
Augusta
Siracusa
6. Plemmirio Marine Reserve
C.Murro di Porco
Porto di Pantelleria
I.Pantelleria
Pantellaria
VHF Ch 16, 22
Scoglitti
Ragusa
Noto
C.Scalambri
Pozzallo
Marzamemi
Porto Palo
Mo(U)Y15s
P.A
Cozzo Spadaro
C.Passero
Fl(2)6s
P.A
Marine/Nature Reserves
1. Zingaro Nature Reserve
2. Capo Gallo - Isola delle Femmine AMP
3. Ustica AMP
4. Laghetti di Marinello
5. Isole Ciclopi AMP
6. Plemmirio AMP
7. Isole Pelagie AMP
8. Isole Egadi AMP
Malta Channel
Campo Lato Alto
VHF Ch 16, 86
Augusta
VHF Ch 16
MF 2182, 2628kHz
Lampedusa
MF 2182, 1876kHz
VHF Ch 16, 25
Chapter VIII Malta
Gozo
Valletta
MALTA
Grecale/Lampedusa
VHF Ch 16, 21
Caltabellotta
VHF Ch 16, 22
Siracusa
VHF Ch 16, 85
Gela
VHF Ch 16, 26
Linosa
Pelagie Is
Lampione
Lampedusa
Porto Lampedusa
Mazara
MF 2182, 2600, 2182kHz
VHF Ch 16, 25
Arrows show prevailing wind direction

Data

PROHIBITED AREAS AND MARINE RESERVES

Marine Reserves (Area Marina Protetta – AMPs)

1. ***Riserva Naturale dell Zingaro*** Nature reserve E of Capo San Vito. There is no designated marine reserve but there have been restrictions reported on anchoring.
2. ***Capo Gallo and Isola delle Femmine*** This recently established marine reserve covers the area around the tiny Isola delle Femmine and Capo Gallo. The harbours of Femmine, Sferracavallo, Fossa del Gallo and Mondello fall within the reserve.
3. ***Ustica*** A marine reserve has been created around Isola Ustica up to three miles off the coast.
4. ***Riserva Naturale Laghetti di Marinello*** A new nature reserve covering the sand dunes on the E side of Capo Tindari. There are restrictions on anchoring in the area.
5. ***Isole Ciclopi*** A marine reserve has been created around Isole Ciclopi stretching from Capo Molini to 1M S of Acicastello.
6. ***Riserva Naturale Plemmirio*** AMP Plemmirio covers the La Maddalena peninsula which forms the S side of the entrance to Siracusa Grand Harbour, and runs S into Baia di Ognina.
7. ***Isole Pelagie Marine Reserve*** Lampedusa, Linosa and the islet of Lampione are all covered within this marine reserve.
8. ***Isole Egadi*** A marine reserve has been created surrounding the islands in this group.

More details and plans of these Marine Reserves are given under the text for each area.

MAJOR LIGHTS

Capo San Vito Fl.5s45m25M & Iso.R.4s12m8M
Castellammare del Golfo Fl(2)10s19m10M
Punta Raisi Aero AlFl.WG.35M

Ustica

Punta Omo Morto Fl(3)15s100m25M & Oc.R.5s95m9M
Punta Gavazzi Fl(4)12s40m16M

Capo Gallo LFl(2)15s40m16M
Palermo (N Mole) Fl(4)15s15m15M
Capo Zafferano Fl(3)WR.10s34m16/12M
Capo Cefalù Fl.5s80m25M
Capo d'Orlando LFl(2)12s27m16M
Capo Milazzo LFl.6s90m16M
Capo Rasocolmo Fl(3)10s85m15M

Aeolian Islands

Stromboli (the red lights from the small eruptions can be visible for up to 40 miles, especially when reflected by clouds).
Strombolicchio Fl(3)15s57m11M
I. Salina. Punta Lingua Fl.3s13m11M
Capo Faro LFl.6s56m18M
Lipari Marina Corta Fl(3)15s11m15M
I. Vulcano. Punta dei Porci Fl(4)20s35m16M
I. Alicudi Fl.3s11m10M
Isola Filicudi, Punta La Zotta Fl(5)15s20m12M

Sicily

Capo Peloro Fl(2)G.10s37m19M (Fl.Y.21M when passage through the Strait of Messina is prohibited). From the same light tower: Iso.R.22m9M (shore-vis-127° over Secche di Capo Rasocolmo)
Punta San Raineri Fl(3)15s41m22M.
Fl.Y.15M (shown when passage through the Strait of Messina is prohibited)
Riposto LFl.5s15m17M
Capo Molini Fl(3)15s42m22M
Catania (harbour) Fl.5s31m22M
Catania (behind the harbour) AlFl.WG.35m(occas) F.R lights mark airport
Brucoli Fl.5s13m11M
Capo Santa Croce LFl(2)12s39m16M
Rada di Augusta, Punta Gennalena Ldg Lts
Front Iso.4s16m12M *Rear* Oc.5s79m17M
Augusta (Magnisi Peninsula) Fl(4)12s10m11M
Siracusa Ldg Lts *Front* Iso.R.2s12m17M
Rear Oc.5s25m17M
Capo Murro di Porco Fl.5s34m17M
Capo Passero Fl(2)10s39m11M
Cozzo Spadaro Fl(3)15s82m24M
Pozzallo Fl(4)12s12m11M
Capo Scalambri Fl(2)8s37m16M
Scoglitti Fl(3)10s15m11M
Licata (E mole) Fl.5s40m21M
Capo Rossello Fl(2)10s95m22M
Capo San Marco Fl(3)15s25m18M
Capo Granitola LFl.10s37m18M
Capo Feto LFl.10s14m11M
Marsala (W mole) Fl(2)10s19m15M
Trapani (Scoglio Palumbo) Fl.5s16m12M & Iso.R.2s8M

Egadi Islands

Capo Grosso (I. Levanzo) Fl(3)15s68m11M
Punta Libeccio (I. Marettimo) Fl(2)15s73m24M
Punta Sottile (I. Favignana) Fl.8s43m25M
Punta Marsala (I. Favignana) Fl(4)15s20m15M

Routes

Routes around Sicily are usually as part of a passage either E-going or W-going. Commonly yachts will leave from Sardinia and make for the NW corner of Sicily to either Trapani or San Vito Lo Capo. If arriving off the W coast of Sicily make sure you do so in daylight as there is a lot of shoal water around Trapani and the Egadi Islands as well as badly marked tuna set-nets. From the W to the E yachts can travel along either the N or S coasts and enjoy favourable winds. When going from E to W it is probably best to go along the N coast.

Yachts on passage to Tunisia will usually leave from somewhere like Marsala or Mazzara del Vallo and proceed straight to the Golfe de Hammamet and one of the marinas there. Yachts can stop off at Pantellaria to break the voyage. Some yachts will make direct for Tunis or Bizerte further west. Yachts on passage to Malta can leave from somewhere like Licata or Porto Palo. Remember it can be worthwhile doing an overnight trip so you arrive in the morning and can clear customs at Msida (not that I ever seem to take my own advice, and end up going into Grand Harbour to clear!).

Yachts on passage to Greece will often leave from Siracusa or Catania to cross to the Greek Ionian. It is worth remembering that conditions up to 20 miles off the coast will not necessarily reflect the weather further out and away from the brisk sea breeze blowing onto the coast you may find less wind.

Quick reference guide

	Shelter	*Mooring*	*Fuel*	*Water*	*Eating out*	*Provisions*	*Plan*	*Charge band*
Sicily N Coast								
San Vito Lo Capo	B	A	A	A	B	B	•	5
Scopello	C	C	O	O	O	O		
Castellammare del Golfo	B	A	A	A	B	B	•	1/5
Balestrate	B	A	O	A	B	B	•	
Terrasini	B	AC	A	A	C	C	•	
Femmine	B	A	B	A	C	C	•	
Sferracavallo	C	AC	B	A	B	B	•	
Fossa del Gallo	B	A	A	A	C	C	•	
Mondello	B	A	B	A	B	A	•	
Addaura	C	A	A	A	C	C	•	
Arenella	B	A	B	B	B	B	•	6
Marina Villa Igiea	A	A	O	A	B	B	•	6
Palermo	A	A	A	A	A	A	•	5
Isola di Ustica								
Cala Sta Maria	B	AB	A	A	B	B	•	1
Sicily N Coast								
Porticello	A	A	B	A	B	C	•	
San Nicola L'Arena	A	A	A	A	B	B	•	3
Termini Imerese	A	A	A	A	A	B	•	
Cefalù	B	AC	A	A	A	A	•	5
Sant' Agata	C	BC	O	B	C	C	•	
Capo d'Orlando	B	A	B	A	C	C	•	4
Tindari	B	C	O	O	C	C	•	
Portorosa Marina	A	A	A	A	B	B	•	6
Milazzo Marina del Nettuno	B	A	A	A	A	A	•	6
Aeolian Islands								
Stromboli	O	C	O	O	C	C	•	
Panarea								
Scalo Ditella	C	AC	O	B	C	C	•	
Punta Milazzese	C	C	O	O	O	O		
Salina								
Santa Marina	B	A	A	A	C	C	•	6+
Rinella	C	AC	O	B	C	C	•	1
Malfa	C	AC	O	B	C	C	•	1
Filicudi								
Porto Filicudi	C	C	O	O	C	C		
Alicudi								
Scalo Palomba	C	C	O	O	C	C	•	
Lipari								
Marina Lunga	B	A	A	B	A	A	•	
Pignataro	B	A	B	A	A	A	•	5
Marina Corta	B	B	B	A	B	A	•	
Vulcano								
Porto di Levante	B	AC	O	O	C	C	•	4
Porto di Ponente	B	C	O	O	C	C	•	
Cala di Maestro Minico	C	C	O	O	C	C	•	
Cala del Cavallo	C	C	O	O	O	O	•	
Gelso	C	C	O	O	C	C	•	
Sicily E Coast								
Messina								
Marina del Nettuno	A	A	B	A	A	A	•	5
Taormina Roads	C	C	O	O	B	A	•	
Naxos (Giardini)	C	AC	B	A	B	B	•	1/3
Riposto Marina	B	A	A	A	B	B	•	5/6
Acireale	C	A	B	A	C	C	•	
Acitrezza	B	A	B	A	B	B	•	
Ognina	B	A	B	A	C	B	•	
Catania	A	A	A	A	A	A	•	4
Brucoli	AC	BC	B	B	B	C	•	
Augusta	A	AB	A	A	B	C	•	
Siracusa	A	AC	A	A	A	A	•	5
La Balata	B	A	O	B	C	C	•	2
Marzamemi	B	A	B	A	C	C	•	2/3
Sicily S Coast								
Porto Palo	B	BC	A	A	C	C	•	
Pozzallo	B	AB	B	B	C	C	•	
Scoglitti	A	AB	A	A	C	C	•	
Gela	B	AB	B	B	B	B	•	
Licata	A	AC	A	A	B	B	•	1/6
Marina di Palma	B	AB	O	B	C	C	•	
San Leone	A	A	A	A	B	C	•	5
Porto Empedocle	A	AC	A	A	B	B	•	3/4
Sciacca	A	A	A	A	B	B	•	5
Palo di Menfi	B	A	B	B	C	C	•	
Isola Pantelleria								
Port Pantelleria	A	A	A	A	B	B	•	3
Scauri	A	A	O	B	C	C	•	1
Cala de Levante	C	C	O	O	C	C	•	
Porto Dietro Isola	C	C	O	O	O	O		
Cala di Tramontana	C	C	O	O	O	O		
Pelagie Islands								
Isola di Lampedusa								
Porto di Lampedusa	B	AC	A	B	B	B	•	1
Cala Pisana	C	C	O	O	O	O	•	
Sicily W Coast								
Mazara del Vallo	A	A	A	A	B	B	•	4
Marsala	B	A	A	A	A	B	•	4/5
Trapani	A	A	A	A	A	A	•	1/2
Isole Egadi								
Isola Favignana								
Cala Grande	C	C	O	O	O	C		
Cala Rotonda	C	C	O	O	O	O		
Favignana	A	A	A	A	B	B	•	5
Isola Levanzo								
Cala Dogana	B	AC	O	B	B	C	•	
Isola Marettimo								
Cala Manione	C	C	O	O	O	O		
Scala Vecchia and Scala Nuovo	C	AC	B	B	C	C	•	5
Cala Cretazzo	C	C	O	O	O	O		
Cala Bianca	O	C	O	O	O	O		

USEFUL WAYPOINTS

Sicily N Coast

⊕1 2M N of Capo San Vito
38°13'·2N 12°43'·9E

⊕2 1M N of Pta. Raisi
38°12'·4N 13°06'·5E

⊕3 0·5M N of Capo Gallo
38°14'·3N 13°19'·00E WGS84

⊕4 1M W of Pta Cavazzi (Ustica)
38°41'·5N 13°08'·0E

⊕5 0·5M N of Capo Zafferano
38°07'·36N 13°32'·25E WGS84

⊕6 1M N of Capo Cefalú light
38°03'·2N 14°01'·7E

⊕7 0·4M N of Capo d'Orlando
38°10'·39N 14°44'·81E WGS84

Aeolian Islands

⊕8 1M N of Strombolicchio
38°50'·0N 15°15'·2E

⊕9 1M S of Capo Monaco (Stromboli)
38°45'·25N 15°13'·0E

⊕10 0·5M N of Pta Palisi (Panarea)
38°39'·3N 15°04'·4E

⊕11 0·5M S of Pta Milazzese (Panarea)
38°36'·9N 15°03'·8E

⊕12 1M N of Capo Faro (Salina)
38°35'·8N 14°52'·2E

⊕13 1M S of Pta Lingua (Salina)
38°31'·1N 14°52'·3E

⊕14 1M E of Capo Graziano (Filicudi)
38°33'·4N 14°36'·9E

⊕15 1M N of Pta La Zotta (Filicudi)
38°36'·0N 14°32'·6E

⊕16 1M N of N end of Alicudi
38°34'·3N 14°21'·2E

⊕17 1M S of S end of Alicudi
38°30'·7N 14°21'·2E

⊕18 1M N of Pta Castagna (Lipari)
38°32'·4N 14°57'·4E

⊕19 0·5M E of Sciarra di Monte Rosa (Lipari)
38°28'·8N 14°59'·4E

⊕20 Mid-channel Bocche di Vulcano
38°26'·1N 14°57'·4E

⊕21 1M S of Pta dei Porci (Vulcano)
38°21'·07N 14°59'·49E WGS84

Sicily N Coast

⊕22 0·75M N of Capo di Milazzo light
38°17'·08N 15°13'·88E WGS84

⊕23 1·1M N of Capo Rasocolmo light
38°19'·99N 15°31'·18E WGS84

Sicily E Coast

⊕24 1·75M E of Capo Peloro
38°15'·86N 15°41'·42E WGS84

⊕25 0·6M W of Pta Pezzo
38°13'·87N 15°37'·31E WGS84

⊕26 1M E of Capo Schiso
37°49'·7N 15°18'·0E

⊕27 0·5M E of Capo Molini
37°34'·49N 15°11'·32E WGS84

⊕28 0·5M E of Capo Santa Croce
37°14'·6N 15°16'·5E

⊕29 0·75E of Capo Murro di Porco
37°00'·10N 15°21'·20E WGS84

⊕30 0·5M E of Capo Passero light
36°41'·23N 15°09'·85E WGS84

⊕31 2M S of I. delle Correnti
36°36'·3N 15°05'·6E

Sicily S Coast

⊕32 2M S of Capo Scalambri
36°45'·1N 14°30'·3E

⊕33 2M S of Licata
37°03'·06N 13°56'·48E WGS84

⊕34 0·8M S of Capo Rossello
37°16'·72N 13°26'·90E WGS84

⊕35 0·5M S of Capo San Marco
37°29'·22N 13°01'·19E WGS84

⊕36 1M S Of Capo Granitola
37°32'·99N 12°39'·62E WGS84

⊕37 2M N of Pta San Leonardo (I. Pantelleria)
36°52'·1N 11°56'·7E

⊕38 3M E of Capo Grecale (I. Lampedusa)
35°31'·0N 12°41'·8E

Sicily W Coast

⊕39 2M S of Capo Feto (Sicily)
37°37'·6N 12°31'·3E

⊕40 0·25M E of Pta Marsala (I. Favignana)
37°55'·09N 12°22'·52E WGS84

⊕41 2M N of Capo Grosso (I. Levanzo)
38°03'·2N 12°20'·0E

Sicily North coast

Riserva Naturale dell Zingaro

A new nature reserve W of Capo San Vito. At present there is no designated marine reserve, but is has been reported that anchoring has been prohibited off the coast here.

✆ 0924 35108 *Fax* 0924 35752
Email info@riservazingaro.it
www.riservazingaro.it

SAN VITO LO CAPO

Approach

This marina is located on the E side of the tip of the cape, less than ½M S of Capo San Vito light. Punta Solanto lies approximately 2M E of the marina, and forms the NW extremity of Golfo di Castellammare.

Conspicuous Capo San Vito lighthouse, a white circular tower 44m (144ft) high, on the low-lying point is conspicuous. From the E the buildings on

The lighthouse at Capo San Vito, looking NW from the harbour *Sandro Bedessi, FOTOTECA ENIT*

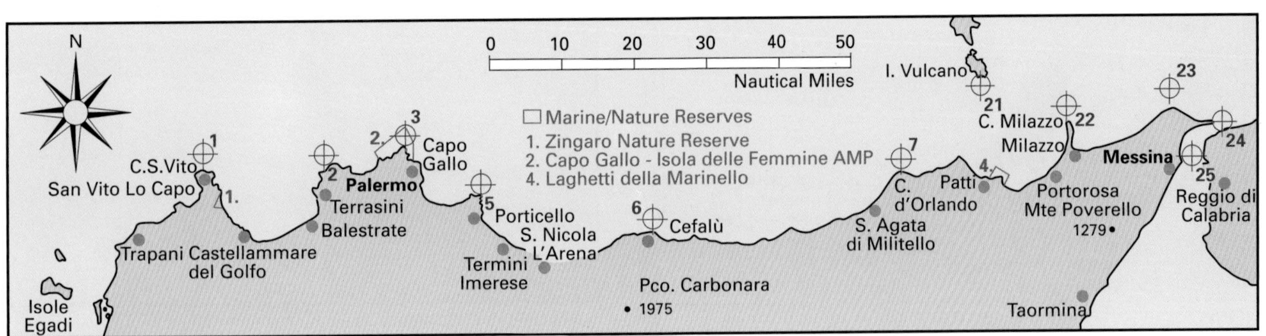

SICILY NORTH COAST

V. SICILY

Food and wine

Specialities in Sicilian cuisine centre around seafood, vegetables such as the aubergine and beans, and sweets. There are, however, a few typical Sicilian meat dishes such as *involtini alla Siciliana*: slices of meat rolled around fillings of ham, salami, cheese, breadcrumbs and onions and cooked over charcoal; or *falso magro:* meat roll filled with sausage, ham, hard-boiled eggs and onions and cooked in tomato sauce. But unlike its seafood, meat is not the region's best produce.

Vegetables introduced by the Saracens, aubergines, pine nuts and others like beans and artichokes are used more often than in other parts of Italy.

Tuna and swordfish are caught off the coasts of Sicily and swordfish steak sprinkled with lemon, capers and herbs and cooked over a charcoal grill is simply the best fish going. Even non-fish-eaters can be tempted by the firm flesh free of bones. Many different succulent fish are found in these waters as are prawns and shrimps called *scampi*, *gamberetti* or *gamberoni*, depending on their size and variety – these are served fried, grilled or in a peppery sauce. Here the Arab influence is felt and *cuscus di pesce*, a dish of semolina and fish, is a favourite. Even the humble sardine gets royal treatment in *sarde a beccofico* where it is filled with breadcrumbs, herbs and currants and baked in the oven with orange juice.

The fertile slopes and plains around Mount Etna produce oranges, lemons, tangerines, grapefruit, grapes, melons and a Japanese fruit called *respole*. The Sicilians are famous for their cakes and ice creams, Sicily being the birthplace of ice cream and *cassata*. The best known dessert is *cassata alla Siciliana*, which is a sponge cake with candied fruits, a dish probably influenced by the Arabs.

Since the best wines have tended to remain on the island rather than be exported, it is not surprising that Sicilian wines are little known outside, although they are now beginning to make an appearance. Corvo, an excellent dry white and red with a pleasant bitterness, is produced near Casteldaccia on the northern coast. Mount Etna produces Etna Bianco, a golden-coloured wine, Etna Rosso which is a deep ruby colour and also Mascalucia, Nicolosi, Trecastagni, Viagrande, Zafferana, Randazzo, Castiglione and Misterbianco. Faro, a red wine, comes from the northeast tip of Sicily and in the highlands reds, white and rosés called Regaleali are produced. The best known wines, apart from the above are Taormina, Villegrande, Pignatello and Marsala.

CAPO SAN VITO TO BALESTRATE

Punta Solanto are also conspicuous. Closer in, the breakwaters of the harbour and the entrance are readily identified.

By night Use Capo San Vito lighthouse Fl.5s45m25M and Iso.R.4s12m8M (165°-R-225° over the 5m shoal N of the cape). Also Punta Solanto Fl.WR.3s25m10/8M (122°-R-144°).

Dangers In bad weather there are heavy confused seas off Capo San Vito. The Admiralty *Pilot* states that these seas can be dangerous to small vessels. A shoal with a least depth of 5m over it lies ¾ mile N of the cape. It is covered by the red light on Capo San Vito and the red light on Punta Solanto between 122° and 144°.

VHF Ch 16, 09, 69 used by the *ormegiattori*.

Note The entrance is silting on the S side and depths are less than charted.

Mooring

Data 200 berths. Visitors' berths. Max LOA 25m. Depths <1–6m.

Berth You will be directed onto one or other of the pontoons where there are laid moorings tailed to the pontoon. Which one you choose is really a matter of luck tempered by a little judgement on wind direction and price. The three pontoons are run by different clubs and in the summer it can be difficult to find a berth at any of them.

Shelter Good shelter although strong NE winds make it uncomfortable.

Authorities The *carabinieri* will sometimes want to look at a yacht's papers. *Ormeggiatori*. Charge band 5. The pontoons all charge a lot in the season for what is offered and the season seems to run from May to October here.

C. Nautico Costa Gaia ☎ 0923 972 037
C. Nautico La Traina ☎ 0923 972 999
D. Nautico Sanvitesse ☎ 0923 974 126

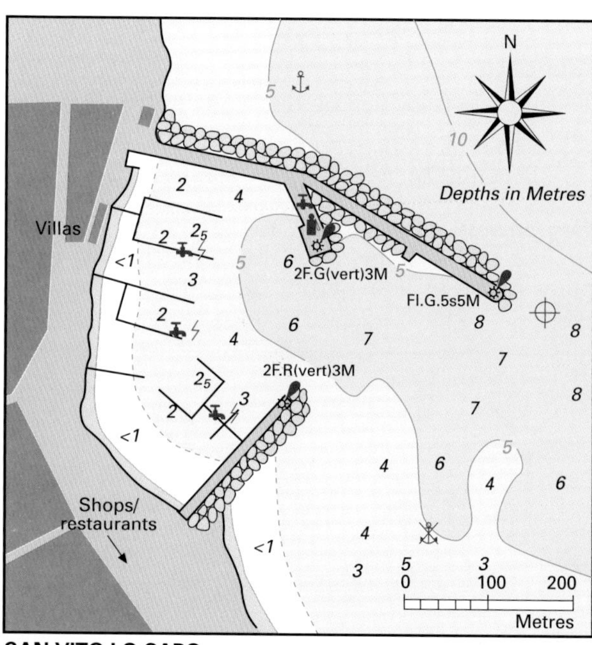

SAN VITO LO CAPO
⊕38°10′·84N 12°44′·23E WGS84

San Vito Lo Capo looking E to the entrance

Anchorage Anchoring is now reported to be prohibited E of harbour, but permitted N of the breakwater, but you must be at least 300m off the beach and outside the buoyed swimming area or the *carabinieri* will come and tell you to move further out. Shelter at anchor is just adequate in settled conditions depending on the wind and swell around. The bottom is sand and good holding.

Facilities

Services Water and electricity on the pontoons. Water on the fuel quay.
Fuel On the spur mole.
Repairs Minor mechanical repairs.
Provisions Most provisions can be bought in the village. Fish can be bought from a building at the root of the N mole where ice can also be obtained.
Eating out Good restaurants, trattorias and pizzerias in the village.
Other PO. Banks. ATMs. Italgaz and Camping Gaz. Buses to Palermo.

General

San Vito Lo Capo is a rapidly developing tourist resort in an exotic setting. On one side there is the low-lying cape and on the other, the red cliffs of a precipitous bluff. Between them is a fine sandy beach and the white houses of the Moorish looking village complete with palms. The sea is a crystal-clear green over a sandy bottom and the rocky headlands on either side of the bay offer good underwater fishing. It sounds like an extract from a package holiday brochure and it attracts a lot of local tourism in the summer. The main street in the village running parallel to the beach is an odd mix of tacky souvenir and other shops and some fine up-market fish restaurants.

Scopello

⊕ 38°04′·7N 12°49′·5E

Lies about four miles to the NW of Castellammare del Golfo and can be recognised by a large square tower and two high rocks (the Faraglioni) lying off it. Local yachts anchor behind the rocks in calm weather off a tunny fishery (no longer used).

CASTELLAMMARE DEL GOLFO

Approach

The town is situated under Mt Inice at the head of the gulf.

Conspicuous The buildings of the town and particularly the retaining wall on the seafront are conspicuous. Closer in the fort and the breakwater are conspicuous.

VHF Ch 16 (0800–1400).

Note Works in progress developing the harbour as shown in the plan.

Mooring

Data c.500 berths. Max LOA c.15m. Depths <1–8m.

Berth Go stern or bows-to where directed or convenient. If possible go close to the town so you don't have to walk too far in and out of town. Otherwise anchor off where convenient.

Shelter Normally good in the summer. With strong E–NE winds it could get uncomfortable at some berths.

Authorities Carabinieri. Ormeggiatori. Charge band 1/5.

Club Nautico ✆ 0924 32511
Lega Navale ✆ 0924 33527

Facilities

Water On the quay.
Fuel On the quay (0800–1900). Recent reports suggest it is difficult to obtain fuel here.
Repairs Mechanical repairs can be carried out in the town. Chandlers.
Provisions Good shopping for all provisions in the town. Small fish market on the beach.
Eating out Restaurants and trattorias in the town around the square. Pizzeria near the harbour.
Other PO. Banks. ATMs. Italgaz and Camping Gaz. Bus to Palermo.

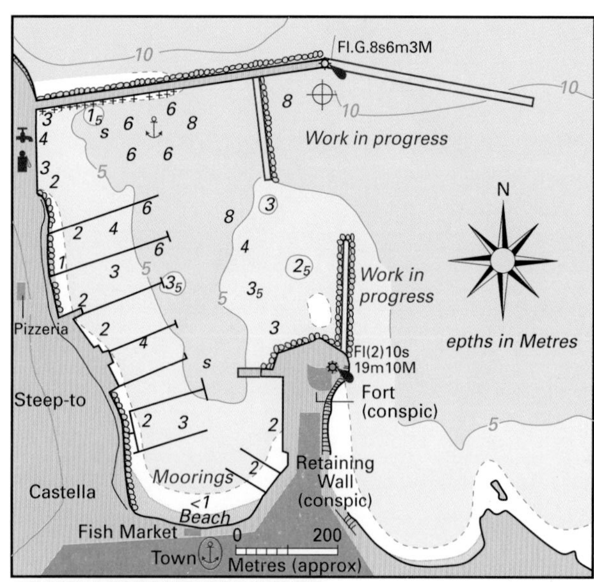

CASTELLAMMARE DEL GOLFO
⊕38°01′·85N 12°53′·0E

General

The old town, built on the steep slopes around the bay, is an attractive huddle of dun-coloured buildings connected by stairways, bridges and steep alleys. On the night I arrived for the first time the locals staged a huge firework display on the mole about 100m off my stern. At times the wind carried the burning cinders over the boat, causing not a little panic. In many Italian harbours summer firework displays are an unusual and exotic danger to consider.

The Doric temple and theatre at Segesta are well worth visiting – about half an hour by taxi. The temple was probably built sometime between 430 and 415BC and its form and construction is superb – many suggest it rivals the Parthenon. It was never finished, there is no roof (though there is the intriguing suggestion that it was built this way deliberately as an open air shrine) and the columns have not been fluted.

BALESTRATE

A harbour in Golfo di Castellamare, just under 6M ENE from Castellammare del Golfo.

Approach

The harbour construction has been completed for several years now, but the development of the port, part of the Italia Navigando Group, has slowed. The harbour is currently closed, but it is hoped that the pontoons and associated infrstructure will get the go ahead in the coming months, rather than years.

The approach is deep and free of dangers.

VHF Ch 16 (24hrs).

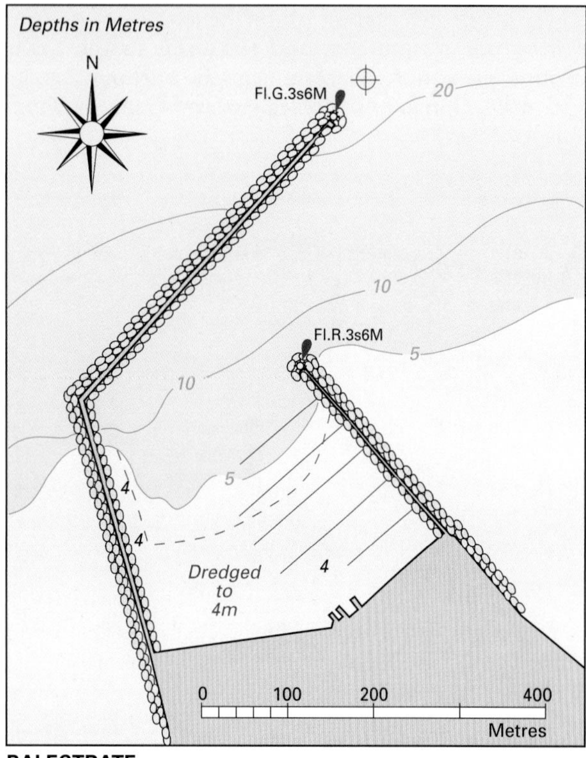

BALESTRATE
⊕38°03′·4N 13°00′·6E

Moorings

Data c.545 berths (when finished). Max LOA 40m. Depths 3–5m.

Berths Go stern or bows-to where directed. Care needed of ballasting along the inside of the breakwaters. Laid moorings to be installed.

Shelter Good shelter from the prevailing winds, although there may be some surge with strong NE winds.

Authorities Harbourmaster. A charge will be made.
Email portodibalestrate@libero.it
www.portodibalestrate.net

Facilities

Water and electricity (220V) to be installed. Slip and travel-lift bay. Most provisions, restaurants and bars in the town.

General

Although there are remains of a 6th-century BC Greek necropolis, Arab tombs and the 8th-century Calatubo castle nearby, the modern town of Balestrate dates from the 17th century when a tunny fishery was established here. The name is believed to date from the early 14th century, when the crossbow (*balestra*) was used to fire an arrow from the shore to determine the limit of the settlement from the state property inland. Balestrate means literally 'the shot from a crossbow'.

TERRASINI

Approach

A small fishing harbour situated approximately 1½ miles NE of Capo Rama.

VHF Ch 16.

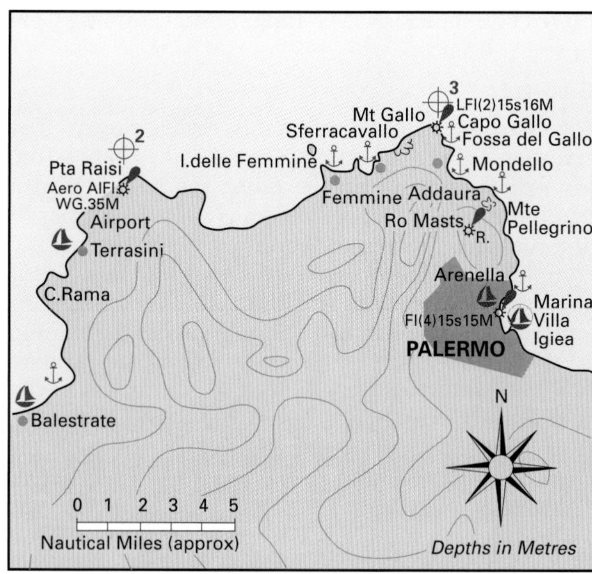

TERRASINI TO PALERMO

⊕2 1M N of Pta. Raisi 38°12′·4N 13°06′·5E
⊕3 1M N of Capo Gallo 38°14′·3N 13°19′·1E

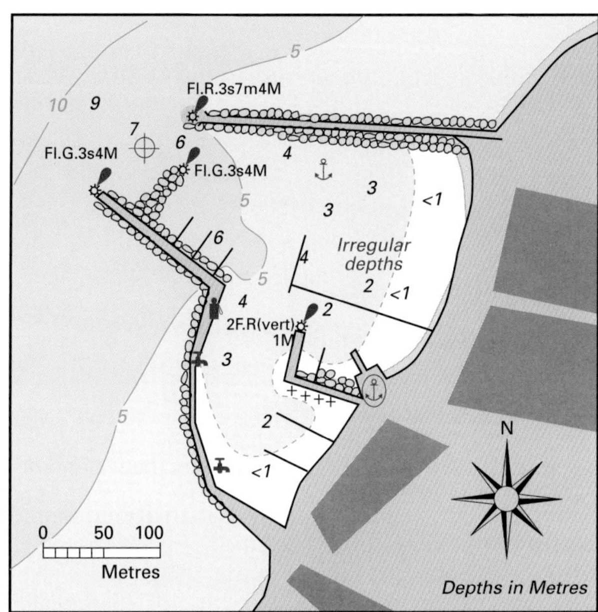

TERRASINI
⊕38°09´·6N 13°04´·8E

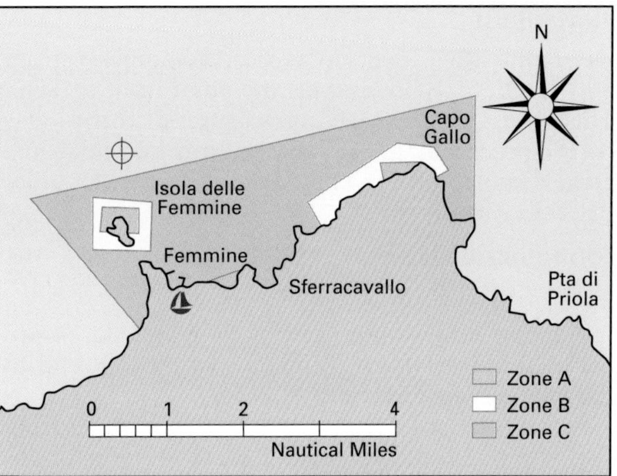

CAPO GALLO - ISOLA DELLE FEMMINE MARINE RESERVES
⊕1M N of I. delle Femmine 38°13′·82N 13°14′·10E WGS84

Dangers Care is needed as the harbour is prone to silting and depths may not be as indicated. Proceed with care.

Mooring

Data 200 berths. Max LOA 12m. Depths <1–6m.

Berth Go stern or bows-to or alongside where possible. The harbour is usually crowded with fishing boats and you may have to go alongside a fishing boat if possible.

Shelter Normally adequate in the summer although with strong W–NW winds there is a surge.

Anchorage It may be possible to anchor under the N breakwater with a long line ashore. Good holding on sand.

Facilities

Water On the quay.
Fuel On the S breakwater.
Repairs 16-ton crane. Mechanical repairs possible.
Provisions Some provisions in the village.
Eating out Restaurants.

Capo Gallo – Isola delle Femmine Marine Reserve

Established in 2003, this marine reserve covers the areas around the tiny Isola delle Femmine and Capo Gallo and is zoned as shown in the plan.
At present the marine reserve is under the authority of the Comune di Palermo and the rules and regulations listed below are provisional.

Zone A
Navigation, anchoring and mooring, swimming, diving and all types of fishing are prohibited.

Zone B
Unregulated navigation, anchoring and mooring are prohibited.
Navigation by sail, oar and motor (up to 5kns) is permitted for access to controlled moorings set out by reserve authorities.
Mooring is permitted in zones where mooring buoys are provided. Swimming, guided underwater diving trips regulated by the reserve authorities, authorised dives, and fishing with static lines and rods are permitted (residents only).

Zone C
Unregulated motor navigation, anchoring and mooring, and all fishing are prohibited.
Navigation by sail, oar and motor (up to 10 knots), and anchoring and mooring in authorised zones are permitted.
Swimming and authorised dives is permitted.
Fishing with static lines and rods, is permitted (residents only; non-residents only if authorised).

Capitaneria di Porto di Palermo ✆ 091 604 3111

AMP Capo Gallo – Isola delle Femmine ✆ 091 584 802
Email Info@ampcapogallo-isola.org
www.ampcapogallo-isola.org

Capo Gallo looking east

Punta Raisi

Off Punta Raisi the depths decrease quickly from 500–800m to 100m and off the point itself to 17m. This abrupt decrease in depths causes disturbed seas off the point and, in bad weather, it is best to keep a good distance off the cape. Behind Punta Raisi lies Palermo Airport.

Torre Pozzillo

⊕ 38°11'·1N 13°08'·2E

A hauling and storage facility is being developed between Terrasini and Femmine, at the NE end of the Palermo airport runway.

A travel-hoist bay and slipway are sheltered from the NW by a stub mole, and there are workshops and hardstanding ashore. The facility is reported to haul yachts up to around 14m, although no details of depths or hauling capacity was available at the time of writing.

FEMMINE (Zone C)

Approach

A small fishing harbour lying approximately three miles W of Capo Gallo. The small islet of I. delle Femmine is easily identified.

Mooring

Data Max LOA c.15m. Depths 1–4m.

Berths Go stern or bows-to or alongside where possible. The harbour is usually crowded with fishing boats and it is often impossible to find a berth.

Shelter Normally adequate in the summer although uncomfortable with NW–W winds.

Note Work is planned to extend the N breakwater.

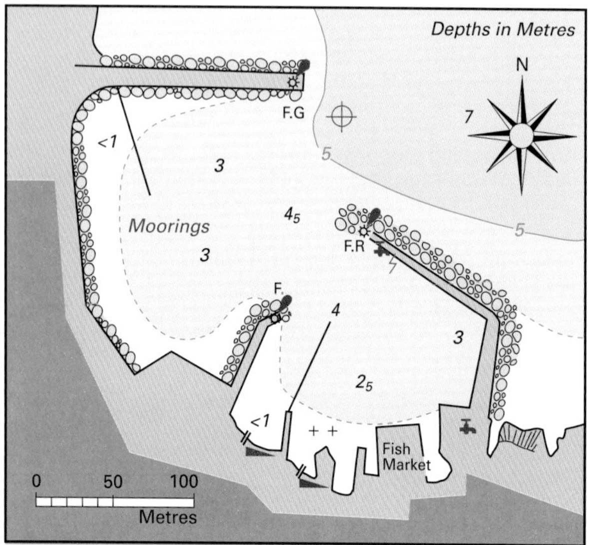

FEMMINE
⊕38°12'·1N 13°14'·1E

Isola delle Femmine looking SE with Femmine harbour behind

Facilities

Services Water on the quay. Electricity at some berths on the inner breakwater.
Provisions Some provisions in the village.
Eating out Restaurants and bars.
Other PO. Bank.

SFERRACAVALLO (Zone C)

Approach

A small harbour about two miles W of Capo Gallo.

By night The end of the mole is lit 2F.R(vert)6m3M.

Note Care is needed under the breakwater where depths are uneven. Yachts drawing more than 1·5m should proceed with caution and berth on the extremity of the breakwater.

Mooring

Data Max LOA 15m. Depths 2–5m.

Berth Go stern or bows-to where possible under the mole. The harbour is usually crowded with fishing boats and it can be difficult to find a berth.

Shelter Adequate in the summer although it can be uncomfortable with W–NW winds.

Facilities

Water On the quay.
Repairs 20-ton crane.
Provisions Most provisions in the village.
Eating out Restaurants and bars ashore.

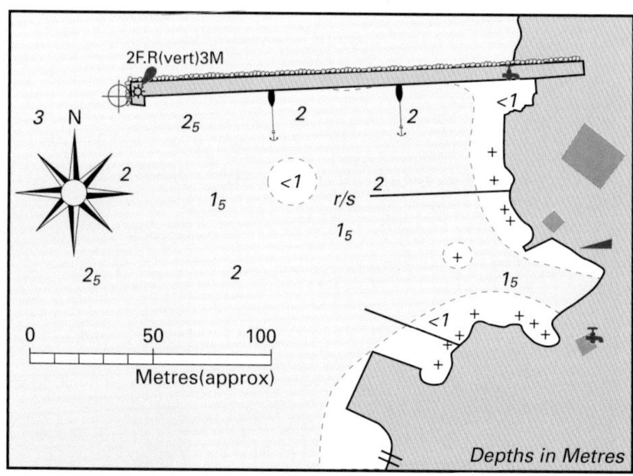

SFERRACAVALLO
⊕38°12'·0N 13°16'·5E

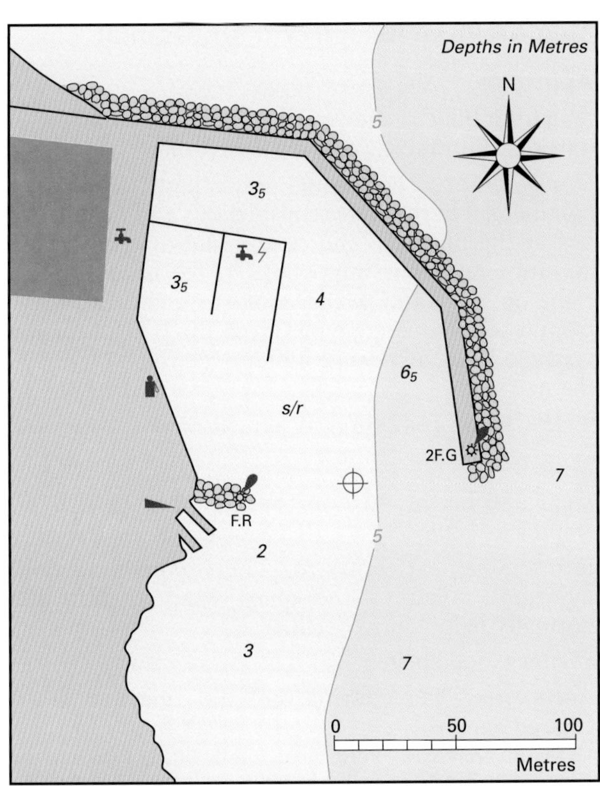

FOSSA DEL GALLO
⊕38°13′·4N 13°19′·4E

FOSSA DEL GALLO (Zone B)

A small harbour directly under Capo Gallo.

Data C.150 berths. Max LOA 15m. Depths 2–6·5m.

Facilities

Water and fuel on the quay. 65-ton travel-lift. Some repairs. Restaurants and bars ashore.

Motomar ☏ 091 453 145
www.motomarcdm.it

BAIA DI MONDELLO (Zone C)

BA 963
Italian 256

The bay lying one mile S of Capo Gallo. Care is needed of the underwater rock in the NE of the bay. Local boats are kept on moorings in the bay. A yacht can anchor in the bay keeping clear of the area where there are permanent moorings.

MONDELLO

A small harbour about half a mile NW of Punta Mondello.

Data Max LOA 12m. Depths 1–2·5m.

The harbour is usually crowded with small power boats and it is difficult if not impossible to find a berth.

Punta Celesi

⊕ 38°11′·5N 13°21′·1E

A small mole extends in a NW direction from the point. It is just 50m long and depths behind it are 1–2m. Anchoring is reported prohibited on the W side of the mole.

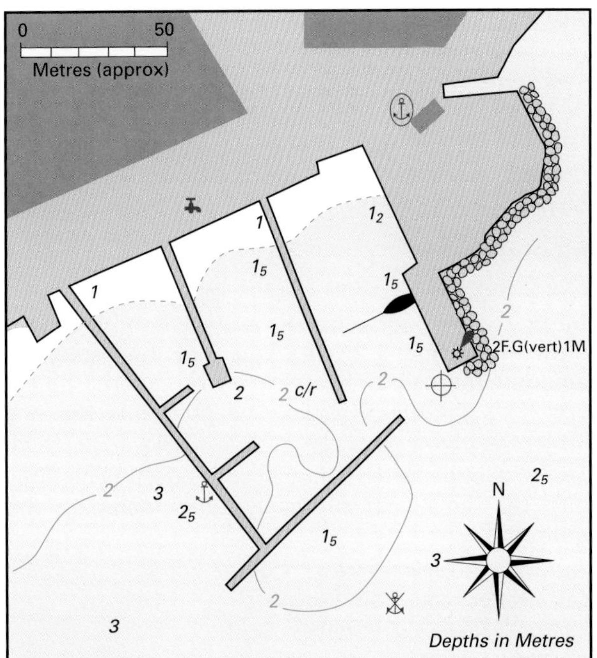

MONDELLO
⊕38°12′·25N 13°19′·75E

ADDAURA

Approach

A small harbour approximately 2½ miles SE of Mondello.

Dangers Care is needed of underwater debris off the end of the breakwater.

Mooring

Data c.75 berths. Max LOA c.12m. Depths 2–8m.

Berth Go stern or bows-to where directed. The harbour is usually full but it it is worth poking your nose in to see if there is a berth.

Shelter Adequate from the summer prevailing winds.

Facilities

Water and fuel on the quay. Restaurant and bar.

Motonautica Addaura ☏ 091 450 111

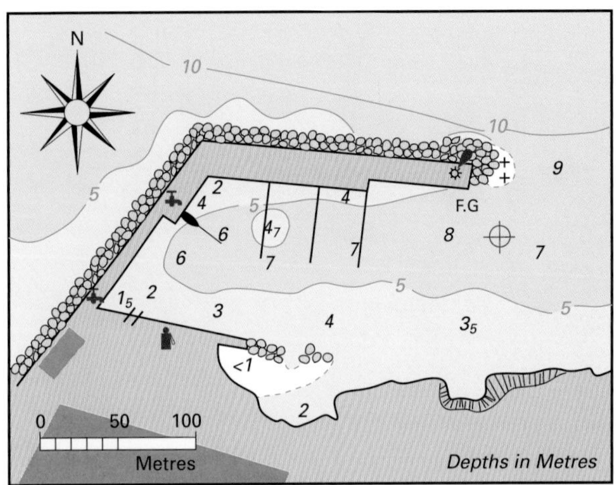

ADDAURA
⊕38°11′·55N 13°21′·3E

V. SICILY

ARENELLA (Cala dei Normanni)

Approach

A small harbour approximately one mile N of Palermo commercial harbour.

By night A night entry is not recommended.

VHF Ch 16, 11 (24hrs).

Mooring

Data Max LOA c.18m. Depths 1–5m.

Berth The harbour is usually crowded and it can be difficult to find a berth. You may find a space amongst the fishing boats or off one of the flimsy pontoons on the W side. The pontoons are not always in place.

Shelter Good shelter although some swell penetrates into the outer part of the harbour including the pontoons.

Authorities Ormeggiatori. Charge band 6.

Cala dei Normanni ✆ 091 540 264
Email info@caladeinormanni.it

Facilities

Water and electricity at most berths. Some provisions and local restaurants.

General

The setting under the fort and faded tenements is most attractive, if a little run-down. Principally geared up to store and launch small local craft, visiting yachts may be able to squeeze in here, although many berths are for max. LOA 10m.

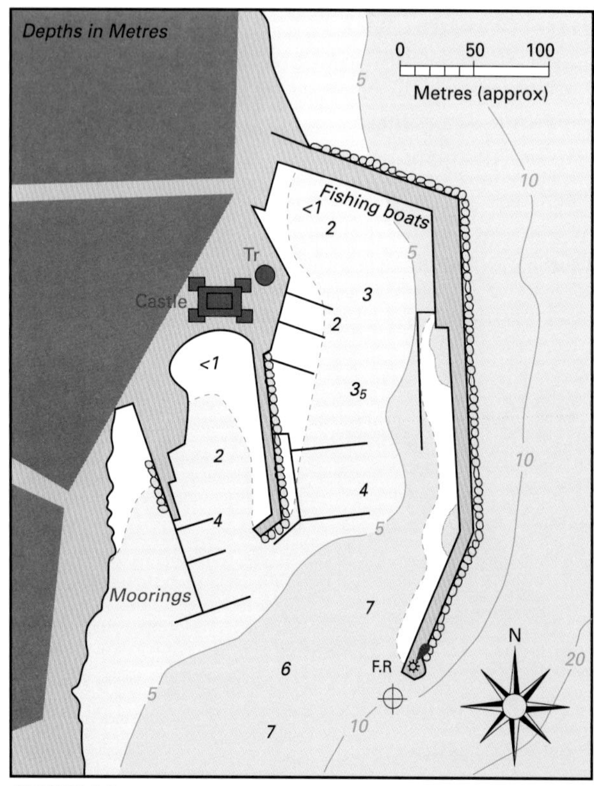

ARENELLA
⊕38°08´·9N 13°22´·5E

MARINA VILLA IGIEA (Porto Acquasanta)

Approach

A marina built at the N end of Palermo commercial harbour. Entrance is easy in all weather.

Conspicuous The cranes and gantries in the commercial harbour are conspicuous and the marina lies at the northern end of the line of cranes. The entrance proper is impossible to see until you are right up to it and yachts seem to enter and leave from a solid concrete wall. From the E head for the Castello Utici, an orange building on the bluff above the marina.

VHF Ch 16, 74 (24hrs).

Mooring

Data 380 berths. Visitors' berths. Max LOA 65m. Depths 2–12m.

Berth Stern or bows-to where directed. Laid moorings tailed to the quay. Marina staff will normally help you to berth.

Shelter Good shelter.

Authorities Harbourmaster and marina staff. Charge band 6.

✉ Marina Villa Igiea, Porto Acquasanta, 90142 Palermo, Sicily ✆ 091 364 123 *Fax* 091 364 225
Email marigiea@tin.it
Email info@marinavillaigiea.com
www.marinavillaigiea.com

Facilities

Services Water and electricity (220/380V) at all berths. WC and shower block (reported to be in poor condition). Laundry service.
Fuel On the quay.
Repairs 50-ton crane. 40-ton boatmover. Slipway. Most mechanical repairs. Other yacht repairs can be arranged. Chandlers nearby.
Provisions Minimarkets and *alimentari* near the marina. Better shopping and a market about 1km away.
Eating out Several local restaurants nearby and at the Hotel Villa Igiea.
Other See Palermo.

General

Marina Villa Igiea has recently become part of a group of marinas, and the facilities have generally improved. Expect pontoon layout to change as the numbers of berths are expanded.

The marina is tucked away under the high walls of the commercial harbour on one side and the decaying suburb of Villa Igiea on the other. It can get a bit airless in the summer heat, but it does offer a secure if expensive base from which to visit Palermo. You can get a bus from Villa Igiea or get a taxi into downtown Palermo.

On the rocky bluff on the northwest side of the marina is the Grand Hotel Villa Igiea. It is a hotel from the grand age of travelling, all faded umber and sandstone, with the most wonderful bar and restaurant looking out over the Bay of Palermo. If you do one thing here you must at least have a drink

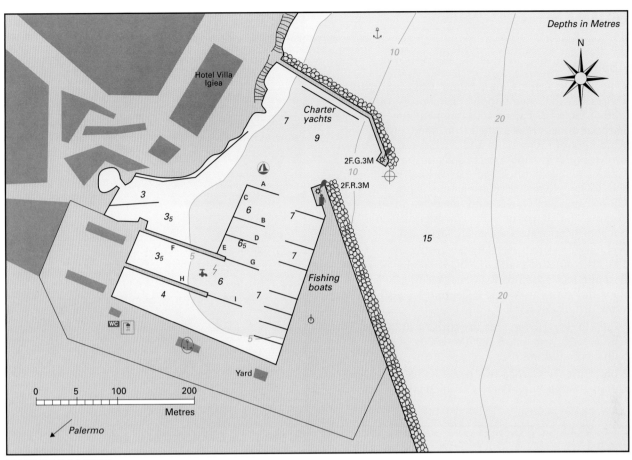

MARINA VILLA IGIEA
⊕38°08′·66N 13°22′·46E WGS84

The approaches to Marina Villa Igiea looking west. The entrance is barely visible

in the bar as the sun goes down and if the mood takes you, stay for dinner as well. It is not overly expensive and the surroundings and service will transport you back to an earlier time of dressing for dinner and 'martinis at six, dear?'

Marina Villa Igiea looking north

PALERMO

BA 963
Italian 255

Approach

Conspicuous Capo Gallo, Monte Gallo and Monte Pellegrino, the mountainous promontory on the W side of Golfo di Palermo and immediately N of the harbour are easily identified from some distance off. A number of radio masts and a white circular tower on Monte Pellegrino are conspicuous and Utreggio Castle, a square brick red 'castle-like' building on the lower slopes, is conspicuous from the east. Closer in, the cranes and derricks in the new commercial harbour are conspicuous and the harbour breakwaters are easily identified.

By night Use the light on Capo Gallo LFl(2)15s40m16M and the light in the N of the harbour Fl(4)15s15m15M. The Aero Fl.R lights on the radio masts on Monte Pellegrino are visible from some distance.

VHF Ch 11, 16 for port authorities (0800–2000). Ch 11, 12 for pilots (0700–1900). Ch 09 for Salpancore (24hrs).

Note Care is needed of ferries and other craft entering and leaving Porto Commerciale.

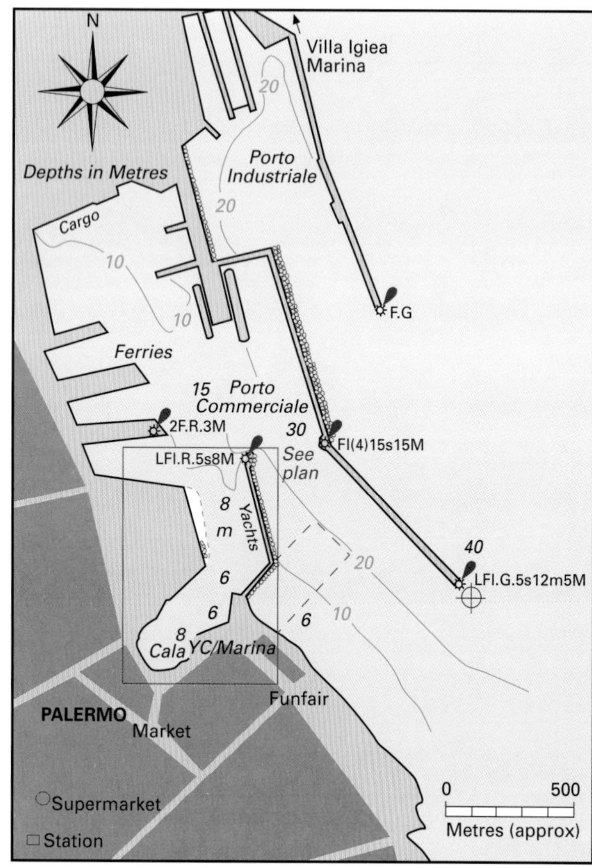

PALERMO
⊕38°07´·3N 13°22´·7E

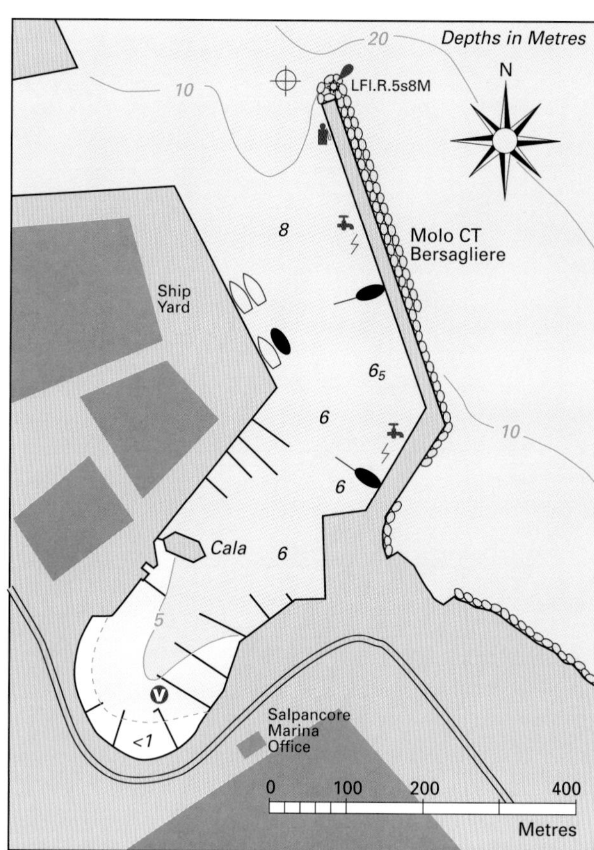

PALERMO - CALA/MOLO BERSAGLIERE
⊕38°07´·55N 13°22´·2E

Mooring

Yachts should head for Molo Bersagliere and the various club berths behind here.

Berth Go stern or bows-to where possible between the club berths. The outer end of the mole from the fuel station is administered by the YC Italiano. From the crook of the mole to the root there are the private berths of the Club Mediterraneo. Most of the SE side of the *cala* beyond the berths on the mole are now also yacht berths and you may be able to negotiate a berth here. Getting a berth here is a matter of fitting in where you can. (Club Salpancore has been recommended.) Laid moorings at most club berths. For an overnight stay you may be able to go on the fuel quay after it closes around 1900. You will have to be off when it opens in the morning. Larger yachts have berthed alongside laid-up tugs and ferries opposite the mole.

Shelter Excellent. Yachts have wintered afloat here.

Authorities Harbourmaster and customs. Papers are regularly checked here. *Ormeggiatori*. Charge band 5.

Salpancore ✆ 091 331 055 / 393 992 2120 *Fax* 091 332 128
Email salpancore@infocom.it

Yacht Club del Mediterraneo ✆ 091 581 837

Nixe Yachting ✆ 091 625 7990 / 338 450 4358

Societa Gianottieri Palermo ✆ 091 328 467 *Fax* 091 582 650

Nautilus Marine ✆ 091 611 8733 / 335 781 7647

Lega Navale ✆ 091 581 940

Palermo looking SSW across Molo Bersagliere towards the city centre *Sandro Bedessi, FOTOTECA ENIT*

Facilities

Services Water and electricity at most berths.
Fuel On the quay.
Repairs A 15-ton crane and mobile crane up to 50 tons. Slipways up to 100 tons. Mechanical and engineering repairs. GRP and wood repairs. Electrical and electronic repairs. Sailmakers. Chandlers. Good hardware and tool shops.
Provisions Excellent shopping for all provisions. There are large supermarkets near the railway station and an excellent street market near the harbour. Ice can be delivered.
Eating out Excellent restaurants, trattorias and pizzerias.
Other PO. Banks. ATMs. Hospital. Italgaz and Camping Gaz. Hire cars. Buses and trains all over Sicily. Ferries to Genoa, Naples, Sardinia and the Aeolian Islands. Internal and international flights to most major European airports.

General

The harbour is oily and dirty, the immediate surroundings seedy and begrimed, but Palermo has such a varied and rich history that scattered here and there are architectural gems, testimony to what once was.

The city was founded by the Phoenicians and became an important Carthaginian stronghold until the Romans conquered it in 254BC. The Saracens (AD831–1072) made Palermo the centre of Arab civilisation in Sicily and bestowed upon it an architectural influence that can be seen today. In the 11th and 12th centuries the Normans added greatly to the architecture and with the accession of the Hohenstaufen dynasty, Palermo reached its zenith under Frederick.

An intelligent, able and kind ruler, he promoted the arts and built many beautiful monuments to his reign. These latter are a unique blend of Norman and Arabic forms. Interested visitors should consult a guidebook for the location of the numerous monuments to the Norman period to be found in and around Palermo. The Aragons and the Bourbons followed the Normans and the city was finally liberated by Garibaldi in 1860. In the Second World War, Palermo was badly damaged by allied air attacks and the post-war buildings are today little more than slums.

Palermo is the power centre of the mafia in Sicily and three days after I left on my first visit here in September 1982 General della Chiesa and his wife were murdered in a mafia ambush. Typically, no witnesses to the murder came forward even though it happened in broad daylight in the middle of Palermo on a crowded street I regularly walked up and down.

Most visitors will see little of mafia activities and apart from the normal precautions against minor criminals like muggers and pickpockets that need to be taken in any large city, you do not need to take special precautions against the mafia here. Their activities are more inclined to big business, getting motorway and harbour contracts, removing the judiciary who cannot be corrupted, and dealing in a few shiploads of Class A drugs.

Isola di Ustica

This small island lies about 36 miles NE of Capo San Vito. The island is not very high (the summit Mt Guardia dei Turchi, is 250m (820ft) high), but is usually visible from some distance off. It is of volcanic origin and consequently a fertile and well-cultivated island. A signal station on the summit and the white tower of the lighthouse on Punta Gavazzi are both conspicuous marks. The harbour Cala Santa Maria is on the NE side.

The history of the island is littered with accounts of massacres and mayhem. It was inhabited around 2000BC though little has been excavated to tell us about the inhabitants. The Greeks called the island Osteodes (island of bones) after the remains of 6,000 mutinous soldiers from Carthage who were abandoned here to die of hunger and thirst. The Romans called it Ustum, 'burnt', from the black basalt of which the island is largely composed. In the 18th century the Bourbons attempted to colonise the island, only to have the entire colony massacred by pirates, all bar two who escaped to tell the awful tale. Towards the end of the 18th century the Bourbons fortified the island and successfully colonised it at last, the venerable forefathers of today's population.

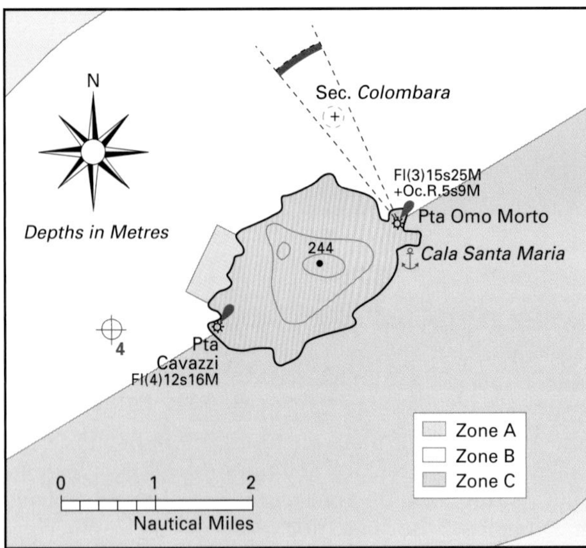

ISOLA DI USTICA MARINE RESERVE

⊕4 1M W of Pta Cavazzi (Ustica)
38°41'·5N 13°08'·0E

Isola di Ustica Marine Reserve

A marine reserve has been established around the Isola di Ustica extending 3M off the coast.

Zone A covers the area between Caletta and Cala Sidoti on the west coast, Zone B the NW coast and Zone C the SE coast.

Zone A
Navigation, access, short and long-term stays and any kind of fishing are all prohibited. Swimming is permitted only in the area of Caletta and Cala Sidoti, which can be reached by land.

Zone B
Navigation, short and long-term stays and sport fishing with static lines are permitted. Underwater fishing is prohibited.

Zone C
The same laws apply as in Zone B.

Capitaneria di Porto di Palermo ✆ 091 604 3111

CALA SANTA MARIA

Approach

Conspicuous The village of Ustica and a small fort-like blockhouse S of the harbour are conspicuous. Closer in, the breakwater is easily identified.

VHF Ch 16.

Mooring

Data Max LOA 15m. Depths 1–7m.

Berth Go stern or bows-to or alongside where there is room leaving the hydrofoil berth clear. The harbour is very crowded with fishing boats and in the summer with yachts. The bottom is sand and rock, but much of it is foul with permanent moorings.

Shelter Good except with SE–E winds which if strong and prolonged could make the harbour dangerous.

Authorities Harbourmaster and customs.

Facilities

Water On the quay. A sign nearby prohibits the use of the water for washing.
Fuel On the quay.
Repairs Limited mechanical repairs.
Provisions Most provisions can be obtained in the village but prices are higher than Sicily, presumably to pay for transport. Fresh fruit and vegetables are limited. Fish is plentiful and varied. Ice from the factory at the harbour.

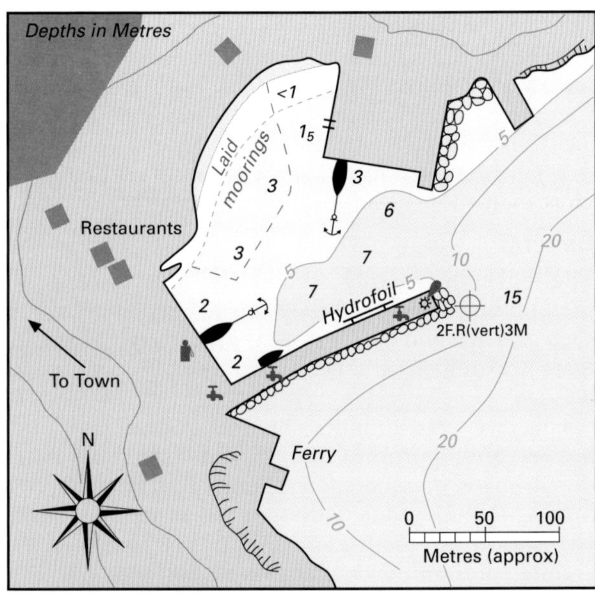

CALA SANTA MARIA (USTICA)
⊕38°42´·4N 13°11´·9E

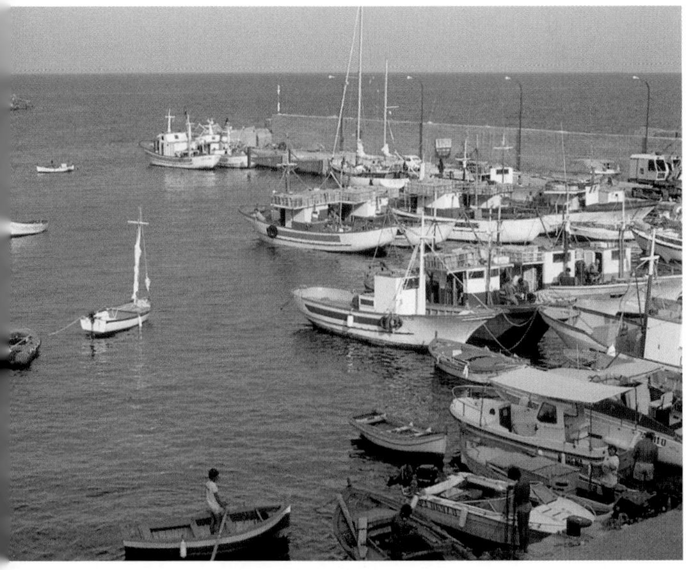
Isola di Ustica. Cala Santa Maria looking NE to the entrance. Sometimes it seems like you could walk across the harbour on the boats moored up inside

Eating out Good restaurants near the harbour and others in the village.
Other PO. Bank. ATM. Camping Gaz. Compressed air station at the harbour for diving bottles. Ferry and hydrofoil to Palermo and Naples.

General

Although the small harbour is crowded in the summer (you can just about walk from one side of the harbour to the other over the boats), Ustica is a delightful place to visit. The island is a green and fertile place and the houses and shops have wonderful murals painted on the outside walls. The surrounding coast offers excellent snorkelling and scuba diving and in July there is an International Festival of Underwater Activities.

Sicily

PORTICELLO (Porticello Santa Flavia, Ponticello)

Approach

Care must be taken of Scoglio Formica lying about one mile E of Porticello. It is awash and easily identified.

Conspicuous Capo Zafferano is a sheer rocky bluff rising to a hill 223m (732ft) high. It appears as an island from a distance. From the E a tower and a large hotel to the S of the harbour are conspicuous and closer in the harbour moles will be seen.

By night Use the light on Capo Zafferano Fl(3)WR.10s34m16/12M (298°-R-344° over Scoglio Formica).

Mooring

Data Max LOA c.15m. Depths 1·5–4·5m.

The harbour is very crowded with fishing boats and it can be difficult to find a place. Try stern or bows-to on the S mole or ask permission to go alongside a fishing boat. In calm weather it may be better to anchor to the S of the harbour in 4–5m. The harbour is very dirty with oil and rubbish.

Shelter Excellent.

Authorities Customs.

Facilities

Water Is rationed in the village.
Fuel On the quay for fishing boats.
Repairs A 60-ton slipway. Mobile crane to 50 tons available. Mechanical repairs. Wood repairs.
Provisions Most provisions can be obtained. Ice from the factory on the quay.
Eating out There is a fish restaurant by the harbour and other restaurants scattered around the village.
Other PO. Bank. Regular bus to Palermo.

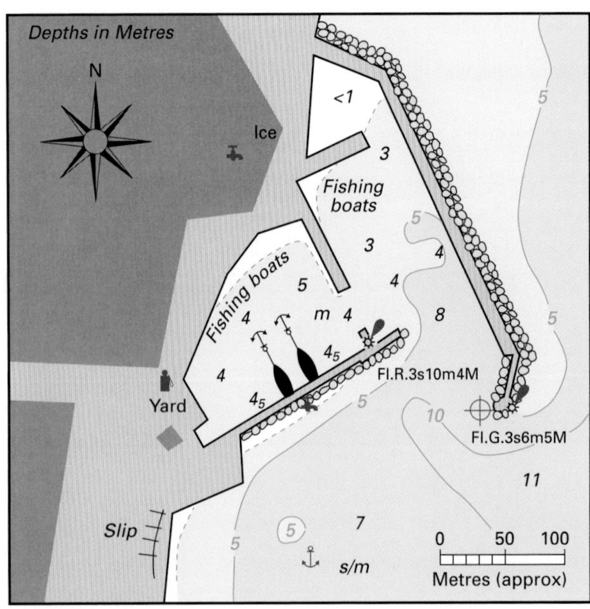

PORTICELLO
⊕38°05′·1N 13°32′·6E

General

A rather plain village in an attractive setting. It is not frequented by tourists in numbers, and its attractions are somewhat diminished for the yachtsman because of the crowded dirty harbour.

SAN NICOLA L'ARENA

Approach

Lies about eight miles SE of Porticello. It is easily recognised by the castle built near the water.

VHF Ch 14, 16 (0800–2000).

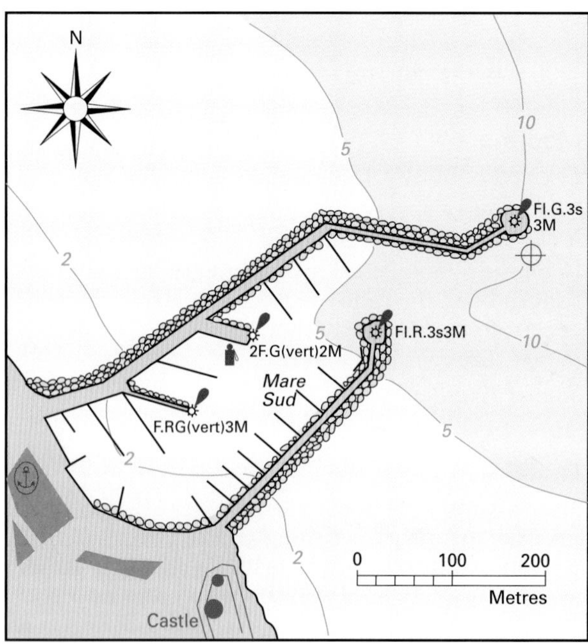

SAN NICOLA L'ARENA
⊕38°01'·1N 13°37'·2E

Mooring

Data 450 berths. 45 visitors' berths. Max LOA 20m. Depths <1–5m.

Berth The harbour is divided up between local fishing boats and the two co-operatives who arrange yacht berths. Mare Sud operates the outer pontoons on the E side. Go stern or bows-to where directed. Laid moorings tailed to the quay.

Shelter Good shelter.

Authorities Customs. *Ormeggiatori*. Charge band 3.

Mare Sud ✆ 091 812 5946 *Fax* 091 810 1207
Email posta@maresud.it
www.maresud.it

Club Nautico ✆ /*Fax* 091 812 5002 ✆ 339 224 6622
Email info@clubnauticomarinasannicola.it
www.clubnauticomarinasannicola.it

Facilities

Services Water and electricity at most berths.
Fuel On the mole running off the NW breakwater.
Repairs 70/15/9-ton cranes. Slipway. Limited mechanical repairs.
Provisions Most provisions can be found.
Eating out Restaurants in the summer.

General

The castle dates back to Arab times and is now a nightclub. The hinterland is attractive – lush orchards backed by high hills.

TERMINI IMERESE

BA 963
Italian 249

Approach

The chimneys of the oil terminal to the E and the apartment blocks of the town are visible from some distance off. Closer in, the outer mole is easily

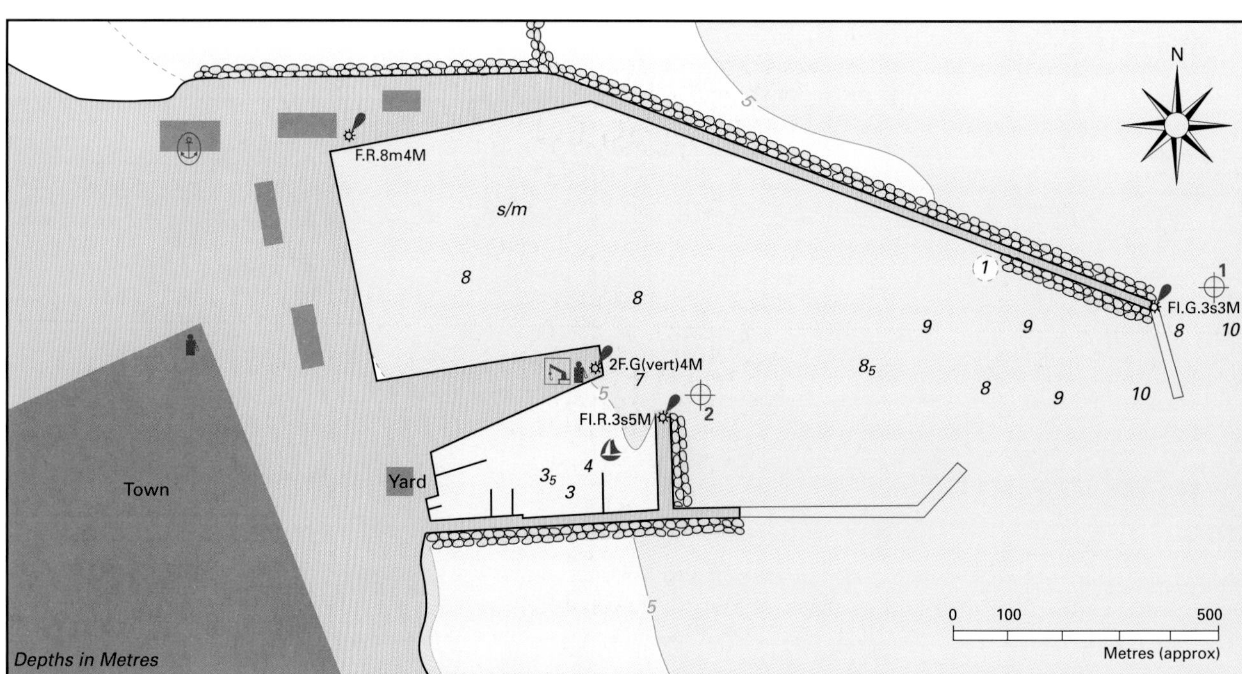

TERMINI IMERESE
⊕1 37°59'·20N 13°43'·49E WGS84
⊕2 37°59'·17N 13°42'·65E WGS84

identified. The oil terminal jetty is over 1M long, and the head lies just under 1·5M E of the main harbour breakwater.

Note Care needed of the piles running down the inside of the E mole.

VHF Ch 14, 16.

Mooring

Data 30 visitors' berths. Max LOA c.25m. Depths 3–5m.

Berth Yachts should head for the S basin tucked under the inner breakwater. Go stern or bows-to where directed or convenient. These pontoons are open to wash from commercial traffic, but tucked inside there is better shelter. Alternatively go alongside on the commercial quay which is somewhat dirty and dusty.

Shelter Good shelter.

Authorities Harbourmaster and customs. *Ormeggiatori*. A charge is made.

Artemar Cantiere Nautico ✆ 091 811 1890
Email info@artemarnautica.it

Mare Sud ✆ /*Fax* 091 819 0370
Email posta@maresud.it

Facilities

Water On the quay.
Fuel On the quay opposite the yacht berths.
Repairs 20-ton cranes. 150-ton slipway. Some mechanical repairs.
Provisions Good shopping for all provisions in the town.
Eating out Restaurants, trattorias and pizzerias.
Other PO. Banks. ATMs. Italgaz and Camping Gaz. Bus and train to Messina and Palermo.

General

Don't be put off by the harbour. And tucked into a desolate spot with a fair walk into town it isn't very inspiring. The Alta Citta (upper city) is an attractive place with a large cathedral. The lower city was a colony of nearby Himera and continued under the Romans as an important spa town. The mineral springs are still here and are said to be beneficial in the treatment of arthritis.

CEFALÙ (Porto Nuovo, Presidiana)

Approach

Conspicuous The precipitous conical hill (269m/822ft high) directly behind the harbour is conspicuous from a considerable distance off. Closer in, the village of Cefalù with the cathedral prominent and the white lighthouse on a rocky spur by the harbour are conspicuous. The harbour mole is easily identified.

By night Use the main light on Capo Cefalù Fl.5s80m25M. An illuminated cross on a cliff behind the cathedral is visible from the north.

VHF Ch 16.

Mooring

Presidiana

Data Limited visitors' berths. Max LOA 18m. Depths 1·5–5m.

Berth Limited berths inside the fuel quay in summer only. Go stern or bows-to, keeping well off the quay. Laid moorings tailed to the quay. Late arrivals may be able to go alongside the fuel quay overnight. Larger yachts berth stern-to on the outside off the pier. Many of the berths are used by fishing boats and there are a lot of laid mooring lines around – care is needed not to get lines around the prop. The hydrofoil uses the end of the pier.

Cefalù town and promontory looking ESE

V. SICILY

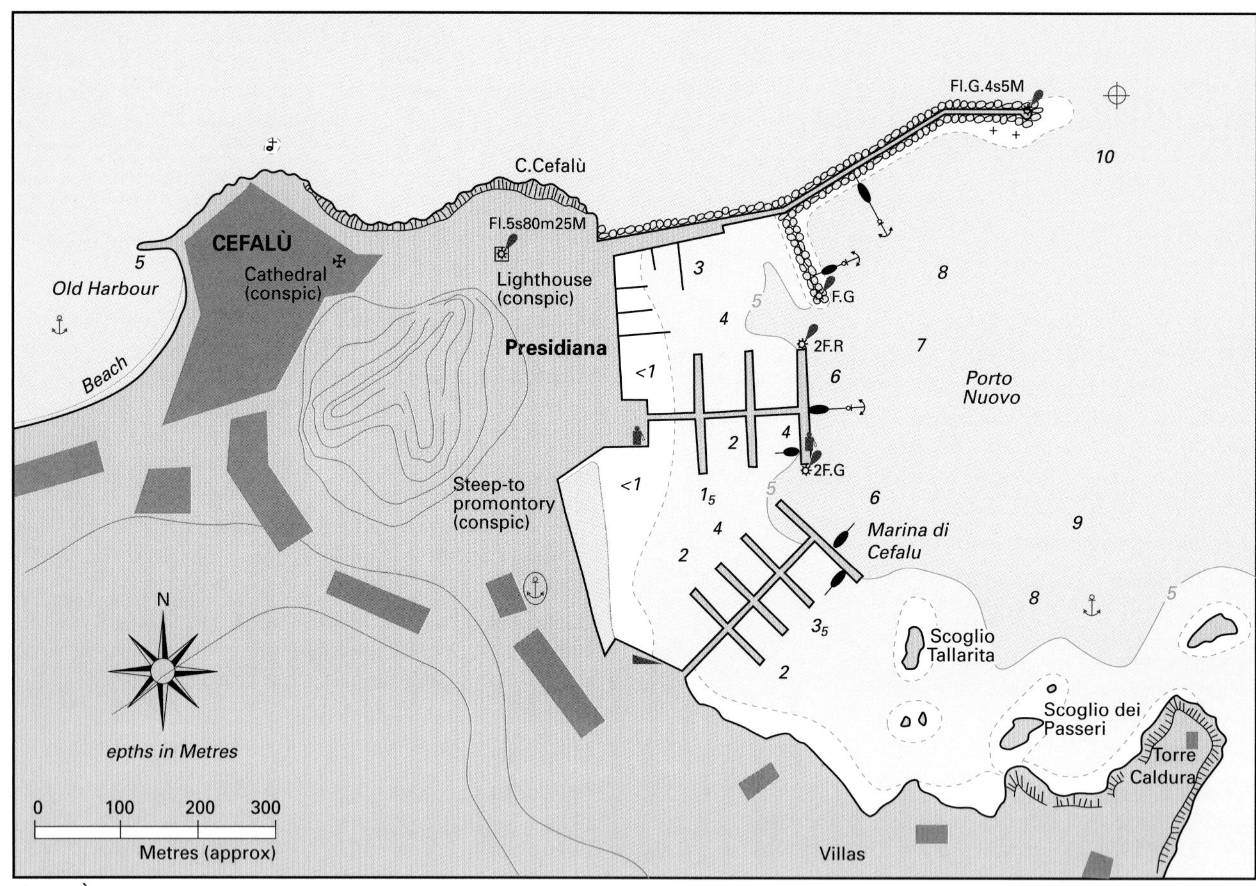

CEFALÙ
⊕38°02´·55N 14°02´·28E WGS84

Marina di Cefalu

Data 150 berths. Max LOA 40m. Depths 2–6m.

Berths Stern or bows-to on the new pontoons in the SW corner of the bay. Laid moorings tailed to the quay.

Shelter Good shelter from the prevailing winds, although NE–E winds can send in a bit of slop at night which can make it uncomfortable in some berths. With strong onshore winds a considerable swell is pushed in here and you may have to vacate the harbour.

Authorities Port police and customs. *Ormeggiatori*. Charge band 5.

Marina Service Cefalu ✆ /*Fax* 366 051 300 ✆ 338 784 9155
Marina di Cefalu ✆ /*Fax* 0921 420 933 ✆ 348 437 5878
Email info@marinacefalu.it
www.marinacefalu.it

Anchorage Anchor off to the E of the marina. Creep in as far as possible as the bottom comes up slowly. It is also possible to anchor and take a long line ashore to the breakwater N of the stub ballast mole. The bottom is mud and weed but not everywhere good holding.

Facilities

Services Water and electricity at most berths. Showers and toilets at the marina.
Fuel On the end of the pier.
Repairs Limited mechanical repairs only.
Provisions Good shopping for all provisions in the town about 20 minutes' walk away.
Eating out Good restaurants, trattorias and pizzerias in the town.
Other PO. Banks. ATMs. Camping Gaz and Italgaz. Rail and bus connections to Palermo and Messina.

General

Cefalù is a bustling tourist resort built about the original picturesque fishing village that juts into the sea under the shadow of the rocky promontory. It possesses a fine Norman cathedral begun by King Roger in 1131 for deliverance from a shipwreck which remains one of the best-preserved examples of its type. The harbour is somewhat remote from the town, but it is well worth a walk around the promontory to see it.

Cefalù old harbour (Porto Vecchio)

A yacht can anchor in 2–5m off the beach under the town in calm weather. It is a pleasant place to be and close to the amenities of the town.

Note The authorities in this area keenly enforce a law which prohibits anchoring or motor-sailing within 300m of the coast. Fines over €100 for a first offence have been applied.

SANTE AGATA (Sant'Agata di Militello)

A new harbour awaiting further development which is presently used by hydrofoils running to the Lipari Islands. It is likely that it has been built as a ferry port for the islands given that Milazzo is now too

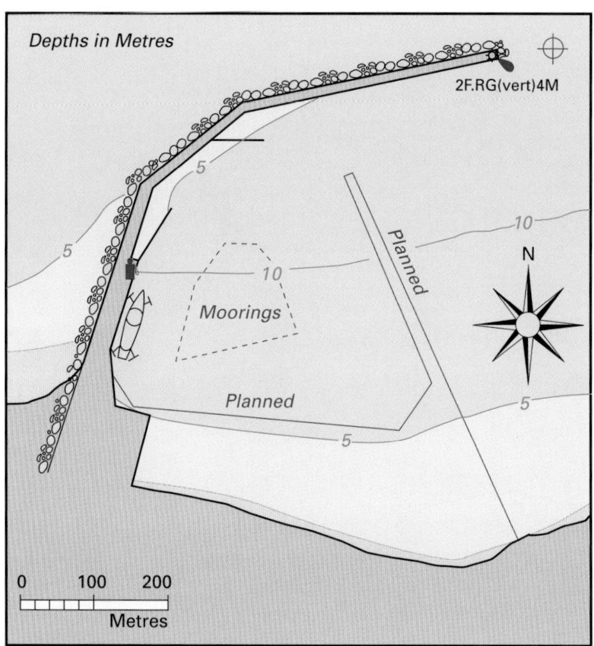

SANT' AGATA DI MILITELLO
⊕38°04'·5N 14°37'·4E

crowded for the number of hydrofoils running services.

Two pontoons have been installed and used by charter companies. Visitors permitted when charter boats out. Care needed of shallows on the N side of each pontoon.

The harbour is not yet complete but affords some shelter. When finished shelter will be nearly all-round and it may be a useful stopover.

There are no services, but there is a fuel quay near the hydrofoil berth.

Sicilmarine ✆ 0941 722 933
Yachting Management ✆ 0941 336 392

CAPO D'ORLANDO (BAGNOLI)

Approach

The lighthouse on Capo d'Orlando and the village on the W side of the cape are easily identified.

By night Use the light on Capo d'Orlando LFl(2)12s16M. A night entry is not recommended.

VHF Ch 09.

Dangers The harbour is subject to silting. The entrance is buoyed and care is needed.

Mooring

Data c.50 berths. Max LOA c.15m. Depths <1–4m.

Berth Where directed. Yachts in transit rely on permanent berth-holders being away. Laid moorings tailed to the quay and mooring lines at some berths.

Shelter Poor at present. Any ground swell outside appears to penetrate into the harbour. Local boats are kept pulled some distance off the pontoons and many use springs on dock lines to minimise the snatching.

Authorities Harbourmaster. Yacht club staff. Charge band 4.

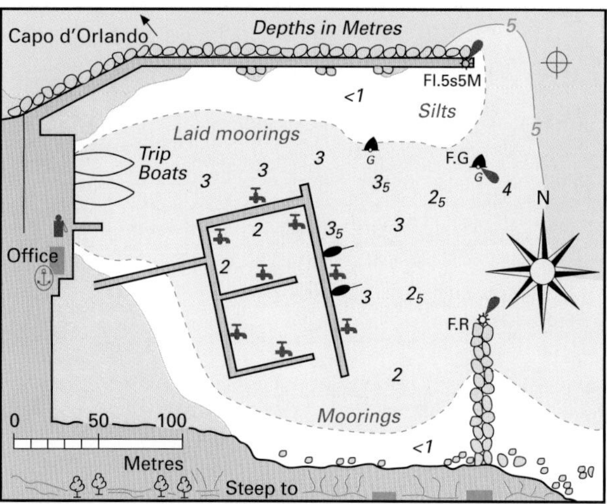

MARINA CAPO D'ORLANDO
⊕38°09'·49N 14°46'·63E WGS84

Anchorage In calm weather a yacht can anchor in the bay E of Capo d'Orlando.

Note There are plans to develop a 600-berth marina here. No details are available at this time.

Facilities

Water on the pontoons. Fuel on the quay, but depths off the fuel quay are mostly shallow and you should reconnoitre first.

General

This small yacht club hums with activity in the summer, and visiting yachts are squeezed in where possible. The village is a hot 20-minute walk away, or just settle for a beer at the yacht club cabin. The harbour is also a base for some of the trip boats running between the north coast of Sicily and the Aeolian Islands.

TINDARI (Zone A/B)

⊕ 1M N of Capo Tindari 38°10'·0N 15°02'·6E

Capo Tindari lies approximately 14 miles west of Milazzo. Between Capo Milazzo on the E side, and Capo Calava on the W, Capo Tindari lies in the SW corner of Golfo di Patti. This large bay is open only to the NE–E and offers good shelter in settled conditions. It is easily recognised by the church with a silver dome and monastery atop a vertical cliff at the NW end. The bay used to be, prior to the marine reserve, one of the best anchorages on the N coast of Sicily.

Anchor off the sandbanks where convenient clear of the marine reserve boundaries. The bottom is sand and good holding. In the event of bad weather, Portorosa Marina is nearby.

Note The authorities in this area keenly enforce a law which prohibits anchoring or motor-sailing within 300m of the coast. Fines over €100 for a first offence have been applied.

The monastery on the cliff-top (about 255m/750ft high) contains a miracle-working Byzantine Black Madonna to which pilgrims flock from all over Sicily, especially for the festival on 8 September. The view from the top is superb, but the walk from the

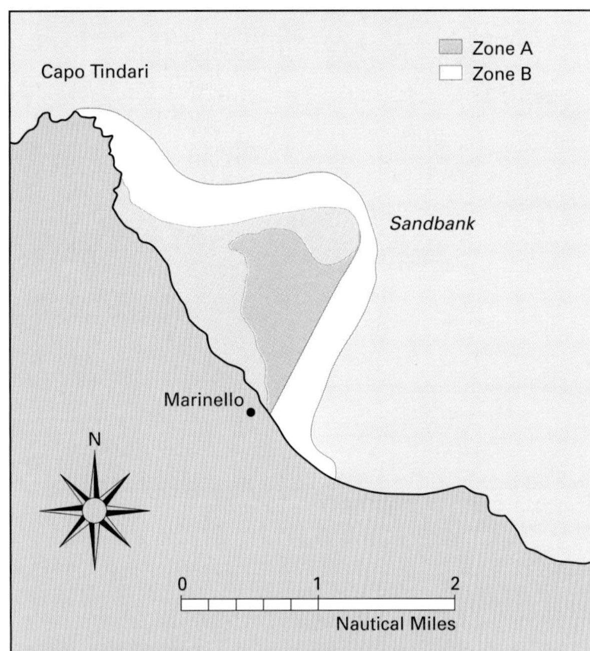

LAGHETTI DI MARINELLO MARINE RESERVE

Laghetti di Marinello Marine Reserve

A new nature reserve (established 2004) on the E side of Capo Tindari. The boundary of Zone A is marked with yellow buoys and lit Fl.Y.4s4M. The area immediately off the sandbank is in Zone A. The near coast is within Zone B.

Zone A
All navigation, short- and long-term stays, anchoring, diving and fishing prohibited.

Zone B
Navigation permitted.
Short- and long-term stays, anchoring, mooring, diving and fishing prohibited.
These boundaries may be extended in the future.

✆ /*Fax* 0907 761 264

bay, especially in the summer, is a killer, and you may well be in need of the Black Madonna's power after attempting it. Below the monastery there are a number of Greek ruins including a theatre and parts of the acropolis.

PORTOROSA MARINA

A marina complex situated close to the ruins of ancient Tindari.

Approach

The harbour lies at the head of the large bay between Capo Tindari and Capo Milazzo. Once into the bay the apartment complex around the marina will be seen and, closer in, the breakwaters will be identified.

VHF Ch 09, 16 (24hrs).

Caution Care needs to be taken in strong NE winds when a swell piles up at the entrance. Once inside there is no problem.

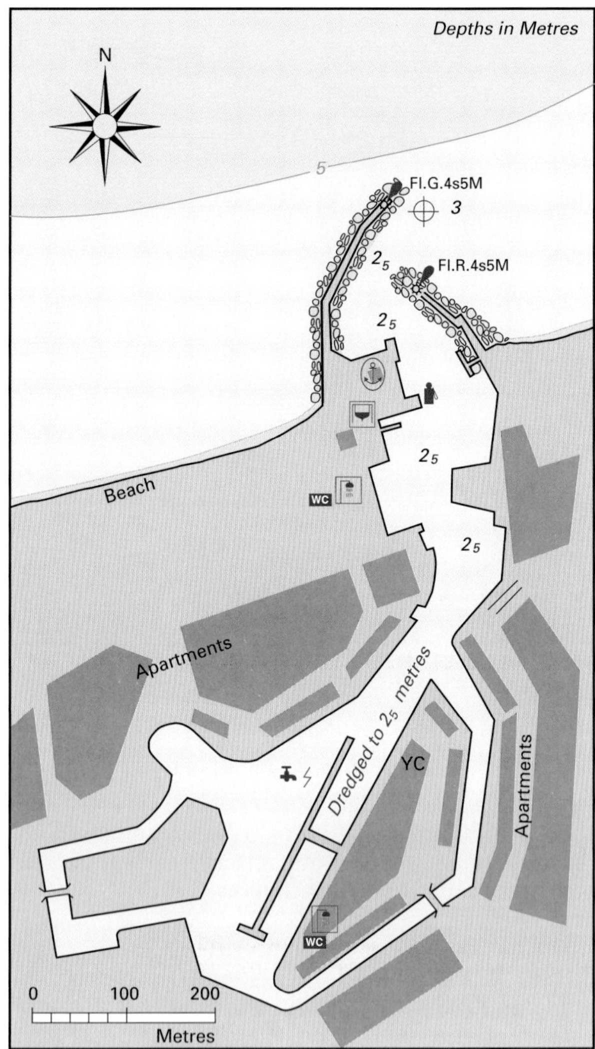

MARINA DI PORTOROSA
⊕38°07′·6N 15°06′·7E

Mooring

Data 700 berths. 50 visitors' berths. Max LOA 40m. Max draught 2m. Depths 2·5–5m.

Berth Near the entrance at the reception quay or where directed. There are laid finger pontoons and some moorings tailed to the quay.

Shelter Excellent all-round shelter.

Authorities Harbourmaster and marina staff. Charge band 6 (June–September).

✉ Marina di Portorosa, Portorosa, 98054 Furnari, Sicily
✆ 0941 874 560 *Fax* 874 655
Email info@marinadiportorosa.com
www.marinadiportorosa.com

Facilities

Services Water and electricity (220/380V) at every berth. Shower and toilet blocks. Laundry service.
Fuel On the quay at the entrance.
Repairs A 50-ton travel-hoist. Mechanical repairs. GRP and wood repairs. Electrical and electronic repairs. Chandlers.
Provisions A minimarket.
Eating out Restaurants and bars.
Other PO. Bank at Furnari.

Marina di Portorosa looking NW across to Tindari
Marina di Portorosa

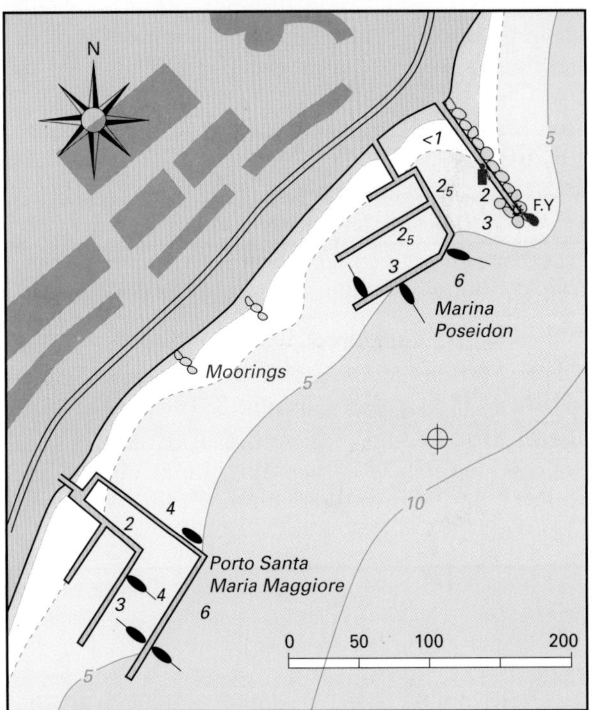

MARINA POSEIDON & PORTO SANTA MARIA MAGGIORE
⊕38°13'·6N 15°14'·9E

General

Portorosa marina has been excavated from the low-lying sandy coast to provide a totally sheltered marina. All around the marina are apartments and the complex now has numerous boutiques, restaurants and cafes. Portorosa is not really my cup of tea, but it is a good place to leave a yacht if you want somewhere safe and secure from which to explore inland. Hire cars can be arranged here and it is well worth while spending a day driving around the interior.

MARINA POSEIDON

A small marina less than a mile N of the entrance to Milazzo harbour.

Approach

The citadel on the headland close to the marina is conspicuous.

By night The end of the breakwater is lit F.Y.

VHF Ch 09.

Mooring

Data 160 berths. Max LOA 35m. Depths 2–5m.

Berths Stern or bows-to where directed on the concrete pontoons. Boats over c.12m berth stern-to on the outside pontoon. Laid moorings tailed to the quay.

Shelter Reasonable shelter from northerlies. Open south.

Authorities Marina staff. Charge band 6 (July–August).

Marina Poseidon ✆ 090 922 2564 / 335 847 2415
Fax 090 924 1091
Email info@poseidonmarina.it

Facilities

Services Water and electricity. Showers and toilets.

Fuel On the quay (0800–2000). Min. depths 2m.
Repairs 60-ton crane. Mechanical and electrical repairs.
Other Provisions, cafes and restaurants in Milazzo.

PORTO SANTA MARIA MAGGIORE

Another new marina close N of Milazzo.

VHF Ch 09.

Mooring

Data 320 berths. Max LOA 100m. Depths 1–6m.

Berths Stern or bows-to on the pontoons where directed. Larger boats use the outer pontoon.

Shelter Little shelter on the outer berths.

Authorities Marina staff. Charge band 6.
✆ /*Fax* 090 922 1002 ✆ 347 634 4620
Email info@portodimilazzo.it
www.portosantamariamaggiore.it

Facilities

Services Water and electricity. Showers and toilets. Wi-Fi.

Repairs Disal Nautica can arrange hauling and repairs.
✆ /*Fax* 090 922 2248
Email info@disalnautica.it

Other Close to the facilities and services of Milazzo.

MILAZZO (Marina del Nettuno)

Approach

Conspicuous The chimneys and storage tanks of the oil refinery about 1½ miles SE of the harbour and the power station chimney further to the E are conspicuous from some distance off. The citadel standing on the peninsula about one mile N of the harbour is also conspicuous. The buildings of the town and the harbour mole are easily identified.

By night Use the light on Capo Milazzo LFl.6s90m16M.

VHF Ch 14, 16 (0600–1800) for port authorities. Ch 09 for Marina del Nettuno-Milazzo.

Note Care must be taken of the ferries and hydrofoils continually coming and going from the port.

Mooring

Data (Marina del Nettuno) 140 berths. Visitors' berths. Max LOA 35m. Depths 8–10m.

Berth Most yachts will proceed to Marina del Nettuno in the NW corner. Yachts may also be able to berth on the town quay although this is likely to be discouraged. At Marina del Nettuno berth where directed. Finger pontoons and laid moorings.

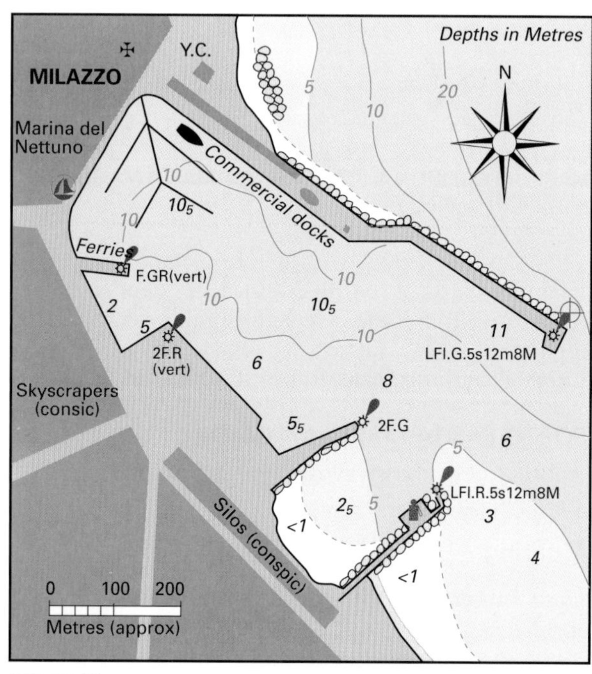

MILAZZO
⊕38°12´·9N 15°15´·0E

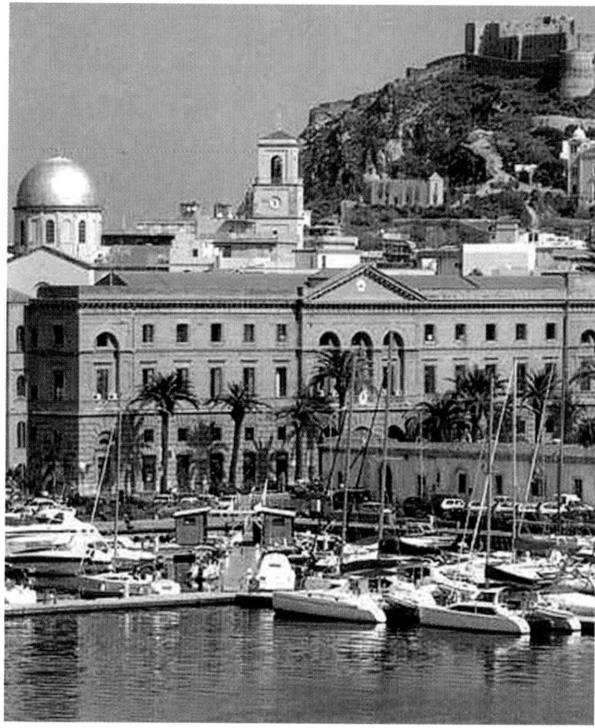

Marina del Nettuno Milazzo *Marina del Nettuno*

Shelter Generally good shelter although a strong *sirocco* (S) is reported to make it uncomfortable in here.

Authorities Harbourmaster and marina staff. Charge band 6 (June–September).
✉ Marina del Nettuno, (COMET) 4 Piazza Nastasi, Milazzo 98057, Sicily
✆ 090 928 1180 *Fax* 090 928 8982
Email info.milazzo@marinadelnettuno.it
www.marinadelnettuno.it/milazzo.html

Facilities

Services Water and electricity (220V) at every berth. Showers and toilets. 24-hour security.
Fuel On the quay in the S of the harbour.
Repairs Travel-hoist. Crane. Mechanical and electrical repairs can be arranged. Chandlers and hardware shops.
Provisions Good shopping for all provisions. Supermarket in town.
Eating out Restaurants nearby and along the waterfront.
Other PO. Banks. ATMs. Camping Gaz and Italgaz. Bus and train to Palermo and Messina. Ferries to the Aeolian Islands.

General

The town was founded as Mylae by the Greeks in 716BC. Today is it a popular resort on account of its nearby beaches and an important ferry port connecting the Aeolian Islands to Sicily.

Isole Eolie (Aeolian Islands)

This archipelago, also called the Lipari Islands after the principal island, lie 35 miles off the coast of Sicily. The islands are peaks of volcanoes and two remain active: Stromboli and Gran Cratere on Vulcano. There are seven islands: Stromboli, Panarea, Filicudi, Alicudi, Salina, Lipari and Vulcano.

The islands have been inhabited from early times and have been the prey of pirates and colonisers from the Carthaginians through to the Spanish. Many fine exhibits from all ages are on display in the Aeolian Museum in Lipari.

Winds

The normal summer winds are from the NW occasionally going around the W. There may also be winds from the NE. Squalls may be encountered among the islands, but they seldom last for long.

The islands take their name from Aeolus, the god of the winds. It was he who gave Odysseus the contrary winds tied up in a bag, but near to Ithaca his sailors opened it believing there was treasure inside and yet again he was blown away from his homeland. (However, Ernle Bradford in *Ulysses Found* believes Ustica to be the home of Aeolus.)

Although there are no really secure harbours, there are sufficient harbours and anchorages sheltered from the prevailing summer winds to make it well worthwhile cruising around the archipelago.

Stromboli, Panarea, Vulcano, Filicudi and Alicudi are all nature reserves. There are no designated marine reserves at this time, but in the future anchorages around the islands may be affected. For more details on National Park regulations see www.parks.it

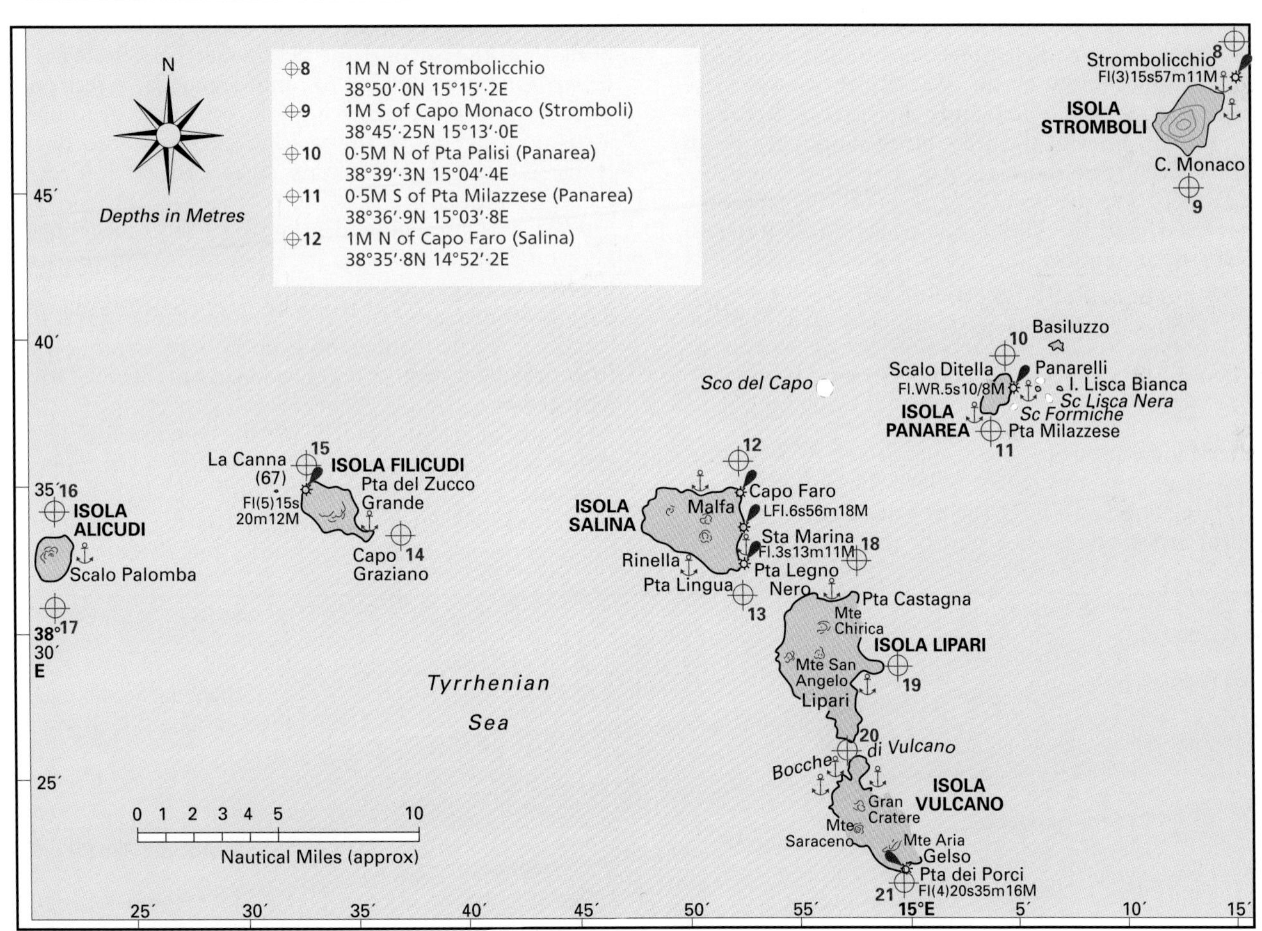

ISOLE EOLIE (Aeolian Islands)

⊕13 1M S of Pta Lingua (Salina) 38°31′·1N 14°52′·3E
⊕14 1M E of Capo Graziano (Filicudi) 38°33′·4N 14°36′·9E
⊕15 1M N of Pta La Zotta (Filicudi) 38°36′·0N 14°32′·6E
⊕16 1M N of N end of Alicudi 38°34′·3N 14°21′·2E
⊕17 1M S of S end of Alicudi 38°30′·7N 14°21′·2E
⊕18 1M N of Pta Castagna (Lipari) 38°32′·4N 14°5′·4E
⊕19 0·5M E of Sciarra di Monte Rosa (Lipari) 38°28′·8N 14°59′·4E
⊕20 Mid-channel Bocche di Vulcano 38°26′·1N 14°57′·4E
⊕21 1M S of Pta dei Porci (Vulcano) 38°21′·07N 14°59′·49E WGS84

Isola Stromboli

Probably the oldest lighthouse in the world, this active volcano has been dubbed 'the lighthouse of the Mediterranean' from ancient times to the present. It guided Odysseus towards the twin perils of Scylla and Charybdis and it has guided me towards the Strait of Messina on a gale-swept winter's night. The island is a conical volcano rising to 925m (3,036ft) and is in almost continuous state of activity. Unlike Vesuvius and Etna, it releases its pressure bit by bit, day by day, instead of building up to a big bang. Small pieces of pumice can be found floating in the sea some distance off the island and on the northwestern slopes a stream of lava, the *sciara del fuoco* or flow of fire, runs into the sea.

In ancient times Stromboli would have been one of the 'sea gates' of the Mediterranean, an unmistakeable signpost for navigating away from and towards the Strait of Messina. Ernle Bradford in *Ulysses Found* identifies Stromboli with the 'Wandering Rocks' Circe described for Odysseus:

> 'Two ways will lie before you, and you must choose between them as you see fit, though I will tell you both. One leads to those sheer cliffs which the blessed gods know as the Wandering Rocks. Here blue-eyed Amphitrite sends her great breakers thundering in, and the very birds cannot fly by in safety. Even from the shy doves that bring Ambrosia to Father Zeus the beetling rock takes toll each time they pass, and the Father has to send one more to make their number up, while for such sailors as bring their ship to the spot, there is no escape whatever. They end as flotsam on the sea, timbers and corpses tossed in confusion by the waves or licked up by tempestuous and destroying flames.'
>
> *The Odyssey, Book 12*

After Homer, the volcano is mentioned by Strabo in his *Geography* and by many later English travellers in Italy. You can climb the volcano, but it is hard work, especially the last part of the ascent which is over jagged scoria (you will need stout shoes) and is hot work in the summer sun (you will need to take a hat and water with you).

There are two indifferent anchorages off the hamlets of San Bartolomeo and San Vincenzo.

Both anchorages are suitable in calm weather only and at the slightest sign of bad weather a yacht should leave.

San Bartolomeo

⊕ 38°48'·5N 15°14'·3E

At San Bartolomeo anchor in 10m on a rocky bottom. There is now a desalination plant here and the water tanker will sometimes need to anchor off the village, taking lines and a pipe ashore to fill up with water. Provisions and restaurants in the delightful village of small cubic white houses set on the edge of the black beach.

San Vincenzo

⊕ 38°48'·0N 15°14'·6E

You can also berth on the E side of Punta della Lena where there are two wharves. Go alongside the N wharf after the day-trip boats leave, around 1800 hours. On the S wharf the best policy is to go stern-to with the bows facing SE, into the usual direction of the swell. During the high season there are now also mooring buoys for visiting yachts in the bay. (Care is needed as pick up lines can be fouled.) Charge band 3.

Alternatively anchor off. Until 1900 yachts must keep more than 300m off the coast. After this time it appears to be permitted to anchor closer in. An after-dark motor around the NW–W side of the island is usually rewarded with a close-up view of Stromboli's fireworks. Oh, and it's a good place to 'trawl' for pumice too.

About one mile NNE of the anchorage lies Strombolicchio, a small steep-to islet with quite fantastic rock formations and a lighthouse (Fl(3)15s11M) on it. A staircase has been cut into the rock to get to the lighthouse, but there are no

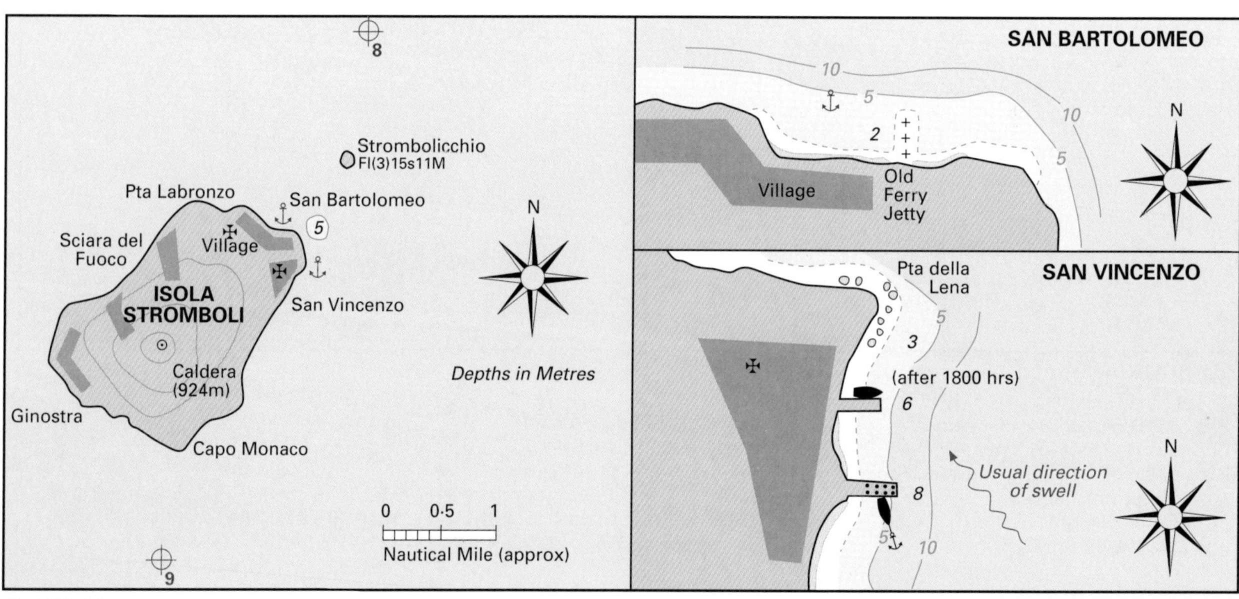

STROMBOLI

suitable depths for anchoring off the islet even in calm weather.

Isola Panarea

Panarea lies on an underwater platform that juts out of the sea at numerous points around the island including the islets of Panarelli, Dattilo, Lisca Bianca and Lisca Nera, Basiluzzo and the Formiche Rocks. It is inhabited and parts of the island are cultivated. At Capo Milazzese on the S of Panarea, a circular hut village dating back to 1500BC has been excavated.

SCALO DITELLA (SAN PIETRO)

Approach

Straightforward from the N or S leaving the outlying islets and rocks to seaward.

Mooring

Berth If you get there in time it is possible to go stern or bows-to the pier on either side depending on the wind direction and sea state. The outer part of the pier is used by hydrofoils. Alternatively anchor to the N of the pier in 5–12m keeping well clear of the laid moorings. You cannot anchor within 200m of the pier, and the water tanker moors to the S of the pier. The bottom is sand and reasonable holding.

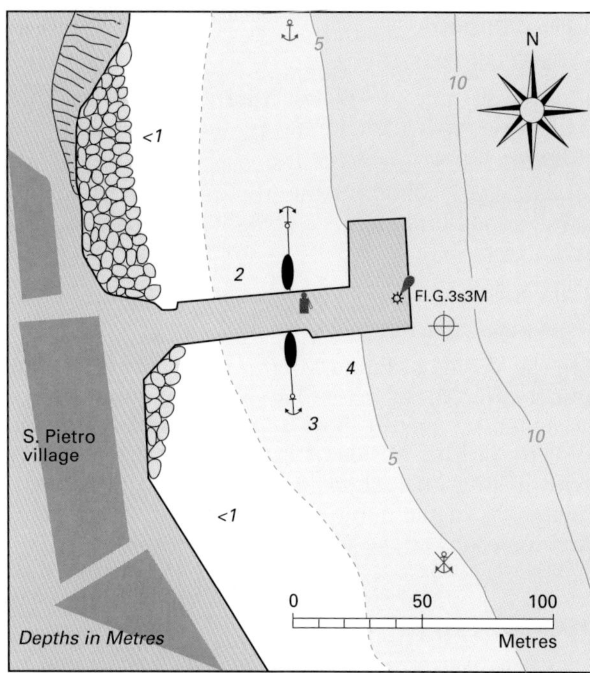

SCALO DITELLA (S. Pietro)
⊕38°38′·1N 15°04′·7E

Shelter Adequate in settled weather but with any fresh winds or moderate seas from anywhere in the E this is not the place to be.

Authorities *Ormeggiatori* who will make a (usually) modest charge on the pier.

Facilities

Fuel Fuel on the quay.

Some provisions and a number of good bars and restaurants.

PUNTA MILAZZESE

On the W and E sides of Punta Milazzese on the southern end of Panarea there are several anchorages. Technically this whole area is off limits and navigating and anchoring in the vicinity is prohibited. This does not always seem to worry the Italians out on the water and so you must just take your chances – with a good possibility that you will be told to move on.

The Aeolian triangle

While the Caribbean has its Bermuda triangle, the Mediterranean has its own 'Aeolian triangle'. In the triangle formed between Ustica off the coast of Sicily, the Aeolian Islands across to the mainland, and the Strait of Messina, an uncommon lot of local bad weather is encountered. My third gale here, like the others, was not forecast at all (the weather forecast was SE 3) and coming suddenly out of nowhere convinced me, along with other accounts of yachtsmen who have spent years sailing in the Mediterranean, that there is an Aeolian triangle.

Some of the accounts read like this. A friend in a 10m yacht was ready to beach his yacht here in bad weather, being unable to weather Lipari Island. He just scraped around the island to anchor in its lee. The only place I have run under bare poles in the Mediterranean was a 14-hour run from off Stromboli to the Strait of Messina in March with 50–55 knots recorded at Reggio weather station. Last year a friend broke his anchor chain on a Swan 44 with gusts up to 60 knots while anchored in the lee of Sicily off the Strait of Messina. Recently, in a modest Force 7, I ran down to Reggio di Calabria again, when a motorboat on passage to Sardinia sank with the loss of two lives. There are numerous other accounts in the same vein.

Perhaps the ancients got it right. The Aeolian islands get their name from Aeolus, god of the winds. In the *Odyssey* he gives Odysseus the contrary winds tied up in a bag, but his curious crew open it and the ship is blown off course to further delay Odysseus' return to Ithaca. If, as many believe, the *Odyssey* is a record of early navigation in the Mediterranean, then those ancient mariners probably muttered among themselves about the dreaded Aeolian triangle and how they 'shouldn't have ever come here with that bloody fool Odysseus'!

The Panarea Ship

Underwater excavation recently began on a trading ship from around 400BC off Panarea. The main problem with the excavation has been coping with the volcanic nature of the island. Hydrogen sulphide gas ('rotten egg' gas) is partially dissolved in the warm volcanic water to form sulphuric acid which makes the job difficult for the divers – as one of them said: it was burning not only the lips and face but 'other delicate parts'. A number of significant finds including black-glazed pottery have been found and there are indications that there is much more to come.

The site is guarded by the *carabinieri* and pleasure boats are not allowed to approach it – a precaution to stop the looting of archaeological sites which is so endemic in Italy.

Cala Zimmari

⊕ 38°37'·6N 15°04'·0E

On the E side of Punta Milazzese and in Baia Milazzese itself. Anchor in 5–10m on sand. Good holding. Open E and south.

Anchorage Anchor off the SE tip of the island on sand, good holding. It is a brisk 30-minute walk into town from here.

Cala Junco

⊕ 38°37'·4N 15°03'·8E

On the W side of Punta Milazzese. Care is needed of underwater rocks in the bay and you should have someone up on the bow conning you in. Anchor directly on the W side of Punta Milazzese in 5–8m with a long line ashore to the point. Alternatively anchor W of the point but not close in where there are numerous above and below-water rocks.

Isola Salina

Lies just over two miles NW of Isola Lipari and is easily identified by its twin peaks. In ancient times it was called Didyma (Greek) and Gemella (Latin) – 'the twins' – on account of the two extinct volcano cones. There is still subterranean activity and at Malfa vapour is given off, and at Rinella sulphuretted hydrogen, the characteristic 'rotten eggs' smell of stink bombs, bubbles up from the seabed. The island is much cultivated, especially with vines, and was famous for its Malvasi (Malmsey) wine. There are several small harbours.

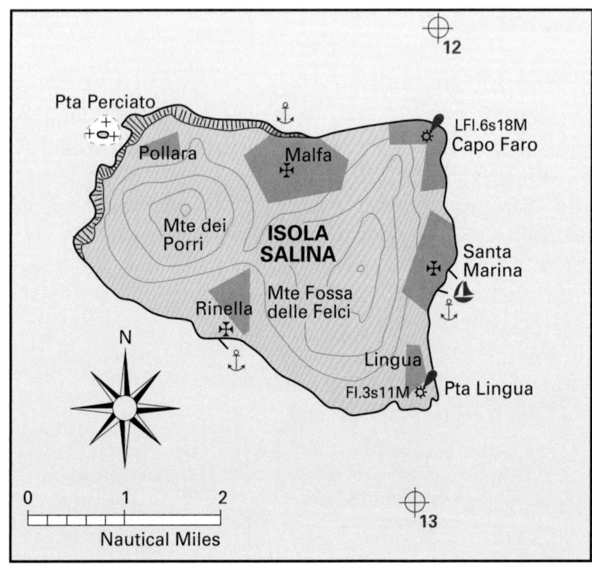

ISOLA SALINA

⊕12 1M N of Capo Faro (Salina) 38°35'·8N 14°52'·2E
⊕13 1M S of Pta Lingua (Salina) 38°31'·1N 14°52'·3E

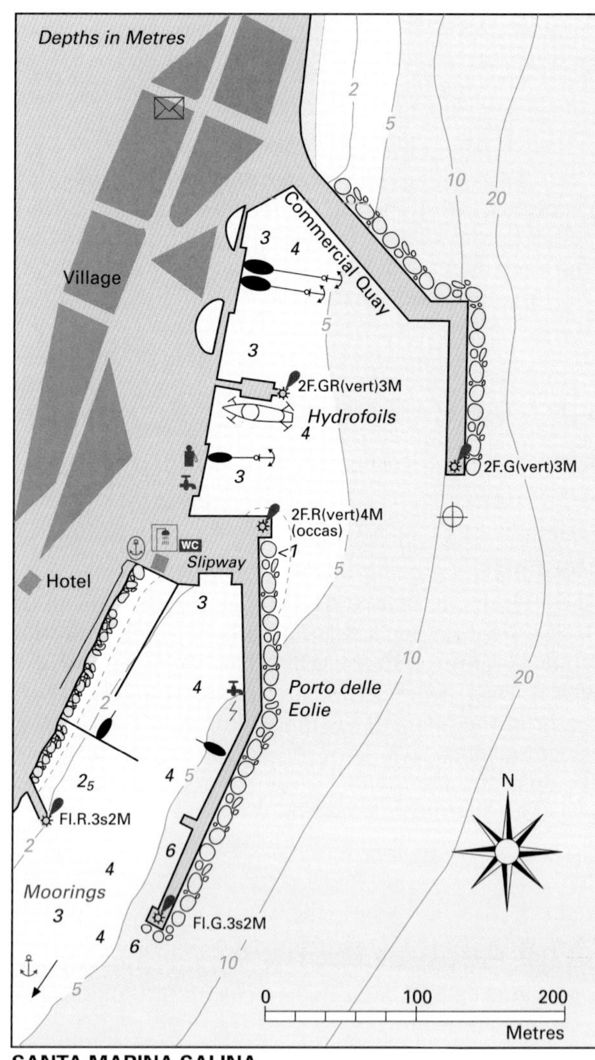

SANTA MARINA SALINA
⊕38°33'·4N 14°52'·6E

SANTA MARINA SALINA

Approach

The harbour lies midway along the E coast off a small settlement.

VHF Ch 16, 11 for Porto delle Eolie.

Mooring

Data Porto Vecchio c.25 berths. Visitors' berths. Max LOA 27m. Depths 3–5m.

Porto Turistico c.130 berths. Visitors' berths. Max LOA c.30m. Depths 1–6m.

Berths Yachts are usually directed to the *porto turistico* in the S basin. Larger yachts over 10m go stern or bows-to along the quay on the inside of the breakwater. Smaller yachts berth on the pontoons on the W side of the basin. The pontoon layout has changed several times recently. The latest reported layout is shown on the plan. Laid moorings tailed to the quay. Alternatively yachts can go on the quay N of the hydrofoil pier in the N harbour.

Shelter Good shelter in settled conditions in both the N and S harbours although the S basin affords the better all-round shelter. Strong southerlies would

Santa Maria Salina looking N into the S basin *Kerr Whiteford*

probably affect the S basin, although whether it would still be tenable is not known.

Authorities Harbourmaster. Charge band 6+ (May–October).
Porto delle Eolie ✆ 090 984 3473 / 346 022 0362
Email info@portodelleolie.com

Facilities

Services Water and electricity at all berths in the S basin. Showers and toilets. Water on the quay in the N harbour.
Fuel On the quay in the N harbour. You need to ring the bell for service.
Repairs 15-ton crane. Some mechanical repairs.
Provisions Minimarket and basic staples.
Eating out Restaurants in the village and at the hotel.

RINELLA

A short mole off a hamlet on the S coast. The end of the mole is lit F.R. Open E–S. There are 1–10m off the mole. If there are no berths on the quay, anchor off. There is limited space to anchor here as there are laid moorings for local boats in depths convenient for anchoring, but outside of the moorings in deeper water (+15m) there is space to anchor. Basic provisions and a restaurant ashore.

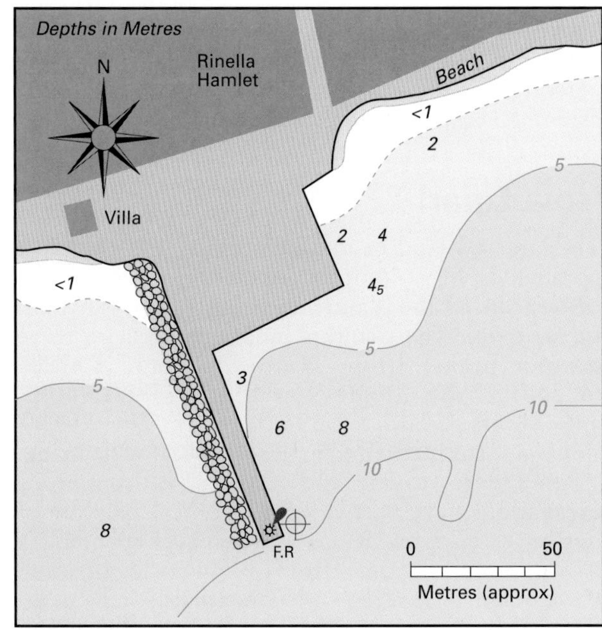

RINELLA
⊕38°32′·7N 14°49′·6E

Malfa (Scalo Galera)

A miniature harbour on the N coast. Two stubby moles run out from the coast. Depths <1–5m. A small yacht may find a berth in here, but it is usually crowded with local boats.

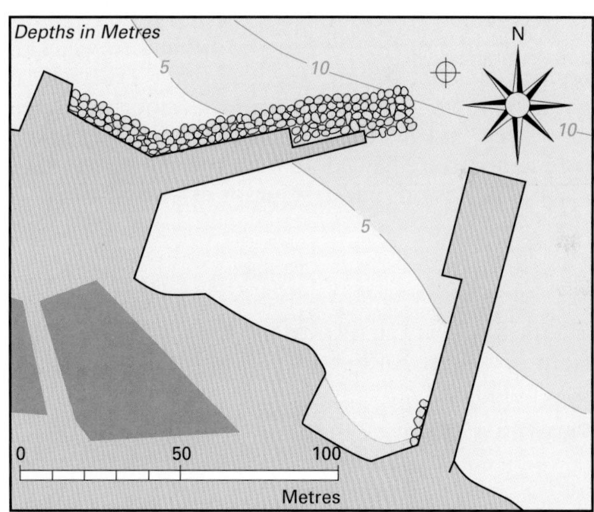

MALFA
⊕38°34′·87N 14°50′·55E

Isola Filicudi

Lies nearly 10 miles W of Salina. It is a high conical peak (Mt Fossa Felci: 775m/2542ft) connected by an isthmus to Capo Graziano. The latter looks like an offlying islet from some angles. The island was at one time well populated and cultivated, but is now only cultivated in parts. It is surrounded by above and below-water rocks, the most striking and conspicuous being La Canna off the NW coast, which is a rock obelisk rising sheer from the sea to 67m.

Porto Filicudi looking ESE towards Salina and Lipari. Note the old groyne running underwater just off the beach
Kevan Lambourne

Porto Filicudi

⊕ 38°33′·7N 14°35′·0E

A short mole off the settlement on the E side of the island. The end of the mole is lit 2F.GR(vert)4M. The mole is reserved for ferries and hydrofoils. Depths <1–5m. Yachts normally anchor off in settled weather, but leave plenty of room near the mole for the ferries to manoeuvre. Care is needed of an old groyne which runs parallel to the beach for approximately 100m SE from the ferry mole. It lies just under the surface and can be difficult to see. The bottom is stoney with weed and not everywhere good holding. Around 20 visitors' moorings have now been laid in the bay. Charge band 2/3. Local fishing boats are hauled up onto the shore.

Basic provisions and restaurant ashore.

Filo di Lorani

⊕**14** 1M E of Capo Graziano (Filicudi)
38°33′·4N 14°36′·9E

On the S side of Capo Graziano there is some shelter from N winds. Anchor in 9–12m on rock, not the best holding.

Pecorini a Mare

⊕ 38°33′·5N 14°34′·0E

A short mole for the hydrofoil on the S side of the island. There is really no room for yachts and in any case you are better off anchoring here as there is nearly always some ground swell.

There are now 12 yellow mooring buoys available. Charge band 3.

Isola Alicudi

The westernmost island of the archipelago lying 8·5M W of Filicudi. It is an extinct volcanic cone rising to 666m (2185ft) and dropping sheer into the sea. The houses were built along the eastern slopes far from the sea so that the inhabitants could escape from the pirates that once infested these waters.

From some distance off Alicudi looks like the quintessential volcanic cone.

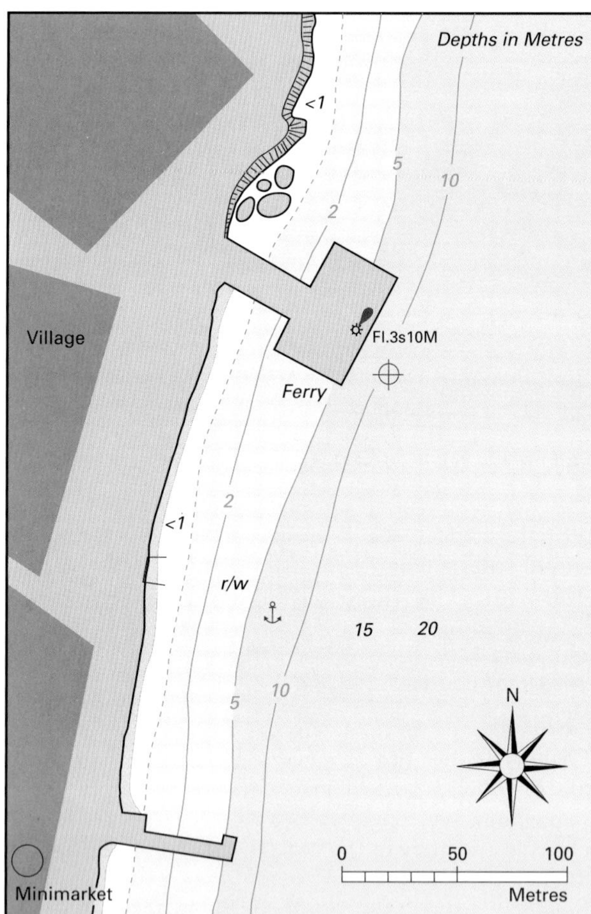

SCALO PALOMBA
⊕38°32′·0N 14°21′·8E

SCALO PALOMBA

On the E coast of Alicudi. There is a short pier used by the ferry and hydrofoil.

In settled weather yachts can anchor off to the S of the pier in 5–15m. There is sometimes room for 2–3 yachts to go stern-to the small pier S of the ferry pier. There are laid moorings in the vicinity, but with care space can be found. In unsettled weather this is not a good place to be. Some provisions and restaurants ashore.

Isola Lipari

The largest island of the archipelago and the most populated. Most of the population lives on the eastern side of the island and about half of it lives in Lipari town. The island is mountainous with three distinct peaks: (from N to S) Monte Chirica (602m/1,975ft), Monte Sant'Angelo (593/1,946ft), and Monte Guardia (369m/1,211ft). The eastern slopes are cultivated and a pleasant local wine made.

At Lipari town and close by, numerous excavations have uncovered a historical panoply of human civilisation. Ruins and remains spanning a dozen ages of man from prehistoric through Phoenician, Greek, Carthaginian, Roman, Byzantine, Norman and the Spanish can be found here and, fortunately, the excellent Aeolian Museum exhibits many of the finds. The latter should not be missed even by those who normally spurn such institutions.

The location of the islands as stepping stones on the trade route through the Tyrrhenian brought colonists to the islands early on. They were settled in 3000BC by settlers from the Near East who prospered trading in the obsidian found around the volcanic islands. This group was replaced by Copper Age settlers and, judging by the indigenous pottery found, the island continued to be important on the trading routes with influences on pottery designs coming from all over the Mediterranean. In the 13th century BC Bronze Age settlers arrived and supplanted the Copper Age colonists, though trade appears to have diminished and, by the 8th century BC, the inhabitants were only just scraping a living on the island.

In 580BC the island was colonised by Greeks from Knidos and Rhodes, who soon organised a small navy to combat the Phoenician and Etruscan pirates who regularly raided the islands. The fleet grew and their skill in these windy waters made them a force to be reckoned with. It must have seemed a logical extension to become pirates themselves and the Liparese boats became feared in the area between the Liparis and the Strait of Messina. The Liparese system of government at this time was an early form of communism that appeared to work. All land, houses, ships, and goods were held communally and redistributed every 20 years in a huge festival. All the pickings from piracy were distributed equally when the ships returned.

Decline started in the Roman era. Lipari sided with Carthage in the Punic Wars and consequently Rome sent a fleet to take the island. Thereafter the islands hobbled along behind Sicily and declined through neglect. In the 20th century many Liparese emigrated to Australia and America. Only in the 1970s and 80s did the fortunes of Lipari revive with tourism, though many, myself included, would say that the chic boutiques and expensive restaurants and bars on Lipari have turned it into a concrete and glass imitation of itself for the smart set from Rome and Naples. I wonder what would happen if the Liparese decided to redistribute everything equally in 20 years' time?

RADA DI LIPARI MARINA LUNGA (Sottomonastero)

Approach

The commercial quay and short mole close to the town immediately N of Punta Scaliddi. Yacht pontoons lie close N of the commercial quay.

VHF Ch 16, 11 (24/24).

Mooring

Berths Stern-to where directed on the yacht pontoons. Yachts are no longer permitted to use the ferry and commercial quay.

Shelter Open NE–SE. With gales from anywhere many berths may become untenable, particularly with southerlies. There is often a ground swell that

Marina Lunga (Lipari) looking north. Note yachts are no longer permitted to moor on the town quay

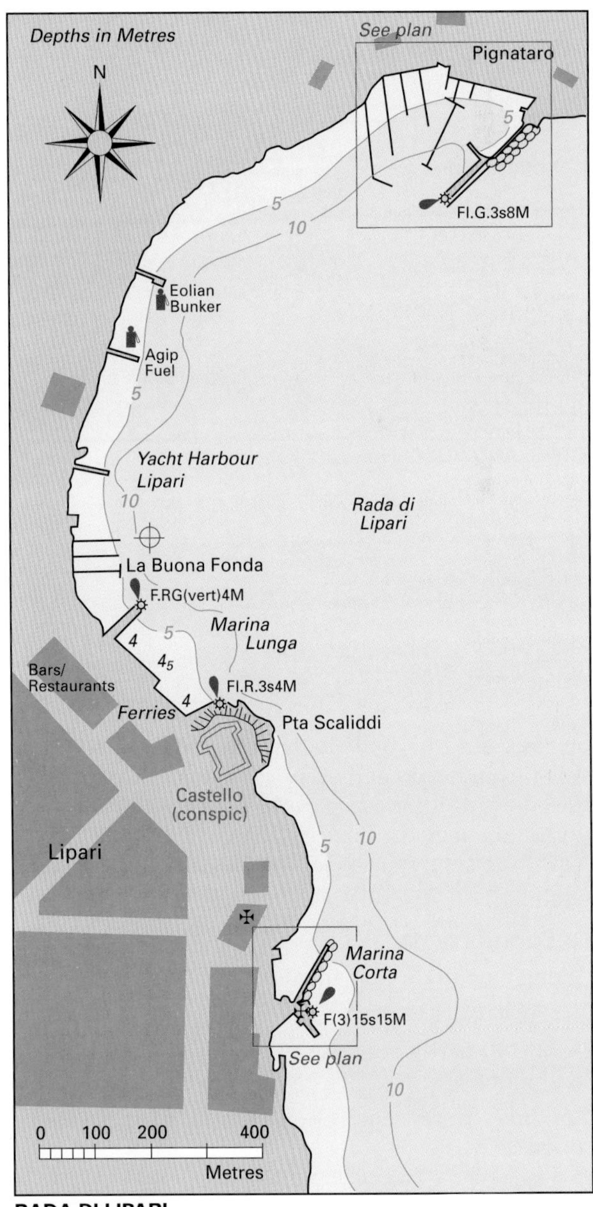

RADA DI LIPARI
⊕38°28′·15N 14°57′·5E

V. SICILY

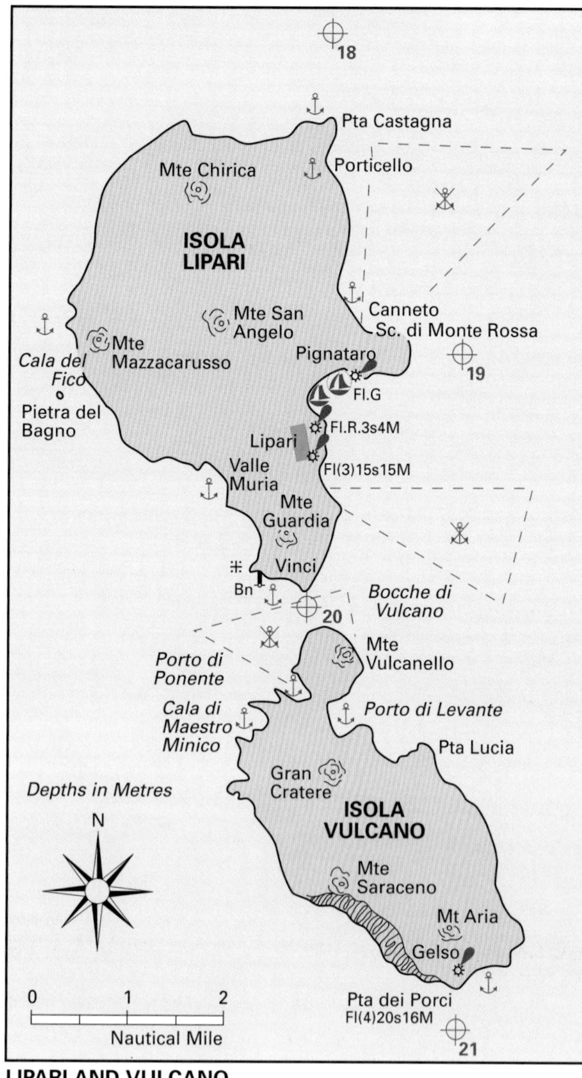

LIPARI AND VULCANO

⊕18 1M N of Pta Castagna (Lipari)
38°32′·4N 14°57′·4E
⊕19 0·5M E of Sciarra di Monte Rosa (Lipari)
38°28′·8N 14°59′·4E
⊕20 Mid-channel Bocche di Vulcano
38°26′·1N 14°57′·4E
⊕21 1M S of Pta dei Porci (Vulcano)
38°21′·07N 14°59′·49E WGS84

creeps round beyond the harbour and the constant wash from ferries and other craft do not do a lot for the comfort of the place. Keep pulled well off so you do not damage the boat from any surge or wash.

Authorities Harbourmaster. *Ormeggiatori*. Charge band 2/3.

La Buona Fonda

A single pontoon immediately N of Marina Lunga.

VHF Ch 16, 13.

Data c.40 berths. Max LOA c.60m. Depths <1–5m. Laid moorings.

Facilities Water and electricity (220V). Laundry service.

La Buona Fonda ✆ /*Fax* 090 982 2342 ✆ 368 274 944
Email info@labuonafonda.it
www.labuonafonda.it

Pontile Portosalvo

Data 40 berths. Max LOA 50m. Depths 4–5m. Pontoons and laid moorings in place.

Filippo Saglimbeni, Pontile Portosalvo ✆ 0368 719 0843
Email portosalvo@virgilio.it

Lipari Services

Single pontoon.

✆ 338 240 2377

Yacht Harbour Lipari

VHF Ch 16, 72.

Data c.40 berths. Max LOA c.60m. Depths 2–6m. Laid moorings.

Facilities

Water and electricity (220/380V). Some repairs can be arranged.

Yacht Harbour Lipari ✆ 090 981 1926 *Fax* 090 981 2677
✆ 338 774 5288
Email info@yachtharbourlipari.it

Fuel On the two pontoons N from Marina Lunga. The pontoons need careful fendering and are unsuitable for dinghies due to protruding metalwork at water level. Attendants can sometimes pull a little too enthusiastically on thrown warps.

Repairs 5/10-ton cranes.

Provisions Good shopping in the town.

Eating out Restaurants, trattorias and pizzerias. Good fish often available.

Other PO. Bank. ATM. Next to the quay is a sign showing the whereabouts of all facilities in the town.

General

You are right in the middle of town here with restaurants and bars just across the road. You should take a wander around the compact capital and if you like shopping this is a good place to be. The yacht berths are beset by wash and any ground swell around, can make for an uncomfortable time, and if going out for dinner make sure that you are pulled well off the pontoon.

MARINA CORTA

Approach

Lies on the S side of Lipari town and Punta Scaliddi.

Mooring

Data Depths <1–5m.

Berth The harbour is normally full of local boats and you will be lucky to find a berth here. Go stern or bows-to where possible.

Shelter Adequate in the summer. Open NE and with strong winds from NE–SE a surge is set up.

Authorities Ormeggiatori.

Facilities

Water on the quay. Otherwise as for Marina Lunga.

The approaches to Marina Corta looking NW

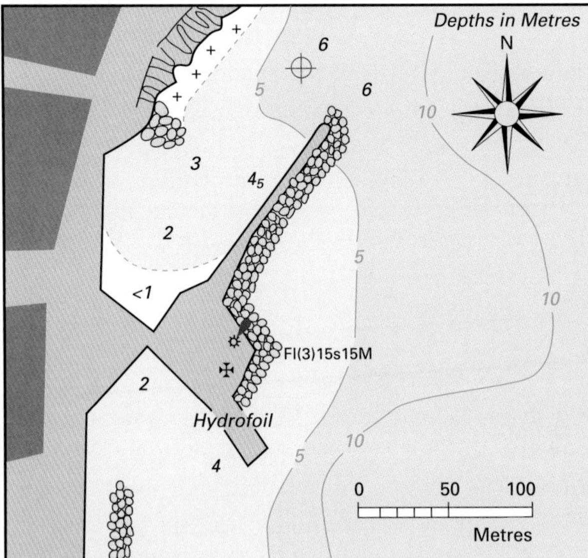

MARINA CORTA
⊕38°27′·8N 14°57′·5E

PIGNATARO

Approach

Lies at the N end of Lipari roadstead.

VHF Ch 11, 16. Ch 74 for Porto Pignatori.

Note The entrance between the moored boats and the breakwater can be a bit tricky if a trawler or tripper boat is coming or going – usually at speed.

Mooring

Data c.150 berths. Visitors' berths. Max LOA c.80m. Depths 3–10m.

Berth The inside of the breakwater is usually busy with fishing boats and harbour authority boats. The main quay has yacht berths with laid moorings (Porto Pignataro), but tends to be reserved for charter and local boats. New pontoons have been installed around the NW side of the harbour and are run as concessions. Go stern or bows-to where directed. Laid moorings tailed to the quay or a small buoy.

Shelter Good shelter in the summer. Open SW for a short distance, but strong southerlies make it untenable here.

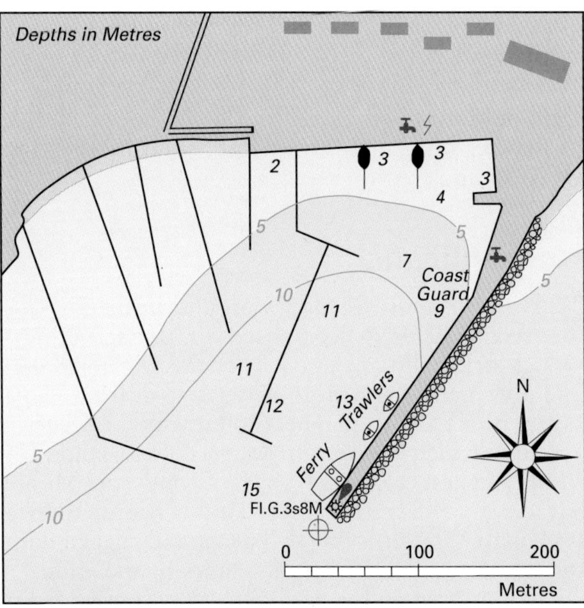

PIGNATARO
⊕38°28′·69N 14°57′·88E WGS84

Authorities Ormeggiatori. Charge band 5.
Porto Pignataro ✆ 333 301 1700 / 333 229 8898
Email portopignataro@virgilio.it
EOL Mare ✆ 090 981 4233 *Fax* 090 981 3534
R Giovanni ✆ 090 981 951

Facilities

Services Water and electricity at most berths on the quay, but water is in short supply in the summer.
Fuel Around the bay on the AGIP or Eolian Bunker pontoons.
Other Facilities as for Marina Lunga. Fresh fruit, bread and water from a man and van. A bus runs to Lipari town from the root of the breakwater in the summer.

General

This is the safest place to be on Lipari and it is a bit more real than downtown Lipari with its boutiques and expensive restaurants. From here you can get a bus or taxi into Lipari or it is a pleasant if somewhat hot walk in summer.

OTHER ANCHORAGES

There are a number of other anchorages around Lipari Island that can be used according to the wind and swell. Clockwise from Punta Castagna there are.

Punta Castagna N side Anchor in 6–10m off the beach. Open to all sectors north.

Porticello Anchor off the jetties running off the beach in 5–10m leaving the large jetty clear. Open E and south.

Canneto Anchor off WSW or E of the huddle of laid moorings. It is quite deep to anchor here and you will usually be in 20m. Open E and south. Bars and restaurants ashore.

Spiaggia di Vinci The small beach immediately W of Punta della Crepazza. Anchor in 10–20m. Open W and south.

Valle Muria Care needed of the reef in the S end of the bay. Anchor in 5–10m towards the N end. Open W and south.

Cala del Fico Care needed of the reef in the middle of the bay. Anchor towards the N end in 10–15m. Open W and south.

Isola Vulcano

The southernmost of the group and in many ways the strangest. It is composed of extinct craters (which originally appeared from the sea in 183BC) and one active crater. It is separated from Isola Lipari by a narrow channel (800m wide), Bocche di Vulcano, which is free from dangers. The island rises to its highest elevation in the south at Monte Saraceno (481m/1,578ft) and Monte Aria (499m/1,637ft). It is mostly barren and rugged with the tufa eroded into fantastic shapes by the wind.

The northern end is dominated by Gran Cratere, an active crater still standing as it appeared in the eruptions in 1888 and 1890. Bubbling mud pools and hot mineral springs bubbling up from the seabed make it a fascinating place. You can select just the temperature you want in the sea by moving closer or further away from one of the numerous springs.

If it looks like a lunar landscape then the impression is only reinforced by the overweight souls who come here and coat themselves in the warm grey mud for its therapeutic effects. One does eventually get used to seeing obese people with overall cracked mudpacks waddling down to the sea, but it takes a while.

PORTO DI LEVANTE

Approach

Lies on the E side of Vulcanello, the northern tip of the island.

Dangers To the N of the ferry pier an unmarked shallow reef extends 80m out from the shore, running southwards to the anchoring area.

VHF Ch 16, 14 (Centro Nautico Baia Levante).

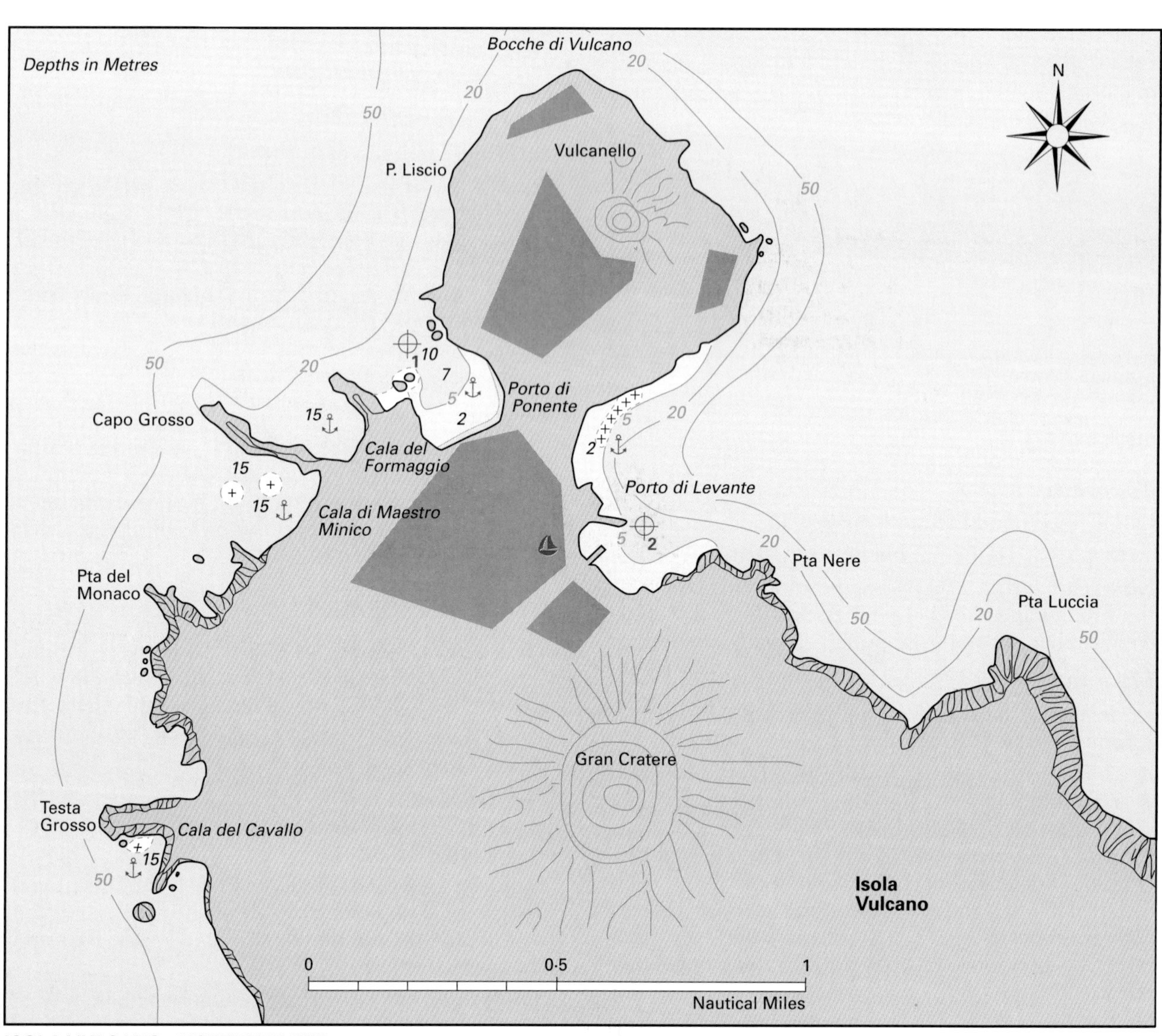

ISOLA VULCANO - NORTHERN END
⊕1 38°25′·31N 14°57′·04E WGS84
⊕2 38°24′·93N 14°57′·80E WGS84

Mooring

Data c.100 berths. Max LOA 70m. Depths 3–5m.

Berth Most yacht berths on new pontoons S of the ferry pier. Laid moorings tailed to the pontoon. Otherwise go stern or bows-to the quay if there is room. Good holding on sand. The mole and the pier should be left clear for ferries and hydrofoils. Charge band 4.

Shelter Adequate in the summer. Open NE–E–SE.

Anchorage Anchor N of the ferry berth clear of the moorings. Care is needed as depths become irregular towards the shore. Alternatively pick up a mooring, although you may have to leave if the owner returns.

Facilities

Services Water and electricity (220V) on the pontoons. Wi-Fi. Mobile crane.

PORTO DI PONENTE

Approach

The approach is straightforward and the pinnacle rocks on either side of the bay are easily identified. Although there are no lights a night approach would be possible with care.

Mooring

Anchor in 5–10m where convenient. Large yachts may have to anchor a bit further out in deeper water. The bottom is coarse sand and the anchor will not always dig in at first. With persistence you can get it to hold.

Shelter Good shelter from all directions except westerlies. In these winds you should go to Porto di Levante or Rada di Lipari.

Facilities

Supermarket. Vegetable stalls. A few restaurants and bars ashore.

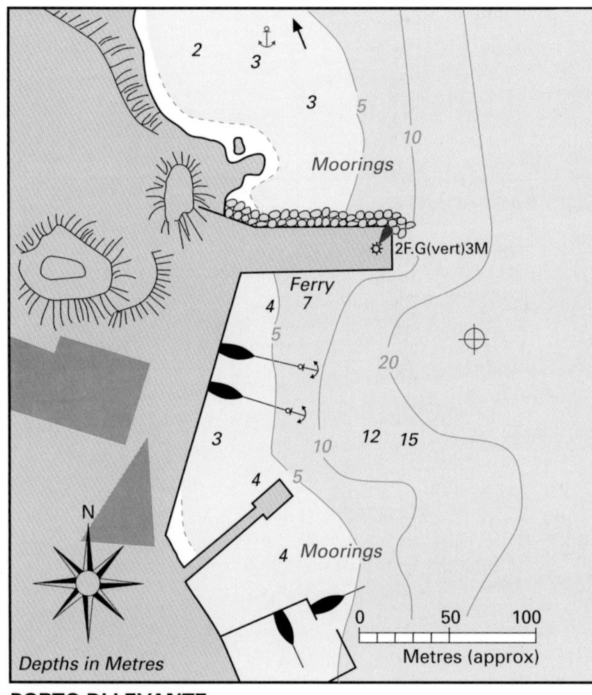

PORTO DI LEVANTE
⊕38°24´·93N 14°57´·80E WGS84

Under the volcano: Porto di Ponente on Vulcano

General

In the anchorage you are sitting right under the cone of the volcano which will occasionally belch a bit of smoke to let you know it is still active. The anchorage here is generally a good one to arrive at from Sicily as there is usually space and reasonable shelter.

Cala del Formaggio

The bay immediately SW of Porto di Ponente. It is fairly deep for anchoring, but might be a useful alternative. Open W–NW.

Cala di Maestro Minico

A small bay NE of Pta del Monaco. Care should be taken of the above-water rocks in the middle. Sheltered from the east. The bottom is sand and rocks and you may need to put a trip line on your anchor.

Cala del Cavallo

A small cove on the S side of Testa Grosso. Care needed of the above and below-water rocks on the N side.

In the mud pools in Porto di Levante
Sandro Bedessi, FOTOTECA ENIT

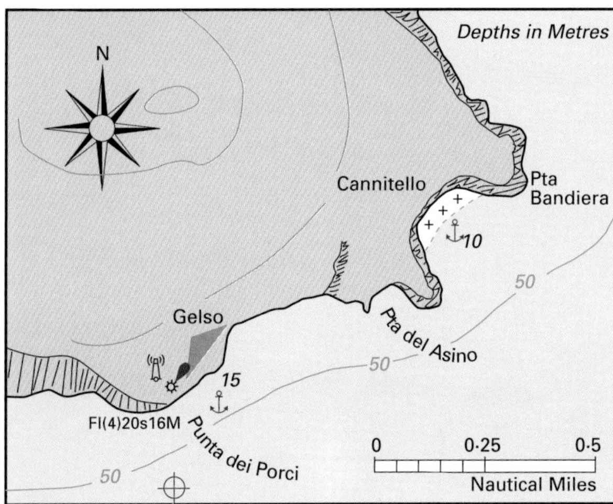

GELSO
⊕38°22′·1N 14°59′·3E

Gelso

An anchorage off the beach and the hamlet of Gelso on the E side of Punta dei Porci. There is a short jetty with 5–6m depths reported off the end. Anchor off the beach to the NE of the jetty in 3–10m. Depths drop off quickly here so you will have to potter around a bit finding the best place. The bottom is coarse sand and adequate holding once the anchor is in.

There is also another anchorage in Cannitello to the NE under Punta Bandiera. Care is needed close in where a reef fringes the coast.

Sicily East coast

Strait of Messina (Stretto di Messina)

BA 1018, 917 and 992
Italian 13, 138, 23

'And all this time, in travail, sobbing, gaining on the current, we rowed into the strait – Skylla to port and on our starboard beam Kharibdis, dire gorge of the salt sea tide. By heaven! when she vomited, all the sea was like a cauldron seething over intense fire, when the mixture suddenly heaves and rises.'

The Odyssey. Book 12 transl. R Fitzgerald.

The Strait of Messina separates Sicily from the mainland of Italy and is much used by yachts on passage to and from the Ionian. At its northern end it is barely 1½ miles across between Capo Peloro and Torre Cavallo, while it is 7½ miles wide at the southern end between Capo Scaletta and Punta Pellaro. Yachts can find shelter at Marina Nettuno off the entrance to Porto Messina or at Reggio di Calabria on the mainland coast opposite.

Although there are strong tides and whirlpools, there is normally no problem in navigating the Strait and a yacht may encounter more problems with squalls blowing off the high land on either side of the

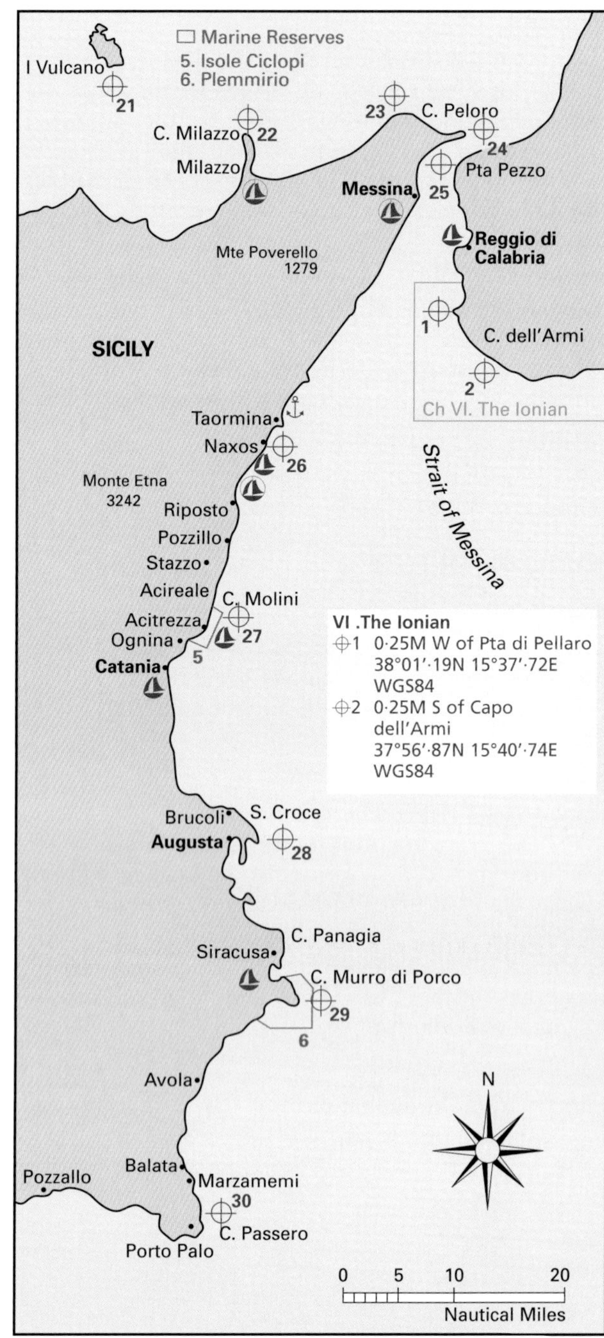

SICILY EAST COAST

⊕**21** 1M S of Pta dei Porci (Vulcano)
38°21′·07N 14°59′·49E WGS84
⊕**22** 0·75M N of Capo di Milazzo
38°17′·08N 15°13′·88E WGS84
⊕**23** 1·1M N of Capo Rasocolmo light
38°18′·99N 15°31′·18E WGS84
⊕**24** 1·75M E of Capo Peloro
38°15′·86N 15°41′·42E WGS84
⊕**25** 0·6M W of Pta Pezzo
38°13′·87N 15°37′·31E WGS84
⊕**26** 1M E of Capo Schiso
37°49′·7N 15°18′·0E
⊕**27** 0·75M E of Capo Molini
37°34′·49N 15°11′·32E WGS84
⊕**28** 0·5M E of Capo Santa Croce
37°14′·6N 15°16′·5E
⊕**29** 0·75M E of Capo Murro di Porco
37°00′·10N 15°21′·20E WGS84
⊕**30** 0·5M E of Capo Passero light
36°41′·23N 15°09′·85E WGS84

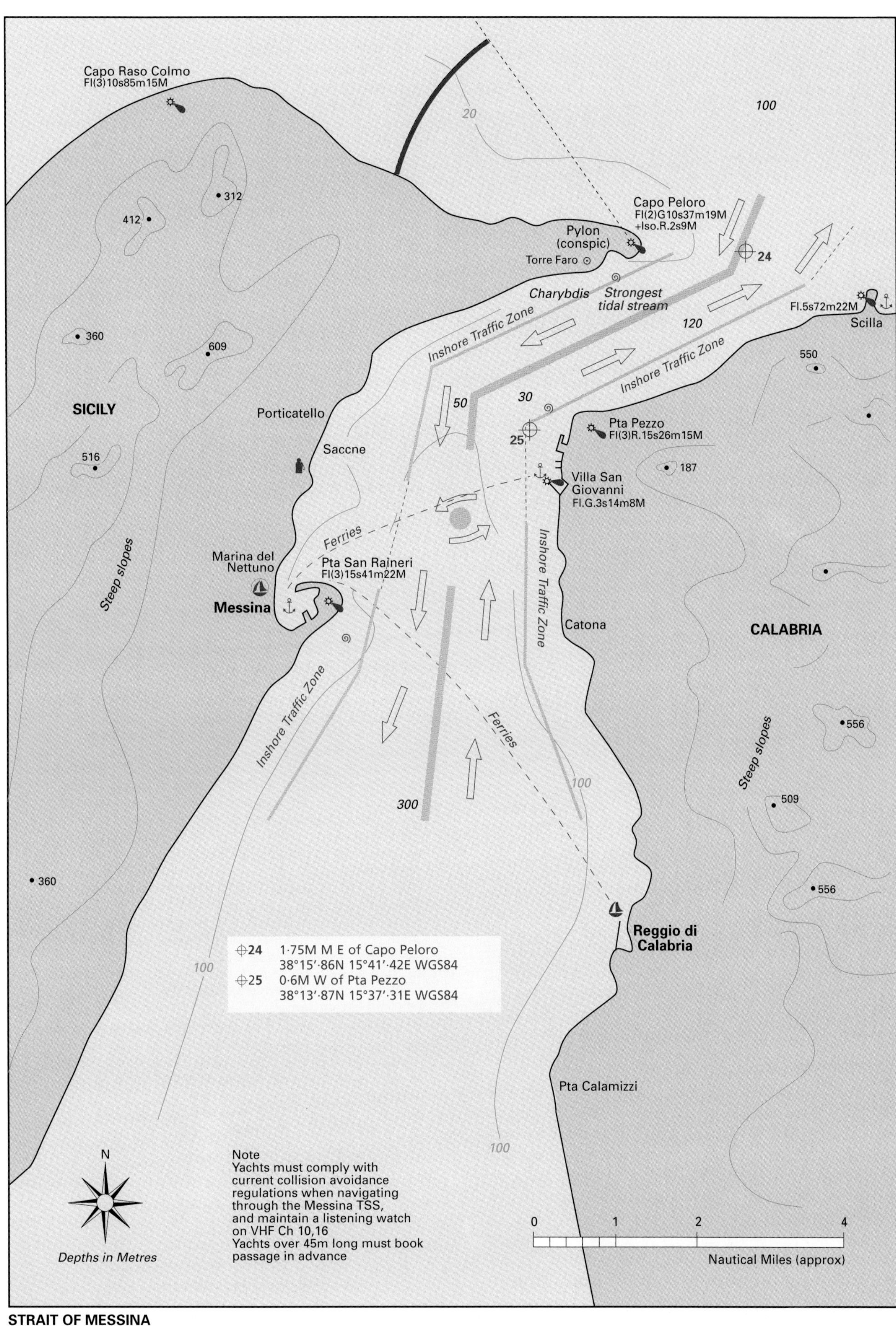
Capo Raso Colmo
Fl(3)10s85m15M
20
100
312
412
Capo Peloro
Fl(2)G10s37m19M
+Iso.R.2s9M
Pylon
(conspic)
Torre Faro
24
Charybdis
Strongest
tidal stream
Fl.5s72m22M
Scilla
120
Inshore Traffic Zone
360
609
550
Inshore Traffic Zone
50
30
SICILY
Porticatello
Pta Pezzo
Fl(3)R.15s26m15M
25
516
Saccne
187
Villa San
Giovanni
Fl.G.3s14m8M
Ferries
Inshore Traffic Zone
Marina del
Nettuno
Pta San Raineri
Fl(3)15s41m22M
Steep slopes
Messina
Catona
CALABRIA
Inshore Traffic Zone
Ferries
556
Steep slopes
100
509
300
360
556
Reggio di
Calabria
24 1·75M M E of Capo Peloro
38°15'·86N 15°41'·42E WGS84
25 0·6M W of Pta Pezzo
38°13'·87N 15°37'·31E WGS84
100
Pta Calamizzi
N
100
Note
Yachts must comply with
current collision avoidance
regulations when navigating
through the Messina TSS,
and maintain a listening watch
on VHF Ch 10,16
Yachts over 45m long must book
passage in advance
0
1
2
4
Depths in Metres
Nautical Miles (approx)

STRAIT OF MESSINA

V. SICILY

Swordfishing boat in the Strait of Messina

Swordfish

Swordfish (and tunny) regularly migrate through the Messina Strait and peculiar boats have evolved there to catch the migrating fish. The swordfish swim southwards in the spring and northwards in June. The old sword fishing boats had perhaps a 10-ft mast with a lookout atop, four rowers, and a harpooner in the bows. These are no longer seen as modern motor boats with immense lattice steel masts and bowsprits have taken their place. The bowsprit is longer than the boat and on the larger craft may be a good 15m (50ft) long. The mast has a chair at the top for the captain who can steer the boat from his perch. An electric winch hoists him up and down. The whole affair is elaborately stayed and the boats operate only in calm weather. Apparently the swordfish 'sleep' on the surface during the day, or at any rate move sluggishly, and the sword fishing boat can creep up and harpoon the unsuspecting fish. Certainly I have surprised swordfish near the Strait which have leapt out of the water barely 50m off my bows. Whatever the theory, the method works.

Scilla and Charybdis

The whereabouts of many of the places visited by Odysseus in the Odyssey have been disputed, but there has never been any doubt that Scilla and Charybdis existed in the Messina Strait, recent popular theories notwithstanding.

In antiquity passage through the Strait was considered perilous in the extreme, but was pursued for the obvious reason that the alternative was to sail all the way around Sicily. In a small craft a yachtsman is in a much better position to understand and appreciate the dangers encountered by Odysseus on passage through the Strait than is, say, the passenger of a large ferry or other ship pushed by powerful engines and untroubled by tidal streams and mountain squalls. To the latter, Scilla and Charybdis are naught but ancient myth, whilst to the yachtsman the dangers are encountered at gut level. Circe warned Odysseus of Scilla and Charybdis: Scilla 'the Render' and Charybdis `the Sucker-down'.

Scilla was said to dwell in a cave atop a sheer cliff on the eastern side of the Strait. She had 12ft which dangled down and six long necks with horrible heads which reached down to pluck dolphin and swordfish from the Strait or sailors from passing ships. At the bottom of the cliff a whirlpool sucked down unwary ships.

Across from Scilla, Charybdis was said to be a giant whirlpool which swallowed ships which strayed too close to it. Today the Strait does not strike terror into the hearts of sailors, but to mariners of old the narrow Strait with its tides and eddies, its whirlpools and violent squalls descending from the mountains, must have appeared frightening.

It is possible that the Strait was more fearsome in antiquity. A whirlpool did exist under Scilla until in 1783 an earthquake altered the local topography. The Admiralty *Pilot* states: 'There is (however), every reason to suppose that a whirlpool did exist off the town of Scilla and that both it and Charybdis were rather more impressive then than the latter is today.' I have read an account of water-spouts in the vicinity of the Strait and the supposition that ancient Scilla was simply Homer's description of such waterspouts. Although I have not seen waterspouts around the Messina Strait, I have seen them elsewhere, and they remain as frightening today as they must have been to Odysseus. Even as late as 1824 the Strait was considered dangerous when Admiral Smyth wrote: 'To the undecked boats of the Rhegians, Locrians, Zancleans and Greeks, it (Charybdis) must have been formidable; for even in the present day, small craft are sometimes endangered by it, and I have seen several men-of-war, and even a 74-gun ship, whirled around on its surface.' This was after the earthquake of 1783 which altered the sea bottom and to some extent tamed Scilla and Charybdis.

Whatever the historians in their comfortable armchairs say, I remember running under bare poles, blown by a winter gale into the Messina Strait, and being all too conscious of Charybdis and squalls and blinding rain and fear.

Strait than with tidal streams. In the words of the redoubtable Admiralty *Pilot*: 'The currents and whirlpools, famous from antiquity, are such as to necessitate some caution in the navigation of the Strait, moreover, in the vicinity of the high land, on either side, vessels are exposed to violent squalls which descend through the valleys with such strength as, at times, to inconvenience vessels.'

Approaches

Since 2008 a VTS Scheme operates through the Straits. All vessels should maintain a listening watch on VHF Ch 10, 16. Vessels moving in the TSS have priority over small craft. The northern approach is straightforward by day and night, but care must be taken of the numerous ships converging on or leaving the Strait.

Capo Peloro is fringed by a bank for a short distance off with depths of less than 5·5m over it, but otherwise the fairway is deep and free of dangers and presents no problems to a yacht entering or leaving.

Tidal streams and whirlpools

Strong tidal streams, such as to cause problems for small yachts, occur only at springs and will only reach an appreciable rate in the narrow northern part of the Strait. Between Punta Pezzo and Capo Peloro the stream can attain 4kns at springs but to the N and S of this narrow section the stream rapidly diminishes in strength. However, I have encountered a slight current (perhaps 1kn) as far away as Capo dell'Armi and Taormina. Under normal conditions the north-going stream begins at about one hour 45 minutes before high water at Gibraltar. The south-going stream starts at four hours 30 minutes after high water at Gibraltar. Both these times are for the streams off Punta Pezzo.

The tidal streams in the Strait are caused by the different times of high and low water between the Tyrrhenian and Ionian Seas such that twice each lunar day there is a maximum slope southward and twice each day a maximum slope northward. Strong winds from an opposite direction can shorten the duration of the tidal stream and conversely strong winds blowing with the stream can cause it to run longer and stronger. The north-going stream is known locally as *montante* and the south-going stream as *scandente*.

The Tyrrhenian sea is warmer and less salty than the Ionian, and the difference in density between the two seas sets up currents which flow southward at the surface and northward below about 30m. At each turn of the tide there is a brief stand followed by one or more bores, or *tagli,* caused by the difference in density between the Tyrrhenian and Ionian seas and by the particular submarine shape of the Strait. In the narrow part of the Strait the *tagli* are accompanied by eddies and whirlpools which can bother small yachts. With wind against tide there are short high breaking seas and with the eddies and whirlpools it is no place for a yacht to be. The eddies are termed *bastardi* (no translation needed) or *refoli* and mostly occur in the following areas:

With the north-going stream:

1. WSW of Capo Peloro off Torre Faro.
2. At the entrance to Porto Messina and for some distance north.
3. NE of Punta Pezzo.

With the south-going stream:

1. From San Salvatore fort and round Messina Harbour and up the NW coast.
2. S of Capo Peloro.
3. Off Acciarello.
4. Between Catona and Punta Calamizzi.

Capo Peloro looking NW from the Strait of Messina

Immediately after the *tagli* small whirlpools well up and disappear in the Strait. They are caused by denser water sinking and are accompanied by smooth oily patches which is the less dense water rising up. There are only three whirlpools of any size which could be a danger to small yachts and these occur in the following positions:

1. Off the beach S of Punta San Raineri.
2. About 200–250m off Torre Faro under Capo Peloro. This is the ancient Charybdis.
3. About 200m W of Punta Pezzo.

For more information on tidal streams see the Admiralty *Mediterranean Pilot Vol I* and *Imray Mediterranean Almanac*.

Winds

Winds normally blow straight up or down the Strait, hemmed in as it is by mountains on either side. In the summer (July and August) winds from the N predominate while in spring and autumn winds from the S can be expected. In unsettled weather there are very strong squalls off high land on either side which can be very violent at times. While waiting for good weather in Reggio di Calabria it is difficult to gauge what the weather is doing outside the Strait. Several times I have left Reggio in squally weather only to discover that, once clear of the Strait, there is an absolute flat calm in the Ionian – an experience shared by many others on passage through the Strait.

Saccne fuel pontoon

At Paradiso approximately 1½M N of Messina is the Saccne Fuel Pontoon with 2–3m depths off it. As well as diesel and petrol there is water and a supermarket close by. In calm weather this makes a useful stop to take on fuel when proceeding through the Strait of Messina.

Saccne ✆ 090 310 221 / 349 596 7075
VHF Ch 16 (0700–2100).

MESSINA

BA 917, 992
Italian 244

Approach

The commercial and ferry port for Messina is easily identified on the W side of the Strait of Messina. There are no useful yacht berths in the commercial harbour and a yacht should make for Marina del Nettuno situated close off the entrance to the commercial harbour.

MARINA DEL NETTUNO (Messina)

Approach

The marina is situated on the coast immediately N of the entrance to Porto Messina.

Conspicuous Ferries are constantly coming and going from Porto Messina day and night. The city of Messina is easily identified and closer in the statue on the E side of the entrance to Porto Messina will be seen. The masts of yachts in the marina will be seen when you are off the N side of Porto Messina.

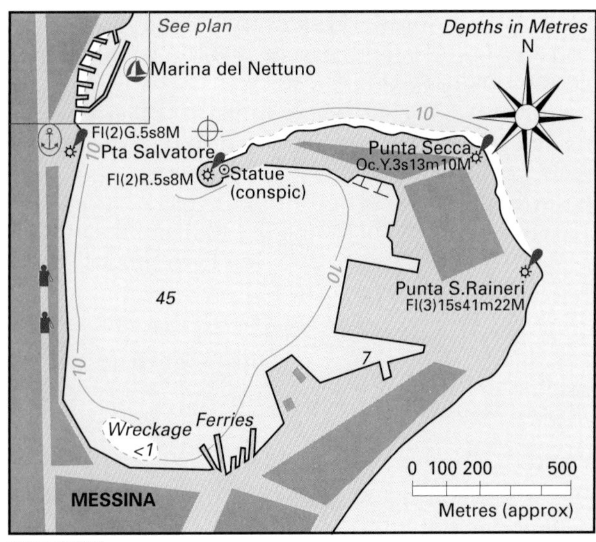

MESSINA
⊕38°11´·8N 15°33´·85E

VHF Ch 09.

Note Any tide running in the Straits of Messina will also effect the marina. S-going tides of up to 3kns have been reported.

Mooring

Data 160 berths. Visitors' berths. Max LOA 35–40m. Depths 5–20m.

Berth Where directed. Marina staff will assist berthing in a RIB. Finger pontoons (low), and laid moorings.

Shelter Good shelter, although there is a near-constant surge on the outer berths. Ferries and pilot boats generate a sizeable wake as they leave and enter the harbour at speed. Mooring warps are reported to chafe rapidly, and so care is needed if leaving a yacht here for any length of time. The marina uses a wave-breaker pontoon to shelter it and it could get a bit bumpy in here with a gale from the E–SE.

Authorities Harbourmaster and marina staff. Charge band 5.

Marina del Nuttuno
⊠ COMET, Via Garibaldi 150, 98122 Messina ✆ 090 344 139
Fax 090 371 0522
Email info.messina@marinadelnettuno.it
www.marinadelnettuno.it

Facilities

Services Water and electricity (220V). Showers and toilets. 24 hour security. Laundry service.
Fuel On the quay at the Saccne Fuel Pontoon 1½M north.
Repairs 70/250-ton travel-hoist. Some repairs can be arranged by the marina. Chandlers.
Provisions Supermarket nearby in Messina.
Eating out Numerous restaurants of all types in Messina.
Other PO. Banks. ATMs. Italgaz and camping gaz. Buses and trains all over Sicily. Ferries to Villa San Giovanni and Reggio di Calabria on the opposite shore.

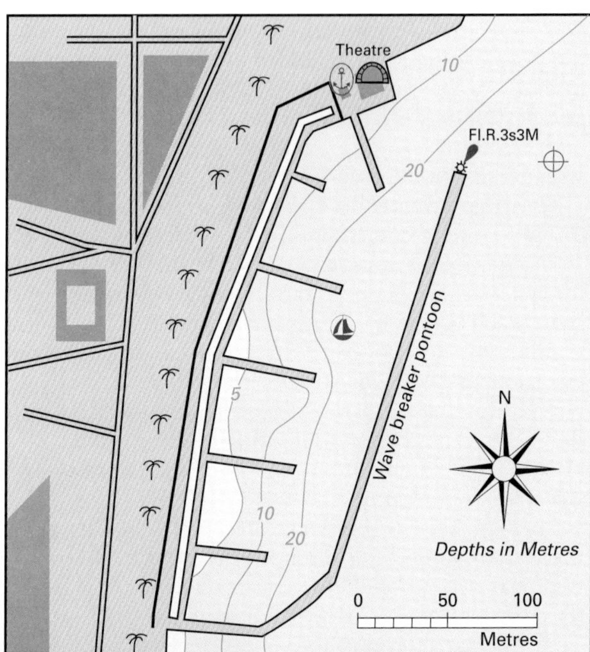

MARINA DEL NETTUNO
⊕38°11′·7N 15°33′·7E

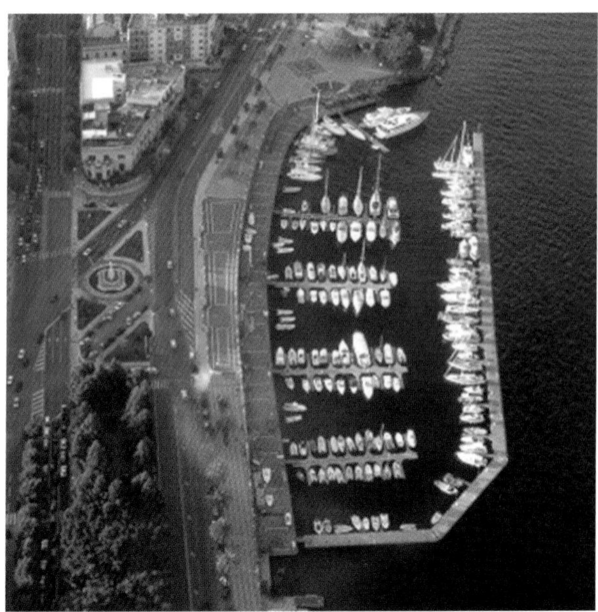

Marina del Nettuno (Messina) *Marina del Nettuno*

General

The first impression of Messina is of a flat city with few skyscrapers. This curious aspect is a result of the numerous earthquakes that have blighted the city and the present buildings are reputed to be 'quake-proof'. The city was devastated and levelled in the 1908 earthquake which also caused the shores of Messina to subside 0.6 of a metre (2ft), drowned hundreds in huge tidal waves and, in Messina alone, caused the death of some 64,000 souls. During the Second World War the city was again devastated by Allied bombing and, once more, had to be rebuilt.

TAORMINA ROADS

Approach

Taormina Roads lies under the old town of Taormina about 25 miles SW of Messina.

Conspicuous The northern end of the roadstead is readily identified by the houses and hotels of Taormina on a rocky spur. Above the town a castle is conspicuous and on Capo Taormina a large brown modern hotel is conspicuous. The southern end of Taormina Roads terminates in Capo Schiso, a low, black ancient lava flow.

By night There are no lights.

Mooring

Around Capo Taormina there are a number of anchorages. They are suitable in settled weather only. Around the beaches are cordoned-off areas for the bathers who are highly visible under the coloured sun umbrellas crowding the beaches in the summer.

Note The anchorages around Isola Bella lie within a Nature Reserve. Formerly managed by the WWF, control has been handed over to the Sicilian authorities. The rules regarding navigation and anchoring are unclear, but certainly the original intention was to prohibit all navigation and anchoring to protect the posidonia beds. During the summer coastguard patrol boats ensure that all craft stay clear of the area. The information below is retained in case the situation changes.

Mazzaro Bay On the N side of Capo Sant'Andrea. The bay must be approached from the ESE passing between Mazzaro Rock and the S side of the bay. Anchor in the S end of the bay and take a line to the above-water rock near the shore. Mooring buoys may also be available.

San Andrea Cove and Isola Bella Nature reserve. The bottom is rocky.

Under Capo Taormina Anchor where convenient under the lee of Capo Taormina. A swell will creep around into the bay with even NW–N winds.

Note The anchorages are crowded in the summer with swimmers, pedalos, sailing dinghies and windsurfers making it difficult to find a spot without disturbing others having fun in the water. You just need to play it by ear.

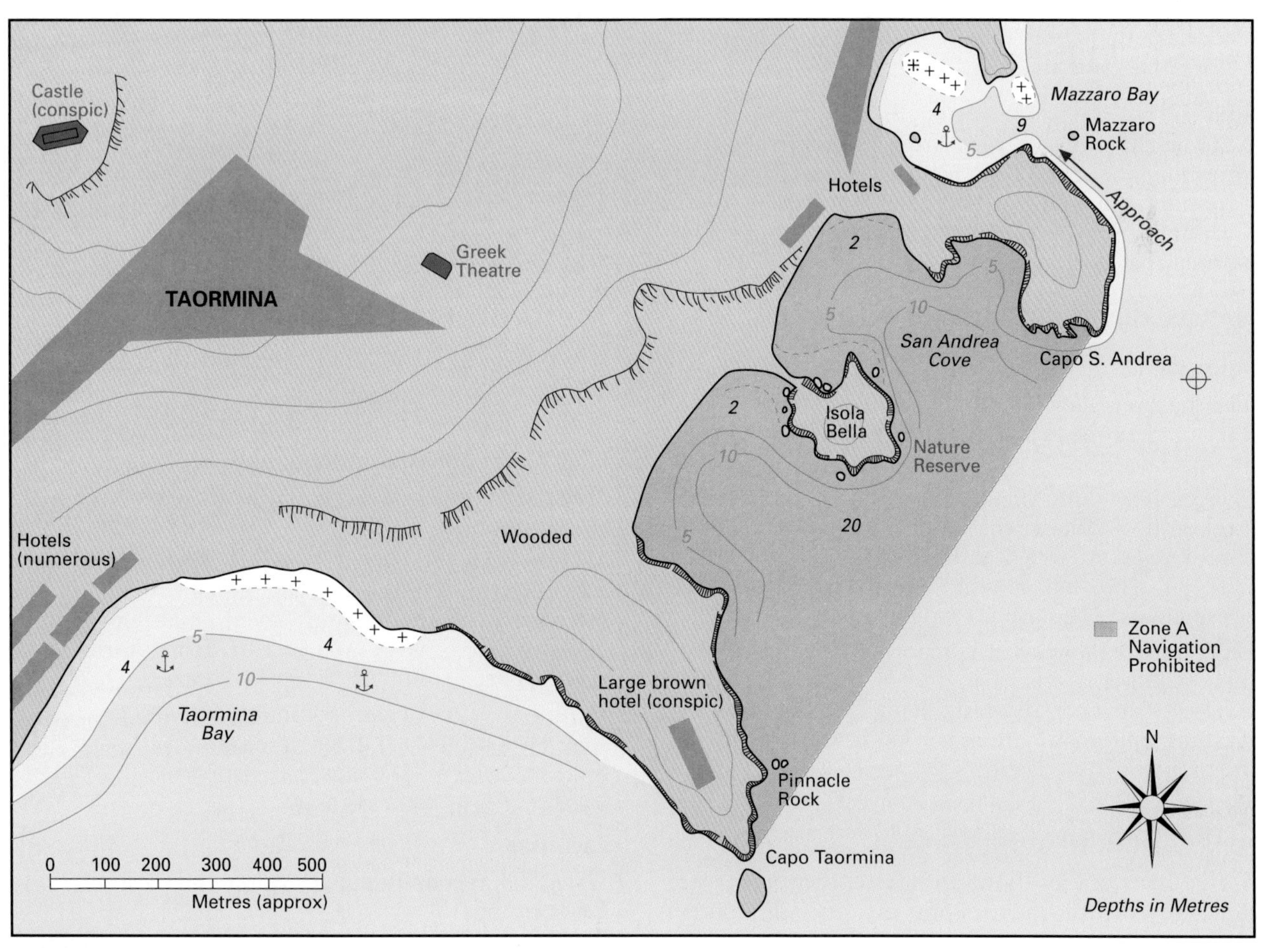

TAORMINA
⊕37°51′·0N 15°18′·4E

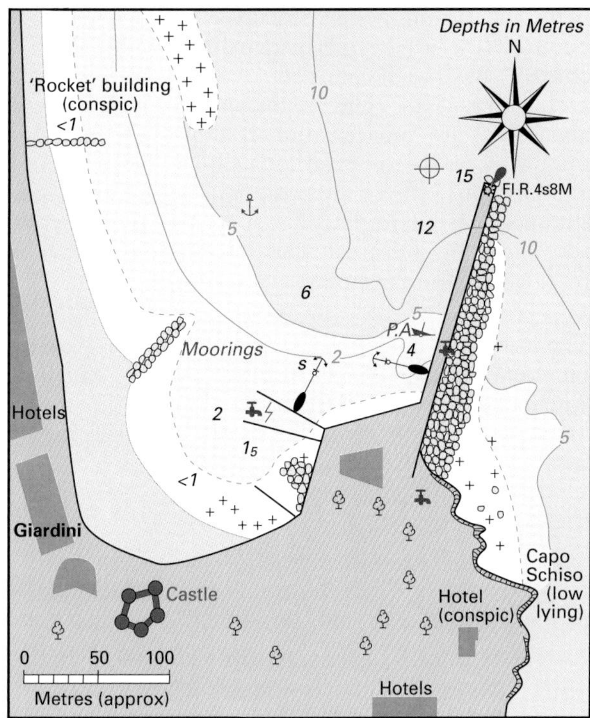

NAXOS (GIARDINI)
⊕37°49´·81N 15°16´·63E WGS84

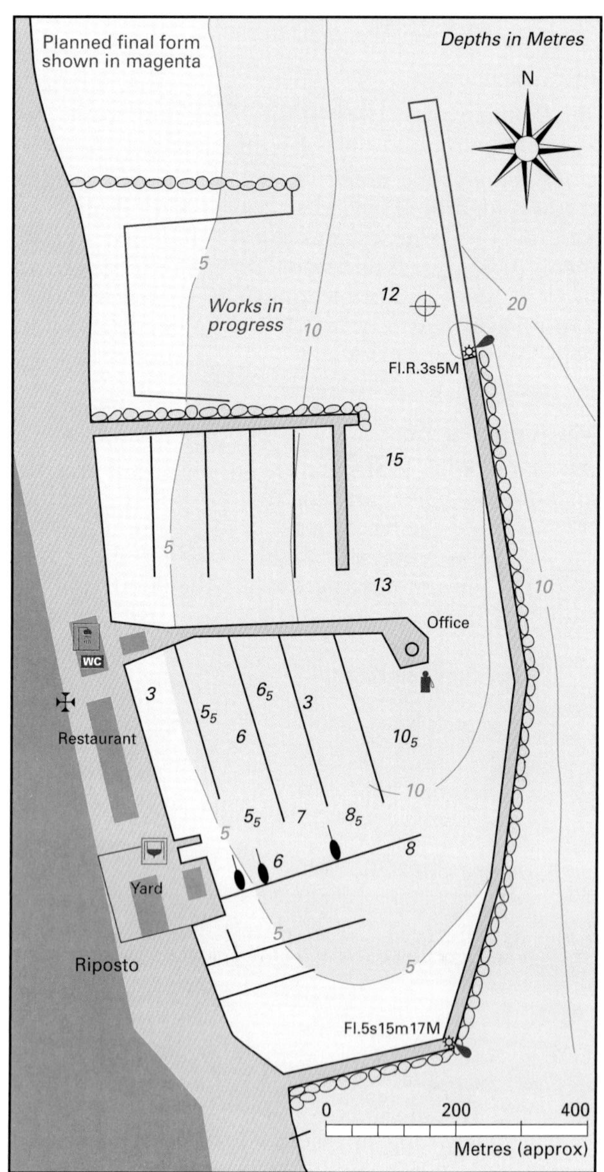

RIPOSTO MARINA DELL'ETNA

Facilities

There are numerous internet cafés and restaurants ashore and some shops for provisioning.

General

A funicular railway runs from Mazzaro Bay to Taormina and a bus runs regularly from all bays to Taormina. It is well worth an excursion ashore to see Taormina itself perched on the rocky bluff, but be warned that it is crowded in the summer.

NAXOS (GIARDINI)

Approach

The harbour lies about 1¾ miles SW of Capo Taormina on the N side of Capo Schiso, a low black ancient lava flow.

Conspicuous The village and a large number of modern hotels lining the beach to the N and S are conspicuous. A large building looking like the nose-cone of a rocket to the N of the harbour is conspicuous. The harbour mole is easily identified.

Dangers Off the quay it is reported (variously) that there is either a shoal patch or a wreck – or both. Whatever is here seriously limits the chances of berthing and great care is needed in the vicinity of the mole.

Mooring

Data Depths <1–6m.

Berth Go stern or bows-to where convenient or directed. Yachts up to 20m can use the outer pontoon. The bottom is coarse sand and not always good holding.

Note Yacht pontoons are not always in place.

Dangers Care needed of rusty protrusions 1m down from top of quay.

Shelter Adequate in the summer and surprisingly good even in light northerlies, though there always seems to be a ground swell making things uncomfortable. With moderate or strong northerlies you will need to move.

Authorities Ormeggiatori. Charge band 1/3.

Scalia Marina ✆ 340 617 2722

Pontoon Walter ✆ 347 621 0852

Marina Yachting ✆ 328 373 8669

Facilities

Services Water on the quay. Water and electricity on the pontoons.
Fuel In the town. You might be able to get a tanker to deliver.

Marina dell'Etna under the brooding bulk of Mount Etna *Marina dell'Etna*

Provisions Most provisions can be found in the town.

Eating out Restaurants, trattorias and pizzerias along the waterfront.

Other PO. Bank. ATM. Bus to Taormina.

General

Naxos (Giardini) is a thriving tourist resort, a sort of hotel suburb of Taormina. But while the hotels are modern and the bars blast out electronic drum beats, the site is the oldest Greek settlement on Sicily.

On the lava flow of Capo Schiso, the original site of Naxos has been excavated and finds are exhibited in the old Bourbon fort nearby. Colonists from Evia and Ionia in Asia Minor settled here around 750BC. Why the site is named after the island of Naxos in the Cyclades is not known. It prospered and in turn established sister colonies, but was destroyed in 403BC when it sided with Athens against Syracuse and was razed by the victorious Syracusans.

RIPOSTO

Approach

Straightforward by day and night.

Conspicuous A cupola in the town is conspicuous and the harbour is easily identified.

VHF Ch 14, 16 (0700–1900). Ch 74 for marina.

Note

1. There are often strong gusts off the slopes of Etna that cause a lumpy sea around Riposto.
2. Works are in progress extending the breakwater and developing the NW side of the harbour. Care needed in the approaches.

Mooring

Marina Porto dell'Etna

Data 360 berths. Visitors' berths. Max LOA 50m. Depths 3–10m.

Berth Where directed. Marina staff will meet you and assist mooring in a RIB. Laid moorings tailed to the pontoons.

Shelter Good shelter inside the marina. The proposed breakwater extension will afford excellent all-round shelter in the marina.

Authorities Harbourmaster and customs. Marina staff. Charge band 5/6 (July–August).

✉ Marina di Riposto Porto dell'Etna, Via Duca del Mare, 95018 Riposto
✆ 095 779 5755 *Fax* 095 779 8200
Email info@portodelletna.com
www.portodelletna.com

Facilities

Services Water and electricity (220/380V) at all berths. WC and shower block. Laundry service.

Fuel Fuel quay at the entrance near the control tower.

Etna

'... then Etna, that wicked witch, resting her thick white snow under heaven, and slowly, slowly rolling her orange-coloured smoke. They called her the Pillar of Heaven, the Greeks. It seems wrong at first, for she trails up in a long, magical, flexible line from the sea's edge to her blunt cone, and does not seem tall. She seems rather low, under heaven. But as one knows her better, oh, awe and wizardry! Remote under heaven, aloof, so near, yet never with us. The painters try to paint, and the photographer to photograph her, in vain!'

D H Lawrence *Sea and Sardinia*

The summit of Mount Etna lies 10 miles W of Riposto. Although the Admiralty *Pilot* describes it as very prominent, this is only true in winter. In summer the mountain is often so obscured by haze that it is difficult to make out its outline even when close to the coast. It should not be relied upon as a conspicuous feature for coastal navigation. Its height, like that of all volcanoes, varies: in 1950 it was 2,798m (9,180ft), in 1,936 about 2,801m (9,190ft) and in 1900 about 3,273·5m (1,0740ft).

The most recent big eruptions were as follows:

1669 Earthquakes began on 8 March, becoming worse over a period of three days. On the third day a deep crack some 14km long opened down the side of Etna and explosions threw rock and ash over a wide area and rivers of lava devastated the surrounding countryside. Catania was destroyed.

1886 Lava flowed to within a hundred metres of the village of Nicolosi where the Veil of Santa Agatha had been brought to save the village.

1892 This eruption formed Mt Silvestri.

1910 Eruption around Mt Silvestri.

1928 Occurred between 12 and 20 November and destroyed a large area of citrus orchards and a number of villages.

1971 Occurred between 4 April and 12 May. This eruption destroyed the old funicular and the observatory. The lava flow stopped about 7km from the sea.

1983 Etna again erupted and remained active for 50 days. Lava destroyed the cable car and numerous houses.

2001 Etna erupted through July and August and lava flows threatened some villages. Ash was blown for hundreds of miles. At the time I was in Siracusa and every morning the decks were covered in a layer of fine black volcanic sand so that the boat resembled a black sand beach.

If possible an excursion should be made up Etna from either Catania or Riposto. A bus travels up to 1,923m from where a gondola-lift takes passengers to 2,608m. From there four-wheel drive vehicles take you to near the summit and guides can escort you to the crater. Although it may be hot at sea-level, be sure to take warm clothes and stout shoes for the summit where it can be very cold even in summer.

Etna *ENIT*

Repairs 160-ton travel-lift. 45-ton crane. Boat-mover. Most work can be arranged, including fibreglass, carpentry and mechanical repairs.

Provisions Good shopping for provisions in the town. Small daily market in the square overlooking the harbour.

Eating out Restaurants, trattorias and pizzerias in the town.

Other PO. Banks. ATMs. Italgaz and Camping Gaz. Bus and train to Catania and Messina. Catania international airport 35km.

General

The town is one of the few not given over to tourism in the summer along this stretch of coast. It is a proper working town and has a pleasant somewhat decayed and dusty feel to it, although the new marina may well bring greater prosperity to the place. Brooding almost overhead is, of course, Etna, though you are unlikely to see her except at sunset because of the haze that envelops the coast in the summer. At night though, you have a ringside view of any glowing lava flows rolling down the mountain. With the new marina here Riposto is a good place to leave a yacht for a trip up to Etna by train via Catania. And with the airport nearby, it is likely to attract over-wintering yachts.

Torre Archirafi

⊕ 37°42'·5N 15°13'·2E

A short breakwater extends in a W to E direction off the hamlet with 1–3m depths reported under it. Suitable in calm weather if you can find a place on it.

Pozzillo

⊕ 37°39'·6N 15°11'·9E

A small fishing harbour approximately 2½ miles S of Riposto. The breakwater is easily spotted when coasting N or south. There are reported to be 5m depths in the entrance decreasing quickly to 2m under the breakwater. A small yacht may find a berth in here among the local boats.

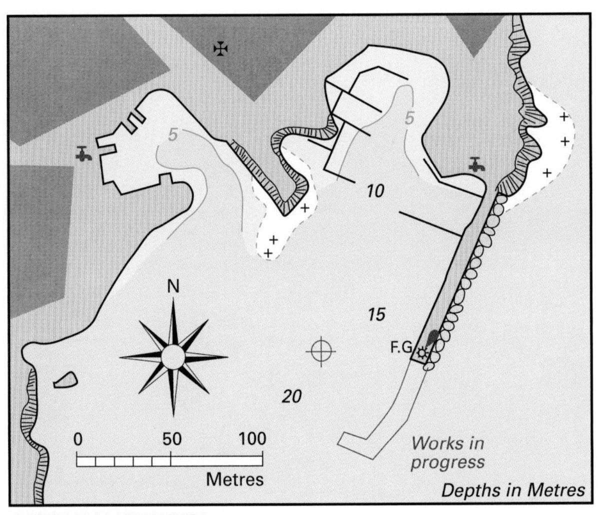

ACIREALE (STAZZO)
⊕37°38′·8N 15°11′·5E

ACIREALE (STAZZO)

A small rock-bound harbour below the town of Acireale. A number of pontoons have been installed under the outer breakwater and a visiting yacht may find a place here. The bottom is rocky, with only indifferent holding, but will easily foul an anchor. Trip line recommended. The harbour is well sheltered except from S winds which are likely to push a swell in.

Water on the quay. Provisions and restaurants ashore. The small harbour is a most attractive place under the steep cliffs and the village around it well worth a visit.

Note Work is in progress extending the outer breakwater and when complete this will provide better shelter.

Santa Maria La Scala

⊕ 37°37′·0N 15°10′·6E

A small fishing harbour where a small yacht may find a berth. Space is tight and you should have everything ready before entering. Go stern or bows-to where directed on the quay along the breakwater. Depths 1–3m. The harbour is open S but has reasonable shelter from N–NW winds.

Nautica Diesel ✆ 095 800 078

ACITREZZA

Approach

Straightforward by day but difficult by night. The approach must be made from the N leaving the northernmost and largest of the Ciclopi (with a red

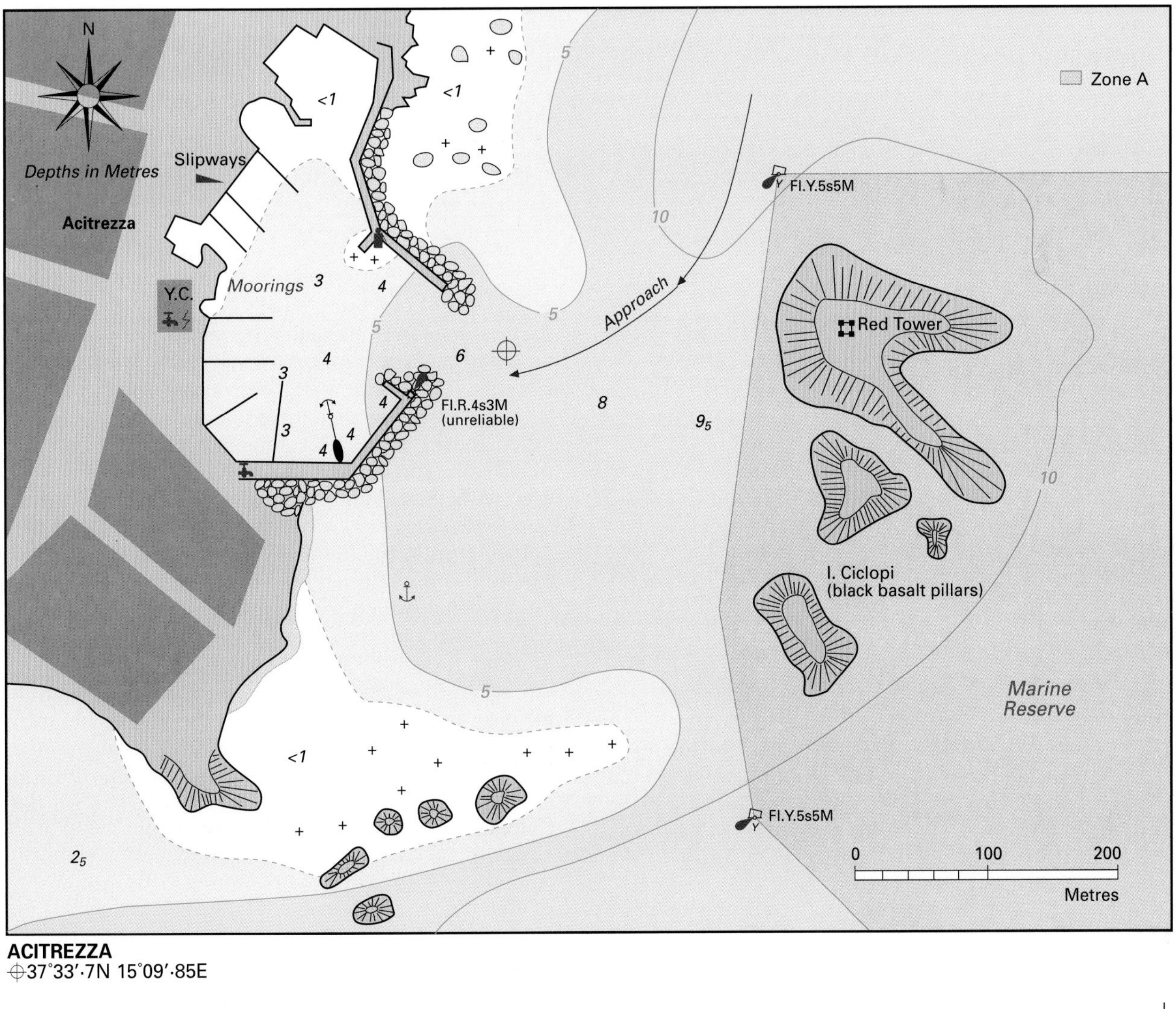

ACITREZZA
⊕37°33′·7N 15°09′·85E

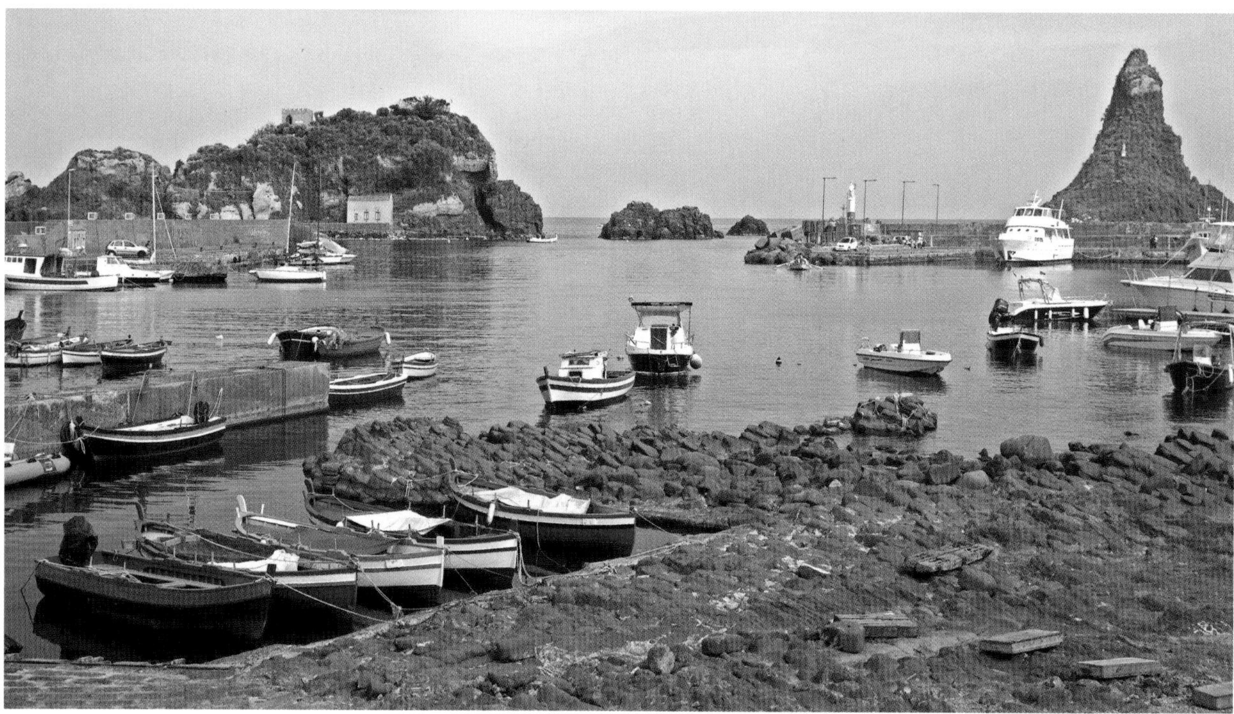

Acitrezza looking E with the red tower and Ciclopi just beyond the harbour *Sandro Bedessi, FOTOTECA ENIT*

tower on it) to port. Closer in the W buoy of the marine reserve will be seen and this can be left immediately to port.

Conspicuous The lighthouse on Capo Molini and the Ciclopi rocks are conspicuous from some distance. The Ciclopi are black basaltic pillars and stand out well against the coast. The harbour moles are easily identified.

By night A night approach is not recommended.

Dangers

The depths around the Ciclopi are variable and a yacht should enter and leave Acitrezza to the N of the Ciclopi. There is a buoyed passage to the SW of Zone A, best attempted in calm weather and in daylight only.

Mooring

Data Max LOA 25m. Depths <1–5m.

Berth Go stern or bows-to wherever you can negotiate a berth. Most of the pleasure craft berths belong to the local yacht club and it is usually full to bursting. The bottom is sand and rock and generally good holding.

Shelter Good shelter, although strong NE winds make the harbour uncomfortable though rarely dangerous.

Anchorage In settled weather anchor off to the S of the harbour, keeping close to the breakwater to avoid entering Zone A of the reserve. Otherwise pick up the white mooring buoy marked *ormeggiatori* and call the telephone number.

Facilities

Water At the small club and a fountain nearby.
Repairs Several small chandlers nearby.
Provisions Most provisions can be obtained nearby. Fish from the stands around the harbour. Ice from the fish van supplying the fishing boats.
Eating out Excellent restaurants around the waterfront.
Other PO. Italgaz and Camping Gaz. Buses to Catania.

General

Acitrezza is an attractive resort town which is crowded at the weekends with the locals from Catania. Acitrezza and nearby Acireale and Aci Castello take their names from Acis, the shepherd killed by the jealous Cyclops Polyphemus, because of his love for the sea nymph Galatea who was in love with Acis. Handel wrote an opera called *Acis and Galatea*.

The Ciclopi, the fantastic black pillars rising from the sea, are said to be the rocks the blinded Polyphemus hurled after Odysseus fleeing with his crew. When Odysseus landed on Sicily the one-eyed monster took him and 12 of his crew prisoner. He ate six and then Odysseus blinded him with a burning stake and escaped with the rest of his men by clinging underneath the Cyclops' sheep when they went out to graze. (However, Ernle Bradford in *Ulysses Found* identified the west of Sicily with the Cyclops.)

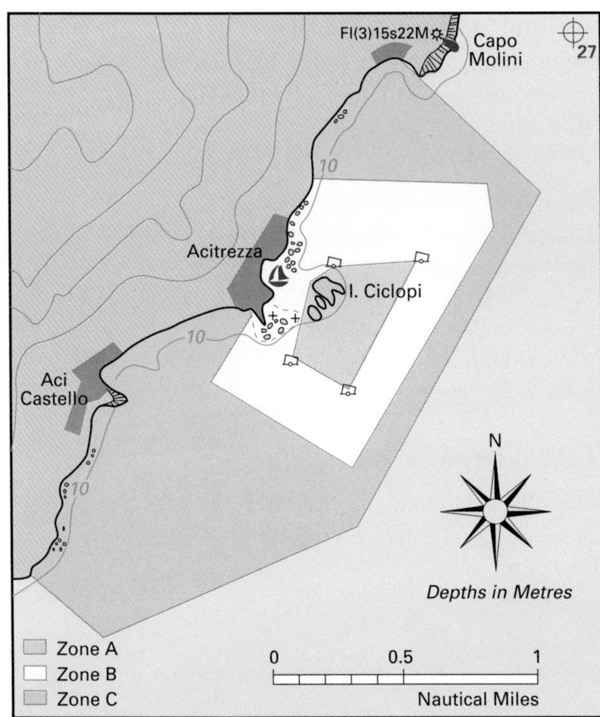

ISOLE CICLOPI MARINE RESERVE

⊕**27** 0·5M E of Capo Molini
37°34′·49N 15°11′·32E WGS84

Isole Ciclopi Marine Reserve

A marine reserve has been created around Isole Ciclopi stretching from Capo Molini to nearly a mile S of Aci Castello. The zone extends up to 1M offshore. Zone A covers an area around Isole Ciclopi marked at the extremities by four yellow buoys (all Fl.Y.5s5M). Access to Acitrezza is immediately W of the NW buoy.

Zone A
Navigation and anchoring prohibited.

Zone B
Fishing prohibited.

Zone C
Commercial fishing prohibited.

✉ Visitors' Centre, Via Provinciale 226, Acitrezza
✆ 095 711 7322 *Fax* 095 711 8358
Email amp@isoleciclopi.it
www.isoleciclopi.it

OGNINA (Porto Ulisse)

Approach

This small fishing harbour lies just N of Catania. It is difficult to identify by day and night.

Conspicuous The slopes around the harbour are lined with apartment blocks. Immediately S of the harbour a buff-coloured mansion can be identified and the harbour mole shows up well.

By night The E breakwater is lit F.R, but it is difficult to see against the lights behind.

Dangers In E winds the harbour may be difficult to enter.

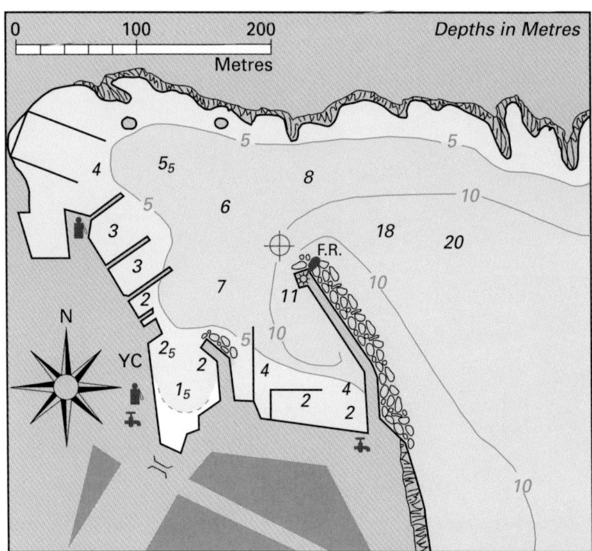

OGNINA (Porto Ulisse)
⊕37°31′·55N 15°07′·3E

Mooring

Data Depths <1–10m.

Berth Go stern or bows-to where directed. The harbour is very crowded with fishing boats and it is difficult to find a place. A *porto turistico* is being developed.

Dangers There are many mooring buoys and floating warps, particularly in the S side of the harbour.

Shelter Good behind the mole but uncomfortable with strong E winds.

Authorities Harbourmaster. charge band 2/3.
Porto Turistico ✆ 095 494 152

Facilities

Water On the quay.
Fuel In the town, although some distance away.
Provisions Limited except for fish which is sold from stands around the harbour. Ice can be obtained from a van which brings it down for the fishing boats.
Eating out Good restaurants around the harbour.

General

Ognina is situated in a rather fashionable suburb of Catania and in the summer the harbour area is a riot of colour and life during the evening *passeggiata*.

CAITO

A small basin N of Catania harbour. It is entered via a narrow canal with depths less than charted at 2·5m in the entrance, shelving rapidly inside the harbour. The entrance is dangerous with strong onshore winds. Berths adjacent to the travel-hoist have just over 2m depths, with less elsewhere. Laid moorings tailed to the quay. Good all-round shelter inside.

Data 250 berths. Max LOA 18m. Depths <1–3m. Charge band 4/5.

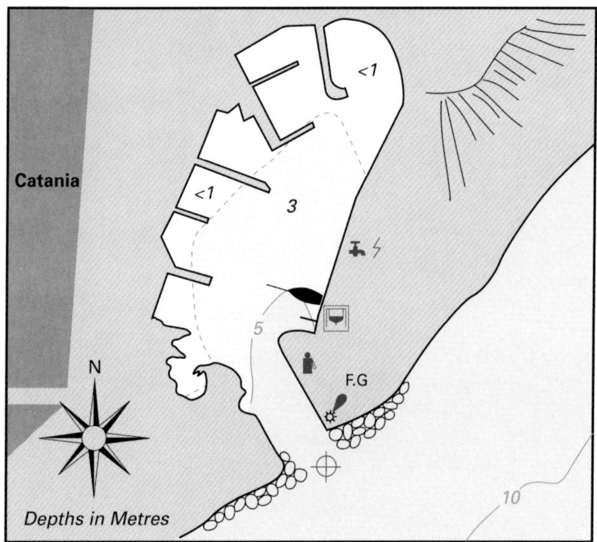

CAITO
⊕37°30′·75N 15°06′·3E

Facilities Water and electricity at most berths. Fuel on the quay. Provisions and restaurants nearby. You are right in the middle of Catania, in fact nearly in Piazza Europa in the middle of town.
Caito MEC ☎ 095 374 966 *Fax* 095 382 995

CATANIA

BA 992
Italian 272

Approach

Straightforward, although there is invariably a ground swell in the approaches to Catania. There may be quite violent gusts off the high ground around Etna. With strong SE winds there is a heavy confused swell at the entrance making entry difficult.

Conspicuous A very tall chimney behind the harbour and a number of smaller chimneys to the N of the harbour are conspicuous. The outer mole with a large crane atop it is also conspicuous from some distance off.

Note There are plans to develop a *porto turistico* to the S of the main harbour.

By night The aerobeacon at the airport AlFl.WG.35m(occas) is also useful.

VHF Ch 12, 16 for port authorities (0700–1900). Ch 12, 14, 16 for pilots. Ch 77 for Club Nautico. Ch 06 for Diporto Nautico Etneo. Ch 09 for Circolo Nautico NIC.
Ch 12, 09 for Mediterraneo YC.

(Note that any of these will answer on Ch 16 if called by name.)

Mooring

A yacht should head for one of the four yacht clubs:

1. Club Nautico

Data 40 berths. Max LOA 25m. Depths 4–8m.

Berth Where directed. Laid moorings. Good all–round shelter.
☎ 095 531 443 *Fax* 095 531 422

2. Diporto Nautico Etneo

Data 90 berths. Max LOA 30m. Depths 4–8m.

Berth Where directed. Laid moorings. Good all–round shelter.
☎ 095 531 347

3. Circolo Nautico NIC

Data 160 berths. Visitors' berths. Max LOA 15m. Depths 6–12m.

Berth Where directed. Laid moorings tailed to buoys. Adequate shelter although uncomfortable with strong SE winds when there is a considerable surge.
☎ 095 531 178

4. Mediterranea Yacht Club

Data 90 berths. Max LOA 30m. Depths 3–10m.

Berth Where directed. Prolonged southerlies make it uncomfortable here.
☎ 095 534 139 *Fax* 095 505 146

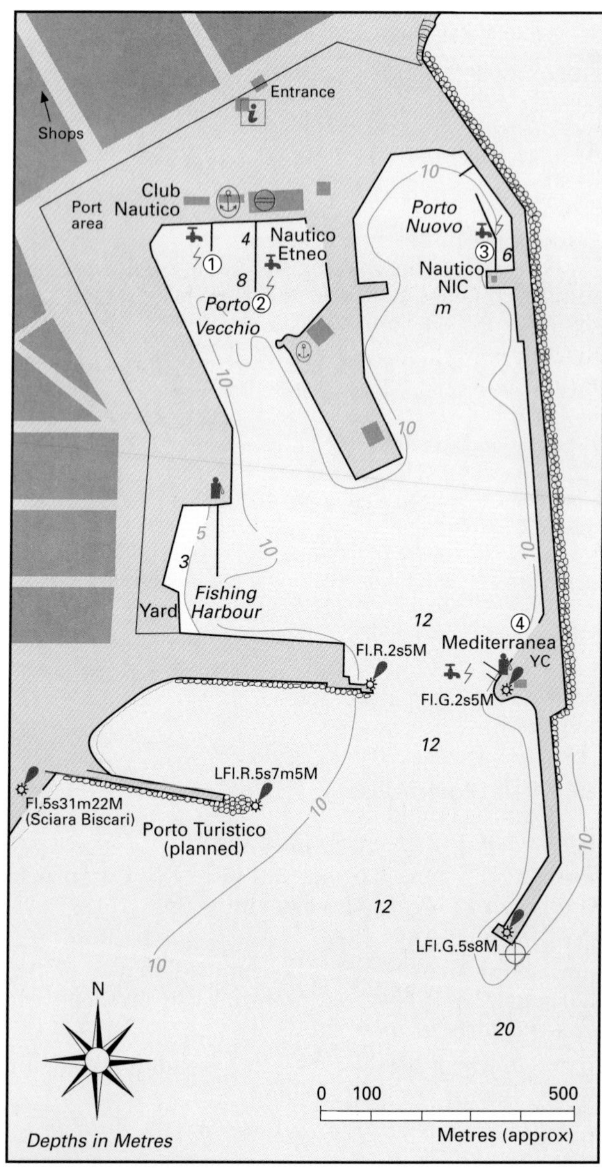

CATANIA
⊕37°29′·1N 15°05′·9E

Catania waterfront

Authorities Harbourmaster and customs. Club officials at all yacht clubs. Charge band 4.

The two outside clubs, Mediterranea and NIC, tend to be cheaper but more uncomfortable than the two inner clubs.

Facilities

Services Water and electricity at or near all berths. Showers and toilets at NIC.
Fuel At Mediterranea YC and can be delivered to the other YCs.
Repairs Slipway to 150 tons. 16 and 40-ton cranes. Mechanical and engineering repairs. GRP and wood repairs. Electrical and electronic repairs. Chandlers. Good hardware and tool shops.
Provisions Excellent shopping for all food supplies. Large daily market near the railway. Good fresh seafood. Ice can be delivered to the quay by a van that supplies the fishing boats.
Eating out Good restaurants including some good little local trattorias immediately behind the harbour.
Other PO. Banks. ATMs. Hospital. Italgaz and Camping Gaz. Hire cars. Bus to Nicolosi for a cable car up to Mt Etna. Buses and trains to Siracusa and Messina. Ferry to Reggio di Calabria and to Malta. Internal flights.

General

Catania is a large grimy industrial harbour surrounded by unattractive buildings. If you manage to penetrate the grime and noise ringing the harbour then the centre of the city comes as a pleasant surprise – slightly cleaner and, here and there, large 18th-century buildings hint at an elegant past. Like Naples, the proximity of Catania to an active volcano seems to breed a race of city-dwellers who care little for their city since at any time it might be flattened by nearby Etna.

In 1669 a mile-wide stream of lava swallowed most of the city and in 1693 an earthquake knocked over all that remained. Rebuilt to an elegant 18th-century style over the solidified lava (much of which was used in the construction), it has gradually sunk under the onslaught of post-war building. It is a safe place from which to organise a tour of Etna. (Staff at the local tourist office at the railway station are helpful.)

BRUCOLI

Approach

Difficult by day and night. The river has silted considerably since earlier surveys and the channel into the river is difficult to identify. A yacht should enter the river only in calm weather and with a careful eye on the depth sounder. A yacht drawing more than 1·5m should not attempt to enter the river. There is reasonable shelter in the adjacent bay with none of the problems of finding the winding channel.

Conspicuous The fort with its crenellated tower, the small lighthouse on the E side, and a large hotel complex on the W side are conspicuous.

By night A red neon light just E of the village has a good range. It would be foolhardy to enter the river by night and a yacht should anchor in the bay.

VHF Ch 09 for Marina di Brucoli.

Dangers The channel into the river appears to change and it is wise to seek local knowledge. With onshore winds it would be dangerous to enter.

Mooring

Brucoli River

After successfully negotiating the channel a yacht has little room to turn before going alongside the cliff where indicated. A new small craft harbour has been dredged out of the silt, but depths here are less than 1m.

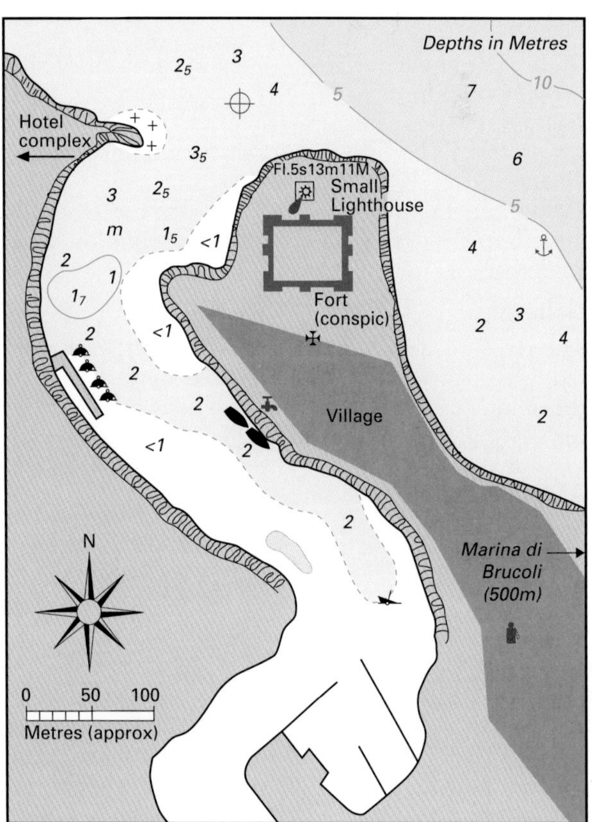

BRUCOLI
⊕37°17′·2N 15°11′·2E

V. SICILY

Brucoli inside the river looking NW

Marina di Brucoli

A new pontoon marina on the E side of the bay to the E of the river.

Data 150 berths. Max LOA c.15m. Depths 2–6m.

Berths Go stern or bows-to where directed. Laid moorings tailed to the pontoon.

Shelter Excellent inside the river. The bay to the E of the village and Marina di Brucoli is open only to the north.

Authorities Ormeggiatori. The local *carabinieri* may ask for your papers.

Marina di Brucoli ✆ 0931 981 808 / 335 782 8354
Email marinadibrucoli@nauticaglem.it

Anchorage Anchor off in the bay where convenient depending on wind and swell.

Facilities

Water Tap above the rough quay in the river. Water on the pontoon.
Fuel On the quay in the marina.
Provisions Basic provisions can be obtained in the village.
Eating out Limited to a few local trattorias unless you go to the expensive restaurants around the bay.
Other PO. Train and bus to Catania.

General

The river anchorage sounds more attractive than it really is, being somewhat dirty and quite smelly in the summer. The new marina provides more berths for visiting craft and the village is pleasant enough.

AUGUSTA

BA 966
Italian 271

Approach

Straightforward by day and night. Augusta is a huge deep water oil port and there are good depths everywhere.

Conspicuous There are a large number of tall chimneys and industrial buildings in the vicinity of the port and usually a number of ships anchored off the harbour. Closer in, the breakwaters are easily identified.

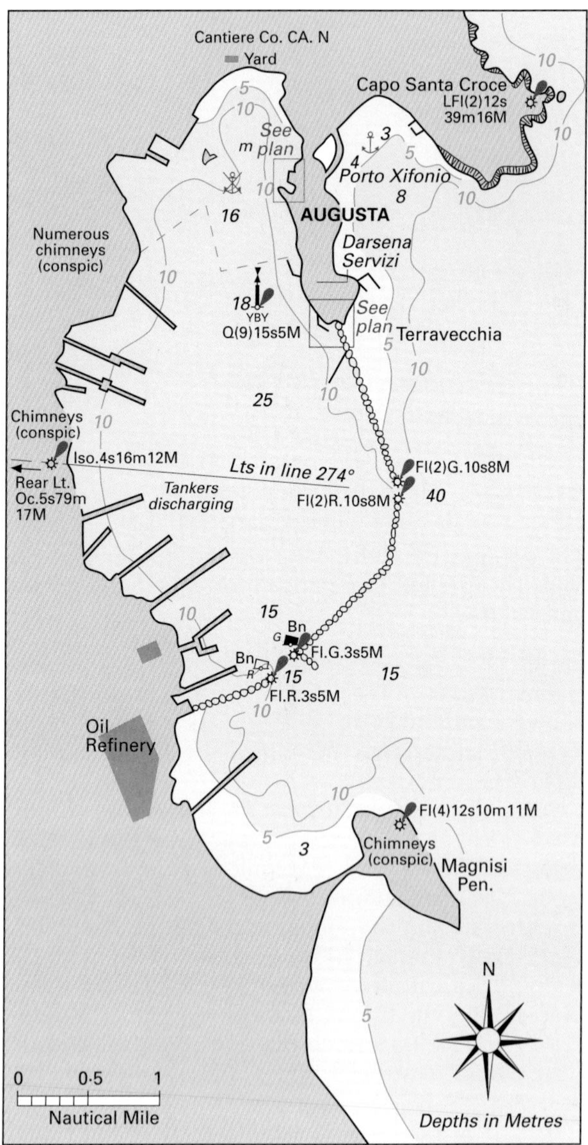

AUGUSTA APPROACHES

By night The piers on the W side of the huge harbour are all lit with various combinations of F/R/G/Y lights. There are also a number of flares on the shoreside refinery.

VHF Ch 11, 16 for port authorities (0700–1900). Ch 12 for pilots. Ch 82 for *ormeggiatori.*

Note There are buoyed deep water channels within Porto Augusta but there are generally sufficient depths (5–6m) outside of the channels.

Mooring

There are a number of possibilities:

Cala del Molo A basin in the NE corner of the harbour. Few visitors' berths. Good shelter.

Terravecchia A basin to the S of Cala del Molo. Go alongside or stern or bows-to where possible. Open S but otherwise good shelter.

Darsena Servizi The basin between Cala del Molo and Terravecchia. Go alongside or stern-to where possible.

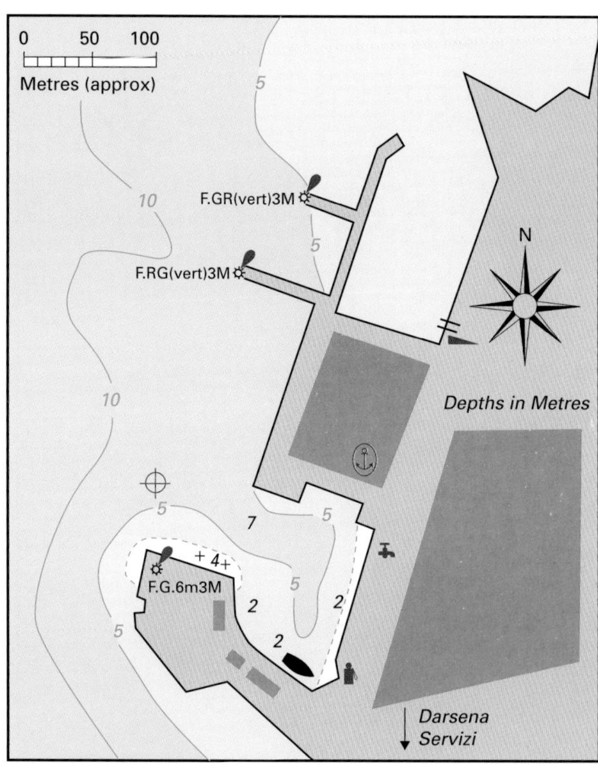

AUGUSTA - CALA DEL MOLO
⊕37°13′·9N 15°13′·1E

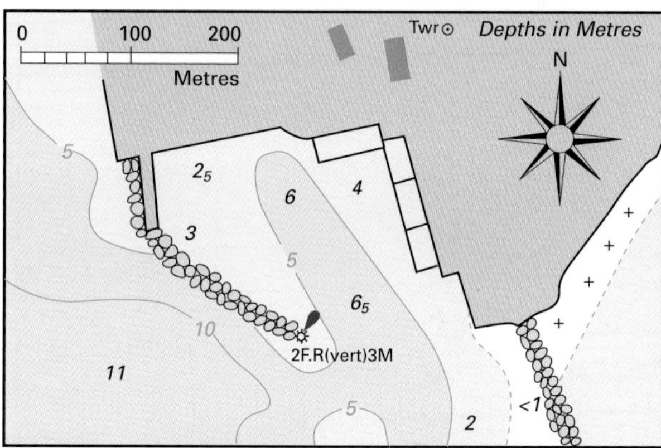

AUGUSTA - TERRAVECCHIA
⊕37°12′·9N 15°13′·5E

Cantiere CO.CA.N A boatyard at the N end of Augusta. Berth where directed. Laid moorings tailed to small buoys. Open south.
✆ 0931 512 352.

Anchorage Under Capo Santa Croce yachts can anchor out in Porto Xifonio. Anchor in 3–5m on mud. Open S so the prevailing wind may blow in here. In the evening it usually dies off so try it and see. There is a small harbour on the NE side of the bay. It is usually full with local boats but a small yacht could investigate the possibility of a berth.

Facilities

Water On the quay at Cala del Molo and Cantiere CO.CA.N.
Fuel On the quay in Cala del Molo.
Repairs The boatyard at the head of the bay has a 16-ton crane and can carry out most repairs.
Provisions Good shopping for most provisions.
Eating out Limited.

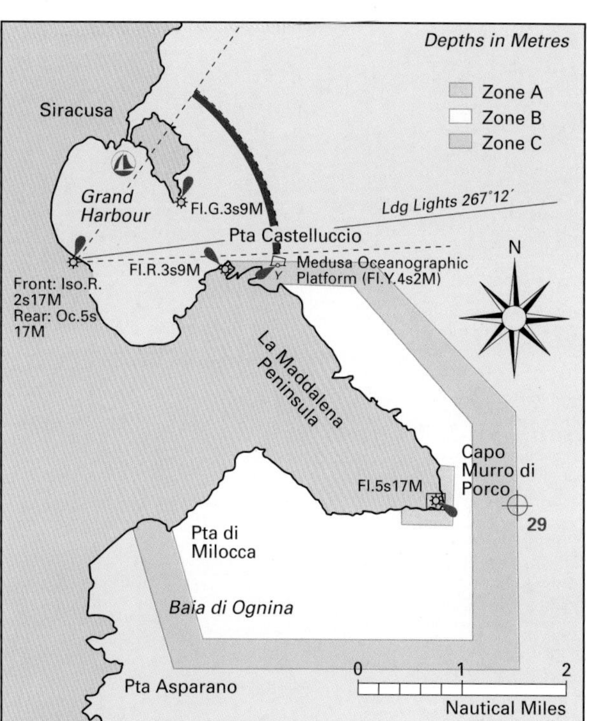

PLEMMIRIO MARINE RESERVE

⊕**29** 0·75E of Capo Murro di Porco
37°00′·10N 15°21′·20E WGS84

Plemmirio Marine Reserve

Plemmirio Marine Reserve was established in 2005 to protect the unusual geological and biological characteristics of the Maddalena Peninsula on the southern side of Siracusa. The perimeter of the Marine Reserve extends for 6½M along the eastern coastline of this tectonic 'horst'. The reserve covers 2,500 hectares of protected sea and has recently been declared a world heritage site by Unesco.

The regulations are not yet clear, but the points below are extracted from the website.

- Anchoring is prohibited.
- Mooring using Marine Reserve authority buoys is permitted.
- Swimming and diving at authorised sites only.
- Fishing under licence only.

The general approach seems to be based on encouraging visitors to experience the park by visiting by boat, swimming and diving. There would seem to be few total restrictions as in other Marine Reserves, but it may be wise to keep out of Zone A in line with the normal Marine Reserve regulations.

✉ Consorzio Plemmirio, Piazza Euripide 21, 96100 Siracusa ✆ 0931 449 310 *Fax* 0931 449 954
Email info@plemmirio.it
www.plemmirio.it

General

Augusta is the main oil port for Italy and is surrounded by industrial development. It cannot be described as attractive by any stretch of the imagination, but does provide good shelter if needed along this stretch of coast. A yacht is recommended to make for Siracusa 12 miles S of Augusta.

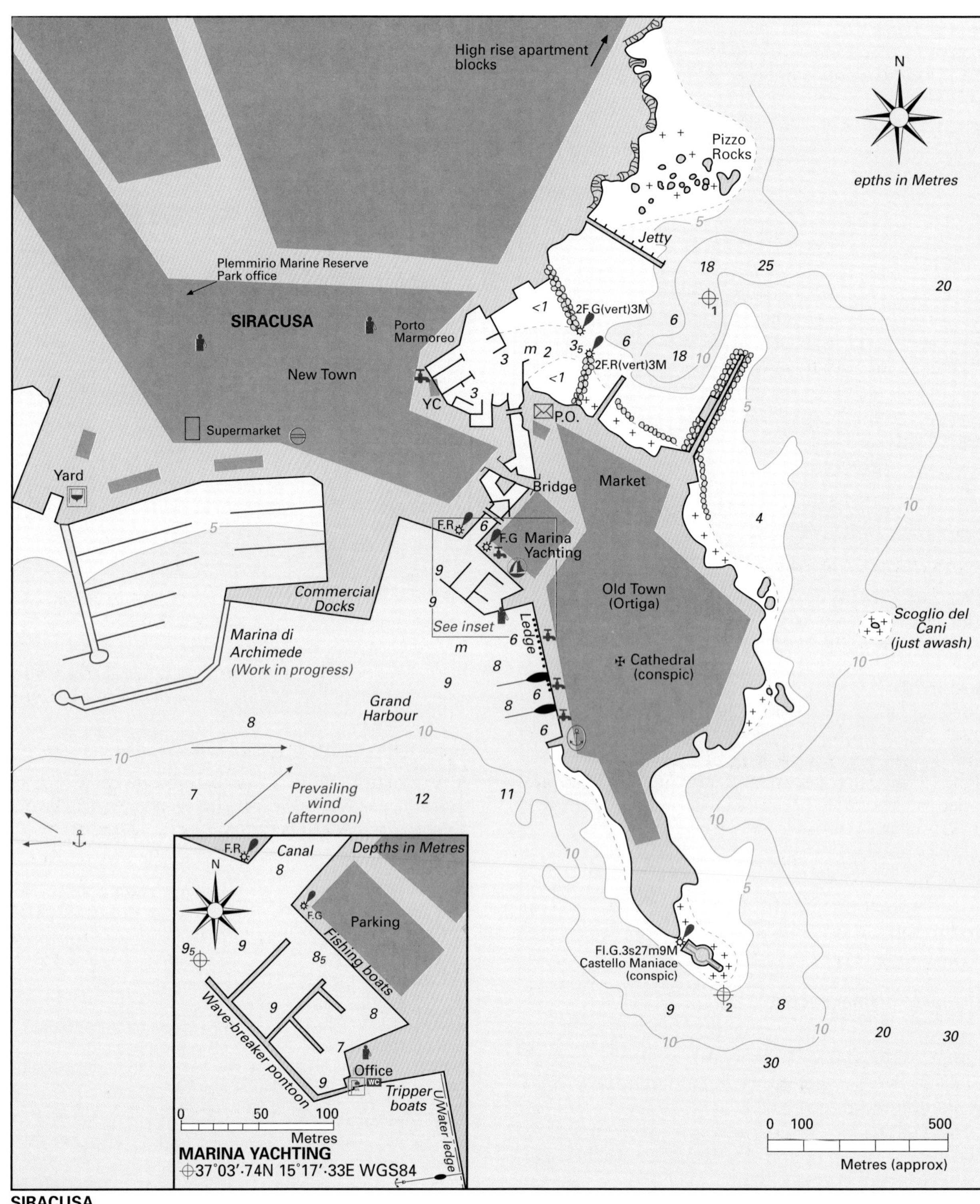

SIRACUSA
⊕1 37°04′·0N 15°17′·9E
⊕2 37°03′·06N 15°17′·77E WGS84

SIRACUSA (SYRACUSE)

BA 966
Italian 269, 270

Approach

Conspicuous The old town of Siracusa (Ortiga) on the peninsula is conspicuous from the E but not from the N or S if a yacht is following the coastline. From the N the recently built high-rise apartment blocks along the coast are conspicuous. From the S the lighthouse on Capo Murro di Porco is conspicuous. Closer in, the conical tower of the modern cathedral in the new town, the lighthouse on Punta Castellucio (with a red tower) and a white minaret immediately W of Castellucio lighthouse are conspicuous. The castle (Castello Maniace) at the tip of the old town is easily identified.

By night Use the light on Capo Murro di Porco Fl.5s34m17M, Punta Castellucio Fl.R.3s21m9M, and Castello Maniace Fl.G.3s27m9M. There are leading lights into Grand Harbour on 267°: front Iso.R.2s12m17M (224°-vis-274°), rear Oc.5s 25m17M (261°-vis-272°).

VHF Ch 09, 11, 16 for port authorities (0700–1900). Ch 14 for pilots. Ch 16, 69 for Marina Yachting.

Dangers Care should be taken of the Pizzo Rocks bordering the coast to the NE of the northern harbour and of the Cani rocks (Scog. de Cani) 300m E of the old town (see plan). The latter are usually just awash but in winds of Force 4 and up are difficult to identify from the whitecaps all around.

Note In the SW corner of Siracusa Bay there is an extensive mussel farm and a yacht should not venture into this area at night.

Mooring

Berth There are four possibilities depending on the wind:

Grand Harbour town quay

Data C.40 berths. Max LOA 50m. Depths 4–8m. Care needs to be taken of a low ledge that borders the quay along Grand Harbour. The quay has recently been upgraded, and has laid moorings at most berths. With prevailing wind in the summer blowing onto the quay it can get uncomfortable for small yachts on here. Generally the afternoon wind does not get up until midday and then dies down at night. It is really a matter of making sure you are pulled off the quay when the afternoon breeze gets up. Good shelter from northerlies.

Note A large concrete wall has been constructed along the quay. It is possible that once the new Marina di Archimede opens, yachts will not be able to berth here.

Marina Yachting

Data 180 berths. Visitors' berths. Max LOA 40m. Depths 7–9m.

A marina built off the fuel quay and the canal leading to Porto Marmoreo. Berth where directed. Laid moorings tailed to the pontoons. With southerlies there is a considerable slop and spray off the wave-breaker pontoon on the outside and a bit of surge inside, more uncomfortable than dangerous. With the prevailing W winds berths stern-to the outside of the wave-breaker are reported to be safe, but with S winds you should either go inside the marina or try in Porto Marmoreo.

Note Some marina pontoons are in disrepair. Visitors usually berth on outside of wave-breaker pontoon.

Siracusa. Castello Maniace in the approaches to Grand Harbour looking NW

Grand Harbour town quay

MARINA DI ARCHIMEDE

A new marina under construction on the W side of the commercial dock. Completion is due in 2011 but no dates are available yet, and it looks optimistic.

Data 550 berths. Max LOA 70m. Depths 4–10m.

Berth Go stern or bows-to where directed. Superyacht berths on the outer quay. Laid moorings at all berths. Looks to provide good all-round shelter inside the marina but the outer berths could get uncomfortable with strong southerlies.

Porto Marmoreo

Data Max LOA 15m. Depths <1–3m.

The yacht harbour on the north side of the old town. Most of the berths on the catwalk in the harbour are private club berths and there are few places for visitors. Try the pontoons in the NE corner. Good shelter and yachts are left here all year round.

There is some feeling that visiting yachts should go on the town quay or in the marina. This harbour can be very smelly from the sewage emptying into it and despite the diverting of some of the sewers, it still smells dreadful in the summer heat.

NW anchorages

Anchor in the NW corner off the beach in 3–5m. The holding on mud is excellent and although the afternoon breeze throws up a bit of a chop, once the anchor is in you are quite safe here. It is also close to dinghy into the customs quay off the new town for provisions. Alternatively you may be able to leave a dinghy up inside the canal.

Marina Yachting, Siracusa

S anchorage

Anchor in the S of the bay. Good shelter from the prevailing summer breeze.

Note There have been several reports of dinghy theft on the quay and at anchor at Grand Harbour. It may be wise to take sensible precautions if leaving a dinghy unattended.

Authorities Harbourmaster, *carabinieri* and customs. The authorities will often ask for papers. Marina staff at Marina Yachting and Marina di Archimede. *Ormeggiatori*. Charge band 5.

Grand Harbour SOGEAS (Societa Gestione Acque Siracusa)
✆ 0931 481 311/335 827 6998 *Fax* 0931 481 321
www.sogeas.it

Marina Yachting (Marina) ✆ 0931 419 002 / 333 413 3344
Fax 0931 412 346 *Email* info@marinayachtingsr.it
www.marinayachtingsr.it

✉ Cantiere Marina Yachting, via Stentinello 9, Siracusa
✆ 0931 756 515

Marina di Archimede
www.marinadiarchimede.it

Facilities

Services Water and electricity on Grand Harbour quay and at Marina Yachting. Showers and toilets to be installed.

Fuel On the quay in the marina (reported weekends only). Fuel by tanker by arrangement.

Repairs A 50-ton slipway. A 10-ton crane at the YC. Mobile crane up to 100 tons. Mechanical and engineering repairs. Wood and GRP repairs. Chandlers. Cantiere Marina Yachting (Targia) 160-ton travel-lift. 25-ton crane. Most repairs can be arranged.

Provisions Excellent shopping for all provisions. Excellent market for produce and fish. There is an excellent market in the old town and large supermarkets in the new town. From the NW anchorage you can take the dinghy across to the customs quay and leave it there. There are two cash-and-carry type shops here and supermarkets and bakeries further into the new town. In Grand Harbour a three-wheeler will visit the quay and can arrange to collect shopping and deliver ice.

Eating out Excellent restaurants, trattorias and pizzerias, particularly in the old town.

Other PO. Banks. ATMs. Hospital. Italgaz and Camping Gaz. Hire cars. Ferry to Malta.

General

The old town, Ortiga, is a delightful warren of alleys and staircases between the baroque limestone mansions now mostly subdivided into apartments. This was once the most powerful city-state of Magna Graecia, rivalling even Athens in power.

It was founded on Ortiga in 734BC by colonists from Corinth and later connected to the mainland by a causeway. It became the largest fortified city of the Greek world containing half a million people and commanding a great fleet. The Athenian expedition to quell the upstart colony attacked in 415BC and was defeated in 413BC when the Siracusean fleet locked the Athenian fleet in the bay and counter-attacked. Thus began Siracuse's great period of power under Dionysius the Elder and Dionysius I.

Siracusa controlled Sicily and the western Mediterranean and enjoyed some 200 years of prosperity until her quarrel with Rome. At the time, the great Archimedes was a resident of the city and he devised huge catapults and, it is said, a system of mirrors and lenses which concentrated the sun's rays and directed them onto the sails of the Roman ships, setting them on fire. The scientist was killed by a Roman soldier despite strict orders to capture his genius alive. Siracusa was bombed by both the Allies and the Germans in the Second World War and was extensively damaged.

Despite the damage suffered during the Second World War there are extensive remains of the old Greek city: the Greek theatre, the best preserved outside Greece; the quarries where Dionysius held the captured Athenians; a large part of the defensive wall built around the city; and, from the Roman period, a well-preserved amphitheatre. The so-called Fountain of Arethusa is at the S end of the town quay and is a pleasant place to relax. The National Archaeological Museum houses local finds from the Greek period. It is located in the Piazza del Duomo (closed on Mondays).

Avola

⊕ 36°53′·8N 15°08′·5E

Approximately 10M N of Balata it is reported a mole has been built at Avola. The mole runs ESE from the coast for approximately 200m. Depths are reported to be 5m at the extremity. Shelter from the N but open south.

North Bay

Approximately 3½ miles N of Balata is a bay which can be used in calm weather. It is sheltered from NW–W–SW. Anchor in 3–5m on sand and weed, good holding.

LA BALATA

Approach

A small harbour immediately N of the more conspicuous Marzamemi.

Dangers Care is needed in the immediate approaches and entrance to the harbour where depths are variable.

Mooring

Data 50 berths. Max LOA 10–12m. Depths <1–3m.

Berth Proceed carefully into the harbour and go stern or bows-to where possible.

Shelter Adequate shelter although brisk southerlies make it uncomfortable and possibly untenable.

Charge band 2.

Anchorage Anchor off under the islet and harbour in 2–3m on sand. Adequate shelter in settled weather.

Facilities

Restaurant and bar.

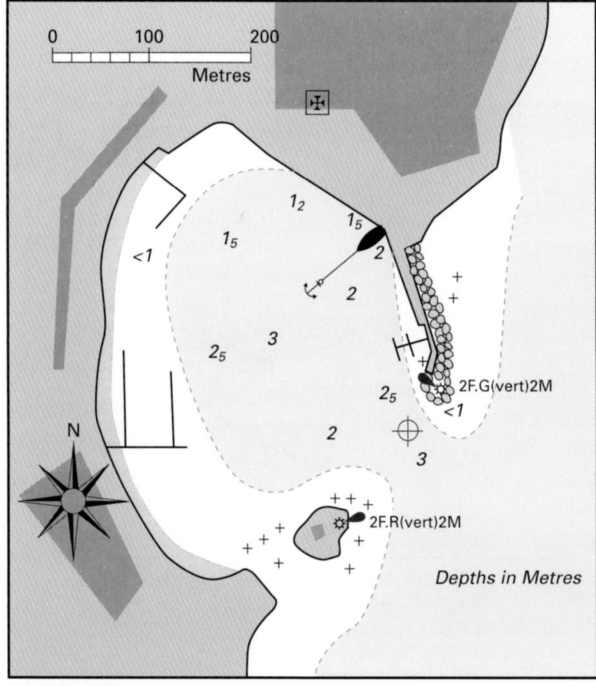

LA BALATA
⊕36°44′·4N 15°07′·2E

MARZAMEMI

Approach

Conspicuous The tall, white Spadaro lighthouse is conspicuous from some distance off. A tower behind the village and a white cement loader and hoppers are conspicuous. Closer in the harbour breakwaters are easily identified.

Note A number of large fish farms are moored in the bay between Marzamemi and Capo Passero. By day it is relatively easy to stay outside the buoyed areas marking off the fish farms, but at night picking out the various lights would be difficult.

By night Because of the fish farms in the vicinity a night approach should be made from the NE and with considerable care.

VHF Ch 16, 06 for Marina Sporting. Ch 09 for Yacht Marzamemi.

Dangers With strong southerlies there is confused swell at the entrance to the harbour. Inside the harbour care should be taken of the above and below-water rocks marked on the plan.

Mooring

Marina Sporting

Data 150 berths. Visitors' berths. Max LOA 20m. Depths 2–8m.

Yacht Marzamemi

A new pontoon marina with visitors' berths.

Data c.130 berths. Max LOA c.50m. Depths 1·5–5m.

Berth Go stern or bows-to where directed at Marina Sporting or Yacht Marzamemi. There are laid

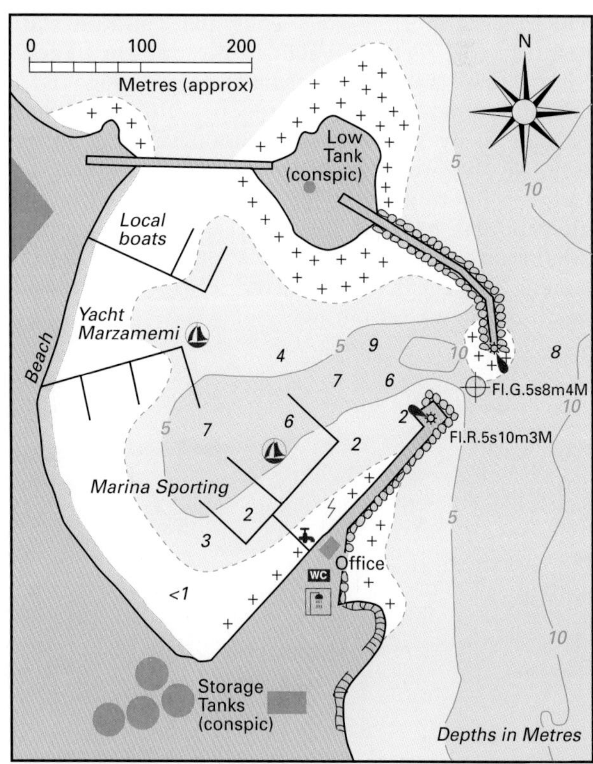

MARZAMEMI
⊕36°43′·99N 15°07′·40E WGS84

V. SICILY

Marzamemi. Looking towards Marina Sporting from the entrance

moorings tailed to the quay.

Shelter Good shelter although strong SE winds may cause a bit of a surge.

Authorities Harbourmaster. Charge band 5.

Marina Sporting ✆ 0931 841 505

Yacht Marzamemi ✆ 0931 841 776 / 331 269 5554
Email info@yachtmarzamemi.it

Facilities

Services Water and electricity at all berths. WC and showers.
Fuel Can be ordered at the marina.
Repairs 7-ton crane. Mechanical and engineering repairs can be organised.
Provisions and eating out Some provisions and restaurant/bar.
Note Nearest ATM is 3km.

General

The Marina Sporting is a friendly place and the staff helpful to visiting yachts. No doubt Yacht Marzamemi are similar. Marzamemi village is a peaceful spot – sometimes too peaceful. This is a part of Sicily where the afternoon siesta is taken seriously and in the small village you could be forgiven for thinking it has been abandoned in the afternoon – at least until the evening when the inhabitants re-emerge for the evening *passeggiata*. Recent work ashore has paved and pedestrianised much of the waterfront.

Capo Passero looking north

South coast

Porto Palo to Mazara del Vallo

PORTO PALO

Approach

Straightforward by day but difficult at night because of the many mooring buoys and ropes for the numerous trawlers using the harbour.

Conspicuous Spadaro lighthouse and Capo Passero and its lighthouse are conspicuous from a considerable distance. Closer in, the mole, the ice factory and two oil storage tanks at the root of the E mole are easily identified.

By night Care is needed of mooring buoys and ropes floating on the surface if entering at night.

VHF Ch 16.

Note Gas platforms and fish pens in the S approaches are not well lit.

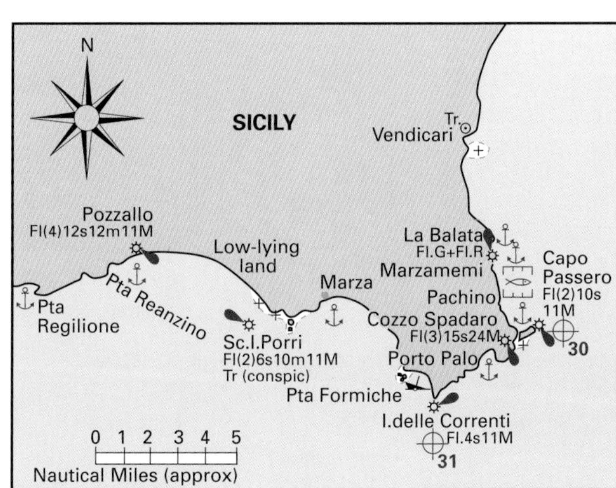

SICILY SE CORNER

⊕**30** 0·5M E of Capo Passero light
36°41'·23N 15°09'·85E WGS84

⊕**31** 2M S of I. delle Correnti
36°36'·3N 15°05'·6E

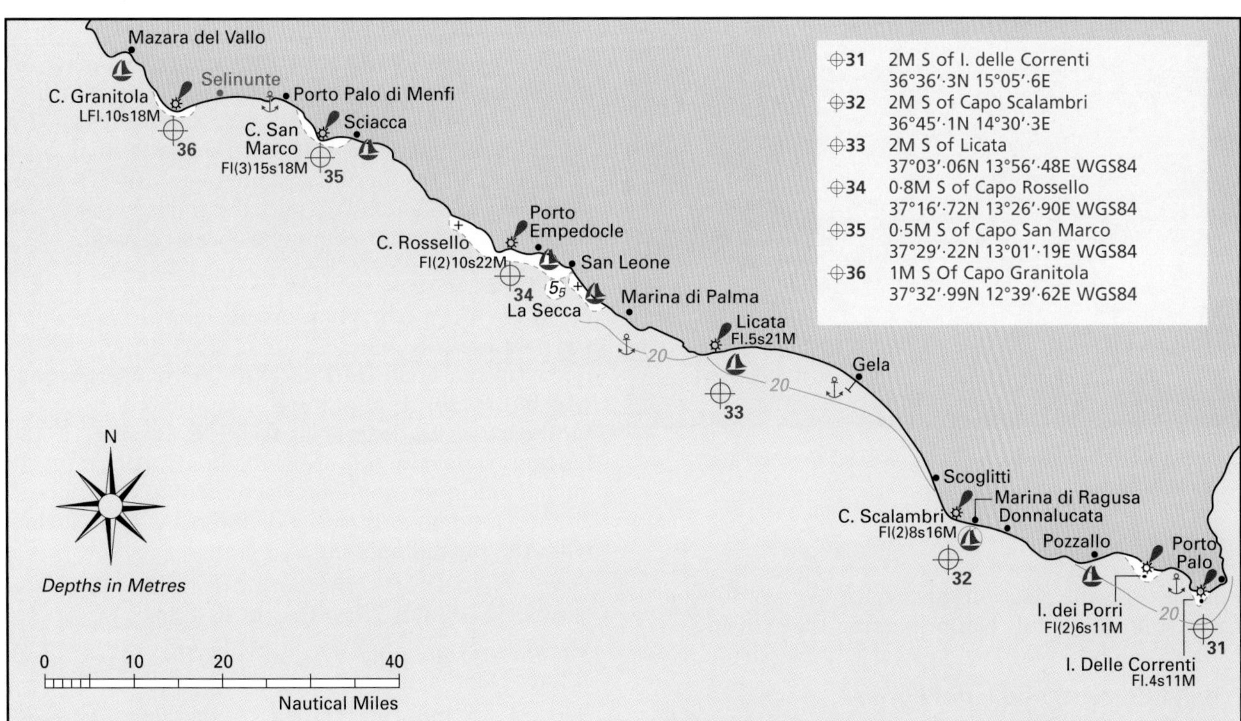

SICILY SOUTH COAST

Mooring

Berth Anchor in the bay clear of the local boats on moorings. Depending on the wind direction there is usually good shelter behind either mole although the E mole affords the best shelter. Under the E mole you must potter around for a bit to find a spot clear of all the permanent moorings. It is difficult to find a big enough spot to swing to an anchor behind the mole. Care is needed of the sunken wreck that is not always easy to see. With old ground tackle a probability a substantial tripping line is recommended. The bottom is sand and weed, good holding. On the W side it can be rock-bound in patches. There are several places a yacht can go bows-to the mole but caution is required because the ballasting extends some distance underwater.

Note A new 600-berth marina is planned, but no further details are available yet.

Shelter Good shelter from W–N–SE. However, with strong SW winds a yacht would be advised to anchor under the lee of the W mole or go to the N side of Capo Passero.

Authorities Customs.

Facilities

Water Limited from a tap near the ice factory.
Fuel On the quay but it is difficult to get to because the quay is crowded with trawlers.
Repairs There is a slip at the harbour for trawlers and an engineering shop nearby. Several yachts have been hauled here.
Provisions Some supplies can be obtained in Spadaro village on the hill. Ice from the factory.
Eating out A fish restaurant at the harbour.

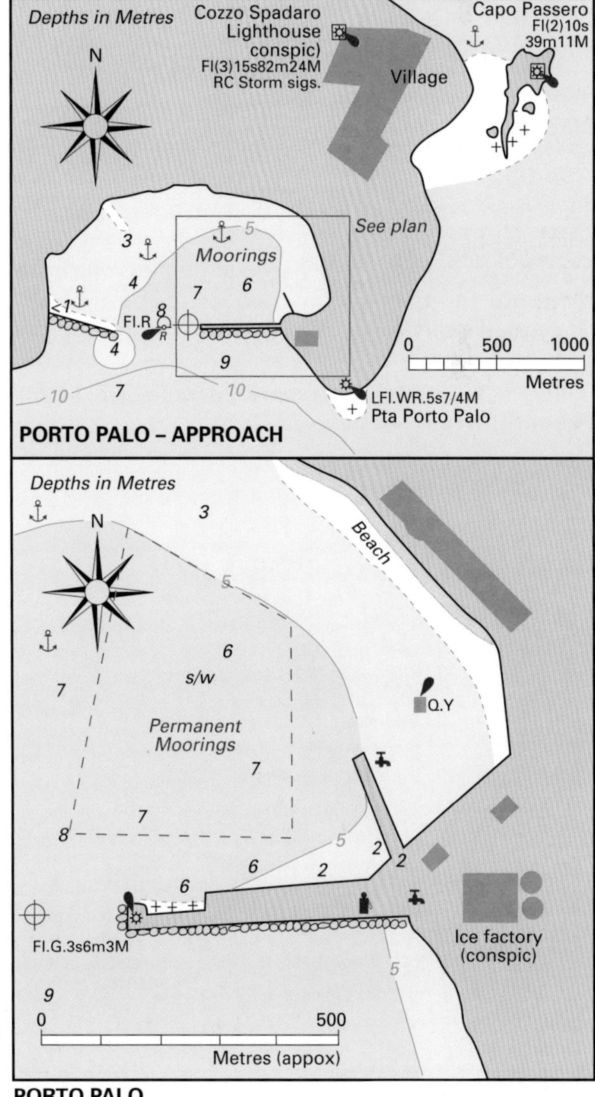

PORTO PALO
⊕36°40′·09N 15°07′·18E WGS84

Cozzo Spadero lighthouse and the village of Porto Palo looking west

General

Porto Palo is the place on this stretch of coast to wait for favourable winds before making the crossing to Malta.

I. delle Correnti and I. dei Porri

The coast around these two islets is shallow and care needs to taken of various above and below-water rocks, wrecks and other obstructions. Both islets are lit Fl.4s16m11M and Fl(2)6s10m11M respectively.

POZZALLO

Approach

The town of Pozzallo is conspicuous and the harbour lies immediately W of the town. The breakwater of the supply harbour running out from the shore and the tall cranes on it are conspicuous. The small craft basin lies on the NE side of the commercial harbour.

VHF Ch 16, 05 for Circomare Pozzallo. Ch 13 for Nautica Serra.

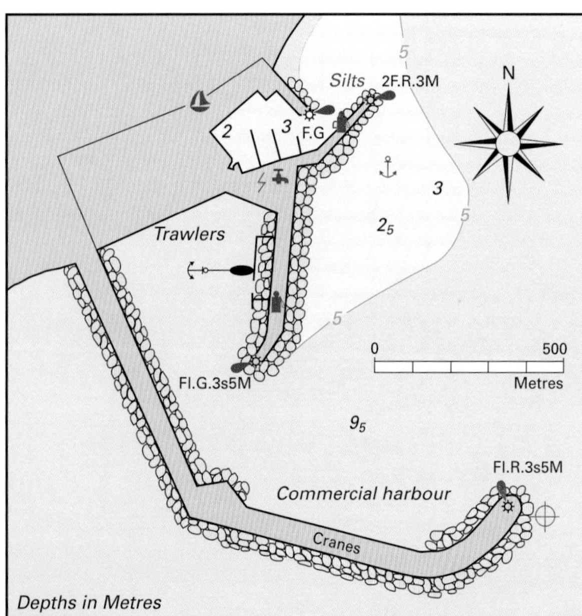

POZZALLO
⊕36°42′·5N 14°50′·6E

Note The small harbour is subject to silting, which reduces depths significantly. Dredging takes place on a remedial basis, so care is needed in the approaches. There is a line of red buoys near the S breakwater which in fact mark the starboard side of a small boat channel. Depths in this channel of just 0·2–0·5m were reported in 2005, and the yachts inside are trapped, although dredging has been planned.

Mooring

Head for the yacht pontoons in main harbour. Go stern or bows-to where there is space. Alternatively make for the small craft harbour (depths permitting) which has three pontoons administered by Serra Outboards and Lega Navale. The N side of the harbour is usually full of fishing boats. Alternatively anchor off in the angle between the two harbours in 2–5m. Good holding on sand, and reasonable shelter from the prevailing wind.

Data Small craft harbour 150 berths. Visitors' berths. Max LOA 25m. Depths 2–4·5m.

Main harbour pontoon c.25 berths. Max LOA c.20m. Depths 4–5m.

Berth Laid moorings tailed to the quay at most berths.

Shelter Adequate in settled weather in the outer harbour. Good shelter in the small craft harbour.

Authorities Harbourmaster.

Note A 400-berth marina is planned for outer harbour.

Ocean Plastic Nautica Pozzallo ☎ 0932 957 344 / 958 606 / 338 548 1683

Nautica Serra ☎ */Fax* 0932 955 520
Lega Navale ☎ 338 991 5019
Email nauticaserra@tiscali.it

Facilities

Services Water and electricity at or near every berth.
Fuel On the quay in both harbours.
Repairs Cantieri Navale Scala 150-ton travel-hoist. 20-ton crane. Some mechanical and electronic repairs. Chandlery.
Provisions Shops and restaurants in Pozzalo town.

Donnalucata

⊕ 36°45′·7N 14°38′·1E

A small and shallow harbour roughly halfway between Pta della Corvo and Capo Scalambri. Depths are everywhere less than 1m, and the narrow harbour is suitable only for small craft less than 6–8m.

MARINA DI RAGUSA

Approach

This new marina lies approximately 15M W of Pozzallo, and 35M SE of Licata. The buildings of the town, and the high breakwaters will be seen from some distance.

VHF Ch 74.

Mooring

Data 800 berths. Visitors' berths. Max LOA c.50m. Depths 2–5m. Min depth reported 2·5m (in 2010).

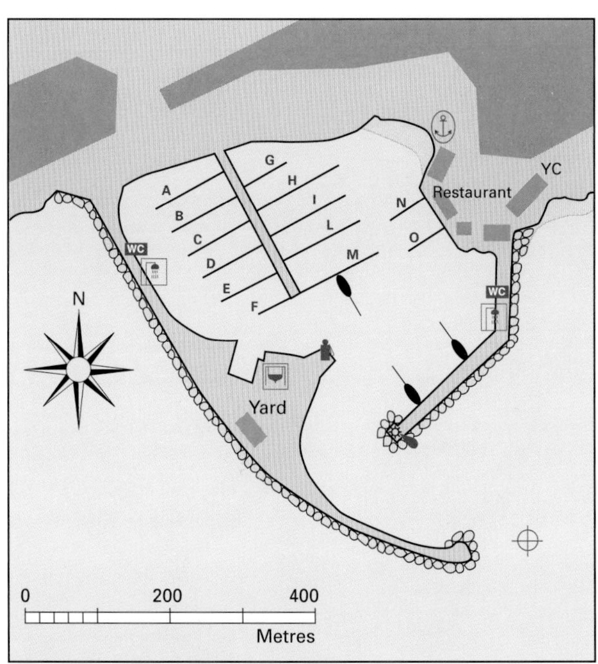

MARINA DI RAGUSA
⊕36°46'·54N 14°32'·94E WGS84

Berth Where directed. Pontoons with laid moorings at all berths. Small red buoys mark concrete mooring blocks which reduce depths to less than 2m in places.

Shelter Good shelter, although some berths may be uncomfortable in strong southerlies.

Authorities Marina staff. Charge band 6 (July–August).

Marina di Ragusa ✆ 0932 230 301 *Fax* 0932 239 466
Email info@portoturisticomarinadiragusa.it

Facilities

Services Water and electricity (220/380V). Showers and toilets. Wi-Fi to be installed.

Fuel On the quay.

Repairs 160-ton travel-lift. Yard and repair facilities due open September 2010.

Other ATM, bars, restaurants and other facilities under development. Good shopping and eating out in the town. Buses to Ragusa and Catania. 20km from the old military airport at Comiso. The airport is due to open to local and international flights sometime soon.

General

During the construction process the marina suffered from silting problems, but with the completion of the breakwaters this seems to have been solved. This new full service marina is a safe place to leave a yacht for travels inland, or over-wintering, and is a handy point to head for from Malta.

Ragusa, the city 20km inland, has been declared a UNESCO world heritage site, with stunning Baroque churches and palaces, museums and historic sites that well reward those few tourists who stop here. The seaside town of Marina di Ragusa was made famous from the late 19th century for its asphalt mines, and exported their 'black gold' to pave roads all over the world. Latterly the town concentrates on attracting tourists to its long sandy beaches, and one of the main attractions, 11km inland, is the 14th-century castle mansion of Donnafugata. Open to the public and accessible by train from Ragusa, this impressive building has been used as a film set for several movies, including the 1963 *Il Gattopado*, (The Leopard) starring Burt Lancaster.

SCOGLITTI

Approach

A large fishing harbour off the fishing village of Scoglitti. Shape a course due E towards the entrance where minimum depths of 3·5m have been reported recently.

By night A night approach should not be attempted without local knowledge.

Dangers Depths in the approaches and inside the outer breakwaters are variable and shallow in places. Silting causes the depths to change and it is advisable to seek local knowledge. Depths can be reduced to less than 1m. The harbour is home to a number of large trawlers that suggest reasonable depths should be maintained in the entrance. With onshore winds an entry over the uncertain depths could be dangerous.

Note Major works in progress on the harbour breakwaters.

The harbour at Scoglitti looking SE along the S breakwater
David Youngman

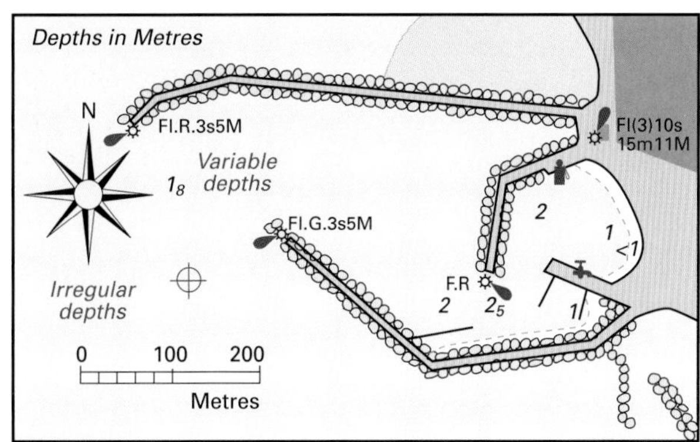

SCOGLITTI
⊕36°53´·4N 14°25´·6E

Mooring

Data 25 berths. Depths <1–2m variable. Max draft 1·5m. Max LOA c.15m.

Berth Local boats are moored along the S breakwater. Scoglitti Beach Club manages berths on pontoons in the entrance to the inner harbour, and a new pontoon in the outer harbour, where there may be the odd visitor's berth. You are advised to call ahead for a berth.

Shelter Good shelter.

Authorities Club staff. Charge band 3/4.

Scoglitti Beach Club ✆ office 393 4382 045 (Piedro)
Docking ✆ 339 5273 045 (Massimo)

Facilities

Services Water and electricity on the pontoons. Showers and toilets.
Fuel On the quay.
Repairs 20-ton crane. Minor mechanical repairs.
Provisions Most provisions can be found in the village.
Eating out Restaurants. One that is reported as being 'worth a special voyage' is Sakello ✆0932 871 688 (only answers during preparation and opening times).

General

The fishing harbour and village are attractive in a homespun, dusty sort of fashion. Great care is needed in the immediate approaches where at least one yacht has nearly come to grief.

GELA

Approach

The long pier of the ANIC oil jetty and the numerous chimneys of the refinery are conspicuous. The large town of Gela behind the harbour is easily identified.

By night Mooring buoys for oil tankers lie some 3M S of Gela Harbour. They are lit Fl.Y.4s. The outer breakwater of the ANIC pier lies 1M NNE of the mooring buoys. The W side is lit Oc.G.4s3M and the E side Oc.R.4s3M.

Dangers The harbour is liable to silting and care is needed in the immediate approaches and in the harbour itself.

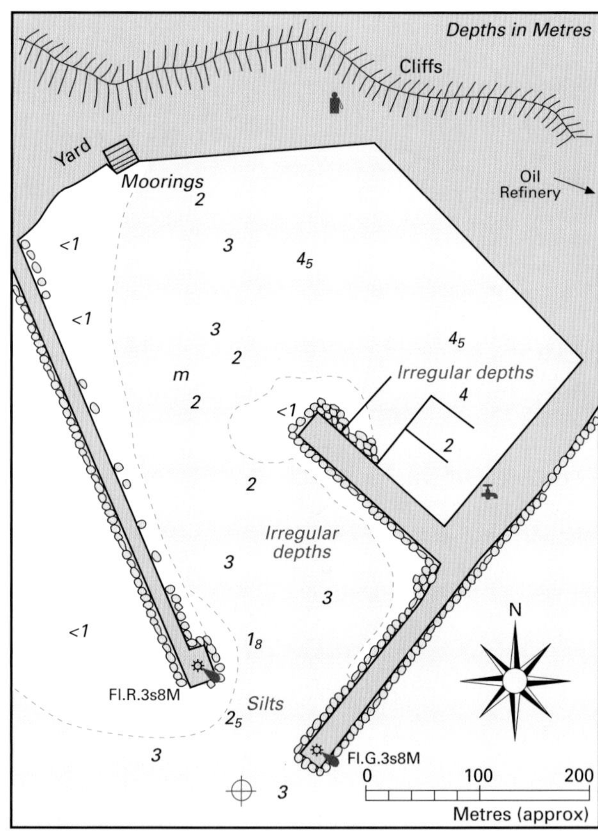

GELA
⊕37°03´·7N 14°13´·8E

VHF Ch 15, 16 for port authorities. Ch 6, 12, 16 for pilots.

Note Local knowledge is essential to determine exactly where the entrance channel into the basin is.

Mooring

Data <1–4m variable.

Berth Go stern or bows-to or alongside where directed or convenient. Care is needed when navigating within the harbour because of variable depths.

Shelter Good shelter although strong S winds may make it uncomfortable.

Authorities Ormeggiatori.

Facilities

Water On the quay.
Fuel Nearby.
Repairs 140-ton slipway. Limited mechanical repairs.
Provisions Good shopping in the town.
Eating out Restaurants in the town.

General

Gela has a reputation as a mafia stronghold and at times the army has been brought in to restore some sort of order to the town. The town behind now largely revolves around the oil refinery and servicing the offshore rigs.

LICATA

BA 965
Italian 267

Approach

Situated at the mouth of the Salso river, Licata is a large trawler port with some commercial traffic.

Conspicuous The large apartment blocks of the town can be seen from some distance. The castle (Sta Angelo) and the cemetery lower down the slopes of the hill behind the harbour are conspicuous, as is the white lighthouse within the harbour. Closer in, the harbour breakwaters and the entrance are easily distinguished.

VHF Ch 14, 16 (0700–1900). Ch 12 for pilots.

Dangers Off the Salso river there is a shifting sandbank but it is not in the approach to the harbour. The harbour is prone to silting but a dredger keeps the approach and inner harbour dredged to good depths.

Mooring

Data Max LOA 20m. Depths 2–8m.

Berth A yacht can moor alongside the W breakwater, or stern or bows-to the mole on the E side of the inner harbour near the fuel quay. The catwalk running down the mole on the W side of the inner harbour is usually full of local boats and is a little run down in recent seasons.

It is likely that visiting yachts will be directed to the new marina Cala del Sole in future.

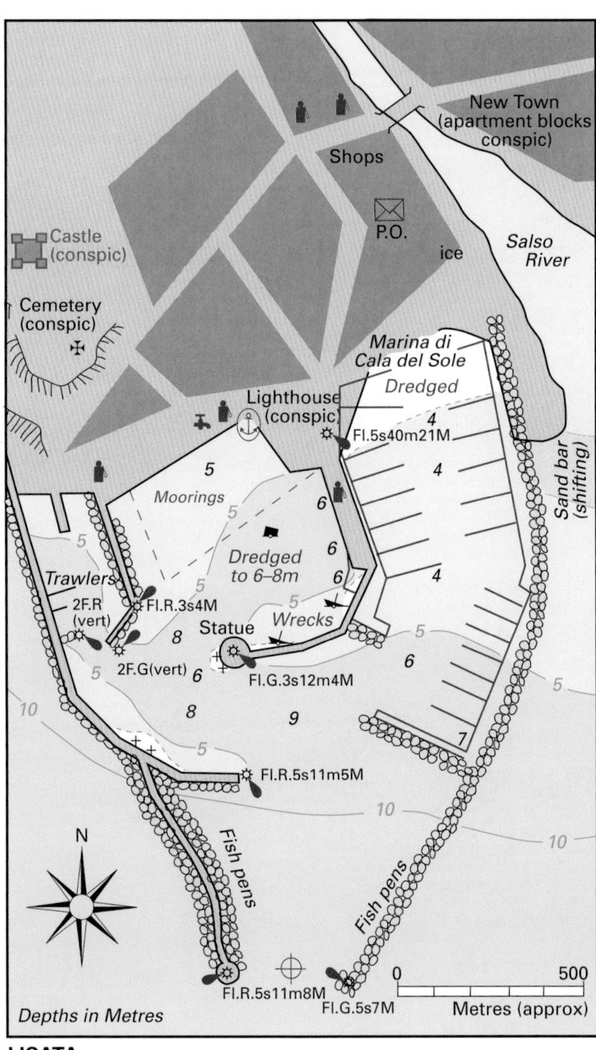

LICATA
⊕37°05′·06N 13°56′·48E WGS84

Licata. The entrance to the inner harbour looking NE to the lighthouse

Licata. The yacht club catwalk looking SSE to the entrance of the harbour

Marina di Cala del Sole

The project is due for completion in 2011. Details below are for the completed marina.

Data 1,500 berths. Visitors' berths. Max LOA 70m. Depths 4–6m (dredged).

Berth Stern or bows-to where directed. Laid moorings tailed to the quay.

Shelter Good all-round shelter can be found from all winds on one side or the other of the harbour.

Authorities Harbourmaster and customs. Charge band 1/6 (Marina Cala del Sole).

Marina Cala del Sole ✆ 0922 774 300
Email info@marinadicaladelsole.it
www.marinadicaladelsole.it

Stella Maris ✆ 0922 770 078

Anchorage It may be possible to anchor in the inner harbour if there is room, but care is needed of the numerous moorings in the area. The bottom is soft mud and not always good holding.

Mausoleums conspicuous on the hillside in the approach to Licata

Facilities

Services Water is limited, but a mini-tanker can deliver to the quay. Water and electricity at the catwalk and in the marina. Wi-Fi, pump-out and laundry planned in the marina.
Fuel On the quay.
Repairs Slipway to 150 tons. Mobile crane to 40 tons. Mechanical and engineering repairs. Chandlers. Most work is concerned with fishing boats. 160-ton travel-lift and repairs planned in the marina.
Provisions Good shopping for most provisions but there is not a wide selection of groceries or fruit and vegetables. Good fish stalls. Ice from the factory near the quay.
Eating out A number of trattorias and restaurants in the town and a large number of bars and cafés on the main street.
Other PO. Banks. ATMs. Hospital. Italgaz and Camping Gaz.

General

Licata is a pleasant if undistinguished town. In the summer it seems as if the entire population takes its *passeggiata* along the yacht mole parading new clothes and eligible daughters for all to see. The cemetery on the hill below the city has many imposing mausoleums which are prominent from seaward. The city seems to specialise in bad Baroque: the mausoleums in the cemetery lead the way, several of the piazzas are hemmed in by it, and the cathedral has been embellished with superfluous bits of it.

The marina is part of a vast new development including houses and apartments, shops, boutiques, extensive leisure facilities, and a desalination plant.

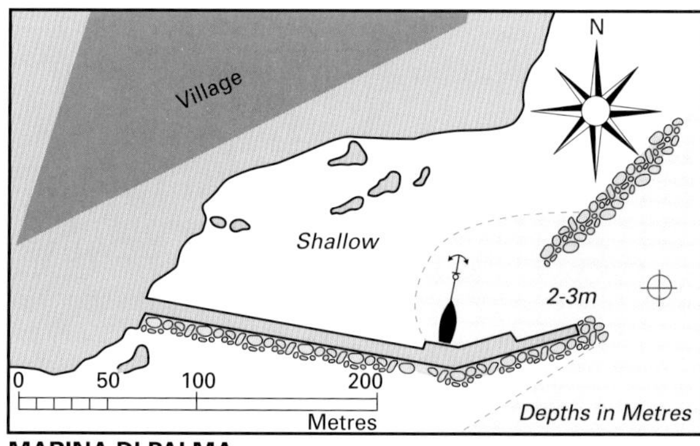

MARINA DI PALMA
⊕37°09´·8N 13°43´·5E

MARINA DI PALMA

A fishing harbour with a mole running obliquely out from the coast and a detached breakwater. The harbour looks as though it would afford useful protection in settled weather. There is little information on depths or facilities ashore.

SAN LEONE

A small pleasure boat harbour three miles SE of Empedocle.

Approach

The village of San Leone near Punta Agragas can be identified and, closer in, the harbour breakwater and a yellow tank immediately behind the harbour are conspicuous. There is often a swell at the entrance.
VHF Ch 74.

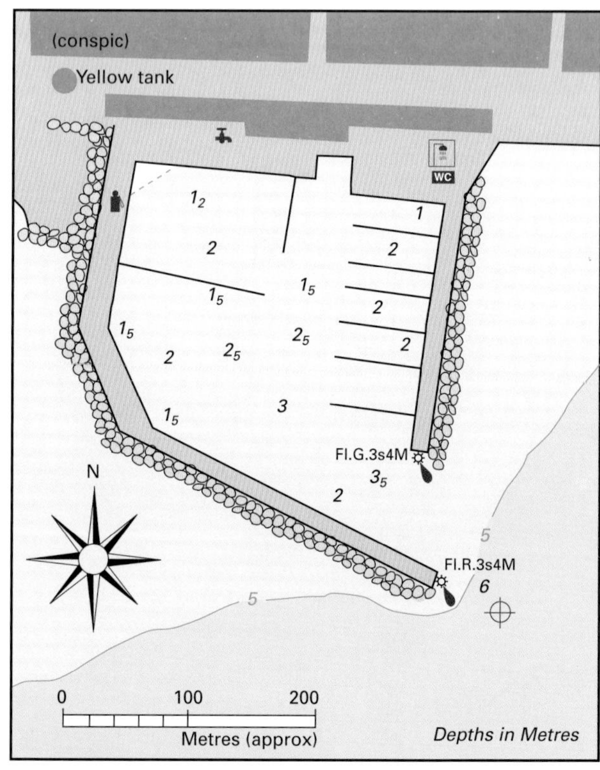

SAN LEONE
⊕37°15´·4N 13°34´·8E

Mooring

Data 200 berths. Max LOA 25m. Depths 1–4m.

Berth Go stern or bows-to where directed or convenient. Porto Turistico run the inner pontoon on the E side where visitors may find a berth.

Shelter Good shelter.

Authorities Ormeggiatori. Charge band 5.

Porto Turistico di S. Leone ✆ 0922 24444 / 0337 303 550
Fax 0922 401 474
Yachting Club S. Leone ✆ 0922 411 243

Facilities

Services Water and electricity.
Fuel On the quay.
Provisions Some provisions in the village.
Eating out Several restaurants.

General

San Leone can be used as an alternative base to Port Empedocle for a visit to the ruins of Agrigento.

PORTO EMPEDOCLE

BA 965
Italian 265

Approach

Straightforward by day and night.

Conspicuous The large town of Agrigento is the most conspicuous landmark, but in summer it can be difficult to see in hazy conditions. Two tall chimneys and a large building behind the harbour are conspicuous. The harbour moles and harbour entrance are easily identified.

By night Use the light on Capo Rossello Fl(2)10s 95m18M. The new mole head is marked by a S cardinal beacon YB Q(6)+LFl.15s7m5M.

VHF Ch 16, 14 for port authorities.

Mooring

Data C.60 berths. Limited visitors berths. Depths 4–8m.

Berth Stern or bows-to the pontoons in the inner basin. Laid moorings at some berths.

Shelter Excellent in the inner port.

The entrance to Empedocle looking NE past the end of the E breakwater

Agrigento

A yacht sailing from Empedocle will see the ruins of Agrigento on a ridge below the town. Agrigento was founded in 582BC when it was known as Akragas to the Greeks; later the Romans called it Agrigentum, the Arabs Girgent, and the Italians Girgenti and, only recently, Agrigento.

The magnificent Doric temples were built below the acropolis, now the modern city, and are well worth an excursion to see. At its height the city attracted poets (like Pindar), artists and, of course, our friend Empedocles. It was sacked by the Carthaginians and later by the Romans who destroyed many of the temples. Nonetheless the remaining ruins, some partially restored, highlight the genius of the Greeks for siting and executing beautiful architecture.

Temple of Neptune at Agrigento
Vito Arcomano, FOTOTECA ENIT

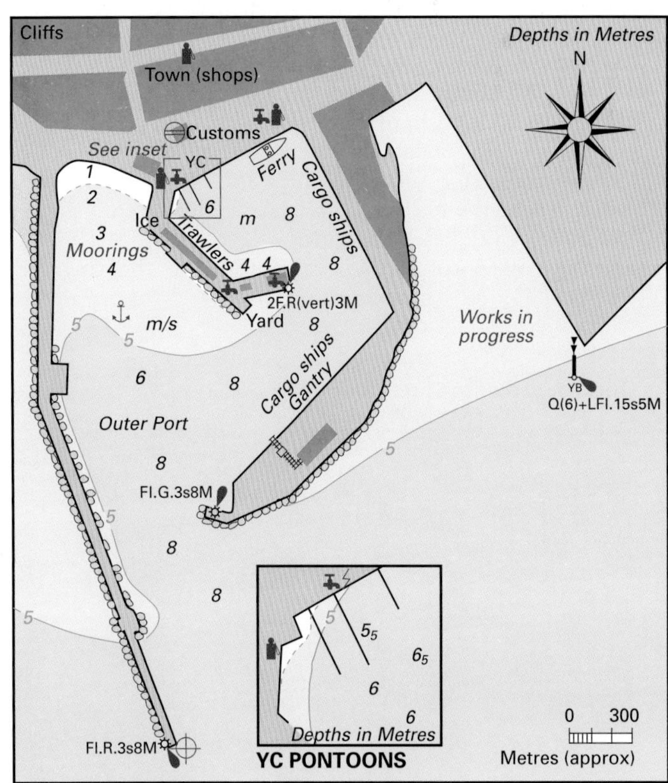

PORTO EMPEDOCLE
⊕37°16′·44N 13°31′·63E WGS84

The yacht club pontoons in the inner basin at Empedocle

Authorities Harbourmaster and customs. Charge band 3/4.

Note Earlier pilot notes refer to 'bothersome urchins' but the police now keep an eye on things and the harbour area appears to be secure.

Anchorage It is possible to anchor to the W of the basin although the surroundings are a bit on the scruffy side. The bottom is soft mud and not always good holding. It can get very rolly if the wind is from the south.

Note Works are in progress developing a new commercial harbour to the E of the E breakwater.

Facilities

Services Water and electricity on the pontoons.
Fuel Near the quay.
Repairs A 50-ton slipway. Mobile crane up to 20 tons. Mechanical and engineering repairs. Chandlers. Good hardware shops.
Provisions Excellent shopping for all provisions. Good fresh fruit and vegetables and fish stalls in a square near the harbour. Ice from the factory on the W mole of the inner harbour.
Eating out A number of restaurants in the town including good seafood restaurants.
Other PO. Banks. ATMs. Hospital. Italgaz and Camping Gaz. Buses to Agrigento. Ferries to Pantelleria and Lampedusa.

General

Porto Empedocle is named in honour of Empedocles (493–433BC), the Greek statesman, philosopher, poet and, some say, magician. The harbour and town are a somewhat scruffy monument to the most illustrious son of Agrigento who ended his days by casting himself in the crater of Etna, so that people might believe he was one of the gods. According to Lucian, Etna spewed out his sandal and so destroyed the illusion.

Siculiana Marina

⊕ 37°19'·9N 13°23'·3E

A small new harbour has been excavated out of the sandbanks off the town of Siculiana Marina. The breakwaters are complete, but there is nothing else here. As with many harbours along this coast, silting looks like it could be a problem here. Italia Navigando is involved in the project to create a 500-berth marina, although no start dates were available at the time of writing.

SCIACCA

Approach

Straightforward by day and night. Care needs to be taken only of the numerous trawlers coming in and out at speed.

Conspicuous From the W a pylon (red and white bands) on Capo San Marco is conspicuous and from the E a large hotel development by the beach is easily seen. A hotel on a high ridge above Sciacca is also prominent. Closer in, the town and the breakwaters are easily identified.

By night Use the light on Capo San Marco Fl(3)15s18M.

VHF Ch 16 (Circomare), Ch 12 (Lega Navale), CB Ch 21 (Circolo Nautico Corallo).

Mooring

Data 250 berths. Max LOA c.20m. Depths 2–7m.

Berth Go on the pontoons inside the W breakwater. The S pontoon is where you are most likely to find a

The approaches to Sciacca looking NE

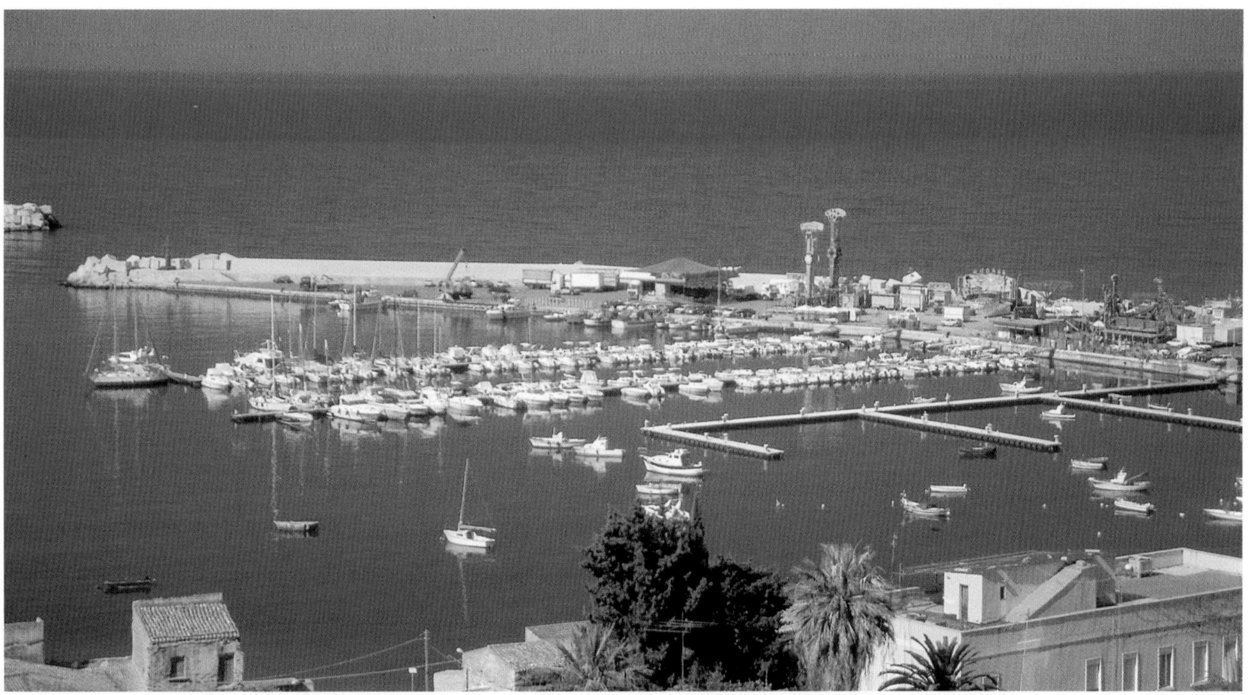

Sciacca yacht pontoons looking SW out over the entrance

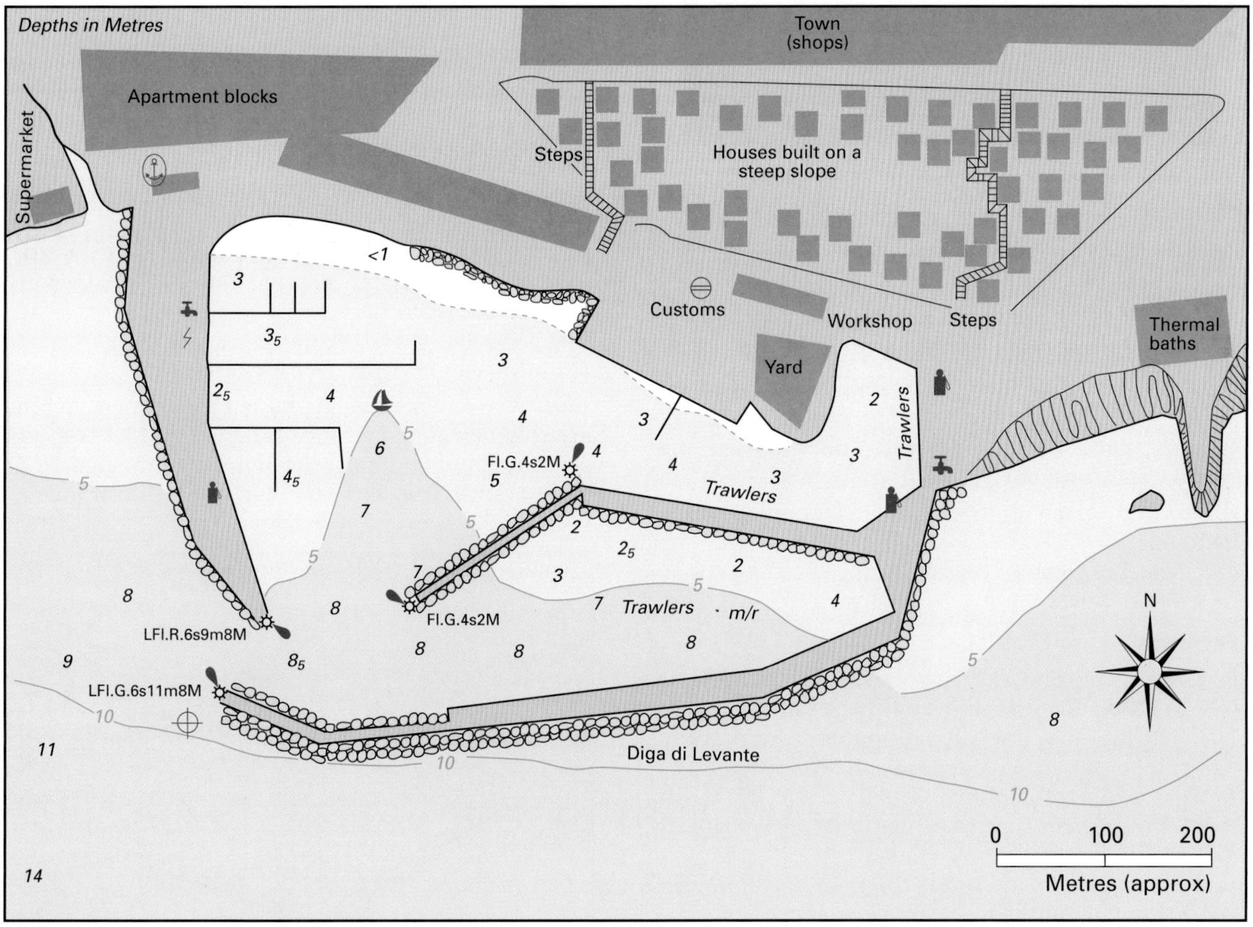

Depths in Metres

Town (shops)

Apartment blocks

Supermarket

Steps

Houses built on a steep slope

Customs

Workshop

Steps

Thermal baths

Yard

Trawlers

Fl.G.4s2M

Fl.G.4s2M

LFl.R.6s9m8M

LFl.G.6s11m8M

Trawlers

Trawlers · m/r

Diga di Levante

N

0 100 200

Metres (approx)

SCIACCA

⊕37°30´·03N 13°04´·49E WGS84

V. SICILY

Selinunte

A yacht sailing along the coastline after Capo Granitola will see the acropolis and complex of temples of Selinunte by the shore. The first temple dates from 600BC and the others were built in the intervening period up until about 400BC. It was founded by colonists from Magna Hyblaea and named after the wild celery (*Gr. selinon*) still to be found growing in the surrounding fields. It grew to be a prosperous city trading all over the eastern Mediterranean. Below the temples there are a few remains of two ancient harbours now completely silted. It was destroyed by Hannibal in 409BC and never recovered.

For my money the site at Selinunte is more satisfying to visit than the site of Agrigento. In calm weather or before the SW breeze gets up (around midday) a yacht can anchor off the site, although it is some distance to the shore as the bottom shelves gently up to the beach. There is a small harbour at Marinella di Selinunte, but it is shallow and not for yachts.

Ruins at Selinunte *Vito Arcomano, FOTOTECA ENIT*

berth. It is administered by both Lega Navale and Circolo Nautico Corallo, both of which offer a helpful service. Laid moorings. The inner harbour is packed with trawlers and the outer basin on the E side is also used by trawlers on laid moorings.

Shelter Good shelter from the prevailing winds on the pontoons. Strong southerlies could make some berths uncomfortable.

Authorities Harbourmaster and customs. Charge band 5.

Circolo Nautico Corallo ✆ 0925 21611
Lega Navale ✆ 0925 85879

Facilities

Services Water and electricity at all berths. WC at CN Corallo. WC and shower at Lega Navale.
Fuel On the quay for large amounts. Alternatively fuel can be jerry-canned from the town.
Repairs A 15-ton slipway. Mobile crane up to 20 tons. A yard here repairs fishing boats. Mechanical and engineering repairs. Chandlers.
Provisions Supermarket near the pontoons and also good shopping in the town above the harbour.
Eating out Good restaurants and trattorias in the town.
Other PO. Banks. ATMs. Italgaz and Camping Gaz. Buses to Agrigento and Selinunte.

General

Sciacca at first glance may look like a rather scruffy, if not downright neglected, fishing port, but it will grow on you. Narrow streets around the harbour lead up to the town via brightly tiled steps. The buildings are a mixture of Moorish, Norman and Spanish influences and a former Jesuit College overlooks the harbour. The local people have a quiet pride in their town and justly so. In June the whole town turns out for the festival of San Pietro – patron saint of the sea. The church dedicated to the saint is down near the harbour, and it is said that if you touch the statue of San Pietro he will bring you fair winds. The climax of the festival is an extraordinary fireworks display that belies the size of this little fishing port.

It is volcanic activity underneath the town that gives rise to the main attraction for many visitors to Sciacca. The Greeks from Selinunte were the first to recognise the healing properties of the volcanic thermal springs and vapours. Legend has it that Daedalus came here from Crete, fleeing the wrath of King Minos, and discovered the theraputic nature of vapours escaping the cliffs. The Greeks carved seats out of the stone, and etched into the rocks the names of particular ailments that might be cured in each seat. The new (1930s) Thermé building stands on the cliff to the E of the town, and the open-air grottoes, spas and baths attract Sicilians and tourists alike to 'take the waters'.

PORTO PALO DI MENFI

Approach

The harbour lies approximately nine miles W of Capo San Marco. It lies on the E side of Capo Scario which has a white tower on it.

Mooring

Data Max LOA 15m. Depths <1–3m.

Berth Care is needed in the harbour where depths are irregular. The entrance is silting and last reports indicated maximum depths of 1·5m in the middle of the entrance. It is likely the harbour will continue to

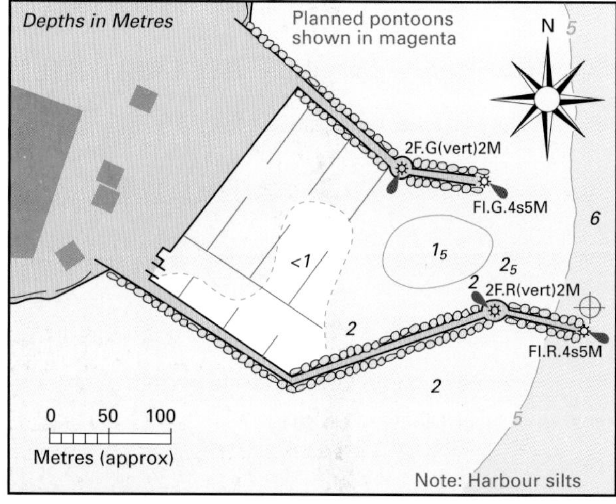

PALO DI MENFI
⊕37°34´·4N 12°54´·6E

silt further so care is needed. On the S side of the harbour there is a large patch where depths are <1–1·3m. Go stern or bows-to the quay where directed or convenient.

Note There are plans to add pontoons to increase the number of berths here.

Shelter Good shelter although strong E winds would probably make it uncomfortable.

Authorities Ormeggiatori.

Facilities

Some provisions and a restaurant ashore.

MARINELLA DI SELINUNTE

A small and shallow fishing harbour off the town of Marinella.

There are depths of around 2m in the entrance and less inside. Depths are uneven and liable to silting; only shoal draught craft should attempt to enter the harbour. In settled weather a yacht could anchor off the beach in 2–5m.

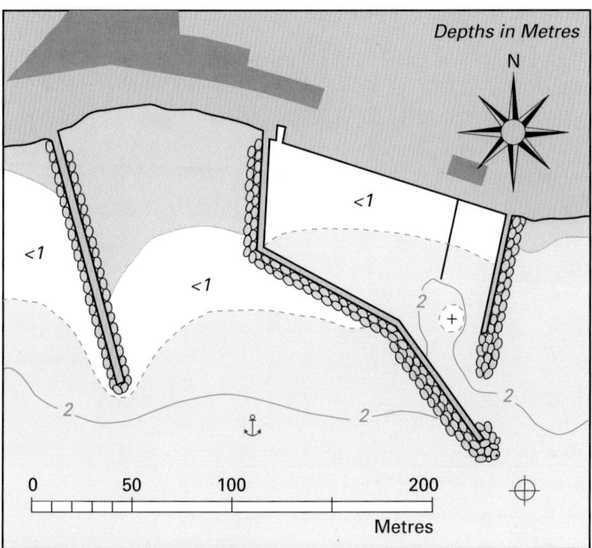

MARINELLA DI SELINUNTE
⊕37°34´·8N 12°50´·5E

Isole Pelagie and Isola Pantelleria

Isola Pantelleria

The island lies about 55 miles SW of Capo Granitola. Of volcanic origin, it is quite high, reaching 836m (2734ft) at the summit of Montagna Grande near the middle of the island. There are numerous extinct volcanic craters on the island and the soil, being of volcanic origin, is fertile and much cultivated. Porto Pantelleria lies at the NW end of the island.

Note Pantellaria is a nature reserve, and marine restrictions may be implemented in the future. For details on the nature reserve see www.parks.it

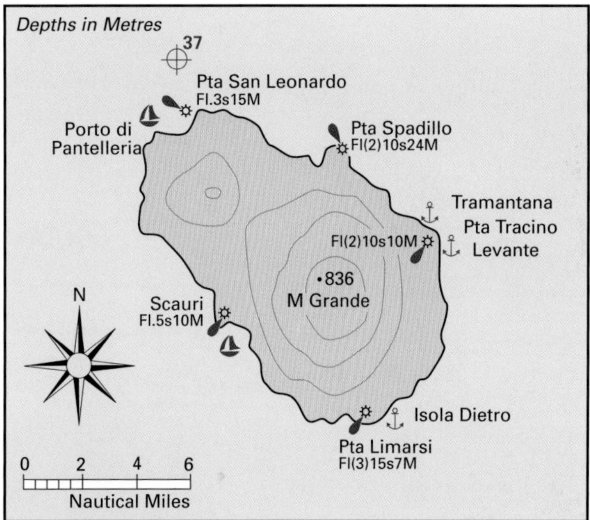

ISOLA PANTELLERIA

⊕**37** 2M N of Pta San Leonardo 36°52′·1N 11°56′·7E

PORTO DI PANTELLERIA

BA 193
Italian 242

Approach

The buildings of the town, particularly a number of tall apartment buildings, are easily identified.

By night Care is needed if making a night approach.

VHF Ch 16.

Danger

1. In Porto Vecchio care must be taken of the above and below-water rocks (the old Punic breakwater) extending out from the town quay

Porto Pantelleria approach looking south *H Williamson*

V. SICILY

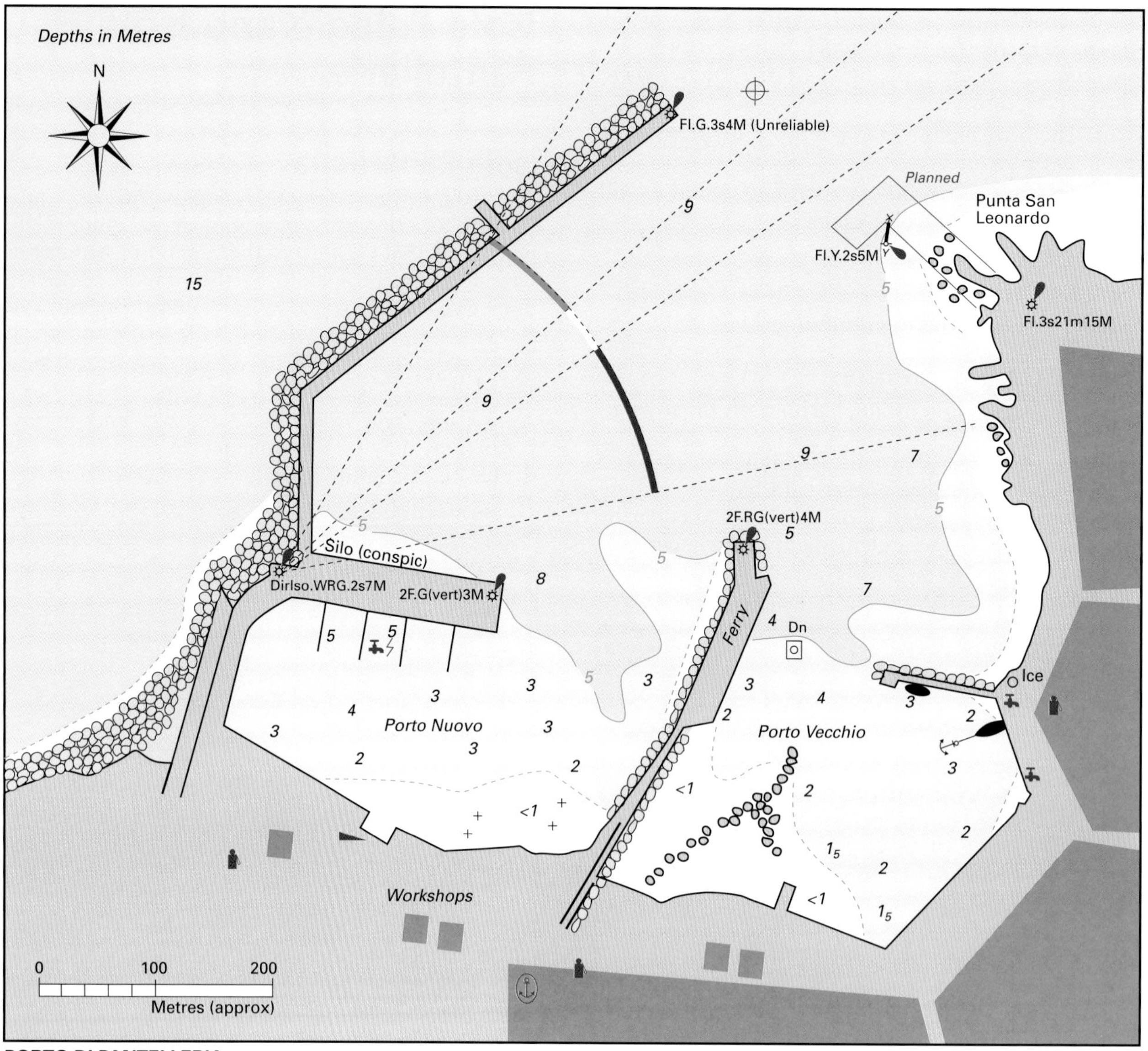

PORTO DI PANTELLERIA
⊕36°50′·2N 11°56′·5E

such as to divide the harbour into two. The N end is marked by E cardinal buoys.

2. An outer breakwater for the E side of the entrance at Pta San Leonardo is planned. It is not known when work will start.

Mooring

Data C.80 berths. 10 visitors' berths. Max LOA 17m. Depths 1·5–6m.

Berth Go stern or bows-to or alongside on the NE corner of Porto Vecchio. Care must be taken of the ballasting which extends underwater from the quay in places. The bottom is coarse sand with some rock and an anchor should have a trip line on it.

The central pontoon area is now designated a military area for the Guardia Costiera and yachts are prohibited. You may also find a berth on the S quay in Porto Nuovo, but play it by ear.

Shelter Good shelter in settled weather. Only with strong northerlies does the harbour become uncomfortable when a swell works its way into both Porto Nuovo and Porto Vecchio.

Pantellaria looking N past the old Punic breakwater, now marked with E cardinal buoys *Luisa Bresciani*

Note During high season do not depend on getting a berth as spaces are very limited.

Authorities Harbourmaster and customs. Charge band 3.

Facilities

Services Water on the quay in Porto Vecchio.
Fuel Near the harbour.
Repairs A 20-ton slipway and 25-ton crane. Limited mechanical repairs.
Provisions Most provisions can be obtained in the town.
Eating out Restaurants and trattorias in the town. Prices in some of the establishments reflect the additional cost of shipping in much of what is consumed, sometimes a more than modest mark-up.
Other PO. Bank. Hospital. Ferry to Porto Empedocle, Trapani and Tunis. Flights to Sicily.

General

The island is fertile and much cultivated with the vine and market gardens. Recently it has become popular for the excellent underwater fishing around its coast. It is a convenient stop-over port on passage between Tunisia and Sicily.

PORTO SCAURI

Approach

A small harbour situated just E of Punta Pietre on the SW side of the island.

By night Use the main light Fl.5s18m10M.

VHF Ch 16, 14.

Note The harbour is small so everything should be ready before you enter.

Mooring

Data 60 berths. Max LOA 15m. Depths 2–7m.

Berth Where directed or convenient. The harbour is crammed full of local boats leaving little room for yachts although a berth can usually be found.

Shelter Good shelter although strong southerlies cause a surge.

Charge band 1.

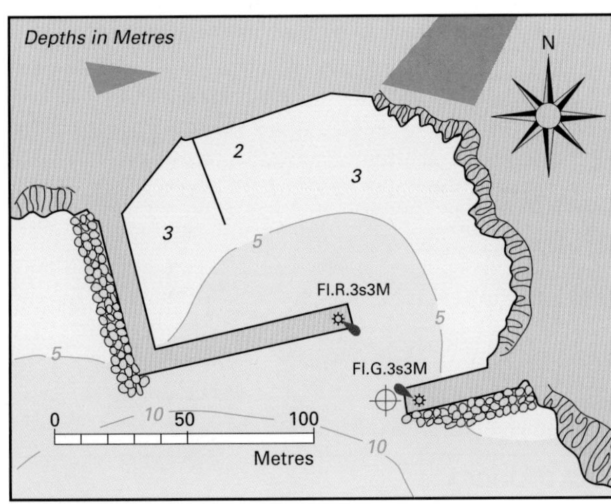

SCAURI
⊕36°46´·0N 11°57´·8E

Facilities

Water On the quay.
Fuel A mini–tanker can deliver.
Provisions In the village about 20 minutes' walk away.

General

It appears that the harbour was built as a small marina, although it is not yet up and running. Other facilities are expected to be added in the future.

PORTO DIETRO ISOLA

⊕ 36°44'·4N 12°02'·5E

A cove on the S end of the island immediately W of Punta Limarsi. Punta Limarsi is lit Fl(3)15s35m7M. Sheltered from W–NW. Anchor in 4–10m.

CALA DI LEVANTE

A cove on the E side of the island under Punta Tracino. Punta Tracino is lit Fl(2)10s49m10M. Sheltered from the west. Anchor in 3–10m. Care is needed of a wreck close inshore. Hamlet ashore.

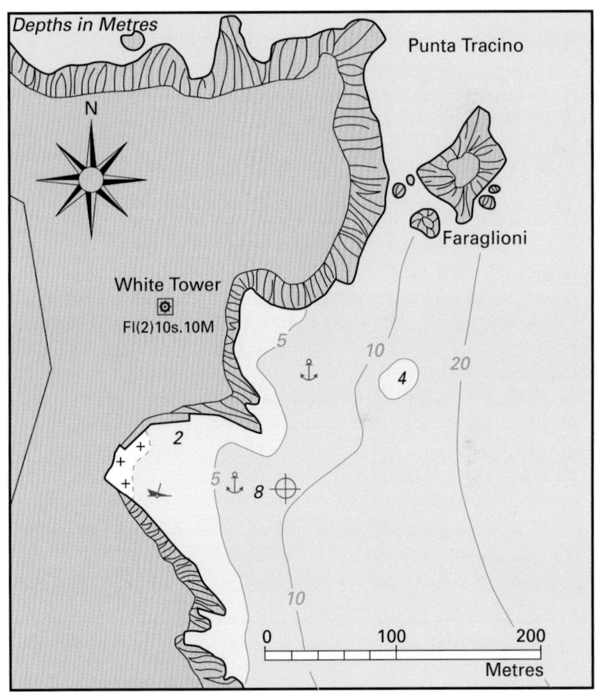

CALA DI LEVANTE
⊕36°47´·7N 12°03´·4E

CALA DI TRAMONTANA

⊕36°47'·9N 12°02'·8E

A miniature cove close W of Cala di Levante. Sheltered from W–SW. Small yachts can anchor in 4–8m. Hamlet ashore.

Isole Pelagie

These consist of Linosa, Lampione and Lampedusa and are situated SSE of Pantelleria and WSW of Malta. Linosa lies about 65 miles SE of Pantelleria, Lampione lies about 32 miles SW of Linosa, and Lampedusa about 10 miles E of Lampione. The islands are all low-lying and, for the most part, bereft of vegetation. There are no secure harbours or anchorages except for Lampedusa.

Isola de Linosa

A volcanic island with elevations of less than 200m. There are two small ports on the island.

SCALO VECCHIO

⊕ 35°51′·2N 12°51′·7E

The principle port for the island, situated on the S coast.

By night The S side of the island is lit on Punta Arena Bianca, W of the harbour, Fl.5s9m9M (276°-vis-150°). The harbour entrance is not lit.

Data Max LOA 10m. Depths 1–8m.

VHF Ch 16, 14.

CALA POZZOLANA DI PONENTE

⊕ 35°51′·8N 12°51′·0E

A small harbour on the West coast of Linosa. The hydrofoil uses the end of the pier.

By night Use the light on Pta Arena Bianca Fl.5s9m9M, and the light on Punta Beppe Tuccio Fl(4)20s32m16M 107°-vis-345°). The harbour entrance is not lit.

Data Max LOA 10m. Depths 1–5m. Provisions and ice in the village.

VHF Ch 16, 14.

Isola di Lampione

A low-lying island (39·5m/130ft) which rises sheer from the sea. There are no anchorages.

Isole Pelagie Marine Reserve (AMP)

Another recently established marine reserve, this covers all the islands in the Isole Pelagie archipelago and its area is at present defined as follows:

Lampedusa
Along the coast from Punta Galera in a westerly direction, including Capo Ponente and round as far as the northern tip of Cala Pisana, including Capo Grecale. Two Zone A areas around Capo Grecale and Isola dei Conigli.

Linosa
From the point to the south of Cala Pozzolana round to Punta Calcarella, including Punta Balata Piatta and Punta Beppe Tuccio. There is one area in Zone A off the N coast.

Lampione
The sea area within approximately 1M of the islet.
The following rules and regulations are provisional.

Zone A
Navigation, access, and anchoring or mooring are all prohibited to any type of craft, as are swimming, diving, commercial, sport and underwater fishing.

Zone B
Unauthorised motor navigation, anchoring and mooring and commercial, sport and underwater fishing are prohibited.
Navigation under sail, oar or motor (max. 5kns), anchoring in authorised zones, guided subaqua trips run by authorised diving centres, and swimming are permitted.

Zone C
Navigation under sail, oars or motor (max. 10 knots), swimming, diving, sport fishing with static line and rod (residents only) and tourist fishing are permitted.

Note
In Zones B and C off Linosa and in Zone C off Lampedusa unlimited access is allowed to the harbours of Pozzolana and Mannarazza (Linosa) and Cala Creta (Lampedusa) in the event of emergencies caused by adverse sea/weather conditions and based on warnings from the local maritime authority.

AMP Pelagie ✆ /*Fax* 0922 975 780
Email amp_pelagie@virgilio.it
www.isole-pelagie.it

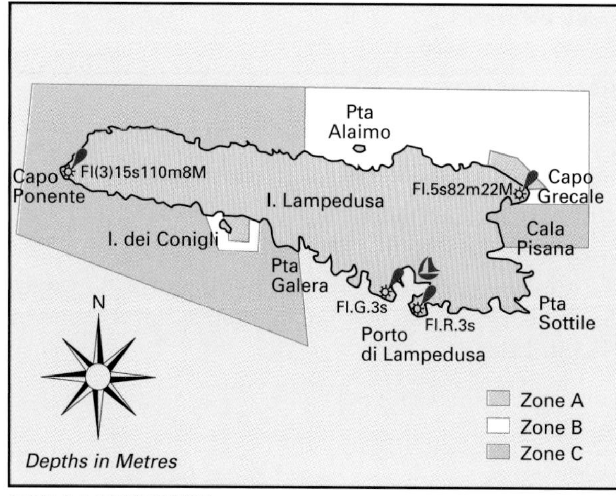

ISOLA LAMPEDUSA

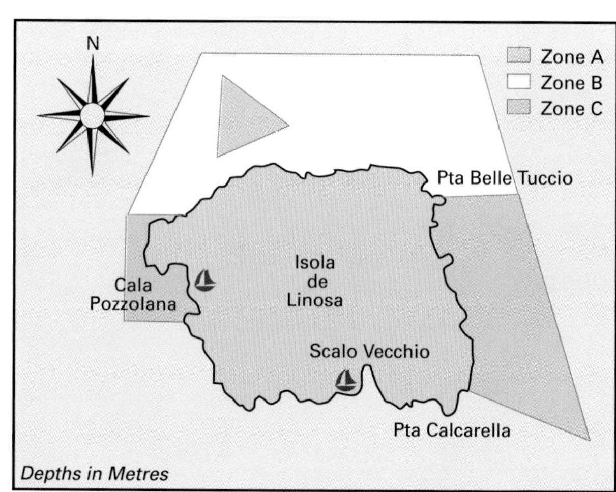

ISOLA DI LINOSA

Isola Lampedusa

The most important of the Pelagie Islands, it supports a small population of about 4,000 inhabitants. It is low-lying, reaching a maximum elevation of only 133m (436ft). Apart from Porto di Lampedusa, small yachts can find shelter in Cala Pisana in 3m depths.

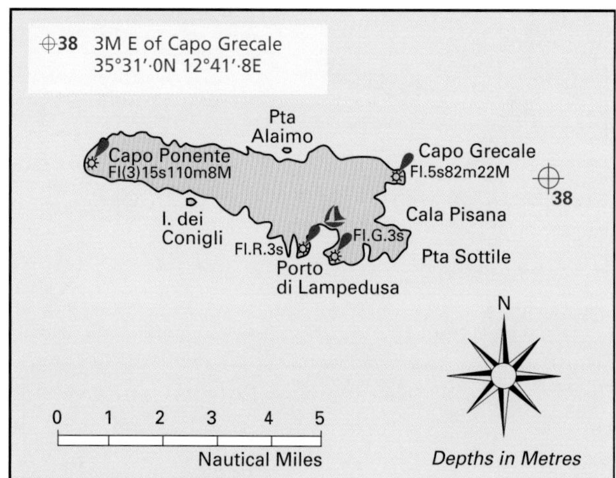

ISOLA LAMPEDUSA

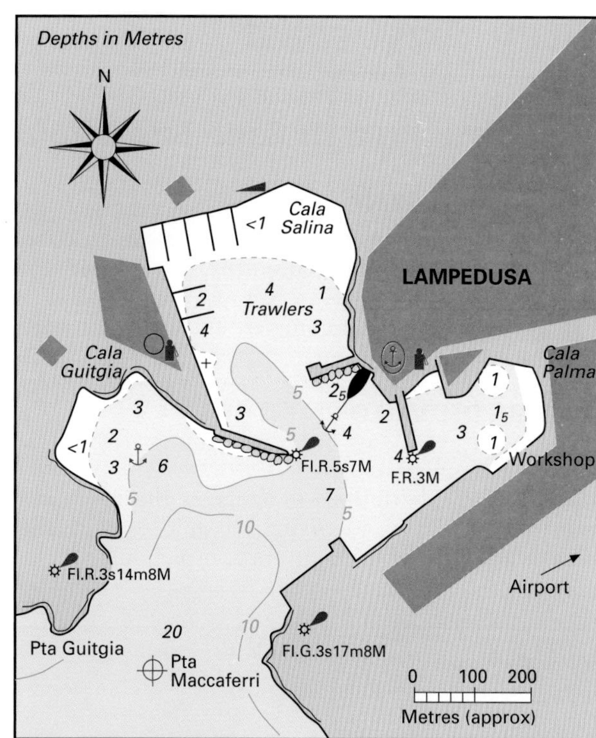

PORTO DI LAMPEDUSA
⊕35°29′·6N 12°36′·0E

PORTO DI LAMPEDUSA

BA 193
Italian 947/05

Approach

The harbour lies about 1½ miles W of Punta Sottile on the SE side of the island.

Conspicuous The town of Lampedusa, the only settlement of any size, is easily identified. A silver storage tank at the root of the mole protecting Cala Salina is conspicuous.

VHF Ch 14, 16 (0700–1900).

Mooring

Berth Go stern or bows-to the quay under the capitaneria office or the mole in Cala Palma. The bottom is sand and weed, good holding. Cala Salina is used by trawlers and it is not recommended you moor here – a yacht was rammed by a trawler in 1989.

Shelter Good shelter in Cala Palma. Strong southerlies send a swell into the harbour which may be dangerous. Cala Palma is the best place to be if there is room.

Note The *marrobio* is said to affect the harbour (see *Mazara del Vallo* below).

Authorities Harbourmaster and customs. Charge band 1/3.

Lungomare ☏ 0922 970 809

Facilities

Water Mini-tanker can deliver.
Fuel Nearby on the quay in Cala Palma.
Repairs A 25-ton slipway. Limited mechanical repairs only.
Provisions Restaurants and trattorias in the town. Prices are said to be high.
Other PO. Bank. Ferry to Porto Empedocle and Trapani. Runway for light aircraft.

General

A barren rocky island, Lampedusa has recently become popular for the good underwater fishing around the coast though that is now restricted by the marine reserve. It is very hot in July and August with a climate similar to that of North Africa.

Cala Pisana

A miniature inlet on the E side of the island. The entrance is little more than 100m wide and only small yachts will be able to use it. Open east. Anchor in 4–10m and take a line ashore. The end of the inlet is shallow.

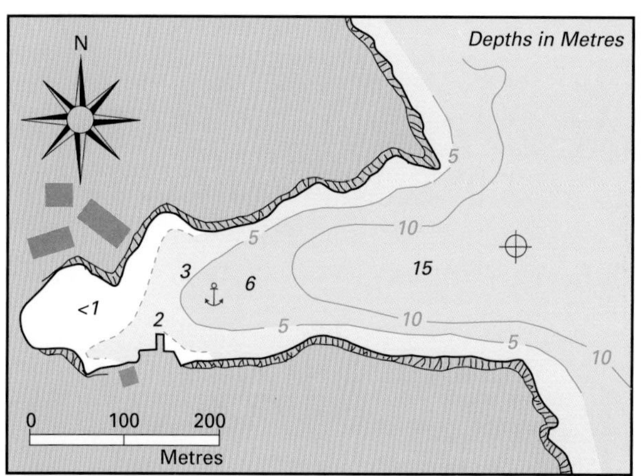

CALA PISANA
⊕35°30′·3N 12°37′·6E

V. SICILY

Sicily West coast

Capo Granitola to Capo San Vito

GRANITOLA MARINA

A new 50-berth *porto turistico* is under construction on the NW side of Capo Granitola, just 600m N of Capo Granitola light.

The breakwaters are complete and pontoons are expected in the near future.

MAZARA DEL VALLO

Approach

Conspicuous The tall skyscrapers of the town are conspicuous on the low-lying coast. Closer in, the breakwaters of the harbour are conspicuous.

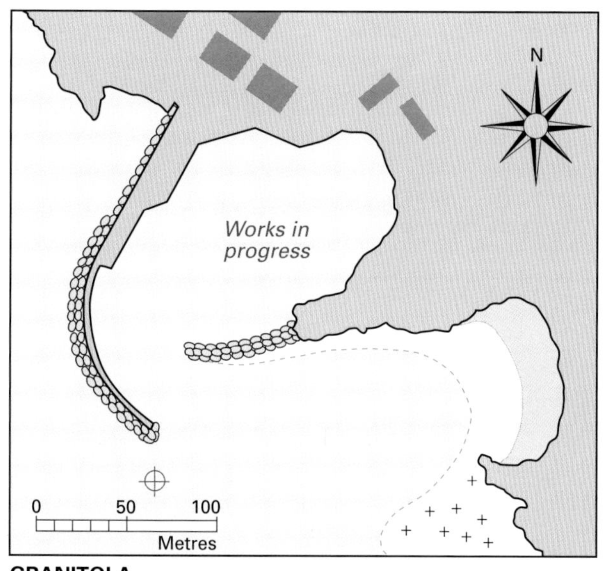

GRANITOLA
⊕37°34'·2N 12°39'·4E

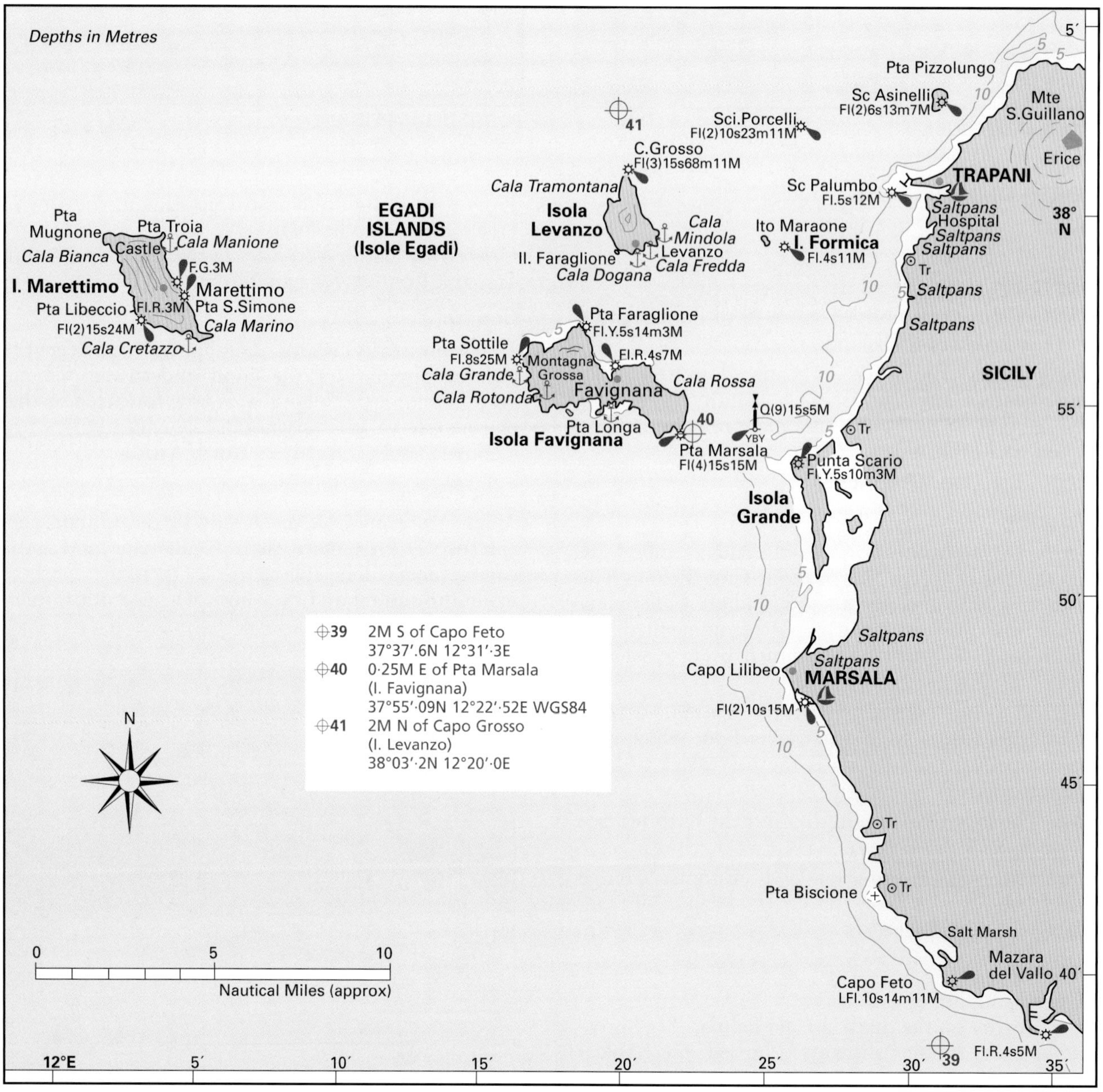

⊕39 2M S of Capo Feto
37°37'.6N 12°31'·3E
⊕40 0·25M E of Pta Marsala
(I. Favignana)
37°55'·09N 12°22'·52E WGS84
⊕41 2M N of Capo Grosso
(I. Levanzo)
38°03'·2N 12°20'·0E

ISOLE EGADI AND THE WEST COAST OF SICILY

VHF Ch 11, 16 for port authorities (0700–1900). Ch 16/CB Ch 10 for Ass. Dipортisti Nautici (Adina).

Dangers Care must be taken of the shoal water fringing the coast. In particular a yacht should take care of the shoal water extending S for about half a mile from Capo Granitola. It can be difficult to see with the sun low in the sky.

Note There is a fish farm reported approximately 2M S of the harbour in position 37°36´·5N 12°36´·1E. It is marked with small yellow buoys and lies in the path of yachts coasting down past Mazara del Vallo.

Mooring

Data 125 berths. Max. LOA 25m. Depths 2–6m.

Berth Mazara del Vallo is the largest trawler port in Italy and, despite the extensions to the outer harbour, it is invariably packed with large trawlers. A yacht may find a place near the *carabinieri* patrol boats at the neck of the river or a place on the new pontoons. Adina runs the single long pontoon. Laid moorings at all pontoon berths.

Shelter Excellent. It is only uncomfortable due to large trawlers entering and leaving the harbour at speed.

Dangers A yacht should be careful of the shallows and above and below-water obstructions on the W side of the entrance to the river.

Authorities Harbourmaster and customs. Charge band 4.

Adina ✆ 0923 940 136 / 906 700

Anchorage In settled weather it is possible to anchor to the E of the harbour in 2–5m. The bottom is mud, good holding.

Facilities

Water On the quay. Water and electricity on the pontoon.

Fuel On the quay, but it is impossible to get to on account of the trawlers. There are pumps near the quay on the E side of the river.

Repairs There is a large shipyard on the W side of the river where large ocean-going trawlers are built. There are good engineering workshops in the vicinity of the yard. Chandlers selling gear for the trawlers can be found on the E side of the river.

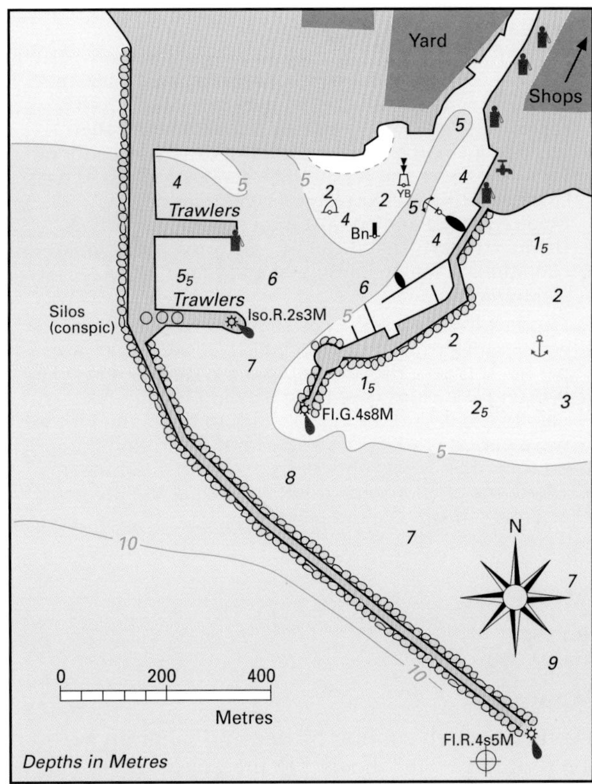

MAZARA DEL VALLO
⊕37°38´·44N 12°35´·04E WGS84

Yacht Service 150-ton slipway. 50-ton travel-hoist. Refits, repairs and call-out service.

✆ 0923 942 864 *Fax* 0923 934 755
Email info@eneayacht.it

Provisions Good shopping for all provisions near the harbour. Ice from a factory near the harbour.

Eating out Good restaurants and trattorias along the waterfront.

Other PO. Banks. ATMs. Italgaz and Camping Gaz.

General

When hemmed-in by trawlers which are often more like small ships, it is difficult to associate Mazara del Vallo with anything else. Much of the town revolves around the boats and the men who go out in them. Many of the boats go over to poach in the rich Tunisian waters and are often arrested. Others go to fish off Libya (I think I would plump for Tunisia myself) and offshore in the Atlantic.

Mazara del Vallo looking NE past the inner breakwater to the yacht pontoon

The Marrobio

This is a form of seiche which is said to affect Mazara del Vallo and Marsala. It is a tidal wave which quickly raises the level of the water up to a metre and then recedes again in a few minutes. The cycle may continue for a few hours and is said to be connected with abrupt changes in the meteorological conditions in the Mediterranean and not just local conditions. HM Denham reports that it can be associated with humid conditions, a falling barometer and the onset of southerlies.

I suspect it is the confluence of two wave trains over comparatively shallow water which, at the right wave period, sets up a rise and fall of the water. For example, if strong SW winds have been blowing for a number of days to the W, and strong SE winds to the E, then if the wave period produces an augmentation around the bottom of Sicily (or other parts of the Mediterranean where the phenomenon is known such as the Balearics or Crete) a *marrobio* can be set up.

MARSALA

BA 964
Italian 258

Approach

Approach with caution by day and night on account of the numerous shoals off the coast. From the N take special care of the shoal water and underwater rocks between Capo Lilibeo and the entrance.

Conspicuous The town with a number of cupolas in it is easily identified. The wine warehouses on Capo Lilibeo show up well but the harbour breakwater can be difficult to make out. The small lighthouse on the NW mole shows up well.

VHF Ch 16 for port authorities (0700–1900).

Dangers The harbour is said to be dangerous to enter with strong SE winds as waves break at the entrance.

Mooring

Note Some care is needed around and between the pontoons where depths are irregular.
Data Max LOA 20m. Depths 2–5m.

Berth Go stern or bows-to where directed or convenient on the pontoons just inside the entrance or on the quay of the S breakwater. Laid moorings.

Shelter Good, although it would be uncomfortable with strong southerlies.

Authorities Harbourmaster and customs. *Ormeggiatori*. Charge band 4/5.

Associazione Sportiva Mothia ✆ 0923 951 201

Cantiere Nautico Polaris ✆ 0923 999 222
Email info@nauticapolaris.com

Club Nautico Lilibeo ✆ 368 348 9203

Facilities

Services Water and electricity at every berth. Showers and toilets in portacabin.
Fuel At the marina and on the town quay.
Repairs 160-ton travel-lift. Slipway to 150 tons. Mobile crane to 10 tons. C.N Polaris can arrange haul out and repairs. Mechanical and engineering repairs. Wood repairs. Chandlers.

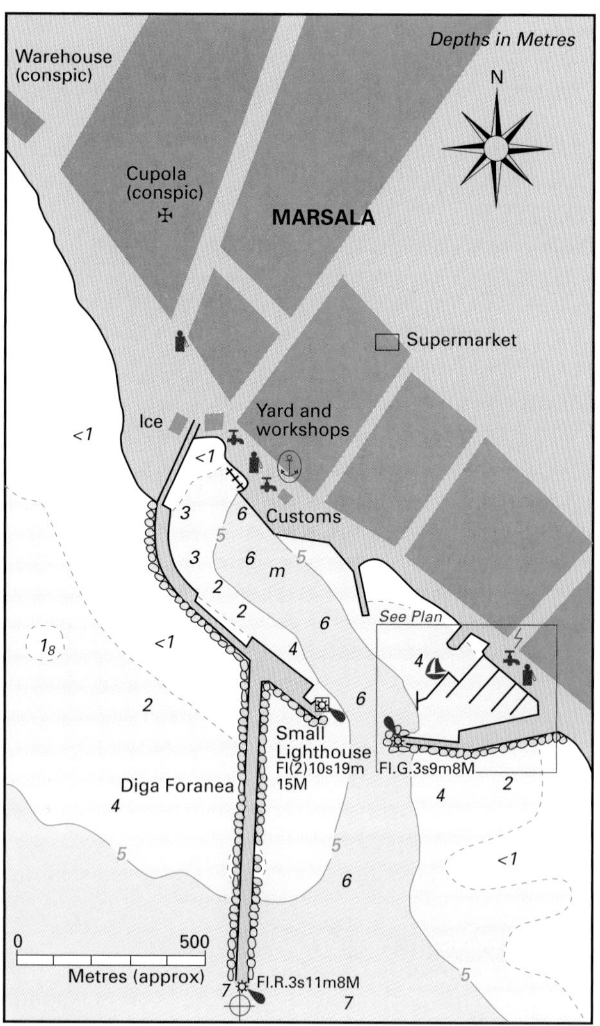

MARSALA
⊕37°46′·95N 12°26′·05E WGS84

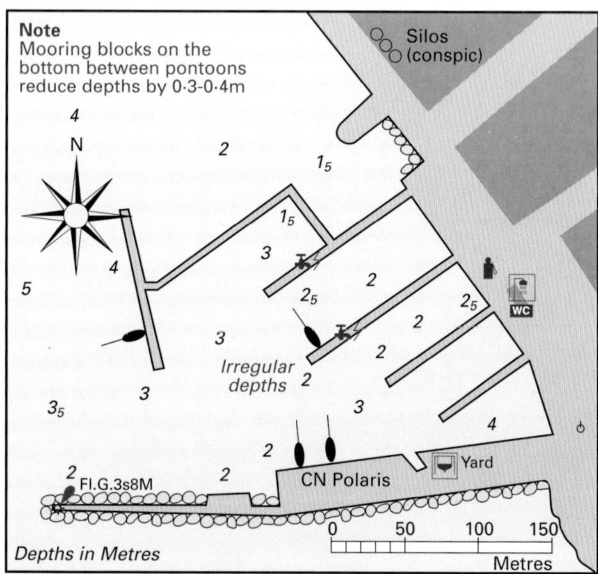

MARSALA - CLUB NAUTICO LILIBEO

The inner entrance to Marsala with the lighthouse conspic looking north

Provisions Good shopping for all provisions, although it is quite a hike to the supermarkets.
Eating out Good restaurants and trattorias in the town and on the waterfront.
Other PO. Banks. ATMs. Italgaz and Camping Gaz. Buses to Trapani. Day trip boat to Favignana.

General

Founded by the Carthaginians, Marsala takes it name from the Arabs who occupied it and called it Marsal – Allah (Harbour of God). It is of course the name bestowed on the honey-coloured dessert wine popular in England in the 19th century. An Englishman, John Woodhouse, began shipping the local wine fortified with alcohol back to England. Today the large hoses you see on the quay pump the local wine into small tankers for export – a considerable amount is said to go to France! Compared with the crowded ports to the east, it is a pleasant relaxed place, especially after a glass or two of fine Marsala Stravecchio. Just north of Marsala behind Isola Grande are the remains of an ancient Phoenician town, Motya, but you need permission from Palermo to visit it.

Lilibeo Marina in Marsala harbour looking SW to the entrance

Isole Egadi

Lying near the W coast of Sicily there are three principal islands: Favignana, Marettimo and Levanzo. Favignana is the main island with a village and a secure harbour.

Currents

Currents flow strongly between the islands. In the summer the current sets predominantly towards the NE and in the winter towards the SW. These currents cause a troublesome popple which is more annoying than dangerous.

Tunny fishing

Tunny fishing was once the economic mainstay of the islands, only to fall victim to both dwindling fish stocks and the lure of the tourist dollar. *Mattanzas* – the static nets laid in the channels between the islands – were gradually replaced with less labour intensive long lines. Only in the last couple of years there appears to be a return to the use of the *mattanzas*. The nets are usually marked with buoys but their boundaries are not always obvious. The reintroduction of the permanent nets also makes navigating around here at night potentially dangerous. Further information is included in the Introduction.

Visibility

In the summer months a haze may obscure the islands so that they are difficult to pick up from even a few miles out. This can cause some anxiety when on passage from Sardinia to the Egadis.

Isola Favignana

This is the largest of the Isole Egadi. In the middle of the island a ridge called Montagna Grossa crosses from N to S and on either side the land is low-lying. On the summit of Montagna Grossa the Aragonese fort of Sta Caterina is conspicuous. At one time there were three Aragonese forts on Favignana but Sta Caterina is the only one to remain intact. In classical times the island was known as 'Aegusa' the 'Goat Island', after a description by Odysseus telling of the large number of goats grazed there. Apparently, up until as recently as 100 years ago, the island had extensive pine forests, but today, apart from a few pines on the slopes above the harbour, it is everywhere barren and dry.

Danger Underwater rocks fringe the N, W and S coasts of the island. A yacht should take special care of those around the N coast between Punta Sottile and Punta Faraglione which appear to be more numerous than shown on Admiralty chart 964.

Cala Grande

⊕ 37°55'·8N 12°16'·4E

This lies at the western tip of Isola Favignana behind the lighthouse. Anchor in 2–3m behind the low spur on which the lighthouse stands or off the hotel. The bottom is sand and good holding. Care must be

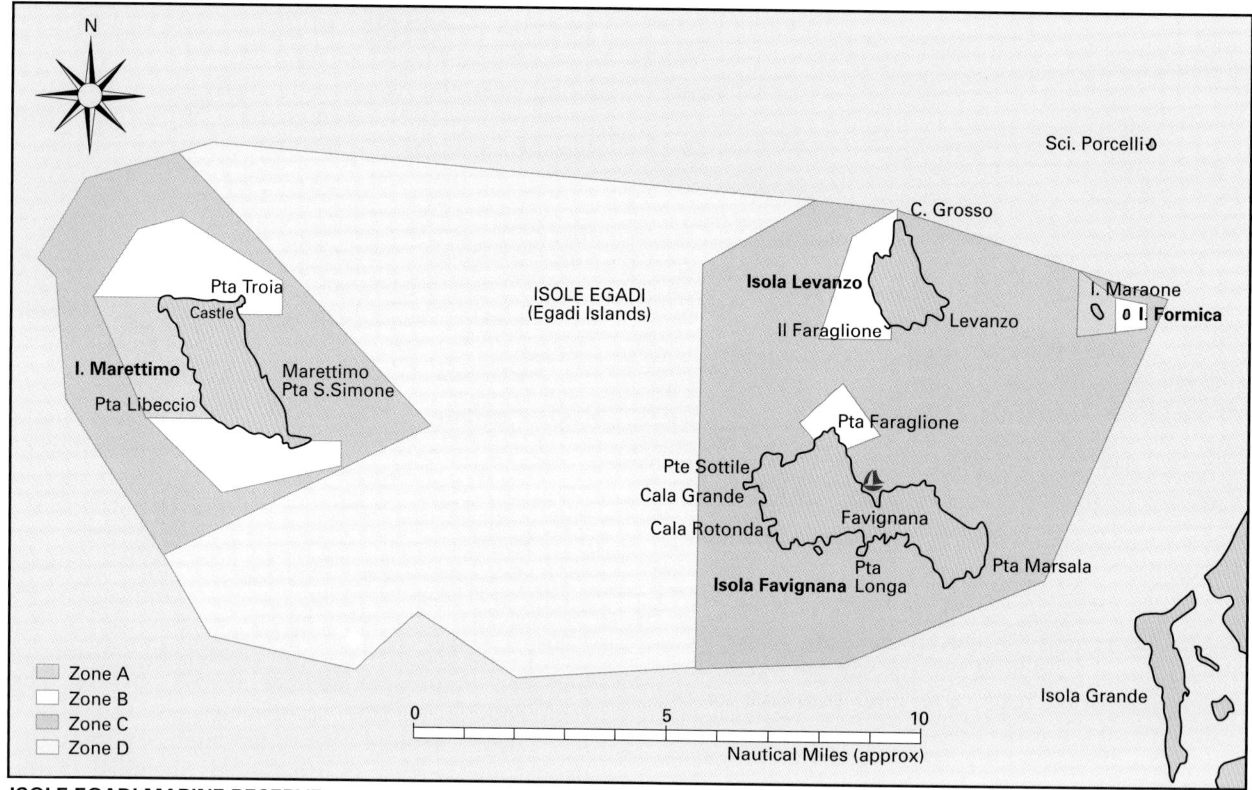

ISOLE EGADI MARINE RESERVE

Isole Egadi Marine Reserve (AMP)

The islands are all enclosed within the marine reserve, which was established in 1991. The W coast of I. Marettimo and the waters around I. Maraone are in Zone A. The borders of Zone A are marked with yellow buoys and by yellow poles on land.

Zone A
Navigation, anchoring, mooring, sport and commercial fishing, and diving are all prohibited. Swimming is permitted.

Zone B
Navigation (over 500m from the coast), swimming, diving with breathing apparatus and authorised fishing are permitted. Underwater fishing and fishing using towed nets are prohibited.

Zone C
Navigation is unregulated. Swimming, diving, sport and authorised commercial fishing all permitted.

Zone D
Commercial and sport fishing allowed subject to certain restrictions. Swimming and diving are permitted.

AMP Egadi ✆ 0923 922 585 / 920 011 *Fax* 0923 921 086
Email info@ampegadi.it
www.ampegadi.it

taken of the underwater rocks in the vicinity. Open to the W and S, the anchorage is somewhat swelly after the normal northerlies.

Restaurant and disco (noisy) at the hotel.

Cala Rotonda

⊕ 37°55′·2N 12°16′·6E

This lies a short distance SE of Cala Grande. Open only to the W and SW, it offers better shelter than Cala Grande. Anchor in 5m in a sandy patch in the middle. A swell usually creeps around into the cove from the normal northerly breeze.

Punta Longa

⊕ 37°54′·8N 12°19′·4E

On the S side of this point on the S side of the island there is a small harbour but it is too shallow for a yacht. However, a yacht can anchor in the lee of the point and be sheltered from the normal northerly breeze. Excellent holding on sand. Good restaurant ashore. A nearby road goes to Favignana town.

FAVIGNANA (CALA PRINCIPALE)

BA 964
Italian 259

Approach

Conspicuous The Aragonese fort with a signal station on Montagna Grossa and the lighthouse on Pta Sottile are both conspicuous from a considerable distance. Closer in, the cupola of the cathedral and the large Florio villa by the harbour are conspicuous.

VHF Ch 16, 11.

Mooring

Data 100 berths. Visitors' berths. Max LOA 50m. Depths <1–4m.

Berth Go stern or bows-to where directed or convenient in the old harbour or in the new S basin. Care needed of a ledge on the waterline on the N side of the S pier. The harbour is very crowded in July and August and it is difficult to find a berth.

Shelter Good shelter. The normal summer northerlies send a swell into the outer harbour.

Authorities Harbourmaster and customs. Charge band 5.

CN Favignana ✆ 0923 922 422
Ormeggiatori Isole Egadi ✆ 0923 922 212

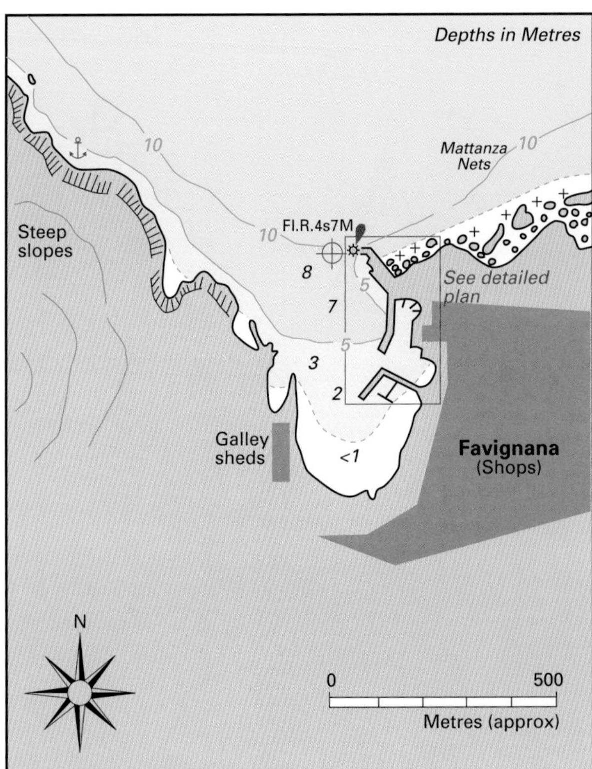

FAVIGNANA APPROACHES
⊕37°56´·09N 12°19·´41E WGS84

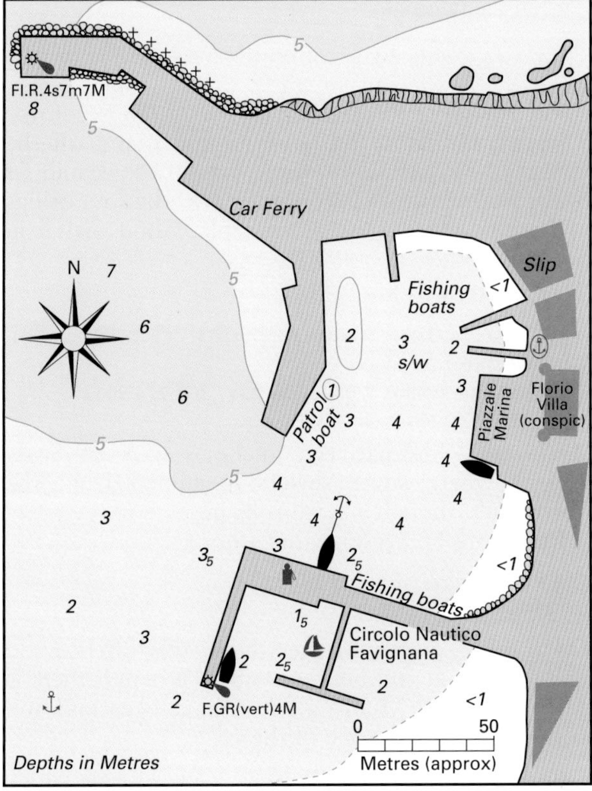

FAVIGNANA

Favignana harbour looking towards the old tunny warehouses

Facilities

Water On the quay. A water man will turn it on but it can be quite expensive. Most of the island's water is brought in by tanker.
Fuel On the quay.
Repairs Slipway to 6 tons. Limited mechanical repairs.
Provisions Several supermarkets and other shops in the village.
Eating out Good restaurants and trattorias in the town catering for the summer hordes.
Other PO. Bank. ATM. Italgaz and Camping Gaz. Hire motor scooters and bicycles in the town. Hydrofoil and car ferries to Levanzo, Marettimo and Trapani.

General

Favignana is a pleasant small town currently riding the crest of a tourist boom. In days gone by it was an important centre for processing the tunny which migrate through the channels between the islands. A Signor Ignazio Flario from Palermo bought the islands 120 years ago and made Favignana the centre of the canning industry. His statue still stands in the town square: a portly gentleman, dressed elegantly in a fashionable 19th-century cut, casually surveying his small empire.

Today the large anchors for the *mattanza* lie abandoned on the foreshore but tunny fishing seems to be undergoing something of a revival. Once again the nets are out, and from April to July the harbour and surrounding waters are given over (in part at least) to the tunny trade. Perhaps this return to traditional methods of tunny fishing has something to do with the Marine Reserve status of the waters surrounding the Egadi Islands. Whatever the cause of this revival, it is essential to maintain a lookout for the nets when navigating around the islands.

Isola Levanzo

This island lies about 3M N of Isola Favignana. Like Marettimo it is steep-to and rugged. It has a number of coves on the S coast sheltered from the normal N–NW wind of the summer, but all are open to the south.

Cala Dogana

This is a cove off the small hamlet of Levanzo. There is a short mole behind which the local fishing boats shelter. Anchor in the bay in 3–5m. Make sure you keep well clear of the approach channel used by the ferries and hydrofoil. The bottom is sand and weed – good holding once through the weed. With the normal summer northerlies the cove is adequately sheltered. Restaurant and limited provisions ashore. Car ferry and hydrofoil to Trapani.

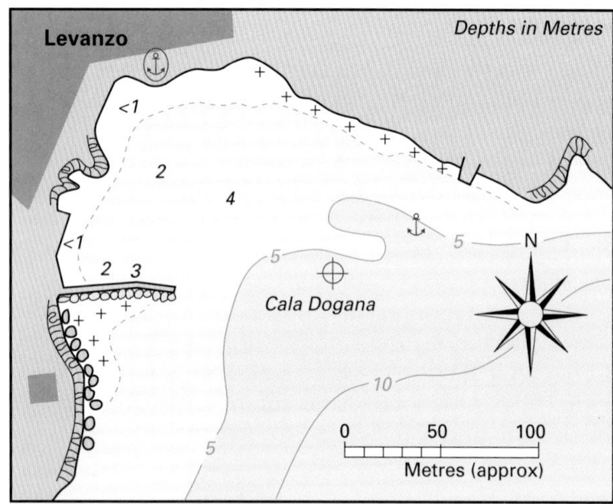

LEVANZO - CALA DOGANA
⊕37°59′·1N 12°20′.4E

Cala Fredda

Adjacent to Cala Dogana. Shelter as for Dogana, only without the ferry wash.

Isola Marettimo

Lying about 18 miles from the coast of Sicily, this is the westernmost of the Isole Egadi. It is everywhere steep-to and rugged with Mount Falcone in the NW rising to about 686m (2,250ft). It has no safe anchorages but, depending on the wind direction and the sea state, there are a number of coves where a yacht can anchor.

Cala Manione

⊕ 37°59′·4N 12°04′·1E

In the NE corner of the island, this anchorage gives some shelter from the NW and west. Anchor in 3–4m on a sand and rock bottom. There is usually a swell in here. With southerlies, there are strong gusts off the high land.

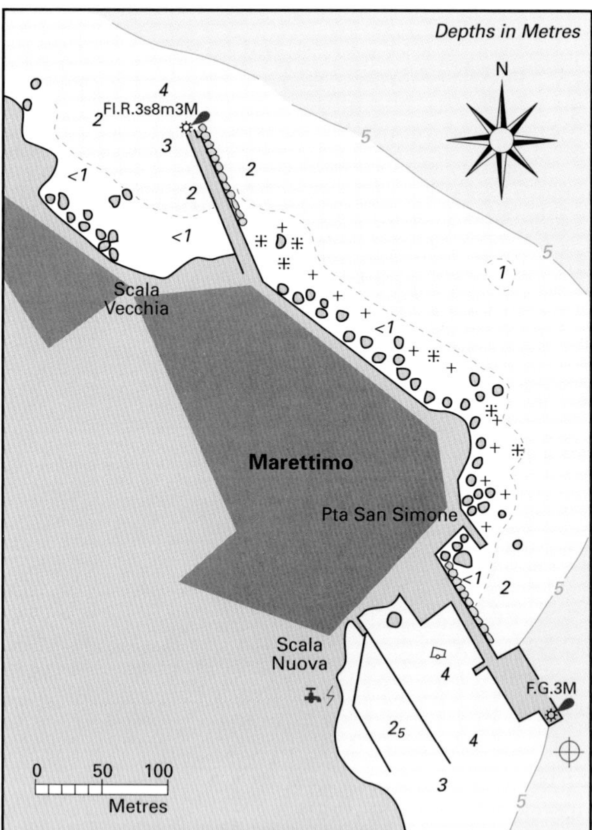

MARETTIMO - SCALA VECCHIA AND SCALA NUOVA
⊕37°58′·8N 12°04′·5E

Scala Vecchia and Scala Nuova

The two miniature harbours of the island off the village of Marettimo on the E side of the island. At Scala Nuova there is a pontoon with laid moorings and water and electricity available. Good shelter in settled weather.

VHF Ch 09 for 'Big Game'.

Data 80 berths. Visitors' berths. Depths 2–5m. Charge band 5.

Big Game Marettimo ✆ 0923 923 231 / 368 774 9613
Email info@biggame-marettimo.it

Anchorage Alternatively, anchor off S of Scala Nuova where some shelter is gained from the northerlies, though a swell rolls in.

Provisions and restaurants ashore.

Cala Cretazzo

⊕ 37°56′·8N 12°04′·16E

On the SW corner of the island, this offers good shelter from N and NE, but with NW winds there is a swell in here. Mooring buoys have been laid and you should pick up one of these.

Cala Bianca

This is very deep, and lies within Zone A of the marine reserve.

Isole Formica

Between Isola Levanzo and Trapani lie the two flat Formica Islets. The more easterly of the two has a tunny factory on it which is conspicuous from some distance off. The buildings are fascinating, appearing as they do to emerge from the sea. In calm weather a yacht can anchor in 6m off the S side for a visit to inspect the buildings. However, someone should be left on board to look after the yacht. Isola Formica is lit Fl.4s28m11M.

Scoglio Porcelli

Lies about three miles N of the Formica Islets. The white lighthouse on it is conspicuous from a considerable distance. Scoglio Porcelli is lit Fl(2)10s23m11M.

Isola Formica looking NW

Sicily

TRAPANI

BA 964
Italian 257

Approach

Although there is no difficulty approaching the harbour by day or night, care must be taken of the shoal water extending nearly a mile off the coast and from the harbour itself. The approach should be made from the SW. It can be difficult to determine just where the coastline is because of the low-lying land along the coast and the dust haze often encountered in the summer.

Conspicuous From the N, Monte Cofana (659m) six miles SSW of Capo San Vito and Monte San Guiliano and Erice with a cluster of communications towers on the summit, immediately NE of Trapani, are conspicuous. From the S the town of Trapani is visible across the low salt pans bordering the coast. Often the white mounds of salt flash in the sun and are conspicuous from a considerable distance. Closer in, the buildings and particularly the red roofs of the hospital to the S of the harbour are conspicuous. Torre Colombaia and the old lighthouse and the breakwaters are easily identified.

By night Use the light on Scoglio Palumbo Fl.5s16m12M/Iso.R.2s9m8M (131°-R-176° over

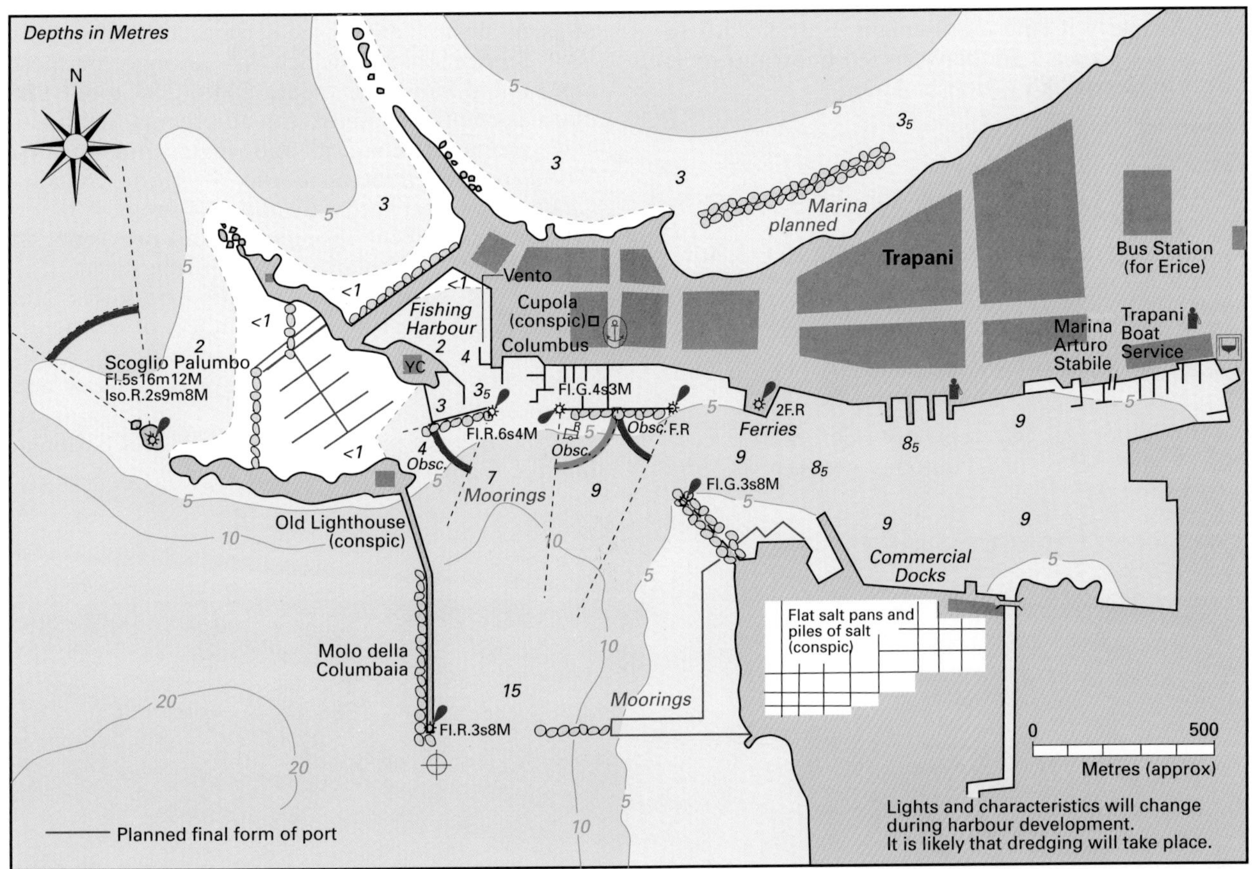

TRAPANI
⊕38°00′·4N 12°30′·0E

Saltpans at Trapani *Vito Arcomano, FOTOTECA ENIT*

Secche La Balata and Balatella). The lights on these breakwaters are partially obscured (*see plan for details*).

VHF Ch 16 for port authorities (0800–0000). Ch 69 for Marina Arturo Stabile.

Dangers

1. The above and below-water rocks fringing the N and W approaches to the harbour should be left some distance off.
2. Ferries and hydrofoils enter and leave the harbour at speed.
3. Work is in progress in the harbour. Care needed, particularly if entering by night. Care needed of shallow area c.1·5m between red buoy and mole off the Guardia Costieri building.

Mooring

Data

Trapani Boat Service 130 berths. Visitors' berths. Max LOA 40m. Depths 2–5m.

Marina Arturo Stabile 100 berths. Max LOA 40m. Depths 2–6m.

Vento di Maestrale c.100 berths. Max LOA c.20m. Depths 1–4m.

Columbus Yachting 80 berths. Max LOA c.20m. Depths 1–4m.

Berths Moorings (free) in NW corner off Lega Navale and SE corner. Pontoons between YC and Guardia Costieri with limited visitors' berths from Vento di Maestrale and Columbus Yachting. Marina Arturo Stabile pontoon off the quay in the NE corner. Limited berths at Trapani Boat Service.

A yacht will be turned away from the fishing harbour which is always full. Try the Lega Navale YC near the fishing harbour. Laid moorings tailed to the quay.

Shelter Good all-round shelter. However, the numerous ferries and hydrofoils cause some wash which is uncomfortable.

Authorities Harbourmaster and customs. Charge band 5.

Trapani Boat Service ✆ 0923 29240 / 28223 / 349 661 8376
Fax 0923 873 334
Email info@boatservicetrapani.it
www.boatservicetrapani.it

Marina Arturo Stabile ✆ 0923 28191 / 3 ✆ 0923 593 967
www.marinaarturostabile.it

Vento di Maestrale ✆ 0923 26874 / 349 627 2840
Email ventodimaestraletp@alice.it
www.marina-postibarca-trapani.it

Columbus Yachting ✆ /*Fax* 0923 28341 ✆ 393 947 7497
Email columbus.tp@me.com
www.columbustrapani.com

Lega Navale ✆ 0923 547 467

Facilities

Services Water and electricity at most berths. Showers and toilets at 'marinas'. Wi-Fi.

Fuel On the waterfront (no water).

Repairs Slipways to 500 tons. Mobile crane to 80 tons. 40/250-ton travel-hoists. There are a number of yards at the E end of the harbour. One of these is Boat Service Trapani which can arrange for most repairs and can haul yachts up to 250 tons. The marinas mentioned above can all organise haul outs and repairs. Mechanical and engineering repairs. Wood repairs. Electrical and electronic repairs. Chandlers. Good hardware and tool shops.

Provisions Excellent shopping for all provisions in the town but particularly in the E of the town.

Eating out Excellent restaurants, trattorias and pizzerias of all types. A number of couscous restaurants reflect the Arabic influence.

Other PO. Banks. ATMs. Hospital. Italgaz and Camping Gaz. Hire cars. Buses and trains to Palermo. Ferries to the Egadi Islands and Sardinia. Internal flights.

Trapani, viewed from Erice

Trapani waterfront with Erice atop Monte Giuliano

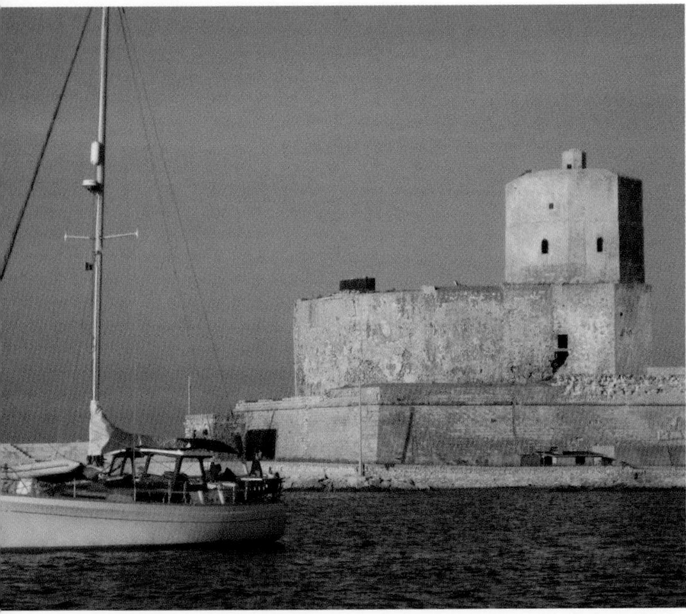

Moorings infront of the old lighthouse

General

Little visited by yachts, Trapani is a bustling harbour which is not unattractive. The arrival of the Americas Cup teams for a regatta in October 2005 did much to accelerate the harbour regeneration. Work on the waterfront quay has made it a much more pleasant place to be, both afloat and ashore. The old quarter of the town reflects the tangled history of this part of Sicily in its hybrid architecture and inhabitants. Arabic influences on the architecture and cuisine are apparent everywhere.

The name Trapani is a corruption of the Greek *dhrepanon* meaning a sickle and referring to the shape of the land jutting out into the sea. Because of its strategic location between North Africa and the Tyrrhenian Sea it was a major Carthaginian colony and later it was important to the Aragonese as a link with Spain.

Behind Trapani, Mte San Giuliano rises to 756m (2,480ft) with the site of Erice on the summit. It can be reached by bus in about 40 minutes or by cable car. It is worth the trip as much for the cool breezes blowing over the top as for the Aragonese village. The village, with its castle and cobbled streets, beautiful as it is, cannot match the view over the surrounding coast and sea. In Greek times the place was known to mariners for its temple of Aphrodite and her sacred courtesans, so it would seem appropriate for modern sailors to make the pilgrimage.

Punta Pizzolungo

⊕ 38°03'N 12°33'E

Just S of this point on the NW corner of Sicily, there is a small harbour used by power boats. A large hotel stands on the shore. The harbour extends in an 'L' from the shore with the entrance at the S end.

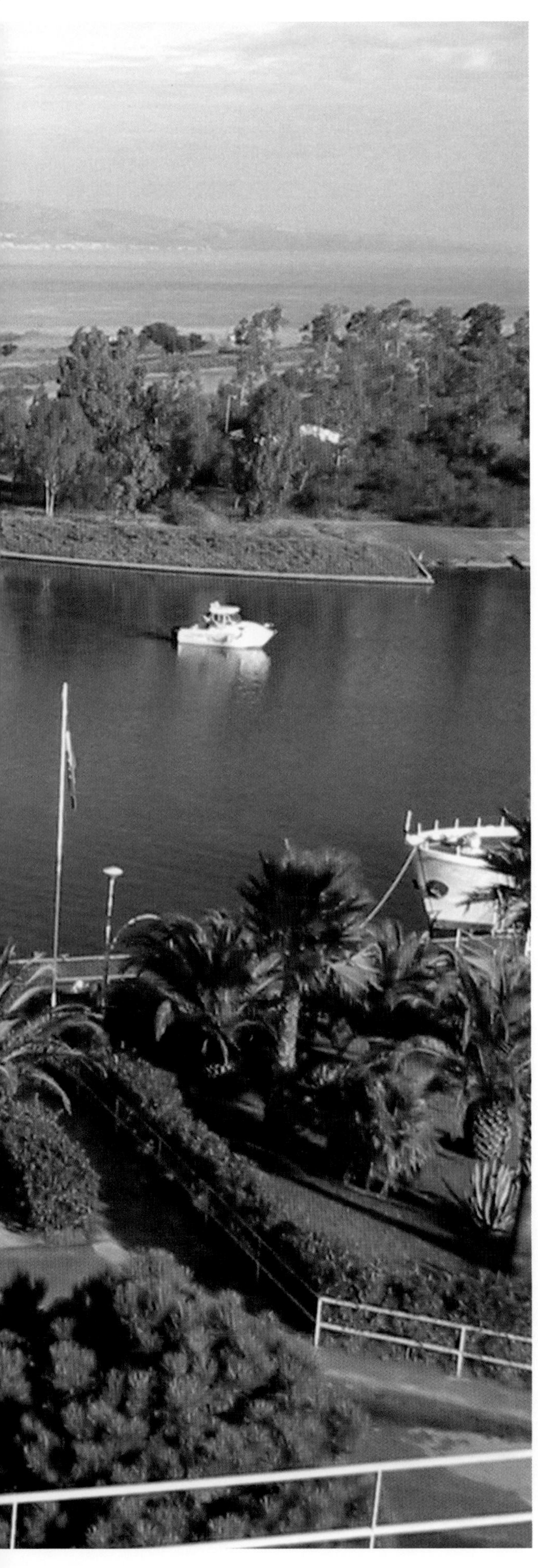

VI.
The Ionian

This chapter covers the coast bordered by the Ionian Sea from Capo dell'Armi on the toe of Italy to Capo Santa Maria di Leuca on the heel of the boot. This is precisely the area known as the Alto or High Ionian on the Italian weather forecast map. There are relatively few harbours along the long coastline, and fewer still in the Golfo di Taranto, that are likely to be visited by a yacht. Most yachts make for Crotone and Santa Maria di Leuca to get a night's rest before turning the corner into the Adriatic or crossing to Greece.

From Capo dell'Armi to Crotone the peninsula of Calabria is mountainous and steep-to. For the most part it is bare and rocky but in the gorges and ravines there are some wooded areas.

In contrast to Calabria, the region of Apulia on the east side of the Golfo di Taranto is composed of plains and rolling hills. It is a very dry region with a low rainfall and consequently is known locally as '*seticulosa*' or 'thirsty'. The whole of the south coast is blessed with long sandy beaches which have only recently attracted growing numbers of tourists.

Although these southern shores were once an important part of Magna Graecia, with the prosperous cities of Crotone, Sibaris and Taras dotted around the Golfo di Taranto, few ancient remains are to be found because successive waves of invaders and earthquakes have battered them down. Indeed, the site of ancient Sibaris has still not been determined with any certainty. Until recently the area was poor and much neglected by the government in Rome, but now the marshes have been drained, hydroelectric schemes initiated and an effort made to attract industry. Tourism too has brought a small measure of prosperity to the coast, but it remains very much the poor cousin of the rich north.

A group called Porto Ulisse have developed a chain of marinas along the alleged route of Odysseus (Ulysses in Latinised form), most of which lie on the Ionian/Adriatic coast of Italy, including Rocella Ionica, Crotone, and Brindisi. There are others in Sicily and the Eastern Sporades and the Dodecanese in Greece. Few of them have anything to do with the traditional ports in Homer's *Odyssey*.

Marina Laghi di Sibari looking across to the Stombi
Casa Bianca Group srl

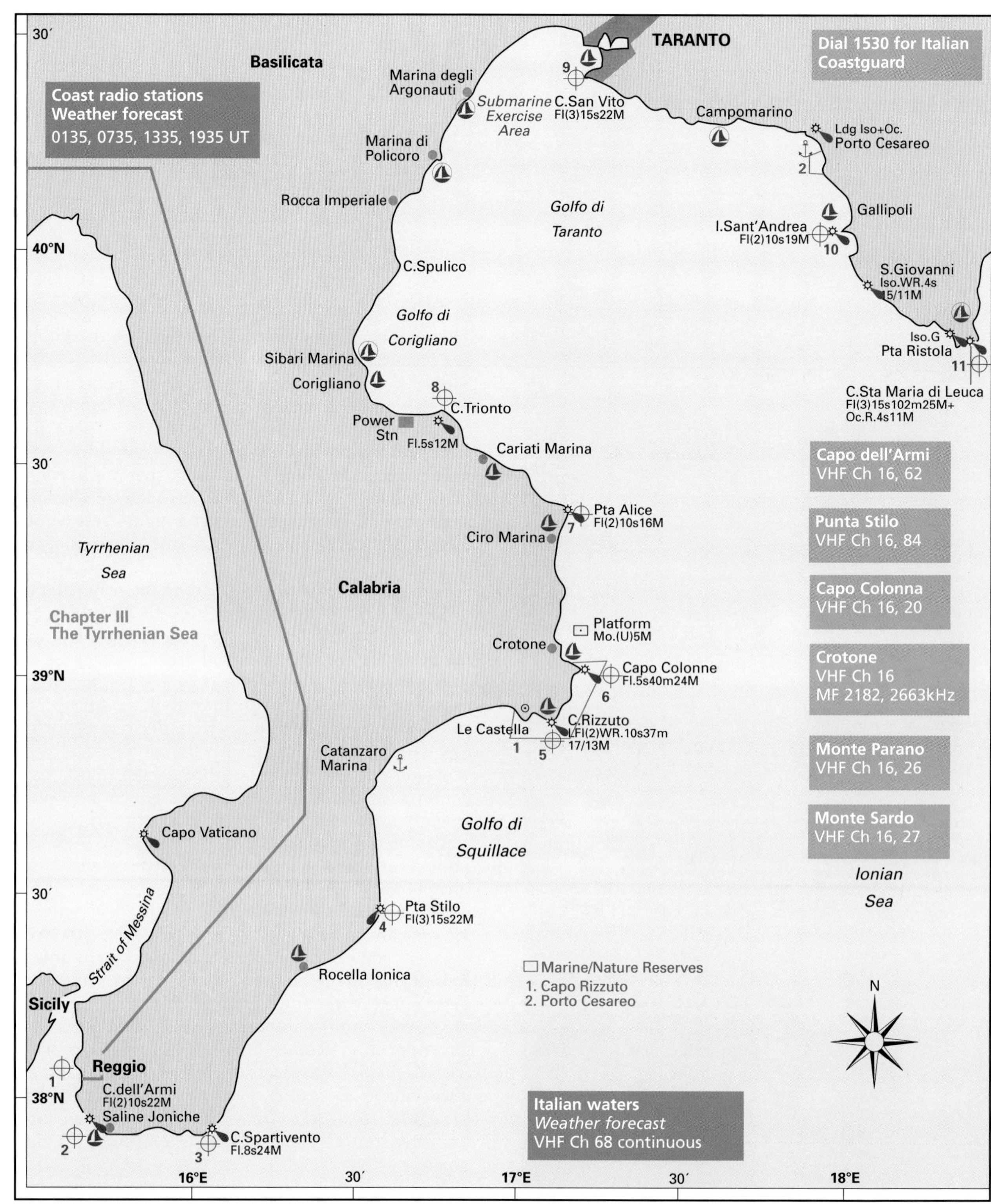

THE IONIAN COAST

USEFUL WAYPOINTS

⊕**1** 0·25M W of Pta. di Pellaro
38°01′·19N 15°37′·72E WGS84

⊕**2** 0·25M S of Capo dell'Armi
37°56′·87N 15°40′·74E WGS84

⊕**3** 0·5M S of Capo Spartivento
37°54′·87N 16°03′·70E WGS84

⊕**4** 1M E of Pta Stilo
38°26′·8N 16°36′·4E

⊕**5** 1M S of Capo Rizzuto
38°52′·8N 17°05′·7E

⊕**6** 1M E of Capo Colonne
39°01′·5N 17°13′·8E

⊕**7** 1M E of Pta Alice
39°24′·0N 17°10′·5E

⊕**8** 1M N of Capo Trionto
39°38′·0N 16°46′·0E

⊕**9** 0·5M W of Capo San Vito
40°24′·7N 17°11′·5E

⊕**10** 1M W of Isola Sant'Andrea
40°02′·8N 17°54′·7E

⊕**11** 1M S of Capo Santa Maria di Leuca
39°46′·7N 18°22′·1E

Weather patterns in the Ionian Sea

The prevailing wind in the summer is from a southerly direction, most often SW. At night there is frequently a light northerly breeze. The Golfo di Squillace is aptly named and here the wind can blow very strongly, usually from the W or NW, and raises a short and uncomfortable sea. A yacht sailing along the S coast will frequently encounter only light winds or calms as far as the Golfo di Squillace and light winds again predominate from Crotone. At night a strong katabatic wind may blow off the land in the Golfo di Squillace. It arrives without warning and may reach Force 6. In winter it is often better to avoid the S coast altogether if bound for Greece as there are frequently SE gales and the coast is a long lee shore with few ports of refuge.

According to the Admiralty *Pilot,* dark clouds on the SE horizon (known locally as *barrata*) indicate strong SE winds and dark clouds over the mountains indicate NE winds. In Crotone a low water level in winter is said to indicate strong northerly winds. In the summer the converse holds and a low water level indicates fine weather and a high water level means the approach of strong southerly winds. In the Golfo di Taranto there is frequently a light northerly wind in the daytime known locally as *borino* or little *bora*. The *bora* proper of the Adriatic may affect the Golfo di Taranto in winter, spring and autumn, and raises a considerable sea.

Currents

There is usually a SW-going current along the south coast, but it rarely reaches one knot and may be reversed by strong SW winds.

When leaving the Straits of Messina heading E, if the tide is against you follow the example of local yachts and go closer inshore to pick up a counter-current, or at least less current against you.

Shoestring cruising in The Ionian

Harbours and Marinas

Most of the marinas and harbours including Rocella Ionica, La Castella, Ciro Marina, Cariati Marina, Sibari Marina, and Gallipoli are all reasonably priced and some are free. Crotone and Santa Maria di Leuca can be expensive and are best visited out of high season.

There are plans to develop some of these places in which case the price band will go up.

Anchorages

There are few good anchorages along this coast. You can anchor off Le Castella or either side of Capo Rizzuto depending on wind and sea. It can blow quite strongly from the S along this stretch of coast, even in summer, so check the weather forecast. In the Golfo di Taranto there is Porto Cesareo on the E side.

Routes

Yachts mostly cruise along this coast en route to or from Greece or the Adriatic. It is pretty much possible to do this section of coast without doing an overnight passage, although there will be one or two long days of 70 miles or so. You will need to leave early in the morning to arrive before dusk on the passage from, say, Reggio di Calabria to Rocella Ionica or from Crotone to Santa Maria di Leuca, and it all assumes you do not meet strong headwinds.

Few yachts head up into the Golfo di Taranto with the exception of yachts headed for Marina Laghi di Sibari. There are now good yacht berths in Taranto, and on the other side of the gulf Gallipoli is well worth a detour and is also a useful port of refuge in strong southerlies.

Data

PROHIBITED AREAS AND MARINE RESERVES

Taranto There are a number of prohibited areas around Taranto. The prohibited area NW of the entrance to Mar Grande is shown on the plan of Taranto.

Marine Reserves (Area Marina Protetta – AMPs)

1. ***Capo Rizzuto*** A marine reserve has been created around Capo Rizzuto from the W of Le Castella to Baie di Crotone. See plan under Le Castella to Crotone.
2. ***Porto Cesareo*** A marine reserve has been created around Porto Cesareo in Golfo di Taranto. See plan under Porto Cesareo.

Major lights

Capo dell'Armi Fl(2)10s95m22M
Capo Spartivento Fl.8s63m24M
Punta Stilo Fl(3)15s54m22M
Capo Rizzuto LFl(2)WR.10s37m17/13M
Red sectors cover Secche de Capo Rizzuto and Secche di La Castella.
Capo Colonne Fl.5s40m24M
Punta Alice Fl(2)10s31m16M
Laghi di Sibari Fl(4)20s23m12M
Capo San Vito Fl(3)15s46m22M
Santa Andrea (Gallipoli) Fl(2)10s45m19M
Torre San Giovanni Iso.WR.4s23m15/11M
Capo Sta Maria di Leuca Fl(3)15s102m25M & Oc.R.4s100m11M over Secche di Ugento

Quick reference guide

	Shelter	*Mooring*	*Fuel*	*Water*	*Eating out*	*Provisions*	*Plan*	*Charge band*
Saline Ioniche	A	C	O	O	O	O	•	
Roccella Ionica	A	A	B	A	C	C	•	2
Catanzaro	C	C	B	B	B	C	•	1
Le Castella	A	AB	B	A	C	C	•	3
Crotone	A/B	A	A	A	A	A	•	3/4
Ciro' Marina	A	AB	B	B	C	C	•	1/2
Cariati Marina	B	B	B	B	C	C	•	1
Corigliano Calabro	A	B	O	B	C	C	•	1
Marina Laghi di Sibari	A	A	A	A	B	B	•	2/3
Marina di Policoro	A	A	A	A	B	C	•	3/4
Porto degli Argonauti	A	A	A	A	C	C	•	3/4
Taranto	A	A	A	A	A	A	•	4
Campomarino	A	A	A	A	C	C	•	
Porto Cesareo	B	C	B	B	B	B	•	1
Gallipoli	A	A	A	A	A	A	•	3
Darsena Fontanelle	A	A	B	A	C	C	•	2/3
Porto Gaio	AC	A	A	A	C	C	•	
Torre Vado	A	A	O	O	C	C	•	
Sta Maria di Leuca	B	A	A	A	B	B	•	3

Capo dell'Armi looking NE

SALINE IONICHE

BA 1941
Italian 23

The entrance to Saline Ioniche has now silted up completely and the entrance is blocked by a shingle bar above water. The N breakwater has now been completely demolished, but depths are unknown. Care needed as silting may reduce depths.

At present yachts anchor where convenient inside the harbour.

Note There have been several incidents of aggravated burglary from yachts anchored in this harbour. It is strongly recommended that yachts do not stop here except in an emergency.

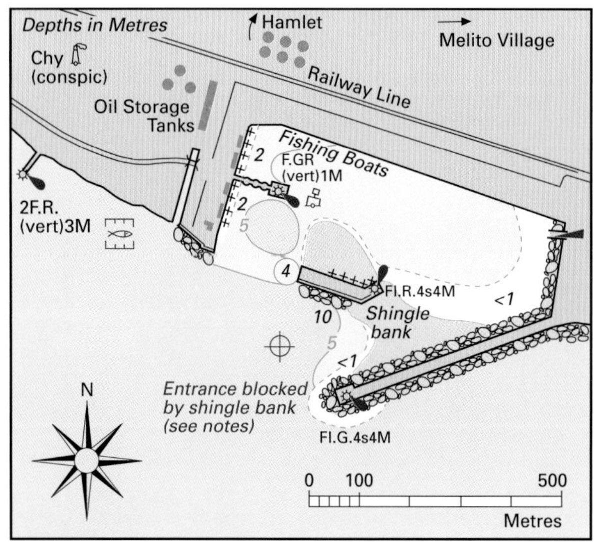

SALINE IONICHE
⊕37°55′·56N 15°43′·88E WGS84

Capo Spartivento looking NE

Fish farm

⊕ 37°53′·7N 15°59′·6E

A large fish farm lies nearly 2M offshore close SW of Capo Spartivento. The four corners are marked by yellow buoys with × topmarks. Yachts coasting between the Straits of Messina and the Ionian can leave it to seaward, but care is needed, particularly if making landfall from the east.

ROCCELLA IONICA

Rocella Ionica is the nearest usable harbour in the E approaches to the Straits of Messina, lying 10M SW of Punta Stilo. The harbour approaches are subject to continuous silting. Care needed.

Approach

The harbour lies to the NE of the village of Rocella Ionica.

Conspicuous From the NE the ruins of the castle and tower on a craggy bluff above the village are conspicuous. From the SW the castle and tower are more difficult to make out. Two small eroded 'peaks' in the cliffs behind the harbour are also conspicuous. Closer in, the breakwater will be seen.

By night The entrance is lit Fl.G.3s11m5M/ Fl.R.3s11m5M.
A night entrance is not advised because of the sandbar at the entrance. See below.

VHF Ch 16, 14 for Guardia Costiera.

Dangers

1. As at Saline Ioniche, the entrance here has silted since my earlier survey. A sandbank under water partially obstructs the entrance, extending out from the extremity of the starboard-hand breakwater. Approach from the S–SE keeping at least 300m SW of the end of the breakwater. Head towards the beach to the W of the groyne until the ruined tower at Rocella Ionica lines up with the port-hand light structure. Keep on this transit and head for the entrance just off the port-hand side. There are 2·5–3m least depths across the sandbar using this dogleg course. Once across the bar there are depths of 3–4m into the marina. It is likely that silting will continue. A small

dredger has been stationed here but it has little chance of keeping pace with the rate of silting. Caution needed as the extent and area of the sandbank is likely to change over time. Latest reports suggest depths can be as little as 2·3m, and that yachts drawing more than 2·2m are prohibited from entering the port. Call ahead on VHF to the coastguard for the latest local advice

2. With onshore winds there are breaking waves at the entrance and with an onshore gale entry would be dangerous. See also the account below.

A very serious incident occurred in 2004 when a yacht attempted to enter the harbour. With his permission, I quote the yachtsman:

'I was entering the port after a 14-hour passage from Reggio Calabria – not particularly rough, about Force 5, but with a large swell that we could hear breaking on the beach all the way along the coast.

Suddenly, over my right shoulder an enormous Malibu Beach-type breaking wave appeared (20ft?), reared up no doubt by the sand bar. It flung us straight over and swept across the harbour entrance taking us with it upside down. The mast-head hit the bottom and I was thrown out into the water but fortunately still attached. The next wave would have finished us off and the boat was already half full of water, but before it hit us my crew had managed to scramble out and taken the helm and pointed us into the wave. The engine, thank God, never stopped and we made it out to sea again. Three hours later, and with the help of the Guardia Costiera we made it safely into port. (The boat was by now too waterlogged to be turned over again but I was again flung into the safety rail with considerable force, slightly injuring my back!)'

Fortunately, this yachtsman recovered and was able to get his yacht, a 37ft Hanse, repaired. We thank him for sending in this horrific account so that others may use his experience.

Mooring

Data 500 berths. Visitors' berths. Max LOA c.30m. Depths 2–4·5m. Max 2·3m in the entrance following the approach described above.

Berth Where directed or convenient. Finger pontoons. Yachts over 14m or so should go on the inside of the outer breakwater as the finger pontoons are too short for larger yachts to moor safely. There can be an appreciable swirling current in here making berthing difficult and you should keep an eye open for the current and take it into account when berthing. It usually flows towards the entrance.

Shelter Good shelter although onshore winds can make some berths uncomfortable, especially near the entrance.

Authorities Harbourmaster. *Carabinieri* and naval personnel who will want to see your paperwork and fill out some forms. Charge band 2.

Facilities

Services Water and electricity points in place. Water from a tap on the pontoon. Showers and toilets.

Fuel Can be delivered. There is a phone number on a notice on the first pier. Don't necessarily expect the fuel truck to arrive straight away. There is also a petrol station on the main coast road not too far from the harbour.

Repairs A crane can be arranged to haul onto the hard. Minor mechanical repairs can be arranged. Hardware shop in the village.

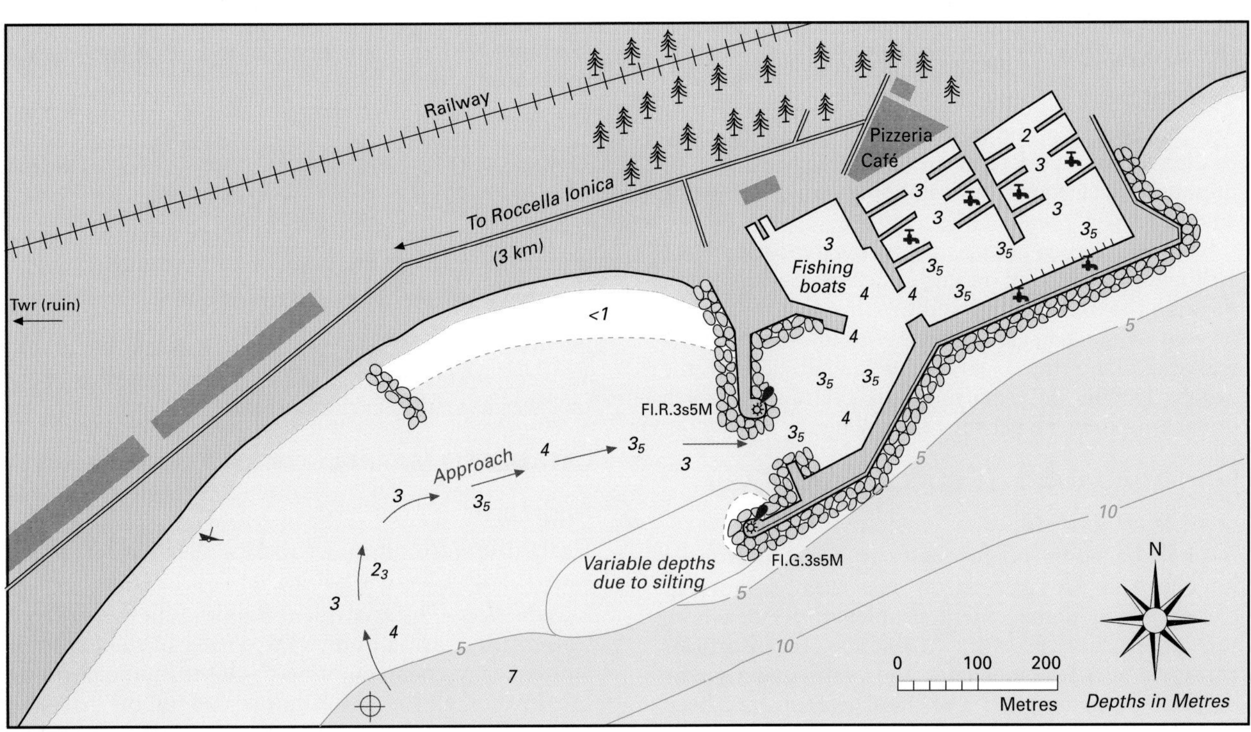

ROCCELLA IONICA
⊕38°19´·45N 16°25´·55E WGS84

The approaches to Roccella Ionica looking NE

Roccella Ionica looking ENE into the marina from the outer breakwater

Provisions In Roccella Ionica village about 3km away. Supermarket on N side of railway around 1.5km along the same road.

Eating out In Roccella Ionica village. There is also a pizzeria near the harbour – highly recommended.

Other Taxis can be ordered. In the village there is a PO and bank with an ATM machine. Buses and trains to Reggio di Calabria and Crotone.

General

The harbour has been built as a *porto turistico* though some work has never been finished. At present it is a convenient stepping stone along the coast between Messina and Crotone.

Roccella Ionica village is a sleepy little place although, sadly, the main coast road runs right through the middle. It is well worth a visit for a meal or provisions. You can avoid the main coast road by walking along the partly gravel road behind the beach. If you have bicycles on board it's worth unpacking them to get into the village.

PORTO BADALATO (LE BOCCE DI GALLIPARI)

⊕ 38°35′·5N 16°34′·4E

A small harbour roughly halfway between Rocella Ioniche and Le Castella. It has been subject to planning and management problems, the beach to the north has erosion problems; the harbour entrance silted completely and subsequently the harbour was closed. New management has been appointed and dredging is reported to have restored 3m depths in the entrance. It is not known when the harbour will officially open again.

Approach

Although dredging has recently restored adequate depths in the entrance and the basin, it is likely to continue silting. Care needed and if in any doubt reconnoitre first.

Mooring

Data c.150 berths. Max LOA c.15m. Depths <1–3m.

Berth Stern or bows-to where directed. Laid moorings tailed to the quay or to pontoons.

Shelter Good shelter in the inner basin.

Facilities

Services Water and electricity to be installed. Few facilities available at the harbour.

CATANZARO MARINA

Approach

Straightforward although there will often be strong squalls with offshore winds.

Conspicuous The apartment buildings in the town of Catanzaro Marina in the NW corner of the Golfo di Squillace are conspicuous and, closer in, the harbour breakwater at the easternmost end of the town is easily identified against the white beach.

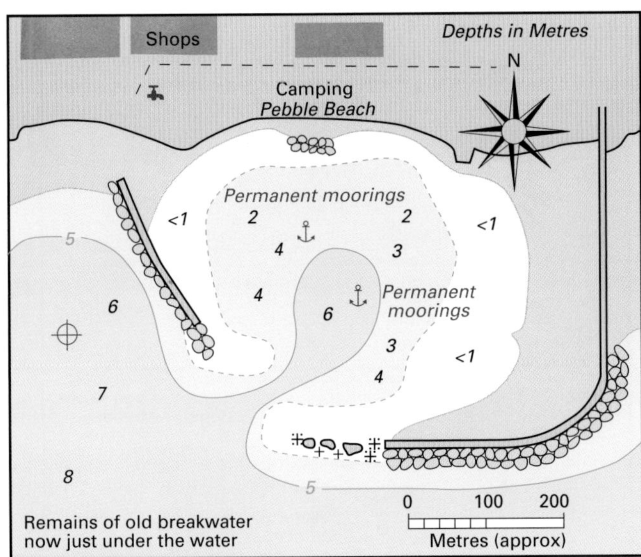

CATANZARO MARINA
⊕38°49´·45N 16°37´·85E

By night Dangerous. The harbour lights were destroyed in a storm some years ago and the underwater rocks fringing the entrance would be difficult to identify by night.

Dangers Half of the breakwater has been destroyed by years of winter storms and reconstruction works are in progress. R/G buoys mark the entrance although care is needed. Within the harbour there are numerous unlit mooring buoys and floating mooring ropes.

Mooring

Berth Anchor where convenient and, if possible, pick up a spare permanent mooring. There are no quayed sections. The bottom is loose shingle and is bad holding.

Shelter Poor now much of the breakwater has been destroyed. Some protection with moderate offshore and light onshore winds. Dangerous in any strong winds.

Authorities The *carabinieri* will often ask for documents.

Facilities

Water Near the harbour in the camping ground.
Fuel In the town.
Repairs A crane can haul a small yacht out in an emergency. Limited mechanical repairs can be carried out.
Provisions Most provisions can be obtained but fresh fruit and vegetables are limited.
Eating out A number of fairly average restaurants.
Other Post office and bank in Catanzaro on the hill behind Catanzaro Marina. Buses from Catanzaro Marina to Catanzaro.

General

Catanzaro Marina is a popular holiday resort for Italians. Behind the harbour there are a number of what appear to be permanent caravan sites and around them a patchwork of multicoloured tents. The attraction is the long shingle and sand beach that sweeps around the bay. Catanzaro Marina is itself an undistinguished collection of apartment blocks, but inland there are interesting villages and fine scenery.

LE CASTELLA (Marina di Capo Rizzuto) (Zone B)

Approach

Straightforward. The castle at the SW end of the village is easily identified and the harbour lies approximately ⅓ mile to the E of it. The entrance to the new marina is narrow but has depths of 2–3m. Rocks just under the surface around the headland to the E of the entrance are difficult to see with any wind but the fairway is free of dangers.

By night A night entrance is not recommended because of the rocks bordering the coast in the final approach. Motion sensitive floodlights illuminate the entrance to the yacht harbour.

Dangers Care needed of the rocks off the coast and the approach should be made from the east.

Mooring

Data Visitors' berths. Max LOA c.20m. Depths 1–3m.

Berth Yachts currently go stern or bows-to or alongside in the marina. Laid mooring chains and ropes are only light and would be inadequate for larger yachts. The pontoons are usually full of small

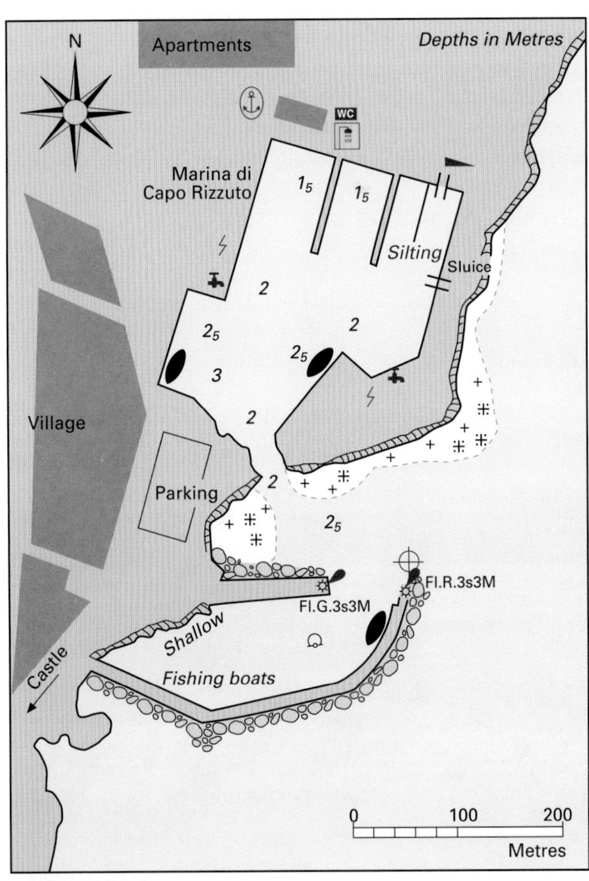

LE CASTELLA
⊕38°54´·51N 17°01´·73E WGS84

Marina di Capo Rizzuto looking S into Le Castella harbour

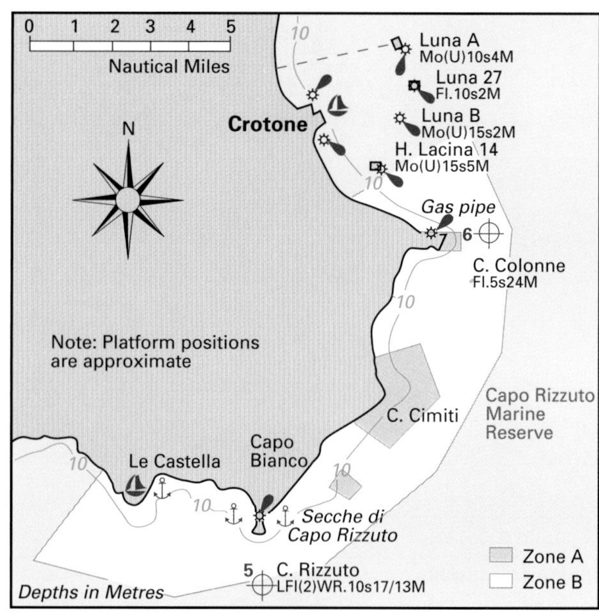

CAPO RIZZUTO MARINE RESERVE

local boats, and in any case depths reduce towards the N quay. Yachts can also go alongside the outer breakwater in the fishing harbour.

Shelter Excellent shelter in the marina. Good shelter in the fishing harbour, although with heavy onshore winds there is likely to be a reflected swell when seas rebound off the coast near the entrance.

Note

1. Sluices open to the sea on the E side of the yacht basin cause a surge with E winds, and are also causing silting here.
2. In heavy weather local boats will take lines right across the basin. The lines will be easily seen in daylight, but care is needed.

Authorities Harbourmaster. *Ormeggiatori.* Charge band 3.

Lega Navale ☎ 0962 795 528
Porto Turistico ☎ 333 989 9986

Marina di Capo Rizzuto looking N from Le Castella harbour

⊕**5** 1M S of Capo Rizzuto 38°52'·8N 17°05'·7E
⊕**6** 1M E of Capo Colonne 39°01'·5N 17°13'·8E

Capo Rizzuto Marine Reserve

A marine reserve has been established around Capo Rizzuto. It extends from the W side of Le Castella right around Capo Colonne into Baia di Crotone.

There are three Zone A areas, around Capo Cimiti, Capo Bianco and Capo Colonne. There is no Zone C. The zones are now as shown on the plan.

Zone A
Navigation, access, mooring and anchoring, sport and commercial fishing, and diving are all prohibited.
Note Yellow buoys mark the boundaries of Zone A.

Zone B
Navigation, access and mooring and anchoring are not subject to regulation. Fishing and diving are permitted with the prior consent of the authorities.

AMP Capo Rizzuto
☎ 0962 795 511/795 623 *Fax* 0962 665 247
Email com@riservamarinacaporizzuto.it
www.riservamarinacaporizzuto.it

Facilities

Services Water and electricity on the quay in the marina. Showers and toilets. Laundry. Chandler nearby.
Fuel Can probably be delivered by mini-tanker.
Provisions Minimarkets and other shops in the village. Supermarket near the marina.
Eating out Several restaurants in the village.
Other PO. Bank. Camping Gaz. Bus to Crotone. International flights from Crotone airport.

General

Le Castella is an intimate little resort, well worth a stop when cruising along the south coast.

The castle the place is named after, Le Castella, the Castello Aragonese, is well worth a visit. Where the marina basin is built is shown on tourist maps as an ancient quarry so it is presumably the same place that the rock for the castle was quarried from.

Capo Rizzuto

⊕5 1M S of Capo Rizzuto 38°52′·8N 17°05′·7E

A yacht can find some shelter either side of Capo Rizzuto from W and E winds. The bottom is sand, mud and rocks and not always good holding.

Capo Colonne

Mooring buoys have been laid on the S side of the cape within the marine reserve and are available to yachts.

CROTONE

BA 140
Italian 146

Approach

Straightforward by day and night. There may be a disturbed swell at the entrance to Porto Vecchio.

Conspicuous Approaching Capo Colonne a tall white tower is conspicuous on a hill behind. The lighthouse and several buildings on the cape are also conspicuous. Rounding Capo Colonne the town of Crotone is conspicuous against the barren hills behind. Closer in, the outer harbour mole and a crane are easily identified.

By night Use the light on Capo Colonne Fl.5s40m24M. For platform lights see below. The harbour lights do not show up well against the loom of the town lights. A night entrance must be made with care because of the gas platforms in the approaches: see below.

VHF Ch 16 for port authorities (24hr). Ch 14, 16 for pilots. Ch 06 for Lega Navale. Ch 72 for YKC.

Gas platforms

Care is needed in the approaches to Crotone of the four gas platforms lying in the sea area off Crotone. From N to S the Luna A platform lies 2½ miles NE of Crotone; Luna B lies just over three miles E of Crotone; Luna 27 lies 3½ miles E of Crotone; and H Lacinia lies two miles SE of Crotone. The approach to Crotone should be made between H Lacinia and Luna B from the SE.

The platforms are lit:

Luna A Mo(U)10s12m4M Horn Mo(U)30s.
Luna B Mo(U)15s15m5M Horn Mo(U)40s.
Luna 27 Fl.10s2M.
Hera Lacinia Mo(U)15s19m5M Horn Mo(U)30s.

Mooring

Data Depths 2–5m.

Berth Yachts will be directed to a berth in Porto Ulisse, as the revamped quay around Porto Vecchio is now styled. Most of the berths are under the direction of various concessions along the quay and on pontoons in Porto Vecchio. There are laid moorings tailed to the quay. There is occasionally a berth for visiting yachts on the Lega Navale pontoons inside YC Kroton.

Natale keeps watch on the harbour wall for approaching yachts and blows a very loud whistle to alert you. He administers a basic toilet and shower block and collects the fees.

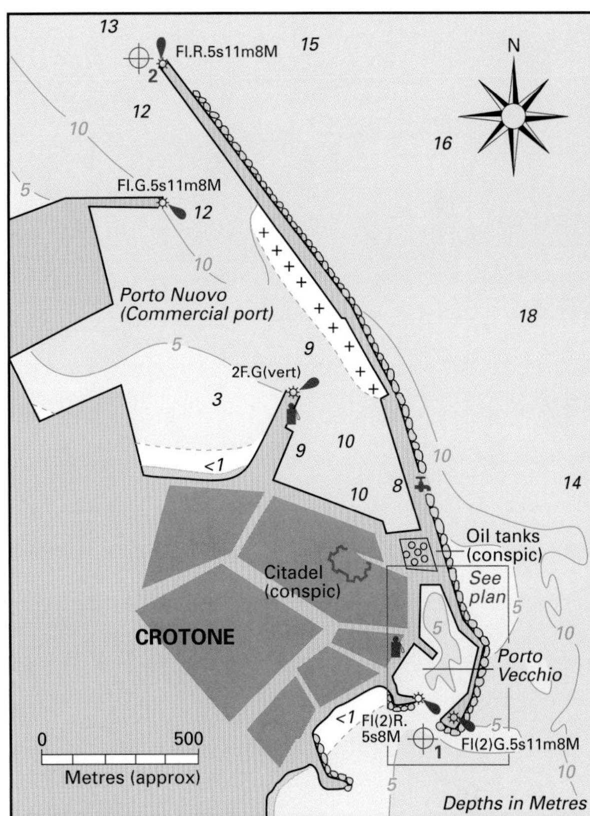

CROTONE
⊕1 39°04′·67N 17°08′·22E WGS84
⊕2 39°05′·7N 17°07′·5E

Shelter Normally adequate in the summer. With strong SW winds a considerable surge develops making it very uncomfortable. With gales from the S it may become untenable and, if possible, a yacht should seek permission to go to Porto Nuovo. Shelter is better in the YC basin.

Authorities Harbourmaster and customs. *Ormeggiatori*. Charge band 3/4. There is a naval college here so you may have cadets coming around to check up on papers.

Yacht Kroton Club ✆ 0962 900 343
Lega Navale ✆ 0962 27240
Autonautico Tricoli, Dr Renato G. Russo
✆ 0962 22852 / 340 832 0909
Blue Ship Charter ✆ 0962 905 526 / 338 705 8723
Email pierluigi@seateam.it
Yachting Club ✆ 333 482 5141
Natale ✆ 329 938 4449
De Santis ✆ 338 686 0494
Paolagest ✆ 0962 900736
Crotone Port Authority ✆ 0962 20721/2

Note There have been reports of aggressive *ormeggiatori* on the town quay.

Facilities

Services Water and electricity on the E quay. Toilets and showers.

Fuel Q8 at the S end of the breakwater. Variable depths off the quay; deeper draught yachts should check with the fuel man where to come alongside.

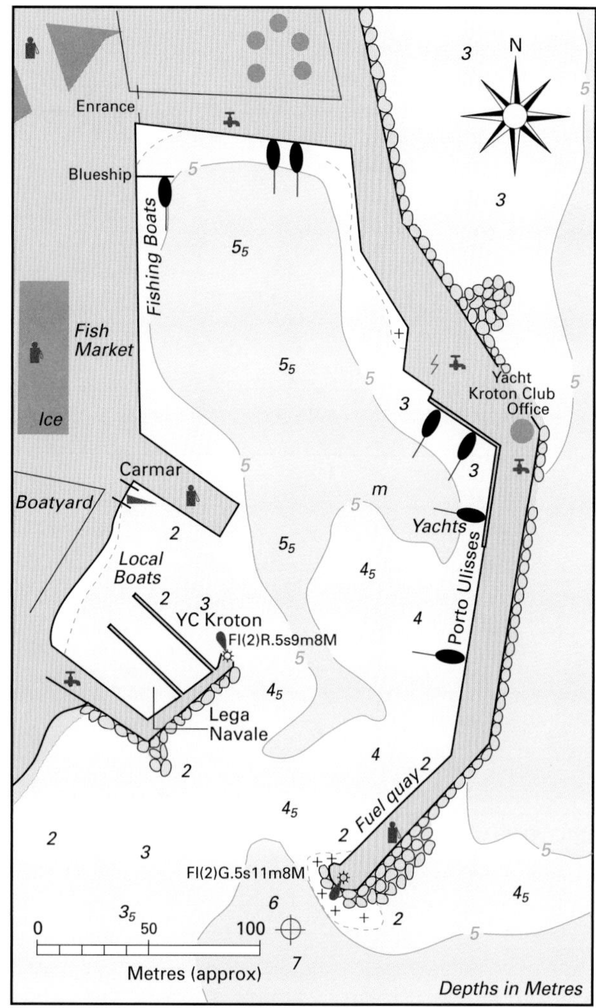

CROTONE – PORTO VECCHIO
⊕39°04´·67N 17°08´·22E WGS84

Carmar have duty free fuel from the pier on the W side of Porto Vecchio, and duty paid fuel on the pier in the commercial harbour.

Carmar ☎ 0962 20156 / 335 740 1734
Email carmarsrl@libero.it

Repairs A boatyard in Porto Vecchio can haul yachts. 150-ton slipway. 75-ton crane. Mechanical and engineering repairs. Electrical repairs. Chandlers.

Provisions Good shopping for all provisions. On the quay there is a fish market (where ice can be bought) and, three streets behind the harbour there is a fruit and vegetable market.

Eating out Restaurants in the town. The seafood restaurant on the waterfront, *Casa di Rosa*, is to be recommended, especially its seafood starters.

Other PO. Banks. ATMs. Hospital. Italgaz and Camping Gaz. Hardware shops and a small chandlery. Hire cars. Buses serve the surrounding area. Internal flights.

General

Crotone, once esteemed for its beautiful women, its art, and its wonderful architecture, today has virtually nothing to show for its ancient glory. Of its temple just one column remains, much of the rest is said to be in the harbour breakwaters. In the museum, fragments of its ancient past are displayed from the age when it controlled much of Magna Graecia. Pythagoras made it his home in the 5th century BC and developed his ascetic-mystic-vegetarian-reincarnation philosophy here for some 30 years before he was ousted along with the oligarchy he supported.

In the Middle Ages it declined substantially and even 15 years ago was a forgotten place. Today it is gradually reviving with the jobs the gas platforms bring, though it is still very much an out-of-the-way place.

Porto Vecchio has now had a new shelf quay built around it and the whole area has been cleaned up and paved to become the new Porto Ulisse. Downtown Crotone has also been getting something of a facelift and the old buildings around the town have had the grime removed, pavement cafés have sprouted and the streets have been cleaned up. It's a far cry from the crumbling seedy place I arrived at in 1976 where any yacht over 10m was likely to be accosted for a lot of lire with not a little menace and very little in the way of service. I remember three very big mafiosi taking *Roulette* to the other side of the harbour during a scirocco and then looking at her diminutive size and growling: 'no problem, the big motorboat pays'. And he did.

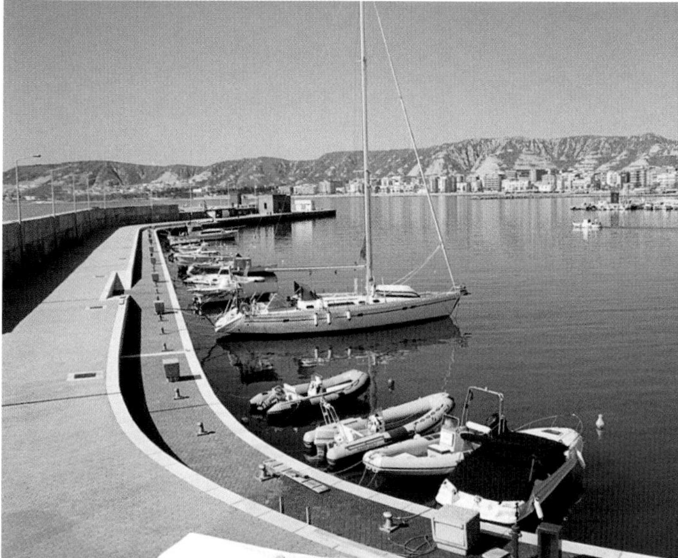

Crotone Porto Vecchio looking S to the entrance

PORTO NUOVO

The large commercial port to the N of Porto Vecchio. If there are strong southerlies Porto Vecchio can become untenable and it is advisable to go to Porto Nuovo in these conditions. Care is needed of rock ballasting under the water along the outer breakwater and yachts normally go alongside the quay in the inner basin wherever space is available. You are likely to be thoroughly checked by the port authorities here and may be asked to produce evidence of insurance, etc.

Porto Nuovo can be contacted on VHF Ch 16.

CIRO' MARINA

A harbour to the N of Crotone.

Approach

The harbour lies approximately 2M S of Punta Alice.

Conspicuous The lighthouse on Pta Alice is conspicuous from some distance. Closer in the harbour breakwaters will be seen.

Mooring

Data 150 berths. Max LOA 15m. Depths (outer and middle basin) 5–6·5m.

Note Depths in the immediate approaches and the outer basin reported 6·5m. Depths in the middle basin reported 5m.

Berth With no designated visitors' berths it can be a problem negotiating a berth here. The pontoons are usually full with local small craft, and the quays are used by fishing boats. Try alongside on the E breakwater in a spot that doesn't have nets and fishing gear on the quay. Otherwise negotiate a berth alongside a fishing boat. Both the Lega Navale and Guardia Costiera will try to help.

Shelter Good all-round shelter.

Authorities Harbourmaster. Charge band 1/2.

Lega Navale ✆ 0962 31766 / 379 007
Ciro' harbour Authority ✆ 0962 611 610
Giovanni Tradico ✆ 0962 31289

Facilities

Services Water and electricity points to be installed.
Fuel Locals will offer to deliver fuel by jerrycan. A fuel station is to be opened on the quay in the SE corner.
Repairs 25-ton travel-hoist.
Provisions Most provisions nearby. Fresh fish available.

General

The harbour was being built as part of the scheme to develop a string of Porto Turisticos around the Calabrian coast to encourage tourism in the area. Like other projects such as Roccella Ionica it is likely to be some time before it is a going concern. Reports describe the town ashore as 'very undistinguished' and while it is true that Ciro is a rather scruffy Calabrian working town, the newly paved quay by the harbour and cafés on the front are beginning to smarten things up, and the locals are friendly and helpful to visiting yachts.

Ciro' Marina looking SW from near the entrance

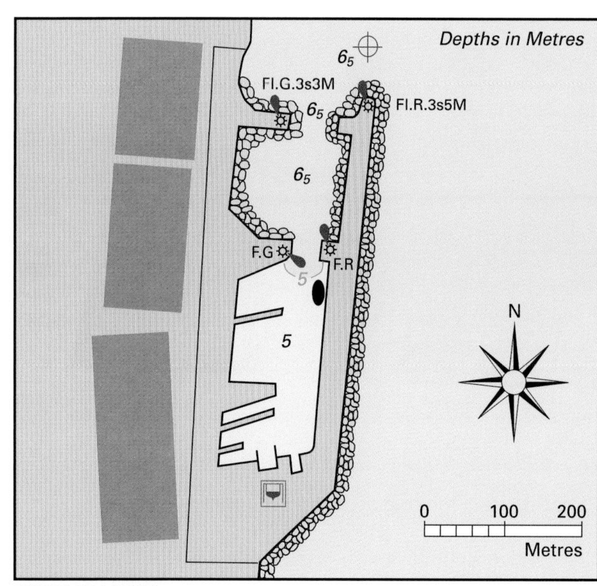

CIRO' MARINA
⊕39°22′·33N 17°08′·19E WGS84

CARIATI MARINA

Approach

This new harbour lies roughly halfway between Punta Alice and Capo Trionto. South of Cariati is Punta Fiume Nica, with a castle and tower on the hill.

Conspicuous From the S the lighthouse on Punta Alice is conspicuous. Closer in a cupola in the town and the harbour breakwaters will be seen.

By night The entrance is not lit and a night approach is not recommended.

Dangers The end of the groynes on the beach to the S of the harbour entrance lie just under the surface and are not easy to see. Keep closer to the breakwater on entry to stay clear.

Mooring

Go alongside or stern or bows-to where convenient or where directed. Further development is underway with pontoons being installed and facilities improved. Depths 2–3m. Reasonable shelter from the prevailing winds.

Facilities

Water On the quay

Fuel Delivery by mini-tanker.

Provisions Most provisions in the town.

Other PO. Gas. Taxi. Bus to Crotone. Train to Crotone/Sibari.

Cariati Marina looking SE to the entrance

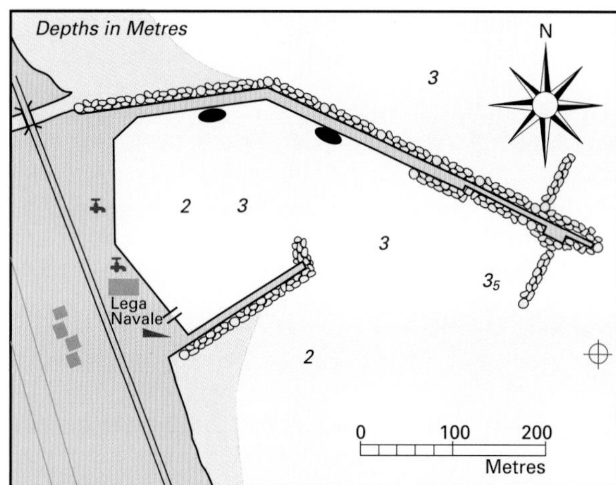

CARIATI MARINA
⊕39°30´·29N 16°56´·79E WGS84

CORIGLIANO CALABRO (Schiavonea)

Approach

Straightforward with no offlying dangers in the approaches.

Conspicuous The power station at Sant Angelo di Rossano is conspicuous (see *Laghi di Sibari Marina* below). The buildings of Schiavonea, particularly a red rectangular tower, are conspicuous. The breakwaters will be seen closer in.

Dangers The entrance is prone to silting but at present is dredged to 12m.

Mooring

Berth Go alongside where convenient in one of the inner basins. The walls are very high and it can be difficult getting on and off.

Shelter Excellent all-round shelter.

Authorities Harbourmaster.

Facilities

Can be found in the town of Schiavonea about 4km away.

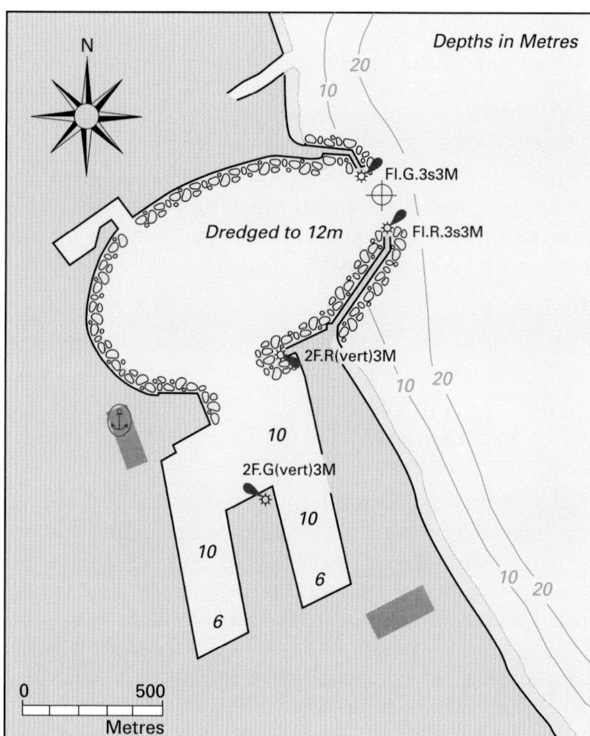

CORIGLIANO CALABRO
⊕39°40´·05N 16°31´·1E

General

The industrial harbour is not the sort of place you would make for, but it could be a useful stop en route. This part of the coast is also a fascinating and little visited area with some wonderful hilltop villages inland. Down in the harbour the high walls restrict air movement in the basin and can make it oppressively hot inside. The surrounding apartments house an assorted collection of urchins – some helpful and some not. The harbour also attracts an impressive collection of mosquitoes in the summer.

MARINA LAGHI DI SIBARI

Approach

The direct approach to the channel has silted and you should head for the entrance buoys to the N of the entrance proper at 39°45´·1N 16°29´·8E. The entrance channel then heads towards the beach until a dog-leg turn to run parallel to the beach (see entrance plan which makes this clearer). The following points should be noted:

1. A dredger works here on a more or less continuous basis, and so the entrance channel may move. It is hoped to re-establish a direct approach channel.
2. A couple of days of strong onshore winds can reduce depths by as much as 1m.
3. The marina will provide a free pilotage service and send someone out in a RIB to guide you in if you call on VHF Ch 09.

Conspicuous The most conspicuous landmark in Golfo di Corigliano is the electricity generating station at Sant Angelo di Rossano. Two chimneys, each 206m high, are visible for a considerable

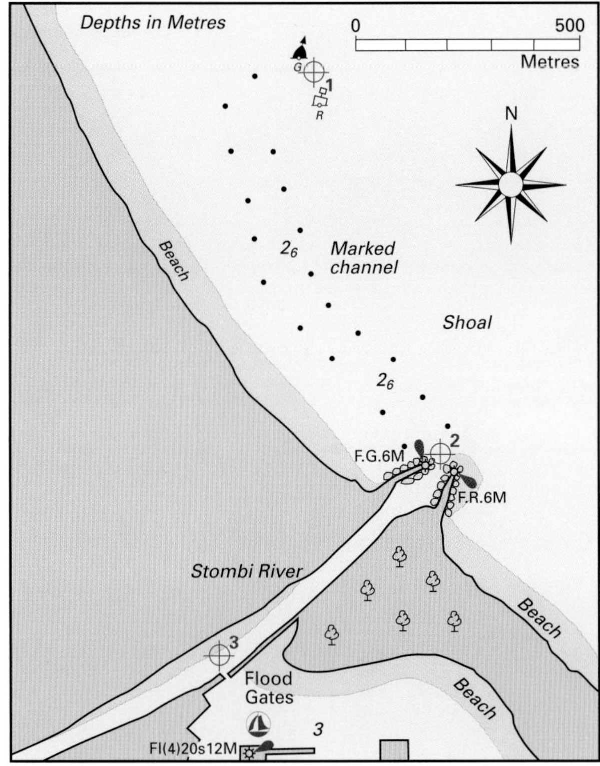

APPROACH CHANNEL TO MARINA LAGHI DI SIBARI
⊕1 39°45´·1N 16°29´·8E
⊕2 39°43´·7N 16°30´·5E
⊕3 39°43´·9N 16°30´·3E

distance. The low-lying coast around the mouth of the Crati river is conspicuous for its lack of buildings. The entrance to the marina lies one mile N of the mouth of the Crati river (but see above). Closer in, the red-roofed two-storey apartments of the marina complex can be distinguished. The two rock breakwaters protecting the entrance to the marina (actually the mouth of the Stombi river) are easily distinguished against the long sandy beach running around the coast. Once into the short Stombi canal, a pair of flood barrier gates will be seen to the left and arrows direct a yacht through the westernmost gate.

By night Use the light at the marina Fl(4)20s23m12M. There are leading lights on 139° front Iso.2s4m4M rear Iso.2s4M. (As the channel is moved these are of little use.)

VHF Ch 09, 16 (24/24 summer; 0730–1700 winter). Ch 09 for pilot (no charge made).

Dangers With strong onshore winds it would be dangerous to enter the river because of the shoals at the entrance. Even with moderate onshore winds I would imagine the entrance channel parallel to the shore could be difficult and possibly dangerous.

Depths The marina is kept dredged to a minimum depth of 3m though the entrance silts.

Note Alleged disputes over responsibility for the access channel resulted in complete silting of the channel in 2004, and several yachts had to leave on a low loader. Check ahead with the marina to get the latest advice.

Mooring

Data 500 berths. 20 visitors' berths. Depths 3m in the basin.

Marina Laghi di Sibari looking across to the Stombi
Casa Bianca Group srl.

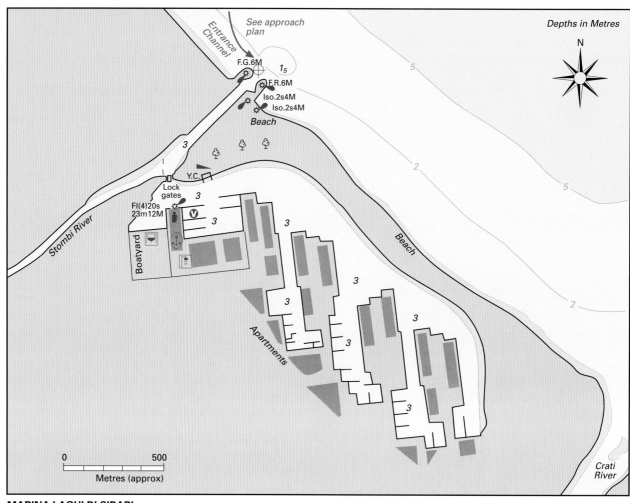

MARINA LAGHI DI SIBARI
⊕39°43′·7N 16°30′·5E

Marina Laghi di Sibari *Casa Bianca Group srl.*

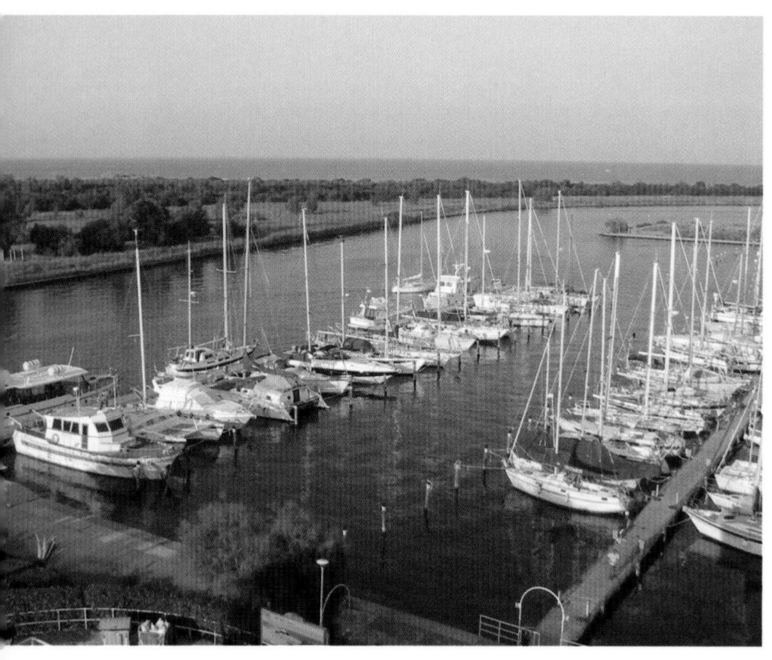

Berth Once into the marina the channel is marked by timber poles with black and white bands. Berth where directed in the first basin inside the flood gates. Go stern or bows-to the pontoons, with posts around which to take a line.

Shelter Excellent.

Authorities Harbourmaster and marina staff. Charge band 2/3.

✉ Cantiere Nautici di Sibari, 87070 Sibari di Cassano Ionio, Cosenza, Italy ✆ 0981 79027, 79051 *Fax* 0981 79147
Email info@marina-sibari.it
www.marina-sibari.it

Facilities

Services Water and electricity at every berth. A shower and toilet block. Laundry block.

Fuel Diesel and petrol at the fuel quay or they can be delivered to the yacht.

Repairs A 50-ton travel-hoist and hardstanding. Mechanical repairs. GRP and wood repairs. Chandlers. The yard here, Cantiere Nautici Laghi di Sibari, has received a lot of compliments over the years for efficiency and work carried out. See *Authorities* for details.

Provisions Most food supplies can be obtained from a minimarket in the marina. Better shopping in Sibari.

Eating out A restaurant and pizzeria in the marina complex.

Other ATM. Telephone, fax and telex facilities at the marina office. Free mini-bus service to Sibari. Hire car. Sailing and sub-aqua facilities. Tennis court and swimming pool. At Sibari, about 4km away, there is a PO and bank. Trains to Naples, Rome. Lamezia international airport 90km.

General

Marina Laghi di Sibari was begun in 1979 and aims to be one of the largest marinas in Italy. The setting is attractive but the residential architecture uninspired compared with similar residential marinas elsewhere. In the summer temperatures in the Sibari region are very high, but as a place to leave the boat for the winter it has much to recommend it.

One hopes the marina will not suffer the same fate as its namesake. The exact site of ancient Sibari – the word which we have absorbed as 'sybaritic', describing what seems to me to have been a wonderful lifestyle in ancient Sibari – has never been positively identified, though it is thought to have been on the left bank of the River Crati. The site was destroyed by the Crotons who diverted the Crati to flood Sibari in 510BC. It remains an archaeological mystery to this day how a large city like Sibari could so completely disappear, though some 2,500 years of silt must amount to an awful lot to dig through. A few descendants of the survivors went on to found Thurii in 443BC near the present day village of Terranova di Sibari. Herodotus died at Thurii around 420BC.

The present-day villages like Terranova di Sibari and other hill villages nearby are fascinating places, still very much cut off from mainstream life and well worth a visit (get a hire car) if you are leaving your boat in Marina Laghi di Sibari.

MARINA DI POLICORO

A huge leisure complex, Marinagri, is under development around the Fiume Agri, 50km SW of Taranto. Part of this development is Marina di Policoro, a new marina and boatyard. Work on the complex began in 2004, and marina berths are now available.

Approach

The marina lies 25M SW of the entrance to Taranto harbour, just S of the Agri rivermouth. The breakwaters and the control tower will be seen closer in.

VHF Ch 16.

Note It is possible that the entrance will silt if not regularly dredged. If in any doubt call ahead before attempting to enter.

Dangers With strong onshore winds entry could be dangerous.

Mooring

Data (when complete) 450 berths. Max LOA 30m. Dredged to 3·5m.

Berth Stern-to where directed. Bow lines are taken to posts.

Shelter Good all-round shelter inside the basin.

Authorities Marina staff. Charge band 3/4.
Marinagri ✆ 0835 910 439
Email info@marinagri.it

Facilities

Services Water and electricity at all berths. Showers and toilets. Pump-out. Laundry. Wi-Fi.

Fuel On the quay.

Repairs 80-ton travel-lift. Some repairs can be arranged.

Other Bar, restaurant, Yacht Club. ATM. The small town of Policoro is about 5km inland.

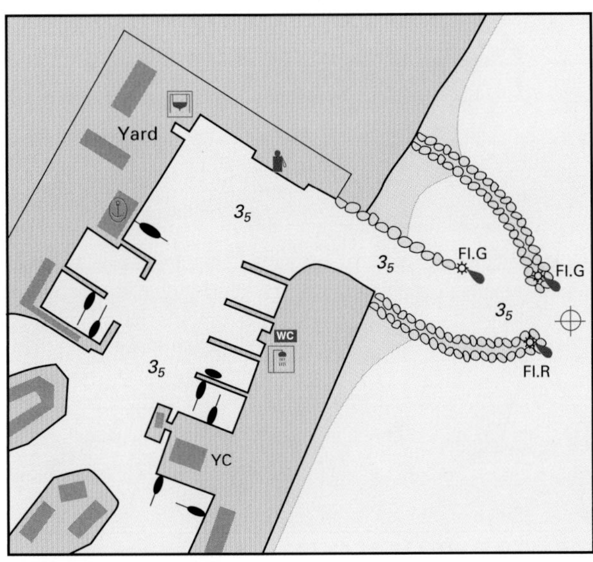

MARINA DI POLICORO
⊕40°12′·3N 16°44′·5E

PORTO DEGLI ARGONAUTI (Marina di Pisticci)

Approach

This new marina lies 17M WSW of the entrance to Taranto harbour.

Care is needed as it is likely the entrance will silt unless dredged regularly. If in any doubt call ahead for advice on depths before entering.

VHF Ch 16.

Dangers With strong onshore winds the entry could be dangerous.

Mooring

Data 450 berths. Max LOA 30m. Depths dredged to 4m.

Berth Stern or bows-to on concrete piers with laid moorings tailed to the pier.

Shelter Good all-round shelter inside the basin.

Authorities Marina staff. Charge band 3/4.
Porto Degli Argonauti ✆ 0835 470 218
Email info@portodegliargonauti.it

Facilities

Services Water and electricity (220/380V). Showers and toilets. Pump-out.

Fuel On the quay.

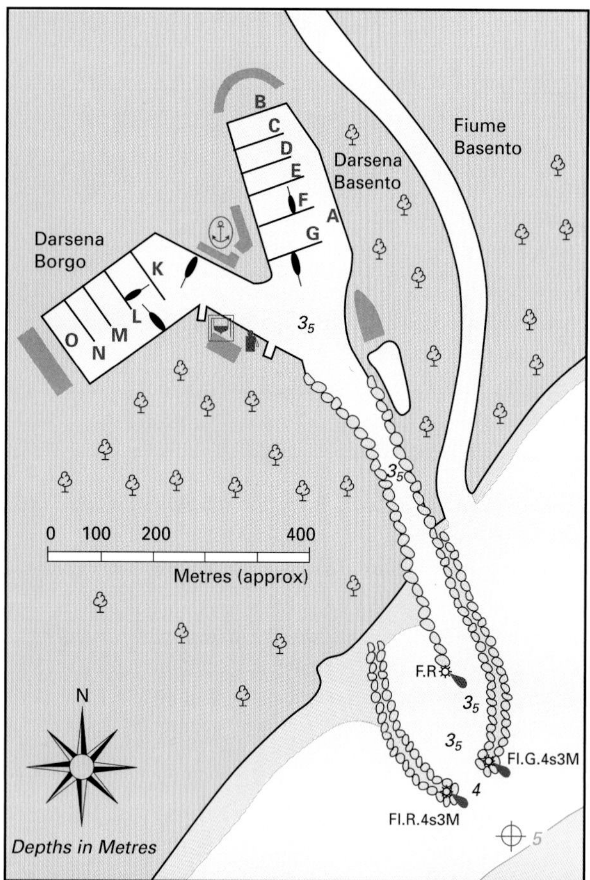

PORTO DEGLI ARGONAUTI
⊕40°20′·0N 16°49′·2E

Repairs Travel-lift. Repairs can be arranged.

Other The associated retail and villa complex will add shops, bars and restaurants within the marina.

TARANTO
(Marina Taranto/Taranto Yacht)

BA 1643
Italian 148

Approach

Straightforward by day and night. A yacht should make for the commercial harbour at the N end of Mar Grande.

Conspicuous From the S the lighthouse on Capo San Vito and San Vito Tower (Torre) are conspicuous. The lighthouse is a white octagonal tower 43m (141ft) high built on top of a white building. San Vito Tower is a large square tower easily distinguished on the low cape. Entering Mar Grande, San Paolo islet and the breakwater running S from it are easily identified. Inside Mar Grande the buildings of Taranto are conspicuous. Steer for the N end of the buildings where the commercial harbour is situated.

VHF Ch 12, 16 for port authorities. Ch 12 for pilots. Ch 11 for Marina Taranto. Ch 12 for Taranto Yacht.

Dangers By day there are no obvious dangers but at night a yacht should be on the lookout for unlit mooring buoys.

Prohibited areas Taranto is an important naval base and there are several prohibited areas shown on the chart. It is also prohibited to take photographs of the naval installations.

Mooring

Data (Marina di Taranto) 250 berths. Max. LOA 30m. Depths 5–12m. (Taranto Yacht pontoon) 200 berths. Max LOA 35m. Depths 2–5m.

Berth Proceed into the Porto Mercantile and head for either Marina Taranto pontoons on the E quay or the Taranto Yacht pontoon on the N side near the entrance to Mar Piccolo. Laid moorings tailed to the pontoons. It appears that the two marinas are merging. Changes in layout may occur. Alternatively it may be possible to secure a berth in the Lega Navale on the E side of Mar Grand, although the basin surrounded by rough stone breakwaters is very small and cramped.

Shelter Good in the Porto Mercantile although strong southerlies can make it bumpy.

Authorities Harbourmaster and customs. Marina staff. Charge band 4 (July–August).

✉ Marina di Taranto, Porto Turistico Molo Sant'Eligio, Corso Vittorio Emanuele, Molo Sant'Eligio, Città Vecchia, 74100 Taranto ☎ 0994 712 115 *Fax* 0994 600 413
Email info@molosanteligio.com
www.molosanteligio.com

Taranto Yacht ☎ 0994 712 115 *Fax* 0994 600 413
Email info@tarantoyacht.it
www.tarantoyacht.it

Lega Navale ☎ 0994 593 801 *Fax* 0994 533 660

Taranto Port Authority ☎ 0994 711 611 *Fax* 0994 706 877
Email authority@port.taranto.it
www.port.taranto.it

Facilities

Services Water and electricity. Showers and toilets.
Fuel Near the quay but large amounts can be delivered.

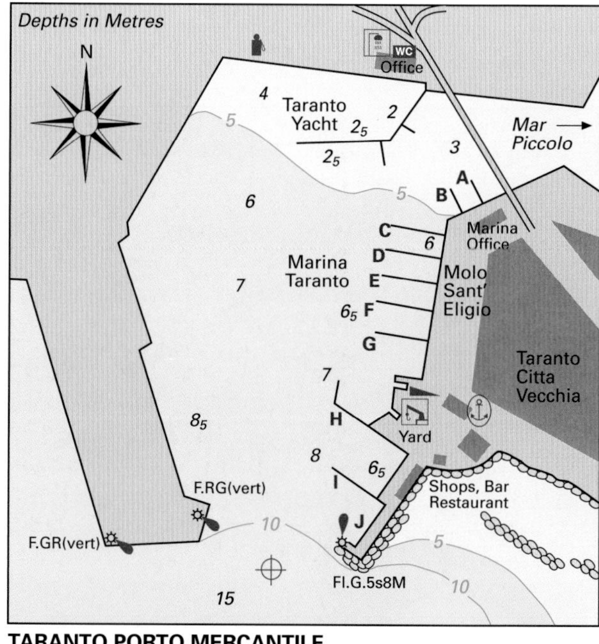

TARANTO PORTO MERCANTILE
⊕40°28′·5N 17°13′·3E

Repairs Both marinas have yards with slipways and mobile cranes to 50 tons. Marina Taranto are to add a travel-lift. Mechanical and engineering repairs. GRP and wood repairs. Rigging and sailmaking. Electrical and electronic repairs. Chandlers.
Provisions Excellent shopping for all food supplies.
Eating out Good restaurants of all types in the town
Other PO. Banks. ATMs. Hospital. Italgaz and Camping Gaz. Good hardware shops. Buses serving the surrounding region and to Rome. Trains to Rome. Brindisi International Airport 50km.

General

The old town (Citta Vecchia) on the island is dominated by the cathedral at the N end and the fort at the S end. Across the bridge to the N is the industrial quarter and across the swing-bridge to the S is the new city. Mar Piccolo is the lagoon extending NE of the town and is used as a naval harbour and for oyster and mussel farms.

Taranto was founded as the Spartan colony of Taras in 708BC and went on to be one of the most powerful cities in Magna Graecia. It gives its name to the Tarantula spider whose bite was reputed to cause a madness cured only by music, wine and dancing. Tarantism was epidemic in southern Europe from the 15th to 17th centuries and was probably an escape from the stranglehold the Catholic church put on pleasures of the flesh. It is remembered today in the national dance of the region, the *tarantella*.

CAMPOMARINO

Approach

A small marina lying approximately three miles E of Capo del Ovo.

Mooring

Data 250 berths. Max LOA 12m. Depths <1–2·5m.

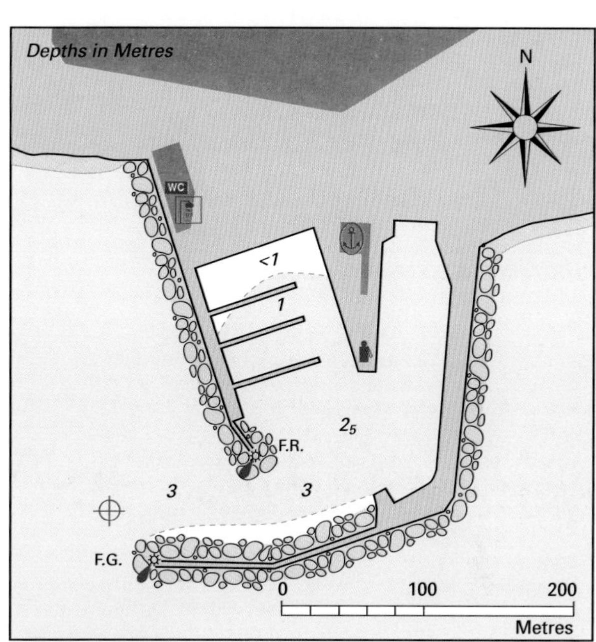

CAMPOMARINO
⊕40°18´·0N 17°35´·1E

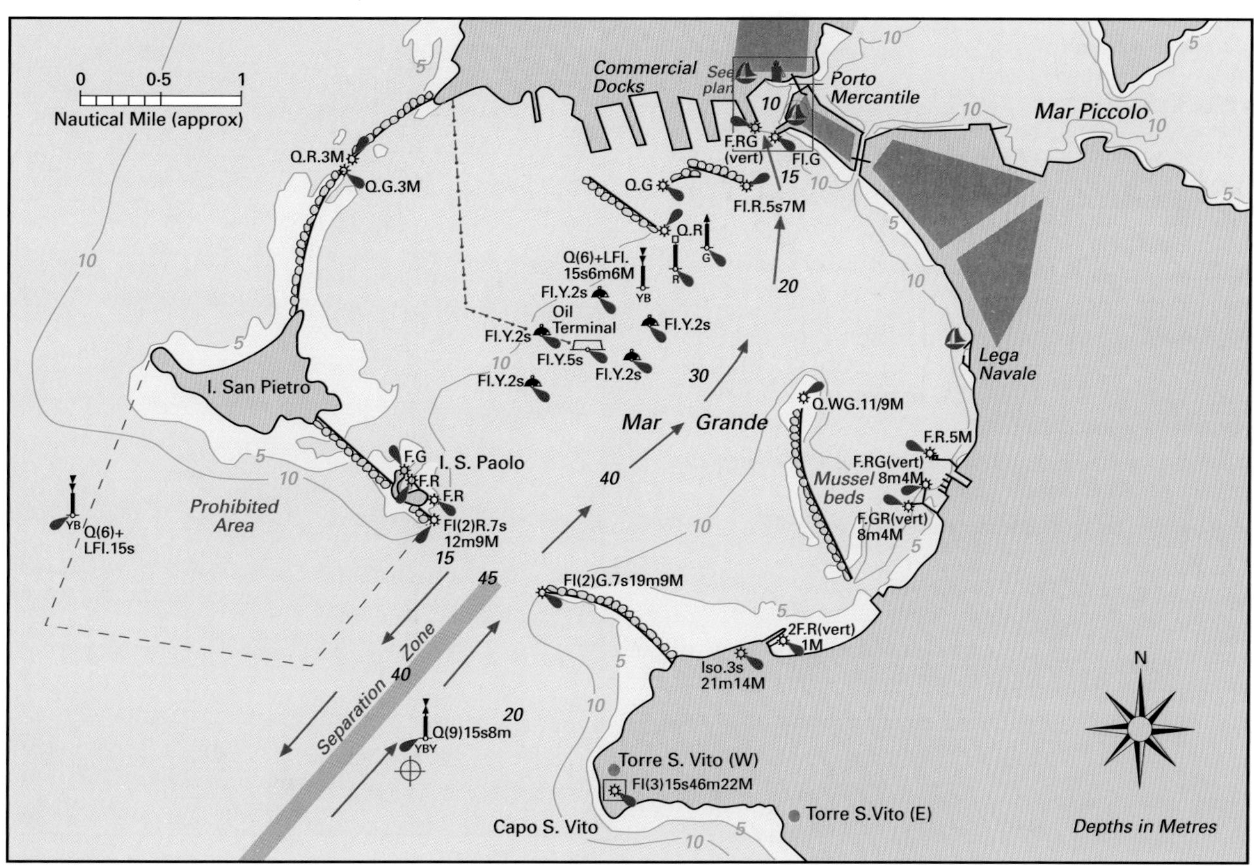

TARANTO
⊕40°25´·3N 17°10´·5E

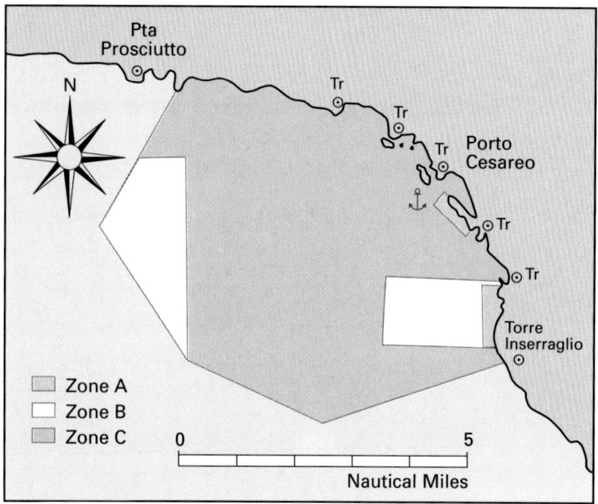

PORTO CESAREO MARINE RESERVE

Porto Cesareo Marine Reserve

A marine reserve has been established around Porto Cesareo. It extends for 7M around the coast on either side of Porto Cesareo. Most of the area is Zone B or Zone C.

There are two Zone A areas: the sea area off the southern coast of Penisola della Strega; and to the south of Porto Cesareo, off the coast between Torre S. Isidoro and Punta Casa Giorgella.

Zone A
Navigation, access, anchoring and mooring, sport and commercial fishing are prohibited. Within 1,000m of the limits of the marine reserve navigation must be below 10 knots.

Zone B
Anchoring and underwater fishing prohibited. Navigation up to 10 knots permitted for authorised vessels. Swimming, subaqua activities, and fishing with rod or line are permitted.

Zone C
Unregulated anchoring and mooring and underwater fishing are all prohibited. Access, transit, swimming, subaqua activities, and mooring on authorised stuctures are permitted.

Berth Where directed. Things are very tight for manoeuvring inside and care is needed. Depths are also variable so any craft drawing over 1–1·5m should exercise care.

Shelter Good shelter although strong westerlies can make some berths uncomfortable.

Authorities Harbourmaster and marina staff.

Facilities

Services Water and electricity. WC and shower block.
Fuel On the central pier.
Provisions Minimarket.
Eating out Several bars and restaurants nearby.

PORTO CESAREO (Zone C)

Approach

Difficult by day and night. By day the leading marks are impossible to identify among the buildings on the shore. By night the rear leading light does not show up well among the lights on the shore. In calm weather the shallow water and underwater rocks fringing the entrance can be clearly seen.

Conspicuous Squillace tower to the S and Cesareo tower in the village are conspicuous.

By night A night approach is not recommended.

Dangers Underwater rocks fringe the coast and the entrance.

Mooring

Southern harbour
Anchor in 2–4m off the town. The bottom is sand and good holding. The quay is fringed with underwater rocks and is unsuitable for even small yachts. The S part of the bay is shallow and is in any case mostly occupied by fish farms. Good shelter from all but strong SW winds.

Northern harbour
Is entered between the two low islets with the light structures on them. Reefs fringe either side of the entrance. Anchor where possible or go on the quay

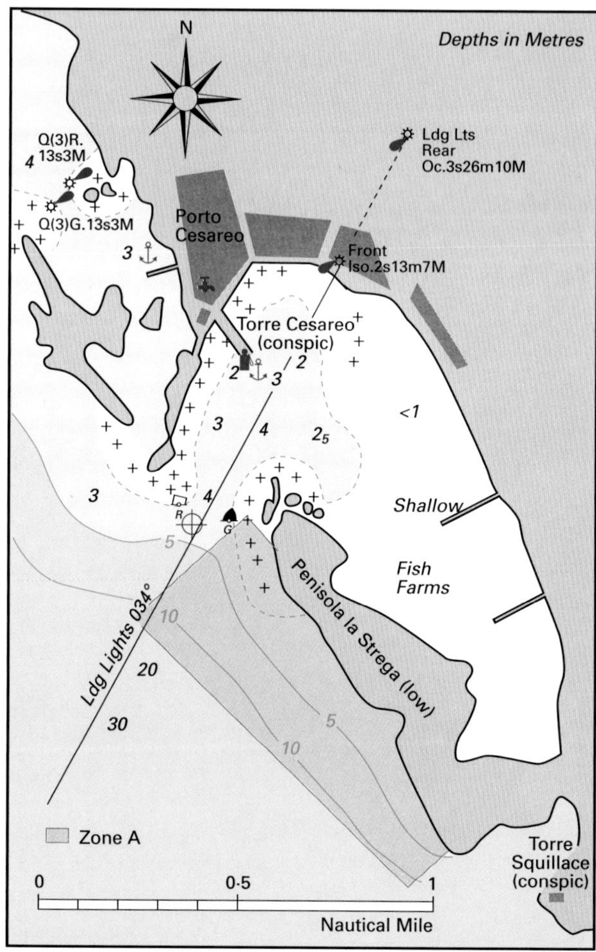

PORTO CESAREO
⊕40°15′·0N 17°53′·5E

if there are sufficient depths. Most spaces are occupied by fishing boats. Shelter appears to be good here.

Facilities

Water From a tap on the quay.
Fuel In the village near the quay.
Repairs Only minor mechanical repairs can be carried out.
Provisions Most supplies can be obtained. Fish can be bought from the fish shop on the quay where ice can also be obtained.
Eating out A number of restaurants in the village.
Other PO. Bank. Italgaz and Camping Gaz.

General

Porto Cesareo is an attractive small tourist resort built around the sandy shore of the bay. The bay is used mostly by sword-fishing boats and is little frequented by yachts.

GALLIPOLI

BA 140
Italian 149

Approach

Straightforward by day and night, although care must be taken of the numerous rocks and islets surrounding the peninsula on which the town is built. A yacht should make for the new marina in the large commercial harbour on the N side of the town. Seno del Canetto on the S side has little room for visiting yachts.

Conspicuous The lighthouse on I. Sant' Andrea is conspicuous from some distance off. The island is very low and the lighthouse, a white octagonal tower 43m (141ft) high, appears to rise from the sea. The old town of Gallipoli on the promontory and a large office building immediately E of the old town are conspicuous.

VHF Ch 11, 16 for port authorities (0700–1900). Ch 16 for pilots.

Dangers The limits of I. Sant' Andrea, being so low-lying, are difficult to distinguish by day or night. I. del Campo and Scoglio del Piccioni, lying close off the promontory of Gallipoli, are easily identified. Rafo Reef (Secca del Rafo) lying approximately 0·2 miles N of Gallipoli promontory has a least depth over it of 2·3m. It is lit Q.5M.

Mooring

Bleu Salento

Yachts are now directed to the new marina pontoons in Porto Mercantile. Marina Bleu Salento is a *Porto Turistico* which has been developed on the S side of the harbour.

VHF Ch 09.

Data 160 berths. Max LOA 60m. Depths 3–8m.

Berth Go stern or bows-to where directed. Laid moorings tailed to the pontoons.

Shelter Good shelter, although strong northerlies and particularly NE winds cause an uncomfortable surge in the harbour.

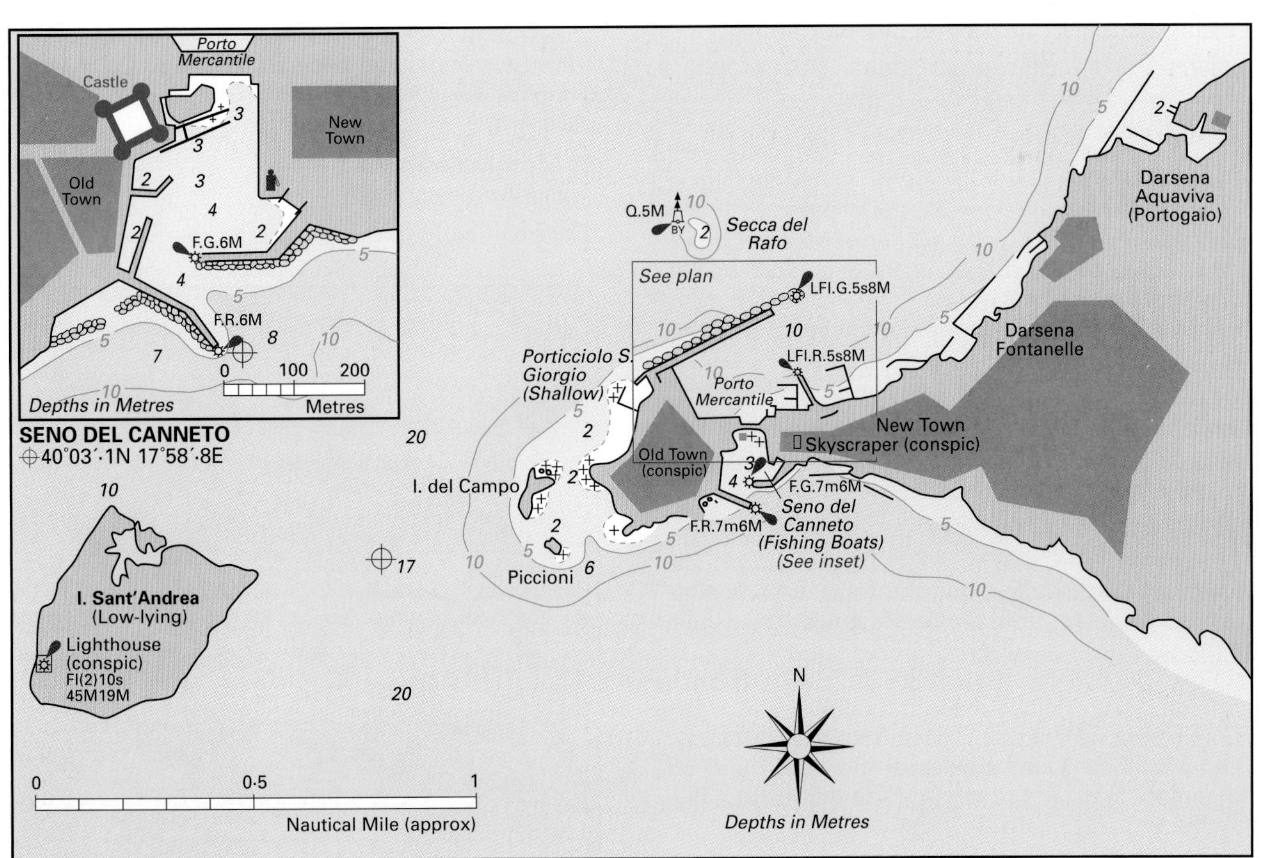

GALLIPOLI APPROACHES
⊕40°03′·0N 17°57′·5E

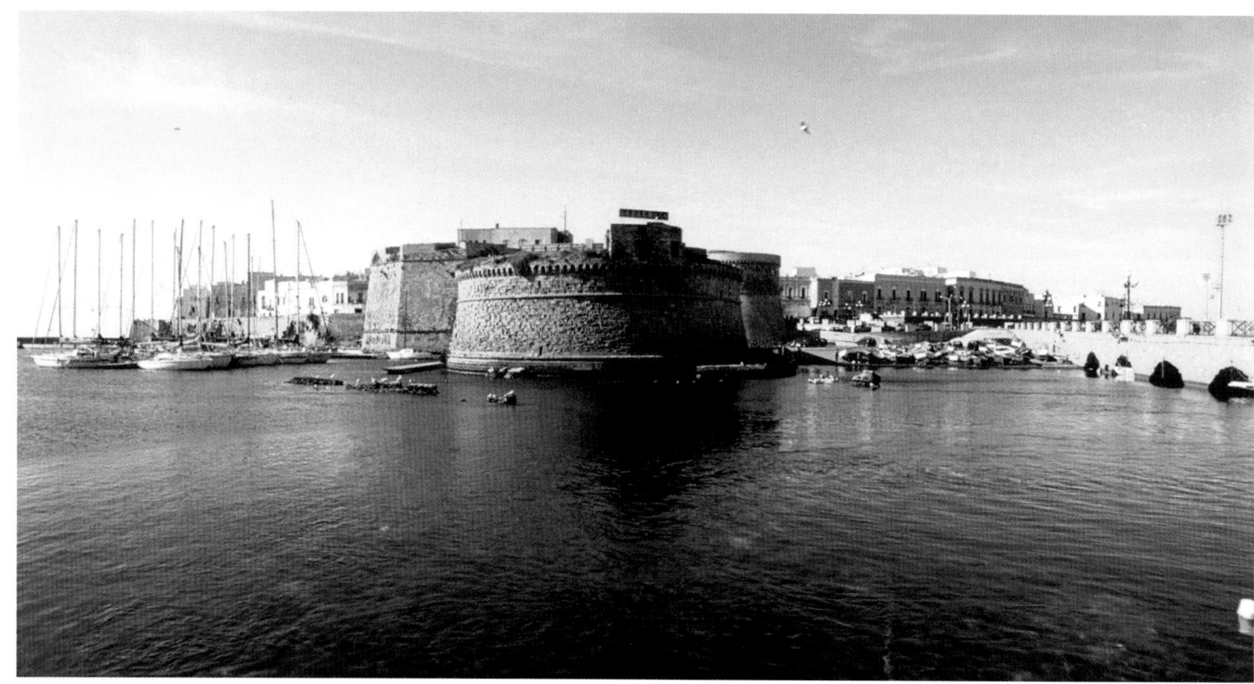

Seno del Canneto, Gallipoli, looking NW to the castle *Vito Arcomano, FOTOTECA ENIT*

Authorities Harbourmaster. Customs. Carabinieri. Marina staff. Charge band 3.
Marina Bleu Salento ✆ 335 601 9017
Email info@bleusalento.com
www.bleusalento.com

Seno del Canneto

Data Max LOA 20m. Depths 1·5–3m.
Yachts are usually directed to Bleu Salente.

Shelter Good shelter in northerlies. Uncomfortable with southerlies.

Facilities

Bleu Salento

Services Water and electricity (220/380V).
Fuel Pumps on the quay in Porto Mercantile are reported to be for fishing boats only. Fuel on the quay in Darsena Fontanelle.
Repairs Travel-lift. Some repairs can be arranged.

Seno del Canneto

Water By arrangement.
Fuel On the E quay for fishing boats only.
Repairs Mechanical and engineering repairs. Also see entry for Fontanelle.

Gallipoli

Provisions Good shopping for all provisions. The fish market is excellent and the fruit and vegetable market good. Ice from the building near the fishing harbour.
Eating out Good restaurants in the old town including several good fish restaurants.
Other PO. Banks. ATMs. Hospital. Italgaz. Camping Gaz. Good hardware shops and a small chandlery in the old town. Buses to the surrounding towns. Internal flights.

General

The old town huddled on the island is a warren of narrow streets and stairways dividing the tightly packed merchant houses which are mostly now apartments. The castle, originally Byzantine but later modified, occupies a key position and was used as late as 1809 when it drove off a British naval squadron. Across the bridge the new town is in bleak contrast – reinforced concrete and non-architecture comparing badly with the crumbling elegance of the old town.

St Giorgio Basin

⊕ 40°03′·4N 17°58′·45E

The small basin backing onto the commercial basin.

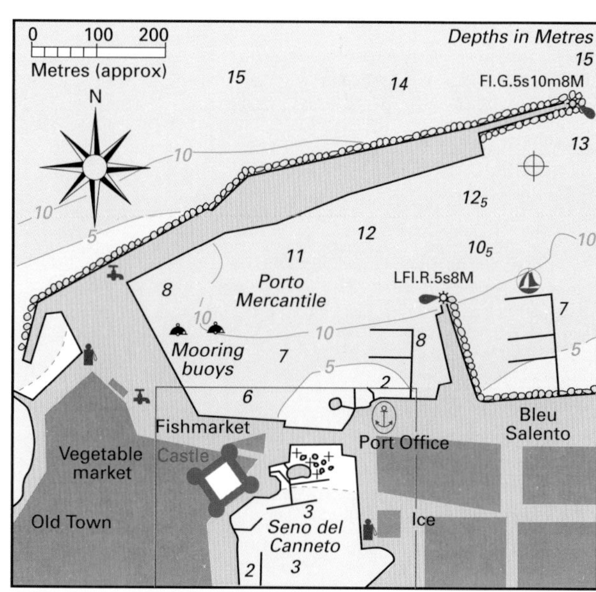

GALLIPOLI - PORTO MERCANTILE
⊕40°03′·6N 17°59′·0E

DARSENA FONTANELLE

Approach

A yacht basin lying immediately NE of Gallipoli commercial harbour.

Mooring

Data 120 berths. Visitors' berths. Max LOA 18m. Depths 1–4m.

Berth Stern or bows-to where directed. Laid moorings.

Shelter Good shelter.

Authorities Yard staff. Charge band 2/3.

✆ 0833 263 535
Email info@darsenafontanelle.it

Facilities

Services Water and electricity. Showers and toilets.
Fuel On the quay.
Repairs Travel-hoist. Crane and slipway. Most yacht repairs can be made.
Eating out Restaurant and bar.

General

The yard staff are reported to be friendly and helpful. It is about ½km into Gallipoli town.

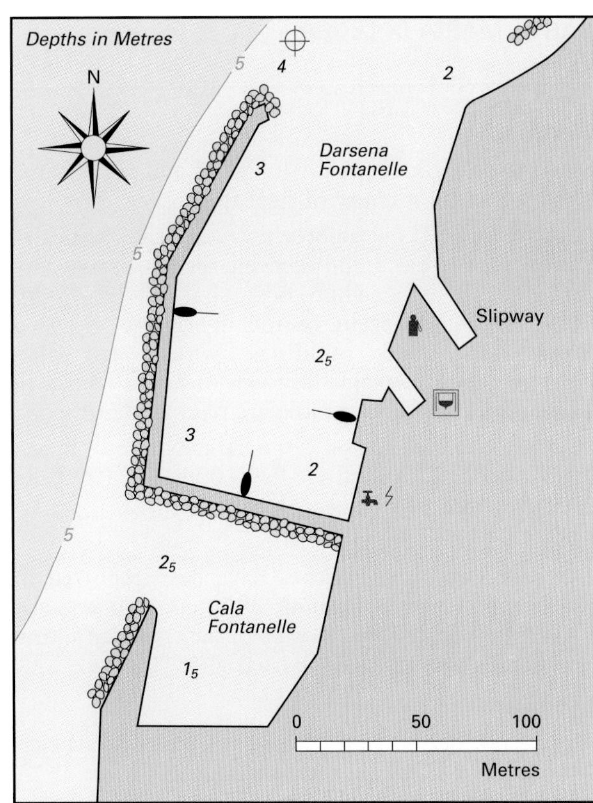

FONTANELLE
⊕40°03′·5N 17°59′·4E

PORTO GAIO

Small marina and boatyard in Darsena Acquaviva, ½M NE of Darsena Fontanelle.

VHF Ch 16, 11.

Mooring

Data c.100 berths. Max LOA c.15m. Depths 1–5m.

Berth Stern or bows-to where directed. The entrance to the inner basin is narrow, with max. depths around 2m. Larger yachts use the pontoon outside the basin. Laid moorings.

Shelter Excellent shelter in the basin. The pontoon offers good shelter from southerlies, but it would be uncomfortable with northerlies, and possibly untenable with strong N–NE winds.

Authorities Marina and boatyard staff.

Porto Gaio, Darsena Acquaviva
✆ 0833 202 204 *Fax* 0833 273 155
Email info@portogaio.it
www.portogaio.it

Facilities

Services Water and electricity. Shower and toilets.
Fuel On the quay in the basin.
Repairs 65-ton travel-lift. Hauling and storage ashore. Mechanical and electrical repairs.
Other It is a 1.5km walk into the centre of Gallipoli.

Secche di Ugento

⊕ Secche di Ugento light 39°49′·7N 18°08′·3E

Between Gallipoli and Sta Maria di Leuca, this reef extends some two miles offshore and a yacht should keep well offshore by day and night. A YBY W cardinal beacon Q(9)15s5M marks the westernmost point of the reef, but it is difficult to see against the land behind and a yacht should not rely on sighting it. The depths N and S of the reef give a useful indication of a yacht's position. By night, the red sector of the light on Torre San Giovanni Iso.WR.4s15/11M 310°-R-013° and the occulting red light on Santa Maria di Leuca Oc.R.4s11M 094°-vis-106° cover the reef and shoal water off Ugento.

Torre San Giovanni d'Ugento

⊕ 39°53′·0N 18°06′·6E

A small harbour 12 miles S of Gallipoli. Details of the approach depths and depths inside the harbour are sparse. Torre San Giovanni light is exhibited at the base of the mole Iso.WR.4s15/11M. The entrance is lit F.R.7m3M (molehead) and Fl(2)G.7m5M (black ⁑ on black post, red band) (La Terra rocks).

Torre Vado

⊕ 39°48′·0N 18°19′·0E

A small harbour off the village of Torre Vado. The entrance is lit Fl(3)G.6s3M/Fl(3)R.6s3M. There are reported to be 1–2m depths in the small harbour.

SANTA MARIA DI LEUCA

BA 187, 188
Italian 28

Approach

Straightforward. Generally the wind and sea become confused in the vicinity of the cape.

Conspicuous The lighthouse on the cape is conspicuous from a considerable distance from any direction. It is a white octagonal tower 48·5m (159ft) high. Adjacent to the lighthouse are two large flat-topped buildings which are also conspicuous. Closer in the town of Santa Maria di Leuca and the harbour mole are readily identified.

By night Use the light on Capo Santa Maria di Leuca Fl(3)15s102m25M and Oc.R.4s100m16M (094°-R-106° over Secche di Ugento).

VHF Ch 12 for Porto Turistico.

Dangers Two shoal patches have been reported in the entrance to the harbour although this has not been corroborated. The N side of the entrance silting and depths are less than charted.

Mooring

Data 700 berths. 250 berths in Porto Turistico Marina di Leuca. 32 visitors' berths. Max LOA 40m. Depths 2–6m.

Berth Where directed. Yachts in transit should head for pontoons on the W quay and off the NE corner which are administered by Porto Turistico Marina di Leuca. Lega Navale has three pontoons in the NW corner. There are laid moorings tailed to the quay. There may be room to go alongside on the S quay but you will have to move if a trawler returns. (One night free.)

Shelter Despite the new inner mole, shelter is on the whole poor here. Any swell around penetrates into the harbour and affects most berths in the harbour except those directly off the inner mole. Shelter is better at the new pontoons further inside the harbour, although there will still be some surge.

Anchorage In calm weather anchor off the village, clear of the harbour entrance in 2–4m. The water is murky here but the holding is adequate. As with outer berths in the harbour, even in calm weather a swell will work around to here.

Authorities Harbourmaster. Marina staff. Charge band 3.

Marina di Leuca ✆ 0833 758 687
Email info@portodileuca.it
Colaci Mare ✆ 0833 758 288

Facilities

Services Water and electricity at every berth. WC and shower block.
Fuel Fuel quay.
Repairs 20-ton crane. Limited mechanical and engineering repairs. Small chandlers.
Provisions A minimarket near the harbour and other provisions in the village.
Eating out Good restaurants near the harbour and others in the village. Lupo de Mare is recommended as being friendly and reasonable.
Other ATM. PO. Pharmacy.

Santa Maria di Leuca looking SW *Claire James*

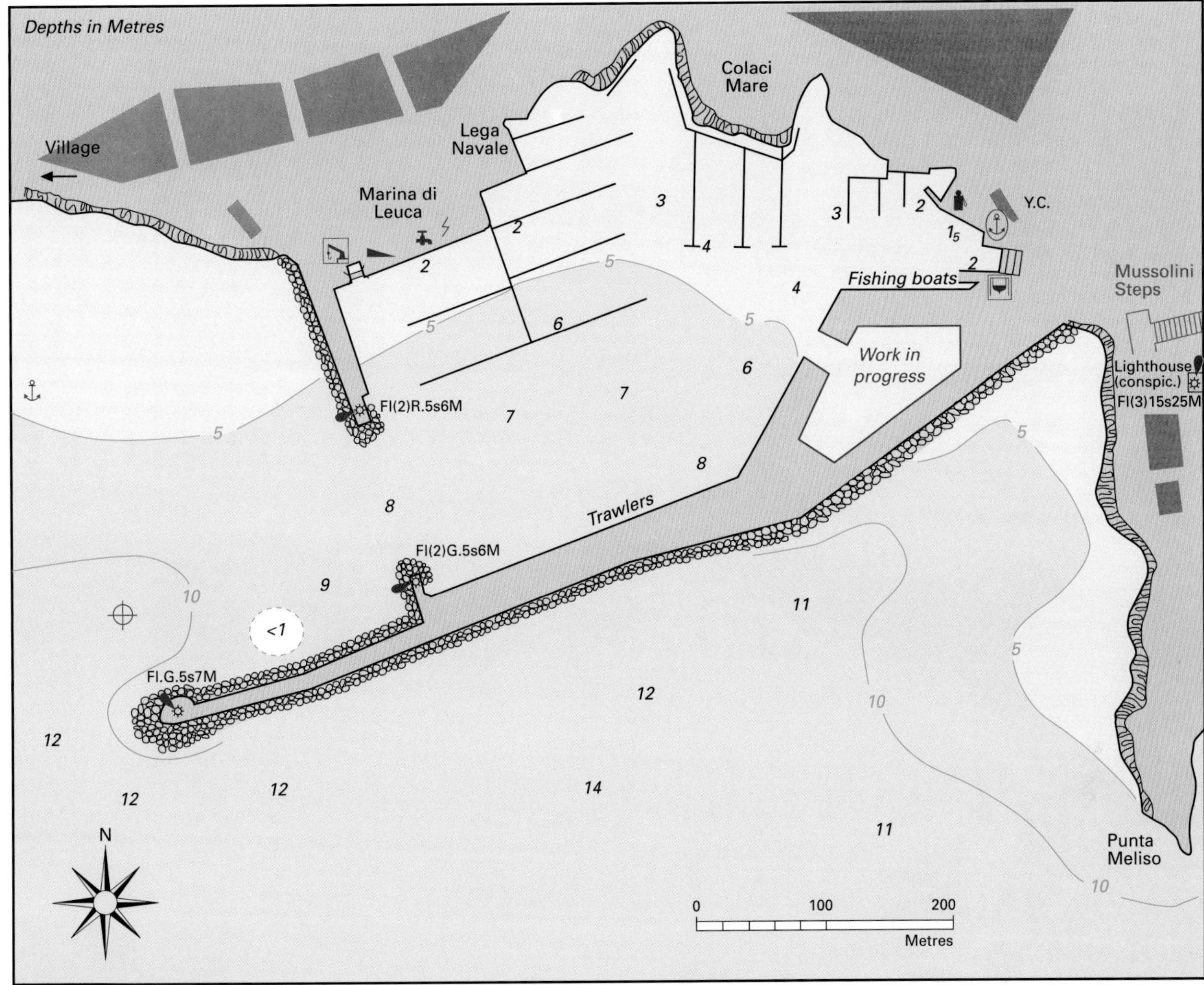

SANTA MARIA DI LEUCA
⊕39°47´·6N 18°21´·5E

General

Santa Maria di Leuca is a rapidly expanding local tourist resort with a number of villas scattered along the shores. Around the nearby coast are a number of impressive caves in the limestone cliffs which can be visited in calm weather. The name of the place comes from its white limestone cliffs, the Greek *leucos* meaning 'white'. The monumental stone staircase by the harbour was built by Mussolini as a ceremonial gateway into Italy.

Crossing to Greece

As a general rule the wind blowing in Santa Maria di Leuca is not a good guide to the wind blowing further out to sea in the Adriatic. In the summer there are often calms or light variable winds in the immediate vicinity whereas, a few miles to the E, there will be a N wind blowing between Force 3–5 and tending to the NW–W nearer to Greece.

There is a S-going current in the Adriatic which may reach one knot in the summer. The visibility around Capo Santa Maria di Leuca and around the Greek island of Corfu and outlying islands can be as little as 1½–2 miles in the summer when a haze obscures the land, so don't be surprised if you don't pick up the islands off Corfu until you are close to them. Do make sure you don't miss them and end up in Albania.

One thing to remember is to advance the time by one hour as Greece is UT+2. DST April–September.

VII.

The Southern Adriatic

Brindisi. Seno di Ponente looking ENE from the boatyard of Navale Balsamo past the yacht pontoons of Assonautica on the N shore
Cantiere Navale Balsamo

This chapter covers just six harbours between Santa Maria di Leuca and Brindisi which a yacht might find helpful en route to Greece or when crossing to Montenegro and Croatia. Only Otranto and Brindisi provide good all-round shelter. Tricase and Castro are very small and suitable for small yachts only. Moreover they are usually packed with local boats and it can be difficult for even a small yacht to find a berth. San Foca is being expanded and may have room for visiting yachts when completed. San Cataldo is fairly shallow and yachts drawing more than 1–1·3m should not attempt to enter.

For additional information on the E coast of Italy see *Adriatic Pilot* by T&D Thompson or the *Imray Mediterranean Almanac.*

Quick reference guide

	Shelter	*Mooring*	*Fuel*	*Water*	*Eating out*	*Provisions*	*Plan*	*Charge band*
Tricase	B	A	A	A	C	C	•	1/2
Castro	C	A	O	B	C	C	•	1/2
Otranto	B	A	A	A	A	B	•	1/3
San Foca	A	AB	O	A	C	C	•	
Brindisi	A	A	A	A	A	A	•	1/2
Brindisi Marina	A	A	A	A	C	C	•	4

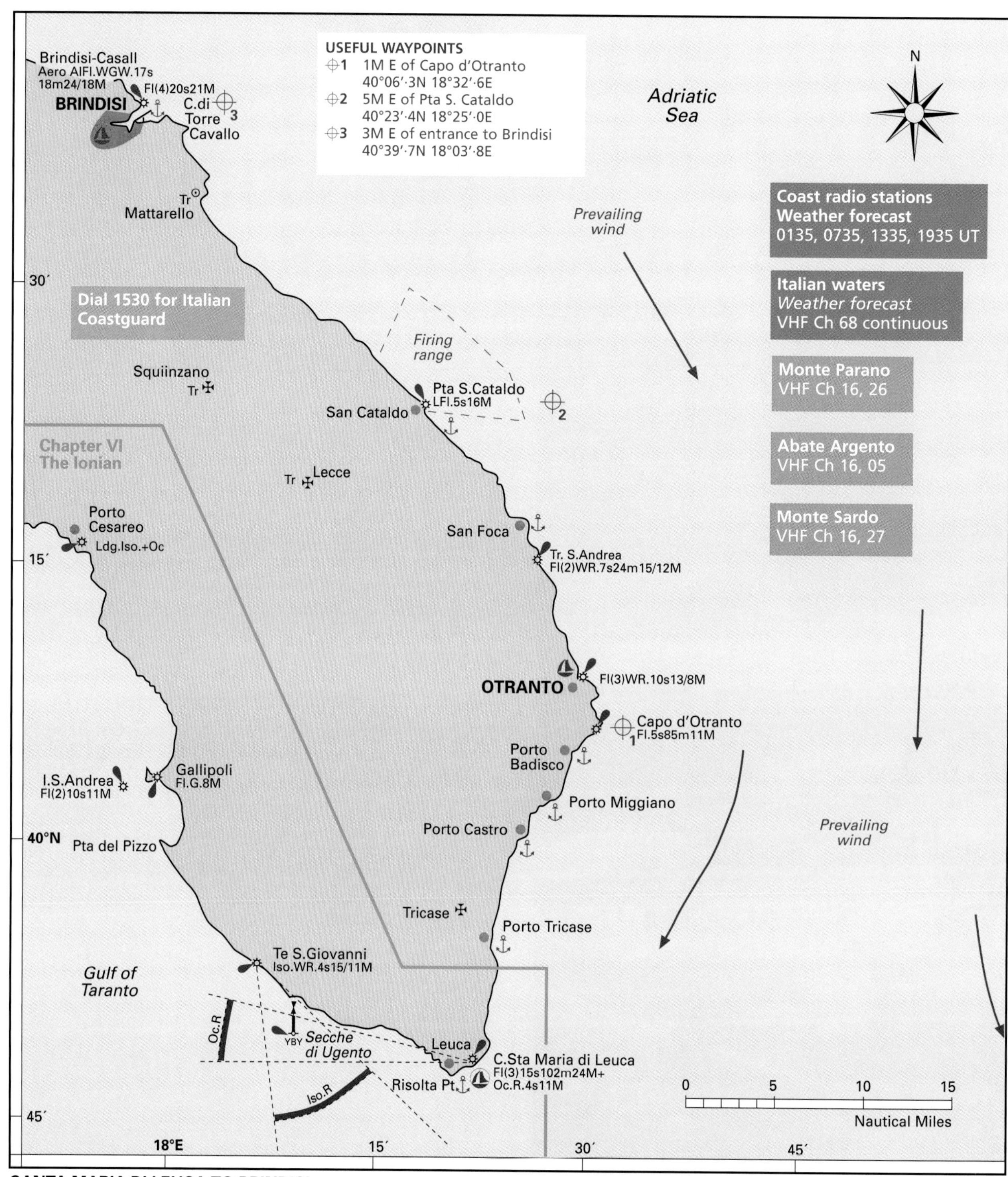

SANTA MARIA DI LEUCA TO BRINDISI

Data

MAJOR LIGHTS

Capo Santa Maria di Leuca Fl(3)15s102m24M+Oc.R.4s100m11M
Capo d'Otranto Fl.5s85m11M
Porto di Otranto (La Punta) Fl(3)WR.10s12m13/8M (R 165°-vis-183° over Secca di Missipezza)
Torre Sant'Andrea Fl(2)WR.7s24m15/12M (R vis. 300°-343° over Secca di Missipezza)
Punta San Cataldo di Lecce LFl.5s25m16M
Castello a Mare Fl(4)20s28m21M
Brindisi Aero AlFl.WGW.17s18m24/18M

Routes

The prevailing wind tends to blow down out of the Adriatic and funnels NW towards Greece and N–NNE around Capo Santa Maria di Leuca. If you are proceeding up the coast it is best to leave early in the morning and motor N during the morning calm. The N–NW breeze usually kicks in around 1000–1100 hours. At times a *scirocco* may blow from the S up the Adriatic and can get up to a Force 6–7.

PORTO TRICASE (Marina di Porto)

A small fishing harbour for the village of Tricase inland. I must emphasise it is very small and generally packed with fishing boats.

Approach

Conspicuous The small village and harbour cannot be easily identified until close in.

VHF Ch 16.

Dangers With strong southerlies it is dangerous to enter.

Mooring

Data 150 berths. Max LOA 11m. Depths <1–3m.

Berth It is difficult to find a place to berth as the harbour is very small and crammed full of local boats. Ask a local if there are any free berths.

Charge band 1/2.

Facilities

Services Water and electricity (220V) near most berths.
Fuel On the quay but it is too shallow for most yachts to go alongside at the fuel quay.
Provisions Some provisions in the village.
Eating out Several restaurants in the summer.

General

A small fishing village that is built on the slopes and attracts a small number of tourists. The harbour can take a few yachts only although it is hoped to expand it in the future.

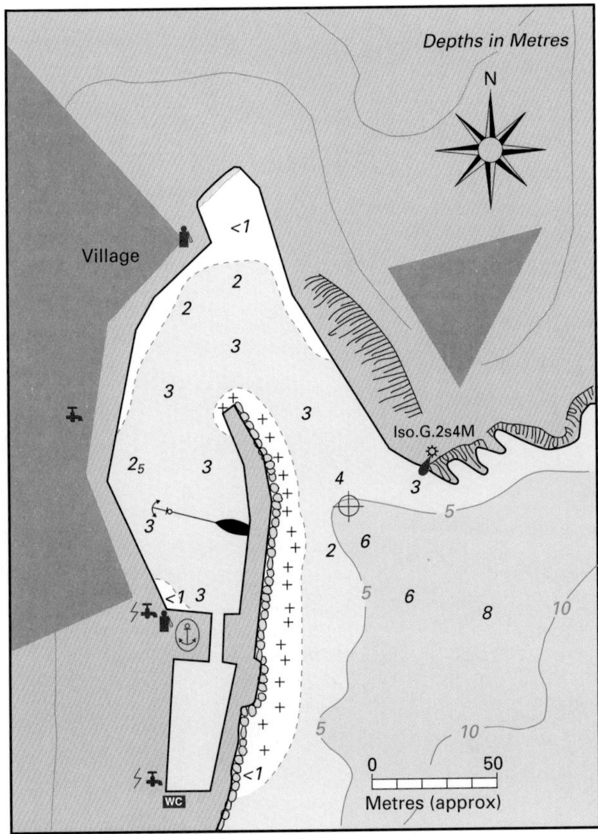

PORTO TRICASE
⊕39°55′·9N 18°23′·8E

Porto di Andrano

⊕ 39°58′·0N 18°24′·5E

A miniature basin, literally 15m wide at the entrance. Only a very small craft (less than 5m) could get in here. There are 2m depths reported inside.

PORTO DI CASTRO

A small port usually crowded with fishing boats.

Approach

The village of Castro and the castle on the hill above are conspicuous from some distance off. With strong winds from the S and E the harbour is dangerous to enter.

VHF Ch 16 (0800–2000).

Mooring

Data 100 berths. Max LOA 8m. Depths <1–4m.

Berth A small yacht may find a place on the mole. With winds from the N a yacht can anchor in the cove to the W of the small harbour. The bottom is sand and weed, good holding.

Charge band 1/2.

Facilities

Water On the quay.
Fuel In the village.
Provisions Limited provisions can be obtained.
Eating out A small *trattoria*.
Other PO. Buses to Gallipoli and Lecce.

General

The small village under the castle is a friendly and attractive place. The local fishermen are generally helpful to the occasional yacht that puts in here.

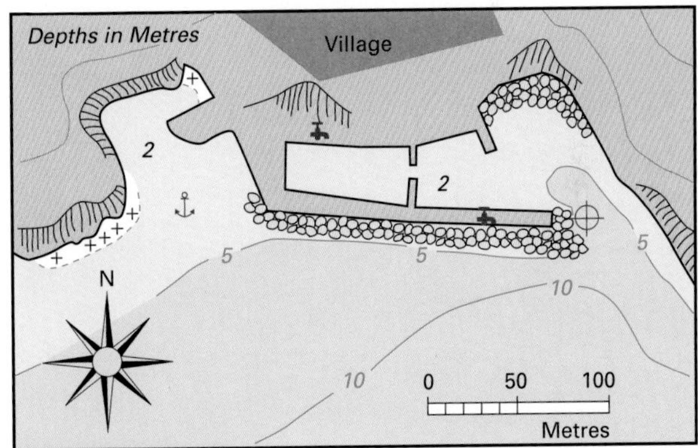

PORTO DI CASTRO
⊕40°00′·0N 18°25′·75E

Porto Miggiano

⊕ 40°01′·7N 18°26′·6E

A small fishing harbour tucked under the tower on the coast at Santa Cesarea Terme. It is mostly full of fishing boats and it is unlikely even very small craft (less than 5m) could get in here.

Porto Badisco

⊕ 40°04′·75N 18°29′·2E

A small fishing harbour lying a little over 3M NE of Miggiano. It is very small inside the basin although small yachts up to 10m may find a berth on the quay outside the basin.

OTRANTO

BA 187, 188
Italian 189

Approach

Conspicuous The town and the breakwater are conspicuous. To the S, Torre del'Orto is easily identified.

VHF Ch 16.

Dangers

1. Care must be taken of the two buoys marking the channel inside the entrance. The buoys may be lit but cannot be relied upon.
2. There are several unlit mooring buoys inside the harbour.

Mooring

Data 80 berths. Max LOA 12/20m. Depths <1–7m.

Berth There are three pontoons in the SE corner: two belonging to the local Lega Navale and the E one to Piccolo Marina. You may find a berth on the end of one of these pontoons (try Andrea at Piccolo first), although they are usually full of local boats. Otherwise berth stern or bows-to in the E corner near the fuel berth. There may also be room to go alongside on the N quay.

Shelter Good, although the harbour is somewhat open to the NE. However, the locals claim that the harbour is secure even with strong winds from that direction.

Authorities Harbourmaster and customs. Charge band 1/3.

Lega Navale ✆ 0836 801 509 *Fax* 0836 804 926

Anchorage It is possible to anchor in the NW corner of the bay in settled weather. Anchor in 2–6m in mud and weed – good holding.

Facilities

Services Water and electricity on the pontoons. Water tap on the quay.

Fuel On the quay, but care is needed of depths off the fuel quay.

Repairs A 7-ton slipway. Mobile crane to 16 tons. Mechanical repairs. Wood repairs. Chandlers.

Provisions Good shopping for most provisions. There is an excellent fish market on the quay where ice can be obtained.

Eating out A number of trattorias and pizzerias in the town.

Other PO. Banks. ATMs. Italgaz and Camping Gaz. Regular train to Lecce where there is excellent shopping. Ferries to Greece (01/06–01/10) and Albania.

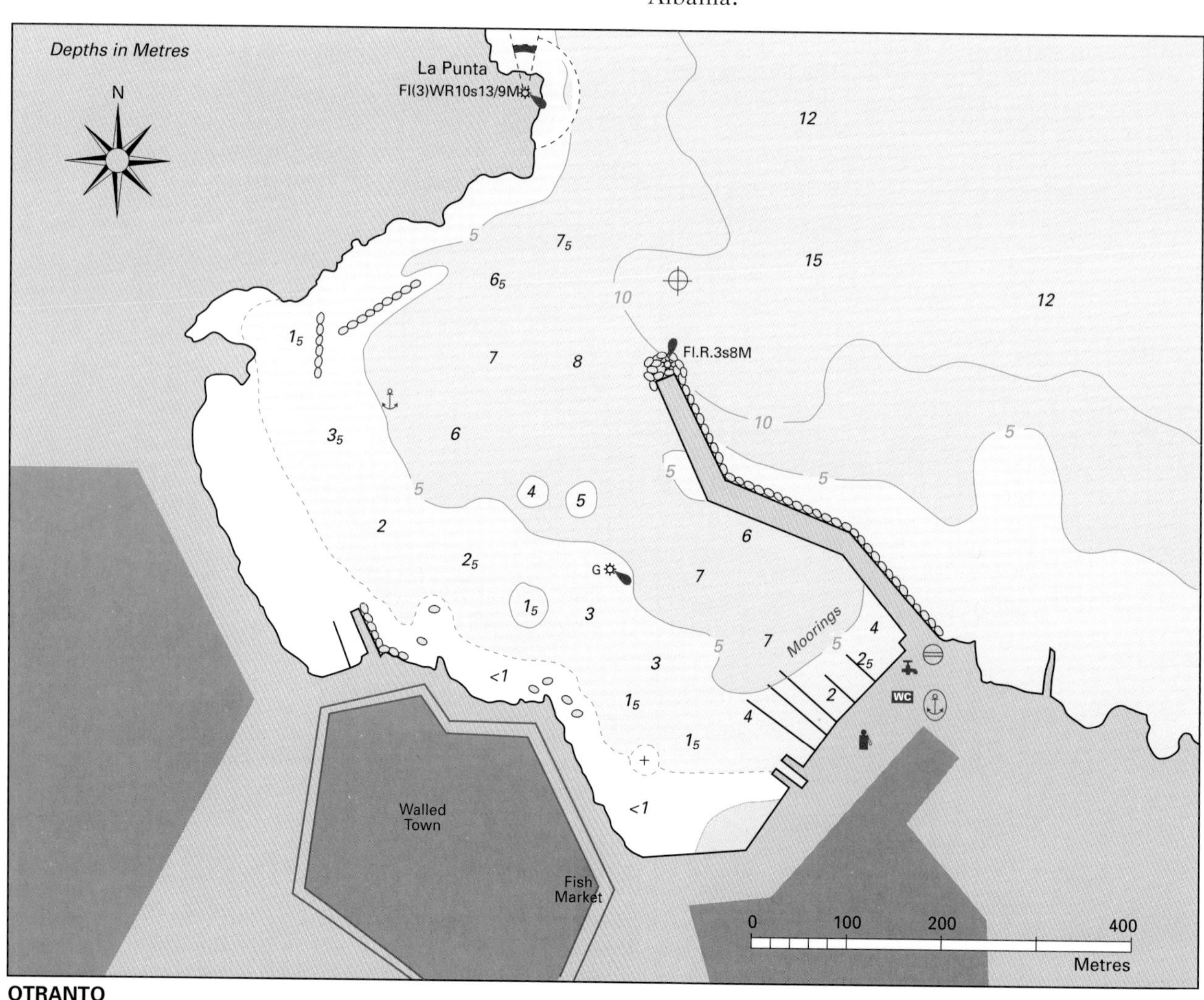

OTRANTO
⊕40°09′·1N 18°29′·6E

Otranto looking SW over the club pontoons

Otranto looking NW along the outer mole

General

At one time this was one of Rome's major east coast harbours and later an important port during the Crusades. It was ruthlessly attacked by the Turks who slaughtered its inhabitants in 1480 and from that the town never recovered. The old town under the Aragonese castle is mostly built of sandstone and is a friendly, attractive place.

Behind Otranto lies Lecce, the chief town of the Salento. Its elegant 17th and 18th-century buildings have earned it the title, the 'Florence of Baroque Art'. It also has some well preserved Roman architecture and is well worth a visit.

SAN FOCA (Melendugno)

Approach

A small harbour to the N of Torre Sant'Andrea. A new breakwater has been built, creating a new outer harbour. The work has not yet been completed and yachts should not depend on finding a berth here. Depths in the approaches and the harbour are variable and great care is needed.

By night Use the light on Torre Sant'Andrea Fl(2)WR.7s24m15/12M (300°-R-343° over Secca di Missipezza). The entrance is lit F.G.5m3M/ Fl.G.3s5M.

VHF Ch 16. CB Ch 10 (Lega Navale).

A reef extends for nearly 400m N from the N breakwater. Approach the entrance from the E–NE.

Mooring

Data 400 berths. Max LOA 12m. Depths <1–2·5m. Depths in the entrance 1·2–5m (reported).

Berth Great care is needed in the harbour where depths are variable. There are only 1·2–1·5m depths in the entrance channel into the basin. A visiting yacht is advised to seek local knowledge.

Shelter Good shelter.

Authorities Harbourmaster. YC staff.
Harbourmaster ✆ 0832 881 103
Legal Naval ✆ 0832 881 218

Facilities

Services Water and electricity (220V) near most berths. Showers and toilets.
Fuel On the quay in the inner basin. Care is needed over depths off the fuel quay.
Repairs 5-ton crane. Mechanical repairs.
Provisions Some provisions nearby.
Eating out Restaurants nearby.

San Cataldo

⊕ 40°23'·7N 18°18'·1E

A small basin that has been dredged out of the sand and an access channel dredged to it. Depths in the access channel are reported to be around 1m and care is needed as the entrance will likely continue to silt.

Data 200 berths. Max LOA 12m. Depths 1–1·5m.

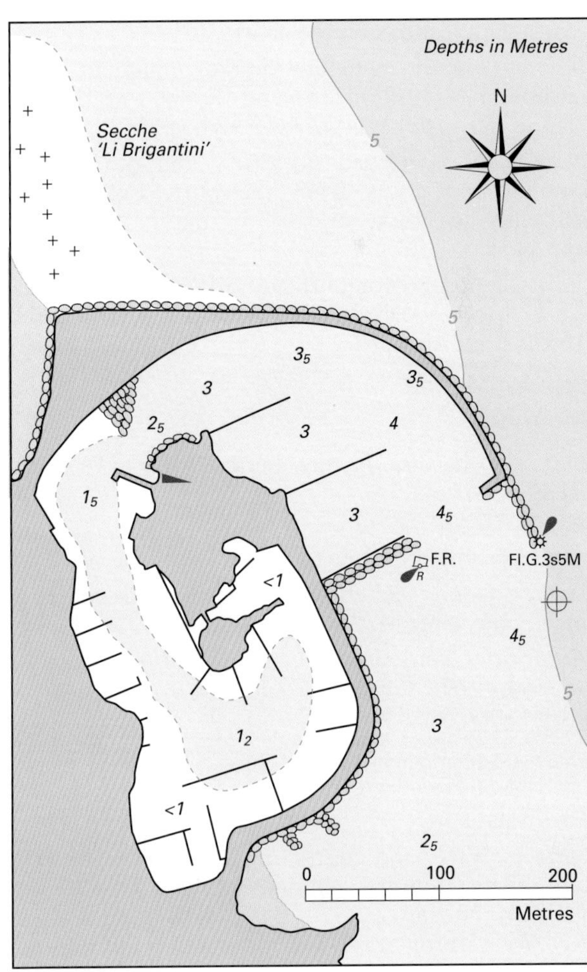

SAN FOCA
⊕40°18'·2N 18°24'·5E

Note There is a firing range off the coast close N of San Cataldo, extending up to 5M off the coast. Call Otranto or Brindisi Capitaneria on VHF Ch 16 for advice on when the ranges are in use.

Porto Frigole

⊕ 40°26'·0N 18°15'·1E N entrance
⊕ 40°26'·2N 18°15'·1E S entrance

Work in progress is reported developing the lagoon near the town of Frigole into a harbour. The lagoon lies just over 3M NW of San Cataldo, and 16M SE of Brindisi. Bridges built over canals linking the lagoon to the sea limit access to all but small motor boats. New concrete quays line access canals and part of the lagoon.

No further information was available at the time of writing.

BRINDISI

BA 1418
Italian 191

Approach

Straightforward by day and night.

Conspicuous The chimneys and buildings of the oil refinery to the E and the island of Sant' Andrea with a fort on it (Fort Castello del Mare) are conspicuous. Once inside the outer harbour, steer for the large stone monument on the N side of the entrance to the inner harbour. In practice the approach is much easier than it looks on the chart.

By night Use the main light on the monument in the harbour Fl(4)20s28m21M and the light at Brindisi Casale Aero AlFl.WGW.17s18m24-18M.

Note Care is needed of ferries and other ships coming and going from the port. Commercial shipping has right of way in the harbour and approaches.

VHF Ch 11, 16 for port authorities (0700–1900). Ch 12 for pilots. Ch 09, 16 for Lega Navale. Ch 08, 16 for Brindisi Marina.

Brindisi Marina

Mooring

Data 640 berths. Visitors' berths. Max LOA 35m. Depths 3–10m.

Berths Stern or bows-to where directed. Laid moorings tailed to the quay.

Shelter Good shelter although strong southerlies may make some berths uncomfortable.

Authorities Marina staff. Charge band 4.

✉ Marina di Brindisi, Bocca di Puglia spa, V. Dardanelli, Rione Casale, 72100 Brindisi
✆ 0831 411 516 *Fax* 0831 414 381
Email info@marinadibrindisi.it
www.marinadibrindisi.it

Facilities

Services Water and electricity (220/380V). Showers and toilets. Laundry facilities.
Fuel On the quay.
Repairs 150-ton travel-lift. Boat-mover and crane. Technical services.
Other Bar, restaurant, pizzeria. ATM. Bus service to central station.

Lega Navale

Mooring

Data 300 berths. Max LOA 18m. Depths 3–6m.

Berth Go stern or bows-to the Lega Navale quay. There are laid moorings tailed to the quay. Alternatively go stern or bows-to the quay SW of the monument, or on the town quay near the harbourmaster's office. Care is needed in places where the quay has a projecting lip just underwater.

Note The town quay is now open to yachts with several concessions operating.

Shelter Excellent, although there is often some chop at the yacht club berths.

Authorities Harbourmaster and customs. YC staff. Charge band 1/2.

Lega Navale ✆ 0831 412 114 *Fax* 0831 414 035

Anchorage Anchoring is prohibited off the N side of the town and is subject to a €300 fine. It is not recommended to anchor anywhere inside the harbour.

Note A small passenger ferry runs across to the town quay from near the monument.

Facilities

Services (Lega Navale) Water and electricity (220V) on the quay. Showers and toilets.
Fuel On the quay to the NW of the town quay. A tanker can be arranged to deliver fuel.
Repairs Yachts can be craned onto the hard at the yacht club. Cantiere Navale Balsamo is based at the W end of Seno di Ponente, past the Lega Navale. 50-ton travel-hoist. 200-ton slipway. Engineering, carpentry, sailmaking and repairs, and paintwork undertaken. Yanmar dealer. Under Punta Riso there are a number of yards with hauling facilities up to 130 tons. Good yacht repairs reported at these yards. Mechanical and engineering repairs possible in and around Brindisi. Also well-stocked chandlers in the town.

Cantiere Navale Balsamo ✆ /*Fax* 0831 451 565
Email info@navalbalsamo.com
www.navalbalsamo.com

Provisions Excellent shopping for all provisions. There is a large Standa supermarket in the town.
Eating out Excellent restaurants, trattorias and pizzerias in the town and also in the suburb near the yacht club. On the waterfront of the town and near the yacht club there are several excellent seafood restaurants.
Other PO. Banks. ATMs. Hospital. Italgaz and Camping Gaz. Ferries to Corfu, Igoumenitsa and Patras. Train connections to most parts of Italy including Rome. Brindisi international airport with flights to other European cities.

General

On the whole Brindisi cannot claim to be an attractive town, but around the harbour it is a lively interesting place and a yacht moored at the yacht club is away from the hustle and bustle of the town centre, yet within easy reach by the small ferries

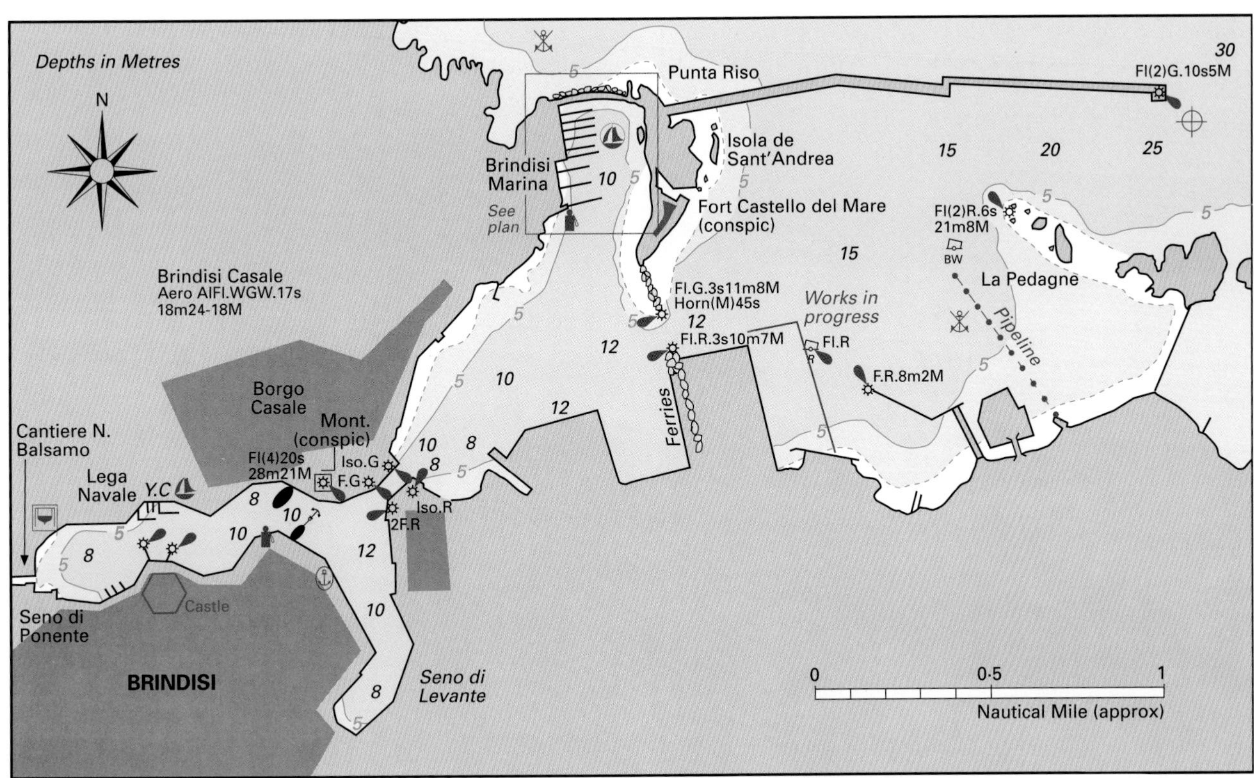

BRINDISI
⊕40°39′·65N 18°00′·1E

running to and fro across the harbour. The harbour is much used by the ferries running to Greece.

With the ferries and the airport close by, the Brindisi Marina and the friendly Lega Navale are becoming popular places for crew changes and overwintering here. The town itself is improving too, with pedestrianised streets and clean and airy squares to sit and relax with a capuccino and take in the atmosphere.

The large column with an elaborate capital by the harbour is said to mark the end of the Appian Way. The monument represents a giant rudder some 50m high dedicated to 'The Italian Sailor'.

Heading north Yachts heading on up the Adriatic either along the east coast of Italy or crossing to Montenegro and Croatia should consult T&D Thompson's *Adriatic Pilot* or the *Imray Mediterranean Almanac.*

Brindisi. The conspicuous monument and lighthouse near the entrance to the inner harbour

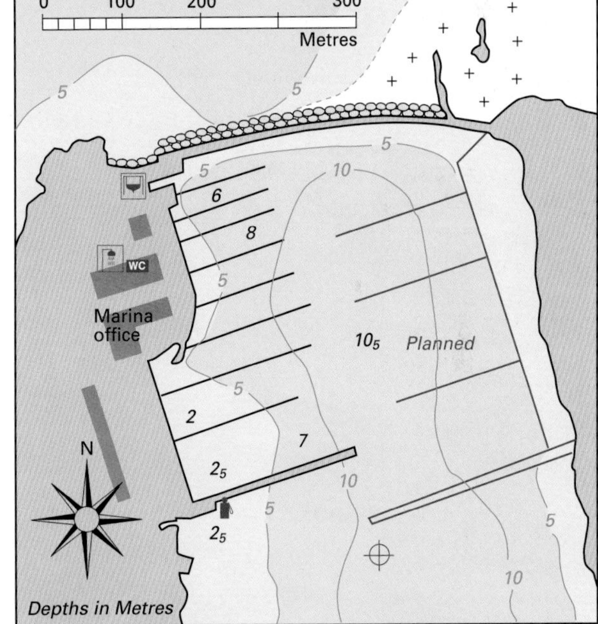

BRINDISI MARINA
⊕40°39′·5N 17°57′·9E

Brindisi looking W into the inner harbour

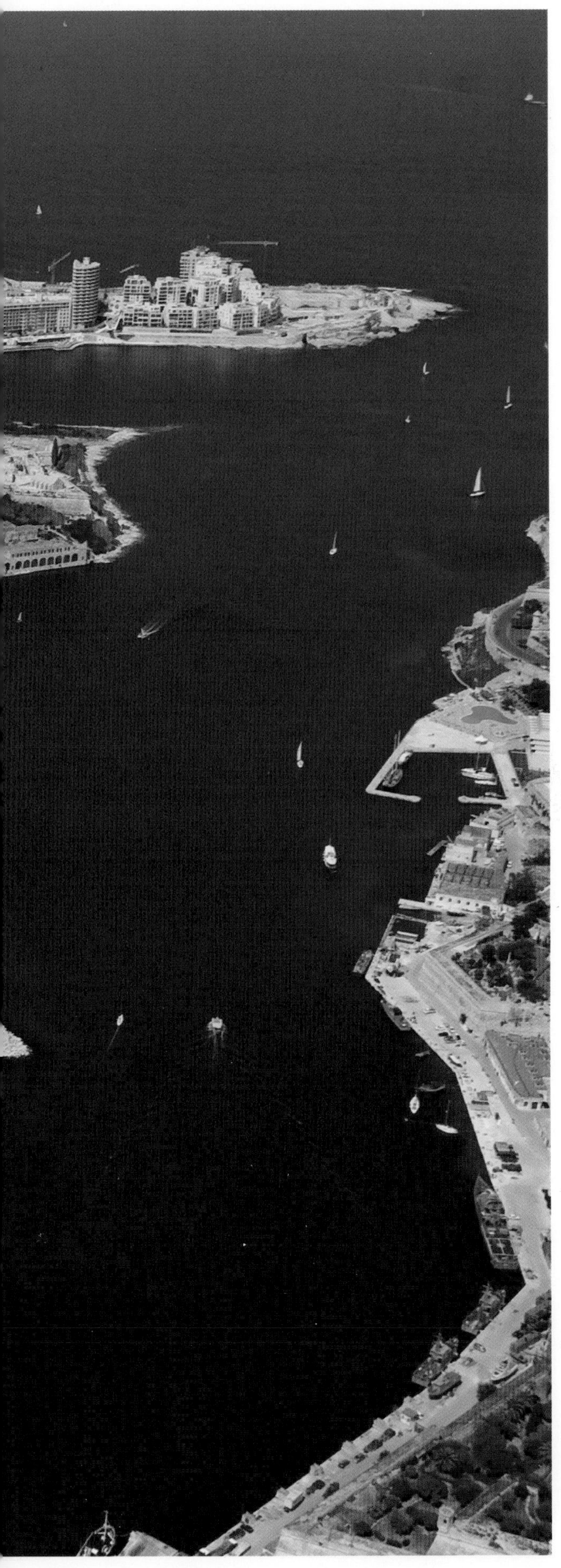

VIII.
Malta

The Republic of Malta consists principally of Malta and Gozo and two other small islands, Comino and Filfla. They lie approximately 60 miles south of Sicily and 220 miles north of the deserts of Libya, in the middle of the channel connecting the western Mediterranean to the eastern half. This strategic position between Africa and Europe has meant that these small arid islands (total area: 122 miles^2) have been coveted by many different nations as a stepping stone between the two continents. The navies and armies of the world have trampled back and forth across Malta, but two great sieges stand apart from the rest. The Great Siege of Suleiman the Magnificent against the Knights of St John in 1565, and the siege of Malta by the Italian and German air forces in 1941 and 1942.

Marsamxett harbour looking NE from Msida Marina over Manoel Island towards Sliema Creek Clive Vella, *MTA*

History

Early prehistory

In the Stone, Copper and Bronze Ages, Malta was inhabited and civilisations of some complexity built temples and had elaborate burial traditions. One of these tombs, the Hypogeum at Paola dating from 2400BC, is a fascinating warren of underground passages and vaults carved out of limestone.

Carthaginians and Romans

In the 9th century BC the Phoenicians arrived and later, in the 6th century, traders from Carthage utilised Malta. The Greeks also visited Malta between the 6th and 7th century BC. The name Malta is thought to be derived from a Phoenician word, *malat*, meaning a safe harbour; or from the Greek word for honey, *meli*, for which the islands are still famous. After the Romans defeated the Carthaginians they occupied Malta, building numerous villas around Medina. In AD60, St Paul and St Luke were shipwrecked in the vicinity of what is now St Paul's Bay. While here, St Paul converted the Roman governor, Publius, and many of the indigenous population. Malta remains staunchly Roman Catholic to this day.

Arabs and Normans

In 870 the Arabs occupied Malta and introduced new crops (cotton and citrus fruit) and influenced the language and architecture. The Maltese (still Christian) and Muslim Arabs lived reasonably amicably side by side. In 1090 Count Roger the Norman took Malta as part of the Kingdom of Sicily. Through various rulers it followed the fates and fortunes of Sicily until the Knights of St John arrived.

The Knights and the Great Siege

In the early 16th century the Turks controlled most of the eastern Mediterranean and were turning their eyes to the west. The Knights of St John, homeless after being ousted from Rhodes in 1523, reluctantly agreed to accept Malta as their new home. In 1530 Grand Master Villiers de l'Isle Adam with 4,000 men moved onto the island and began building fortifications at what is now Valletta. The Grand Master died in 1534 and in 1557 Jean Parisot de la Vallette became Grand Master. The Turks, knowing of Malta's strategic location, decided to rid themselves of this thorn in their side once and for all and on 19 May, 1565, a Turkish fleet of 138 ships, 38,000 men, and much heavy artillery reached Malta. Combined with the ships and forces of the North African pirate, Dragut, this force faced only 600 Knights and 9,000 troops.

The besieged Knights fought on through the summer of 1565 and lost Fort St Elmo, until finally they were holed up in Birgu, Senglea and Fort St Angelo. There were many dead and numerous atrocities on both sides. The Turks tied the dead bodies of the Knights to crosses and floated them across to the defenders while the Knights retaliated by bombarding the Turks with the heads of their fallen troops.

Eventually a relief force arrived from Sicily and the Turks retreated after losing, it is estimated, some two-thirds of their troops. Fort St Elmo was rebuilt and Valletta, named after the brave and stout Grand Master, was developed from 1566 onwards. For two centuries the Knights prospered, until Napoleon arrived in 1798 and the once valiant Knights meekly departed. French rule was unpopular. Napoleon had looted the churches of Malta to finance his Egyptian Campaigns. As a result he quickly fell out of favour and the British aided the Maltese in a revolt in 1800. Malta became a crown colony in 1814, with the autocratic governor Sir Thomas 'King Tom' Maitland. Grand Harbour was developed as a naval base and shipyard in the latter half of the 19th century and propped up a sagging economy. In 1921, after the 1919 riots, the Maltese were given local autonomy under a British governor.

The second Great Siege

In the early part of the Second World War, Malta was a vital Allied naval base separating Europe from Rommel's troops in North Africa. The Italians began a fierce blitz on Malta in 1941 and, unable to subdue it, were joined by German bombers. Throughout 1942 until November, Malta was bombed incessantly and the Maltese were reduced to living in rubble-strewn towns in near-starvation conditions. The Allies, well aware of how vital Malta was to them, attempted to keep the island supplied by convoys which failed to get through. In August 1942 a convoy with the tanker *Ohio* carrying much-needed oil, passed Gibraltar and, despite five days of fierce bombing in which many ships were sunk and the *Ohio* badly damaged, managed to limp into Grand Harbour where huge crowds had gathered to cheer it in and welcome the breaking of the blockade. For their bravery the islanders were collectively awarded the George Cross.

After the war a new constitution made the island self-governing and in 1964 Malta became an independent member of the British Commonwealth. In 1971 the Labour Party with Dom Mintoff as Prime Minister was voted into office and remained in power until 1984. Malta became a Republic in 1974, and proclaimed its neutrality in 1979. The island treasures its independence and under Dom Mintoff's leadership a wide range of affiliations were pursued: with Libya, China, North Korea and the USSR as well as with EU members and the USA. Mintoff was much criticised but he must have been one of the few politicians in the world who could bring together China, the USSR, the USA and Libya in a country as small as Malta. During the 1990s the Nationalist Party, under Prime Minister (and now President) Adami, and then PM Gonzi, led Malta into the EU, gaining full membership in 2004.

Useful books

The Great Siege of Malta 1565 Ernle Bradford (Penguin). Very readable.
The Kapillan of Malta Nicholas Monserrat. Perhaps his best book.
Blue Guide to Malta Peter McGregor Eadie.

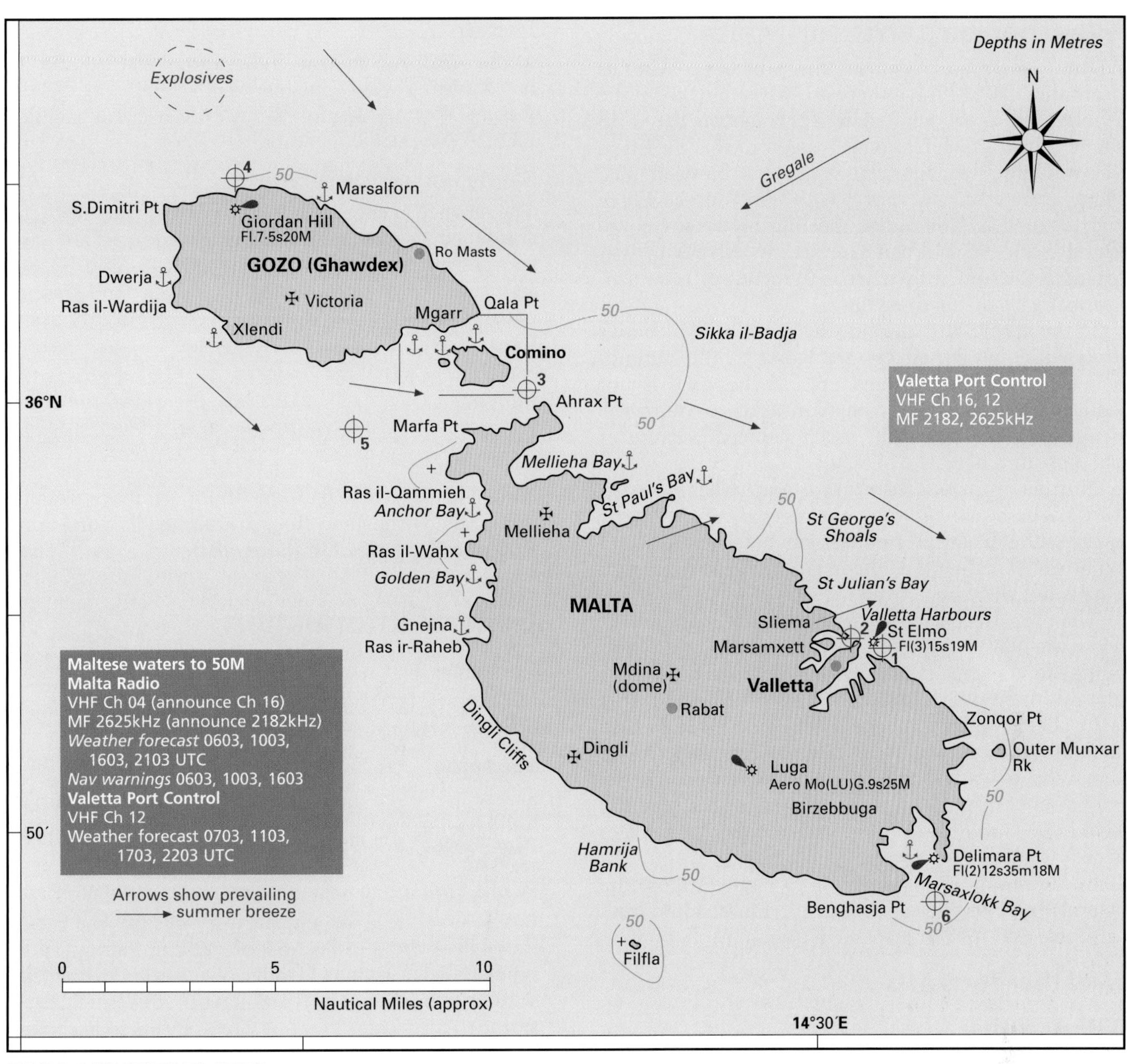

MALTA AND GOZO ISLANDS

USEFUL WAYPOINTS

⊕**1** Entrance to Grand Harbour
35°54′·17N 14°31′·58E WGS84

⊕**2** Entrance to Marsamxett
35°54′·30N 14°30′·98E WGS84

⊕**3** Mid-channel between Comino and Ahrax Pt
36°00′·3N 14°21′·63E

⊕**4** 2M N of Giordan Hill light (Gozo)
36°06′·4N 14°13′·1E

⊕**5** Mid-channel between Ras in-Newwiela and Ras Il-Qammieh
35°59′·4N 14°17′·35E

⊕**6** 2M S of Delimara Pt light (Marsaxlokk)
35°47′·3N 14°33′·5E

Data

MAJOR LIGHTS

Malta I
Valletta Grand Harbour St Elmo Fl(3)15s34m19M
Luqa Airport Aero Mo(LU)G.9s104m25M
Marsaxlokk Fl(2)12s35m18M

Gozo (Ghawdex)
Giordan Hill Fl.7.5s180m20M

Useful telephone numbers

Police	191
Ambulance	196
Fire Service	199

Malta International dialling code +356

Maritime Rescue Coordination Centre MRCC (AFM) ✆ 2180 9279

Valetta Port Control/Turetta ✆ 2124 1363 / 4

Immigration Authority (Yachting) ✆ 2134 2396

Customs (Yachting Centre) ✆ 2133 5691

Port Health Inspector ✆ 2122 0003

Port Medical Officer ✆ 2122 4810

Weather patterns for Malta

In the winter and summer, the prevailing wind is from the NW although there are also winds from the N and NE. In the winter the NE *gregale* is the wind to be feared as Marsamxett is open to this direction (as is Grand Harbour). It will often blow at gale force and sometimes more, with winds up to Force 9/10 recorded. The famed meeting between George Bush (Snr) and Mikhail Gorbachov off Malta was partially disrupted by a strong *gregale*. It is said to normally blow for three days.

In the spring and autumn the *scirocco* (SE) blows frequently but its effects are worst in the autumn when the sea has warmed up and the wind is not cooled on its passage from North Africa. With the *scirocco*, visibility can be much reduced because of the dust in the air.

Northerlies are called *rih fuq*; southerlies *rih isfel*; the *scirocco xlokk*; and the prevailing NW the *majjistral*. The latter is commonly believed in Malta to be the same wind as the *mistral* in France though this is not the case.

The prevailing wind in the summer is a sea breeze from the NW that gets up around midday and blows until the evening. It usually gets up to a Force 4–5 though there can be stronger gusts off the land. It is also channelled by the land to blow through and around the high land so its direction at times can be from the W–N. At times it may blow through the night depending on pressure differences between the two large land masses of Tunisia and Sicily on either side.

In the middle of summer in July and August the islands are very hot, the temperature sometimes reaching 38–40°C (over 100°F).

Weather forecasts

VHF forecasts

Valetta Radio broadcasts weather forecasts for Maltese waters up to 50M offshore on VHF Ch 11 at:

Summer time 0903, 1303, 1903, 2303 LT
Winter time 0803, 1203, 1803, 2303 LT

Malta Radio broadcasts the same forecast on VHF Ch 04 one hour ahead of Valetta Port Control.

Telephone forecasts

✆ 5004 3848

24-hour local forecast and 3-day 50M offshore forecast (costs 21c for the first five minutes).

Navtex

Station identifier O. Transmissions every four hours at 0220, **0620**, 1020, 1420, **1820**, 2220.
(Weather forecasts in bold.)

Marinas All the marinas post a daily weather forecast, usually from an internet source.

Meteorological Office The Met office at Malta Airport can supply forecasts
✆ 356 249 600 *Fax* 356 249 563.

Internet

Malta Airport Synoptic chart, radar picture and 3-day forecasts www.maltairport.com
Balzan Weather Station 5-day forecast and satellite picture www.maltaweather.com

Safety and rescue services

The Armed Forces Malta (AFM) is the Maltese combined forces military organisation. They are responsible for all maritime security and safety services. AFM coordinate all search and rescue operations from the Maritime Rescue Coordination Centre (MRCC).

MRCC (AFM) ✆ 2180 9279 or 2182 4220 (after hours).

For distress calls on VHF: Valetta Port Control VHF Ch 12 or 09.

Note The initials MRCC in Malta are more usually associated with Malta Rock Climbing Club or Malta Rod and Custom Club (hot-rods!)

General information

Currency

In January 2008 Malta adopted the Euro as its official currency.

Shopping

Shops are open daily (except Sunday and public holidays) from 0900–1300 and 1530–1900. Some shops are open all day and stay open until 2200.

Public transport

Buses serve all areas and are very cheap. The buses themselves are a collection of varying vintages and types (Ford, Commer, Dodge, Bedford, Leyland) in varying condition. Nearly all have a votive picture or statue to the Virgin Mary or Christ inside to keep you safe along the way. Unfortunately many of the older buses are being replaced with sleek new models.

Taxis

Are available everywhere. Fares are reasonable.

Flights

One of the advantages of wintering in Malta is the availability of flights to most major European

So that would be the fuel truck then?

airports. Charter flights and standby flights are readily available. Good deals on international flights to the USA or Australia can also be arranged.

Customs

Malta now comes under EU laws on customs and VAT such that goods imported from within the EU are not subject to additional tax or restrictions and should be delivered to you without problems. Goods imported from outside the EU may be subject to duty. Extracting these items can be tricky and many will employ an agent to help. It is better to have goods air-freighted than brought by ship as customs clearance on the former is more easily facilitated. A tip: have the goods addressed to your yacht with these three simple but all-important words on the label: 'Yacht in transit'.

Pets

There is a total ban on the unauthorised introduction of dogs, cats and all pets onto the island. If you have a pet on board and you enter Maltese waters you can anchor off *as long as your pet does not go ashore*. If it does go ashore it may be destroyed by the authorities.

Pets from EU countries with microchips and Pet Passports may be admitted once they have been seen by the Health Department vet.

For more information see notes in the *Introduction*, and contact the Port Health Department.
✆2122 4810

Security

For the most part Malta has few problems with theft, but around the marina it does pay to keep all easily removable items, especially push-bikes and yachting shoes, out of reach. In the yacht yard there is a rash of break-ins from time to time, so keep your yacht well and truly secured and take easily removed equipment off the deck.

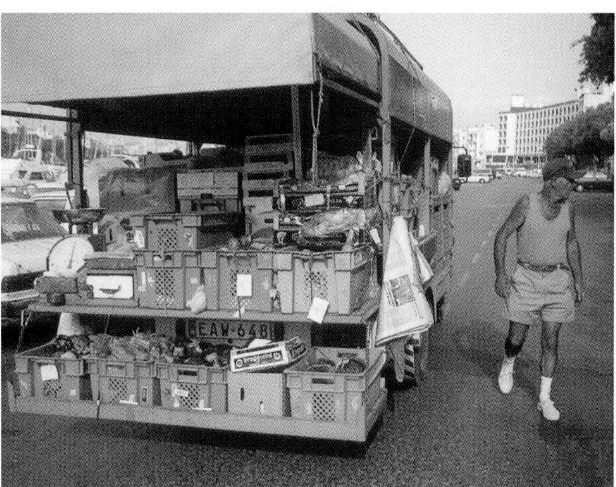

Friendly mobile fruit and veg at Msida Marina

Food

Shopping in Malta for foodstuffs can be a treat as you will find imported delights such as English Marmite and Rose's lime juice as well as Italian pesto and parmesan cheese. There are lots of small shops and a number of larger supermarkets. Opening times are from 0800–1200 and 1600–1900.

Fruit and vegetables are seasonal and limited in supply and, whilst the shops will have a small section of pre-weighed and packed produce, you will also come across mobile fruit and veg vans that will often call at the various marinas or just be parked on a street corner. But be early, as anytime after 1100 you will end up with a second-rate selection.

Sometimes during the weekdays and always on Saturdays you will find small vans carrying cages of live rabbits and chickens. Some will have a regular corner but mostly they will drive slowly through the streets and from them you can buy a chicken or rabbit fresh off the claw or paw! They say that death is instant and painless, yet this method of selling does not appeal to me and, if I wish to eat either of these meats, I still prefer to buy it from the butcher or supermarket.

Frozen beef from the Antipodes is inexpensive, and excellent for making stews and casseroles. Fish when in season is good value. The *lampuki* (*dorada*) season is in November and December and in the springtime tuna and swordfish are migrating. Seafood in Malta cannot be compared to Italy's and unfortunately, in between these seasons, the choice is poor and expensive. When ordering prawns, cod or plaice from a restaurant they are more than likely to be from a deep freeze cabinet.

There is an indoor market at the back of the Phoenicia Hotel (which is just outside the main gates of Valletta) where you will find fruit, vegetables, fish and foodstuffs, but again you will have to be early, otherwise all you will find are the leftovers.

The cost of eating in Malta is very reasonable. Most of the restaurants and snack bars cater for British tourists, making it hard to find traditional Maltese dishes. You will see *timpani* which is a macaroni pie or *bragioli* (beef olives), stuffed fillets of beef, but should you wish to sample the true dishes of Malta you will have to search around for a restaurant. Try the area around Sliema and St Julian's for good restaurants of all types.

Approach to the islands

The two principal islands, Gozo and Malta, are low-lying and difficult to see from a distance. There are no mountains or peaks to make identification easy: Gozo is a slightly undulating island reaching 194m (638ft) at its western end and Malta is a wedge sloping from the SW (240m/786ft) to the east. Modern developments have obscured many of the older marks and the most conspicuous object is now the tall Hilton skyscraper at St Julian's. In addition Nadur Church on Gozo, the spire of St Paul's in Valletta and a cluster of communication masts on the eastern end of the island stand out. There is often a bit of haze over the islands and even close-to it can take some time before you can visually identify where you are. Off St Paul's Bay there are now tuna pens which are marked at the seaward end by buoys. Also see note below.

When on passage between Malta and Sicily you can expect to have a lumpy old sea most of the time. In the summer you will usually leave Malta with some wind, then run out of it in the middle though there will still be a sea running, and then pick up wind again as you get towards Sicily. In the spring and autumn, southerlies, usually SE, often blow which is good for going from Malta to Sicily, but can make the trip from Sicily to Malta difficult. In the channel between Malta and Sicily there is usually an E-going current of at least one knot unless easterlies have been blowing for some time to stop or reverse it.

Tuna pens

There are several tuna pens in the approaches to Valetta. They are easily seen by day and are lit Fl.Y. New tuna pens have been established in the following positions off Marsaxlokk Bay. For more details check *Notices to Mariners* on the MMA website www.mma.gov.mt

A 35°53'·58N 14°38'·58E
B 35°53'·58N 14°40'·62E
C 35°52'·77N 14°40'·62E
D 35°52'·77N 14°38'·58E

Entry Formalities

A yacht entering Malta should fly a Maltese courtesy ensign and a 'Q' flag. Although Malta is now part of the EU, customs and immigration checks are still an entry requirement for those arriving by yacht.

Those with EU/EEA passports arriving from an EU/Schengen country, with no pets or declarations may proceed directly to a marina. Check in advance to agree that you may berth before going to Valetta to complete the paperwork.

All others, and everyone who arrives from outside the EU must complete full customs and immigration clearance in Valetta before proceeding to a marina berth. Yachts may anchor in the fairway off Msida Marina before being allocated a berth.

When 10 miles off Malta call Valetta Port Control (Turetta) on VHF Ch 12 to advise them of your arrival. They will probably ask you to call again when you are 1M off.

The main customs and immigration office is in Valetta, Grand Harbour, although the high quay here really isn't an easy place for small yachts to moor. Attend carefully to warps and fenders as the quay is open to wash from all passing traffic. Unfortunately the customs and immigration office at Msida closed in October 2008. The good news is that since 2008 the customs and immigration office in Mgarr Marina on Gozo has stayed open 24/7 all year round. It is hoped this will continue, although change at short notice is possible. Call ahead to ensure you can clear in here.

Valetta Port Control (Palace Tower Signal Station PTSS)
VHF Ch 12 ✆ 229 144 91 / 92

Depending on where you are the following procedure applies:

Mgarr Office hours are 24/7. Berth where directed and clear in. If you arrive at night berth where possible and clear in in the morning.

Grand Harbour The customs quay in Grand Harbour is far from convenient, with only a very high quay to tie up on if you cannot get on the lower sections of quay used by the customs boats.

Note

1. Yachts which have agreed a berth in Grand Harbour Marina or Msida Marina may find it possible to arrange to clear in at the marina.
2. Before leaving Maltese waters all yachts must 'clear out' with customs and immigration. This will include presenting proof of payment of harbour dues or marina fees.

Malta Maritime Authority (MMA)

Malta Maritime Authority (MMA) used to regulate all yacht berths in Maltese waters, although recently all marinas have been privatised, and new marinas are opening.

Grand Harbour Marina looking NW across to Valetta
Clive Vella, MTA

Looking E over Valetta to Rinella, Kalkara and Dockyard Creeks *Clive Vella, MTA*

VALETTA

Approach

There are numerous shipyards through the harbour, although yachts should call ahead to arrange services in advance.

GRAND HARBOUR MARINA

A marina on the east side of Dockyard Creek in Grand Harbour.

Approach

From the entrance to Grand Harbour proceed to Dockyard Creek which is the third inlet on the E side.

The approaches to the marina are buoyed with port and starboard hand buoys. Small yellow buoys mark small craft channels to the inner moorings and slips on the Senglea side of the creek. Care needed at night of small craft moorings close to the channel.

VHF Ch 13 Callsign *Grand Harbour Marina.*

Dangers Large ships and ferries regularly arrive and depart from Grand Harbour. The harbour entrance is quite restricted for large ships to manoeuvre so you should keep well clear and if necessary give way to commercial ships.

Mooring

Data 285 berths. Max LOA 85m. Depths 4–15m.

Berth Where directed. There are laid moorings tailed to the quay or to a buoy or finger pontoons for smaller yachts. Marina staff help arriving yachts to berth.

Shelter Good all-round shelter although there can be some wash from work-boats.

Authorities Harbourmaster and staff. Marina staff can arrange customs and immigration clearance for EU passport holders. Very helpful and attentive staff. Charge band 4/5.

Grand Harbour Marina ✆ 2180 0700 *Fax* 2180 6148
Berth enquiries ✆ 7920 0849
Email info@ghm.com.mt
www.ghm.com.mt

Facilities

Services Water and electricity (220/380V) at all berths. Telephone connections. Shower and toilet block.

Fuel Can be delivered by tanker.

Repairs Most repairs can be arranged. Kalkara Boatyard on the NE side of Kalkara Creek have 42-ton travel-lift, 50-ton boat-mover, max LOA 22m and can carry out most repairs.

Provisions Shops in Vittoriosa. Minimarket to be opened.

Eating out Several restaurants in Vittoriosa. Others in Valletta across the water. The roof-top restaurant at the Hotel Castille in Valletta is good value with superb views. Restaurant and bar to be built in the marina.

General

Grand Harbour must be one of the most impressive harbours in the Mediterranean, with the imposing walls of Valetta on the N side, and Kalkara and the three cities of Cospicua, Vittoriosa and Senglea on the south.

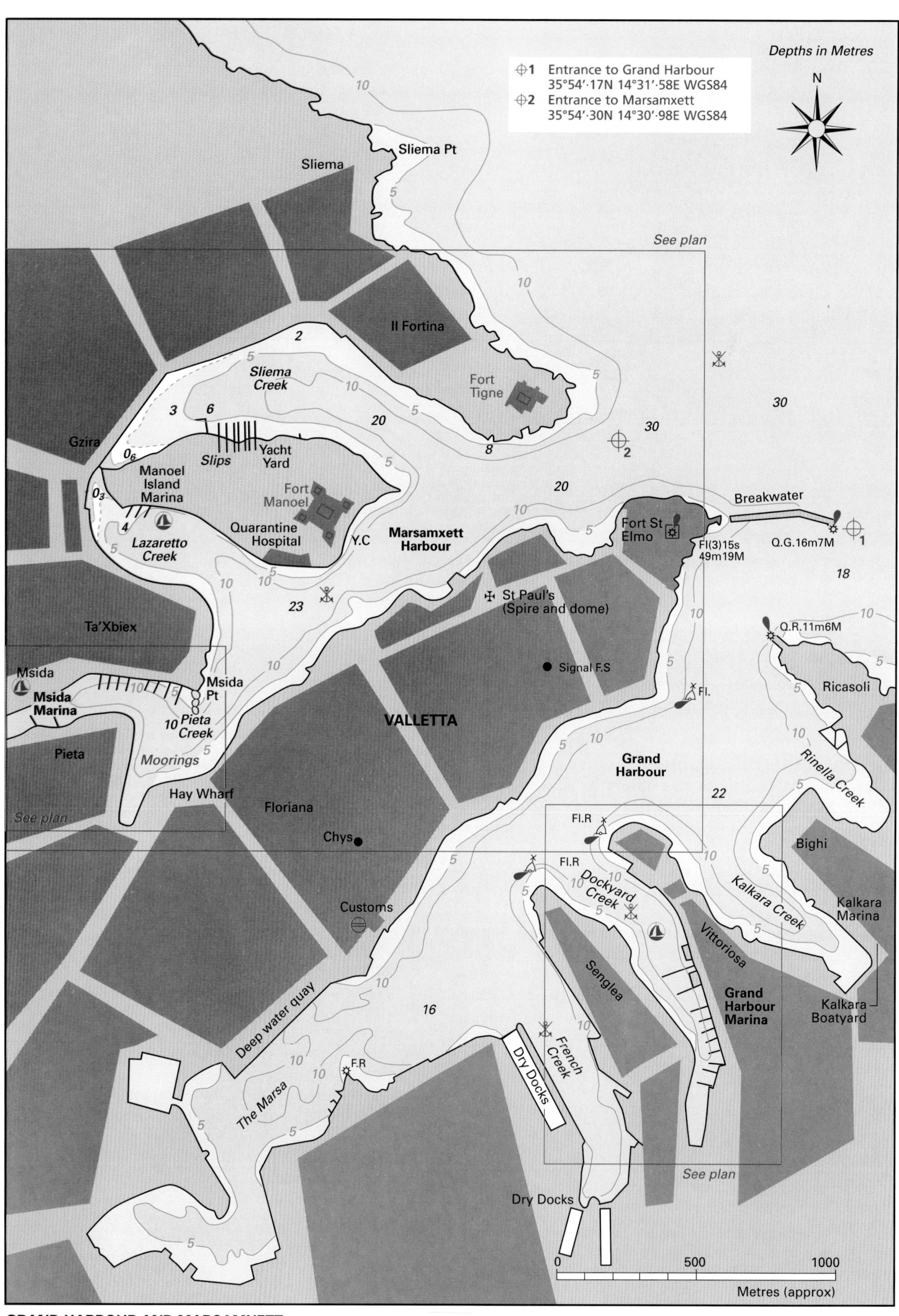

GRAND HARBOUR AND MARSAMXETT

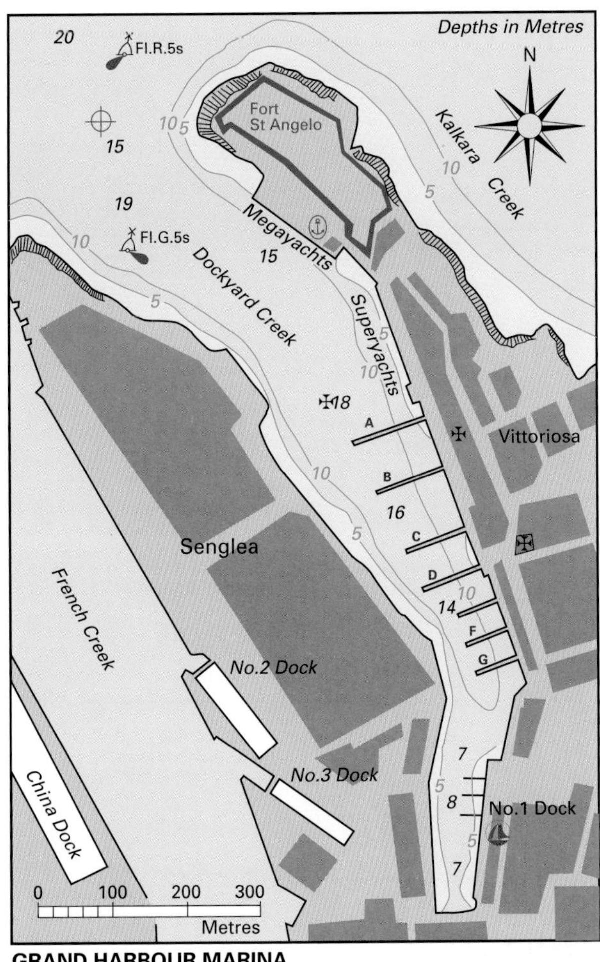

GRAND HARBOUR MARINA
⊕35°53'·6N 14°30'·95E

The Camper and Nicholsons-managed GHM was officially opened in 2006, and provides berths for all, from small yachts to mega-yachts, in the imposing surroundings of Dockyard Creek.

No.1 Dock

The old No.1 Dock at the head of Dockyard Creek is to be re-developed into a 60 berth marina. It is likely to be open in 2011, and GHM is applying for the franchise.

Data 60 beths on pontoons. Max LOA 20m.

Kalkara Marina

A new marina is to be developed in Kalkara Creek, alongside Kalkara boatyard. There will be three pontoons and quayside berths with laid moorings and ancillary services, and should be open from 2011.

Data 120 berths. Max LOA c.20m. Depths 5–10m.
Kalkara Marina ✆ 2166 1306 / 9942 5999

Kalkara Boatyard

A well established yard providing most services for yachtowners near the head of Kalkara Creek.
Kalkara Boatyard, Kalkara Wharf, Kalkara KKR 1501
✆ 21 661 306 fax 21 690 420
Email info@kalkaraboatyard.com
www.kalkaraboatyard.com

MARSAMXETT

BA 177
Italian 917

Approach

Marsamxett lies immediately N of Valletta and Grand Harbour. A yacht should make for here and clear in at the customs office at Msida Marina.

Conspicuous The spire and dome of St Paul's is conspicuous. On either side of the harbours the

Grand Harbour: Valetta on the right, Dockyard Creek to the left *Mario Galea, MTA*

VIII. MALTA

coast is extensively developed with no conspicuous features. Closer in, the breakwater protecting Grand Harbour from northerly winds and particularly St Elmo lighthouse on the eastern extremity is conspicuous. It is difficult to pinpoint the entrance to Marsamxett as neither Fort Tigne (Il-Fortizza Ta'Tigne) nor Fort St Elmo (Il-Fortizza Sant'Iermu), on the N and SE sides respectively, show up well. Once into the entrance, Fort Manoel and the old Quarantine Hospital can be identified. There is usually an ocean-going tug or two berthed at the N entrance to Lazzaretto Creek.

By night The lights are difficult to pick up against the loom of the lights of the town and a night approach is not easy for the first time.

VHF Ch 09 for MMA Yacht Centre.

Dangers

1. With strong northerlies and particularly northeasterlies there is a heavy confused swell at the entrance. With a gale from the NE (*gregale*) great care is needed in the entrance.

Marsamxett harbour, looking NE from Msida Marina over Manoel Island towards Sliema Creek *Clive Vella, MTA*

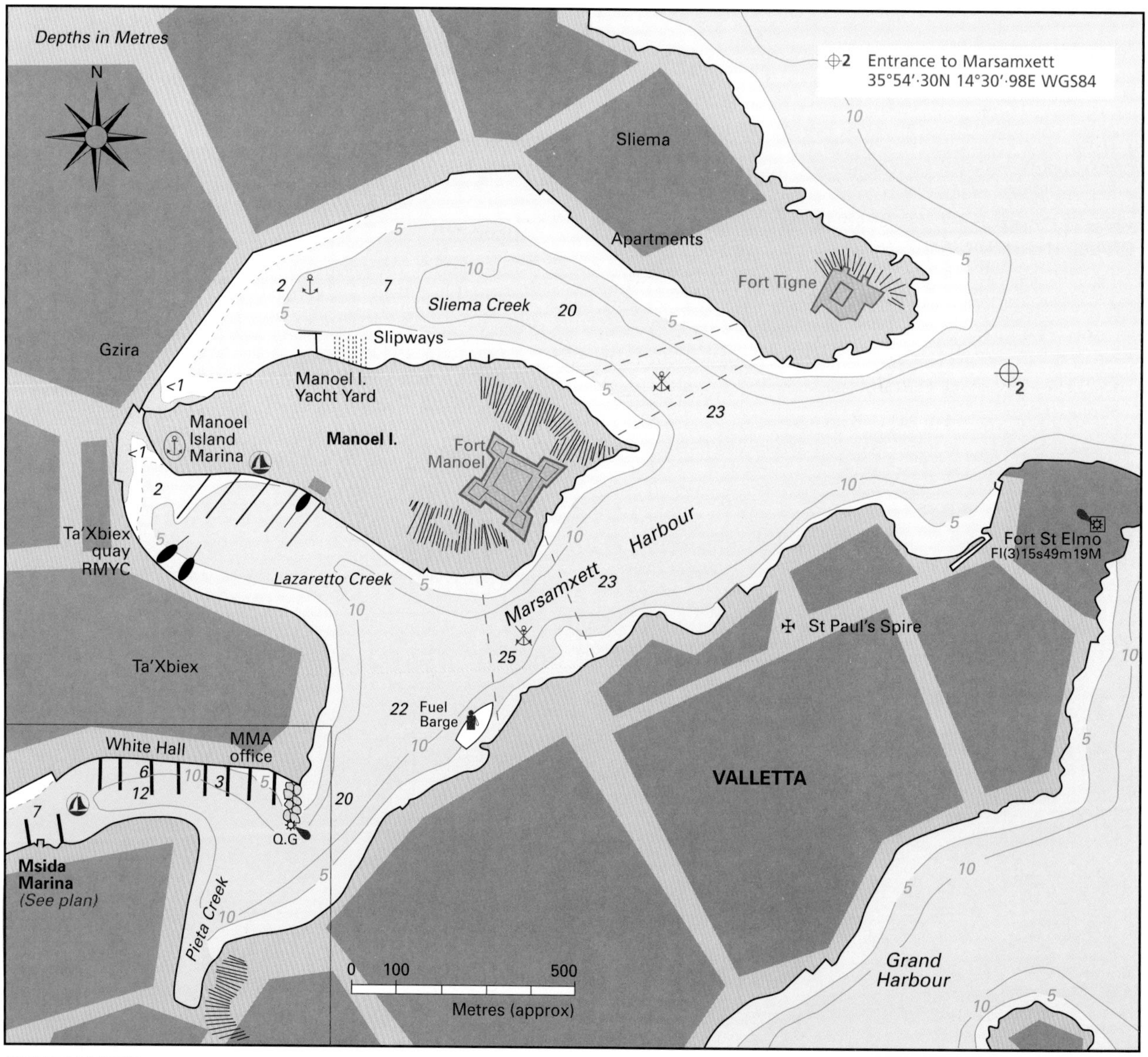

Depths in Metres
⊕2 Entrance to Marsamxett
35°54'·30N 14°30'·98E WGS84
Sliema
Apartments
Fort Tigne
Sliema Creek
Slipways
Gzira
Manoel I. Yacht Yard
Manoel Island Marina
Manoel I.
Fort Manoel
Ta'Xbiex quay RMYC
Lazaretto Creek
Marsamxett Harbour
Fort St Elmo
Fl(3)15s49m19M
St Paul's Spire
Ta'Xbiex
Fuel Barge
White Hall
MMA office
Q.G
Msida Marina
(See plan)
Pieta Creek
VALLETTA
Grand Harbour
Metres (approx)

MARSAMXETT

2. In Sliema Creek there are numerous small craft moorings and often several large ships laid up. These are not lit. On the S side of Lazaretto Creek there are also some small craft moorings.

Mooring

Once you have cleared customs, there are several berthing options in Marsamxett.

Msida Marina
Manoel Island Marina
Ta'Xbiex quay
Sliema Creek anchorage

Note Yachts may only remain on anchor in mid-stream within the Yachting Centre until a specific berth has been allotted by the berthing master who must be contacted on VHF Ch 09.

MSIDA CREEK MARINA

In Msida Creek running WSW from Marsamxett Harbour.

Note Msida Marina has been privatised and is now run by a berth-holder's association.

VHF Ch 09, callsign *Msida Marina.*

Mooring

Data 700 berths. Visitors' berths. Max LOA 18m. Depths 4–14m.

Note Msida Marina is a popular place and consequently it gets crowded. The marina staff do their best to provide berths to visitors, although that may mean that you get swapped around a bit when owners return to their berths after a cruise.

Berth Where directed. There are laid moorings tailed to the quay or the pontoon, but between the pontoons it can be a bit tight to manoeuvre into a berth. Visiting yachts will usually have to go on the more exposed berths near the outside of the marina.

Shelter Good all-round shelter. There is better protection here from the *gregale* than in Lazaretto Creek so naturally berths are at a premium.

Msida Marina *MMA*

Authorities Marina staff. Charge band 2.

✉ Msida Marina, Ta'Xbiex Seafront, Ta'Xbiex, XBX 1028, Malta ✆ 2133 2800 / 7992 7215 *Fax* 2133 2141

Facilities

Services Water and electricity at or near every berth. A shower and toilet block in the office block.

Fuel Can be delivered by mini-tanker. This means you will usually have to go alongside the quay in between the pontoons. As this is very narrow you need to be prepared.

Provisions Good shopping nearby. The Gala Centre up the hill from the N side of the marina has a good selection of most things. Fruit and vegetable vans call daily.

Eating out Numerous restaurants nearby.

Other Buses into Valetta.

General

Msida Marina is a good place to be in Malta, with good all-round protection and friendly and helpful staff. You can walk around to Gzira and Sliema or get a bus into Valletta from the square at the western end of the marina.

At the entrance sits the *Black Pearl*, an old Baltic trading ship. The *Black Pearl* was built in 1909 in Sweden and originally christened the *Black Opal.* At around 150ft LOA she was built with a hull of two layers of oak to withstand ice and for 69 years carried cargo around the Baltic. In 1969 she was converted to barquentine rig and refitted below for passengers. Re-named *Aeolus,* she cruised to Australia on the normal trade route via the Atlantic and Pacific. For a number of years she cruised with paying passengers around the Pacific until 1974, when the hull was found to be so infested with gribble and teredo, that it was decided to return her to England for repairs. In Suez a fire broke out in the engine room and she sailed to Malta for repairs. In Marsamxett she sank settling in 70ft of water. In 1979 she was refloated by the Vella brothers, rechristened *Black Pearl*, and used in the film *Popeye*. She sank again in 1981 and was refloated and taken to Grand Harbour. Eventually it was decided to put her ashore at Msida. The bar and restaurant based in the old schooner *Black Pearl* has recently come under new management. The restaurant is now called Mare Nostrum and the chef, Elias Francheschi, was previously at the Royal Malta Yacht Club. Great food and wine in an unusual setting, with a superb view over the water.

TA'XBIEX QUAY

Yacht berths on the quay opposite Manoel Island.

Mooring

Data 55 berths. Visitors' berths. Max LOA 40m. Depths 2–8m.

Note Berths here are generally for larger yachts and are mostly occupied by annual berth-holders.

Berth Stern or bows-to on the quay where directed. Laid moorings at all berths.

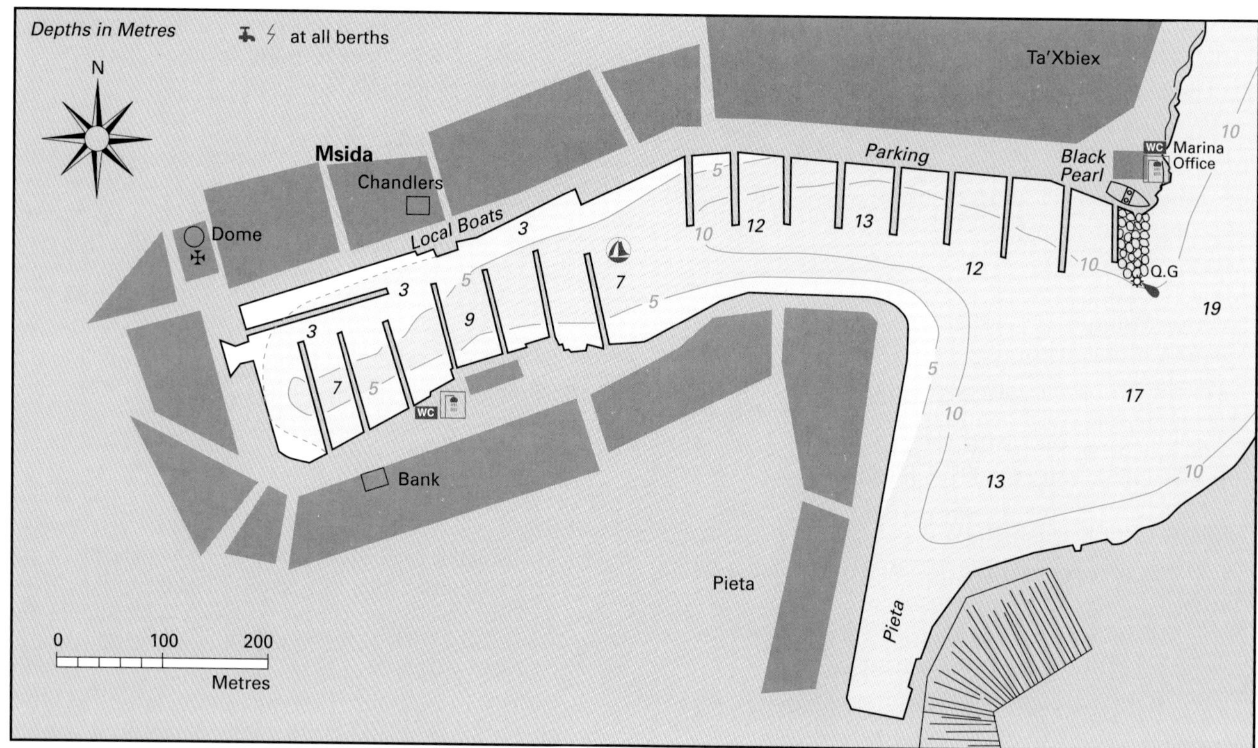

MSIDA MARINA

Shelter Good all-round shelter although with a strong Gregale (NE–E) there is a considerable surge and yachts should keep well pulled off the quay. At times yachts here have attached old car tyres to their mooring warps to ease the snatching on them. There are numerous tyres lying along the quay for just such a purpose.

Authorities Transport Malta. Charge band 2/3.

Berth manager: Chris Schembri ✆ 2122 2203 *Fax* 2133 2141
Email info.tm@transport.gov.mt
www.transport.gov.mt

Royal Malta YC ✆ 2133 3109 / 2131 8417
Fax 356 2133 1131
Email info@rmyc.org

The quay at the entrance to Msida Marina

Anchorage The anchorage in Lazaretto Creek is now very limited by yachts on Ta'Xbiez quay and the pontoons of Manoel Island Marina. Anchoring is no longer encouraged here as it is difficult to keep out of the fairway. The bottom is mud and not everywhere good holding. If you anchor here you must still go to Customs House on Manoel Island to pay marina fees.

Alternatively anchor off clear of the laid moorings at the W end of Sliema Creek. Technically you are not supposed to do this, but in the summer it is possible as long as you do not obstruct the slipways at Manoel Island Yacht Yard or the access for the tripper boats running from the quay at Sliema. It can be very noisy in this anchorage.

Facilities

Services Water near every berth. A deposit must be paid to be connected and the supply is metered. The water quality in Malta has improved with the new reverse osmosis plants in operation, but it still has a brackish taste to it. Electricity points near every berth. A shower and toilet block at the RMYC club house near Msida Marina.

Fuel A mini-tanker does the rounds of the marina every day in the summer. There is a petrol station in Gzira just over the bridge to Manoel Island. There is also a fuel barge on the port side under the city walls. The barge makes a £M3 service charge regardless of quantity.

Repairs See separate section. Numerous chandlers nearby.

Provisions Good shopping close by and excellent shopping once you have scouted around. The

Marsamxett harbour looking SW over fort Manoel and Sliema Creek *MTA*

supermarket (Gala Centre) on Testaferrata St has a good choice. Some items, particularly fresh fruit and vegetables, are often in short supply. Ice from the 'ice-man' who drives around every day in the summer.

Eating out Good restaurants of all types close by. Most serve anglicised meals in one form or another. For more choice head for Sliema and St Julian's.

Other PO. Banks with ATMs. Hospital. Gas containers can be filled in 24 hours. Paraffin is available from small tankers which come round on a more or less regular route. Hire cars and motor bikes. Ferries to Italy. International flights to most European airports.

General

This old established club was based at Fort Manoel and visiting yachtsmen are welcome to join as temporary members. They have recently moved to the old Yachting Centre building at Msida and offer berths on Ta'Xbiex quay. The club organises the Middle Sea Race, usually run in late September or early October.

The quay is a short walk from the quay back to Msida, and most facilities are easily found nearby. There are cinemas in St Julian's showing mostly British films and several newsagents stocking a good range of British daily newspapers and magazines. Several bars nearby cater for yachts although allegiances to one or another bar change over the years. There are several good restaurants nearby and a *KFC* if you like cardboard food. Buses (Nos 61, 62, 63) run regularly into Valletta from just across the bridge.

MANOEL ISLAND MARINA

A new marina on the S side of Manoel Island.

VHF Ch 13.

Mooring

Data 200 berths. Visitors' berths. Max LOA 125m. Depths 2–10m.

Berth Where directed stern or bows-to on pontoons. Larger yachts (>16m) go stern or bows-to the quay. Laid moorings at all berths.

Shelter Good shelter from the prevailing winds although with a strong *gregale* (NE–E) a considerable surge is set up and you will need to keep well pulled off the quay or pontoon.

Note It is intended to build a breakwater at the entrance to Lazaretto Creek which should improve the shelter from the *gregale*.

Authorities Marina staff. Charge band 3.

✉ Manoel Island Marina, Gzira GZR03, Malta
✆ 2133 8589 *Fax* 2131 1714
Email info@manoelislandmarina.com
www.manoelislandmarina.com

Facilities

Services Water and electricity (110/220/380V). Showers and toilets. Pump-out.

Fuel At the fuel barge in Marsamxett harbour.

Repairs 40-ton travel-hoist 550-ton floating dock. Extensive refit and repair facilities. Most repairs can be arranged.

MANOEL ISLAND YACHT YARD

This large yard, inherited from the Admiralty, now deals almost exclusively with yachts. It is owned by Malta Dry Docks and, although it has many fine facilities and skilled craftsmen, it suffers from a surfeit of workers (unemployment is high in Malta). Nonetheless its charges are reasonable and provided a close eye is kept on the yard costings for jobs and, where necessary, an outside costing is available for comparison (although no outside contractors can do work inside the yard), then I can recommend this yard's work.

It should be noted that, for short periods, the yard does not like the owner or crew to carry out work on the yacht that the yard can do. For longer stays and in some cases for shorter stays this is interpreted with some flexibility and in practice it all works out amicably. As an informal policy the owner and crew are allowed to live on board for one week after coming out and for one week before going into the water again.

The following facilities are available:

1. The yard operates seven slipways capable of slipping vessels up to 50m in length 3·9m draught and up to 500 tons. The yard should be contacted for the latest rates.
2. A 35-ton travel-hoist is operated and about 250 boats can be stored in the yard boat park.
3. Engineering. Repairs and rebuilding of all types of marine engines and installation carried out. All welding and machining work.
4. Hull repairs. All steel, GRP and wood repairs. Renewal and repairs to teak decks. Shot blasting and spray painting (including epoxy and polyurethane paints).
5. Textiles and rigging. Surveys, servicing and repairs to life-rafts and inflatables.
6. Electrics and electronics. Major electrical repairs (to generators, transformers, alternators) and minor repairs carried out. A battery shop where batteries are trickle-charged over the winter.
7. Surveys and classification. *Lloyd's Register of Shipping*. London Salvage Association. US Salvage Association. Det Norske Veritas.
8. Malta Superyacht Services MSYS dry dock facility for 140m MAX LOA, 8m draught vessels, and all associated technical services.

✉ Manoel Island Yacht Yard, Manoel Island, Gzira, GZR 03, Malta ✆ 22 33 4453 *Fax* 21 34 3900
Email info@yachtyard-malta.com
www.yachtyard-malta.com

Manoel Island and Tigne Point Project

A huge development project which in addition to complete regeneration of Manoel Island, vast apartment and retail complexes, will include a new 400 berth marina.

No plans were available at the time of writing but further details will be included in future supplements.

Yacht services in Malta

Several yacht agencies exist, including:

✉ Ripard Larvan & Ripard, 156 Ta'Xbiex Seafront, Ta'Xbiex, Malta ✆ 21 33 5591 *Fax* 21 33 1563
Email darins@rlryachting.com

✉ S & D Yachts Limited, Sea Breeze, Triq Giuseppe Cali, Ta'Xbiex MSD 14, Malta
✆ 21 32 0577 / 33 1515 / 339 908 *Fax* 21 33 2259
Email info@sdyachts.com

These agencies will undertake to look after a yacht afloat over the winter, checking warps, airing the boat, running the engine, pumping bilges, and carrying out any other work (painting, varnishing, mechanical, engineering and wood work according to a contract or on a time basis). A yachtsman new to Malta should enquire among other yachtsmen as to the merits or otherwise of one or other of the agencies.

Kalkara Boatyard, Manoel Island Yacht Yard and several other yards can haul yachts including:

✉ Cassar Enterprises, Marsa Cross Rd, Marsa
✆ 21 225 764/624 500 *Fax* 21 229 761.

✉ Bezzina Ship Repair Yard, 1/3 Church Wharf, Marsa
✆ 21 2624 613/234 411.

✉ Guzi Azzopardi, 52 Church Wharf, Marsa
✆ 21 2234 200.

Other useful services and addresses are as follows:

Chandlers In Gzira on the waterfront and in the streets immediately behind there are numerous chandlers. Similarly, around Msida Marina there are numerous chandlers. With a little persistence it is possible to find almost everything, though some items may have to be ordered.

✉ D'Agata Marine, 152 Ta'Xbiex Wharf, Gzira, Malta
✆ 21 341 533 *Fax* 21 340 594
Email info@dagatamarine.com

✉ Medcomms LTD, 4 Msida Road, Gzira GZR 1401, Malta
✆ 21 335 521/330 147 *Fax* 21 310 820
Email admin@medcomms.com.mt

✉ Gauci Borda & Co Ltd, 53 Msida Rd, Yacht Marina, Gzira GZR 03, Malta ✆ 2131 3748 *Fax* 21 343 604
Email gborda@digigate.net

Yachting in Malta is a magazine with listings for the marine industry in Malta
www.yachtinginmalta.com.mt

Cruising around Malta

Malta is more a place to hole up for the winter or just visit rather than a cruising area. However, there is enough to see and do for a short cruise of a week or so around Malta and Gozo. Below I have outlined the principal harbours and anchorages, though by no means all the possible anchorages.

Note When the British navy was here it must have been something of a problem to keep all those midshipmen and ratings occupied and out of trouble. Evidently one of the little occupations allotted to them was to chart the waters around Malta and, consequently, the coves and inlets around the islands have been extensively charted. Even tiny places like Xlendi and Dwejra on Gozo, that could have been of little or no use to the navy, have wonderful harbour plans in considerable detail.

Thus, for the yachtsman wanting to explore the coasts of the islands, there is a formidable battery of Admiralty charts.

No. 194	Approaches to Malta and Gozo
No. 2538	Malta
No. 177	Valletta harbours
No. 2537	Ghawdex (Gozo), Kemmuna (Comino), and the northern part
No. 2623	Channels between Malta and Ghawdex (Gozo)
No. 36	Marsaxlokk
No. 195	St Paul's Bay, Xlendi, Dwejra, and Marsalforn

St Julian's Bay

⊕ 35°55'·25N 14°29'·85E

Lies just over a mile NW of the entrance to Marsaxmett. Anchor where convenient. Open to the NE–E. Here you are not very far away from it all, with restaurants and rowdy bars everywhere.

PORTOMASO MARINA

A new marina on the W side of St Julian's Bay, built right under the towering Hilton Hotel.

Approach

The entrance is difficult to identify, but the tower of the Hilton and the new apartment blocks around the marina are readily identified.

By night The southern entrance point to St Julian's is lit Fl.G.6s4M.

VHF Ch 16, 13 callsign *Portomaso.*

Dangers

1. If Merkanti, an offlying reef, lies approximately 500m NE of the entrance to the marina. The reef is marked with an E cardinal buoy and is lit Q(3)10s.
2. Care is needed with strong NE winds which pile up at the entrance to the marina. An entrance channel of 4m is marked by orange buoys.

Mooring

Data 150 berths. Visitors' berths. Max LOA c.20m. Depths 3–3·5m.

Berth Where directed. Laid moorings tailed to the quay.

Shelter Good shelter although a strong gregale (NE) is reported to cause a surge in the harbour.

Authorities Harbourmaster and staff.

Charge band 4.

✉ Portomaso Marina, St Julian's PTMOI, Malta
✆ 2138 7803 *Fax* 2138 9655
Email info@portomasomarina.com
www.portomasomarina.com

Facilities

Services Water and electricity at every berth. Showers and toilets.

Provisions Shops in Sliema and St Julian's.

Eating out Restaurants and bars in the marina. A wide choice in St Julian's and Sliema.

Other Exchange facilities. Fax and internet facilities.

Looking S over Portomaso Marina in St Julian's bay *Clive Vella, MTA*

VIII. MALTA

General

The marina sits surrounded by luxury apartments and the Hilton Hotel. It is a friendly enough place and definitely very up-market, but it is not a place where you can hang your washing out and do some varnishing on the quay.

Salina Bay

⊕ 35°57'·55N 14°26'·0E

Lies just under Qawra Point, the S entrance to St Paul's Bay. The head of the bay is mostly shallow. Reasonable shelter from the prevailing winds. It takes its name from the salt pans at the head of the bay. Can get smelly in the summer.

Note Permission has just been granted to develop mooring facilities for yachts in the bay. Further details will be included in future supplements.

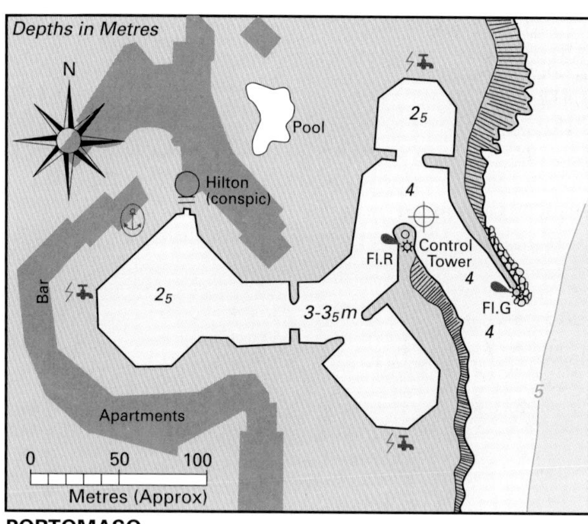

PORTOMASO
⊕35°55'·26N 14°29'·69E WGS84

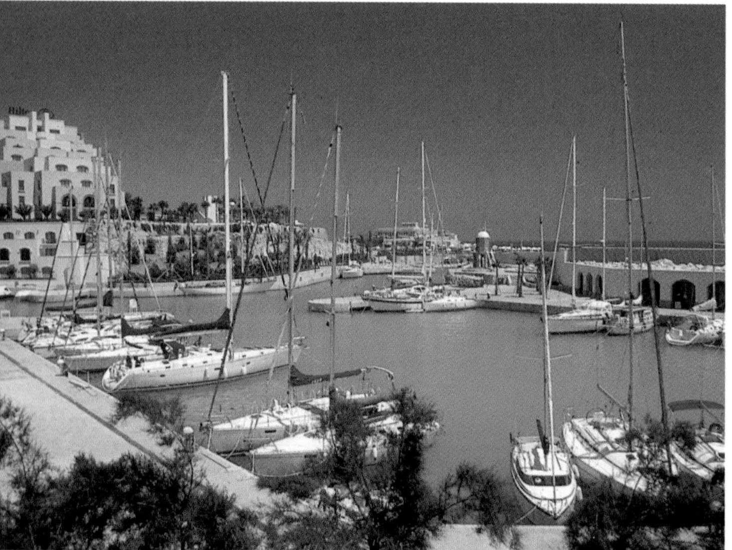

Portomaso looking E towards the control tower

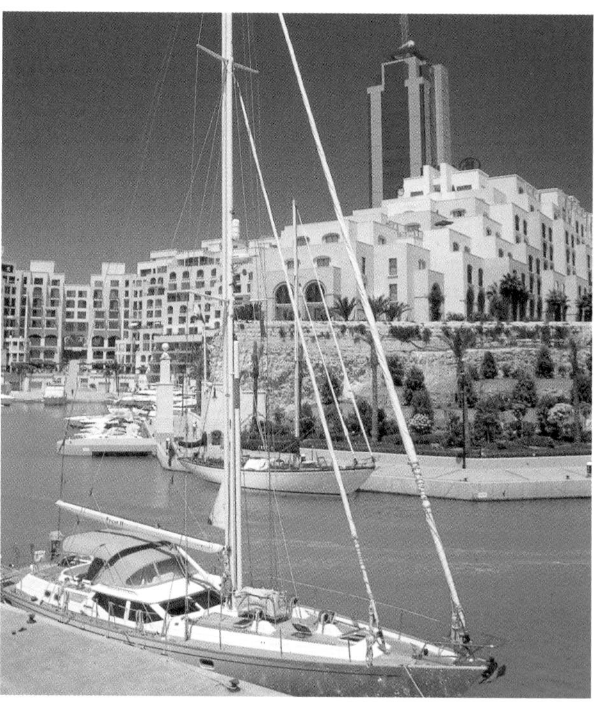

Portomaso at St Julian's looking in from the entrance. The tall blue Hilton Hotel in the background is now the most conspicuous object in the approaches to Malta *Lu Michell*

ST PAUL'S BAY (XEMXIYA BAY)

A popular anchorage well protected from the prevailing winds though there are gusts out of the bay. A yacht can anchor in a number of places:

1. Off Bugibba on the S side. There is a small harbour here though it is mostly shallow.
2. Towards the head of the bay in 3–6m before it shallows.
3. In Mistra Bay on the N side though the cove itself is fringed by rocks around the edges and at the head. Shelter here is not as good as it looks.
4. Immediately N of Ras il-Misgnuna under the cliffs. There is a good lee from the prevailing wind here and clear water.

St Paul's Bay, Xemxija looking south *Clive Vella, MTA*

5. Under St Paul's Island. Reasonable protection and clear water.

   The bottom is sand and weed at the NE end and mud and weed near the head of the bay. At Bugibba and St Paul on the S side there are shops for provisions, restaurants and bars.

Note

1. In recent years tuna pens have been anchored off St Paul's Island to keep captured tuna alive before exporting them. The pens are marked by buoys which are usually lit with a Q although this cannot always be relied on.
2. Permission has just been granted to develop mooring facilities for yachts in the bay. Further details will be included in future supplements, although there is some local opposition to the plans.

Mellieha

⊕ 35°59'·0N 14°22'·7E

The large bay immediately N of St Paul's. Care needs to be taken of Mellieha Rock in the middle of the bay. The normal NW wind gusts out of here and, though the bay looks good on the chart, it is rather a desolate and windy spot. Anchor in 4–8m where convenient near the head of the bay. On the S side the village of Mellieha has sprawled down the slopes to the waterfront and there are restaurants and bars ashore.

Marfa

⊕ 35°59'·5N 14°19'·8E

The ferry harbour for ferries to Mgarr on Gozo.

Anchorages on the W side of Malta

On the W side of Malta between Marfa and Ras ir-Raheb there are a number of anchorages suitable in calm weather or with light easterlies, but most of them are exposed to the prevailing NW wind. The popular anchorages are at: Paradise Bay, Anchor Bay, Golden Bay, and Gnejna Bay.

Mellieha, Ghadira Bay looking south *MTA*

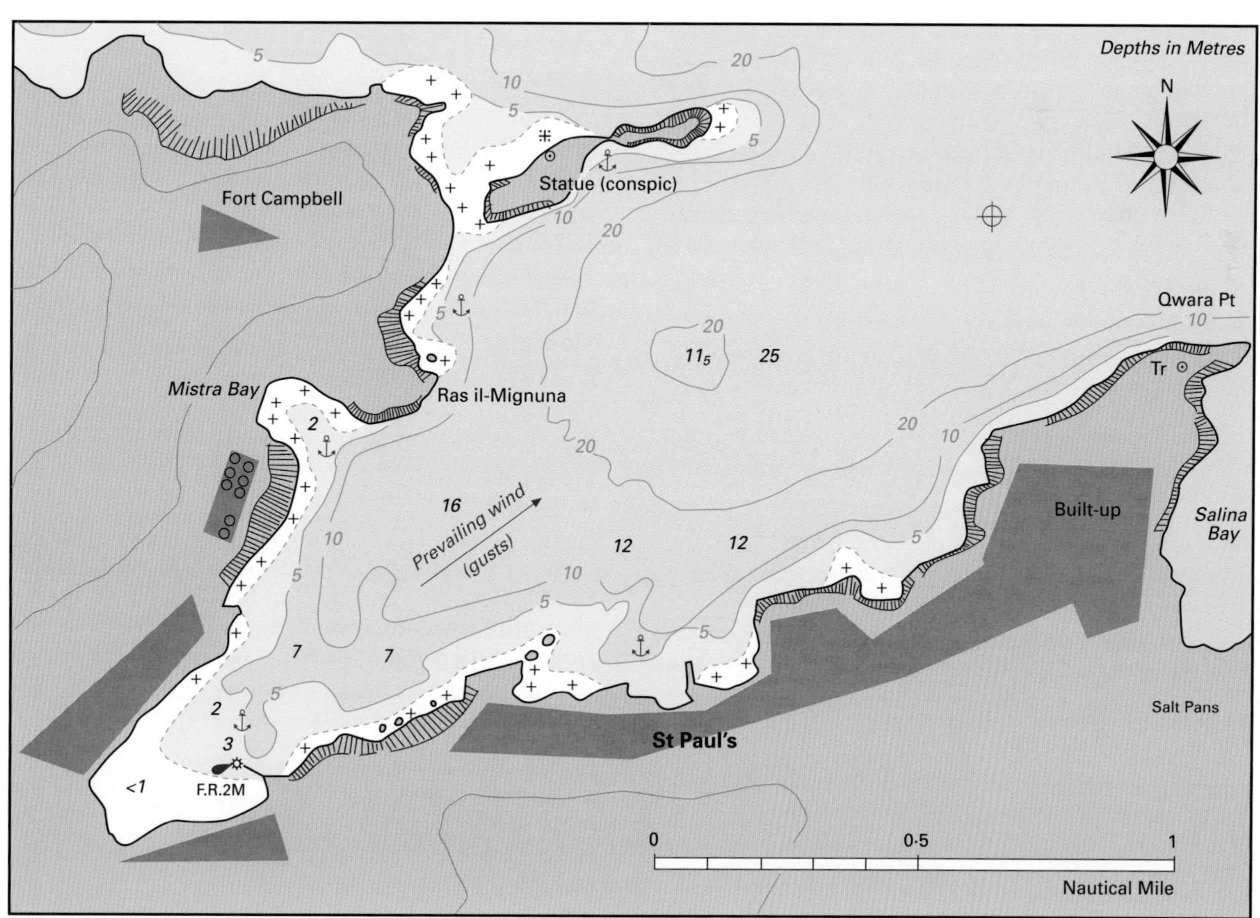

ST PAUL'S BAY
⊕35°57'·85N 14°25'·1E

Fishing harbour at Marsaxlokk *Michele Pesante, MTA*

Marsaxlokk

A large three-headed bay on the SE end of Malta with Malta's main fishing harbour in the N bay head. Care needs to be taken of the shoal water running out for a short distance on either side of the entrance.

Anchor off Birzebbuga at the head of the W cove or you may find a place in the basin on the W side. Below the resort town of Birzebugga the whole of the W side of the bay is given over to the commercial port including tankers and Ro-Ro. The NE side off Marsaxlokk fishing port and town is taken up with the Delimara power station but, offers the best anchorage and shortest, dinghy ride to the charming port town.

Note Works in progress extending the quay to the S of the small fishing boat basin of Marsaxlokk.

Most provisions and restaurants and bars at Marsaxlokk. A good Sunday market here also.

St Peters Pool

⊕ 35°50'·3N 14°34'·0E (Xrobb il-Ghagin)

Two large horseshoe coves with chalky cliffs on the SE corner of Malta. A natural arch in the S side of the bay is conspicuous. Anchor in 5·8m on sand.

Comino Island

The small island in the Comino Channel between Malta and Gozo. It is entirely barren although the brown rock is relieved on the W side by the impressively eroded cliffs with natural arches, caves, and striated rock. There is a hotel at San Niklaw and a few villas at Santa Maria. There are several anchorages around the island.

Blue Lagoon A much-frequented anchorage between Comino and Cominotto on the NW tip. Care needs to be taken of the reef running out from the N of Cominotto. Anchor in 3–10m wherever you can squeeze in. The bottom is soft sand, not everywhere good holding. Good shelter from the prevailing winds.

The bay is constantly churned up by day with tripper boats and everyone else charging around and anchoring in impossibly tight spaces. By night a couple of tripper boats run disco boats to the lagoon which boom out mindless bubble gum music until the wee hours. Unless you feel like an all-night party I suggest you pop in here for a look and then go over to Mgarr for the night.

Note The shallow S entrance is now blocked off by a line of small buoys marking off the swimming area.

San Niklaw On the N side with the hotel on its W side. Anchor in 4–10m. Good shelter from the prevailing winds. This bay is also popular, taking the overflow from Blue Lagoon.

Santa Maria To the E of San Niklaw. Anchor in 6–10m in the outer part of the bay. Shelter here is not quite as good as in the other two anchorages.

MGARR

The harbour for Gozo on the N side of the Comino Channel. Note that Mgarr is now a port of entry, with the relevant officials stationed here all year round.

Note The marina may be privatised in the near future.

Approach

Straightforward. The breakwaters show up well and the numerous ferries coming and going pinpoint the entrance.

VHF Ch 13 for Gozo Marina. Call ahead for assistance.

Dangers Care is needed of the ferries running to Marfa. Before entering see if any of the ferries on the quay are moving, and likewise when leaving keep an eye out for an approaching ferry.

Note Gozo Marina is now run by Harbour Management Ltd who also run the Manoel Island Marina.

Mooring

Data 300 berths. Visitors' berths. Max LOA 80m. Depths 1·5–5m.

Berths Call ahead to book a berth. Pontoons F or I usually have space for visitors. Laid moorings tailed to the quay.

Shelter Good shelter although strong southerlies can cause a bit of a surge. With E–SE winds a substantial swell enters the harbour and makes most berths uncomfortable, and even dangerous.

Authorities Harbourmaster. Customs. Immigration. Charge band 3. (Check out before 1100.)

✉ Mgarr Marina, Harbour Management Ltd, Manoel Island Marina, Manoel Island GZR 3010
Docking ✆ 9924 2501 Office ✆ 2099 2051
Email info@gozomarina.net
www.gozomarina.net

Note Yachts may complete entry formalities here as an alternative to Valetta.

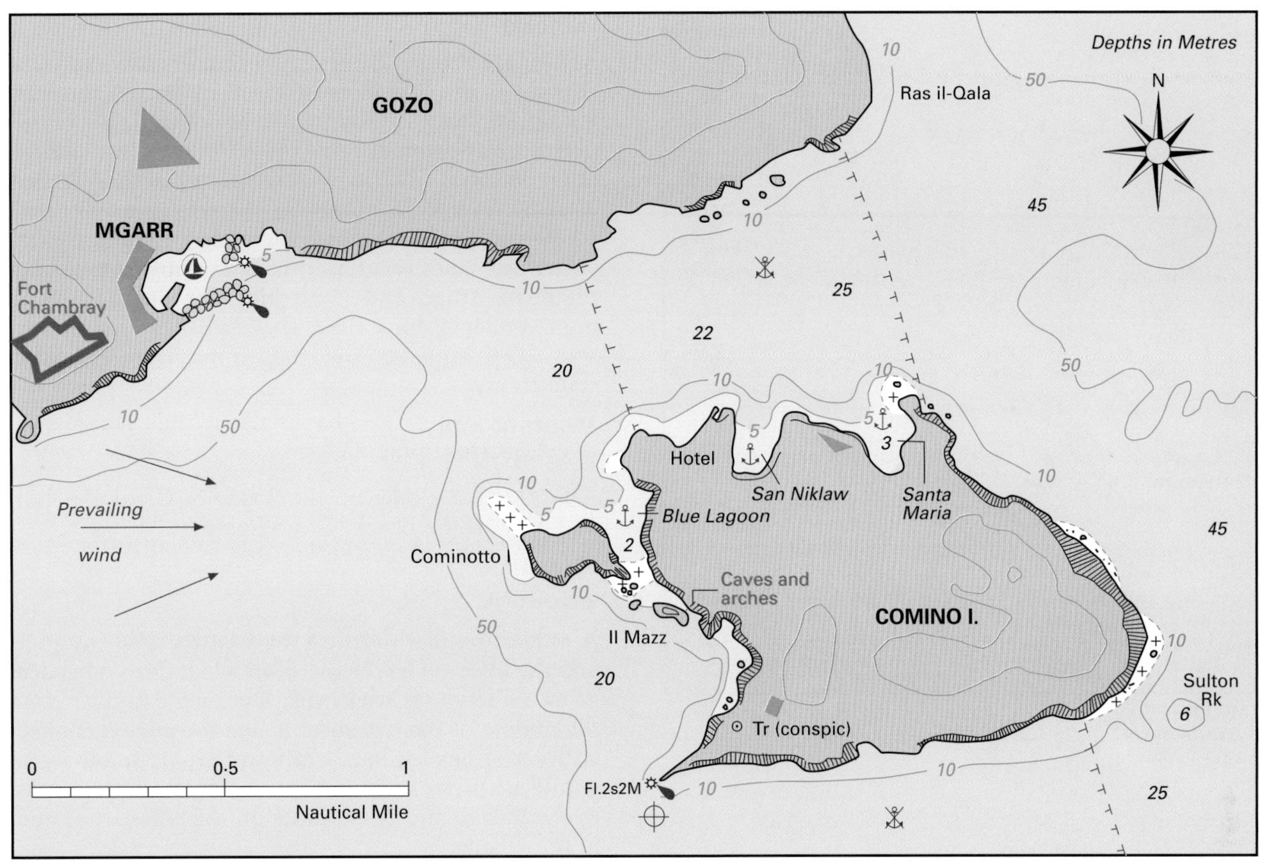

MGARR AND COMINO ISLAND
⊕36°00'·2N 14°19'·5E

Cominotto Island and Blue Lagoon on Comino *MTA*

Facilities

Services Water and electricity on the pontoons. Showers and toilets.
Fuel From the petrol station nearby.
Provisions Most provisions can be found in the village.

Eating out Restaurants and bars near the harbour.

Other ATM in ferry terminal. Hire cars, mo-peds and bicycles. Ferry from Gozo to Cirkewwa every 45minutes. Cirkewwa is 30–40minutes from Valetta by car. Ferry from Gozo to Valetta once a day Monday–Thursday, except holidays.

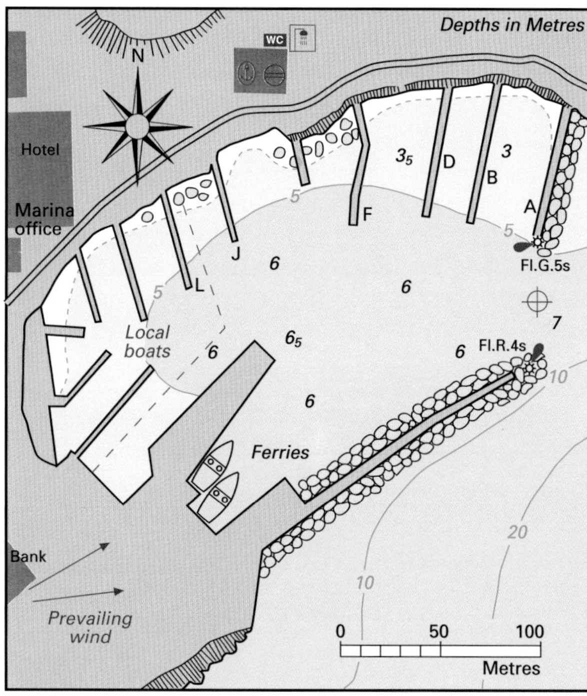

MGARR
⊕36°01´·41N 14°17´·93E WGS84

Mgarr *Mario Galea, MTA*

General

Mgarr used to be this sleepy little port town, barely stirring as the odd ferry dropped by. In the summer heat it was easy to fall in with the soporific air of the place, away from the hustle of Valetta, but things have changed. The new ferry terminal has ferries arriving every 45 minutes, waters churning and passengers bustling along the quay to regularly lift you from your reverie. Still, it remains a pleasant place to stop, and with the new management improvements look like they will get underway soon. Oh, and the town has some quite excellent restaurants.

Mgarr Ix-Xini

⊕ 36°01'·2N 14°16'·5E

A long narrow inlet on the S side of Gozo. Anchor in 5–6m off the beach. Good holding.

Xlendi

⊕ 36°01'·8N 14°12'·8E

A miniature inlet on the SW of Gozo. The entrance and the inlet are less than 100m wide. Care is needed of an underwater rock with less than 1m over it in the middle of the entrance. Inside the inlet is choked with moorings for local craft and even a small yacht would be lucky to find a spot to anchor. Provisions in the village and restaurants on the waterfront and in the village.

Xlendi Bay, Gozo *Jurgen Scicluna, MTA*

Dwejra

⊕ 36°02'·8N 14°11'·4E

An almost circular bay on the W of Gozo. It is partially protected by Fungus Rock in the middle of the entrance. Yachts normally anchor on the N side with a long line ashore. With the normal NW wind a bit of a surge is set up in here, usually more uncomfortable than dangerous. With strong NW–SW winds it would not be a good place to be.

The place is rather forbidding with high cliffs all around it. Fungus Rock is so named because the type of fungus that grows on it was gathered for its medicinal properties, perhaps as an antiseptic dressing or for a potion with antibacterial properties?

Marsalforn

⊕ 36°04'·5N 14°15'·7E

A small bay on the N side of Gozo. The miniature harbour is too shallow as well as too small for all but the smallest runabouts. It is open N and the prevailing NW winds send a swell in.

Dwejra on the W coast of Gozo

Dwejra is partialy protected by Fungus Rock *MTA*

Appendix

I. USEFUL ADDRESSES

Embassies

Australia Via Antonio Bosio, 5, Rome ✆ 06 852 721 *Fax* 06 852 72300
Austria Via G. Pergolesi 3, 00198 Rome, Italy ✆ 06 844 0141 *Fax* 06 854 3286 *Email* rom-ob@bmaa.gv.at or bmlv.vait@pronet.it
Belgium Via dei Monti Parioli 49, 00197, Rome, Italy ✆ 06 360 9511 *Fax* 06 322 6935 *Email* rome@diplobel.org or ambelrom@tin.it
British Embassy Via XX Settembre 80a I-00187 Rome RM ✆ 06 4220 0001
British Consulate Via Saluzzo 60, Torino 10125, Italy ✆ 11 6509202, *Fax* 11 6695982 *Email* beturin@yahoo.com
There are also British missions in Bari, Cagliari, Catania, Florence, Genoa, Milan, Naples, Palermo, Trieste and Venice.
Canadian Embassy Via Zara 30, Rome 00198, Italy ✆ 06 85444 2911 *Fax* 06 85444 2912 *Email* rome.citizenservices@international.gc.ca
Denmark Via dei Monti Parioli 50, Rome, Italy 00197 ✆ 06 3200441 *Fax* 06 3610290 *Email* romamb@um.dk
Finland Via Lisbona 3, Rome, Italy 00198 ✆ 06 852231, *Fax* 06 68540362 *Email* sanomat.roo@formin.it
France Piazza Farnese 67, Rome, Italy 00186 ✆ 06 686 011 *Fax* 06 686 015
Germany Via San Martino della Battaglia 4, Rome, Italy 00185 ✆ 06 492131, *Fax* 06 4452672 *Email* mail@deutschebotschaft-rom.it
Greece Viale G. Rossini 4, Rome, Italy 00198 ✆ 06 853755, *Fax* 06 8415927, *Email* gremroma@tin.it
Ireland Piazza di Campitelli 3, Rome, Italy 00186 ✆ 06-6979121, *Fax* 06-6792354 *Email* irish.embassy@esteri.it
Netherlands Via Michele Mercati 8, 00197 Rome, Italy ✆ 06 3221141, *Fax* 06-3221140, *Email* rom@minbuza.nl or nlgovrom@tin.it
Norway Via delle Terme Deciane 7, 00153 Rome, Italy ✆ 06 5717031 *Fax* 06 57170326 *Email* emb.rome@mfa.no
Portugal Viale Liegi 23, 00198 Rome, Italy ✆ 06 844801, *Fax* 06-8417404 *Email* embptroma@virgilio.it
Spain Palazzo Borghese - Largo Fontanella Borghese 19, 00186 Rome, Italy ✆ 06 6840401 *Fax* 06-6872256 *Email* ambespit@mail.mae.es
Switzerland Via Barnaba Oriani 61, 00197 Rome, Italy ✆ 06 809571 *Fax* 06 808851 *Email* vertretung@rom.rep.admin.ch
United States Embassy Via Vittorio Veneto 121-00187, Rome ✆ 06 467 41 *Fax* 06 4674 2244 *Email* uscitizensrome@state.gov

II. USEFUL BOOKS AND CHARTS

(Not a bibliography, just the most useful books I have come across).

Admiralty Pilots

Mediterranean Pilot Vol. I (NP45) Covers West Mediterranean to the heel of Italy excluding France, Corsica, Sardinia and West Italy.
Mediterranean Pilot Vol. II (NP46) Cover France, Corsica, Sardinia and West Italy

List of Lights and Fog Signals

List of Lights. Vol. E (NP78) Mediterranean Black Sea.

Radio Publications

ALRS Small Craft NP289 United Kingdom and the Mediterranean (Admiralty)

Yachtman's pilots

Imray Mediterranean Almanac (Biennial) editor Rod Heikell (Imray). All lights, radio signals, harbour information and other associated information.
Mediterranean Cruising Handbook Rod Heikell (Imray). General primer on cruising in the Mediterranean.
The Tyrrhenian H M Denham (John Murray). Covers Corsica, Sardinia, Sicily and the mainland Italian coast. Although out of date it contains interesting material on naval history.
Porticcioli d'Italia. Bruno Ziravello. Handy Italian Pilot. In Italian.
Pagine Azzure. Covers all harbours in Italy in some detail. Issued annually. In Italian.
Navigare Lungocosta Mauro Mancini. Five volumes cover western Italian waters.
Navigare Lungocosta *No 1.*
Navigare Lungocosta *No 2.*
Navigare Lungocosta *No 3.*
Navigare Lungocosta *No 4.*
Navigare Lungocosta *No 5.*
A set of detailed pilots with pen and ink sketches of approaches, harbours, boats, in an inimitable style. In Italian.
*156 Porti d'Italia (*Instituto Geografico de Agostini). Good colour photographs but only covers a limited number of ports. In Italian.
Coste Porti e Approdi della Sardegna. A Capitanio and G Premoselli. Good but incomplete. Covers Sardinia only. In Italian.
Adriatic Pilot T & D Thompson (Imray, Laurie Norie & Wilson). Covers the east coast of Italy.

Other guides

Baedeker's Italy (Baedeker/AA).
Blue Guides. Northern Italy. Rome and Environs. Southern Italy. Sicily (A & C Black). Classic guides.
Companion Guides. Tuscany Archibald Lyall. *Southern Italy* Peter Gunn re-issued by Taurus Parke paperbacks. Readable guides.

Berlitz Guides. Italian Riviera. Rome. Sicily. Malta. Handy pocket-sized guides that are surprisingly good for their size.
A Concise History of Italy Vincent Cronin (Cassell).
Sardinia Virginia Waite (Batsford).
Sea and Sardinia D H Lawrence (Penguin).
The Penguin Atlas of Ancient History. The Penguin Atlas of Medieval History. The Penguin Atlas of Modern History Colin McEvedy.
The Mediterranean and the Mediterranean World in the Age of Philip II. Vols I and II. Fernand Braudel (Fontana). Don't be put off by the title or the hefty size of these tomes. Most of it is very readable.
Sicily: An Archaeological Guide. Margaret Guido (Faber).
The Portable Roman Reader Ed. Basil Davenport (Penguin). Useful compact volume of some of the classics.
Naples, Pompeii and Southern Italy Anthony Pereira (Batsford).
Rough Guide to Italy (Rough Guides).
Sardinia Russell King (David & Charles).

General

Italy: The Unfinished Revolution Matt Frei (Arrow Books).
Midnight in Sicily Peter Robb (The Harvill Press).
Lugworm Homeward Bound Ken Duxbury (Pelham Books). O.P. An amusing account of a voyage in an open boat from Greece to England which takes in the Italian coast.
The Story of S. *Michele* Axel Munthe (Mayflower). Some admire him, some detest him.
The Poems of Catullus transl. Peter Whigham (Penguin).
Ulysses Found. Ernle Bradford (Sphere). A delightful book tracing the track of Ulysseus by the author who has sailed his own yacht around the area.
The Wind off the Island Ernle Bradford (Hutchinson) O.P.
The Plundered Past Karl E Meyer (Penguin). Readable book on the traffic in art treasures including the losses from Italy.
I, Claudius and *Claudius the God* Robert Graves (Penguin)
Old Calabria Norman Douglas (Century). A classic.
Along the Way Aldous Huxley (Paladin).
Isabel and the Sea George Millar (Century – reprint by Dovecote Press).

Flora

Flowers of the Mediterranean Anthony Huxley and Oleg Polunin. Excellent colour photographs and line drawings for identification.

Marine life

Hamlyn Guide to the Flora and Fauna of the Mediterranean Sea. Comprehensive compact guide.
Mediterranean Seafood Alan Davidson (Penguin). Contains excellent line drawings and descriptions of many fish – prior to the pot.
The Yachtsman's Naturalist M Drummond and P Rodhouse (Angus and Robertson). About Britain and northern Europe but many of the species are common to the Mediterranean.
Dangerous Marine Animals Bruce Halstead. The standard reference work.

Food

Italian Food Elizabeth David (Penguin). Excellent.
Food in History Reay Tannahill Contains much on Italian food as part of a general history.
Mediterranean Seafood Alan Davidson (Penguin). Excellent.

IMRAY CHARTS

Imray and British Admiralty charts are available from:

Imray Laurie Norie & Wilson Ltd
www.imray.com
Wych House The Broadway St Ives
Cambridgeshire PE27 5BT England
+44(0)1480 462114 *Fax* +44(0)1480 496109
Email orders@imray.com

Below are details of Imray charts.

Chart	*Title*	*Natural Scale*
M16	Ligurian Sea *Plans* San Remo, Approaches to Genoa, Golfo Marconi, Approaches to La Spezia, Viareggio, Approaches to Livorno, Livorno	1:325,000
M17	North Tuscan Islands to Rome *Plans* Scarlino to Punta Ala, Approaches to Giglio Marina, Approaches to Civitavecchia, Approaches to Fiumocino and Fiuma Grande, Approaches to Anzio	1:325,000
M18	Capo d'Anzio to Capo Palinuro *Plans* Rada di Gaeta, Golfo di Pozzuoli and Rada di Napoli, Approaches to Acciaroli, Capo Palinuro	1:325,000
M19	Capo Palinuro to Punta Stilo *Plans* Golfo di Policastro, Approaches to Vibo Valentia, Isole Alicudi, Stretto di Messina	1:325,000
M20	Eastern Mediterranean – Sardinia to Cyprus and Port Said	1:2,750,000
M21	Eastern Mediterranean Passage Chart – South Coast of Turkey, Syria, Lebanon & Cyprus *Plans* Larnaca Marina, Mersin, Alanya Limani	1:768,000
M22	Eastern Mediterranean Passage Chart – Egypt to Israel, Lebanon & Cyprus *Plans* Jounie, Larnaca, Hefa, Bur Sa'id	1:788,000
M23	Northern Adriatic Passage Chart – Golfo di Trieste to Bar and Promontario del Gargano	1:750,000
M29	Golfo di Taranto *Plans* Approaches to Brindisi, Approaches to Otranto, Approaches to Gallipoli, Approaches to Crotone	1:375,000
M30	Southern Adriatic and Ionian Sea – Dubrovnik to Kerkira and Sicilia *Plans* Approaches to Brindisi, Approaches to Sicilia	1:220,000
M31	Sicilia *Plans* Approaches to Marsala, Approaches to Favignana, Approaches to Trapani, Approaches to Palermo	1:400,000
M40	Ligurian and Tyrrhenian Seas *Plans* Monte Argentario, Bonifacio Straits, Golfo di Salerno	1:950,000
M45	Tuscan Archipelago *Plans* Approaches to Porto Capraia, Approaches to Portoferraio, Bastia, Talamone, Approaches to Porto S. Stefano	1:180,000
M46	Isole Pontine to the Bay of Naples *Plans* Approaches to Ponza, Approaches to Porto d'Ischia, Approaches to Sorrento, Approaches to Marina Grande (Capri)	1:180,000
M47	Aeolian Islands *Plans* Approaches to Lipari, Bocche di Vulcano	1:140,000
M50	Sardegna to Ionian Sea *Plan* Stretto di Messina	1:1,100 000

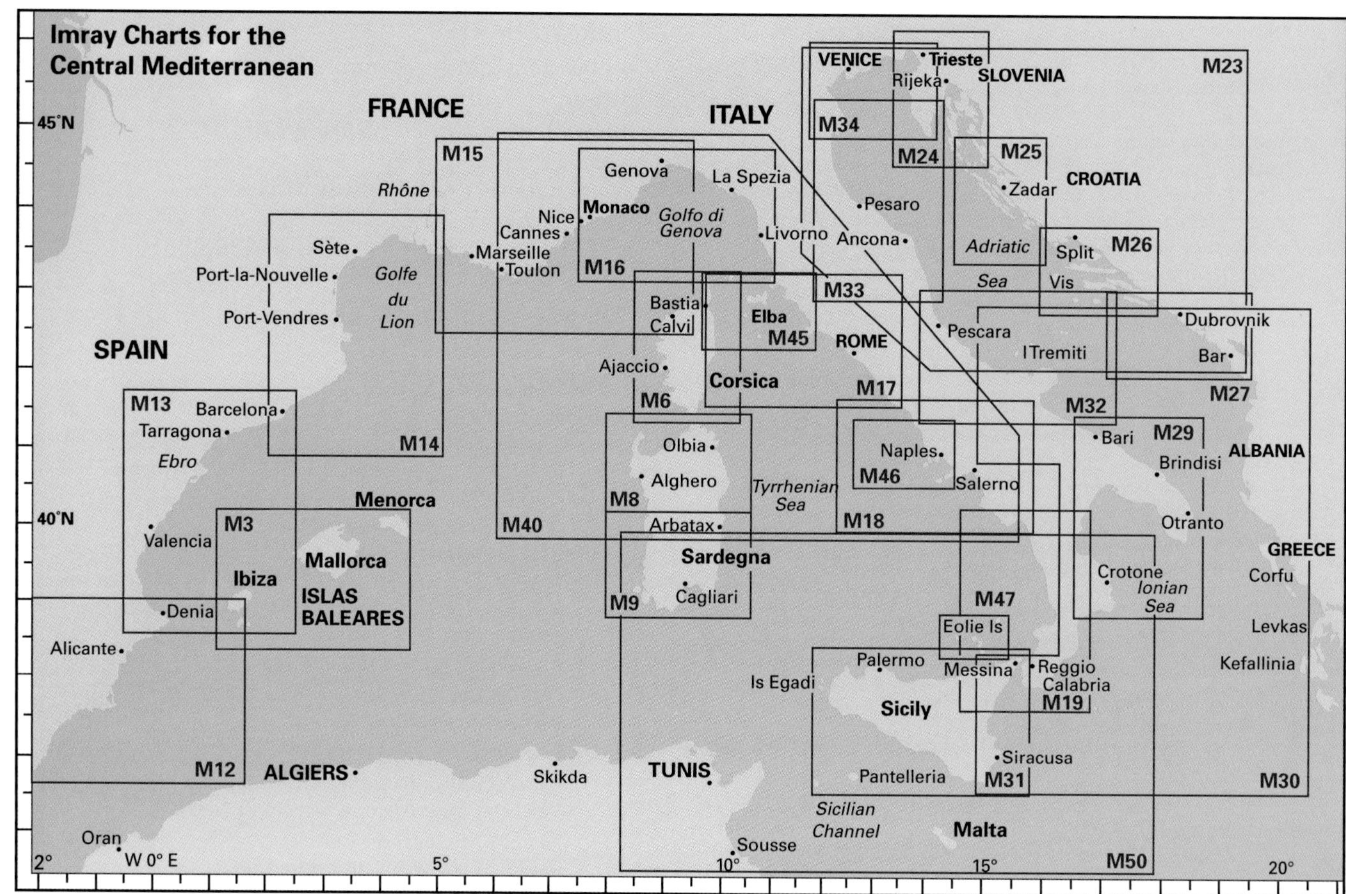

IMRAY DIGITAL CHARTS

Imray Digital Charts are electronic editions of standard Imray charts published in PC format with integrated GPS plotter software.

The plotter enables high-resolution raster images of Imray charts to be used for simple navigation. The clear interface provides an ideal starting point for electronic navigation and provides the navigator with all the essential tools for using charts on a PC.

Their clear and simple format of Imray Digital Charts has come to be regarded as one that has set standards for entry level electronic charting.

The range now covers the British Isles and Coasts of NW Europe from the North of Scotland to Gibraltar, the Western Mediterranean and the Eastern Caribbean.

There area covered by this pilot is:

ID50 The Western Mediterranean

See www.imray.com for full details of charts offered

ADMIRALTY CHARTS

For details of Admiralty charts for Italy and Malta see www.ukho.gov.uk

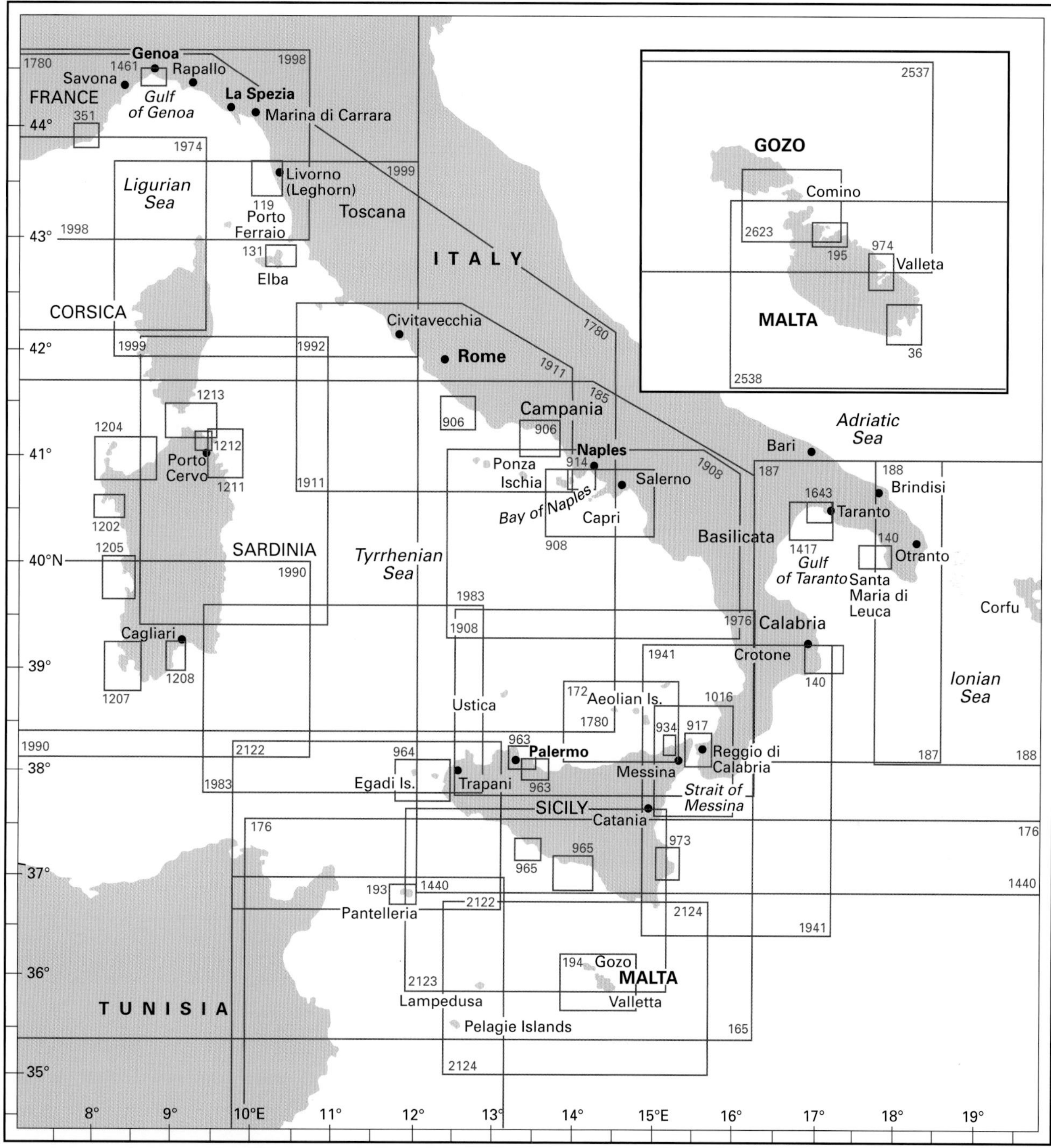

ITALY: SMALLER SCALE ADMIRALTY CHARTS

ITALIAN CHARTS

Italy: Istituto Idrografico del la Marina, www.marina.difesa.it

Italian charts are available from Edizioni il Frangente www.frangente.com

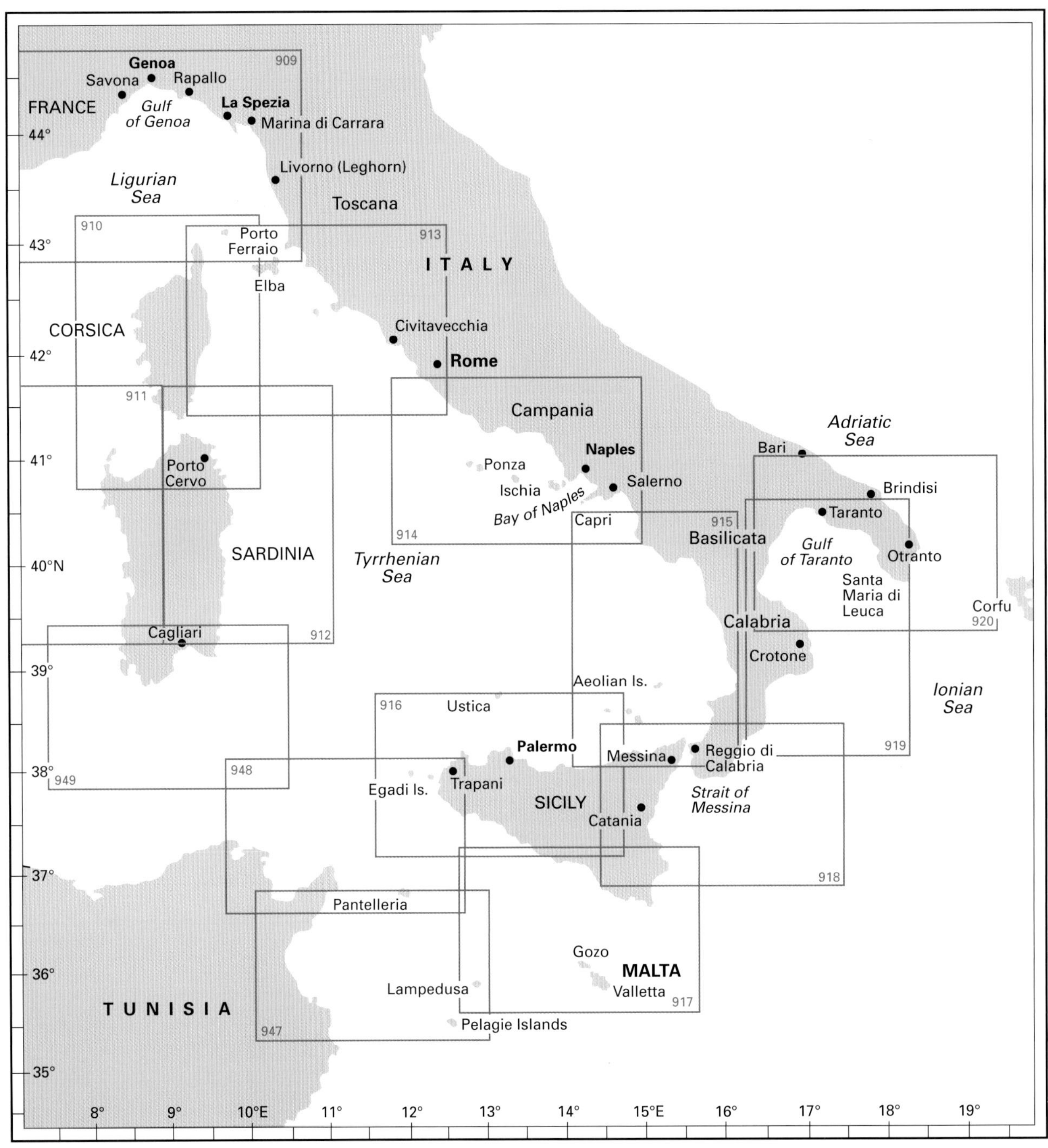

ITALIAN CHARTS

III. USEFUL CONVERSIONS

1 inch = 2·54 centimetres (roughly 4in = 10cm)
1 centimetre = 0·394 inches

1 foot = 0·305 metres (roughly 10ft = 3 metres)
1 metre = 3·281 feet

1 pound = 0·454 kilograms (roughly 10lbs = 4·5kg)
1 kilogram = 2·205 pounds

1 mile = 1·609 kilometres (roughly 10 miles = 16 km)
1 kilometre = 0·621 miles

1 nautical mile = 1·1515 miles
1 mile = 0·8684 nautical miles

1 acre = 0·405 hectares (roughly 10 acres = 4 hectares)
1 hectare = 2·471 acres

1 gallon = 4·546 litres (roughly 1 gallon = 4·5 litres)
1 litre = 0·220 gallons

Temperature scale

t°F to t°C: $\frac{5}{9}$(t°F–32) = t°C

t°C to t°F: $\frac{9}{5}$(t°C+32) = t°F

So 70°F = 21.1°C   20°C = 68°F
80°F = 26.7°C   30°C = 86°F
90°F = 32.2°C   40°C = 104°F

IV. GLOSSARY

GENERAL

yes *si*
no *no*
please *per favore*
thank you *grazie*
excuse me *scusi*
you're welcome *prego*
where? *dove*?
when? *quando*?
how? *come?*
today *oggi*
tomorrow *domani*
left *sinistra*
right *destra*
big *grande*
small *piccolo*
open *aperto*
closed *chiuso*
goodbye *arrivederci*
good morning *buon giorno*
good evening *buona serra*
good night *buona notte*
I don't understand *non capisco*

zero *zero*
one *uno*
two *due*
three *tre*
four *quattro*
five *cinque*
six *sei*
seven *sette*
eight *otto*
nine *nove*
ten *dieci*
twenty *venti*
one hundred *cento*
one thousand *mille*

Sunday *domenica*
Monday *lunedi*
Tuesday *martedi*
Wednesday *mercoledi*
Thursday *giovedi*
Friday *venerdi*
Saturday *sabato*

IN THE RESTAURANT

aglio garlic
agnello lamb
albicocche apricots
al forno baked
anitra duck
antipasto hors d'oeuvre
arrosto roast
braciola chop
carciofi artichokes
cipolle onions
coniglio rabbit
cozze mussels
crostacei shellfish
fegato liver
formaggio cheese
fragole strawberries
fritto fried
frutto di mare seafood
funghi mushrooms
gamberi prawns
gnocchi dumplings
insalata salad
melanzana aubergine
peperoni peppers
pesca peach
pesce fish
pollo chicken
pomodoro tomato
prosciutto ham
risotto rice dish
salsa sauce
uovo egg
vitello veal
vongole clams
zuppa soup

SHOPPING

apples *mela*
apricots *albicocche*
aubergines *melanzana*
bakery *panetteria*
beans *fagioli*
beef *manzo*
biscuits *biscotto*
bread *pane*
butcher *macellaria*
butter *burro*
carrots *carote*
cheese *formaggio*
chicken *pollo*
chocolate *cioccolata*
coffee *caffe*
cucumber *cetriolo*
eggs *uovi*
fish shop *pescheria*
flour *farina*
garlic *aglio*
grocer *drogheria*
ham *prosciutto*
honey *miele*
jam *marmellata*
lamb *agnello*
lemon *limone*
meat *carne*
melon *anguria*
milk *latte*
oil *olio*
onions *cipolle*
oranges *arance*
peaches *pesche*
pepper *pepe*
pork *carne*, *maiale*
potatoes *patate*
rice *riso*
salt *sal*
sugar *zucchero e*
tea *te*
tomatoes *pomodori*
water *acqua*
wine *vino*

ITALIAN TERMS FOUND ON CHARTS

alto high
ancorraggio anchorage
arcipelago archipelago
bacino basin, dock
baia bay
banchina quay
bassafondo shoal
bocca mouth of river
bocche strait
cala small bay
canale canal, channel
capo cape
castello castle
darsena basin
diga breakwater, mole
fiumara, *fiume* river
forte fort
golfo gulf
insenatura cove, inlet
isola, isole island, islands
isolotto islet
lago lake
mare sea
marina beach, landing place
mezzo middle
molo mole
monte mount, mountain
passagio passage
passo pass, channel
piano plain
ponte bridge
pontile pier
porto port
punta point
rada roadstead
sabbia sand
scali steps
scalo landing place
scoglio rock, reef
scogliera ridge of rocks
secca shoal, sandbank
secche group of shoals, reef
spiaggia beach
stretto strait
torre tower
valle valley
vecchio old
vortici eddy, whirlpool

Index

INDEX

INDEX